RECORDS OF THE REFORMED DUTCH CHURCH OF ALBANY, NEW YORK
1683-1809

Marriages, Baptisms, Members, Etc.

Excerpted from
Year Books of The Holland Society
of New York

With an Introduction by
LOUIS DUERMYER

Baltimore
GENEALOGICAL PUBLISHING CO., INC.
1978

Excerpted from Year Books of
The Holland Society of New York
for 1904, 1905, 1906, 1907, 1908,
1922/23, 1924/25, 1926/27

Reprinted
with new front matter
and with the permission of
The Holland Society of New York

Genealogical Publishing Co., Inc.
Baltimore, 1978

Library of Congress Catalogue Card Number 78-54063
International Standard Book Number 0-8063-0808-7

Made in the United States of America

Publisher's Note

This book consists of eight continuous sections, or parts, each excerpted from a different volume of the *Year Book of The Holland Society of New York*. Each section is complete in itself for a designated period and is indexed according to an independent sequence of page numbers. Thus there are eight sets of page numbers and eight indexes. This should not occasion much difficulty, however, as the sections succeed one another in chronological order. We have added half-title pages before each section to indicate the period of coverage and to identify the *Year Book* from which the section was excerpted.

Preface

A very large number of past and present members of The Holland Society, and indeed of many of our sister patriotic and hereditary societies, can trace their descent from Dutch pioneers who at one time or another made their homes in the vicinity of Albany. The undersigned is one of these.

The re-publication of the records of Albany's Reformed Dutch Church is a benefit to many families. The recent growth of interest in genealogical study and the proliferation of research libraries all across America have created a need for these records to be made available once again, since copies of the original *Year Books* in which this material appeared were acquired by relatively few institutions.

From its original organization nearly a century ago, The Holland Society has dedicated itself to preserving and publishing contemporary records relating to the exploration and settlement of America. Reprints such as the Albany Church Records enhance the Society's efforts and supplement its program of publishing new works relating to the accomplishments of the Dutch founders.

CARL A. WILLSEY

Introduction

It is common to think of Albany as an important source both of migration and pioneer leadership throughout the entire period of the westward expansion of America. An examination of the history of its settlement and a study of some of the demographic factors can help provide an understanding of just how great, indeed, was that influence, providing, as well, an understanding of the consequent need for genealogists and historians to turn to the records of the Albany area when seeking to identify the colonial origins of many American families.

One of the oldest permanent settlements in America, Albany first saw Dutch navigators upon the Hudson River in 1610; these came to traffic with the Indians, and built small trading houses. A fort was built on a nearby island in 1614, but when destroyed by an unusually heavy storm, it was replaced by a stockade fort inside the present city limits, in 1623. (This was three years earlier than the Dutch decision to form a settlement on Manhattan Island.) An unbroken tide of immigration can be traced from that period.

Owing principally to the European demand for furs, Albany prospered. The steady growth of its fur industry provided a base for subsequent colonization and the creation of a local agriculture and commerce. There was only minimal English influence until about the time of the French and Indian Wars, say about 1754, although there was an Episcopal minister at Albany by 1710.

Until late in the 19th century Albany ranked among the most populous cities of America. When the patriots organized against George III, Albany was allotted the greatest number of delegates in the Colony of New York. With the expectation of eventual independence, the first New York State Assembly included ten delegates from Albany City and County. No other county was allowed that many. In 1786, only five cities in the United States (Philadelphia, New

York, Boston, Baltimore, and Charleston) had a larger number of houses or greater population.

Changing economic realities eventually favored the greater growth of major seaport cities, and Albany lost its relative viability. The same virility that had characterized the first Albany pioneers now led their descendants to undertake the massive migrations to each of the inland areas opened to settlement. Family names long prominent in Albany are found associated with the expanding frontier, notably in government, commerce, and education. No seasoned student of America's local history can have overlooked the frequency with which the old Dutch and Walloon names recur.

It is unfortunate that the records of The Albany Reformed Protestant Dutch Church which have been preserved lack details of the first forty-odd years of the settled ministry, although commencing with the arrival of Domine Megapolensis in 1642, the residents of Albany and surrounding Rensselaerswyck had access to the religious ordinances of baptism and marriage and the privilege of Christian burial. Civil marriages were also sometimes performed by the Patroon's agents.

The recruitment of the Reverend Domine Johannes Megapolensis in 1642 was financed entirely by the patroon Kilian Van Rensselaer, who guaranteed a house, an annual salary, outfitting expenses, and support of his wife and children if the Domine should die before the end of the contract period of six years. There was even an added provision for support money and ransom if he should be captured by Holland's enemies while in passage. This man became the first minister to preach to the Indian natives, and his success among them can be assessed by the great number of Indians later found among the Albany church members. He learned their language and later wrote a scholarly study of the Mohawks, published in Holland. Completing six years as contracted, Megapolensis left his first post and proceeded downriver to New Amsterdam, intending to return to The Netherlands. Instead, Governor Stuyvesant was able to persuade him to remain, and he served twenty years as senior pastor at the port settlement.

Little is known of the Rev. Wilhelmus Grasmeer, who officiated for only one year. The next minister of the Church at Albany was the Rev. Gideon Schaats, who arrived in 1652 and served more than thirty years. Albany's second church structure was built for him, in 1656, and was used until about 1715. Midway in the Rev. Schaats' tenure he was assisted by the Rev. Mr. Wilhelmus Niewenhuyt, whom the Governor attempted to replace in favor of a Rev. Nicholas Van Rensselaer, but the congregation resisted this usurpation.

In 1683 the Rev. Goddefridus Dellius arrived to serve as the aide to the now elderly Rev. Schaats. Eventually he succeeded to the pastorate, returning to Holland only in 1699, after sixteen years of service. During his ministry he carried the church sacraments to outlying settlements, as far away as Schenectady.

Domine Johannes Petrus Nucella served Albany from 1699 until 1702. The next minister, again noted for his special zeal in Indian missionary efforts, was the Rev. Johannes Lydius, whose untimely death in 1710 left the church without a minister. Some services were held during the ensuing two-year vacancy by the Rev. Gualterus Du Bois of the New Amsterdam church and by the Rev. Petrus Vas of Kingston.

The Rev. Petrus Van Driessen was called to the congregation in 1712. Once again the members found that the decrepit condition of the church building and a growth in membership demanded a new structure.

The new and more massive edifice was built over and around the old church, which was then dismantled and carried out piecemeal, so that worship was disrupted for only three Sabbaths. This, the third church structure, continued in use until well after the end of the events recorded in this present volume.

Succeeding pastors whose records are included in this volume were the Rev. Cornelius Van Schie, Rev. Theodorus Frelinghuysen, Rev. Eilardus Westerlo, Rev. John Bassett, and Rev. John B. Johnson. Ministers who served as occasional assistants, and for only short periods during this era, were the Rev. Dr. John H. Livingston and the Rev. Mr. Linn.

The very fine transcripts from which these published Albany records are taken were made from numerous ancient journals and loose sheets by the late Dr. John H. Trotter. His excellent scholarship and the completeness of those records after 1683 help offset the serious research difficulties arising from the loss of any earlier church books. These records, in fact, commence with an introductory note by Domine Dellius noting that no previous list had been kept.

Complementing, and to some extent supplementing, the Albany Church Records, are two other volumes which, until quite recently, had long been out of print, and it is well to draw the reader's attention to them. These are the efforts of Professor Jonathan Pearson: *Genealogies of the First Settlers of the Ancient County of Albany, from 1630 to 1800* (1872) and *Genealogies of the Descendants of the First Settlers of the Patent and City of Schenectady, from 1662 to 1800* (1873), both reprinted by the Genealogical Publishing Company in 1976. Professor Pearson augmented the church records with studies of the land and probate records, court minutes, records of the patroons, and other private family papers.

Another important source is the list of burials at Albany recorded by Barent Brat for the years 1722 to 1757 and published in Volume I of Joel Munsell's *Annals of Albany*.

LOUIS DUERMYER
February 4, 1978

(Louis Duermyer is Genealogist and Librarian of the National Society of Colonial Dames in the State of New York, Librarian of The Holland Society of New York, and author of materials on genealogy and local history.)

Records of the Reformed Dutch Church of Albany, New York

Part 1
1683-1700

Excerpted from
Year Book of The Holland Society
of New York (1904)

NAMES OF THE MEMBERS OF THE CHURCH OF JESUS CHRIST AT NEW ALBANY, AT THE END OF THE YEAR 1683, AND AFTERWARD.

"And because no list has been kept of them, the names have not been put down in their proper places and order of succession, but have been put down promiscuously."

Juriaen Teunisz.
Ariaentje Teunisz.
Abraham Staets.
Tryntje Staets.
Willem Teller.
Marretje Teller.
Jan Becker.
Mari Becker.
Aarnout Cornelisz Vilen.
Gerrigje Vilen.
Andries Teller.
Sephia Teller.
Johannes Provoost.
Cornelis Van Dyck.
Lysbet Van Dyck.
Catryn Rutgers.
Annetje Lieves.
Jochum Staats.
Lysbet Bancker.
Margariet Schuyler.
Richart Pritti.
Lysbet Pritti.
Annetje Staats.
Jan Tomesz.
Geertruyt Tomesz.
Jacob Schermerhoorn.
Jannetje Schermerhoorn.
Meindert Hermansz.
Heleen Hermensz.

Evert Wendel, the father.
Marritje Wendels.
Johannes Wendell.
Lysbet Wendell, now Schuyler.
Hendrick Cuyler.
Annetje Cuyler.
Henderick Roosenboom.
Gysbertje Roosenboom.
Jan Ouderkerck.
Dirck Wesselse Ten Brouck.
Styntje Ten Brouck.
Marten Krygier.
Jannetje Krygier.
Adriaan Gerritsz.
Jannetje Gerritsz.
Gerrit Swart.
Antonia Swart.
Wouter Van den Uythoff.
Leendert Phlipsen.
Agnietje Leendertsz.
Anna Van der Heyden.
Arien Van Elpendam.
Gerrit Van Esch.
Marietje Van Esch.
Hermen Tomesz.
Catelyntje Tomesz.
Anna Ketel.
Grietje Gouws, deceased.

Taakel Dirckz.
Marritje Taakels.
Wynand Gerritsz.
Tryntje Wynands.
Pieter Loockerman.
Marritje Lookermans.
David Schuyler.
Catelyntje Schuyler.
Pieter Meesz Vrooman.
Folckje Vrooman.
Jacob Meesz Vrooman.
Lysbeth Vrooman.
Aalbert Ryckman.
Nelletje Ryckman.
Sybrant Van Schayck.
Lysbet Van Schayck, now
  Corlaar.
Jacob Staats.
Ryckje Staats.
Willem Percker.
Maria Percker.
Robbert Levinckston.
Alida Levinckston.
Phlip Freest.
Tryntje Freest.
Gerrit Hardenberch.
Jaapje Hardenberch.
Abraham Van Tricht.
Lysbeth Van Tricht, now
  Van der Poel.
Symen Schermerhoorn.
Wilmje Schermerhoorn, now
  Winnen.
Johannes De Wandelaar.
Sara De Wandelaar.
Johannes Van Sandt.
Margariet Van Sandt.
Melchert Wynandtsz (Van
  der Poel).
Ariaantje Wynandtsz.
Laurens Van Alen.
Elbertje Van Alen.
Tryntje Rutten, now Rose-
  boom.
Jan Jansz Bleecker.
Grietjen Bleecker.
Jan Byvang.
Belie Byvang.

Gerrit Lansing.
Elsje Lansing.
Hendrick Lansing.
Lysbet Lansing.
Jan Lansing.
Geertje Lansing.
Jan Nack.
Jan Vinhagel.
Marretje Vinhagel.
Geertje Bout.
Willem Bout.
Luycas Gerritsz.
Antje Lucasz.
Isaac Verplanck.
Abigael Verplanck.
Johannes Beeckman.
Nicolaas Van Rotterdam
  or Groesbeek.
Machtelt Beeckman.
Lysbet Van Rotterdam.
Harmen Bastiaansz (Vis-
  scher).
Hester Bastiaansz.
Robbert Sandersz (Glenn).
Elsje Sandersz.
Jacob Sandersz (Glenn).
Caatje Sandersz, now Douw.
Nicolaas Ripsz.
Marie Nicolaasz Ripsz.
Jacob Coenraatsz.
Geertje Jacobsz.
Johannes Roosenboom.
Margeriet Roosenboom.
Jan Cloet.
Bata Cloet.
Pieter Davidsz Schuyler.
Alida Schuyler.
Gysbert Marselisz.
Barbar Marselisz.
Willem Claesz Croesbeeck.
Geertruyt Croesbeeck.
Johannes Roos.
Cornelia Roos.
Jan Gilbert.
Cornelia Gilbert.
Evert Wendel, the son.
Lysbeth Wendel.
Cornelis Scherluyn.

Geertruyt Scherluyn.
Rachel Retle.
Jacob Loockerman.
Tryntje Loockerman.
Caatje Loockerman, now Ten Broeck.
Jacob Abrahamsz.
Catelyntje Jacobsz.
Nicolaes Van Elslant.
Aaltje Fransz Pruyn.
Johannes Appel.
Annetje Appel.
Johannes Tomesz Mingaal.
Mari Jansz Mingaal.
Jacobus Turck.
Caatje Turck.
Levinus Van Schayck.
Margeriet Van Schayck.
Henderick Bries.
Marie Bries, now Loker-mans.
Reinier Barents.
Bastiaan Harmensz Vis-scher.
Dirkje Bastiaansz.
Maas Cornelisz.
Jacomyn Maasz.
Willem Gysbertsz.
Catryn Willemsz.
Cornelis Gysbertsz.
Pieter Winnen.
Tanne Winnen.
Levinus Winnen.
Jan Salomonsz.
Caatje Jansz Salomonsz.
Barbar Salomonsz.
Dirck Bensing.
Tysje Bensing.
Lysbet Herris, now Kaer.
Huybertje Jeedts.
Pieter Schuyler.
Engeltje Schuyler.
Arent Schuyler.
Maria Van Renselaar.
Ciliaan Van Renselaar.
Anna Van Renselaar.
Teunis. Van der Poel.
Catryn Van der Poel.

Anna Van der Poel.
Hendrick Van Esch.
Annetje Van Esch.
Luycas Pietersz.
Ariaantje Luycasz.
Adam Winnen.
Anna Winnen, now wife of Jacob Teunisze.
Marten Jansz.
Jannetje Martensz.
Marritje Quakelbosch.
Douwe Jelisz, died Nov. 24, 1700.
Rebecca Douws.
Wouter Quakelbosch.
Neeltje Quakelbosch.
Jan Quakelbosch.
Machtelt Quakelbosch.
Reinier Quakelbosch.
Lysbet Quakelbosch.
Folckje Brabanders.
Margriet Ketel.
Ysbrant Elders.
Jan De Noorman, Sr.
Marretje Noormans, now Carbith.
Jan Douw.
Catryn Douw.
Aries Appel.
Wouter De Rademaecker.
Grietje Woutersz.
Gerrit Reyersz.
Annetje Reyersz.
Marretje Van Schayck.
Geertje Brickers.
Marretje Zacharias.
Robbert Sickels.
Cornelis Van der Hoeve.
Metje Van der Hoeven.
Mercelis Jansz.
Annetje Marselis.
Pieter Bogardus.
Wyntje Bogardus.
Marten Gerritsz.
Jannetje Martensz.
Teunis Cornelisz.
Hester Teunisse.
Geertje Van der Hoeven.

Jurrien Coller.
Lysbeth Coller.
Andries De Sweed.
Neeltje Andriesz.
Teunis Slingerlandt.
Celia Slingerlant.
Jan Hendricksz.
Maria Jansz.
Jan Van der Hoeven.
Jannetje Van Wey.
Sara Ketel.
Sella Ketel, now Rachel Van der Heyden.
Antje Crass.
Paulyn Jansz.
Wyntje Paulyns.
Ryck Michielsz.
Jannetje Paulyns.
Anna Pietersz * Van Slyk.
Hendrick Maesz.
Lysbeth Hendricksz.
Gerrit Gysbertsz Van den Berg.
Teuntje Gerritsz.
Frerick De Drent.
Jannetje Vries, now Salsberry.
Hendrick Marselisz.
Barent Pietersz.
Jacob Salomonsz.
Lyntie Salomonsz.
Geertruyt Rinckhout.
Mattys Hooghteeling.
Maria Hoochteeling.
Jan Jacobsz Van Oost Strant.
Agniet Van Oostrant.
Philp Leendertsz.
Wyntie Phlipsz.
Gerrit Lambertsz.
Marie Jochemsz.
Dirck Teunisz Van dr Vechten.
Jannetie Dircksz, *rather* Van dr Vechten.

Gerrit Teunisz Van dr Vechten.
Grietie Gerritsz Van der Vegten.
Magdaleen Quakelbosch.
Andries Jansz Witbeek.
Jan Bronck.
Commertje Bronck.
Melchert Abramsz.
Engeltie Abramsz.
Hendrick Abels.
Sophia Abels, now Nak.
Johannes Oothout.
Hendrick Oothout.
Jacobus Jansz.
Jannetje Jacobsz.
Mayken Jacobusz.
Abraham Van Breemen.
Marretje Van Breemen.
Johannes Jansz Witbeek.
Lysbet Jansz Witbeek.
Cornelis Teunisz Van Vechten.
Annetje Cornelisz.
Claes Van Petten.
Itje Van Petten.
Marten Cornelisz.
Marretje Martensz.
Cornelia Martensz, now Van Deuse.
Engeltje Andriesz Witbeek.
Geertje Gysbertsz.
Hendrick Verwey.
Teunis De Metselaer.
Egbertje Teunisz.
Wilmje Teunisz, now Bratt.
Symen Schouten.
Eypjen Schouten.
Andries Hansz.
Gerritje Andriesz.
Itje Hans.
Jacob Van Oostrant.
Mees Hogenboom.
Catryn Hogenboom.
Ariaantje Hoogenboom.

* This Pietersz had been crossed out, and Van Slyk added in a different (but ancient) handwriting.

Antoni Van Schayck.
Marietje Van Schayck.
Roeloff Gerritsz.
Geertruyt Roeloffsz, wife of
Roelof Gerritse.
Jan Gruttersz.
Herman Lievensz.
Marretje Hermensz Lievense.
Jan Van Esch.
Aaltje Van Esch.
Barent Bratt.
Susanna Bratt.
Geurt Hendriksz.
Marretje Geurten.
Andries Carstelsz.
Harman Jansz Knickelbacker.
Lysbet Harmensz.
Wessel Ten Broeck.
Elsje Ten Broeck, now Cuyler.
Lambert Van Valkenborgh.
Alida Vinhagel, now Visscher.
Gysje Van der Heyden, now
Geesje Kip.
Cornelia Van der Heyden.
Jan Teyszen Hoes.
Styntje Hoes.
Jochum Lambertsz.

Eva Jochumsz.
Pieter Vosburgh.
Jannetje Pietersz Vosburg.
Geertruyt Vosburgh.
Mara Jacobsz, now Van
Vechten.
Jan Martensz.
Dirckje Jansz.
Aalbert Gerdenier.
Marretje Aalbertsz.
Jannetje Lambertsz.
Tam Greeve or Kreeve.
Immetje Kreeve.
Aaltje Adamsz.
Teunis Cool.
Marretje Teunisz.
Ariaantje Hendricksz.
Teuwis Abramsz.
Helena Teuwisz.
Samson Bensing.
Tryntje Samsonsz.
Johannis Bensing.
Mattys Hoogteeling, dead.
Nanning Harmensz Visscher.
Cornelis Stephens.
Hilletje Cornelisz.
Caspar Leendertsz.
Aletta Casparsz.
Mayken Martensz.
Isabella Dellius.

These were accepted as members at the end of the year
1683, and so on.

Dorethe Volkensz.
Catrynte Volkensz.
Maria Schuyler, now Van
Dyck.
Mayken Jacobsz.
Annigje Jansz.
Phlip Wendel.
Bastiaan Harmansz Visscher.
Rebecca Evertsz, wife of
Jeroon Hansse.
Hester Brickersz, now Slingerland.

Aaltje Arentsz.
Andries Jansz.
Barentje Jansz.
Jonas Volkensz Douw.
Chiliaan Winne.
Thomas Winne.
Barentje Wollewever, alias
Schaats.
Jacob Teuniszen Van
Schoonderwoert.
Margriet Van Dam.
Hester Harmensz.
Willemyntje Nack.

Sara Cuyler, now Van Brugge.
Maria Sanders, now Roseboom.
Gerritje Costers, now Roseboom.
Alida Evertsz, now Oothout.
Paulus Martenszen Van Benthuysen.
Wouter Pietersz Quakelbosch.
Pieter Hendricksz De Haes.
Pieter Tomesz Mingaal.
Helena Byvang.
Rebecca Claesz, now Van Schaak.
Catelyntje Ten Brouck.
Martina Bicker, now Hooges.
Susanna Wendel.
Benony Van Corlar.
Jan Ratlife.
Antje Van Esch, now Ridder.
Martina Teunisz.
Cornelia Ten Broeck.
Susanna Barents.
Sara Sandersz, now Grevenraat.
Maria Keteluym, now Bratt.
Dirckje Luykensz.
Antje Becker.
Abraham Staats, Jr.
Elbert Gerritsz.
Jan Huybertsz.
Johannes Bleycker, Jr.
Antoni Bries.
Gerrit Lansing, Jr.
Herbert Jacobsz Van Deuse.
Hendrick Rosenboom, Jr.
Jan Abeel.
Maria Parckar.
Catryn Villeroy.
Sara Hardenberch.
Annetje Lives.
Hermen Rutgersz.
Abraham Cuyler.
Dirck Barentsz Bratt.

Salomon Fredericks Booch.
Elizabeth Van Gelder.
Symon Van Esch.
Catharina Van Schayck.
Debora Van Dam, wife of Hendrick Hanse.
Margriet Jurries.
Zytje Marselis, wife of Joseph Janse.
Evert De Ridder.
Cornelis Martensz.
Jacob Vosburch.
Isaac Vosburch.
Abraham Jansz.
Lambert Jansz.
Isaac Jansz.
Dorothe Vosburch.
Teuntje Jansz, now Winnen.
Marietje Vosburch.
Anna Vosburch.
Geertruy Sickels.
Evert Bancker.
Elizabeth Bancker.
David Christiaansz.
Abraham Isaacsz.
Anna Sickels.
Cornelia Van Male.
Johannes Schuyler.
Margriet Schuyler.
Cornelia Vroman.
Lysbeth Lansingh, now Bratt.
Judick Marselis, wife of Lucas Lucasz.
Andries Hansz Huyck.
Catryn Andriesz.
Cornelia Tysz.
Geertruy Jansz, now wife of Barent Gerritse.
Marretje Hendericksz, now Schermerhoorn.
Ariaantje Gerritsz.
Lyntje Winne, now Witbeek.
Lysbeth Rosenboom, now Van Deuse.
Johanna Bratt, now Keteluyn.

Henderickje Van Schoonhove, now Poppi.
Ariaantje Van Schoonhove.
Frans Pietersz Clauw.
Elsje Franse Clauw.
Adam Dingman.
Geertje Martensz.
Geertruy Ten Broeck, now Schuyler.
Anna De Peyster.
Annetje Gerritsz.
Eytje Pietersz.
Caatje Bleycker, now Cuyler.
Eva Vinhagel, now Beekman.
Willem Jacobsz Van Deuse.
James Willet.
Maria Wendell.
Abraham Kip.
Henderick Greefraadt.
Johannes Pruyn.
Jan Jansz Post.
Johannes Bratt.
Huybert Gerritsz.
Rut Melchertsz.
Cornelis Gerritsz.
Anna Sanders.
Maria Van Rensselaer, now Schuyler.
Jacomyntje Vile.
Mayken Oothout, wife of Thomas Harmensz.

Caatje Melchertsz, now Witbeek.
Jannetje Cobus.
Rachel Melchertsz.
Cornelia Coljer.
Catarina Van Alen, now Van d Poel.
Nelletje Quakelbosch.
Francyntje Hendericks.
Geertruy Hogenboom.
Neeltje Slingerlandt.
Engeltje Lives.
Geertruy Jansz.
Margriet Brickers.
Susanna Lansing.
Hester Davids.
Cornelia Van Vreedenburch, Van Yselsteyn.
Weyntje Fransen.
Judick Van Houten.
Henderick Van Renselaar.
Joseph Jansz.
Jan Fondaas.
Marretje Van Petten, now Van Alen.
Cateleyntje Van Pette, Van Vechten.
Ariaantje Van der Heyden.
Margriet Hansz, now Visscher.
Henderick Van Dyck.
Abraham Schuyler.
Cornelia Van Olinde.

On July 11, 1690, the following 3 proselytes from among the heathens (after having been taught by us the mysteries of the faith and of the doctrines of Jesus Christ, and they had made a public confession of the same in the church) were admitted to the communion of the Lord's holy and most worthy Supper, and consequently on the 13th participated with the congregation in the communion.

Paulus, dead; Laurens (dead) and Maria, married people. The first named was baptized by us, Dec. 26, 1689, and the two last mentioned were baptized by the Jesuits, but had been afterward instructed by us in the Christian religion.

On October 22, 1691, the following proselytes from among the heathens, after having been instructed by us in the mysteries of the faith and of the doctrines of Jesus Christ, and after making a public confession received baptism, were admitted to the Lord's Supper, and consequently on the 25th participated with the congregation in the communion: David, dead,—and Rebecca, married people; Lidia. On the same date at the same time with the above were accepted:

Sara Harmensz.	Jannetje Blyker.
Marretje Gerritsz.	Marretje Vinhagel.

Anna Coster.

On March 24, 1692, the following proselytes were admitted and on the 27th participated with the congregation in the Lord's Supper:

Isak (dead) bapt. July 11, 1690.	Rachel, bapt. July 11, 1690.
	Rebecca, bapt. July 11, 1690.

Eunice, bapt. Aug. 6, 1690.

On the same date were admitted:

Meindert Schuyler.	Marietje Pruym, wife of Elbert Gerritse.
Jacobus Van Dyk.	Rachel Cuyler, now Schuyler.
Johannes Rykman.	Tryntje Rykman, now Bries.
Willem Van Alen.	Marritje Bogardus, now Van Vechten.
Tammus Noxen.	Grietje Takel.
Lucas Jansz Witbeek.	Martje Lookerman, now Fonda.
Andries Douw.	Barber Jansz, wife of Gerrit Rykse.
Pieter Lucasz Kooyman.	Elsje Wendell, now Staats.
Debora Staats, now Roseboom.	Jannetje Oothout, Van Schaak.
Elsje Rutgers, now Schuyler.	
Maria Banker.	
Anna Gansevoort.	
Christine Ten Broek.	
Antje Van der Heyden.	

On September 17, 1692, after confession of faith in the principles of the Christian religion was accepted as member Canastasji, who on the 18th partook with the congregation of the Lord's Supper.

Gerrit Rosenboom.	Pieter Verbrugge.

Stephaanus Croesbeek.

On December 23, 1692, after confession of faith in the principles of the Christian religion was accepted as member Henderik, who on the 25th partook with the congregation of the Lord's Supper.

On April 13, 1693, these following persons were admitted as members:

Antoni Coster.
Johannes Gerritsz Van Vechten.
Marten Winnen.
Melchert Van der Poel.
Elisabeth Kreigier.
Tryntie Wendell, now Millington.

Neeltje Schermerhoorn, now Ten Eyk.
Elisabet Ten Broek, now Coster.
Catrina Nak.
Geertruy Van Benthuysen, now Becker.
Maria Van der Poel, died at Neoboracum.

At the same time with the above was accepted as member, after previous confession, Cornelis, a proselyte, and bapt. by us Feb. 7, 1692.

Also admitted Claas Jansz.

On October 25, 1693, these following persons were accepted as members:

Johannes Harmensz.
Moeset, a proselyte, and bapt. by us March 28, 1692.

Marta, a proselyte, and bapt. by us Aug. 15, 1692.

On Dec. 30, 1693, the following proselytes, after previous confession of faith, were admitted as members:

Sara, bapt. Jan. 1, 1693. | Iosine, bapt. Aug. 6, 1690.

On April 6, 1694, were accepted as members:

Pieter Hoogenboom.
Johannes Kip.
Jacobus Van Schoonhoven.
Geertruy Van Schoonhoven.
Jacomyntje Van Schoonhoven, now Van Deuse.
Geertje Willems.
Anna Bogardus.
Lydia Ten Broek.
Lysbeth Slingerlant.
Christine Pruyn.
Catelyntje Schuyler, now Abeel.

Susanna Wendell.
Claartje Bratt.
Elsje Hansz.
Jannetje Swart, now Van d^r Zee.
Alida Fondaas, now Van Vechten.
Hester Fondaas, wife of Jan Dirckse.
Lysbeth Jansz.
Geertje Quakkelbosch, now Groesbeek.

1694, July 6, were admitted Gideon and Alida. The first mentioned was bapt. by us Oct. 29, 1693. The second was bapt. Aug. 6, 1690.

Dec. 26 were accepted as members:

Neeltje Van Bergen, now Douw.

Dirk Van der Heyden.
David Schuyler.

Also at the same time the following proselytes:

Margriet, bapt. Dec. 31, 1693.
Eva, dead, bapt. Apr. 6, 1694.
Maria, Elsie, these two were bapt. by the Jesuits, but were by us instructed with the others in the principles of the Christian religion whereupon they made confession of their faith before the Rev. Consistory of N. Albany.

At Kinderhook on Jan. 20 were accepted as members:

Ariaantje Barents, wife of Pieter Martensz.

Robbert Teuisz Van Deuse.
Johannes Van Alen.

1695, this 21st of March were admitted as members after a previous confession of the principles of the religion:

Thomas Harmensz.
Hendrik Hansz.
Tam Williams and wife, Agnietje Gansevoort.
Frans Winne.
Elsje Gansevoort Winnen.
Claas Sivers.
Albert Rykman.
Gerrit Ryksz.
Rachel Winne, died at Senechtade.
Hendrik Pruym.

Tryntje Cornelisz, wife of Pieter Walderon.
Sara Foreest.
Claartje Quakelbosch, wife of Dirk Takelse.
Annetje Hogenboom.
Rachel Slingerlant.
Maria Wendell.
Diwertje Van Petten.
Anna Van Petten, wife of Claas Siwerse.
Daniel Bratt.

1695, Dec. 26. The following proselytes were accepted after confession:

Pieter, dead; bapt. Oct. 26, 1694; Joseh; Tierk, went to Canada and turned papist.
Agniet, the wife of Tjerk, was bapt. Dec. 31, 1693.
Lea, bapt. Aug. 6, 1690.
Susanna, June 23, 1695.

Cornelis Bogardus.
Brant, a proselyte, who was bapt. Dec. 26, 1694.
Jacob, He was bapt. by the Jesuits but was by us instructed in the Christian religion.

The number of members, as found at the end of the year 1683, and afterward.

A.

Adriaan Gerritsz Papendorp.
Abraham Staats.
Aarnout Corn. Vielen.
Andries Teller.
Annetje Van Schayck.
Annetje Staats.
Annetje Cuyler.
Antonia Swart.
Anna Van der Heyden.
Agnietje Leendertsz.
Arien Van Elpendam.
Anna Ketel.
Aalbert Ryckman.
Alida Levingston.
Abraham Van Tricht.
Ariaantje Wynantsz Van der Poel.
Antie Luycasz.
Abigael Verplanck.
Alida Schuyler.
Aaltje Fransz.
Annetje Appel.
Arent Schuyler.
Anna Van Renselaar.
Anna Van der Poel.
Annetje Van Esch.
Ariaantje Luycasz.
Adam Winnen.
Anna Winnen.
Arien Appel.
Annetje Reyersz.
Annetje Marselis.
Andries De Sweed.
Antje Cross.
Anna Pietersz.
Agniet Van Oostrant.
Andries Jansz.
Abraham Van Breemen.
Annetje Cornelisz.
Andries Hansz.
Ariaantje Hoogeboom.
Antoni Van Schayck.
Aaltje Van Esch.
Andries Carstelsz.

Alida Vinhagel.
Aalbert Gardenier.
Aaltje Adams.
Ariaantje Hendricksz.
Annigje Jansz.
Aaltje Arensz.
Andries Jansz.
Antje Van Esch.
Abraham Staats, Jr.
Antoni Bries.
Annetje Lives.
Abraham Cuyler.
Abraham Jansz.
Anna Vosburch.
Abraham Isaacksz.
Anna Sickels.
Andries Hansz Huyck.
Ariaantje Gerritsz.
Ariaantje Van Schoonhoven.
Adam Dingman.
Anna De Peyster.
Annetje Gerritsz.
Anna Sanders.
Ariaantje Van der Heyden.
Abraham Schuyler.
Anna Coster.
Andries Douw.
Anna Gansevoort.
Antje Van der Heyden.
Antoni Koster.
Alida. This is one of the proselytes and was bapt. Aug. 6, 1690, and was accepted as a member, on July 6, 1694, after examination in the Christian religion, and with the congregation partook of the Lord's Supper on the 8th.
Ariaantje Barents.
Agnietje Gansevoort.
Albert Rykman.
Annetje Hogenboom.
Anna Van Pette.

Abram Lansing.
Anna Glenn.
Annetje Schaats.

Belie Byvang.
Bata Cloet.
Barbar Marselisz.
Bastiaan Harmensz.
Barber Salomonsz.
Barent Pietersz.
Barent Bratt.
Bastiaan Harmansz.
Barentje Jansz.

Cornelis Van Dyck.
Catryn Rutgers.
Catelyntje Tomesz.
Catelyntje Schuyler.
Caatje Sandersz.
Cornelia Roos.
Cornelia Gilbert.
Cornelis Scherluyn.
Caatje Loockerman.
Catelyntje Jacobsz.
Caatje Turck.
Catryn Willemsz.
Cornelis Gysbertsz.
Caatje Jansz Salomonsz.
Chyliaan Van Renselaar.
Catryn Van der Poel.
Catryn Douw.
Cornelis Van der Hoeve.
Celia Slingerlant.
Commertje Bronck.
Cornelis Teunisz.
Claas Van Petten.
Cornelia Martensz.
Catryn Hogenboom.
Cornelia Van der Heyden.
Cornelis Stephensz.
Caspar Leendertsz.
Colette Casparsz.
Catryntje Volkensz.
Chiliaan Winne.
Catelyntje Ten Brouck.
Cornelia Ten Brouck.
Catarina Villeroy.

Antoni, a proselyte, bapt.
Oct. 29, 1693.
Arent, a proselyte.

B.

Barentje Schaats.
Benoni Van Corlaar.
Barber Jansz.
Brant, proselyte, bapt. Dec.
26, 1694. Member, Dec.
26, 1695. Communicant,
Dec. 29.
Barent, proselyte, bapt.
Jan. 1, 1696. Dead.

C.

Catarina Van Schayck.
Cornelis Martensz.
Cornelia Van Male.
Cornelia Vroman.
Cornelia Tysz.
Catryn Andriesz.
Caatje Bleycker.
Cornelis Gerritsz.
Caatje Melchertsz.
Cornelia Coljer.
Catarina Van Alen.
Cornelia Van Vreedenburch.
Catelyntje Van Petten.
Cornelia Van Olindt.
Christine Ten Broek.
Canastasji, heathen woman,
accepted as member Sept.
17, 1692.
Catrina Nak.
Cornelis, heathen, bapt.
Sept. 7, 1692, member
Apr. 13, 1693, communi-
cant Apr. 16.
Claas Jansz.
Claas Sivers.
Claartje Quakelbosch.
Cornelis Bogardus.
Catelyntje Teuwisz.
Catrina Staats.
Catrina Van Schayk.
Catrine, a proselyte.
Catelina Wendel.

D.

Dirck Wesselsz Ten Broeck.
David Schuyler.
Dirck Bastiaansz.
Dirck Bensing.
Douwe Jelisz, died Nov. 22, 1700.
Dirck Teunisz or Teuwisz.
Dirckje Jansz.
Dorete Volkensz.
Dirckje Luyckensz.
Dirck Barentsz Bratt.
Debora Van Dam.

Dorethe Vosburch.
David Christiaansz.
David, proselyte, accepted Oct. 22, 1691, communicant Oct. 25.
Debora Staats.
Dirk Van der Heyden.
Daniel Brat.
Diwertje Van Petten.
Dorcas, proselyte, bapt. Dec. 26, 1694.
Dirkje Winnen.

E.

Evert Wendell, Sr.
Elbertje Van Alen.
Elsje Lansing.
Elsje Sandersz.
Evert Wendell, Jr.
Engeltje Abramsz.
Engeltje Andriesz.
Egbertje Teunisz.
Eypje Schouten.
Engeltje Schuyler.
Elsje Ten Broeck.
Eva Jochumsz.
Elbert Gerritsz.
Elizabeth Van Gelder.
Evert De Ridder.
Evert Bancker.
Elizabeth Bancker.
Elizabeth Lansing.
Elsje Fransen Clauw.

Eva Vinhagel.
Eytje Pietersz.
Engeltje Lives.
Elsje Rutgers.
Elsje Wendell.
Eunice, heathen, bapt. Aug. 6, 1690, accepted March 24, 1692, communicant March 27.
Elisabeth Kreigier.
Elisabeth Ten Broek.
Eva, bapt. Apr. 6, 1694, accepted Dec. 26, 1694.
Elsie, proselyte, bapt. by the Jesuits; accepted Dec. 26, 1694.
Elsje Gansevoort.
Elisabeth Lansing.

F.

Folckje Vrooman.
Folckje Brabanders.
Frerick De Drent.

Frans Pietersz Clauw.
Francyntje Hendericksz.
Frans Winne.

G.

Gerrigje Vilen.
Geertruyt Tomesz.
Gysbert Roosenboom.
Gerrit Swart.
Gerrit Van Esch.

Grietje Gouws.
Gerrit Hardenbergh.
Grietje Bleecker.
Gerrit Lansing.
Geertje Lansing.

Geertje Bout.
Geertje Jacobsz.
Gysbert Marselisz.
Geertruyt Croesbeeck.
Geertruyt Scherluyn.
Grietje Woutersz.
Gerrit Reyersz.
Geertje Brickers.
Geertje Van der Hoeven.
Gerrit Gysbertsz.
Geertruyt Rinckhout.
Gerrit Lambertsz.
Gerrit Teunisz.
Grietje Gerritsz.
Geertje Albertsz.
Geertje Gysbertsz.
Gerritje Andriesz.
Geertruyt Roelofsz.
Gerrit Hendricksz.
Gysje Van der Heyden.
Geertruyt Vosburgh.
Gerritje Costers.
Gerrit Lansing, Jr.

Geertruy Sickels.
Geertruy Jansz.
Geertje Martensz.
Geertruy Ten Broeck.
Geertruy Hogenboom.
Geertruy Jansz.
Grietje Takel.
Gerrit Rosenboom.
Geertruy Van Benthuysen.
Gideon; this is one of the proselytes, and was baptized Oct. 29, 1693, and after a more thorough examination in the Christian religion was accepted as a member, July 6, 1694, and partook of the Lord's Supper, July 8.
Gerrit Rycksz.
Gysbert Scharp. In lead pencil was added much later: Andriessen.

H.

Heleen Harmensz.
Hendrick Cuyler.
Hendrick Roosenboom.
Harmen Tomesz.
Hendrik Lansing.
Harmen Bastiaansz.
Hendrick Bries.
Huybertje Jeedts.
Hendrick Van Esch.
Hester Teunisz, or Teuwisz.
Hendrick Maesz.
Hendrick Marcelisz.
Hendrick Abelsz.
Hendrick Oothout.
Hendrick Verwey.
Harmen Lievensz.
Harmen Jansz Knickelbacker.
Helena Teuwisz.
Hilletje Cornelisz.
Hester Brickersz.
Hester Harmensz.

Helena Byvang.
Herbert Jacobsz.
Hendrick Rosenboom, Jr.
Hendrickje Van Schoonhoven.
Henderick Greefraadt.
Huybert Gerritsz.
Hester Davids.
Henderick Van Renselaar.
Henderick Van Dyck.
Henderik, heathen, bapt. July 11, 1690; accepted Dec. 23, 1692; communicant Dec. 25.
Hendrik Hansz.
Hendrik Pruyn.
Hagar, proselyte, bapt. Sept. 6, 1696.
Hendrik Jansz.
Hasueros Marselis.
Harman Rykman.
Helena Pruyn.

I [and J].

Jannetje Gerritsz Papendorp.
Jurriaan Teunisz.
Jan Becker.
Johannes Provoost.
Jochom Staats.
Jan Tomesz.
Jacob Schermerhoorn.
Jannetje Schermerhoorn.
Johannes Wendell.
Jan Ouder Kerck.
Jannetje Krygier.
Jacob Meesz Vrooman.
Jacob Staats.
Jaapje Hardenbergh.
Johannes De Wandelaar.
Johannes Van Sant.
Jan Jansz Bleecker.
Jan Byvang.
Jan Lansing.
Jan Nack.
Jan Vinhagel.
Isaack Verplanck.
Johannes Beeckman.
Jacob Sandersz.
Jacob Coenraatsz.
Johannes Rosenboom.
Jan Cloet.
Johannes Roos.
Jan Gilbert.
Jacob Loockerman.
Jacob Abramsz.
Johannes Appel.
Johannes Tomesz.
Jacobus Turck.
Jacomyn Maasz.
Jan Salomonsz.
Jannetje Martensz.
Jan Quakelbosch.
Jan De Noorman, Sr.
Jan (Andriesz) Douw.
Jannetje Martensz Van Bergen.
Jurriaan Coller.
Jan Hendricksz.
Jan Van der Hoeven.
Jannetje Paulyns.

Jannetje Vries.
Jacob Salomonsz.
Jan Jacobsz Van Oostrant.
Jannetje Dirckz.
Jan Bronck.
Johannes Oothout.
Jacobus Jansz.
Jannetje Jacobusz.
Johannes Jansz.
Itje Van Petten.
Jan Gruttersz.
Jan Van Esch.
Jan Tysz.
Jochum Lambertsz.
Jannetje Pietersz.
Jan Martensz.
Jannetje Lambertsz.
Immetje Kreeve.
Johannes Bensing.
Isabelle Dellius.
Iphje Hans.
Jacob Van Oostrant.
Jonas Volkensz.
Jacob Teunisz Van Schoonderwoert.
Jan Rateliff.
Jan Huybertsz.
Johannes Bleycker, Jr.
Jan Abeel.
Isaack Vosburch.
Isaack Jansz.
Jacob Vosburch.
Johannes Schuyler.
Judick Marzelis.
Johanna Bratt.
James Willet.
Johannes Pruyn.
Jan Jansz Post.
Johannes Bratt.
Jacomyntje Vile.
Jannetje Cobus.
Judick Jansz.
Joseph Jansz.
Jan Fondaas.
Jannetje Blyker.
Isak, heathen, bapt. July 11, 1690, member March

24, 1692, communicant
March 27.
Jacobus Van Dyk.
Johannes Rykman.
Jannetje Oothout.
Johannes Gerritsz.
Johannes Harmensz.
Iosine, heathen woman,
bapt. Aug. 6, 1690, member Dec. 30, 1693, communicant Dec. 31.

Johannes Van Alen.
Jacob, heathen, bapt. by the
Jesuits in Canada. Member Church at N. Albany,
Dec. 26, 1695. Communion, Dec. 29.
Jan Teuwisz.
Jannetje Jochumsz.
Johannes, proselyte.
Iacomine, proselyte, bapt.
Aug. 6, 1690.

L.

Lysbeth Van Dyck.
Lysbeth Bancker.
Lysbeth Pritti.
Lysbeth Wendell.
Leendert Phlipsz.
Lysbeth Vrooman.
Lysbeth Van Tricht.
Lysbeth Van Schayck.
Laurens Van Alen.
Lysbeth Lansing.
Luycas Gerritsz.
Lysbeth Van Rotterdam.
Levinus Van Schayck.
Levinus Winne.
Lysbeth Herris.
Luycas Pietersz.
Lysbeth Quakelbosch.
Lysbeth Coller.

Lysbeth Hendriksz.
Lyntje Salomonsz.
Lysbeth Jansz.
Lysbeth Harmensz.
Lambert Van Valkenborgh.
Lambert Jansz.
Lyntje Winne.
Lysbeth Rosenboom.
Laurens, a heathen, bapt. by
the Jesuits. Member at
N. Albany, July 11, 1690
Lidia, bapt. July 11, 1690
Member Oct. 22, 1691.
Lord's Supper, Oct. 25.
Lucas Jansz.
Laurens Claasz.
Lucas Lucasz.
Lammertje Lookerman.

M.

Marretje Teller.
Marie Becker.
Margriet Schuyler.
Meindert Hermansz.
Marietje Wendell.
Mattys Hoogteeling.
Marten Krygier.
Marietje Van Esch.
Marietje Takels.
Marretje Loockerman.
Maria Perker.
Margriet Van Sant.
Melchert Wynandtsz.
Marretje Vinhagel.

Magtelt Beeckman.
Marie Nicolaesz Ripsen.
Margriet Roosenboom.
Marie Jansz.
Margriet Van Schayck.
Marie Bries.
Maas Cornelisz.
Marten Jansz.
Marretje Quakelbosch.
Magtelt Quakelbosch.
Margriet Ketel.
Marretje Noormans.
Marretje Van Schayck.
Marretje Zachariasz.

Metje Van der Hoeven.
Marselis Jansz.
Marten Gerritsz.
Maria Jansz.
Maria Hooghteeling.
Marie Jochemsz.
Melchert Abramsz.
Magdaleen Quakelbosch.
Mayken Jacobusz.
Marretje Van Breemen.
Marten Cornelisz.
Marretje Martensz.
Mees Hogenboom.
Marietje Van Schayck.
Marretje Harmensz.
Marretje Geurten.
Maria Jacobsz.
Marretje Aalbertsz.
Marretje Teunisz or Teu-
wisz.
Mayken Martensz.
Martina Bekker.
Maria Schuyler.
Mayken Jacobsz.
Margriet Van Dam.
Maria Sandersz.
Martina Bicker.
Martina Teunisz.
Maria Barentsz.
Maria Keteluym.
Maria Barcker or Parcker.
Margriet Jurries.
Marietje Vosburch.
Margriet Schuyler.
Marretje Hendricksz.
Maria Wendell.
Maria Van Renselaar.
Mayken Oothoudt.
Margriet Brickers.
Marretje Van Petten.

Margriet Hansz.
Maria, bapt. by the Jesuits
July 11 . . . .; accepted
as member of R. D.
church July 13.
Marritje Gerritsz.
Marretje Vinhagel.
Maria Banker.
Marietje Pruym.
Marritje Bogardus.
Marietje Lokerman.
Marten Winne.
Melchert Van der Poel.
Maria Van der Poel.
Moeset, heathen woman, ba.
March 28, 1692. Member
Oct. 25, 1693.
Marta, heathen woman,
bapt. Aug. 15, 1692, mem-
ber Oct. 25, 1693.
Margriet, heathen woman,
bapt. Dec. 31, 1693, mem-
ber Dec. 26, 1694.
Maria, heathen woman,
bapt. by the Jesuits,
member Dec. 26, 1694.
Maria Wendell.
Marritje Jansz.
Meindert Rosenboom.
Maria Salisburry.
Mayke Van Esch.
Margrietje Pels.
Margriet Rycksz.
Margriet Schuyler.
Marritje Jansz.
Maas Ryksz.
Margriet Levingston.
Margriet Blyker.
Margriet Harmansz.
Marretje Lokermans.

N:

Nelletje Ryckman.
Nicolaes Van Rotterdam.
Nicolaes Ripsen.
Nicolaes Van Elslant.
Nanning Harmensz.
Neeltje Quakelbosch.

Nelletje Quakelbosch.
Neeltje Slingerlandt.
Neeltje Schermerhoorn.
Neeltje Van Bergen.
Neeltje Gerrits.

P.

Pieter Loockerman.
Pieter Meesz Vrooman.
Phlip Freest.
Pieter Davidsz Schuyler.
Pieter Winne.
Pieter Schuyler.
Paulyn Jansz.
Phlip Leendertsz.
Pieter Vosburgh.
Phlip Wendell.

Paulus Martensz Van Ben-
thuysen.
Pieter Hendricksz De Haas.
Pieter Tomesz Mingaal.
Paulus, heathen, bapt. Dec.
26, 1689. Member July
11, communicant July 13.
Pieter Lucasz Koeman.
Pieter Verbrugge.

R.

Richart Pritti.
Ryckje Staats.
Robbert Levingston.
Robbert Sandersz.
Rachel Retle.
Reinier Barens.
Rebecca Douws.
Reinier Quakelbosch.
Robbert Sickels.
Ryck Michielsz.
Rebecca Evertsz.
Rebecca Claasz.
Rut Melchertsz.

Rachel Melchertsz.
Rebecca, heathen, member
Oct. 22, 1691.
Rachel and Rebecca, hea-
thens, bapt. July 11, 1690.
Members March 24, 1692.
Communicants March 27.
Rachel Cuyler.
Robbert Teuisz.
Rachel Winne.
Rachel Slingerlant.
Robbert Levingston, Jr.

S.

Sephia Teller.
Styntje Ten Broeck.
Sybrant Van Schayck.
Symen Schermerhoorn.
Sara De Wandelaar.
Sara Ketel.
Sella Ketel.
Sephia Abels.
Symen Schouten.
Styntje Jansz.
Samson Bensing.
Sara Cuyler.
Susanna Wendell.
Susanna Barents.
Sara Sandersz.
Sara Hardenberch.

Salomon Fredericksz Booch.
Symon Van Esch.
Susanna Lansing.
Sara Harmensz.
Stephanus Croesbeek.
Sara, proselyte, bapt. Jan. 1,
1693. Member Dec. 30.
Communicant Dec. 31,
1693.
Sara Foreest.
Sara Bratt.
Sara Van Deusen.
Sara Van Alen.
Sara Jansz.
Salomon Cornelisz.
Sara Marselis.

T.

Tryntje Staats.
Tryntje Wynants.
Takel Dirks.
Tryntje Freest.
Tryntje Rutten.
Tryntje Loockerman.
Tysje Bensing.
Teunis Van der Poel.
Teunis Cornelisz.
Teunis Slingerlant.
Teuntje Gerritsz.
Teunis De Metselaar.
Tanne Winne.

Tam Kreese.
Teunis Cool.
Teunis Abramsz.
Tryntje Samsonsz.'
Thomas Winne.
Teuntje Jansz.
Tammus Noxen.
Tryntje Rykman.
Tryntje Wendell.
Thomas Harmensz:
Tam Williams.
Tryntje Cornelisz.

W.

Willem Teller.
Wouter Van den Uythoff.
Weynand Gerritsz.
Willempje Schermerhoorn.
Willem Bout.
Willem Claesz Croesbeeck.
Willem Gysbertsz.
Wouter Quakelbosch.
Wouter De Rade Maecker
(the wheelright).
Weinte Bogardus.

Weintje Paulyns.
Weintje Phlipsz.
Willempje Teuwisz or Teu-
nisz.
Wessel Ten Broeck.
Willemyntje Nack.
Wouter Pietersz Quakel-
bosch.
Willem Jacobsz.
Weyntje Fransz.
Willem Van Alen.

Y.

Ysbrant Elders.

Z.

Zytje Marselis.

Members accepted since the year 1696:

Jan. 22, Jan Teuwisz.
Marietje Van Deuse.
Laurens Claasz Van Schaak.
Jannetje Jochumsz, wife of
Isaac Jansz.
Catelyntje Teuwisz.
April 9. Meindert Rosen-
boom.
Abram Lansing.
Catrina Staats, now Schayk.
Saartje Bratt, wife of Rey-
nier Meyndertsz.
Anna Glenn, now Wendel.
Maria Salisburry.

Mayke Van Esch, now Wen-
del.
Saartje Van Deusen.
Margrietje Pels.
June 26 the following prose-
lytes were admitted:
Antoni, bapt. Oct. 29, 1693.
Dorcas, bapt. Dec. 26, 1694.
Barent, bapt. Jan. 1, 1696.
Catrina, aged about 30 yrs.,
was bapt. by the Jesuits.
Sept. 18. Johannes and
Arent, both bapt. by the
Jesuits.

1697, April 1. Mayken Van
Esch, now Ouderkerk.
Annetje Schaats.
Margriet Ryksz.
Elisabeth Lansing, now
Groesbeek.
Susanna Wendell, now
Wyngaard.
Margriet Schuyler, now Lev-
ingston.
Catrina Van Schayk, now
Quakkenbosch.
Dec. 27. Sara Van Alen.
1698, Jan. 15. Gysbert
Scharp.
Hendrik Jansz.
Sara Jansz.
Marretie Jansz.
April 21. Hagar, proselyte,
bapt. Sept. 6, 1696.
Iacomine, proselyte, bapt.
Aug. 6, 1690.
Luycas Lucasz.
Salom Cornelisz Van Vech-
ten.
Hasueros Marselis.
Maas Ryksz.
Harme Rykman.
Robbert Levingston, Jr.
Margriet Levingston.
Margriet V. Trigt.
Margriet Blyker.
Margriet Harmensz.
Catelina Wendell, now
Schuyler.
Neeltje Gerrits.
Dirkje Winne.
Sara Merselis.
Marritje Roelofs-Kidni.
Helena Pruyn.
Lammertje Lokerman-
Oothout.
1699, Jan. 8. The following
persons were admitted as
members at Kinderhoek:

Evert Van Alen.
Stephanus Van Alen.
Manuel V. Schaak.
Lysbeth Arnoutsz V. Eli.
Apr. 6. These following
persons were admitted as
members:
Reyer Gerritsz.
Jacobus Schuyler.
Andries Nak.
Hendrik Douw.
Jan Jansz V. Aarnem.
Wouter Quakkelbosch.
Mathys Nak.
Maria Verplank.
Geertje Gerrits Van den
Berg.
Lysbeth Gansevoort.
Margrietje Rykman.
Lysbeth Viele, died Neo-
boracum.
Helena Fonda.
Antje Quakelbosch.
Josina Maasz.
Hilletje Gansevoort.
Maria Quakelbosch.
Neeltje Marinus.
Rachel Douw.
Cornelia Quakelbosch.
Anna Pruyn.
Canastaji, proselyte, aged
about 36 years.
Bata, proselyte, bapt. 1696.
1699, Sept. By Rev. Nu-
cella: Jonathan Braad-
horst.
1700, Jan. 5. Susanna Wen-
dels.
May 8. Claes Fonda.
Daniel Winnen.
Isack Ouderkerck.
Lysbet Wendels.
Mary Ingolsbie.
Rachel Bogardus.
Susanna Trujex.

MARRIAGE RECORD, COMMENCED IN THE YEAR 1683.

[For list of abbreviations see page in front of index.]

Were united in marriage after 3 banns in the church:

1683, Nov. 14. Jonas Volkersz Douw, y. m., and Magdalena Pietersz Quakelbosch, y. d., both b. and l. at N. A.

1684, Feb. 24. 1st banns. Gerrit Lubbertsz, y. m., of N. Y., and Alida Everts, y. d., of N. A. Marr. March 12.

Apr. 2. Wessel Tenbroek, y. m., and Catharina Lookerman, both b. and l. at N. A.

Apr. 9. Antoni Slingerlandt, widᵣ of Engeltie Albertsz Bratt, and Geertje Fondaas, wid. of Jan. Bicker, both l. here.

Apr. 9. Hieronimus Hansz, y. m., of N. A., and Rebecka Evertsz, y. d., l. here.

Apr. 9. Pieter Willemsz, y. m., and Johanna Hansz, y. d., both l. here.

Apr. 30. Henderik J. Van Oothout, y. m., and Catarina Folkerse Douw, both l. here.

Oct. 1. Johannes Jansz Quisthout, y. m., of N. Y., and Albertje Barentsz, y. d , of N. A.

Nov. 2. Johannes Cuyler, y. m., and Elsje Ten Broek, y. d., both b. and l. at N. A.

Nov. 26. Arent Schuyler, y. m., and Jenneke Teller, y. d., both l. at N. A.

Dec. 17. Johannes Bikker, y. m., and Anna Van der Zee, y. d., both l. at N. A.

1685, Feb. 4. Douwe Aukens, y. m., of Schenegtade, and Maria Vile, wid. of Mathys Vroman, of N. A.

Feb. 11. Symon Jansz, y. m., and Jannetje Paulusz y. d., both l. here.

June 28. Adriaan Appel, widᵣ of Maria Reyverding, and Folkje Pietersz, wid. of Pieter Meese Vroman, both l. here.

Oct. 14. Henderik Fransz, y. m., and Cornelia Andriesz, y. d., both l. in the country [landschap] of N. A.

Oct. 21. Mathys Jansz, y. m., and Cornelia Mattheusz, y. d., both l. in the neighborhood [landschap] of N. A.

Nov. 15. Pieter Tomesz Mingaal, y. m., and Margriet Roosenboom, y. d., both l. here.

Dec. 9. Antoni Brat, y. m., and Willemje Teunisz, y. d., both l. here.

1686, Jan. 1. Salomon Frederiksz Boogh, y. m., and Anna Bratt, y. d., both of N. A.

Jan. 6. Nanning Harmensz Visser, y. m., and Alida Vinhagel, y. d., both of N. A.

Jan. 20. Bartholomeus Henderiksz Vroman, y. m., of Sch., and Cornelia Jansz Helmer, y. d., of N. A.

Jan. 21. Marte Gerritsz Van Bergen, wid: of Jannetje Teunisz, and Neeltje Myndertsz, y. d., both l. at N. A.

Feb. 10. Lucas Lucasz Van Hooghkerken, y. m., and Henderikje Jansz, y. d., both of N. A.

Apr. 5. Robbert Sikkels, y. m., and Geertruy Riddenhaas, y. d., both l. in the vicinity of N. A.

May 4. Henderik Greefraad, y. m., of N. Y., and Sara Sanders, y. d., of N. A.

June 2. Benoni Van Corlar, y. m., and Elizabeth Van der Poel, wid. of Sybrant Van Schayk, both l. here.

June 16. Arie Tomesz, y. m., and Mayke Jacobsz, y. d., both l. in the vicinity of N. A.

July 2. Johannes Van der Linde, y. m., and Neeltje Dirksz, y. d., both l. near N. A.

July 18. Kiliaan Van Renselaar, y. m., and Anna Van Renselaar, y. d.

Aug. 1. First banns. Isaac Vosberge, y. m., and Anneke Jans, both from the vicinity of N. A.

Aug. 8. First banns. Juriaan Henderiksz Bries, y. m., of L. I., and Agnietje Barents, y. d., of N. A.

Aug. 18. Johannes Teller, y. m., and Susanna Wendell, y. d., of N. A.

Sept. 12. First banns. Dirk Barentsz Bratt, y. m., and Anna Teunisz, both of N. A.

Sept. 12. Banns. Evert Banker, y. m., and Elizabeth Abeel, y. d., both of N. A.

Oct. 31. First banns. Michiel Dirksz, y. m., and Maria Parker, y. d., of N. A.

Nov. 7. First banns. Dirk W. Van Slyk, y. m., and Anneken Jans, y. d., both l. near N. A.

1687, March 9. Dirk Van der Heyden, y. m., and Rachel Jochumsz, y. d., both of N. A.

March 16. Barent Gerritsz, y. m., and Geertruy Jansz, y. d., living in the vicinity of N. A.

July 1. Gerrit Marselisz, y. m., and Bregtje Hansz, y. d., both of N. A.

Aug. 7. First banns. Dirk Van der Karre, y. m., and Feytje Claasz, from Kinderhook.

Oct. 16. D. Laurentius Van den Bosch and Cornelia Ten Broek, y. d., of N. A.

Oct. 16. First banns. Jacobus Van Deurse, y. m., of N. Y., and Catarina Borgert, y. d., of N. A.

Oct. 16. First banns. Abraham Kip, y. m., and Geesje Van der Heyde, y. d., both l. at N. A.

Dec. 25. First banns. Helmig Jeralimans, y. m., and Anneke Lucasz, wid. of Frans Mennoury, both l. near N. A.

1688. Feb. 5. First banns. Pieter B. Kool, wid: of Henderikje Jansz, and Yanneke Dingmans, y. d., both from Kinderhook.

Apr. 1. First banns. Evert De Ridder, y. m., and Anna Van Esch, y. d., both 1. here.

May 6. First banns. Pieter Jansz Bosch, y. m., of N. Y., and Susanna Barents, y. d., of N. A.

June 3. François Gaignon, y. m., and Ariaantje Jansz, y. d., of N. A.

June 17. Phlip Wendell, y. m., and Maria Harmensz, y. d., both from N. A.

June 19. First banns. Karel Robbertsz, y. m., and Anneke Jansz, y. d., both 1. here.

July 5. Willem Nickols, y. m., of N. Y., and Anna Van Renselaar, wid. of Kiliaan Van Renselaar.

July 5. First banns. Joseph Jansz, y. m., and Seytje Marselis, y. d., of N. A.

Aug. 26. Jacob Jacobsz Van Oostrant, y. m., and Anna Croesbeek, y. d., both 1. here.

Aug. 26. First banns. Leendert Arentsz, y. m., of N. Y., and Janneke Willemsz Van Slyk, y. d., of N. A.

Aug. 26. First banns. Coenraad Mattysz Hoogteeling, y. m., and Tryntje Willemsz Van Slyk, y. d., of N. A.

Sept. 22. First banns. Jacobus La Methe [?], y. m., of N. Haarlem, and Geertie Martensz, y. d., of Sch.

Sept. 22. First banns. Johannis Jorisz, y. m., from L. I., and Aaltje Kobusz, y. d., of N. A.

Oct. 7. Johannes Legget, y. m., of N. Y., and Catelina Ten Broek, y. d., of N. A.

Oct. 7. First banns. Henderik Pydt, y. m., of L. I., and Maria Verwey, y. d., of N. A.

Oct. 7. First banns. Arent Slingerlandt, y. m., and Geertruy Jacobusz, y. d., both of N. A.

Oct. 10. Johannes De Peyster, y. m., of N. Y., and Anna Banker, y. d., of N. A.

Nov. 18. Benjamin Hygeman, y. m., of L. I., and Barentje Jansz, y. d., of N. A.

Nov. 18. Johannes Roosenboom, y. m., and Gerritje Koster, y. d., both of N. A.

Nov. 25. Henderik Van Esch, wid! of Annetje Evertsz, and Catarina Van Dam, y. d., of N. A.

1689, Feb. 3. Henderik Van Dyk, y. m., and Maria Schuyler, y. d., both of N. A.

Apr. 4. Lucas Jansz Van Sasberge, y. m., and Maria Evertsz Van Wesel, y. d., of N. A.

May 5. Johannes Oothout, y. m., and Aaltje Evertsz, wid. of Gerrit Lubbertsz, both 1. near N. A.

May 12. Francois Winnen, y. m., and Elsje Gansevoort, both of N. A.

June 3. Cornelis Teunisz Van Vegten, wid: of Annetje Leendertsz, and Maria Lucasz, wid. of Jacob Claasz.

Sept. 22. Robbert Mateuisz, y. m., and Cornelia Martensz, y. d., both l. near N. A.

Sept. 22. Cornelis Martensz, y. m., and Ariaantje Gerritsz, y. d., both l. near N. A.

Oct. 13. First banns. Evert Willer, y. m., from N. E., and Josyntje Gardenier, y. d., from Kinderhook.

Oct. 20. Thomas Winne, y. m., and Tryntje Jansz, y. d., both l. near N. A.

Oct. 20. Isaac Jansz Van Alstyn, y. m., and Maria Abbedis, y. d., both l. under the jurisdiction of N. A.

Nov. 17. Abraham Cuyler, y. m., and Catarina Bleyker, y. d., both of N. A.

Nov. 24. Gerrit Rosenboom, y. m., and Maria Sanders, y. d., both of N. A.

Dec. 20. Hillebrant Lootman, y. m., and Anna Elbur, wid. of Antoine Barroa, both l. under the jurisdiction of N. A.

1690, Jan. 15. Adam Antonisz Swart, y. m., of Sch., and Metje Willemsz Van Slyk, y. d., of N. A.

Jan. 22. Willem Boin [?], y. m., and Seyke Jansz, y. d., both l. at N. A.

June 26. Jean Span, y. m., of N. Y., and Ariaantje Hogenboom, y. d., of N. A.

Aug. 3. Gerrit Symonsz, y. m., and Catryn Helmertsz, y. d., both l. at N. A.

1691, June 21. Johannes Glenn, wid: of Annetje Peek, and Diwertje Wendell, wid. of Meindert Wimp.

June 28. Lucas Jansz, y. m., and Catarina Melchersz, y. d., both of N. A.

Sept. 8. Jacobus Verplank, y. m., of N. Y., and Margareta Schuyler, y. d., of N. A.

Sept. 14. Piter Schuyler, wid: of Engeltje Van Schayck, and Maria Van Renselaar, y. d., both l. at N. A.

Oct. 14. Wouter Van den Uythoff, wid: of Elizabeth Henderiksz, and Elizabeth De Lint, wid. of Jacob Meesz Vrooman, both l. at N. A.

Oct. 18. Jacob Teunisz, wid: of Catryn Claasz, and Annetje Lookerman, wid. of Adam Winne, both l. at N. A.

Oct. 29. George Bradschaff, wid: of Mary Warran, and Elizabeth Beek, wid. of Cornelis Van Dyk, l. at N. A.

Nov. 11. Abraham Schuyler, y. m., and Geertruy Ten Broek, y. d., both l. at N. A.

Dec. 10. Hermannus Vedder, y. m., and Grietje Cornelisz, wid. of Andries Bratt, both l. at Sch.

Dec. 23. Tammus Noxen, y. m., and Geertruy Hogenboom, y. d., both l. at N. A.

1692, Jan. 13. Frederik Harmensz Vischer, y. m., and Margriet Hansz, y. d., both l. at N. A.

Jan. 13. Willem Jacobsz, y. m., and Elizabeth Rosenboom, y. d., both l. at N. A.

March 9. Jan Danielsz, y. m., and Jannetje Paulusz, wid. of Symen Jansz Post, both l. at N. A.

March 25. Fil Harrit, y. m., and Annetje Tjerks, wid. of Frans Harmensz, both l. at Sch.

March 26. Henderik Willemsz Brouwer, y. m., and Marritje Pietersz Bosboom, wid. of Teunis Karstensz, both l. at Sch.

June 29. Melchert W. Van der Poel, wid* of Ariaantje Verplank, and Elisabeth Teller, wid. of Abraham Van Trigt, both l. at N. A.

Aug. 7. Tomas Willemsz, y. m., of N. Y., and Agnietje Gansevoort, y. d., of N. A.

Aug. 17. Simon Westfall, y. m., of Kingston, and Nelletje W. Quakelbosch.

Aug. 21. Gerrit Lansing, Jr., y. m., of N. A., and Catrina Sandersz Glenn, wid. of Cornelis Barentsz, of Sch.

Sept. 3. Wilhem Hooge, y. m., of Bosinylant, in Kings Co., and Martina Bekker, y. d., of N. A.

Sept. 11. Rut Melchertsz, y. m., and Weyntje Harmensz, y. d., both of N. A.

Sept. 20. Jacobus De Warrum, y. m., of N. Y., and Anna Gansevoort, y. d., of N. A.

Sept. 20. Marte Beekman, y. m., of N. Y., and Neeltje Slingerlant, y. d., of N. A.

Sept. 21. Jacobus Van der Spiegel, y. m., of N. Y., and Anna Sanders, y. d., of N. A.

Sept. 21. Antoni Bries, y. m., and Catarine Rykman, y. d., both of N. A.

Sept. 21. Henderik Hansz, y. m., and Debora Van Dam, y. d., both of N. A.

Oct. 16. Geraldus Kampfoort, wid* of Antje Raal, l. at Sch., and Ariaantje Uldrik, wid. of Gerrit Claasz, l. at N. A.

Oct. 16. Benjamin Van der Water, l. on L. I., and Engeltje Harmensz, y. d., l. at N. A.

Oct. 26. Johannes Beekman, wid* of Maghtelt Schermerhoorn, and Eva Vinhagel, y. d., both of N. A.

Nov. 13. Andries Jacobsz Gardenier, y. m., and Eytje Ariaansz, wid. of Henderik Gerritsz Van Wyen, both l. near N. A.

Nov. 20. Thomas Harmensz, y. m., and Mayken Jansz Oothout, y. d., both of N. A.

Nov. 23. Lucas Lucasz, wid* of Henderikje Jansz, and Judik Marselis, y. d., of N. A.

Dec. 6. Jan Nak, wid: of Caterina Roemers, and Sophia Wykersloot, wid. of Henderik Abelsz Riddenhaas.

1693, Jan. 15. Pieter Martensz, y. m., and Ariaantje Barents, y. d., both l. near N. A.

Jan. 30. Jan Henderiksz Van Sasbergen, wid: of Emmeke Lucasz, and Janneke Jansz, wid. of Ryk Ridderson.

March 28. Lambert Jochumsz Van Valkenborgh, y. m., and Jannetje Fransz Clauw, y. d., both l. at Kinderhook.

Apr. 6. William Hilte, wid: of Sara Ebb, and Antje Berkhove, of N. Y.

May 7. Johannes Barentsz Bratt, y. m., and Maria Ketelheim, v. d., both of N. A.

May 7. Martes Cornelisz, wid: of Marretje Quakkelbosch, and Tanneke Adams, wid. of Pieter Winnen.

June 16. Teunis Vile, y. m., and Lysbeth Van Eps, y. d., both of Sch.

June 17. Gerrit Jacobsz, y. m., and Lysbeth Aarnoutsz Eli, both l. at Kinderhook.

June 28. Coenraadt Elmendorff, y. m., of Kingston, and Ariaantje Gerrits, wid. of Cornelis Martensz Van Bueren, l. near N. A.

July 2. Elbert Gerritsz, y. m., and Maria Pruyn, y. d., both l. at N. A.

July 23. Gerrit Gysbertsz * Van Brakel, wid: of Reyntje Stephens, and Elisabeth Jans, wid. of Jan Van Eps, both l. at Sch.

July 24. Jonathan Stephens, y. m., from N. E., and Lea, wid. of Claas Willemsz, both l. at Sch.

Oct. 29. Capt. Benjamin Phips, wid:, l. at N. A., and Hanna Deen, wid., l. at N. Y.

Oct. 29. Jacob Supplisoo, y. m., and Eytje Hendriksz, wid. of Dirk Hesseling, both l. at Sch.

Oct 29. Johannes Bleyker, Jr., y. m., and Anna Coster, y. d., both of N. A.

Dec. 13. Piere Simon, wid: of Elisabeth Du Peis, l. at N. Rochelle, and Marie Everts, wid. of Lucas Jansz, l. at N. A.

Dec. 13. Cornelis Claasz, y. m., and Susanna Ouwerkerk, y. d., both l. at N. A.

Dec. 20. Huybert Gerritsz, y. m., and Maria Lansing, y. d., both l. here.

1694, Jan. 1. David Schuyler, y. m., and Elsje Rutgers y. d., both l. at N. A.

Jan. 17. Abram Jansz Van Alsteyn, y. m., and Marietje. Van Deuse, y. d., both l. near N. A.

---

*A note in lead pencil in the original says: " This should be Gysbert Gerritse V. B."

Apr. 11. Johannes Abeel, y. m., and Catelina Schuyler, y. d., both of N. A.

July 12. Jean Kerr, aged 31 years, y. m., of Londonderry, Ireland, last from Southampton, and Elisabeth Claassen, wid. of Jean Harrits, of N. A.

Oct. 25. Jacobus Van Dyk, y. m., and Jacomyntje Glenn, y. d., both l. at Sch.

Nov. 1. Hendrik Rosenboom, y. m., and Debora Staats, y. d., both l. at N. A.

Nov. 4. Willem Van Alen, y. m., and Marietje Van Petten, y. d., both l. at N. A.

Nov. 4. Gerrit Luycasz Wingaart, y. m., and Sara Harmensz Visscher, y. d., both l. at N. A.

Nov. 25. Johannes Andriesz Scherp, y. m., and Geertruy Rees, y. d., both l. near N. A.

Nov. 28. Teunis Dirksz, y. m., and Catrina Van Petten, y. d., both l. near N. A.

Dec. 5. Jan Fondaal, y. m., and Marritje Lookerman, y. d., both l. at N. A.

1695, Jan. 24. Harbart Jacobsz, y. m., and Marritje Gerrits, y. d., both l. at N. A.

March 14. Jan Teuwisz Van Deussen and Marietje Martensz, y. d., both l. near N. A.

March 21. Cornelis Schermerhoorn, y. m., and Marritje Hendriksz, y. d., both l. near N. A.

March 31. David Kitteluym, y. m., and Johanna Bratt, y. d., both l. at N. A.

Apr. 13. William Haal, y. m., and Tryntje Claasen, wid. of Elias Van Gyseling, both l. at Sch.

Apr. 25. Johannes Schuyler, y. m., and Elisabeth Staats, wid. of Johannes Wendell, both l. at N. A.

Apr. 25. Johannes Lucasse Wingaardt, y. m., and Susanna Wendell, y. d., both l. at N. A.

May 20. Johannes Ouwerkerk, y. m., and Neeltje Claasz, wid. of Hendrik Gardenier, both l. at N. A.

July 2. Wouter Van der Zee, y. m., and Jannetje Swart, y. d., both l. at N. A.

July 17. Cornelis Van Esch, y. m., and Marietje Van den Bergh, y. d., both l. at N. A.

Aug. 16. Daniel Keteluym, y. m., l. at N. A., and Debora Vile, y. d., l. at Sch.

Sept. 10. Henri Possi, y. m., b. in England at Boorton, and Antje Hogenboom, y. d., both l. at N. A.

Sept. 10. Jacob Bastiaansz De Wit, wid: of Barbar Gysbertsz, and Saartje Jansz, wid. of Jan Jacobsz Gardenier.

Nov. 21. Jonathan Deyer, y. m., from Weels [Wales] in England, and Maria Dirksz, wid. of Harmannus Hagendoorn, both l. at Sch.

Dec. 5. Hendrik Rosenboom, Sr., wid. of Gysbertje Lansing, and Trynte Jansz, wid. of Rut Jacobsz, both l. at N. A.

Dec. 11. Jillis Fondaa, y. m., and Rachel Winne, y. d., both l. at N. A.

1696, Feb. 5. Teunis Willemsz Van Slyk, y. m., and Jannetje Hendriksz, y. d., both l. here.

Feb. 10. Cornelis Van Slyk, y. m., of Sch., and Claartje Bratt, y. d., of N. A.

Apr. 15. Abram Groot, y. m., and Anna Wimp, wid. of Sander Glenn, both l. at Sch.

Feb. 23. Jonathan Braathorst, y. m., from Derington, Eng., and Cathrine Bensing, wid. of Reinier Schaats, both l. here.

Apr. 24. Jonas Douw, wid^r of Magdalena Quakelbosch, and Catrina Van Witbeek, wid. of Jacob Sandersz Glenn.

May 3. Isak Ouderkerk, y. m., and Mayken Van Esch, y. d., both l. here.

May 17. Melchert Van der Poel, Jr., y. m., and Caterina Van Alen, y. d., both l. here.

June 2. Marten Van Benthuysen, y. m., and Feitje Bosboom, y. d., both l. here.

June 4. Jean Fein, y. m., from Waterfort, Ireland, and Jopje Claasz Van Slyk, y. d., from N. A.

June 8. Warner Carstens, y. m., and Anna Pruyn, y. d., both l. here.

June 11. Daniel Van Olinde, y. m., and Elisabeth Kreigier, y. d., both l. here.

July 3. Abraham Staats, y. m., and Elsje Wendel, y. d., both l. here.

July 24. Daniel Wilkenson, y. m., and Anna Bratt, both l. here.

Aug. 21. Jacob Lookerman, wid^r of Tryntje Claasen, and Maria De Hooghes, wid. of Hendrik Bries, both l. here.

Sept. 4. Teunis Rappaille, y. m., from the Walebout, L. I., and Sara Dirksz, y. d., from N. A.

Sept. 27. Gerrit Ryksz, y. m., and Barbar Jansz, y. d., both l. here.

Oct. 4. Wouter Quakkelbosch, J., y. m., and Cornelia Bogaart, y. d., both l. here.

Oct. 7. Jacobus Winne, y. m., and Marritje Bronk, y. d., both l. here.

Oct. 14. Jan Jansz Van Aarnem, y. m., and Hester Fonda, y. d., both l. here.

Dec. 14. Pierre Benoy, y. m., from Rochelle, and Hendrikje Schoonhoven, both l. here.

1697, Jan. 1. Andries Rees, y. m., and Ariaantje Andriesse Scharp, y. d., both l. near N. A.

Jan. 7. Jonatan Jansz, y. m., and Catelyntje Martensz, y. d., both l. near N. A.

Jan. 13. Adam Vroman, wid: of Grietje Rykman, l. at Sch., and Grietje Takels, y. d., l. at N. A.

March 28. Omi De la Grange, y. m., and Elsje Van Loon, y. d., both l. at N. A.

Apr. 18. Daniel Bratt, y. m., and Elisabeth Lansing, y. d., both l. at N. A.

May 2. Ritchart Hill, y. m., from Sarry in O. Eng., and Emmetje Claasz, wid. of Pieter Bogi, both l. here.

May 4. Patrik Magrigari, y. m., from Scotland, and Zytje Hooghteeling, wid. of Frank Marrits.

May 23. Willem Jansz, y. m., and Feytje Dirksz, y. d., both l. in N. A. county.

May 23. Abraham Van Deurse, y. m., and Jacomyntje Van Schoonhoven, y. d., both l. in the city and county of A.

June 24. Andries Douw, y. m., and Elsje Hansz, y. d., both l. here.

July 3. Johannes Van Alen, y. m., and Sara Dingman, y. d., both l. at Kinderhook.

July 21. Moses De Puis, y. m., from Canada, and Annetje Christiaansz, y. d., both l. here.

Aug. 26. Robbert Levingston, Jr., y. m., and Margareta Schuyler, y. d., both l. here.

Sept. 2. Lambert Andriessen, y. m., from L. I., and Lea Harmensz, y. d., both l. here.

Oct. 3. Hendrik Douw, y. m., and Neeltje Meynderts, wid. of Marten G. Van Bergen, both l. here.

Nov. 1. Jan Evertsz, y. m., and Martine Simonsz, y. d., l. here.

Nov. 12. Coenraadt Borgaart, y. m., and Geesje Van Wye, y. d., both l. at Kinderhook.

Nov. 19. Johannes Simonsz, y. m., and Susanna Wimp, y. d., both l. at Sch.

Dec. 8. Ahasueros Marselisz and Sara Heemstraat, both l. here.

1698, Jan. 26. Pieter Hogenboom, y. m., and Jannetje Muller, y. d., both l. here.

Feb. 20. Isak Jansz Van Alstyn, wid: of Maritje Vosburgh, and Jannetje Jochums Van Valkenborg, y. d., both l. at Kinderhoek.

Feb. 22. Arent Claasz Van Schaak, y. m., and Maria Van Loon, y. d., both l. here.

March 16. Daniel Winnen, y. m., and Dirkje Van Esch, y. d., both l. here.

Apr. 12. Abram Wendell, y. m., and Mayken Van Esch, y. d., both l. here.

May 1. John Kidni, y. m., from Barbados, and Marritje Roelofs, y. d., from N. A.

July 24. Mathys Nak, y. m., and Susanna Lansing, y. d., both l. here.

Aug. 6. Folkert Simonsz, y. m., and Jannetje Schermerhoorn, y. d., both l. at Sch.

Nov. 6. Hendrik Jansz Van Sasberry, y. m., and Cornelia Claasz Van Schaak, wid. of Hans Jurriaansz, both l. at Claverak.

Nov. 12. Bartholemy Pikkart, y. m., from Lesterchier in O. E., and Eechje Claasz, y. d., from Sch.

Nov. 17. Gerrit Hendriksz Van Wyen, y. m., and Agnietje Conyn, y. d., both l. here.

Dec. 11. Johannes Glenn, y. m., and Jannetje Bleyker, y. d., both l. here.

Dec. 15. Antoni Coster, y. m., and Elisabeth Ten Broek, y. d., both l. at N. A.

1699, Jan. 18. Adriaan Quakkelbosch, y. m., and Catrina Van Schayk, y. d., both l. at N. A.

Feb. 17. Dominicus Van Schaak, y. m., and Rebecca Croesbeek, both l. here.

Feb. 22. James Parkar, y. m., and Geertruy Van Benthuysen, y. d., both l. at N. A.

March 15. Manasse Saksby, y. m., from London, and Pietertje Jansz Jonker, y. d., from Sch., both l. there.

March 15. Benjamin La Noy, y. m., from Picardie, and Feitje Jansz Jonker, y. d., from Sch., both l. there.

March 19. Johannes Van Vegten, y. m., and Maria Bogardus, y. d., both l. here.

June 18. Barent Vroman, y. m., b. in Albany Co., l. at Sch., and Tryntje Taakels Hemstraat, y. d., b. and l. at A. Marr. in Sch. by Joh. Sandsen Glen, Justice.

June 20. Levinus Winne, widr of Teuntje Martens, and Willemje Viele, wid. of Symon Schermerhoorn, both l. here. Marr. in A. by Joh. Schuyler, Justice.

July 9. Abraam Groot, widr, l. at Sch., and Hester Hermanse Visscher, y. d., l. here. Marr. at Sch. by Joh. Sandsen Glen, Justice.

July 16. Jilles Van Vorst, y. m., l. here, and Elisabeth Van Eps, wid. of Teunis Viele, l. at Sch. Marr. at Sch. by Joh. Sanderse Glen, Justice.

July 16. Stephanus Groesbeek, y. m., and Elisabeth Lancing, y. d., both b. and l. here. Marr. in A. by Peter Schuyler, Justice.

July 26. Claes Siversen, y. m., b. in Denmark, l. at A., and Annetje Van Putten, y. d., b. and l. at A. Marr. at A. by Dirck Wesselse and Albert Ryckman, Justices.

Aug. 13. Jan Fyn, widr of Jobje Van Schaak, and Alida

Gardenier, y. d.   Marr. by Pieter Vosburg, Justice, at Kinderhoek.

Sept. 1.   Sam Docksje, y. m., b. on L. I., l. in Colony Rensselaarswyck, and Barber Janss, y. d., b. and l. at A. Marr. by Gerrit Teunissen, Justice, in Col. R.

Sept. 17.   Thomas Millington, y. m., b. in O. E., and Tryntje Wendels, b. at A., both l. here.   Marr. at A. by Pieter Schuyler, Justice.

Sept. 7.   Reynier Meynertsen, y. m., and Sara Brat, y. d., both b. and l. at A.

Sept. 17.   Maas Hendricksen Van Buuren, y. m., and Ariaantje Van Weye, y. d., both b. and l. in R.   Marr. in A. by Jan Vinhagen, Justice.

Nov. 10.   Salomon Van Vegten, y. m., and Alida Vonda, y. d., both b. and l. in the Col. R.   Marr. by Dirrick Wesselse and Albert Ryckman, Justices.

Nov. 13.   Richard Janssen, y. m., b. in Col. R., and Tryntje Hoogteeling, y. d., b. in A. Co., both l. in A. Co. Marr. in the Colony by Gerrit Teunissen, Justice.

Nov. 26.   Eduwart Carbert, y. m., b. in E., and Maria Post, wid. of Jan Brat, b. in Brazil, both l. at A.   Marr. in A. by Dirrick Wesselse and Albert Ryckman, Justices.

Dec. 19.   Laurens Van Schaak, y. m., b. and l. at Kinderhook, and Jannetje Oothout, y. d., b. and l. at A.   Marr. in A. by Albert Rykman, Justice of the Peace.

Dec. 10.   Goossen Van Schayk, y. m., and Catharina Staats, y. d., both b. and l. at A.   Marr. in A. by Peter Schuyler, Justice of the Peace.

Dec. 17.   Johannes Claasse Groesbeek, y. m., and Geertruy Quakkenbosch, y. d., both b. and l. in A. Co.   Marr. in A. by Pieter Schuyler, Justice of the Peace.

BAPTISMAL RECORD OF ALBANY, BEGUN IN THE YEAR 1683.

[For list of abbreviations, see page fronting index.]

1683
Aug. 5.   Nicolaes and Johannes, twins, children of Gysbert Marselis.   Witnesses: the father, Nicolaes Jacobsz, Marcelis Jansz.   Presented for baptism by Cathryn Claasz and Huybertje Marselis.

Aug. 12.   Wouter, of Gerrit Lansing.   Wit.: Evert Wendell.   By Elizabeth Wendell.

Aug. 19.   Jannetje, of Gabriel Tomesz Stridles.   Wit.: father, Richart Pritty.   By Jannetje Martensz.

1683

Aug. 26. Catelyntje, of Jacob Korenbeurs. Wit.: Jacob Jansz Koorenbeurs, Dirk W. Ten Broek. By Elizabeth Henderiksz.

Marretje, of Albert Rykman. Wit.: father, Pieter Schuyler. By Maria Van Esch.

Sept. 9. Arien, of Gerrit Arisz. Wit.: Cornelis Teunisz, Jan Verbeek. By Lysbeth Van der Linden.

Leendert, of Phlip Leendertsz. Wit.: Leendert Phlipsz, Johannes Jansz. By Jannetje Martensz.

Sept. 16. Cornelis, of Jan Van der Hoeve. Wit.: the father, Jurriaan Caillardt. By Geertruy Cornelisz.

Sept. 19. Leendert, of Harmen Gansevoort. Wit.: Leendert Phlipsz. By Annetje Leendertsz.

Sept. 23. Annetje, of Jan Salomonsz. Wit.: the father, Salomon Frederiksz. By Anna Van Renselaar.

Isaac, of Johannes Provoost. Wit.: the father. Johannes Wendell. By Annetje Staats.

Sept. 28. Robbert, of Evert Wendell. Wit.: the father, Johannes Wendell. By Elsje Barents.

Frans, of Frans Jansz Pruyn. By Bata Slegtenhorst.

Cornelis, of Jacob Corn Voss. Wit.: Albert Rykman. By Jannetje Cornelis.

Oct. 7. Catarina, of Johannes Roos. Wit.: Melchert Wynandsz, Gerrit Roos. By Tryntje Arensz.

Oct. 14. Wynand, of Melchert Wynandsz Van der Poel. Wit.: the father, Gerrit Wynandsz Van der Poel. By Catryn W. Van der Berch.

Barent, of Gerrit Reyersz. Wit.: the father. By Cornelia Cornelisz.

Jacob, of Jacobus Turk. By Catalyntje Paulusz.

Oct. 21. Magdalena, of Abraham Van Trigt. By Maria Van Esch.

Oct. 28. Barendine, of Gerrit Hardenberch. Wit.: father, Jacob Sandersz. By Styntje Wessels.

Oct. 31. Antoine, of Antoine Lepinar. By Tryntje Rutgers.

Aalbert, of Jan Van Loon. Wit.: Zybrand Van Schayk. By Tryntje Melchertsz.

Nov. 21. Helena, of Jacob Sandersz Glen. Wit.: father, Robbert Sandersz. By Jannetje Dongues.

Dec., 16. Petrus, of Livinus Winne. Wit.: Pieter Winne. By Mayken Martensz.

Dec. 23. Wynand, of Johannes Van Sant. Wit.: father, Wynand Gerritsz Van der Poel.

Dec. 25. Pieter, of Cornelis Stephensz Muller. Wit.: Pieter Lookerman, Chiliaan Van Renselaar. By Anna Van Renselaar.

Dec. 30. Bartholomeus, of Meuwis Hogenboom. Wit.: Chiliaan Van Renselaar. By Anna Van Renselaar.

1684

Jan. 6. Anna, of Caspar Leendertsz. Wit.: Adam Winne. By Tanne Winne.

Jan. 13. Johannes, of Hieronimus Wendell. Wit.: Evert Wendell, Bastiaan Harmensz. By Geertruy Harmensz.

Jan. 23. Weintje, of Johannes Kleyn. Wit.: Jan Gilbornsz. By Cornelia Gilbornsz.

Jan. 27. Johannes, of Johannes Beekman. Wit.: father, Hendrik Beekman. Pres. by Metje Beekman.

Feb. 3. Philippina Johanna, of Robbert Levingston. Wit.: father, David Schuyler, Arent Schuyler. By Engeltje Schuyler.

Johannes, of Jan Albertsz Bratt. By Martje Elbertsz.

Feb. 6. Cornelis, of Maas Cornelisz. Wit.: Albert Rykman. By Lysbeth Gardenier.

Feb. 13. Rachel, of Pieter Bogardus. Wit.: father, Dirk W. Ten Broek. By Elsje Ten Broek.

Feb. 20. Hendericus, of Johannes Byvang. By Margrietje Bleyker.

Feb. 24. Richardt, of Dirk Evertsz. Wit.: Richard Willemsz. By Lysbeth Douwe.

Thomas, of Harmen Livesz. Wit.: Andries Hansz. By Dirkje Thomasz.

March 2. Johannes, of Johannes Wendell. Wit.: father, Jacob Staats, Johannes Lansing. By Annetje Staats.

March 9. Isaac, of Douwe Jelisz. Wit.: Jacob Salomonsz. By Anna Renselaar.

March 23. Jurriaan, of Symon Schouten. Wit.: father, Johannes Wendell. By Margriet Schuyler.

Apr. 1. Susanna, of Phlip De Foreest. Wit.: father, Johannes Wendell. By Elizabeth Wendell.

Apr. 6. Brant, of Jacobus Jansz. Wit.: father. By Engeltje Melchertsz.

Apr. 13. Nicolaes, of Jacob Claesz Egmont. Wit.: father, Lucas Van Hooghkerken. By Antje Lucasz.

Samson, of Samson Bensing. Wit.: Robbert Martensz. By Weintje Harmensz.

Apr. 16. Christoffel, of Joseph Peth. Wit.: Jan Karten, Christoffel Cheef. By Anneken Marselis.

Apr. 20. Alida, of Cornelis Van Dyk. Wit.: for the father, Godefridus Dellius. Dirk W. Ten Brook. By Isabella Dellius.

Apr. 23. Andries, of Andries Jansz. Wit.: Andries Jansz. By Dorethee Folkersz.

Apr. 27. Christoffel, of Joseph Jedts. Wit.: father, Jan Karter. By Anneke Marselis.

May 7. Martje, of Wouter Quakelbosch. Wit.: father, Robbert Sandersz. By Nelletje Rykman.

1684

May 10. Geertruy, of Johannes Pietersz Quakelbosch. Wit.: father, Reinier Quakelbosch. By Martje Pietersz.

Barent, of Egbert Anthonisz. Wit.: Barent Bratt. By Antje Bratt.

May 17. Grietje, of Zacharias Sickels. Wit.: Lambert Van Valkenborg, Robbert Sickel. By Rachel Lambertsz.

Hester, of Bastiaan Harmensz. Wit.: Tjerk Harmensz. By Ariaantje Harmensz.

June 3. Nicolaes, of Jacob Teunisz. Wit.: Jan Thomasz, Claas Ripse Van Dam. By Maria Claasz.

June 21. Jacob, of Isaac Verplank. Wit.: father, Jacob Ten Eyk. By Ariaantje Verplank.

June 28. Neeltje, of Thomas Creeve. Wit.: Henderik Abelsz Riddenhaas. By Jannetje Laamme.

July 6. Dirk, of Corn. Scherluyn. Wit.: Johannes Scherluyn. By Hester Tjerks.

July 13. Elsie, of Robbert Sandersz. Wit.: father, Myndert Harmenszen Van den Bogaard, Arent Schuyler. By Elizabeth Wendell.

July 23. Johannes, of Simon Jacobsz Schermerhoorn. Wit.: father, Jacob Schermerhoorn, Jan Andriesz. By Gerritje Gertsz Vyle.

Aug. 10. Margriet, of Jan Andriesz Douw. Wit.: father, Wilhelm Appel, Willem Gysbertsz. By Anna Van Renselaar.

Aug. 24. Johannes, of Barent Jansz Wimp. Wit.: father, Sweer Teunisz. By Janneke Martens.

Aug. 31. Lidia, of Adam Winnen. Wit.: father, Marten G. Van Berge.

Sept. 7. Teunis, of Esaias. Wit.: father, Cornelis Teunisz. By Anna Maria Cornelisz.

Sept. 10. Andries, of Claes Van Petten. Wit.: father.

Sept. 14. Alida, of Jan Cloet. Wit.: father, Pieter D. Schuyler. By Margareta Schuyler.

Sept. 21. Abeltje, of Antoine Lepinar. By Tryntje Rutten.

Sept. 28. Claartje, of Christoffel. Wit.: Jacob Vosburg. By Eva Vroman.

Josyntje, of Adam Dingman. Wit.: father. By Jacomina Maasz.

Thomas, of Gabriel T. Stridles. Wit.: father, Cornelis Teunisz. By Elizabet Pritty.

Oct. 5. Philippus, of Pieter Schuyler. Wit.: father, Arent Schuyler, Levinus Van Schayk. By Margaretha Schuyler.

Gosen, of Anthony Van Schayk. Wit.: father, Sybrant Van Schayk. By Anna Van Schayk.

Oct. 15. Anna, of Pierre Villeroy. Wit.: father, Jacob Lookerman. By Gysje Van der Heyden.

1684–1685
Oct. 19. Jannetje, of Lucas Pietersz. Wit.: father, Maas Cornelisz. By Aaltje Gardeniers.

Jacob, of Isaac Caspersz. Wit.: Henderik Lansing. By Lysbeth Lansing.

Marietje, of Jonas Folkersz. Wit.: father, Henderik Martensz. By Dorethe Folkersz.

Nov. 2. Geertruy, of Johannes Lansing. Wit.: father, Henderik Lansing. By Gysbertje Roos.

Henderikje, of Jan Van Esch. Wit.: father, Henderik Oothout. By Jannetje Cobusz.

Nov. 9. Jochum, of Willem Kitteluym. Wit.: father, Wouter Van den Uythoft, Henderik Roosenboom. By Annetje Jochumsz.

Dec. 3. Saartje, of Jan Spoor. By Jacomyntje Maasz.

Johannes, of Pieter D. Schuyler. Wit.: father. Abraham Schuyler, Willem Claesz. By Maria Schuyler.

Dec. 7. Jannetje, of Takel Dirksz. Wit.: father, Jan Corn. Vyselaar, Jacob Lookerman. By Tryntje Lookerman.

Dec. 28. Rachel, of Matthys Hooghteeling. Wit.: father, Henderik Marselis. By Weinte Dirksz.

Tanne, of Caspar Leendertsz. Wit.: father, Phlip Leendertsz. By Maria Leendertsz.

1685, Jan. 1. Jacobus, of Jacobus Turk. By Catelyntje Paulusz.

Jan. 4. Gerrit, of Zybrant Van Schayk. Wit.: father, Johannis Lansing, Levinus Van Schayk. By Maria Van Schayk.

Grietje, of Gerrit Lubbertsz. By Rebecca.

Jan. 7. Tryntje, of Jochum Staats. Wit.: father, Levinus Van Schayk. By Rykje Staats.

Jan. 18. Johannes, of Meindert Harmensz Van den Bogaard. Wit.: father, Jacob Sandersz Glenn, Johannes Wendell. By Elsje Sanders.

Jan. 21. Jannetje, of Roeloff Gerritsz. Wit.: father, Jean Villette. By Lysbeth Jacobs.

Jan. 25. Josyntje, of Albert Jacobsz Gardenier. Wit.: Jan Salomonsz, Jacob Salomonsz. By Syntje Adams.

Feb. 1. Marretje, of Marten Jansz. Wit.: Jacob Ten Eyk. By Ariaantje.

Feb. 8. Johannes, of Andries Hansz. Wit.: Johannes Bekker. By Annetje Teunisz [?], Anna Bekker [?].

Feb. 15. Maria, of Lucas Gerritsz. Wit.: father. By Magteltje Jacobs.

March 1. Folkert, of Henderik Jansz Oothout. Wit.: Johannes Jansz Oothout. By Dorothee Folkertsz.

Marten, of Cornelis Van der Hoeven. By Susanna Barens.

1685

March 8. Magdalena, of Jacob Cornelisz Van den Bogaard. Wit.: father, Wouter Pietersz Quakelbosch. By Antje Pietersz Quakelbosch.

Marretje, of Cornelis Gysbertsz. Wit.: Willem Gysbertsz. By Margriet Gysbertsz.

March 15. Janneke, of Abraham Jansz. Wit.: Jacob Jansz. By Lysbeth Jacobsz.

March 22. Maria, of Evert Wendell. Wit.: father, Jeronimus Wendell. By Marretje Wendell.

Ulderik, of Gerrit Claesz. Wit.: Jan Vinhagel. By Barentje Schaats.

Abraham, of Johannes De Wandelaar. Wit.: father, Albert Rykman. By Sara Cuyler.

Apr. 17. Johannes, of Jacob Martensz. By Barentje Schaats.

Apr. 19. Dirk, of Phlip Leendertsz. Wit.: Michiel Dirksz. By Neeltje Dirks.

Heyltje, of Broer Jansz. Wit.: Jeames Parkar. By Maria Parkar.

Apr. 26. A ch. of Wessel Ten Broek. Wit.: father, Dirk W. Ten Broek, Jacob Lookerman. By Tryntje Lookerman.

Mayken, of Jacob Ten Eyk. Wit.: Johannes Roos. By Ariaantje Gardenier.

May 3. Anna, of Antoine Barroa. Wit.: father, Albert Rykman. By Jannetje Crygier.

Magdalena, of Melchert Abrahamsz Van Deursz. Wit.: father, Gysbert Cornelisz, Marten Cornelisz. By Caatje H. Oothout.

May 10. Johannes, of Antoni Van Slingerland. Wit.: Douw Jelisz, Johannes Appel. By Maria Jansz.

May 13. Magdalena, of Albert Rykman. Wit.: father, Henderik Beekman, Jacob Cornelisz. By Lysbeth Quakelbosch.

May 17. Gelyn, of Melckert Wynandsz Van der Poel. Wit.: father, Pieter D. Schuyler. By Tryntje Schuyler.

May 24. Maria, of Jan Gilbert. Wit.: father, Evert Wendell. By Lysbet Wendell.

June 3. Ephraim, of Johannes Wendell. Wit.: father, Godefridus Dellius, Phlip Wendell. By Lysbet Wendell.

July 3. Alida, of Henderik Lansing. Wit.: father, Wouter Van den Uythoff, Johannes Rosenboom. By Hilletje Kitteluym.

July 5. Marretje, of Gysbert Cornelisz. Wit.: Marten Jansz. By Tryntje Lookerman.

July 12. Willem, of Willem Gysbertsze. Wit.: Cornelis Gysbertsz, Johannes Van Sandt. By Margriet Wynandsz.

1685

July 26. Marten, of Livinus Winne. Wit.: Marten Cornelisz, Kiliaan Winnen. By Tanne Winne.

July 29. Jochum, of Andries Hansen. Wit.: Lambert Van Valkenborgh. By Anna Sachariasz.

Aug. 2. Ariaantje, of Willem Abrahamsz. Wit.: Jan Verbeek, Jacob Meesz. By Catelyntje Jacobsz.

Aug. 12. Jacobus, of Johannes Beekman. Wit.: father, Myndert H. Van den Bogaard. By Antje Beekman.

Aug. 16. Leendert, of Johannes Jansz. Wit.: Henderik Jansz. By Maria Gansevoort.

Aug. 26. Lysbeth, of Jan Salomonsz. Wit.: Gerrit Van Esch. By Anneken Adams.

Sept. 16. Cornelis, of Willem Rees. Wit.: Phlip Leendertsz. By Agnietje Henderiksz.

Abigael, of Cornelis Swarts. Wit.: Melchert Wynandsz. By Geertruy Schuyler.

Sept. 20. Willem, of Pieter Willemsz. Wit.: Willem Neefje. By Barentje Neefje.

Sept. 27. Margareta, of Arent Schuyler. Wit.: Andries Teller. By Margareta Schuyler.

Oct. 4. Margriet, of Hieronimus Hansz. Wit.: father, Wouter Aartsz.

Oct. 14. Jan, of Reyer Jacobsz Schermerhoorn. Wit.: Jacob Schermerhoorn, Meyndert H. Van den Bogaardt. By Helena Van den Bogaardt.

Oct. 18. Christina, of Adam Vrooman. Wit.: Robbert Sandersz. By Maria Sanders.

Oct. 21. Cateline, of Willem Groesbeek. Wit.: father, David Schuyler, Pieter D. Schuyler. By Cateline Schuyler.

Oct. 25. Jeane, of Godefridus Dellius. Wit.: Robert Levingston, Levinus Van Schayk. By Engeltje Schuyler.

Oct. 28. Cornelis, of Stephen Mulder. Wit.: Gerrit Van Esch. By Maria Van Esch.

Nov. 1. Johannes, of Jan Buys. Wit.: father, Symon De Groot. By Lysbeth Wendell.

Nov. 11. Neeltje, of Christiaan Christiaansz. Wit.: Jan Vinhagel. By Geertruy Scherluyn.

Nov. 15. Sander, of Jacobus Sandersz Glenn, deceased. Wit.: Sander Glen, Andries Jansz. By Elizabeth Van Trigh.

Mariken, of Johannes Bekker. Wit.: father, Willem Keteluyn. By Martina Bekker.

Nov. 22. Marie, of Jan Harris. Wit.: Robbert Sandersz. By Gerritje Vile.

Nov. 29. Anna, of Johannes Cuyler. Wit.: father, Henderik Cuyler, Dirk W. Ten Broek. By Anna Cuyler.

Olivier Stephen, of Andries Teller. Wit.: father, Willem Teller, Arent Schuyler. By Maria Van Renselaar.

1685–1686

Dec. 6. Anneken, of Gerrit Gysbertsz. Wit.: Pieter Schuyler. By Engeltje Schuyler.

Dec. 9. Livertje and Claas, twins, of Reinier Quakelbosch. Wit.: Jacob Vos. By Nelletje Rykman and Janneke Albertsz.

Dec. 13. Roeloff (bo. after his father's death), of Roelof Kersten. Wit.: Cornelis Gysbertsz. By Anna Van Schayk.

Dec. 20. Jan, of Maas Cornelisz. Wit.: father, Jan Gauw. By Ariaentje Lucasz.

Dec. 27. Jacob (bo. after his father's death), of Jacob Claesz. Wit.: Jacob Schermerhoorn. By Magtelt Beekman.

Jacob, of Jacob Schermerhoorn, Jr. Wit.: father, Jacob Schermerhoorn, Henderik Cornelisz. By Helena Van den Bogaard.

Marretje, of Lambert Jansz. Wit.: Jan Martensz. By Marritje Wendell.

1686, Jan. 1. Robbert, of Samson Bensing. Wit.: Mathys Jansz. By Cornelia Martensz.

Laurens, of Harme Jansz Van Bommel. Wit.: Antoni Van Schayk. By Marietje Van Schayk.

Jan. 10. Marie, of Piere Bogy. Wit.: father, Tam Greeve. By Emmetje Greeve.

Andries and Pieter, twins, of Jan Albertsz Bratt. Wit.: Antoni Bratt. By Annetje Bratt and Antje Cross.

Anna, of Jan Redly. Wit.: Jochum Lambertsz. By Marretje Zachariasz.

Jan. 20. Feytje, of Jacob Van der Slyk. By Sara Cuyler.

Rachel, of Jan Van Rotterdam. Wit.: Henderik Cuyler. By Anna Bakker.

Pieter, of Jan Pietersz. Wit.: Abraham Van Trigt. By Lysbeth Van Trigt.

Jan. 24. Sander, of Phlip Phlipsz. By Catryn Sanders.

Gerretje, of Benoni Arentsz. Wit.: Jacob Meesz Vrooman. By Aartje Arents.

Jan. 27. Johannes, of Jan Mangels. Wit.: Johannes Lansing. By Geertruy Lansing.

Jan. 31. Dirk, of Gabriel Tomesz Stridler. Wit.: Dirk Teunisz. By Anneke Cornelisz.

Feb. 3. Lysbeth, of Dirk Arents Bratt. Wit.: Evert Banker. By Elizabeth Banker.

Evert, of Dirk Evertsz. Wit.: Gerrit Arentsz. By Barentje Schaats.

Eva, of Dirk Bensing. Wit.: Leendert Phlipsz. By Lysbeth Harris.

Feb. 10. Gerrit, of Gysbert Marselis. Wit.: father, Gerrit Marselis. By Rebecca Claasz.

1686
Feb. 21. Antje, of Jan Bronk. Wit.: father. By Agnietje Phlipsz.

March 7. Susanna, of Henderik Beekman. Wit.: father, Albert Rykman. By Nelletje Rykman.

Gosen, of Gerrit Reyersz. Wit.: father. By Anna Van Schayk.

March 10. Henderik, of Henderik Oothout. Wit.: Henderik Van Esch. By Mayke Oothout.

March 17. Gerrit, of Jan Byvang. Wit.: Harme Rutgers. By Helena Byvang.

Jannetje, of Johannes Van Sant. Wit.: Gerrit Wynandsz, Abraham Isaacksz. By Catarina Van Sant.

Rebecca, of Douwe Jelisz. By Aaltje Everts.

March 21. Margriet, of Douwe Aukens. Wit.: Aarnout Vile, Symon Schermerhoorn. By Willemje Schermerhoorn.

March 28. Benjamin, of Egbert Teunisz. Wit.: Dirk Barentsz. By Anna Teunisz.

Apr. 2. Lea and Rachel, twins, of Anthoni Bratt. Wit.: Barent Brat, Egbert Teunisz. By Susanna Bratt and Egbertje Teunisz.

Baatje, of Johannes Klyn. By Willemje Vile.

Egbertje, of Harmen Livisz. By Anna Van Schayk..

Apr. 11. Jacomyntje, of Elias Van Gyseling. Wit.: father, Myndert Harmensz Van den Bogaardt.

Henderik, of Johannes Bleyker. Wit.: Cornelis Van Dyk, father. By Maria Vinhagel.

Barentje, of Frans Pruym. By Antje Pruym.

Apr. 14. Margriet, of Gosen Van Oort. Wit.: Symon Schermerhoorn. By Willemje Schermerhoorn.

Apr. 18. Jan, of Symon Schouten. Wit.: Jan Cloet. By Maria Teunisz.

Apr. 25. Margriet, of Samuel Arentsz Bratt. Wit.: father, Albert Rykman. By Helena Van de Bogaardt.

Apr. 28. Catelyntje, of Henderik Lambertsz. Wit.: Henderik Roosenboom. By Willemje Schermerhoorn.

Isaac, of Omi De la Grange. By Tryntje Rutte.

May 4. Johannes, of Tam Creeve. By Catryn Jacobsz.

May 9. Lysbeth, of Claas Laurentsz. Wit.: Jan Verbeek, Jacob Meesz Vrooman. By Barentje Schaats.

Johannes, of Jan Cornelisz Van der Hoeven. Wit.: Jonge Jan. By Maria Jansz.

May 23. Pieter, of Jacob Vosburg. Wit.: Lucas Pietersz Coeyman, father. By Marretje Martensz.

Willem, of Isaak Tjerks. Wit.: Johannes Wendell. By Elsje Lansing.

Marie, of Piere Vileroy. Wit.: Albert Rykman. By Cornelia Van der Heyde.

1686

May 30. Helena, of Abraham Van Trigt. Wit.: father, Arent Schuyler. By Jenneken Schuyler.

June 20. Neeltje, of Carel Hansz. Wit.: Jacob Schermerhoorn. By Geertruy Rinkhout.

Rachel, of Harmen Gansevoort. Wit.: Caspar Leendertsz. By Aaltje Winne.

July 2. Cornelis and Michiel, twins, of Christoffel Crussy. Wit.: Mathys Hooghteeling.

July 4. Isaac, of Jochum Van Valkenborg. Wit.: Jacob Vosburg. By Anna Jans.

July 14. Ludovicus, of Jacobus Peek. Wit.: father, Ludovicus Cobes. By Catarina Van Dam.

July 25. Philippus, of Robbert Levingston. Wit.: David Schuyler, Phlip Schuyler. By Cornelia Schuyler.

Metje, of Phlip Foreest. Wit.: Jesse Kip. By Ariaantje Jeremiasz.

Aug. 15. Grietje, of Gerrit Lubbertsz. By Rebecca Hieronimus.

Hester, of Cornelis Van Scherluyn. Wit.: Tjerk Harmensz. By Ariaantje Harmensz.

Aug. 18. Henderik, of Henderik Jacobsz. Wit.: Cornelis Van der Berg. By Cornelia Roos.

Jan, of Henderik Gerritsz. By Catelyn Van Elslandt.

Aug. 22. Elizabeth, of Cornelis Van Dyk. Wit.: father, Johannes Bleyker. By Elizabeth Wendell.

Sept. 12. Frederik, of Salomon Frederiksz. Wit.: father, Barent Salomonsz, Jacob Salomonsz. By Susanna Salomonsz.

Anna, of Pieter Schuyler. Wit.: father, David Schuyler, Robbert Levingston. By Margareta Van Schayk.

Sept. 19. Johanna, of Marten Krygier. Wit.: Robbert Levingston. By Anna Van Renselaar.

Hester, of Hieronimus Wendell. Wit.: father, Evert Wendell. By Elizabeth Wendell.

Dirkje, of Isaac Verplank. Wit.: David Schuyler. By Geertje Ten Eyk.

Oct. 10. Catelina, of Pieter D. Schuyler. Wit.: father, David Schuyler. By Margareta Schuyler.

Johannes, of Hans Jurriaanse. Wit.: Jan Verbeek. By Anne Marie.

Maria, of Bastiaan Harmensz. Wit.: Cornelis Scherluyn. By Marretje Harmensz.

Johannes, of Jan Andriesz Douw. Wit.: Johannes Appel. By Annetje Appels.

Oct. 24. Gerrit, of Jacob Jansz. By Aaltje Jacobsz.

Oct. 27. Tobias, of Albert Rykman. Wit.: Godefridus Dellius. By Isabella Dellius.

1686–1687

Nov. 7. Aarnout, of Symon Jacobsz Schermerhoorn. Wit.: father, Myndert H. Van den Bogaardt. By Helena Van den Bogaardt.

Johannes, of Jan Van Esch. Wit.: Symon Van Esch. By Antje Van Esch.

——, of Laurens Van Alen. Wit.: Isaac Verplank. By Sara De Wandelaar.

Frans, of Henderik Franse Clauw. Wit.: Frans Pietersz Clauw, Jan Cornelisz Van der Hoeven. By Neeltje Van der Hoeve.

Nov. 14. Jan, of Symon Jansz. Wit.: Wouter Quakelbosch. By Rebecca Douw.

Johanna, of Joseph ——. Wit.: Gysbert Marselis. By Zytje Marselis.

Nov. 21. Manasse and Ephraim, twins, of Dirk W. Ten Broek. Wit.: father, Wessel Ten Broek, Albert Rykman. By Catarina Ten Broek and Catalina Ten Broek.

Lucas, of Lucas Gerritsz. Wit.: father. By Lysbeth Lansing.

Nov. 24. Rachel, of Adam Winne. Wit.: Kiliaan Winne. By Lyntje Winne.

Dec. 5. Dirk, of Wessel Ten Broek. Wit.: father, Pieter Lookerman, Marten Cornelisz.

Dec. 15. Cornelis, of Meyndert H. Van den Bogaardt. Wit.: father, Henderik Cuyler. By Elizabeth Banker.

Dec. 25. Lysbeth, of Henricus Greefraad. Wit.: father, Robbert Sanders. By Elsje Sanders.

1687, Jan. 12. Catarina, of Roelof Gerritsz. Wit.: father, Jacob Jacobsz Van Oostrant. By Catryn Harmensz.

Jan. 16. Gerrit, of Adam Dingman. Wit.: Teunis Cool, father. By Marretje Teunisz.

Lucas, of Andries Jansz. Wit.: Melchior Abrahamsz. By Caatje Folkersz.

Folkert, of Jonas Folkensz. Wit.: Henderik Oothout. By Lysbet Pietersz.

Maria, of Jacob Martensz. By Marie Slingerlandt.

Jan. 23. Isaac, of Johannes Wendell. Wit.: father, Pieter Schuyler, Abraham Staats. By Elsje Lansing.

Feb. 6. Agnietje, of Phlip Leendertsz. Wit.: Gabriel Tomesz. By Maria Leendertsz.

Feb. 13. Magtelt, of Jan Quakelbosch. Wit.: father, Myndert H. Van den Bogaardt. By Folkje Pietersz.

Helena, of Jan Floddersz. Wit.: Jacob Abrahamsz, Maas Cornelisz. By Neeltje Martensz.

Feb. 23. Elsje, of Evert Wendell. Wit.: father, Henderik Greefraadt. By Ariaantje Wendell.

Anneke, of Lucas Lucasz. Wit.: Jan Henderiksz. By Anneke Lucasz.

1687

March 9. Jacobus, of Melchert Wynandsz. Wit.: Abraham Schuyler, father.

March 16. Elizabeth, of Jan Cloet. Wit.: father, Frederik Cloet. By Gysberte Roosenboom.

March 20. Leendert, of Caspar Leendertsz Conyn. Wit.: Leendert Phlipse Conyn, Kiliaan Winne. By Tanne Winne.

March 27. Lysbeth, of Albert Jacobsz. Wit.: Johannes Roos, Lambert Jansz. By Ariaantje Jacobsz.

Apr. 3. Sara, of Johannes De Wandelaar. Wit.: father, Godefridus Dellius, Abraham Cuyler. By Isabella Dellius.

Apr. 10. Agniet, of Cornelis Tomesz. Wit.: Johannes Tomesz. By Metje Martensz.

Apr. 17. Salomon, of Jan Salomonsz. Wit.: father, Adam Winne. By Marietje Van Esch.

Geertruy, of Claas Van Petten. Wit.: father, Jacob Staats. By Antje Staats.

Rutgert, of Jacob Tomisz. Wit.: Rutger Tomisz. By Geertruy Schuyler.

Apr. 24. Jan, of Andries Jansz. Wit.: father, Andries Jansz, Wouter Van den Uythoff. By Aaltje Jansz.

Marietje, of Isaac Casparsz. Wit.: Henderik Lansing. By Lysbet Violet.

May 1. Jacobus, of Jan Tysz. Wit.: father, Pieter Schuyler. By Engeltje Schuyler.

Johanna, of Benoni Van Corlar. Wit.: father, Teunis Corn. Van der Poel, Adriaan Gerritsz Papendorp. By Jannetje Van Papendorp.

May 5. Susanna, of Cornelis Van der Hoeve. Wit.: Johannes Beekman. By Dorethee Jansz.

Barent, of Antoni Bratt. Wit.: Teunis Teunisz, Egbert Teunisz. By Martina Teunisse.

May 8. Lea, of Zacharias Sikkels. Wit.: Lambert Van Valkenborg, Abraham Isaaksz. By Folkje Pietersz.

May 16. Johannes, of Jacobus Turk. Wit.: father, Paulus Martensz. By Elsje Sandersz.

Willem, of Willem Gysbertsz. Wit.: Gerrit Wynandsz By Catarina Van Santen.

May 22. Engeltje, of Melchert Abrahamsz. Wit.: father, Pieter Tomesz, Jonas Folkersz.

Jan, of Abraham Jansz. Wit.: father, Jean Violette. By Rebecca Douwe.

July 10. Henderik, of Pieter Barendsz Cool. Wit.: Adam Dingman, Teunis Barendsz Cool. By Aaltje Dingman.

July 17. Magdalena, of Michiel Cailljer. Wit.: Gabriel T. Stridles. By Cornelia Caillier.

1687

July 24. Storm, of Willem Kitteluym. Wit.: Henderik Lansing. By Anna Van der Zee.

Aug. 7. Jan, of Mattys Jansz Goes. Wit.: father, Jan Tysz Goes. By Styntje Goes.

Nicolaes, of Nicolaas Laurentsz. Wit.: Laurens Van Alen. By Sophia Van Wykersloot.

Aug. 14. Ephraim, of Pieter Bogardus. By Antje Staats.

Antoni, of Antoni Brockholt. Wit.: Arent Schuyler. By Maria Teller.

Aug. 28. Agniet, of Dirk Van der Heyden. Wit.: Willem Keteluym, Peter D. Schuyler. By Anna Van der Heyden.

Sept. 4. Johannes, of Johannes Lansing. Wit.: father, Levinus Van Schayk. By Margriet Van Schayk.

Sept. 11. Gerritje, of Antoni Van Schayk. Wit.: Adriaan G. Papendorp, Pieter Schuyler. By Geertje Lansing.

Daniel, of Libarté. Wit.: Jean Rogier. By Lysbeth Rogier.

Bata, of Livinus Winne. Wit.: Jacob Salomonsz. By Anna Lookerman.

Philippus, of Arent Schuyler. Wit.: Pieter Schuyler. By Maria Teller.

Barent, of Jan Bratt. Wit.: Barent Albertsz Bratt, Egbert Teunisz. By Susanna Jansz.

Sept. 18. Jacob, of Jacob Van den Bogaard. Wit.: father, Isaak Verplanck. By Marretje Hendriksz.

Sept. 25. Nathaniel, of Frerik Ellis. By Tryntje Melchertsz.

Susanna, of Johannes Beekman. Wit.: father, Symon Schermerhoorn. By Helena Van den Bogaard.

Christina, of Johannes Cuyler. Wit.: father, Abraham Cuyler. By Syntje Ten Broek.

Hans, of Pieter Willemsz. Wit.: Hieronimus Hansz. By Rebecca Everts.

Oct. 2. Cornelis, of Cornelis Gysbertsz. Wit.: Wouter Pietersz Quakelbosch. By Anna Van Schayk.

Geertje, of Marten Jansz. Wit.: Symon Van Esch. By Dirkje Lucasz.

Oct. 16. Abraham, of Isaac Vosburg. Wit.: Pieter Vosburg. By Marietje Vosburg.

Henderik, of Jacob Schermerhoorn. Wit.: father, Marte Cornelisz. By Marretje Martensz.

Oct. 30. Willem, of Samson Bensing. Wit.: Jacob Isaacs. By Margriet Rosenboom.

Nov. 13. Elizabeth, of Cornelis Swart. Wit.: Isaac Verplank. By Maria Schuyler.

1687–1688

——, of Michiel Dircksz. Wit.: father, Marten Gerritsz Van Bergen. By Engeltje Schuyler.

Nov. 27. Gerrit, of Marten Gerritsz. Wit.: Gabriel Tomesz. By Anna Van Renselaar.

Dec. 4. Jeremias, of Egbert Teunisz. Wit.: Gerrit Reyers. By Anna Van Renselaar.

Dec. 18. Adam, of Johannes Van Sante. Wit.: Jacob Abrahamsz. By Barentje Schaats.

Dorethee, of Henderik Oothout. Wit.: Gerrit Van Esch. By Tryntje Rutten.

Dec. 23. Jeane Alette, of Godefridus Dellius. Wit.: father, Pieter Schuyler.

1688, Jan. 8. Jacob, of Cornelis Stephensz. Wit.: father, Jacob Lookerman. By Marie Lookerman.

Willem, of Dirk Willemsz Van Slyk. Wit.: Jan Henderiksz Van den Bergh. By Geertje Willemsz.

Jan, of Symon Jansz. Wit.: Wouter Quakelbosch. By Neeltje Wouters.

Jan. 11. Margriet, of Jan Jacobsz Van Oostrant. Wit.: father, Jacob Van Oostrant. By Antje Van Oostrant.

Jan. 15. Isaac, of Joachim Staats. Wit.: father, Reinier Barentz. By Elizabeth Banker.

Jan. 25. Arent, of Dirk Evertsz. Wit.: father, Wouter Quakelbosch. By Lysbeth Gerritsz.

Feb. 12. Gerardus, of Evert Banker. Wit.: father, Adriaan G. Papendorp, Johannes Abeel. By Elizabeth Banker.

Maria, of Jan Byvang. Wit.: Johannes Hooghlandt. By Eva Vinhagel.

Feb. 19. Jacob, of Maas Cornelisz. By Dirkje Lucasz.

March 4. Rebecca, of Gerrit Lubbertsz. Wit.: father, Douwe Jelisz. By Jannatje Martensz.

March 11. Maria, of Robbert Sikkels. Wit.: father, Hendrik A. Riddenhaas. By Maria Sikkels.

Cornelis, of Andries Hansz Huyg. Wit.: Lambert Van Valkenborg. By Judik Verwey.

March 14. Isaac, of Abraham Isaaksz. Wit.: Johannes Van Sante. By Marretje Lambertsz.

March 18. Pieter, of Wouter Quakelbosch. Wit.: father, Douwe Jelisz. By Rebecca Douwe.

March 25. Andries, of Jacob Ten Eyk. Wit.: Andries Coeman. By Elsje Cuyler.

March 29. Geertruy, of Jan Van der Hoeve. Wit.: Johannes Mingaal. By Tryntje Rykman.

May 6. Cornelia, of Johannes Roos. Wit.: Jacob Ten Eyk. By Maria Schuyler.

May 24. Arent, of Frans Pruyn. By Anna Pruyn.

1688

June 4. Barent, of Gerrit Reyersz. Wit.: father. By Anna Van Schayk.

June 10. Janneke, of Dirk Van der Kerre. Wit.: Benoni Van Corlar. By Lysbeth Cailjer.

June 17. David, of Willem Claasz Croesbeck. Wit.: David Schuyler, Abraham Schuyler. By Catryn Jacobsz.

July 8. Engel, of Henderik Fransen. Wit.: Andries Hansz. By Dorothea Jansz.

July 15. Rykert, of Jan Redly. Wit.: Abraham Isaaksz. By Judik Verway.

Gerrit, of Gerrit Gysbertsz. Wit.: Wouter Pietersz Quakelbosch. By Sara Henderiksz.

July 29. Robbert, of Robbert Levingston. Wit.: Johannes Schuyler. By Margareta Schuyler.

Tileman, of Cornelis Scherluyn. Wit.: Frederik Harmensz. By Hester Harmansz.

Aug. 22. Ytje, of Jacob Martensz. Wit.: father. By Annetje Vosburg.

Thomas, of Lambert Jansz. Wit.: Pieter Thomasz Mingaal, father. By Dorothea Jansz.

Sept. 2. Cornelis, of Harmen Jansz. Wit.: father, Jacob Cornelisz. By Jannetje Jacobsz.

Sept. 30. Johannes, of Roeloff Gerritsz. Wit.: father, Harme Livisz. By Lysbeth Violet.

Elizabeth, of Myndert Harmensz Van den Bogaardt. Wit.: father, Evert Banker. By Elizabeth Pritty.

Oct. 7. Anneke, of Adam Winne. Wit.: Wessel Ten Broek. By Anna Van Renselaar.

Cateline, of Johannes Bensing. Wit.: Jacob De Cuyper. By Caatje Melchertsz.

Oct. 10. Christina, of Omi De la Grange. Wit.: Johannes Lansing. By Cornelia Croesvelt.

Oct. 28. Jacob, of Isaac Verplank. Wit.: Jacob Ten Eyk, the father. By Ariaante Van der Poel.

Nov. 11. Pieter, of Jan Bratt. Wit.: Johannes Appel. By —— Appel.

Robbert, of —— Jedts. By Judik Marselisz.

Isaac and Sara, twins of Johannes Wendell. Wit.: father, also Meyndert Wimp and Abraham Staats for the son, Samuel Staats for the daughter. By Diwertje Wimp and Jannetje Staats.

Nov. 14. Rachel, of Johannes Bleyker. Wit.: father, Godefridus Dellius. By Catarina Bleyker.

Nov. 18. Isaac, of Abraham Kip. Wit.: father, Dirk Van der Heyden. By Tryntje Foreest.

Dec. 26. David, of Pieter D. Schuyler. Wit.: father, David Schuyler, Wouter Van den Uythoff. By Catelina Schuyler.

1688–1689

Dec. 30. Susanna, of Dirk B. Bratt. Wit.: Egbert Teunisz. By Marretje Egbertsz.

1689, Jan. 1. Anna, of Dirk Van der Heyden. Wit.: Johannes Van der Heyden, David Keteluyn. By Cornelia Van der Heyden.

Jan. 13. Helena, of Johannes Beekman. Wit.: father, Jacob Schermerhoorn. By Wilmje Schermerhoorn.

Jan. 20. Elizabeth, of Gerrit Lansing. Wit.: father, Wouter Van den Uythoff. By Gysbertje Roosenboom.

Susanna, of Egbert Teunisz. Wit.: father, Gerrit Reyersz. By Susanna Bratt.

Jan. 23. Harmanus, of Nanning Harmensz Visser. Wit.: father, Harmen Bastiaansz. By Marretje Vinhagel.

Hilletje, of Johannes Becker. Wit.: Wouter Van den Uythoff. By Hilletje Keteluyn.

Jan. 27. Antje, of Phlip Leendertsz. Wit.: Pieter Winn.

Feb. 6. Laurens, of Laurens Van Alen. Wit.: father, Gerrit Van Esch. By Catarina Van Alen.

Feb. 17. Ephraim, of Evert Wendell. Wit.: father, Phlip Wendell. By Sara Greefraadt.

Feb. 20. Hilletje, of Jan Salomonsz. Wit.: father, Wessel Ten Broek. By Tryntje Lookerman.

Isaac, of Phlip Foreest. Wit.: father, Frederik Hansz. By Geesje Kip.

Tobias, of Dirk W. Ten Broek. Wit.: father, Johannes Cuyler. By Catarina Ten Broek.

Feb. 24. Barent, of Salomon Frederiksz Bouw. Wit.: Antoni Bratt. By Wilmpje Tomesz.

March 3. Neeltje, of Evert Banker. Wit.: father, Johannes Abeel. By Annetje Papendorp.

Maria, of Jan Van Esch. Wit.: Gerrit Van Esch. By Catarina Van Esch.

March 17. Arent, of Dirk Evertsz. Wit.: father, Johannes Paulusz. By Jannetje Paulusz.

Henderik, of Henderik Gerritsz Verwey. By Rykje Staats.

March 24. Eytje, of Pieter Jansz Bosch. Wit.: father, Pieter Vosburg. By Jannetje Vosburg.

Magdalena, of Albert Rykman. Wit.: father, Pieter Schuyler. By Engeltje Schuyler.

March 29. Jacobus, of Pierre Vileroy. Wit.: Abraham Kip, Dirk Van der Heyden. By Celle Van der Heyden.

Jacobus, of Johannes Roos. Wit.: Jacob Ten Eyk. By Maria Van Dyk.

Apr. 4. Jacob, of Jochum Lammertsz. Wit.: father, Jan Tysz. By Styntje Jansz.

Geertruy, of Isaak Vosburg. Wit.: father, Pieter Vosburg. By Jannetje Vosburg.

1689
Apr. 7. Willem, of Jan Harris. Wit.: Harmen Tomesz. By Catarina Borger.

Apr. 14. Annetje, of Evert De Ridder. Wit.: father, Henderik Van Esch. By Catarina Van Esch.

Apr. 21. Rachel, of Dirk Bensing. Wit.: Jan Harris. By Weyntje Harmensz.

Apr. 28. Jonas, of Jan Bronk. Wit.: father, Henderik Bries. By Marretje Bries.

Elsje, of Hieronimus Wendell. Wit.: father, Gerrit Lansing, Meyndert Wimp. By Diwer Wimp.

May 12. Elizabeth, of Gabriel T. Stridley. Wit.: father, Henderik Van Dyk. By Elizabeth Pritty.

Jan, of Jan Jacobsz Gardenier. Wit : Maas Cornelisz. By Rebecca Jeroons.

Angenetie, of Caspar Leendertsz Conyn. Wit.: Leendert Phlipsz, Pieter Winne. By Tanne Winne.

May 19. Dorethee, of Jurriaan Cailljer. Wit.: Jan Corn Oeff. By Cornelia Cailljer.

Gysbertje, of Leendert Arentsz Grauw. Wit.: father, Pieter Willemsz Van Slyk. By Barentje Willemsz VanSlyk.

June 2. Lidia, of Henderik Beekman. Wit.: father, Reinier Quakelbosch. By Susanna Jansz.

Henderik, of Melchert Wynandsz Van der Poel. Wit.: father, Gerrit Wynandsz. By Catryn Van Santen.

Elsje, of Jan Andriesz Douw. Wit.: Adriaan Appel, Teunis Slingerlandt. By Catryn Van der Poel.

June 16. Alida, of Jacobus Turk. Wit.: father, Marten Van Benthuysen. By Maria Sandersz.

Johannes, of Tam Creeve. Wit.: father, Isaac Verplank. By Margriet Van Santen.

Isaac, of Jacob Vosburg. Wit.: father, Marten Jansz. By Jannetje Lambertsz.

June 22. Geertruy, of Maes Cornelisz. Wit.: father, Gerrit Reyersz. By Dirkje Koeman.

June 30. Folkje, of Frerik Gerritsz. Wit.: father, Henderik Bries. By Maria Bries.

Annetje, of Gysbert Marselisz. Wit.: father, Jacob Teunisz. By Geertruy Croesbeek.

Evert, of Phlip Wendell. Wit.: father, Evert Wendell, Harme Bastiaansz.

Hilletje, of Andries Jansz. Wit.: father, Jan Andriesz, Wouter Van den Uythoff. By Aaltje Jansz.

Jonathan, of Henderik Reydt. Wit.: Henderik Lansing. By Antje Verwey.

July 14. Abraham, of Evert Jansz. Wit.: Melchert Wynandsz. By Albertje Van Alen.

Abraham, of Melchert Abrahamsz. Wit.: father, Johannes Bleyker. By Caatje Bleyker.

48

1689

Aug. 4. Henderik, of Johannes Rosenboom. Wit.: father, Henderik Rosenboom. By Geertruy Lansing.

Gerardus, of Jan Cloet. Wit.: Frederik Cloet. By Alida Levingston.

Aug. 11. Jannetje, of Joseph Jansz. Wit.: father, Marselis Jansz. By Jannetje Marselis.

Aug. 17. Geertruy, of Pieter Schuyler. Wit.: father, Stephanus Van Cortlant, Livinus Van Schayk. By Alida Levingston.

Catarina, of Johannes De Wandelaar. Wit.: father, Johannes Cuyler. By Elsje Cuyler.

Aug. 25. Anna, of Tomas Weekfilt. Wit., Jan Gilbert.

Johannes, of Cornelis Van der Hoeve (dec^d). Wit.: Johannes Van der Hoeve. By Cornelia Cailljer.

Sept. 1. Dorethee, of Jonas Folkersz. Wit.: father, Albert Rykman. By Caatje H. Oothout.

Meyndert, of Marte G. Van Bergen. Wit.: Claas Siwers, the father. By Neeltje Cornelisz.

Sept. 8. Jacob, of Abraham Jansz. Wit.: father, Roeloff Gerritsz. By Agniet Jansz.

Tryntje, of Joachim Staats. Wit.: father, Jacob Staats, Reinier Barents. By Elizabeth Banker.

Agniet, of François Gaignon. Wit.: father, Helmert Jansz. By Agniet Jansz.

Sept. 15. Claas, of Ryn Pietersz Quakelbosch. Wit.: father, Henderik Beekman. By Nelletje Woutersz.

Sept. 22. Cornelis, of Jacob Schermerhoorn. Wit.: father, Cornelis Schermerhoorn. By Marretje Henderiksz.

Pieter, of Jacob Van den Bogaard. Wit.: father, Henderik Cornelisz. By Tryntje Rykman.

Oct. 6. Jan, of Barent Gerritsz. Wit.: father, Huybert Gerritsz. By Caatje Sandersz.

Maria, of Arent Schuyler. Wit.: father, Nicolaes Beyer. By Judith Beyer.

Oct. 13. Catarina, of Willem Gysbertsz. Wit.: Jan Van Sant, Gerrit Wynandsz. By Catarina Van Sant.

Elizabeth, of Samson Bensing. Wit.: Reynier Schaats, Ruth Melchertsz. By Agniet Leendertsz.

Geertruy, of Andries Hansz. Wit.: Lucas Jansz. By Grietje Folkersz.

Oct. 20. Christina, of Wessel Ten Broek. Wit.: Jacob Lookerman, Johannes Cuyler. By Styntje Wessels.

Oct. 27. Maria, of Lucas Lucasz. Wit.: Helmer Jansz. By Dorethee Jansz.

Nov. 10. Engeltje, of Arent Slingerlandt. Wit.: father, Antoni Van Slingerlandt, Jacobus Gerritsz Van Vorst. By Geertruy Slingerlandt.

1689–1690

Nov. 17. Henderik, of Coenraad Hoogteeling. Wit.: Henderik Marselis. By Zeytje Hoogteeling.

Cornelis, of Henderik Van Dyk. Wit.: father, David Schuyler. By Catalina Schuyler.

Dec. 1. Folkert, of Cornelis Vile. Wit.: Aarnout Vile. By Ariaantje Wendel.

Dec. 4. Christina, of Johannes Cuyler. Wit.: father, Abraham Cuyler, Wessel Ten Broek. By Caatje Ten Broek.

Maria, of Nanning Harmensz. Wit.: father, Johannis Vinhagel. By Hester Harmensz.

Margriet, of Robbert Berrit. Wit.: Willem ——. By Anneke Kros.

Dec. 15. Pieter, by Harmen Livisz. Wit.: father, Pieter Schuyler. By Jannetje Davids.

Dec. 27. Paulus. After a previous public confession was baptized a certain heathen who had become blind a number of years ago, and whose name among his nation had been Ock-Kweese. He is about 40 years old, and the name Paulus was given to him. The interpreters of the confession were Aarnout Cornelisz Vile and Hilletje Cornelisz.

1690, Jan. 8. Barbar, of Albert Gardenier. Wit.: Andries Gardenier, Jan Byvang. By Helena Byvang.

Ariaantje, of Dirk Van der Kerre. Wit.: Johannes Abeel. By Jannetje Papendorp.

Jan. 12. Storm, of Jan Bratt. Wit.: father, Antoni Bries. By Antje Becker.

Jan. 26. Jonathan, of Andries Rees. Wit.: Dirk Ten Broek. By Styntje Ten Broek.

Dirk, of Michiel Dirksz Van Vegten. Wit.: father, Jeames Parker. By Alida Levingston.

Feb. 2. Anna, of Douwe Jelisz. Wit.: father, Teunis Slingerlandt. By Hester Jansz.

Lysbeth, of Pieter Van Slyk. Wit.: Leendert Arentsz. By Elizabeth Pritty.

Feb. 5. Lidia, of Marte Jansz. Wit.: father, Jacob Vosburg. By Marietje Vosburg.

Feb. 12. Catarina, of Mathieu Beaufils. Wit.: father, Henderik Lansing. By Lysbeth Lansing.

Marie, of Abraham Isaacksz. Wit.: Gerrit Wynandsz. By Catryn Van Sante.

Feb. 16. Marretje, of Gerrit Claasz. Wit.: father. By Caatje Cuyler.

Teunis, of Antoni Bratt. Wit.: father, Egbert Teunisz. By Susanna Bratt.

Feb. 23. Claas, of Cornelis Dykman. Wit.: father. By Ariaantje Melchertsz.

4

1690

Feb. 26. Lucas, of Cornelis Teunisz Van Vegten. Wit.: father, Gabriel T. Stridles. By Anna Helmertsz.

March 2. Isaac, of Isaac Ter Jeuks. Wit.: Hieronimus Wendell. By Elizabeth Wendell.

Jacob, of Symon Schouten. Wit.: father, Jacob Staats. By Elizabeth Wendell [sic].

March 5. Gysbert, of Robbert Levingston. Wit. Godefridus Dellius, Livinus Van Schayk. By Jenneken Schuyler.

March 9. Johannes, of Cornelis Stephensz. Wit.: father, Henderik Van Renselaar. By Sophia Teller.

Matheus, of Tys Jansz. Wit.: Thomas Winne. By Tryntje Winne.

March 12. Marietje, of Henderik Oothout. Wit.: father, Andries Volkersz Douwe. By Jannetje Cobusz.

March 23. Abraham, of Jan Pietersz Quakelbosch. Wit.: father, Myndert Harmensz. By Rebecca Douwe.

Dirk, of Samuel Gardenier. Wit.: Maas Cornelisz. By Cornelia Roos.

Matthys, of Cornelis Gysbertsz. Wit.: father, Antoni Van Schayk. By Maria Van Schayk.

Apr. 6. Claas, of Claas Van Petten. Wit.: father, Jochum Staats. By Catelyn Van Petten.

Apr. 13. Jannetje, of Jacobus Isaacsz. Wit : father, Jan Harris, Abraham Isaacsz. By Lysbeth Harris.

Apr. 27. Nicolaas, of Jan Weyer. Wit.: father. By Pietertje Fransz.

Marietje, of Dirk Willemsz. Wit.: father, Pieter Willemsz Slyk. By Henderikje Lucasz.

Geertruy, of Cornelis Swart. Wit.: father, Adam Swart. By Abigael Verplank.

May 4. Pieter, of Frans Winnen. Wit.: father, Pieter Winnen. By Agnietje Leendertsz.

May 11. Johannes, of Johannes Dykman. Wit.: father. By Folkje Barentsz.

Emmetje, of Lucas Jansz. Wit.: father, Cornelis Teuisz. By Hilletje Cornelisz.

Geraldus, of Geraldus Canfoort. Wit.: Leendert Claasz. By Catryn Jansz.

May 16. Margriette, of Christoffel Brussy. By Ariaantje Wendell.

Willem, of Gosen Van Oort. Wit.: father, Johannes De Wandelaar. By Marietje Van Esch.

May 18. Ariaantje, of Claas Laurensz. Wit.: father, Jacob M. Vrooman. By Antje Sanders.

Pieter, of Thomas Winne. Wit.: Pieter Winne. By Marietje Van Esch.

June 8. Sander, of Jan Jansz Van Rotterdam. Wit.: Sander Glenn, Jan Pirot. By Diwer Wimp.

1690

Jochum, of Michiel Cailjer. Wit.: Thomas Winnen By Judic Jansz.

June 22. Louys, of Gerrit Jansz Ruyting. Wit.: father. By Elsje Cuyler.

July 11. These following persons, after having been instructed in the Christian religion and having made, on the before-mentioned date, a public confession in the church of N. A., were ba.:

A heathen called among his people Swongara, i. e., Little Board, aged about 40 years, now called David.

A heathen woman, the wife of Swongara, now David, called among her people Kowajatense, about 30 years old, now called Rebecca.

Tekaniadaroge, that means Division of the wax [?], (lack-scheydinge), old about 22 years, now called Isac.

Tejonihokarawa, i. e., Open the door, about 30 years old, now called Henderick.

A heathen woman, Karanondo, i. e., Lifter [opligster, which may also mean sharper], about 50 years old, now called Lidia.

A ch. 12 years old, of whom this Karanondo, now Lydia, is the grandmother, and who, after the ch.'s mother (her daughter) died, adopted him as her own. The name of this ch. among its people was Kaadsjihandasa, i. e., Runner from the fire (* vier-uyt loper), now called Seth.

A heathen woman, Sion heja, i. e., Lively, about 25 years old, now called Rachel.

Her husband was ba. by the Jesuits and called Joseph, but was thereafter instructed by us in the faith of J. C. His name among his people was Skanjodowanne, i. e., Eagle's beak.

Their ch. about 4 years old was also ba. and called Manasse.

Two chn. of Kanastasis. This woman was thus called at her baptism by the Jesuits, but thereafter was instructed by us in the Christian religion. Her husband is dead. The oldest ch., about 8 years old, was called Jacob, and the youngest, about 3 years old, was named Sara.

A ch., 12 years old, called among its people Sagonorasse, i. e., Fastener (Vast-binder), whose parents are dead. He was adopted by his relatives, Laurens and Maria (who have been admitted to the Lord's holy and high-worthy Supper) and who promised to have him educated in the doctrines of Christ. He was named Adam.

July 13. Johannes, of Robbert Teuisz. Wit.: father, Marte Cornelisz, Teuis Abrahamsz. By Marritie Martensz.

---

* Vier at present is the numeral *four* in Dutch, but two centuries ago meant also *fire;* at present it is written vuur.

1690

July 20. Lidia, of Harmen Gansevoort. Wit.: Dirk Bensing. By Weintje Phlipsz.

July 27. Sophia, of Robbert Sikkels. Wit.: father, Lambert Van Valkenborch. By Sophia Riddenhaas.

Neeltje, of Daniel Jansz (sick). Wit.: Johannes Bekker in place of father. By Ariaantje Wendell.

Aug. 3. Johannes, of Johannes Van Santen (absent). Wit.: Henderik Bries, representing father. By Geertruy Ten Broek.

Pieter, of Isac Vosburg. Wit.: father, Jan Tysz. By Styntje Jansz.

Tobias, of Cornelis Martensz. Wit.: father, Marten Cornelisz, Albert Rykman. By Marritje Martensz.

Jacobus, of Dirk Van der Heyden (absent). Wit.: Abraham Kip, for father. By Anna Keteluym.

Aug. 6. Were ba. the following persons, after having been instructed by us in the Christian religion and having made, on the before-mentioned date, a public confession in the church at Albany:

A widow from the heathen, about 60 years old, named among her nation Kwaowarate, i. e., Transition or Passage (Overgang), but now called Lea.

A widow from the heathen, about 40 years old, named among her nation Wanika, i. e., Loaned, but now called Iosine. She is the sister of Lea. The dau. of this Iosine, about 9 years old, was also ba. and called Jakomine. The son of Josine, about 7 years old, was also ba. and called Josua.

A married heathen woman, whose husband was ba. on the 11 and called Isak. She is about 16 years old and the dau. of Lea. Among her nation she was called Karehodongwas, i. e., a Plucker of trees (Boomplukster), but now named Eunice. Her son, about 9 months old, was now likewise ba. and called Simon.

A married heathen woman, about 30 years old (but her husband has not yet been ba.), the dau. of Lea, called among her nation Karehojenda—Fallen tree,—and now named Alida.

The interpreter at the Confession was Hilletje Cornelisz.

Aug. 10. Marietje, of Symon Jansz Post. Wit.: father. By Nelletje Quakelbosch.

Catarina, of Meindert H. Van den Bogaardt. Wit.: father, Jacob Staats. By Caatje Cuyler.

Aug. 17. Engeltje, of Johannis Lansing. Wit.: father. By Gerritje Rosenboom.

December. Lysbet, of Henderik and Catarina, both proselytes from among the heathen, and after previous instruction and confession bapt. in the church at A.

1691–1692

1691, Apr. 30. Petrus, of Pieter Bogardus and Wyntje Corn. Bosch. Wit.: Catarina Van Renselaar.

May. Pieter, of Jan Salomonsz and Caatje Lookerman. Wit.: Hendrik Van Renselaar, Maritje Lookerman.

May 22. Willem, of Claas Willemsz and Lea. Wit.: Harme Vedder, Divertje Wimp.

May 31. Caspar, of Jacob Casparsz and Henderikje Dreeper. Wit.: Gerrit Lansing, Marietje Lansing.

June 1. Maria, of Joseph and Rachel, proselytes. Wit.: Laurens and Rebecca.

June 7. Styntje, of Frerik Gerritsz and Lysbeth Carstersz. Wit.: Claes Teunisz, Gillis Gerritsz.

Annetje, of Jan Wibesz and Anne Marie. Wit.: Rebecca Douwe.

Lysbeth, of Frans Merrit and Zytje Mathysz. Wit.: Henderik Marselis, Tryntje Rutgers.

June 14. Gerardus, of Evert Banker and Elizabeth Abeel. Wit.: Abraham De Peister, Johannes De Peister, Elizabeth Banker.

June 21. Engeltje, of Arent Slingerlant and Geertruy Van Vorst. Wit.: Johannes Appel, Teunis Slingerlant, Anna Appel.

June 28. Isaak, of Joachim Staats and Antje Barens. Wit.: Reinier Barens, Wyntje Bogardus.

Pieter, of Caspar Leendertsz and Aletta Winnen. Wit.: Livinus Winne, Lyntje Winne.

July 5. Henry, of Laurens and Maria, proselytes. Governor Henry Slougter was his godfather.

July 12. Geertruy, of Tjerk Harmensz and Femmetje Jans. Wit.: Johannes Harmensz, Marietje Harmensz.

July 28. Isaak, of Isack Swits and Susanna Groot. Wit.: Elisabeth Banker.

Aug. 4. Jan, of Pieter Jansz Bosch and Susanna Barents. Wit.: Jan.P. Bosch, Jannetje Barents.

Isaac, of Claas Graaf and Lysbet Willemsz. Wit.: Tjerk Harmens, Lysbet Rinkhout.

Johannes, of Johannes Bekker and Anna Van der Zee. Wit.: Johannes Bekker, Martina Bekker.

Wouter, of Jeronimus Hansz and Rebecca Evertsz. Wit.: Douwe Jelisz, Aaltje Evertsz.

Aug. 11. Daniel, of Carel Hansz and Lysbeth Rinkhout. Wit.: Gysbert Merselis, Caatje Cuyler.

Willem, of Willem Barent and Lysbet Sikkels. Wit.: Anna Sikkels.

Jacobus, of Johannes Wendell and Elizabeth Staats. Wit.: Reinier Barent, Susanna Teller.

Aug. 17. Johannes, of Lambert Jansz and Jannatje Mingal. Wit.: Johannes T. Mingal, Jannetje Mingal.

1691–1692

Gerrit, of Evert Ridder and Anna Van Esch. Wit.: Gerrit Van Esch, Aaltje Van Esch.

Aug. 24. Meindert, of Barent Wimp and Folkje Symensz. Wit.: Johannes Wendell, Caatje Sandersz.

Sept. 6. Lambert and Margerite, twins of Jean Ratli and Rachel Van Valkenbork. Wit.: Jean Gilbert, Abr. Isaaksz, Anna Abramsz, Judik Verwey.

Willem, of Jean Harris and Lysbeth Claasz. Wit.: M⁺ Kint, Benoni Van Corlar, Lysbeth Van der Poel.

Emmetje, of Piere Bogi and Emmetje Claasz. Wit.: Abraham Schuyler, Tryntje Rykman.

Sept. 13. Marretje, of Wouter Quakelbosch and Neeltje Gysbertsz. Wit.: Elbert Gerritsz and Annetje Gerritsz.

Sept. 20. Phlip, of Jan Bronk and Commertje Leendertsz. Wit.: Dirk Teunisz, Anna Gansevoort.

Catelyntje, of Melchert Abrahamsz and Engeltje Rutgertsz. Wit.: Herbert Abrahamsz, Jannetje Blyker.

Oct. 11. Cornelia, of Jan Gardenier and Sara Van Bremen. Wit.: Jacob Ten Eyk, Aaltje Oothout.

Wynand, of Gerrit Wynandsz Van der Poel and Catryn Van Sant. Wit.: Wynand Gertsz, Johannes Van Sant, Margriet Van Sant.

Oct. 18. Gerrit, of Barent Gerritsz and Geertruy Jansz. Wit.: Cornelis Gerritsz and Ariaantje Gerritsz.

Johannes, of Cornelis Stephensz and Hilletje Lookerman. Wit.: Henderik V. Renselaar, Sophia Teller.

Oct. 23. Jacobus, of Laurens Van Alen and Elbertje Evertsz. Wit.: Johannes Van Alen, Catrina Van Alen.

Oct. 25. Rebecca, of Arent Vedder, and Sara Groot. Wit.: Phlip Foreest, Rebecca Groot.

Meindert, of Elias Van Gyseling and Tryntje Claasz. Wit.: Johannes Beekman, Symen Schermerhoorn, Helena Van den Bogaardt.

Anna, a heathen woman, was bapt. after previous instruction in the mysteries of the faith and after a public confession. She is about 21 years old, and was named among her own nation Skonwakwani.

Nov. 1. Mattheus, of Robbert Teuwisz and Cornelia Martensz. Wit.: Pieter Martensz, Catelyntje Jacobsz.

Dec. 6. Gerretje, of Egbert Teunisz and Marritje Barentsz. Wit.: Harmen Livisz, Martyn Teunisz.

Dec. 13. Tymen, of Cornelis Tymesz and Marretje Ysbrants. Wit.: Geertje Lansing.

Dec. 16. Sara, of Esias Teunisz Swart and Eva Teunisz. Wit.: Wouter Van den Uythof, Mari Van Dam.

Dec. 20. Anna, of Abraham Kip and Geesje Van der Heyden. Wit.: Phlip Foreest, Anna Van der Heyden.

1691–1692
Geertje, of Cornelis Gysbertsz and Cornelia Wynandsz. Wit.: Ariaantje Cornelisz.
Dec. 26. Jan, of Henderik Jansz and Lyntje Winnen. Wit.: Live Winnen and Geertruy Jansz.
Dec. 27. Marie, of Christoffel Brussi and Christine Claasz. Wit.: Cornelis Scherluyn, Ariaantje Wendell.
1692, Jan. 1. Catarine, of Henderik V. Renselaar and Catarine Verbrugge. Wit.: Pieter Verbrugge, Maria Schuyler.
Jacobus, of Johannes Sandersz and Diwer Wendell. Wit.: Gerrit Lansing, Marritje Wendell.
Andries, of Andries Jansz, and Engeltje Folkersz. Wit.: Jonas Folkersz, Tryntje Rutger.
Elisabeth, of Roelof Gerritsz and Geertruy Jacobsz. Wit.: Jan Jacobsz, Lysbeth Regi.
Jan. 3. Machtelt, of Jacob Schermerhoorn and Geertje Henderiksz. Wit.: Johannes Beekman, Jannetje Schermerhoorn.
Lidia, of Brechje. Wit., Eytje Pietersz.
Jan. 6. Cornelis, of Harmen Jansz and Lysbet Jansz. Wit.: Takel Dirksz, Aaltje Van Esch.
Jan. 10. Henderik, of Johannes Cuyler and Elsje Ten Broek. Wit.: Abraham Schuyler, Sara Verbrugge.
Sacharias, of Abraham Isaksz and Anna Sikkel. Wit.: Isak Isaksz, Catelyntje Abramsz.
Reinier, of Folkert Van Hoesen and Marietje Bensing. Wit.: Gerrit Teunisz, Tryntje Schaats.
Jan. 13. Rachel, of Harmen Livesz and Marretje Teunisz. Wit.: Engeltje Harmensz.
Jesse, of Phlip Foreest and Tryntje Kip. Wit.: Johannes Kip, Elsje Lansing.
Jan. 17. Willem, of Coenraadt Hooghteling and Tryntje Van Slyk. Wit.: Pieter V. Slyk, Metje V. Slyk.
Gerrigje, of Franc Hardig and Catrine Jansz. Wit.: Gerrit Lucasz, Claas Lucasz, Lucas Gertsz.
Jan. 20. Gysbert, of Jan Van der Hoeven and Dorethe Jansz. Wit.: Antoni Bries, Maria Mingaal.
Jan. 31. Lysbeth, of Gysbert Marselis, Barber Claasz. Wit.: Marselis Jansz, Rebecca Claasz.
Feb. 7. Anna, of Johannes De Wandelaar and Sara Schepmoes. Wit.: Pieter Verbrugge, Caatje Cuyler.
Maria, of Johannes Bleyker, S^r, and Margriet Rutsz. Wit.: Abraham Cuyler, Sara Verbrugge.
Feb. 7. The following pros. were ba.:
Rebecca, among the heathens Jokeyha, i. e., She who shells (Uytdopster), aged 20 years.
Eunice, among the heathen Honiskoö, i. e., Paralysed in the back, aged 14 years.

1692
Sara, a ch. 3 or 4 months old.
Cornelis, among the heathen Aanasjadago, i. e., Plucker of feathers, 22 years old.
Jan, among the heathen Onodaka, i. e., Koddens [game-keeper ?], 16 years old.
Daniel, among the heathen Sognihöa, i. e., Sprig, 15 years old.
Abraham, among the heathen Hojadio, i. e., Own body, 10 years old.
Jan, among the heathen Etsje ni ser, i. e., Sleeper on branches, 12 years old.
Elias, a child, one year old.
Feb. 14. William, of William Nobel and Marritje Pietersz. Wit.: Andries Teller, William Schaats [?], Jacomeintje Sanders.
Feb. 18. Abraham, of Jacob Van den Bogaardt and Jannetje Quakelbosch. Wit.: Albert Rykman, Tryntje Rykman.
Feb. 28. Jacob, of Wessel Ten Broek and Caatje Lookerman. Wit.: Jacob Lookerman, Johannes Cuyler, Styntje Ten Broek.
March 6. Geertruy, of Lucas Jansz and Catrine Melchertsz. Wit.: Melchert Abrahamsz, Caatje Sandersz.
March 13. Henderik, of Isak Casparsz and Dorethee Bosch. Wit.: Albert Rykman, Lysbet Lansing.
Judik, of Arent Schuyler and Jenneken Teller. Wit.: Wilhem Teller, Johannes Schuyler, Elisabeth Van Trigt.
March 20. Willem, of Robbert Levingston and Alida Schuyler. Wit.: Pieter Schuyler, Kiliaan Van Renselaar, Maria Schuyler.
Agniet, of Pieter De Germeau and Caatje Van der Heyden. Wit.: Dirk Van der Heyden, Abraham Kip, Antje Van der Heyden.
March 25. Tammus, of Robbert Barrit and Wyntje Jansz. Wit.: Jan Gilbert, Elisabeth Tymesz.
March 27. Margriet, of Jacobus Peek and Elisabeth Teunisz. Wit.: Jacob Teunisz, Grietje Bleeker.
Antje, of Harmanus Vedder, Jr., and Margriet Jacobsz. Wit.: Dirk W. Ten Broek, Tryntje Rykman.
March 28. Marten, of Marten Gerritsz Van Bergen and Neeltje Meyndertsz. Wit.: Kiliaan Van Renselaar, Maria Schuyler.
The following pros. were ba.:
Eva, called among the heathen Jawaandasse, i. e., Who has not any too much to eat, aged 35 years, mother of the following 3 chn., who were also ba. at the time:
Catarina, among the heathen Tokwanaharonne, i. e., Who stands in the midst of the people, 18 years old.

1692

Noach, among the heathen Tetsjohoniodaon, i. e., Erected poles, 9 years old.

Anna, among the heathen Tiosseroage, i. e., Who clings to a dress.

Moeset, called among the heathen Tsudtakkwe, i. e., Repulsed, 30 years old, mother of the following 3 chn., who were ba. at the same time:

Magdalene, among ·the heathen Koanadakkarrie, i. e., Who has left—or run away from—her castle, 11 years old.

Debora, among the heathen Tsionesse, i. e., Lowered again, 8 years old.

Christine, among the heathen Skanjadaradi, i. e., Across the river, 4 years old.

Grietje, among the heathen Shohwason, i. e., One who always covers herself, aged 20 years.

Martyn, among the heathen Sinonda, i. e., A small mountain, 13 years old.

Dorkas, among the heathen Tionaktiago, i. e., One who breaks her sleeping place, 13 years old.

Rut, among the heathen Hoa, i. e., Owl, 12 years old.

Henderik, among the heathen Waäms or [Waänis], i. e., Long bow, 1 year old.

Cornelia, the ch. of Canastasji, 6 weeks old.

Apr. 6. Johannes, of David Willemsz and Rachel Hansz. Wit.: Jacobus Peek, Jannetje Jacobsz.

Maria, of Henderik Van Esch and Catryn Van Dam. Wit.: Claas R. V. Dam, Maria Van Dam.

Apr. 16. Jacob, of —— Gardenier and Lena ——. Wit.: Pieter Koeman and Geertje Koeman.

Apr. 23. Johannes, of Johannes Rosenboom and Gerritje Coster. Wit.: Gerrit Rosenboom and Gysbertje Rosenboom.

Elisabeth, of Henderik Van Dyk and Maria Schuyler. Wit.: Jacob Staats, Cateline Schuyler.

David, of Willem C. Croesbeek, Geertruy Schuyler. Wit.: Abraham Schuyler, Catelina Schuyler.

Jacob, of Dirk Van der Heyden and Rachel Jochumsz. Wit.: Anna V. d. Heyden.

Jacob, of Omi De la Grange and Annetje De Vries. Wit.: Tryntje Rutten.

May 8. Johannes, of Mathys Jansz and Cornelia Teuisz. Wit.: Marritje Wendell, Johannes T. Mingaal.

Maria, of Pieter Schuyler and Maria Van Renselaar. Wit.: Arent Schuyler, Henderik Van Renselaar, Margareta Schuyler.

Pieter, of Jonas Folkertsz and Magdalena Quakelbosch. Wit.: Andries Folkertsz, Nelletje Rykman.

1692

May 15. Egbertje, of Dirk Bratt and Anna Teunisz. Wit.: Egbert Teunisz, Barent A. Bratt, Susanna Bratt.

June 5. Henderik, of Henderik Beekman and Annetje Quakelbosch. Wit.: Marten Beekman, Tryntje Rykman.

Reyer and François, twins of Meyndert H. V. Bogaart and Helena Schermerhoorn. Wit.: Johannes De Wandelaar, Jacob Staats, Elisabeth Wendell, Sara Cuyler.

Jochum, of Jochum Lambertsz and Eva Henderiksz Vroman. Wit.: Pieter Martensz, Ariaantje Barens.

Hanna, of Samuel Bratt and Susanna J. Van Slyk. Wit.: Pieter Schuyler and Elsje Rutgersz.

June 12. Wilhelmus, of Willem Gysbertsz and Catryn V. d. Poel. Wit.: Johannes V. Santen, Margriet Van Santen.

June 19. Dirk, of Harmannus Hagen and Margriet Dirksz. Wit.: Johannes Appell, Jannetje Bleyker.

July 3. Leendert, of Johannes Jansz and Lysbeth Leendertsz. Wit.: Frans Winnen, Elsje Winnen.

Rebecca, of Symon Groot and Geertruy Rinkhout. Wit.: Phlip Wendell, Susanna Groot.

Johannes, of Samson Bensing and Tryntje Matheusz. Wit.: Johannes Teller, Collette Caspersz.

Lysbeth, of Isak Trujeks and Maria Willemsz. Wit.: Phlip Foreest, Ariaantje Wendell.

Aug. 14. Antje, of Gosen Van Oort and Maria Peek. Wit.: Jacobus Peek, Catryntje Glenn.

Aug. 15. Marta, a heathen woman, about 48 years old, called among her nation Teianjeharre, i. e., Two heights.

Alette, her dau., about 10 years old, called among her nation Quaktendiatha, i. e., One who is being driven.

Catarine, a widow, about 33 years old, called among her nation Sadiogwa, i. e., She has as much, or An equal share.

Aug. 21. Elsje, of Jan Albertsz and Geesje Jansz. Wit.: Antje Staats.

Hester, of Nanning Harmensz and Alida Vinhagel. Wit.: Eva Vinhagel, Tjerk Harmensz.

Aug. 28. Jan, of Isak Vosburg and Anna Jansz. Wit.: Judic Jansz, Johannes Lucasz.

Geertruy, of Claas Frederiksz and Ifje Arents. Wit.: Antje Staats.

Sept. 4. Jacob, of Willem Jacobsz and Elisabeth Rosenboom. Wit.: Harbart Jacobsz, Gysbertje Rosenboom.

Sept. 7. Phlip, of Jan Bronk and Commertje Leendertsz. Wit.: Caspar Leendertsz, Jonas Volkertsz, Wyntje Phlipz.

Sep. 11. Jan, of Evert Wiler and Josine Jansen. Wit.: Maas Cornelisz, Sara Jansz.

1692–1693

Sep. 16. Maria, of Thomas Willemsz and Agnietje Gansevoort. Wit.: Frans Winne, Antje Gansevoort.

Sep. 18. Styntje, of Thomas Winne and Teuntje Jans. Wit.: Jan Tysz, Judik Jansz.

Oct. 23. Maria, of Franc Marris and Zytje Matthysz. Wit.: Henderik Marris [?], Hilletje Corn.

Folkert, of Henderik Oothout and Caatje Folkertsz. Wit.: Andries Folkertsz, Jannetje Oothout.

Pieter, of Jacob Teunisz and Anna Lookerman. Wit.: Henderik Hansz, Catrina Renselaar.

Folkje, of Michiel Coljer and Titje Jurriaans. Wit.: Claas Lucasz, Lysbeth Lansing.

Maria, of Frans Winnen and Elsje Gansevoort. Wit.: Leendert Phlipsz, Tanne Winne.

Oct. 30. Grietje, of Abraham Cuyler and Caatje Bleyker. Wit.: Jan Jansz Bleyker, Johannes Cuyler, Grietje Bleyker.

Nov. 20. Teunis, of Pieter Willemsz Van Slyk and Johanna Hansz. Wit.: Jan Hansz, Elsje Rutgersz.

Maria, of Evert Ridder and Anna Van Esch. Wit.: Jan Van Esch, Maria Van Esch.

Nov. 27. Alida, of Jacob Turk and Catrina Van Benthuysen. Wit.: Marten Van Benthuysen, Elisabeth Wendell.

Caterina, of Johannes Van Santen and Margriet Van der Poel. Wit.: Isac Isaksz, Willem Gysbertsz, Catrine Van der Poel.

Nov. 30. David, of Abraham Schuyler and Geertruy Ten Broek. Wit.: Dirk W. Ten Broek, Cateline Schuyler.

Dec. 4. Jacob, of Marten Jansz and Jannetje Cornelisz. Wit.: Phlip Foreest, Tryntje Foreest.

Dec. 18. Rachel, of Albert Rykman and Nelletje Quakelbosch. Wit.: Henderik Bries, Catryn Rutgers.

Dec. 23. Antoni, of Antoni Bratt and Wilmje Teunisz. Wit.: Johannis Bratt, Johanna Bratt.

Dec. 25. Rebecca, of Daniel Jansz Van Antwerpen and Marietje Groot. Wit.: Johannes Sandersz, Elisabeth Wendell.

Dec. 26. Anna, of Cornelis Teunisz Van Veghten and Mara Lucasz. Wit.: Henderik V. Renselaar, Elisabeth Wendell.

1693, Jan. 1. Arent, of Reyer J. Schermerhoorn and Ariaantje Arentsz. Wit.: Jacob Staats, Elisabeth Wendell.

Sara, Dekajagentha, i. e., Who leaves by two doors, about 40 years old.

Abraham, son of the above, formerly Wagwagton, i. e., Pushed over, about 17 years old.

1693

Isak, also a son of the above, formerly Sirware, i. e., Puts the cloth in the water, about 4 years old.

Jacob, of Isack and Eunice, married proselytes.

Jan. 15. Feytje, of Phlip Leendertsz and Weyntje Dirksz. Wit.: Frans Winnen, Agniet Thomasz.

Jan. 18. Engeltje, of Jan Vroman and Geesje Symonsz. Wit.: Johannes Appell, Tryntje Schaats.

Jan. 21. Alida, of Pieter D. Schuyler and Alida Slegtenhorst. Wit.: Pieter Schuyler, Geertruy Groesbeek.

Feb. 1. Jan, of Antje Jansz Bratt. Wit.: Claartje Jansz Bratt.

Matheuis, of Johannes Bensing and Lysbeth Matheuisz. Wit.: Johannis Tomesz, Marretje Mattheuisz.

Feb. 12. Ariaantje, of Claas Laurentsz and Marietje Swart. Wit.: Wouter V. Uythoff, Jannetje Swart.

Johannes, of Henderik Brouwer and Marritje Pietersz. Wit.: Gysbert Marselis, Rebecca Claasz.

Antje, of Gerrit Jansz and Marritje Lowysz. Wit.: Pieter Mingall, Cornelia V. Olinda.

Feb. 19. Isak, of Jan Quakelbosch and Magtelt Jansz. Wit.: Tryntje Rykman.

Margareta, of Johannes Teller and Susanna Wendell. Wit.: Gerrit Lansing, Lysbet Teller.

March 1. Maria, of Wilhem Peeren and Lysbeth Sikkell. Wit.: Abram Isaksz, Rachel Rattelis.

March 5. Lucretia, of Lucas Jansz Van Sasberge * and Marietjen Evertsen. Wit.: Jan Lansing, Elsje Rutgers.

March 19. Wilhelm, of Melchert W. Van der Poel and Elisabeth Van Trigt. Wit.: Arent Schuyler, Jenneken Schuyler.

March 26. Anna, of Simon Van Esch and Rachel Melchertsz. Wit.: Henderik Van Esch, Catryn Van Esch.

Apr. 2. Abraham, of Evert Wendell, Jr, and Elisabeth Sanders. Wit.: Gerrit Lansing, Maria Roseboom.

Apr. 9. Jeuriaan, of William Hooge and Martina Bekker. Wit.: Jan Bekker, Sr, Joh. Bekker, Jr, Elisabeth Wendell.

Sara, of William Hilten and Anna Berkhoven. Wit.: Jan Visscher, Sara Visscher.

Apr. 16. Annetje, of Jan Pietersz Mebi and Antje P. Bosboom. Wit.: Jan Hendriksz Vrooman, Cornelia Pietersz Van Olinda.

Apr. 17. Tietje, of Johannes Oothout and Aaltje Evertsz. Wit.: Gerrit Van Esch, Jannetje Van Es.

May 7. Selia, of Joseph Jets and Huybertje Marselis. Wit.: Haseverus Marselis, Antje Huybertsz.

* Note in the record: "The father was killed, Feb. 17, in an encounter with his enemy."

1693

May 4. Anna, of Joseph Jansz and Seitje Merselis. Wit.: Hasueros Merselis, Judik Merselis.

May 14. Catelyntje, of Rut Melchertsz and Wyntje Harmensz. Wit.: Harmen Tomesz, Engeltje Abrahamsz.

Cornelis, of Pieter Martensz and Ariaantje Barents. Wit.: Cornelis Hendriksz, Marte Martensz, Ariaantje Gerrits.

May 21. Robbert, of Gerrit Rosenboom and Maria Sanders. Wit.: Robbert Sanders.

May 25. Jannetje, of Hendrik Fransz and Cornelia Andriesz. Wit.: Jan Cornelisz, Marietje Jansz.

June 11. Johannes, of Cornelis Van Scherluyn and Geertje Harmensz. Wit.: Johannes V. Scherluyn, Johannes Harmensz, Sara Harmensz.

Eytje, of Pieter Vosburg and Jannetje Barents. Wit.: Isak Vosburg, Anna Jansz.

June 18. Gelyna, of Isak Verplank and Abigail Uytenbogaart. Wit.: Hendrik Van Dyke, Geertruy Kroesbeck.

July 2. Elisabeth, of Christiaan Christiaansz and Marritje Elders. Wit.: Jacob Coenraad, Catelyntje Jacobsz.

Maria, of Benoni Van Corlar and Elisabeth Van der Poel. Wit.: Jan Abeel, Maria Van Schayk.

Harmannus, of Phlip Wendell and Maria Visscher. Wit.: Nanning Harmensz, Evert Wendell, J:, Elsje Lansing.

Margareta, of Jan Cloet and Bata Slogtenhorst. Wit.: Henrik Rosenboom, Alida Schuyler.

July 9. Rebecca, of Harme Gansevoort and Marietje Leendertsz. Wit.: Leendert Phlipsz, Agnietje Leendertsz.

Geertruy, of Marten Krygier and Jannetje Hendrix. Wit.: Elisabeth Banker, Dirk W. T. Broek.

July 23. Eva, of Frerik Harmensz and Margriet Hansz. Wit.: Hendrik Hansz, Hester Hansz.

Aug. 20. Elisabeth, of Everard Banker, Elisabeth Abeel. Wit.: Johannes Abeel, Catrina Van der Poel.

Jacob, of Roelof Gerritsz and Geertruy Jacobsz. Wit.: Jean Rogi, Lysbet Rogi.

Jenneken, of Jacob Ten Eyk, and Geertje Koeyman. Wit.: Johannes Cuyler, Caatje Cuyler.

Debora, of Hendrik Hansz and Debora Van Dam. Wit.: Claas R. V. Dam, Maria Van Dam.

Geertruy, of Bastiaan Harmensz and Dirke Teunisz. Wit.: Nanning Harmensz, Evert Teunisz, Hester Tjerks.

Henderikje, of Lucas Lucasz and Judik Marselis. Wit.: Gysbert Marselis, Annetje Marselis.

Gerrit, of Gerrit Lansing, J:, and Catryntje Sanders. Wit.: Gerrit Lansing, S:, Elsje Lansing.

Aug. 25. Maria, of Antoni Bries, Catrine Rykman. Wit.: Harme Rutgersz, Albert Rykman, Maria Bries.

Aug. 27. Jan, of Dirk Arentsz and Marietje Van Eps. Wit.: Jan Abeel, Lysbeth Teunisz.

1693

Engeltje, of Gerrit Symonsz and Tryntje Helmertsz. Wit.: Jan H. Vrooman, Ariaantje Barents.

Antje, of Claas Grave and Lysbeth Rinkhout. Wit.: Geertruy De Groot, Jᵣ

Jacob, of Phlip Phlipsz and Lysbeth Gansevoort. Wit.: Isak Swits, Diwer Sanders.

Sep. 3. Marietje, of Jacob Jansz and Judik Fransz. Wit.: Jacob Staats, Antje Staats.

Elsje, of Lambert Jochumsz Van Valkenborgh and Jannetje Klauw. Wit.: Mathys Nak, Catryntje Lucasz.

Catelyntje, of Thomas Harmensz and Mayke Oothout. Wit.: Harmen Thomasz, Jannetje Oothout.

Sep. 10. Jacob, of Jan Salomonsz and Caatje Lookerman. Wit.: Jacob Teunisz, Maria Schuyler.

Hilletje, of Johannes Bekker, Jᵣ, and Anna Van der Zee. Wit.: Willem Hooge, Hilletje Van der Zee.

Sept. 24. Christyntje, of Gillis De la Grànge and Jenneke Adriaans. Wit.: Johannes Appell, Annetje Appell.

Oct. 1. Anna, of Hendrik Van Renselaar and Catrina Verbrugge. Wit.: Pieter Schuyler, Sara Verbrugge.

Oct. 15. Barent, of Andries Hansz and Grietje Gysbertsz. Wit.: Wouter Quakelbosch, Johanna Pietersz.

Oct. 22. Andries, of Andries Gardenier and Eytje Ariaansz. Wit.: Jan Hendriksz, Jacomyntje Maasz.

Sara, of Johannes Cuyler and Elsje Ten Broek. Wit.: Dirk W. Ten Broek, Pieter Verbrugge, Styntje Ten Broek.

Oct. 29. Engeltje, of Barent Wimp and Folkje Symonsz. Wit.: Jacobus Peek, Maratje Mingal.

Jacob, of Isak Swits and Susanna Groot. Wit.: Evert Banker, Elisabeth Banker.

The following pros. were ba.:

Tonidoge, i. e., Split Moon, now called Gideon, about 23 years old.

Akerrijehe, i. e., One who continually turns something around, now Antoni, about 15 years old.

Thomas, a ch. of Rebecca, who was ba. by us, Sept. 7, 1692.

Anna, of Joseph and Jacomine, marr. people among the pros.

Nov. 19. Pieter, of Johannes De Wandelaar and Sara Schepmoes. Wit.: Pieter Verbrugge, Sara Cuyler.

Christoffel, of Cornelis Stephensz and Hilletje Lookerman. Wit.: Pieter Schuyler, Catrina Van Renselaar.

Johannes, of Lucas Jansz and Catryn Melchertsz. Wit.: Jan Andriesz, Margriet Bleyker.

Nov. 26. David, of Hendrik Van Dyk and Maria Schuyler. Wit.: David Schuyler, Rykje Staats.

Dec. 3. Susanna, of Johannes Bratt and Maria Keteluyn. Wit.: Willem Keteluyn, Susanna Bratt.

1693-1694
Dec. 20. Thomas, of Robbert Broun and Maria Hujes. Wit.: Thomas Charp, Betti Perens.
Dec. 24. Tanneke, of Hendrik Jansz and Lyntje Winnen. Wit.: Marten Cornelisz, Tanneke Martensz.
Dec. 31. Josina, of Samuel Gardenier and Helena Dirksz. Wit.: Maes Cornelisz, Aaltje Gardenier.
Sara, of Jacob Teunisz and Anna Lookerman. Wit.: Hendrik V. Renselaar, Marritje Lookerman.
Casparus, of Casparus Leendertsz and Alette Winnen. Wit.: Frans Winne, Eva Winne.
Andries, of Andries Huyk and Catryn Valkenborg. Wit.: Wilhem Peer, Lysbet Sikkels.
Dirk, of Jacob Vosburg and Dorethe Jansz. Wit.: Marte Cornelisz, Abigael Verplank.
Agniet, formerly known as Kajaidahje, about 40 years old, wife of Tjerk.
Susanna, her ch., 2 months old.
Margriet, formerly Kviethentha, 17 years old.
1694, Jan. 7. Dirck, of Dirk Van der Heyden and Rachel Keteluym. Wit.: Johannes Te Neur, David Schuyler, Maria Van Dyk.
Jan. 14. Geertruy, of Christoffel Brussi and Styntje Niclaasz. Wit.: Claas Rust, Hester Harmensz.
Jan. 17. Annetje, of Andries Albertsz Bratt and Cornelia Teunisz Verwey. Wit.: Dirk Bratt, Barent Bratt, Maria Bries.
Johanna, of Jacob Casparsz and Hendrikje Hansz. Wit.: Huybert Gertsz, Maria Lansing.
Roeloff, of Jan Albertsz and Geesje Jansz. Wit.: Antje Cross.
Geertruy, of Isak Vosburg and Annetje Jansz. Wit.: Tys Jansz, Elisabeth Beek.
Jan. 21. Marietje, of Barent Gerritsz and Geertruy Jansz. Wit.: Cornelis Claasz, Geertje Gerritsz.
Jan. 28. Pieter, of Teunis Pietersz and Margriet Laurentsz. Wit.: Helmert Jansz, Antje Laurents.
Feb. 7. Benjamin, of Wilhelm Rees and Catryn Jansz. Wit.: Robbert Levingston, Alida Levingston.
N. B.—The parents belonging to the Lutheran Church, the witnesses promised to educate the child in the confession of our church.
Feb. 11. Agnietje, of Arent Vedder and Sara Groot. Wit.: Gerrit Lansing, Sr, Susanna Lansing.
Geertruy, of Pieter Schuyler and Maria Renselaar. Wit.: Robbert Levingston, Richart Engelsby, Catrina Renselaar.
Feb. 14. Helena, of Samson Bensing and Tryntje Matheusz. Wit.: Thomas Harmensz, Engeltje Melcherts.

1694
Feb. 18. Jacob, of Abram Isaksz and Anna Sikkels.
Wit.: Herbert Jacobsz, Tryntje Wendell.
Feb. 21. Pieter, of Marten G. V. Bergen and Neeltje
Meyndertsz. Wit.: Gerrit Teunisz, Catrina Van Renselaar.
Marten, of Robbert Teuwisz and Cornelia Martensz.
Wit.: Rut Melcheltsz, Catelyntje Martensz.
March 11. Hendrik, of Hendrik Gardenier and Neeltje
Claasz. Wit.: Willem Gysbertsz, Cornelis Claasz Van den
Berch, Susanna Ouwerkerk.
March 18. Teunis, of Arent Slingerlant and Geertruy
Van Vosch. Wit.: Teunis Slingerland, Johannes T. Min-
gal, Maria Mingal.
Apr. 1. Alida, of Tammus Noxen and Geertruy Hogen-
boom. Wit.: Meuis Hogenboom, Hendrik V. Renselaar,
Antje Hogenboom.
Apr. 6. Johannes, of Piere De Germeau and Catrina
Van der Heyde. Wit.: Wessel Ten Broek, Catrine Ten
Broek.
Apr. 11. The following pros. were ba. after previous
confession:
Eva, 49 years old, called among the heathen Sowasthoa,
i. e., Little one.
Seli, Eva's adopted dau., 9 years old, called among the
heathen Tejononnaron.
Anna; her heathen name was Sajogerenha, i. e., Little
chaser (opdryvertje); about 26 years old.
Gerrit, Anna's little ch.
Moses, ch. of Gideon (the mo. is not yet ba.).
Helena and Hester, twins of Joseph and Rachel.
Dorothe, of Grietje, who was ba. March 28, 1692.
Apr. 15. Thomas, of Johannes Jansz and Lysbeth Leen-
dertsz. Wit.: Caspar Leendertsz, Alette Pietersz.
Marietje, of Coenraat Hooghteeling and Tryntje Wil-
lemsz. Wit.: Wouter Van den Uythoff, Jannetje Swart.
Apr. 22. Rebecca, of Jan Wibusz and Anne Marie
Hansz. Wit.: Maas Cornelisz, Rebecca Evertsz.
Apr. 29. Johannes, of Johannes Rosenboom and Ger-
ritje Coster. Wit.: Johannis Lansing, Margriet Mingal.
Gosen, of Antoni Van Schayk and Maria Van der Poel.
Wit.: Johannes Abeel, Elisabeth Corlar.
Mathys, of Mathys Hooghteeling and Maria Hendriksz.
Wit.: Annetje Harmensz, Marte Gerritsz.
May 6. Claas, of Dirk Van der Karre and Feytje Van
Schaak. Wit.: Johannes Abeel, Catryntje Van der Poel.
Claas, of Hansz Jurriaansz and Cornelia Claasz. Wit.:
Hendrik Lansing, Catryntje Van Alen.
Anna, of Elbert Gerritsz and Maria Pruyn. Wit.: Jo-
hannes Pruyn, Jannetje Gerritsz.

1694
Jannetje, of Jacob Schermerhoorn and Gerritje Hendriksz. Wit.: Dirk W. Ten Broek, Johannes Cuyler, Neeltje Schermerhoorn.

May 20. Johannes, of Johannes Beekman and Eva Vinhagell. Wit.: Jan Vinhagell, Alida Vinhagell.

May 27. Sara, of Evert Wile and Josine Jacobsz. Wit.: Jacob Winnen, Eva Winnen.

June 17. Anna, of Abraham Kip and Geesje Van der Heyden. Wit.: Johannes Kip, Anna Van der Heyden.

Maria, of Robbert Barrit and Wyntje Jansz. Wit.: Ritchart Weyt, Elisabeth Jansz.

Christine, of Wessel Ten Broek and Catrina Lookerman. Wit.: Johannes Cuyler, Christina Ten Broek.

June 24. Wynand, of Cornelis Gysbertsz and Cornelia Wynandsz. Wit.: Willem Gysbertsz, Maria Melchertsz.

July 1. Claas, of Cornelis Claasz and Susanna Ouwerkerk. Wit.: Jan Ouwerkerk, Neeltje Claasz.

July 8. Helena, of a proselyte.

July 29. Phlip, of Phlip Leendertsz and Weyntje Dirksz. Wit.: Teunis Dirksz, Caspar Leendertsz, Feytje Dirksz.

Lysbeth, of Huybert Gerritsz and Maria Lansing. Wit.: Cornelis Gerritsz, Lysbeth Lansing.

Johannes, of Jan Casparsz and Rachel Willemsz. Wit.: Hendrik Lansing, Lysbeth Verwey.

Aug. 19. Johannes, of Jan Redly and Rachel Lambertsz. Wit.: Johannes Rosenboom, Gerritje Rosenboom.

Aug. 26. Johannes, of Abram Jansz and Marritje Van Deusen. Wit.: Jacob Van Deusen, Catelyn Bensing.

Johannes, of Johannes Blyker, Jr, and Anna Koster. Wit.: Johannes Blyker, Geertje Lansing.

Sept. 11. Anna, of Jean Gilbert and Cornelia Van den Bergh. Wit.: Abraham Cuyler, Gerritje Rosenboom.

Hermannus, of Nanning Harmansz and Alida Vinhagel. Wit.: Johannes Vinhagel, Johannes Harmensz, Maria Vinhagel.

Oct. 21. Jannaatje, of Frans Winne and Elsje Gansevoort. Wit.: Jacob Winne, Eva Winne.

Oct. 28. Phlip, of Pieter D. Schuyler, Alida Slechtenhorst. Wit.: Johannes Abeell, Bata Slegtenhorst.

Nov. 4. Hermannus, of Thomas Willemsz and Agnietje Gansevoort. Wit.: Leendert Phlipsen, Tryntje Schaats.

Nov. 25. Catrina, of Phlip Foreest and Tryntje Kip. Wit.: Phlip Wendell, Margrietje Harmensz.

Catrina, of David Schuyler and Elsje Rutgers. Wit.: Harme Rutgers, Abram Schuyler, Catrina Rutgers.

Dec. 9. Isak and Jacob, twins of Jan Van der Hoeve and Dorethe Jansz. Wit.: Lucas Lucasz, Marietje Bries, Albert Rykman, Marietje Jansz.

1694–1695

Dec. 14. Anna, of Hendrik Van Esch and Catrina Van Dam. Wit.: Evert Ridders, Debora Van Dam.

Dec. 16. Johanna, of Robbert Levingston and Alida Schuyler. Wit.: Piter Schuyler, Richart Engelsby, Isabella Dellius.

Dec. 26. Geertruy, of Andries Jansz and Engeltje Volkertsz. Wit.: Andries Douw, Caatje Melchertsz.

The following pros. were ba.:

Pieter, formerly Kanarongwe, i. e., Drawer out of arrows, about 20 years old.

Sander, formerly Anoniachtha, i. e., Dancer, about 20 years old.

Brant, formerly Thowariage, i. e., One whose fence has been broken, about 21 years old.

Dorcas, formerly Sakkoherriho, i. e., One who re-enters the bushes, about 23 years old.

Christine, formerly Tsike, i. e., Seer, about 18 years old.

Amirant, formerly Kanianaundon, i. e., One who lifts cones (Kegel steenen), about 20 years old.

1695, Jan. 6. Gerrit, of Evert Ridders and Antje Van Esch. Wit.: Kiliaan Van Renselaar, Maria Schuyler.

Jan. 9. Marietje, of Hendrik Beekman and Antje Quakkelbosch. Wit.: Johannes Beekman, Eva Vinhagel.

Jan. 20. Breechje, of Mathys Jansz and Cornelia Teuisz. Wit.: Jan Tysz, Lena Teuisz.

Abraham, of Pieter Vosburgh and Jannetje Barents. Wit.: Ariaantje Barens.

Barent, of Pieter Martensz and Ariaantje Barents. Wit.: Pieter Vosburg, Jannetje Barents.

Abigael, of Marte Jansz and Jannetje Cornelis. Wit.: Abraham Jansz, Doretje Jansz.

Jochum, of Lambert Valkenborch and Jannetje Fransz. Wit.: Bartel Valkenborg, Catryn Van Alen.

Abigael, of Gerrit Jacobsz and Elisabeth. Wit.: Andries Scharp, Aaltje Jansz.

Jan. 23. Anna, of William Hilten and Anna Berkhove. Wit.: Jean Kint, Catrine Wendell.

Isak, of Jacob Vosch and Jannetje Quakelbosch. Wit.: Isak Vosburgh, Geertje Quakelbosch.

Feb. 20. Jacob, of Jacob Aartsz and Sara Pels. Wit.: Pieter Schuyler, Maria Schuyler.

Feb. 24. Pieter, of Hendrik Jansz and Lyntje Winnen. Wit.: Jan Andriesz, Catrina Sanders.

March 10. Daniel, of William Hooge and Martina Bekker. Wit.: John Visscher, Elsje Wendell.

Johannes, of Gerrit Lansing, Jr., and Catrina Glenn. Wit.: Johannes Glenn, Diwer Wendell.

March 17. Nelletje, of Antoni Bries and Catrina Rykman. Wit.: Jan Rykman, David Schuyler, Nelletje Rykman.

1695

Joseph, of Joseph Jets and Huybertje Marselisz. Wit.: Antje Bekker.

Hester, of Phlip Wendell and Marietje Visser. Wit.: Johannes Visser, Ariaantje Wendell.

Maria, of Kanastasi, a proselyte.

March 31. Catelyntje, of Jan Salomonsz and Catelyntje Lookerman. Wit.: Jan Fonda, Catrina Ten Broek.

Dirck, of Antoni Bratt and Willemje Teunisz. Wit.: Dirck Bratt, Anna Bratt.

Apr. 7. Sara, of Jacobus Turk and Catrina Van Benthuysen. Wit.: Gerrit Roosenboom, Catelyntje Van Benthuysen.

Jan, of Hendrik Oothout and Caatje Volkerts. Wit.: Jan Van Esch, Grietje Bleyker.

Apr. 14. Neeltje, of Johannes Abeell and Catalina Schuyler. Wit.: Everard Banker, Catelina Schuyler.

Anna, of Abraham Cuyler, Catarina Bleyker. Wit.: Johannes Cuyler, Johannes Bleyker, Sara Verbrugge.

David, of Isak Verplank and Abagael Uytenbogaardt. Wit.: Meindert Schuyler, Margriet Verplank.

Margriet, of Wilhem Jacobsz and Elisabeth Rosenboom. Wit.: Hendrik Rosenboom, Cataline Jansz [?].

Apr. 28. Lucas, of Johannes Lucasz Wyngaart and Susanna Wendell. Wit.: Nicolaas Lucasz, Anna Lucasz.

Helena, of Jan Bronk and Commertje Leendertsz. Wit.: Leendert Phlipsz, Tomas Harmensz, Elsje Winne.

May 2. Hasueros, of Everard Wendell, Jr., and Elisabeth Sanders. Wit.: Catelyntje Van Benthuysen, Gerrit Rosenboom.

May 16. Jacob, of Andries Jacobsz and Eytje Ariesz. Wit.: Jacob Staats, Geertje Ten Eyk.

May 19. David, of Dirk Van der Heyden and Rachel Keteluym. Wit.: Daniel Keteluym, Alida Levingston.

May 26. Johannes, of Gysbert Marselis and Barbar Groesbeek. Wit.: Willem Groesbeek, Judik Marselis.

Dirkje, of Lambert Jansz and Jannetje Mingaal. Wit.: Johannes Teller, Tryntje Wendell.

Jurriaan, of Michiel Coljer and Tite Jurriaansz. Wit.: Huybert Gerritsz, Maria Lansing.

Johanna, of Pieter W. Van Slyk and Johanna Hansz. Wit.: Hendrik Van Dyk, Jannetje Swart.

Teuntje, of Barent Gerritsz and Gertruy Lansing. Wit.: Wouter P. Quakelbosch, Marritje Gerritsz.

June 16. Helena, of Tjerk Harmensz and Emmetje Jansz. Wit.: Cornelis Van Scherluyn, Sara Harmensz.

Pieter, of Isak Jansz Alestyn and Marietje Abbedis. Wit.: Isak Verplank, Alida Van Wey.

Jeremias, of Jacob Teunisz and Anna Lookerman. Wit.: Gerrit Van Esch, Hilletje Lookerman.

1695

June 21. Marietje, of Willem Van Alen and Marietje Van Petten. Wit.: Gerrit Van Esch, Marietje Van Esch.

June 23. Lysbeth, of Isak Casparsz and Dorethe Bosch. Wit.: Jean Rogi, Maria Lansing.

Susanna, formerly Nikajada, i. e., Thin waist, about 30 years old.

Jonas, 3 years old, Diwer, 5 months old, chn. of Susanna.

Dirk, formerly Rode, i. e., Stupid, about 80 years old.

June 30. Hans, of Hendrik Hansz and Debora Van Dam. Wit.: Johannes Hansz, Elsje Hansz.

July 7. Neeltje, of Karel Hansz and Lysbeth Rinkhout. Wit.: Johannes Beekman, Neeltje Schermerhoorn.

July 14. Jacob, of Henderik Rosenboom and Debora Staats. Wit.: Jacob Staats, Margriet Mingaal.

July 21. Christine, of Abraham Schuyler and Geertruy Ten Broek. Wit.: Pieter D. Schuyler, Wessel Ten Broek, Styntje Ten Broek.

Cornelia, of Cornelis Van Scherluyn and Geertruy Harmensz. Wit.: Phlip Wendell, Alida Vinhagel.

Cornelia, of Harmen Knikkelbacker and Lysbeth Bogart. Wit.: Evert Van Esch, Cornelia Bogart.

Aug. 4. Jochum, of Johannes Bratt and Maria Keteluym. Wit.: Barent Bratt, Rachel Van der Heyden.

Aug. 18. Harmannus, of Frerik Harmansz and Margriet Hansz. Wit.: Tjerk Harmensz, Ariaantje Harmensz.

Aug. 25. Elsje, of Johannes Cuyler and Elsje Ten Broek. Wit.: Meindert Schuyler, Cornelia Ten Broek.

Sep. 8. Jannetje, of Johannes Andriesz Schaap and Geertruy Rees. Wit.: Jan Salomonsz, Neeltje Schaap.

Marten, of Johannes Beekman and Eva Vinhagell. Wit.: Claas Rust, Marietje Vinhagell.

Sep. 15. Catrina, of Johannes Bensing and Lysbeth Teuwisz. Wit.: Thomas Harmensz, Cornelia Robberts.

Elsje, of Gerrit Rosenboom and Maria Sanders. Wit.: Johannes Rosenboom, Margriet Mingal.

Sept. 29. Dirk, of Teunis Dirksz and Caatje Van Petten. Wit.: Dirk Teunisz, Marten G. Van Bergen, Hendrik Oothout, Marritje Van Alen.

Oct. 4. Gerrit, of Joseph Jansz and Zytje Marselis. Wit.: Gysbertje Marselis.

Wilhem, of Johannes Teller and Susanna Wendell. Wit.: Johannes Tomesz, Elisabeth Schuyler.

Johannes, of Marten G. V. Bergen and Neeltje Meinders. Wit.: Dirk Teunisz, Weintje Bogardus.

Oct. 6. Elisabeth, of Jelis De la Grange and Jenneke Adriaansz. Wit.: Johannes Tomesz, Marietje Mingal.

Catelina, of Henderik Van Dyk and Maria Schuyler. Wit.: Abraham Schuyler, Geertruy Croesbeek.

1695–1696
Oct. 13. Johannes, of Johannes Tomesz and Mayken Oothout. Wit.: Johannes Oothout, Wyntje Tomesz.
Rebecca, of Ariaantje Van der Heyden. Wit.: Marietje Egberts.
Nov. 17. Jacob, of Jan Quakelbosch and Machtelt Post. Wit.: Abram Schuyler, Geertruy Schuyler.
Christoffel, of Everard Banker and Elisabeth Abeel. Wit.: Wilhelm Banker, Marte Kreigier, Catelyntje Abeel.
Rebecca, of Johannes Oothout and Aaltje Everts. Wit.: Jan Hansz, Alida Fondaas.
Ariaantje, of Melchert W. Van der Poel and Elisabeth Teller. Wit.: Gerrit Van Esch, Marietje Van Esch.
Jannetje, of Abram Isaksz and Anna Sikkels. Wit.: Melchert Abramsz, Rachel Van Valkenborch.
Nov. 24. Engeltje of Jochum Lambertsz and Eva Vroman. Wit.: Abram Isaks, Jacomyn Nak.
Dec. 1. Anna, of Gerrit Lucasz and Sara Harmensz Visser. Wit.: Lucas Gerritsz, Ariaantje Wendell.
Dec. 4. Annetje, of Lucas Lucasz and Judic Marselis. Wit.: Marcelis Jansz, Huybertje Marselis.
Dec. 8. Anna, of David Keteluyn and Johanna Bratt. Wit.: Barent Bratt, Dirk Van der Heyden, Rachel Van der Heyden.
Dec. 18. Alida, of Johannes De Wandelaar and Sara Schepmoes. Wit.: Meindert Schuyler, Rachel Schuyler.
Dec. 25. Philp, of Johannes Schuyler and Elisabeth Staats. Wit.: Alida Levingston, Pieter Schuyler, Jacob Staats.
1696, Jan. 1. Marietje, of Caspar Konyn and Alette Winnen. Wit.: Jacob Winnen, Elsje Winnen.
The following pros. were also ba.:
Zacharias, a little ch. of Joseph and Kanastasi, both previously ba. in Canada.
Lucas, about 21 years old, son of Eva, 50 years old. His name among the heathen was Sondagerakwe, i. e., Who digs up the soil.
Barent, 19 years old. His former name was Tarogiagetho, i. e., Who scrapes the air.
Isak, 17 years old, formerly Sognaondje, i. e., Who defeats the skeleton.
Jacob, 22 years old, formerly Kajingwirago, i. e., Large arrow.
Hester, 35 years old, formerly Toaddoni, i. e., One who cradles.
Debora, 13 years old, dau. of Hester, formerly Kahusje, i. e., Long wooden shaft.
Frans, 6 years old, son of Hester.
Gerrit, also a little ch. of Hester.

1696
Agniet, 50 years old, formerly Katerakse, i. e., Root-eater.

Abraham, 17 years old, son of Agniet, formerly Sadig-niadode, i. e., They are alike.

Marie, a small child of Brant and Margriet, both pros.

Celie, 30 years old, her name among the heathen Waka-jesha, i. e., In vain.

Seth, a little child of Celie.

Jan. 12. Catrine, of Henri Possi and Antje Hogen-boom. Wit.: Hendrik V. Renselaar, Aaltje Oothout.

Alida, of Elbert Gerritsz and Maria Pruyn. Wit.: Jo-hannes Gerritsz, Alida Pruyn.

Jan. 15. Philippus, of Pieter Schuyler and Maria Van Renselaar. Wit.: Johannes Schuyler, Kiliaan V. Rense-laar, Elisabeth Dellius.

Jan. 19. Storm, of Johannes Bekker and Anna Van der Zee. Wit.: Gerrit Lansing, Wouter Van der Zee, Catrine Rutgers.

Matheus, of Jan Teuwisz Van Deursen, Marretje Mar-tensz. Wit.: Albert Rykman, Nelletje Rykman.

Jan. 22. Margriet, of Jan Albertsz and Geesje Dirksz. Wit.: Andries Scharp, Neeltje Scharp.

Philippus, of Johannes Tomesz and Lysbeth Conyn. Wit.: Abraham Jansz, Marritje Teuisz.

Hendrik, of Samuel Gardenier, Helena Dirksz. Wit.: Evert Wieler, Josyne Gardenier.

Feb. 2. Anna, of Hendrik Van Renselaar and Catrine Verbrugge. Wit.: Kiliaan V. Renselaar, Wyntje Bogar-dus.

Feb. 5. Maria, of Samson Bensing and Tryntje Ma-theuisz. Wit.: Johannis Bensing, Agnietje Schaats.

Feb. 12. Elsje, of Jacob Van Hoese and Judik Fransz. Wit.: Johannes Schuyler, Abraham Staats, Elsje Wendell.

Margriet, of Cornelis Van Slyk and Claartje Bratt. Wit.: Albert Rykman, Antoni Bries, Elsje Rutgers.

Feb. 16. Gosen, of Antoni Van Schayk and Maria Van der Poel. Wit.: Johannes Abeell, Elisabeth Corlar.

Hendrik, of Willem Rees and Catrina Jansz. Wit.: Jacob Staats, Elsje Cuyler.

Feb. 18. Coenraat, of Hans Juriaansz and Cornelia Claasz. Wit.: Laurens Claasz, Dirk Van der Kerre, Lysbet Lansing.

March 8. Geertruy and Alida, twins of Nanning Visser and Alida Vinhagel. Wit.: Bastiaan Visser, Johannes Beekman, Geertruy Scharluyn, Marietje Vinhagel.

Marritje, of Pieter Martensz and Ariaantje Barents. Wit.: Marte Cornelisz, Albert Rykman, Catelyntje Mar-tens.

1696
March 11. Abraham, of Isak Vosburgh and Anna Jansen. Wit.: Hendrik Hanse, Debora Van Dam.
March 22. Engeltje, of Rut Melchertsz and Weintje Harmensz. Wit.: Jan Jansz Bleyker, Tryntje Schaats.
Apr. 5. Storm, of Wouter Van der Zee and Jannetje Swart. Wit.: Johannes Bekker, Adriaan Bratt, Margriet Schuyler.
Apr. 13. Willem, of Mathys Warmond and Susanna Heghs. Wit.: William Hyde, Hendrikje Van Schoonhoven.
Moeset, about 20 years old, kept her original name.
Neeltie, about 24 years old, formerly Kawachkerat, i. e., One who is whitish.
Catrina, about 2 years old, Neeltie's child.
Sara, about 15 years old, formerly Sukkorio, i. e., One who has beautiful hair.
Jan, about 22 years old, formerly Juthori, i. e., Cold.
Elias, of Joseph and Jacomoni, bapt. pros. Wit.: David, Gideon, and Josine.
Apr. 19. Arent, of Benoni V. Corlar and Elisabeth Van der Poel. Wit.: Antoni V. Schayk, Egbert Teunisz, Elisabeth Banker.
Apr. 26. Anna, of Bastiaan Harmensz and Dirkje Teunisz. Wit.: Johannes Harmensz, Hester Harmensz.
May 10. Breechje, of Evert Wiler and Josina Gardenier. Wit.: Johannes Oothout, Hendrik Hansz, Hester Fonda.
Johannes, of Jan Casparsz and Rachel Willemsz. Wit.: Teunis Dirksz, Catrine Van Petten.
Rebecca, of Johannes Fonda and Marritje Lookerman. Wit.: Douwe Fonda, Rebecca Fonda.
May 17. Jeremie, of Jacob Teunisz and Anna Lookerman. Wit.: Kiliaan Van Renselaar, Marietje Van Es.
June 1. Mathieu, of Piere De Garmeau and Catrina Van der Heyden. Wit.: Abram Kip, Phlip Foreest, Christine Ten Broek.
June 7. Breechje and Evert, twins of Evert Pels and Grietje Van Deusen. Wit.: Melchert Abramsz, Symon Van Esch, Wyntje Van Deuse, Antje Ridders.
June 14. Mathys, of Coenraat Hooghteeling and Tryntje W. Van Slyk. Wit.: Claas Siwersz, Tryntje Hooghteling.
Matheus, of Abraham Jansz and Marietje Van Deuse. Wit.: Hendrik Hansz, Marritje Harbarts.
June 21. Maria, of Johannes Ouderkerk and Neeltje Claassen. Wit.: Egbert Teunisz, Mayke Van Esch.
June 28. Andries, of Hendrik Fransen and Cornelia Andriesz. Wit.: Melchert Van der Poel, Catrina Van der Poel.

1696

Meesje, of Gerrit Jacobsz and Lysbet Eli. Wit.: Barent Brat, Susanna Brats.

Salomon, of Dirk Van der Kerre and Feitje Claasz. Wit.: Antoni Van Schayk, Johannes Abeel, Elisabet Banker.

The following from among the pros. were ba.:

Thomas, 5 years old, ch. of Gideon and Catrina.

Antonette, 2 years old, ch. of Gideon and Catrina.

Johannes, about 26 years old, Owajadatferrio, i. e., He has been found.

Judik, a ch. of Anne.

Blandine, about 37 years old, formerly Koatkitsquanni.

Agnis, about 15 years old; Clara, about 12 years old; Jephta, about 10 years old; Isai, about 6 years old, chn. of Blandine.

July 12. Caspar, of Jan Bronk and Commertje Leenderts. Wit.: Caspar Leenderts, Feitje Dirks.

July 19. Ariaantje, of Cornelis Stephensen and Hilletje Lookerman. Wit.: Wessel Ten Broek, Catrina Ten Broek.

Johannes, of Albert Slingerlandt and Hester Brikkers. Wit.: Antoni Slingerlant, Arent Slingerlant, Geertje Brikkers.

Aug. 2. Anna, of Dirk Bratt and Anna Teunisz. Wit.: Daniel Bratt, Martyn Teunisz.

Aug. 9. Pieter, of Pieter D. Schuyler and Alida Slegtenhorst. Wit.: David Schuyler, Myndert Schuyler, Geertruy Schuyler.

Tryntje, of Harbert Jacobsz and Marritje Gerrits. Wit.: Elbert Gerrits, Catelyntje Jacobs.

Aug. 16. Tobias, of Robbert Teuwisz and Cornelia Martensz. Wit.: Antoni Bries, Tryntje Bries.

Aug. 23. Douwe, of Jelis Fonda and Rachel Winnen. Wit.: Douwe Fonda, Rebecca Fonda.

Elisabeth, of Wessel Ten Broek and Catrina Lookerman. Wit.: Abram Schuyler, Maria Lookerman.

Sep. 6. Elisabeth, of Simon Jongs and Anna Ro. Wit.: William Heid, Elisabeth Fletscher.

Anna, of Johannes Harmensz Visser and Elisabet Nottingam. Wit.: Tjerk Harmensz Visser, Hester Visser.

Sep. 13. Anna, of Daniel Keteluyn and Debora Vile. Wit.: Johannes Bratt, Maria Bratt.

Sep. 20. The following pros. were ba.:

Jonatan, about 20 years old, formerly Takaradi.

Bata, about 36 years old, formerly Tejoderondat.

Hagar, about 17 years old, formerly Dekarogwendats.

Sara, the ch. of Rut and Hester, both pros.

Natan, the ch. of Gideon and Dorcas, both pros.

Sep. 27. Hester, of Frerik Harmensz and Margriet Hansz. Wit.: Tjerk Harmensz, Elsje Hansz.

1696–1697
Hendrik, of Harme Gansevoort and Marie Leenderts.
Wit.: Jan Bronk, Caspar Leenderts, Kommertje Bronk.
Oct. 4. Jacob, of Cornelis Schermerhoorn and Marritje
Hendriks. Wit.: Cornelis Hendriks, Jan Rykman, Neeltje
Schermerhoorn.
Nov. 8. Pieter, of Daniel Van Olinda and Lysbeth
Kreigier. Wit.: Marten Kreigier, Susanna Bratt.
Nov. 11. Marretje, of Andries Hansz and Catrina Lambertsz. Wit.: Cornelis Scherluyn, Lysbeth Wendell.
Pieter, of Lambert Jochumsz and Jannetje Fransz. Wit.:
Wouter Storm, Jannetje Woutersz.
Nov. 15. Beertje, of Teunis Willemsz and Jannetje Hendriks. Wit.: Gerrit Hendriks, Aaltje Hendriks.
Geertruy, of Johannes Bleyker, J^r, and Anna Coster.
Wit.: Jan Lansing, Grietje Bleyker.
Nov. 26. Sara, of Robbert Barrit and Wyntje Jansz.
Wit.: Judik Lucasz.
Nov. 30. Elsje, of Frans Winne and Elsje Gansevoort.
Wit.: Tam Williams, Agniet Gansevoort.
Dec. 10. Elisabeth, of William Hilten and Antje Berkhoven. Wit.: Wouter Van der Zee, Sara Melchertsen.
Matheus, of Jean Van Loon and Maria Albertsz. Wit.:
Maria Gansevoort.
Dec. 16. Johannes, of Isak Terjeks and Maria Willemsz.
Wit.: Gerrit Lansing, Elisabeth Schuyler.
Dec. 27. Geertruy, of Barent Gerritsz and Geertruy
Jansz. Wit.: Cornelis Van Esch, Geertruy Jansz.
Jean Baptiste, of Moyse Depuis and Anna. Wit.: Abigael Verplank.
Johannes, of Moeset. Wit.: Hilletje Olinda.
[These last 2 chn. are illegitimate. The first of a semiblack mother and a Christian father; the other of a pros.
from among the heathen and a Christian father.]
Debora, of Jacob, ba. Jan. 1, 1696. The mother not yet
ba., but receives instruction.
Willem, after confession. Formerly Toadakje, One who
is being led.
1697, Jan. 3. Pieter, of Pieter and Canastasji, pros.
Wit.: Rebecca. The father was killed a few months
ago.
Jan. 6. Aaltje, of Cornelis Van Es and Marritje Gerrits.
Wit.: Isak Overkerk, Aaltje Van Es.
Jan. 10. Catelyntje, of Jan Salomonsz and Caatje
Lookerman. Wit.: Jan Fonda, Catrine Ten Broek.
Mathys, of Dirk Van der Heyden and Rachel Kitteluyn.
Wit.: Pieter Schuyler, Maria Schuyler.
Jan. 17. Hendrik, of Evert Ridders and Anna Van Esch.
Wit.: Hendrik Van Renslaar, Mayke Van Es.

1697

Jan. 31. Rachel, of Jan Wibesz and Anna Hansz. Wit.: Caspar Liendertsz, Cate . . . Winne.

Martin, of Jacob Vosburgh and Dorethe Jansz. Wit.: Dirk W. Ten Broek, Christine Ten Broek.

Feb. 3. Elbertje, of Melchert Van der Poel, Jr, and Catrine Van Alen. Wit.: Laurens Van Alen, Catelyntje Schuyler.

Feb. 17. Gerrit, of Johannes Rosenboom and Gerritje Coster. Wit.: Pieter Mingall, Antje Blyker.

Anna, of Tammus Williams and Agnietje Gansevoort. Wit.: Jonatan Bradhorst, Elsje Winne.

Feb. 21. Barent, of David Keteluyn and Johanna Bratt. Wit.: Willem Keteluyn, Antoni Brat, Marretje Egberts.

Feb. 28. Anna, of Meindert Schuyler and Rachel Cuyler. Wit.: Abram Cuyler, Cateline Schuyler.

March 14. Hester, of Gerrit Lucasz and Sara Harmensz. Wit.: Tjerk Harmensz, Hester Tjerk.

March 21. Susanna, of Simon Groot and Geertruy Rinkhout. Wit.: Gerrit Lansing, Ariaantje Wendell.

Apr. 2. Maria, of Johannes Beekman and Eva Vinhagel. Wit.: Nanning Visser, Alida Visser.

Apr. 4. Geertruy, of Hendrik Jansz and Lyntje Winnen. Wit.: Jelis Fonda, Rachel Fonda.

The following chn. of pros. were ba.:

Daniel, aged 7 years; Adam, aged 6 weeks, chn. of Neeltje, ba. Apr. 13, 1696.

Christine, 4 weeks old, ch. of Johannes and Rebecca.

Brant, 2 months old, ch. of Marie, ba. in Canada, formerly Senehanawith, i. e., Who boils maize.

Jacob, 2 months old, ch. of Christine, ba. Dec. 26, 1694. Her husband has not yet been ba.

Jan, 4 weeks old, ch. of Jan and Maria. She was ba. in Canada, and he at A., Apr. 13, 1696.

Apr. 5. Johannes, of Isak Ouwerkerk and Mayke Van Esch. Wit.: Jan Van Esch, Aaltje Van Esch.

Apr. 11. David, of David Schuyler and Elsje Rutgers. Wit.: Abram Schuyler, Pieter Schuyler, Cateline Schuyler.

Daniel, of Christiaan Christiaansz and Maria Isbrantsz. Wit.: Johannes Mingal, Nelletje Rykman.

Evert, of Phlip Wendell and Maria Visser. Wit.: Bastiaan Visser, Hester Visser.

Apr. 18. Maria, of Hendrik Hansz and Debora Van Dam. Wit.: Frerik Harmens, Margriet V. Dam.

May 2. Henderikje, of Hendrik Oothout and Caatje Volkers. Wit.: Jonas Volkers, Maria Schuyler.

Gerrit, of Arent Slingerlant and Geertruy Cobes. Wit.: Albert Slingerlant, Hester Brikkers.

1697

May 9. Catryntje, of Andries Rees and Ariaantje Andriesz. Wit.: Gysbert Merselis, Caatje Jansz.

May 13. Reinier, of Tjerk and Agniet, both pros.

May 16. Dirk, of Tys Jansz and Cornelia Teuisz. Wit.: Claas Lucasz, Catelyntje Teuisz.

May 23. Maria, of Cornelis Van Slyk and Clara Bratt. Wit.: Jan Bratt, Dirk W. T. Broek, Geertruy Van Slyk.

Isak, of Jacob Casparsz and Hendrikje Hansz. Wit.: Benoni V. Corlar, Ariaantje Wendell.

May 30. Johannes, of Adam Vroman and Grietje Takels. Wit.: Lucas Gerritsz, Takel Dirksz, Margriet Levingston.

Abraham, of Abraham Staats and Elsje Wendell. Wit.: Gerrit Lansing, Johannes Schuyler, Elisabeth Schuyler.

June 6. Elisabeth, of Hendrik Rosenboom, J^r, and Debora Staats. Wit.: Hendrik Rosenboom, S^r, Rykje Staats.

Maria, of William Hooge and Martine Bekker. Wit.: Dirk W. Ten Broek, Christine Ten Broek.

July 4. Susanna, of Johannes Bratt and Maria Keteluyn. Wit.: Antoni Bratt, Alida Levingston.

July 25. Tryntje, of Patrik Magrigari and Zytje Hooghteeling. Wit.: Hendrik Marselis, Tryntje Hooghteling.

Pieter, of Hendrik Beekman and Antje Quakelbosch. Wit.: Jacob Bogaart, Lysbeth Quakelbosch.

Aug. 1. Marretje, of Andries Bratt and Cornelia Verwey. Wit.: Antoni Bratt, Marritje Teunisz.

Arent, of Jan Gilbert and Cornelia V. der bergh. Wit.: Abram Schuyler, Elsje Cuyler.

Casparus, of Warnar Casparsz, Anna Pruyn. Wit.: Johannes Pruyn, Helena Pruyn.

Sara, of Jacob Teunisz and Anna Lokerman. Wit.: Jan Fonda, Debora V. Dam.

Aug. 8. Catelyntje, of Abraham Kip and Geesje Van der Heyde. Wit.: Hendrik Hansz, Cornelia V. der Heyden.

Aug. 15. Cornelis, of Evert Wendell and Elisabeth Sanders. Wit.: Abraham Wendell, Elsje Staats.

Sara, of Jan Jansz Van Haarlem and Hester Fonda. Wit.: Douwe Fonda, Rebecca Fonda.

Aug. 22. Tryntje, of Harbart Jacobsz and Marritje Gerritsz. Wit.: Willem Jacobsz, Annetje Gerritsz.

Neeltje, of Wouter Quakkelbosch and Cornelia Lauw. Wit.: Wouter Quakkelbosch, Neeltje Quakkelbosch.

Sep. 12. Johannes, of Phlip Foreest and Tryntje Kipp. Wit.: Gerrit Lansing, Elsje Hansz.

Sep. 19. Piere, of Piere Benoy and Hendrikje Van Schoonhoven. Wit.: Jacobus Van Schoonhoven, Geertruy Van Schoonhoven.

1697

Sep. 25. Johannes, of Johannes Lucasz and Susanna Wendell. Wit.: Phlip Wendell, Ariaantje Wendell.

Oct. 31. Johannes, of Johannes Schuyler and Elisabeth Staats. Wit.: Robbert Levingston, Jacob Staats, Maria Schuyler.

Susanna, of Daniel Bratt and Elisabeth Lansing. Wit.: Barent Bratt, Susanna Bratt.

Hendrik, of Antoni Bries and Catrine Rykman. Wit.: Jacob Lookerman, Pieter Rykman, Elsje Schuyler.

Nov. 7. Pieter, of Hendrik Van Dyk and Maria Schuyler. Wit.: Jacobus Van Dyk, Meyndert Schuyler, Geertruy Schuyler.

Styntje, of Isak Vosburgh and Annetje Jansz. Wit.: Evert Wendell, Elisabeth Wendell.

Eva, of Willem V. Alen and Maria V. Petten. Wit.: Claas V. Petten, Teunis V. Vechten, Catrina V. Petten.

Tobias, of Pieter Martensz and Ariaantje Barents. Wit.: Wessel Ten Broek, Catrina Ten Broek.

Barent, of Pieter Vosburgh and Jannetje Barents. Wit.: Jacobus Turk, Catrina Turk.

Pieter, of Jan Fondaa and Marritje Lokerman. Wit.: Jacob Lookerman, Maria Lookerman.

Nov. 14. Ahasueros, of Jacobus Turk and Catrine Benthuysen. Wit.: Geertruy Benthuysen.

Rachel, of Willem Jansz and Feitje Dirksz. Wit.: Teunis Dirksz, Caatje Teunisz.

Tryntje, of Pieter Van Slyk and Johanna Jansz. Wit.: David Schuyler, Elsje Staats.

Nov. 21. Catelyntje, of Willem Jacobsz and Elisabeth Rosenboom. Wit.: Johannes Rosenboom, Margriet Mingal.

Nov. 24. Jochum, of Jan Ratelief and Rachel Jochumsz. Wit.: William Hilton, Maria Rosenboom.

Harmen, of Thomas Harmensz and Mayken Oothout. Wit.: Hendrik Oothout, Trynte Braades.

Dec. 5. Johannes, of Jonathan Jansz and Caatje Martensz. Wit.: Dirk Wessels, Styntje Wessels.

Dec. 12. Rykart, of Gerrit Rykertsz and Barbar Jansz. Wit.: Maas Rykartsz, Grietje Rykartsz.

Dec. 15. Gysbert, of Gerrit Rosenboom and Maria Sanders. Wit.: Pieter Mingal, Barent Sanders, Elisabeth Wendell.

Dec. 25. Lysbeth, of Caspar Conyn and Aletta Winnen. Wit.: Pieter Bronk, Wyntje Dirksz.

Amos, formerly Harogiechta, i. e., One who descended dead from heaven, 40 years old.

Asa, formerly Onasiadikha, i. e., Pasture burner, about 35 years old.

1698
1698, Jan. 1. Dorethe, of Andries Witbeek and Engeltje Volkertsz. Wit.: Hendrik Douwe, Elsje Douwe.

Harmen, of Harmanus Vedder and Grietje V. Slyk. Wit.: Albert Rykman, Jʳ, Maria Vinhagel.

Jan. 2. Maria, of Joseph Jansz and Zytje Marselis. Wit.: Hasueros Marselis, Sara Marselis.

Jan. 12. Jeremias and Pieter, twins of Pieter Schuyler and Maria V. Renselaar. Wit.: Kiliaan Van Renselaar, Godefridus Dellius, Elisabeth Schuyler, Alida Livingston.

Jan. 16. Antje, of Lambert Jansz and Jannetje Mingall. Wit.: Abram Van Alstyn, Maritje Van Alstyn.

Arent, of Hans Bekker and Cornelia Schayk. Wit.: Laurens Van Schayk, Cornelia Van Schayk, Zytje Van der Karre.

Pieter, of Jan Albertsz. Wit.: Pieter Vosburg, Jannetje Vosburgh.

Jan. 19. Catelyntje, of Isak Verplank and Abigail Uytenbogaart. Wit.: David Schuyler, Geertruy Schuyler.

Feb. 6. Rachel, of Isak Casparts and Dorethe Bosch. Wit.: Daniel Bratt, Marritje Van Alen.

Feb. 13. Jannetje, of Cornelis V. Vegte and Mara Lucasz. Wit.: Salomon V. Vegte, Hendrik Douw, Catrina V. Renselaar.

Willem, of Jhon Fine and Jopje Claasz. Wit.: William Hoge, Jan Van der Kerre, Martina Hoges.

Feb. 16. Gerrit, of Gysbert Marselis and Barbar Croesbeek. Wit.: Steph Croesbeek, Huybertje Jouets [?].

Feb. 20. Wilhelm, of Cornelis V. Scherluyne and Geertruy Harmensz. Wit.: Gerrit Lucasz, Lysbet Nottingam.

Feb. 27. Maritje, of Coenraadt Burgaart and Geesje Van Wyen. Wit.: Gerrit Lucasz, Ariaantje Van Wye.

March 6. Pieter, of Jacob Winne and Marretje Bronk. Wit.: Pieter Bronk, Catrina Staats.

Sara, of Joseph Yets and Huybertje Marselis. Wit.: Hasueros Merselis, Sara Merselis.

March 9. Benjamin, of Jacob Vos and Jannetje Quakelbosch. Wit.: Harme Van Bommell, Lysbeth Bogart.

Tanneke, of Jelis Fonda and Rachel Winne. Wit.: Levinus Winne, Elsje Winne.

March 16. Grietje, of Daniel Keteluym and Debora Vile. Wit.: Douwe Aukens, Margriet Levingston.

Apr. 3. Benjamin, of Johannes Jansz and Lysbeth Leendertsz. Wit.: Andries Jansz, Tamus Williams, Tryntje Bradis.

Apr. 10. Geertje, of Willem Gysbertsz and Catryn Wynandsz. Wit.: Wouter Quakelbosch, Geertruy Gysbertsz.

Apr. 25. Jacob, 2 months old, of Brant and Margriet, pros. Wit.: Canastasji.

1698

Neeltje, about 10 weeks old, of Nadikansha and Catrine, pros. Wit.: Dorcas.

Marcus, about 4 months old, adopted by Josina. Wit.: Martha.

May 1. Benjamin, of Antoni Bratt and Willemje Teunisz. Wit.: Elbert Harmensz, Sara Bratt.

May 8. Elisabeth, of Hendrik V. Renselaar and Catrina Verbrugge. Wit.: P. Schuyler, G. Dellius, Isabella Dellius.

Simon, of Carel Hansz and Lysbet Rinkhout. Wit.: Willem Claasz, Rebecca Claasz.

June 26. Johannes, of Abraham Cuyler and Catrina Blyker. Wit.: Meyndert Schuyler, Jannetje Blyker.

Johannes, of Hasueros Marselis and Sara Heemstraat. Wit.: Takel Heemstraat, Tryntje Marselis.

Folkert, of Hendrik Douwe and Neeltje Myndertsz. Wit.: Andris Douw, Grietje Gertsz.

Marietje, of Eduward Wieler and Josyntje Gardenier. Wit.: Jan Fondaas, Marretje Fondaas.

Maria, of Wessel Ten Broek and Catrine Lokerman. Wit.: Samuel Ten Broek, Geertruy Schuyler.

July 10. Elisabeth, of Wouter V. d. Zee and Jannetje Swart. Wit.: Albert V. d. Zee, Hilletje Keteluyn.

Maria, of Lucas Lucasz and Judic Marselis. Wit.: Willem Croesbeek, Sytje Marselis.

Engeltje, of Albert Slingerlant and Hester Brikker. Wit.: Johannes Appell, Annetje Appell.

Willem, of Willem Scharp and Geertruy Rees. Wit.: Hasueros Marselis, Sara Heemstraat.

Maria, of Hendrik Clauw and Cornelia Scharp. Wit.: Antoni Bratt, Wilmje Bratt.

July 15. Jacobus, of Johannes Teller and Susanna Wendell. Wit.: Johannes V. Alen, Tryntje Wendell.

July 16. Elisabeth, adopted by Rebecca, pros. Wit.: Marie, pros.

July 17. Engeltje, of Robbert Levingston, Jr., and Margareta Schuyler. Wit.: Maria Schuyler.

Saartje, of Phlip Leendertsz and Wyntje Dirks. Wit.: Tam Williams, Elsje Winne.

Catrine, of Robbert Levingston and Alida Schuyler. Wit.: Brant Schuyler, Abram De Peyster, Catrine, Countess of Bellomont.

Abram, of Marten Jansz and Jannetje Cornelisz. Wit.: Abram Verplank, Maritje Verplank.

Aug. 14. Arie, of Andries Gardenier and Eytje Ariesz. Wit.: Samuel Gardenier, Aaltje Gardenier.

Evert, of Abram Wendell and Mayken Van Esch. Wit.: Hendrik Van Esch, Marritje Wendell.

1698
Johannis, of Nanning Visser and Alida Vinhagel. Wit.:
Frerik Visser, Maria Vinhagel.
Eduward, of Mettys Warmond and Susan Hiks. Wit.:
Eduward Reems, Annetje Reyers.
Aug. 28. Cornelis, of Jacobus Van Dyk and Jacomine
Glenn. Wit.: Hendrik Van Dyk, Catrine Staats.
Elisabeth, of Jacob Schermerhoorn and Gerritje Hendriks. Wit.: Albert Rykman, Margriet Levingston.
Sep. 4. Alida, of Isak Hendriksz and Judik Jansz. Wit.:
Jan Goes, Claas Lucasz, Sara Gerritsz.
Sep. 25. Nicolaas, of Hendrik Hansz and Debora Van
Dam. Wit.: Claas R. Van Dam, Hendrik Van Esch,
Catrina Van Esch.
Oct. 2. Dirk, of Piere Villeroy and Catrine Van der
Heyde. Wit.: Catrine Ten Broek, Robbt Levingston, Jr
Oct. 9. Pieter, of Coenraad Hooghteeling and Tryntje
Van Slyk. Wit.: Jan Bronk, Elsje Winne.
Gerrit, of Johannes Bekker and Anna Van der Zee.
Wit.: Johannes Mingall, Maria Mingall.
Oct. 23. Willem, of Teunis Willemsz and Jannetje Hendriks. Wit.: Evert Banker, Elisabeth Banker.
Maria, of Abraham Staats and Elsje Wendell. Wit.:
Jacob Staats, Marietje Wendell.
Oct. 30. Annetje, of Johannes Ouwerkerk, and Neeltje
Claasz. Wit.: Johannes Schuyler, Elysebeth Wendell.
Jacob, of Jacob Teunisz, or Tainisz, and Anna Lokerman.
Wit.: Hendrik Van Esch, Catrina Van Esch.
Nov. 6. Mauris, of Johannes Van Alen and Sara Dingman. Wit.: Melchert Wynandsz, Catryn V. Alen.
Nov. 20. Johanna, of Johannes Beekman and Eva
Vinhagel. Wit.: Jan Vinhagel, Ariaantje Wendell.
Mary, of William Hilten and Antje Berkhoven. Wit.:
Jan Ratly, Judik Marselis.
Nov. 27. Harmannus, of Johannes Visscher and Elisabeth Nottingham. Wit.: Bastiaan Visser, Ariaantje Wendell.
Nov. 30. Marie, of Piere Benoye and Hendrikje V.
Schoonhoven. Wit.: Abram V. Deurse, Jacomyntje V.
Deursen.
Dec. 4. Dirkje, of Abram Alstyn and Marietje V.
Deusen. Wit.: Jacob Vosburgh, Helena V. Deusen.
Dec. 18. Harmannus, of Tjerk Harmansz and Femmetje Jansz. Wit.: Gerrit Lucasz, Ariaantje Wendell.
Dec. 25. Arent and Laurens, twins of Dirk Van der
Karre and Feitje Claasz. Wit.: Antoni Van Schayk, Evert
Banker, Anna V. Stryen, Catrine V. Schayk.
Claas, of Arent V. Schaak and Marietje V. Loon. Wit.:
Hendrik Sasberry, Cornelia V. Schaak.

1699

1699, Jan. 1. Pieter, of Daniel Winnen and Dirk V. Esch. Wit.: Livinus Winne, Rachel Winne.

Jan. 4. Elisabeth, of Willem Croesbeek and Geertruy Schuyler. Wit.: Steph. Croesbeek, Rebecca Croesbeek.

Jan. 8. Jochum, of Isak V. Alstyn and Jannetje V. Valkenborgh. Wit.: Jochum V. Valkenborgh, Maritje V. Valkenborgh.

Cornelis, of Gerrit Jacobsz and Lysbeth Aarnoutse Eli. Wit.: Lambert Staringh, Lena Fonda.

Jacob, of Johannes V. Hoesen, Jannetje Cornelisz. Wit.: Jan Tysz, Geesje Coenraadt.

Jan. 18. William, of Robbert Barrith and Wyntje Jansz. Wit.: William Hilten, Cornelia Gilberts.

Feb. 19. Eva, of Lambert Jochumsz and Jannetje Fransen. Wit.: Melchert Melchertsz, Geertruy Harmensz.

Johannes, of Johannes Cuyler and Elsje Ten Broek. Wit.: Antoni Coster, Geertruy Schuyler.

Johannes and Gerrit, twins of Mathys Nak and Susanna Lansing. Wit.: Gerrit Lansing, Elsje Lansing, Sofia Nak.

Feb. 22. Johannes, of Jan Salomonsz and Catelyn Lokerman. Wit.: Kiliaan Van Renselaar, Catrine Van Renselaar.

Feb. 26. Lucas, of Gerrit Lucasz and Sara Harmansz. Wit.: Lucas Gerritsz, Geertruy Scherluyn.

March 19. Catrine, of Evert Ridder and Anna Van Esch. Wit.: Hendrik Oothout, Jannetje Oothout.

March 26. Anna, of Dirk Van der Heyden and Rachel Keteluyn. Wit.: Abraham Kip, Margriet Levingston.

Ariaantje, of Barent Gerritsz and Geertruy Jansz. Wit.: Johannes Gerritsz, Neeltje Gerritsz.

Apr. 9. Andries, of Andries Rees and Ariaantje Scherp. Wit.: Tomas Harmensz, Mayjen Oothout.

Johannes, of Michiel Calljer and Titje Van Hoesen. Wit.: Daniel Bratt, Maria Van Housen.

Sep. 3. The following chn. were ba. by P. Nucella: Elsje, of Frederik Hermenssen and Margrietje Hanssen. Wit.: Joannes Hanssen, Hester Tjercks.

Eduwart, of Thomas Willemsse and Agnitje Gansenvoos. Wit.: Thomas Hermensse, Elisabet Gansevoos.

Hendrick, of Antoni Coster and Elisabet Ten Broeck. Wit.: Jan Lancing, Christina Ten Broeck.

Marytje, of Hendrick Janssen and Lyntje Winnen. Wit.: Joannes Galen, Antje Galen.

Cathryntje, of Pieter Hoogeboom and Jannetje Mullers. Wit.: Meeuwis Hoogeboom, Hilletje Mullers.

Alida, of Gerrit Rycks and Barber Janss. Wit.: Thomas Jansse, Lena Pruym.

1699–1700

Saartje, of Samuel Gardenier and Helena Hendrickse.
Wit.: Wessel Dirriks, Sara Dingemans.
Evart, of Hermen Jansse and Lysbet Boogert. Wit.:
Evart Ridder, Antje Ridders.
Jacob, of Isack Vosburg and Annetje Goes. Wit.: Jan
Goes, Teuntje Goes.
Volckert, of Hendrick Douw and Neeltje Meynerts.
Wit.: Andries Douw, Grietje Teunisse.
Isack, of Jan Fort and Margriet Rinckhout. Wit.:
Maas Rykse, Geertruy Groot.
Cornelis, of Isack Ouderkerck and Mayke Van Es. Wit.:
Gerrit Van Es, Jannetje Oothout.
Hendrickje, of Hendrick Oothout and Caatje Douw.
Wit.: Jonas Douw, Margriet Schuyler.
Ariaantje, of Melcher Van der Poel and Catharina Van
Alen. Wit.: Melchert Wynantse Van der Poelen, Abigail
Van den Vos.
Elisabat, of Daniel Brat and Elisabet Lancing. Wit.:
Hendrick Lancing, Lysbet Casperse.
Cornelia, of Wouter Quackelebosch and Cornelia Boogert.
Wit.: Albert Rykman, Jr., Antje Quackelebosch.
Joannes, of Daniel Van der Linde and Lysbeth Crugier.
Wit.: Marten Crugier, Jannetje Crugier.
Sep. 8. Hendrick, of Johannes Bleecker and Anna
Coster. Wit.: Antony Coster, Cathryna Cuyler.
Catharina, of Johannes Glen and Jannetje Bleyckers.
Wit.: Jan Jansse Bleyker, Grietje Bleycker.
Mary, of Matthys Bofie and Cathryn Barroa. Wit.:
Bennoni Corlaer, Marta.
Sep. 10. Margriet, of Asag and Maria, pros. Wit.:
Arent, Eva.
Dirrick, of Willem Janssen and Feytje Van Vegten.
Wit.: Daniel Brat, Santje [?] Brat.
1700, Jan. 5. Arent, of Hendrick Van Dyck and
Maria Schuylers. Wit.: Willem Groesbeek, Rachel Schuy-
lers.
Thomas, of Eduwart Whiler and Josyna Jacobsen. Wit.:
Jaen Fyn, Alida Fyn.
Geertruy, of Gerrit Roelofsen and Marytje Jans. Wit.:
Roelof Gerritsen, Geertruy Roelofsen.
Lysbet, of Francoys Winnen and Elsje Gansevoort.
Wit.: Leving Winnen, Willemje Winnen.
Lysbet, of Jan Van Strey and Annaatje Van d. Poele.
Wit.: Antony Van Schayck, Lysbet Correlaar.
Dirrick, of Ahasueros Marseelis and Sara Heemstraat.
Wit.: Gysbert Marseelis, Barber Marseelis.
Annaatje, of Johannes Van Vegten and Maria Bogardus.
Wit.: Pieter Bogardus, Margrietje Van Vegten.

1700
Abraam, of Jacob and Jacomyn, pros. Wit.: Elisabet Wendels.

Willem, of Evert Banckert and Elisabeth Abeel. Wit.: Pieter Schuyler, Antoni Van Schayck, Sibilla Bankerts.

Hermanus, of Bastiaan Hermanse and Dirrickje Teunisse. Wit.: Frederik Hermesse, Hester Hermesse.

Gerrit, of Herbert Jacobsen and Marritje Gerrits. Wit.: Jan Gerritse, Catalyntje Van Elsland.

Catharina, of Anthoni Bries and Catharina Rykmans. Wit.: Albert Rykman, Jr, Antoni Rutgers, Catharina Rutgers.

Jan. 7. Roelof, of Jan Cittene and Marritje Roelofse. Wit.: Roelof Gerritsen, Geertruy Roelofsen.

Annaatje, of Jacob Bastiaanse De Wit and Saartje Jans. Wit.: Pieter Schuyler, Maria Van Renselaar.

Lena, of Mathys Hoes and Cornelia Van Deusen. Wit.: Abraam Janssen, Marritje Van Deusen.

Margrietje, of Andries Hansen Huyk and Cathryn Lammertsen. Wit.: Robbert Levingston, Jr, Margrietje Levingston.

Bernardus, of Johannes Brat and Maria Keetel. Wit.: David Keetel, Robbert Levingston, Marritje Brat.

Jannetje, of Dominicus Van Schayck and Rebecca Groesbeek. Wit.: Johannes Groesbeek, Geertruy Groesbeek.

Adam, of Jacob Dingemans and Eva Swartwoud. Wit.: Adam Dingemans, Aaltje Dingemans.

Maria, of Jan Fonda and Marritje Loockermans. Wit.: Jillis Fonda, Landje Loockermans.

Eytje, of Pieter Martissen and Ariaantje Barens. Wit.: Marten Martisse, Judickje Barens.

Magtel, of Adriaan Quackelbosch and Catharina Van Schayck. Wit.: Jan Quackelbosch, Magtel Quackelbosch.

Hendrick, of Maas Van Beuningen and Ariaantje Van Weye. Wit.: Jacob Schermerhoorn, Marritje Hendriks.

Anna, of Abraam Wendell and Mayke Van Es. Wit.: Evert Wendel, Marritje Wendel.

Elsje, of Philip Wendel and Marytje Visscher. Wit.: Gerrit Lancing, Geertruy Van Schaluynen.

Ifje, of Andries Brat and Cornelia Verwey. Wit.: Antoni Bries, Elsje Schuylers.

Jan, of Johannes Oothout and Aaltje Evertse. Wit.: Evert Ridder, Antje Ridders.

Apr. 28. Elisabeth, of Johannes Rooseboom and Gerritje Costers. Wit.: Antoni Coster, Elisabet Rooseboom.

Maria, of Leving Winnen and Willemje Viele. Wit.: Johannes Beekman, Margrietje Levingston.

Catharina, of Stephanus Groesbeek and Elisabet Lancing. Wit.: Claes Jacobse Groesbeeck, Geertje Lancing.

Ahasueros, of Gerrit Rooseboom and Maria Sanders.

1700
Sara, of Abraam Cuyler and Catharina Bleyckers. Wit.:
Pieter Van Brugg, Antje Blykers.
Sara, of Johannes Groenendyck and Delia Cuyler. Wit.:
Abraam Cuyler, Sara Van Brugg.
Pieter, of Pieter Van Slyck and Johanna Hanssen. Wit.:
Cornelis Van Nes, Marritje Van Nes.
Alida, of Gerrit Van Wey and Agnitje Casperssen. Wit.:
Marten Dell, Cathryn Van Wey.
Abraam, of Jan Jansse Van Aarnheym and Hester
Fonda. Wit.: Claes Fonda, Helena Fonda.
Meynert, of Reynier Meynertsen and Saartje Brat. Wit.:
Antoni Brat, Neeltje Douw.
Marycke, of Thomas Willinton and Tryntje Wendels.
Wit.: Johann Mingael, Elsje Lancing.
Willem, of Pieter Walderen and Tryntje Van den Berg.
Wit.: Jacob Lancing, Cornelia Van den Berg.
Thomas, of Samuel Daxie and Barbar Janss. Wit.: Jan
Fonda, Marritje Fonda.
Pieter, of Hendrick Hanssen and Debora Van Dam.
Wit.: Claes Ripse Van Dam, Andries Douw, Elsje Hen-
dricksen.
May 9. Margriet, of Patrick Magrickerie and Sije Hoog-
teelen. Wit.: Hendrick Van Dyk, Tryntje Wandelaar.
May 12. Adam, of Arent and Agniet, pros. Wit.: Re-
becca.
Johannes, of Johannes Cloet and Baata Van Slegtenaats.
Wit.: Robbert Levingston, Jr, Lysbet Schuyler.
Sybrand, of Anthoni Van Schayck and Marytje Van dr
Poel. Wit.: Evert Bancker, Grietje Van Schayk.
Gerrit, of Isack Casperssen and Dorothe Bos. Wit.:
Jacobus Lancing, Maritje Van Hoese.
Eva, of Teunis Dirricksen and Cathalina Van Petten.
Wit.: Willem·V. Haalen, Grietje Volkets.
Jan, of Hendrick Janssen and Cornelia Claessen. Wit.:
Willem Groesbeek, Jan Fyn, Jannetje Oothout.
Hendrick, of Coenraad Hendriksen and Geesje Hendrick-
sen. Wit.: Maas Hendriksen, Ariaantje Hendriksen.
Maria, of Richard Janssen and Tryntje Hoogteelen.
Wit.: Hendrick Douw, Neeltje Douw.
Kommertje, of Caspar Conyn and Alettico Winnen.
Wit.: Tam Willemse, Sara Van Brugg.
Johannes, of Dirrick Janssen Goes and Lybetje Luy-
cassen Wyngart. Wit.: Claes Luycassen Wyngart, Mayke
Jansse Goes.
Rachel, of Isack Verplancke and Abigail Uyt den Boo-
gert. Wit.: Abraam Schuyler, Melchert Van der Poel, Jr,
Racheltje Schuyler.
Kiliaan, of Cornelis Stevissen and Hilletje Loockermans.
Wit.: Pieter Van Brugg, Marritje Schuylers.

LIST OF ABBREVIATIONS.

A., Albany (same as N. A.).
A. Co., Albany County.
b., born.
bapt., ba., baptized.
ch., child; chn., children.
Col. R., Colony Rensselaerswyck.
dau., daughter.
dec^d, deceased.
E., Eng., England.
J. C., Jesus Christ.
l., living.
L. I., Long Island.
marr., married.
mo., mother.
N. Albany, N. A., New Albany.
N. E., New England.
N. Haarlem, New Haarlem.
N. Rochelle, New Rochelle.
N. Y., New York.
O. E., O. Eng., Old England.
pros., proselyte, proselytes.
R., Rensselaerswyck.
Sch., Schenectady
wid., widow.
wid^r, widower.
wit., witness, witnesses.
y. d., unmarried woman.
y. m., unmarried man.
Wouter, of Gerrit Lansing, means Wouter, *child* of Gerrit Lansing.
By Elizabeth Wendell means *presented for baptism* by Elizabeth
Wendell, etc., etc.

INDEX.

There was some question as to the best mode of preparing this index, inasmuch as there are so many variations in spelling the cognomens as well as the baptismal names in these records. Those entering the names in the records appear to have exercised their own judgment as to orthography, and frequently varied it without apparent reason. If all the names were indexed separately, just as they appear in the records with the original spelling, it is evident that the work of tracing family lineages by the unskilled searcher would be greatly increased. It was concluded therefore that it would facilitate reference by embracing under one heading all names evidently belonging to one family, and indexing them, as far as practicable, under that form which now seems to be in most common use.

It is also to be observed that most of the early Dutch families were not regularly entered under their family name until many years later. They were mostly known by their patronymic. For instance the Heemstraats will have to be looked for, sometimes, under Dirks or Takels, the Groesbeeks under Claasze, the Van der Poels under Wynandtsz, the Van Deusens under Teuisz, the Van Beurens and Vroomans under Meesz or Maas, the Van Bergens under Gerrits, etc., etc.

Appended will be found a list of the most numerous variations in the surnames that appear in these records:

Barens, Barents, Barentsz, Barent.
Bleecker, Blyker, Blykers, Bleycker, Bleyker, Bleyckers.
Borgert, Borger, Borgaart, Burgaart.
Brickers, Brikkers, Brickersz, Brikker.
Carstens, Carstelsz, Carstersz, Karstensz.
Casperssen, Casparsz, Caspersz, Casparts, Casperse.
Claasz, Claasen, Claessen, Claassen, Claesz.
Cobes, Cobus, Kobusz, Cobusz.
Coeman, Koeman, Koeyman, Coeyman, Kooyman.
Coljer, Cailler, Cailljer, Coller, Caillardt, Cailjer, Calljer.
Creeve, Kreeve, Greeve, Kreese.
Crygier, Kreigier, Crugier, Krygier.
De Ridder, Ridders, Ridder, Riddert.
Dirksz, Dirks, Dirckse, Dirricksen, Dirriks.
Evertsz, Everts, Evertsen, Evertse.
Fonda, Fondaas, Vonda, Fondaal, Fondaa.
Gerritsz, Gerrits, Gerritse, Gertsz, Gerritsen.
Groesbeek, Croesbeek, Croesbeeck, Kroesbeck, Croesbeck. [Also Van Rotterdam.]

Harmensz, Harmansz, Hermanse, Harmens, Hermenssen, Hermesse, Hermensz, Hermensse.

Harrits, Harris, Herris, Harrit.

Hendriks, Henderiksz, Hendricksz, Hendriksen, Hendriksz, Hendricksen, Hendericks, Hendrickse, Hendrix.

Hoogteeling, Hooghteling, Hoogteelen, Hooghteeling, Hoochteeling.

Isaacksz, Isaaksz, Isaacsz, Isaksz.

Jansz, Janssen, Jans, Jansen, Janss, Jansse, Janse.

Jurriaans, Jurriaanse, Jurriaansz, Jurries, Juriaansz.

Keteluym, Keteluyn, Kitteluym, Ketelheim, Kitteluyn.

Lieves, Lives, Lievensz, Livesz, Livisz, Lievense.

Lookerman, Lokerman, Loockerman, Loockermans.

Lucasz, Luycasz, Luykensz, Luyckensz.

Maesz, Mees, Maasz, Meesz.

Marselis, Marselisz, Merselis, Marseelis, Marcelisz, Marzelis.

Mattheusz, Matheuisz, Mateuisz, Matheusz, Mathysz, Matthysz.

Mingal, Mingaal, Mingall, Mingael.

Myndertsz, Meyndertsz, Meynderts, Meinders, Meynerts, Meynertsen.

Ouderkerk, Ouderkerck, Overkerk, Ouwerkerk.

Parkar, Parker, Percker, Parckar, Perker, Parcker.

Quakkenbosch, Quakelbosch, Quakkelbosch, Quackelebosch.

Ratlife, Rateliff, Redly, Ratli, Ratelief, Ratly, Retle, Rattelis.

Roelofsz, Roeloffsz, Roelofsen, Roelofs, Roelofse.

Rutgers, Rutgersz, Rutger, Rutgertsz.

Rykse, Ryksz, Rycksz, Rykertsz, Rycks, Rykartsz.

Sickels, Sikkels, Sikkel, Sikkell, Sickel.

Simonsz, Symensz, Symonsz, Symens.

Sivers, Siwerse, Siversen, Siwers, Siwersz.

Slegtenhorst, Slechtenhorst, Slogtenhorst, Van Slegtenaats.

Stephens, Stevens, Stephensen, Stevissen.

Ten Broek, Ten Brouck, Ten Broeck, Ten Brook, T. Broek, Tenbroek.

Trujeks, Ter Jeuks, Terjeks, Trujex.

Van Alsteyn, Van Alstyn, Alstyn, Alestyn, V. Alstyn.

Van Corlar, Van Corlaar, V. Corlar, Corlaer, Corlar, Correlaar.

Van den Bergh, Van der Berch, Van den Berg, V. der Bergh, Van den Berch, Van Bergen, V. Bergen.

Van den Bogaardt, Bogaart, Bogart, Boogert, Van den Bogaard, Van de Bogaardt, Van den Boogaardt, Van den Boogaard, V. Bogaart.

Van Deurse, Van Deusen, V. Deusen, V. Deursen, Van Deursen, Van Deursz, Van Deuse.

Van Hoesen, Van Hoese, V. Hoesen, Van Housen.

Van Olinde, Van Olindt, V. Olinda, Van der Linde, Van der Linden.

Van Renselaar, Renselaar, V. Renselaar, Van Rensselaer.

Van Sant, Van Santen, Van Sante, Van Sandt, V. Santen.
Van Sasbergen, Sasberry, Van Sasberge, Van Sasberry.
Van Schayck, Van Schayk, V. Schayk, Van Schaak, V. Schaak, Schayk.
Van Scherluyn, Scherluyn, V. Scherluyne, Scharluyn, Van Schaluynen, V. Scherluyn.
Van Schoonhove, Van Schoonhoven, V. Schoonhoven, Schoonhoven.
Van Slyk, V. Slyk, Van der Slyk, Van Slyck, Slyk.
Van Tricht, Van Trigt, Van Trigh, V. Trigt.
Van Valkenborgh, Valkenborg, Van Valkenborg, V. Valkenborgh, Van Valkenborch, Valkenborch, Van Valkenbork.
Van Vechten,'Van Vegten, Van Veghten, V. Vegte, Van dʳ Vechten.
Van Wey, Verwey, Van Weye, Van Wye, Van Wyen, Verway.
Vielé, Vilen, Vile, Vyle, V. Eli.
Volkerts, Folkertsz, Folkersz, Volkers, Volkensz, Volkets, Volkertsz.
Vos, Van den Vos, Van Vosch, Voss.
Vosburg, Vosburch, Vosburgh, Vosberge.
Wieler, Whiler, Willer, Wiler, Wile.
Willemsz, Willems, Willemsse, Willemse.
Wynandtsz, Wynands, Wynants, Wynandsz.
Wyngart, Wingaart, Wingaardt, Wyngaart, Wyngaard.

Abbedis, Maria, Marietje, 24, 67.
Abeel, Abeell, Catelyntje, 69.
  Elizabeth, 22, 53, 61, 69, 82.
  Jan, 6, 15, 61.
  Johannes, 27, 44, 46, 49, 61, 64, 65, 67, 70, 72.
Abels, Abelsz, Hendrick, 4, 14.
  Sophia, Sephia, 4, 18.
Abramsz, Abrahamsz, Anna, 54.
  Catelyntje, 55.
  Engeltie, 4, 13, 61.
  Herbert, 54.
  Jacob, 3, 15, 41, 44.
  Melchert, Melchior, 4, 17, 41, 42, 47, 54, 56, 69, 71.
  Teunis, 19.
  Teuwis, Teuis, 5, 51.
  Willem, 37.
Adamsz, Adams, Aaltje, 5, 11.
  Anneken, 37.
  Syntje, 35.
  Tanneke, 26.
Albertsz, Aalbertsz, Geertje, 14.
  Jan, 58, 63, 70, 77.
  Janneke, 38.
  Maria, Marretje, 5, 17, 73.
Andriesz, Andriessen, Ariaantje, 75.
  Catryn, 6, 12.
  Cornelia, 21, 61, 71.

Engeltje, 13.
Gerritje, 4, 14.
Jan, 34, 47, 62, 66.
Lambert, 29.
Neeltje, 4.
Anthonisz, Egbert, 34.
Appel, Appels, Appell, Anna, Annetje, 3, 11, 40, 53, 62, 78.
Aries, Adriaan, Arien, 3, 11, 21, 47.
  Johannes, 3, 15, 36, 40, 45, 53, 58, 60, 62, 78.
  Wilhelm, 34.
Arensz, Arentsz, Aartsz, Aaltje, 5, 11.
Aartje, Ariaantje, 38, 59.
Benoni, 38.
Dirk, 61.
Gerrit, 38.
Ifje, 58.
Jacob, 66.
Leendert, 23, 49.
Tryntje, 32.
Wouter, 37.
Ariaansz, Adriaans, Ariesz, Arisz, Eytje, 25, 62, 67, 78.
Gerrit, 32.
Jenneke, 62, 68.
Aukens, Douwe, 21, 39, 77.

Bakker, Anna, 38.
Bancker, Banker, Banckerts,
Anna, 23.
Elisabeth, Lysbet, 1, 6, 13,
16, 38, 41, 44, 48, 53, 61,
62, 71, 72, 79.
Evert, Everard, 6, 13, 22, 38,
44, 45, 46, 53, 61, 62, 67,
69, 79, 82, 83.
Maria, 8, 17.
Sibilla, 82.
Wilhelm, 69.
Barentsz, etc., Agnietje, 22.
Albertje, 21.
Antje, 53.
Ariaantje, 10, 11, 26, 58, 61,
62, 66, 70, 76.
Cornelis, 25.
Dirk, 39.
Elsje, 32.
Folkje, 50.
Jannetje, 53, 61, 66, 76.
Judickje, 82.
Maria, Marritje, 17, 54.
Reinier, 3, 18, 44, 48, 53.
Susanna, 6, 18, 23, 35, 53.
Willem, 53.
Barrit, Barrith, Berrit, Robbert,
49, 56, 65, 73, 80.
Barroa, Antoine, 24, 36.
Cathryn, 81.
Bastiaansz, Dirck, 13.
Dirkje, 3.
Harmen, 14, 46, 47.
Hester, 2.
Beaufils, Bofie, Mathieu, Mat-
thys, 49, 81.
Becker, Bekker, Antje, Anna, 6,
35, 49, 67.
Jan, 1, 15, 60.
Johannes, Joh., Hans, 35,
37, 46, 52, 53, 60, 62, 70,
71, 77, 79.
Mari, Marie, 1, 16.
Martina, 17, 25, 37, 53, 60,
66, 75.
Beek, Elizabeth, 24, 63.
Beekman, Beeckman, Antje, 37.
Hendrik, 33, 36, 39, 47, 48,
58, 66, 75.
Johannes, 2, 15, 25, 33, 37,
42, 43, 46, 54, 55, 65, 66,
68, 70, 74, 79, 82.
Machtelt, Magtelt, 2, 16,
38.
Marten, 25, 58.
Metje, 33.
Bellomont, Catrine, Countess of,
78.
Benoy, Pierre, 28, 75, 79.

Bensing, Catelyn, 65.
Cathrine, 28.
Dirck, 3, 13, 38, 47, 52.
Johannis, 5, 15, 45, 60, 68,
70.
Marietje, 55.
Samson, 5, 18, 33, 38, 43, 48,
58, 63, 70.
Tysje, 3, 19.
Berkhoven, Anna, Antje, 26, 60,
66, 73, 79.
Beyer, Judith, 48.
Nicolaes, 48.
Bicker, Bikker, Jan, 21.
Johannes, 21.
Martina, 6, 17.
Bleecker, Blyker, etc., Antje, 74,
83.
Caatje [see Catarina], 7, 12,
47, 59.
Catarina [see Caatje], 24, 45,
67, 78, 83.
Jan, 2, 15, 59, 71, 81.
Jannetje, 8, 15, 30, 54, 58,
78, 81.
Johannes, 6, 15, 26, 39, 40,
45, 47, 55, 65, 67, 73, 81.
Margriet, Grietjen, 2, 13, 17,
20, 33, 56, 59, 62, 67, 73,
81.
Bogardus, Anna, 9.
Cornelis, 10, 12.
Maria, Marritje, 8, 17, 30, 81.
Pieter, 3, 33, 43, 53, 81.
Rachel, 20.
Wyntje, Weinte, 3, 19, 53,
68, 70.
Bogy, Bogi, Pieter, Piere, 29, 38,
54.
Boin, Willem, 24.
Booch, Boogh, Bouw, Solomon,
6, 18, 21, 46.
Boogert. See Van den Bogert.
Borgert, etc., Catarina, 22, 47.
Coenraadt, 29, 77.
Bosboom, Antje, 60.
Feitje, 28.
Marritje, 25.
Bosch, Bos, Dorethee, 56, 68, 77,
83.
Jan, 53.
Pieter, 23, 46, 53.
Wyntje, 53.
Bout, Geertje, 2, 14.
Willem, 2, 19.
Braathorst, Bradhorst, Jona-
than, 20, 28, 74.
Brabanders, Folckje, 3, 13.
Bradis, Braades, Trynte, Tryn-
tje, 76, 77.

Dirksz, Dirriks, etc., Feitje,
  Feytje, 29, 65, 72, 76.
Geesje, 70.
Helena, 63, 70.
Jan, 9.
Jannetie, 4, 15.
Margriet, 58.
Maria, 27.
Michiel, 22, 36, 44.
Neeltje, 22, 36.
Sara, 28.
Taakel, 2, 19, 35, 55, 75.
Teunis, 27, 65, 68, 71, 76, 83.
Weinte, Weyntje, 35, 60, 65,
  76, 78.
Wessel, 81.
Docksje, Daxie, Sam., Samuel,
  31, 83.
Dongues, Jannetje, 32.
Douw, Douwe, Douws, Andries,
  Andris, 8, 11, 29, 50, 66,
  78, 81, 83.
Caatje, 81.
Catarina, Catryn, 3, 12, 21.
Elsje, 77.
Hendrik, 20, 29, 77, 78, 81,
  83.
Jan, 3, 15, 34, 40, 47.
Jonas, 5, 21, 28, 81.
Lysbeth, 33.
Neeltje, 83.
Rachel, 20.
Rebecca, 3, 18, 41, 42, 44,
  50, 53.
Dreeper, Henderikje, 53.
Du Peis, Elisabeth, 26.
Dykman, Cornelis, 49.
Johannes, 50.
Ebb, Sara, 26.
Egbertsz, Egberts, Marretje,
  Marietje, 46, 69, 74.
Egmont, Jacob, 33.
Elbertsz, Martje, 33.
Elbur, Anna, 24.
Elders, Marritje, 61.
Ysbrant, 3, 19.
Eli [see also Vielé], Lysbeth, 26,
  72, 80.
Ellis, Frerik, 43.
Elmendorff, Coenraadt, 26.
Evertsz, Evertse, Alida, Aaltje,
  6, 21, 23, 39, 53, 60, 69, 82.
Annetje, 23.
Dirk, 33, 38, 44, 46.
Elbertje, 54.
Jan, 29.
Marie, Marietjen, 26, 60.
Rebecca, 5, 18, 21, 43, 53, 64.
Fletscher, Elisabeth, 72.
Floddersz, Jan, 41.

Fonda, Vonda, Alida, 9, 31, 69.
Claes, 20, 83.
Douwe, 71, 72, 75.
Geertje, 21.
Helena, Lena, 20, 80, 83.
Hester, 9, 28, 71, 75, 83.
Jan, 7, 15, 27, 67, 73, 75, 76,
  78, 82, 83.
Jillis, Jelis, 28, 72, 74, 77, 82.
Johannes, 71.
Marretje, 78, 83.
Rachel, 74.
Rebecca, 71, 72, 75.
Foreest, Freest, De Foreest,
  Phlip, 2, 18, 33, 40, 46, 54,
  55, 58, 59, 65, 71, 75.
Sara, 10, 18.
Tryntje, 2, 19, 45, 59.
Fort, Jan, 81.
Fransz, Fransen, Aaltje, 11.
Henderik, 21, 45, 61, 71.
Jannetje, 66, 73, 80.
Judik, 62, 70.
Pietertje, 50.
Weyntje, 7, 19.
Frederiksz, Claas, 58.
Salomon, 32, 40.
Fyn, Fein, Fine, Alida, 81.
Jan, Jhon, Jean, 28, 30, 77,
  81, 83.
Gaignon, François, 23, 48.
Galen, Antje, 80.
Joannes, 80.
Gansevoort, Gansevoos, Agniet,
  Agnietje, 10, 11, 25, 59, 65,
  73, 74, 80.
Anna, Antje, 8, 11, 25, 54,
  59.
Elisabet, Lysbeth, 20, 62, 80.
Elsje, 10, 13, 23, 59, 65, 73,
  81.
Harmen, 32, 40, 52, 61, 73.
Hilletje, 20.
Maria, 37, 73.
Gardenier, Gardeniers, Gerde-
  nier, —— 57.
Aalbert, 5, 11, 35, 49.
Alida, Aaltje, 31, 35, 63, 78.
Andries, 25, 49, 62, 78.
Ariaantje, 36.
Hendrik, 27, 64.
Jan, 27, 47, 54.
Josyntje, Josyne, Josina, 24,
  70, 71, 78.
Lysbeth, 33.
Samuel, 50, 63, 70, 78, 81.
Gauw, Gouws, Jan, 38.
Grietje, 1, 13.
Gerritsz, Gertsz, Adriaan, 1.
Annetje, 7, 11, 54, 75.

Records of the Reformed Dutch Church of Albany, New York

Part 2
1700-1724

Excerpted from
Year Book of The Holland Society
of New York (1905)

RECORDS OF THE R. D. CHURCH OF ALBANY.

[For list of abbreviations see page fronting index.]

Names of the persons who, since my arrival at Albany, having had their banns published, were united in marriage:

1700, Sept. 30. Barent Ten Eyk, y. m., and Neeltje Schermerhorn, y. d., both b. and l. at A.

Oct. 20. Johannes Quakkenbosch, y. m., and Anna Cloet, y. d., both of A.

At Kingston. Gysbert Van den Berg, y. m., b. and l. at A., and Dievertje Masten, y. d., b. and l. at Kingston.

Oct. 27. Evert Van Esch, y. m., and Geertje Gerritse Van den Berg, y. d., both b. in Col. R.

Willem Stout, y. m., b. in London, Eng., and Geertruy Geurtse Schoonhoven, y. d., both l. here.

Thomas Eechars, y. m., b. and l. at N. Y., and Elisabeth Slingerland y. d., b. and l. at N. A.

Nov. 3. Adriaan Oothout, y. m., b. in Col. R., and Lammertje Lokermans, y. d., b. at N. A., both l. at N. A.

Jacobus Lucasse Wyngaard, y. m., and Maria Quakkenbosch, y. d., both b. and l. here.

Dirk Heemstraat, y. m., b. in Col. R. and Claartje Quakkenbosch, y. d., b. at N. A.

Richart Moor, y. m., b. in West India, and Geesje Jansse Salsberry, y. d., b. at C., both l. at C.

Dec. 4. Wynand Willemse Van den Berg, y. m., b. and l. at A., and Volkje Volkertse Van Hoesen, y. d., b. at R.

Dec. 20. L. by Gov. Bellamont. Samuel Vetch, y. m., b. at Edinburg, Scotland, l. at N. Y., and Margareta Levingston, y. d., b. and l. at N. A. Ma. at bride's.

1701, Jan. 10. Caspar Van Hoese, y. m., and Racheltje Slingerlant, y. d., both b. and l. here. Ma. at the h. of the bride's br. in law, Johannes Mingaal.

Apr. 6. Johannes DeWandelaar, y. m., and Lysbeth Gansevoort, y. d., both b. and l. here.

May 3. Reg. Jan Herris, y. m., b. in O. E., and Moeset Tassama, b. in N. E., both l. in A. Co. Ma. after three B. by Alderman Wessel Ten Broek.

June 13. Reg. Bartholomeus Van Valkenburg, y. m., and Catharina Van Aalsteyn, y. d., both b. and l. at K. Ma., July 6, at h. of Johannes Thomse Mingaal.

Reg. Cornelis Van den Berg, y. m., b. at N. A., and Maria Winnen, y. d., b. in Col. R., both l. at N. A. Ma., July 6, at h. of Col. Pr. Schuyler.

July 6. Reg. Johannes Berheith and Catharina Gilbert, y. d., both b. and l. here. Ma., July 27, in the Chu.

July 13. First B. Elbert Harmensz, y. m., of N. A., and Catharina Bogaert, y. d., of N. H. Ma., Aug. 10, at h. of Egbert Teunisse, after 3 pr. at N. A., N. Y., and N. H.

Aug. 16. Reg. Thomas Thomasse, y. m., b. and l. at Bergen, and Sara Van Deuse, y. d., b. and l. in Col. R. Recd. cert., Sept. 1, to be ma. at Bergen.

Sept. 27. Reg. Johannes Harmense Knikkelbakker and Annetje Quakkenbosch, both b. and l. in Col. R. Ma. Oct. 19.

Reg. Jacob Lanssing, y. m., and Helena Pruyn, y. d., both b. and l. at A. Ma., Oct. 19, at h. of Frans Pruyn, bride's father.

Oct. 11. Reg. with permission of Capt. John Bennit, John Appelstoun, y. m., b. at Leicester, O. E., and Annetje Casparus, y. d., b. and l. at A. Ma. Nov. 2.

Oct. 21. Reg. Gysbert Andriesse Scharp, y. m., b. in R., l. at K., and Lysbeth Jansse Goewey, y. d., b. in R., l. at A. Ma. Nov. 16.

Nov. 1. Reg. Pieter Quakkenbosch, y. m., b. at A., and Neeltje Marens, y. d., bo. at Sch., both l. at A. Ma. Nov. 19.

Reg. Matthys Pars, y. m., b. and l. at King., and Theuna Winnen, y. d., b. in Col. R., l. at A. Ma. at King.

Nov. 16. Volkert Douwe, y. m., b. and l. in Col. R., and Margarita Van Tricht, y. d., b. and l. at A. Ma. with L. at bride's h.

Nov. 22. Reg. Andries Davidse, y. m., b. at A., and Cornelia Van Vliet, y. d., b. at Mormeltown, both l. at King. Recd. cert. to be ma. at King.

Dec. 15. With L. Barent Staats, y. m., b. in Col. R., and Neeltje Van den Berge, b. at N. A., both l. at N. A.

Dec. 30. With L. Johannes Van Alen, y. m., and Christina Ten Broek, y. d., both b. and l. at N. A. Ma. at the bride's father's.

1702, March 22. With L. Johannes Hansse, y. m., and Sara De Forest, y. d., both b. and l. at N. A. Ma. at the bride's father's h.

May 3. Reg. with the consent of Capt. Bennet. John Woodcock, y. m., b. in Yorkshire, O. E,. and Ariaantje Gardeniers, y. d., b. at K. Ma., May 19, in the Chu. at K.

July 2. Stephanus Van Alen, y. m., b. at A., l. at K., and Maria Cornelisse Muller, y. d., b. and l. in Col. R.

Aug. 26. With L. Volkert Van Vechten, y. m., l. in Col. R., and Lydia Ten Broek, y. d., b. and l. at A. Ma. at bride's father's h.

Sept. 5. Reg. Thomas Witbeek, y. m., and Jannetje Van Deuse, y. d., b. and l. in Col. R. Ma., Sept. 24, at the bride's brother's, Ruth Van Deuse's, h.

Oct. 9. Reg. Cornelis Swits, y. m., b. and l. at Sch., and Hester Visscher, y. d., b. at A. Ma., Nov. 8, at bride's father's h.

Reg. Jan. Rees, y. m., b. and l. in Col. R., and Maria Janse Goewey, y. d., b. and l. at N. A. Ma., Nov. 1, in bride's father's h.

Oct. 17. Reg. Ritchart Brewer, b. in O. E., and Katharina Scharp, y. d., b. in N. E. Ma., Nov. 22, at groom's h.

Nov. 7. Reg. Jan Van Hoesen, y. m., b. at A., l. at R., and Jannetje Van Schaak, y. d., b. and l. at K. Ma. upon a cert. of Aug. 23, 1703, to be ma. by a J. P.

Reg. Ma. Nov. 15. William Turner, y. m., b. in O. E., l. here, and Abigael Bogaert, l. at Katskil in A. Co.

Nov. 14. Reg. Ma. Dec. 2. Marten Jacobse Delmont, y. m., b. in Col. R., and Lysbeth Vile, b. at Sch., both l. here.

Nov. 21. Reg. Cornelis Gerritse Van den Berg, y. m., and Maria Van Bueren, wid. of Jan Teewisse Van Deuse, both b. and l. in Col. R. Ma., Dec. 20, at h. of Mayor, Albert Rykman.

Dec. 5. Reg. Ma. Dec. 22. Matthys Nak, widr. of Susanna Lanssing, b. at N. A., and Agnietje Schaats, y. d., b. at Sch., both l. at N. A.

Dec. 26. Reg. Ma. Jan. 27, 1703. Cornelis Henrikse Van Bueren, y. m., b. and l. in Col. R., and Hendrikje Van Esch, y. d., b. and l. in A. Co.

1703, Feb. 21. Reg. Ma. March 10. Willem Van Esch, y. m., b. and l. at Half Moon, and Lena Fonda, y. d., b. and l. in Col. R.

March 20. Reg. John Collinson, y. m., b. at London, O. E., here in garrison, and Rebecca Bratt, wid. of Claas Borgart, l. at A. Ma., March 31, at bride's sister's h.

Apr. 17. Reg. Arent Van Putten, y. m., b. in A. Co., l. at Sch., and Jannetje Conyn, y. d., b. and l. at Koxhakki. Recd. cert. May 12.

May 15. Reg. Ma. June 6. Cornelis Martense Van Aalstein, y. m., and Marretje Van den Berg, y. d., both b. and l. in Col. R.

June 11. Reg. Emanuel Van Schaak, y. m., b. at K., and Margarita Lucasse Wyngaard, y. d., b. at A., both l. at K. Ma., July 2, at h. of Gerrit Lucasz Wyngaard.

June 27. With L. Isaac Lanssing, y.m., and Jannetje Beekman, y. d., both b. and 1. at A. Ma. at bride's father's.

July 31. Reg. Frans Langet, y. m., b. at Esopus, 1. at N. Y., and Maria Van Schaak, y. d., b. and 1. at K. Ma., Sept. 6, at Gerrit Van Esch's h.

Oct. 2. Reg. Borger Huik, y. m., and Maeyke Goes, y. d., both b. and 1. at K. Ma., Oct. 22, at h. of Lucas Gerritse Wyngaard.

Nov. 19. Reg. Harmen Van Salsberry and Tanna Konyn, y. d., both b. and 1. at R. Recd. cert. Dec. 4.

Nov. 20. Reg. Ma. Dec. 5. Dirk Van Vechten, y. m., b. in R., 1. at A., and Margarita Luwes, y. d., b. and 1. in Col. R.

Nov. 28. With L., at bride's h. Abraham Lanssing, y. m. and Magdalena Van Tricht, y. d., both b. and 1. at A.

1704, Jan. 15. Reg. Samuel Pruin, y. m., and Maria Bogaard, y. d., both b. and 1. at A. Ma., Feb. 6, at the bride's father's h.

Jan. 20. Reg. Jan Hendrikse Bout, y. m., and Jannetje Scharp, y. d., both 1. at C. Recd. cert. Feb. 1.

Jan. 29. Reg. Jan Huybertse, y. m., b. at A., 1. in Col. R., and Elisabeth Van Klinkenberg, b. in Ulster Co. 1. at K. Ma., March 1, by a J. P.

March 4. Reg. Ma. March 22. Henrik Lanssing, y. m., b. at A., and Jannetje Knikkelbakker, y. d., b. in Col. R., both 1. in Col. R.

Apr. 23. With L. Reyer Gerritsen, y. m., and Geertruy Lanssing, y. d., both b. and 1. at A. Ma. at bride's father's h.

May 31. Reg. Pieter Van Oostrant, y. m., b. and 1. in Ulster Co., and Rachel Dingmans, y. d., b. and 1. at K.

June 3. Reg. Jacobus Schuiler, widr. of Catelyntje Wendel, and Susanna Wendel, y. d., both b. and 1. at A. Ma., June 11, at bride's mother's h.

June 10. Reg. Oyje Oyjens, y. m., b. at Cork, Ireland, and Maria Wendel, y. d., b. at A., both 1. at A. Ma., June 29, at bride's father's h.

July 15. Reg. Ma. Aug. 6. Albert Roelofse Van der Werke, y. m., b. at A., 1. in A. Co., and Dirkje Van Aalstein, y. d., b. at K., 1. in Col. R.

Aug. 26. Reg. Barent Egbertse, y. m., and Maria DeGarmo, y. d., both b. and 1. at A. Ma., Sept. 27, at bride's grandmother's.

Sept. 19. With L. Barent Sanders, y. m., and Maria Wendel, y. d., both b. and 1. at A. Ma., Sept. 19, at Mayor Joh. Schuyler's.

Sept. 20. With L. Johannes Lanssing, y. m., and Helena Sanders, y. d., both b. and 1. at A. Ma., Sept. 20, at bride's mother's h.

Sept. 24. Reg. Coenraat Ten Eyck, y. m., and Gerritje Van Schaik, y. d., both b. and l. at A. Ma., Oct. 15, at bride's father's h.

Oct. 28. Reg. Ma. after three B. Pieter Lanssing, Jr., b. at A., l. at Lange Rak, and Cornelia Rees, y. d., b. at Koxhakki, l. at C. in R.

Dec. 9. Reg. Ma. Dec. 26. Thomas Doksi, y. m., b. at Newtown, L. I., and Antje Jansse Goewey, y. d., b. and l. at A.

Dec. 30. Reg. Pieter Van Alen, y. m., b. at A., and Josina Dingmans, y. d., b. at K., both l. at K. Ma., Jan. 7, 1705, at bride's father's h.

1705, Feb. 10. Reg. Jeremias Muller, y. m., b. and l. in Col. R., and Lysbeth Halenbeek, y. d., b. at A., l. at Klinkenburg. Ma., Feb. 21, at bride's father's h.

Apr. 7. Reg. Jan Witbeek, y. m., b. and l. in Col. R., and Agnietje Bronk, y. d., b. and l. in A. Co. Ma. by Jonas Douw, J. P., at bride's father's h.

Sept. —. With L. Johannes Pruin, y. m., and Emilia Sanders, y. d., both b. and l. at A. Ma. at bride's mother's.

Oct. 20. With L. Samuel Kip, y. m., b. at N. Y., l. at Kipsberry, and Margarita Rykman, y. d., b. and l. at A. Ma. at bride's parents' h.

Oct. 27. Reg. Jacobus Turk, widr. of Catharina Van Benthuysen, l. at A., and Teuntje Hoes, wid. of Thomas Winnen, l. at K. Recd. cert., Nov. 5.

Nov. 10. Reg. Ma. Dec. 5. Marten Jansse Van Aalstede, b. and l. in Col. R., and Cornelia Van den Berg, y. d., b. at A., l. in Col. R.

Meyndert Roseboom, y. m., and Maria Vinhagen, y. d., both b. and l. at A. Ma., Nov. 30, at bride's parents' h.

Nov. 17. Reg. Pieter Bronk, y. m., b. at Koxhakki, l. at Katskill, A. Co., and Anna Bogardus, y. d., b. and l. at A. Ma., Dec. 2, at bride's h.

Dec. 1. Ma. Jan. 6, 1706. Abraham Ouderkerk, y. m., bo. at A., and Elisabeth Cloet, y. d., b. at Can., both l. at Can.

Dec. 15. Reg. Frederik Harmansse Visscher, widr. of Margarita Hansse, and Elisabeth Sanders, wid. of Evert Wendel, Jr., both l. at A. Ma. Jan. 5, 1706 at bride's h.

1706, Jan. 1. Reg. Jan Van Hoesen, y. m., b. at C., and Engeltje Jansse, y. d., b. at Koxhakki, both l. there. Recd. cert.

Jan. 20. Reg. Albert Van der Zee, y. m., b. at A., l. Col. R., and Hilletje Ganssevoort, y. d., b. and l. at A. Ma., Feb. 10, at bride's parents' h.

Jan. 23. Reg. John Thorn, y. m., b. at N. Y., l. at A., and Geertje Bresser, y. d., b. at King. Ma., Feb. 7, at P.

Feb. 2. Reg. William Hale, y. m., b. at N. Y., l. at A., and Maria Çasparus, y. d., l. at A. Ma. Feb. 20, in the chu. Reg. Pieter Vroman, y. m., b. and l. at Sch., and Geertruy Van Aalstein, y. d., b. and l. in Col. R.

March 21. With L., at bride's mother's h. Johannes Vinhagen, y. m., and Maria Van Tricht, y. d., both b. and l. at A.

Apr. 21. With L., at bride's parents'. Pieter Winnen, y. m., and Maria De Forest, y. d., both b. and l. at A.

May 8. With L., at bride's father's. Johannes Gerritsen, y. m., and Christina Pruyn, y. d., both b. and l. at A.

May 11. Reg. Jan Dufour, y. m., b. at N. Y., l. at Bloemendaal, and Katharina Roelofse Van der Werke, y. d., b. at A., l. in Col. R. Ma., June 5, at Gerrit Roelofse's.

May 18. Reg. Abraham Van Valkenburg, y. m., b. and l. at K., and Catelyntje Schermerhoorn, y. d., b. and l. in A. Co. Recd. cert., June 2.

June 8. Reg. Gerrit Wibusse, y. m., b. and l. in A. Co., and Maria Gilbert, y. d., b. and l. at A. Ma., July 14, in the Chu.

July 3. Reg. William Rogers, soldier in Capt. Weemes' Co., and Mary Johnson, b. at Boston, N. E., l. at A. Ma., July 16, at bridegroom's.

July 12. Reg. Christoffel Yeads, y. m., b. and l. at A., and Catalyna Winnen, y. d., b. in Col. R., l. at A. Ma., July 28, in the Chu.

Aug. 17. Reg. Wynand Van der Poel, y. m., b. and l. at A., and Catharina De Hooges, y. d., b. in Ulster Co., l. here. Ma., Sept. 8, at P.

Nicolaas Brusy, y. m., b. in A. Co., l. in Ulster Co., and Catelyntje Bout, y. d., b. at Sch., l. at C. Ma., Sept. 8, at P.

Oct. 9. Reg. Frederik Meyndertse, y. m., and Sara De Wandelaar, y. d., both b. and l. at A. Ma., Dec. 1, at P.

Isaac Van Deuse, y. m., and Bata Van Yselstein, y. d., both b. and l. at C. Ma., Dec. 3, at P.

Nov. 17. Reg. Jan Van Esch, y. m., b. and l. in Col. R., and Catelyntje Groesbeek, y. d., b. and l. at A. Ma., Dec. 10, at P.

Nov. 28. With L. at P. Henrik Ten Eyk, y. m., and Margarita Bleeker, y. d., both b. and l. at A.

Nov. 30. Jan Hardiks, y. m., b. and l. at C., and Maria Bekker, y. d., b. at A., l. in Col. R. Ma., Dec. 22, at P.

Dec. 13. After B. at Sch. Victor Pootman, y. m., and Margarita Mebi, y. d., both l. at Sch.

Dec. 22. After B., at Sch. Simon Danielse, y. m., and Maria Peek, y. d., both l. at Sch.

1707, Feb. 1. Reg. Ma. Feb. 26. Johannes Van Valkenburg, y. m., b. and l. at K., and Margarita Barheit, y. d., b. and l. in Col. R.

Feb. 8. Reg. Alexander MecCaisland, soldier in Capt. James Weemes' Co., and Sara Jenkins, y. d., l. at A. Ma., Feb. 27, at P.

March 15. Reg. Patrick Martyn, drummer in Col. Ingolsby's grenadiers, and Mary Cox, y. d., b. and l. at A. Ma., March 30, at P.

Apr. 5. Reg. Ma. Apr. 20. Jan Borgaart, y. m., b. and l. at K., and Catharina Van Wie, y. d., b. in Col. R., l. at K.

Apr. 12. Reg. Ma. May 25. Jacob Cloet, y. m., b. at A., l. at Can., and Geertruy Van Franke, y. d., b. and l. at Can.

May 3. Reg. Ffrancois Pace, soldier in Capt. James Weemes' Co., and Anna Flensburg, wid. of Ogleby, l. at A. These persons' B. had been published three times without opposition, but they were not married because said widow's husband returned from the sea, and thus proved not to be dead, as averred.

May 4. With L. Johannes Dellomont, y. m., b. in Col. R. l. at A., and Johanna Clara Kleyn, wid. of N. N. Metselaar.

May 17. Reg. Ma. June 7. Charles Berwoir, y. m., b. at Mt. Royal, Canada, l. in Ulster Co., and Aaltje Roelofse Van der Werke, y. d., b. and l. at A.

June 27. Reg. Andries Brusy, y. m., b. at Koxhakki, l. at Tochkanik, and Engeltje Claeuw, y. d., b. at K., l. at Tochkanik. Ma. July 13, at Jan Salomonse Goewey's.

Aug. 3. Reg. Lambert Huyk, y. m., b. at K., and Anna Ratteliffe, y. d., b. at A., both l. at A. Ma., Aug. 28, at Col. Pieter Schuyler's.

Aug. 29. Reg. Ma. Sept. 27. Henrik Jansse Witbeek, widr. of Lyntje Winnen, bo. at C., and Helena Bout, y. d., b. at A., l. at C.

Thomas Edwards, soldier in Col. Ingolsby's Co., and Aaltje Tipping, l. at K. Ma., Sept. 14, at P.

Sept. 16. Reg. at Bergen, N. J., and also had their B. here. Dirk Philipse Conyn, y. m., b. and l. in A. Co., and Rachel Andriesse, y. d., b. at N. Y., l. at Bergen, N. J.

Oct. 8. With L., at bride's father's. Cornelius Bogaart, y. m., and Dorothea Oothout, y. d., both b. and l. at A.

Oct. 19. With L., at bride's father's. Anthony Van Schayk, Jr., y. m., and Anna Catharina Ten Broek, y. d., both b. and l. at A.

Dec. 6. Reg. James Davis, Sergt. in Col. Ingolsby's Co., and Elisabeth, wid. of John Owens. Ma., Dec. 15, at P.

Dec. 16. With L., at bride's parents'. Anthony Van Schayk, A. F., Jr., y. m., and Susanna Wendel, y. d., both b. and l. at A.

1708, Jan. 17. Reg. Antoine Rouwville, y. m., b. at

Vienne, Dauphiné, and Heyltje Dekker, y. d., b. A. Co., both l. at Livingston Manor.

May 2. Reg. Ma. May 20. Pieter Van Bueren, y. m., b. and l. in Col. R., and Geertruy Vosburg, y. d., b. and l. at K.

May 29. Reg. Samuel Doksi, widr. of Barbara Goewey, l. at A., and Lysbeth Bas, y. d., b. at Midwout, L. I., l. here.

June 5. With L. Johannes Wendel, son of Hieronymus, y. m., and Susanna Viele, y. d., both b. and l. at A.

Sept. 18. Reg. Andries Brat, y. m., b. in A. Co., and Weintje Rosa, y. d., b. and l. in Ulster Co.

Sept. 19. With L. Philip Livingston, y. m., and Catharina Van Brug, y. d., both b. and l. at A.

Sept. 24. Reg. Ma. Oct. 17. Wouter Vroman, y. m., b. and l. at Sch., and Maria Halenbeek, y. d., b. and l. at A.

Oct. 22. Reg. Ma., Nov. 26, at A. Pieter Clement, y. m., b. at New Utrecht, l. at Sch., and Anna Ruytter, y. d., b. and l. at Sch.

Oct. 31. Reg. Jonathan Rumbly, y. m., b. at London, E., and Johanna Corlar, y. d., b. and l. at A. Ma., Nov. 7, by Rev. John Barclay.

Nov. 7. With L., at Harbert Jacobse's. Harbert Van Deuse, y. m., b. and l. at C., and Helena Van Deuse, y. d., b. and l. in Col. R.

Nov. 27. Reg. Ma. Dec. 15. Nicolaas Van Woerd, y. m., b. and l. at A., and Dirkje Barheit, y. d., b. in Col. R., l. at A.

Dec. 18. Reg. Ma., Dec. 3. Isaac Fonda, y. m., and Alida Lanssing, y. d., b. and l. in Col. R.

1709, Jan. 29. Reg. Ma. Feb. 9. Cornelis Laurentse Van Wurmerik, y. m., b. in Col. R., and Annaatje Van Petten, wid. of Claas Sieverse.

Feb. 18. Reg. Ma. March 3. Cousset Vedder, y. m., b. at A., and Margarita Berrit, y. d., b. and l. at A.

Feb. 19. Reg. Ma. March 6. Anthony Bogardus, y. m., b. and l. at A., and Jannetje Knikkelbakker, wid. of Henrik Lansing, b. in Col. R., l. at A.

June 11. Reg. Ma. June 30. Johannes Christiaanse, y. m., b. at Sch., l. at Can., and Neeltje Cornelisse, y. d., b. at N. Y., l. at Can.

June 12. With L. Gerrit Van Nes, y. m., and Catelyntje De Forest, y. d., both b. and l. at A.

June 18. With L. Johannes Ten Broek, y. m., and Elisabeth Wendel, y. d., both b. and l. at A.

June 19. B. Johannes Van Hoese, widr., and Willempje Viele, wid. of Levinus Winnen, l. at A.

June 21. With L. Jacob Visscher, y. m., and Susanna Egbertse, y. d., both b. and l. at A.

July 17. Reg. Ma. July 19. Dirk Jansse, y. m., b. in

Westchester Co., l. here, and Maria Cornelisse, y. d., b. in A. Co., l. here.

Oct. 1. Reg. Ma. Oct. 23. Daniel Le Fort, y. m., b. and l. at Can., and Gerritje Van den Berg, y. d., b. and l. in Col. R.

Oct. 6. Reg. Jan Wimp, widr. of Catelyntje Schermerhoorn, and Ariaantje Swits, y. d., both b. and l. at Sch. Ma., Nov. 4, at P.

Oct. 28. Reg. Eldert Cornelisse, y. m., b. and l. at Can. and Hester Visscher, y. d., b. and l. at A. Ma., Nov. 7, at P.

Oct. 29. Reg. Evert Rykse Van Franke, y. m., and Maria Visscher, y. d., both b. and l. at A. Ma., Nov. 14, at P.

Dec. 10. Reg. Hendrik Valkenburg, y. m., and Anna Huyk, y. d., both b. and l. at K.

1711, March 4. Reg. Ma. March 11. Korset Veder, widr. of Marragrita Berret, l. at Half Moon, and Neeltje Christiaans, y. d., l. at Can.

1712, Feb. 10. Reg. Jan Goes, y. m., and Margrietje Wyngaarts, wid. of Manuel Van Schayk, both l. at K.

The two last named couples were married by Rev. Peter Vas.

MARRIAGES BY REV. PETRUS VAN DRIESSEN.

1712, Apr. 18. Harmen Philipsen and Anna Urzula Lapp. Had their B. at Sch.

May 11. Leendert Ganzevoord and Catryna Wandelaars. After three B. here.

May 26. With L. Rutgher Bleeker, y. m., and Catalyna Scuyler, wid. of Jan Abeel.

June 24. With L. Anthony Van Schayck and Anna Cuyler.

June 26. With L. Thomas Williams and Helena Bronk.

July 24. Reg. Jan Gardenier and Anna Engelen Van Sweits. Ma. by Rev. Haeger, V.D.M., in Germany.

July 28. With L. Joannes Evertsen and Barentie Bruyne.

Aug. 26. After three B. Joannes Van Deusen and Christyna Van Alen.

Aug. 26. With L. Petrus Van Driessen and Eva Cuyler.

Oct. 16. After three B. Abram Van Vechten and Agnitie W. Meek [?].

Nov. 7. With L. Samuel Ten Broek and Maria Van Rensselaar.

Nov. 20. After three B. Jacob Schermerhoorn and Margarita Tellers.

Nov. 25. With L. Andries Van Petten and Moycka Ten Eik.

1713, Jan. 13. After three B. Abraham Van der Poel and Antie Van den Berg.

Feb. 6. After three B. Cornelis Scermerhoorn and Margritie Albertti.

Feb. 23. After three B. Jochum Van Valkenburg, widr. of Eva Vroman, and Jannetie Mingaal, wid. of Lamberd Van Aalsteyn.

Apr. 29. After three B. Andries Huyck and Maria Oudekerk.

May 23. After three B. Meyndert Marselis and Tyke Oothout.

July 4. After three B. Jacob Van Valkenburg and Christyna Wenne.

July 4. After three B. Johannes Huyck and Eva Van Aalsteyn.

Aug. 13. After three B. Nicolaes Gardenier and Rachel Wenne.

Oct. 5. With L. Pieter Cojeman and Elizabeth Greveraad.

Oct. 26. After three B. Levynus Harmensen and Catryna Van den Berg.

Nov. 5. With L. Andries Nack and Jannetie Le Gransie.

Dec. 27. After three B. Thomas Berrit and Barentie Spoor.

1714, Jan. 15. With L. Joannes Beekman and Hester Wendel.

Feb. 6. Three B. Leendert Conyn and Henderikie Kool.

Feb. 15. Three B. Kilyaen Wenne and Marretie Kool.

Feb. 17. With L. Jacobus Schoonhoven and Susanna Brath.

Apr. 16. Three B. Arent Scermerhoorn and Antie Fonda.

June 4. Three B. Philip Van Vechten and Engeltie Van Deusen.

June 13. With L. Joannes Lansingh and Geertruy Scuyler.

June 23. Three B. Jacob Scermerhoorn and Agnietie Van Vegten.

July 24. Three B. Elderd Ouderkerk and Helena Sophia Knipping.

Aug. 22. Three B. Andries Gardenier and Sara Van Woert.

Aug. 28. Three B. Dirck Hagedoorn and Maria Matysen.

Sept. 22. Gerrit Dingmans, b. and l. at K., and Cornelia Gardeinier, b. in Westchester Co., l. at K.

Sept. 24. Three B. Nicolaas Bossy and Cornelia Pietersen Brouwer.

Oct. 15. Three B. Joannes Becker and Cornelia Uzile.

Oct. 24. With L. Tobias Ten Broeck and Marretie Van Stryen.

Nov. 4. Three B. Jacob Gardenier, y. m., and Cornelia Van der Schuive, wid. of Antony Bassaleyn.

Nov. 6. With L. Theunis Harmensen and Rachel Gansevoord.

Nov. 9. With L. Juryaan Hoghen and Maria Beekman.

Nov. 13. With L. Pieter Conyn and Alida De Wandelaar.

Nov. 21. With L. Arent Pruim and Catharyna Gansevoord.

Nov. 26. With L. Dirck Ten Broeck and Margarita Cuyler.

Dec. 2. With L. Nicolaes Schuyler and Elsie Wendel.

Dec. 18. With L. Sander Glen and Rebecka Swits.

Dec. 18. With L. Jacob Beekman and Debora Hansen.

Dec. 28. With B. Barent Bratt and Maria Rykmans.

Dec. 29. With L. Joannes Ten Broeck and Catharina Van Renselaar.

1715, Jan. 8. With B. Joannes Roelefsen Van der Werke and Margarieta Baar.

March 11. With B. Hendrik Van Wie and Hilletie Beckers.

March 18. With B. Willem Ketelhuin and Maria Ridder.

March 28. With L. Walter Barheit and Rachel Wenne.

May 8. With B. Claes Egmond, y. m., and Marretie Bronck, wid. of —— Wenne.

May 13. With L. Arnout DeGraaf and Ariaentie Van der Volge.

May 24. With B. Petrus Van Woerd and Ariaentie Van den Bergh.

May 31. With B. Joannes Kool and Rachel Bon.

June 5. With B. Joannes Muller and Elizabeth Halenbeek.

June 7. With L. Marten Van Bergen and Catryna De Mejer.

Aug. 18. With L. Tobias Ryckman and Helena Beekman.

Oct. 27. With L. Gerrit Lansingh and Elizabeth Banker.

Nov. 18. With L. Jacob Halenbeek and Maria Vischer.

Nov. 20. With B. Wynant Van den Bergh and Aaltie Van Ness.

Nov. 24. With L. Joannes De Peyster and Anna Schuyler.

Dec. 13. With B. Hieroon V. Vlieren and Margarita Huygh.

Dec. 31. With L. Andries Gardenier and Syntie Gardenier.

1716, Jan. 15. With B. Abram Fort and Anna Barbara Knoet.

Feb. 3. With B. Pieter Bratt and Cristina Bouman.

Feb. 10. With B. Matheus Vlensburgh and Maria Van Zanten.

Feb. 28. With L. Theunis Eghbertsen and Engeltie Beekman.

Apr. 22. With B. Dirck Van der Heyde and Ekbertie Bratt.

Apr. 29. With B. Lucas Van Vechten and Tanna Woedes.

Apr. 30. With B. Jephta Cornelissen and Cristina Martensen.

Apr. 30. With L. Hendrik Anthony and Eva Visscher.

May 20. With B. Samuel Criegier and Geertruy Visscher.

June 2. With B. Matheus Van Deusen and Engeltie Slingerlant.

July 1. With L. Rutgert Melchersen and Margariet Roseboom.

July 22. With L. Anthony Bratt and Rebecka Van der Heyde.

Aug. 12. With L. Jacob Roseboom and Geertruy Lidius.

Oct. 19. With B. Jacob Egmond and Anna Lansingh.

Oct. 24. With L. Wilhelmus Van den Bergh and Gerretie Van den Bergh.

Nov. 9. With B. Willem Hoogtelinck and Helena Uzile.

Nov. 16. With L. Claes Fonda and Anna Marcelis.

Nov. 29. With L. Joannes Wendel and Anna Kip.

Dec. 7. With B. Barent Barhayt and Cornelia Quackenbosch.

1717, Jan. 20. With B. John Tannson and Maria Huygh.

Feb. 18. With B. Pieter Vosburgh and Dirckie Van Aalsteyn.

Feb. 26. With L. Leendert Bronck and Anna De Wandelaar.

March 24. With B. Joannes Redly and Selia Jets.

Apr. 6. With B. Jakob Brouwer and Maria Bovy.

May 24. With L. Mathias Van den Bergh and Catalyna Van Deusen.

Sept. 6. With B. Joannes Van der Wilge and Catharina Heyps.

Oct. 8. With L. Petrus Douw and Anna Van Renselaar.

Oct. 14. With B. Simon Vrooman and Eytie Delmond.

Nov. 13. With B. Joannes Beckingh and Sara Van Arnhem.

Nov. 28. With L. Isaak Wendel and Catelyna Van Dyck.

Dec. 15. With L. Jacob Glen and Sara Wendel.

1718, March 23. With B. Joannes Barhayt and Catalyna Dinghsmans.

Apr. 10. With L. David Van Dyck and Christyna Ten Broeck.

May 14. With L. Jacob Schermerhoorn and Johanna Beekman.

May 16. With L. Lambert Kool and Catalyna Van Deusen.

May 20. With B. Joannes Van Zanten and Sara Kiltens.

May 30. With L. Ruben Van Vegten and Geertruy Witbeck.

May 30. With B. Hendrik Gardenier and Margarita Van Woerd.

June 29. With L. Meindert Wimph and Alida De Wandelaar.

June 30. With L. Joannes Symonsen and Susanna Wendel.

Aug. 21. With L. Robbert Tewezen and Geertruy Van Benthuysen.

Aug. 22. With L. Jessey De Forest and Neeltie Quakkenbosch.

Sept. 4. With L. Joannes Maazen and Rebecka Fonda.

Sept. 12. With B. Hans Jurryaen Gunterman and Anna Elizabeth Melchior.

Sept. 25. With B. Dirck Van der Karre and Magdalena Baart.

Oct. 19. With L. Dirk Nieukerk and Anna Vischer.

Oct. 23. With L. Gerrit Lansingh and Engel Van Deusen.

Nov. 8. With B. David Foreest and Abigael Van Aalsteyn.

Nov. 30. With L. Jan Wimph and Helena Van Tricht.

Dec. 2. With B. Hendrik Halenbeek and Susanna Bratt.

Dec. 12. With L. Thomas Van Aalsteyn and Maria Van Alen.

1719, Jan. 16. With B. Claes Van den Bergh and Anna Hooghkerk.

May 18. With L. John Nieuwkerk and Dorothe Douw.
May 18. With B. Moses Ingerson and Tryntie Van Slyk.
May 19. With B. Capt. Phillip Schuyler, widr. of Elizabeth De Mejer, and Catryna Scherph, wid. of Ritsiert Bruuwer.
May 23. With B. Cornelis Sluyter and Anna Woedkook.
May 25. With B. John Reypel and Catryna Eshoven.
May 28. With B. Joseph Jets and Hendrickie Hooghkerk.
June 10. With L. Anthoni Kip and Catalyna Kip.
June 19. With B. John Zeegers and Brechie Wielaars.
July 14. With L. Marten Van Buuren and Maria Van den Bergh.
Aug. 5. With L. Jan Van Aalsteyn and Maria Staats.
Sept. 6. With B. Dirk Bratt, Jr., and Cornelia Walderom.
Sept. 6. With B. Stoffel Muller and —— Halenbeek.
Sept. 20. With B. Jacob Quakkenbosch and Geertruy Van der Werken.
Sept. 21. With B. Daniel Brodhead and Hester Wyngaart.
Oct. 4. With B. Theunis Slingerland and Elizabeth Van der Zee.
Oct. 9. With B. Joannes De Garmoy and Eckbertie Visser.
Oct. 11. With B. Abraham Vosburgh and Geertie Van den Bergh.
Oct. 21. With L. Marten Vosburgh and Eytie Van Buuren.
Nov. 8. With B. Christyaan Syansch and Catryna Van Buuren.
Nov. 21. With L. John Bassett and Susanna Beekman.
Dec. 20. With B. Phillip Witbeek and Anna Williaems.
Dec. 25. With B. Marten Van Deusen and Elbertie Van der Poel.
Dec. 29. With L. Barent Van Buuren and Maria Wenne.
1720, Jan. 19. With B. Willem Walderom and Elizabeth Beekman.
Jan. 21. With B. Pieter Wenne, Jr, and Rachel Van Alen.
Jan. 30. With B. Pieter Vosburgh, J., and Helena Goes.
May 3. With L. Jacob Van der Heyden and Hesther Visser.

May 15. With B. Joannes Ouderkerk and Jannetie Viele.

July 7. With L. Cornelis Van Hoorn and Joanna Livingston.

July 17. With L. David Schuyler and Anna Brad.

Aug. 22. With L. Uldrik Van Franken and Geertruy Criegier.

Sept. 15. With L. Gozen Van Schayck and Neeltie Abeel.

Sept. 23. With B. Ephraim Bogardus and Agnietie De Garmoy.

Sept. 23. With L. Christophel Abeel and Margarita Bries.

Oct. 10. With B. Abraham Van Deusen and Anna Myrryn.

Nov. 13. With L. Thomas Sharp and Maria Dewarran.

Nov. 27. With L. Benjamin Bratt and Magdalena Ryckman.

Dec. 4. With L. Gysbert Rooseboom and Christina Bries.

Dec. 16. With B. Williaem Liddeson and Elizabeth Bouman.

Dec. 29. With L. Phillip Schuyler and Margarita Schuyler.

1721, Jan. 10. With B. Tobias Van Buuren and Anna Goes.

Jan. 11. With B. Barent Vosburg and Jannetie Van Schayk.

Feb. 3. With L. John Van Aalsteyn and Cathrina Foreest.

Feb. 7. With B. William Rogiers and Susanna Foreest.

Feb. 26. With B. Benjamin Van Vlek and Anna Gilberts.

March 20. With B. Wynant Van den Bergh and Anna Wendels.

June 16. With B. Jochum Calliers and Christina Vosburgh.

June 18. With B. Roelef Kidny and Engel Burger.

July [?] 1 [?]. With L. Cornelis Van Dyck and Maria Bries.

July 10. Abraham and Christina (Pros.).

July 11. With B. Abraham Van Arnhem and Alida Lansingh.

July 15. With L. John Oothout and Chathalyna Van Deusen.

Aug. 20. With L. Henry Beekman and Jennit Livingston.

Oct. 8. With L. John Walters and Sara Winne.

Oct. 21. With B. Caspar Ham and Anna Leych.

Nov. 5. With B. Jonas Bronk and Antie Conyn.
Nov. 6. With B. Akes Bratt and Margarita Knoet.
Nov. 8. With L. John Walrave and Anna Ridder.
Nov. 12. With B. Harmen Van Aalsteyn and Dorothee Van Slyck.
Dec. 2. With B. Meyndert Van Iveren and Ariaentie Wyngaert.
Dec. 26. With B. Williaem Garland and Mary Lues.
Dec. 28. With L. Marten Beekman and Geertruy Visser.
1722, Jan. 2. With B. Charles Cunstable and Mary Askley.
Jan. 3. With B. Gerrit Ridder and Anna Van den Bergh.
Apr. 22. With B. Augustinus Turk and Anna Ketelluyn.
May 24. With B. Johannes Vosburgh and Maria Van Buuren.
June 5. With L. Joh. Schoonmaker and Johanna Van Vegten.
June 9. With B. Jacob Sneyder and Elizabeth Feek.
June 25. With B. Gerrit Vanden Berg and Alida Van Wie.
June 26. With B. Thomas Wyllaer and Chath. Haver.
July 24. With B. Jan Evertsen and Elizabeth Bouman.
July 29. With B. John Robberts and Susanna Lyster.
Sept. 18. With L. Laurens Claassen and Susanna Wellive.
Sept. 19. With B. John Schuts and Maria Kool.
Sept. 20. With L. Frederick Van Cortlandt and Maria Van Rensselaar.
Nov. 2. With B. Isack Van Arnhem and —— Salisbury.
Nov. 4. With L. Pieter Schuyler, Jr., and Chatharina Groesbeek.
Nov. 16. With L. Arent Van Dyck and —— Van Alen.
Dec. 1. With L. Harmannus Schuyler and Jane Bancker.
Dec. 9. With L. Henry Cuyler, Jr., and Margarita Van Deusen.
Dec. 22. With L. Dirk Scherluyn and Maria Van Ness.
1723, Jan. 8. With B. Arien Gardenier and Elyzabeth Van Slyk.
March 7. With B. Pieter Bennewe and Anna Fort.
Apr. 25. With L. John Hansen and Sara Cuyler.
May 11. With B. David Quackkenbosch and Anna Schoth.
June 9. With L. Johannes Marselis and Johanna Beekman.

June 17. With B. Joh. Jac. Eahl [?] and Johanna Van Slyk.

July 8. With B. Williaem Halenbeek and Cornelia Goes.

July 16. With B. David Verplank and Ariaentie Kojemans.

Oct. 5. With B. —— Van Aalsteyn and ——. At John Beekman's.

Oct. 7. With L. Jacobus Van Alen and Helena Van Aalsteyn.

Oct. 10. With B. Jacob Van Aalsteyn and Pietertie Van Yveren.

Oct. 17. With B. Jacob V. Woert and Hendrikkie Oothoud.

Nov. 1. With L. John Bensley and Lidia Van Benthuysen.

1724, Jan. 4. With B. Lambert Rettelyf and Anna Van Santen.

Jan. 15. With B. Mathew Fanine and Mary Patrik.

Jan. 16. With L. Joh. V. D. Heyde and Rachel V. D. Heyde.

Jan. 24. With B. Abr. Ouderkerk and Ariaentie Van Ness.

Jan. 24. With B. Joh. Slingerlant and Anna Slingerlant.

Feb. 4. With B. Caspar Conyn and Hendrickie Van Schayk.

March 7. With B. Pieter Fonda and Maria Beekman.

Apr. 1. With L. John Dunbaarr and Maria Van Hoesen.

Apr. 8. With B. Martinus Van Olinde and Jannetie Van der Werke.

Apr. 20. With B. Claes Becker and Jannetie Van der Karre.

Apr. 20. With L. Johannes Goes and Jannatie Van Schayk.

May 13. With B. Joh. Huyk and Madel Van Vlieren.

June 4. With B. Pieter Uzile and Anna Ackerson.

July 4. With B. Rejer Schermerhoorn and Geertie Ten Eyk.

July 5. With L. Th. Slingerlant and Cornelia Kip.

July 7. With B. John Sithnem and Volkie Van Hoesen.

Aug. 20. With B. Gerrit Van Nes and Sara Van den Berg [see Sept. 11].

Sept. 8. With B. Cornelis Van Buuren and Maria Litser.

Sept. 11. With B. Gerrit Van Nes and Sara Van Den Bergh [see Aug. 20].

Oct. 12. With B. Theunis Viele and Maria Fonda.

2

Oct. 25. With L. Hendr. Rooseboom and Elsie Cuyler.
Oct. 30. With B. Jacobus Gardenier and Johanna Tippen.
Nov. 10. With L. Petrus Van Bergen and Christina Coster.
Nov. 11. With B. David Groesbeek and Maria V. D. Poel.
Nov. 13. With B. Daniel Hoioson and Jane Pouwel.
Dec. 11. With B. Giliaen Verplank and Ariaentie V. d. Poel.
Dec. 13. With L. Joh. Bleeker and Jenn. Ten Eyck.
Dec. 15. With B. Adam V. D. Bergh and Maria Spoor.
Dec. 20. With B. Pieter Schuyler and Hendrickie Hun.
Dec. 29. With L. Samuel Cojemans and Chatharina Van Schayk.

REGISTER OF THE CHILDREN THAT HAVE BEEN BAPTIZED SINCE JULY 21 OF THIS YEAR 1700.

[For list of abbreviations, see page fronting index.]

1700. July 21. Adam, ch. of Johannes Van Alen and Sara. Witnesses: Adam and Aeltje Dingmans.

Cornelis, of Thomas Harmense and Mekke Thomasze. Wit.: Gerret Van Nes, Weyntje Van Deusen.

Henrikje, of Laurens Van Schayk and Jannetje Othout. Wit: Manuel Van Schayk, Maria Van Nes.

Rachel, of Willem Van Alen and Maria Van Petten. Wit.: Johannes Van Alen, Elisabeth Van der Poel.

Hermannus, of David Schuyler and Elsje Rutgers. Wit.: Anthony Rutgers, Anthony Bries, Henrikje Rutgers.

Johannes, of Jacob Schermerhoren and Gerritje Henriks. Wit.: Reyer Schermerhoorn, Grietje Rykmans.

Margariet, of Jacob Teunisz and Annigje Lokermans. Wit.: Jan Jansz Bleyker, Grietje Bleyker.

Sara, of Arent Slingerlant and Geertruy Van Voust. Wit.: Johannes Thomasz, Anna Van Voust.

Elisabeth, of Henrik Van Renselaar and Catharina Verbruggen. Wit.: Johannes Schuyler, Sara Verbruggen.

Augustinus, of Jacob Turk and Catharina Van Benthuysen. Wit.: James Peeruker, Margariet Levingston.

Johan, of Jacob and Marretje Conynen. Wit.: Felix and Weintje Leendersz.

July 28. Annaetje, of Thomas Van Alsteyn and Jannigje Mingaal. Wit.: Pieter Mingaal, Margariet Roseboom.

Dirk, of Abraham and Geertruy Schuyler. Wit.: Jacobus Schuyler, Elsje Kuyler.

Abraham, of Abraham and Elsje Staats. Wit.: Jochem and Antje Staats.

1700

Aug. 4. Margaret, of Willem Hoogen and Martina Bekker. Wit.: Pieter Schuyler, Maria Van Renselaar.

Anna, of [no parents given, perhaps the above]. Wit.: Abraham Wendel and sister.

Aug. 11. Ephraim, of Johannes Lucasz Wyngaard and Susanna. Wit.: Hermannus Wendel, Sara Wyngaard.

Jacob, of Wessel Ten Broek and Katharina Lokermans. Wit.: Jacob and Maria Lokermans.

Susanna, of David Ketelaar and Johanna Bratt. Wit.: Dirk and Susanna Bratt.

Aug. 25. Ariaantje, of Hermanus and Anna Wendel. Wit.: Tjerk Hermansz, Ariaantje Wendel.

Sept. 1. Laurens, of Gideon and Dorcas, pros. Wit.: Pieter and Rachel Schuyler, Canastasi, a pros.

Samuel, of Jonathan Braadhazt and Cathalyntje Bensing. Wit.: Harmen Thomasz, Thomas Harmensz, Agnietje Van Vecht.

Marytje, of Willem Jacobse Van Deuse and Lysbeth Roseboom. Wit.: Pieter Mingaal, Gerritje Roseboom.

Robert, of Robert Teewisz Van Deuse and Cornelia. Wit.: Marten and Marrytje Van Bueren.

Sept. 8. David, of Philip and Tryntje Freest. Wit.: Abraham Lansing, Maria Wendel.

Sept. 15. Gideon, of Benoni Van Korlaar and Lysbeth Van der Poel. Wit.: Anthony Van Schayk, Catharina Van der Poel.

Jurriaan, of Claas Siewerts and Antje Claasse. Wit.: Henrik and Neeltje Douw.

Jochem, of Dirk and Rachel Van der Heyden. Wit.: Johannes Bratt, Cornelia Van der Heyden.

Sept. 22. Cornelis, of Evert Wendel and Lysbeth Sanders. Wit.: Capt. Sanders from Sch., and Emilia Sanders.

Rykje, of Goosse Van Schayk and Katharina Staats. Wit.: Jacob Staats, Benoni Van Korlaar, Rykje Staats.

Oct. 13. Rykje, of Hendrik Roseboom and Debora Staats. Wit.: Johannes Roseboom, Catharina Staats, wife of Goossen Van Schayk.

Oct. 27. Anthony, of Joseph Janse and Sytje Marcelis. Wit.: Henrik Van Rensselaar, Maria Josephs.

Nov. 3. William, of Jan Redly, alias Rattelife, and Rachel. Wit.: Henrik and Catharina Rensselaar.

Hendrik, of Teunis Willemse and Annetje Hendriks. Wit.: Henrik and Marytje Van Dyk.

Gysbert, of Henrik Franse Klaeuw and Cornelia. Wit.: Gysbert Andriesse Scherp, Margarita Livingston.

Cornelis, of Salomon Van Vechten and Alida Fonda. Wit.: Dirk Van Vechten, Helena Fonda.

Cornelis, of Daniel and Debora Ketelen. Wit.: David and Anna Ketelen.

1700–1701

Nov. 10. Jonas, of Andries Janse Witbeek and Engeltje Volkertse. Wit.: Henrik Rensselaar, Neeltje, wife of Nikes Douw.

Harmen, of Isaac and Jannetje Janse. Wit.: Anthony and Marytje Van Schayk.

Dec. 8. Teunis, of Albert Slingerland and Hester Brikkers. Wit.: Johannes Mingaal, Geertruy Slingerland.

Dec. 15. Christina, of Antony Coster and Elisabeth Ten Broek. Wit.: Dirk Wesselse Ten Broek, Geertje Lanssing.

Dec. 26. Harmen, of Nanning Harmense Visscher and Alida Vinhagel. Wit.: Johannes and Maria Harmense Visscher.

Dec. 29. Catharyn, of Jan Feyn and Alida Gardeniers. Wit.: Johannes Abeel, Margareta Vetch.

Beertje, of Coenraad Hoogteeling and Tryntje Van Slyp. Wit.: Tames Williamse, Hilletje Gansevoort.

1701, Jan. 1. Catharina, of Gysbert Marselis and Barbar Groesbeek. Wit.: Ahasueros Marselis, Lysbeth Lanssing.

Marretje, of Maarten Martense Van Buuren and Judikje Barentse. Wit.: Albert Rykman, Marytje Van Bueren.

Andries, of Barent Gerritse and Geertruy Janse. Wit.: Goossen Van Schayk, Katharina Staats.

Jan. 5, at Kinderhook:

Jacob, of Johannes and Jannetje Van Hoesen. Wit.: Isaac and Antje Vosburg.

Andries, of Johannes and Geertruy Scharp. Wit.: Andries Scharp, Agnietje Jansse.

Sander, of Abraham Van Aalsteyn and Maria Van Deuse. Wit.: Teeuwis Van Deuse, Cornelia Tysse.

Cornelis, of Pieter Meesse Hogeboom and Jannetje. Wit.: Cornelis and Jannetje Mulder.

Jan. 8. Johannes, of Johannes Beekman and Eva Vinhagels. Wit.: Henrik Hansse, Neeltje Ten Eyk.

Jan. 12. Margarita, of Johannes Schuyler and Lysbeth Staats. Wit.: Jochem Staats, Margareta Schuyler.

Geurt, of Willem Hont and Geertruy Geurtse Schoonhoven. Wit.: Antony Bratt, Anna Andriesse.

Jan. 26. Johannes, of Ahasueros Marselis and Sara Heemstrate. Wit.: Dirk Takelse Heemstraat, Claartje Quackenbosch.

Laurens, of Melchert Van der Poel and Catharina Van Alen. Wit.: Willem and Marrytje Van Alen.

Jan. 29. Timotheus, of Abigael Bogerds. Wit.: Huybertje Jeeds.

Feb. 5. Dorothee, of Gerrit Schouten and Lysbeth Aarnolds. Wit.: Philip Bosi, Dorothee Friddi.

Feb. 9. Mary, of Henry Holland and Jenny Sehly. Wit.: Capt. James Wimps [Weems], Capt. Bennit, wid. Ingolsby.

1701
Feb. 16. Egbert, of Antony and Willempje Bratt.
Wit.: Egbert Teunisse, Marytje Bratt.
Feb. 23. Henrik, of Cornelis Schermerhoorn and Marrytje Henriks. Wit.: Wessel and Lidia Ten Broek.
March 2. Richard, of William and Anneke Hilten.
Wit.: John Bennit, Ritchard Bruyas, Marry Ingolsbie.
March 19. Johanna, of Evert Van Esch and Geertje Van den Berg. Wit.: Hendrik and Catharina Van Esch.
March 23. Jannetje, of Barent Ten Eyk and Neeltje Schermerhoorn. Wit.: Coenraad Ten Eyk, Johannes and Jannetje Beekman.
Caspar, of Johannes Jansse and Lysbeth Leendertse.
Wit.: Thomas Harmanse, Hilletje Gansevoort.
Dorothea, of Henrik Douw and Neeltje Meyndertse.
Wit.: Reynier Meyndertse, Saartje Bratt.
March 26. Johannes, of Richart Moor and Geesje Jansse Salsberry. Wit.: Johannes and Gerritje Roseboom.
Lysbeth, of Johannes Claasse Groesbeek and Geertje Quakkenbosch. Wit.: Claas Jacobse Groesbeek, Antje Quakkenbosch.
March 30. Neeltje, of Johannes Abeel and Cathelina Schuyler. Wit.: Abraham Schuyler, Lysbeth Banker.
Apr. 6. Jacob, of Maas Cornelisze and Jacomyntje Gardeniers. Wit.: Albert Rykman, Marytje Lokermans.
Apr. 13. Rebecca, of Jan Salomonse Goewey and Caetje Lokermans. Wit.: Arien Oothout, Marytje Lokermans.
Apr. 20. Casper, of Caspar Melchertse and Jannetje Schermerhorn. Wit.: Levinus Winnen, Neeltje Schermerhoorn.
Apr. 27. Jan, of Willem Janse and Fytje Dirks Van Vechten. Wit.: Gerrit Teunisse Van Vechten, Grietje Van Vechten.
Rachel, of Cornelis Bogardus and Rachel Tjerks. Wit.: Johannes Van Alen, Margrietje Van Tricht.
May 4. Taakel, of Dirk Taakelse! Heemstrate and Claartje Quakkenbosch. Wit.: Taakel Dirkse, Saartje Taakels, wife of Ahasuerus Marselis.
May 11. Anna, of Jacobus Lucasse Wyngaard and Maria Quakkenbosch. Wit.: Claas Lucasze Wyngaard and Geertruy Schuylers.
Elisabeth, of Lucas Lucasze Hoogkerke and Judith Marselis. Wit.: Ahasuerus Marselis, Geertruy Groesbeek.
June 1. Anne, of Matthys and Susanna Warmond.
Wit.: Jan Hanse Berheit, Alida Oothout.
Frans, of Jurrien Fransen and Marrytje Jansse. Wit.: Caspar and Racheltje Van Hoesen.
Ariaantje, of Johannes Ouderkerk and Neeltje Claasse.
Wit.: Egbert Teunisse and wife Marytje.

1701
Alida, of Elbert Gerritse and Marytje Pruyn. Wit.:
Reyer Gerritse, Aaltje Pruym.
June 8. Elisabeth, of Johannes and Johanna Bekker.
Wit.: Pieter Mingaal, Annetje Appels.
June 15. Johannes, of Philip Leendertse and Weyntje
Dirks. Wit.: Ruth Melchertse, Neeltje Meyndertse, alias
Douw.
June 22. Lyntje, of Henrik Janse and Lyntje Winnen.
Wit.: Levinus and Willempje Winnen.
June 29. Lysbeth, of Jan Harris and Moeset Tassama.
Wit.: Philip Schuyler, Lambertje Oothout.
July 6. Claas, of Dominicus and Rebecca Van Schayk.
Wit.: Cornelis and Jannetje Van Schayk.
Jannetje, of Henrik and Cornelia Van Salsberry. Wit.:
Emanuel and Rebecca Van Schayk.
Neeltje, of Andries Lees and Ariaantje Scharp. Wit.:
Henrik and Debora Hansse, Gysbert Scherp.
July 13. Margariet, of Henrik Oothout and Catharina
Douw. Wit.: Gerrit Teunisse Van der Vechte, Grietje
Van Vechten.
July 20. Jacob and Cornelia, chn. of Abraham Kip and
Geesje Van der Heyden. Wit.: Johannes and Lysbeth
Schuyler, Johannes Hansse, Rachel Van der Heyden.
Isaac, of Jochum Staats and Antje Reyndertse. Wit.:
Johannes Schuyler, Rykje Staats.
Sara, of Johannes D'Wandelaar and Lysbeth Gansevoort.
Wit.: Johannes De Wandelaar, Hilletje Gansevoort.
Cornelis, of Evert De Ridder and Anna Van Esch. Wit.:
Thomas Harmanse and wife Mayke.
Aug. 3. Storm, of Wouter Van der Zee and Jannetje
Swart. Wit.: Barent Bratt, Maria Van der Volge.
Aug. 24. Harmen, of Frederik Harmensse Visscher and
Margareta Hansse. Wit.: Tjerk Harmensse Visscher,
Marytje Wendels.
Anna, of Gerrit Lucasse Wyngaard and Sara Visscher.
Wit.: Johannes Lucasse Wyngaard, Ariaantje Wendel.
Aug. 31. Jannetje, of Evert Banker and Elisabeth
Abeel. Wit.: Henrik Van Rensselaar, Marta Duyking.
Magdalena, of Robbert and Wyntje Berrith. Wit.:
Lucas Lucasze Hoogkerke, Racheltje Schuyler.
Sept. 7. Ariaantje, of Dirk and Fytje Van der Karre.
Wit.: Anthony Van Schayk, Maria Duyking, Geesse Van
Schayk.
Pieter, of Johannes Groenendyk and Delia Cuyler. Wit.:
Pieter Van Brugge, Racheltje Schuyler.
Marrytje, of Dirk Bratt and Anna Teunisse. Wit.:
Isaac Bratt, Anna Van der Boog.
Willem, of Cornelis Van den Berg and Maria Winnen.
Wit.: Willem Gysbertse Van den Berg and Catharina.

1701

Sept. 14. Abraham, of Isaac Ouderkerk and Maeyke Van Esch. Wit.: Daniel Winnen, Marrytje Van den Bogaart.

Sept. 28. Marta, of Hendrik Van Dyk and Marytje Schuyler. Wit.: Johannes and Cathalyntje Abeel.

Margarita, of Anthony Bries and Tryntje Rykman. Wit.: Harmen and Margarita Rykman.

Margrietje, of Tames Williams and Agnietje Gansevoort. Wit.: Johannes De Wandelaar, Jr., Hilletje Gansevoort.

Anna, of Gerrit and Agnietje Van Wyen. Wit.: Levinus and Willempje Winnen.

Douwe, of Jan Fonda and Matje Lokermans. Wit.: Claas and Alida Fonda.

Oct. 3. Anna, of Johannes and Maria Bratt. Wit.: Dirk and Antje Bratt.

Oct. 5. Jan, of Daniel Winnen and Dirkje Van Esch. Wit.: Cornelis and Hendrikje Van Esch.

Susanna, of Reynier Meyndertse and Saartje Bratt. Wit.: Barent and Susanna Bratt.

Magdalena, of Henrik and Annetje Matteuse. Wit.: Albert Rykman, Jr., Marytje Martense.

Jacobus, of Willem Claesse Groesbeek and Geertruy Schuyler. Wit.: Johannes Groesbeek, Jacobus Schuyler, Geertje Groesbeek.

Oct. 12. Jacob, of Edward and Josyntje Whiler. Wit.: Ariaantje and Jacob Janse Gardenier.

Oct. 26. Catharina, of Wynand Willemse Van den Berg and Volkje Van Hoese. Wit.: Willem Gysbertse Van den Berg, Catharina.

Nov. 2. Catharina, of Caspar Van Hoesen and Racheltje Slingerland. Wit.: Johannes Thomasze Mingaal, Maria.

Heyltje, of Jacob Teunisse and Annetje Lokermans. Wit.: Aryen Oothout, Lammertje Lokermans.

Nov. 19. Margarita Johanna, of Johannes Lydius and Isabella Rachels. Wit.: Col. Pieter Schuyler, Margarita Selyns, Maria Schuyler.

Jacob, of Herbert Jacobse Van Deuse and Marrytje Reyertse. Wit.: Willem Jacobse Van Deuse, Lysbeth Van Deuse.

Dec. 21. Jacobus, of Robbert Livingston, Jr., and Margarita Schuyler. Wit.: Robbert Livingston, Sr., Johannes Schuyler, Alida Levingston.

Teunis, of Albert and Hester Slingerland. Wit.: Arent and Geertruy Slingerland.

Dec. 28. Tjerk Harmense, of Philip Wendel and Maria Visschers. Wit.: Frederik Harmense Visscher, Lysbeth Schuyler.

Marten, of Pieter Van Buere and Ariaantje Barents. Wit.: Jonathan Jansse, Marrytje Van Buere.

1702
Henrik, of Maas Van Buere and Ariaantje Van Wie. Wit.: Jacob and Catelyntje Schermerhoorn. Racheltje, of Kaspar and Alette Conyn. Wit.: Daniel and Willempje Winne.

1702, Jan. 4. Meyndert, of Pieter Vosburg and Jannetje Barents. Wit.: Marten Van Bueren, Judith Barents.

At K. Caspar, of Michiel Kaljer and Tiete Van Hoesen. Wit.: Jan Hoes, Maeyeke Goes.

At K. Styntje, of Coenraat Borgat and Geesje Verwey. Wit.: Dirk Goes, Styntje Hoes.

At K. Antje, of Isaac Vosburg and Anna Goes. Wit.: Henrik Rensselaar, Catharina Van Rensselaar, Jannetje Van Alen.

Jan. 11. Sybrant, of Goosse Van Schayk and Catharina Staats. Wit.: Antony Van Schayk, Jr., Lysbeth Van Corlaar.

Jan. 18. Susanna, of Cornelis Claasse Van den Berg and Susanna Ouderkerk. Wit.: Antony Van Schayk, Sr., Marytje Van Schayk.

Jan. 21. Thomas, of Thomas Millington and Tryntje Wendel. Wit.: Thomas and Marrytje Wendel.

Gerrit, of Daniel Brat and Lysbeth Lanssing. Wit.: Antony Brat, Alida Lanssing.

Feb. 1. Marrytje, of Claas Siwers and Annetje Van Petten. Wit.: Willem Van Alen, Sara Meynderts.

Feb. 15. Engeltje, of Henrik and Geertruy Vrooman. Wit.: Henrik Van Valkenburg, Jannetje Vrooman.

Feb. 24. Reyer, of Jacob Schermerhoorn and Gerritje Henriks. Wit.: Cornelis Van Buere, Jannetje Beekman.

March 22. Johannes, of Gerrit Roseboom and Maria Sanders. Wit.: Willem Jacobse Van Deuse, Sara Grevenraad.

March 25. Rebecca, of Jan Janse Van Aarnhem and Hester Fonda. Wit.: Jan Fonda, Marretje Lokermans.

March 29. Johannes, of John Appelstown and Annetje Casparus. Wit.: Willem Hondt, Geertruy Schoonhoven.

Apr. 3. Abraham, of Pieter DeGarmo and Catharina Van der Heyden. Wit.: Philip Schuyler, Johannes Thomasse Mingaal, Lysbeth Schuyler.

Teunis, of Bastiaan Harmense Visscher and Dirkje Teunisse. Wit.: Antony and Anna Bratt.

Apr. 11. Pieter, of Willem Van Alen and Marrytje Van Petten. Wit.: Gerrit Van Esch, Melchert Van der Poel and Christina Van Alen.

Apr. 19. Pieter, of Harmen Knikkelbakker and Lysbeth Bogert. Wit.: Wouter and Antje Quakkenbosch.

Maria, of Wouter Quakkenbosch and Cornelia Bogert. Wit.: Elbert Harmense and wife Catharina.

May 3. Joachim, of Barent Staats and Neeltje Van den Berg. Wit.: Jochem and Antje Staats.

1702
May 10. Bartholomaus, of Pieter Hogeboom and Jannetje Muller. Wit.: Jeremias Muller, Catharina Ten Broek.

Cornelis, of Gysbert Van den Berg and Dievertje Masten. Wit.: Cornelis and Cornelia Van den Berg.

Sara, of Salomon Van Vechten and Alida Fonda. Wit.: Henrik and Catharina Van Rensselaar.

May 17. Antje, of Ritchart Janse Van den Berk and Tryntje Hoochteeling. Wit.: Helmer Janse Jeraleman, Antje Jeraleman.

May 19. At K. Jochem, of Bartholomeus Van Valkenburg and Catharina Van Aalsteyn. Wit.: Jochem Lambertse Van Valkenburg, Eva Van Valkenburg.

At K. Bartholomaeus, of Isaac Van Aalsteyn and Jannetje Van Valkenburg. Wit.: Abraham Van Aalsteyn, Margarita Van Valkenburg.

At K. Lysbeth, of Samuel Gardeniers and Helena Bye. Wit.: Burger Huyck, Rachel Dingmans.

May 24. Weyntje, of Johannes Van Vechten and Marytje Bogardus. Wit.: Volkert Van Vechten, Antje Bogardus.

June 14. Hermanus, of Frans Winnen and Elsje Gansevoort. Wit.: Henrik Hansse, Hilletje Gansevoort.

Sybrand, of Adriaan Quakkenbosch and Catharina Van Schayk. Wit.: Goosse Van Schayk, Lysbeth Corlaar.

June 21. David, of Pieter Quakkenbosch and Neeltje Marens. Wit.: Dirk and Claartje Van Heemstrate.

June 28. Ida, of Teunis Van Slyk and Jannitje Hendrikse. Wit.: Levinus Winnen, Catharina Van Schayk.

July 5. Claas, of Arent Schayk and Maria Van Loon. Wit.: Wynand Van den Berg, Lysbeth De Wandelaar.

Harbert, of Thys Janse Hoes and Cornelia Van Deuse. Wit.: Ruth and Catelyntje Van Deuse.

Johannes, of Jan and Geesje Albertse. Wit.: Willem Claasse Groesbeek, Geertruy Groesbeek.

July 26. Egbert, of Antony Bratt and Willempje Teunisse. Wit.: Egbert Teunisse and wife Marrytje.

Alida, of Jacob Lanssing and Helena Pruyn. Wit.: Henrik Lanssing, Antje Yverse.

Aug. 2. Maria, of Kiliaan Van Rensselaar and Maria Van Cortland. Wit.: Pieter Schuyler, My Lady Cornbury.

Aug. 9. Pieter, of Lambert Van Alstein and Jannetje Mingaal. Wit.: Pieter Mingaal, Margarita Roseboom.

Aug. 16. Dorothea, of Volkert Douw and Margarita Van Tricht. Wit.: Willem Teller, Elisabeth Van der Poel.

Margarita, of Pierre Benoit and Hendrikje Schoonhoven. Wit.: Hendrik and Maria Van Schoonhoven.

Rachel, of Patrik Magrigeri and Sydje Hoogteeling. Wit.: Albert Rykman, Lysbeth Rosier.

1702
Pietertje, of Henrik Douw and Neeltje Meynders. Wit.:
Volkert Van Vechten, Lydia Ten Broek.
Aug. 30. Gerrit, of Laurens Van Schayk and Jannetje
Oothout. Wit.: Gerrit and Maria Van Esch, Maeyke
Oothout.
Sara, of Levinus Winnen and Willempje Vile. Wit.:
Francois Winnen, Agnietje Conyn.
Geertje, of Barent Ten Eyck and Neeltje Schermerhoorn.
Wit.: Cornelis Schermerhoorn, Geertje Ten Eyck.
Andries, of Gysbert Andriesse Scharp and Lysbeth
Jansse Goewey. Wit.: Aryen and Lammertje Oothout.
Sept. 6. Edward, of Herry Holland and Jenny Sehly.
Wit.: My lord Cornbury, Maria Van Rensselaar.
Barent, of Marten Van Bueren and Judith Barents.
Wit.: Johannes and Elsje Cuyler.
Sept. 20. Nicolaas, of Johannes Bleeker, Jr., and Anna
Coster. Wit.: Nicolaas Bleeker, Gerretje Roseboom.
Henrikje, of Thomas Harmense Hun and Mayke Ooth-
out. Wit.: Ruth Melchertse Van Deuse, Kaatje Oothout.
Sept. 27. Jannetje, of Gerrit Roelofse Van der Werk
and Maria De Voor. Wit.: Albert and Aaltje Van der
Werk.
Geurt Henrikse, of Abraham Van Deuse and Jacomyntje
Van Schoonhoven. Wit.: Jacobus and Marytje Van
Schoonhoven.
Marrytje, of Abraham Wendel and Maeyke Van Esch.
Wit.: Henrik Van Esch, Anna Ridders.
Oct. 4. Anna, of John Whoodkok and Ariaantje Gar-
denier. Wit.: Jonathan Braadhast, Aaltje Fyn.
Helena, of Henrik Van Rensselaar and Catharina Van
Brug. Wit.: Ciliaan and Maria Van Rensselaar.
Oct. 18. Jacobus, of Johannes Van Alen and Sara Ding-
mans. Wit.: Laurens and Maria Van Alen.
Jan, of Jan Fyn and Alida Gardenier. Wit.: Jan
Woodkok, Ariaantje Gardenier.
Oct. 25. Johannes, of Dirk Taakelse Heemstrate and
Claartje Quakkenbos. Wit.: Pieter Quakkenbos, Maria
Wyngaard.
Nov. 1. Katharina, of Abraham Staats and Elsje Wen-
del. Wit.: Johannes Schuyler, Rykje Staats.
Lysbeth, of Johannes Knikkelbakker and Anna Quack-
enbosch. Wit.: Harmen and Lysbeth Knikkelbakker.
Nov. 4. Elisabeth, of William Hond and Geertruy
Schoonhoven. Wit.: Henrik Van Schoonhoven, Maria
Casparus.
Nov. 22. Maria, of Jacob Van Hoese and Judith Claeuw.
Wit.: Hendrik Hansse, Racheltje Van Hoese.
Jacob, of Harmanus Wendel and Anna Glen. Wit.:
Jonas Douw, Maria Van Vechten.

1702–1703
Nov. 25. Maria, of Johannes Cuyler and Elsje Ten Broek. Wit.: Johannes Van Alen, Katharina Cuyler.
Harmen, of Johannes De Wandelaar and Lysbeth Gansevoort. Wit.: Thomas Williams, Sara Van Brug.
Nov. 29. Alida, of Johannes Beekman and Eva Vinhagel. Wit.: Johannes Vinhagel, Debora Hansse.
Johannes, of Adriaan Oothout and Lammertje Lokermans. Wit.: Thomas Harmensse Hun, Maeyke Hun.
Dec. 2. Maria, of Samuel Doksi and Barbar Goewey. Wit.: Jan Salomonse Goewey, Maria Van Rensselaar.
Cornelia, of Pieter Walderon and Tryntje Van den Berg. Wit.: Cornelis and Maria Van den Berg.
Dec. 6. Anna Margarita, of Antony Van Schayk and Maria Van der Poel. Wit.: Evert Banker, Gerritje Van Schayk.
Cornelis, of Daniel Keteluyn and Debora Vile. Wit.: Kornelis Vile, Johannes Dykman, Anna Kaneel.
Dec. 20. Gerrit, of Cornelis Van Esch and Maria Van den Berg. Wit.: Cornelis and Gerritje Van den Berg.
Dec. 25. Jannetje, of Barent Gerritse Van den Berg and Geertruy Janse Witbeek. Wit.: Johannes Claasse, Geertje Quakkenbosch.
Margarita, of Johannes Hansse and Sara De Foreest. Wit.: Henrik Hansse, Catelina De Foreest.
Dec. 27. Geertruy, of Johannes Roseboom and Gerritje Coster. Wit.: Henrik Roseboom, Jr., Elisabeth Groesbeek.
1703, Jan. 3. At K. Frans, of Lambert Valkenburg and Jannetje Claeuw. Wit.: Jochem Valkenburg, Tryntje Van Aalstein.
Barentje, of Pieter Slyk and Anna Hansse. Wit.: Lambert Huyck, Rachel Dingemans.
Jan. 10. Maria, of Melchert Van der Poel, Jr., and Catharina Van Ale. Wit.: Gerrit Wynandse Van der Poel, Willem Gysbertse, Catharina Van den Berg.
Jan. 27. Teunis, of Andries Bratt and Cornelia Verwey. Wit.: Johannes and Maria Mingaal.
Tames, of Jan Herris and Moeset Tassama. Wit.: Col. Pieter Schuyler, Maria Van Rensselaar.
Feb. 7. Maria, of Johannes Van Alen and Christina Ten Broek. Wit.: Willem Van Alen, Styntje Ten Broek.
Feb. 10. Elisabeth, of William Hilten and Anna Barko. Wit.: James Parker, Caatje Oothout.
Feb. 21. Abraham, of Philip De Foreest and Tryntje Kip. Wit.: Levinus Winnen, Maria Wendel.
Feb. 28. Judith, of William Hogen and Anna Bekker. Wit.: Colonel Staats, Jacobus and Catharina Turk.
Lyntje, of Hendrik Witbik and Lyntje Winne. Wit.: Jeremias Mulder and Teuntje Janse.

1703
March 3. Hendrik, of Hendrik Roseboom and Debora
Staats. Wit.: Gerrit and Gerritje Roseboom.
March 21. Elisabeth, of Willem Van Deuse and Lys-
beth Roseboom. Wit.: Gerrit Roseboom, Marytje Van
Deuse.
Jannetje, of Ritchard Moor and Geesje Salsberry. Wit.:
Jan Lanssing, Anna Coster.
March 26. Johannes, of Stephanus Groesbeek and Elisa-
beth Lansing. Wit.: Jan Lanssing, Barbar Marselis.
Apr. 4. Maria, of Abraham Cuyler and Catharina
Bleeker. Wit.: Nicolaas Bleeker, Rachel Schuyler.
Apr. 25. Marten Cornelisse, of Jonathan Witbeek and
Catharina Van Bueren. Wit.: Henrik Rensselaar, Mag-
dalena Van Bueren.
Gerrit Teunisse, of Volkert Van Vechten and Lydia Ten
Broek. Wit.: Dirk Wesselse Ten Broek, Grietje Van
Vechten.
Pieter, of Cornelis Claasse and Susanna Ouderkerk.
Wit.: Wouter Quakkenbosch, Neeltje Van den Berg.
Pieter, of Jacob Winnen and Maria Bronk. Wit.: Leen-
dert Bronk, Susanna Wendel.
May 16. Johannes, of Johannes Barheith and Catharina
Gilbert. Wit.: Jan Gilbert, Albert Rykman, Cornelia
Gilbert.
May 30. David, of Gideon and Dorcas, pros.. Wit.:
Stephanus Groesbeek, Isabella Lydius.
William, of Johannes Harmanse Visscher and Elisabeth
Nottingham. Wit.: Bastiaan Harmanse Visscher, Geertruy
Scherluyn.
Johannes, of Jacobus Lucasse Wyngaard and Maria
Quakkenbosch. Wit.: Pieter and Machtilda Quakkenbosch.
June 6. Jannetje, of Johannes Abeel and Catelyntje
Schuyler. Wit.: Willem Groesbeek, Jacobus Schuyler,
Catharina Van der Poel.
June 13. Lucas, of Henrik Van Salsberg and Cornelia
Van Schaak. Wit.: Cornelis Teeuwisse Mulder, Hilletje
Mulder.
Rachel, of Jurriaan Claeuw and Maria Jansse. Wit.:
Wessel Ten Broek, Maria Claeuw.
Samuel, of Willem Jansse and Fytje Dirkse Van Vechten.
Wit.: Philip Leendertse Conyn, Anna Van Vechten.
Laurens, of Teunis Pieterse and Margarita Laurensse.
Wit.: Hendrik Jansse Witbeek, Lyntje Witbeek.
Franciscus, of Johannes Van Hoesen and Jannetje
Jansse. Wit.: Jan Harding, Fytje Van Schaak.
Sara, of Jan Van Hoesen and Jannetje Van Schaak.
Wit.: Pieter and Jannetje Vosburg.
June 20. Hendrik, of Coenraad Hoogteeling and Tryntje
Van Slyk. Wit.: Henrik and Debora Hansse.

1703
Isaac, of Marten Van Aalstein and Jannetje Cornelisse.
Wit.: Cornelis and Maria Bogaart.
Anna, of Gerrit Rykse and Barbara Jansse. Wit.: Claas
Gerritse, Antje Pruyn.
June 27. Henrik, of Gerrit Van Wie and Annetje Conyn.
Wit.: Johannes Van Wie, Tanna Conyn.
July 2. Isaac, of Cornelis Swits and Hester Visscher.
Wit.: Isaac and Susanna Swits.
July 11. Neeltje, of Johannes Ouderkerk and Neeltje.
Wit.: Cornelis and Marytje Van Esch.
July 25. Christiaan, of Jillis De la Grange and Jenneke
Adriaanse. Wit: Johannes and Eva Beekman.
Aug. 1. Alida, of Nanning Harmense Visscher and
Alida Vinhagel. Wit.: Johannes Vinhagel, Johannes
Beekman, Sara Wyngaard.
Celia, of Joseph Jansse and Sytje Marselis. Wit.: Gys-
bert Marselis, Johanna Yeads.
Aug. 8. Christina, of Roelof De Duytscher and Jannetje
Brissi. Wit.: Claas and Antje Brissi.
Pieter, of Henrik Fransse Claeuw and Cornelia Scharp.
Wit.: Henrik and Debora Hansse.
Aug. 15. Abraham, of Abraham Van Aalsteyn and
Maria Van Deuse. Wit.: Pieter and Margarita Mingaal.
Jannetje, of Dirk Van der Karre and Sophia Van Schaak.
Wit.: Goosse and Gerritje Van Schayk.
Rykaart, of Henrik Hansse and Debora Van Dam.
Wit.: Johannes Beekman, Sara Hansse.
Aug. 22. Pietertje, of Reynier Meyndertse and Sara
Bratt. Wit.: Egbert and Marrytje Teunisse.
Aug. 29. Abraham, of Lucas Janse Witbeek and Cathar-
ina Van Deuse. Wit.: Ruth and Weyntje Van Deuse.
Bernardus, of Johannes Bratt and Maria Keteluin. Wit.:
Daniel Keteluin, Marrytje Egbertse.
Sept. 5. Adam, of Cornelis Van den Berg and Maria
Winne. Wit.: Jacob Teunisse, Catelyntje Winne.
Neeltje, of Johannes Claasse Groesbeek and Geertje
Quakkenbosch. Wit.: Wouter and Neeltje Quakkenbosch.
Sept. 12. Jacobus, of John Rattelief and Rachel Valken-
burg. Wit.: Lambert Huyk, Geertruy Scherluyn.
Sept. 19. Henrik, of Johannes Groenendyk and Delia
Cuyler. Wit.: Meindert Schuyler, Catharina Cuyler.
Rachel, of Dirk Van der Heyden and Rachel Keteluyn.
Wit.: Coenraet Ten Eyk, Margarita Colins.
Jan, of Ritchart Jansse and Tryntje Hoogteeling. Wit:
Coenraat and Rachel Hoogteeling.
Gerrit, of Cornelis Van den Berg and Maria Van Buere.
Wit.: Reyer Gerritse, Marretje Van Deuse.
Oct. 1. Pieter, of Maarten Delmont and Lysbeth Viele.
Wit.: Abraham and Catharina Cuyler.

1703
Oct. 3. Laurens, of Stephanus Van Alen and Maria Muller. Wit.: Laurens Van Alen, Hilletje Muller.

Jacob, of Herbert Jacobse Van Deuse and Marretje Gerritse. Wit.: Elbert and Marytje Gerritse.

Oct. 10. Geertruy, of Kiliaan Van Rensselaar and Maria Van Cortland. Wit.: Henrik and Catharina Van Rensselaar, Olof Van Cortland.

Ariaantje, of Gerrit Lucasze Wyngaard and Sara Visscher. Wit.: Bastiaan Visscher, Maria Wendel.

Oct. 17. Adrianus, of Evert Banker and Elisabeth Abeel. Wit.: Kiliaan Van Rensselaar, Isabella Lydius.

Jacobus, of William Turner and Abigail Bogard. Wit.: Albert Rykman, Sr., Anna Gansevoort.

Eva, of Antony Bries and Tryntje Rykman. Wit.: Wessel and Catharina Ten Broek, Harmen Rutgers.

Oct. 24. Eva, of Claas Siwers and Antje Van Putten. Wit.: Reynier Meyndertse, Maeyke Hun.

Katharina, of Matthys Nak and Agnietje Schaats. Wit.: Jan Nak, Sampson Bessing, Sophia Nak.

Oct. 31. Ariaantje, of Evert Van Esch and Geertje Van den Berg. Wit.: Cornelis Van Esch, Gerritje Van den Berg.

Willem, of Willem Rees and Maria Goewey. Wit.: Samuel Doksi, Saartje Goewey.

Nov. 7. Thomas, of Tames Williams and Agnietje Gansevoort. Wit.: Johannes De Wandelaar, Maria Gansevoort.

Johannes, of Jan Fonda and Matje Lokermans. Wit.: Jacob Teunisse, Hester Fonda.

Nov. 24. Jannet, of Robbert Livingston, Jr. and Margarita Schuyler. Wit.: Antony Van Schayk, John Colins, Geertje Lanssing.

Dec. 1. Henrik, of Jacob Lanssing and Helena Pruyn. Wit.: Johannes Pruyn, Huybert Van den Berg, Lysbeth Lanssing.

Dec. 12. Magtel, of Isaac Lanssing and Jannetje Beekman. Wit.: Gerrit and Elsje Lansing.

Dec. 15. Jannetje, of Emanuel Van Schaak and Margarita Wyngaard. Wit.: Gerrit Lucasse Wyngaard, Sara Wyngaard.

Anna, of Henrik Oothout and Catharina Douw. Wit.: Jan Jansse Bleeker, Lydia Van Vechten.

Martinus, of Cornelis Van Aalstein and Maria Van den Berg. Wit.: Marten and Jannetje Van Aalstein.

Dec. 19. Catharina, of David Schuiler and Elsje Rutgers. Wit.: Harmen Rutgers, Isaac Verplanke, Maria Lokermans.

Johannes, of John Colinson and Rebecca Brat. Wit.: Barent Brat, Maria Slingerlant.

1703–1704
Dec. 24. Anna, of Barent Staats and Neeltje Van den Berg. Wit.: Jochem and Anna Staats.

Rykje, of Goosse Van Schayk and Catharina Staats. Wit.: Jacob and Rykje Staats.

Dec. 25. Albertus, of Johannes Bekker and Anna Van der Zee. Wit.: Barent Bratt and Maria Lokermans.

Kiliaan, of Evert De Ridder and Anna Van Esch. Wit.: Kiliaan and Maria Van Rensselaar.

1704, Jan. 1. Geertruy, of Thomas Witbeek and Jannetje Van Deuse. Wit.: Johannes Van Vechten, Engeltje Van Deuse.

Jan. 2. Albertus, of Arent Slingerland and Geertruy Van Voste. Wit.: Albert and Hester Slingerland.

Johannes, of Caspar Van Hoesen and Racheltje Slingerland. Wit.: Johannes and Maria Mingaal.

Jan. 5. Antony, of Wouter Van der Zee and Jannetje Swart. Wit.: Antony Brat, Johannes Lansing, Jr., Elsje Lansing.

Jan. 8. Ytje, of Coenraad Borgert and Geesje Van Wie. Wit.: Burger Huyk, Catharina Van Wie.

Andries, of Johannes Scharp and Geertruy Rees. Wit.: Gysbert and Neeltje Scharp.

Abraham, of Cornelis Martense and Cornelia Van Vredenburg. Wit.: Abraham and Marrytje Van Aalstein.

Hilletje, of Pieter Hogeboom and Jannetje Muller. Wit.: Stephanus Van Alen, Hilletje Muller.

Jan. 12. Andries, of Johannes Witbeek and Lysbeth Conyn. Wit.: Andries Douw, Anna Gansevoort.

Jan. 19. Kiliaan, of Daniel Winne and Dirkje Van Esch. Wit.: Albert Rykman, Jr., Maria Rykman.

Jan. 30. Suster, of Daniel Keteluyn and Debora Viele. Wit.: Dirk and Rachel Van der Heyde.

Johannes, of Lucas Lucasse Van Hoogkerke and Judith Marselis. Wit.: Evert Banker, Rachel Schuyler.

Feb. 6. John, of John Whoodkok and Ariaantje Gardenier. Wit.: Gerrit Roseboom, Lysbeth Wendel.

Aaltje, of Isaac Ouderkerk and Maeyke Van Esch. Wit.: Thomas Harmense Hun, Lena Van Esch.

Jacob, of Barent Ten Eyk and Neeltje Schermerhoorn. Wit.: Coenraad Ten Eyk, Jannetje Lanssing.

Feb. 16. Harmen, of Dirk Van Vechten and Margarita Luwes. Wit.: Robbert Levingston, Elbert Luwes, Margarita Levingston.

Feb. 19. Margarita, of David Keteluyn and Johanna Bratt. Wit.: Antony and Daniel Bratt, Margarita Keteluyn.

Johannes, of Philip Wendel and Maria Visscher. Wit.: Johannes Schuyler, Lysbeth Wendel.

1704

Feb. 13, at K.: Evert, of Edward Wieller and Josina Jansse. Wit.: Evert Van Alen, Helena Gardenier.

Dirkje, of Isaac Van Aalstein and Jannetje Van Valkenburg. Wit.: Bartholomeus and Jannetje Van Valkenburg.

Isaac, of Isaac Vosburg and Anna Goes. Wit.: Burger Huyk, Teuntje Winnen.

Johannes, of Jacob Dingmans and Eva Swartwoud. Wit.: Johannes and Sara Van Alen.

Anna, of Dirk Goes and Elisabeth Wyngaard. Wit.: Jan Goes, Margarita Van Schaak.

March 1. Henry, of Henry Holland and Jenny Sehly. Wit.: Capt. Mattheus, Capt. Shenks, Mad. Wimps.

Abraham, of Joseph Yeads and Huybertje Marselis. Wit.: Christoffel and Johanna Yeads.

March 5. Thomas, of Albert Slingerland and Hester Brikkers. Wit.: Johannes and Maria Mingaal.

Catelyntje, of Johannes Schuyler and Elisabeth Staats. Wit.: Jacobus Schuyler, Antje Staats.

March 8. David, of Thomas Nobel and Catharina Marris. Wit.: Pieter and Neeltje Quakkenbosch.

March 15. Franciscus, of Samuel Pruyn and Maria Bogert. Wit.: Jacob Bogert and Antje Van Yvere.

March. 22. Jillis, of Pieter De Garmo and Catharina Van der Heyden. Wit.: Antony Bries, Maria De Garmo.

Apr. 16. Christina, of Johannes Van Alen and Christina Ten Broek. Wit.: Dirk Wesselse Ten Broek, Gerrit Van Esch, Marrytje Van Alen.

Engeltje, of Jacobus Mol and Lydia Winnen. Wit.: Levinus and Catelyntje Winnen.

Machtel, of Dirk Taakelse Van Heemstrate and Catharina Quakkenbosch. Wit.: Pieter and Machtel Quakkenbosch.

Apr. 23. Anna, of Thomas Millington and Tryntje Wendel. Wit.: Pieter and Maria Mingal.

Lysbeth, of Cornelis Van Bueren and Hendrikje Van Esch. Wit.: Albert Rykman, Lysbeth Van Bueren.

Apr. 30. Gerrit, of Elbert Gerritse and Maria Pruin. Wit.: Reyer Gerritse, Marrytje Van Deuse.

May 7. Lucas, of Johannes Lucasse Wyngaard and Susanna Wendel. Wit.: Claas Lucasse Wyngaard, Evert and Hester Wendel.

Isaac, of Jan Janse Van Aarnhem and Hester Fonda. Wit.: Salomon and Alida Van Vechten.

May 14. Abraham, of Abraham Lanssing and Magdalena Van Tricht. Wit.: Gerrit Lanssing, Lysbeth Van der Poel.

May 21. Gerrit Cornelis, of Willem Van Alen and Marrytje Van Putten. Wit.: Laurens and Johannes Van Alen, Catharina Van der Poel.

June 4. Maria, of Teunis Dirkse Van Vechten and

1704
Catelyntje Van Putte. Wit.: Johannes and Maria Van Vechten.

Gysbert, of Ahasueros Marselis and Sara Van Heemstrate. Wit.: Lucas Lucasse Hoogkerke and Huybertje Jeads.

June 18. Maria, of Willem Hond and Geertruy Schoonhoven. Wit.: Jacobus and Maria Schoonhoven.

Samuel, of Samuel Gardenier and Lena Dirkse By. Wit.: Cornelis Maasse, Catelyntje Dingmans.

Lysbeth, of Andries Rees and Ariaantje Scharp. Wit.: Jan and Maria Rees.

June 25. Johannes, of Henrik Douw and Neeltje Meyndertse. Wit.: Henrik and Maria Rensselaar.

July 9. Johannes, of John Kidney and Maria Van der Werke. Wit.: Albert Van der Werke. Dirkje Van Aalstein.

Johannes Henricus, of Johannes Lydius and Isabella Rachel. Wit.: Kiliaan Van Rensselaar, Elisabeth Banker.

July 16. Lidia, of Hendrik Van Dyk and Maria Schuyler. Wit.: Jacobus Schuyler, Jacomina Van Dyk.

July 23. Elisabeth, of Gerrit Roseboom and Maria Sanders. Wit.: Jacobus Turk, Emilia Sanders.

July 30. Edward, of John Colins and Margarita Schuiler. Wit.: My lord and My lady Cornbury, Maria Schuyler.

Aug. 6. David, of Joseph Jansse and Sydje Marselis. Wit.: Kiliaan and Catharina Van Rensselaar.

Christina, of Matthys Goes and Cornelia Van Deuse. Wit.: Pieter and Margarita Mingaal.

Alida, of Warner Van Ivere and Anna Pruyn. Wit.: Samuel Pruyn, Maria Gerritse.

Aug. 13. Johannes, of Harmen Van Salsberry and Tanna Conyn. Wit.: Gerrit and Agnietje Van Wie.

Johannes, of Maas Van Buere and Ariaantje Van Wie. Wit: Wessel and Catharina Ten Broek.

Aug. 20. Catharina, of Gysbert Scharp and Lysbeth Goewey. Wit.: Jan Rees, Sara Goewey.

Andries, of Burger Huyk and Mayeke Goes. Wit.: Lambert Huyk, Teuntje Winne.

Pieter, of Patrik Magrigeri and Sydje Hoogteeling. Wit: Jan Rosier, Lieut. Bruwer, Anna Hoges.

Aug. 27. Abraham, of Abraham Schuiler and Geertruy Ten Broek. Wit.: David and Rachel Schuiler.

Sept. 17. Hester, of Johannes Harmensse Visscher and Lysbeth Nottingham. Wit.: Nanning Harmensse Visscher, Ariaantje Wendel.

Dirk, of Thomas Harmensse Hun and Maeyke Oothout. Wit.: Aryen and Lammertje Oothout.

Andries, of Teunis Van Slyk and Jannetje Henrikse Van Wie. Wit.: Johannes Beekman, Maria Mingaal.

34

1704–1705

Sept. 24. Bernardus, of Daniel Bratt and Lysbeth Lanssing. Wit.: Jacob Lanssing, Susanna Egbertse.

Johannes, of Abraham Staats and Elsje Wendel. Wit.: Barent Sanders, Susanna Wendel.

Oct. 1. Lambert, of Bartholomeus Van Valkenburg and Catharina Van Aalstein. Wit.: Johannes Mingaal, Jannetje Van Aalstein.

Oct. 22. Johannes, of Johannes De Wandelaar and Lysbeth Gansevoort. Wit.: Leendert Gansevoort, Sara De Wandelaar.

Nov. 19. Abraham, of Pieter Quakkenbosch and Neeltje Marens. Wit.: Jan and Machtel Quakkenbosch.

Nov 26. Catharina, of Andries Douw and Lydia De Meyer. Wit.: Henrik Douw, Margarita Van Vechten.

Nov. 29. Henrik, of Oyje Oyjens and Maria Wendel. Wit.: Thomas and Lysbeth Wendel.

Dec. 6. Adriaan, of Adriaan Quakkenbos and Catharina Van Schayk. Wit.: Dirk and Claartje Van Heemstrate.

Dec. 17. Pieter Lokerman, of Adriaan Oothout and Lammetje Lokerman. Wit.: Jan and Marrytje Fonda.

Volkert, of Wynand Van den Berg and Volkje Van Hoesen. Wit.: Ruth and Weyntje Van Deuse.

Dec. 24. Catharina, of Jacobus Teunisse Van Woerd and Anna Lokermans. Wit.: Cornelis Teeuwisse Muller, Hilletje Muller.

Isaac, of Abraham Van Deuse and Jacomyntje Van Schoonhoven. Wit.: Teeuwis and Marrytje Van Deuse.

Johanna, of Cornelis Kierstede and Sara Elswaart. Wit.: Kiliaan Van Rensselaar, Maria Schuiler.

Dec. 31. Evert, of Gerrit Lanssing, Jr., and Catharina Glenn. Wit.: Abraham Lanssing, Jacomina Van Dyk.

Maria, of Samuel Doksi and Barbara Goewey. Wit.: Thomas Doksi, Marrytje Fonda.

1705, Jan. 7, at K.: Elbertje, of Johannes Van Alen and Sara Dingmans. Wit.: Laurens and Jannetje Van Alen.

Elisabeth, of Jacob and Jannetje Hoogteeling. Wit.: Jochem Valkenburg, Jannetje Vosburg.

Stephanus, of Dominicus Van Schaak and Rebecca Groesbeek. Wit.: Laurens Van Schaak, Catharina Van Petten.

Helmer Johannes, of William Turner and Abigail Bogaart. Wit.: Helmer Jansse and wife Anna.

Maria, of Johannes Van Hoesen and Jannetje Jansse De Ryk. Wit.: Dirk and Fytje Van der Kar.

Maria, of Lambert Valkenburg and Jannetje Van Aalstein. Wit.: Bartholomaeus Valkenburg, Maria Claeuw.

Caspar, of Willem Jansse Casparsse and Fytje Dirkse Van Vechten. Wit.: Jurrien Claeuw, Weyntje Conyn.

Jan. 10. Catharina, of Stephanus Groesbeek and Elisa-

1705
beth Lanssing. Wit.: Willem Groesbeek, Geertruy Lanssing.

Catharina, of Harmanus Wendel and Anna Glen. Wit.: Evert and Susanna Wendel.

Jan. 13. Femmetje, of Cornelis Swits and Hester Visscher. Wit.: Tjerk Harmensse Visscher, Antje Visscher.

Egbert Teunisse, of Barent Egbertse and Maria De Garmo. Wit.: Antony Bratt, Marrytje Egberts.

Jan. 31. Lyntje, of Frans Winnen and Elsje Gansevoort. Wit.: Leendert Gansevoort, Anna De Worm.

Feb. 18. Jobje, of Henrik Jansse Van Salsberry and Cornelia Van Schaak. Wit.: Thomas Harmansse Hun, Maeyke Hun.

Eva, of Bernhardus Swartwoud and Rachel Schepmoes. Wit.: Pieter Van Brugge, Maria Lokermans.

Catelyntje, of Jacob Kip and Rachel Swartwoud. Wit.: Abraham Kip, Catelyntje De Foreest.

Tecla, of Evert Wynkoop and Geertje Elmendorp. Wit.: Cornelis and Jenneke Cool.

Nicolaas, of Gerrit Wynkoop and Hilletje Gerritse. Wit.: Moses and Maria Du Puis.

Catharina, of Abraham Le Foy and Anna Maria Tower. Wit.: Henrik and Katharina Oothout.

Jannetje, of Cornelis Bogaart and Cornelia La Maitre. Wit.: Levinus Winne, Aaltje Bogaart.

March 4. Johannes, of Melchert Van der Poel and Catharina Van Alen. Wit.: Johannes Van Alen, Geertruy Groesbeek.

March 25. Jeremy, of Kiliaan Van Rensselaar and Maria Van Cortlandt. Wit.: Henrik Rensselaar, Maria Schuyler.

Apr. 5. Jannetje, of Laurens Van Schaak and Jannetje Oothout. Wit.: Elias Van Schaak, Lammertje Oothout.

Margareta, of Gerrit Rykse and Barbara Jansse. Wit.: Johannes Pruyn, Margarita Rykse.

Apr. 8. Alida, of Jan Huibertse and Lysbeth. Wit.: Henrik Douw, Antje Staats.

Heyltje, of Stephanus Van Alen and Maria Muller. Wit.: Johannes Van Alen, Catharina Van der Poel.

Apr. 29. David, of Johannes Abeel and Catelyntje Schuyler. Wit.: Meindert Schuyler, Geertruy Groesbeek.

Jacob, of Coenraat Ten Eyck and Gerritje Van Schayk. Wit.: Antony Van Schayk, Geertje Ten Eyck.

Jeremy, of Henrik Van Rensselaar and Catharina Van Brug. Wit.: Kiliaan Van Rensselaar, Anna Nicols.

Johannes, of Johannes Brat and Maria Keteluin. Wit.: Daniel Brat, Margarita Caneel.

May 6. Catharina, of Gerrit Roelofse Van der Werke

1705
and Marytje Jansse Diffoer. Wit.: Jan Jansse Diffoer,
Catharina Van der Werke.
May 13. Elisabeth, of Johannes Cuyler and Elsje Ten
Broek. Wit.: Pieter and Sara Van Brugge.
Ariaantje, of Pieter Hoogeboom and Jannetje Muller.
Wit.: Henrik Rensselaar, Antje Hogeboom.
Sara, of Cornelis Claasse and Susanna Ouderkerk. Wit.:
Antony and Lysbeth Coster.
May 17. Neeltje, of Dirk Van der Kerre and Fytje Van
Schayk. Wit.: Coenraat Ten Eyk, Katharina Quakken-
bosch.
May 20. Catharina, of Matthys Nak and Agnietje
Schaats. Wit.: Jonathan Braadhorst, Elsje Lanssing.
May 27. Neeltje, of Johannes Beekman and Eva Vin-
hagel. Wit.: Isaac Lanssing, Catharina Cuyler.
June 3. Eva, of Caspar Leendertse Conyn and Aletta
Winnen. Wit.; Pieter Winnen, Anna Gansevoort.
June 24. Geertruy and Catharina, twins of Abraham
Kip and Geesje Van der Heyden. Wit.: Johannes and
Lysbeth Schuiler, Barent Egbertse, Sara Hansse.
Geurt and Jacob, twins of Pierre Benoit and Henrikje
Van Schoonhoven. Wit.: William Hont, Hilletje Mulder,
Jacobus Van Schoonhoven, Maria Casparus.
July 15. Marten Cornelis, of Marten Van Bueren and
Judith Barents. Wit. : Pieter and Magdalena Van
Bueren.
Robbert, of Barent Sanders and Maria Wendel. Wit.:
Johannes Schuyler, Elsje Sanders.
Christoffel, of Roelof De Duytser and Jannetje Bressy.
Wit.: Andries Bressi and Hester Wendel.
July 22. Johannes, of Anthony Bratt and Wilmpje
Teunisse. Wit.: Teunis Egbertse, Hester Visscher, Jr.
July 29. Abraham, of Jacobus Lucasze Wyngaard and
Maria Wyngaart. Wit.: Abraham Schuyler, Sara Wyn-
gaart.
Aug. 5. Lysbeth, of Henrik Lanssing, Jr., and Jannetje
Knikkelbakker. Wit.: Johannes Knikkelbakker, Lysbeth
Lanssing.
Aug. 12. Samuel, of Teunis Pietersse Sardam and Mar-
garita Laurensse. Wit.: Samuel and Antje Van Vechten.
Joachim, of Daniel Keteluyn and Debora Vile. Wit.:
Dirk and Rachel Van der Heyden.
Aug. 19. Jacobus, of William Hilten and Anna Barko.
Wit.: Henrik Oothout, Anna Delmont.
Sept. 9. Cornelis, of Cornelis Schermerhoorn and Mar-
rytje Van Bueren. Wit.: Albert Rykman, Johannes and
Elsje Cuyler.
Sara, of Lucas Lucasse Van Hoogkerke and Judith Mar-
selis. Wit.: Evert Banker, Rachel Schuyler.

1705

Gerrit, of Johannis Lanssing and Helena Sanders. Wit.: Gerrit and Elsje Lanssing.

Sept. 22. Melchert, Abraham, of Thomas Witbeek and Jannetje Van Deuse. Wit.: Jonas and Catharina Douw.

Sept. 29. Jacobus, of Abraham Vosburg and Claartje Bressy. Wit.: Isaac Verplanke, Margarita Vetch.

Teunis, of Coenraat Hoogteeling and Tryntje Van Slecht [?]. Wit.: Frans Winnen, Anna Gansevoort.

Henrik, of Herbert Jacobse Van Deuse and Marrytje Gerritse. Wit.: Reyer Gerritse, Geertruy Gerritsen.

Oct. 7. Omphry, of Ritchart Moor and Geesje Salsberry. Wit.: William and Anna Hoogen.

Gerrit, of Claas Gerritsen Van Frank and Geertruy Quakkenbosch. Wit.: Maas Rykse, Ariaantje Van Frank.

Oct. 14. Jesje, of Henrik Hansse and Debora Van Dam. Wit.: Frederik Visscher, Eva Beekman.

Gerrit, of Henrik Fransse Claeuw and Cornelia Scharp. Wit.: Andries Rees, Geertruy Scharp.

Maria, of Henrik and Geertruy Vroman. Wit.: Levinus and Wilmpje Winnen.

Roelof, Gerrit, of Albert Van der Werke and Dirkje Van Aalstein. Wit.: Roelof Gerritse and wife Geertruy.

Oct. 21. Douwe, of Salomon Van Vechten and Alida Fonda. Wit.: Jan Fonda, Hesther Van Aarnhem.

Oct. 28. Abraham, of John Whoodkoks and Ariaantje Gardenier. Wit.: John Pray, Maria Roseboom.

David, of Cornelis Martense and Cornelia Vredenburg. Wit.: Levinus and Wilmpje Winnen.

Dirk, of Pieter Van Slyk and Johanna Barheit. Wit.: Pieter Van Brug, Grietje Barheit.

Nov. 4. Henrik, of Tames Williams and Agnietje Gansevoort. Wit.: Leendert and Hilletje Gansevoort.

Nov. 11. Cornelis, of Emanuel Van Schaak and Margarita Wyngaard. Wit.: Claas and Maria Wyngaard.

Elisabeth, of Goosse Van Schayk and Catharina Staats. Wit.: Antony Van Schayk, Lysbeth Corlaar.

Nov. 18. Cornelis, of Pieter Walderon and Tryntje Van den Berg. Wit.: Cornelis and Maria Van Aalstede.

Lena, of Abraham Van Aalstede and Maria Van Deuse. Wit.: Mattheus Van Deuse, Maria Wendel.

Catharina, of Johannes Groesbeek and Geertje Quakkenbosch. Wit.: Stephanus Groesbeek, Barbar Marselis.

Nov. 25. Nicolaas, of Nanning Visscher and Alida Vinhagen. Wit.: Johannes Vinhagen, Jr., Lysbeth Visscher.

Nov. 28. Gerrit, of Abraham Lanssing and Magdalena Van Tricht. Wit.: Gerrit Lanssing, Jr., Elsje Lanssing.

Dec. 9. Margarita, of Johannes Van Vechten and Maria Bogardus. Wit.: Jonas Douw, Lydia Van Vechten.

1705-1706

Jonas, of Henrik Oothout and Catharina Douw. Wit.: Volkert and Margarita Douw.

Dec. 12. Jannetje, of Barent Ten Eyk and Neeltje Schermerhoorn. Wit.: Andries and Maeyke Ten Eyk.

Gerrit, of Isaac Lanssing and Jannetje Beekman. Wit.: Johannes and Eva Beekman.

Dec. 21. Benjamin, of Levinus Winnen and Wilmpje Viele. Wit.: Henrik Vrooman and Sara Van Brug.

Dec. 25. Henrik, Lysbeth, of Willem Van Deuse and Lysbeth Roseboom. Wit.: Henrik and Debora Roseboom, Marrytje Van Deuse.

Dec. 30. Machtelt, of Pieter Quakkenbosch and Neeltje Marens. Wit.: Jan and Machtelt Quakkenbosch.

1706, Jan. 6. Lucas, of Gerrit Lucasse Wyngaard and Sara Visschers. Wit.: Nanning and Dirkje Visscher.

Barent, of Reynier Meyndertse and Sara Brat. Wit.: Daniel and Lysbeth Brat.

Blandina, of Abraham Gaasbeek Chambers and Sara Bayard. Wit.: Francois Salsbury, Maria Gaasbeek.

Laurentia, of Wessel Ten Broek and Jacomina Gaasbeek. Wit.: Cornelis Vernoy, Sara Gaasbeek.

Cornelis, of Cornelis Vernoy and Sara Ten Broek. Wit.: Cornelis Vernoy, Elsje Cuyler.

Pieter, of Robbert Levingston, Jr., and Margarita Schuyler. Wit.: Pieter and Maria Schuyler.

Jenneke, of Coenraad Elmendorp and Blandina Kierstede. Wit.: Jan Gerritse, Antje Kierstede.

Jan. 8. Willem, of Johannes Trephagen and Aagje Winnen. Wit.: Levinus and Elsje Winnen.

Magdalena, of Barent Borhans and Margarita Jansse. Wit.: Jan and Magdalena Matthysse.

Jan. 13, at K.: Kiliaan, of Jacob Winnen and Maria Bronk. Wit.: Leendert Philipse Conyn, Antje Van Vechten.

Henricus, of Johannes Spoor and Maria Singer. Wit.: Henrik and Jannetje Singer.

Johanna. The father deceased, the mother Alida Tippings. Wit.: Andries and Ydje Gardenier.

Alette, of Harmen Jansse Salsberry and Tanna Conyn. Wit.: Leendert Conyn, Lysbeth Scharp.

Barbara, of Bastiaan Dewit and Margarita Pearson. Wit.: Jan Pearson and Antje Post.

Apollonia, of Willem Van Vredenburg and Heyltje Van Etten. Wit.: Cornelis Martensse, Cornelia Vredenburg.

Adam, of Matthys Pars and Tanna Winnen. Wit.: Jacob Winnen, Hilletje Muller.

Rebecca, of Pieter Van Oostrande, Jr., and Rachel Dingmans. Wit.: Adam and Aaltje Dingmans.

1706
Jacob, of Pieter Van Oostrande, Sr., and Rebecca Trop-hagen. Wit.: Pieter and Geesje Ploeg.

Johannes, of Burger Huyg and Maeyke Hoes. Wit.: Jan Hoes, Catharina Huyg.

Matthys, of Jan Henrikse Bout and Jannetje Scharp. Wit.: Matthys Jansse, Styntje Hoes.

Magdalena, of Thomas Jansse and Maeyke Bogert. Wit.: Jan and Magdalena Matthysse.

Jan, of Coenraat Borger and Geesje Van Wie. Wit.: Jan Borger, Lysbeth Hoes.

Matthys, of Rykaart Jansse and Tryntje Hoogteeling. Wit.: Claas Siwers, Anna Van Pette.

Johanna, of Adam Swart and Metje Van Slyk. Wit.: Pieter and Johanna Van Slyk.

Jan. 23. Catharina, of Jan Fonda and Matje Loker-mans. Wit.: Antony Van Schaik, Johanna Van Stryen.

Feb. 3. Cornelis, of Jeremias Muller and Lysbeth Halen-beek. Wit.: Cornelis Teeuwisse Muller, Hilletje Muller.

Feb. 20. Sybrand of Gerrit ·Van Schayk and Sara Goewey. Wit.: Goosse Van Schayk, Lysbeth Corlaar.

Feb. 24. Lysbeth, of Simon Groot, Jr., and Geertruy Rinkhout. Wit.: Cornelis Swits, Abraham Cuyler, Lys-beth Schuyler.

Johannes, of Johannes Glen, Jr., and Jannetje Bleeker. Wit.: Johs. Bleeker, Jr., Catharina Cuyler.

Feb. 27. Evert, of Abraham Wendel and Maeyke Van Esch. Wit.: Thomas Wendel, Tryntje Millington

March 3. Margarita, of Volkert Van Vechten and Lydia Ten Broek. Wit.: Johannes Van Vechten, Elsje Cuyler.

March 10. Ariaantje, of Philip Wendel and Maria Vis-scher. Wit.: Harmanus and Susanna Wendel.

Cornelis, of Wessel Ten Broek and Catharina Lokermans. Wit.: Antony Coster, Tryntje Bries.

Maria, of Cornelis Van Esch and Marrytje Van den Berg. Wit.: Wouter Quakkenbos, Sr., Maeyke Ouderkerk.

March 17. Catharina, of Barent Gerritse Van den Berg and Geertruy Witbeek. Wit.: Willem Gysbertse Van den Berg, Antje Van den Berg.

March 24. Anna, of Isaac Casparse Halenbeek and Dorothea Ten Bosch. Wit.: Caspar Van Hoesen, Daniel Bratt, Alida Lanssing.

Jan Salomon, of Gysbert Scharp and Lysbeth Goewey. Wit.: Laurens Scharp, Catelyntje Winnen.

Apr. 7. Gerardus, of Evert Banker and Elisabeth Abeel. Wit.: Johannes Banker, Goosse Van Schayk, Maria De Peyster, Lysbeth Van Corlaar.

Barent, of Andries Bratt and Cornelia Verwey. Wit.: Daniel and Lysbeth Bratt.

Apr. 21. Margarita, Anna, of Johannes Roseboom and

1706

Gerritje Coster. Wit.: Meyndert and Debora Roseboom, Geertruy Gerritse.

Catelyntje, of Jacob Schuyler and Susanna Wendel. Wit.: David and Catelyntje Schuyler, Geertruy Groesbeek.

Apr. 28. Rachel, of Evert Ridder and Antje Van Esch. Wit.: Evert Van Esch, Weyntje Van Deuse.

May 5. Annaatje, of Johannes Bekker and Anna Van der Zee. Wit.: David Schuyler, Lysbeth Lansing.

May 13. Ariaantje, of Barent Staats and Neeltje Van den Berg. Wit.: Gysbert Van den Berg, Marrytje Van Esch.

May 19. Laurens, of Pieter Van Alen and Josina Dingmans. Wit.: Melchert and Catharina Van der Poel.

Gerrit, of Teunis Van Slyk and Jannetje Van Wie. Wit.: Jan and Agnietje Van Wie.

June 2. Henrik, of Johannis Bleeker, Jr., and Anna Coster. Wit.: Abraham Cuyler, Elisabeth Groesbeek.

Sara, of Abraham Staats and Elsje Wendel. Wit.: Abraham and Jannetje Provoost.

June 9. Margarita, of John Ratteliff and Rachel Van Valkenburg. Wit.: Jochem Van Valkenburg, Catharina Barheit.

Eva, of Isaac Van Aalstein and Jannetje Van Valkenburg. Wit.: Jochem Van Valkenburg, Anna Rattelif.

Pieter, of Wouter Quakkenbos and Cornelia Bogert. Wit.: Jan Fonda, Geertje Quakkenbos.

June 16. Catharina, of Henrik Roseboom and Debora Staats. Wit.: Meyndert Roseboom, Lysbeth Van Deuse.

June 30. Henrik, of Isaac Henrikse Burger and Judith Hoes. Wit.: Jacobus and Teuntje Turk.

Elisabeth, of Jacob Lanssing and Helena Pruyn. Wit.: Daniel and Elisabeth Bratt.

Neeltje, of Johannes Knikkelbakker and Anna Quakkenbosch. Wit.: Wouter Quakkenbosch, Jr., Neeltje Quakkenbosch.

July 14. Maria, of Caspar Van Hoesen and Racheltje Slingerland. Wit.: Johannes and Maria Mingaal.

Hans, of Johannes Hansse and Sara Foreest. Wit.: Pieter Winnen, Debora Hansse.

Hanna, of Evert Van Esch and Geertje Van den Berg. Wit.: Gerrit Van Esch, Jr., Maeyke Wendel.

July 28. Nicolaas, of Claas Siwers and Antje Van Petten. Wit.: Coenraat Ten Eyck, Marrytje Van Alen.

Willem, of Cornelis Van Bueren and Henrikje Van Esch. Wit.: Cornelis and Aaltje Van Esch.

Geertruytje, of Anthony Coster and Lysbeth Ten Broek. Wit.: Wessel Ten Broek, Elsje Cuyler.

Aug. 4. Elisabeth, of Johannes Harmense Visscher and Elisabeth Nottingham. Wit.: Gerrit Lucasse Wyngaard, Alida Visscher.

1706

Cornelia, of Cornelis Van Aalsteyn and Marrytje Van den Berg. Wit.: Cornelis Gysbertse Van den Berg, Tryntje Walderon.

Aug. 18. Pieter, of Johannes Van Alen and Christina Ten Broek. Wit.: Wessel Ten Broek, Elsje Cuyler.

Nicolaas Frederik, of William Van Alen and Marrytje Van Petten. Wit.: Gerrit Van Esch, in the father's absence; Willem Teller, Elsje Schuyler.

Aug. 25. Hilletje, of Wouter Van der Zee and Jannetje Swart. Wit.: Dirk Van der Heyden, Hilletje Van der Zee.

Sept. 1. Pieter, of Pieter Bronk and Antje Bogardus. Wit.: Johannes Andriesse Witbeek, Marytje Van Vechten.

Tryntje, of Thys Hoes and Cornelia Van Deuse. Wit.: Paulus Van Vleq, Maria Van den Berg.

Sept. 22. Isaac, of Cornelis Swits and Hester Visscher. Wit.: Isaac and Susanna Swits.

Levinus, of Pieter Winnen and Maria De Forest. Wit.: Levinus and Willemina Winnen.

Martinus, of Martinus Van Aalstein and Cornelia Van den Berg. Wit.: Cornelis Van Aalstein, Dirkje Van der Werke.

Cornelis, of Isaac Ouderkerk and Maeyke Van Esch. Wit.: Cornelis Van Esch, Dirkje Van Bueren.

Gerrit, of Ahasueros Marselis and Sara Van Heemstrate. Wit.: Christoffel and Catelina Yeads.

Sept. 29. Tobias, of Jonathan Witbeek and Catharina Van Deuse. Wit.: Anthony and Lysbeth Coster.

Rebecca, of Johannes De Wandelaar, Jr., and Lysbeth Gansevoort. Wit.: Albert Van der Zee, Marytje Gansevoort.

Oct. 6. Cornelia, of Jan Barheit and Catharina Gilbert. Wit.: Gerrit and Mary Wibusse.

Sara, of Abraham Cuyler and Catharina Bleeker. Wit.: Johannes Bleeker, Jr., Elsje Cuyler.

Nov. 17. Abraham, of Volkert Dou and Margarita Van Tricht. Wit.: Jonas Douw, Grietje Van Vechten.

Rachel, of John Johnson Van Aarnhem and Hester Fonda. Wit.: Isaac and Rebecca Fonda.

Alida, of Samuel Pruyn and Maria Bogert. Wit.: Elbert Gerritse, Barentje Pruyn.

Abraham, of Herbert Jacobse Van Deuse and Marrytje Gerritse. Wit.: Christina Gerritse.

Dec. 15. Anthony, of Cornelis Van Slyk and Claasje Bratt. Wit.: David Schuyler, Maria Rykman.

Cornelis, of Dirk Van Vechten and Margarita Harmense. Wit.: Teunis Van Vechten, Anna Gansevoort.

Hendrikje, of Adriaan Oothout and Lammetje Lokermans. Wit.: Henrik and Catharina Oothout.

1706-1707

Johannes, of Samuel Doksi and Barbara Goewey. Wit.: Gerrit and Sara Van Schayk.

Dec. 22. Elisabeth, of William Hont and Geertruy Schoonhoven. Wit.: William Hogen, Anna Corlaar.

Gysbert, of Joseph Jansse and Zytje Marselis. Wit.: Gysbert and Barbara Marselis.

Jacob, of Gerrit Lanssing, Jr., and Catharina Glen. Wit.: Jacob and Lena Lanssing.

Dec. 25, b. Sept. 17. Edward Whieller and Josina Gardenier. Wit.: Cornelis and Geertruy Maasse.

Henrik, of Henrik Brouwer and Marrytje Bosboom. Wit.: Jesse and Aaltje De Graaf.

Catharina, of Albert Vedder and Maria Glen. Wit.: Stephanus and Lysbeth Groesbeek.

Claas, of Jesse De Graaf and Aaltje Akkermans. Wit.: Caspar Van Hoesen, Annetje Akkermans.

Maria, of Arent Danielse and Sara Van Eps. Wit.: Symon Danielse and Maria Peek.

Marrytje, of Dirk Taakelse Van Heemstrate and Catharina Quakkenbosch. Wit.: Takel Van Heemstrate and Grietje Vroman.

Lysbeth, of Claas Gerritse Van Franke and Geertruy Quakkenbosch. Wit.: Jan and Machteld Quakkenbosch.

Dec. 29. Cornelis, of Stephanus Van Alen and Maria Muller. Wit.: Cornelis Teeuwisse Muller, Marrytje Van Alen.

1707, Jan. 5. Sealy, of Henry Holland and Jeanny Sehly. Wit.: Robbert Levingston, Sr., Margarita Levingston.

Maria, of Coenraad Ten Eyk and Gerritje Van Schayk. Wit.: Barent Ten Eyk, Maria Van Schayk.

Henrikje, of Johannes Oothout and Aaltje. Wit.: Cornelis Van Esch, Lammertje Oothout.

Jan. 12. Robbert, of Johannis Lanssing and Lena Sanders. Wit.: Gerrit Roseboom, Lysbeth Visscher.

Engeltje, of Samuel Gardenier and Lena By. Wit.: Nicolaas Gardenier, Josina Dingmans.

B. Sept. 17, 1706. Jesje, of Jacob Dingmans and Eva Swartwouds. Wit.: Cornelis Maasse Van Bloemendaal, Catelyntje Dingmans.

Jan. 12, 1707. Johannes, of Pieter Ouderkerk and Alida Cloet. Wit.: Robbert Livingston, Jr, Anna Quakkenbosch.

Jan. 19. Evert, of Harmanus Wendel and Anna Glen. Wit.: Evert Wendel, Catharina Dou.

Pieter, of Bartholomeus Van Valkenburg and Catharina Van Aalstein. Wit.: Johannes and Margarita Mingaal.

Jan. 29. Rachel, of Bartholomeus Pikkart and Aagje Claasse. Wit.: Wynand Van den Berg, Anna Gansevoort

1707

Feb. 2. Anna, of Oyje Oyjens and Maria Wendel. Wit.: Johannes Mingaal, Maria Wendel.

Feb. 5. Alida, of Johannes Laurensse Van Alen and Sara Dingmans. Wit.: Johannes Pieterse Van Alen, Jacomyntje Van Bloemendaal.

Feb. 9. Abraham, of Melchert Van der Poel, Jr., and Catharina Van Alen. Wit.: Abraham, Wynand and Catharina Van der Poel.

Feb. 16. Lysbeth, of Cornelis Schermerhoorn and Marrytje Van Bueren. Wit.: Barent Ten Eyk, Pieternella Rykman.

Margarita, of Marten Van Slyk and Margarita Van Franken. Wit.: Robbert Livingston, Jr., Margarita Livingston.

Feb. 19. Susanna, of William Rodgers and Mary Johnson. Wit.: Evert Ridder, Henrik Lanssing, Catharina Van den Berg.

Sara, of Frederik Cloet and Francyntje Dumont. Wit.: Gysbert Marselis, Neeltje.

Maria, of Pieter Symonse and Neeltje Van der Volge. Wit.: Marten and Lysbeth Delmont.

Jean, of Jean Du Four and Catharina Van der Werke. Wit.: Henrik and Jannetje Van der Werke.

Marrytje, of David Keteluyn and Anna Bratt. Wit.: Daniel Keteluyn, Susanna Egbertse.

Sybrand, of Gerrit Van Schayk and Sara Goewey. Wit.: Jan Salomonse Goewey, Katharina Quakkenbos.

Feb. 26. Juriaan, of Lambert Van Valkenburg and Jannetje Claeuw. Wit.: Henrik Van Valkenburg, Helena Beekman.

March 2. Johannes, of Dirk Van der Heyden and Rachel Keteluyn. Wit.: Pieter De Garmo, Margarita Kanneel.

March 9. Michiel, of Willem Jansse Halenbeek and Fytje Van Vechten. Wit.: Reynier Meyndertse Van Yveren, Alida Lanssing.

March 16. Jacobus, of Abraham Van Valkenburg and Catelyntje Schermerhoorn. Wit.: Jacob and Gerritje Schermerhoorn.

Ruth, of Thomas Harmensse Hun and Maeyke Oothout. Wit.: Ruth Melchertse Van Deuse, Aertje [?] Ridder.

March 23. Jacobus, of Abraham Schuyler and Geertruy Ten Broek. Wit.: Johannes Cuyler, Johannes and Catharina Ten Broek.

Stephanus, of Kiliaan Van Rensselaar and Maria Van Cortlandt. Wit.: Philip and Lysbet Schuyler, in place of Geertruy Van Cortland.

Maria, of Pieter Hoogeboom and Jannetje Muller. Wit.: Pieter Van Brug, Catharina Van Rensselaar.

1707
Alida, of Johannes Pruyn and Emilia Sanders. Wit.:
Barent Sanders, Antje Van Yvere.

March 30. Henricus, of Johannes Beekman and Eva
Vinhagen. Wit.: Meyndert and Maria Roseboom.

Apr. 6. Gerrit, of Jan Gerritson and Christina Pruyn.
Wit.: Johannis Pruyn, Annetje Reyers.

Jacob, of Jan Dekker and Tysje Bogert. Wit.: Helmer
Jansse and wife Antje.

Apr. 20. Catharina, of Marten Delmont and Lysbeth
Viele. Wit.: Jan Delmont and Caatje Cuiler.

Maria, of Daniel Bratt and Elisabeth Lanssing. Wit.:
Dirk and Susanna Bratt.

B. Nov. 8, 1706. Joseph, of Christoffel Yeads and
Catelyntje Winnen. Wit.: Jacob Teunisse, Huybertje Yeads.

1707, Apr. 27. Catelyntje, of Jan Rees and Maria Goewey. Wit.: Gerrit Van Schayk, Lammertje Lokerman or
Oothout.

Meyndert, of Frederik Meyndertse Van Yvere and Sara
De Wandelaar. Wit.: Reynier Van Yvere, Catharyna
De Wandelaar.

May 11. Geertruy, of Andries Rees and Ariaantje
Scharp. Wit.: Ahasueros and Sara Marselis.

Debora, of Goosse Van Schayk and Catharina Staats.
Wit.: Gerrit Van Schayk, Debora Roseboom.

May 22. Ariaantje, of Albert Van der Zee and Hilletje
Gansevoort. Wit.: Leendert Gansevoort, Anna De Warm.

June 1. Teunis, of Teunis Van Vechten and Catharina
Van Putten. Both died before the baptism. Wit.: Johannes Van Vechten, F. van Dirk [meaning probably "son
of Dirk"], Reynier Meyndertse Van Yveren, Marrytje Van
Alen.

June 2. Jacob, of John Herris and Moeset Tassama.
Wit.: Kiliaan Van Rensselaar, Anna Van Stryen.

June 8. Cornelis, of Cornelis Van den Berg, dec^d, and
Maria Winnen. Wit.: Willem Gysbertse and Wynand
Van den Berg, Margarita Van Sant.

Hermanus, of Johannes Vedder and Maria Fort. Wit.:
Jan Fort, Elsje Cuyler.

Margarita, of Johannes Meyndertse Van Yveren and
Geertruy Van Slyk. Wit.: Albert Rykman, Sr., Hermanus
Rykman, Saartje Van Yveren.

June 15. Christoffel, of Nicolaas Bressy and Catelyntje
Bont. Wit.: Abraham Kip, Lena Bont.

Henrik, of Abraham Van Deuse and Jacomyntje Van
Schoonhoven. Wit.: Pierre and Henrikje Benoit.

June 22. Lucas, of Dirk Hoes and Lysbeth Van Wyngaarde. Wit.: Caspar and Racheltje Van Hoese.

Thomas, of Jacobus Turk and Teuntje Hoes. Wit.:
Pieter and Bata Winnen.

1707
June 29. Hendrik, of Jan Borgaart and Katharina Van Wie. Wit.: Gerrit and Agnietje Van Wie.

Margarita, of Johannes Bratt and Maria Keteluyn. Wit.: David Keteluyn, Margarita Vetch.

July 4. Andries, of Jan Witbeek and Agnietje Bronk. Wit.: Volkert and Engeltje Witbeek.

Isaac, of John Whoodkok and Ariaantje Gardenier. Wit.: Patrik Martin, Rebecca Fonda.

July 6. Neeltje, of Johannes Scharp and Geertruy Rees. Wit.: Laurens Scharp, Hilletje Goewey.

July 13. Harmanus, of Abraham Groot and Hester Visscher. Wit.: Johannes Visscher, Sara Wyngaard

Susanna Catharina, of Johannes Lydius and Isabella Rachels. Wit.: Henrik Van Rensselaar, Johannes and Elisabeth Schuyler.

July 27. Elisabeth, of Patrik Martin and Mary Cox. Wit.: John and Ariaantje Whoodkok.

Aug. 3. Jacob, Mees, of Adam Vroman and Margarita Heemstraat. Wit.: Wessel Ten Broek, Dirk Van Heemstrate, Alida Levingston.

Mattheus, of Isaac Van Deuse and Bata Van Ysselsteyn. Wit.: Cornelis Martense Van Ysselsteyn, Marrytje Van Deuse.

Johannes, of Wynand Van der Poel and Catharina De Hooges. Wit.: Melchert Van der Poel, Sr., Tryntje Rutgers.

Cornelia, of Victor Pootman and Grietje Mebi. Wit.: Arent Pootman, Jacomyntje Van Dyk.

Abraham, of Johannes Spoor and Maria Singer. Wit.: Gerrit and Marytje Spoor.

Martha, of Pierre Benoit and Hendrikje Van Schoonhoven. Wit.: Ariaan Oothout, Maeyke Ouderkerk.

Aug. 17. Elisabeth, of Stephanus Groesbeek and Elisabeth Lanssing. Wit.: Anthony Coster, Geertruy Groesbeek.

Adriaan, of Adriaan Quakkenbosch and Catharina Van Schayk. Wit.: Gerrit Van Schayk, Albert Rykman, Neeltje Quakkenbosch.

Aug. 24. Cornelia, of Pieter Martense Van Bueren and Ariaantje Barentse. Wit.: Johannes and Elsje Cuyler.

Sept. 7. Dorothea, of Abraham Vosburg and Claartje Brussy. Wit.: Abraham Kip, Lydia Van Vechten.

Sept. 14. Catharina, of William Van Alen and Marrytje Van Putten. Wit.: Laurens Van Alen, Maria Vinhagen.

Sept. 21. Hendrik, of Meyndert Roseboom and Maria Vinhagen. Wit.: Jan Vinhagen, Sr., Margarita Mingaal.

Niclaas, of Jan Thorn and Geertje Bresser. Wit.: Wynand Van der Poel, Sara Hansse.

Rachel, of Johannes Cuyler and Elsje Ten Broek. Wit.: Volkert Van Vechten, Rachel Schuyler.

1707–1708

Sept. 28. Franciscus, of Jan Hardinks and Maria Bekker. Wit.: William Hooges, Tames Carter, Antje Bekker.

Oct. 5. Jan, of Jan Huybertse, dec^d, and Lysbeth. Wit.: Baltus Van Benthuysen, Isabella Lydius.

Henrik, of Pieter Cool and Jannetje Dingmans. Wit.: Cornelis Maasse, Aaltje Dingmans.

Douwe, of Daniel Keteluin and Debora Viele. Wit.: Dirk Brat, Hilletje Keteluin.

Oct. 12. Andries, of Dirk Bratt and Maria Van Eps. Wit.: Evert and Elisabeth Banker.

Helena, of Meyndert Bogart and Neeltje Palmentier. Wit.: Cornelis Schermerhoorn, Neeltje Ten Eyk.

Oct. 19. Anna Maria, of Gerrit Wibusse and Maria Gilbert. Wit.: Johannes and Dirkje Barheit.

Jan, of Daniel Winnen and Dirkje Van Esch. Wit.: Jan and Aaltje Van Esch.

Antoine, of Matthieu Beaufils and Catharina Barrois. Wit.: Carel and Aaltje Barrois.

Cornelis, of Hendrik Jansse Van Salsberry and Cornelia Van Schaak. Wit.: Jan Lanssing, Lysbeth Groesbeek.

Nov. 16. Cornelis, of Dominicus Van Schaak and Rebecca Groesbeek. Wit.: Willem Claasse Groesbeek, Stephanus and Geertje Groesbeek.

Pieter, of Pieter Bronk and Anna Bogardus. Wit.: Jan Witbeek, Sara Van Brug.

Nov. 19. Tames, of Tames Luwes and Mary Tebuch [?] Wit.: Abraham Broeks, Susanna Wyngaard.

Nov. 23. Henrik, of Jan Van Esch and Catelyntje Groesbeek. Wit.: Henrik Van Esch, Geertruy Groesbeek.

Dec. 3. Maria, of Barent Sanders and Maria Wendel. Wit.: Gerrit Roseboom, Elisabeth Schuyler.

Dec. 7. Robbert, of Charles Olver and Margarita Schuyler. Wit.: Henry Holland, John Colins, the mother.

Bata, of Johannes Quakkenbos and Anna Cloet. Wit.: Jan and Bata Cloet.

Claas Laurense, of Laurens Van Schaak and Jannetje Oothout. Wit.: Johannes Oothout, Aaltje Van Esch.

1708, Jan. 1. William, of Frederik Harmense Visscher and Elisabeth Sanders. Wit.: Johs. Harmense Visscher, Helena Lanssing.

Jan. 4. Gerrit, of Jacob Cloet and Geertruy Van Franke. Wit.: Jan Cloet, Ariaantje Camfort.

Johannes, of Reynier Meyndertse Van Yvere and Sara Bratt. Wit.: Fredrik Meinderse, Willempje Bratt.

Jan. 11. Johannes, of Abraham Ouderkerk and Lysbeth Cloet. Wit.: Anthony Coster, Bata Cloet.

Johannes, of Hendrik Van Rensselaar and Catharina Van Brug. Wit.: Pieter Schuyler, Johannes Lydius, Catharina Van Brug.

1708

Jan. 18. Geesje, of Jan Henrikse Bont and Jannetje Scharp. Wit.: Johannes Beekman, Annetje Ryerts.

Abraham, of Jan Fonda and Matje Lokermans. Wit.: Kiliaan and Maria Van Rensselaar.

Coenraat, of Coenraat Borgert and Geesje Van Wie. Wit.: Marten and Lysbeth Delmont.

Jan. 25. At Esopus. Pieternelle, of Jacobus Dubois and Susanna Leg. Wit.: Jan Leg, Antje Fynhout.

At Esopus. Catharina, of Pieter Ploeg and Aaltje Peld. Wit.: Henrik and Jannetje Beekman.

Jacob, of Henrik Ten Eyk and Margarita Bleeker. Wit.: Jan Janse Bleeker, Geertje Ten Eyk.

Johannes, of Roelof De Duytser and Jannetje Brussy. Wit.: Barent and Matje Sandertse.

Jannetje, of Cornelis Bogert and Dorothea Oothout. Wit.: Jacob Bogert, Grietje Van Vechten.

Jan. 28. At Esopus. Tjaatje, of Tjerk Matthyse and Maria Ten Eyk. Wit.: Cornelis Wynkoop, Barbara Matthysse.

At Esopus. Anna Catharina, of Cornelis La Maitre and Margarita Van Steenbergen. Wit.: Thomas and Maria Van Steenbergen.

Isaac, of Abraham Van Aalstein and Marrytje Van Deuse. Wit.: Harbert Teeuwisse Van Deuse, Lena Van Deuse.

Machtelt, of Jacobus Lucasse Wyngaard and Maria Quakkenbosch. Wit.: Adriaan and Caatje Quakkenbosch.

Marytje, of Arent Van Schaak and Maria Van Loon. Wit.: Caspar Van Hoesen, Anna Gansevoort.

Neeltje, of Barent Gerritse Van den Berg and Geertruy Witbeek. Wit.: Wynand and Gerritje Van den Berg.

Feb. 1. At Esopus. Jacob, of Bernardus Swartwoud and Rachel Schepmoes. Wit.: Jacob Kip, Willem Schepmoes, Elsje Schuyler.

At Es. Cornelis, of Salomon Dubois and Tryntje Gerritse. Wit.: Daniel and Lea Dubois, Harmen and Maria Rykman.

At Es. Louis, of Abraham Bevier and Rachel Vernoy. Wit.: Louis and Hester Bevier, Jan Bevier, Maria Horenbeek.

At Es. David, of Pieter Usile and Cornelia Dauw Wit.: Cornelis Schermerhoorn, Maria Roseboom.

At Es. Blandina, of Jonas Le Roy and Maria Usile. Wit.: Johannes Van Kleek, Lena Lanssing.

Feb. 8. Johannes, of Johannes Wendel and Elisabeth Walters. Wit.: Johannes and Elisabeth Schuyler.

Feb. 11. Mary, of William Rodgers and Mary Johnson. Wit.: Johannes Hansse, Agnietje Nak.

Feb. 15. Antje, of Charles Barrois and Aaltje Van der Werke. Wit.: Albert and Jannetje Van der Werke.

1708

Sara, of Gerrit Lucasse Wyngaard and Sara Visscher. Wit.: Frederik Harmense Visscher, Alida Visscher.

Feb. 22. Sybrand, of Gerrit Van Schayk and Sara Goewey. Wit.: Goosse Van Schayk, Lysbeth Van Corlaar.

Marytje, of Isaac Vosburg and Annetje Hoes. Wit.: Johannes and Catelyntje Abeel.

Racheltje, of Ritchart Jansse and Tryntje Hoogteeling. Wit.: Pieter Bronk, Judith Hoogkerke.

Feb. 29. Tjerk, of Cornelis Swits and Hester Visscher. Wit.: Jacob and Elisabeth Visscher.

Apr. 4. Dirk, of Gideon and Dorcas. Wit.: Wessel Ten Broek, Geertruy Schuyler.

May 2. Margrietje, of Tames Williams and Agnietje Gansevoort. Wit.: Pieter Bronk, Rachel Gansevoort.

May 16. William, of William Hilten and Antje Barko. Wit.: Pieter Schuyler, Margrita Colins.

Johannes, of Abraham Lanssing and Magdalena Van Tricht. Wit.: Volkert and Margarita Douw.

Martinus, of Albert Roelofse Van der Werke and Dirkje Van Aalstein. Wit.: Cornelis and Marrytje Van Aalstein.

May 23. Engeltje, of Pieter Walderon and Tryntje Van den Berg. Wit.: Gysbert Willemse Van den Berg, Cornelia Van Aalstein.

May 24. Betty, of Tames Kadman and Margarita Yvens. Wit.: Daniel Killy, Annaatje Hogen.

May 30. Cornelis, of Gysbert Scharp and Lysbeth Goewey. Wit.: Henrik and Catharina Van Rensselaar.

Marytje, of Barent Ten Eyk and Neeltje Schermerhoorn. Wit.: Jacob Schermerhoorn, Gerritje Ten Eyk.

Caspar, of Harmen Van Salsberry and Tanna Conyn. Wit.: Dirk Philipse Conyn, Alida Lanssing.

June 6. Johannes, of Coenraat Hoogteling and Tryntje Van Slyk. Wit.: Johannes and Eva Beekman.

Robbert, of John Kidni and Marrytje Van der Werke. Wit.: Carel and Aaltje Barrois.

June 13. Anna, of Evert Banker and Elisabeth Abeel. Wit.: Johannes Lydius, Maria Van Rensselaar.

Eva, of Johannes Van Valkenburg and Margarita Barheit. Wit.: Hieronymus and Rebecca Barheit.

Ida, of Marten Van Bueren and Judith Barentse. Wit.: Pieter Van Bueren, Ariaantje Barentse.

July 4. Johannes, of Lambert Joachimse Van Valkenburg and Jannetje Claeuw. Wit.: Reinier Meyndertse, Agnietje Nak.

Johannes, of Pieter Meesse Hoogeboom and Jannetje Mulder. Wit.: Jan Salomonse Goewey, Lammertje Lokermans.

Hendrikje, of Jeremias Mulder and Lysbeth Halenbeek. Wit.: Jacob Lanssing, Lysbeth Bratt.

49

1708

Elsje, of Johannes G. F. Lanssing and Helena Sanderse.
Wit.: Gerrit G. F. and Catharina Lanssing.

Francyntje, of John Herris and Moeset Tassama. Wit.:
Johannes Knikkelbakker, Jannetje Lanssing.

July 9. Johannes, of Thomas Witbeek and Jannetje Van
Deuse. Wit.: Melchert Abrahamse Van Deuse, Caatje
Witbeek.

July 11. Hendrik, of Hendrik Claeuw and Cornelia
Scharp. Wit.: Jan Salomonse and Hilletje Goewey.

July 18. Tjerk Harmen, of Philip Wendel and Maria
Visscher. Wit.: Tjerk Harmense Visscher, Alida Visscher.

Franciscus, of Jacob Lanssing and Helena Pruyn. Wit.:
Samuel and Barentje Pruyn.

Aug. 1. Weintje, of Dirk Philipse Conyn and Rachel
Andriesse. Wit.: Leendert Bronk, Anna Gansevoort.

Sybrand, of Antony S. F. Van Schayk and Anna Catharina Ten Broek. Wit.: Wessel Ten Broek, Lysbeth Van
Corlaar.

Aug. 8. Ritchard, of Ritchard Moore and Geesje Salsbury. Wit.: Henrik and Debora Hansse.

Aug. 15. Catharina, of Henrik Witbeek and Lena Bout.
Wit.: Frans and Elsje Winnen.

Maria, of Johannes Vinhagen and Maria Van Trigt. Wit.:
Johannes Vinhagen, Sr., Lysbeth Van Trigt.

Adam, of Christoffel Yeads and Catelyntje Winnen.
Wit.: Joseph Yeads, Anna Winnen.

Aug. 15. Wouter, of Johannes Groesbeek and Geertje
Quakkenbosch. Wit.: Wouter Quakkenbosch, Jr., Geertruy Groesbeek.

Daniel, of Anthony Bratt and Willempje Teunisse. Wit.:
Reynier Van Yvere, Dirkje Barheit.

Sept. 19. Johannes, of Willem Van Oostrande and
Marytje De Hooges. Wit.: Wynand and Catharina Van
der Poel.

Abraham, of Pieter Quakkenbos and Neeltje Marinus.
Wit.: Pieter Rykman, Caatje Quakkenbos.

Johannes, of Balthazar Van Benthuysen and Lidia
Dealy. Wit.: Barent Sanders, Catelyntje Van Benthuysen.

Lena, of Johannes Van Alen and Christina Ten Broek.
Wit.: Samuel Ten Broek, Henrik Van Balen, Catharina
Ten Broek.

Pieter, of Barent Egbertse and Maria De Garmo. Wit.:
Dirk and Cornelia Van der Heyden.

Henrik, of Abraham Wendel and Maeyke Van Esch.
Wit.: Henrik Van Es, Maria Mingaal.

Sept. 26. Catharina, of Borger Huyk and Maeyke Hoes.
Wit.: Reinier Van Yvere, Sara Wyngaard.

Geertruy, of Jean Du Fou and Catharina Van der Werke.
Wit.: Johannes Van der Werke Marrytje Kidni.

1708

Pieter, of Johannes Bekker and Annetje Van der Zee. Wit.: Johannes Roseboom, Lysbeth Van Deuse.

Henrik, of Evert Whieller and Josina Gardenier. Wit.: Henrik and Catharina Van Rensselaar.

Cornelis, of Marten Van Aalstein and Cornelia Van den Berg. Wit.: Gysbert Van den Berg, Marrytje Van Aalsteyn.

Pieter, of Teunis Van Slyk and Jannetje Van Wie. Wit.: Johannes Mingal, Marrytje Visscher.

Isaac, of Abraham Staats and Elsje Wendel. Wit.: Johannes and Elisabeth Wendel.

Oct. 1. Hester, of Johannes Visscher and Lysbeth Nottingham. Wit.: Nanning and Lysbeth Visscher.

Oct. 3. Gerrit, of Niclaas Gerritse Van Franke and Geertruy Quakkenbosch. Wit.: Maas Rykse, Ariaantje Kampvoord.

Willem, of Wynand Van den Berg and Volkje Van Hoesen. Wit.: Gysbert and Marytje Van den Berg.

Ephraim, of Stephanus Van Alen and Maria Mulder. Wit.: Melchert Van der Poel, Jr., Emmetje Van Alen.

Marrytje, of Jan Dekker and Tysje Bogerd. Wit.: Ritchard Van den Berk, Rachel Hoogteeling.

Jan Dirk, of Jan Janse Van Aarnhem, dec^d, and Esther Fonda. Wit.: Jan Fonda, in place of the father; Cornelis Maasse, Anna Fonda.

Oct. 24. Johannes, of Gerrit Rykse Van Franke and Barbara Jansse. Wit.: Warnar Karstense, Marrytje Van Deuse.

Oct. 31. Maria, of Isaac Van Aalstein and Jannetje Van Valkenburg. Wit.: Jan and Rachel Ratteliffe.

Catharina, of Marten Delmont and Lysbeth Viele. Wit.: Johannes Bleeker, Jr., Maria Schuyler.

Nov. 7. Henrik, of Jan Van Es, and Catelyntje Groesbeek. Wit.: Henrik Van Es, Geertruy Groesbeek.

Nov. 14. Petrus, of Pieter Rykman and Cornelia Keteltas. Wit.: Harmen and Maria Rykman.

Nov. 21. Joachim, of Abraham Van Valkenburg and Catelyntje Schermerhoorn. Wit.: Lambert Huyk, Maria Rykman.

Philip, of Pieter Winnen and Maria De Foreest. Wit.: Hans and Sara Hansse.

Dec. 8. Maria, of Adriaan Oothout and Lammertje Lokermans. Wit.: Jan and Matje Fonda.

Dec. 12. Johannes, of Kiliaan Van Rensselaer and Maria Van Cortlandt. Wit.: John Colins, Philip Cortlandt, Maria Van Rensselaar in place of Anna Nickols.

Catharina, of Barent Staats and Neeltje Van den Berg. Wit.: Abraham Staats, Lysbeth Schuyler.

Dec. 15. Andries, of Johannes De Wandelaar, Jr., and

1708–1709
Lysbeth Gansevoort. Wit.: Frederik Meyndertse, Catharina De Wandelaar.
Dec. 19. Sybrand, of Goosse Van Schayk and Catharina Staats. Wit.: Henrik Roseboom, Catharina Quakkenbosch.
Douwe, of Daniel Keteluyn and Debora Viele. Wit.: Joachim Keteluyn, Antje Kaneel.
Dec. 25. Isaac, of Jacob Anonsfontje and Jacomyn Kwanogweech. Wit : Robbert Wendel, Rachel Kajodarontje.
Robbert, of Philip Livingston and Catharina Van Brug. Wit.: Robbert Livingston, Sara Van Brug.
Dec. 26. Henrik, of Pieter Van Buere and Geertruy Vosburg. Wit.: Cornelis Van Buere, Cornelis and Marrytje Schermerhoorn.
1709, Jan. 1. Catharina, of Wouter Van der Zee and Jannetje Swart. Wit.: Joachim Keteluyn, Elsje Schuyler.
Takel, of Ahazueros Marselis and Zara Van Heemstraat. Wit.: Takel Van Heemstraat, Pieter Van Brug, Grietje Vroman.
Johannes, of Arent Brat and Jannetje Vroman. Wit.: Reyer Schermerhoorn, Tryntje Bries.
January 9, at Kinderhook: Ephraim, of Tys Jansse Goes and Cornelia Van Deuse. Wit.: Jan Goes, Magdalena Van Bueren.
Catharina, of Jacobus Turk and Teuntje Goes.
Marrytje, of Emanuel Van Salsdyk and Rebecca Westfaeling. Wit.: Pieter Cool, Jannetje Dingmans.
Annaatje, of Isaac Ouderkerk and Maeyke Van Es. Wit.: Johannes and Neeltje Ouderkerk.
Andries, of Jan Rees and Maria Goewey. Wit.: Cornelis Stevense Muller, Hilletje Muller.
Abraham, of Willem Jansse Halenbeek and Fytje Van Vegten. Wit.: Dirk Conyn, Antje Van Vegten.
Gerardus, of Jacob Dingmans and Eva Swartwoud. Wit.: Pieter Van Alen, Josyntje Dingmans.
Neeltje, of Stephanus Hiesoor and Sara Hoornbeek. Wit.: Jacob and Eva Dingmans.
Jan. 12. Johannes, of Volkert Dou and Margarita Van Trigt. Wit.: Volkert Jonasse Dou, Helena Van Trigt.
Johannes, of Dirk Van Heemstrate and Catharina Quakkenbos. Wit.: Jacobus Wyngaard, Neeltje Quakkenbos.
Rebecca, of Salomon Van Vegten and Alida Fonda. Wit. Isaac Fonda, Alida Lanssing, now Fonda.
Jan. 23. Johannes, of Mattheus Nak and Agnietje Schaats. Wit.: Thomas Harmanse Hun, Weyntje Van Deuse.
Jan. 26. Christoffel, of Andries Brussy and Engeltje Claeuw. Wit.: Abraham and Geesje Kip.

1709
Jan. 30. William, of Francois Salisbury and Maria Gaasbeek. Wit.: Jacob Marius Groen, Maria Salisbury.
Catharina, of Teunis Pieterse and Margarita Laurensse. Wit.: Jacob and Dorothea Vosburg.
Margarita, of Antoine Rowville and Heyltje Dekker. Wit.: Cornelis Teeuwisse Mulder, Jurriaan Dekker, Hilletje Mulder.
Feb. 6. Petrus, of Pieter Oostrander and Rachel Dingmans. Wit.: Bernhardus Swartwoud, Rachel Schepmoes.
Feb. 9. Anna, of Harmanus Wendel and Anna Glen. Wit.: Johannes and Hester Wendel.
Grietje, of Claas Fransse and Barbara Heemstraat Wit.: Dirk and Caatje Heemstraat.
Feb. 13. Abraham, of Wynand Van der Poel and Catharina De Hooges. Wit.: Melchert Van der Poel, Jr., Catharina Van der Poel.
Feb. 20. Catharina, of Abraham Cuyler and Katharina Bleker. Wit.: Henrik and Margarita Ten Eyk.
Alexander, of Albert Vedder and Maria Glen. Wit.: Gerrit Lanssing, Jacomina Van Dyk.
Feb. 27. Abraham, of Gerrit Lanssing and Catharina Glen. Wit.: Jan and Magdalena Lanssing.
Andries, of Lambert Huyk and Anna Ratteliffe. Wit.: Jan and Rachel Ratteliffe.
Cornelis, of Cornelis Van Aalstein and Marrytje Van den Berg. Wit.: Pieter Walderon, Dirkje Van der Werke.
March 6. John, of Robbert Levingston, Jr., and Margarita Schuyler. Wit.: Philip Levingston, Margarita Vetch.
Stephanus, of Jacobus Cromwel and Maria Philips. Wit.: Harmen Philipse, Elsje Cuyler.
Ariaantje, of Johannes Wendel and Susanna Viele. Wit.: Harmanus and Ariaantje Wendel.
March 9. Rachel, of Lucas Lucasse Hoogkerke and Judith Marselis. Wit.: Willem Van Alen, Barbara Marselis.
March 13. Margarita, of Johannes Bleeker, Jr., and Anna Coster. Wit.: Ruth Bleeker, Margarita Ten Eyk.
March 16. Anna, of Herbert Jacobse Van Deuse and Marrytje Gerritse. Wit.: Johannes and Maria Mingaal.
March 20. Hieronimus, of Jan Barheit and Catharina Gilbert. Wit.: Hieronimus and Rebecca Barheit.
Eva, of Bartholomeus Van Valkenburg and Catharina Van Aalstein. Wit.: Johannes and Eva Beekman.
March 27. Lena, of Jan Witbeek and Agnietje Bronk. Wit.: Pieter and Antje Bronk.
Apr. 10. Jurriaan, of Caspar Van Hoesen and Racheltje Slingerlandt. Wit.: Albert and Hester Slingerlandt.
Apr. 17. Christoffel, of Abraham Vosburg and Claartje Brussy. Wit.: Cornelis Bogert, Alida Levingston.

1709
Jacobus, of Melchert Van der Poel and Catharina Van Alen. Wit.: Abraham Schuyler, Maria Van Dyk.

Apr. 22. Jacobus, of Johannes Meyndertse and Geertruy Van Slyk. Wit.: Henrik Douw, Reynier Meyndertse, Margarita Kip.

Apr. 25. Antje, of Victor Pootman and Grietje Mebi. Wit.: Johannes and Maria Mingal.

Lysbeth, of Johannes Van Alen and Sara Dingmans. Wit.: Willem Van Alen, Geertruy Maasse.

Coenraad, of Jan Borgaart and Catharina Van Wie. Wit.: Jan and Catharina Van Wie.

Aaltje, of Cornelis Van Bueren and Hendrikje Van Esch. Wit.: Jan and Catelyntje Van Esch.

June 12. Engeltje, of Wouter Vroman and Maria Halenbeek. Wit.: Albert Rykman, Jannetje Van Slyk.

Martinus, Barent, twins of Pieter Vroman and Geertje Van Aalstein. Wit.: Marten Van Aalstein, Dirkje Van der Werke, Cornelis Bogert, Abigail Verplanke.

Jannetje, of Arent Pootman and Lysbeth Akkermans. Wit.: Johannes Mingal, Tryntje Bries.

Johannes, of Johannes Pruyn and Emilia Sanders. Wit.: Frederik Visscher, Sara Grevenraad.

Celia, of Joseph Jansse and Sydje Marselis. Wit.: Pieter and Sara Van Brug.

Ephraim, Johannes, twins of Volkert Van Vegten and Lidia Ten Broek. Wit.: Samuel and Catharina Ten Broek, Jonas Douw, Marytje Van Vegten.

Sara, of Frederik Meyndertse and Sara De Wandelaar. Wit.: Johannes and Lysbeth De Wandelaar.

June 19. Maria, of Willem Marinus and Bata Klein. Wit.: Jan and Johanna Clara Delmont.

Simon, of Caspar Springsteen and Jannetje Schermerhoorn. Wit.: Jacob Schermerhoorn, Susanna Beekman.

June 26. Claas, of Teunis Van der Volge and Sara Freer. Wit.: Claas and Maria Van der Volge.

Margriet, of Jan De Koning and Geertruy Jansse. Wit.: Jacob Pearson.

Antony, of Johannes Bratt and Maria Keteluyn. Wit.: Dirk Van der Heyden, Anna Bratt.

Magdalena, of Frederik Cloet and Francyntje Du Mont. Wit.: Jacob and Lena Lanssing.

Storm, of Albert Van der Zee and Hilletje Gansevoort. Wit.: Willem and Hilletje Keteluyn.

Pieter, of Pieter Symonse, dec^d, and Neeltje Van der Volge. Wit.: Johannes Symonse, Sara Van der Volge.

Lydia, of Andries Douw and Lydia De Meyer. Wit.: Jonas Douw, Philip and Lysbeth Schuyler.

July 3. Adam, of Johannes Tejasse and Rebecca Oodsdjchouwe. Wit.: Ezras, Neeltje Tewagkerat.

1709

Marytje, of Johannes Christiaanse and Neeltje Cornelisse. Wit.: Bastiaan Visscher, Neeltje Christiaanse.

Cornelia, of Isaac Van Deuse and Bata Van Yselstein. Wit.: Abraham Van Aalstein, Lena Van Deuse.

July 10. Gerrit, of Jacob Cloet and Geertruy Van Franke. Wit.: Robbert Livingston, Jr., Ariaantje Campfort.

Teunis, of Dirk Cornelisse Van Vechten and Margarita Harmensse. Wit.: Levinus and Egbertje Harmensse.

July 24. Adriaan, of Thomas Harmensse Hun and Maeyke Oothout. Wit.: Jan and Catelyntje Van Esch.

Douwe, of Isaac Fonda and Alida Lanssing. Wit.: Jan and Rebecca Fonda.

Aug. 21. Adam, of Pieter Laurentse Van Alen and Josina Dingmans. Wit.: Johannes Maasse Bloemendaal, Geertruy Bloemendaal.

Yda, of Jan Van Wie and Catharina Huyck. Wit.: Gerrit and Agnietje Van Wie.

Catharina, of Dirk Hogeboom and Maria Delmont. Wit.: Johannes and Maria Mingaal.

Sept. 11. Maria, of Andries Bratt and Weyntje Rosa. Wit.: Storm and Maria Bratt.

Johannes, of Isaac Lanssing and Jannetje Beekman. Wit.: Gerrit Lanssing, Susanna Beekman.

Oct. 16. Jan, of Pieter Bronk and Anna Bogardus. Wit.: Leendert Gansevoort, Maria Van Rensselaar.

Emanuel, of Dirk Van der Karre and Fytje Van Schaak. Wit.: Evert Banker, Maria Van Schayk.

Gerrit Teunis, of Johannes Van Vechten and Maria Bogardus. Wit.: Pieter Van Brugh, Jannetje Bogardus.

Oct. 23. Cornelis, of Abraham Groot and Hester Visscher. Wit.: Evert Wendel, Lysbeth Visscher.

Nicolaas, of Dirk Groot and Lysbeth Van der Volge. Wit.: Abraham Groot, Maria Van der Volge.

Maria, of Meyndert Roseboom and Maria Vinhagel. Wit.: Johannes Roseboom, Alida Visscher.

Maria, of Abraham Wendel and Maeyke Van Esch. Wit.: Johannes and Maria Mingaal.

Gerardus, of Stephanus Van Groesbeek and Lysbeth Lanssing. Wit.: Johannes Groesbeek, Gerritje Roseboom.

Jacobus, of Charles Barrois and Aaltje Van der Werke. Wit.: Johannes and Geertruy Van der Werke.

Philippus, of Johannes Hansse and Sara De Forest. Wit.: Henrik Hansse, Catelyntje Van Esch.

Oct. 30. Hendrik, of Samuel Gardenier and Helena Bey. Wit.: Andries and Josina Gardenier.

Simon, of Johannes Symonse Vedder and Susanna Wimpel. Wit.: Volkert Symonse Vedder, Neeltje Van der Volge.

1709–1710

Magdalena, of Volkert Symonse Vedder and Jannetje Schermerhoorn. Wit.: Johs. Symonse Vedder, Neeltje Slingerland.

Petrus, of Marten Van Slyk and Margarita Van Franke. Wit.: Aldrik and Maria Van Franke.

Weyntje, of Arent Van Petten and Jannetje Conyn. Wit.: Tames Williams, Anna De Warm.

Jesaias, of Jesaias Swart and Eva Teunisse Van Schoonderwoert. Wit.: Rutger Bleeker, Debora Hansse.

Robbert, of Jonathan Rumney and Johanna Van Corlaar. Wit.: John Colins, Goosse Van Schayk, Elisabeth Van Corlaar.

Hendrik, of Cornelis Bogert and Dorothea Oothout Wit.: Henrik Oothout, Maria Pruyn.

Geertruy, of Cornelis Van Slyk and Claartje Bratt. Wit.: Tobias Rykman, Maria Bries.

Nov. 13. Laurens, of Cornelis Laurentse Van Wurmerink and Annaatje Van Petten. Wit.: Lucas Hoogkerke, Marrytje Bronk.

Johannes, of Wouter Quakkenbos and Cornelia Bogert. Wit.: Johs. Knikkelbakker, Abigail Verplanke.

Benjamin, of Barent Van den Berg and Geertruy Witbeek. Wit.: Tames Williams, Anna De Warm.

Nov. 20. Robbert, of John Dunbar and Bata Winnen. Wit.: Evert and Sara Wendel.

Nov. 27. Neeltje, of Henrik Douw and Neeltje Van Yvere. Wit.: Jonas and Catharina Douw.

Rachel, of Johs. Cuyler and Elsje Ten Broek. Wit: Johannes Ten Broek, Rachel Schuyler.

Johannes, of Barent TenEyk and Neeltje Schermerhoorn. Wit.: Johs. Beekman, Jr. Marrytje Schermerhoorn.

Robbert, of Johs. Wendel and Elisabeth Walthers. Wit.: Robbert and Catharina Walthers.

Dec. 4. William, of William Rodgers and Mary Johnson. Wit.: John Dunbar, William Hoges, Sara Hanssene.

Dec. 18. Henrik, of Elbert Gerritse and Maria Pruyn. Wit.: Samuel Pruyn, Antje Van Yvere.

Henricus, of Daniel Bratt and Lysbeth Lanssing. Wit.: Isaac Fonda, Jannetje Bogardus.

Dec. 25. Harmen, of Johs. Knikkelbakker and Anna Quakkenbosch. Wit.: Kiliaan and Maria Van Rensselaar.

Catharina, of Gerrit S. Van Schayk and Sara Goewey. Wit.: Salomon Goewey, Catharina Quakkenbosch.

1709–10, Jan. 8. Alida, of Samuel Doksi and Lysbeth Bas. Wit.: Frans and Elsje Winnen.

Jacob, of Nicolaas Van Woerd and Dirkje Barheit. Wit.: Jacob Teunisse, Barbar Marselis.

Anna Margarita, of Cousset Vedder and Margarita Barrith

1709–1710

(died the day before the ch.'s bapt.). Wit.: Jan Dellemont, Johanna Clara Delmont.

Antony, of Reynier Van Yvere and Sara Brat. Wit.: Dirk and Anna Brat.

Jan. 15. Barent, of Henrik Vroman and Marrytje Wimp. Wit.: Barent and Volkje Wimp.

Gabriel, of Claas Brussy and Catelyntje Bont. Wit.: Barent and Maria Egbertse.

Helena, of Harmen Van Slyk and Jannetje Vrooman. Wit.: Albert Rykman, Barent Vroman, Geertruy Van Yveren.

Lysbeth, of Simon Danielse and Maria Peek. Wit. Jacobus and Lysbeth Peek.

Joachim Lambert, of Isaac Valkenburg and Lydia Van Slyk. Wit.: Henrik Vroman, Rachel Ratteliffe.

Gerritje, of Gerrit Lucasse Wyngaard and Sara Visscher. Wit.: Johs. Visscher, Claas Lucasse, Susanna Wyngaard.

Jan. 22. Geertruy, of Pieter Hogeboom and Jannetje Mulder. Wit.: Stephanus Van Alen, Matje Fonda.

Willem, of Andries Rees and Ariaantje Scharp. Wit.: Johs. Scharp, Hilletje Goewey.

Anna, of John Hardinx and Maria Bekker. Wit.: Johs. Bekker, Nicolaas Wyngaard, Anna Hoges.

Hermanus, of Harmen Salsberry and Tanna Conyn. Wit.: Reuben Van Vechten, Anna Warm.

Jan. 29. Johannes, of Albert Van der Werke and Dirkje Van Aalstein. Wit.: Johs. Van Aalstein, Geertje Vroman.

Feb. 5. Johannes, of Laurens Van Schaak and Jannetje Oothout. Wit.: Henrik and Caatje Oothout.

Claas Frederik, of Willem Van Alen and Marrytje Van Petten. Wit.: Claas Van Petten, Elsje Schuyler.

Feb. 15. David, of Jillis Van Vorst and Lysbeth Van Eps. Wit.: Arent Slingerland, Rebecca Fonda.

Maria, of Gerrit Gysbertse and Catharina Van der Volge. Wit.: Claas and Maria Van der Volge.

Cornelia, of Mattheus Goes and Jannetje Bries. Wit.: Johannes Cuyler, Cornelia Goes.

BAPTISMS BY DO. G. DU BOIS.

1710, Apr. 23. Johannes, of Evert Banker and Elisabeth Abeel. Wit.: Johs.ˈ De Peyster, Johs. and Magdalena Abeel, Neeltje Banker.

Cornelis, of Cornelis Claasz and Susanna Ouwderkerk. Wit.: Johs. Roseboom, Gerretje Costers.

Willemyntje, of Matthys Nak and Aggenietje Schaats. Wit.: Andries Nak, Wyntje Harmensz.

Maria, of Wynant Van den Berg and Folkje Van Hoese. Wit.: Gysbert and Cathalyna Van den Berg.

1710
Jacobus, of Abraham Lanse and Magdalena Van Trigt.
Wit.: Joh. Lanse, Catharina Geele.

Jannetje, of Cornelis Schermerhoorn and Maria Van
Buuren. Wit.: Jacob Schermerhoorn, Susanna Beekman.

Apr. 28. Catharina, of Cornelis Slingelant and Eva
Mebie. Wit.: Caspar Van Hoese, Maria Slingelant.

Neeltje, of Arend Danielsz and Sara Van Eps. Wit.:
Dirk Bradt, Aggenietje Vedders.

Isaak, of Louis Fiele and Maria Freer. Wit.: Abraham
Cuiler, Catharina Bleekers.

Mettje or Nieltje, of Jan Danielse and Aggenietje Vedders. Wit.: Robbert Levingston, Margritha Schuilers.

Margrita, of Johs. Vedder and Maria Fort. Wit.: Albert
Vedder, Eva Vinnagels.

Magdalena, of Gerrit Simons and Tryntje Helmes. Wit.:
Pieter Van Brugge, Jannetje Fromman.

Johannes, of Evert Van Eps and Eva Tol. Wit.: Jan
Baptist Van Eps, Heleena Geele.

Apr. 30. Cornelis, of Johs. Scherp and Geertruy Rees.
Wit.: Hendrik Van Renselaar, Catharina Van Brugge.

Jannetje, of Coenraat Hoogteeling and Tryntje Van
Slyk. Wit.: Isaac Lansen, Jannetje Beekman.

Lammert, of Isaac Van Aalstein and Jannetje Valkenburg. Wit.: Johs. and Catharina Vrooman.

Andries, of Lambert Van Valkenburg and Anna Huik.
Wit.: Lammert Huik, Anna Raedelif.

Elisabeth, of Jesse De Graaf and Aaltje Helston. Wit.:
Abraham and Maria De Graaf.

Thimotheus, of Jan Leenderdsz and Eliaan Jans. Wit.:
Corset Vedder, Judik Marcellus.

Dirkje, of Abraham Aalstyn and Maria Van Deuse.
Wit.: Johs. and Jannetje Mingal.

Evert, of Hendrik Bont and Jannetje Evertsz. Wit.:
Hieronimus Barheit, Aaltje Everts.

Dirk, of Johannes Spoor and Maria Singer. Wit.: Claas
Van Woert, Dirkje Barheit.

Pieter, of Pieter Kool and Jannetje Dinansse. Wit.:
Samuel Pruin, Maria Bogaart.

Margrita, of Daniel Fort and Gerritje Van den Berg.
Wit.: Cornelis Van Nes, Maria Van Berg.

Tobias, of Marte Van Buuren and Judikje Barens. Wit.:
Tobias and Magdalena Rykman.

Oct. 27. Gerrit Lucasse, of Jacobus Wyngaart and
Maria Kwakkenbos. Wit.: Lucas Wyngaart, Susanna
Wendels.

Catharina, of Baltus Van Benthuise and Lidia Daely
Wit.: Johs. and Alida Turk.

Neeltje, of Joh. Beekman and Eva Vinhagen. Wit
Johs. Lansing, Maria Visser.

1710

Johannes, of Joh. Vinhagen and Maria Van Trigt. Wit.: Johannes Teller, Alida Vinhage.

Rykaart, of Evert Van Franken and Marytje Vissers. Wit.: Bastiaan Visser, Grietye Van Franke.

Johannes, of Adriaan Kwakkenbos and Catharina Van Schaajk. Wit.: Dirk Takelse, Claartj Kwakkenbos.

Johannes, of Hendrik Ten Eyk and Grietje Bleekers. Wit.: Coenraat Ten Eyk, Caatje Bleekers.

Nicolaas, of Johs. Groesbeek and Geertje Kwakkenbos. Wit.: Willem and Barber Groesbeek.

Teuntje, of Evert Van Es and Geertje Van den Berg. Wit.: Kiliaan Van Renselaar, Maria Van Kortlant.

Dirk Wesselsse, of Johs. Van Alen and Christina Ten Broek. Wit.: Gualtherus Du Bois, Dirk Ten Broek, Anna Kuilers.

Lena, of Jan Fonda and Marytje Lokermans. Wit.: Adriaan Oothouwt, Maria Schuiler.

Oct. 30. Rebekka, of Johs. Van Valkenburg and Margrita Barheit. Wit.: Wouter Barheit, Fietje Oothoudt.

Doretea, of Ritgart Jansse and Tryntje Hoogteeling. Wit.: Lucas Lucasse, Lena Sanders.

Benjamin, of Abraham Ouderkerk and Elisabeth Kloete. Wit.: Eldert and Susanna Ouwderkerk.

Jacobus, of Thomas Witbeek and Jannetje Van Deuse. Wit.: Lucas Witbeek, Wyntje Hun.

Philp, of Matthys Bovie and Catharyn Barwee. Wit.: Claas Bovie and Marytje Van der Werke.

Dirk, of Dirk Bradt and Marytje Van Eps. Wit.: Dirk Barendse Brad, Marytje Bries, Jr.

Adriantje, of Claes Van Franke and Geertruy Kwakkenbos. Wit.: Ulderik and Marytje V. Franke.

Marytje, of Eldert Cornelisse and Hester Visser. Wit.: Bastiaan Visser, Marytje Timesse.

Anna, of Gerrit Van Es and Cathalyntje Foreest. Wit.: Henderik Van Es, Catharyntje Voreest.

Philip, of Gysbert Scherp and Elisabeth Goewy. Wit.: Hendrik Hansse, Debora Van Dam.

Jonathan, of Jonathan Witbeek and Cathalyntje Van Buure. Wit.: Wessel Ten Broek, Catharyna Lokermans.

Nov. 3. Abraham, of Johs. Kwakkenbos and Anna Kloete. Wit.: Adriaan and Marya Kwakkenbos.

Simon, of Evert Ridder and Antje Van Es. Wit.: Simon Van Es, Cathalyntje Groesbeek.

Nov. 5. Pieter, of Philp Livenston and Catharina Van Brugge. Wit.: Pieter Van Brugge, Alida Schuilers.

Geertruy, of Jan Du Voe and Tryntje V. dr. Werke. Wit.: Carel Barrewee, Aaltje Van der Werken.

Dorethe, of Eduard Wiler and Josyntje Gardenier. Wit.: Claas Gardenier, Mayke Ten Eyk.

1710–1711

Jannetje, of Pieter Van Buure and Geertruy Vosburg. Wit.: Cornelis V. Buure, Ytje Vosburg.

Alida, of Teunis Van Slyk and Jannetje Van Wye. Wit.: Hendrik Van Wye, Elisabeth Van Dyk.

BAPTISMS BY D°· PETRUS VAS.

1711, March 4. Gerardus, of Gerrit Roelofsz and Maria Gerrits. Wit.: Evert Ridder, Annetje Ridders.

Catrina, of Pieter and Maria Winne. Wit.: Frans Winne, Catalyntje Van Nes.

Jannetjen, of Jacob Bogaard and Catalyntjen Schuylders. Wit.: Jacob Bogaard, Jannetjen Kwakkenbos.

Barent, of Anthony Levis and Jannetjen Morenes. Wit.: Gosen Van Schayk, Johanna Van Strey.

Egbert Theunisz, of Benjamin Egbers and Annetjen Vissers. Wit.: Barent and Marretje Egberts.

Angenietjen, of Johannes and Elisabeth De Wandelaar. Wit.: Johannes Kuyler, Rachel Gansevoort.

Gerrit, of Jacob and Helena Lansen. Wit.: Isaak and Alida Vonda.

Harmen, of Albert Van der Zee and Hilletjen Gansevoort. Wit.: Frans Winne, Elsjen Gansevoort.

Catrina, of Abraham Wendel and Mayke Van Es. Wit.: Gerrit and Marytjen Van Es.

Pieter, of Schibolet and Anna Bogardus. Wit.: Johannes and Marytje Van Vechten.

Anna Catryna, of Adriaan and Lammertjen Oothoud. Wit.: Wessel and Catryntje Ten Broek.

Jeronimus, of Flip and Marytjen Wendel. Wit.: Johannes Glen, Elisabeth Schuyler.

Willem, of Jan and Cathalina Van Es. Wit.: Willem Groesbeek, Catryn Van Es.

Melchert, of Wynant and Catryntjen Van der Poel. Wit.: David Schuylder, Tryntje Waldere.

March 11. Ephraim, of Pieter Martens Van Buuren and Adriaantjen Barents. Wit.: Johannes and Elisabeth Ten Broek.

Rachel, of Lammert Huyk and Annaatjen Roelofs. Wit.: Pieter and Maria Schuylder.

Johannes, of Marten Van Aalsteede and Cornelia Van den Berg. Wit.: Johannes and Lidia Van Aalsteede.

Geertruy, of Barent Staats and Neeltje Van den Berg. Wit.: Gerrit Van den Berg, Marretje Schuylders.

Abraham, of Abraham Van Valkenburg and Catlina Schermerhorn. Wit.: Jacob Schermerhorn, Magdalena Van Buure.

Susanna, of Johannes and Elisabeth Wendel. Wit.: Anthony Van Scheyk, Elsje Staats.

1711

Christina Maria (Aborigine). Wit.: Abraham Schuylder and Rebecca (Aborigine).

Oct. 7. Jacob, of Abraham and Elsjen Staats. Wit.:
Jacob and Isabella Staats.

Jacob, of Gosen Van Schayk and Catrina Staats. Wit.:
Jacob and Isabella Staats.

Margrita, of Meyndert and Marya Rooseboom. Wit.:
Johannes Vinhagen, Elisabeth Van Deusen.

Meyndert, of David Schuylder and Elsjen Rutgers. Wit.:
Meyndert Schuylder, Harmanus Rutgert, Geertruy Groesbeek.

Theunis, of Casper Van Hoesen and Rachel Slingerland.
Wit.: Johannes Appel, Arent Slingerland, Annetjen Appels.

Petrus, of Arent Oostrander and Geertruy Van Bloemendaal. Wit.: Pieter Oostrander, Jacomyntje Masen.

Geertruy, of Evert and Engeltje Wendel. Wit.: Jan
and Geertruy Lansen.

Maria, of Johannes and Helena Lansen. Wit.: Abraham Lansen, Maria Sanders.

Johannes, of Harmanus and Anna Wendel. Wit.: Johannes and Elsjen Wendel.

Pieter, of Marten and Lysebet Delmond. Wit.: Louwis
Viele, Susanna Wendel.

Catalina, of Christoffel and Catalina Jets. Wit.: Hendrik and Debora Hansen.

Rykert, of Maas and Anna Rykse. Wit.: Gerrit and
Margrietje Rykse.

Gerrit, of Jacob and Lena Lansen. Wit.: Jonas Douw,
Elsjen Lansen.

Willem, of Isaak Ouderkerk and Mayke Van Es. Wit.:
Hendrik Oothout, Caatjen Douw.

Johannes, of Frederik and Sara Meenders. Wit.: Hendrik Douwe, Sara Verbrugge.

Oct. 12. Hillegont, of Gerrit Ryksz and Barbara Jans.
Wit.: Johannes Pruym, Milia Sanderse.

Catrina, of Jan and Catrina Van Wie. Wit.: Isaak and
Alida Vonda.

Oct. 14. Dina, of Dirk Jansz and Marretje Jans. Wit.:
Jefta Cornelise, Dina Cornelis.

Barentje, of Johannes and Catrina Barheyd. Wit.: Willem Gillebart, Cornelia Gillebartse.

Angenietjen, of Matheus Goes and Jannetjen Bries.
Wit.: Pieter Van Bueren, Geertruy Vosburg.

Jerimias, of Pieter Hoogeboom and Jannetjen Mulders.
Wit.: Ariaen Oothoud, Marytjen Wenne.

Christyntjen, of Burger Huyk and Maayke Goes. Wit.:
Klaas Wyngaart, Christyntjen Wenner.

Ysaak, of Melgert and Catrina Van der Poel. Wit.:
Stephanus and Marytje Van Aalen.

1711–1712

Antonies, of Karel Berwe and Aaltjen Van der Werke. Wit.: Anthoy Koster, Tryntjen Bries.

Elisabeth, of iDirk Van der Kar and Fytjen Van Schayk. Wit.: Louweres Van Schayk, Annaatjen Rommeli.

Jannetjen, of Pieter Bogaart and Rebekka Vonda. Wit.: Jacob Bogaart, Antjen Vonda.

Oct. 24. Sara, of Johannes and Bethte Visscher. Wit.: Nanning Visscher.

Catrina, of Pieter Walderen and Catrina Van den Berg. Wit.: Willem and Catrina Van den Berg.

Elisabeth, of Volkert Douwen and Margrietjen Van Trigt. Wit.: Andries Douwen, Madalena Van Trigt.

1712, Feb. 10. Isaak, of Korset Vedder and Neeltjen Christiaans. Wit.: Corn. and Marytjen Christiaansz.

Anna, of Dirk Van Vegten and Margrietjen Harmens. Wit.: Leendert Gansevoort, Antjen Van Vegten.

Catalyntjen, of Cornelis Van Buuren and Hendrikjen Van Nes. Wit.: Pieter and Marretjen Van Buuren.

Roelof, of Albert Roelofse and Dirkjen Van Aalstee. Wit.: Karel Broewee, Aaltjen Roelofs.

Wessel, of Anthony Van Schayk and Anna Catryn Ten Broek. Wit.: Dirk Wessels Ten Broek, Gosen Van Schayk, Caatjen Ten Broek.

Margriet, of Daniel Fort and Gerritjen Van ᴧden Berg. Wit.: Gerrit Van den Berg, Margriet Fort.

Marretjen, of Baren Egberts and Maria De Garmo. Wit.: Benjamin and Marretjen Egbertse.

Thomas, of Samuel Dakse and Lysebeth Jans. Wit.: Jan Fonda, Marretjen Lookerman.

Elysabeth, of Jacob Kloet and Geertruy Van Franken. Wit.: Olderik V. Franken, Anna Kloet.

Jacob, of Samuel Pruyn and Marretje Bogaart. Wit.: Jacob and Dorethe Bogaart.

Catharina, of Corn. and Dorethe Bogaart. Wit.: Pieter Bogaart, Marytjen Oothoud.

Hendrik, of Johannes and Zara Hansen. Wit.: Gerrit Van Es, Tryntjen Frees.

Johannes, of Anthony and Catrina Abrahams. Wit.: Johannes and Margrieta Van Vegten.

Marya, of Anthony and Jannetjen Bogardes. Wit.; Johannes and Annetjen Knikkerbakker.

Catalina, of Harpert Jacobsz and Marretjen Harpers. Wit.: Willem Jacobsz, Elysabet Rooseboom.

Feb. 17. Wyntjen Francen, of Lammert V. Valkenburg and Jannetjen Klauw. Wit.: Johannes Lansen, Lena Zanders.

Elbertjen, of Pieter and Jesyna Van Alen. Wit.: Stefanus Van Aalen, Zara Dingman.

Pieter, of Jacob Van Olinda and Eva De Graaff. Wit.: Robbert Jets, Maria De Graaff.

1712

Willem, of Niclaas Groesbeek and Marytjen Kwakken-
bos. Wit.: Willem and Geertruy Groesbeek.
Marretjen, of Thys Hoes and Cornelia Theuwese. Wit.:
Melgert Van Deusen, Engeltjen Rutse.

BAPTISMS BY DOM. PIETER VAN DRIESSEN.

Apr. 20, (Easter). Maghter, of Claes Van Franke and
Geertruy Quakkenbosch. Wit.: Isack Van den Bosch.
Anna, of Joannes Bleecker and Anna Coster. Wit.:
Gerrit Lancen, Elisabeth Coster.
Dirckie, of Heldert Teimesen and Hester Vischers.
Wit.: Evert Rycksen, Dirckje Vischers.
Joannes, of Gerrit Van Schaick and Sara Goe. Wit.:
Anthoni Van Schaik, Catrina Staets.
Annatie, of Hannes Hansen and Neeltie Cornelissen.
Wit.: Cornelis Gertilianse.
Jenneke, of Cornelis Van Alstee and Marretie Van den
Berg. Wit.: Marten Van Alstee, Geertruy Van den Berg.
Pieter, of Philip and Catrina Liphfeston. Wit.: Pieter
Van Brug, Alida Liphfeston.
Jannetie, of Marten and Judith Van Buren. Wit.:
Barend Sandersen, Maria Sanders.
Cornelia, of Gerrit and Marretie Spoor. Wit.: Willem
and Cornelia Gilberd.
Catryntie, of Maars Van Buren and Maddelena Bogaer d
Wit.: Abraham Bogaerd, Catalyntie Scuyler.
Cornelis, of Salomon Vechter and Alida Van Vechter.
Wit.: Joannes Van Vechter, Elssie Cuylers.
Lucas, of Lucas Hoogkerke and Judith Marselis. Wit.:
Stoffer Jerres, Catalyna Wenna.
Susanna, of Folkert Symense and Janneke Scermerhorn.
Wit.: Barend and Marretie Sandersen.
Gerretie, of Nicolaes and Gerretie Van Woerdt. Wit.:
Barend and Susanna Brad.
Hendrik, of Henrie and Catrina Van Renselaar. Wit.:
Jacob Van Cortland, Maria Staets.
Gerretie, of Joannes and —tie Wendel. Wit.: Philip
Wendel, Willempie Van House.
Pieter, of Frederik and Francyntje Kloet. Wit.: Bar-
ber and Gerrit Ryxsen.
Jonathan, of Koenraed and Tryntie Hoogteeling. Wit.:
Rachel Hoogteeling, Ritser Van den Berg.
Frederik, of Nicolaes Claessen Van Petten and Rebecca
Groot. Wit.: Willem and Maria Van Alen.
Eva, of Hendrik Valkenburg and Anna Huek [?]. Wit.:
Jochem Van Valkenburg.
Adam, of Hendrik Vrooman and Marretie Wenn. Wit.:
Jan and Catryna Vrooman.

1712

Teuntie, of G. Gerritsen Van den Berg and Egbertie Harmsen. Wit.: Geertry Van den Berg, Theunis Harmsen.

Pieter, of Thomas and Clara Langh. Wit.: Dirk and Anna Bratt.

Harmen, of Leendert Gansevoord and Catrina Wandelaars. Wit.: Hannes Wandelaar, Maria Gansevoord.

Gerrit Lukesen, of Jacobus and Maria Wyngaard. Wit.: Isak Quakenbosch, Maria Wyngaart.

Annatie, of Jacob and Jannetie Persen. Wit.: Jan and Elisabeth Rosy.

Frederik, of Cornelis Laurensen and Ana Van Petten. Wit.: Hendrik Ten Eyk, Jacob Egmontsen.

Cornelis, of Laurens and Jannetie Van Schaik. Wit.: Thomas Harmsen, Dorothe Oothoud.

Tjerk Harmsen, of Benjamin and Antie Everson. Wit.: Cornelis Wit, Hester Witsen.

June 13. Anna, of Jan and Geertruy De Graeff. Wit.: Abraham and Christina Truex.

Harmen, of Harmen Meinderts and Geertruy Meindertsen. Wit.: Freryck Meindertsen, Jannetie Van Slyck.

Catryna, of Hermann and Jannetie Van Slyck. Wit.: Hendrik Vroman, Catrina Lucassen.

Anthony, of Coenraat and Gerretie Ten Eyck. Wit.: Anthoni and Catryna V. Schaik.

— 12. Reynier, of Reinier and Sara Meinderssen. Wit.: Barent Egbertse, Sara Meindertsen.

Folkert, of Gysbert and Catalyntie Van den Bergh. Wit.: Willem and Catryn Gysbertsen.

Klaes, of Gerrit and Catryna Van Brakel. Wit.: Cornelis Van der Volgen, Elisabeth Graaf.

Oct. 19. Hendrick, of Ryckert and Tryntie Jansen. Wit.: Isack Lansing, Annatie Gansevoord.

Annatie, of Pieter and Jannetie Hogeboom. Wit.: Jan Gerritsen, Antie Hogeboom.

Catryna, of Joannes and Elisabeth Wendel. Wit.: Joann Walter, Epraim and Sara Wendel.

Jaroon, of Joan and Margaritie Van Valkenburg. Wit.: Joch. Valkenburg, Rebecca Funda.

Gosen, of Adriaen and Catryna Quakkenbosch. Wit.: Antoni Van Schaik, Johanna Rumblis.

Isack, of Abrah. Van Valkenburgh and Cataleyntie Valkenburg. Wit.: Isack Lansing, Susanna Beeckman.

Dirck, of Folkert and Lidia Van Vechten. Wit.: Pieter Douw, Geertry Scuyler.

Margarieta, of Hendrik and Debora Rosenboom. Wit.: Gosen Van Schaick.

Wouter, of Joannes and Geertie Groesbeeck. Wit.: Nicolaes and Marretie Groesbeeck.

1712–1713

Wouter, of Joannes and Antie Knickerbakker. Wit. Wouter and Cornelia Quackenbosch.

Laurens, of Gysbert and Lysbeth Scerph. Wit.: Wessel and Catie Ten Broeck.

Catryna, of Gerrit and Catalyntie Van Nes. Wit.: Joannes Hansen, Catryna Van Nes.

Cataleyna, of Christoffel and Catalyna Jeits. Wit.: Hendrik and Debora Hansen.

Abram, of Joannes and Marretie Vinhagel. Wit.: Nanning Harmsen, Madelena Lansingh.

Anna, of Cornelis and Hesther Swits. Wit.: Tierik Harmsen, Rebecca Swits.

David, of Daniel and Deborah Helmig. Wit.: Jacob Van der Heide, Annatie Ketelaer [?].

Dec. 6. Reynier Schaats, of Matthias and Agnitie Nack. Wit.: Thomas Hun, Bartholomeus Schaats, Maeyke Hun.

1713, Jan. 4. Isack, of Pieter and Marretie Wenne. Wit.: Jesse and Tryntie Freest.

Elizabeth, of Abram and Elzie Staats. Wit.: Joannis Schuyler, Elizabeth ——.

Jan. 7. Pieter, of Abram and Maria Staats. Wit.: Col Pieter Scuyler, Margariet Levesthon.

Jan. 18. Marytie, of Evert and Anke [?] Ridder. Wit.: Gerrit and Hendrik Van Nest, Caty Rynselaar.

Wilhelmus, of Wynant and Volkie Van den Bergh. Wit.: Wilhelmus and Catryna Van den Berg.

Geertie, of Hendr. and Grietie Ten Eick. Wit.: Joannes Bleeker, Neeltie Ten Eick.

Jan. 27. Isack, of Hannes and Anna Quackenbosch. Wit.: Robbert Livveston, Geertr. Van Franken.

Sara, of Dirck and Marretie Jansen. Wit.: Jacob Staats, Elizabeth Staas.

Feb. 8. Joannes, of Rutgert and Cataleyna Bleeker. Wit.: Jan Jansen Bleeker, Catryna Cuyler.

Feb. 22. Pieter, of Pieter and Geertruy Van Buren. Wit.: Harmen and Mary Ryckman.

Feb. 27. Jannetie, of Barent and Neeltie Staats. Wit.: Cornelis Gerritsen, Samuel Staats, Geertruy Nygel.

March 1. Cornelia, of Willem and Sara Sluyter. Wit.: Robbert Wielaar, Rosyna Gardenier.

Geertruy, of Hendrik and Marytie Roelefs. Wit.: Geertruy and Joannes Roelefsen.

Hendrik, of Cornelis and Hendrikie Van Buren. Wit.: Dirck and Christyntie Ten Broeck.

Dirck, of Teunis and Janetie Van Slyck. Wit.: Joannes and Sara Hansen.

Pieter Lookkerman, of Ariaen and Lammetie Oothoud. Wit.: Wessel and Catryntie Ten Broeck.

1713

Ariaentie, of Wynant and Catryntie Van der Poel. Wit.: Abram and Antie Van der Poel.

March 8. Frans, of Daniel and Dickie Winne. Wit.: Frans and Elsie Wenne.

Elsie, of Abram and Magdalena Lansing. Wit.: Joannes and Maria Vinnagel.

Marretie, of Asheur. and Sara Marselis. Wit.: Lukas ᐧ Lukassen, Judith ——.

March 23. Cornelis, of Jan and Cataleintie Van Nes. Wit.: David Groesbeek, Marretie Van Nes.

March 30. Anna, of Jan and Marretie Gerritsen. Wit.: Antoni Van Schaik, Marretie Van Deusen.

Apr. 3. Jacobus, of Col. and Maria V. Renselaar. Wit.: Jac. and Philip Cortlant, Hendrik V. Renselaar, Margarita Bayert, Margarita Liveston.

Folkert, of Andries and Lidia Douw. Wit.: Folkert Van Vechten, Catryna De Meyer.

Apr. 25. Jannetie, of Evert and Geertie Van Nes. Wit.: Gerrit Van den Berg, Antie Ridders.

Marretie, of Jan and Catryna Borgaet. Wit.: Hendrik Van Wie, Hilletie Bickker.

May 17. Dirckie, of Evert and Marretie Rycksen. Wit.: Theunis Egbertsen, Dirckie Visschers.

May 24. Maria, of Storm and Sophia Brat. Wit.: Joannes Appel, Maria Bratt.

Pieter, of Samuel and Elyzabeth Dackzy. Wit.: Jacob and Agnietie Muller.

Maria, of Pieter and Annatie Bronk. Wit.: Jonas Bronk, Marritie Willems.

May 25. Pieter, of Jacob and Anna Snyder. Wit.: Pieter Spys.

Francoy, of Mattheus Bouphi [?] and Catrina Barrowa. Wit.: Wouter Quakkenbosch, Old Rebecca Douw.

Christian Willem, of Nicolaes Roul and Dort. Marg. Royl. Wit.: Christ. Willem Walborn, Ann. Doret. Mary Roul.

May 31. Harmen, of Thomas and Hilletie Williaems. Wit.: Jan Witbeek, Catharina Gansevoort.

June 2. Alida, of Jacob and Chataleintie Bogaart. Wit.: Cornelis Bogaart, Alida Scuyler.

June 21. Magdalena, of Arent and Jannetie Bratt. Wit.: Hendrik Vroman, Engeltie Veeder.

Anna, of Hannes and Marytie Vedder. Wit.: Jacobus and Jacomyn Van Dyck.

June 28. Joannes, of Evert and Engeltie Wendel. Wit.: Joannes and Gerritie Roseboom.

July 5. Jannetie, of Willem and Feytie Halebeek. Wit.: Jacob Mulder, Philip Conyn, Catie Renselaar.

Marretie, of Jonathan and Catalyna Witbeek. Wit.: Mart. and Judithie Van Buren.

1713
July 26. Cornelis, of Elderd and Hesther Tymenzen.
Wit.: Dirk and Anna Bratt.
Aug. 2. Catryna, of Joannes and Geertruy Scerp. Wit.:
Pieter Ver Brugge, Maria Ten Broek.
Aug. 7. Anna, of Cortzett and Neeltie Vedder. Wit.:
Arent Vedder, Catryna Cuylers.
Mattheus, of Mattheus and Joanna Goes. Wit.: Claes
Lukassen, Annatie Gansevoort.
Engel, of Pieter Vrooman and Geertry Vroman. Wit.:
Joannes and Abigael V. Aalsteyn.
Antony, of Daniel and Elisabet Bratt. Wit.: Teunis
Bratt, Sara Renjejz [?].
Joanna, of Abraham and Cristina Truex. Wit.: Abra-
ham Cip, Sara Hansen.
Sept. 20. Pieter, of Joannes and Elizabeth Wandelaar.
Wit.: Frans Wenne, Racheltie Scuyler.
Marretie, of Samuel and Marretie Pruyn. Wit.: Cor-
nelis and Cataleyntie Bogaart.
Cornelia, of Marten and Cornelia Van Aalsteyn. Wit.:
Wynant Van de Berg, Tryntie Van Aelstein.
Alida, of Meindert and Maria Roseboom. Wit.: Gerrit
Roseboom, Eva Beekman.
Sept. 24. Joannes, of Joannes and Elizabet Visscher.
Wit.: Frerik Visscher, Ariaentie Wendel.
Hendrik, of Jan and Catryntie Van Wie. Wit.: Agnitie
Van Wie.
Sep. 27. Robbert, of Joannes and Styntie Van Deusen.
Wit.: Harpert Van Deusen, Tryntie Bries.
Engeltie, of Hendrik and Maria Vrooman. Wit.: Barent
Vroman, Cristyna Swarts [?] or V. Wart [?].
Jan Petist, of Jan Petist and Helena Van Ness. Wit.:
Robbert Wendel, Catrintie Lansing.
Catyrna, of Lambert and Anna Huyck. Wit.: Stoffel
and Cathalyna Jets.
Marytie, of Isack and Maycke Ouderkerk. Wit.: Hen-
drik and Aaltie Van Nes.
Margaritie, of Isak and Lidia Volkenburg. Wit.: Rob-
bert Liveston, Margaritie Livingston.
Tryntie, of Dirk and Claartie Heemstraat. Wit.: Pieter
Quackenbosch, Maretie Pruym.
Teuntie, of Daniel and Gerretie Fort. Wit.: Evert and
Marretie Van Nes.
Jan, of Jan and Agnitie Witbeek. Wit.: Andries and
Lydia Douw.
Catryna, of Antony and Anna Catryna Van Scayck.
Wit.: Dirck and Cristina Ten Broeck.
Oct. 8. Maria, of [Joannes Pruym] Joannes and Bar-
entie Evertsen. Wit.: Joannes and Amelia [?] Pruym.
Nicolaes, of Andries Van Putten and Mayke Van Petten.
Wit.: Claes Frerikse Van Petten, Geertie Ten Eik.

1713–1714
Oct. 12. Catryntie, of Abram and Marretie Van Aal-steyn. Wit.: Ruth and Catalyntie Van Deusen.
Neeltie, of Teunis and Sara Van der Volge. Wit.: Rob-bert and Margarietie Liveston.
Joannes, of Jan and Rebekka Fort. Wit.: Joannes Beekman, Margarietie Fort.
Thomas, of Bartholomeus and Catryna Van Volkenburg. Wit.: Abram Van Valkenburg, Lisebeth Van Deusen.
Oct. 19. Hendrik, of Abram and Majeke Wendel. Wit.: Hendrik Van Nes, Catalyntie Freest.
Melchert, of Harpert and Lena Van Duese. Wit.: Ruth Van Deusen, Catie Witbeek.
Jacobus, of Stephanus and Marretie Van Alen. Wit.: Jan Fonda, Agnitie Mullers.
Oct. 26. Eva, of Jacob and Christina Valkenburg. Wit.: Joannes Beekman, Gritie Valkenburgh.
Jeremias, of Pieter and Neeltie Quakkenbosch. Wit.: Joannes Visscher, Geertruy Scuyler.
Nov. 1. Gerrit, of Meindert and Titie Marselis. Wit.: Gysberd Marselis, Alida Oothoud.
Ephraim, of Ephraim and Anna Wendel. Wit.: Frerik Visscher, Elizabeth Visschers.
Nov. 29. Joannes, of Gerrit and Marretie Spoor. Wit.: Joannes Cuyler, Annatie Gilberd.
Jacob, of Jacob and Helena Lansing. Wit.: Arent and Barentie Pruym.
Dec. 6. Antony, of Antony and Anna Van Scayck. Wit.: Antony and Marretie Van Schayk.
Dec. 12. Samuel, of Edderd and Josyne Wiele. Wit.: Obedias and Cornelia Couper.
Dec. 27. Abraham, of Abram and Catryna Cuyler. Wit.: Petrus Van Driessen, Sara Van Brugh.
1714, Jan. 10. Jacob, of Visschert and Elsie [?] Moor. Wit.: Joannes Bykman, Eva Beekman.
Elbertie, of Leendert [?] and Emmetie Conyn. Wit.: Melchert and Catryna Van der Poel.
Emmetie, of Hendrik and Cornelia Salsberi. Wit. Harmen and Hanna Salsberi.
Jan. 17. Petrus, of Petrus, Jr., and Eva Van Driessen. Wit.: Joannes Cuiler in place of Petrus Van Driesen, Sara Verbrughe in place of Johanna Van Driesen.
Jan. 31. Joannes, of Albert and Dirckie Van der Werke. Wit.: Jacob and Abigael Van Aalst.
Jacob, of Ruth and Elizabeth Van Woerd. Wit.: David Groesbeek, Elizabeth Marselis.
Feb. 7. Christina, of Samuel and Maria Ten Broeck. Wit.: Hendrik and Catryna Van Renselaar.
Neeltie, of Joannes and Maria Van Vechten. Wit.: Antony Bogaardus, Neeltie Douw.

1714

Melchert, of Abram and Antie Van der Poel. Wit.: Melchert and Catryna Van der Poel.

Feb. 14. Petrus, of Fredrick Meindertsen and Sara Meyndertsen. Wit.: Leendert Gansevoort, Annatie Wandelaar.

Joannes, of Barent and Geertruy Gerritsen. Wit.: Lucas and Geertruy Witbeek.

Elsie, of Joannes and Amilia Pruym. Wit.: Gerrit Roseboom, Elyzabeth Vischer.

Feb. 21. Jan Tyssien, of Jan and Margarita Goes. Wit.: Hendrik Hansen, Teuntie Goes.

Geertruy, of Joannes and Marretie Fonda. Wit.: Isak Fonda, Hester Slingerlant.

Sara, of Claes and Geertruy Van Franken. Wit.: Samuel Crieger, Annatie Quakkenbosch.

Eizabeth, of William and Elizabeth Poel. Wit.: Elizabeth Scuyler.

March —. Marretie, of Volkert [?] and Antie Ekbersen. Wit.: Jacob and Janna [?] Visscher.

Rebecca, of Isack and Alida Fonda. Wit.: Claas and Anna Fonda.

March 21. Dirck, of Dick [?] and Marretie Jansen. Wit.: Hendrik and Debora Roseboom.

March 26. Marritie, of Levynus and Catryna Harmensen. Wit.: Theunis and Marretie Harmensen.

March 28. Benjamin, of Salomon and Alida Goewyck. Wit.: Gosen Van Schaik, Lysebeth Van Corlaar.

Apr. 11. Harmannus, of Harmanus and Anna Wendel. Wit.: Jacob Lansingh, Sanna Wendels.

Eva, of Pieter Walderingh and Catrina Waldering. Wit.: Gerrit Van den Berg, Engeltie Beekman.

Joannes, of Philip and Catryna Livingston. Wit.: Joannes Cuyler, Joannes Livingston, Margarieta Collins.

Joseph, Catryna, of Nicolaes and Catryna Staring. Wit.: Joseph and Catryna Essching, Catryna Engelspreken.

May 2. Symon, of Dirk and Elizabeth Grood. Wit.: Barent Zanders, Susanna Swits.

May 16. Andries, of Laurens and Hilletie Scerp. Wit.: Gysbert Scerp, Agnitie Mullers.

May 23. Joannes, of Folkert and Jannetie Symensen. Wit.: Joannes Symensen, Anna De Waaran.

June 13. Joannes, of G [?] R. and Maria G. Van der Werke. Wit.: Joannes R. Van der Werk, Mally Van Hoogen.

Petrus, of Marten and ——ike Van Buren. Wit.: Antony Coster, Geertruy Scuyler.

July 12. Eva, of Cornelis and Eggie Slingerlant. Wit.: Albert Slingerlant, Neeltie Beekmans.

Joseph, of Robert and Merry Jojets. Wit.: Joseph Jojets.

1714
Jacob, of Jacob and Lena Lansing. Wit.: Abram Lansing, Antie Wendels.

Joannes, of Barent and Maria Zanders. Wit.: Joannes Wendel, Elizabeth Visscher.

Aug. 14. Elize Margarieta, of Pieter and Elizabart Knyskerk. Wit.: Hannes and An. Marg. Gremmer, Elizabeth Hanghin.

Eliza Barber, of Hannes and A. Marga Gremmer. Wit.: Pieter and Elizabeth Knyskerk, Elizabeth Hoanghin.

Abram, of Joannes and Elizabeth Wendel. Wit.: Abram Wendel, Merry Walter.

Tierk Harmsen, of Cornelis and Hester Swits. Wit.: Benjamin Ekbertsen, Geertruy Visscher.

Aug. 29. Alida, of Pieter and Jesyna Van Alen. Wit.: Cornelis Maarsen, Cornelia Gardenier.

Wouter, of Nicolaes and Marretie Groesbeek. Wit.: Wouter Quakkenbosch, Geertruy Groesbeek.

Ariaentie, of Joannes and Hessi Beekman. Wit.: Harmanus and Ariaentie Wendel.

Sept. 12. Isack, of Joannes and Sara Hansen. Wit.: Joannes Hendriksen, Sanna Schermerhoorn.

Sep. 19. Jonas, of Jonas and Marretie Lerway. Wit.: Storm Bratt, Cornelia Uzile.

Maycke, of Pieter and Elizabeth Kojeman. Wit.: Andries Kojeman, Anna Greveraad.

Sep. 20. Eduward, of Willem and Sara Sluiter. Wit.: Hendrik Hansen, Breghie Wielaar.

Oct. 3. Geertruy, of Kilyaen and Maria Van Renselaar. Wit.: Stephanus and Geertruy Cortlant, Robbert Livingston, Jr.

Barend, of Coenraad and Gerretie Ten Eik. Wit.: Tobias and Neeltie Ten Eik.

Dorethee, of Wouter and Marretie Vroman. Wit.: Daniel and Elisabeth Brat.

Oct. 8. Margariete, of Ruthgert and Catalyna Bleeker. Wit.: Abram Senyly, Maria Van Dyck.

Oct. 10. Catalyntie, of Arent and Antie Schermerhoorn. Wit.: Joannes Beekman, Neeltie Ten Eik.

Oct. 17. Goosen, of Gerrit and Sara Van Schaik. Wit.: Gysbert Scherph, Maria Van Corlaar.

Oct. 31. Jannetie, of Joannes and Margaritie Valkenburg. Wit.: Hendrik and Margarietie Ten Eick.

Hester, of Jesse and Aaltie De Graaf. Wit.: Abram Truex, Marretie Wendels.

Nov. 7. Hubertie, of Christoffel and Catalyntie Jets. Wit.: Joannes and Eva Beekman.

Hendrik, of Claes and Rachel Gardenier. Wit.: Hendrik and Syntie Gardenier.

Nov. 29. Robberd, of Thomas and Barentie Berrit. Wit.: Claes Van Woerd, Wyntie Berrit.

1714–1715

Dec. 12. Engeltie, of Harpert and Lena Van Deusen. Wit.: Melchert Abramsen, Catalyntie Van Deusen.

Dec. 25. Jannetie, of Jan and Catryna Du Fou. Wit.: —— Kitni, Marretie Kitni.

Anna, of Cornelis and Antie Lanzensen. Wit.: Helmer and Antie Jansen.

Jacob, of Reinier and Sara Meindertsen. Wit.: Hendrik Douw, Zanna Visscher.

Gideon, of Adriaen and Catryna Quakkenbosch. Wit.: Gozen Van Schaik, Maria Van Corlaar.

Margarieta, of Wynant and Catryna Van der Poel. Wit.: Willem Claassen, Marytie Bries.

1715, Jan. 1. Maria, of Gerrit and Eckbertie Van den Bergh. Wit.: Cornelis Van den Bergh, Eckbertie Bratt.

Jan. 5. Anna, of Eldert and Hester Tymensen. Wit.: Tierck and Eckbertie Visscher.

Jan. 9. Abraham, of Hendrik and Debora Roseboom. Wit.: Willem Jacobsen, Maria Roseboom.

Jan. 23. Agnietie, of Thomas and Hilletie Williams. Wit.: Jonas Bronck, Agnietie Witbeek.

Catryna, of Barent and Maria Eckbertsen. Wit.: Abram Kip, Agnietie Germoor.

Anna, of Eldert and Lena Ouderkerk. Wit.: Abram Ouderkerk, Mettie Jansen.

Jan. 26. Maria, of Joannes and Elizabeth Oostrander. Wit.: Jacob Lansingh, Maria Van den Bergh.

Jan. 30. Hendrik, of Gerrit and Catalyna Van Nes. Wit.: Jan Van Nes, Sara Hansen.

Feb. 4. Ysack, of Isack and Ammerency Verplanck. Wit.: Jacob Bogaard, Abigail Verplanck.

Feb. 13. Elsie, of Joannes and Zuzanna Wendel. Wit.: Evert Wendel, Zuzanna Wyngaard.

Marten, of Pieter and Marretie Wenne. Wit.: Abram and Geesie Kip.

Feb. 20. Catryna, of Epraim and Anna Wendel. Wit.: Hendrik and Marretie Van Ness.

March 2. Jacob, of Joannes and Anna Bleeker. Wit.: Hendrik Bleeker, Geertruy Gerritsen.

Rebecka, of Jan and Annetie Danielsen. Wit.: Symon Danielsen, Marretie Peeks.

Harmen, of Isack and Lidia Valkenburgh. Wit.: Harmen and Madalena Ryckman.

March 6. Rachel, of Cornelis and Dorothe Bogaard. Wit.: Jacob Bogaard, Madelena Ryckmans.

Apr. 7. Joannes, of Joannes and Geertruy Lansingh. Wit.: Joannes Lansingh, Margarieta Livingston.

Maria, of Jan and Rebecca Fort. Wit.: Simon and Marretie Danielsen

1715

Apr. 24. Anna, of Dirck and Marretie Hagedoorn. Wit.: Joannes and Anna Appel.

Lidia, of Ritser and Tryntie Jansen. Wit.: Willem Hoogtelink, Marretie Wenne.

Grietie, of Daniel and Debora Ketelhuin. Wit.: Willem Ketelhuin, Sanna Bratt.

Abraham, of Evert and Engeltie Wendel. Wit.: Antony Coster, Hester Beekmans.

May 1. Aryaantie, of Jacob and Geertruy Knoet. Wit.: Gerrit Van Franken, Catie Cuyler.

Dirck Wessels, of Samuel and Maria Ten Broeck. Wit.: Hendrik and Catryna V. Renselaer.

May 8. Elbertie, of Joannes and Christina Van Deusen. Wit.: Willem and Maria Van Alen.

May 10. Margarita, of Hendrik and Margarieta Ten Eick. Wit.: Tobias Ten Eick, Rachel Bleeker.

Joannes, Heyltie, of Jeremias and Elizabeth Muller. Wit.: Joannes and Agnietie Muller, Jacob Muller and Maritie Van Alen.

Alida, of Meindert and Fytie Marselis. Wit.: Wouter Barhait, Rebecca Oothout.

May 23. Cristyna, of Frans and Margarita Pruim. Wit.: Jacob and Lena Lanzingh.

May 27. Elberd, of Dirck and Margarita Van Vegten. Wit.: Theunis and Rachel Harmensen.

Jacob, of Joannes and Geertruy Groesbeek. Wit.: Gysberd Marselis, Catalyna Van Ness.

July 10. Willem, of Jan Barhajck and Catryna Barhaik. Wit.: Willem Gilbert, Christina Cuylers.

Catryna, of Jacob and Zuzanna Schermerhoorn. Wit.: Jesse and Tryntie Freest.

July 30. Abraham, of Albert and Dirckie Roelefsen. Wit.: Pieter Walderingh, Tryntie Van Aalsteyn.

Elsie, of Anthony and Anna Van Schayck. Wit.: Joannes and Elsie Cuyler.

Aug. 7. Bastyaen, of Evert and Marretie Rycksen. Wit.: Elderd and Hessie Tymensen.

Andries, of Gerrit and Barber Rycksen. Wit.: Elberd Gerritsen, Anna Van Franken.

Aug. 27. Teunis, of Jan and Catryna Barhait. Wit.: Balthus and Lidia Van Benthuisen.

Harmen, of Teunis and Rachel Harmensen. Wit.: Bastyaen Harmensen, Maria Gansevoort.

Sept. 4. Catryna, of Dirck and Margarita Ten Broeck. Wit.: Abram Cuyler, Catryna Ten Broek.

Teuntie, of Kilyaen and Maretie Wenne. Wit.: Pieter Wenne, Emilia Pruim.

Sara, of Willem and Feytie Halenbeek. Wit.: Daniel and Elizabeth Bratt.

1715
Elizabeth, of Joannes and Maria Vinhagel. Wit.
Joannes and Eva Beekman.
Sept. 18. Jan, of Cornelis and Hendryckie Van Buren.
Wit.: Daniel and Dirckie Wenne.
Elizabeth, of Nicolaas and Elsie Schuyler. Wit.: Philip
Schuyler, Margarita Livingston.
Geertruy, of Jan and Catalyntie Van Ness. Wit.: Symon
Van Ness, Geertruy Groesbeek.
Pieter, of Jacob and Catalyntie Bogaard. Wit.: Samuel
Pruym, Alida Schuyler.
Joannes, of Daniel and Gerretie Fort. Wit.: Abram
Fort, Bethi Van den Bergh.
Sept. 26. Catryna Johanna, of Tobias and Marretie
Ten Broek. Wit.: Wessel Ten Broeck, Johanna Van
Stryen.
Abraham, of Lowys and Marritie Viele. Wit.: Simon
Danielsen, Marretie Peeks.
Oct. 9. Pieter, of Dirck and Maretie Jansen. Wit.:
Pieter Cornelissen, Elsie Staats.
Sara, of Pieter and Alida Comyn. Wit.: Frans Wenne,
Anna De Wandelaar.
Oct. 16. Debora, of Gerrit and Anna Van Bergen.
Wit.: Petrus Van Bergen, Dorothe Douw.
Oct. 30. Henderik, of P. and Eva Van Driessen. Wit.:
Joannes Cuyler, Sara Van Brugh.
Dirck Wessels, of Joannes and Catryna Ten Broek.
Wit.: Hendrik and Catryna Van Renselaar.
Machtel, of Jacob and Debora Beeckman. Wit.: Joannes and Eva Beekman.
Anthony, of David and Elsie Schuyler. Wit.: Ruth
Bleeker, Anthony Rutgers.
Anneke, of Maas and Anna Rycksen. Wit.: Jacob
Teunissen, Maria Gerritsen.
Jacob, of Joannes and Anna Quakkenbosch. Wit.:
Gerardus Kloet, Alida Ouderkerk.
Nov. 13. Marritie, of Harpert and Marretie Jacobsen.
Wit.: Ruth Melchersen, Maria Gerritsen.
Susanna, of Isack and Jannetie Lansingh. Wit.: Joannis and Catryntie Lansingh.
Nov. 20. Engeltie, of Joannes and Margariet Roelefsen.
Wit.: Hendrik and Barber Roelefsen.
Nov. 27. Sara, of Gozen and Cataryna Van Schayck.
Wit.: Antony and Anna Cataryna Van Schayck.
Dec. 3. Laurens, of David and Susanna Littelriel.
Wit.: Robb. Livingston, Jr., Lysbeth Groesbeek.
Dec. 11. Anna, of Joannes and Cornelia Becker. Wit.:
Storm Becker, Lybetie Van Deusen.
Dec. 18. Maria, of P. M. and Ariaentie Van Buren.
Wit.: Joannes and Elsie Cuyler.

1715–1716
Willempie, of Barent, Jr., and Maria Bratt. Wit.: Albert Ryckman, Willempie Bratt.

Dec. 23. Joannes, of Jacob and Lena Lansingh. Wit.: Joannes and Catryna Lansingh.

Dec. 25. Abraham, of Bartholomeus and Cataryna V. Valkenburgh. Wit.: Thomas Van Aalsteyn, Maria Mingaals.

Rachel, of Claes and Geertruy Van Franken. Wit.: Jacob Quakkenbosch, Grietie Van Franken.

Maria, of Joannes and Lysebeth De Wandelaar. Wit.: Joannes Witbeek, Grietie Van Vegten.

1716, Jan.1. Anna, of Adriaen and Lammetie Oothout. Wit.: Kilyaen and Maria Van Renselaar.

Jan. 15. Joannes, of Meyndert and Marya Roseboom. Wit.: Hendrik and Gerretie Roseboom.

Wilhelmus, of Levinus and Catryna Harmensen. Wit.: Wynant and Catryna Van den Bergh.

Agnitie, of Jan and Catryna Van Wie. Wit.: Harmen Ryckman, Alida Van Wie.

Jan. 22. Rachel, of Pieter and Neeltie Quackenbosch. Wit.: Wynant Van der Poel, Neeltie Ten Eick.

Jacob, of Joannes and Elizabeth Wendel. Wit.: Jacob and Sara Wendel.

Anna, of Andries and Lidia Douw. Wit.: Folkert Douw, Gerrit Van Bergen, Anna Mejers.

Feb. 12. Wilhelmus, of Gerrit and Maria Spoor. Wit.: Thomas and Barentie Berrit.

Hieronimus, of Wouter [?] and Rachel Barhayt. Wit.: Jan Barhayt, Grietie Van Valkenburg.

March 11. Elizabeth, of Joannes and Neeltie Cristyaensen. Wit.: Joannes and Elsie Cuyler.

Alida, of Arent and Catlyna Pruim. Wit.: Joannes Pruim, Elsie Wenne.

March 18. Andries, of Nicolaes and Dirckie Van Woerd. Wit.: Bastyaen Visscher, Rachel Schuyler.

March 31. Maria, of Henderik and Maria V. der Werken. Wit.: Jan and Maria Kithni.

Geurt, of Jacob and Susanna Schoonhoven. Wit.: Dirck Bratt, Maria and Henderikie Schoonhoven.

Apr. 8. Anna, of Jan and Margarita Goes. Wit.: Evert Wendel, Hessie Wyngaart.

Apr. 15. Marritie, of Evert and Geertie Van Ness. Wit.: Abram Van der Poel, Marretie Van Ness.

Ariaentie, of Cornelis and Hester Swits. Wit.: Jacob and Sanna Visscher.

Apr. 22. Willem, of Daniel and Dirckie Wenne. Wit.: Gerrit Van Ness, Marytie Wenne.

Cornelis Andriessen, of Isack and Bata Van Deusen Wit.: Willem Yselsteyn, Lybetie Van Deusen.

1716
May 10. Hester, of Benjamin and Rachel De Mess. Wit.: Joannes and Anna Van Vegten.

Evert, of Joannes and Barentie Evertsen. Wit.: Samuel Pruym, Antie Van Yveren.

May 13. Sara, of Simon and Maria Danielsen. Wit.: Lowys and Maria Viele.

Tobias, of Pieter and Geertruy Van Buren. Wit.: Jacob Scermerhoorn, Maria Bries.

Gysbert, of Cornelis and Maria Van Aalsteyn. Wit.: Joannes and Cornelia Van Aalsteyn.

May 20. Albert, of Wouter and Johanna Van der Zee. Wit.: Isack and Lena Lansingh.

Joachim, of Abram and Elsie Staats. Wit.: Hendrik and Debora Roseboom.

May 21. Pieter, of Anthony and Johanna Bogardus. Wit.: Pieter and Sara Van Brugh.

June 3. Andries, of Frerik and Sara Meyndertsen. Wit.: Pieter Conyn, Sara Reynier.

Martin Gerretsen, of Marten and Catryna Van Bergen. Wit.: Hendrik and Neeltie Douw.

Nelletie, of Tobias and Helena Ryckman. Wit.: Albert and Nelletie Ryckman.

June 24. Jonas, of Jonathan and Maria Larway. Wit.: Pieter and Helena Uzile.

Omphry, of Ritsert and Gesie Moor. Wit.: Stephanus Groesbeek, Engeltie Wendel.

Abraham, of Harmanus and Anna Wendel. Wit.: Nicolaas Schuyler, Engeltie Wendels.

June 28. Nicolaas, of Abram and Catrina Cuyler. Wit.: Ruth and Catalyna Bleeker.

Elizabeth, of Salomon and Alida Goewey. Wit.: Arent and Maria Van Corlaar.

June 31 [sic]. Susanna, of Abram and Maycke Wendel. Wit.: Philiph and Maria Wendel.

July 15. Maritie, of Theunis and Engeltie Eckbertsen. Wit.: Barent Bratt, Maritie Eckbertsen.

Anna, of Jacob and Helena Lansingh. Wit.: Frans Pruyn, Anna Van Yveren.

Henderik, of Isack and Alida Fonda. Wit.: Jacob Lansingh, Susanna Bratt.

July 22. Jacob, of Pieter and Rebecca Bogaardt. Wit.: Cornelis Bogaardt, Sara Van Arnhem.

July 29. Cornelia, of Isack and Amarencie Verplanck. Wit.: Gelyn and Marritie Verplanck.

Rachel, of Dirck and Eckbertie Van der Heyde. Wit.: Jacob and Rachel Van der Heyde.

Aug. 13. Alida, of Mathys and Agnietie Nack. Wit.: Ruth Van Deusen, Jenneke Nack.

Aug. 19. Hendrik, of Leendert and Catrina Gansevoort. Wit.: Frans and Elsie Wenne.

1716

Jacobus, of Burger and Maicke Huyck. Wit.: Joannes and Mia Vinhagel.

Sept. 23. Gerrit, of Mathias and Maria Bovy. Wit.: Dirck Ten Broeck, Catie Cuyler.

Willem, of Jan and Tryntie Du Four. Wit.: Cornelis and Hendrikie Van Buuren.

Ephraim, of Anthoni and Elizabeth Coster. Wit.: Gerrit Lansingh, Gerrittie Roseboom.

Elizabeth, of Anthony and Catrina Van Schaik. Wit.: Gerrit and Catrina Van Schaick.

Isack, of Isack and Maycke Ouderkerk. Wit.: Abram and Meytie Ouderkerk.

Johanna, of Joannes and Margarita Valkenburgh. Wit.: Lambert and Rachel Rately.

Anna Maria, of Thomas and Barentie Berrit. Wit.: Gerrit and Maria Spoor.

Thomas, of Jacob and Christina Valkenburgh. Wit.: Wouter and Rachel Barhayt.

Cornelis, of Gerrit and Tryntie Van den Bergh. Wit.: Matheus Van den Bergh, Marretie Van Aalsteyn.

Ariaentie, of Abram and Anna Van der Poel. Wit.: Wynant and Ariaentie Van der Poel.

Oct. 12. Jan, of Pieter and Christina Bratt. Wit.: Wouter and Elizabeth Van der Zee.

Oct. 14. Sara, of Samuel and Elsie Bebbington. Wit.: Isack Greveraad, Maria Roseboom.

Joannes, of Christophel and Catalyna Jets. Wit.: Jan and Maretie Gerretsen.

Oct. 21. Cornelia, of Joannes and Antie Knikkerbakker. Wit.: Antony and Jannetie Bogardus.

Oct. 27. Lysebeth, of Pieter and Lysbeth Koyeman. Wit.: Pieter Van Brughe, Geertie Ten Eick.

Catalyna, of Wynant and Folkie Van den Bergh. Wit.: Gerrit and Geertie Van den Bergh.

Nov. 4. Joannes, of Matheus and Maria Vlensburgh. Wit.: Daniel Killy, Annetie Van Zanten.

Neeltie, of Gerrit, Jr., and Elizabeth Lansingh. Wit.: Evert and Elizabeth Banker.

Nov. 12. Petrus, of Joannes and Elizabeth Oostrander. Wit.: Gerrit and Gerrittie Van den Bergh.

Dec. 9. Jacobus, of Ruth and Catalyna Bleecker. Wit.: Joannes Bleeker, Rachel Schuyler.

Dec. 16. Catryna, of Melchert and Catryna Van der Poel. Wit.: Jacobus Van Alen, Arientie Van der Poel.

Salomon, of Laurens and Hilletie Scerph. Wit.: Salomon Goewey, Agnietie Germoy.

Elbertie, of Joannes and Christina Van Deusen. Wit. Jan Van Aalsteyn, Engeltie Van Ness.

1716–1717

Dec. 21. Geertruy, of Nicolaas and Maria Groesbeek. Wit.: David Groesbeek, Catalyna Van Ness.

Dec. 23. Gysbert, of Marten and Cornelia Van Aalsteyn. Wit.: Mathias and Aaltie Van den Bergh.

1717, Jan. 6. Catryna, of Joannes and Catryna Ten Broeck. Wit.: Dirck, Wessel, and Christina Ten Broeck.

Jan. 13. Sara, of Jacob and Geertruy Roseboom. Wit.: Jacob Staats, Debora Roseboom.

Jan. 16. Phillip, of Philip and Catryna Livingston. Wit.: Meindert Schuyler, Johanna Livingston.

Franciscus, of Frans and Anna Pruym. Wit.: Arent and Catryna Pruym.

Jennetie, of Benjamin and Antie Eckbertsen. Wit.: Tjerk and Femmetje Visschers.

Wilhelmus, of Wilhelmus and Geertie Van den Bergh. Wit.: Gysbert and Folkie Van den Bergh.

Jan. 20. Hendrik, of Hendrick and Hilletie Van Wie. Wit.: Storm Becker, Eytie Delmont.

Feb. 3. Jan Petist, of Kilyaen and Maria Van Renselaar. Wit.: Alida Livingston, John Collins.

Catryna, of Coenraed and Gerretie Ten Eick. Wit.: Anthoni and Anna Van Schayck.

Feb. 10. Abraham, of Marten and Elizabeth Delmond. Wit.: Lowys and Maretie Viele.

Roelef, of Joannes and Margariet Roelefsen. Wit.: Albert and Dirckie Roelefsen.

Feb. 27. Sophia, of Eldert and Lena Ouderkerck. Wit.: Anthoni and Elizabeth Coster.

Joannes, of Matheus and Engeltie Van Deusen. Wit.: Harpert Van Deusen, Geertruy Slingerlant.

March 3. Jannetie, of Samuel and Geertruy Criegier. Wit.: Bastyaen Visscher, Jannetie Criegier.

March 6. Catryn, of Ruth and Elizabeth Van Woerdt. Wit.: Willem and Geertruy Groesbeeck.

Maria, of Jacob and Antie Schermerhoorn. Wit.: Philip and Jannetie Van Vegten.

Geertruy, of Thomas and Jannetie Witbeeck. Wit.: Ruth and Catalyna Van Deusen.

March 10. Anna, of Hendrick and Catryna Caarn. Wit.: Joannes and Anna Appel.

March 20. Barent, of Abram and Maria Staats. Wit.: Geertruy and Joannes Lansingh.

March 24. Hendrik, of Samuel and Maria Ten Broeck. Wit.: Dirck Wessels, Wessel and Cristyna Ten Broeck.

March 31. Anna Maria, of Philip and Madalena Laucks. Wit.: Andries Bratt, Wyntie Roos.

Petrus, of Claes and Cornelia Bovy. Wit.: Matheus and Maria Bovy.

1717

Apr. 14. Margarita, of Folkert and Margarita Douw. Wit.: Hendrik and Lidia Douw.

Dirck, of Tobias and Marretie Ten Broek. Wit.: Dirck Wessels Ten Broeck, Cristyna Ten Broeck.

Anna, of Abraham and Cristina Truex. Wit.: Hans Hansen, Sara Wendels.

Apr. 18. Wouter, of Wouter and Cornelia Barhayt. Wit.: Wouter and Neeltie Quackenbosch.

Apr. 21. Jacobus, of Albert and Dirckie Roelofsen. Wit.: Jesse and Catryna Freest.

Jacobus, of Abram and Maria Van Aalsteyn. Wit.: Thomas Van Aalsteyn, Engeltie Van Vegten.

Isack, of Cornelis and Geertruy Huygh. Wit.: Ruth and Catalyna Bleeker.

Lucas, of Pieter and Josyna Van Alen. Wit.: Willem and Maria Van Alen.

Joannes, of Abram and Catalyna Valkenburgh. Wit.: Jacob and Elizabeth Schermerhoorn.

Wyntie, of Scibboleth and Anna Bogardus. Wit.: Hendrik Renselaar, Catryna Van Renselaar.

Apr. 28. Ariaentie, of Daniel and Gerritje Fort. Wit.: Nicolaes Fort, Antie Van der Poel.

May 19. Ariaentie, of Evert and Engeltie Wendel. Wit.: Joannes Lansingh, Jr., Antie Bleekers.

May 26. Pieter, of Pieter and Alida Conyn. Wit.: Gerrit and Agnietie Van Wye.

May 30. Maria, of Jan and Maria Gerritsen. Wit.: Stoffel and Catalyntie Jets.

June 2. Petrus, of Jefta [?] and Maria Cornelissen. Wit.: Barent Staats, Dina Cornelissen.

June 9. Lucas, of Jacobus and Maria Lucassen. Wit.: Wynant Van den Bergh, Cristina Cuyler.

Cornelis, of Joannes and Lybetie Muller. Wit.: Jacob and Agnietie Muller.

Joannes, of Joannes, Jr., and Esther Beekman. Wit.: Joannes and Eva Beekman.

Tryntie, of Harpert and Helena Van Deusen. Wit.: Lucas and Catie Witbeek.

Anna, of Dirk and Margarita Ten Broeck. Wit.: Wessel Ten Broeck, Catie Cuyler.

June 10. Breghie, of Meindert and Titie Marselis. Wit : Gysbert Mazelis, Alida Oothout.

June 16. Commertie, of Pieter and Antie Bronk. Wit.: Joannes Van Vegten, Agnietie Witbeek.

June 31 [sic]. Joannes, of Joannes and Zelia Redly. Wit.: Lambert and Rachel Redly.

Jms [sic], of William and Marretie Letteson. Wit.: Jan De Graaf, Blandyna Tyssen.

Robbert, of Ritser and Tryntie Van den Berck. Wit.: Gerrit Van Bergen, Hendrickie Hooghkerk.

1717

Susanna, of Reynier and Sara Meindertsen. Wit.: Theunis Eckbertsen, Maria Bratt.

Eva, of Lucas and Tanneke Van Vegten. Wit.: Daniel and Dirkie Wenne.

Simon, of Casper and Jannetie Van Steents. Wit.: Isack and Johanna Lansingh.

July 13. Anhtoni, of Anthoni, Jr., and Anna Van Schayck. Wit.: Anthoni and Maria Van Schayck.

Anna, of Jan and Maria Tannson. Wit.: Hieroon and Margariet Van Vlieren.

July 19. Isack, of Pieter and Maria Wenne. Wit.: Jesse and Catrina Foreest.

July 26. Jan, of Storm and Sophia Bratt. Wit.: Albert Slingerlant, Maria Barway.

Pieter, of Pieter and Tryntie Walderon. Wit.: Wilhelm and Geertie V. den Bergh.

Alida, of Matheus and Agnitie Nack. Wit.: Ruth Van Deusen, Jenneke Nack.

Aug. 4. Elizabeth, of Gerrit and Sara Van Schayck. Wit.: Kiliaen and Maria Van Renselaer.

Aug. 11. Jacob, of Dirk and Clara Takelsen. Wit.: Isack Quakkenbosch, Lena Ryckman.

Aug. 18. Anthoni, of Wynant and Catryna Van der Poel. Wit.: Meindert Schuyler, Catryna Bries.

Tobias, of Hendrik and Griettie Ten Eyck. Wit.: Ruth Bleeker, Jenneke Ten Eyck.

Bata, of Jacob and Geertruy Knoet. Wit.: Joannes and Bata Knoet.

Aug. 25. Elizabeth, of Joannes and Anna Wendel. Wit.: Abram Kip, Elizabeth Visscher.

Coenraet, of Willem and Lena Hoogtelink. Wit.: Coenraet and Tryntie Hoogtelink.

Sept. 4. Elizabeth, of Thomas and Hilletie Williaems. Wit.: Arent and Catryna Pruym.

Gerardus, of Gerrit and Eckbertie Van den Bergh. Wit.: Barent Staats, Antie Van der Poel.

Teuntie, of Wouter and Rachel Barhayt. Wit.: Daniel and Dirckie Wenne.

Sept. 15. Joachim, of Barent and Neeltie Staats. Wit.: Joannes and Elyzabeth Schuyler.

Sept. 22. Adam Wenne, of Nicolaes and Rachel Gardenier. Wit.: Pieter Van Woerdt, Sara Gardenier.

Sept. 29. Joannes, of Petrus and Eva Van Driessen. Wit.: Abram Cuyler, Joannes Van Driessen, Rachel Schuyler.

Oct. 6. Jochum, of Hendrik and Anna Valkenburgh. Wit.: Joannes and Emilia Pruym.

Maria, of Theunis and Rachel Harmensen. Wit.: Thomas Williaems, Grietie Van Vegten.

1717–1718

Agnietie, of Leendert and Jennietie Conyn. Wit.: Jacob Muller, Antie Conyn.

Oct. 13. David, of Caspar and Rachel Van Housen. Wit.: Theunis Eckbertsen, Neeltie Beekman.

Catryna, of Joannes and Geertie Groesbeek. Wit.: Joannes Knikkerbakker, Anna Fonda.

Anthoni, of Adriaen and Catryna Quakkenbosch. Wit.: Goozen and Catryna Van Schayk, Robbert Livingston.

Oct. 20. Cornelia, of Matheus and Jannetie Goes. Wit.: Harp. V. Deusen, Lena Van Deusen.

Oct. 27. Philiph, of Nicolaes and Elzie Schuyler. Wit.: Harmannus and Ariaantie Wendel.

Nov. 3. Catryna, of Andries and Maria Fuyck. Wit.: Jan and Catie Verwie.

Nov. 10. Elizabeth, of Abraham and Magdalena Lansingh. Wit.: Jacob Lansingh, Lena Van Tricht.

Elizabeth, of Epraim and Anna Wendel. Wit.: Robbert Wendel, Susanna Schuyler.

Nov. 17. Cornelia, of Joannes and Cornelia Becker. Wit.: Pieter and Cornelia Uzile.

Maria, of Jacob and Catalyna Bogaard. Wit.: Pieter Schuyler, Marretie Pruym.

Nov. 27. Kiljaen, of Hendrik and Catryna Van Renselaar. Wit.: Joannes and Catryna Ten Broeck.

Dec. 4. Maria, of Joannes and Geertruy Lansingh. Wit.: Pieter Schuyler, Gerretie Roseboom.

Dec. 8. Anna, of Jan and Catalyna Van Ness. Wit.: Stephanus and Elyzabeth Groesbeek.

Adam, of Maes and Anna Rycksen. Wit.: Jan Fonda, Catalyna Joeyts.

Phillippus, of Gerrit and Catalyna Van Ness. Wit.: Kilyaen and Maria Van Renselaar.

Dec. 11. Catalyna, of Cornelis and Henderikie Van Buuren. Wit.: Barent and Maria Bratt.

Dec. 29. Catryna, of Jacob and Maria Brouwer. Wit.: Cornelis and Dorothee Bogaard.

1718, Jan. 11. Wilhelmus, of Marten and Catryna Van Bergen. Wit.: Gerrit Van Bergen, Lidia Douw.

Anthony, of Joannes and Anna Bleeker. Wit.: Joannes Lanzingh, Rachel Bleeker.

Catryna, of Ariaen and Lammetie Oothout. Wit.: Cornelis and Dorothe Bogaart.

Elizabeth, of Pieter and Geertruy Van Buuren. Wit.: Maas and Madalena Van Buuren.

Jan. 28. Elsie, of Jacob and Anna Egmont. Wit.: Gerrit and Catryna Lansingh.

Harmen, of Levinus and Catryna Harmensen. Wit.: Gysbert V. den Berg, Catalyna V. Hoesen.

Feb. 2. Abraham, of Gerrit and Maria Spoor. Wit.: Joannes Spoor, Cornelia Gilbert.

1718

Feb. 6. Jannatie, of Pieter and Geertruy Vroman. Wit.: Jacob and Lidia Van Aalsteyn.

Feb. 16. Harmen, of Joannes and Elizabeth De Wandelaar. Wit.: Thomas Williaems, Catryna Gansevoort.

Catryna, of Joannes and Elizabeth Wendel. Wit.: Robbert and Catryna Walters.

Joannes, of Jurjaen and Maria Hoogen. Wit.: Joannes and Eva Beekman.

March 2. Johanna, of Joannes and Maria Vinhagel. Wit.: Folkert and Margariet Douw.

March 9. Hendrik, of Joannes and Catryna Ten Broeck. Wit.: Joannes and Elsie Cuyler, Samuel Ten Broek.

March 16. Jacob, of Anthoni and Anna C. Van Schayk. Wit.: Jacob Ten Broek, Maria Van Corlaar.

Apr. 6. Susanna, of Barent and Maria Ekbertsen. Wit.: Jacob and Susanna Visscher.

Apr. 11. Geurt, of Jacobus and Susanna Schoonhoven. Wit.: Dirk and Anna Bratt.

Wilhelmus, of Andries and Lidia Douw. Wit.: Kilyaen Van Renselaar, Petrus Douw.

Neeltie, of Gerrit and Elizabeth Lansingh. Wit.: Evert Banker, Gerritie Roseboom.

Apr. 13. Marten Gerritsen, of Gerrit and Anna Van Bergen. Wit.: Kilyaen and Maria Van Renselaar.

Cornelis, of Mathias and Catalyna Van den Bergh. Wit.: Ruth and Margarita Van Deusen.

Elizabeth, of Nicolaes and Maria Van der Werken. Wit.: David and Christyna Van Dyk.

Apr. 14. Rebecka, of Claes and Annetie Fonda. Wit.: Jan Fonda, Barber Marselis.

Apr. 20. Jannetie, of Jan Tyssen Goes and Eytie Goes. Wit.: Joannes and Hessie Beekman.

Apr. 27. Jacob, of Isack and Johanna Lansingh. Wit.: Joannes Beekman, Jr., Neeltie Ten Eyck.

May 4. Jacob, of Phillip and Madalena Lauxs. Wit.: Andries Bratt, Wyntie Roos.

Hendrik, of Jacob and Debora Beekman. Wit.: Hendrik and Debora Hansen.

May 11. Nicolaes, Catryna, of Claes and Dirckie Van Woerd. Wit.: Willem, Joannes, Geertruy, Geertie Groesbeek.

May 18. Margariet, of Joannes and Catryna V. der Wilge. Wit.: Storm Beckers, Elysabeth Van der Zee.

May 22. Maria, of Elderd and Lena Ouderkerk. Wit.: Isack and Mayke Ouderkerk.

June 2. Ysack, of Isack and Bata Van Deusen. Wit.: Melchert and Lena Van Deusen.

June 30. Elizabeth, of Balthus and Lidia Van Benthuysen. Wit.: Marten Van Benthuysen, Elizabeth Greveraat.

1718

Joannes, of Joannis and Lena Lansingh. Wit.: Pieter Schuyler, Joannes and Emilia Pruym.

Hillegon, of Andries and Wyntie Bratt. Wit.: Theunis Bratt, Geertruy Visscher.

Joannes, of Daniel and Johanna Flensburgh. Wit.: Daniel and Margariet Killy.

Joannes, of Jan and Chatarina Van Wie. Wit.: Ariaen De Gardenier, Susanna Bratt.

Willempie, of Anthoni and Rebekka Bratt. Wit.: Theunis and Willempie Bratt.

Joannes Appel, of Dirck and Maria Hagedoorn. Wit.: Joannes and Anna Appel.

Neeltie, of Theunis and Engel Egbertsen. Wit.: Jacob Schermerhoorn, Neeltie Beekman.

Elsie, of Abraham and Elsie Staats. Wit.: Barent and Neeltie Staats.

July 20. Cornelis, of Wynant and Aaltie Van den Bergh. Wit.: Pieter and Tryntie Walderom.

Alida, of Jacob and Maria Halenbeek. Wit.: Nanningh and Alida Visscher.

July 27. Joseph, of Joannes and Sara Van Zanten. Wit.: Joseph and Zetie Van Zanten.

Maria, of Jeremias and Elizabeth Muller. Wit.: Joannes and Elizabeth Muller.

Aug. 3. Cornelia, of Anthoni and Jannetie Bogardus. Wit.: Joannes Van Vegten, Susanna Bratt.

Marretie, of Jan and Catryna Du Foy. Wit.: Jacob and Jannetie Peersen.

Magdalena, of Petrus and Anna Douw. Wit.: Jonas Douw, Catryna Van Renselaar.

Teuntie, of Abram and Anna Van der Poel. Wit.: Gerrit Van den Berg, Maria Van Alen.

Aug. 10. Folkert, of Jan and Agnitie Witbeek. Wit.: Folkert Witbeek, Margarieta Douw.

Abraham, of Isack and Alida Fonda. Wit.: Salomon Van Vegten, Hessie Van Arnhem.

Aug. 24. Catalyna, of Laurens Scerp and Hilletie Scherp. Wit.: Gerrit Van Schayk, Catalyna Goewey.

Catryna, of Matheus and Maria Vlensburg. Wit.: Daniel Vlensburgh, Anneke Broecks.

Aug. 31. Joannes, of Hendrik and Elsie Schermerhoorn. Wit.: Jacob and Gerretie Schermerhoorn.

Rebecca, of Joannes and Elizabeth Oostrander. Wit.: Gerrit and Eckbertie Van den Bergh.

Sept. 7. Catryna, of Jacob and Lena Lansingh. Wit.: Isack and Magdalena Lansingh.

Sept. 14. Pieter, of Pieter and Rebekka Bogaard. Wit.: Samuel Pruym, Catalyna Bogaardt.

Sept. 21. Rebecka, of Jacob and Elizabeth Evertsen. Wit.: Ysack and Barentie Fonda.

1718
Sept. 28. Hendrik, of Cornelis and Dorothee Bogaard. Wit.: Hendrik Oothout, Maria Pruym.
Oct. 5. Ephrajm, of Stephanus and Maria Van Alen. Wit.: Pieter and Johanna Hogeboom.
William, of Obedie Cuoper and Cornelia Couper. Wit.: Cornelis and Jacomyn Maassen.
Anneke, of Christoffel and Catalyna Jets. Wit.: Pieter and Ariaentie Van Woerd.
Oct. 10. Ysack, of Abram and Jannetie Provoost. Wit.: Jacob Staats, Elizabeth Schuyler.
Rachel, of Barent, Jr., and Maria Bratt. Wit.: Pieter and Nelletie Ryckman.
Oct. 12. Anna, of Joannes and Catryna Zeller. Wit.: Willem and Geertruy Groesbeek.
Marretie, of Jacob Corn. and Anna Schermerhoorn. Wit.: Joannes Beekman, Marretie Schermerhoorn.
Oct. 19. Abraham, of Isack and Amerency Verplank. Wit.: David Verplank, Maria Daevids.
Jan, of Jona [?] and Maria Larway. Wit.: Joannes Beekman, Elizabeth Uzile.
Maria, of Gysbert and Catalyna Van den Berg. Wit.: Joannes Hun, Geertie Van den Berg.
Pieter, of Willem and Lena Hoogtelink. Wit.: Pieter and Cornelia Uzile.
Joannes, of Jacob and Helena Lansing. Wit.: Joannes and Elizabeth Oostrander.
Nov. 1. Geertruy, of Joannes and Margarieta Van der Werke. Wit.: Robbert and Margarieta Livingston.
Tanneke, of Daniel and Dirckie Wenne. Wit.: Isack and Maycke Ouderkerk.
Nov. 9. Joannes, of Anthony, Jr., and Anna Van Schayk. Wit.: Joannes and Elsie Cuyler.
Nov. 15. Sara, of Joannes and Neeltie Christyaensen. Wit.: Dirck Ten Broeck, Elizabeth Marselis.
Joannes, of Ysack and Catalyne Wendel. Wit.: Joannes and Elizabeth Schuyler.
Nov. 23. Philip, of Dirck and Grietie Van Vegten. Wit.: Philip Van Vegten, Maria Williaems.
Nov. 30. Anna, of Joannes and Zelia Redly. Wit.: Stoffel and Hubertie Jojets.
Dec. 6. Catryna, of Schibboleth and Anna Bogardus. Wit.: Joannes Garnoy, Cornelia Van der Heyde.
Dec. 17. Andries, of Coenraet and Gerretie Ten Eyk. Wit.: Hendrik and Grietie Ten Eyck.
Dec. 21. Eva, of Daniel and Gerretie Fort. Wit.: Abram and Antie Van der Poel.
Dec. 28. Neeltie, of Nicolaes and Rachel Gardenier. Wit.: Maas Van Franken, Rebekka Bloemendaal.
Sara, of Leendert and Catryna Gansevoort. Wit.: Joannes De Wandelaar, Sara Meyndertsen.

1719

1719, Jan. 1. Christyna, of Dirck and Margarita Ten Broek. Wit.: Hendrik Cuyler, Anna Catryna V. Schayk.

Anna, of Ruben and Geertruy Van Vegten. Wit.: Philip Van Vegten, Antie Schermerhoorn.

Cornelis, of Jacob, Jr., and Antie Schermerhoorn. Wit.: Ruben and Engeltie Van Vegten.

Breghie, of Gerrit and Tryntie Van den Berg. Wit.: Cornelis V. Aalsteyn, Dirckie Van der Werken.

Jan. 4. Anna, of Kiliaan and Maria Van Renselaar. Wit.: Samuel Bajart, Catryna Van Renselaar, Anna De Lance.

Jan. 18. Eva, of Abraham and Catalyna Valkenburgh. Wit.: Johannes and Eva Beekman.

Jan. 21. Abraham, of Cornelis and Marretie Van Aalsteyn. Wit.: Mathias and Catalyna V. den Berg.

Feb. 1. Joannes, of Joannes and Sara Becker. Wit.: Laurens Becker, Rebecca Van Arnhem.

Geessie, of Joannes E. and Anna Wendel. Wit.: Ephrajm Wendel, Geessie Kip.

Feb. 4. Joannes, of Jacob and Geertruy Roseboom. Wit.: Hendrik Roseboom, Isabella Staats.

Feb. 11. Nicolaas, of Evert and Marretie Rycksen. Wit.: Maas and Anna Rycksen.

Feb. 26. Styntie, of Jan and Grietie Goes. Wit.: Joannis and Hessie Beekman.

Martynus, of Samuel and Geertruy Cregier. Wit.: Harmen Visscher, Anna Criegier.

Philip, of David and Abigael Foreest. Wit.: Joannes Van Aalsteyn, Catryne Foreest.

March 8. Maria, of Frans and Margarieta Pruym. Wit.: Elbert and Anna Gerritsen.

Margarita, of Thomas and Barentie Berrit. Wit.: Joannes and Amilia Pruym.

Catryna, of Claes and Cornelia Bovy. Wit.: Ulrich V. Franken, Maria Brouwers.

Maria, of Jacob and Catelyna Bogard. Wit.: Pieter Schuyler, Marretie Pruym.

Apr. 5. Geertruy, of Jacob and Jannetie Peersen. Wit.: Roelef and Geertruy Gerritsen.

Joannes, of Joannes and Annetie Paree. Wit.: Claes Van Woerden, Maria Spoor.

Hendrik, of Philip and Catryna Livingston. Wit.: Pieter and Rachel Schuyler.

Ephraim, of Evert and Engeltie Wendel. Wit.: Joannes Bleeker, Elyzabeth Groesbeek.

Apr. 12. Jan, of Thomas and Hilletie Williams. Wit.: Jan Bronk, Catryna Gansevoort.

Ysack, of Hendrik and Susanna Halenbeek. Wit.: Joannes Muller, Lybetie Bratt, Jr.

1719

Neeltie, of Frerik and Sara Meyndertsen. Wit.: Joannes Van Vegten, Maria De Warant.

Apr. 19. Rachel, of Theunis and Rachel Harmensen. Wit.: Leendert Gansevoort, Elsie Wenne.

Wyntie, of Pieter and Antie Bronk. Wit.: Sciboleth and Jannetie Bogardus.

Arent, of Tewys and Engeltie Van Deusen. Wit.: Theunis Slingerlant, Maria Mingaal.

Maria, of Gerrit Dinghmans and Cornelia Dingmans. Wit.: Cornelis Maassen, Sara Van Alen.

May 3. Marten, of Abram and Marretie Van Aalsteyn. Wit.: Gerrit, Jr., and Catalyna Lansingh.

Jacob, of Albert and Dirckie Roelefsen. Wit.: Cornelis Bogaard, Geertruy V. den Berg.

Hendrik, of David and Christyna Van Dyk. Wit.: Cornelis and Maria Van Dyk.

May 7. Abraham, of Gosen and Catryna Van Schayk. Wit.: Jacob Roseboom, Maria Van Corlaar.

Ysack, of Joannes and Elysabeth Muller. Wit.: Ysack Fonda, Susanna Bratt.

May 17. Christyna, of Tobias and Marretie Ten Broek. Wit.: Dirck and Christyna Ten Broeck.

Christyna, of Jacobus and Maria Wyngaart. Wit.: David Schuyler, Elsie Cuyler.

May 24. Jannetie, of Cornelis and Griettie Schermerhoorn. Wit.: Joannes Schermerhoorn, Geertie Ten Eyk.

May 31. Arientie, of Joannes and Sanna Symensen. Wit.: Barent Sanders, Sara Luyckassen.

Maas, of Joannes Maassen and Rebecka Massen. Wit.: Cornelis Massen, Jacomyntie Maassen.

Catryna, of Jesse and Neeltie D. Foreest. Wit.: Sara Hansen, Gerrit Van Ness.

Maria, of Arent and Catryna Pruym. Wit.: Samuel Pruym, Anna Kitsenaar.

June 7. Cornelia, of Storm and Sophia Bratt. Wit.: Barent Bratt, Cornelia Uzile.

June 21. Jacob, of Lowys and Maria Viele. Wit.: Ysak and Mayke Ouderkerk.

June 28. Antie, of Hendrik and Hilletie Van Wie. Wit.: Wouter V. der Zee, Antie Beekers.

Catalyna, of Gerrit and Sara Van Schayk. Wit.: Arent V. Corlaar, Catalyna Goewey.

Joannes, of Joannes and Zantie Wendel. Wit.: Joannes and Hassie Beekman.

Jochum, of Joannes Valkenburgh and Margarita Valkenburg. Wit.: Barent and Maria Sanders.

July 19. Maria, of Lucas and Tanneke Van Vegten. Wit.: Jacob and Anna Egmond.

1719
July 26. Gerrit, of Gerrit, Jr., and Engeltie Lansingh. Wit.: Gerrit and Catryna Lansingh.

Aug. 22. Machtel, of Tobias and Helena Rykman. Wit.: Joannes and Eva Beekman.

Jannetie, of Marten and Cornelia Van Aalsteyn. Wit.: Gerrit Van den Bergh, Margariet Van Zanten.

Aug. 30. Rebecca, of Pieter and Tryntie Walderon. Wit.: Wynant Van der Poel, Catryna Gilbert.

David, of Wynant and Tryntie Van der Poel. Wit.: Harmanus Schuyler, Margarieta Van Zanten.

Cornelis, of Cornelis and Hessie Swits. Wit.: Jacob and Lena Visser.

Sept. 6. Jacob, of Joannes and Elizabeth Wendel. Wit.: Isack and Jacob Wendel, Merry Zanders.

Cornelis, of Jacob and Agnietie Muller. Wit.: Joannes Muller, Antie Konyn.

Sept. 13. Anna, of Casper and Rachel Van Hoesen. Wit.: Albert and Engeltie Slingerlant.

Sept. 20. Joannes, of Joannes and Catryna Ten Broek. Wit.: Tobias Ten Broek, Petrus and Anna Douw.

Sept. 27. Christyna, of Ruth and Elizabeth Van Woerdt. Wit.: Pieter and Ariaentie Van Woerdt.

Hendrykus, of Marten and Catryna Van Bergen. Wit.: Henricus Douw, Anna Van Bergen.

Oct. 4. Cornelis, of Claes and Antie Van den Bergh. Wit.: Pieter and Ariaentie Van Woerdt.

Oct. 9. Cornelis, of Mathias and Catalyna Van den Bergh. Wit.: Cornelis and Marretie Van Aalsteyn.

Oct. 11. Gerrit Hendriksen, of Jan and Catryna Burger. Wit.: Gysbert Van den Bergh, Alida Van Wie.

Cornelia, of Anthony and Jannatie Bogardus. Wit.: Joannes and Anna Van Vegten.

Oct. 18. Jacob, of Pieter and Dirckie Vosburgh. Wit.: Joannes Mingaal, Maretie Beekman.

Elizabeth, of Adriaan and Catryna Quakkenbosch. Wit.: Gozen, Jr., and Margarieta Van Schayk.

Oct. 25. Alida, of Joannes and Catalyna Barhayt. Wit.: Cornelis Maassen, Anna Warms.

Catryna, of Mathias and Maretie Boffy. Wit.: Hendrik Cuyler, Neeltie Beekman.

Margarieta, of Pieter and Maretie Wenne. Wit.: Jesse De Foreest, Sara Hansen.

Eva, of Joachim and Elsie Van Valkenburg. Wit.: Joannes Mingaal, Jannetie Valkenburgh.

Joannes, of Claes and Geertruy Van Franken. Wit.: Joannes and Elizabeth Schuyler.

Nov. 1. Elizabeth, of Gerrit and Anna Nieukerke. Wit.: Joannes and Elizabeth Visser.

Nov. 8. Maria, of Jacob and Anna Egmond. Wit.: Claes Egmond, Judith Hooghtelink.

1719–1720

Nov. 15. Jannetie, of Joannes, Jr., and Hester Beekman. Wit.: Jacob Beekman, Jannetie Lansingh.

Joannes, of Jacob and Geertruy Knoet. Wit.: Dirk Ten Broek, Neeltie Beekman.

Elsie, of Anthoni and Anna Van Schayk. Wit.: Joannes and Elsie Cuyler.

Anna, of Petrus and Eva Van Driessen. Wit.: Pieter Van Brugh, Hendrik and Elsie Cuyler, Maria Cruger.

Nov. 22. Neeltie, of Anthoni and Catryna Abrams. Wit.: Joannes and Neeltie Ouderkerk.

Neeltie, of Hendrik and Margarita Gardenier. Wit.: Claes and Rachel Gardenier.

Nov. 29. Pieter, of Nicolaes and Maria Groesbeek. Wit.: Joannes and Antie Knikkerbakker.

Wouter, of Wouter and Jannetie Van der Zee. Wit.: Theunis Van Slingerlant, Jannetie Beekman.

Dec. 26. Geertruy, of Gerrit and Elizabeth Lansingh. Wit.: Joannes Lansingh, Jannetie Bankers.

Dec. 27. Joannes, of Joannes and Cornelia Becker. Wit.: Gerrit and Maryke Becker.

Melchert, of Harpert and Lena Van Deusen. Wit.: Philliph and Engeltie V. Vegten.

1720, Jan. 7. Christyaen, of Corset and Neeltie Vedder. Wit.: Nicolaes Bleeker, Catie Cuyler.

Jan. 14. Geertruy, of Marten and Maria Van Buuren. Wit.: Maas Van Buuren, Geertruy Van den Bergh.

Jan. 27. Jacob, of Samuel Dokzy and Elizabeth Dockzy. Wit.: Jan Maassen, Anna Ridders.

Feb. 3. Abraham, of Joannes and Sara Becker. Wit.: Abraham and Hester Van Arnhem.

Anthoni, of Dirck and Cornelia Bratt. Wit.: Theunis and Willempie Bratt.

Feb. 7. Dirk Bratt, of Jacobus and Susanna Van Schoonhoven. Wit.: Dirk and Anna Bratt, Pieter Bennewa.

Feb. 21. Cornelis, of Wilhelmus and Geertie Van den Bergh. Wit.: Pieter and Tryntie Walderom.

March 6. Jannetie, of Thomas and Maria Van Aalsteyn. Wit.: Willem Van Alen, Jannetie Van Valkenburgh.

March 9. Jochum, of Jacob and Styntie Van Valkenburgh. Wit.: Isack and Lena Lansingh.

Joseph, of Joseph and Hendrikie Jets. Wit.: Lucas Hooghkerk, Huybertie Jets.

March 13. Susanna, of Theunis and Engeltie Eckbertsen. Wit.: Jacob and Susanna Visser.

Nelletie, of Jacob and Maria Brouwer. Wit.: Joannes and Eckbertie De Garmoy.

March 20. Teuntie, of Barent and Neeltie Staats. Wit.: Isack Staats, Margarita Schuyler.

1720

March 27. Folkert, of Pieter and Anna Douw. Wit.: Hendrik Van Renselaar, Catryna Ten Broek.

Apr. 3. Anna, of Jurryaan and Maria Hoogen. Wit.: Daniel and Maria Hoogen.

Jacob, of Isack and Maycke Ouderkerk. Wit.: Joannes and Catalyntie Hun.

Margarita, of Andries and Wyntie Bratt. Wit.: Wynant and Catryna Van der Poel.

Joannes, of Jephta [Cornelisse *] and Maria Christ'na [Martensen *]. Wit.: Jacob Roseboom, Margar'ta Schuylers.

Apr. 10. Catalyna, of Jan and Catalyna Van Ness. Wit.: Nicolaes and Maria Groesbeek.

Joannes, of Eldert and Lena Ouderkerk. Wit.: Jesse Foreest, Anna Van den Bergh.

Joannes, of Phillip and Anna Witbeek. Wit.: Thomas and Hilletie Williaems.

Isack, of Pieter and Margarieta Van Aalsteyn. Wit.: Jochum Van Aalsteyn, Engeltie Valkenburgh.

Apr. 24. Abraham, of Jacob and Helena Lansingh. Wit.: Samuel and Maria Pruym.

Arent, of Theuis and Elizabeth Slingerlant. Wit.: Albert Slingerlant, Anna Appels.

May 7. Phillip, of David and Abigael Foreest. Wit.: Jacob Van Aalsteyn, Catryna Foreest.

Pieter, of Joannes and Eckbertie De Garmoy. Wit.: Pieter Garmoy, Anna Bogardus.

Hendrik, of Hendrik and Margarita Ten Eyck. Wit.: Abraham Cuyler, Antie Bleekers.

May 8. Catharina, of Ephraim and Anna Wendel. Wit.: Joannes Wendel, Maria Van Ness.

Alida, of Joannes and Chatharina Van der Wilge. Wit.: Joannes and Antie Appel.

Pieter, of Pieter and Alida Ouderkerk. Wit.: David Schuyler, Jentie Livingston.

May 15. Anneke, of Nicolaes and Rachel Gardenier. Wit.: Jacob and Hyltie Van Woert.

Philliph, of Leendert and Immetie Conyn. Wit.: Leendert Gansevoort, Agnietie Mullers.

Marretie, of Isack and Bata Van Deusen. Wit.: Abram and Marretie Van Aalsteyn.

Anna, of Gerrit and Anna Van Bergen. Wit.: Nicolaes Mejer, Elsie Schoonmaker.

Margarita, of Wouter and Rachel Barhayt. Wit.: Barent and Mattie Sanders.

May 22. Lena, of Benjamin and Antie Eckbertsen. Wit.: Barent Eckbertsen, Lena Visser.

* These patronymics had been added in lead pencil probably a century or more after the entries were originally made.

1720

June 12. Barent, of Jan Tyssen Goes and Eytie Goes. Wit.: Gozen and Catie Van Schayk.

June 19. Jacob, of Bartholomeus and Catharina V. Valkenburg. Wit.: Joannes and Sara Hansen.

Effie, of Jacob and Debora Beekman. Wit.: Joannes Becker, Jr., Maria Hansen.

Dirck, of Jacob and Hester Van der Heyde. Wit.: Dirk and Anna Van der Heyde.

Agnietie, of Theunis and Jannetie Van Slyck. Wit.: Isack and Alida Fonda.

June 26. Pieter Meessen, of Pieter and Geertie Vroman. Wit.: Cornelis Van Aalsteyn, Marretie Van den Bergh.

July 3. Jacobus, of Cornelis and Margarita Schermerhoorn. Wit.: Cornelis Schermerhoorn, Hester Beekman.

Jannetie, of Jochum and Elsie Van Valkenburg. Wit.: Lamberd Redly, Eva Beekman.

Meyndert, of Ruthger and Chathalyna Bleekers. Wit.: Meyndert Schuyler, Margarita Ten Eyk.

Rebecka, of Meindert and Fytie Marselis. Wit.: Claes and Antie Fonda.

July 10. Chatharina, of Ruben and Geertruy Van Vegten. Wit.: Lucas and Chatharina Witbeek.

July 15. Huybert, of Joannes and Elizabeth Van Oostrant. Wit.: Isack and Alida Fonda.

Pieter, of Willem and Elizabeth Walderom. Wit.: Pieter and Tryntie Walderom.

Cornelis, of Levinus and Chatharina Harmensen. Wit.: Wilhelmus Van den Berg, Marretie Gerritsen.

Isack, of Abraham and Geertie Vosburg. Wit.: Gerrit Van den Berg, Neeltie Abeel.

Aug. 20. Jacobus, of Joannes and Maria Vinhagel. Wit.: Meindert and Maria Roseboom.

Catharina, of Joannes and Christina Van Deusen. Wit.: Melchert and Chatharina Van der Poel.

Aug. 28. Anna, of Pieter and Lena Vosburgh. Wit.: David and Christina Van Dyck.

Sept. 4. Johannes, of Samuel and Maria Ten Broek. Wit.: Johannes and Christina Ten Broek.

Levinus, of Anthoni and Chatharina Van Schayk. Wit.: Anthoni Coster, Margarita Ten Broek.

Cornelia, of Laurens and Hilletie Scherp. Wit.: Jacob Goewey, Alida Fonda.

Joseph, of Johannes and Sara Van Santen. Wit.: Joseph and Setie Jansen.

Sept. 11. Nanningh, of Jacob and Maria Halenbeek. Wit.: Johannes Visser, Hester Van der Heyde.

Cornelis, of Claes and Antie Van den Bergh. Wit.: Cornelis Claessen, Susanna Van den Bergh.

1720

Marten, of Jacob C. and Anna Schermerhoorn. Wit.: Theunis Eckbertsen, Neeltie Beekman.

Sara, of Gerrit and Chathalyna Van Ness. Wit.: Hendrik De Ridder, Neeltie Foreest.

Sep. 18. Hans Hendrik, of Dirk and Maria Hagedoorn. Wit.: Hans Hendrik Matyssen, Neeltie Beekman.

Benjamin, of Dirck and Grietie Van Vegten. Wit.: Benjamin and Engeltie Van de Waater.

Gerrit, of Daniel and Gerretie Fort. Wit.: Gerrit Van den Bergh, Ariaentie Van Ness.

Sept. 25. Gysbert, of Claes and Anna Fonda. Wit.: Gysbert and Elizabeth Marselis.

Oct. 2. Marytie, of Thomas and Elizabeth Ecker. Wit.: Johannes Appel, Marytie Mingaal.

Anna Maria, of Philliph and Madelena Laucks. Wit.: Casper Ham, Anna Leybin.

Eytie, of Andries and Josyna Gardenier. Wit.: Nicolaes and Rachel Gardenier.

Schibboleth, of Scibboleth and Anna Bogardus. Wit.: Ephraim Bogardus, Maria Eckberts.

Oct. 9. Obedie, of Obedie and Cornelia Couper. Wit.: Jan and Rebecca Maassen.

Oct. 14. Philliph, of Jesse and Neeltie Foreest. Wit.: Johannes and Chatharina Foreest.

Joseph, of Matheus and Maria Flensburg. Wit.: Joseph, Jr., and Hendrickie Jets.

Oct. 30. Hendrik, of Joannes and Margariet Van de Werke. Wit.: David and Christyna Van Dyk.

Hendrik, of Dirk and Madalena Van der Karre. Wit.: Anthoni and Catharina Van Schayk.

Abigael, of Isack and Amarency Verplank. Wit.: Jacobus, Cornelis and Catalyna Verplank.

Nov. 6. Williaem, of Edmond and Antie Groen. Wit.: William Baalden, William Poel, Elyzabeth Corlaar.

Nov. 13. Abraham, of Jacob and Lena Lansing. Wit.: Meindert and Lena Lansing.

Nov. 20. Daniel, of Pieter and Rachel Wenne. Wit.: Daniel and Dirckie Wenne.

Andries, of Jan and Catharina Van Wie. Wit.: Johannes and Catalyna Hun.

Nov. 22. Geessie, of Hendrik and Elsie Schermerhoorn. Wit.: Joannes Beekman, Geertie Ten Eyck.

Joannes, of Jacob and Jannetie Peersen. Wit.: Harmanus and Antie Wendel.

Folkie, of Wynant and Folkie Van den Berg. Wit.: Gysbert and Catalyna Van den Berg.

Dec. 11. Ysack, of Jan and Catrina De Fou. Wit.: Isack and Alida Fonda.

Joannes, of Joannes and Geertie Groesbeek. Wit.: David and Elizabeth Groesbeek.

1720–1721

Dec. 23. Joseph, of Johannes and Zelia Redly. Wit.: Joseph and Huybertie Jets.

Dec. 25. Jacob, of Hendrik and Margarita Gardenier. Wit.: Andries and Sara Gardenier.

Hendrik, of Robbert and Catharina Wieler. Wit.: Claes and Rachel Gardenier.

Tryntie, of Willem and Lena Hoogtelink. Wit.: Mathias and Maria Hoogtelink.

Gerretie, of Abraham and Catalyna Valkenburg. Wit.: Jacob Schermerhoorn, Geertie Ten Eyk.

Dec. 26. Jannetie, of Stephanus and Maria Van Alen. Wit.: Stephanus and Ariaentie Muller.

1721, Jan. 1. Catharina, of Hendrik and Maria Van der Werken. Wit.: Jacob Beekman, Elizabeth Groesbeek.

Jan. 8. Petrus, of Leendert and Hendrikkie Conyn. Wit.: Willem Kool, Maria Wenne.

Elizabeth, of Tobias and Marretie Ten Broek. Wit.: Folkert and Lidia Van Vegten.

Jan. 11. Magdalena, of Frans and Margariet Pruym. Wit.: Casparus Van Yveren, Alida Gerritsen.

Ryckert, of Claes and Cornelia Bovy. Wit.: Ryckert and Bethsie Hilten.

Susanna, of Joannes and Anna Wendel. Wit.: Isack and Susanna Kip.

Jan. 15. Ephraim, of Johannes and Catharina Ten Broek. Wit.: Antoni and Elizabeth Costers.

Jacobus, of Phillip and Geertruy Verplank. Wit.: John Collins, Gleyn Verplank, Maria Van Renselaar.

Jan. 18. Jannetie, of Willem and Feytie Iselsteyn. Wit.: Johannes and Maria Van Vegten.

Feb. 1. Isack, of Cornelis and Marritie Van Aalsteyn. Wit.: Gerrit and Cathrina Van den Bergh.

Feb. 5. Elizabeth, of Hendrik and Susanna Halenbeek. Wit.: Dirk and Elizabeth Bratt.

Feb. 12. Catharina, of Christyaen and Catharina Schans. Wit.: Barent Bratt, Maria Huyser.

Alida, of David and Anna Schuyler. Wit.: Meindert and Alida Schuyler.

Elizabeth, of Ahasuerus and Anna Wendel. Wit.: Ephraim Wendel, Susanna Schuylers.

Maria, of Anthoni, Jr., and Anna Van Schajk. Wit.: Anthony and Maria Van Schayk.

Elizabeth, of Johannes and Elizabeth Wendel. Wit.: Phillip and Margariet Schuylers.

Feb. 15. Anna Margarieta, of Coenraat and Gerretie Ten Eyck. Wit.: Gozen Van Schayk, Jenneke Ten Eyck.

Feb. 26. Rachel, of Gerrit and Echbertie Van den Bergh. Wit.: Jacob and Susanna Visser.

1721

March 1. Johannes, of Johannes and Rebecca Maassen. Wit.: Johannes and Maria Fonda.

Albert, of Albert and Dirckie Roelefsen. Wit.: Samuel and Maria Pruym.

Ariaentie, of Anthoni and Rebecka Bratt. Wit.: Dirck Bratt, Cornelia Van der Heyde.

Catharina, of David and Christina Van Dyck. Wit.: Wessel and Chatharina Ten Broek.

Harmannus, of Gerrit and Catrina Van den Berg. Wit.: Marten and Cornelia Van Aalsteyn.

Apr. 7. Johannes, of Leendert and Catharina Gansevoort. Wit.: Pieter Wenne, Anna Kitsenaar.

Apr. 9. Reyer, of Jacob, Jr., and Antie Schermerhoorn. Wit.: Jacob and Elizabeth Schermerhoorn.

Frederyk, of Abraham and Anna Fort. Wit.: Walrave Knoet, Emilia Pruym.

Apr. 10. Petrus, of Ephraim [?] and Agnietie Bogardus. Wit.: Schibboleth Bogardus, Maria Van Vegten.

Rebecka, of Pieter and Rebecka Bogard. Wit.: Jan and Marretie Fonda.

Apr. 16. Pieter, of Thomas and Hilletie Williaems. Wit.: Jan Witbeek, Anna Wenne.

Apr. 23. Anna, of Daniel and Johanna Flensburg. Wit.: Joseph and Huibertie Jets.

Maria, of Dirk and Margarita Ten Broeck. Wit.: Jacob Ten Broek, Maria Cuyler.

Cornelis, of Wilhelmus and Geertie [or Geessie] V. d. Berg. Wit.: Pieter and Tryntie Walderom.

May 7. Jannetie, of Reyk and Geertruy Van Franken. Wit.: Joh. Van O. Linde, Jennetie Criegier.

Sarah, of Phillip and Chatharina Livingston. Wit.: John Collins, Chatharina Van Rensselaer.

May 14. Maria, of Isack and Cathalina Wendel. Wit.: Cornelis and Maria Van Dyck.

Abraham, of Jacob and Geertruy Quakkenbosch. Wit.: Isack Quakkenbosch, Anna Wyngaard.

Adriaen, of Pieter and Christina Bratt. Wit.: Albert and Hester Slingerlant.

May 18. Johannes, of Matheus and Jannetie Goes. Wit.: Joh. Beekman, Jr., Lybetie Wenne.

May 28. Hendrik, of Jacob and Geertruy Rooseboom. Wit.: Joh. Lydius, Elisabeth Rooseboom.

Antoni, of Gozen and Neeltie Van Schayk. Wit.: Antoni Van Schayk, Catalyna Bleeker.

June 4. Maria, of Isack and Alida Fonda. Wit.: Joh. and Elizabeth V. Oostrande.

Maria, of Jonas and Maria Larway. Wit.: Piete Uzile, Geertruy Visser.

June 11. Jannetie, of Jeremias and Elizabeth Muller. Wit.: Jan and Maria Fonda.

1721

Gerrit, of Abraham and Anna V. D. Poel. Wit.: Cornelis and Theuntie V. D. Bergh.

June 18. Nicolaes, of Jan and Antie Parys. Wit.: Math Flensburg, Barentie Barrit.

Rachel, of Wilhelmus Rykman and Anna Van der Heyde. Wit.: Dirk and Rachel Van der Heyde.

Catharina, of Gysbert and Catalyna V. D. Berg. Wit.: Wilhelm and Geertie V. D. Berg.

July 2. Lidia, of Antoni and Chatharina Abrahams. Wit.: Barent Staats, Lydia Douw.

Maria, of Cornelis Van Buuren, Hendrikkie Van Ness. Wit.: Benjamin Bratt, Madalena Rykman.

July 7. Johannes, of Salomon and Alida Goewey. Wit.: Pieter Schuyler, Maria Van Rensselaar.

July 9. Phillip, of Jacob and Agnitie Muller. Wit.: Cornelis Muller, Jannetie Meessen.

July 16. Maria, of Balth and Lidia V. Benthuysen. Wit.: Augustinus Turck, Maria Rooseboom.

Pieter, of Tobias and Anna V. Buuren. Wit.: Lucas and Anna Wyngaart.

Jacob, of Joh. and Elyzabeth Muller. Wit.: Jacob and Anna Van Woerdt.

Catalyna, of Jacob of Catah. Bogardt. Wit.: Meyndert Schuyler, Anna Peyster.

July 30. Jannetie, of Hieroon and Margariet Van Vlieren. Wit.: Robbert and Margarieta Livingston.

Anna, of Abraham and Methy Ouderkerk. Wit.: Joh. Ten Broek, Maria Van Ness.

Aug. 6. Pieter, of Joh., Jr., and Geertruy Lansingh. Wit.: Philip and Margarita Schuyler.

Fytie, of Stoffel and Rachel Muller. Wit.: Joh. and Elizabeth Muller.

Aug. 13. Dirkie, of Samuel and Geertrui Criegier. Wit.: Barent Bratt, Dirckie Visser.

Neeltie, of Willem and Elizabeth Walderom. Wit.: Teunis Eckbertsen, Neeltie Beekman.

Cornelia, of Joh. and Sara Becker. Wit.: Abram and Alida V. Arnhem.

Sept. 17. David, of Wynant and Catrina V. D. Poel. Wit.: Harmannus and Catharina Schuyler.

Oct. 1. Margarita, of Simon and Maria Van Antwerpen. Wit.: Robbt. and Margarita Livingston.

Jannetie, of Claes and Dirkie Van Woerdt. Wit.: Theunis Eckberts, Susanna Visser.

Cornelia, of Marten Van Buuren and Maria V. D. Bergh. Wit.: Isack and Madalena Bogaardt.

Oct. 8. Harmen, of Joh. and Elizabeth Vissers. Wit.: Tierk Visser, Maria Wendels.

Oct. 22. Lena, of Theunis and Engeltie Ekbertsen. Wit.: Willem Walderom, Susanna Basset.

1721–1722

Oct. 29. Maria, of Daniel and Dirckie Wenne. Wit.: Ephraim and Anna Wendel.

Nov. 5. Elizabeth, of Jems and Margariet Bort. Wit.: John Makinthos, Grees Garrits.

Arientie, of Hendrik and Hilletie Van Wie. Wit.: Hendrik Van Buuren, Mally Hoogen.

Nov. 20. Maria, of Gysbert and Catharina Rooseboom. Wit.: Gerrit and Maria Rooseboom.

Nov. 23. Merry, of Gzysyn and Merry Weydt. Wit.: John and Zara Walters.

Nov. 25. Elsie, of Thomas and Maria Barth. Wit.: Joseph and Hendrickie Jojets.

Nanningh, of Jacob and Hester V. D. Heyde. Wit.: Math. V. D. Heyde, Geertruy Visser.

Nov. 30. Lucas, of Jacobus and Maria Wyngaart. Wit.: Gysbert and Catalyna V. D. Bergh.

Dec. 10. Willem, of Thomas and Maria Van Aalsteyn. Wit.: Johannes and Marretie Van Alen.

Dec. 17. Tryntie, of Dirk and Cornelia Bratt. Wit.: Pieter and Tryntie Walderom.

Wyntie, of Mathias and Catalyna V. D. Bergh. Wit.: Gerrit and Engeltie Lansingh.

Phillip, of Joh. and Cath. V. D. Wilge. Wit.: Wouter and Hilletie V. D. Zee.

Ariaentie, of Mart and Eytie Vosburgh. Wit.: David Van Dyk, Marytie Van Buuren.

Johannes, Jacob, of Abrah. and Alida V. Arnhem. Wit.: Jacob Lansingh, Joh. Becker, Lena Lansing, Hester V. Arnhem.

Cornelis, of Pieter and Geertruy V. Buuren. Wit.: Hendr. and Marritie V. Buuren.

Dec. 31. Marretie, of Roelef and Engel Kidny. Wit.: Wynant and Catharina V. D. Poel.

Pieter, of Joh. and Cornelia Becker. Wit.: Pieter Uzile, Maria Larway.

Johannes, of Lucas and Tanna V. Vegten. Wit.: Leendert and Geertruy V. Vegten.

1722, Jan. 7. Samuel, of Akes and Margarita Bratt. Wit.: Jacobus Van Slyk, Margarita Bratt.

Hartman, of Abram and Cath. V. Deusen. Wit.: Harpert and Lena V. Deusen.

Margariet, of Williaem and Rachel Naarten. Wit.: Math and Geertie V. D. Bergh.

Elizabeth, of Nicolaas and Catharina Kithel. Wit.: Christ and Cath. Schayns.

Jan. 24. Meyndert, of Abraham and Madalena Lansingh. Wit.: Meyndt Lansingh, Ariaentie V. D. Poel.

Pieter, of Math and Rebecka Garmoy. Wit.: Joh. Garmoy, Anna Bogardus.

1722
Christina, Lidia, of Arent and Catharina Pruym. Wit.
Hendr. and Emilia Pruym, Leend. and Mar. Ganse-
voort.

Margarita, of Daniel and Debora Kithel. Wit.: Jacob
V. D. Heyden, Susanna Bratt.

Jan. 28. Maria, of Benjamin and Madalene Bratt. Wit.:
Albert Ryckman, Willempie Bratt.

Isack, of Jacob and Lena Lansing. Wit.: Casparus and
Alida Van Iveren.

Huibert, of Joannes and Elizabeth Oostrander. Wit.:
Pieter V. D. Lyn, Antie V. D. Poel.

Feb. 28. Albert, of Andries and Wyntie Brat. Wit.:
Hendr. Douw, Tryntie Bries.

William, of John and Sara Bromly. Wit.: Jeremias
Pamerton, Anna Heyne.

Jacob, of Jacob and Anna Egmond. Wit.: Joh. Lansingh, Jacomyna Van Dyk.

March 4. John, of Jems and Anna Wilson. Wit.:
Gryphyn Wyet, Charles and Rachel Bockly.

March 11. Johannes, of Marten and Geertruy Beekman.
Wit.: Jacob Visser, Eva Beekman.

Cornelia, of Wynant and Anna V. D. Berg. Wit.: Gerrit V. D. Bergh, Marretie Van Aals—.

William, of Isack and Elizabeth Tryer. Wit.: Andries
Douw, Sara Walters.

Jannetie, of David and Abigael Foreest. Wit.: Abraham Foreest, Lidia Van Aalst.

March 18. Sara, of Meindert and Ariaentie Van Iveren.
Wit.: Reinier and Sara Van Iveren.

Christina, of Joh. and Cath. Ten Broek. Wit.: Folkert
V. Vegten, Elizabeth V. Rensselaar.

Adriaen, of Storm and Sophia Bratt. Wit.: Pieter
Uzile, Jr., Engeltie Slingerlant.

Ruthgert, of Gerrit and Engeltie Lansingh. Wit.: Ruthgert and Margarita V. Deusen.

Apr. 1. Abraham, of Frederyk and Sara Meyndertsen.
Wit.: Petrus and Eva Van Driessen.

Susanna, of Eldert and Lena Ouderkerk. Wit. Ephraim
and Anna Wendel.

Apr. 8. Johannes, of Christ. and Margarita Abeel. Wit.:
Ruth Bleeker, Catharina Bries.

Martha, of Jurriaen and Maria Hoogen. Wit.: Joh.
Beekman, Jannetie Lansingh.

Goozen, of Mart. and Corn. V. Aalsteyn. Wit.: Wilh.
and Geertie V. D. Bergh.

Apr. 15. Hendrik, of Petrus and Anna Douw. Wit.:
Hendr. Douw, Elizabeth V. Rensselaar.

Heyltie, of Steph. and Maria Muller. Wit.: Cornelis
and Agnietie Muller.

1722

Teuntie, of Jacob and Styntie V. Valk. Wit.: Pieter and Anna Wenne.

Apr. 22. Johannes, of Andries and Lidia Douw. Wit.: Jan Witbeek, Margarita Douwe.

Luycas, of Joseph and Hendrikie Jets. Wit.: Claes and Antie Van den Bergh.

Apr. 29. Petrus, of Jacob and Maria Brouwer. Wit.: Isack Fonda, Maria Hilten.

Chatharina, of Joan and Catalina Oothout. Wit.: Hendr. Oothout, Elizabeth Van Deusen.

Maria, of Christoffel and Chathalina Joets. Wit.: Abraham Joets, Zara Bosch.

Benjamin, of Pieter and Maria Wenne. Wit.: John and Sara Waaters.

May 3. Maria, of Joh. and Christina V. Deusen. Wit.: Pieter and Lydia Van Dyk.

Gerrit, of Math. and Maria Bovy. Wit.: Joh. V. O. Linde, Geertruy V. Franken.

May 6. Pieter, of Jan and Agnietie Witbeek. Wit.: Lucas Witbeek, Hilletie Williaems.

Michiel, of Jochum and Christ. Calliers. Wit.: Abraham and Geertie Vosburg.

Maycke, of Joh. and Jann. Ouderkerk. Wit.: Daniel and Dirkie Wenne.

May 13. Dirck, of Burger and Mayke Huyck. Wit.: Lambert and Rachel Redly.

Agnietie, of Theunis and Rachel Harmensen. Wit.: Gerrit V. D. Bergh, Math. Williams.

Wilhelmus, of Gerrit and Anna Van Bergen. Wit.: Marten Van Bergen, Lidia Douw.

May 19. Adriaan, of Joh. and Elyzabeth De Wandelaar. Wit.: Arent Pruym, Anna Kitsenaar.

May 27. Marytie, of Joh. and Marg. Valkenburgh. Wit.: Ysack and Alida Fonda.

June 3. Gerrit, of Barent and Neeltie Staats. Wit.: Ritsert and Anna Staats.

June 10. Laurens, of Leendert and Immetie Conyn. Wit.: Ruben V. Vegten, Lybetie Wenne.

Nicolaes, of Nicolaas and Merry Saxburry. Wit.: Isack and Jannetie Lansingh.

Evert, of Anthony and Jannetie Bogardus. Wit.: Joh. Schoonmaker, Wyntie V. Vegten.

June 17. Neeltie, of Hendr. and Marg. Gardenier. Wit.: Andr., Jr., and Josyna Gardenier.

Maria, of Co. and Maria V. Dyk. Wit.: David and Maria V. Dyk.

Margarita, of Daniel and Gerritie Fort. Wit.: Hendr. Ten Eyck, Anna Staats.

July 1. Cornelia, of Schibboleth and Anna Bogardus. Wit.: Math. De Garmoy, Agnietie Bogardus.

1722

July 22. Maria, of Epraim and Anna Wendel. Wit.: Abr. Wendel, Maria V. Renss, Jr.

July 29. Elsie, of Joh., Jr., and Hester Beekman. Wit.: Evert Wendel, Elsie Schuylers.

Aug. 12. Cornelis, of Ruben and Geertr. V. Vegten. Wit.: Joh. Witbeek, Engeltie V. Vegten.

Bastyaen, of Joh. and Eck. De Garmoy. Wit.: Bast. and Dirckie Vissers.

Maria, of Jak. and Susanna V. Schoonhoven. Wit.: Isack Bratt, Eckbert V. D. Heyden.

Jacobus, of Thom. and Maria Scherph. Wit.: Leendt Gansevoort, Eliz. De Warran.

Petrus, of Jacob and Geertruy Knoet. Wit.: Joh. and Eliz. Schuyler.

Aug. 26. Thomas, of Thomas and Mary Davids. Wit.: Joh. and Sara Hansen.

Sept. 2. Maria, of Carel and Aaltie Barreway. Wit.: Hendr. V. D. Werke, Maria Corlaar.

Jochum, of Pieter and Grietie V. Aalsteyn. Wit.: Joch. and Jany Valkenburg.

Isack, of Harm. and Dorothe V. Aalsteyn. Wit.: Jan and Dirkie V. Aalsteyn.

Goozen, of Anth. V. Schajk and Anna C. Ten Broek. Wit.: David V. Dyck, Ryckie V. Schayk.

Barent, of Hendr. and Marg. Ten Eyk. Wit.: Nicol. Bleeker, Gerr. Ten Eyck.

Sept. 16. Maria, of Petrus and Eva Van Driessen. Wit.: John Cruger, Meyndert Schuyler, Maria Van Driessen, Catie Cuylers.

Rachel, of Jan and Catalyna Van Nes. Wit.: Meyndert and Rachel Schuyler.

Catalyna, of Gerrit and Catalyna Van Nes. Wit.: Abraham and Geessie Kip.

Chatharina, of Ephraim and Agnietie Bogardus. Wit.: Joh. Garmoy, Corn. V. D. Heyde.

Sept. 23. Cornelis, of Jacob and Anna Schermerhoorn. Wit.: Corn. and Elyzabeth Schermerhoorn.

Tryntie, of Isack and Batha Van Deusen. Wit.: Isack Yselsteyn, Engeltie Van Ness.

Tryntie, of Willem and Elyzabeth Walderom. Wit.: Pieter and Tryntie Walderom.

Cornelia, of Willem and Lena Hooghtelink. Wit.: Pieter Uzile, Maria Larway.

Oct. 7. Elyzabeth, of Jacob and Jann. Peers. Wit.: Carel and Aaltie Barway.

Elyzabeth, of Sam. and Elsie Bibbingthon. Wit.: Joh. Pruym, Helena Lansingh.

Mathias, of Pieter and Lena Vosburg. Wit.: Sander Van Aalsteyn, Christ. Goes.

1722
Ritsert, of Benjamin and Elizabeth Woud. Wit.:
Luuk Hackings, Sara Boel.

Oct. 14. Chatharina, of Marten and Elbertie Van
Deusen. Wit.: Laurens and Ariaentie V. D. Poel.

Oct. 21. Antie, of Walderom and Anna Knoet. Wit.:
Cornelis and Chatharina Ridder.

Gerrittie, of Pieter and Charloth Kojemans. Wit.:
Bern. Freeman, Gerr. Drajers.

Sara, of Obedie and Cornelia Couper. Wit.: Isack and
Alida Fonda.

Anna, of Anth. and Anna V. Schayk. Wit.: Cornelis
and Christ. Cuyler.

Nov. 4. Wouter, of Theunis and Eliz. Slingerlant.
Wit.: Wouter and Jann. Van D. Zee.

Maria, of Wyn. and Chath. V. D. Poel. Wit.: Harm.
and Chath. Schuyler.

Johannes, of Jacob and Debora Beekman. Wit.: Joh.
Hansen, Jann. Lansingh.

Nov. 11. Jacob, of Joh. and Marg. V. D. Werke. Wit.:
Joh. Beekman.

Maas, of Maas and Anna Rycksen. Wit.: Dirk and
Marg. Ten Broek.

Nov. 18. Ysack, of Joh. and Marr. Vosburgh. Wit.:
Mart. and Marr. V. Buuren.

Nov. 25. Anna, of Joh. and Sara V. Santen. Wit.:
Ryckert and Maria Hilten.

Dec. 2. Patrick, of Charles and Mary Connstable. Wit.:
John Bromley, Elizabeth Stevens.

Margarita of Matth. and Maria Flensburgh. Wit.: Jos.
and Zytie V. Santen.

Cornelis, of Joh. and Rebekka Maassen. Wit.: Jac.
Maassen, Maria Fonda.

Willem, of Abr. and Geertie Vosburgh. Wit.: Wyn.
and Alida V. D. Bergh.

Dec. 9. Maria, of Pieter, Jr., and Rachel Wenne. Wit.:
Will. and Marya V. Alen.

Routh, of Wilh. and Routh Tuck. Wit.: Charl Wikkenson, Mary Couck.

Rachel, of Joh. and Zelia Redly. Wit.: Willem and
Elyzabeth Redly.

Katryn, of Tho. and Helena Story. Wit.: Christ Kan-
neda, Elizabeth Stevens.

Dec. 16. Gerrit, of Jan and Maria Gerritsen. Wit.:
Harpert Jacobsen, Geertruy Lansingh.

Ritzart, of Rogier and Zara Jeems. Wit.: Abraham
and Meetie Ouderkerk.

Maria, of [names of parents blank]. Wit.: Ree and
Zara Freely.

Elizabeth, of [names of parents blank]. Wit.: Will and
Elyzabeth Steevens.

1723
1723, Jan. 6. Maria, of Dirk and Maria Hagedoorn.
Wit.: Hendrik Koorn, Maria Beekman.

Maria, of Joh. and Elyz. Wendell. Wit.: Arent, Joh.,
Jr., and Maria Schuyler.

Jan. 8. Johannes, of Jems and Elyz. Wils. Wit.: Joh
D. Garmoy, Anna Bogardus.

Margarita, of Dan. and Joh. Flensburg. Wit.: Math
and Maria Flensburgh.

Jan. 9. Catalyna, of Gozen, Jr., and Neeltie V. Scayk.
Wit.: Rutg. Bleeker, Maria V. Schayk.

Jan. 13. Evert, of Evert and Engeltie Wendel. Wit.:
Steph. and Elyz. Groesbeek.

Jan. 20. Jannetie, of Jan and Cat. De Fou. Wit.:
Corn. and Marr. V. Nesch.

Eduard, of Thom. and Cath. Wyllaar. Wit.: Obedia
and Corn. Couper.

Hilletie, of Joh. and Brechie Zeeger. Wit.: Joh. Ten
Broeck, Elyz. Rensselaar.

Jan. 24. Jacob, of Edmond and Aaltie Gruum. Wit.:
Jacob and Elyzabeth Sneyder.

Jan. 30. Isack, of Pieter and Geertruy Vroman. Wit.:
Barent and Marytie Sanders.

Agnietie, of Gerr. W. and Alida V. D. Berg. Wit.:
Gerrit and Ann. Van Wie.

Maria, of Jacob, Jr., and Antie Schermerh. Wit.: Ph.
and Jann. V. Vegten.

Feb. 10. Mayke, of Arien and Lamb. Oothout. Wit.:
Joh. and Catal. Hun.

Feb. 17. Maria, of David and Christ. Van Dyk. Wit.:
Dirk Ten Broek, An. Cath. V. Schayck.

Jacobus, of Nicol and Maria Groesbeek. Wit.: Jacob
Groesbeek, Elyzab. Marselis.

Feb. 20. Pieter, of Pieter, Jr., and Cath. Schuyler.
Wit.: Steph. Groesbeek, Geertruy Lansingh.

Johannes, of Ph. and Geertr. V. Plank. Wit.: Joh.
Schuyler, Corn. Cortlant.

Cornelia, of Jesse and Neeltie D. Freest. Wit.: Joh.
Knikkerbacker, Maria Quakkenbosch.

Johannes, of Casper and Anna Ham. Wit.: Jan and
Rebecka Maassen.

March 3. Ariaentie, of Ulryck and Geertruy V. Franken. Wit.: Claes V. Franken, Maria Bovy.

Hendrik, of Claes and Corn. Bovy. Wit.: Petrus
Brouwer, Hendr. Oothout.

March 6. Chatharina, of Levinus Harmensen and Cath.
Van den Bergh. Wit.: Abram Vosburg, Geertie V. D.
Berg.

March 10. Volkie, of Wynant and Folkie V. D. Bergh.
Wit.: Levinus Harmensen, Maria Gerritsen.

1723
Pieter, of David and Anna Schuylers. Wit.: Dirck
Bratt, Alida Schuyler.

March 13. Anna, of Evert and Marr. Ryksen. Wit.:
Ryck and Anna V. Franken.

Isack, of Joh. and Sara Becker. Wit.: Isack and Jann.
V. Arnhem.

March 17. Antie, of Gerrit and Anna Ridders. Wit.:
Corn. and Antie Ridders.

Anna, of Andries and Maria Huyck. Wit.: Isack and
Alida Fonda.

March 24. Johannes, of Joh. and Antie Knikkerbacker.
Wit.: Nicol. and Maria Groesbeek.

Cornelis, of Abrah. and Catal. Valkenburg. Wit.: Joh.
and El. Schermerhoorn.

David, of Christ. and Chath. Schyans. Wit.: Jac.
Lansingh, Marg. Douw.

Antie, of Frans and Marg. Pruym. Wit.: Hendr. Lansing, Alida V. Iveren.

Matheus, of Harp. and Lena V. Deusen. Wit.: Gerr.
V. D. Berg, Engelt. V. Nes.

March 31. Catalyntie, of Joh. and Anna Visser. Wit.:
Barent Sanders, Cornelia Kip.

Anna, of John and Anna D. Peyster. Wit.: Meindt
and Rachel Schuyler.

Neeltie, of Isack and Jann. Lansing. Wit.: Jac. Lansing, Geer. T. Eyk, Jr.

Apr. 7. Gerrit, of Pieter and Tryntie Walderom. Wit.:
Gerr. V. D. Bergh, Chath. V. D. Poel.

Apr. 12. Johannes, of Sam. and Bethi Docks. Wit.:
Pieter and Anna Bennewe.

Jannetie, of John and Zara Waaters. Wit.: John Tumbaar, Elzie Wenne.

Apr. 28. Eva, of Joch. and Elsje Valkenburg. Wit.:
Joch. V. Aalsteyn, Marg. Redly.

Gerrit, of Jan and Cath. Van Wie. Wit.: Hendr. and
Anna V. Wie.

Gysbert, of Gerrit and Tryntie V. D. Berg. Wit.: Goz.
and Geertr. V. D. Berg.

Wessel, of Dirk and Marg. Ten Broek. Wit.: Anth.
Van Schayk, Christ. V. Dyk, Jr.

May 5. Gerrit, of Jacob and Anna Egmond. Wit.:
Gerrit and Sanna Lansing.

Elyzabeth, of Hendr. and Elsie Schermerhoorn. Wit.:
Corn. and Marretie Schermerhoorn.

Rebecka, of Roelef and Engeltie Kidny. Wit.: Math.
Flensburg, Maria Burger.

Willempie, of Eckbert and Elyzeb. Bratt. Wit.: Barent
and Willempie Bratt.

Margarita, of Wouter and Rachel Barhayt. Wit.: Bar.
and Mattie Sanders.

1723

May 12. Margarita, of Joh. and Maria Vinhagel. Wit.: Abr. Lansingh, Ariaentie V. D. Poel.

Jacob, of Gerr. and Sara Van Schayk. Wit.: Jacob Goewey, An. Catr. V. Schayk.

May 19. Tobias, of Coenraad and Gerretie Ten Eyk. Wit.: Gozen and Marg. Van Schayk.

Catharina, of Benjamin and Geertruy Rees. Wit.: Daniel and Dirckie Wenne.

May 23. Maria, of Gysbert and Elyzab. Scerp. Wit.: Jacob and Catalyna Goewey.

Catharina, of Gysbert and Catal. V. D. Bergh. Wit.: Wilh. and Geertie V. D. Bergh.

May 26. David, of Jems and Marg. Bath. Wit.: Jeems and Elyz. Wellews.

June 2. Joohne, of Benj. and Elyz. Wood. Wit.: Will. Liedts, Zara Jeims.

June 9. Maria, of Leendt. and Cath. Gansevoort. Wit.: Arent Pruym, Rachel Harmensen.

Fytie, of Dirck and Comm. Halenbeek. Wit.: Jan Halenbeek, Lybetie Conyn.

William, of Will. and Jenne Haylingh. Wit.: Eduard Holland, Anna D. Peyster.

Andries, of Nicol. and Rachel Gardenier. Wit.: Hend. and Cath. V. Rensselaer.

June 16. Anthony, of Benj. and Madal. Bratt. Wit.: Barent Bratt, Nelletie Rykmans.

Andries, of Hieroon and Marg. V. Vlieren. Wit.: Daniel Flensburgh, Lena V. Vlieren.

Eckbert, of Teunis and Engeltie Eckbertsen. Wit.: Dirk Brat, Dirkie Vissers.

June 19. Elyzabeth, of Isack and Catarina Wendel. Wit.: Jacob and Sara Wendel.

Cornelia, of Wilh. and Geertie V. D. Berg. Wit.: Pieter and Tryntie Walderon.

Isack, Jacob, of Isack and Alida Fonda. Wit.: Pieter Bogaart, Alida Van Vegten, Jacob and Lena Lansingh.

July 14. Dorothee, of Hendr. and Susanna Halenbeek. Wit.: Isack Fonda, Anna Halenbeek.

Catharina, of Hendr. and Margar. Cuyler. Wit.: Abrah. and Cath. Cuyler.

Jan, of Leendt. and Anna Bronk. Wit.: Claes and Marr. Egmond.

Johannes, of Sam. and Marr. Pruym. Wit.: Arent and Cath. Pruym.

Aug. 5. Andries, of Andries and Engeltie Witbeek. Wit.: Albert and Hester Slingerlant.

Aug. 18. Sander, of Jacob and Lena Lansing. Wit.: Jacob and Cath. Wendell.

Catalyna, of Vincent and Cat. Mettens. Wit.: Goz., Jr., and Neeltie V. Schayk.

1723

Aug. 25. Thomas Garton, of Daniel and Hester Brodhead. Wit.: Ritser Piek, Anna Garton.

Anthoni, of Corn. and Maria V. Dyk. Wit.: Albert Ryckman, Tryntie Bries.

Abraham, of Wyn. and Anna V. D. Bergh. Wit.: Abr. and Maycke Wendell.

Sept. 29. Gerrardus, of Joh. and Geertruy Lansingh. Wit.: Anth. Coster, Antie Bleeker.

Lena, of Tob. and Lena Rykman. Wit.: Joh. Beekman, Jr., Cath. Bries.

Anthoni, of Anth. and Rebekka Bratt. Wit.: Bar. and Corn. Bratt.

Oct. 6. Adam, of Jan and Catal. Barhayt. Wit.: Claes and Rachel Gardenier.

David, of Jonas and Maria Larway. Wit.: David and Corn. Uzile.

Oct. 20. Hendrik, of John and Sara Hansen. Wit.: Hendr. and Debora Hansen.

Dirck, of Dirk and Madal. V. D. Karre. Wit.: Ger., Jr., and Neeltie V. Schayk.

Pieter, of Laur. and Hilletie Scherph. Wit.: Jan and Rebecka Bloemendaal.

Nov. 3. Madalena, of Jeremias and Susanna Schuyler. Wit.: Pieter Schuyler, Madal. Bajen.

Theuntie, of Abrah. and Anna V. D. Poel. Wit.: Gerr. V. D. Bergh, Geertr. Groesbeek.

Johannes, of Math. and Reb. D. Garmoy. Wit.: Abr. and Bessie V. Arnhem.

Nov. 10. Bastyaen, of Sam. and Geertr. Criegier. Wit.: Theunis and Anna Visser.

Lidia, of Isak and Elyz. Fryer. Wit.: Joh. and Zelia Redly.

Nov. 22. Jannetie, of Jak. and Pietert. V. Aalsteyn. Wit.: Joh. V. Aalsteyn, Abigael D. Freest.

Dec. 8. William, of Philip and Cath. Livingston. Wit.: Robert Livingston, Albany; Robert Livingston, N. Y.; Anna D. Peyster.

Dec. 15. Johannes, of Salomon and Alida Goewey. Wit.: Pieter Schuyler, Maria Van Rensselaar.

Dec. 18. Alida, of Rykert and Maria Van Franken. Wit.: Ger. R. and Barbar. Van Franken.

Abraham, of Pieter and Rebecka Bogaart. Wit.: Ysack Fonda, Sara Van Vegten.

Jacob, of Corn. and Marr. V. Aalsteyn. Wit.: Alb. V. D. Werke, Lidia V. Aalsteyn.

Dec. 21. Adam, of Pieter and Christina Bratt. Wit.: Storm and Sophia Bratt.

Dec. 26. Petrus, of Marten and Maria Van Buuren. Wit.: Jacob Lansingh, Teuntie Van D. Bergh.

1724

1724, Jan. 8. Ulderyck, of Math. and Maria Bovy. Wit.: Christ. and Catalyna Yoets.

Jacob, of Jacob and Hendr. V. Woert. Wit.: Jacob and Zara V. Woert.

Jan. 12. Adam, of Daniel and Dirckie Wenne. Wit.: Hendr. and Cath. V. Rensselaer.

Jan. 15. Eva, of Harm. and Dorothee Van Aalsteyn. Wit.: Isack and Alida Fonda.

Jan. 18. Hendrickie, of Piet and Anna Bennewe. Wit.: Jac. V. Schoonhoven, Maria Bennewe.

Jeremias, of Joh. and Cath. Ten Broek. Wit.: Jeremias and Lena V. Rensselaar.

Storm, of Joh. and Corn. Becker. Wit.: Albert Becker, Lidia Beasely.

Jan. 22. Chatharina, of Marten and Cath. V. Bergen. Wit.: Jan and Dorothee Nieuwkerk.

Anthony, of Christ. and Marg. Abeel. Wit.: Hendr. and Nell. Bries.

Maria, of Joh. and Cath. V. D. Wilge. Wit.: Jon. Larway, Mally Williaems.

Ariaentie, of Hendr. and Hill. Van Wie. Wit.: Jan and Cath. Van Wie.

Jan. 26. Jacob, of Joh. and Eckbertie Garmoy. Wit.: Math. Garmoy, Maria Eckbertsen.

Maria, of Arent and Heyltie V. Dyk. Wit.: Corn. and Maria V. Dyk.

Feb. 2. Douwe, of Claes and Anna Fonda. Wit.: Isack and Rebecka Fonda.

Franciscus, of Arent and Cath. Pruym. Wit.: El. Gerritsen, Cath. Gansevoort.

Feb. 12. Lea, of Joh. and Elyz. V. Oostrander. Wit.: Will. Borhans, Alida Fonda.

Ephraim, of Schibb. and Anna Bogardus. Wit.: Pieter V. Brugh, Geessie Kip.

Feb. 23. Neth Ethweth, of Neth and Marg. Telleth. Wit.: Albert and Eva Bratt.

Ritsert, of Will. and Rachel Northen. Wit.: John and Judy Marroew.

Feb. 26. Maria, of Tho. and Eleon. Story. Wit.: Will. Williams, Mary Mahane.

Johannes, of Joh. and Neeltie Christyaen. Wit.: Corn. and Maria Cuyler.

Lucas, of Th. and Jann. Witbeek. Wit.: Gerr. and Engeltie V. D. Bergh.

March 1. Philip, of Th. and Hill. Williaems. Wit.: Phill. and Engeltie V. Vegten.

Anna, of Lucas and Tanna V. Vegten. Wit.: Joh. and Anna Schermerhoorn.

Daniel, of Nic. and Cath. Kittel. Wit.: Gerr. and Cath. Lansingh.

1724

March 8. Frerik, of Wald. and Anna Knoet. Wit.: Frerik and Francyntie Knoet.

Maria, of Jacob and Maria Halenbeek. Wit.: Jacob V. D. Heyde, Geertruy Visser.

Wyntie, of Ephr. and Agnietie Bogardus. Wit.: Anth. Bogardus, Antie Bronk.

March 15. Gerrit, of Jac. and Geert. Quakkenbosch. Wit.: Gerr. and Mar. V. D. Werken.

Rachel, of Claes and Dirkie Van Woert. Wit.: Jan and Catal. Van Nes.

Sara, of Joh. and Sara V. Santen. Wit.: Sam and Anna Redly.

March 29. Gysbert, of Joh. and Anna Marselis. Wit.: Gysbert and Anna Marselis.

Catharina, of Petr. and Anna Douw. Wit.: Joh. Ten Broek, Lena Van Rensselaar.

Apr. 25. Hendrik, of Joh. and Brechie Zeeger. Wit.: Hendr. and Griettie Gardenier.

Jeremias, of Joh. and Elyz. Muller. Wit.: Hendr. and Anna Halenbeek.

May 3. Abraham, of Eldert and Helena Ouderkerk. Wit.: Andries and Sara Gardenier.

Isack, of Abrah. and Ariaentie Ouderkerk. Wit.: Isack and Mayke Ouderkerk.

Heyltie, of Jacob and Agnietie Muller. Wit.: Joh. and Catal. Goewyk.

Geertruy, of Andries and Wyntie Bratt. Wit.: Barent and Maria Bratt.

May 14. Marten, of David and Abigael Freest. Wit.: Joh. and Sara Hansen.

May 17. Maria, of John and Zelia Brunly. Wit.: Jems Davids, Mary Constable.

Jacobus, of Simon and Mar. V. Antwerpen. Wit.: Jacob and Sara Glen.

Jannetie, of John and Maria Tumbarr. Wit.: John and Sara Waaters.

May 24. Cornelia, of Math. and Cat. Van Den Bergh. Wit.: Pieter and Tryntie Walderon.

Wyntie, of Tho. and Mary Barth. Wit.: Will. Berrit, Geertr. Verplank.

May 31. Maria, of Joh. and Jann. Ouderkerk. Wit.: Lowys and Maria Viele.

June 7. Philip, of Ph. and Cath. Conyn. Wit.: Jacob and Agnietie Muller.

Henry, of John and Lidia Beasely. Wit.: Ro. and Elsie Rooseboom.

Pieter, of Dirk, Jr., and Corn. Brat. Wit.: Anth. and Rebecca Bratt.

Maria, of Pieter and Mar. Fonda. Wit.: Joh. and Mar. Mingaal.

1724

Antie, of Jacob and Maria Brouwer. Wit.: Math. and Chath. Bovy.

June 28. Jesse, of Pieter and Maria Wenne. Wit.: Joh. and Neeltie Foreest.

Isack, of Dan. and Gerr. Fort. Wit.: Isack Fort, Geertruy V. Der Lyn.

July 5. Maria, of Will. and Anna Hooghtelink. Wit.: Pieter Hooghtelink, Jane Lansingh.

Hendrik, of Corn. and Dorothee Bogaart. Wit.: Hendr. and Hendrikie Oothout.

Cornelia, of Pieter, Jr., and Anna Uzile. Wit.: Pieter and Corn. Uzile.

Onar, of Math. and Mary Fanine. Wit.: Dan Flensburgh, Anna Hoogen.

July 26. Petrus, of Gerr. and Anna Van Bergen. Wit.: David and Christ. Van Dyk.

Mettie, of Jeems and Elyz. Walles. Wit.: Cath. Leyster.

Hester, of Joh. and Anna Slingerlant. Wit.: Alb. and Hest. Slingerlant.

Mary, of Sam. and Corn. Borghtal. Wit.: John Dumbar, Mary Banks.

Johannes, of Jacob and Matnamskwaa Sinhoo.

Elyzabeth, of Gerrit and Corn. Dinghmans. Wit.: Jacob Goewey, Sara Gardenier.

Aug. 9. Tjerk Harmensen, of Mart. and Geert. Beekman. Wit.: Tjerk H. Visser, Antie Eckbertsen.

Elyzabeth, of Isack and Bata V. Deusen. Wit.: Teunis V. Aalsteyn, Elyz. V. Rensselaar.

Susanna, of Ab. and Mad. Lansingh. Wit.: Jan B. Wemp, Jann. Lansingh.

Marten, of Joh. and Marr. Vosburgh. Wit.: Jan and Marr. V. Aalsteyn.

Aug. 16. Samuel, of John and Judy Morrow. Wit.: Samuel Bortsen, Mary Van der Lin.

Hester, of Isack and Jann. V. Arnhem. Wit.: Abr. and Ha. Van Arnhem.

Maria, of Jan and Rebecca Maassen. Wit.: Pieter and Cath. Fonda.

Aug. 23. Abraham, of Christ. and Catal. Joets. Wit.: Dan Flensburg, Sara Gardenier.

Elyzabeth, of Obedy and Corn. Couper. Wit.: Joh. and Elizabeth Van Oostrander.

Sept. 13. David, of Tho. and Mary Davids. Wit.: John and Lidia Beasely.

Jacob, of Bar. and Maria Eckbertsen. Wit.: Joh. D. Garmoy, Geessie Kip.

Susanna, of Ephr. and Anna Wendell. Wit.: Dirk V. Scherluyn, Catal. Schuyler.

1724

Sept. 20. Catharina, of Gerr. and Alida V. D. Bergh. Wit.: Wilh. and Geertie V. D. Bergh.

Johannes, of Math. and Rebecka Garmoy. Wit.: Abrah. and Hessie V. Arnhem.

Helena, of Abr. and Alida V. Arnhem. Wit.: Jacob and Helena Lansingh.

Jacob, of Jacob and Elyz. Evertsen. Wit.: Jacob Lansingh, Elyz. Bratt.

Johannes, of Roel and Engeltie Kidny. Wit.: Joh. and Maretie Kidny.

Mayke, of Gerr. and Catal. V. Nes. Wit.: Gerr. and Engeltie V. D. Bergh.

Sept. 27. Elyzabeth, of John and Catal. Oothout. Wit.: Will. V. Deusen, Dorothee Bogaart.

Eckbert, of Petr. and Sara Bogardus. Wit.: Jonas Douw, Catl. Schoonmaker.

Thomas, of Tho. and Maria Scherp. Wit.: John and Marg. Olyvier.

Lambert, of Tho. and Marr. V. Aalsteyn. Wit.: Joh. Mingaal, Eva Van Aalsteyn.

Oct. 4. Albertus, of Joseph and Hendr. Jets. Wit.: Math. Flensburgh, Zelia Rettelyf.

Margarita, of Dan. and Joh. Flensburgh. Wit.: Math. Flensburgh, Anna Rettelyf.

Jacob, of Abr. and Metty Ouderkerk. Wit.: Ephraim and Anna Wendel.

Hendrick, of Eckbert and Elyz. Brat. Wit.: Anth. and Jann. Bogardus.

Oct. 9. Johannes, of Gerrit and Elyz. Lansingh. Wit.: Anth. Coster, Elyz. Groesbeek.

Oct. 11. Wessel, of David and Christ. Van Dyk. Wit.: Francis Harrisson, Arent Van Dyk, Joh. Harrisson, Catal. Wendell.

Gerretie, of Jak. and Antie Schermerhoorn. Wit.: Hend. and Marr. Schermerhoorn.

Commertie, of Ph. and Sara Bronk. Wit.: Th. and Hilletie Williams.

Abraham, of Mart. and Corn. V. Aalsteyn. Wit.: Jac. Lansingh, Abigael De Foreest.

Oct. 25. Catharina, of Fr. and Sara Meindertsen. Wit.: Ph. and Cath. Livingston.

Jan, of Jonas and Antie Bronk. Wit.: Ph. and Cath. Conyn.

Luycas, of Rub. and Geertr. V. Vechten. Wit.: Sal. and Jan. V. Vegten.

Gerrit Lucas, of Dan. and Hester Broadheat. Wit.: Lucas and Sara Wyngaart.

Catharina, of Anth. and Anna V. Schayk. Wit.: Goz. Van Schayk, Gerretie Ten Eyk.

1724

Nov. 8. Ariaentie, of Barent and Maria Van Buuren. Wit.: Leend. Gansevoort, Aryaentie Van Buuren.

Nicolaas, of Joh. and Sara Becker. Wit.: Nicol. Van Schayk, Rachel V. Arnhem.

Nov. 22. Levynus, of Kiliaan and Maria Wenne. Wit.: Corn. and Rebecka Bloemendal.

Marten, of Will. and Elyz. Walderom. Wit.: Pieter Fonda, Neeltie Beekman.

Nov. 29. Catharina, of Casp. and Anna Ham. Wit.: Casp. Leyb [?], Sara Gardenier.

Anthony, of Math. and Maria Flensburg. Wit.: Jos. and Zytie V. Santen.

Elyzabeth, of Ev. and Eng. Wendell. Wit.: Joh. Beekman, Elyz. Coster.

Sept. [sic] 27. Anna, of Jacobus and Susanna Schoonhoven. Wit.: Dirk, Jr., and Marr. Bratt.

William, of Joh. and Immetie Gaaf. Wit.: Eduard and Zeely Hollant.

LIST OF ABBREVIATIONS.

A., Albany (same as N. A.).
A. Co., Albany County.
b., B., born or banns.
br., brother.
C., Claverack.
Can., Canistagioene.
cert., certificate.
ch., chn., child; children.
Chu., chu., Church.
Col. R., Colony Rensselaerswyck.
dec^d., deceased.
Eng., E., England.
Es., Esopus.
h., house.
J. P., Justice of the Peace.
K., Kinderhook.
King., Kingston.
L., Licence.
l., living.
L. I., Long Island.
Ma., ma., Married.
N. A., New Albany.
N. E., New England.
N. H., New Haarlem.
N. Y., New York.
O. E., Old England.
P., the Parsonage.
pr., proclamations.
Pros., Proselyte, proselytes.
R., Rensselaerswyck.
Recd. cert., Received Certificate.
Reg., Registered.
Sch., Schenectady.
V. D. M., Verbi Divini Minister (Minister of the Word of God).
Wid., widr., widow; widower.
Wit., Witness, witnesses.
y. d., unmarried woman.
y. m., unmarried man.
Cornelis, of Thomas Harmense, means Cornelis, *child* of Thomas Harmense, etc., etc.

INDEX.

There was some question as to the best mode of preparing this index, inasmuch as there are so many variations in spelling the cognomens as well as the baptismal names in these records. Those entering the names in these records appear to have exercised their own judgment as to orthography, and frequently varied it without apparent reason even in the same entry. If all the names were indexed separately just as they appear in the records, with the original spelling, it is evident that the work of tracing family lineages by the unskilled searcher would be greatly increased. It was concluded, therefore, that it would facilitate reference to embrace under one heading all names evidently belonging to the same family, indexing them, as far as practicable, under that form which now seems to be in commonest use.

It is also to be observed that most of the early Dutch families were not regularly entered under their family name until many years had passed. They were mostly known by their patronymics. For instance, the Heemstraats will have to be looked for, sometimes, under Dirks or Takels, the Groesbeeks under Claasze, the Vander Poels under Wynandtsz, the Van Deusens under Teuisz or Harpers, the Van Beurens and Vroomans under Meesz or Maas, the Van Bergens under Gerrits, etc., etc.

Appended will be found a list of the most numerous variations in the surnames that appear in these records:

Barheit, Barhayt, Barheith, Barheyd, Barhaik, Barhajck, Barhait, Berheit, Berheith.

Barrit, Berrit, Barrith, Berret, Berrith.

Barrois, Barreway, Barway, Berwoir, Barrewee, Berwe, Broewee, Barwee, Barrowa.

Beaufils, Bovy, Boffy, Bouphi, Bossy, Bovie, Bosi.

Becker, Beckers, Beekers, Beckingh, Bekker.

Beekman, Beeckman, Bykman, Beekmans.

Bleecker, Bleeker, Bleekers, Bleker, Bleyker.

Bogaert, Bogert, Bogaart, Bogard, Bogerds, Bogaerd, Bogaard, Bogaardt, Bogardt, Vanden Bogaart, Bogart, Bogerd.

Borgert, Borgaet, Borgart, Borgat, Borger, Borgaart.

Bratt, Brat, Brad, Brath.

Brussy, Brusy, Brissi, Bressy, Bressi.

Christiaansz, Christyaen, Christyaensen, Cristyaensen, Christiaanse, Chrystiaensen, Christiaans.

Claas, Claasse, Claessen, Claassen.

Cojeman, Cojemans, Kojeman, Kojemans, Koyeman.

Conyn, Comyn, Conynen, Konyn.

Cornelis, Cornelise, Cornelisse, Cornelissen, Cornelisze.

Cuyler, Cuylers, Cuiler, Kuilers, Kuyler.

Davids, Davidse, Daevids, Davis.

De Fou, De Four, Diffoer, Du Fou, Du Four, Dufour, Du Foy, De Voor, Du Voe.

De Garmo, De Garmoy, Germoy, Garmoy, Garnoy, D. Garmoy.

De Graaf, Graaf, De Graaff, De Graeff.

Delmond, Delmont, Dellemont, Dellomont.

De Wandelaar, Wandelaar, Wandelaars, D'Wandelaar.

De Warran, De Waaran, De Warm, De Warant, De Worm, Warms.

Dingman, Dingmans, Dinghsmans, Dinghmans, Dingemans, Dinansse.

Dockzy, Dackzy, Dakse, Docks, Doksi, Dokzy.

Douw, Douwen, Dou, Dauw, Douwe.

Dunbar, Dunbaarr, Dumbar, Tumbaar, Tumbarr.

Egberts, Egbertse, Eckbertse, Ekbertse, Eckbertsen, Ekbertsen, Egbers, Egbertsen, Eckberts, Eghbertsen, Ekbersen.

Everson, Everts, Evertsen, Evertsz.

Flensburg, Flensburgh, Vlensburg, Vlensburgh.

Foreest, De Foreest, D. Freest, Freest, Frees, Voreest, De Forest, D. Foreest.

Gansevoort, Gansevoord, Ganssevoort, Ganzevoord.

Gerritsen, Gerritse, Garrits, Gerretsen, Gerritson.

Gilbert, Gilberts, Gilberd, Gillebartse, Gillebart.

Goewey, Goe, Goewyck, Goewyk, Goewy.

Harding, Hardinks, Hardiks, Hardinx.

Harmensz, Harmensen, Harmsen, Harmensse, Harmens, Harmense, Harmanse, Hermansz.

Heemstraat, Van Heemstraat, Heemstrate, Van Heemstrate.

Hendriks, Hendrikse, Hendriksen, Henriks.

Hoges, Hogen, Hoogen, Hoghen, Hooges.

Hoogteeling, Hoogtelinck, Hooghtelink, Hoogtelink, Hoogteling, Hoochteeling.

Huyck, Huyk, Huik, Huek, Huyg, Huygh.

Jansz, Jansse, Jansen, Jans, Janse, Janssen.

Jeeds, Joets, Yoets, Jeits, Yeads, Joeyts, Jojets, Jets, Jeads.

Ketelluyn, Ketelen, Keteluyn, Keteluin, Ketelhuin.

Kidny, Kidni, Kidney, Kithni, Kitni.

Knickerbacker, Knikkerbakker, Knikkelbakker, Knikkenbakker.

Lansing, Lanssing, Lansingh, Lanse, Lansen, Lanzenzen, Lanzensen, Lancen, Lanzingh.

Livingston, Levingston, Liphfeston, Levesthon, Liveston, Livenston.

Lucassen, Lukassen, Lucasse, Luyckassen.

Maassen, Maasse, Maarsen, Massen, Meessen, Maazen.

Marselis, Marcelis, Mazelis, Marcellus.

Matteuse, Matthysse, Matyssen, Matysen, Matthyse.

Meyndertse, Meinderse, Meenders, Meindertsen, Meinderts, Meynders, Meindersen, Meynderts.

Muller, Mullers, Mulder, Mulders.

Oothout, Othout, Oothoud, Oothouwt, Oothoudt.

Ouderkerck, Ouderkerk, Ouwderkerk, Oudekerk.

Pearson, Peersen, Peers, Persen.

Pruyn, Pruim, Pruin, Pruym.

Quackenbosch, Quackkenbosch, Quakkenbosch, Quakkenbos, Kwakkenbos, Quakenbosch.

Ratteliffe, Rattelif, Raedelif, Redly, Rettelyf, Ratteliff, Rattelief, Rately.

Roelofs, Roelefsen, Roelofsen, Roelofsz, Roelofse.

Rommeli, Rumbly, Rumblis, Rumney.

Ryckman, Ryckmans, Rykman, Rykmans.

Rykse, Ryksen, Rycksen, Ryxsen, Rykse, Ryksz.

Sanders, Sandersen, Sanderse, Sandertse, Zanders.

Schans, Schayns, Schyans Syansch.

Scharp, Scherp, Scherph, Scerph, Scerp, Sharp.

Schermerhoorn, Schermerh., Scermerhoorn, Schermerhorn, Schermerhoren, Scermerhorn.

Schuyler, Schuiler, Schuylder, Schuilers, Scuyler, Schuylers, Schuylders.

Slingerland, Slingerlandt, Slingerlant, Slingelant.

Symense, Symensen, Simons, Symonse, Symonson.

Ten Eyk, Ten Eyck, Ten Eick, Ten Eik, T. Eyk.

Tymensen, Teimesen, Timesse, Tymenzen.

Van Alen, Van Aalen, Van Ale, V. Alen.

Van Aalsteyn, Van Aalst, V. Aalsteyn, Van Aalstein, Van Aalstede, Aalstyn, Van Aelstein, Van Aalstee, Van Aalsteede, Van Alstein, Van Aals.

Van Benthuysen, Van Benthuise, Van Benthuisen, V. Benthuysen.

Van Brug, Van Brugge, Van Brugh, Ver Brugge, Van Brughe, V. Brugh, Verbrughe.

Van Bueren, V. Buuren, Van Buuren, Van Buren, Van Buure, Van Buere, V. Buure, Van Beuren.

Van Corlaar, V. Corlaar, Van Korlaar, Corlaar, Corlar.

Van Cortlant, Van Cortlandt, Van Cortland, Cortlant, Van Kortlant, Cortlandt.

Van den Bergh, V. D. Bergh, V. D. Berg, Van den Berg, Van Bergen, V. den Berg, Van den Berck, V. Bergen, V. den Bergh, Van Berg, Van den Berge, Van den Berk, Van de Berg.

Van der Heyde, Van der Heyden, V. D. Heyde, V. D. Heyden, Van der Heide.

Van der Karre, Van der Kar, Van der Kerre, V. D. Karre.

Van der Werke, Van der Werk, Van der Werken, V. D. Werke, V. D. Werken, V. dr Werke, V. der Werken.

Van der Zee, Van D. Zee, V. D. Zee, V. der Zee.

Van Deusen, Van Deuse, V. Deusen, Van Duese.

Van Dyck, Van Dyk, V. Dyck, V. Dyk.

Van Eps, see Van Ness.

Van Franken, V. Franken, Van Frank, Van Franke, V. Franke.

Van Hoesen, V. Hoesen, Van Hoese, Van House, Van Housen.

Van Iveren, V. Iveren, Van Ivere, Van Yvere, Van Yveren.

Van Ness, Van Esch, Van Nes, Van Es, V. Nes, V. Nesch, Van Eps, Van Nest.

Van Petten, Van Pette, Van Putten, Van Putte.

Van Renselaar, Rensselaar, Van Rensselaar, Rynselaar, Renselaar, V. Renselaer, V. Rensselaer, V. Renselaar, V. Rensselaar, Van Renselaer, V. Renss.

Van Salsberry, Salsberi, Salsbury, Salsberry, Van Salsberg.

Van Santen, Van Zanten, V. Santen, Van Sant.

Van Schayck, Van Scayck, Van Schayk, Van Schajk, V. Schayk, V. Schayck, Van Schaik, Van Scheyk, V. Schaik, V. Schajk, Schayk, Van Schaak, Van Schaajk, V. Scayck, Van Schaick, V. Scayk.

Van Slyk, Van Slyck, Slyk, Van Slyp, Van Slecht.

Van Valkenburg, Van Valkenburgh, Valkenburgh, Valkenburg, Van Volkenburg, V. Valkenburgh, V. Valkenburg, V. Valk., Volkenburg.

Van Vechten, Van Vecht, Van Vegten, Van Vechter, V. Vegten, V. Vechten, Van der Vechte, Vechter.

Van Woerd, Van Woert, V. Woert, Van Schoonderwoert, Van Woerdt, Van Woerden.

Van Wyen, Van Wie, Van Wye, V. Wie, Verwei, Verwey.

Van Yselstein, Van Ysselsteyn, Yselsteyn, Iselsteyn.

Verplanck, Verplanke, Verplank, V. Plank.

Vinhagel, Vinhagen, Vinhage, Vinhagels, Vinnagels, Vinnagel.

Visscher, Vischer, Visser, Visschers, Vissers, Vischers.

Walderon, Waldere, Waldering, Walderom, Walderen, Walderingh.

Walthers, Walters, Walter, Waaters.

Wielaars, Wielaar, Wieller, Whiler, Wyllaar, Wyllaer, Wieler, Wiler, Wiele, Whieller.

Wimp, Wimph, Wemp, Wimpel.

Winnen, Wenn, Wenne, Wenna, Wenner, Winne.

Witbeek, Witbeeck, Witbeck, Witbik.

Woodcock, Woedkook, Whoodkoks, Whoodkok, Woodkok.

Wyngaard, Wyngaart, Wyngaert, Van Wyngaarde,Wyngaarts.

Staats, Staas—*Continued.*
Isack, 86.
Jacob, 19, 31, 60, 64, 76, 82.
Jochem, Jochum, 18, 20, 22,
24, 31.
Maria, 14, 62, 64, 76.
Neeltie, 64, 78, 81, 86, 95.
Ritsert, 95.
Rykje, 19, 22, 26, 31.
Samuel, 64.
Staring, Catryna, 68.
Nicolaes, 68.
Stevens, Steevens, Elizabeth, 97.
Will., 97.
Story, Eleon, 102.
Helena, 97.
Tho., 97, 102.
Stout, Willem, 1.
Swart, Swarts, Adam, 39.
Cristyna, 66.
Jannetje, 22, 31, 41, 51.
Jesaias, 55.
Swartwoud, Bernhardus, Bar-
nardus, 35, 47, 52.
Eva, 32, 42, 51.
Rachel, 35.
Swits, Ariaantje, 9.
Cornelis, 3, 29, 35, 39, 41, 48,
64, 69, 73, 85.
Hesther, Hester, Hessie, 64,
69, 73, 85.
Isaac, 29, 41.
Rebecka, Rebecca, 11, 64.
Susanna, 29, 41, 68.
Symense, Folkert, 62, 68.
Gerrit, 57.
Jannetie, 68.
Joannes, Johannes, 13, 53,
68, 84.
Pieter, 43, 53.
Sanna, 84.
Takelsen, Takelse, Taakels,
Clara, 78.
Dirk, 58, 78.
Saartje, 21.
Tannson, John, Jan, 12, 78.
Maria, 78.
Tassama, Moeset, 1, 22, 27, 44, 49.
Tebuch, Mary, 46.
Tejasse, Johannes, 53.
Teller, Tellers, Johannes, 58.
Margarita, 9.
Willem, 25, 41.
Telleth, Marg., 102.
Neth., 102.
Ten Bosch, Dorothea, 39.
Ten Broek, Ten Broeck, Anna
C., 96.
Anna Catharina, 7, 49, 61.
Catharina, Catryntje, Caat-
jen, Cat Cathie., 25, 30, 33,

43, 49, 53, 59, 61, 64, 71, 72,
76, 79, 80, 85, 87, 90, 91, 94,
102.
Christina, Styntje, 2, 13, 27,
32, 41, 49, 58, 64, 66, 76,
77, 84, 88.
Dirck, Dirk, 11, 20, 28, 32,
58, 61, 64, 66, 71, 75, 76,
77, 82, 83, 84, 86, 91, 97,
98, 99.
Elisabeth, Elsje, Lysbeth,
20, 27, 36, 40, 45, 55, 59.
Geertruy, 33, 43.
Jacob, 80, 91.
Johannes, Joh., 8, 11, 43, 55,
59, 72, 76, 79, 80, 85, 88,
90, 92, 94, 98, 102, 103.
Lydia, Lidia, 3, 21, 26, 28,
39, 53.
Margarita, Marg., 71, 77, 83,
88, 91, 97, 99.
Maria, Marretie, 66, 67, 71,
72, 76, 77, 84, 88, 90.
Samuel, 9, 49, 53, 67, 71, 76,
80, 88.
Sara, 38.
Tobias, 11, 72, 77, 84, 85, 90.
Wessel, 1, 19, 21, 28, 30, 33,
38, 39, 40, 41, 45, 48, 49,
58, 59, 64, 72, 76, 77, 91.
Ten Eyk, Andries, 38.
Barent, 1, 21, 26, 31, 38, 42,
43, 48, 55.
Coenraat, Coenraad, 5, 21,
29, 31, 35, 36, 40, 42, 58,
63, 69, 76, 82, 90, 100.
Geertie, Geertje, Geer., 17,
26, 35, 47, 66, 75, 84, 89,
90, 99.
Gerritje, Gerretie, Gerr., 48,
63, 69, 76, 82, 90, 96, 100,
105.
Henrik, Hendrik, Hendr., 6,
47, 52, 58, 63, 64, 69, 71,
78, 82, 87, 95, 96.
Jenn., Jenneke, 18, 78, 90.
Margarita, Griettie, Marg.,
52, 64, 69, 71, 78, 82, 87,
88, 96.
Maria, 47.
Moycka, Mayke, Maeyke, 10,
38, 58.
Neeltje, Neeltie, 20, 46, 64,
69, 73, 80.
Tobias, 69, 71.
Teunisse, Teunissen, Teunisz,
Anna, 22.
Dirkje, 24.
Egbert, 2, 21, 25, 29.
Jacob, 18, 23, 29, 30, 44, 55,
72.

9

Van Vechten, Vechter, Abram, 9.
Agnietie, 10, 19.
Alida, 32, 62, 100.
Anna, Antje, 28, 36, 38, 51, 61, 74, 85.
Dirk, Dirck, 4, 19, 31, 41, 54, 61, 71, 82, 89.
Engeltie, 77, 83, 86, 96, 102.
Fytje, 21, 28, 34, 43, 51.
Geertruy, Geertr., 83, 88, 93, 96, 105.
Gerrit, 21, 22.
Johanna, Jannetie, Jann., 16, 76, 98, 105.
Johannes, Joannes, 25, 31, 33, 37, 39, 44, 54, 59, 61, 62, 67, 74, 77, 81, 84, 85, 90.
Leendert, 93.
Lucas, 12, 78, 84, 93, 102.
Lydia, Lidia, 30, 37, 45, 63, 90.
Margarita, Grietje, 21, 22, 28, 34, 41, 47, 61, 71, 73, 78, 82, 89.
Maria, Marytje, 26, 33, 41, 53, 59, 67, 90, 91.
Philip, Phill., Ph., 10, 76, 82, 83, 86, 98, 102.
Ruben, Rub., 13, 56, 83, 88, 95, 96, 105.
Salomon, Sal., 19, 25, 32, 37, 51, 62, 81, 105.
Samuel, 36.
Sara, 101.
Tanneke, Tanna, 78, 84, 93, 102.
Teunis, 32, 41, 44.
Volkert, Folkert, 3, 25, 26, 28, 39, 45, 53, 63, 65, 90, 94.
Wyntie, 95.
Van Vlek, Van Vleq, Benjamin, 15.
Paulus, 41.
Van Vlieren, V. Vlieren, Hieroon, 12, 78, 92, 100.
Madel., Lena, 17, 100.
Margariet, Marg., 78, 92, 100.
Van Vliet, Cornelia, 2.
Van Vorst, Van Voust, Van Voste, Anna, 18.
Geertruy, 18, 31.
Jillis, 56.
Van Vredenburg, Vredenburg, Cornelia, 31, 37, 38.
Willem, 38.
Van Woerdt, Van Schoonderwoert, Anna, 92.
Ariaentie, 82, 85.

Dirckie, Dirkie, 73, 80, 92, 103.
Elizabeth, 67, 76, 85.
Eva, 55.
Gerretie, 62.
Hendr., 102.
Hyltie, 87.
Jacob, 17, 87, 92, 102.
Jacobus, 34.
Margarita, 13.
Nicolaas, Claas, 8, 55, 57, 62, 69, 73, 80, 83, 92, 103.
Petrus, Pieter, 11, 78, 82, 85.
Ruth, 67, 76, 85.
Sara, 10, 102.
Van Wurmerik, Van Wurmerink, Cornelis, 8, 55.
Van Wyen, Verwei, Agnietje, 23, 33, 40, 45, 54, 66, 77.
Alida, 16, 73, 85.
Ann, Anna, 98, 99.
Ariaantje, 24, 33.
Catharina, Katharina, Catryntie, Catie, Cath., 7, 31, 45, 53, 60, 66, 73, 79, 81, 89, 99, 102.
Cornelia, 27, 39.
Geesje, 24, 31, 39, 47.
Gerrit, 23, 29, 33, 45, 54, 77, 98.
Hendrik, Hendr., 11, 59, 65, 76, 84, 93, 99, 102.
Hilletie, 76, 84, 93, 102.
Jan, 40, 53, 54, 60, 66, 73, 79, 81, 89, 99, 102.
Jannetje, 33, 40, 50, 59.
Johannes, 29.
Van Yselstein, Iselsteyn, Bata, 6, 45, 54.
Cornelis, 45.
Feytie, 90.
Isack, 96.
Willem, 73, 90.
Vas, Peter, Petrus, 9, 59.
Vedder, Vedders, Veder, Aggenietje, 57.
Albert, 42, 52, 57.
Arent, 66.
Cousset, Korset, Cortzett, 8, 9, 55, 57, 61, 66, 86.
Johannes, Hannes, Johs., 44, 54, 55, 57, 65.
Marytie, 65.
Neeltie, 66, 86.
Volkert, 54, 55.
Veeder, Engeltie, 65.
Verbruggen, Verbrugge, Catharina, 18.
Sara, 18, 60.
Vernoy, Cornelis, 38.
Rachel, 47.

Walderon,—*Continued.*
Willem, Will., 14, 88, 92, 96, 106.
Walrave, John, 16.
Walthers, Waaters, Catharina, Catryna, 55, 80.
Elisabeth, 47, 55.
John, Joann, 15, 63, 93, 95, 99, 103.
Merry, 69.
Robbert, 55, 80.
Zara, Sara, 93, 94, 95, 99, 103.
Warmond, Matthys, 21.
Susanna, 21.
Weemes, Wimps, Capt., 6.
James, 7, 20.
Mad., 32.
Wellive, Susanna, 16.
Wendel, Wendell, Wendels, Abraham, Abram, Abr., 19, 26, 39, 49, 54, 59, 67, 69, 74, 96, 101.
Ahasuerus, 90.
Anna, Antie, 15, 19, 60, 67, 68, 69, 70, 74, 78, 79, 83, 87, 89, 90, 93, 94, 96, 104, 105.
Ariaantje, 19, 22, 33, 52, 66, 69, 79.
Catarina, Tryntje, Cath., 24, 32, 100.
Cathalina, Catelyntje, Catal., 4, 82, 91, 105.
Elisabeth, Elsie, Lysbeth, Elyz., 8, 11, 26, 31, 34, 40, 50, 59, 60, 63, 69, 73, 80, 85, 90, 98.
Engeltje, Eng., 60, 65, 71, 74, 77, 83, 98, 106.
Ephraim, Epraim, Ephr., 63, 67, 70, 79, 83, 87, 90, 93, 94, 96, 104, 105.
Evert, Ev., 5, 19, 32, 35, 42, 54, 55, 60, 65, 70, 71, 73, 77, 83, 96, 98, 106.
Hermannus, Harmanus, 19, 26, 35, 39, 42, 52, 60, 68, 69, 74, 79, 89.
Hester, 10, 32, 36, 52.
Isaak, Ysack, 13, 82, 85, 91, 100.
Jacob, 73, 85, 100.
Johannes, Joannes, Joh., 8, 12, 47, 50, 52, 55, 59, 60, 62, 63, 69, 70, 73, 78, 80, 83, 84, 85, 87, 90, 98.
Maeyke, Majeke, 40, 67, 74, 101.
Maria, Marretie, Marytje, 4, 19, 22, 24, 27, 30, 34, 36, 37, 43, 46, 59, 69, 74, 92.

Philip, Flip, 23, 31, 39, 49, 59, 62, 74.
Robbert, 51, 66, 79.
Sara, 13, 55, 63, 73, 77, 100.
Susanna, Sanna, Zantie, 4, 7, 13, 28, 32, 34, 35, 39, 40, 57, 60, 68, 70, 84.
Thomas, 24, 34, 39.
Wessels, Dirck, 76.
Westfaeling, Rebecca, 51.
Weydt, Gzysyn, 93.
Merry, 93.
Wibusse, Gerrit, 6, 41, 46.
Mary, 41.
Wielaars, Whiler, etc., Brechie, 14, 69.
Catharina, Cath., 90, 98.
Edward, Edderd, 23, 32, 42, 58, 67.
Evert [see Edward], 50.
Josyntje, Josyne, 23, 67.
Robbert, 64, 90.
Thomas, Thom., 16, 98.
Wikkenson, Charl., 97.
Willems, Willemse, Marritie, 65.
Teunis, 19.
Williams, Williaems, Williamse, Anna, 14.
Hilletie, Hill., 65, 70, 78, 83, 87, 91, 95, 102, 105.
Maria, Mally, 82, 102.
Math., 95.
Thomas, Tames, Th., 9, 20, 23, 27, 30, 37, 48, 55, 65, 70, 78, 80, 83, 87, 91, 102, 105.
Will., 102.
Wils, Walles, Wellews, Elyz., 98, 100, 104.
Jems, 98, 100, 104.
Wilson, Anna, 94.
Jems, 94.
Wimp, etc., Barent, 56.
Jan, 9, 13, 104.
Marrytje, 56.
Meindert, 13.
Susanna, 54.
Volkje, 56.
Winnen, Aagje, 38.
Aletta, 36.
Anna, 49, 91, 95.
Bata, 44, 55.
Catalyna, Lyntje, 6, 7, 22, 27, 29, 32, 39, 44, 49, 62.
Christyna, Christyntjen, 10, 60.
Daniel, 23, 24, 31, 46, 65, 72, 73, 78, 82, 89, 93, 95, 100, 102.
Dickie, Dirckie, 65, 72, 73, 78, 82, 89, 93, 95, 100, 102.

Records of the Reformed Dutch Church of Albany, New York

Part 3
1725-1749

Excerpted from
Year Book of The Holland Society
of New York (1906)

RECORDS OF THE R. D. CHURCH OF ALBANY.

MARRIAGES.

[For list of abbreviations see page fronting index.]

1725, Jan. 8. With Banns. Jochum Van der Heyde and Anna Ketelluyn.

Feb. 8. **B.** Sybrant Quakkenbosch and Elyz. Knikkerbacker.

Feb. 10. **B.** Evert Ylingh and Maria Veeder.

Feb. 13. **B.** Will. Rettelief and Martha Bennewe.

Feb. 15. **B.** Theunis Van Slyk, Jr., and Anna Vosburgh.

May 2. **B.** Willem Huygh and Anna Ouderkerk.

May 4. With Licence. Joh. Hun and Anna [?] Wenne.

May 23. **B.** ———Knikkerbacker and Geertruy Vosburgh.

May 28. **B.** Gerr. Knoet and Machtel Heemstraat.

July 4. **B.** William Williams and Mary Hicky.

July 8. **B.** Dirk Goes, Jr., and Elsie Van Valkenburg.

Aug. 3. **B.** William Tuisely and Chaterina Evans.

Aug. 18. **B.** Andr. Mackans and Hagar Pycket.

Sept. 17. **B.** Lambert Van Valkenburgh and Leah Lauw.

Oct. 3. **B.** Jasowe Perre and Elyz. Leenyn.

Oct. 12. **B.** Joh. D. Foreest and Maria Quakkenbosch.

Nov. 22. **B.** Johannes Wyngaart and Maria Huyser.

Nov. 23. **B.** Corn. Ridder and Susanna Van den Berg.

Nov. 25. **L.** Isack Bogaart and Hendrickie Oothout.

Nov. 25. **L.** Ahasuerus Rooseboom and Maria Brat.

Dec. 26. **L.** David V. D. Heyde and Geertruy Visser

Ditto 2. Were ma. *in pres.* [?] *of Mr. Scriba Vengete.** [?] David Schuiler and Maria Hansen; quod attestor Eiland Westerlo, Eccl. Alban, Aug. 17, 1761.

1726, Jan. 2. **L.** Barent Vosburgh and Elyz. Wenne.

Jan. 2. **B.** Jan Wenne and Rachel Verplank.

Jan. 9. **L.** Jan Witbeek and Maria Williams.

* The clause in italics was poorly written in the original and may mean that the Scriba (*clerk*) had forgotten (*vergeten*) to record the entry at the time.

1

Jan. 13. **L.** Hendr. Bries and Wyntie Van Vegten.
Jan. 14. **B.** Jacob Fort and Sara d' Wandelaar.
Jan. 26. **B.** Joh. Van den Bergh and Maria Van Nes.
June 11. **B.** Will. Crellen and Marg. Bennewe.
July 15. **L.** Frans Pruym and Alida [?] Van Yveren.
Oct. 23. **B.** Gerr. Bekker and Ariaentie V. D. Kar.
Oct. 29. **B.** Laur. V. D. Poel and Ariaentie V. D. Berg.
Oct. 30. **B.** Joh. Goewey and Jann. V. D. Berg.
Dec. 9. **L.** Cornelis Cuyler and Catalyna Schuyler.
Dec. 9. **L.** Joh. Lansing and Catalyna Hun.
Dec. 17. **B.** Rykert Hilten and Maria Benewe.
1727, Jan. 10. **B.** Teunis [?] Visser and Machtel [?]
Lansingh.
Jan. 25. **B.** ——— Becker and ——— Van Slyk.
Feb. 20. **B.** Benj. Bogaard and Anna Halenbeek.
March 2. **B.** Douwe Fonda and Aaltie Ouderkerk.
March 6. **B.** Mart. V. Aalsteyn and Cath. V. D. Berg.
Apr. 11. **L.** Pieter Van Alen and Anna Van Wie.
Apr. 13. **B.** Jonath. Brooks and Rebecka Tattein.
Apr. 17. **B.** Sam. Thomson and Grietie Brass.
July 8. **L.** Johannes Van Driessen and Marg. V. Stryen,
Wid. Ten Broek.
Oct. — **B.** Cornelis Veeder and Elyzabeth Visser.
Oct. 28. **L.** John A. Cuyler and Chath. Wendel.
Oct. 31. **B.** Lod. Schreyder and Heyltie Van Woerd.
Nov. 11 **L.** Isaac Greveraad and Alida Gerritsen
Nov. 16. **B.** Jacob Knoet and Maria Brouwer.
Nov. 18. **B.** Gerr. V. Zanten and Anna V. d. Berk.
1728, Jan. 23. **B.** Isaac Van Aalsteyn and Maria V. D.
Bergh.
Feb. 12. **B.** Joch. V. Aalsteyn and Eva Van Valkenburgh.
Feb. 13. **B.** Roelef Jansen and Elyz. Schermerh.
Feb. 13. **B.** Hugert Viele and Cath. Van Woerdt.
Feb. 14. **B.** Jacob Van Vorst and Anna Beek.
Feb. 16. **L.** Joh. Visser and Anna Staats.
Feb. 25. **B.** Isaac Swits and Maria Vroman.
Feb. 26. **B.** Nic. V. Schayk and Dorothee Witbeek.
Apr. 10. **L.** Nic. Bleeker and Marg. Rooseboom.
Apr. 18. **L.** M. Basseth and Elyz. Schermerh.
June 15. **B.** Salomon Goewey and ———.
June 17. **L.** Jac. Ten Eyk and Alida Visser.
June 23. **B.** Pieter [?] Viele and Cath. V. Schayk.
June 28. **L.** Isaac [?] Staats and Maria [?] Van Deusen.
July 4. **B.** Zach. Zichelson and Anna [?] ———.
July 8. **B.** Baz. V. Yveren and Corn. V. Aalsteyn.
Oct. 24. **B.** Coenraat Rightmeyer and Catharina Hooft-
mensch.
Nov. 1. **L.** Do. John Miln and Maria Van Rensselaar.
Nov. 13. **L.** P Livingston and Sealy Hollant.

Dec. 14. **L.** Henry Hollant and Alida Beekman.
Dec. 19. **L.** Jacob Wendel and Helena Van Rensselaar.
Dec. 27. **L.** Jonas Witbeek and Dorothee Douwe.
1729, Jan. 15. **L.** Lancaster Symes, Jr., and M. Lydius.
Apr. 3. **L.** H. H. Rooseboom and Cat. Schuyler.
Apr. 3. **L.** G. Fielding and Cat. Rooseboom.
May 12. **B.** J. G. Lansingh and J. V. Vechten.
June 23. **B.** Jan Oothout, Jr., and M. Wendel.
July 5. **L.** St. Van Rensselaer and ———— Groesbeek.
July 6. **L.** John [?] Beekman and Sara Cuyler.
July 12. **L.** G. Van Benthuysen and Maria Van Alen.
July 15. **L.** G. C. [or Gl.] V. Den Bergh and M. V. Vegten.
July 18. **B.** Jan D. Van Arnhem and E. Lansingh.
Sept. 5. **L.** Johs. Glandorff and Maria Van Corlaar.
Sept. 7. **B.** Isaac Fort and Jac. Viele.
Sept. 12, **B.** Hendr. Hoogteelink and Hester Pricker.
Sept. 17. **B.** Nic. Groesbeek and Anna Corlaar.
Dec. 9. **L.** James [?] Stevens and Sara Groenendyk.
Dec. 13. **B.** Abr. Wyngaart and Elyz. V. Franken.
1730, Jan. 6. **L.** Abm. [?] Douw and Lyntie Wenne.
Mar. 28. **B.** Mart. V. Buren, Jr., and Th. V. D. Berg.
June 16. **B.** Kilyaen Wenne and Reb. Fonda.
June 23. **B.** John Heyton and M. V. Hoogkerk.
Aug. 1. **L.** Barent Brat and ———— Marselis.
Dec. 10. **B.** C. Langh and B Hooghtelink.
Dec. 17. **L.** M. V. d. Heyde and ———— Brat.
Dec. 17. **L.** Simon [?] Veeder and Geetruy [?] Kip.
Dec. 22. **L.** G. Marcelis and ———— Bleeker.
Dec. 22. **B.** Johs. Quackenbos and Elyz. Rumbly.
1731, Jan. 9. **L.** Richd. Garmoy and R. Evertsen.
Jan. 28. **B.** P. Van d. Berg and ———— V. D. Berg.
Feb. 5. **B.** J. M. V. Bloemendaal and Sara Gardenier.
Mar. 5. **B.** W. Teller and C. V. Alen.
Apr. 3. **B.** H. Bunsing and ———— Goewey.
Apr. 24. **L.** J. Bichard and Eliz. Van Rensselaar.
June. **B.** ———— Rycksen and ————.
Aug. 1. **B.** Jac. Bennewe and ————.
Aug. 4. **B.** Harm. Visser and Sara Wyngaart.
Oct. 1. **B.** Jam. Davis and ————.
Oct. 3. **B.** W. [?] Brat and ———— Hoogtelink.
Oct. 7 **B.** ———— Van Buuren and A. Wenne.
1732, Jan. 26. **B.** ————V. D. Berg and Maria Vinhagel.
Feb. 10. **B.** J. Brat and M. V. Franken.
Feb. 13. **B.** Abr. Lansing and R. Van Schayk.
March 21. Cert. from **Sch.**: B. A. Brat and A. V. D. Heyde.
March 27. **B.** Abr. D. Foreest and R. Symensen.
Apr. 23. **B.** James Davis and ———— Hoogkerk.

May 15. **B.** Nic. Groesbeek and ——— d. Wandelaar.
May 23. **B.** H. V. Deusen, Jr., and Th. Van Aalsteyn.
July 17. **B.** Daniel Brat and Wyntie Bogardus.
Sept. 7. **L.** Abr. Schuyler and Cath. Staats.
Sept. 16. **B.** James Stenhouse and A. M. Vedder.
Sept. 22. **B.** G. Knoet and M. Heemstrate.
Sept. 26. **L.** C. Walderom and ——— Jones.
Oct. 6. **L.** Ro. Wendel and C. Wenne.
Oct. 8. **B.** R. Tumbarr and Cor. Spoor.
Oct. 18. **B.** Johs. Van Buuren and Eytie Van Buuren.
Oct. 21. **L.** Hendr. V. Wie and Corn. Walderom.
Oct. 29. **L.** D. Fonda and A. V. Nes.
Nov. 30. **B.** Jacobus Van Valkenburg and Marg. Rettelief.
Dec. 3. **L.** Jochum Brat and Neeltie Groesbeek.
Dec. 29. **L.** Jacob Glenn and Elyz. Cuyler.
1733, **B.** Jan. 17. Albertus Becker and Cath. V. d. Zee.
Feb. 7. **B.** P. Becker and Sara Slingerlant.
March 13. **B.** C. V. D. Berg and R. Ridder.
Apr. 21. **B.** ——— Lansing and L. V. Deusen.
May 26. **L.** Levinus Wenne and ——— Wendel.
June 2. **L.** Adam Jates, y. m., and Annaatje Gerritse,
y. d., A.
May 12. **Reg.** Anthony Crispel, Jr., y. m., b. at Horly,
l. at King, and Catharina Van Benthuyse, y. d., b. and l.
at A. Ma. June 14.
July 7. **L.** Corn. De Ridder, y. m., and Gerritje Van
Noezen, y. d., both of A.
Aug. 19. **B.** Sybrant Van Schaik, y. m., and Jannetje
Bogaart, y. d., both b. and l. here.
Aug. 19. Jan Winne, y. m., b. in Col. R., and Catha-
lyntje Van Buren, b. here, both l. in Col. R.
Oct. 12. **L.** Corns Ten Broek and Maria Cuyler. Ma.
at bride's h.
Oct. 29. ——— Van Aalsteyn and ——— Van Val-
kenburg.
Nov. 3. **L.** Jac. Verplank and Lidia Van Aalsteyn.
Nov. 25. **L.** G. M. Weiss, Minister at Katskil, and Anna
Bronk.
Dec. 9. **L.** Edwaerd Collins and Marg. Bleeker.
Dec. 19. **L.** M. Veeder and Elyz. Douw.
Dec. 27. **L.** Pieter Quackenbos and Anna Oothout.
Oct. 16. [sic] **Reg.** Andries Logen, y. m., b. at Enter, Ire.,
and Alida Pruyn, y. d., b. in Col. R., both l. at Stairtoge.
Ma. Oct. 29.
Oct. 27. [sic] **Reg.** Jacobus Hilten, y. m., and Judith
Maarten, y. d., both b. and l. here. Ma. Nov. 11.
Oct. 30. [sic] **Reg.** Pieter Magriegrie, y. m., b. here, l.
at, 'sHairtoge, and Annatje Broidts, y. d., b. and l. here.
Ma. Nov. 12.

1734, Jan. 3. **L.** John Van Renselaar, y. m., and Enge-
lina Levingston, y. d., both b. and l. here.
Jan. 11. **B.** Simon Ridder and N. V. D. Zee.
Jan. 15. **L.** P. Groenendyk and N. V. Yvere.
Feb. 23. **B. L.** Witbeek and Cat. Verplank.
March 3. **B.** Sam. Morrel and Alida Dockzie.
March 17. Reg., Ma. Apr. 7. Dirck Janse, y. m., b.
here, and Cornelia Sluyter, y. d., b. at K., both l. at C.
May 12. **B. R.** Van Woerdt and M. Eckbertsen.
Aug. 11. **L.** Lucas Van Hoogkerk, y. m., and Rebecca
Fonda, y. d.
Aug. 30. **L.** Goossie Van Schaik, widr., and Debora
Van Schaick, y. d.
Aug. 7. [sic] **L.** Gerr. J. Lansing and Eytie Van Wie.
Oct. 29. **L.** Johs. Van Vegten, Jr., and Neeltie Beekman.
Oct. 29. **B.** Ritsert Olfert and Martha Benewe.
Nov. 4. **B.** Storm V. D. Zee and Lena Slingerlant.
Nov. 29. **L.** Gerr. J. Lansing and Maria Evertson.
Oct. [sic] 29. **L.** Hendrik Myndertsé Rozeboom, y. m.,
and Marytje Ten Eyck, y. d.
Dec. 5. **L.** Robbert Lansing, y. m., and Margrietje
Rozeboom, y. d.
1734/5, Jan. 9. **L.** Wouter Knickerbakker, y. m., and
Elizabeth Fonda, y. d.
Feb. 7. **B.** Reg. Jan. 25. Claas Bovy, y. m., l. in Col.
R., and Machtelt Van Franken, y. d., l. at Nist.
1735, March 20. **L.** Sybrandt Van Schaick, Jr., y. m.,
and Anna Rozeboom, y. d.
Jan. [sic] 7. **L.** F. Oothout and C. Ridder.
Jan. 17. **L.** B. Brat and C. V. Vegten.
Feb. 23. **L.** H. Lansing and A. Ouderkerk.
May 17. **B.** Jan D. Fou and Feytie Van D. Karre.
May 26. **B.** John Speysser and Mary Schia.
July 29. **L.** Cornelius Van Buren and Twenky Van den
Bergh, y. d.
Aug. 3. **B.** Jan Courtnie, y. m., b. in Ire., and Marytje
Vander Linde, wid. of Jan Olivier.
Sep. 5. **B.** Storm Van der Zee, y. m., and Elizabeth
Slingerlandt, y. d.
July 13. **B.** Johs. Ouderkerk and Helena Fonda.
July 27. **B.** J. Smith and G. D'Garmoy.
Aug. 15. **B.** John Dret and M. D. Fou.
Sep. 6. **L.** Will. Teller and Anna Schoonmaker.
Sep. 23. **B.** Abr. Vroman and M. Verplank.
Oct. 5. **B.** A. Van Woerdt and El. Becker.
Nov. 7. **L.** Abr. Fonda and Sus. Wendel.
Nov. 24. **B.** R. Springsteen and M. Borner.
Dec. 6. **L.** Harmen Hun and Elsie Lansing.
Dec. 11. **L.** Sybr. Van Schayck and Alida Roseboom.

Oct. [sic] 12. **B.** Anthony Van der Zee, y. m., and Maria Ridder, y. d.

Oct. 17. **B.** Casparus Witbeek and Antje Van der Zee, y. d.

Nov. 12. **L.** Jacobus Schuylder, y. m., and 's Jeertje Staats, y. d.

Dec. 25. **L.** Dirk Van Schelluyne, widr., and Elizabeth Rozeboom, y. d.

Dec. 28. **B.** Jonathan Bantly, y. m., and Orseltje Bayly, wid.

1736, Jan. 18. **L.** Johannes Provoost, y. m., and Catharyna Staats, y. d.

March 7. **B.** Patrik Macarti, y. m., and Greesje Rhee, wid.

Apr. 2. **B.** Hendrik Gerritse, y. m., and Dirckje Symense, y. d.

May 23. **L.** Ro. Schot and Agnietie Williams.

May 23. **B.** P. Doxy and Geertr. Du Fou.

June 29. **B.** Evert Ph. Wendell and Sus. Lansing.

June 11. **B.** Samuel Guardenier, y. m., and Barentje Barith, y. d.

June 18. **L.** at K. Dirck Van Alen, y. m., and Catharyna Johanna Ten Broek, y. d.

July 3. **B.** Joh. Van Schaik, y. m., and Alida Bogaart, y. d.

July 9. **B.** Adriaen Quackenbos, y. m., and Elizabeth Knoet, y. d.

July 27. **B.** P. Van O'Linde and C. Leischer.

Aug. 5. **B.** G. Viele and H. Oothoudt.

Aug. 17. **L.** Jac. T. Eyck and Cath. Cuyler.

Aug. 23. **B.** C. Decker and J. Schermerhoorn.

Aug. 31. **L.** Kil. Muller and Anna Brat.

Sep. 15. **L.** G. Brat and Maria Ten Eyck.

Oct. 31. **L.** Will. Hilten and Margr. Jones.

Nov. 2. **B.** S. Valkenburg and Jac. Born.

Nov. 13. **B.** H. Van Buuren and A. Salsberry.

Oct. 16. **B.** at Scha. Philippus Winne, y. m., and Zara Van Antwerpen.

Oct. 24. **L.** Abraham Wendel, y. m., and Geertruy Bleeker, y. d.

Dec. 26. **B.** John Morris, y. m., and Iefje Brad, y. d.

1736/7, Jan. 6. **L.** Franciscus Lansingh, y. m., and Marytje Livenston, y. d.

Feb. 12. **L.** Barnardus Harzen, y. m., and Catharina Pruyn, y. d.

March 1. **B.** Johannes Van der Werken, y. m., and Christyna Pruyn, y. d.

1737, May 28. **B.** Isaac Van Valkenburg, y. m., and Jannetje Klemet, y. d.

June 1. **L.** Corn. Van den Bergh, y. m., and Anneke Rykse, y. d.

June 22. **B.** Jan Bel, y. m., and Rachel Abramse, y. d.

Aug. 11. **L.** Abraham Wyngaart, widr., and Lybetje Van Aalsteyn, wid.

Sep. 5. **B.** Joseph Jets, y. m., and Maria Dumbaer.

Sep. 15. **B.** Geurt Brad, y. m., and Elizabeth Karn, y. d.

Sep. 28. **B.** Zacharias Haas, y. m., and Geesje Witbeek, y.d

Oct. 21. **L.** H. V. Slyk and ——— Visser.

Oct. 23. **B.** Jac. Kidny and Anna Hagedoorn.

Nov. 11. **B.** Storm Van d. Zee and Eva Slingerlant.

Nov. 21. **B.** John Magee and Cath. Oliver.

Nov. 28. **B.** Johs. Jetz and Rebecka Walderom.

Oct. 22. **B.** Mattheus Van Deuse, y. m., and Suzanna ———, y. d.

Oct. 27. **B.** Isaac Quackenbos, y. m., and Rebecca DeGroot, y. d.

Nov. 30. **L.** Jacob H. Ten Eyck, y. m., and Anna Wendel, y. d.

Dec. 5. **B.** Johannes Hoogh, y. m., and Catharyna Ruyter, y. d.

Dec. 23. **B.** Barent Van Buren, y. m., and Margrietje Van Vegte, y. d.

1737/8, Feb. 6. **B.** Frederik Ruyter, y. m., and Engeltje Van der Werken, y. d.

Feb. 15. **B.** Broeks Farmer, y. m., and Rachel Ryckman, y. d.

Feb. 17. **B.** Jacobus Groesbeek, y. m., and Zara Van Vegten, y. d.

Feb. 19. **B.** William Radtgert, Jr., y. m., and Mary Weith, y. d.

Feb. 22. **B.** William Crooks, y. m., and Margrieta Anderson, wid.

1738, March 4. **B.** 's Jeems Flemming, y. m., and Lena Gardenier, y. d.

March 19. **B.** Corns. Van Aalsteyn, y. m., and Theuntje Fort, y. d.

Apr. 1. **B.** Jonathan Witbeek, Jr., y. m., and Magtel Wyngaard, y. d.

Apr. 25. **B.** Robbert Barreith, y. m., and Maria Maarten, y. d.

Apr. 30. **B.** Volkert Van Hoezen, y. m., and Alida Marcelis, y. d.

May 13. **B.** Japik Jap. Lansing, y. m., and Huybertje Jaets, y. d.

May 13. **B.** Japik Van Woerd, y. m., and Annaatje Ouderkerk, y. d.

June 21. **B.** Franciscus Winne, y. m., and Agnietje Van Wie, y. d.

June 21. **B.** Willem Groesbeek, y. m., and Catharyna Van Es, y. d.

July 2. **B.** Harmen Vedder, y. m., and Tryntje Van Heemstraat, y. d.

July 5. **L.** Ritchard Hanszen, widr., and Catharyna Ten Broeck, y. d.

July 7. **B.** Gerrit Van Francken, y. m., and Marytje Fort, y. d.

Sep. 9. **B.** Douwe Ketelheyn, y. m., and Nelletje Brouwer, y. d.

Oct. 17. **B.** Adriaan Brad, y. m., and Zelia Van Zanten, y. d.

Nov. 3. **L.** Hendrik Van Buren, y. m., and Geertruy Witbeek, y. d.

Nov. 16. **L.** Abraham Van der Poel, y. m., and Elizabeth Koeymans, y. d.

Nov. 16. **B.** Johannes Vinnagel, Jr., y. m., and Neeltje Van den Bergh y. d.

Dec. 2. **L.** Cornelis Van Nes, y. m., and Suzanna Swits, y. d.

Dec. 9. **B.** William Seksby, y. m., and Annaatje Ratdelief y. d.

Dec. 15. **L.** Killiaan Winne and Geertruyda Coster, y. d.

1738/9, Jan. 18. **L.** Gerrit H. Lansing, y. m., and Magtel Beekman, y. d.

Jan. 19. **L.** Corns. Ouderkerk, y. m., and Catharyna Huyck, y. d

Jan. 20. **L.** Tjerk Switz, y. m., and Jannetje Waters, y. d.

Jan. 22. **B.** Abraham Viele, y. m., and Francyntje Fort, y. d.

Jan. 26. **L.** Willem Van den Bergh, y. m., and Suzanna Van Iveren, y. d.

Jan. 30. **L.** James Pat Blado, y. m., and Zara Bath, y. d.

Feb. 3. **L.** Willem Clauw, y. m., and Christina Huyk, y. d.

Feb. 17. **L.** Hendrik Fonda, y. m., and Anna Van Vegten, y. d.

Feb. 24. **L.** Harmen Vischjer, y. m., and Rachel Van der Heyden, Jr., y. d.

March 8. **L.** Gerardus Groesbeek, y. m., and Maria Ten Broeck, y. d.

1739, Apr. 24. **B.** Franciscus Belvil, y. m., and Neeltje Abramse, y. d.

May 12. **L.** Joachim Staats, y. m., and Elizabeth Schuyler, y. d.

June 7. **L.** Theunis Van Slyck, Jr., widr., and Cathalyna Goewey, y. d.

June 28. **B.** Jan Baptist Van Vorst, y. m., and Catryna Marcelis, y. d.

June 28. **B.** Ephraim Smit, y. m., and Elizabeth Jets, y. d.

Aug. 14. **B.** Johannes Abramse, y m., and Catharyna Schjans, y. d.

Aug. 26. **B.** Salomon Meyer, widr., and Anna Margriet Covel, wid.

Aug. 31. **B.** Willem Brad, y. m., and Elizabeth Van Vorst, y. d.

Aug. 31. **B.** Andries Scherp, y. m., and Elizabeth Goewyck, y. d.

Sep. 6. **L.** Johannes Livingston, y. m., and ·Catharyna Ten Broeck, y. d.

Sep. 7. **B.** Cornelis Groot, y. m., and Elizabeth Potman, y. d

Oct 4. **L.** Hendricus Brad, y. m., and Rebecca Van Vegten, y. d.

Oct. 18. **L.** Wouter Groesbeek, y. m., and Marytje Bogardus, y. d.

Nov. 6. **L.** Gerrit Theunisze Van Vegten, y. m., and Lena Witbeek, y. d.

Nov. 24. **B.** Corns. Huyck, y. m., and Nelletje Bovie, y. d.

Nov. 24. **B.** Johannes Huyk, y. m., and Catharina Bovie, y d.

Nov 30. **L.** Johannes G. Rozeboom, y m. and Elsje Lansing, y. d.

Dec. 6. **L.** Johannes Zandertse, y. m., and Debora Glen, y. d.

Dec. 7. **L.** Douwe Bogaert, y. m., and Willemtje Brad, y. d.

Dec. 14. **B.** Wouter Groesbeek, y. m., and Jannetje Bogaart, y. d.

1739/40, Jan. 11. **B.** Abram Quackenbos, y. m., and Bata Ouderkerk, y. d.

Jan. 17. **L.** William Hogan, Jr., y. m., and Suzanna Lansingh, y. d.

Feb. 9. **B.** William Boets [?], y. m., and Maria Christiaanse, y. d.

Feb 16. **L.** Philip Hanzen, y. m., and Geertruy Van Nes, y. d.

Feb. 18. **B.** Isaak Huygh, y. m., and Neeltje Knoe , y. d.

Feb. 22. **B.** Gysbert Van Zanten, y. m., and Margriet Kaarn, y. d.

Feb. 25. **B.** Samuel Born, y. m., and Magdalena Pruyn, y. d.

March 8. **L.** Gerrit Is. Lansing, y. m., and Ariaantje Beekman, y. d.

March 10. **L.** John Van Buren, y. m., and Agnietje Conyn, y. d.

1740, March 27. **L.** William Salisbury, y. m., and Theuntje Staats, y. d.

Apr. 14. **L.** Philip Livingston, Jr., y. m., and Christyna Ten Broeck, y. d.

May 8. **L.** Japik Harzen, Jr., y. m., and Marytje Pruym, y. d.

May 9. **L.** Johannes F. Witbeek, y m., and Eva Walderon, y. d.

May 14. **L.** Gerrit Johnse Lansing, y. m., and Elsje Lansingh, y. d.

May 23. **L.** Anthony Van Yveren, y. m., and Marrietje Van den Bergh, y. d.

May 24. **B.** Johannes Van Yveren, y. m., and Maria Oostrande, y. d.

May 25, **L.** John Jacobse Rozeboom, y. m., and Magtel Rykman, y. d.

May 29. **L.** Harmen Ganzevoort, y. m., and Magdalena Douw, y. d.

June 21. **L.** Hendrik Van Slyk, y. m., and Elisabeth Van Benthuysen, y. d.

July 11. **B.** Hendrik Nicol. Gardenier, y. m., and Eva Van Valkenburg, y. d.

July 11. **B.** Abram Van Valkenburg, y. m., and Neeltje Gardenier, y. d.

Aug. 29. **L.** Jacob J. Schermerhoorn, y. m., and Catharina Van Buren, y. d.

Sep. 27. **L.** Abraham H. Wendel, y. m., and Elizabeth Wendel, y. d.

Oct. 16. **L.** Jacobus Van der Poel, y. m., and Neeltje Huyck, y. d.

Oct. 18. **L.** Jacobus Groesbeek, y. m., and Cathalina Jaets, y. d.

Oct. 19. **L.** Jan Brad, y. m., and Catharina Fonda, y. d.

Oct. 30. **L.** Bernardus Bradt, y. m., and Margrieta Williams, y. d.

Nov. 1. **B.** Andries Van Woerd, y. m., and Elizabeth Vander Werken, y. d.

Dec. 6. **B.** Staats Zeger, y. m., and Suzanna Bradt, y. d.

Dec. 6. **L.** Robbert Sandertse, y. m., and Maria Lansingh, y. d.

1740/1, Jan. 9. **B.** Adam Brad, y. m., and Lydia Zeger, y. d.

Jan. 10. **L.** Johannes Bleeker, widr., and Eva Bries, y. d.

Jan. 27. **B.** Dirck Maarten, y. m., and Catharyna Brouwer, y. d.

Feb. 6. **B.** James Parker Benthuysen, y. m., and Zara Cooper, y. d.

Feb. 27. **B**. Abraham Vinhagel, y. m., and Jannetje Van Buren, y. d.

March 4. **L**. James Elswood, widr., and Maria Flensburgh, wid.

1741, March 20. Phillip Ruyter, y. m., and Geertruy Van der Werke, y. d.

March 30. **L**. Jonas Oothout, y. m., and Elizabeth Lansing, y. d.

Apr. 20. **B**. Abram G. Lansing, widr., and Catharina De Foreest, wid. of Jan Van Aalsteyn.

May 1. **B**. Albert Van der Zee, y. m., and Antje Van Wie, y. d.

May 8. **B**. Dirk Bradt, widr., and Antje Barroway, y. d.

May 21. **L**. Dirck Van Vegten, y. m., and Elizabeth Ten Broek, y. d.

Aug. 14. **L**. Johannes Jac. Lansingh, y. m., and Rachel Lievense, y. d.

Aug. 22. **B**. Johannes Flensburgh, y. m., and Cornelia Hooghteling, y. d.

Aug. 26. **L**. Cornelius Van den Bergh, y. m., and Rachel Brad, y. d.

Sep. 10. **B**. Jacob Doxs, y. m., and Marretje De Vous, y. d.

Oct. 5. **B**. Johan Casparse Geefhart, y. m., and Elizabeth Zeger, y. d.

Oct. 17. **L**. Abraham Melchertse Witbeek, y. m and Marrietje Van Deuse, y. d.

Oct. 23. **B**. Roelof De Vous, y. m., and Bethje Goelding, y. d.

Oct. 24. **B**. Jacob Bogaard, Jr., y. m., and Maria Jaets, y. d.

Nov. 20. **B**. Benjamin Van den Bergh, y. m., and Johanna Vinnagel, y. d.

Dec. 20. **L**. Isaac Halenbeek, y. m., and Gerritje Van Woerd, y. d.

Dec. 20. **B**. Hendrik Zandertsen, widr., and Anna Miller.

1741/2, Jan. 8. **B**. Samuel Staats, y. m., and Neeltje Staats, y. d.

Jan. 14. **B**. Abraham Doxs, y. m., and Rebecca Marcelis, y. d.

Feb. 9. **B**. Johan Jurry Criger, y. m., and Margariet Schoemaker, y. d.

Feb. 20. **B**. Omphry Hitkok, widr., and Zara Thammes, wid.

Feb. 21. **B**. Corn. C. Van Aalsteyn, y. m., and Catharyna Wendel, y. d.

March 6. **L**. Hermanus Wendel, Jr., y. m., and Catharina Van Vegten, y. d.

March 13. **L.** Thomas Williams, Jr., y. m., and Maria Van Hoesen, Jr., y. d.

May 20. **L.** Volkert P. Douw, y. m., and Annaatje De Peyster, y. d.

May 21. **L.** Jabes Doty, y. m., and Maria Anne Prys, y. d.

June 1. **B.** Willem Brommely, y. m., and Lena Boom, y. d.

June 14. **B.** Eduard Hogil, y. m., and Maria Egmond, y. d.

June 22. **B.** Thomas Marl, y. m., and Hester De Mes, y. d.

June 25. **L.** Gerrit Van Alen, y. m., and Catharina Van Wie, y. d.

July 4. **B.** Jacob Viele, y. m., and Eva Fort, y. d.

July 17. **B.** Abraham Bekker, y. m., and Elizabeth Van Olinda, y. d.

July 31. **B.** Jan Brad, y. m., and Zantje Zeger, y. d.

Sep. 24. **B.** Benjamin Hilten, y. m., and Maria Prys, y. d.

Oct. 4. **B.** Thomas Couper, y. m., and Elizabeth Van Buren, y. d.

Oct. 14. **L.** John Van Wie, Jr., y. m., and Gerritje Wendel, y. d.

Oct. 15. **L.** Casparus Conyn, widr., and Eva Van Alen, y. d.

Oct. 22. **L.** Cornelis Schermerhoorn, y. m., and Maria Winne, y. d.

Oct 30. **B.** Patrik Regil, y. m., and Elizabeth Prys, y. d.

Nov. 6. **L.** Jacob Jac. Lansing, y. m., and Maria Egbertse, y. d.

Nov. 19. **B.** Abraham Van Vranken, y. m., and Dirkje Crigier, y. d.

Dec. 9. **B.** Willem Lievense, y. m., and Maria Fonda, y. d.

Dec. 11. **L.** Isaac Hanze, y. m., and Maria Brad, y. d.

Dec. 25. **L.** Jacob Witbeek, y. m., and Cathalyna Van Deuse, y. d.

Dec. 29. **B.** John Dilling, y. m., and Maria Miller, y. d.

Dec. 29. **B.** Abraham Delmont, y. m., and Suzanna Egbertse, y. d.

1743, Feb. 3 **L.** Geurt Van Schoonoven, y. m., and Annaatje Lansing, y. d.

Feb. 17. **B.** Cornelis Muller, y. m., and Maria Van Hoezen, Jr., y. d.

Feb. 19. **B.** Joseph Radelief, y. m., and Margrieta Brad, y. d.

Feb. 24. **L.** Isaac Ouderkerk, y. m., and Annetje Knoet, y. d.

Feb. 27 **L.** Jacob Clement, y. m., and Jannetje Van Woerd, y. d.

March 4. **B.** Obedia Couper, y. m., and Maria Fonda, y. d.

Apr. 14. **B.** Samuel Green, y. m., and Judith Brommely, y. d.

May 5. **L.** Johannes Van der Poel, widr., and Annaatje Staats, y. d.

May 29. **L.** Jacob Vroman, y. m., and Rachel Van Woerd, y. d.

June 9. **B.** Pieter David Schuyler, y. m., and Eliza Barbara Herchemer, y. d.

June 16. **L.** Jacob Mynd. Van Yveren, y. m., and Wyntje Van den Bergh, y. d.

June 28. **L.** Dirk Wess. Ten Broek, y. m., and Catharina Conyn, y. d.

July 7. **L.** Bastiaan Tymense, y. m., and Mayken Ouderkerk, y. d.

July 23. **B.** John Welsch, y. m., and Annaatje Thiel, y. d.

July 23. **B.** Pieter Merschel, y. m., and Annaatje Flensburgh, y. d.

Aug. 5. **L.** John Rutgerse Bleeker, y. m., and Elizabeth Staats, y. d.

Sep. 5. **B.** Ryckert Bovie, y. m., and Marytje Huyk, y. d.

Sep. 8. **L.** Abraham Fonda, y. m., and Maria Van Schoonoven, y. d.

Oct. 2. **B.** Benjamin Goewyk, y. m., and Catharina Van den Bergh, y. d.

Oct. 2. **L.** Omie Le Gransie, y. m., and Maria Van Brakel, y. d.

Oct. 14. **L.** Hendrik Ten Broek, y. m., and Anna Van Schaik, y. d.

Nov. 2. **L.** Barent Staats, y. m., and Magdalena Schuyler, y. d.

Nov. 3. **L.** Wessel Van Schaik, y. m., and Marytje Gerritse, y. d.

Nov. 21. **B.** Hendrik Van den Berk, y. m., and Tryntje Hooghtelingh, y. d.

Nov. 24. **B.** Albert Brad, y. m., and Annaatje Kaarn, y. d.

Dec. 3. **L.** Peter Walderon, y. m., and Neeltje Lansing, y. d.

Dec. 9. **B.** Hendrik Bloem, y. m., and Elizabeth Gardenier, y. d.

Dec. 17. **L.** Robbert Rozeboom, y. m., and Rykje Rozeboom, y. d.

Dec. 30. **B.** Lambert Kool, y. m., and Marytje Kitnie, y. d.

1744, Jan. 3. **L.** Ephraim Van Vechten, y. m., and Catharina Ten Broeck, y. d.

Jan. 4. **L.** Willem Van Aalsteyn, y. m., and Christina Van Alen, y. d.

Jan. 15. **L.** John Williams, y. m., and Cornelia Bogardus, y. d.

Jan. 21. **B.** Johannes Radelief, Jr., y. m., and Geertruy Brad, y. d.

Jan. 21. **L.** Pieter Williams, y. m., and Zara Van Yveren, y. d.

Jan. 24. **B.** Hendrik Jongh, y. m., and Catharina Landman, y. d.

Jan. 29. **B.** Jacob Egmond, y. m., and Mary Lewis, y. d.

Feb. 29. **L.** Theunis Van Vechten, y. m., and Cornelia Knickerbakker, y. d.

March 2. **L.** Hendrik Jansze Van Wie, y. m., and Cornelia Van den Bergh, y. d.

March 8. **B.** Adam Van Vranken, y. m., and Ariaantje Knoet, y. d.

Apr. 21. **B.** Evert Zeger, y. m., and Zara Aarscherd, y. d.

May 5. **L.** Abraham Cuyler, Jr., y. m., and Jannetje Beekman, y. d.

May 20. **L.** Abraham Jac. Lansing, y. m., and Elizabeth Couper, y. d.

June 1. **B.** Symeon Springsteen, y. m., and Maria Zeger, y. d.

June 11. **B.** Gysbert Van Aalsteyn, y. m., and Antje Ridders, y. d.

June 15. **L.** Daniel P. Winne, y. m., and Jannetje De Foreest, y. d.

June 20. **L.** Abraham Kip, y. m., and Elsje Pruyn, y. d.

June 21. **L.** Matthias Bovie, widr., and Elenor Bennewe, wid.

June 22. **B.** David Schans, y. m., and Maria Immerik, y. d.

July 2. **L.** Hendrik Van Hoezen, y. m., and Cathalina Van den Bergh, y. d.

Oct. 20. **L.** John Jacobs Lansing and Catlyna Van Schaik, spinster, both of A. Co.

1744/5, Jan. 6. **L.** Jacobus Bleeker and Margreta Ten Eik, spinster, both of A. Co.

1745, Apr. 19. **L.** John Van Deusen, Carp'r., and Maria Winne, spinste , both of A.

Apr. 19. **L.** Jacob Bellieur, yeoman, and Catharina Van den Bergh, spinster, both of A. Co.

Apr. 20. **L.** Arent Van Deusen, mason, and Catharina Waldrom, spinster, both of A.

Apr. 20. **B.** David Van Zanten, y. m., and Rachel Hooghteeling, y. d., both of A. Co.

Apr. 21. **L.** Barent H. Ten Eik, merchant, and Helena Rykman, spinster, both of A. Co.

May 4. **L.** Philip De Freest of A. Co., and Maria Bloemendal, spinster, of A.

May 11. **L.** Nikolaas Cuyler, merchant, of A. City, and Maria Schuyler, spinster, of A. Co.

1746/7, Jan. 11. **B.** John Davie, l. in the Great Bend, and Elizabeth Wyngaart of A.

Jan. 11. **L.** Robert Sanders and Elizabeth Schuyler, both of A.

Jan. 12. **B.** Johannes, son of Seth, and Maria, dau. of Aaron, pros.

Joseph, son of Hendrick, and Christina, dau. of Seth, pros.

Jan. 17. **L.** Petrus Van Hoesen of A. Co. and Helena Fonda of A.

1747. Dec. 2. **L.** Staats Van Sandvoort of Sch. and Willemtje Brat of A.

Dec. 31. **L.** Cornelius Van Santvoord, Jr., of Sch. and Ariaantje Brat of A.

1747/8, Jan. 9. **L.** Johannes Perry of C. and Francyntje Knoet of Col. R.

1748, Oct. 30. **L.** Peter Jones and Abigael Winne, both of A.

Nov. 5. **Ma.** Reynier Van Aalsteyn and Cornelia Van den Berg.

Nov. 6. **Ma.** Gozen Van Schaick and Majeke Van den-Berg.

Nov. 13. **Ma. L.** Robert Crannel and Ariaantje Bovie.

Nov. 19. **Ma.** Ephraim Bogardus, y. m., and Anatje Halenbeek, y. d.

Nov. 28. Michael Philips, y. m., b. in Rhode Island, and Margarita Wyngaard, y. d., b. at A., both l. here.

Dec. 3. **L.** William Merryday and Hilleke Lewis, wid., both of A.

BAPTISMAL RECORD SINCE THE YEAR 1725.

[For list of abbreviations see page fronting Index.]

1725, Jan. 3. Elyzabeth, ch. of Pieter and Cath. Schuyler. Witnesses: Ph. Schuyler, Elyz. Groesbeek.

Jan. 17. Johannes, of Sam. and Anna Rettelief. Wit.: Joh. and Rachel Rettelief.

Jan. 20. Margarita, of Ph. and Geerte Verplank. Wit.: Ro. Livingston, Jr., Gerrt Drajer, Marg. Freeman.

Jan. 24. Elyzabeth, of Mart. and Jann. Van Olinde. Wit.: Pieter and Elyz. V. Olinde.

Feb. 3. Theunis, of Ruth and Bethy Van Woerdt. Wit.: Andries and Sara Gardenier.

Feb. 3. Chatharina, of Dirk and Maria Hagedoorn. Wit.: Will. and Elyz. Walderom.

Feb. 7. Cathalyna, of Isack and Cath. Wendell. Wit.: David and Maria Van Dyk.

1725

Feb. 7. David, of Harm. and Jann. Schuyler. Wit. : Evert and Elyz. Banker

Feb. 10. Johannes, of Joh. and Marg. V. D. Werke. Wit.: Dirk and Marg. Ten Broek.

Feb. 17. Marytie, of Joh. and Zelia Rettelief. Wit.: Joseph and Hendr. Yets.

Anna, of Anth. and Jann. Bogardus. Wit.: Jisse and Neelt. Foreest.

Feb. 21. John, of John and Elyz. Teller. Wit.: Georgh Wilson, Elyz. Brouw.

Feb. 24. Maria, of Corn. and Hendr. V. Buuren. Wit.: Corn. and Marr. Schermerhoorn.

Albert, of Andr. and Eng. Witbeek. Wit.: Folk. and Marg. Douw.

Elyzabeth, of Meind. and Titie Marselis. Wit.: C. Hansen Tol, Elyz. Marselis.

Mar. 6. Barent, of Gerr. and Eng. V. D. Bergh. Wit.: Andr. and Theuntie V. D. Bergh.

John, of John Waters and Sara Waters. Wit.: Pieter and Lyntie Wenne.

Susanna, of Gerrit and Susanna Ridder. Wit.: Pieter and Ariaentie V. Woert.

Evert, of Joh. and Anna Wendell. Wit.: Theunis Slingerland, Catalyna Kip.

Jacob, of Jac. and Hest. [?, V. d. Heyde. Wit.: Joh. Visser [?].

Mar. 21. Hilletje, of Evert and Marr. Rycksen. Wit.: Joh. and Eckb. D. Garmoy.

Elsie, of Joh. and Sara Hansen. Wit.: Joh. and Elsie Cuyler Joseph, of Moses and Alida, pros. Wit.: Hendrick Cuyler and Jacomyn, a pros.

Jacob, of Symon and Josina, pros. Wit.: Petr. Van Driesen and Christina, a pros.

Apr. 4. Reynier, of Jacob and Pietertie V. Aalsteyn. Wit.: Reynier and Sara V. Yveren.

Mary, of Willem and Rous [?] Turk or Tuck. Wit.: George Wilson, Sara Rylief.

Mary, of Are [?] and Mary Gunner. Wit.: John and Mary Turnbarn.

Josyna, of Evert and Maria Wielaar. Wit.: Roelef Clark, Helena Wielaar.

Dirk, of Anth. and A. Chath. V. Schayk. Wit.: Corn. T. Broek, Lydia V. Vegten.

Johannes, of Goz. and Neeltie V. Schayk. Wit.: Christ. Abeel, Gerr. Ten Eyk.

Apr. 11. Rachel, of Will. and Martha Rettelief. Wit.: Jac. and Rachel Rettelief.

Anth. Bries, of Christ. and Marg. Abeel. Wit.: Goz. V. Schayk, Catal. Bleeker.

1725

Ysack, of P. and M. V. Aalsteyn. Wit.: Jan and El.
V. Aalsteyn.
Anna Marg., of Pieter and Charl. Cojeman. Wit.:
Sam. Cojeman, Anna Barckley.
Jeems, of Will. and Jeen Hellingh. Wit.: Jeems Banks,
Jeen Hollant.
May 2. Jeremias, of Will. Schyarh and Mary Schyarch.
Wit.: John and Judy Morrow.
May 16. Epraim, of Joh. and Elyz. Wendell. Wit.:
Epram and Cath. Wendell.
Tytie, of Wouter Barhayt and Rachel Barheyt. Wit.
Meyndt and Tytie Marselis.
May 17. Barent, of Reyer and Geertie Schermerhoorn.
Wit.: Hendr. and Jann. T. Eyk.
May 30 Pieter, of Corn. V. Buuren and Maria Van
Buuren. Wit.: Joh., Jr., and Maria Cuyler.
Marten, of Dirk and Maria Hogeboom. Wit.: Mart.
Delmond. Rest illegible.
Sara, of Dirk and Mary Ten Broek. Wit.: David Van
Dyk, Marg. Cuyler.
Sara, of Leendert and Anna Bronk. Wit.: Frerik and
Sara Meyndertsen.
Catharina, of Corn. and Maria Van Dyk. Wit.: Isack
Wendell Nell Bries.
Nicolaes, of Jacob and Geertruy Knoet. Wit.: Nicol.
and Rachel Bleeker.
June 6. Catharina, of Hendr. and Marg. Cuyler. Wit. :
Abrah. Cuyler and Elyz. V. Deusen.
Cornelia, of Wyn. and Anna V. D. Bergh. Wit.: Wilh.
and Geertie V. D. Berch.
June 13. Jacob, of Hendr. and Elsie Schermerhoorn.
Wit.: Joh. and Elyz. Schermerhoorn.
Neeltie, of Nicolaas and Marr. Groesbeek. Wit.: Piet.
and Maria Quakkenbosch.
Elyzabeth, of Frans and Marg. Pruym. Wit.: Abr. V.
Aarnheim, Elyz. Lansingh.
June 26. Zacharias, of Ezras and Elyzabeth, pros.
Wit.: Ezras and Josyna, pros.
Pieter, of Aquarith and Christina, pros. Wit.: Quarant
and Jacomyn, pros.
Neeltie, of Hendrik and Anna, pros. Wit.: Ezras and
Margariet, pros.
Maas, Maddalena, of Pieter and Geerte V. Buuren.
Wit.: Maas and Madel. Van Buuren, Benjamin and
Madelena Bratt.
July 4. Geertruy, of Dirk and Maria Van Schelluyn.
Wit.: Corn. and Geertruy Van Schelluyn.
July 25. Catharina, of Hieroon and Grietie Van Vlieren.
Wit.: Ysack Fonda, Anna Valkenburg.

1725

Pieter, of Leend. and Chath. Gansevoort. Wit.: Thom. and Hill. Williams.

Aug. 1. Andries, of Christ. and Cath. Schyans. Wit.: Jan Gerritsen, Maria Quakkenbosch.

Joseph, of Hendrik and Margarita, pros. Wit.: Joseph and Zelia, pros.

Willem, of David and Maria Groesbeek. Wit.: Melch. V. D. Poel, Geertruy Groesbeek.

Aug. 16. Matheus, of Claes and Corn. Bovy. Wit.: Anth. and Cath. Bovy.

Marretie, of Adam and Maria V. D. Berg. Wit.: Claes V. Woert, Maretie Spoor.

Aug. 22. Johannes, of Joh., Jr., and Jenneke Bleeker. Wit.: Johannes and Anna Bleeker.

Aug. 30. Lena, of Th. and Eng. Eckbertsen. Wit.: John Basset, Rach. Beekman.

Lowys, of Th. and Maria Viele. Wit.: Lowys and Maria Viele.

Sep. 5. Willem, of Joh. and Zara V. Santen. Wit.: Ysaak and Jann. Lansingh.

Helena, of Jac. and Anna Gardenier. Wit.: Sam. and Jesyna Gardenier.

Ariaantie, of Ryk and Geerte V. Franken. Wit.: Will. Banker, Maria V. Olinde.

Catharina, of Sybr. and Elyz. Quakkenbosch. Wit.: Anth. V. Schayk and Cath. Quakkenbosch.

Marget, of Daniel and Elyz. Jenschen. Wit.: Joseph Heyns, Zelia Hollant.

Robert, of Arens and Sara, pros. Wit.: John and Eliza Rosie, Zara Kidny.

Christina, of Joh. and Cath. Ten Broek. Wit.: Folk. and Lidia V. Vegten.

Hendrik, of Hendr. and Marg. Ten Eyk. Wit.: Henkr. Bleeker, Cath. Gleyn.

Jan, of Jan and Cat. Van Nes. Wit.: John D. Peyster, Elyz. Groesbeek.

Sep. 26. Gerrit, of Gerr. and Eck. V. D. Berg. Wit.: Daniel and Gerretie Fort.

Chatharina, Ariantie, of Jan and Chath. Du Fou. Wit.: Joh. Roelofsen, Aaltie Barrewey, Isack Lansingh, Marr. Kidny.

Oct. 1. Ysack, of Gelyn V. Plank and Ariaentie Verplank. Wit.: Folk. Douw, Abigael V. Plank.

Dirk, of Willem and Catalyna Barheyt. Wit.: Johann and Elyz. Bratt.

Oct. 3. Elyzabeth, of Barent and Neeltie Staats. Wit.: Jacob and Isabelle Staats.

Elyzabeth, of Hendr. and Susanna Halenbeek. Wit.: Gerrit and Elyz. Bratt.

1725

Fytie, of Jan and Cath. Halenbeek. Wit.: H. V. Deusen, Agnietie Muller.

Oct. 10. Marten Gerritsen, of Petr. and Christ. V. Bergen. Wit.: Hendr. Douw, Elyz. Koster.

Nicolaas, of Jacob and Anna Egmond. Wit.: Zander and Engeltie Lansing.

Johannes, of Willem and Anna Huyck. Wit.: Meindt and Fytie Marselis.

Oct. 24. Margarita, of Math. and Maria Bovy. Wit.: Joh. and Margarita Knoet.

Neeltie, of Mart. and Cath. V. Bergen. Wit.: Andries Douw, Lidia V. Vegten.

Ysack, Elsie, of Jacob and Lena Lansingh. Wit.: Gerr. and Jann. Lansingh, Bar. and Maria Sanders.

Dirck, of Joch. and Anna V. D. Heyde. Wit.: Math. and Anna V. D. Heyde.

Catharina, of Wilh. and Geertie V. D. Bergh. Wit.: Wyn. and Cat. V. D. Bergh.

Nov. 7. Henderickus, of Eckbert and Elyz. Bratt. Wit.: Ant. and Jann. Bogardus.

Catalyna, of Pieter and Maria Fonda. Wit.: Jan and Maria Fonda.

Willem, of Pieter and Rachel Wenne. Wit.: Pieter and Eva V. Alen.

Sara, of Ph. and Cath. Levingston. Wit.: Abr. Cuyler, Cath. V. Rensselaar.

Johannes, of Jacob and Hendr. V. Woert. Wit.: Jan and Aaltie Oothout.

Nov. 14. Wouter, of Jesse and Neeltie D. Foreest. Wit.: Pieter and Corn. Quakkenbosch.

Anna, of Nath. and Mar. Eylleth. Wit.: Jeremiah and Marr. Pemlethon.

Johannes, of Joh. and Rachel V. D. Heyde. Wit.: David and Rachel V. D. Heyde.

Nov. 21. Johannes, of Marten and Maria V. Buuren. Wit.: Andr. V. D. Bergh, Geertr. V. Vegten.

Maria, of Abr. and Antie V. D. Poel. Wit.: Glyn V. Plank, Maria Groesbeek.

Nov. 25. Anna, of Abr. and Geertie Vosburgh. Wit.: Levinus Lieves, Cath. V. D. Berghe.

Isack, of Isack and Elyz. Fryer. Wit.: Jerm. Ten Brooks, Maria Bennewe.

Maria, of Petrus and Anna Douw. Wit.: Sam. and Maria Ten Broek.

Nov. 26. Margarita, of Piet. and Anna Bennewe. Wit.: Isack Fort, Marg. Bennewe.

Theunis, of Anth. and Rebecka Brat. Wit.: Abr. and Geesje Kip.

1725-1726

Elyzabeth (illegitimate), of Elyzabeth Martyn. (Father, Charles Danielson.) Wit.: John Brownley, Marr Pemmetshon.

Anthony, of Joseph and Agniet, pros. Wit.: Anthony and Sara, pros.

Aaron, of Tierk and Katharina, pros. Wit.: Ezras and Neeltje, pros.

Pieter, of Johannes and Margariet, pros. Wit.: Pieter and Maria, pros.

Chatharina, of Johannes and Margariet, pros. Wit.: Chatharina, pros.

Jacob, of Johannes and Maria, pros. Wit.: Jacomina.

Catharina, Sara, of Margariet, pros. Wit.: Ezras and Margariet, pros.

1726, Jan. 1. Christiaen, of Joh. and Neeltie Christiaensen. Wit.: Corn. and Maria Cuyler.

Eva, of Joh. and Johanna Marselis. Wit.: Joh. and Eva Beekman.

Jan. 2. Catharina, of Andries and Wyntie Bratt. Wit.: Gysb. and Chath. Rooseboom.

Rachel, of Nicolaes and Rachel Gardenier. Wit.: Jer. and Maria V. Rensselaer.

Jan. 9. Gerretie, of Joh. and Elyz. Oostrander. Wit.: Harm. Oostrander, Lena Lansingh.

Madalena, of Pieter and Rebecca Bogaart. Wit.: Maas and Madal. Van Buuren.

Jan. 16. Thomas, of Joh. and Brechie Zeeger. Wit.: Evert and Cath. Wielaar.

Jan. 19. Johannes, of Hendr. and Elsie Rooseboom. Wit.: Joh. and Gerretie Rooseboom.

Cornelis, of Gerr. and Sara Van Nes. Wit.: Joh. and Maria V. D. Bergh.

Feb. 6. Meyndert, of B. and Jann. Vosburgh. Wit.: Claes Lucassen, Maria V. Dyk.

Andries, of Andr. and Maria Huyck. Wit.: Lamb. Rettelief, Ariaentie Ouderkerk.

Feb. 16. Elyzabeth, (illeg.), of Maria Burger. Wit.: Roelof Kidny, Dirkie Van Woert.

Pieter, of Joh. and Rebecka Maassen. Wit.: Pieter and Maria Fonda.

Sara, of Tho. and Mary Archel. Wit.: George and Helena Wilson.

Feb. 23. Geertruy of Casper and Anna Ham. Wit.: Jan and Agnietie Witbeek.

Feb. 27. Evert, Francyntje, of Walderom and Anna Knoet. Wit.: Willem and Maria Ketelluyn, Joh. and Grietie Knoet.

Volkie, of Gysbert and Cat. V. D. Bergh. Wit.: Wyn. and Volkie V. D. Bergh.

1726

March 13. Johanna, of John and Lidia Beasely. Wit.: Joh. and Lena Lansingh.

Petrus, of Pieter and Geertruy V. D. Lyn. Wit.: Petr. Van Driessen, Maria Van Rensselaar.

Dirckie, of Joh. and Eckbertie Garmoy. Wit.: Harm. Visser, He ter Tymensen.

March 27. Rachel, of Levinus and Cath. Harmensen. Wit.: Gerrit and Alida V. D. Bergh.

Engeltie, of Dirk and Lena V. D. Karre. Wit.: Anth. V. Schayk, Feyte V. d. Karre.

Arientie, of Evert and Maria Wielaar. Wit.: Jan and Rachel Woutkok.

Willempie, of Benj. and Mad. Brat. Wit.: Bar. Brat, Nell. Rykmans.

Apr. 3 Richard, of Daniel and Hester Brodhead. Wit.: Richard and Wyntie Brodhead.

Jacob Salomons, of Laurens and Hilletie Scherp. Wit.: Jacob and Alida Goewey.

Apr. 17. Melchert, of Marten and Elbertie Van Deusen. Wit.: Melchert Van Deusen, Maria Groesbeek.

Maria, of Jeremias and Susanna Schuyler. Wit.: Phillip and Marg. Schuyler.

Jacob, of Obedy and Corn. Couper. Wit.: Jacob Maassen, Sara Gardenier.

Hester, of Abr. and Alida V. Arnhem. Wit.: Claes Fonda, Sara Becker.

Elyzabeth, of Eldert and Helena Ouderkerk. Wit.: Pieter and Ariaentie Van Woerdt.

Maria, of Daniel and Susanna, pros. Wit.: Hendrik and Rebecka, pros.

Joseph, of Abraham and Maria, pros. Wit.: Hendrik and Elyzabeth, pros.

Jannetie, of Philip and Cath. Conyn. Wit.: Joh. Muller, Antie Hogeboom.

Robert, of Tobias and Ariaentie Van Deusen. Wit.: Ro. and Geertruy V. Deusen.

Jeremias, of Christ. and Rachel Muller. Wit.: Jeremias and Elyzabeth Muller.

Apr. 24. Johannes, of Gerrit and Elyz. Lansingh. Wit.: Joh. and El. Groesbeek.

Lucas, of Harm. and Geesie V. Hoesen. Wit.: Folk. Gysb. and Catal. V. D. Bergh.

May. 1. Anna, of Sam. and Geertr. Criegier. Wit.: Evert and Marr. Rycksen.

Wyntie, of Ph. and Zara Bronk. Wit.: Jacob and Agnietie Muller.

May 8. Maria of Pieter and Christ. Bratt. Wit.: Andr. and Wyntie Bratt.

1726

May 15. Cornelia, of Gerr. and Cath. V. D. Bergh.
Wit.: Evert Pels, Tryntie Walderom.
Johannes, of Seth and Margariet. Wit.: Ezras, Anna
Wendell.
June 19. Johannes, of Goz. and Neeltie V. Schayk.
Wit.: Chr.st. and Maria Abeel.
Hillegon, of Maas and Anneke Ryksen. Wit.: Piet.
V. Woerdt, Marr. Fonda.
Judy, of John and Zara Bromly. Wit.: Sam. Bortsel,
Zely Rely.
John, of Will. and Rachel Northen. Wit.: John Lednys,
Elyz. Waals.
Levinus, of Kilyaen and Maria Wenne. Wit.: Benjamin
Wenne, Zara Waaters.
Madlena, of Tho. and Mary Bart. Wit.: Ysack Fryer
Maddel. Barheyt.
Thomas, of Joh. and Anna Hun. Wit.: Dirk and
Mayke Hun.
July 3. Frank, of Frank and Sara. Wit.: John Rosie,
Sara Kidny.
Johannes, of Hendr. and Hill. V. Wie. Wit.: Gerr.
Beeker, Marike Hardyk.
Pieter, of Abr. and Elyz. Vosburgh. Wit.: Pieter
Wenne, Maria V. Buuren.
Johannes, of Dirk Brat and Corn. Bratt. Wit.: Corn.
and Engeltie Walderom.
Jannetie, of Harm. and Dor. V. Aalsteyn. Wit.: Isack
Lansing, Jann. Lansingh.
John, of John and Jann. Gaaf. Wit.: Tho. Hollant,
Judy Hoogen.
July 10. Lyzabeth, of Paulus and Hester, pros. Wit.:
Ezras and Maria, pros.
Neeltie, of Pieter and Chatarina, pros. Wit.: Hendrik
and Zara, pros.
Pieter, of Philip and Zaria, pros. Wit.: Ezras and
Canistazy, pros.
Jacob, of Ezras and Chatarina, pros. Wit.: Hendrik
and Eva, pros.
Maria, a heathen woman, bapt. after confession of faith.
Robert, of Will. and Marg. Crellen. Wit.: Rob. Cren-
nen, Maria Bennewe.
Aug. 7. Jeems, of John and Mary Pareois. Wit.:
Jems Banks, Zelia Hollant.
Ephraim, of Eph. and Agn. Bogardus. Wit.: Joh.
D. Garmoy, Anna Bogardus.
Jannetie, of J. and Elsie V. Valkenburgh. Wit.: Jacob
and Grietie Rettelief.
Jurryaen, of Lamb. and Lea V. Valkenburg. Wit.:
Isack and Alida Fonda.

1726

Elyzabeth, of Joh. and Mar. Wyngaart. Wit.: Ab. and Anna Wyngaart.

Anna, of Th. and Mar. Scherp. Wit.: Jos. Heyns, Cat. Pruym.

Jacob, of Isack and Hendr. Bogaart. Wit.: Hendr. Oothout, Mar. Pruym.

Aug. 28. Evert, of Harm. and Jann. Schuyler. Wit.: Meyndt Schuyler, Elsie Vas.

Antie, of Corn. and Sus. Ridder. Wit.: Hendr. and Anna Ridder.

Jannetie, of Joh. and Jann. Goes. Wit.: Laur. V. Schayk, Mayeke Hun.

Rutgert, of Math. and Catal. V. D. Berg. Wit.: Rutg. and Marg. V. Deusen.

Johannes of Gerr. and Eng. Lansingh. Wit.: Joh. Lansingh, Anna Egmont.

Sep. 4. Henr. Jacobus, of Jacob and Geerte Rooseboom. Wit.: Hendr. Rooseb., Jr., Maria Lydius.

Cornelis, of Joh. and Sara Becker. Wit.: Coenraat Becker, Sara Van Vechten.

Sep. 11. Elyzabeth, of David and Christ. V. Dyk. Wit.: Jacob and Margar. Ten Broek.

Susanna, of Will. and Elyz. Walderom. Wit.: John and Susanna Basset.

Sep. 25. Maria, of Ahas. and Marr. Roseboom. Wit.: Gerr. and Maria Rooseboom.

Hendrik, of Jacob and Antie Schermerhoorn. Wit.: Sal. and Sara V. Vegten.

Elyzabeth, of Hendr. and Marg. Cuyler. Wit.: Will. V. Deusen, Marg. (or Mary) Ten Broek.

Engeltie, of Evert and Engeltie Wendell. Wit.: Nicolaes Schuyler, Geertruy Lansingh.

Oct. 8. Jacomyn, of Joh. and Jann. Ouderkerk. Wit.: Hugo and Jacom. Viele.

Ephraim, of Schiboleth and Anna Bogardus. Wit.: Pieter Verbrugh, Geessie Kip.

Philip, of Jonas and Antie Bronk. Wit.: Jacob and Agnietie Muller.

Hendrik, of Joh. and Lyz. Muller. Wit.: Hendr. and Susanna Halenbeek.

Hendrik, of Corn. and Maria V. Dyk. Wit.: Hendr. Bries, Catal. Wendell.

Debora, of Jacob and Debora Beekman. Wit.: Tobias Rykman, Sara Hansen.

Oct. 23. Cornelis, of Daniel and Dirckie Wenne. Wit.: Gerr. and Marr. V. D. Bergh.

Antie, of Lucas and Tanneke Van Vegten. Wit.: Joh. Schermerh., Jann. V. Vegten.

1726-1727

Elsie, of Bar. and Maria V. Buuren. Wit.: Dan. and Elsie Wenne.

Oct. 30. Marretie, of Jan and Rachel Wenne. Wit.: Claas and Marr. Egmond.

Dirk, of David and Geertr. V. D. Heyde. Wit.: Math. and Rach. V. D. Heyde.

Maria, of Lamb. and Antie Rattelief. Wit.: Jos. and Zytie V. Santen.

Anna, of Frans and Alida Pruym. Wit.: Casp. V. Jeveren, Alida Pruym.

Nov. 6. Cornelis, of Johan and Maria V. D. Berg. Wit.: Gerr. and Sara Van Nes.

Catharina, of Joseph and Maria, pros. Wit.: Maria, pros.

Hendrik, of Jan and Cath. Van Salsbergen. Wit.: Jan Bekker, Rach. V. Arnhem.

Margarita, of Nicolaes and Cath. Kittel. Wit.: Bar. and Marr. Sanders.

Engeltie, of Ruben and Geertr. V. Vegten. Wit.: Leendr. Gansevoort, Sara Van Vegten.

Hilletie, of Roel [?] and Lena Clark. Wit.: Eduard Holl., Cath. Wielaar.

Nov. 27. Johanna, of Andr. and Hagar Makansch. Wit.: John Dumbar, Marg. Levingston.

Sara, of Isack and Catal. Wendell. Wit.: Phill. and Marg. Schuyler.

Dec. 5. Rachel, of Gerr. and Eng. V. D. Berg. Wit.: Gerr. V. D. Bergh, Eng. V. Vegten.

Magdalena, of Phil. and Magd. Louk. Wit.: Corn. V. Dyk, Bar. Spoor.

Dec. 13. Anna, of Gerr. W. and Alida V. D. Bergh. Wit.: Hendr. and Agnietie V. Wie.

Stephanus, of Arent and Hyltie V. Dyk. Wit.: Steph. and Maria V. Alen.

1727, Jan. 1. Geertruy, of Joh. and Geerte Lansing. Wit. : Jer. Schuyler, Elyz. Groesbeek.

Catharina, of David and Maria Groesbeek. Wit.: Nicolaes Groesbeek, Cat. Van Ness.

Gerrit, of Meynd. and Fytie Marselis. Wit.: Jan Oothout, Hendr. V. Woert.

Jan. 8. Maria, of Christ. and Cath. Schyaensch. Wit.: Caspar Ham, Marg. Pruym.

Pieter, of Christ. and Catal. Yets. Wit.: Robert Yets, Hyltie V. Woerdt.

Chatharina, of Math. Garnoy and Rebecka Garmoy. Wit.: Jillis Garmoy, Agnietie Bogardus.

Jan. 15. Roelef, of Hendr. and Elsie Schermerh. Wit.: Roelef Albertsen, Elyz. Schermerhoorn.

Matheus, of Jac. and Maria Brouwer. Wit.: Anth. and Maria Bovy.

1727
Jan. 22. Maria, of Pieter and Cath. Schuyler. Wit.:
John Groesbeck, Marg. Livingston.

Eva, of Jurr. and Maria Hoogen. Wit.: Will. Hoog,
Jr., Judic Hoogen.

Egie, of Joh. and Anna Slingerl. Wit.: Joh. and Anna
Appel.

Johannes, of Symen D. and Maria V. Antwerp. Wit.:
Joh. and Sara Hansen.

Jan. 29. Maria, of Evert and Maria Ryksen. Wit.:
Sam. and Geertr. Criegier.

Anthony, of Eckb. and Elyz. Bratt. Wit.: Barent
and Willempie Bratt.

Feb. 1. Jeremias, of Sam. and Maria T. Broek. Wit.:
Jer. V. Rensselaar, Jr., Chat. Ten Broek.

Christina, of Claude and Christ. D. Lamether. Wit.:
Gerr. T. and Marg. V. Vegten.

Feb. 12. Maria, of Gerr. and Anna Ridder. Wit.:
Edmond and Marr. Blodt.

Catalyna, of Joh. and Jann. Goewey. Wit.: Sal. and
Cat. Goewey.

Ma garita, of Math. and Maria Flensburg. Wit.: L.
Rettelief, Joh. Flensburgh.

Judic, of Joseph and Hendr. Yets. Wit.: L. and J.
V. Hooghkerke.

Joseph, of Jems and El. Wels. Wit.: John Upers,
M. Marmer.

Christina, of Anth. and Anna V. Schayk. Wit.: Joh.
Jerm. [?] Cuyler, Sara Hansen.

Feb. 22. Anthony, of Hendr. and Wyntie Bries. Wit.:
Joh. V. Vegten, Tryntie Bries.

Maria, of Cousart and Jannetie, pros. Wit.: Hendrik
and Rebecca, pros.

Maria, of Symen and Josyne, pros. Wit.: Thomas
and Canasthazy, pros.

March 5. Gerardus, of Math. and Jann. V. Olinde.
Wit.: Ulryk V. Franken, Judick Hoogen.

Neeltie, of G. and Anna V. Bergen. Wit.: Folk. and
Pietertie Douw.

Gerrit, of Joh. and Zara V. Zanten. Wit.: Gerr. V.
Zanten, Maria Hilten.

Hessie, of Meind. and Ar. V. Yveren. Wit.: Luc. and
Sara Wyngaart.

Geertie, of Joh., Jr., and Jenneke Bleeker. Wit.:
Coen. and Geertie Ten Eyk.

Catharina, of Laur. and Ariaentie V. d. Poel. Wit.:
Melch. and Ar. V. D. Poel.

March 26. Margarita, of Dirk and Marg. Ten Broek.
Wit.: Joh. Ab. and Sara Cuyler.

1727

Apr. 2. Brant (adopted by Jacomyn), of Johannes and Mary, pros. Wit.: Hendrik and Josyne, pros.

Aaron, of Sander and Margariet, pros. Wit.: Jan and Mary, pros.

Gerretie, of R. and Geertie Schermerhoorn. Wit.: J. Schermerhoorn, Maria Ten Eyk.

Hieroon, of Joh. and Lena Huyck. Wit.: Hier. and Grietie V. Vlieren.

Apr. 9. Margarita, of John and Mar. Fitscherler. Wit.: Jacob and Marg. Rettelief.

Susanna, of Cornelis and Josyna, pros. Wit.: Jacob and Josyna, pros.

Apr. 16. Marten, of Fred. [?] and Sara Meyndertsen. Wit.: Meynd. Schuyler, Anna Peyster.

Nicolaes, of Roel. and Eng. Kidny. Wit.: Andr. and Wyntie Bratt.

Apr. 23. Jonathan, of Joh. and Rachel Witbeek. Wit.: Mart. Witbeek, Maria Conyn.

Elyzabeth, of Jacob and Sara Fort. Wit.: Leendt and Cath. Gansevoort.

Hendrik, of Hendr. and Marg. Gardenier. Wit.: Nic. and Rachel Gardenier.

Elyzabeth, of Will. and Lena Hooghtelink. Wit.: Jan and Elyz. Van Aalsteyn.

May 6. David, of Jan and Maria, pros. Wit.: Hendrik, of Isack Kip, and Rebecka, pros.

Hendrik, of Jacobus and Susanna Schoonhoven. Wit.: Theunis Harmensen, Maria Hilten.

Maria, of Jan and Catalyna Oothout. Wit.: Corn. and Marg. Bogaart

May 13. Catharina, of Ephr. and Anna Wendell. Wit.: Joh. and Anna Wendell.

Elyzabeth, of Claes and Annetie Fonda. Wit.: Joh. and Anna Marselis.

Cornelis, of Wyn. and Anna V. d. Bergh. Wit.: Corn. and Tryntie Walderom.

Elyzabeth, of Marten and Cath. Van Bergen. Wit.: Folkert Douw, Christina Van Dyk.

Johannes, of Jac. Corn. and Anna Schermerhoorn. Wit.: Joh. and Susanna Basset.

May 22. Cornelis, of Johannes and Catharina Ten Broek. Wit.: Johannes Van Alen, Lydia Van Vegten.

Cornelis, of Petr. and Sara Bogardus. Wit.: Philip and Engeltie Van Vegten.

Albert, of Joh. and Marg. V. D. Werke. Wit.: Abr. and Antie Van Der Poel.

June 4. Catharine, of Joh. and Mar. D. Foreest. Wit.: Joh. and Sara Hansen.

Elyzabeth, of Jonath. and Rebecka Broek. Wit.:
Isack Fryer, Femmetie Tatteyn.

Maria, illeg., of Chat. Fyn (father, John Johnson).
Wit.: William Roetsels, Jannetie Makluys.

Sara, of Jacob and Pietert. V. Aalsteyn. Wit.: Corn.
and Marr. V. Aalsteyn.

Catharina, of Jacob and Christ. Ten Broek. Wit.:
Dirck and Christina Ten Broek.

Annie, of Math. and Maria Bovy. Wit.: Ant. Bovy,
Elyz. V. Franken.

Magdal. Mary, of Eduard and Magd. Hollant. Wit.
Henry Hollant, Magdal. Bojen.

Johannes, of Phill. and Geerte Verplank. Wit.: Eduard
and Marg. Collins.

June 9. Joseph, of ―――― and Sara, pros. Wit.:
Ezra and Canasthazy, pros.

Moses, of Pieter and Elyzabeth, pros. Wit.: Anthony
and Sara, pros.

Jan, of ―――― and Hilletie, pros. Wit.: Simon and
Josyna, pros.

Jannitje, of Benj. and Anna Bogaart. Wit.: Corn.
Bogaart, Magdel. Van Buuren.

July 23. Christina, of Joseph and Maria, pros. Wit.:
Brant and Chatharina, pros.

Robert, of Will. and Cat. Berryt. Wit.: Thom. and
Maria Beth.

Anthony, of Gysb. and Cath. Rooseboom. Wit.: Anth.
Rutgers, Cath. Bries.

Elyzabeth, of Peter and Cat. V. Bergen. Wit.: Anth.
Coster, Pietertie Douw.

Wyntie, of Jacob and Agnitie Muller. Wit.: Joh.
Conyn, Alida V. D. Bergh.

Aug. 13. Roelef, of Joh. and Brechie Zeeger. Wit.:
Roelef and Helena Klerk.

David, of Christ. and Marg. Abeel. Wit.: Hendr.
Bries, Maria V. Dyk.

Johannes, of Joh. and Sara Hansen. Wit.: Ryck and
Debora Hansen.

John, of John and Zara Waters. Wit.: Joh. Hun,
Elyz. Ritsenaa.

Zeth, of David and Lydia, pros. Wit.: Seth and Sara, pros.

Sep. 3. Margarita, of Sam. and Elyz. Doxy. Wit.:
Pieter and Engel Livingston.

Susanna, of Corn. and Susan Ridder. Wit.: Claes
V. D. Berg, Ariaentie V. Woert.

Sep. 10. Commertie, of Leendt and Lena Bronk.
Wit.: Th. and Hilletje Williaems.

Femmetie, of Mart. and Geert. Beekman. Wit.: Joh.
Beekman, Maria Hoogen.

1727

Sep. 17. John, of Th. and Maria Viele. Wit.: Jan and Maria Fonda.

Elsie, of Leendt and Cath. Gansevoort. Wit.: Petr. V. Driesen, Cathar. Pruyn.

Sep. 24. Jen., of Nath. and Marg. Elleth. Wit.: Henri Holland, Elyz. Bratt.

Cornelis, of Mart. and Cath. V. Aalsteyn. Wit.: Corn. and Marr. V. Aalsteyn.

Barber, of Ryk and Maria V. Franken. Wit.: Joh. Pruym, Anna V. Franken.

Anna, of Ryk and Mally Hilten. Wit.: Joh. and Sara V. Santen.

Thomas, of Joh. G. and Catal. Lansingh. Wit.: Gerr. Lansing, Mayke Hun.

Barber, of Joh. and Johanna Marselis. Wit.: Gerr. and Elyz. Marselis.

Oct. 1. Jan, of Gerr. and Sara V. Nes. Wit.: Petr. V. D. Bergh, Eng. Livingston.

Ann, of Dan. and Hest. Brodhead. Wit.: Jacob Wendel, Sara Wyngaart, Jr.

Abraham, of Pieter and Maria Wenne. Wit.: Abr. and Abigael Foreest.

Anna, of Th. and Eng. Eckbertsen. Wit.: Bar. and Anna Bratt.

Oct. 6. Samuel, of Frans and Alida Pruym. Wit.: Samuel and Maria Pruym.

David, of Frans and Marg. Pruym. Wit.: Christ. Schiaensch, Emilie Pruym.

Daniel, of Ezras and Elysabeth, pros. Wit.: Ezras and Neeltie, pros.

Jan, of Moses and Alida, pros. Wit.: Jan and Maria, pros.

Oct. 8. Abrabam, of Joh. and Anna Wendel. Wit.: Anth. and Geertruy Kip.

Lena, of Piet. and Maria Fonda. Wit.: Th. Eckbertsen, Neeltie Beekman.

Agnietie, of Jan and Maria Witbeek. Wit.: Thom. and Hilletie Williams.

Oct. 18. Harmen, of Arent and Cath. Pruym. Wit.: Sam. Pruym, Anna Dwarrant.

Nov. 5. Anneke, of Jacob and Hendr. V. Woerd. Wit.: Ruth V. Woerd, Maria Gerritsen.

Nov. 12. Lidia, of Isaac and Elyz. Fryer. Wit.: Jac. Rettelief, Lidia Douw.

Nov. 19. Willem, of Glen and Ariaentie Verplank. Wit.: Jac. V. Plank, Marg. Douw.

Rachel, of Joh. and Rachel V. D. Heyde. Wit.: James Banks, Anna V. D. Heyde.

Catharina, of Jacob and Anna Egmont. Wit.: Isaac and Jann. Lansingh.

1727-1728

Dec. 6. Maria, of Mart. and Mar. V. Buuren. Wit.: Gerr. and Engelt. V. D. Bergh.

Dec. 10. Chatharina, of Joh. and Elyz. V. Oostrander. Wit.: Steph. and Elyz. Groesbeek.

Daniel, of Hendr. and Sus. Halenbeek. Wit.: Barn. Brat, Elyz. Muller.

Johannes, of Meyn and Tine [?] Marselis. Wit.: Jan Oothout, Hendr. V. Woert.

Dec. 17. Elsie, of Hendr. and Elsie Rooseboom. Wit.: Joh. and Elsie Cuyler.

Johannes, of Andr. and Eng. Witbeek. Wit.: Th. and Corn. Slingerland.

Dec. 24. Charlotte Amelia, of Pieter and Charl. Em. Kojeman. Wit.: Dav. and Ariaentie Verplank.

Dec. 28. Elyzabeth, of Ruth. and Elyz. V. Woerd. Wit.: Step. Groesbeek, Anna Fonda.

Anne, of Hosonjonda and Madalena, pros. Wit.: Hendrik and Eva, pros.

Petrus, of Daniel and Elyzabeth, pros. Wit.: Jacomyn, pros.

Ezras, of Jooticke and Maria, pros. Wit.: Thomas and Canastazy, pros.

Laurens, of Kenunksies and Anna, pros. Wit.: Hendr. and Margariet, pros.

Maria, of Thomas and Alida, pros. Wit.: Ezra and Maria, pros.

1728, Jan. 10. Cornelia or Cornelis, of Willem and Elyz. Walderon. Wit.: Corn. and Engeltie Walderon.

Jan. 14. Anna, of Gerrit and Ariaentie Becker. Wit.: Joh. and Elyz. Bekker.

Jan. 17. Isaac, of Douwe and Aaltie Fonda. Wit.: Joh. Ouderkerk, Rebecka Maassen.

Lidia, of Th. and Rach. Harmensen. Wit.: Arent Pruym, Maria Gansevoort.

Jan. 21. Margarita, of Jan and Rebekka Fort. Wit.: Dan. and Gerr. Fort.

Susanna, of Evert and Maria Jansen. Wit.: Ryer and Debora Wimp.

Pieter, of Will. and Martha Rettelief. Wit.: Pieter Bennewe, Mally Hilten.

Feb. 10. Cornelis, of Adam and Maria V. D. Bergh. Wit.: Wyn. V. D. Bergh, Maria Gerritsen.

Petrus, of Will. and Marg. Grennel. Wit.: Will. and Martha Rettelief.

Feb. 21. Abraham, of Obedie and Corn. Couper. Wit.: Claes and Antie Fonda.

Abraham, of Abr. and Christ. Truex. Wit.: Hendr. Coster, Cath. Ten Broek.

1728

Jacob, of Nic. and Rachel Gardenier. Wit.: Jacob Maassen, Marr. Bloth.

Feb. 25. David, of Jan and Cat. Van Nes. Wit.: Gerr. and Elyz. Marselis.

Jannetie, of Jac. and Ant. Schermerh. Wit.: Corn. Schermerh., Anna V. Deusen.

Eva, of Joh. and Neeltie Van Eps. Wit.: Jacob and Sara Gleyn.

Anna, of Sybr. and Elyz. Quackenbosch. Wit.: Piet. Quakkenbosch, Neeltie Knikkerbakker.

March 17. Hendrik, of Rits. and Sara Hansen. Wit. John Hansen, Maria Sc' uyler.

March 24. Bastyaen, of Th. and Mach. Visser. Wit.: Bast. and Dirckie Visser.

Apr. 7. Margarita, of Abr. and Magd. Lansingh. Wit.: Gleyn Verplank, Dorothe Douw.

Apr. 14. Elyzabeth, of Pieter and Geertr. V. D. Lyn. Wit.: Step. Groesbeek, Sara Hansen.

Apr. 21. Isaac, of Jac. Quakkenbos and Geert. Quakkbos. Wit.: Jac. and Jann. Pearson.

Maria, of Sam. and Geert. Criegier Wit.: Joh. and Elyz. V. Olinda.

Catharina, of Abr. and Geertd. Vosburg. Wit.: Gysb. and Cath. V. D. Berg.

Antie, of Jac. and Eng. La Gransie. Wit.: Arie D. Meulen., Antie Meulenaar.

May 15. Engeltie, of Nic. and Dor. V. Schayk. Wit.: Corn. Bogaart, Geertr. Groesbeek.

Elsie, of Joh. and Anna Hun. Wit.: Pieter and Lyntie Wenne.

May 30. Cornelis, of John and Maria Ackerson. Wit.: Pieter and Maria Fonda.

Nicolaes, of Jurryaen Syverwsen and Elyzabeth Syverssen. Wit.: Hendr. Douw, Sara Cuyler.

Rachel, of Johs. and Anna D. Peyster. Wit.: Evert Banker, Anna D. Peyster at N. Y.

Cornelis, of Corn. and Hendr. V. Buuren. Wit.: David and Maria Schuyler.

June 9. Magdalena, of Hendr. Klock and Jacom. Klok. Wit.: Ph. and Magdal. Louk.

Sara, of Isaac and Alida Greveraat. Wit.: Elbert and Maria Gerritsen.

June 16. Nelletie, of Benj. and Magd. Brat. Wit.: Pieter and Lena Rykman.

Dirck, of David and Christ. P. V. Dyk. Wit.: Pieter and Maria C. Van Dyk.

June 30. Ryckert, of Johs. and Zelia Rittelief. Wit.: Joch. and Marg. Rettelief.

1728

Rutgert, of Harp. and Lena V. Deusen. Wit.: Will. and Bata V. Deusen

Cornelia, of Anth. and Rebekka Bratt. Wit.: Jillis D. Garmoy, Geertruy Kip.

July 7. Nicolaes, of Walder and Anna Knoet. Wit.: Nicol. and Rachel Bleeker.

Willempie, of Dirk and Corn. Brat. Wit.: Benjam. and Lena Bratt.

July 14. Eva, of J. and Heyltie Schreydel. Wit.: M. Schuyler, Sara Gardenier.

Catharina, of Johs. and Cath. Cuyler. Wit.: Abr. and Cath. Cuyler.

Jacob, of Ephr. and Agn. Bogardus. Wit.: Jill. D. Garmoy, Marg. V. Veghten.

Aug. 10. Jacomina, of Jan and Reb. Maassen. Wit.: Douwe and Aaltie Fonda.

Mikkel, of Mich. and Elyz. Basteth. Wit.: Step. Basteth, Lena Symons.

Barent, of Eck. Eckbersten and Rach. Eckbertsen. Wit.: Benj. and Marr. Eckbertsen.

Aug. 18. Hieroon, of Hieroon and Grietie V. Vlieren. Wit.: Jan Vojelle, Maria Yerkes.

Alida, of Johs. and Anna Visser. Wit.: Harm. and Alida Visser.

Gerretie, of Coenr. and Gerr. Ten Eyk. Wit.: Johs. Bleeker, Jr., Elyz. V. Corlaar.

Alida, of Phill. and Cath. Livingston. Wit.: Johs. Schuyler, Marg. Leetsch.

Sep. 15. Johannes, of Johs. and Anna Knoet. Wit.: Jacob and Bata Knoet.

Jenneke, of Abr. and Mettie Ouderkerk. Wit.: Wyn. and Anna V. D. Bergh.

Eytie, of Hendr. and Hill. V. Wie. Wit.: Gerr. and Agnietie V. Wie.

Catharina, of Da. and Abig. Foreest. Wit.: Johs. and Cath. V. Aalsteyn.

David, of David and Maria Groesbeek. Wit.: Jac. Groesbeek, Ariaent. V. Plank.

Samuel, of Frans and Alida Pruym. Wit.: Sam. and Mar. Pruym.

Elsie, of Johs., Jr., and Cath. Cuyler. Wit.: Johs. and Elsie Cuyler.

Sep. 22. Pieter, of Jerem. and Susanna Schuyler. Wit.: Thom. Bayen, Marg. Schuyler.

Jacob, of Johs., Jr. and Jennie [?] Bleeker. Wit.: Nic. and Geertr. Bleeker.

Sep. 29. Isaac, of Jesse and Neeltie D. Foreest. Wit.: Abr. and Sara D. Foreest.

32

1728-1729
Marretie, of Johs. and Maria Wyngaart. Wit.: Corn.
Bogaart, Macht. Wyngaart.
Oct. 3. Stephanu , of P. and Cath. Schuyler. Wit.:
Jer. Schuyler, Elyz. Groesbeek.
Oct. 13. Sara, of Johs. and Elyz. Wendell. Wit.:
Corn. Cuyler, Jacoba Walters.
Nelletie, of Jacob and Maria Knoet. Wit.: Jacob and
Maria Brouwer
Rachel, of Sam. and Antie Rettelief. Wit.: Johs.
Rettelief, Rachel Rittelief.
Oct. 20. Abraham, of Claes and Corn. Bovy. Wit.
Abr. Schuyler, Eng. Livingston.
Nanningh, of Math. and Geertr. V. D. Heyde. Wit.:
Nann. and Alida Visser.
Eva, of Jurr. and Maria Hoogen. Wit.: Joh. J. Beek-
man, Judick Hoog n.
Oct. 27. Alida, of Jac b and Hester V. D. Heyde.
Wit.: Nicolaes and Alida Visser.
Nov. 3. Cornelis, of Wilh. and Geertie V. D. Bergh.
Wit.: Corn. and Engeltie Walderom.
Nov. 10. Abraham, of G. Corn. and Tryntie V. D
Bergh. Wit. Abr. and Rach. Pels.
Jannetie, of Js. and Mar. V. Aalsteyn. Wit.: Jac.
and Abig. V. Aalsteyn.
Petrus, of R. and Mar. Hilten. Wit.: Will. and Marg.
Grennie.
Nov. 17. Wouter, of Johs. and Maria D. Foreest. Wit.:
P. and C. Quakkenbosch.
Pieter, of Johs. and Cath. Ten Broek. Wit.: P. Van
Brugh, Maria Ten Broek.
Dec. 1. Abigael, of Jan and Rach. Wenne. Wit.:
Gl. and Ab. V. Plank.
Dec. 4. Reynier, of M. and A. V. Yveren. Wit.:
Benj. and Antie Eckbertsen.
Dec. 8. Willem, of Piet. and Rach. Wenne. Wit.:
Piet. and Eva V. Alen
Willem, of Piet. and Anna V. Alen. Wit.: Will. and
Maria V. Alen.
Johannes, of Johs. and Sara V. Santen. Wit.: Math.
Flensburg, Antie V. Santen.
Anna Maria, of Mart. and Catr. V. Bergen. Wit.:
Hendr. Douw, Cath. V. Bergen.
Willem, of G. and Alida V. D. Bergh. Wit.: F. V. D.
Bergh, Maria Conyn.
1729, Jan. 1. Maria, of Nicol. and Maria Groesbeek.
Wit.: Pieter Quakkenbosch, Elyz. Groesbeek.
Jan. 5. Neeltie, of Johs. and Neeltie Christiaensen.
Wit.: Ph. and Cath. Livingston.

1729

Folkie, of Mart. and Cath. V. Aalsteyn. Wit.: W. and Folkie V. D. Bergh.

Jan. 12. Johannes, of Jac. and Zara Fort. Wit.: Pieter Wenne, Anna Kitsenaar.

Maria, of Hendr. and Wyntie Bries. Wit.: Alb. Rykman, Maria V. Veghten.

Johannes, of Johs. and Sara Hansen. Wit.: Corn. Cuyler, Anna V. Schayk.

Jan. 15. Neeltie, of Jac. and Alida T. Eyk. Wit.: Johs. Visser, Jann. T. Eyk.

Claes, of Math. and Maria Bovy. Wit.: Nic. Fort, Sara Cuyler.

Jan. 19. Hester, of Th. and Corn. Slingerlant. Wit.: Abr. Kip, Hester Slingerlant.

Dirk, of Johs. and Rach. V. D. Heyde. Wit.: Math. and Anna V. D. Heyde.

Jan. 22. Lowys, of Pieter and Cath. Viele. Wit.: Lowys Viele, Sara V. Schayk.

Jan. 29. Johannes, of Corn. and Cath. Cuyler. Wit.: Johs. and Elsie Cuyler.

Feb. 2. Geertruy, of R. and E. Kidny. Wit.: R. Kidny, Ors [?] Jansen.

Catharina, of Dirk and Mar. V. Schelluyn. Wit.: Til [?] V. Schelluyn, Anna Wendels.

Philippus, of Rub. and Geertr. V. Vechten. Wit.: Abr. Witbeek, Anna V. Deusen.

Feb. 9. Maria, of Andr. and Hagar Mackans. Wit.: Corn. and Hendr. V. Buuren.

Santie, of G. and Sara V. Nes. Wit.: C. and Antie V. D. Bergh.

Johannes, of Jac. and Christ. T. Broek. Wit.: Johs. V. Alen, Cath. V. Schayk.

Feb. 19. Mathias, of W. and Lena Hooghteelingh. Wit.: H. and Beertie Hooghteelingh.

Rachel, of Jac. Rittelief and Cath. Rettelief. Wit.: S. or L. and R. Rettelief.

Feb. 23. John, of Nath. and Margr. Elleth. Wit.: John Armstrongh, Catal. Goewey.

Philip, of Johs. and Geertr. Lansingh. Wit.: Piet. Schuyler, Engelt. Wendel.

March 16. Hendrick, of Isaac and Cat. Wendel. Wit.: Ph. and Marg. Schuyler.

Petrus, of Casper and Anna Ham. Wit.: Petrus Ham, Cath. Leyth.

March 30. Lena, of Jac. and Maria Brouwer. Wit.: Jac. Brouwer, Elyz. Lansingh.

Apr. 6. Maria, of Jan and Elyz. V. Aalsteyn. Wit. P. and M. V. Aalsteyn.

Abraham, of Dirk and Marg. Ten Broeck. Wit.: Corn. Ten Broek, Cath. Cuylers.

Engeltie, of Johs. and Anna Slingerlant. Wit.: Th. and Engeltie Slingerlant.

Apr. 20. Lodewicus, of Hugo and Cath. Viele. Wit.: Lowys and Maria Viele.

David, of Corn. and Maria V. Dyk. Wit.: Pieter V. Dyk, Nelletie Bries.

Joachim, of Isaac and Maria Staets. Wit.: Barent Staets, Elyz. V. Deusen.

Johannes, of Coenraet and Cath. Richtmeyer. Wit.: Piet. and Leentie Wenne.

Maria, of Gerr. and Antie V. Santen. Wit.: Jos. and Zeytie V. Santen.

Maria, of Math. and Jann. V. Olinda. Wit.: Jan D. Fou, Anna Peers.

May —. Reynier, of B. and C. V. Yveren. Wit.: M. and Sara V. Yveren.

Johannes, of Sybr. and El. Quackenbosch. Wit.: Jesse and Neeltie D. Foreest.

Gysbert, of Math. and Cat. V. D. Bergh. Wit.: Gysbert and Dievertie V. D. Bergh.

Leendert, of J. and Agn. Muller. Wit.: L. and Jann. Conyn.

May 25. Abraham, of H. and M. Cuyler. Wit.: Jan and Cat. Oothout.

Catharina, of M. and Mar. Flensburg. Wit.: Johs. and Zara V. Santen.

June 9. Alida, of Sal. and Mary Goewey. Wit.: Step. V. Rensselaer, Elyz. Ramsly.

Maria, of Harm. and Elyz. V. Vegten. Wit.: Dirck V. Veghten, Marg. V. Vegten.

Ariaentie, of Abr. and Antie V. D. Poel. Wit.: Rutg. Bleeker, Anna D. Peyster.

June 14. Hendrik, of Chr. Schiaey and Cath. Schiaens. Wit.: Abr. and Alida V. Arnhem.

Johannes, of Sam. and Elyz. Dockzy. Wit.: Joh. and Elyz. Schuyler.

June 21. Evert, of Jac. and Anna Egmond. Wit.: Evert and Jan. Lansingh.

Antie, of Gerr. and Anna Ridder. Wit.: Evert and Cath. Van Nes.

Debora, of H. A. and Cat. Rooseboom. Wit.: H. and Debora Rooseboom.

Maria, of Zach. Zilchelson and Anna Zichelson. Wit.: Abr. and Mach. Wyngaart.

Willempie, of Dirck, Jr., and Corn. Brat. Wit.: Benj. and Mad. Brat.

1729

July 13. Jacob, of Symen and Josyna, pros. Wit.: Thomas and Canastazy, pros.

Hendrick, of Fredr. and Sara Meyndertsen. Wit.: G. and Marg. V. D. Bergh.

Dirck, of Assuerus and Marr. Wendel. Wit.: Dirck and Eckb. Bratt.

Jannetie, of D. and M. V. D. Karre. Wit.: Isaac and Alida Fonda.

July 27. Robert, of Pieter Livingston and Zelia Hollant. Wit.: Ph. Schuyler, Marg. Livingston.

Geertruy, of Joh. and Jann. Goewey. Wit.: Gerr. V. D. Bergh, Catie Witbeeck.

Maria, of Jac. and P. V. Aalsteyn. Wit.: M. V. Yveren, Lidia V. Aalsteyn.

Mayeke, of Wyn. and Anna V. D. Berg. Wit.: Jan, Jr., and Marretje Oothout.

Hester, of Math. and Reb. D. Garmoy. Wit.: Jan and Alida V. Arnhem.

Aug. 23. Catharina, of Anth. and Cath. Bovy. Wit.: Jac. and Maria Brouwer.

Maria, of Js. and Alida Greveraad. Wit.: Hend. and Anna Gerritsen.

Folkert, of G. and Cat. V. D. Berg. Wit.: Lev. and Cath. Harmensen.

Sep. 7. Petrus, of P. and Anna Bennewe. Wit.: W. and Martha Rettelief.

Willempje, of Benjamin and Rachel Wenne. Wit.: John Dumbarr, Sara Waaters.

Catharina, of Leend. and Anna Bronk. Wit.: Leend. and Cath. Gansevoort.

Jannetie, of Eckbert and Elyz. Brat. Wit.: Anth. and Jannetie Bogardus.

Johannes, of Johs. and Johanna Marselis. Wit.: Johs. J. Beekman, Maria Hoogen.

Geertruy, of G. and Eng. V. D. Bergh. Wit.: Bar. V. D. Bergh, Jann. Goewey.

Johannes, of Jos. and Hend. Yoets. Wit.: L., Jr., and Mar. V. Hooghkerk.

Margarita, of Petr. and Anna Douw. Wit.: Jac. Wendel, Marg. Douw.

Pieter, of Liv. and Catr. Harmensen. Wit.: Harm. V. Vegten, Elyz. V. Buuren.

Henricus, of Mart. and Geert. Beekman. Wit.: Johs. Johs. Beekman, Helena Visscher.

Cornelia, of Johs. and Mar. D. Foreest. Wit.: P. and Corn. Quakkenbosch.

Nov. 9. Johannes, of Johs. and Brechie Seeger. Wit.: Johs. and Sara V. Santen.

1729-1730

Andreas, of Joh. and Dor. Witbeek. Wit.: Folkert and Marg. Douw.

Maria, of Obedie and Cornelia Couper. Wit.: Abr. and Alida Van Arnhem.

Rebecka, of P. and M. Fonda. Wit.: Jan and Reb. Bloemendaal.

Barber, of Claas and Antie Fonda. Wit.: Isaac and Alida Fonda.

Hendrick, of Isaac and Hendr. Bogaart. Wit.: Corn. and Dorothe Bogaart.

Nov. 19. Lankaster, of Lank. and Mary Symes. Wit.: Jacob Staats, Cath. Symes.

Alexander, of J. and Elyz. Denninson. Wit.: L. Gansevoort, Cath. Pruym.

Hendrickie, of William and Marg. Kennall. Wit.: Will. and Martha Rettelief.

Dec. 2. Dorothe, of B. and A. Bogaart. Wit.: Jac. Bogaart, El. Muller.

Maria, of Goz. and Neeltie V. Schayk. Wit.: Anth. V. Schayk, Jr., Gerr. Ten Eyck.

Alida, of J. and H. V. Woert. Wit.: M. and Fytie Marselis.

Dec. 8. Kiliaen, of Step. and Elyz. Rensselaar. Wit.: Step. and Eliz. Groesbeek.

Abigael, of G. and A. V. Plank. Wit.: D. V. Plank, M. and Ariaentie V. D. Poel.

Dec. 13. Catharina, of Chr. and Marg. Abeel. Wit.: M. Schuyler, Elyz. Banker.

Marretje, of Johs. and Maria V. D. Berg. Wit.: Abr. and Antie V. D. Poel.

Gerrit, of Johs. and Elyz. V. Oostrandt. Wit.: Isaac and Elyz. Fonda.

Stephanus, of Pieter and Cath. Schuyler. Wit.: Johs. Lansingh, Marg. Schuyler.

Eliaz, of Moses and Alida, pros. Wit.: Maria, pros. Nikes and Sara, ma. christians.

Abraham, Cornelis and Catharina, pros.

1730, Jan. 4. Maria, of Douw and Aaltie Fonda. Wit.: Jan and Maria Fonda.

Maria, of Th. and Eng. Eckbertsen. Wit.: P. and M. Fonda.

Sara, of Isaac and Bata V. Deusen. Wit.: H. and Lena V. Deusen.

Jan. 7. Christina, of Sam. and Maria Ten Broek. Wit.: Johs. Ten Broek, Geertr. Schuyler.

Anthony, of P. and Christ. Van Bergen. Wit.: H. and Geertr. Coster.

Jan. 22. Leendert, of Ph. and Cat. Conyn. Wit.: L. and Cath. Gansevoort.

Jacob, of J. V. B. and Dirkie Van Hoesen. Wit.: Isaac and Alida Fonda.

Feb. 1. Maria, of Th. and Maria Viele. Wit.: Johs. and Jann. Ouderkerk.

Johannes, of J. and El. V. Arnhem. Wit.: Abr. and Alida V. Arnhem.

Catherina, of Gerrit and Anna Ridder. Wit.: H. and Cath. Ridder.

Abraham, of Sam. and Geertr. Crieger. Wit.: Johs. and Eck. D. Garmoy.

Feb. 4. Stephanus, of N. and D. V. Schayk. Wit.: Jan and Agnietie Witbeek.

Cornelis, of G. and M. V. D. Berg. Wit.: C. V. D. Bergh, Lydia V. Vegten.

Agnietie, of L. and Cat. Gansevoort. Wit.: Eduard and Marg. Williams.

Feb. 13. Margarita, of Jan and Cat. Oothout. Wit.: H. V. Deusen, Maria Staats.

Anna, of Hendrik and Anna, pros. Wit.: Symen and Catharina, pros.

Feb. 18. Catharina, of E. and Agn. Bogardus. Wit.: M. D. Garmoy, M. Eckbertsen.

Feb. 22. Engeltie, of Andr. and Eng. Witbeek. Wit.: Jan and Agn. Witbeek.

Fredericus, of Jac. and Mar. Knoet. Wit.: Fr. Knoet, Neeltie Foreest.

Johannes, of M. and Marg. V. D. Werke. Wit.: Jesse Foreest, Lidia V. Aalsteyn.

Johannes, of Joch. and Hill. Rettelief. Wit.: Lam. and Rach. Rettelief.

Feb. 28. Susanna, of Jan and Maria. Wit.: Hendrik and Christina.

Cornelis, of Daniel and Elyzabeth. Wit.: Hendr. and Maria.

March 11. Adam, of Petrus and Elyzabet. Wit.: Catharina.

Johannes, of Lucas and Sara. Wit.: Eva.

March 28. Neeltie, of Johs. and Anna Visser. Wit.: Barent and Neeltie Staats.

Andries, of Jer. and Marr. Pammerton. Wit.: Albert Brat, Maria Flensburgh.

Harmanus, of Jac. and Hel. Wendell. Wit.: Harm. and Anna Wendel.

Maria, of Wald. and Anna Knoet. Wit.: Will. and Rachel Ketelluyn.

Apr. 18. Susanna, of H. and Sus. Halenbeek. Wit.: Benjam. and Marg. Brat.

May 3. Maria, of Dav. and Maria Groesbeek. Wit.: Laur. and Cath. V. D. Poel.

1730

Harmanus, of Johs., Jr., and Cath. Cuyler. Wit.: Harm. and Anna Wendel.

May 10. Gerrit, of M. and Fytie Marselis. Wit.: Jac. V. Woerdt, Cat. Cuyler.

May 17. Engeltie, of Math. and Cat. V. D. Berg. Wit.: Gerr. Lansing, Engelt. Lansingh.

Hendrickie, of R. and Maria Hilten. Wit.: Jac. Hilten, Martha Rettelief.

June 5. Gerrit, of Johs. and Mary V. D. Werken. Wit.: Jan D. Fou, Jr., Neeltie V. Schayk.

Hendrik, of Ephr. and Anna Wendel. Wit.: Jac. and Debora Beekman.

Fytie, of Arent and Charl. V. D. Kar. Wit.: Piet. and Hendr. Schuyler.

Catharina, of Johs. G. and Jann. Lansingh. Wit.: G. Lansing, Jr., Cath. Lansingh.

June 14. Machtel, of Joh. and Mar. Wyngaart. Wit.: Tob. and Lena Rykman.

Dirk, of Ger. and Ar. Becker. Wit.: Gysb. and Elsie Rooseboom.

Elyzabeth, of H., Jr., and Elsie Rooseboom. Wit.: Johs., Jr., and Antie Rooseboom.

June 18. Jannetie, of Isaac and Mar. V. Aalsteyn. Wit.: J. and Cath. V. Aalsteyn.

Marretie, of Abr. and Anna Witbeek. Wit.: L. and Cath. Witbeek.

Abraham, of Johs. and Cath. T. Broek. Wit.: D. and Geert. Schuyler.

Anna, of Jur. and Elyz. Sywertsen. Wit.: W. Valen or V. Alen, S. V. Yveren.

Aug. 2. Mayke, of F. and Cath. V. D. Berg. Wit.: W. and Cat. V. D. Berg.

Phillip, of Nic. and Corn. Bovy. Wit.: Ph. Bovy, Elyz. Knoet.

Sara, of P. and Cat. Viele. Wit.: Sybr. V. Schayk, Jann. Ouderkerk.

Jacob, of Hugo and Catr. Viele. Wit.: P. and Ariaent. V. Woerdt.

Catharina, of Sal. and Marg. Goewey. Wit.: Sybr. and El. Quakkenbosch.

Aug. 22. Rachel, of D. and Geertr. V. d. Heyde. Wit.: Johs. Visser, Jr., Anna V. D. Heyde.

Cornelia, of W. and El. Walderom. Wit.: Gerr. V. D. Bergh, Engelt. Walderom.

Catalyna, of Hendr. and Marg. Cuyler. Wit.: John, Jr., and Cath. Cuyler.

Aug. 30. Maria, of Hendrik and Maria. Wit.: Joseph and Maria.

1730

Johanna, of Johs. and Elyz. Quakkenbos. Wit.: Nic. and Anna Groesbeek.

Gerrittje, of Nic., Jr., and Marg. Bleeker. Wit.: Johs. and Gerr. Rooseboom.

Jacob, of Abr. and Alida V. Arnhem. Wit.: Gerr. Lansingh, Elyz. V. Arnhem.

Eva, of Johs. J. and Sara Beekman. Wit.: Johs. and Eva Beekman.

Sep. 13. Dirck, of H. and Elyz. V. Vegten. Wit.: Dirck and Eng. V. Vegten.

Folkie, of Mart. and Tryntie V. Aalsteyn. Wit.: W. V. D. Bergh, El. Denninson.

Sep. 25. Jacobus, of Piet. and Geert. V. D. Lyn. Wit.: Christ. and Neeltie Tappen.

Henry Holland, of Rich. [?] or Piet. [?] and Zelia Livingston. Wit.: Henry and Jenny Holland.

Hester, of Brand and Catharina. Wit.: Symen and Jacomyne.

Susanna, of Cahousouwane and Catharina. Wit.: Hendrik and Maria.

Oct. 3. Anna, of Barth and Hendr. Hogeboom. Wit.: Isaac and Alida Fonda.

Matheus, of Jac. and Cath. Rettelief. Wit.: Jac. and Maria Brouwer.

Rachel, illeg., of (Daniel Hoogen and) Rachel Beekman. Wit.: Piet. Teunis, Engeltje Eckbertsen.

Oct. 17. Maria, of Is. and Mar. La Gransie. Wit.: Andr. and Hagar Makans.

Petrus, of Abr. and G. Vosburg. Wit.: W. and Geert. V. D. Berg.

Oct. 24. Johannes, of W. and M. Rettelief. Wit.: L. and M. Rettelief.

Johannes, of N. [?] and W. Bries. Wit.: F. V. Vegten, M. V. Dyk.

Nov. 1. Catalyna, of Joh. and Zelia Rettelief. Wit.: Christ. and Cat. Jets.

Cornelia, of J. and M. D. Foreest. Wit.: P. Quackenbos, Anna V. Nes.

Nov. 8. Johannes, of Sam. and Antie Rettelief. Wit.: Johs. V. Santen, Marg. Rittelief.

Isaac, of Th. and Mach. Visser. Wit.: Is. and Jann. Lansing.

Nov. 15. Alida, of Jac. and Alida T. Eyck. Wit.: Jac. Koenr. T. Eyck, Geertr. V. D. Heyde.

Maria, of P. and Anna Bennewe. Wit.: Ryk. and Marie Hilten.

Nov. 22. Daniel, of Anth. and Rebecka Brat. Wit.: Dan. and Elyz. Brat.

Nov. 25. Coenraat, of Coenr. and Cath. Rigtmeyer. Wit.: Jan and Cat. Van Nes.

Nov. 29. Maria, of R. and Geertr. V. Vegten. Wit.: Jac. Lansingh, Anna Kitsenaar.

Abraham, of Th. and Corn. Slingerlant. Wit.: Johs. E. Wendel, Geessie Kip.

Dec. 12. Catharina, of John and Catr. Armstrong. Wit.: P. D. Garmoy, Grietie Garmoy.

Cornelis, of Bar. and Corn. V. Yveren. Wit.: Mart. and Cath. V. Aalsteyn.

Walter, of Ritsert and Sara Hansen. Wit.: Dav. Abr. Schuyler, Debora Beekman.

Dec. 20. Abraham, of Jos. and Hendr. Jets. Wit.: John Eyton, Johanna Flensburg.

Dec. 25. Canastazy, Rebecka, Abraham, Rachel, pros. Sara, of Rebecka. Wit.: Abraham and Josyna.

Catharina, of Josyna. Wit.: Abraham and Catharina.

Lena, of Madelena. Wit.: Seth and Maria.

Joseph, of Abraham and Grietie. Wit.: Adam and Grietie.

David, of David and Margarita. Wit.: Symen and Esther.

Nikes, of Nikes and Elizabeth. Wit.: Seth and Lydia.

Joseph, of Rachel. Wit.: Joseph and Maria.

Joseph, of Rebecka. Wit.: Gideon and Madalena.

Lidea, of Laurens and Rachel. Wit.: Seth and Sara.

1731, Jan. 3. Gerrit, of Johs. and Sara Van Santen. Wit.: Gerr. Van Santen, Mally Hilton.

Jan. 6. Johannes, of Jan and Marr. Oothout. Wit.: Johs. and Aaltie Oothout.

Geertruy, of Roel. and Eng. Kidny. Wit.: Ro. Kidny, Orseltie Jansen.

Jan. 10. Jan, of Douwe and Aaltie Fonda. Wit.: Pieter Fonda, Maria Viele.

Gerrit, of Ulrich and Geertr. V. Franken. Wit.: Meind. Schuyler, Maria V. Olinda.

Jan. 17. Catalyna, of Jos., Jr., and Eva Joets. Wit.: Chr. and Catal. Joets.

Feb. 3. Abraham, of Jacob and Sara Fort. Wit.: Abr. and Anna Fort.

Gerrit, of Ant. Boy [sic] and Cath. Bovy. Wit.: Jac. and Cath. Rettelief.

Debora, of Johs. and Sara Hansen. Wit.: Johs. Cuyler, Maria Schuyler.

Jan, of E. and M. Jansen. Wit.: Simon and G. Veeder.

Feb. 21. Maria, of G. and Alida V. D. Berg. Wit.: Pieter Winne, Anna Kitsenaar.

William, of Rens. and Elyz. Nichols. Wit.: Fr. and Maria Salisbury.

1731

Feb. 25. Lowys, of Simon and Marr. V. Antwerpen. Wit.: David A. and Maria Schuyler.

John, of Eck. Eckberts and Rach. Eckbertsen. Wit.: J. D. Garmoy, Cat. Goewey.

March 14. Johannes, of Jac. and Anna Egmond. Wit.: Abr. and Elsie Lansingh.

Geertruy, of Sam. and Geertr. Criegier. Wit.: Johs. and Eckb. D. Garmoy.

Catalyna, of Piet. and Geertr. V. Buuren. Wit.: Johs. and Catar. V. Buuren.

Johannes, of Jac. and Agnietie Muller. Wit.: Jan. Fonda, Elyz. Muller.

Barent [?], of M. Cos. [?] and Th. V. Buuren. Wit.: Gerr. and Maria V. D. Bergh.

Apr. 4. Christina, of Dav. and Chr. V. Dyk. Wit.: Corn. T. Broek, Maria Cuyler.

Daniel, of Kil. and Reb. Wenne. Wit.: Dan. and Dirkie Wenne.

Margarita, of Jur. and Mar. Hoogen. Wit.: Johs. and Johanna Marselis.

Apr. 16. Elyzabeth, of Js. and Maria Staets. Wit.: W. V. Deusen, Neeltie Staets.

Philip, of P. and S. Bronk. Wit.: Joh. Conyn, Agn. Muller.

Apr. 18. Grietie, of Sara. Wit.: Joseph and Maria.

Catharina, of Anna. Wit.: Abraham and Josyna.

Cornelis, of Margariet. Wit.: Simon and Maria.

Susanna, of Jac. and Sus. Schoonhoven. Wit.: Ahas. Rooseboom, Margr. Rennie.

Agnietie, of P. and Anna V. Alen. Wit.: Gerr. and Agn. V. Wie.

Adam, Sara, Isaac, Abraham, pros.

May 9. Lena, of J. and Maria Brouwer. Wit.: J. and Elyz. V. Arnhem.

Anna, of M. and Ar. Van Yveren. Wit.: B. V. Yveren, Sara Wyngaart.

Johannes, of Johs., Jr., and Jenn. Bleeker. Wit.: Johs. and Anna Bleeker.

May 15. Jacob, of Johs. and Rachel V. D. Heyde. Wit.: Jeems Banks, Eckb. V. D. Heyde.

May 12. [sic] Cornelis, of Petr. and Mar. V. D. Berg. Wit.: P. and A. V. Woerdt.

Jacobus, of Z. and R. [?] [or A?] Zichelson. Wit.: Johs. and M. Wyngaart.

Commertie, of J. and A. Bronk. Wit.: A. and Catr. Pruym.

Maria, of D. and H. V. Vechten. Wit.: G. Corn. and Eva V. Alen.

1731

Barber, of Bar. and Elyz. Brat. Wit.: Gysb. Marselis, Madelena Bart.

May 20. Albert of Johs. and Anna Slingerlant. Wit.: Th. and Hest. Slingerlant.

Catharina, of J. and N. [?] Foreest. Wit.: Ph. Wendel, Anne V. Nes.

June 8. Franciscus, of Fr. and M. Pruym. Wit.: Hendr. Gerritsen, Cath. Pruym.

June 10. Grietie, of Carroragiera and Susanna. Wit.: Adam and Margriet.

Rebecca, Jan, of Elyzabeth. Wit.: Hendrik and Rebecca.

Jacob, of Rebecka. Wit.: Gideon and Margariet.

Pieter, of Sal. and Margr. Goewey. Wit.: Lowys and Heyltie Schreyddel.

July 2. Catharina, of Zyte [?] and R. D. Garmoy. Wit.: Johs. D. Garmoy, Marr. Eckbertsen.

Geertruy, of Mart. and Jann. V. Olinda. Wit.: Jac. Rooseboom, Cat. V. Schayk.

Harmannus, of E. and Eng. Wendel. Wit.: Jacob Wendel, Cath. Cuyler.

Alida, of Johs. and Anna Knoet. Wit.: G. and Barb. Rycksen.

Maria, of Is. and Alida Greveraat. Wit.: H. and Anna Gerritsen.

Aug. 8. Geertruy, of J. and Maria Halenbeek. Wit.: D. and G. V. D. Heyde.

Elyzabeth, of H. and Hill. V. Wie. Wit.: A. and El. Becker.

Jacobus, of H. and C. Roseboom. Wit.: J. Roseboom, Sus. Schuyler.

Elyzabeth, of Corn. and Cat. Cuyler. Wit.: Johs. and Elyz. Schuyler.

Aug. 22. Paulus, of Joseph and Catharina. Wit.: Simon and Sara.

Rykert, of G. and Antie V. Zanten. Wit.: R. and Catr. V. D. Berck.

Folkert, of G. C. and M. V. D. Berg. Wit.: F. V. Vegten Neeltie Staets.

Elsie, of Abr. and L. Douw. Wit.: P. Wenne, M. Douw.

Sep. 5. Maria, of Johs. and J. Goewey. Wit.: Johs. Witbeek, Reb. Goewey.

Margarita, of Ephr. [?] and Anna Wendel. Wit.: R. Hansen, Mar. Schuyler.

Johannes, of John and Jann. Macluur. Wit.: Obed. and Anna Couper.

Catharina, of Corn. and Maria V. Dyk. Wit.: G. Rooseboom, Chr. V. Dyk.

1731

Gerrit, of W. and C. [or G.] V. D. Bergh. Wit.: G. W. and Alida V. D. Berg.

Sep. 24. Johannes, of Johs. and Cath. Cuyler. Wit.: Jac. Glen, Rachel Bleeker.

Sep. 26. Sara, after previous confession. Wit.: Hendrik and Christina.

Gysbert, of G. and Marg. Marselis. Wit.: G. Marselis, Anna Fonda.

Pieter, of Simon and G. Veeder. Wit.: Isaac Kip, Anna Wendel.

Susanna, of D. and A. Foreest. Wit.: W. and Sus. Rodgiers.

Oct. 2. Maria, of Jac. and Geertr. Quackenbosch. Wit.: D. and Christ. V. Dyk.

Sara, of J. and H. V. Woerdt. Wit.: P. V. Woerdt, Sara Gardenier.

Oct. 10. Geertie, of H. and Anna Ridder. Wit.: G. V. D. Berg, Geertie Van Nes.

Margarita, of Dirk and Marg. T. Broek. Wit.: Johs. J. Beekman, Maria Cuyler.

Willem, of W. and Ant. Knoet. Wit.: W. Ketelluyn, Maria D. Ridder.

Oct. 17. Philip, of John and Corn. Schuyler. Wit.: Johs. and Elyz. Schuyler.

Oct. 24. Elyzabeth, of G. and Cath. Rooseboom. Wit.: R. and Elsie Rooseboom.

Benjamin, of M. and Mar. V. Buuren. Wit.: G. V. D. Bergh, Elyz. Coster.

Oct. 31. Anna, of Johs. and Anna Visser. Wit.: Nic. Visser, Alida Ten Eyk.

Pieter, of Jacob and Maria Knoet. Wit.: Claes and Nelletie Bovy.

Nov. 7. Philip, of Johs. and Maria D. Foreest. Wit.: Jan and Cath. V. Aalsteyn.

Johs., of J. and Bata V. D. Heyde. Wit.: Johs. and Anna Knoet.

Anthony, of Benj. and M. Brat. Wit.: B. and Elyz. Brat.

Maas, of J. and Sara Maassen. Wit.: C. Maassen, G. Oostrander.

Nov. 13. Aaltie, of W. and A. [?] V. D. Berg. Wit.: H. and A. [?] Ridder.

Neeltie, of Andr. and Sara Gardenier. Wit.: J. Lowys Schrodel, Hyltie Schrodel.

Maria, of Abr. and Ely. Wyngaart. Wit.: Johs. and Anna Wyngaart.

Nov. 21. Maria, of Johs. and Cath. T. Broek. Wit.: J. Ritsert, M. V. D. Bergh.

Catharina, of Jac. and Cath. Rettelief. Wit.: Jac. and Maria Brouwer.

Ritsert, of John and Maria Liethen. Wit.: Joseph and Hendr. Yets.

Dec. 5. Melchert, of G. and A. Verplank. Wit.: A. V. D. Poel, D. Witbeek.

Dec. 12. Lena, of Mich. and Lyb. Basset. Wit.: Jac. and Deb. Beekman.

Elyzabeth, of Johs. and Anna V. Franken. Wit.: Johs. Knoet, Marg. V. Franken.

Jannetie, of D. and Mad. V. D. Karre. Wit.: Isaac and Alida Fonda.

Hester, of B. and R. Wenne. Wit.: Abr. and Hest. V. Arnhem.

Dec. 23. Thomas, of H. and Hest. Hoogtelink. Wit.: C. Hoogteelink, Hest. Slingerlant.

Dec. 25. Hester, of M. and R. D. Garmoy. Wit.: J. V. Arnhem, Reb. Fonda.

1732, Jan. 9. Gerrit, of Ahas. and Marr. Rooseboom. Wit.: Ro. Rooseboom, Sus. Visser.

Lucas, of Abr. and Anna Witbeek. Wit.: Ha. and Catal. V. Deusen.

Petrus, of Will. and Marg. Grannie. Wit.: Will. and Martha Rettelief.

Jan. 23. Petrus, of G. and Sara V. Nes. Wit.: P. and A. V. Woerdt.

Ariaentie, of G. and Anna Ridder. Wit.: C. V. D. Bergh, Elyz. Fonda.

Anna, of Johs. E. and Anna Wendel. Wit.: Abr. and Anna Wendel.

Catharina, of M. and M. Flensburg. Wit.: G. and A. V. Santen.

Bastyaen, of H. and S. [or L. ?] Visser. Wit.: C. [or B. ?] and D. Visser.

Feb. 5. Johannes, of G. and M. V. Benthuysen. Wit.: Joh. and Ch. V. Alen.

Abraham, of D. and Anny Quakkenbos. Wit.: R. Hansen, M. Wyngaart.

Rutgert, of Chr. and M. Abeel. Wit.: Cor. V. Dyk, Marg. Bleeker.

Anna, of Petr. and Anna Douw. Wit.: Johs. V. Rensselaar, Lydia Douwe.

March 8. Elyzabeth, of H., Jr., and El. Rooseboom. Wit.: Corn. and Christ. Cuyler.

Dirckie, of M. and M. V. D. Werke. Wit.: J. V. Aalsteyn, M. Verplank.

Willem, of R. and M. Hilten. Wit.: W. Hilten, Cat. Goewey.

March 12. Elyzabeth, of H. and A. V. Deusen. Wit.: B. Staats, Elyz. V. Deusen.

1732

March 18. Cornelis, of H. and C. Bunsing. Wit.: Sal. Goewey, Elyz. V. Corlaar.

Adriaen, of S. and El. Quackenbos. Wit.: Adr. and Catr. Quackenbos.

Harmanus, of Jac. and Hel. Wendel. Wit.: H. V. Rensselaar, Cath. Ten Broek.

March 27. Elyzabeth, of Johs. and El. V. Oostrander. Wit.: G. and Elyz., Jr., Brat.

Apr. 2. Stephanus, of Pieter and Catr. Schuyler. Wit.: Step. V. Rensselaar, Marg. Schuyler.

Gerrit, of H. and S. Halenbeek. Wit.: G. Halenbeek, Elyz. Brat.

Apr. 7. Gerrit, of Johs. and Joh. Marselis. Wit.: Mart. Beekman, Marg. Marselis.

Apr. 9. Kiliaen, bapt. upon confession; former name Canadagaje.

Catharina, of Jan and Anne. Wit.: Aaron and Christina.

Apr. 10. Sara, of Abr., and Alida V. Arnhem. Wit.: Jan D. V. Arnhem, Reb. Garmoy.

Apr. 16. Goosen, of Abr., Jr., and Ryckie Lansing. Wit.: Abr. Lansingh, Catr. Van Schayck.

Melchert, of Dav. and Maria Groesbeek. Wit.: Melch. V. D. Poel, Geertruy Groesbeek.

Anna, of Frank and Alida Pruym. Wit.: Casp. V. Yveren, Cath. Pruym.

Apr. 30. Gerretie, of Johs. and Eng. Schermerhoorn. Wit.: Will. V. Buuren, Elyz. Schermerhoorn.

Margareta, of Chr. and Catr. Schyans. Wit.: Frans and Catr. Pruym.

May 7. Engeltie, of G. and Eng. V. D. Berg. Wit.: Abr. and Catr. Witbeek.

Hilletie, of R. and L. Klerk. Wit.: Joh. and B. Zeeger.

Rachel, of J., Jr., and E. Jets. Wit.: Adam Jets, Lena Fonda.

Wynant, of F. [?] and C. V. D. Berg. Wit.: G. V. D. Berg, Chr. Huyck.

Maria, of Eph. and Agn. Bogardus. Wit.: D. Garmoy, Eck. D. Garmoy.

The following persons were bapt. after a previous confession: Petrus, Moses, Hester, Antony, Margarita, Maria, Catharina, Nicolaes, Jannetie, Brand, Catharina, Anna, Jacomyn, Christina, Margarieta, Elyzabeth, Maria, Margarieta, Gideon.

Lourens, of Jonathan and Maria, pros. Wit.: Hendrik and Josyna, pros.

Thomas, of Nicolaes and Jannetie, pros. Wit.: Nikes and Sara, pros.

May 14. Dirck, of Math. and Marg. V. D. Heyde. Wit.: David and Rach. V. D. Heyde.

1732

Andries, Willem, of Jeremy and Marr. Pammerton. Wit.: Andr., W., Eckb., and Yvy [?] Brat.

May 21. Tryntie, of Dirck and Corn. Brat. Wit.: Corn. and Cath. Walderom.

June 4. Maria, of G. [or P.] and Cath. Viele. Wit.: G. Van Schayk, Reb. Goewey.

July 2. Jacob, of Nic. and Corn. Bovy. Wit.: Jac. and Maria Brouwer.

Margarieta, of Pieter and Zelia Livingston. Wit.: John [?] and Margr. Livingston.

Hester, of Andr. and Eng. Witbeek. Wit.: Johs. and Anna Slingerlant.

July 9. Catharina, of Jac. and Catr. Bennewe. Wit.: Mart. and Elyz. Delmont.

Stephanus, of John and Elyz. Ritsert. Wit.: Henr. [?] V. Rensselaer, Catr. Ten Broeck.

Tanneke, of P. and Rachel Wenne. Wit.: Kil. and Rebecka Wenne.

July 16. Johannes, of N. V. and G. V. Lier. Wit.: H. and Eytje Verwie.

July 23. Barent, of Andr. and M. V. d. Berg. Wit.: Bar. V. d. Berg, M. Vinhagel.

Persons bapt. after a previous confession of their faith: Adam, Paulus, Catharina, Dyvertie, Margarieta, Sara, Elyzabeth, Thomas, Kiliaen, Petrus, Jacob, Johannes, Joseph.

Rachel, of Sweerath and Catharina, pros. Wit.: Abraham and Josyna.

Aug. 6. Henricus, of Folk. and Anna Douw. Wit.: H. and N. Douw.

Catharina, of R. and M. Livingston. Wit.: Ph. and Cath. Livingston.

Margarita, of Johs. and M. Wyngaart. Wit.: G. V. Franken, M. Wyngaart.

Ariaentie, of H. and A. V. Buuren. Wit.: M. and Madl. V. Buuren.

Aug. 13. Maria, of B. and A. Bogaert. Wit.: Sam. and M. Pruyn.

Maria, of Steph. and Elyz. V. Rensselaar. Wit.: Jeremias V. Rensselaar, Maria Milt.

Cornelis, of Johs. and Neeltie Christiaensen. Wit.: Daniel Ketelluyn, Engeltie Livingston.

Wynant, of Mart. and Catr. V. Aalsteyn. Wit.: Wyn. V. D. Berg, Maria V. Aalsteyn.

Andries, of Nic. and Dorothee V. Schayk. Wit.: Andr. and Dor. Witbeek.

Catalyntie, of Dirk and Marg. Hun. Wit.: Johs. and Maike Hun.

1732

Sep. 3. Anna, of G. and M. Banker. Wit.: E. Banker, A. D. Peyster.

Wouter, of J. and M. Quackenbos. Wit.: P. and C. Quackenbos.

Abraham, of Jo. and Cha. Cuyler. Wit.: H. Cuyler, M. Ten Broek.

Sep. 10. Christina, of Da. and Christ. V. Dyk. Wit.: Corn. Ten Broek, Maria Cuyler.

Maria, of C. and A. Ham. Wit.: L. Schreydel, H. Scheyldel. [sic]

Johannes, of Johs. and Sara Hansen. Wit.: Jac. Beekman, Chr. Cuyler.

Sep. 17. Catharina, of Jac. and Anna Egmont. Wit.: Evert and Elsie Lansingh.

Sep. 24. Marike, of Jan and M. Oo hout. Wit.: Abr. and M. Wendel.

John, of John and Sara Waters. Wit.: E. Collins, Jer and Elyz. Rensselaar.

Oct. 1. Rachel, of Will. and M. Rettelief. Wit.: Jac. and Rachel Rettelief.

Maria, of Hendr. and Wyn. Bries. Wit.: Johs. V. Vegten, Anna Schoonmaker.

Oct. 8 Nicolaes, Jacob, of Johs. and Genevieve Lydius. Wit.: Nic. Lydius, Jacob and Isabella Staets.

Oct. 13. Anna, of James and Neeltie Bonting. Wit.: Abr. and Alida Van Arnhem.

Alida, of Jacob and Alida T. Eyck. Wit.: N. Groesbeek, Maria T. Eyk.

Thomas, of Edward and Maria Williams. Wit.: Th. and Grietie Williams.

Isaac, of Th. and M. Visser. Wit.: G. and Elsie Lansing.

Ann, of Edoald and Magdal. Holland. Wit.: Rits. Holland, Ann Groesbeek.

Oct. 30. Andries, of M. and T. Marselis. Wit.: B. Barheyt, Antje V. d. Poel.

Johannes, of J. and Sara Beekman. Wit.: Mart. Beekman, Johanna Marselis.

Rebecca, of Th. and M. Viele. Wit.: Jan Maassen, Catr. Fonda.

Jacob, of Jac. and A. V. Arnhem. Wit.: G. and Antie Lansingh.

Nov. —. Maria, of G. and Alida V. d. Berg. Wit.: Arent and Cath. Pruym.

Jacobus, of Johs. and Sara V. Santen. Wit.: Jac. Hilton, Zelia V. Zanten.

Gysbert, of G. and Marg. Marselis. Wit.: Gysb. Marselis, Elyz. Brat.

Anna, of W. and A. V. d. Berg. Wit.: Evert and Susanna Wendel.

1732-1733

Nov. 19. David, of D. and G. V. D. Heyde. Wit.: Jac. V. D. Heyde, Alida Ten Eyck.

Jacob, of Z. and R. D. Garmoy. Wit.: Jacob and Elyz. Evertsen.

Jillis, of K. and R. Wenne. Wit.: Jillis and Rachel Fonda.

Nov. 22. Catharina, of Johs. and Jann. Lansing. Wit.: G. and Eng. Lansingh.

Nov. 27. Anna Cath., of Sal. and M. Goewey. Wit.: Dirk T. Broek, Anna Groesbeek.

Douwe, of Claes and Anna Fonda. Wit.: G. Marselis, Rebecka Bogart.

Albert, of Th. and C. Slingerlant. Wit.: Johs. Slingerlant, Eng. Witbeek.

Dec. 3. Sara, of P. and Sara Douwning. Wit.: Jeems Maclaeny, Marg. Stoor.

Dec. 10. Johannes, of Rub. and Geertr. V. Vegten. Wit.: Johs. G. Lansingh, Jann. Goewey.

Antony, of Dan. and Wyntie Brat. Wit.: Ant. and Reb. Brat.

Dec. 13. Philip, of Math. and Maria Bovy. Wit.: Jac. and Cath. Rettelief.

Dirck, of H. V. Vechten and L. V. Vegten. Wit.: Douwe and Aaltie Fonda.

Dec. 17. Nannink, of John and Anna Visser. Wit.: H. and Ariaentie Van Deusen.

Dec. 24. Anna, of L. and Anna Rettelief. Wit.: Will. Rettelief, Maria Flensburg.

Philip, of Johs. and Maria D. Foreest. Wit.: G. and C. V. Nes.

Gerrit, of M. and Cat. V. D. Berg. Wit.: H. and Tryntie V. Deusen.

Neeltie, of W. and Elyz. Walderom. Wit.: Th. and Eng. Eckbertsen.

Abraham, of Jos. and Hendr. Jets. Wit.: John Jeton, Joh. Flensburg.

Dec. 29. Henricus, of Eck. and Elyz. Brat. Wit.: Ant. and Reb. Brat.

Dec. 31. Catie, of G. and M. Knoet. Wit.: D. and Catie Heemstrate.

Johannes, of N. and M. Roseboom. Wit.: J. Bleker, Jr., G. Bleeker.

1733, Jan. 7. Geertruy, of Johs. and Geertr. Lansing. Wit.: Steph. Groesbeek, Elyz. V. Rensselaar.

Catharina, of —— Van Zanten and Antie. Wit.: R. and Cath. Van d. Berg.

Margarita, of Ananias and Sara. Wit.: Hendrick and Margarita.

Jan. 14. Jacob, of Isaac and Hendr. Bogaart. Wit.: Hendr. Oothout, Maria Pruym.

1733

Pieter, of David and Eng. Uzile. Wit.: P. and Geertie Vroman.

Catharina, of Abr. and Anna Witbeek. Wit.: Abr. and R. V. Deusen.

Feb. 4. Maria, of Is. and Alida Greveraad. Wit.: Arent Pruym, Anna Gerritse.

Feb. 25. Andries, of J. and Jany Makluur. Wit.: Johs. and Breggie Zeeger.

March 4. Johannes, of P. and M. Fonda. Wit.: Douwe and Reb. Fonda.

March 7. Albert, of J. and A. Slingerlant. Wit.: Andr. Witbeek, Eva Slingerlant.

Anna, of P., Jr., and A. Uzile. Wit.: H. and Elyz. Groesbeek.

March 11. Catharina, of Abr. and Reb. Foreest. Wit.: J. and Sara Hansen.

Lena, of Th. and Eng. Eckbertsen. Wit.: Anth. Brat, Rachel Beekman.

March 18. Petrus, of Eck, and Rachel Eckbertsen Wit.: Johs. D. Garmoy, Anna Bogardus.

Gerrit, of Johs. and Maria V. d. Berg. Wit.: Abr. and Antie V. D. Poel.

Nicolaes, of R. and Eng. Kidny. Wit.: Jan and Maria Brat.

Elsie, of Johs. and Anna Hun. Wit.: Pieter and Lyntie Wenne.

March 23. Abraham, of Douwe and A. Fonda. Wit.: Johs. and Anna Ouderkerk.

Folkert, of G. and M. V. D. Berg. Wit.: G. T. V. Vegten, Anna Schoonmaker.

March 31. Joseph, of Daniel and Elyzabeth, pros. Wit.: Joseph and Josyna, pros.

Jacobus, of C. and C. Richtmeyer. Wit.: —— V. Franken, M. Olphert.

Apr. 8. John, of Ro. and Corn. Tumbarr. Wit.: John and Maria Tumbarr.

Apr. 15. Catharina, of Ph. and Cath. Livingston. Wit.: Pieter Van B. Livingston, Eva Van Driessen.

Elyzabeth, of Johs. and Anna Knoet. Wit.: Johs. Ouderkerk, Dirkie V. Franken.

Apr. 22. Folkie, of Isaack and Maria V. Aalsteyn. Wit.: Wyn. and Folkie V. D. Bergh.

May 13. Pieter, of R. and Sara Hansen. Wit.: Nic. Hansen, Mar. Livingston.

Andries, of Jer. and M. Pemberton. Wit.: Andr. and Yvie Brat.

May 20. Maria, of Ant. and Catr. Bovy. Wit.: Adam Jets, Eng. V. D. Werk.

Jan, of D. and Maria Housie. Wit.: Jan and Maria Brat.

1733

At Schag. May 27. Maria, of Jochum Bradt and Neeltje Groesbeek. Wit.: Bernardus and Maria Bradt.

Maria, of Hugo Viele and Catharyna Van Woerd. Wit.: Johannes Ouderkerk, Jannetje Viele.

Hannes, of Nicolaas Groesbeek and Agnietje De Wandelaars. Wit.: Hannes Groesbeek, Geertje Quackenbos.

June 6. Cornelia, of Obedia Couper and Cornelia Gardenier. Wit.: Douwen, Jr., and Elizabeth Fonda.

Suzanna, of Hendrik Hendrikse Roseboom and Cathalyna Schuyler. Wit.: Myndert and Suzanna Schuyler.

June 20. Christina, of Abr. and Cath. Schuyler. Wit.: David and Geertr. Schuyler.

June 24. Maria, of R. and Elyz. Nichols. Wit.: H. V. Rensselaar, Frenkie Nichols.

July 15. Aron, of Ruth and Elyzabeth, pros. Wit.: Abraham and Margarieta, pros.

Maria, of Jan and Susanna, pros. Wit.: Brand and Josina, pros.

Aug. 5. Abraham, of Hendrik Cuylder and Margrietje Van Deuse. Wit.: Dirk Ten Broek, Marytje Staats.

Aug. 8. Elyzabeth, Annaatje, of Zacharias Zikkels and Annaatje Wyngaards. Wit.: Gerrit Wyngaart, Elizabet Koddelaar, Andries Bradt, Margrietje Wyngaardt.

Aug. 12. Johannes, of Japik Beekman and Debora Hansen. Wit.: Rykert Hansz, Suzanna Beekman.

Aug. 15. Ephraim, of Hannes Ten Broek and Catharyna Van Renzelaar. Wit.: Johannes Van Renzelaar, Elizabeth Coster.

Aug. 19. Agnietje, of Hendrik Van Wie and Catharyna Walran. Wit.: Gerrit Van Wie, Agnietje Conyn.

Maas, of Jacob Maasze Bloemendaal and Zara Gardenier. Wit.: Corn. Maasze Bloemendaal, Geertruy Oostrander.

Aug. 26. Wilhelmus, of Corn. Van Schie and Josyna Prys. Wit.: Petrus Van Driess, Henricus Douw, Eva Cuylder.

Aug. 29. Philip, of Corn. Cuylder and Cathalyna Schuylder. Wit.: Johannes Cuylder, Jr., Annaatje Van Schaik.

Sep. 16. Maria, of Hannes and Rachel Van der Heyde. Wit.: Isaac Kip, Maria Schutze.

Sep. 30. Corn., of Petrus and Maritje Van den Bergh. Wit.: Pieter Van Woerdt, Ariaantje Van ———.

Oct. 5 [?] Thomas, of Pieter Livingston and Zelie Hollandt. Wit.: Henry Holland, Jr., Alida Beekman.

Oct. 2. Geertie, of Johs., Jr., and Jenn. Bleker. Wit.: Hendr. and Geertie T. Eyck.

Geertie, of Abr. and Geertie Vosburg. Wit.: W. G. Van d. Berg, Reb. Fonda.

1733

Lydia, of Jac. and M. V. Valkenburg. Wit.: J. and L. V. Valkenburg.

Francyntie, of J. and Mar. Knoet. Wit.: Abr. and Anna Fort.

Oct. 3. Ann, of J. and A. Stenhouse. Wit.: P. V. B. Livingston, M. Bath.

William, of J. and R. Potton. Wit.: W. Teyllier, W. Heyllin, Eleanor Teyllier.

Ann, of Ch. and W. Forbeliol. Wit.: J. Waters, Rachel Johnson.

Oct. 7. Gerrit, of M. and A. V. Yveren. Wit.: H. Visser, Piet. V. Aalsteyn.

Alida, of D. and A. Fonda. Wit.: —— and Alida Fonda.

Catharina, of G. and C. Roseboom. Wit.: Abr. Roseboom, Eva Bries.

Maria, of J. and M. Brouwer. Wit.: D. and M. Schuyler.

Hester, of S. and G. Criegier. Wit: Corn. Tymensen, Marr. Groot.

Oct. 14. Fytie, of Jac. and H. V. Woert. Wit.: Sand. V. Woert, Alida Marselis.

Oct. 21. Albertus, of Johs. and Brechie Zeeger. Wit.: Jac. M. and Sara V. Bloemendaal.

Neeltie, of Jesse and Neeltie D. Foreest. Wit.: Joh. and M. Quackenbos.

Nov. 4. Joh. Catharina, of Sal. and Marg. Goewey. Wit.: D. Ten Broek, Anna Groesbeek.

Hendrik, of Ar. and Ch. V. d. Karre. Wit.: R. and Geertr. V. D. Werke.

Nov. 11. Philip, of Joh. and Corn. Schuyler. Wit.: Jer. Van Rensselaar, Maria Miln.

Jannetie, of Jacob and M. Gleyn. Wit.: Johs. and Jannetie Gleyn.

Dec. 21 [Sic.]. Anna, of Johannes and Maria. Wit.: Seth and Anna.

Maria, of Cornelis and Anna. Wit.: Thomas and Canastazie.

Elyzabeth, of Petr. and Anna Douwe. Wit.: Folk. V. Vegten, Eng. Livingston.

Philip, of J. and Maria D. Foreest. Wit.: Abr. and Reb. D. Foreest.

Dec. 8 [sic] Abraham, of Jan and Marr. Oothout. Wit.: Abr. and Maicke Wendel.

Dec. 12. Johs., of M. and M. V. D. Heyde. Wit.: Joch. and Maria Brat.

Dec. 16. Gerrit, of P. and Anna V. Alen. Wit.: Gerr. Van Alen, Maria Conyn.

Folkert, of Abr. and Lyn. Douw. Wit.: Folk. Douwe, Anna Hun.

1733-1734

Dec. 19. Johannes, of Alb. and Cath. Becker. Wit.: Gerr. Becker, Antie V. d. Zee.

Susanna, of Ezras and Maria, pros. Wit.: Abraham and Christina, pros.

Hendrick, of Frans and Marg. Pruym. Wit.: Fransc. Lansing, Maria Evertsen.

Oct. [sic] 15. Hendrik, of Jacob Wendel and Helena Renzelaar. Wit.: Evert Wendel, Jr., Wid. Anna Wendel.

Oct. 22. Anna, of Isaac Staats and Maria Van Deusen. Wit.: Hendrick Cuylder, Margrietje Van Deusen.

Oct. 28. Maas, of Johannes and Ida Van Buren. Wit.: Hendrik and Cathalyna Van Buren.

Geesje, of Symen Veder and Geertruy Kip. Wit.: Hannes Evertse Wendel, Annaatje Wendel.

Nov. [sic] 18. Maria, of Thomas Van Aalsteyn and Marytje Van Alen. Wit.: Pieter Winne, Jr., Rachel Van Alen.

Nov. 25. Maria, of Thomas and Diana, negroes. Wit.: Willem.

Maria, of Jan Aremstran and Catharina Gardemo. Wit.: Egbert Egbertse, Gerritje Van Woerdt.

Dec. —. Waters, of Corn. De Ridder and Gerritje Van Hoesen. Wit.: Jan Waters, Zelia Winne.

1733/4, Jan. 6. Salomon, of Hendrik Bulsin and Cathalyna Goewey. Wit.: Anthony S. Van Schayk, Elizabeth Goewey.

Johannes, of Johannes Van der Werke and Margriet Baart. Wit.: Stev. Renzelaar, Elizabeth Groesbeek.

Jan. 30. Pieter, Jenneke, of Gerrit Van Benthuysen and Marytje Van Alen. Wit.: Willem and Lena Van Alen, Barent and Lena Zandertse.

Feb. 3. Mary of John Iets and Maria Houwkerk, Wit.: Claas Van den Bergh, Mary Clodt.

Feb. 20. Johannes, of Joh. Van Oostrander and Elizabeth Van den Bergh. Wit.: Douwe and Rebecca Fonda.

Jan. [sic] 6. Johannes, of Jac. and Cath. Rettelief. Wit.: Petr. Van Driessen, Rachel Rittelief.

Jan. 9. Pieter, of Lev. and Sus. Wenne. Wit.: Johs. Hansen, Maria Wenne.

Jan. 20. Alida, of Jurr. and Maria Hoogen. Wit.: M. Beekman, Marg. Hun.

Jan. 23. Johannes, of Johs. and Jann. Goewey Wit.: Sal. and Cat. Goewey.

Feb. 29. Johannes, of David Groesbeek and Maria Van der Poel. Wit.: Johannes Van der Poel, Annaatje Groesbeek.

March 6. Jeptha, a negro, bapt. upon confession.

Feb. [sic] 13. Eva, of Mart. and Geertr. Beekman. Wit.: Hendr. Beekman, Hester Swits.

1734

Feb. 21. Matheus, of M. and Reb. D. Garmoy. Wit.: Dirk and Eckb. D. Garmoy.

March 3. Jannetie, of Dan. and W. Brat. Wit.: Ant. and Jann. Bogardus.

March 6. Meyndert Schuyler, of John and Anna D. Peyster. Wit.: M. Schuyler, P. Van Brugh, Maria Banker. Gerardus, of M. and Jann. Van Olinde. Wit.: G. Van de Werke, Anna Ouderkerk.

March 10. Gysbert, of Johannes Van Zanten and Zara Hilten. Wit.: Gysbert Van Zanten, Juditje Hilten. Catharyna, of Johannes Wendel and Annaatje Kip. Wit.: Japik Millar, Geertruy Kip.

March 24. At H. M., Margrieta, of Jacob De Fort and Zara De Wandelaar. Wit.: Jacob Van der Heyden, Hester Visscher.

March 31. Marritje, of Abraham Van Deusen and Rachel Pels. Wit.: Harpert Japikse, Annaatje Witbeek.

Apr. 11. Chatharina, of Abr., Jr., and Helena Lansing. Wit.: H. and Cath. V. Deusen.

Apr. 21. Maria, of David and Abigael Foreest. Wit.: Js. and Mar. Van Alsteyn.

May 5. Johannes, of Rob. and Cath. Wendel. Wit.: Johs. Schuyler, Elyz. Wendel.

Hendrick, of D. and Madal. V. Der Karre. Wit.: D. and Aaltie Fonda.

Roelef, of M. and M. V. D. Werke. Wit.: Alb. V. D. Werke, Ab. Foreest.

Elsie, of Isaac and Alida Greveraat. Wit.: Elbert Gerritsen, Lena Lansingh.

May 12. Maria, of Ro. and Corn. Tumbarr. Wit.: Johs., Jr., and Maria Spoor.

Catharina, of Johs. F. [?] [or H. ?] and Cath. Cuyler. Wit.: Dirck Ten Broek, Anna Wendel.

Casparus, of Frans S. Pruyn and Alida Van Yveren. Wit.: Jacob and Marritje Pruyn.

May 19. Marritje, of Hannes Witbeek and Racheltje Cernyn. Wit.: Tobias and Cathalyntje Witbeek.

Johannes, of Andries Van den Berg and Marrytje Vinhagel. Wit.: Agnietje Witbeek, Johannes Vinhagel.

Cathalyna, of Hannes Wyngaart and Maria Cuyler. Wit.: Corn. Cuylder, Cathalyna Schuylder.

Abraham, of Dirck Ten Broek and Margrieta Cuylder. Wit.: Abraham Cuylder, Jr., Catharina Ten Broek.

Maragriet, of Johannes Henr. Lydius and Geneveva Maste. Wit.: Jacob Rozeboom, Geertruy Isabella Lydius.

May 22. Neeltje, of Hendr. Van Deuse and Ariaantje Staats. Wit.: Jan Oothoudt, Neeltje Staats.

June 3. Anthony, of Hendr. and Wyntje Bries. Wit.: Harm. Rykman, Tryntie Bries.

1734

Hendrik, of Ahazueros Rozeboom and Maria Bradt. Wit.: Gysbertus and Elsje Rozeboom.

June 9. Dirkje, of Hendrik and Aaltje Van Buren. Wit.: Daniel and Dirkje Winne.

Cathalyna, of Christoffel and Margrietje Abeel. Wit.: Gysbertus and Catharyna Rozeboom.

June 23. Geertruy, of R. and M. Hilten. Wit.: Pieter Bennewe, Hoop Hunt.

Pieter, of Carel [?] and Jannetie Walderom. Wit.: Willem Walderom, Corn. Brat.

Elsie, of Isack and Mary. Wit.: Andr. Bratt, Corn Busscher.

Madalena, of Chr. and Beertie Lang. Wit.: Ph. and Madl. Louck.

June 29. Mally, of Jac. [?] and Maria Lins. Wit.: Hendr. and Catal. Buntingh.

Johannes, of M. and El. Veeder. Wit.: J. S. Veeder, Maria Evertsen.

John, of J. Creddisch and Corn. Buscher. Wit.: Nath. and Edl. Edwards.

July 12. Elyzabeth, of Gleyn and Ar. Verplank. Wit.: Isaac Verplank, Madl. Wimp.

Sara, of Benj. and Rachel Wenne. Wit.: Kil. Wenne, Gerrittie Ridder.

Abraham, after a confession of faith. Formerly a heathen.

July 7. [sic] Annaatje, of Mattheus Flensburg and Maria Van Zanten. Wit.: Jeremias Pamerton, Zelia Van Zanten.

Johannes, of Hendrik Logen and Alida Pruyn. Wit.: Frans and Catharyna Pruyn.

Phillip, of Evert and Engeltje Wendel. Wit.: Johannes Wendel, Geertruyda Lansing.

July 12. Elizabeth, of Stevanus Van Renzelaar and Elizabeth Groesbeek. Wit.: Stevanus and Elizabeth Groesbeek.

July 29. Hendrik, of Hendrik and Suzanna Halenbeek. Wit.: Hendricus Brat, Catharyna Van Vegte.

July 31. Neeltje, of William Hogen, Jr., and Pietertje Douw. Wit.: Henricus and Neeltje Douw.

Aug. 14. Cornelis, of Machiel and Lybetje Bestid. Wit.: Isaac and Jannetje Lansing.

Isaac, of Theunis Slingerland and Cornelia Kip. Wit.: Isaac Kip, Geertruy Veder.

Aug. 18. Willem, of Jacobus Hilten and Judith Maarten. Wit.: Hannes and Zara Van Zanten.

Aug. 28. Alida, of David and Geertruy Van der Heyden. Wit.: Harm. and Annaatje Visscher.

Sep. 1. Maria, of Hendrik Van Wie and Hilletje Becker. Wit.: Hannes and Ydtje Van Buren.

1734

Sep. 29. Lena, of Isaac Van Deusen and Bata Van Yselsteyn. Wit.: Harpert and Tryntje Van Deusen.

Oct. 6. Johannes, of Pieter Van Alen and Annaatje Van Benthuysen. Wit.: Johannes Van Alen, Catharyna Van Benthuysen.

Aug. [sic] 10. Evert, of Gerr. and Mar. Banker. Wit.: Chr. and Elyz. Banker.

Sara, of Bar. and Corn. Meyndertsen. Wit.: Anth. Meyndertsen, P. Van Yveren.

Aug. 28. Nicolaes, of J. and M. Quackenbos. Wit.: Jesse D. Foreest, Marg. Bogaart.

Folkie, of F. and Cath. V. d. Berg. Wit.: M. and Cath. Van Aalsteyn.

Willem, of D. and M. Hun. Wit.: Will. and Martina Hoogen.

Sep. 1. Cornelia, of Dav. and Eng. Uzile. Wit.: J. and Elyz. Van Aalsteyn.

Isaac-Valk, of L. and M. V. Aalsteyn. Wit.: J. and M. V. Valkenburg.

Sep. 8. Daniel, of Anth. and Reb. Brat. Wit.: Daniel and Elyz. Brat.

Sep. 22. Isaac, Sara, of Isaac and Cath. Wendel. Wit.: M., J., and C. Schuyler, Cath. Cuyler.

Anthonie, of Chr. and C. Schians. Wit.: R. and G. V. Vegten.

Jacob, Catharina, of Is. and Hendr. Bogaart. Wit.: J. Bogaart, F. Oothoudt, Dor. and Jann. Bogaart.

Johannes, of G. and M. Marsselis. Wit.: Johs. and Anna Bleeker.

Barent, of Jac. and A. T. Eyck. Wit.: Johs. T. Eyck, Anna Visser.

Frans, of Kil. and Reb. Wenne. Wit.: J. and Cat. Wenne.

Oct. 6. Hendrick, of H. and Reb. Klauw. Wit.: Sal. and Cat. Goewey.

Anna, of Ephr. and Agn. Bogardus. Wit.: H. and W. Bries.

Gerrit, of H. and Sara Visser. Wit.: M. and Ar. Van Yveren.

Oct. 10. Abraham, slave of M. Hun, bapt. after confession.

Oct. 27. Anna, of Simon and Hilletie Ridder. Wit.: Hendr. and Cath. Ridder.

Nov. 10. Elyzabeth, of Leend. and Cat. Witbeek. Wit.: Jan and Elyz. Witbeek.

Rachel, of Benj. and Anna Bogaart. Wit.: Abr. and Dor. Bogaart.

Elyzabeth, of Abr. and Alida V. Arnhem. Wit.: Fr. and Anna Lansingh.

56

1734-1735

Dec. 15. Thomas, of Jeremias and Susanna Schuyler. Wit.: Edw. Hollant, Margr. Schuyler.

Abraham, of Dav. and Maria Schuyler. Wit.: Johs. Hansen, Geertr. Schuyler.

Oct. [sic] 10. Cathalyna, of Sybrant and Jannetje Van Schayck. Wit.: Japik and Alida Bogaart.

Oct. 27. Brit, of Jephta and Clara. Wit.: Henry and Bric Pieperaas.

Nov. 3. Catharyna, of Johannes Van Renzelaar and Engeltje Livingston. Wit.: Hendrik Van Renzelaar, Margrietje Livingston.

Nov. 17. Elizabeth, of Cornelis Van Schie and Josyna Prys. Wit.: Stevanus Groesbeek, Elizabeth Lansing.

Lucas, of Lucas Hooghkerk and Rebecca Fonda. Wit.: Lucas Hooghkerk, Hendrika Jaits.

Adriaan, of Johannes Quackenbos and Elizabeth Romblic. Wit.: Goze and Debora Van Schaik.

Dec. 1. Barent, of Gerrit and Engeltje Van den Bergh. Wit.: Japik and Geertruy Witbeek.

Dec. 15. Cornelia, of Petrus Rykman and Catharyna Van Kierstede. Wit.: Pieter Rykman, Neeltje Ryckman.

1734/5, Jan. 5. Annaatje, of Sybrand and Elizabeth Quackenbos. Wit.: Harmen and Neeltje Knickerbakker.

Jan. 29. Barber, of Johannes and Margrieta Bradt. Wit.: Gerrit and Barber Rykse.

Maria, negress, bapt. after a confession.

Feb. 9. Thomas, of Johannes and Jannetje Makluur. Wit.: Pieter Livingston, Annaatje De Peyster.

Johannes, of Jillis and Rachel De Garamo. Wit.: Johannes De Garamo, Agnietje Bogardus.

Cornelis, of Harme and Elizabeth Van Vegte. Wit.: Corn. and Hendrikje Van Buren.

March 23. Willem, of Pieter Danielse Winne and Rachertje Van Alen. Wit.: Pieter Van Alen, Annaatje Van Wie.

1735, March 30. Alida, of Johannes and Annaatje Visscher. Wit.: David and Geertruy Van der Heyden.

Jan. [sic] 8. Hilletie, of Johs. and Breggie Zeeger. Wit.: Jan and Maria Brat.

Maria, of Isaak and Jac. Fort. Wit.: Th. and Maria Viele.

Engeltje, of Dirk, Jr., and Corn. Brat. Wit.: Daniel Brat, Engeltie Walderon.

Jan. 18. Margrieta, of Lamb. and Anna Rettelief. Wit.: G. and A. Van Zanten.

Johannes, of Nicolaes and Agnietie Groesbeek. Wit.: St. and Elyz. Rensselaar.

Elizabeth, of Joch. and Neeltie Brat. Wit.: Steph. Groesbeek, Antie Fonda.

1735
Feb. 14. Cornelis, of C. and Rach. Van d. Berg. Wit.:
G. V. d. Berg, M. Gerritsen.
Hester, of Jan and E. V. Arnhem. Wit: J. and H.
V. Arnhem.
Feb. 21. Evert, of H. and Anna Ridder. Wit.: S.
Ridder, Cath. Oothout.
Pieter, of Johs. and Sara Hansen. Wit.: Corn. Cuyler,
Deb. Beekman.
Mar. 3. Nicolaes, of J. and M. V. Woert. Wit.: Nic.
and Dirckie V. Woert.
Jacobus, of R. and Eng. Kidny. Wit.: J. Kidny,
El. V. d. Werken.
March 9. Lucas, of A. and A. Witbeek. Wit.: H. J.
and Cat. V. Deusen.
March 23. Jan Gerritsen, of Adam and Anna Yets.
Wit.: Chr. Yets, M. Gerritsen.
Jan, of Abr. and Elb. Fonda. Wit.: Jan and Maria
Fonda.
March 30. Gerrit, of G. and A. V. d. Berg. Wit.:
H. and Cath. V. Wie.
Apr. 4. Dirckie, of Th. and M. Visser Wit.: H.
Visser, Eck. D. Garmoy.
Lidia, of Jacob and Diever, pros. Wit.: Seth and Sara.
Sara, of Abraham and Dina, pros. Wit.: Hendrick
and Rebecka.
Apr. 13. Jacob, of Jac. and Geertr. Quackenbos. Wit.:
Abr. Quackenbos, Geertr. d. Fou.
Antie, of An. and Catr. Bovy. Wit.: Johs. V. D.
Werke, Ariaentie Bovy.
Rebecka, of Eck. and Rach. Eckbertsen. Wit.: Jac.
Van Woerdt, Susanna Eckbertsen.
May 4. Patrick, of Andr. and Hagar Makans. Wit.:
Pieter and Zelia Livingston.
Maria, of G. C. and M. V. d. Berg. Wit.: Johs., Jr., and
Neeltje V. Vegten.
May 15. Margrieta, of Sal. and M. Goewey. Wit.:
Jer. Van Rensselaar, Cath. Ten Broek.
Christina, of G. and M. V. Benthuysen. Wit.: Johs.
Ten Broek, Elyz. Coster.
May 18. Willempie, of Dan. and Wyntie Brat. Wit.:
Barent and Elyz. Brat.
May 26. Meyndert, of H. M., and Maria Rooseboom.
Wit.: Jacob T. Eyck, Mary Rooseboom.
June 2. Ariaentie, of Evert and Maria Jansen. Wit.:
Johs. Sym., and Susanna Vedder.
Stephanus, of Th. and Maria Viele. Wit.: Abr. and
Elbertie Fonda.
Ariaentie, of Storm and Lena V. d. Zee. Wit.: L.
Gansevoort, Anna Kitsenaar.

Isaac, of M. and C. V. Aalsteyn. Wit.: B. and Corn.
V. Yveren.

June 8. Helena, of G. J. and Eytie Lansing. Wit.:
Fr. and Anna Lansing.

June 22. Anna, of W. and Elyz. Walderom. Wit.:
Isaac and Jann. Lansing.

Mally, of Syaack and Mally, pros. Wit.: Thomas and
Diana, pros.

July 2. Johannes, of Jacob and Elyz. Glen. Wit.:
Johs. and Elsie Cuyler.

Petrus and Brant, pros. from among the heathen, after
confession.

Apr. 13. [sic] Salomon, of Hendrick and Cathalyna
Bulsen. Wit.: Anthony and Elizabeth Van Schaick.

Judichje, of Johannes and Ydtje Van Buren. Wit..
Marten and Marytje Van Buren.

Elizabet, of Pieter and Annaatje Magriegrie. Wit.:
Corns. and Catharyntje Cuylder.

Apr. 27. Jonathan, of Daniel and Alida Maarten.
Wit.: Pieter and Ariaantje Van Wourdt.

Fydtje, of Gerardus and Ariaantje Becker. Wit.:
Arent and Scherlotte Van der Kar.

Barbar, of Johannes and Annaatje Knoet. Wit.: Hannes and Annaatje Van Francken.

June 1. Wynandt, of Wynand Van den Bergh and
Annaatje Wendel. Wit.: Jan and Cathalyna Van Es.

June 4. Gerritje, of Nicolaas Bleecker, Jr., and Margrieta Rozeboom. Wit.: Johannes Rozeboom, Anna
Van Schaik.

Gooze, of Gooze and Debora Van Schaik. Wit.:
Anthony, Jr., and Chataryna Van Schaik.

June 14. Johannes, of Japik and Marytje Knoet.
Wit.: Frederik Knoet, Anna Catryn.

June 18. Jane, of Pieter Livingston and Zelia Hollandt.
Wit.: Henricus Beekman, Engeltje Renzelaar.

Agnieta, of Hendrik, Jr., and Catharyn Van Wie. Wit.:
Gerrit and Agnieta Van Wie.

July 6. Cobus, a negro of Johannes Van Buren, bapt.
after confession.

July 23. Catharyna, of Jacob Wendel and Helena
Renzelaar. Wit.: Johannes Renzelaar, Annaatje Douw.

July 30. Lammert, of Zaccharias Sikkel and Annaatje
Wyngaart. Wit.: Lammert Raadly, Rachel Raedtly.

Annaatje, of Reyer and Mary Sjoos. Wit.: Jan Joons,
Anna Couper.

Aug. 3. Volkje, of Volkert and Catharyna Van den
Berg. Wit.: Marting and Catharyntje Van Aalsteyn.

Aug. 13. Maria, of Douwe and Aaltje Fonda. Wit.:
Harme and Elizabeth Van Vegten.

1735

Aug. 24. Rachel, of Jochum and Bata Van der Heyden. Wit.: Hannes and Rachel Van der Heyden.

Aug. 31 Maria, of Johannes and Johanna Marcelius. Wit.: Hendricus Beekman, Alida Hollandt.

July [sic] 9. Margrieta, of R. and M. Olfer. Wit.: W. Hilten, M. Olfert.

Cortlant, of J., Jr., and Corn. Schuyler. Wit.: Ph. Schuyler, G. Beekman.

July 27. Rachel, of J. and M. Valkenburg. Wit.: L. and R. Rettelief.

Aug. 18. Catalina, of M. and C. V. d. Berg. Wit.: W. and G. V. d. Berg.

Wouter, of P. and A. Quackenbos. Wit.: H. Oothoudt, M. Foreest.

Maria, of D. and A. Fonda. Wit.: Johs. and C. Fonda

Aug. 22. Femmetie, of J. and M. Switz. Wit.: B. and T. Vroman.

Elizabeth, of C. and El. Rigtmyer. Wit.: Johs. and Anna Hun.

Hendrik, of Corn. and C. Cuyler. Wit.: Ph. J. and M. Schuyler.

Aug. 26. Folkert, of J., Jr., and H. V. Vegten. Wit.: F. and L. V. Vegten.

Willem, of J. and M. Pemperton. Wit.: Andr. and Yvie Brat.

Sep. 7. Johannes, of P., Jr., and R. Bronk. Wit.: H. Bries, C. Bronk.

Sep. 14. Eggie, of J. and A. Slingerlant. Wit.: S. and El. V. d. Zee.

Hendrik and Christina, after foregoing confession. Ch. of Hendrik and Christina. Wit.: Lucas and Maria.

Oct. 19. Gerardus, of Ger. and Mach. Knoet. Wit.: Pieter and Cath. Schuyler.

Cornelis, of Johs., Jr., and Cath. Cuyler. Wit.: Corn. Cuyler, Anna V. Schaik.

Oct. 26. Stephanus, of Hugo and Cath. Viele. Wit.: P. and Cath. Viele.

Philip, of Jac. and Cath. Rettelief. Wit.: J. and Cath. V. Aalsteyn.

William, of F., Jr., and Anna Douwe. Wit.: Will. and Anna Hoogen.

Nov. 2. Pieter, of Abr. and Lyntie Douwe. Wit.: Johs. Hun, Margr. Williams.

Ryckert, of G. and A. V. Zanten. Wit.: J. and M. V. d. Berg.

Nov. 9. Mercy of W. and —— Joungh. Wit.: Jac. Hilten, Bar. Siabbets.

Gerrit, of Ro. and C. Tumbarr. Wit.: Adam Jetz, Sara Waters.

1735-1736
Petrus, of J. and H. V. Woerdt. Wit.: P. and A. V. Woerdt.

Nov. 23. Nicolaes, of J. and M. V. d. Berg. Wit.: Cl. and Antie V. d. Bergh.

Nov. 26. Wouter, of J. and M. D. Foreest. Wit.: J. and M. Quackenbos.

Dec. 10. Cornelis, of Jan and M. Oothout. Wit.: C. and D. Bogaardt.

Cornelis, of Obed. and Corn. Couper. Wit.: Johs. and Anna Hun.

Dec. 14. Albertus, of Jac. Maessen and Sara Maassen. Wit.: A. H. and Sara Gardenier.

Dec. 25. Abraham, of David and Maria Schuyler. Wit.: Jac. Schuyler, Debora Beekman.

Nov. [sic] 2. Maria, of Robbert and Margrieta Lansing. Wit.: Johannis and Helena Lansing.

Nov. 9. Anna, of Wouter and Elizabeth Knikkerbakker. Wit.: Hannes Knickerbakker, Elizabeth Quackenbos.

Nov. 19. Lena, of Mynkel and Lybetje Bestidt. Wit.: Corn. and Hendrikje Van Buren.

Nov. 23. Adam, of Robbert Flindt and Susanna Flind. Wit.: Marten [?] and Maria Flensburgh.

Oct. [sic] 12. Johannes, of Pieter and Maria Fonda. Wit.: Douwe Fonda, Rebecca Blommendaal.

Suzanna, of Jan Moen and Christina Logen. Wit.: Roelof Lindts, Geertruy Hondt.

Oct. 19. Dorethe, of Johannes and Elizabeth Valckenburg. Wit.: Hendrik and Elizabeth Halenbeek.

Oct. 26. Catharyna, of Hannes and Elizabeth Quackenbos. Wit.: Adriaan and Catharyn Quackenbos.

Dec. 7. Anna Catharyna, of Sybrand, Jr., and Anna Van Schaik. Wit.: Anthony and Anna Catharyna Van Schaik.

Dec. 28. Margriet, of Nathaniel and Ida Engels. Wit.: Mathys and Margrieta Van der Heyden.

1735/6, Jan. 7. Rachel, of William and Rachel Narden. Wit.: Abraham and Geertruy Witbeek.

Anna, of Renzelaar and Elizabeth Nikkels. Wit.: Jeremias Van Renzelaar, Patroon, Maria Mil.

Jan. 11. Geertje, of Japik and Alida Ten Eyck. Wit.: Hendrik Myndert Rozeboom, Geertruy Van der Heyde.

Jan. 14. Isabella Margrieta, of Johannis Henricq Lydius and Genevieva Mazee. Wit.: Lancaster Symes, Margrieta Johanna Lydius.

Feb. 8. Geertruidtje, of Abraham Vroman and Marytje Verplanck. Wit.: Japik Verplanck, Lydia Van Aalsteyn.

Feb. 25. Johannes, of Dirk and Magdalena Van der Kar. Wit.: Laving Londer Zee, Engeltje Van der Werken.

1736

Geertruy, of David and Engeltje Uziele. Wit.: Willem and Lena Hooghtelinck.

Pieter, of Robbert and Catharyna Wendel. Wit.: Laving and Zuzanna Winne.

Feb. 29. Margriet, of Thomas and Elizabeth Wilkenson. Wit.: Jacobus and Judick Hilten.

Lena, of Abraham and Helena Lansing. Wit.: Gerrit and Suzanna Lansing.

Rachel, of Petrus and Annaatje Douw. Wit.: Hendrik, Jr., and Elizabeth Van Renzelaar.

Thomas, of Johannes and Annaatje Hun. Wit.: Dirck and Mayke Hun.

1736, March 7. Margriet, of Sjems and Margriet De Long. Wit.: Manes and Mary Kerl.

Thomas, of Jonathan and Orsel Bankly. Wit.: Sjeems and Margrietje Smidt.

Symen [or Tymen], of Daniel Hortje and Marie Horttie. Wit.: Tymen [or Symen] Danielse Edwaard, Marytje Edwaardt.

Apr. 4. Jacob, of Gerrit Japikse Lansing and Marytje Lansing. Wit.: Japik and Lena Lansing.

Catharyna, of Hendrik and Wyntje Bries. Wit.: Bernardus Brat, Catharyna Rozeboom.

Apr. 22. Philip, of Pieter and Catharyna Schuyler. Wit.: Johannes Schuylder, Elizabeth Renzelaar.

Jan, of Jan and Catharyn Harenstrong. Wit.: Sjeems and Margriet Smit.

Apr. 25. Marritje, of Gerrit Cornelisse Van Es and Zara Van Es. Wit.: Hendrik and Annaatje Ridder.

May 2. Willem, of Isaac and Maria Staats. Wit.: —— V. Deusen, Anna Staats.

Geertruy, of Jac. Schuyler and Geertr. Schuiler. Wit.: Bar. Staats, Geertr. Schuyler.

Rachel, of Johs. and R. V. d. Heyde. Wit.: J. E. Wendell, R. D. V. d. Heyde.

Jan. [sic] 7. Harmen, of T. and Mar. V. Buuren. Wit.: Pieter Wenne, Anna Hun.

Jan. 18. Jacobus, of Ger. and M. Knoet. Wit.: Johs. and Geertr. Knoet.

Jan. 25. Jan, of John and Anna Dret. Wit.: R. and G. Du Fou.

Elyzabeth, of J. and M. Courtir. Wit.: Ulrick V. Franken, Elyz. V. d. Linde.

Feb. 8. Elyzabeth, of Johs. and Hel. Ouderkerk. Wit.: J. and Anna Knoet.

Tryntie, of Chr. and Dor. Langh. Wit.: Isaac and Jann. Lansing.

Marten, of J. and Mar. V. Aalsteyn. Wit.: Dav. and Abigael Foreest.

1736

March 7. Catalyna, of Johs. and Jann. Goewey. Wit.:
Abr. and Antie V. d. Poel.

Cornelis, of Will. and T. V. Buuren. Wit.: H. and
Elyz. V. Vegten.

Apr. 4. Jacob, of Abr. and An. V. Arnhem. Wit.:
H. and Anna Lansingh.

Apr. 11. Willem, of H. and Ariaent. V. Deusen. Wit.:
Hendr. and A. Cuyler.

Apr. 25. Barber, of J. and Anna V. Franken. Wit.:
Gerr. and Ann V. Franken.

May 9. Elyzabeth, of Ger. and Maria Banker. Wit.:
Johs. and Anna D. Peyster.

May 16. Jacob, of Roel. and Elyz. Jansen. Wit.:
J. Schermerh., Jr., Antie Schermerhoorn.

Jacob, of Johs. and Eng. Schermerhoorn. Wit.: J.
and M. Schermerhoorn.

Machtel, of Abr. and Antje Springsteen, Wit.: J.
Beekman, Macht. Springsteen.

Dirck, of Dirck and Margr. Ten Broek. Wit.: Nic.
Cuyler, Cath. Sybr. V. Schayck.

Rebecka, of John and M. Heaton. Wit.: Ji. Jets,
Sara Hoogkerk.

Pieter, of Th. and Mar. V. Aalsteyn. Wit.: Piet. and
Anna V. Alen.

May 23 Maria, of Abr. and Rebecka Foreest. Wit.:
D. and Sara V. Antwerpen.

June 13. Maas, of H. and A. V. Buuren. Wit.: P. V.
Buuren, Mad. Huyck.

June 16. Maria, of N. and A. V. d. Kar. Wit.: H.
and A. V. Wie.

Huybertie, of Jos. and H. Jets. Wit.: J. and Zytie
V. Zanten.

June 20. Jochum Brat, of M. and M. V. d. Heide.
Wit.: B. and Anna Brat.

June 23. Margarita, of R. and Zely Livingston. Wit.:
Edw. Holland, G. Lansingh.

June 27. Eva, of Henry and Alida Hollant. Wit.:
Jac. and Eva Beekman.

July 11. Margarita, of Abr. and Rachel Van Deusen.
Wit.: Evert Pels, Breggie Goelet.

May 9. [sic] Eva, of Pieter and Anna Bennewe.
Wit.: Arent Van Coddelaar, Theuntje Fort.

Pieter, of Jacobus and Elizabeth Bennewe. Wit.:
Abraham and Elizabeth Delmont

Evert, of Corn. and Jannitje Walran. Wit.: Evert
Van Es, Eva Walron.

May 19. Thomas, of Dirck and Margrietje Hun. Wit.:
Adriaan and Hendrikje Hun.

May 23. Rachel, of Johannes and Elizabeth Van Oosterandt. Wit.: Hendrik Ridder, Rachel Ter Williger.

May 26. Jenneke, of Pieter and Annaatje Van Alen. Wit.: Gerrit and Maria Van Benthuysen.

June 3. Marten, Jacob, of Theunis and Engeltje Ebbertse. Wit.: Jacob Visscher, Elizabeth Walran, Jacob Schermerhoorn, Marytje Ebberts.

June 6. Maas, of Hendrik and Aaltje Van Buren. Wit.: Pieter Van Buren, Magdalena Huyk.

Abraham, of David and Maria Groesbeek. Wit.: Abraham and Ariaantje Van der Poel.

June 30. Gerrit, of Evert and Annaatje Lansing. Wit.: Gerrit Lansing, Suzanna Wendel.

July 1. Stevanus, of Theunis and Maria Viele. Wit.: Pieter and Lybetje Viele.

July 18. Maria, of Corn. Van Schie and Josyna Prys. Wit.: Anthony S. Van Schaik, Joh. and Catharyna Ten Broek, Neeltje Isaacs.

Wouter, of Albert Becker and Catharyntje Bekker. Wit.: Storm Van der Zee, Hilletje Ridders.

Aug. 1. Rutger, of Alexander and Elizabeth Van Woerd. Wit.: Rutger and Elizabeth Van Woerd.

Caspar, of Reyer and Marytje Sprinksteen. Wit.: Benjamin and Catharyna Bogert.

Aug. 11. Stevanus, of Abraham and Elbertje Fonda. Wit.: Stevanus and Maria Van Alen.

Aug. 29. Lena, of Hendrik and Annaatje Lansing. Wit.: Franciscus and Annaatje Lansing.

Cathalyna, of Johannes and Maria Wyngaart. Wit.: Corn. and Catalyna Cuylder.

Catharyna, of Joh., Jr., and Sara Beekman. Wit.: Abraham Cuylder, Margrieta Ten Broek.

Sep. 12. Margriet, of Darby Greedy and Ariaantje Symense. Wit.: Roelof Kirnie, Rachel Sparten [?].

Geesje, of Theunis and Cornelia Slingerland. Wit.: Symen Veder, Geesje Kip.

Jonathan, of Willem and Lena Hooghtelingh. Wit.: Jonathan Hoogteling, Antje Van Zanten.

Daniel, of Barnardus Brat and Catharyna Brad. Wit.: Gerrit and Elyzabeth Bradt.

Gerrit Reyersse, of Hendrik Gerritse and Dirkje Symense. Wit.: Elbert and Anna Gerritse.

Sep. 26. Nanning, of Nicolaas and Annaatje Visscher. Wit.: Joh. Visscher, Geertruy Van der Heyden.

Sjene, of Richart and Elizabeth Millar. Wit.: Tobias Ryckman, Mary Blodt.

Oct. 3. Elizabeth, of Johannes and Margrieta Bradt. Wit.: Rykert Van Franken, Elizabeth Bradt.

64

Hendricus, of William, Jr., and Pietertje Hogen. Wit.:
Hendricus Douw, Judikje Pels.
Cathalyne, of Matthys and Cathalyntje Van den Berg.
Wit.: Wilhelmus and Geertje Van den Bergh.
Margrieta, of Johannes and Engeltje Renzelaar. Wit.:
Pieter Livingston, Christyna Ten Broek.
Volkert, of Myndert and Elizabeth Viele. Wit.: Vol-
kert and Margrieta Douw.
Maria, of Barent and Cornelia Van Yveren. Wit.:
Johannes and Catharyna Van Aalsteyn.
Maarten Cornelisze, of Johannes and Rachel Witbeek.
Wit.: Jonathan Witbeek, Jannetje Van Buren.
Oct. 8. Suzanna, of Isaac and Cathalyna Wendel.
Wit.: Japik and Zara Glen.
July [sic] 26. Wouter, of Storm and Elyz. V. d. Zee.
Wit.: Ger. Groesbeek, Elyz. Slingerlant.
Franciscus, of Hendr. and Alida Hogin. Wit.: Fr.
Pruym, Anna Lansing.
Catharina, of Jacob, pros. Wit.: Jac. Hilten, Elyz.
Goewey.
Aug. 8. Sara, of Jesse and N. D. Foreest. Wit.:
—— D. Foreest and Abigael D. Foreest.
Aug. 22. Johs. Jansen, of Casp. and Antie Witbeek.
Wit.: Jan Witbeek, M. Williams.
Sep. 5. Johannes, of H. C. and R. Lauw. Wit.: J.
and Jann. Goewey.
William, of J. and Elyz. Reyel. Wit.: W. and Eleon.
Teiller.
Anna, of J. A. and Catr. Cuyler. Wit.: Jac. Wendell,
M. Cuyler.
Mayke, of D. and Elyz. Hun. Wit.: Johs. and Mayeke
Hun.
Douwe, of H. and D. Wenne. Wit.: Douwe Bogaart,
Sara Fonda.
Gozen, of Sybr. and W. V. Schaick. Wit.: D. and G.
V. Schayck.
Rachel, of M. and R. V. d. Berk. Wit.: J. and N. V.
d. Berk.
Jan, of Johs. and M. Fonda. Wit.: P. and M. Fonda
Jeremias, of Chr. and Catr. Schians. Wit.: —— V.
Rensselaar and E. V. Rensselaar.
Antie, of C. and Rach. V. d. Berg. Wit.: Symon and
M. V. d. Berg [?].
Oct. 31. Henriette, of Hitsen and Mary Holland.
Wit.: Edw. Holland, Marg. Collins.
Willempie, of E. and E. Brat. Wit.: B. and W. Brat.
Jacob, of J. and B. Zeeger. Wit.: J. and —— Maassen.
Nov. 14. Cornelis, of N. and D. V. Schaick. Wit.:
Step. Groesbeek, Dor. Bogaart.

1736
Eva, of C. and El. Rigtmeyer. Wit.: L. and Catr. Gansevoort.

Willempie, of B. and Zach. Wenne. Wit.: Dan. Wenne, Sara Waters.

Isaac, illeg., of (J. J. Lansing and) Rebecca Oostrandt. Wit.: Johs. and M. Oostrander.

Nov. 20. Marretie, of Johs. and Geertr. [?] Kidney. Wit.: Nath. Flensburgh, Marr. Kidny.

Nov. 28. Jacobus, of H. and Cat. Rooseboom. Wit.: Ephr. Wendel, Elyz. V. Schelluyne.

Stephanus, of P. and El. Landman. Wit.: Step. and Elyz. V. Rensselaar.

Maria, of Jac. and Marr. V. Woerdt. Wit.: B. and Sus. Eckbertsen.

Dec. 12. Maria, Elyzabeth, of Ar. and Charl. V. D. Karre. Wit.: N., El., and W. V. Schaick, Mar. V. D. Werke.

Sara, of James and Sara Stevenson. Wit.: P. V. Brugh, Delia Groenendyk.

Oct. 16. [sic] Johannes, of Isaac and Jakemyntje Fort. Wit.: Johannes and Jakemyntje Fort.

Pieter, of Laving and Suzanna Winne. Wit.: Maarten Winne, Catharyna Wendel.

Oct. 29. Barent, of Hendrik Myndertse Rozeboom and Maria Rozeboom. Wit.: Coenraad and Jannetje Ten Eyck.

Gerrit, of Hendrik and Suzanna Halenbeek. Wit.: William Halenbeek, Marytje Bradt.

Nov. 7. Maria, of Jacobus and Judith Hilten. Wit.: Dirk and Maria Maarten.

Nov. 21. Elbert, of Isaac and Alida Grevenraad. Wit.: Elbert and Anna Gerritsen.

Dec. 5. Petrus, of Johannes and Margrietje Quackenbos. Wit.: Johannes and Marytje Foreest.

Dec. 17. Sjeems, of Sjon and Mary Linds. Wit.: Cherl. Dennel, Edi Englis.

Dec. 26. Margrietje, of Jan and Jannetje Maklier. Wit.: Frans and Margrietje Pruyn.

At H. M. 1736/7, Jan. 8. Harmen, of Japik and Saartje Fort. Wit.: Pieter and Maria De Wandelaar.

Philip, of Pieter and Grietje Macarti. Wit.: Abraham Viele, Cornelia Knickerbakker.

Jan. 12. Abigil, of Dennis and Mary Springer. Wit.: Gerrit and Marytje Van der Werken.

Aafje, of Tobias, Jr., and Marytje Ryckman. Wit.: Harmen Ryckman, Eva Bries.

Jacob, of Benjamin and Anna Bogaart. Wit.: Andries Huyck, Jannetje Bogaert.

Margrieta, of Sjeems and Anna Margrieta Steenhuysen. Wit.: Robbert, Jr., and Anna Maria Barreith.

1736-1737

Maria, of Rykert and Maria Hilten. Wit.: Geurt and Nelly Bennewe.

Jan. 26. Jan, of Robbert and Agnietje Schot. Wit.: Casparus Bronk, Hilleken Williams.

Jacobus, of Christoffel and Margrietje Abeel. Wit.: Jacobus Bleeker, Eva Bries.

Feb. 13. Mary, of David and Rebecca Mahanney. Wit.: Sjeems Grandt, Idey English.

Pieter Symense, of Symen and Geertruy Veders. Wit.: Isaac and Wid. Geesje Kip.

Feb. 20. Suzanna, of Myndert and Ariaantje Van Yveren. Wit.: Japik and Suzanna Van Yveren.

Cornelis, of Gerrit, Jr., and Engeltje Van den Bergh. Wit.: Ephraim and Annaatje Wendel.

Feb. 27. Pieter, of Hendrik, Jr., and Catharyna Van Wie. Wit.: Willem and Elizabeth Walrau.

Johannes, of Georgius and Margriet Lubkens. Wit.: Jan Olivert, Catharyna Schuyldert.

Abraham, of Marten and Dirkje Van Buren. Wit.: Abraham Douw, Marytje Van Buren.

1737, March 2. Harmen, of Nicolaas, Jr., and Agnietje Groesbeek. Wit.: Hannes and Rebecca De Wandelaar.

Margrieta, of Cherl. and Elizabeth Donnels. Wit.: Mettis Flensburg, Margriet Maarten.

Isaac, of Lucas Hoogkerk, Jr., and Rebecca Fonda. Wit.: Isaac and Alida Fonda.

March 13. Phillip, of Johannes and Mary De Foreest. Wit.: Hannes and Sara Hanse.

Theunis, of Harmen and Sara Visscher. Wit.: Hannes and Ebbertje De Garamo.

March 27. Barent, of Johannes and Annaatje Visscher. Wit.: Joachim and Neeltje Staats.

1736/7, Jan. 5. Echje, of Storm and Lena V. d. Zee. Wit.: Th. and Eva Slingerlant.

Daniel, of Joj. and Eva Ketelluyn. Wit.: Math. and Marg. V. D. Heyde.

Jan. 9. Geertruy, of Andr. and Marg. V. d. Berg. Wit.: Benj. V. d. Berg. Maria V. Buuren.

Jan. 22. Mary, of Th. and El. Evans. Wit.: John and Cath. Jones.

Maria, of J. G. and Jann. Lansing. Wit.: Sal. and Sara V. Vegten.

Hendrick, of Henry and El. V. Rensselaar. Wit.: H. and Mar. V. Rensselaar.

Ann, of J. and Reb. Brooks. Wit.: P. and Ann Magriegerie.

Feb. 6. Sara, of Sal. and M. Goewey. Wit.: P. Wenne, A. V. Vegten.

1737

March 3. Sara, of J. and A. V. Schaick. Wit.: G. and Sara V. Schaick.

Anna Maria, of W. and R. Barheyt. Wit.: G. and Elz. Lansingh.

Jacob, of D. and A. Foreest. Wit.: J. D. Foreest, Piet. V. Aalsteyn.

John, of J. and A. Springer. Wit.: J. and W. Bennewe.

March 19. David, of M. and M. Flensburg. Wit.: D. and Z. V. Zanten.

1737. Apr. 3. Ariaentie, of P. and Cath. Ryckman. Wit. :H. Ryckman, A. Kiersteede.

Andries, of R. and Eng. Kidny. Wit.: J. and Cath. Rettelief.

Apr. 8. Jacob, of D. and G. V. D. Heyde. Wit.: Johs. and Margr. V. D. Heyde.

Elsie, of Jac. and Elyz. Glen. Wit.: John, Jr., and Cath. Cuyler.

Apr. 10. Elyzabeth, of Moses and Margariet, pros. Wit.: Simon and Maria, pros.

Elsie, of Corn. and Cat. Cuyler. Wit.: John Schuyler, Jr., Sara Hansen.

Apr. 11. Jinny and Elizabeth, negresses, after a foregoing confession.

Apr. 17. Kiliaen, of Stev. and Elyz. V. Rensselaar. Wit.: Jer. V. Rensselaar, Corn. Schuyler.

Philip, of Jac. and Antie Schermerhoorn. Wit.: Johs. Schermerhoorn, Zuz. Lansingh.

Wouter, of Kil. and Hill. Ridder. Wit.: Ant. V. D. Zee, Rach. V. d. Bergh.

Apr. 31. [sic] Daniel, of Mart. and Jann. V. Olinde. Wit.: Johs. and Geertr. Barreway.

Barber, of Gerr. and Marg. Marselis. Wit.: Johs. and Joh. Marselis.

Eckbertis, of Petr. and Marr. V. d. Berg. Wit.: Gerr. V. d. Berg. Eckb. V. D. Heyde.

May 15. Dirck, of H. and Elyz. V. Vegten. Wit.: D. and Sara V. Vegten.

May 28. Machtel, of J. and G. Quackenbos. Wit.: G. V. D. Werke, A. V. Franken.

Susanna, of H. and A. Lisser. Wit.: J. Witbeek, M. Wyngaart.

June 19 Catharina, of Cornelis and Anna, pros. Wit.: Aaron and Canastazy, pros.

Johannes, of Johs., Jr., and Neeltie V. Vegten. Wit.: Mart. and Eva Beekman.

Rachel, of Jan and Anna Dret. Wit.: Johs. and Eckb. D. Garmoy.

Gideon, of Brant and Rebecka, pros. Wit.: Joseph and Maria, pros.

1737
Apr. [sic] 24. Richart, of Sjeems and Elizabeth Grand. Wit.: Richart Millar, Annetje Schot.

May 8. Jannetje, of Jacob and Catharyna Valkenburg. Wit.: Japik and Margrit Beekman.

Cathalyntje, of David and Maria Groesbeek. Wit.: Jan and Cathalyntje Van Nes.

May 14. Maria, of Hugo and Catharyna Viele. Wit.: Isaac and Jakemyntje Fort.

May 15. Elizabeth, of Pieter and Geertruy Dokse. Wit.: Jan Livingston, Susanna Bradt.

Margrieta, of Daniel and Alida Maren. Wit.: Willem and Theuntje Van Buren.

May 19. Catharyna, of Cornelis and Maria Ten Broek. Wit.: Dirk and Margrieta Ten Broek.

May 22. Tobias, of Maarten and Maria Van Buren. Wit.: Barent and Jannetje Van Buren.

June 5. Jacob, of Abraham and Maria Vroman. Wit.: Cornelis Verplank, Racheltje Winne.

Johannes, of Leendert and Cathalyntje Witbeek. Wit.: Cornelis and Dirkje Verplank.

Reyer, of Reyer and Geertje Schermerhoorn. Wit.: Japik and Alida Ten Eyk.

Willemtje, of Dirk and Cornelia Brad. Wit.: Benjamin Brad, Magdalena Bradt.

June 12. Abraham, of Zacharias and Annaatje Sikkels. Wit.: David Schuylder, Christyna Wyngaart.

Anna, of Japik and Helena Wendel. Wit.: Johannis H. Wendel, Catharyna Cuylder.

July 3. Jacobus, of Laurens and Ariaantje Van der Poel. Wit.: Jacobus Van der Poel, Elizabeth Van Schaik.

Maria, of Jacobus and Helena Van Alen. Wit.: Mattheus and Sara Van Aalsteyn.

Maria, of Isaac and Hendrikje Viele. Wit.: Louis and Marytje Viele.

Maria, of Thomas and Maria Schjerp. Wit.: Johannes and Annaatje Hun.

July 10. Samuel, of Samuel and Barentje Gardenier. Wit.: Johannes Schermerhoorn, Zara Gardenier.

Ch. of a negress, Mary, a slave. Wit.: Jephta, a negro.

July 16. Jan, of Jan and Fytje De Vous. Wit.: Roelof DeVous, Marytje Van der Werke.

July 17. Daniel, of Pieter and Suzanna Van Olinde. Wit.: Martinus and Elizabeth Van Olinde.

July 27. Clara, a negress of Joh. Lansingh, after a previous confession.

July 31. Isaac, of Martinus and Catharyntje Van Aalsteyn. Wit.: Willem and Cathalyna Van den Bergh.

Aug. 10. Lydia, of Gerrit C. and Margrieta Van der Bergh. Wit.: Ephraim Van Vegten, Elizabeth Ten Broek.

1737

Aug. 19. Ezras, of Pieter and Zelia, pros.
Cornelia, of Barent A. and Annaatje Brad. Wit.:
Barent Brad, Ebbetje Van der Heyde.
Ann, of Daniel Huzzon and Mary Huzon. Wit.: Adri-
aan and Hillegont Brad.
Stevanus, of Johannes, Jr., and Cornelia Schuyler.
Wit.: Stevanus Van Renzelaar, Cathalyna Cuyler.
Aug. 28. Catharyna, of Gerrit Japikse Lansing and
Yda Lansing. Wit.: Hendrik Janse Van Wie, Catharyna
Van Wie.
Sep. 4. Isaac, of Jacobus and Margriet Valkenburg.
Wit.: Isaac and Jannetje Valkenburg.
Sep. 11. Wilhelmus, of Corn. Van Schie and Josyna Prys.
Wit.: Johannes Ten Broek, Catharyna Van Renzelaar.
Cornelis, of Dirck and Elizabeth Van Schelluyne. Wit.:
Japik and Debora Rozeboom.
Elizabeth, of Gerrid Brad and Maria Bradt. Wit.:
Bernardus, Jr., and Elizabeth Brad.
Elizabeth, of Sybrand and Elizabeth Quackenbos.
Wit.: Johannis and Cornelia Knickerbakker.
Sep. 18. Jannetje, of Johannes and Anna Van Franken.
Wit.: Japik and Jannetje Paarsen.
Neeltje, of Petrus and Christyna Van Bergen. Wit.:
Johannes, Jr., and Neeltje Douw.
Jannetje, of Anthony and Marytje Van der Zee. Wit.:
Symeon and Hilletje Ridder.
Marytje, of Evert, Jr., and Suzanna Wendel. Wit.:
Philip and Suzanna Wendel.
Sep. 18. Johannes, of Jochem and Christyna Cailver.
Wit.: Hendrik Halenbeek, Elizabeth Hillen.
Aug. [sic] 15. Anna, of Nicol. and Margrieta Bleeker,
Wit.: Hendrik Rozeboom, Jr., Margrieta Marcelius.
David, of Dan. and Mary Yorck. Wit.: Will. Helmer.
Oct. 6. Jacob, of Gerr. and Maria Lansing. Wit.:
Jac. and Lena Lansingh.
Pieter, of Hans and Sara Hansen. Wit.: Dav. Schuyler,
Elsie Rooseboom.
Johannes, of Abr. and G. Vosburg. Wit.: W. and
Cat. V. D. Bergh.
Oct. 16. Elyzabeth, of Andr. and Hag. Maknans.
Wit.: H. and Elyz. Van Vegten.
Oct. 21. Johannes, of Anth. and Rebecka Brat. Wit.:
Johs. and Rach. V. d. Heyde.
Lidia, of Is. and Jann. Valkenburg. Wit.: Jac. and
Margr. Valkenburg.
Geertruy, of Jac. Schuiler and Geertr. Schuyler. Wit.:
Dav. and Geertr. Schuyler.
Mayke, of Douwe and Aaltwe Fonda. Wit.: Corn.
Ouderkerk, Geertr. Fonda.

1737-1738
Oct. 30. Elyzabeth, of W., Jr., and Maria Hilten. Wit.: R. and Zara Hilten.

Oct. 23 [sic]. John, of John and Ietje Morris. Wit.: Hugo and Catharyna Viele.

Nov. 6. Harpert, of Abraham and Anna Witbeek. Wit.: Johannes Witbeek, Geertruy Van Vegten.

JaAlexander, of Robbert and Susanna Flind. Wit.: Wn and Suzanna Brad.

Alida, of Gerrit W. and Alida Van den Bergh. Wit.: Francis and Marritje Lansing.

Nov. 20. Isaac, Alida, of Wouter and Elizabeth Knickerbakker. Wit.: Isaac, Alida, Hendrik, and Marytje Fonda.

Jannetje, of Theunis and Maria Fiele. Wit.: Douwe and Aaltje Fonda.

Dec. 4. Maria, of Jurriaan and Maria Hogen. Wit.: Hendrik Beekman, Annaatje Douw.

Jan, of Johannes and Helena Ouderkerk. Wit.: Jan and Marytje Fonda.

Dec. 23. Jannetje, of Anthony and Catharyna Bovie. Wit.: Isaac and Alida Fonda.

Hendrik, of Robbert and Margrieta Lansing. Wit.: Jacob and Debora Rozeboom.

Francis, of Renzelaar and Elizabeth Nickels. Wit.: Sylvester and Laurenna Salisbury.

Wyntje, of Jan and Antje Olvert. Wit.: Hendrik Brad, Wyntje Bradt.

Dec. 26. Hendrik, of Isaac and Alida Greveraad. Wit.: Ephraim Wendel, Elsje Rozeboom.

1737/8, Jan. 1. Engeltje, of Jonas and Dorethe Witbeek. Wit.: Abraham and Lyntje Douwe.

Elizabeth, of Thomas and Elizabeth Willekens. Wit.: Thomas Scherp, Elizabeth Karenwel.

Jan. 11. Maria, of Gerrit and Maria Van Benthuysen. Wit.: Pieter and Annaatje Van Alen.

Cornelia, of Evert and Annaatje Lansing. Wit.: Obedias and Cornelia Couper.

Louis, of Japik and Hendrikje Van Woerd. Wit.: Louis and Hiltje Credel.

Jan. 15. Elizabeth, of Isaac and Maria, pros. Wit.: Joseph and Catharyna, pros.

Jan. 22. Diana, of Thomas and Diana, pros. Wit.: Willem and Mary, pros.

Feb. 5. Dirck, of Gerrit and Marritje Knoet. Wit.: Gerardus and Machtel Knoet.

Rachel, of Gerrit and Annaatje Ridder. Wit.: Corns. and Rachel Van den Bergh.

Gerrit, of Theunis and Machtel Visscher. Wit.: Johannes and Zantje Lansing.

1738

Cherles, of Jan Kjerreith and Catharyn Kartreith.
Wit.: Jan Wendel, Gerritje Van Woerd.

Anna, of Willem and Elizabeth Walran. Wit.: Isaac
and Jannetje Lansing.

Feb. 8. Jacobus, of Joachim and Bata Van der Heyden.
Wit.: Johannis Van der Heyden, Lena Ouderkerk.

Margrieta, of Johannes and Christyna Van der Werken.
Wit.: Stevanus and Elizabeth Van Renzelaar.

Feb. 8. Hendrik, of Abram A. and Maria Schuyler.
Wit.: Johannes and Sara Hanze.

Pieter, of Marin and Sara Jordan. Wit.: English and
Mary Grand.

Petrus, of Pieter and Annaatje Uziele. Wit.: Abraham
and Elizabeth Wyngaard.

Adam, of David and Engeltje Uziele. Wit.: Adam
and Blandina Vroman.

Feb. 11. Robbert, of Laving and Suzanna Winne.
Wit.: Robbert and Elizabeth Wendel.

Marytje, of Philippus and Zara Winne. Wit.: Lavinus
and Suzanna Winne.

Feb. 12. Marritje, of Johannes and Marytje Van den
Bergh. Wit.: Petrus and Marritje Van den Bergh.

Feb. 15. Hester, of Hendrik and Dirkje Gerritse.
Wit.: Eldert and Hester Symense.

Christyna, of Japik and Christina Ten Broek. Wit.:
Pieter and Lena Van Alen.

Barber, of Johannes and Anna Knoet. Wit.: Ryckert
and Maria Van Franken.

Feb. 22. Johannes, of Gerardus and Maria Banker.
Wit.: Willem Banker, Neeltje Lansing.

William, of Jan and Hopie Donnowa. Wit.: Ryckert
Hilten, Anna Kitzenaar.

Melchert, of Marten and Elbertje Van Deusen. Wit.:
Abraham and Antje Van der Poel.

Japik, of Barnardus and Catharyna Harzen. Wit.:
Johannes S. and Annaatje Wendel.

March 1. Hendrikje, of Douwe J. and Aaltje Fonda.
Wit.: Hendrik and Cathalyna Van Buren.

Margriet, of Daniel and Ida English. Wit.: William
Paal, Mally Hutje.

Ariaantje, of Japik and Maria Brouwer. Wit.: Douwe
and Ariaantje Van Vegten.

1738, March 26. Antje, of Alexander and Elizabeth
Van Woerd. Wit.: Japik and Catharyna Van Woerd.

Lydia, of Jan and Rachel Bel. Wit.: Japik Abramse,
Catharyna Bel.

Catryn, of Jan and Christyna Moen. Wit.: Richart
Millar, Betje Kitzenaar.

March 31. Jannetje, negress of Isaak Fonda, bapt.
after a foregoing confession.

Apr. 2. Ebbetje, of Willem and Theuntje Van Buren. Wit.: Gerrit Van den Bergh, Anna Visscher.

Elizabeth, of Johannes, Jr., and Catryna Van der Heyden. Wit.: Matthys and Rachel Van der Heyden.

Apr. 3. Lena, of Christiaan and Baartje Lange. Wit.: Wynand and Volkje Van den Bergh.

Apr. 16. Willem, of Jacobus and Catharyna Radelif. Wit.: Jacobus and Margrieta Van Valkenburg.

Alida, of Johannes and Margrieta Brad. Wit.: Andries Van Franken, Marytje Brad.

Lena, of Jeroen and Margrieta Van Vlier. Wit.: Jan and Catharyna Van Aalsteyn.

Anna, of Gerrit and Antje Van Zanten. Wit.: Lambert and Annetje Radelif.

Stevanus, of Abraham and Elbertje Fonda. Wit.: Stevanus and Marytje Van Alen.

Apr. 23. Wynand, of Isaac and Marytje Van Aalsteyn. Wit.: Willem and Cathalyntje Van den Bergh.

Gerritje, Elizabeth, of Sybrand, Jr., and Annaatje Van Schaik. Wit.: Johannes Rozeboom and wife, Gerritje, Johannis Rozeboom, Elizabeth Van Schaik.

George, of George and Margrieta Lubkens. Wit.: Thomas Sijerp, Geertruy Coster.

Jurriaan, of Coenraad and Elizabeth Regtmeyer. Wit.: Jurriaan and Ann [?] Mary Regtmeyer.

Christyna, of Volkert and Catharyna Van den Bergh. Wit.: Wilhelmus and Geertje Van den Bergh.

Cornelis, of Isaac and Maria Switz. Wit.: Tjerk and Susanna Switz.

David, of Andries and Alida Logen. Wit.: Barnardus Harzen, Marytje Pruyn.

Apr. 30. Jacob, Helena, of Franciscus and Maria Lansing. Wit.: Hendrik and Annaatje Lansing, Abram and Alida Van Aarnem.

Mayke, of Jan and Maria Oothout. Wit.: Evert Wendel, Annaatje Van den Bergh.

May 7. Catharyna, of Hendrik and Hilletje Van Wie. Wit.: Robbert and Elsje Rozeboom.

Cornelis, of Hannes and Annaatje Slingerland. Wit.: Storm Van der Zee, Cornelia Slingerland.

Cornelis, of Cornelis and Anneke Van den Bergh. Wit.: Claas and Suzanna Van den Bergh.

May 11. Johannes, of Hendrik and Christina, pros. Wit.: Johannes E. and Elizabeth Wendel.

May 14. Lena, of Mykel and Elizabeth Bessed. Wit.: Johannes Bessid, Jannetje Ten Eyck.

May 22. Elizabeth, of Abram and Elizabeth Wyngaard. Wit.: Isaac and Alida Fonda.

May 28. Johannes, of Johannes and Catharyna Hogh. Wit.: Lodewyck and Hiltje Schriddel.

1738

Catharyna, of Jillis and Rachel De Garamo. Wit.: Anthony Brad, Rebekka Bradt.

Annaatje, of Abraham G. and Lena Lansing. Wit.: Harmen and Elsje Hun.

June 4. Gerrit, of Cornelis and Jannetje Walran. Wit.: Dirck Bradt, Engeltje Walran.

Zara, of Johannes and Marytje De Foreest. Wit.: Fillip Hansen, Catharyna Van Es.

June 18. Symen, of Zacharias and Geesje Haas. Wit.: Thomas Vlyd, Antje Vlydt.

June 21. Jacobus, of Johannes and Maria Wyngaart. Wit.: Gerrit and Christyntje Wyngaard.

June 28. Aalbert, of Harmen and Eva Van der Zee. Wit.: Storm and Hilletje Van der Zee.

Catharyna, of Gysbert and Catharyna Rozenboom. Wit.: Hendrik Bries, Corns. and Maria Van Dyk.

July 2. Jan, of Pieter and Geertruy Doxsie. Wit.: David and Geertruy Van der Heyden.

Samuel, of Johannes and Engeltje Schermerhoorn. Wit.: Dirk and Zara Guardenier.

July 7. Zara Maria, of Johannes Lydius and Geneveva Mazee. Wit.: Johannes Jan [?] Rozeboom, Geertruy Isabella Lydius.

Elisabeth, of Robbert and Catharyna Wendel. Wit.: Jan Schuylder, Elizabeth Wendel.

July 23. Hendrik, of Jan and Elizabeth Van Aarnem. Wit.: Hendrik and Anna Lansing.

July 26. Gerritje, of Hendrik, Jr., and Elsje Roseboom. Wit.: Gerrit, Jr., and Margrieta Rozeboom.

Dirck, of Dirk and Margrieta Ten Broeck. Wit.: Japik Ten Eyck, Maria Ten Broeck.

July 31. Anthony, of Dirck and Cornelia Brad. Wit.: Benjamin Brad, Magdalena Bradt.

Josyntje, of Johannes and Bregje Zeger. Wit.: Douwe and Aaltje Fonda.

Aug. 27. Josyna, of Samuel Wiele and Margrieta Wieler. Wit.: Obadias Couper, Josyna Wieler.

Christoffel, of Johannes Jets and Rebekka Walran. Wit.: Christoffel and Cathalyna Jets.

Maria, of Sybrand and Alida Van Schaik. Wit.: Hendrik M. and Maria Rozeboom.

Jeremias, of Johannes and Engeltje Van Renzelaar. Wit.: Jan Livingston, Annaatje Douwe.

Elizabeth, of Roelof and Lena Clerk. Wit.: Japik Maarse, Elizabeth Wielaer.

Sep. 3. Margrieta, of Jeremias and Suzanna Schuyler. Wit.: Johannes Schuyler, Margrieta Livingston.

Abraham, of Alexander and Elbertje Van Aalsteyn. Wit.: Johannes and Marytje Van Aalsteyn.

1738
Abraham, of Dirck and Magdalena Van der Kar. Wit.: Arent and Charlotte Van der Kar.

Catharyna, of Gerrit Theunisse Van Slyk and Annaatje Van der Slyk. Wit.: Pieter and Catharyna Van Slyk.

Elizabeth, of Abraham and Geertruy Wendel. Wit.: Ephraim Wendel, Suzanna Schuyler.

Johannes, of Barnardus and Catharyna Brad. Wit.: Johannes Van Vegten, Wyntje Bries.

Sep. 10. Elizabeth, of Johannes and Elizabeth Quackenbos. Wit.: Benjamin Rommelie, Elizabeth Quackenbos.

Coenraad, of Jurriaan and Barbara Sijerp. Wit.: Abraham and Bata Fort.

Dennis, of Danis and Mary Springer. Wit.: Jan and Jannetje Makler.

Debora, of Joachim and Eva Ketelheyn. Wit.: Douwe and Nelletje Ketelheyn.

Jan, of David and Rebecka Mohennie. Wit.: Symen and Matje Danielse.

Sep. 17. Cornelis, of Cornelis and Rachel Van den Bergh. Wit.: Adam Van den Bergh, Marytje Gerritse.

Elizabeth, of Japik Van Woerd and Annaatje Ouderkerk. Wit.: Louis Scherrette, Catharyna Van Woerd.

Johannes, of Jacob and Annaatje Kithnie. Wit.: Isaac Bogaart, Hendrikje Bogaert.

Rebecka, of Benjamin and Rachel Wenne. Wit.: Jan and Elizabeth Van Aarnem.

Alida, of Gerrit J. and Marytje Lansing. Wit.: Barentje Hanzen, Jacob J. Lansingh.

Willem, of Jacobus and Zara Groesbeek. Wit.: David and Geertruy Groesbeek.

Maria, of Robbert and Maria Barreith. Wit.: Dirk Maarten, Barentje Savits.

Sep. 24. Harmen, of Volkert and Alida Van Hoezen. Wit.: Harmen and Geesje Van Hoezen.

Dirkje, of Killiaan and Rebecka Winne. Wit.: Willem and Marytje Winne.

Barent, of Japik and Alida Ten Eyck. Wit.: David and Hester Van der Heyden.

Oct. 1. Barent, of Pieter and Annaatje Van Alen. Wit.: Jacob Van Benthuysen, Lena Van Alen.

Margrieta, of Japik H. and Annaatje Ten Eyck. Wit.: Hendrik and Margrieta Ten Eyck.

Oct. 6. Jan, of Richart and Martha Oliver. Wit.: Thom. Sjerp, Hoop Dolvin.

Oct. 8. Elizabeth, of Johannes, Jr., and Cornelia Schuyler. Wit.: Isaac Wendel, Margrieta Schuyler.

Oct. 22. Marten Corneliszen, of Barent and Margrietje Van Buren. Wit.: Marten and Maria Van Buren.

1738

Mattheus, of Frans and Magtel Bovie. Wit.: Matthys and Marytje Bovie.

Marytje, of Evert and Elsje Seskby. Wit.: Willem and Marrytje Seskby.

Nov. 5. Bata, of Gerardus and Magtel Knoet. Wit.: Hannes and Annaatje Knoet.

Johannes, of Hendrik and Annaatje Beekman. Wit.: Marten and Eva Beekman.

Hilletje, of Robbert and Agnietje Schot. Wit.: Thomas and Margrieta Williams.

Nov. 12. Neeltje, of Hendrik and Ariaantje Van Deusen. Wit.: Jochem Staats, Annaatje Visscher.

Dec. 3. Elizabeth, of Johannes and Zara Van Zanten. Wit.: Willem, Jr., and Margriet Hilof.

Barent, of Johannes Goewyck and Jannetje Van den Bergh. Wit.: Japik Bloemendal, Marytje Goewyck.

Lucas, of Jan Item and Marytje Iten. Wit.: Lucas and Zara Hoogkerk.

Dec. 6. Japik, of Jacobus and Maria, black pros. Wit.: Charl. Danniels, Judith Hilten.

Harmen, of Sybrand and Elizabeth Quackenbos. Wit.: Wouter and Elizabeth Knickerbakker.

Dec. 10. Margrieta, of Cornelis and Cathalyna Cuyler. Wit.: Phillip Schuyler, Elsje Rozeboom.

Dec. 17. Aegje, of Storm and Lybetje Van der Zee. Wit.: Hannes and Aegje Slingerland.

Catharyna, of Hendrik Scheber and Marytje Schever. Wit.: Nicolaas and Catharyn Kittel.

Frans, of Hendrik and Rebecca Klauw. Wit.: Frans and Alida Pruyn.

Hendrik, of Johannes and Lysbet Valk. Wit.: Gerrit Brad, Marytje Bogardus.

Alexander, of Sjems and Magdalena Flemming. Wit.: Roelof Kirniel, Brefje Zeger.

Dec. 20. Maria, of Pieter and Catharyna Schuyler. Wit.: Gerardus Groesbeek, Annaatje Staats.

Abraham, of Gerrit Corn. Van Nes and Zara Van Nes. Wit.: Abraham and Antje Van der Poel.

Laurens, of Arent and Hiltje Van Dyck. Wit.: Abraham Fonda, Cathalyna Wendel.

Anthony, of Hendrik and Suzanna Halenbeek. Wit.: Anthony Brad, Marytje Van Oostrandt.

Dec. 24. Jan, of Josua and Geesje Broeks. Wit.: Zacharias and Geesje Haas.

Martina, of William, Jr., and Pietertje Hogen. Wit.: Jurriaan and Maria Hogen.

Jannetje, of Abraham and Marytje Vroman. Wit.: Pieter and Grietje Van Aalsteyn.

1738-1739

Johannes, of Dirk and Margrietje Hun. Wit.: Johannes and Annaatje Hun.

Dec. 25. Engeltje, of Theunis and Cornelia Slingerland. Wit.: Johannes Van der Heyden, Elizabeth Wendel.

Dec. 30. Judikje, of Lucas Hooghkerk, Jr., and Rebecca Hoogkerk. Wit.: Nicolaas and Antje Van den Bergh.

Dec. 31. Johannes, of Evert and Marytje Ryder. Wit.: Johannes and Bregje Zeger.

1738/9, Jan. 10. Geertruy, of Andries, Jr., and Engeltje Witbeek. Wit.: Petrus and Annaatje Douw.

Abraham, of Pieter and Elizabeth Landman. Wit.: Abraham and Alida Van Aarnem.

Anna, of Barent A. and Anna Brad. Wit.: Schibboleth and Anna Bogardus.

Daniel, of Frans and Agnietje Winne. Wit.: Daniel Winne, Catharyna Van Wie.

Japik, of Japik Valkenburgh and Catharyna Valkenburg. Wit.: Johannes and Annaatje Hogen.

Tryntje, of Abraham and Rachel Van Deusen. Wit.: Abraham Witbeek, Cathalyntje Van Deusen.

Jan. 14. Sjems, John, of Jan and Catharyna Mackie. Wit.: George and Margriet Lubkens, John and Mary Olivert.

Mayke, of Douwe and Aaltje Fonda. Wit.: Abraham and Elbertje Fonda.

Jan. 17. Debora, of Ryckert and Catharyna Hanzen. Wit.: Nicolaas Hanzen, Debora Beekman.

Jan. 21 Jeremias, of Philip and Catharyntje Conyn. Wit.: Johannes and Commertje Conyn.

Abraham, of Matthys and Rebecca De Garamo. Wit.: Benjamin and Rachel Winne.

Jan. 24. Phillip, of Lavinus and Suzanna Winne. Wit.: Philip and Zara Winne.

Frans, of Johannes and Christina Van der Werken. Wit.: Frans and Margriet Pruyn.

Johannes, of Dirck and Catharina Johanna Van Alen. Wit.: Pieter and Lena Van Alen.

Jan. 28. William Windslo, of William and Margrieta Crannill. Wit.: Rykert Hilten, Hoop Donnowac.

Nicolaus, of Cornelis Van Schie and Josyna Prys. Wit.: Johannes Ten Broek, Catharyna Van Renzelaar.

Feb. 4. Obedia, of Evert and Annaatje Lansing. Wit.: Thomas and Zara Couper.

Maria, of Jonathan and Rebekka Broeks. Wit.: Jan Freyer, Marytje Lewis.

Feb. 11. Anna Catharyna, of Johannes and Maria Geertruy Poin. Wit.: Jan Livingston, Catharyna Ten Broek.

1739

At Schag. Feb. 17. Catharyna, of Richard and Grees Weith. Wit.: Louis and Marytje Viele.

Anna, of Hugo and Catharyna Viele. Wit.: Johannes and Jannetje Ouderkerk.

Symen, of Abraham and Rebecca Foreest. Wit.: Gysbert and Maria Van Brakel.

At Sch. Jan. 18. Mayke, of Willem and Marytje Ouderkerk. Wit.: Cornelis and Catharyna Ouderkerk.

Geertruy, of Hendrik and Annaatje Lisjer. Wit.: Willem Lievense, Magiel Quackenbos.

Geertruy, of Arent and Scharlotta Van der Kar. Wit.: Hendrik Van der Werken, Fydje Van der Kar.

Feb. 25. Japik, of Pieter and Suzanna Van Olinda. Wit.: Johannes Van Olinda, Zaartje Maartzen.

Gerrit, of Hendrik, Jr., and Catharyna Van Wie. Wit.: Gerrit Willemse Van den Bergh, Alida Van den Bergh.

Pieter, of Jacobus and Judith Hilten. Wit.: Johannes and Zelia Livingston.

Symen, of Myndert and Elizabeth Veder. Wit.: Symen Veder, Debora Wimp.

Elizabeth, of Symen Groot and Bata Knoet. Wit.: Cornelis and Cathalyntje Cuyler.

Zara, of Hannes and Aaltje Schaik. Wit.: Pieter and Cathalyntje Bogaart.

1739, March 18. Neeltje, of Hendrik and Wyntje Bries. Wit.: Pieter and Annaatje Douw.

March 25. Elizabeth, of Wouter and Elizabeth Knickerbakker. Wit.: Lucas and Rebecca Hooghkerk.

Apr. 15. Maria, of Jacob and Helena Wendel. Wit.: Abraham H. Wendel, Annaatje Ten Eyck.

Abraham, of Andries and Marytje Van den Bergh. Wit.: Abraham and Elizabeth Vinagel.

Apr. 22. Christoffel, of Adam and Annaatje Jaits. Wit.: Christoffel and Catharyna Jaits.

Jacob, of Isaac and Cathalyna Wendel. Wit.: Cornelis Cuyler, Elizabeth Wendel.

Apr. 23. Johannes, of Johannis and Annaatje Visscher. Wit.: Japik and Rachel Visscher.

May 6. Jannetje, of Reyer Sprinksteen and Marytje Springsteen. Wit.: Tobias Rykman, Marytje Schermerhoorn.

Martina, of Eduart and Maria Williams. Wit.: Jurriaan Hogen, Margrietje Hun.

Isaac, of Hendrik and Annaatje Lansing. Wit.: Douwe and Aaltje Fonda.

Geertruy, of David and Maria Groesbeek. Wit.: Stevanus Groesbeek, Elizabet Renzelaar.

Abraham, of Glen and Ariaantje Verplank. Wit.: Abraham Lansing, Jr., Elisabeth Lansingh.

May 13. Maria, of Isaac and Jacomyntje Fort. Wit.: Theunis and Marytje Viele.

May 27. Margriet, of Frederick and Engeltje Ruyter. Wit.: Roelof and Geertruy Van der Werken.

Hilletje, of William and Margriet Kruck. Wit.: Benjamin Winne, Hilletje Ridder.

Judick, of Daniel and Alida Marl. Wit.: David Schuyler, Cathryna Ten Broeck.

Maria, of Robbert and Cornelia Tum Bar. Wit.: Louis and Hilletje Schrodel.

May 31. Annaatje, of Ryckert and Annaatje Van Francken. Wit.: Maas and Annaatje Van Franken.

Myndert, of Barent and Cornelia Van Iveren. Wit.: Myndert and Ariaantje Van Iveren.

June 3. Johannes, of Bartholomeus and Agnietje Van Aalsteyn. Wit.: Pieter and Grietje Van Aalsteyn.

Isaac, of Leendert and Cathalyntje Witbeek. Wit.: Glen Verplanck, Rachel Winne.

Alida, of John and Jannetje Maklur. Wit.: John Waters, Jannetje Swits.

Jannetje, of Harmen and Elsje Hun. Wit.: Isaac and Jannetje Lansing.

Barent, of Isaac and Marytje Staats. Wit.: Joachim and Theuntje Staats.

June 17. Johannes, of Sjeems and Anna Margrietje Steenhuysen. Wit.: Harmen, Jr., and Marytje Vedder.

Salomon, of Douwe and Ariaantje Van Vegten. Wit.: Salomon Van Vegten, Zara Groesbeek.

Catharyna, of Samuel and Barentje Gardenier. Wit.: Cornelis Maarze, Josyna Guardenier.

Ariaantje, of Hieronymus and Marytje Van Valkenburgh. Wit.: Johannes and Annaatje Hun.

Maria, of Johannes and Neeltje Vinnagel. Wit.: Johannes and Maria Vinnagel.

Johannes, of Cornelis and Zanneke Van Nes. Wit.: Johannes and Cathalyntje Van Nes.

Catharyna, of Jan and Annaatje Dereth. Wit.: Jan and Fydtje De Vous.

June 24. Johannes, of Johannes, Jr., and Neeltje Van Vegten. Wit.: Marten and Eva Beekman.

July 1. Hiltje, of Gysbert and Neeltje Klauw. Wit.: Andries Sijerp, Elizabeth Goewey.

July 8. Elizabeth, of Gerardus and Maria Groesbeek. Wit.: Stevanus Groesbeek, Margrieta Ten Broek.

Eva, of Johannes, Jr., and Zara Beekman. Wit.: Hendrik Cuyler, Eva Beekman.

July 13. Hendrik, of Jacob and Elizabeth Glen. Wit.: Cornelis Cuyler, Zara Hansen.

1739

July 15. Maria, of Douwe and Nelletje Ketelheyn. Wit.: Japik and Maria Brouwer.

Catharyn, of Franciscus and Neeltje Belvil. Wit.: Anthony and Catharyna Abramse.

Roelof, of Roelof and Engeltje Kitnie. Wit.: Bernardus Brad, Zara Kitney.

July 29. Elizabeth, of Andries and Mayke Witbeek. Wit.: Pieter Coeymans, Scherlotte Cojemans.

Aug. 5. Annaatje, of Isaac and Alida Grevenraad. Wit.: Hendrik and Dirckje Gerritse.

Annaatje, of Isaac and Jannetje Van Valkenburg. Wit.: Lammert and Annetje Radelief.

Cathalyntje, of Willem G. and Zantje Van den Bergh. Wit.: Gysbert and Cathalyntje Van den Bergh.

Aug. 12. Jan, of William and Rachel Nordin. Wit.: Isaac and Marytje Credit.

Neeltje, of Joachim and Elizabeth Staats. Wit.: Barent and Neeltje Staats.

Hendrik, of Johannes and Elizabeth Van Oostrandt. Wit.: Wouter Knickerbakker, Jannetje Bogardus.

Volkert, of Johannes V. and Jannetje Douw. Wit.: Volkert Douw, Dorothe Bogaart.

Aug. 19. Maria, of Stevanus and Elizabeth Van Renzelaar. Wit.: Johannes Arense Schuyler, Maria Millin.

Nicolaus, of Willim and Anna Seskby. Wit.: Johannes and Zelie Radelif.

Aug. 26. Johannes, of Nicolaas, Jr., and Margrieta Bleeker. Wit.: Jacob Bleecker, Anna Van Schaik.

Sep. 2. Hendrik, of Hendrik H. and Catharyna Rozeboom. Wit.: Jacob Rozeboom, Catharyna Vielde.

Myndert Schuyler, of Johannes and Anna De Peyster. Wit.: Myndert Schuyler, Anna De Peyster.

Sep. 9. Mattheus, of Anthony and Catharyn Bovie. Wit.: Matthys and Marytje Bovie.

Anna, of Sjems and Elizabeth Ryon. Wit.: Thomas and Annaatje Schjerp.

Hieronymus, of Hendrik and Rebecca Spoor. Wit.: Johannes Spoor, Johanna Valkenburgh.

Aelbertus Meinert, of George and Margrieta Lubcken. Wit.: Thomas Scharp, Catharina Schuyler.

Anna, of Benjamin and Anna Bogaart. Wit.: Pieter and Rebecka Bogaart.

Sep. 23. Margrieta, of Gerrit C. and Margrieta Van den Bergh. Wit.: Dirck Van Vegten, Lena Witbeek.

Marritje, of Jacob and Annaatje Kitnie. Wit.: Johannes and Geertruy Kitnie.

Anna, of Abraham and Alida Van Aernem. Wit.: Johannes Jac. and Anna Lansing.

1739
Hendricus, of Johannes and Johanna Marcelius. Wit.: Nicolaas Fonda, Neeltje Van Vegten.

Oct. 7. Jacobus, of Johannes and Eva Valkenburgh. Wit.: Akes Valkenburgh, Annetje Radelif.

Johannis, of Abraham and Elizabeth Vosburgh. Wit.: Harmen Ganzevoort, Annaatje Hun.

Anna, of Rynert and Marytje Van Franken. Wit.: Andries Brad, Elsje Bradt.

Oct. 14. Dirckje, of Pieter Danielse Winne and Rachel Winne. Wit.: Jan and Cathelyntje Winne.

Johannes, of Hendrik M. and Maria Rozeboom. Wit.: Johannes M. and Margrieta Rozeboom.

Sep. [sic] 29. Wouter, of Nicolaas and Agnietje Groesbeek. Wit.: Wouter and Elizabeth Groesbeek.

Oct. 28. Abraham, of Johannes and Helena Ouderkerk. Wit.: Abraham and Elbertje Fonda.

Rachel, of Jacobus Valkenburg and Margriet Valkenburgh. Wit.: Lambert and Rachel Radelief.

Pieter, of Sjaack and Maria, black pros. Wit.: Jephta and Claar, black pros.

Nov. 4. Gerrit, of Petrus and Marytje Van den Bergh. Wit.: Hendrik, Jr., and Elsje Rozeboom.

Japik, of Japik, Jr., and Hubertje Lansing. Wit.: Hannes and Annaatje Lansing.

Nov. 11. Johannes, of Johannes and Marytje Foreest. Wit.: Johannes and Margrieta Quackenbos.

Nov. 18. Bata, of Johannes and Anna Knoet. Wit.: Robbert Rozeboom, Alida Pruyn.

Nov. 25. Johannes, of Jacob Aarhnout and Margrieta Aarnhout. Wit.: Coenraadt and Elizabeth Regtmeyer.

Jacobus, of Jonathan and Magtel Witbeek. Wit.: Johannes Wyngaerd, Christyna Wyngaard.

Matthys, of Matthys and Margrieta Van der Heyden. Wit.: Japik and Rachel Van der Heyden.

Dec. 2. Nanningh, of Harmen and Rachel Visscher. Wit.: Japik and Ebbitje Van der Heyden.

Dec. 12. Maria, of Egbert and Rachel Ebbertse. Wit.: Petrus, Jr., and Wyntje Bogardus.

Dec. 19. Johannes, of Isaac and Marytje Van Aalsteyn. Wit.: Gerrit and Jannetje Foreest.

Catharyna, of Evert and Zantje Wendel. Wit.: Gerrit Lansingh, Annaatje Egmond.

Zara, of Harmen B. and Zara Visscher. Wit.: Johannes Visscher, Zara Van Yveren.

Dec. 23. Eva, of Wouter and Rachel Barreith. Wit.: Andries and Gerritje Van Woerd.

Marytje, of Willem and Catharyntje Groesbeek. Wit.: Gerrit Van Nes, Geertruy Groesbeek.

1739–1740

Willem, of Jacobus and Catharyna Radelief. Wit.: Akes and Margrieta Van Valkenburgh.

Johannes, of Franciscus S. [?] and Alida Pruyn. Wit.: Johannes and Elsje Pruyn.

1739/40, Jan. 9. Hendrik Van Nes, of Hendrik and Anna Ridder. Wit.: Ephraim and Annaatje Wendel.

Hilletje, of Storm and Lena Van der Zee. Wit.: Johannes and Annaatje Slingerland.

Marrietje, of Abram and Geertje Vosburgh. Wit.: Franciscus and Marritje Lansing.

Maria, of Hendrik and Dirkje Gerritse. Wit.: Isaac and Alida Grevenraad.

Jan. 16. Antje, of Anthony and Marytje Van der Zee. Wit.: Storm Van der Zee, Rachel Van den Bergh.

Martinus, of Martinus and Jannetje Van Olinde. Wit.: Hannes and Rachel Van der Heyden.

Jan. 20. Anthony, of Jan and Rachel Bel. Wit.: Anthony and Catharyna Abramse.

Jan. 23. Lammetje, of Isaac and Hendrikje Fiele. Wit.: Ary and Lammetje Oothout.

Mayke, of Willem and Christyntje Klauw. Wit.: Volkert and Catharyna Van den Bergh.

Margrieta, of Thomas and Eva Turk. Wit.: Johannes and Lybetje Valkenburgh.

Feb. 3. Hendrik, of Matthias and Margreta Jonghans. Wit.: Hendrik Ridder, Elizabeth Landman.

Willem, of Willem and Margrietje Hilten. Wit.: Jacobus and Judith Hilten.

Feb. 17. Gerrit, of Zaccharias and Anna Zikkels. Wit.: Gerrit and Margriet Wyngaart.

Myndert, of Japik and Hendrikje Van Woerd. Wit.: Myndert and Rebecca Marcelis.

Feb. 24. Suzanna, of Jurriaan and Maria Hogan. Wit.: Willem Hogan, Alida Hollandt.

Frederick Blom, of John and Antje Olphert. Wit.: Geurt and Nelletje Bennewe.

1740, March 2. Benjamin, of Hendrik and Cathalyna Bulsen. Wit.: Benjamin Goewyk, Hilletje Ridder.

Wouter, of Casparus and Antje Witbeek. Wit.: Albertus and Catharyntje Bekker.

March 8. Balthazar, of Johannes H. and Geneve Lydius. Wit.: John J. and Rykje Rozeboom.

Cornelia, of John and Elizabeth Couper. Wit.: Obedia and Cornelia Couper.

Petrus, of Abraham and Elbertje Fonda. Wit.: Petrus and Marytje Fonda.

March 16. Robbert, of John and Catharyna Livingston. Wit.: Dirk Ten Broeck, Margrieta Livingston.

1740

Dirk, of Jacobus and Geertruy Schuyler. Wit.: Dirk Schuyler, Neeltje Staats.

Marytje, of Jesse and Neeltje De Foreest. Wit.: Philip and Geertruy Hanze.

March 23. Dirck, of Johannes and Engeltje Schermerhoorn. Wit.: Jacob and Zara Bloemendaal.

Anthony, of Johannes and Catharyna Abramse. Wit.: Anthony and Catharyna Abramse.

Anneken, of Cornelis and Anneken Van den Bergh. Wit.: Ryckert and Anna Van Franken.

March 30. Jan, of Laurens and Ariaantje Van der Poel. Wit.: Jan Van den Bergh, Antje Van der Poel.

Gerrit, of Johannes and Anna Van Vranken. Wit.: Rykert and Maria Van Vranken.

Hendrik, of Hendrik and Frena Marking. Wit.: Hannes and Elizabeth Duyvendorp.

Maria, of Japik and Christina Ten Broek. Wit.: Anthony Van Schaik, Gerrit Van Benthuysen, Margrieta Ten Broek.

Apr. 6. Jacob, of Johannes and Elizabeth Duyvendorp. Wit.: Jacob and Margriet Ernhoud.

Johannes, of Evert and Marytje Evertse. Wit.: Isaac and Maria Switz.

Apr. 20. Myndert, of Jan and Maria Oothoud. Wit.: Myndert and Fiedje Marcelis.

Christiaan, of Coenraad and Elizabeth Regtmeyer. Wit.: Lowies and Hilletje Schrodel.

Margrieta, of Johannes A. and Catharyna Cuyler. Wit.: Evert H. and Helena Wendel.

Samuel, of Pieter and Geertruy Doxs. Wit.: Wouter Knickerbakker, Geertruy Groesbeek.

Hendrik, of Andries and Alida Logen. Wit.: Japik Harzen, Jr., Maria Pruyn.

Apr. 27. David, of Joseph and Catharyna, pros. Wit.: Killiaan, pros., Elizabeth E. Wendel.

Hendrik, of Gerrit W. and Alida Van den Bergh. Wit.: Gerrit J. and Idtje Lansing.

David, of Johannes and Rachel Van der Heyden. Wit.: Dirck and Hester Van der Heyden.

Maria, of Christoffel and Margrieta Abeel. Wit.: Barent and Rachel Brad.

May 4. Gerrit, of Willem and Theuntje Van Buren. Wit.: Hendrik and Geertruy Van Buren.

Cathalyna, of Johannes and Margrietje Brad. Wit.: Johannes and Annaatje Knoet.

May 11. Maria *Lisbet, of Barent and Margrietje Van Buren. Wit.: Johannes Van Vegten, Wyntje Bries.

---

* This Lisbet had been added in a different handwriting.

1740

May 18. Hendrik, of Hendrik and Suzanna Meyer. Wit.: Jacobus and Margriet Aarnhoud.

Suzanna, of Hannes and Anna Worgsmans. Wit.: Hannes Hun, Anna Muller.

Volkert, of Martenus and Catharyna Van Aalsteyn. Wit.: Volkert and Volkje Van den Bergh.

May 25. Nikolaas, of Gerrit and Margrieta Marcelis. Wit.: Johannes Bleeker, Geertruy Wendel.

May 26. Johannes, of Rykert and Catharyna Hanzen. Wit.: Johannes and Catharyna Ten Broek.

Robbert, of William Kruks and Margriet Kroeks. Wit.: Sjeems Doin, Cathalyna Bulsen.

June 1. Thomas, of Willem Badt and Elisabeth Bedt. Wit.: Thomas and Maria Bidt.

Maria, of Thomas and Elizabeth Wilkenson. Wit.: Wynand and Cathalyna Van den Bergh.

Geertruy, of Pieter and Adriana Knoet. Wit.: Abraham and Zara Van Francken.

At Schag. June 14. Maria, of Joachim and Eva Kittelheyn. Wit.: Barnardus Bradt, Catharyna Groesbeek.

Willem, of Douwe and Neeltje Kittelheyn. Wit.: Willem and Maria Kittelheyn.

Rebecca, of David and Rebecca Mohennie. Wit.: Richart Weith, Elizabeth Delmond.

Margriet, of Johannes and Marya Geertruy Boam. Wit.: Walran and Anna Knoet.

Benjamin, of Daniel and Maria Springer. Wit.: Hugo and Catharyna Viele.

June 17. Catharyna, of Jacobus and Catharyna Van Valkenburgh. Wit.: William, Jr., and Zantje Hogan.

Catharyna, of Renzelaar and Elizabeth Nickels. Wit.: Abraham and Rachel Salisbury.

Jannetje, of Theunis and Magtel Visscher. Wit.: Isaac and Jannetje Lansing.

Cornelia, of Johannes and Margrieta Quackenbos. Wit.: Wouter Knickerbakker, Neeltje Foreest.

June 22. Laurens, of Andries, Jr., and Elizabeth Scherp. Wit.: Louw and Hilletje Schrodel.

Debora, of Lambert and Jacomyntje Van Valkenburg. Wit.: Johannes and Debora Hanzen.

Geertruy, of Gerrit and Marritje Knoet. Wit.: Olderick and Jannetje Van Vrancken.

June 29. Cornelis, of Hannes and Catharina Huyk. Wit.: Cornelis and Catharina Ouderkerk.

Francis of Johannes, and Catharyna Hogen. Wit.: Ryckert and Annaatje Van Vrancken.

Johannes, of Theunes and Cathalyna Van Slyck. Wit.: Laurens Schjerp, Jannetje Goewyck.

1740

Obedia, of Evert and Anna Lansing. Wit.: Thomas and Zara Couper.

Hendrik, of Hannes Jochem Maak and Frena Mook. Wit.: Jacob and Margrieta Aarnoud.

July 16. Rachel, of David and Geertruy Van der Heyden. Wit.: Japik Van der Heyden, Rachel Visscher.

Maria, of William, Jr., and Zusanna Hogan. Wit.: Jurrian and Maria Hogan.

July 23. Jacob, of Lavinus and Suzanna Winne. Wit.: Jacob Wendel, Catharina Winne.

Margrietje, of Abraham and Rachel Van Deusen. Wit.: Raphiel and Breggie Golet.

July 27. Eldert, of Japik and Anna Van Woerd. Wit.: Andries and Zara Guardenier.

Volkert, of Gerrit Theunisse Van Vegten and Lena Van Vegten. Wit.: Johannes and Lydia Van Vegten.

July 30. Johannes, of Cornelis and Maria Ten Broeck. Wit.: Cornelis Cuyler, Zara Hanzen.

Aug. 3. Burger, of Volkert and Catharina Van den Bergh. Wit.: Burger Huyck, Marytje Gerritse.

Aug. 10. Cornelis, of Harmen and Eva Van der Zee. Wit.: Theunis and Rachel Slingerland.

Geertruy, of Johannes and Neeltje Vinnagel. Wit.: Gerrit B. Van den Bergh, Ariaantje Van der Poel.

Aug. 17. Hiltje, of Samuel and Margrieta Wielar. Wit.: Johan Lewis and Hiltje Schrodel.

Aug. 31. Johannes, of Pieter and Anna Bennewe. Wit.: Johannes and Eva Fort.

Lena, of Zacharias and Geesje Haas. Wit.: Johannes and Jannetje Goewyck.

Anna, of Japik H. and Anna Ten Eyck. Wit.: Jacob and Anna Wendel.

Alida, of Nicolaas and Anna Visscher. Wit.: Jacob Van der Heyden, Rachel Visscher.

Judith, of Robbert Berrith and Maria Barrith. Wit.: Jacobus and Judith Hilten.

Alida, of Hendrik and Anna Fonda. Wit.: Isaac and Alida Fonda.

Daniel, of Hendrik M. and Aaltje Van Buren. Wit.: Willem and Maria Winne.

Sep. 7. Harpert, of Abraham G. and Helena (decd.) Lansing. Wit.: Evert and Annaatje Lansing.

Barent, of Japik and Alida Ten Eyck. Wit.: Japik H. Ten Eyck, Rachel Visscher.

Zara, of Philip and Geertruy Hanzen. Wit.: Johannes and Sara Hansen.

Willem, of Willem and Lena Hooghteling. Wit.: Abraham and Elizabeth Wyngaart.

1740
Sep. 14. Pieter, of Hendrik and Annaatje Van Buren.
Wit.: Pieter and Geertruy Van Buren.
Jacob, of Ryckert and Maria Hilten. Wit.: Japik and
Catharina Brouwer.
Sep. 21. Zara, of William and Maria Botz. Wit.:
Sjems Stenhuys, Aafje Beekman.
Maria, of Bernardus and Catharina Bradt. Wit.:
Henricus Brad, Suzanna Halenbeek.
Sep. 28. Catalina, of Japik and Maria Brouwer. Wit.:
Jan and Cathalina Winne.
Catharina, of Theunis and Maria Viele. Wit.: Pieter
and Maria Fonda.
Abraham, of Jan and Elizabeth Van Aarnem. Wit.:
Abraham and Alida Van Aarnem.
Mykel, of Mykel and Elisabeth Bestid. Wit.: Hendrik
M. and Maria Rozeboom.
Catharina, of Franciscus and Marritje Lansing. Wit.:
Willem and Catharina Londerzee.
Elizabeth, of Wouter and Elizabeth Knickerbakker.
Wit.: Abraham Fonda, Cornelia Knickerbakker.
Oct. 5. Elizabeth, of Frederik and Engeltje Ruyter.
Wit.: Hendrik and Catharina Van der Werken.
Johannes, Abraham, of Volkert, Jr., and Annaatje Douw.
Wit.: Isaac and Hendrikje Bogaart, Dirk and Margrietje
Hun.
Elizabeth, of Johannis and Christina Van der Werken.
Wit.: Bernardus and Marytje Harzen.
Cornelis, of Storm and Elizabeth Van der Zee. Wit.:
Aalbert Van der Zee, Rachel Slingerlandt.
Elizabeth, of Hendricus and Rebecca Brad. Wit.:
Gerrit Brad, Elizabeth Bradt.
Maria, of Douwe and Willemtje Bogaart. Wit.: Barent
Brad, Rachel Bradt.
Oct. 12. Simeon, of Philippus and Zara Winne. Wit.:
Hans, Jr., and Margrietje Hanse.
Johannes, of Abraham and Anna Witbeek. Wit.:
Cornelis Van Vegten, Marritje Van Deusen.
Oct. 19. Jacob, of Johannis and Alida Van Schaik.
Wit.: Cornelis Bogaart, Catharina Van Schaik.
Zara, of Sybrand and Jannetje Van Schaik. Wit.:
Johannes Van Schaik, Jannitje Groesbeek.
Johannes, of Egbert and Elizabeth Brad. Wit.: Evert
and Cornelia Bogardus.
Willem, of Hendrik, Jr., and Catharyna Van Wie. Wit.:
Johannes Th. and Eva Witbeek.
Oct. 26. Willem, of Reyer and Marytje Sprinksteen.
Wit.: Johannes Schermerhoorn, Aefje Beekman.
Willemtje, of Dirck and Cornelia Brad. Wit.: Johannes
Jaets, Willemtje A. Bradt.

1740-1741
Nov. 2. Isaac, of Gerrit Is. and Ariaantje Lansing.
Wit.: Isaac and Jannetje Lansing.
Bo. Oct. 31. Cornelis, of Cornelis and Cathalyna
Cuyler. Wit.: Isaac Wendel, Maria Ten Broek.
Nov. 9. Bregje, of Volkert and Alida Van Hoesen.
Wit.: Myndert and Fiedtje Marcelis.
Rinier, of Anthony and Maria Van Yveren. Wit.:
Rinier and Zara Van Yveren.
Nov. 16. Anna, of Isaac and Alida Grevenraad. Wit.:
Robert Zanders, Dirkje Gerritse.
Nov. 23. Margrietje, of Abraham and Lyntje Douwe.
Wit.: Johannes V. Douw, Dorethe Witbeek.
Jacob, of John Jac. and Margret Rozeboom. Wit.:
Jacob and Geertruy Isab. Rozeboom.
Jannetje, of Benjamin and Rachel Winne. Wit.:
Jacobus Van Renzelaar, Catharina Tam Baarn.
Rachel, of Killiaan and Rebecca Winne. Wit.: Abra-
ham and Zara Fonda.
Dirk, of Cherl Danielse and Elizabeth Dennielse. Wit.:
Dirck Maerten, Judith Hilten.
Dec. 3. Elizabeth, of Alexander and Elizabeth Van
Woerd. Wit.: Cornelis and Wyntje Van den Bergh.
Dec. 14. Margrieta, of Robbert and Agnietje Schot.
Wit.: Pieter and Elizabeth Williams.
Joachim, of Johannis and Anna Visscher. Wit.: Gerrit
and Elizabeth Staats.
Dec. 26. Robbert, of Johannes and Engeltje Van
Renzelaar. Wit.: Killiaan Van Renzelaar, Zelia Living-
ston.
Dec. 28. Catharina, of Frans and Agnieta Winne.
Wit.: John Van Wie, Maria Winne.
Tryntje, of Johannes and Rebekka Jaets. Wit.: Gerrit
and Engeltje Walran.
1740/1, Jan. 4. Frans, of Samuel and Magdalena Born.
Wit: Frans and Margarita Pruyn.
Ryckje, of Sybrand and Alida Van Schaik. Wit.:
Johannis M. Rozeboom, Debora Van Scaick.
Jan. 7. John, of Sjeems and Lena Flemmingh. Wit.:
Pieter Lodewyk, Agnietje Rous.
Jan. 11. Joseph, of Gysbert and Margrietje Van Zanten.
Wit.: Joseph and Zydtje Van Zanten.
Mattheus, of Pieter and Johanna Klauw. Wit.: Hans
and Zara Hanse.
Pieter, of Andries and Nelletje Huyk. Wit.: Stevanus
and Elizabeth Van Renzelaar.
Evert, of Cornelis and Gerritje Ridder. Wit.: Symen
and Hilletje Ridder.
Jan. 11. Anna, of Evert and Elsje Siskby. Wit.:
Japik and Annaatje Egmond.

1741

Jan. 21. Elizabeth, of Gerardus and Magtel Knoet. Wit.: Johannes and Lena Ouderkerk.

Maria, of Dirck and Catharina Van Alen. Wit.: Johannes T. and Elizabeth Ten Broek.

Bata, of Mattheus and Rachel Van Deusen. Wit.: David Esselsteyn, Catharina Hanszen.

Hendrik, of Evert and Marytje Wielaar. Wit.: Evert Zeger, Josyna Aartsier.

Jan. 27. Sylvester, of William and Theuntje Salisbury. Wit.: Francis and Maria Salisbury.

Feb. 1. Abraham and Jacob, of Lucas, Jr., and Rebecca Hoogkerk. Wit.: Abram, Lybetje, Douwe and Aaltje Fonda.

Maria, of Cornelis and Catharina Ouderkerk. Wit.: Douwe and Aaltje Fonda.

Feb. 8. Rachel, of Gerrit and Anna Van Zanten. Wit.: Johannes and Zara Van Zanten.

Alida, of Jacobus and Zara Groesbeek. Wit.: Salomon Van Vegten, Rebecca Bradt.

Feb. 15. Elizabeth, of Pieter and Elizabeth Landman. Wit.: Stevanus and Elizabeth Van Renzelaar.

Jeems, of Sjeems and Zara Bacblado. Wit.: Douwe Fonda, Elsje Badt.

Christina, of Ryckert, Jr., and Annaatje Van Franken. Wit.: Isaac Truax, Jannetje Van Slyk.

Feb. 22. Oliverr, of Johannes, Jr., and Cornelia Schuyler. Wit.: Cornelis Cuyler, Elizabet Skinner.

Maria, of Cornelis and Josyna Van Schie. Wit.: John De Peyster, Margarita Schuyler.

Anna, of Theunis and Cornelia Slingerland. Wit.: Abraham H. Wendel, Neeltje Douw.

March 1. Cornelia, of Jacobus, Jr., and Maria Harzen. Wit.: Bernardus Harzen, Alida Grevenraadt.

March 15. Catharina, of Caspar and Rachel Cailjer. Wit.: Richard and Lydia Van den Berck.

Jannetje, of Johan and Anna Dret. Wit.: Isaac and Jannetje De Vous.

Geertje, of Cornelis and Jannetje Walderon. Wit.: Hendrik and Anna De Ridder.

Philip, Gerrit, of Evert, Jr., and Zusanna Wendel. Wit.: Hermanus and Maria Wendel, Evert and Anna Lansing.

Johannes, of Johannes and Maria De Foreest. Wit.: David and Abigail Foreest.

Anna, of Bernardus and Catharina Harzen. Wit.: Franciscus S. and Alida Pruyn.

March 22. Geertruy, of Sybrand, Jr., and Anna Van Schaik. Wit.: Hendrik Rozeboom, Jr., Catharina Van Schaik.

1741

Gerrit, of Staats and Suzanna Zeger. Wit.: Gerrit and Maria Zeger.

Cornelis, of Jacob and Zara Maarse Bloemendaal. Wit.: Johannes and Maria Maarse Bloemendaal.

March 29. Jacob, of Douwe and Aaltje Fonda. Wit.: Cornelis and Catharina Ouderkerk.

1741 Apr. 5. Annaatje, of Abraham H. and Elizabeth Wendel. Wit.: Jacob and Annaatje Wendel.

Apr. 26. Thomas, of Johannes Th. and Eva Witbeek. Wit.: Melchert A. and Jannetje Witbeek.

May 7. Dirkje, of Andries and Elizabeth Van Woerd. Wit.: Nicolaas and Dirkje Van Woerd.

Maria, of Pieter and Catharina Schuyler. Wit.: Gerardus and Maria Groesbeek.

Andries, of Johannes and Jannatje Goewyk. Wit.: Johannes Van Schaik, Catharina Van de Bergh.

Zara and Josua, pros. Wit.: Joseph, Catharina, Symon, Maria, pros.

Zara, of Johannes and Maria Van Yveren. Wit.: Abraham and Zara Van Yveren.

May 13. Elsje, of Gysbert and Catharina Rozeboom. Wit.: Johannes G. and Maria Rozeboom.

May 24. Christina, of Abraham and Lydia Brad. Wit.: Pieter and Christina Brad.

Johannes, of Hans, Jr., and Margrieta Hanze. Wit.: Johannes and Zara Hanze.

May 31. bo. May 28. Phillip, of Phillip, Jr., and Christina Livingston. Wit.: Phillip and Catharina Livingston.

Gerrit, of Gerrit and Maria Van Franken. Wit.: Gerrit R. and Barbera Van Franken.

June 7. Zusanna, of Johannes and Maria Van den Bergh. Wit.: Cornelis and Suzanna Van den Bergh.

Christina, of Hendrik and Maria Schuver. Wit.: Adam Gardinier, Lena Kittel.

Catharyna, of Hendrik and Annaatje Lisjer. Wit.: Andries Huyk, Elizabeth Van Renzelaar.

June 10. Jacob, of Gerrit J. and Ida Lansing. Wit.: Abraham and Alida Van Aarnem.

June 14. Adriaan, of Anthonie and Catharina Bovie. Wit.: Jacob C. Ten Eyk, Zelia Livingston.

Isaac, of Isaac and Hendrikje Bogaart. Wit.: Abraham Bogaart, Marytje Pruyn.

June 17. Zara, of Harmen and Magdalena Ganzevoort Wit.: Leendert and Catharina Ganzevoord.

June 21. Jacobus, of Matthys and Rebecca De Garamo. Wit.: Jacobus and Catharina Bogardus.

June 24. Geertruy, of Frans and Magtel Bovie. Wit.: Hannes and Rachel Van Vranken.

1741
June 28. Zelotte, of Andries and Mayke Witbeek.
Wit.: Gerrit and Cathalyntje Witbeek.
Pieter, of Sjeems and Zara Stevense. Wit.: Pieter and
Marg. [or Mary] Groenendyk.
William, of Hendrik and Suzanna Halenbeek. Wit.:
Isaac and Dorethea Halenbeek.
Nelletje, of Wilhelmus and Anna Rykman. Wit.:
Pieter and Cornelia Rykman.
July 8. Elizabeth, of Dirk and Alida Vosburgh. Wit.:
Sybrand and Zara Van Schaik.
July 12. Willem, of Jacobus and Catharina Radelief.
Wit.: Johannes, Jr., and Rachel Radelief.
Johannes, of David and Maria Groesbeek. Wit.: Abra-
ham and Antje Van der Poel.
July 19. Rachel, of Hendrik N. and Eva Gardenier.
Wit.: Nicolaas and Rachel Gardinier.
July 22. Marytje, of Barent and Margrieta Van Buren.
Wit.: Hendrik and Wyntje Bries.
July 26. Maria of Wouter and Jannetje Groesbeek.
Wit.: Willem and Catharina Groesbeek.
Aug. 9. Adam, of Jacobus and Judith Hilten. Wit.:
Willem and Margrieta Hilten.
Maria, of Harmen and Elizabeth Van Vegten. Wit.:
Hendrik and Geertruy Van Buren.
Aug. 16. Laurens, of Gysbert and Neeltje Klauw.
Wit.: Wessel and Elizabeth Van Schaik.
Christina, of Thomas and Theuntje Valkenburg. Wit.:
Jack Valkenburg, Christina Barreith.
Lydia, of Johannes, Jr., and Neeltje Van Vegten. Wit.:
Gerrit F. Van Vegten, Margrieta Van den Berg.
Johannes, of Bernardus and Margrieta Brad. Wit.:
Johannes Brad, Maria Bradt.
Elizabeth, of Willem and Elizabeth Walran. Wit.:
Pieter Walran, Rachel Beekman.
Petrus, of Abraham and Elizabeth Wyngaart. Wit.:
Pieter Uziele, Christina Wyngaardt.
Aug. 23. Aaltje, of Gerrit and Zara Van Es. Wit.:
Melchert Van der Poel, Catharina Van den Berg.
Aug. 30. Geertruy, of Isaac and Neeltje Huyk. Wit.:
Hendrik and Anna Litsyer.
Margrietje, of Johannes and Zara Beekman. Wit.:
Hendrik Beekman, Margrieta Cuyler.
Suzanna, of Levinus and Suzanna Winne. Wit.:
Benjamin Winne, Annaatje Staats.
Cathalyna, of Jonathan and Magtel Witbeek. Wit.:
Johannes and Rachel Witbeek.
Sep. 13. Marytje, of Willem and Marie Ouderkerk.
Wit.: Arent and Scherlotte Van der Kar.
Sep. 20. Hendrik, of Isaac and Maria Staats. Wit.:
Barent Staats, Jr., Ryckje Rozeboom.

1741

Dirck, of Johannes and Margrieta Brad. Wit.: Cornelis Maarsen, Annatje Bradt.

Zara, of Harmen Seb. and Zara Visscher Wit.: Johannes Visscher, Zara Van Yveren.

Sep. 27. Samuel, of John and Elizabeth Couper. Wit.: Obediah, Jr., and Elizabeth Couper.

Sep. 28. Jacob, of Johannes and Catharina Cuyler. Wit.: Johannes and Elizabeth Glen.

Pieter, of Dirck and Margrieta Hun. Wit.: Harmen Hun, Annaatje Douw.

Oct. 4. Eva, of Isaac and Jannetje Valkenburgh. Wit.: Harmen and Jannetje Valkenburgh.

Anthoni, of Adriaan and Zelia Brad. Wit.: Gysbert and Catharina Rozeboom.

Oct. 11. Zara, of James and Elizabeth Ryan. Wit.: Thomas Willekens, Maria Lewis.

Pieter, of Nicolaas and Agnietje Groesbeek. Wit.: Harmen and Helena Ganzevoort.

Marytje, of Jacob and Neeltje Van der Poel. Wit.: Andries and Magdalena Huyk.

Oct. 16. Jacobus, of Frans Belleville and Neeltje Belville. Wit.: Barent Staats, Annaatje Douw.

Abraham, of Myndert and Elizabeth Veder. Wit.: Abraham and Lyntje Douw.

Pieter, of Rykert and Catharina Hanse. Wit.: Hendrik Ten Broek, Marytje A. Schuyler.

Hester, of Hendrik and Annaatje Beekman. Wit.: Isaac and Hester Switz.

Oct. 25. Tjerk Harmense, of Cornelis and Suzanna Van Nes. Wit.: Isaac and Hester Switz.

Mykel, of Mykel and Elizabeth Bessid. Wit.: Japik B. and Alida Ten Eyk.

Nov. 1. Jacob, of Jacob, Jr., and Cathalyntje Schermerhoorn. Wit.: Cornelis, Jr., and Marytje Schermerhoorn.

Cornelis, of Jacob and Elizabeth Glen. Wit.: Johannis and Jannetje Glen.

Nov. 15. Neeltje, of Hendrik M. and Maria Rozeboom. Wit.: Sybrant Van Schaik, Geertje Schermerhoorn.

Nov. 29. Barent, of Joachim and Elizabeth Staats. Wit.: Barent and Neeltje Staats.

Coenraad, of Jacob C. and Catharyna Ten Eyk. Wit.: Coenraad and Gerritje Ten Eyk.

Dec. 13. Robbert, of Jems and Margrieta Steenhuysen. Wit.: Douwe J. and Aaltje Fonda.

Helena, of Gerrit Joh. and Elsje Lansingh. Wit.: Johannes and Helena Lansingh.

Dec. 16. Jannetje, of Barent and Catharina Lewis. Wit.: Hendrik, Jr., and Catharyna Van Wie.

91

1741-1742

Dec. 25. Martinus, of Barent and Cornelia Van Yveren. Wit.: Wilhelmus and Cornelia Van den Bergh.

1741/2, Jan. 1. Abraham, of Johannes Boom and Anna Burger. Wit.: Abraham and Geertruy Wendel.

Jan. 6. Ryckert, of Matthys and Rebecka Van der Berk. Wit.: Ryckert and Tryntje Van der Berk.

Jacobus, of John and Antje Olivert. Wit.: Jacobus La Gransie, Engeltje Veeder.

Jan. 10. Geertruy, of Isaac and Maria Switz. Wit.: Jacob and Suzanna Visschjer.

Laurens, of Abraham and Hendrikje Fonda. Wit.: Arent and Hilletje Van Dyk.

Jan. 13. Joseph, of Adam and Anna Jates. Wit.: Joseph Jates, Cathalyna Groesbeek.

Jan. 20. Cornelis, of John and Bata Ligged. Wit.: Cornelis and Cathalyna Cuyler.

Jacobus, of Adam and Catharyna Van Alen. Wit.: Isaac and Elizabeth Van Aalsteyn.

Jan. 24. Christiaan, of Johannes and Catharina Abramse. Wit.: Christiaan Schans, Marytje Harzen.

Leendert, of Johannes and Racheltje Witbeek. Wit.: Cornelis, Jr., and Geertruy Van Buren.

Feb. 14. Nicolaas, of Johannes and Catharina Huyk. Wit.: Pieter and Nelletje Bovie.

Hendrik, of Philip and Geertruy Ruyter. Wit.: Frederik and Engeltje Ruyter.

Johannes, of Johannes, Jr., and Neeltje Vinnagel. Wit.: Abraham Vinnagel, Maria Van den Bergh.

Elizabeth, of Anthony D. and Christina Brad. Wit.: Gerrit Brad, Suzanna Halenbeek.

Johannes, of Wouter and Maria Groesbeek. Wit.: Nicolaas and Geertje Groesbeek.

Zara, of Abraham and Rebecca Foreest. Wit.: Robbert Rozeboom, Annaatje Van Nes.

Mattheus, of Mattheus and Margrieta Van der Heyden. Wit.: Matthias and Suzanna Van Deusen.

Anna, of Johannes and Anna Knoet. Wit.: Gerrit and Marytje Van Franken.

Catharina, of Evert and Anna Lansing. Wit.: Johannes G. and Engeltje Lansing.

Zara, of Hugo and Catharina Viele. Wit.: Andries and Zara Gardenier.

Feb. 28. Neeltje, Elizabeth, of Sybrand and Elizabeth Quackenbos. Wit.: Johannes, Jr., and Corna. Knickerbacker, Anthony and Catharina Quackenbos.

Maria, of Johannes and Maria Geertruy Boom. Wit.: Dirk Ten Broek, Maria Groesbeek.

Feb. 28. Gerrit, of Willem and Catharina Groesbeek. Wit.: Wouter Groesbeek, Anna Van Es.

1741-1742

March 7. Anna, of Johannes Bleeker and Eva Bleecker. Wit.: Jacob and Anna Bleeker.

Eva, of Jacobus and Catharina Van Valckenburgh. Wit.: Johannes and Gerritje Van Valkenburg.

Engeltje, of Barent A. and Anna Brad. Wit.: Mattheus and Margrieta Van der Heyde.

Gerritje, of Johannes and Engeltje Schermerhoorn. Wit.: Corns. and Gerritje Schermerhoorn.

Johannis, of Johannes and Margrietje Quackenbos. Wit.: Philip and Cornelia Foreest.

March 14. Levinus, of Robbert and Cornelia Tombaar. Wit.: Pieter Winne, Jannetje Swits.

Alida, of Lucas and Rebecca Hoogkerke. Wit.: Douwe and Aaltje Fonda.

Marytje, of Cornelis M. and Rachel Van den Bergh. Wit.: Barent Brad, Willemtje Bogaart.

Jan, of Philip and Geertruy Hanze. Wit.: Jan and Cathalyntje Van Es.

1742, March 28. Belshazar, of Jacobus P. and Zara Van Benthuysen. Wit.: John and Lydia Bezely.

Apr. 4. Joseph, of Johan Caspar and Elizabeth Geefhart. Wit.: Robbert and Maria Rozeboom.

Theunis, of Hendrik and Elizabeth Van Slyk. Wit.: Theunis and Jannetje Van Slyk.

Alida, of Henricus and Rebecca Brad. Wit.: Douwe Van Vegten, Zara Groesbeek.

Apr. 4. Hendrik, of Hendrik and Wyntje Bries. Wit.: John and Engeltje Van Renzelaar.

Jacob, of Hendrik and Anna Lansing. Wit.: Abram and Alida Van Aarnem.

Elizabeth, of Anthony and Maria Van der Zee. Wit.: Cornelis Ridder, Cathalyna Van Hoezen.

Apr. 11. Maas, of Cornelis and Anneke Van den Bergh. Wit.: Adam and Anna Van Franken.

Abraham, of Cornelis and Cathalina Cuyler. Wit.: Anthony Van Schaik, Zara Glen.

Jan, of Pieter and Anna Quackinbos. Wit.: Volkert Oothout, Cornelia Foreest.

Apr. 18. Jannetje, of Albert and Antje Van der Zee. Wit.: Storm and Lybetje Van der Zee.

Apr. 25. Nicolaas, of Nicolaas, Jr., and Margrieta Bleeker. Wit.: Johannes Rozeboom, Anna Bleeker.

Maria, of Isaac and Elizabeth Muller. Wit.: Nicolaas and Maria Kittel.

Johanna, of Thomas and Eva Turk. Wit.: Johannes Pruyn, Jr., Johanna Valkenburg.

Gerrit, of Andries and Marytje Van den Berg. Wit.: Laurens and Ariaantje Van der Poel.

Maria, of Abram Vinnagel and Jannetje Van Buren. Wit.: Johannes Vinhagel, Maria Vinnagel.

1742

May 2. Catharina, of Isaac and Anna Van der Poel. Wit.: Cornelis and Catharina Ouderkerk.

Dirk, of Arent and Scherlotta Van der Kar. Wit.: Gerrit and Adriana Bekker.

Zara, of Willem Gysb. and Zuzanna Van den Bergh Wit.: Renier and Zara Van Yveren.

May 9. Stevanus, of Gerardus and Maria Groesbeek. Wit.: Dirck Ten Broek, Elizabeth Groesbeek.

May 16. Hendrik, of Jonas and Elizabeth Oothout. Wit.: Abraham Lansing, Dorethe Van den Bogaart.

Thomas, of Willem and Margrieta Hilten. Wit.: Pieter Joons, Annaatje Van Zanten.

Rebecca, of Jacob and Hendrikje Van Woerd. Wit.: Ruth and Elizabeth Van Woerd.

Evert, of Corns. and Rachel Van den Bergh. Wit.: Killiaan De Ridder, Marytje Gerritse.

Cathalyntje, of Johs. G. and Jannetje Lansing. Wit.: Johs. Hun, Hendrikje Schuyler.

May 23. Barent, of Johannes and Christina Van der Werken. Wit.: Barent Brad, Catharina Harzen.

Matthias, of Johannes and Cornelia Flensburgh. Wit.: Joseph and Margrieta Flensburgh.

June 2. Stevanus, of Stevanus and Elizabeth Van Renzelaar. Wit.: Stevanus and Elizabeth Groesbeek.

Elizabeth, of Hendrik H. and Cathalina Rozeboom. Wit.: Abraham and Rykje Rozeboom.

June 6. Hermanus, of Hermanus Th. and Catharina Wendel. Wit.: Jacob and Anna Wendel.

Gerrit Theunisse, of Gerrit C. and Margrieta Van den Bergh. Wit.: Gerrit Van den Bergh, Catharina Ten-Broek.

June 13. Petrus, of Petrus and Christyna Van Bergen. Wit.: Johannes and Catharina Ten Broek.

Lena, of Roelof and Engeltje Kitnie. Wit.: Daniel Hawson, Hillegond Bradt.

June 20. Hendrikje, of Willem and Theuntje Van Buren. Wit.: Gerrit Van den Bergh, Agnietje Lievense.

Abraham, of Symen and Geertruy Véder. Wit.: Teunis Slingerland, Suzanna Wendel.

Wyntje, of Jan and Catharina Brad. Wit.: Andries Brad, Maria Bradt.

June 23. Maria, of Bernardus and Catharina Brad. Wit.: Hendrik Bries, Elizabeth Hilten.

June 27. Evert, of Jan and Maria Oothoud. Wit.: Cornelis and Catharina Van Aalsteyn.

July 4. Jannitje, of Samuel and Lena Born. Wit.: Eduard and Margreta Collings.

July 11. Storm, of Harmen and Eva Van der Zee. Wit.: Johannes and Hester Slingerland.

1742.

July 18. Johannes, of Abraham H. and Annaatje Wendel. Wit.: Ephraim and Anna Wendel.

July 21. Willem, of Isaac and Maria Van Aalsteyn. Wit.: Willem and Volkje Van den Bergh.

July 25. Cornelis, of Abraham and Maria Vroman. Wit.: Hendrik G. and Catharina Van Wie.

July 28. Johannes, of Johannes and Maria Van den Bergh. Wit.: Cornelis and Catharina Van den Bergh.

Aug. 1. Anna, of Zaccharias and Geesje Haas. Wit.: Lambert Kool, Willemtje Bradt.

Anna, of Andries and Alida Logen. Wit.: Johannes Bruyn, Elsje Pruyn.

Aug. 8. Rebecca, of Jacob, Jr., and Maria Bogaart, Wit.: Pieter and Rebecca Bogaart.

Aug. 15. Zara, of Gerrit F. and Annaatje Van Sliyk Wit.: Johannes Van Wie, Agnietje Van Slyk.

Neeltje, of Jacobus and Geertruy Schuyler. Wit.: Barent and Neeltje Staats.

Sep. 12. Jacob, of Gerret and Margrieta Marcelis. Wit.: Nicholaas and Margrieta Bleecker.

Annaatje, of Jacob and Anna Kitnie. Wit.: Pieter and Elizabeth Walran.

Anna, of Jacob H. and Annaatje Ten Eyk. Wit.: Jacob and Anna Wendel.

Anna, of Hendrik and Dirkje Gerritse. Wit.: Cornelis Tymense, Anna Visscher.

Sep. 19. Jan, of Roelof Vous and Bechje De Vous. Wit.: Jan and Fydtje De Vous.

Cornelis, of Cornelis and Catharina Van Aalsteyn. Wit.: Dirk Brad, Cornelia Bradt.

Sep. 26. Hendrik, of Frederik and Engeltje Ruyter. Wit.: Volkert, Jr., and Annaatje Douw.

Johannes, of Christiaan and Baartje Lange. Wit.: Phillip Louk, Magdalena Loek.

Maria, of Johannis and Annaatje Slingerland. Wit.: Harmen and Rachel Van der Zee.

Antje, of Hendrik and Annaatje Ridder. Wit.: Cornelis and Jannetje Walran.

Agnietje, of Andries and Mayke Witbeek. Wit.: Thomas Witbeek, Anna Margrieta Koeymans.

Oct. 10. Margrieta, of John and Catharina Livingston. Wit.: Jeems and Margrieta Ten Broek.

Oct. 24. Petrus, of Abraham and Rebecca Doxs. Wit.: Jacobus Van Renzelaar, Ariaantje Van Woerd.

Hendrik, of Johannes and Engeltje Van Renzelaar. Wit.: Johannes Ten Broek, Helena Wendel.

Hendrik, of Gysbert and Margrietje Van Zanten. Wit.: Hendrik and Anna Koorn.

1742-1743

Dorethe, of Johannes and Jannetje Douw. Wit.: Cornelis Bogaart, Margareta Douw.

Jannetje, of Melchert A. and Marritje Witbeek. Wit.: Johannes Th. and Jannetje Witbeek.

Gerrit, of Johannis and Anna Visscher. Wit.: Jacobus Schuyler, Elizabeth Staats.

Oct. 31. Hendricus, of Johannis and Johanna Marcelis. Wit.: Barent Brad, Catharina Marcelis.

Juliana, of Johannis and Catharina Hogil. Wit.: Francis Hogil, Catharina Landman.

Francis, of Renzelaar and Elizabeth Nicolls. Wit.: Eduart Holland, Francis Hollandt.

Nov. 7. Thomas, of Robbert and Maria Barrit. Wit.: Petrus Maarten, Maria Barrith.

Gerrit, of Gerrit and Maria Knoet. Wit.: Pieter D. and Hendrikje Schuyler.

Nov. 14. Isaac, of Willem, Jr., and Suzanna Hogan. Wit.: Isaac and Jannetje Lansing.

Nov. 28. Dirck, of Pieter and Annaatje Van Alen. Wit.: Dirk Van Alen, Franckje Van Benthuysen.

Dec. 1. Mattheus, of Johannis and Rachel Van der Heyden. Wit.: Gerrit and Frankje Van Benthuysen.

Dec. 5. Casparus, of Hendrik, Jr., and Catharina Van Wie. Wit.: Leendert Ganzevoort, Agnietje Van den Bergh.

Alexander, of Hendrik and Cathalena Bulsen. Wit.: Pieter and Maria Fonda.

Johannes ,Margrieta, of Jacobus and Margrieta V. Valkenburg. Wit.: Jacobus and Annetje Radelief, Harm and Jannetje Van Valkenburg.

Pieter, of Staats and Suzanna Zeger. Wit.: Pieter and Christina Brad.

Magdalena, of Benjamin and Anna Bogaart. Wit.: Jan and Cathalina Winne.

Dec. 8. Tobias, of Jan and Anna Dret. Wit.: Johannes Jac. and Anna Lansing.

Dec. 12. Mayke, of Cornelis and Catharina Ouderkerk. Wit.: Hendrik and Annaatje Lansing.

Dec. 18. Hillegond, of Rykert, Jr., and Anna Van Franken. Wit.: Cornelis and Anna Van den Berg.

Dec. 25. Zara, of Johannes and Maria Van Yveren. Wit.: Abraham and Catharina Van Yveren.

Isaac, of Jacob and Margriet Aarnold. Wit.: Isaac and Marytje Cradik.

1742/3, Jan. 2. Maria, of Sybrand and Jannetje Van Schaik. Wit.: Pieter Schuyler, Maria Pruyn.

Johannes, of Alexander and Elizabeth Van Woerd. Wit.: Theunis and Christina Van Woerdt.

Jan. 12. John, of John and Rachel Bel. Wit.: Stevanus and Elizabeth Van Renzelaar.

1743

Gerrit, of Philip and Margrieta Van Es. Wit.: Gerrit and Anna Van Es.

Jan. 16. Petrus, of Harmen and Magdalena Ganzevoort. Wit.: Petrus and Anna Douwe.

Jan. 23. Tobias, of Hendrik and Anna Van Buren. Wit.: Thomas and Elizabeth Couper.

Christyna, of Pieter and Elbertje Van Buren. Wit.: Robbert Van Deusen, Jannetje Goes.

Hannes Jacobs, of Hannes and Anna Wurgsmans. Wit.: Johannes Douw, Johanna Hun.

Philip, of Hendrik and Maria Schieber. Wit.: Marten Corn. and Geertruy Van Buren.

Rebecca, of Douwe and Willemtje Bogaart. Wit.: Pieter and Rebecca Bogaart.

Volkert Van Hoezen, of John and Anna Mekkentosch. Wit.: Martinus Van Aalsteyn, Suzanna Wendel.

Jan. 30. Willem, of Omphri and Zara Hitkok. Wit.: Willem and Maria Kittelheyn.

Debora, of Evert and Maria Jansze. Wit.: Myndert and Elizabeth Veder.

William, of David and Rebecca Mahanni. Wit.: Peter and Anna Magriegrie.

Christoffel, of Jacob, Jr., and Huybertje Lansing. Wit.: Christoffel and Catalyna Jaits.

Feb. 6. Gerrit, of Adam and Lydia Brad. Wit.: Gerrit and Maria Zeger.

Barent, of Robbert and Maria Sandertz. Wit.: Barent and Geertruy Sandertz.

Ariaantje, of Dirk and Zara Woedkok. Wit.: Johannes and Anna Gardenier.

Lena, of Jacob Jac. and Marretje Lansing Wit.: Jacob and Lena Lansing.

Jacob, of Abraham and Catharina Lansing. Wit. Hendrik and Anna Lansing

Jannetje, of Jeremias and Jannetje Hogeboom. Wit.: Pieter Hogeboom, Geertruy Van Es.

Catharina, of Pieter and Anna Magiegrie. Wit.: John and Catharina Stevense.

Feb. 20. Myndert, of Folkert and Alida Van Hoezen. Wit.: Abraham Dogs, Rebecca Doxs.

Feb. 27. Maria, of Jacob and Alida Ten Eyk. Wit.: Johannes Beekman, Anna Ten Eyk.

March 3. Marritje, Cathalyntje, of Martinus and Catharyna Van Aalsteyn. Wit.: Barent and Cornelia Van Yveren, Adam Yeets, Catelyntje Van den Berg.

March 20. Catharyna, of Volkert and Catharina Van den Bergh. Wit.: Willem Van den Berg, Maria Gerritse.

1743, March 27. Geertruy, of Benjamin and Anna Van den Bergh. Wit.: Johannis and Maria Vinnagel.

Helena, of Robbert and Margrietje Lansing. Wit.: Gerrit Lansing, Elsje Rozeboom.

Agnietje, of Gerrit T. and Lena Van Vegten. Wit.: Jan and Agnietje Witbeek.

Anna, of Volkert P. and Anna Douw. Wit.: John De Peyster, Anna Douw.

Apr. 1. Ludovicus Biblicus Jacobus, of Isaac and Hendrikje Viele. Wit.: Pieter and Catharina Viele.

Apr. 3. Johannes, of Wouter and Elizabeth Knickerbakker. Wit.: Wouter Groesbeek, Neeltje Bradt.

Catharina, of Evert and Elsje Seskby. Wit.: Abraham G. Lansing, Catharina Lansingh.

Apr. 10. Albert, of Storm and Elizabeth Van der Zee. Wit.: Albertus and Catharina Bekker.

Ariaantje, of Jacob and Helena Wendel. Wit.: Killiaan and Engeltje Van Renzelaar.

Apr. 17. Cathalyntje, of Harmen and Elsje Hun. Wit.: Dirk and Hendrikje Hun.

Elizabeth, of Eduart and Maria Hogil. Wit.: Pieter Hogil, Rebecca Kitnie.

Apr. 24. Pieter, of Nicolaas and Agnietje Groesbeek. Wit.: Harme and Lena Ganzevoort.

Johannes, of Philip and Geertruy Ruyter. Wit.: Roelof Van der Werken, Catrina Landman.

Ephraim, of Johannes and Neeltje Van Vegten. Wit.: Ephraim Van Vegten, Margrieta Van den Bergh.

Cornelis, of Jacob, Jr., and Cathalyna Schermerhoorn. Wit.: Jan Van Buren, Zara Livingston.

Dirk, of Richart and Catharina Hanze. Wit.: Dirk and Catharina Ten Broek.

May 1. Johannes, of Evert and Anna Lansingh. Wit.: John and Elizabeth Couper.

Marritje, of Gerardus and Magtel Knoet. Wit.: Jacob Heemstraat, Margriet Wyngaart.

Tryntje, of Johannis Thomasse Witbeek and Eva Witbeek. Wit.: Willem Walran, Corn. Bradt.

May 8. Jacob, of Hendrik and Frena Springer. Wit.: Barent Gans, Barbara Gansch.

Jacob, of Cornelis and Maria Muller. Wit.: Jacob and Agnietje Muller.

Rachel, of Thomas and Theuntje Valkenburgh. Wit.: Jacob H. Muller, Rebecca Barheyt.

May 15. Barent, of John and Catharina Van den Bergh. Wit.: Gerrit Van den Bergh, Jr., Maria Van Buren.

Lavinus, of Willem and Maria Lievense. Wit.: Lavinus and Catharina Lievense.

May 22. Martha, of Jacobus and Elsje Bennewe. Wit.: Theunis Viele, Martha Olivert.

Margriet, of Hendrik and Elizabeth Luyks. Wit.: Coenraad Richtmeyer, Elizabeth Rigtmeyer.

1743

May 29. Christina, of Jan and Suzanna Brad. Wit.: Adriaan and Maria Brad.

Anneke, of Anthony and Catharina Bovie. Wit.: Corns. N. and Anneke V. d. Bergh.

Nicolaas, of Andries, Jr., and Nelletje Huyk. Wit.: Hendrik Bovie, Catharina Huyk.

June 5. Cornelis, of Cornelis and Jannetje Walran. Wit. : Hendik, Jr., and Catharina Van Wie.

Dirk, of Dirk and Greesje Weith. Wit.: Jacob Doksie, Alida Maria.

Margrieta, of Jacob and Maria Harzen. Wit.: Hendrik Gerritse, Catharina Harzen.

June 8, bo. June 6. Dirk, of Philip, Jr., and Christina Livingston. Wit.: Dirk and Margrieta Ten Broek.

June 12. Willem, of Gerrit and Catharina Van Alen. Wit.: Pieter and Rachel Winne.

Jacob, of Cornelis and Maria Schermerhoorn. Wit.: Reyer and Maria Schermerhoorn.

June 15. Dirk, of Johannes and Margrieta Brad. Wit.: Robbert Rozeboom, Anna Bradt.

Rachel, of Franciscus and Marretje Lansing. Wit.: Harmen and Rachel Lievense.

June 26. Coenraad, of Jurriaan and Anna Koen or Korn. Wit.: Coenraad and Margriet Korn or Koen.

July 3. Elizabeth, of Lavinus and Zusanna Winne. Wit.: Abraham and Catharina Wendel.

Douwe, Pieter, of Killiaan and Rebecca Winne. Wit.: Douwe and Willimtje Bogaart, Pieter and Rachel Winne.

July 6. Abraham, of Ebbert and Maria Ebbertse. Wit.: Jacob Visscher, Zara Van Aalsteyn.

July 10. Agnietje, of Bernardus and Margrietje Brad. Wit.: Thomas and Hilletje Williams.

Alida, of Isaac and Alida Grevenraad. Wit.: Ahazueros and Marritje Rozeboom.

July 17. Hester, of Gerrit Isaacse Lansing and Ariaantje Lansing. Wit.: Johannes, Jr., and Hester Beekman.

Marritje, of Abraham and Rachel Van Deuzen. Wit.: Abraham and Annaatje Witbeek.

July 24. Maria, of John and Lena Reynlie. Wit.: Isaac and Maria Creddok.

July 27. Myndert, of Sybrand and Alida Van Schaik. Wit.: Abraham Van Schaik, Maria Rozeboom.

Cathalyntje, of Anthony and Maria Van Yveren. Wit.: Gysbert and Cathalina Van den Bergh.

July 31. Elizabeth, of Hieronymus and Zara Barheyt. Wit.: Roelof and Elizabeth Janse.

Jannetje, of Wouter and Maria Groesbeek. Wit.: Anthony and Jannetje Bogardus.

1743

Elbertje, of Laurens and Cornelia Van Alen. Wit.: David and Marytje Groesbeek.

Margrieta, of Hieronymus and Maria Van Valkenburgh. Wit.: Joh. and Joha. Valkenburgh.

Aug. 7. Mattheus, of Jacob and Maria Brouwer. Wit.: Jacobus Radelief, Jannetje Van Vranken.

Christyna, of Zaccharias and Annaatje Sikkels. Wit.: Gerrit Van Vranken, Margrietje Wyngaart.

Aug. 14. Johannes, of Pieter and Catharina Schuyler. Wit.: Gerardus and Maria Groesbeek.

Pieter, of Wouter and Jannetje Groesbeek. Wit.: Pieter and Rebekka Bogaart.

Lavinus, of Benjamin and Rachel Winne. Wit.: Pieter Winne, Marytje Gerritse.

Joseph, of Adriaan and Zelia Brad. Wit.: Joseph and Zydtje Van Zanten.

Aug. 21. Abraham, of Abraham and Anna Witbeek. Wit.: Melchert A. Witbeek, Catharina Wendel.

Pieter, of Pieter W. and Anna Van Alen. Wit.: Casparus and Eva Conyn.

Jannetje, of John and Jannetje Makluur. Wit.: Corn. and Rachel Van den Bergh.

Aug. 28. Maria, of John and Elizabeth Wielaar. Wit.: Evert Zeger, Zara Aalschirt.

Jannitje, of Mykel and Elizabeth Bessed. Wit.: Jacob and Annaatje Schermerhoorn.

Sep. 25. Catharina, of Johannis and Jeneveva Lydius. Wit.: Johannes Jac. and Magtel Rozeboom.

Cornelis, of Hendricus and Annaatje Beekman. Wit.: Johannes Beekman, Maria Hogan.

Geertruy, of Theunis and Cornelia Slingerland. Wit.: Theunis Corn. and Hester Jr. Slingerland.

Oct. 2. Johannes, of Willem and Lena Brommely. Wit.: Johannes and Barbara Boom.

Johannes, of Joseph and Margriet Radelief. Wit.: Akes and Margrieta Van Valkenburg.

Nicolaas, of Joachum and Elizabeth Staats. Wit.: Nicolaas and Elsje Schuyler.

Philip, of Jeems and Elizabeth Ryen. Wit.: William Tellar, Elizabeth Welkens.

Oct. 16. Mary, of John and Hopie De Levil. Wit.: Jacob and Catharina Groesbeek.

Cornelis, of Gerrit W. and Alida Van den Bergh. Wit.: Corns. Van den Bergh, Marytje Gerritse.

Willem, of Jacob and Zara Groesbeek. Wit.: David Groesbeek, Cathalina Van Es.

Johannes, of Isaac and Maria Hanse. Wit.: Johannes and Zara Hanse.

Marritje, of Pieter and Geertruy Doxsie. Wit.: David Schuyler, Jannetje De Vous.

1743-1744

Johannes, of Jan and Catharina Brad. Wit.: Pieter and Geertruy Fonda.

Oct. 23. Johannes, of Hendrik and Suzanna Meyer. Wit.: Hendrik and Fryna Springer.

Elizabeth, of Coenraad and Elizabeth Richtmeyer. Wit.: Lodewyk Richtmeyer, Antje Vlydt.

Jannetje, of Jacob and Elizabeth Glen. Wit.: Johannes Cuyler, Elsje Rozenboom.

Zara, of Matthys and Rebecca De Garamo. Wit.: Johannes Bekker, Lena Van Aarnhem.

Oct. 30. Rutger, of Jacob R. and Annaatje Van Woerd. Wit.: Pieter Van Woerd, Fydtje Ouderkerk.

Nov. 6. Johannes, of Hendrik and Aaltje Van Buren. Wit.: Johannes and Yda Van Buren.

Jannetje, of Reyer and Marytje Sprinksteen. Wit.: Tobias Rykman, Marytje Schermerhoorn.

Obedya, of Thomas and Elizabeth Couper. Wit.: Obedia and Corna. Couper.

Abraham, of David and Maria Groesbeek. Wit.: Hendrik and Johanna Van Es.

Nov. 27. Johannis, of Gerrit and Maria Van Vranken. Wit.: Daniel and Annaatje Fort.

Zara, of Johannes and Alida Van Schaik. Wit.: Jacob Bogaart, Hendrikje Schuyler.

Dec. 4. Marytje, of Thomas and Hester Marl. Wit.: Petrus, Jr., and Marytje Bogardus.

Abraham, of Jacob C. and Catharina Ten Eyk. Wit.: Hendrik Cuyler, Margrieta Ten Broek.

Dec. 7. Geertruy, Anna, of Hermanus, Jr., and Catharina Wendel. Wit.: Abram Witbeek, Geertruy Van Vegten, Abraham Wendel, Catharina Cuyler.

Dec. 11. Ariaantje, of Johannes and Neeltje Vinnagel. Wit.: Andries Van den Bergh, Catharina Van der Poel.

Dec. 14. Cathalina, of Abraham and Rebecca Foreest. Wit.: Hendrik, Jr., and Anna Van Es.

1743/4, Jan. 1. Hendrik, of Johannes and Maria Geertruyd Boom. Wit.: Cornelis and Rachel Van den Bergh.

Jan. 8. Jannetje, of Hendrik and Elizabeth Van Slyk. Wit.: Gerrit F. and Anna Van Slyk.

Cornelia, of Obedia and Maria Couper. Wit.: Thomas and Cornelia Couper.

Jan. 11. Marytje, of Hendrik and Annaatje Lisjer. Wit.: Hendrik Bovie, Catharina Huyk.

Jan. 18. Abraham, of Abraham and Elbertje Fonda. Wit.: Theunis and Marytje Viele.

Thomas, of Richart and Martha Olivert. Wit.: George Lubkens, Marg. Olivert.

Sjeems, of Sjeems and Annaatje Wells. Wit.: Barent and Catharina Lewis.

1744

Jan. 22. Elizabeth, of Jacob and Frena Moogh. Wit.: Pieter and Christina Brad.

Gerrit, of Johannes Casper and Elizabeth Caspar. Wit.: Johannes and Maria Zeger.

Jan. 25. Gerrit Theunisse, of Hendrik and Wyntje Bries. Wit.: Gerrit Theunisse Van Vegten, Catharina Brad.

Catharina, of Abraham B. and Ariaantje Van Valkenburgh. Wit.: Jacob Vosburgh, Ariaantje Van Buren.

Zara, of Gerrit and Antje Van Zanten. Wit.: David and Anna Van Zanten.

Rykert, of Theunis and Dorethea Hooghteling. Wit.: Rykert and Tryntje Van den Berk.

Jan. 29. Ariaantje, of Wilhelmus and Anna Rykman. Wit.: Harmen B. Visjer, Ariaantje Van Yveren.

Feb. 12. John, of John and Maria Courtnie. Wit.: Benjamin Brad, Neeltje Bennewe.

Lena, of Johannes and Corna. Flensburgh. Wit.: Willem and Lena Hooghtelingh.

Theunis, of Theunis and Magtel Vischjer. Wit.: Johannes De Garamo, Anna Vischjer.

Cathalina, of Johannes and Rebecca Jaets. Wit.: Jacob and Cathalina Groesbeek.

Feb. 26. Johannes, of Frederik and Engeltje Ruyter. Wit.: Johannes Van der Werken, Engeltje Van der Kar.

Maria, of Jacobus and Catharina Radelief. Wit.: Matthys and Ariaantje Bovie.

Hilletje, of Albert and Antje Van der Zee. Wit.: Hendrik and Ariaantje Van Wie.

Annaatje, of Jacobus and Judith Hilten. Wit.: Pieter and Jenneth Maarten.

Maria, of Gerrit and Anna Ridder. Wit.: Symen and Hilletje Ridder.

Isaac, of Jan and Elizabeth Van Aarnem. Wit.: Isaac Jac. and Hubertje Lansing.

March 4. Jacobus, of Geurt and Anna Van Schoonhoven. Wit.: Dirk Brat Van Schoonoven, Maria Fonda.

Antje, of Anthony and Maria Van der Zee. Wit.: Corns. and Rachel Van den Bergh.

March 11. Gerrit, of Johannes and Anna Knoet. Wit.: Andries Van Vranken, Elsje Pruyn.

Eva, of Jacob and Hendrikje Van Woerd. Wit.: Lodewyk and Hiltje Schredel.

Cathalyntje, of Philip and Geertruy Hansse. Wit.: Corns. and Suzanneke Van Es.

1744, March 18. Johannes, of Johannes and Zara Beekman. Wit.: Johannes A. Cuyler, Maria Hogan.

March 23. Abraham, of Robbert and Catharina Wendel. Wit.: Abraham Wendel, Anna Van Es.

1744
Apr. 8. Elizabeth, of Abraham and Rebecca Dox.
Wit.: Volkert and Alida Van Hoezen.
Apr. 15. Bernardus, of Hendrik and Suzanna Halenbeek. Wit.: Bernardus Brad, Elizabeth Halenbeek.
Gerritje, of Jacobus and Catharina Van Valkenburgh.
Wit.: Abraham and Neeltje Van Valkenburg.
Catharina, of Coenraad and Catharina Hooghteling.
Wit.: Theunis Van der Volgen, Maria Hooghtelingh.
Isaac and Rebecca, of Douwe and Aaltje Fonda. Wit.:
Wouter and Elizabeth Knickerbakker, John Maarzen,
Maria Maartzen.
Margrietje, of Johannes L. and Eva Van Valckenburgh.
Wit.: Corns. and Catharina Ouderkerk.
Suzanna, of Myndert and Elizabeth Veder. Wit.:
Lucas Joh. Wyngaard, Annaatje Hun.
May 13. Nicolaas, of Pieter and Adriana Knoet. Wit.:
Gerrit and Maria Van Vranken.
Augustinus, of Jurriaan and Barbara Scherp. Wit.:
Isaac and Maria Van Aalsteyn.
Anna, of Frans and Neeltje Belville. Wit.: John and
Rachel Bel.
Margrieta, of Samuel and Magdalena Born. Wit.:
Bernardus and Catharina Harzen.
May 20. Gerardus, of Johannes and Christyna Van der
Werken. Wit.: Johannes and Hester Van Aarnem.
Margrieta, of Andries and Alida Logen. Wit.: Abraham Jac. and Catharina Lansing.
Andries, of Johannes and Catharina Huyk. Wit.:
Bernardus and Catharina Brad.
Samuel, of Hendrik and Maria Gardenier. Wit.:
Johannes and Engeltje Schermerhoorn.
Hermanus, of Abraham H. and Elizabeth Wendel.
Wit.: Evert Wendel, Jr., Catharina Cuyler.
May 27. Gozen, of Johannes A. and Elizabeth Quackenbosch. Wit.: Anthony G. and Cathalyntje Van Schaik.
Abraham, of Jonas and Elizabeth Oothoudt. Wit.:
Abraham Lansing, Jr., Lena Lansingh.
Volkert, of Johannes V. and Jannetje Douw. Wit.:
Volkert Douw, Dorethe Bogaart.
Elizabeth, of Isaac and Elizabeth Muller. Wit.: Jeremias Muller, Jr., Elizabeth Valk.
Pieter, of Philip and Zara Winne. Wit.: Pieter Winne,
Jannetje Switz.
June 3. Hendrik Van Nes, of Hendrik and Anna
Ridder. Wit.: Ephraim and Anna Wendel.
June 10. Geesje, of Cornelis and Maria Muller. Wit.:
Harmen and Geesje Van Hoesen.
Margrieta, of Gerardus and Maria Groesbeek. Wit.:
John and Catharina Livingston.

1744

Frederik, of Staat and Suzanna Zeger. Wit.: Adam and Lydia Brad.

June 17. Nicolaas, of Gerrit C. and Zara Van Nes. Wit.: Corns. Nic. Van den Bergh, Zantje Ridder.

Marten, of Abraham and Jannetje Vinnagel. Wit.: Johannes and Ida Van Buren.

Cathalyntje, of Jacob, Jr., and Marytje Bogaart. Wit.: Christoffel and Cathalyntje Jaats.

Christina, of Gerrit C. and Margrieta Van den Bergh. Wit.: Dirk Ten Broek, Zara Hanzen.

Obedia, of Jacobus and Zara Van Benthuysen. Wit.: Thomas and Cornelia Couper.

Nicolaas, of Willem and Catharina Groesbeek. Wit.: Pieter Groesbeek, Zara Van Nes.

June 24. Carel, of Claas and Magtel Bovie. Wit.: Jacob and Aaltje Barroway.

Hendrik, of Isaac and Gerritje Halenbeek. Wit.: Hendrik and Suzanna Halenbeek.

June 27. Marritje, of Jacob and Cathalyna Witbeek. Wit.: Melchert A. and Marritje Witbeek.

Cornelis, of Johannes W. and Margrieta Quackenbos. Wit.: Cornelis and Cornelia Bogaart.

July 1. Margrietje, of Roelof and Engeltje Kidnie. Wit.: Hendrik Van der Werken, Rebecca Kidnie.

Johannes, of Anthony D. and Christina Brad. Wit.: Bernardus and Catharina Brad.

July 6. Leendert, of Jacob and Zara Fort. Wit.: Hendrik Ganzevoort, Agnietje Lievense.

July 8. Mary, of John and Hillegont Leuwis. Wit.: William Teller, Maria Bradt.

Gerrit, of Frans and Agnietje Winne. Wit.: Pieter D. and Rachel Winne.

Johannes, of Johannes and Gerritje Van Wie. Wit.: Johannes and Zuzanna Wendel.

Maria, of Jan and Suzanna Brad. Wit.: Christiaan Lang, Baartje Langh.

Marten Cornelisse, of Jonathan and Magtel Witbeek. Wit.: Tobias Witbeek, Margrieta Wyngaart.

July 15. Nicolaas, of Dirck and Magdalena Van der Kar. Wit.: Gerrit and Ariaantje Bekker.

Wilhelmus, of Robbert and Cornelia Dunbar. Wit.: Jacob and Helena Wendel.

Gysbert, Catharina, of Wynand and Anna Van den Bergh. Wit.: Matthys and Cathalina Van den Bergh, Corn., Jr., and Catharina Van Aalsteyn.

July 18. Nicolaas, of Evert and Elsje Seskby. Wit.: Nicolaas Seskby, Maria Hogil.

July 22. Jacob, of Franciscus S. and Alida Pruyn. Wit.: Bernardus Harzen, Cathalina Winne.

1744
Aug. 5, bo. Aug. 1. Wilhelmus, of Cornelis Van Schie and Josyna Prys. Wit.: Phillip, Jr., and Catharina Livingston.

Obedia, of Abraham Jac. and Elizabeth Lansing. Wit.: Obedia and Cornelia Couper.

Hendrik, of Killiaan and Ariaantje Van Renzelaar. Wit.: Johannes Van Renzelaar, Anna Douw.

Rebecca, of Hendricus and Rebecca Spoor. Wit.: Pieter and Rebecca Bogaart.

Eduart, of William and Zara Groin. Wit.: Jacob Groin, Catarina Caddenton.

Oct. 19. Henrik, of Jacob Henr. Ten Eik and Anna Wendel. Wit.: Joh. and Margreta Ten Eik.

Gysbert, of Anthony Van Ieveren and Maria Van den Bergh. Wit.: Gysbert and Catlyna Van den Berg.

Dirk, of John Levingston and Catharina Ten Broek. Wit.: Johs. Van Renselaar, Sely Levingston.

Geertruyd, of Abrah. Witbeek and Anna Van Deusen. Wit.: Melchert Abrs. Witbeek, Catharina Wendel.

Catharina, of Johannes Bleiker and Eva Bries. Wit.: Henrik and Nelletje Bries.

Lydia, of Ephraim Van Veghte and Catharina Ten Broek. Wit.: Gerrit Teunisz Van Veghte, Lydia Van Veghte.

Obadia, of Thomas Cooper and Elisabet Van Duren. Wit.: Obadia and Cornelia Cooper.

Abraham, of Lucas Hooghkerk and Rebecca Fonda. Wit.: Abraham Fonda, Elisabet Knikkerbakker.

Maria, of Adam Yeats and Anna Gerritzen. Wit.: Adam Van den Bergh, Maria Bogaard.

Reinier, of Jacob Van Jeveren and Wyntje Van den Bergh. Wit.: Reinier and Sara Van Ieveren.

Maria, of Barent Staats and Maghdalena Schuyler. Wit.: Jeremie and Margreta Schuyler.

Alida, of Jan Oothout and Marritje Wendel. Wit.: Jacob and Henrikje Van Woert.

Elisabeth and Maria, twins, of Johannes Ouderkerk and Helena Fonda. Wit.: Johannes and Annatje Cloet, Pieter and Geertruyd Fonda.

Petrus, of Johannes Van den Bergh and Maria Van Nes. Wit.: Pieter and Ariaantje Van Woert.

Anthony, of Wessel Van Schayk and Maria Gerritzen. Wit.: Anthony Van Schayk, Maria Gerritzen.

Pieter, of Adam Bratt and Lydia Zegers. Wit.: Adriaan and Marytje Bratt.

Anna, of Harmen Ganzevoort and Magdalena Douw. Wit.: Petrus and Anna Douw.

Oct. 21. Lena, of Jan De Voe, Jr., and Fytje Van der Kar. Wit.: Dirk, Jr., and Engeltje Van der Kar.

1744-1745

Pieter, of Teunis Vile and Maria Fonda. Wit.: Pieter and Catharina Vile.

Suzanna Baker, of William Rodgers, Jr., and Mary White. Wit.: William Rodgers, Jane Walte.

Johannes and Eva, twins, of Thomas Turk and Eva Valkenburg. Wit.: Jaques and Margrietje Valkenburg, Isak and Gerritje Halenbeek.

Anna, of Zacharia Haas and Geesje Witbeek. Wit.: Anthony and Willempje Brat.

Elisabet, of Daniel Morall and Alida Doxat. Wit.: Jacob Doxat, Ann Flight.

Thomas, of John Williams and Cornelia Bogardus. Wit.: Thomas and Hilletje Williams.

Johannes, of Jacobus Van Alen and Lena Van Alstein. Wit.: Johannes Hun, Anna Hunn.

Albertus, of Henrik Blom and Elisabet Gardenier. Wit.: Jan and Barber Gardenier.

1744/5, Jan. 3. Benjamin, of Jacob Lansing, Jr., and Marretje Ebberts. Wit.: Benjamin Ebberts, Antje Fisher.

Jan. 4. Johanna, of Pieter Busie Marshal and Annatje Glensburgh. Wit.: Johannes Glensburgh, Catlyntje Yeats.

Willem, of Gerrit Van Alen and Catharina Van Wie. Wit.: Pieter Daniels Winne, Rachel Winne.

Elisabet, of Tobias Mackee and Sara Cas. Wit.: Coenraad and Elisabet Rechsmider.

Catharina, of Henrik Van den Berg and Catharina Hooghteeling. Wit.: Gerrit Van Zanten, Antje Van den Berg.

Barent, of Douwe Bogaard and Willempje Brat. Wit.: Barent Bratt, Elisabet Marcelis.

Jan. 4. Johannes, of Johannis Ratlif and Geertruyd Bratt. Wit.: Johannis Ratlif, Sr., Maria Ratliff.

Johannes, of Egbert Bratt and Elisabet Lansing. Wit.: Harmen and Annatje Bogardus.

Arent, of Jan Oliver and Antje Blom. Wit.: Cornelis and Elisabet Van den Bergh.

Alida, of Benjamin Goewey and Catharina Van den Bergh. Wit.: Henrik and Catlina Bulsem.

Magdalena, of Isaak Hanszen and Maria Bratt. Wit.: Benjamin and Magdalena Bratt.

Lucas, of Harmen Fisher and Sara Wyngaard. Wit.: Albert and Sara Rykman.

Mayke, of Henrik Lansing and Anna Ouderkerk. Wit.: Corn. Ouderkerk, Maria Cloet.

Mayke, of Isak Ouderkerk and Anna Cloet. Wit.: Walran and Francyntje Cloet.

Jan. 6. Tryntje, of Henrik Van Wie, Jr., and Catharina Waldron. Wit.: Dirk Bratt and Cornelia Waldron.

Debora, of Rykhart Hanssen and Catharina Ten Broek. Wit.: David Abrahamsz Schuyler, Aefje Beekman.

1745
Feb. 17. Rachel, of Volkert Petr. Douw and Annatie De Peister. Wit.: Meyndert and Annatie Schuyler.

Maria, of Roelof Devou and Elisabeth Goeldin. Wit.: Willem and Jantie Devou.

Maria, of Willem Van Buire and Theuntje Van den Berg. Wit.: Douwe and Alida Fonda.

Alida, of Abraham Isaacse Fonda and Maria Van Schoonhooven. Wit.: Isaac and Alida Fonda.

Tobias, of Hendrick Van Buire and Annatie Van Saltzberg. Wit.: Thomas and Elisabeth Koeper.

Isaac, of Cornelis Ouderkerk and Catharina Heuck. Wit.: Isaac Ouderkerk, Anneke Knoet.

Maria, of Andrees Van den Bergh and Marytie Pinhaarn. Wit.: Johannes and Johanna Finnagel.

Dirck, of Theunis Van Vegten and Cornelia Knickerbackker. Wit.: Benjamin Van Vegten, Catharina Wendel.

Elisabeth, of Jacob Wendel and Helena Van Rentzlaar. Wit.: Hendrick Van Rentzlaar, Elisabeth Richard.

Hilliye, of Pieter Williams and Sara Van Yvere. Wit.: Thomas and Hilleye Williams.

Piter, of William Hildon and Margarith Jones. Wit.: Peter Jones, Margarith Oliver.

Elisabeth, of Piter Walrom and Neeltie Lansing. Wit.: Willem and Elisabeth Walrom.

Annatie, of Jacob Eggemond and Maria Lewis. Wit.: Gerrit Landsing, Annatie Yaets.

Johannes, of Evert Zeeger and Sara Ochert. Wit.: Johannes and Bregye Zeeger.

Silvester, of Rentzlaar Nicles and Elisabeth Saltzberg. Wit.: William Saltzbergh, Theuntie Staats.

1745, Apr. 19. Maria, of Isak Van Aalstein and Maria Van den Berg. Wit.: Jurien Sharp, Barber Smit.

Johannes, of Lambert Cool and Marritje Kidney. Wit.: Johannes Kidney, Geertruyd Van der Werpe.

Jacobus Schuyler, of Henrik Henriks Rozeboom and Catlyntje Schuyler. Wit.: Dirk V. Schelluyne, Margrietje Lansing.

Catlina, of David Groesbeek and Maria Van der Poel. Wit.: Meindert Schuyler, Rachel Van Es.

Elisabet, of Johannes Meinderts, Jr., and Maria Oostrandt. Wit.: Johannes and Elisabet Oostrand.

Lucas, of Johannes Fisher and Anna Staats. Wit.: Lucas I. Wyngaart, Alida Fisher.

Rebecca, of Wouter Groesbeek and Jannetje Bogaard. Wit.: Pieter and Rebecca Bogaard.

Isaak, of Abraham V. Arnhem and Alida Lansing. Wit.: Pieter Schuyler, Alida Van Ieveren.

Apr. 21. Rykert, of Jan Bronk and Lydia Van den Bergh. Wit.: Jan and Maria Van den Bergh.

1745

Maas, of Adam Van Vranken and Ariaantje Cloet. Wit.: Maas and Annatje Van Vranken.

Anna, of Jacobus Schuyler and Geertruyd Staats. Wit.: Jochum Staats, Anna Schuyler.

Jannetje, of Wouter Groesbeek and Maria Bogardus. Wit.: Harmen and Jannetje Bogardus.

Geesje, of Volkert Van Hoesen and Alida Marcelis. Wit.: Reinier and Elsje Van Hoezen.

Gerrit, of Isaak Greveraart and Alida Gerritzen. Wit.: Johannis Gerritze, Maria Wendell.

Adriaan, of Adriaan Bratt and Celia Van Zanten. Wit.: Hans and Marytje Locks.

Susanna, of Henrick and Susanna Meyer. Wit.: Ludowick and Marya.

May 5. Christiaan, of David and Maritje Schants. Wit.: Christiaan and Catharina Schants.

Abraham, of Gerrit Johannis and Elsje Lansing. Wit.: Abraham and Magdalena Lansing.

Eva, of Johannis Van Vegten and Neeltje Beekman. Wit.: Johannes Beekman, Maria Hogen.

Claartje, of Gerardus Clut and Magtel Heemstraat. Wit.: Gerrit and Maritje Clut.

May 12. Elisabeth, of Johannis Vinhagen, Jr., and Neeltje Van den Berg. Wit.: Jakobus and Elisabeth Vinhagen.

Hendrik, of Cornelis Waldron and Jannetje Van Nes. Wit.: Ephraim Wendel and wife Anna.

Isaac, of Hendrik Funda and Chatharina Groesbeek. Wit.: Wouter Knikkebakker and wife Elisabeth.

Jakobus, of Thomas Valkenburg and Teuntje Berheit. Wit.: Corn. Joh. Muller and wife Teuntje.

Dirk, of Cornelis Cuyler and Cathalina Schuyler. Wit.: Hans Hansen, Cornelia Van Cortland, wid. of Joh. Schuyler.

Sep. 8. Goossen, of Johannis Jacobse Lansing and Cathalyna Van Schaick. Wit.: Anthony, Jr., and Debora Van Schaick.

Lena, of Barent Ten Eyck and Lena Ryckman. Wit.: Tobyas Ryckman, Magtel Roseboom.

Cornelis, of Harmanus Wendell, Jr., and Catharina Van Vegte. Wit.: Cornelis and Geertruy Van Vegte.

Cristina, Maragrieta, of Zacharias Sikkelson and Anna Wyngaert. Wit.: Luykas, Maragrieta, Gerrit, and Maragrieta Wyngaert.

Catharina, of Sybrant Van Schaik and Alida Roseboom. Wit.: Abraham Lansing, Sara Van Schaick.

Cornelis, of Michell Bessett and Elizabeth Schermerhorn. Wit.: Jan and Cathalyna Winne.

Cornelis, of Johannis V. Douw and Jannetje Bogardt. Wit.: Abraham Douw, Rachel Bogardt.

1745-1746

Alieda, of Hendrick Buusen and Cathalyna Goewyck. Wit.: Johannes and Alieda Goewyk.

Johannis, of William Bromly and Lena Boom. Wit.: Mattys and Catharina Boom.

Sep. 28. Zophia, of William Pieterson and Lena Van Eps. Wit.: Jacob Visher, Cathrina Van Eps.

Maria, of Johannis and Anna Slingerlandt. Wit.: Johannis De Peyster, Anna Douw.

Rebecca, of Gysbert Van Brakele and Maria Van Antwerpe. Wit.: Abraham and Rebecca De Foreest.

Catharina, of Johannes Van Wie and Gerretje Wendell. Wit.: Gerrit and Catharina Van Alen.

William, of Johannes Flensburg and Cornelia Hoogtelinck. Wit.: William Hoogtelink, Lena Hoogetelink.

Oct. 6. Johannis, of Johannis and Eytje Van Bueren. Wit.: Barent and Maretje Van Bueren.

Helena, of Robert and Maragrieta Lansing. Wit.: Lysbeth V. Schelluyne, Gerrit Johs. Lansingh.

Mattheus, of Alexander and Elizabeth Van Woert. Wit.: Cornelia and Rutger V. den Berg.

1745/6, Jan. 10. Catharina, of Fredrik Ruyter and Engeltje Van dr Werriken. Wit.: John Hog, Catharina Ruyter.

Margareta, of Roelof Van der Werriken, Jr., and Annatje Vosburg. Wit.: Albert, Jr., and Engeltje Van der Werriken.

Catharina, of Abrah. Cuyler, Jr., and Jannetje Beekman. Wit.: Henrik Cuyler, Jr., Margareta Ten Broek.

Margareta, of Gerhardus Groesbeek and Maria Ten Broek. Wit.: John Livingston, Sara Ten Broek.

Henrik, of Roelof Van der Werken and Geertruyd Fonda. Wit.: Joh. and Geertruyd Kidney.

Maria, of Gerrit Luc. Wyngaard and Christina Van Woert. Wit.: Lucas Jac. and Christina Wyngaard.

Catharina, of Nicolaas Cuyler and Maria Schuyler. Wit.: Henrik Cuyler, Margareta Ten Broek.

Susanna, of Nicolaas Cuyler and Maria Schuyler. Wit.: Jeremie and Susanna Schuyler.

Marten, of Henrik Beekman and Anna Swits. Wit.: Cornelis and Susanneke Van Es.

Jacob, of Abrah. Jac. Lansing and Elisabet Cooper. Wit.: Jacob and Lena Lansing.

Volkert, of Gerrit Teunis V. Veghten and Lena Witbeek. Wit.: Joh. Van Veghte, Margareta Van den Berge.

Catharina, of Isak Swits and Maria Vroman. Wit.: Henricus and Anna Beekman.

Jacob, of Johannes Abr. Cuyler and Catharina Wendell. Wit.: Abraham Cuyler, Jr., Jannetje Beekman.

Sanneke, of Abraham Harm. and Elisabet Wendell. Wit.: Evert Hs. and Geesje Wendell.

1746-1745

Abraham, of Cornelis V. Alstein and Catharina Wendel.
Wit.: Wynand and Annatje Van den Bergh.
Pieter Waldron, of Johannes Thomasz Witbeek and Eva
Waldron. Wit.: Cornelis and Engeltje Waldron.
Pieter, of Jacob Bogaard, Jr., and Maria Yeats. Wit.:
Pieter Prs., Jr., and Rebecca Bogaart.
Maria, of Henrik Gerritz and Dirkje Tymes. Wit.:
Isak and Alida Greverard.
Maria, of Matthys Van dr Heiden and Margareta Bratt.
Wit.: Killiaan Muller, Egbertje Van der Heiden.
Jan. 12. Jacobus, of Johannes Mol and Rebecca Bar-
heit. Wit.: Jacob and Margrietje Muller.
Jannetje, of Barent Luwis and Catharina Van Slyk.
Wit.: Richard and Anna Cartwright.
Maria, of James Wales and Annatje Broom. Wit.:
Petrus, Jr., and Catharina Bogardus.
Ytje, of William Groom and Sarah Coddington. Wit.:
Dirk and Margreta Hun.
Joseph, of David Van Zanten and Rachel Hooghteel-
ing. Wit.: Joseph Van Zanten, Annetje Redley.
Jannetje, of Johannes Goest and Geertruyd Van Buren.
Wit.: Mattheus and Jannetje Goest.
Jannetje, of Thomas Cooper and Elisabet Van Buren.
Wit.: Henrik P. and Geertruyd V. Buren.
Elsje, of Coenraad Rechtmayer and Elisabet Houst.
Wit.: Coenraad and Elsje Ricker.
Pieter, of Obadiah Cooper and Maria Fonda. Wit.:
Pieter and Catlina Fonda.
Anna, Isaak, of Benjamin Bogaard and Anna Halen-
beek. Wit.: Pieter and Rebecca Bogaard, Wouter
Vroman, Maria Halenbeek.
Jannetje, of Willem Van Slyk and Catharina Van Schaik.
Wit.: Jacob Van Schaik, Annatje Bekkers.
Harpert, of Melchert Van Deuzen and Neeltje Quakken-
bosch. Wit.: Rutger Lansing, Cornelia Van den Bergh.
Maria, of Benjamin Van den Bergh and Annatje Vinnagel.
Wit.: Gerrit Van den Bergh, Jannetje Goewey.
Pieter, of Hugo Vile and Catharina Van Woert. Wit.:
Johan Lodewyk Schrattel, Catharina Van Woert.
Levinus, of Abrah. Jacobs Lansing and Catharina
Lievens. Wit.: Franciscus and Marretje Lansing.
Johannes, of Abraham Vile and Francina Fort. Wit.
Jacob and Eva Vile.
Cornelia, of Johannes Yeats and Rebecca Waldron.
Wit.: Dirk and Cornelia Bratt.
Anna, of Gerrit Lansing, Jr., and Annatje Yeats. Wit.:
Christoffel and Catlena Yeats.
1745 [sic], July 5. Levinus, of Benjamin Winne and
Rachel V. Aarnheim. Wit.: Piter Winne, Marytje
Gerritse.

1745-1746

Rachel, of Volkert Van d. Bergh and Catharina Huyck. Wit.: Corn. and Catharina Ouderkerk.

Rutger, of John Ruths Bleeker and Elizabeth Staats. Wit.: Rutger and Catlyna Bleeker.

Gysbert, of Willem Van d. Bergh and Susanna Van Yeveren. Wit.: Corn. and Marytje Van den Bergh.

July 7. Henrik, of Isaac Haalenbeek and Gerritje Van Woerden. Wit.: Henr. and Susanna Halenbeeck.

Geurt, of Jacobus Bennewe and Elsje Marten. Wit.: Geurt V. Schoonhoven, Maria Fonda.

Diana Malli, negress of Elsje Roseboom. Wit.: Abraham, serv. of Mayke Hun, Marie, negress of J. Schuyler.

Casparus, of Simon Sprincksteen and Maria Zeeger. Wit.: Staats Zeegers, Susanna Brats.

Isaac, of Johan Duret and Annatje De Vous. Wit.: Pr. Fonda, Maria Barrewe.

Johannes, of Gr. Teun. V. Slyk and Annatje Turk. Wit.: Henry Janz. V. Wyen, Ariaantje V. Wyen.

Saar, of Diana, negress of Hesth. Van Schelluynen. Wit.: Isack Joh. Rozeboom, Beth, negress of Isaac Kip.

Aug. 25. Jacob, of Niclaas Kroesbeek and Angenitje Wandelaar. Wit.: Jacob Kroesbeek, Catlyntje Yaets.

Abraham, of Jacob Viele and Eva Fort. Wit.: Abraham Fort, Anna Barb. Knoet.

Isaac, of Piter Doxe and Geertruid D. Vou. Wit.: Daniel Morrel, Alida Doxe.

John Piter, of Hendrik Loux and Anna Elis. Coen. Wit.: Hannes and Anna Barb. Boom.

Isaac, of John V. Aarnheim and Elisabeth Landzing. Wit.: Isaac and Huibertje Landzing.

Margaritha, of Benjamin V. Vegten and Annatje Bgardus. Wit.: Gerrit V. den Berg, Margaritha V. Vegte.

Elisabeth, of Jacobus V. Valkenburg and Margarith Redlef. Wit.: Jacobus and Catharina Redlef.

Piter, of Daniel Piter Winne and Jantje D. Vreest. Wit.: Piter Danielse Winne, Rachel Winne.

Jurrian, of Willem Hogin, Jr., and Susanna Landzing. Wit.: Johannes and Annatje Hogin.

Anthony, of Sybrand V. Schaick, Jr., and Annatie Roseboom. Wit.: Wessel V. Schaick, Margaretha Bleeker.

Catharina, of Phil. Livingston, Jr., and Christyna Ten Broek. Wit.: John and Catharina Livingston.

1745/6 [sic], Feb. 16. Robbert, of Jacobus Hilden and Judy Marten. Wit.: Robbert Merrit, Elisabeth Daniels.

Cornelia, of Johannes Huick and Catharina Bovi. Wit.: Peter V. Slyck, Racheltje Redly.

Neeltje, of Samel and Neeltje Staats. Wit.: Barent and Neeltje Staats.

1746

Anna, of Jacob Bleeker and Margarith T. Eyk. Wit.: Hendrick T. Eyck, Anna Bleekers.

Anna, of Franciskus Landzing and Markje Liverse. Wit.: John and Elis. V. Aarnheim.

Margarithje, of Philip Hansen and Geertruid V. Ess. Wit.: Hans Hansen Jumd [?], Elsie Mombroed.

Magdalena, of Isaac Hansen and Maria Bratt. Wit.: Benjamin and Magdalena Bratt.

Matheus, of Hannes V. Deuse and Marytje Winne. Wit.: Arent and Geertruid V. Deuse.

Johannes, of Jacob Quackenbosch and Catharina Huick. Wit.: Geerardus Quackenbosch, Cornelia Vreest.

1746, Apr. 25. Maria, of Jonathan Widbeeck, Jr., and Magdel. Wyngaard. Wit.: Gerrit Luk. Wyngaard, Christintje V. Woerd.

Marte, of Marte Cornl. V. Buire and Lena Hus. Wit.: Hannes and Heitye Van Buire.

Catharina, of Jacob C. Ten Eyck and Catharina Cuiler. Wit.: Anthony and Gerritye T. Eyk.

Jacomyntie, of Sam. Born and Lena Bruin. Wit.: Hendrick and Annatye Gerritse.

Annatye, of Egbert Egberson and Malli Lents. Wit.: Jacob Landsing, Markie Egberson.

Marytye, of Johannis V. der Werken and Christina Bruin. Wit.: Theunis V. Woerd, Catharina Vosburgh.

Annatye, of Benjamin Goe and Catharina Van d. Berg. Wit.: Gerrit Wils V. d. Berg, Alida V. d. Bergh.

Apr. 27. Jesse, of Lavynus Winne and Susanna Wendel. Wit.: Jesse and Sara Winne.

Barbara, of Gerrit Van Vranke and Maria Fort. Wit.: Rykert Van Franke, Maria Bradt.

Margaritha, of Jacob Harse and Maria Bruin. Wit.: Jan Van Aarnheim, Elisabeth Landsing.

Lena, of Jacob Rutsche Van Woerd and Annatje Ouderkerk. Wit.: Hannes Ouderkerk, Catharina V. Woerd.

Jacob, of Reyer Sprinckstien and Maria Torner. Wit.: Hendrik Mynds. Roseboom, Maria Zeeger.

Christyntje, of Jacobus Valkenburg and Catharina Durik. Wit.: Hendrikus and Annatje Beekman.

Niclaas, of Henderik Gardenier and Eva V. Valckenburg. Wit.: Abram and Neeljie V. Valckenburg.

May 25. Harmanus, of Cornelis Muller and Maria Van Hoesen. Wit.: Hendrick Van Hoesen, Cathlyntje V. d. Berg.

Myndert, of Jacob Van Woerd and Hendrickje Oothoud. Wit.: Myndert Muselis, Rebecca Dox.

Rachel, of Gysbert Van Aalstyn and Annatje Gardenier. Wit.: Gerhardus Kroesbeek, Rachel Quack.

1746

Johannes, of Harme Knickkerbackker and Rebecca Wandelaar. Wit.: Johannes and Cornelia Knickkerbackker.

July 26. Maria, of Henderick Bloem and Elisabeth Cornier. Wit.: Casper and Anatje Ham.

Eldert, of Bastiaan and Majeke Thymonsen.

Geertruy, of Jacobus and Sara Chroesbeek.

Cornelia, of Pieter, Jr., and Geertruy Schuyler.

Pieter, of Wouter and Jannetje Chroesbeek.

Willem, of Johannes and Maria Van den Berg. Wit.: Gerrit and Anna Ridder.

Levinus, of Levinus and Catharina Liverson.

Maria, of Wessel and Maria Van Schaick. Wit.: Corn. Van Bergen, Eliz. Van Schaick.

Johannes, of Joh. Johannissen Lansing and Ariaantje Lansing. Wit.: Joh. and Geertruy Lansing.

Anatje, of Jacob and Mareytje Lansing. Wit.: Benjamin and Anatje Ecberts.

Harmen, of Reynier and Cornelia Van Hoesen. Wit.: Folkerd Van Bergen, Elsje Van Hoesen.

Maria, of Pieter and Elizabeth Lansing. Wit.: Johan Lansing, Margarita Schuyler.

Willem, of Willem and Catharina Chroesbeek. Wit.: Hend. Van Nes, Eliz. Chroesbeek.

Barent, of Barent and Cornelia Van Iveren. Wit.: Joh. and Engeltje Van Renselaar.

Maria, of Henderick Meynert Roseboom and Maria Roseboom. Wit.: Joh. M. Roseboom, Alida Van Schaick.

Elizabeth, of Pieter and Ariaantje Knoet. Wit.: Jesse and Neeltje D. Freest.

Aug. 3. Maria, of Adam Brat and Lydia Zeeger. Wit.: David Brat, Anatje Zeeger.

Gerrit, of Gerrit Jacobsen Lansing and Elizabeth Van Schaick. Wit.: Abram and Alida Van Arnem.

Henderickje, of Jan Van Buren and Angenietje Conyn. Wit.: Willem and Teuntje Van Buren.

Aug. 10. Geesjen, of Henderick Van Hoezen and Catalyntje Van den Berg. Wit.: Ecbert and Elsjen Van Hoesen.

Abram, of Isaac and Anatje Van der Poel. Wit.: Hannes and Anatje Van der Poel.

Anna, of Hannes Casper Gibhart and Elizabeth Zeger. Wit.: Staats Zeger, Susanna Brat.

Aug 17. Elizabeth, of Henderick Springer and Frena Keyzer. Wit.: Henderick and Sussanna Meyer.

Matthew, of Matthew Schot and Mary Hue. Wit.: Adam Winne, Mareytje Schermerhorn.

Pieter, of Hannes Quackenbosch and Racher Gardenier. Wit.: Abram and Neeltje Valkenburg.

1746
Cilliaan, of Cornelius Van den Berg and Rachel Ridder.
Wit.: Adam and Anatje Jeets.
Jeremie, of Reydert Hansen and Catharina Ten Broeck.
Wit.: Hannes Van Renselaar, Engeltje Renselaar.
Aug. 24. Teunis, of Arent Slingerland and Jacameyntje
Van der Volgen. Wit.: Teunis Slingerland, Engeltje
Van Deusen.
Johannes, of Dirck and Mareytje Bratt. Wit.: Andries
and Mareytje Bratt.
Teunis, of Storm Van der Zee and Elizabeth Slingerland.
Wit.: Antony and Anatje Van der Zee.
Dirkje, of Harmen and Sara Fischer. Wit.: Corns.
Tymonsen, Maretje Van Vrancken.
Aug. 31. Anna, of William Burch and Mareytje
Christiaansen. Wit.: Andries and Dirckje Van Vliet.
Nicholaas, of Jacob Vrooman and Rachel Van Woert.
Wit.: Nicholaas and Dirckje Van Woert.
Nov. 16. Christina, of Pieter Van Alen and Anatje
Van Benthuizen. Wit.: Hannes Van Vegten, Alida
Holland.
Maria, of Gerrit Van Vrancken and Susanna Ebbers.
Wit.: Jacob and Maritie Ebberse.
Elisabeth, of Lucas Witbeek and Geertruy Lansen
Wit.: Gerret and Neeltie Lansen.
Yennet, of Livingston's Pomp and Mrs. Hunner's Sara.
Wit.: Lanscin's Henry, Mr. Kep's Elisabeth.
Johannes, of Wouter Knikkabakker and Elisabeth
Fonda. Wit.: Harmen and Neeltie Knikkaback.
Susanna, of Barent Staats and Magdalena Schuyler.
Wit.: Abram Staats, Susanna Schuyler.
Jannetie, of Ryker Van Vranken and Annatie Trueax.
Wit.: Cornelius Van Slyk, Saertie Trueax.
Jan, of Jan Brat and Catrina Fonda. Wit.: Abrah.
and Geertruy Fonda.
Albert, of Hendrik Bries and Wyntie Van Vegten.
Wit.: Gysbert Roseboom, Maragrita Abeel.
Magdalena, of Abraham and Cathrina Lansen. Wit.:
Gerret Lansen, Elisabet Oothout.
Cornelius, of Johannes Douw and Jannetie Bogert. Wit.:
Cornelius Bogert, Maragrita Douw.
Elisabeth, of Derrik Van der Heiden and Elisabet
Wendel. Wit.: Jacob and Catharina Wendel.
Nov. 23. Johannes, of Andries Van Wie and Lena Van
Aarnoms. Wit.: Henderick Van Wie, Hesje Van Aarnoms.
Pieter, of Hendrick Jong and Catrina Landman. Wit.:
Pieter Hogel, Catrina Vos.
Nov. 30. Susanna, of Hendericus Brat and Rebecca
Van Vegten. Wit.: Bernardus Brat, Jr., Susanna Halen-
beek.

1746-1747

Dec. 7. Maria, of Jurrian Hoes and Cornelia Van Buren. Wit.: Pieter and Maretje Van Buren.

Dec. 14. Meynert Schuyler[?] [or Pets Douw?] of Folkert Pet. Douw and Anna De Peyster. Wit.: Pets Douw [or Mynert Schuyler ?], Rachel Schuyler.

Jacob, of Isaac Lansing and Anatje Van Woerdt. Wit.: Abram and Alida Van Arnham.

Johannes, of Teunis and Magtle Fisscher. Wit.: Samuel Cregier, Neeltje Waldron.

Meyndert, of Meyndert Feder and Elizabeth Douw. Wit.: Joh. Folk. and Jan. Douw.

Dec. 21. Lena, of Henderick Van den Berg and Catharina Hoogteeling. Wit.: W. and Lena Hoogteeling.

Burger, of Johannes Huyck and Engeltje Van Hoezen. Wit.: Burger and Rachel Huyck.

Elizabeth, of Andries Huyck and Maretje Van Deuzen. Wit.: Lamberth Redley, Mareg. Cuyler.

Jacobus, of Abram Izack Funda and Maria Van Schoonhoven. Wit.: Geurt and Anatje V. Schoonhoven.

Dec. 25. Pieter, of Jan Bratt and Saintje Zeger. Wit.: Pieter Bratt, Christina Bouwman.

1747, Jan. 11. Hendrick, of Hendrik Van Weed and Catharina Waldren. Wit.: Corns. Waldren, Angenietie Van Es.

Pieter, of Adam Van Alen, Jr., and Anatje Vosburg. Wit.: Joh. Ger. and Elsje Rozeboom.

Jannetje, of Gerrit I. Lansing and Ariaantje Beekman. Wit.: Teunis Fisscher, Elsje Hun.

Jan. 18. Pieter, of Jan Bronck and Lydia Van den Berg. Wit.: Pieter Bronck, Hillitje Willems.

Rebecca, of Antony A. Bratt and Wyntje Bogardus. Wit.: Antony and Rebecca Bratt.

Jan. 19. Elizabeth, of Robbert Berret and Maria Masten. Wit.: Johannes Schever, Elizabeth Danielson.

Maria, of Adam Jets and Anatje Gerritsen. Wit.: Jacob Bogert, Maria Boogert.

Feb. 1. Johannes, of Henderick and Susanna Meyer. Wit.: Hendrick and Frena Springer.

Ariaantje, of Hendrick Van Buuren and Aaltje Winne. Wit.: Jan and Catalyntje Winne.

James, of Johannes Renselaar and Engeltje Livingston. Wit.: Phillip and Maragrieta Schuyler.

Feb. 8. Maria, of Jacobus Clement and Jannetie Van Woert. Wit.: Josep and Antie Clement.

Feb. 15. Catharina, of Hendrick Van Renselaar and Elizabeth Van Brug. Wit.: Petrus and Anna Douw.

Daniel, of Pieter Marchal and Anatje Vlensburg. Wit.: Johannes and Margrietje Vlensburgh.

1747

Feb. 22. Maria, of Henderik Hoogtieling and Hester Bricker. Wit.: Joh. S. Bratt, Marytje Hoogteeling.

Engeltje, of Arent Van Deusen and Cathareyntje Waldron. Wit.: Jan and Engeltje Van Deusen.

Anatje, of Pieter Van Buuren and Mareytje Van der Poel. Wit.: Abram and Antje Van der Poel.

Lena, of Coenraad Hoogteeling and Cornelia Bratt. Wit.: Willem and Lena Hoogteeling.

March 1. Janetje, of Andries Van Slyk and Maria Benthuyzen. Wit.: Jacobus and Sara V. Benthuysen.

March 15. John, of Richard and Mary Shuckburgh. Wit.: Henry Holland, Mary Butler.

Marten, of Robert Wendel and Catarina Winne. Wit.: Marten and Sara Winne.

March 29. Thomas, of Thomas Wilkenson and Elizabeth Codman. Wit.: Jacobus and Judith Hilton.

Hendrick, of Andries Van Woerdt and Elizabeth Van der Werken. Wit.: Hendrick V. dr. Werken, Elizabeth Wendel.

Harmanus, of Jacob H. Ten Eyk and Anatje Wendel. Wit.: Evert, Jr., and Helena Wendel.

Jacob, of Antony Van Iveren and Maria Van den Berg. Wit.: Meyndert V. Iveren, Wyntje Van Iveren.

Hendericus, of Johannes Van Vegten, decd., and Neeltje Beekman. Wit.: Hendericus Beekman, Johanna Muzzelius.

Apr. 11. Wouter, of Antony Van der Zee and Anatje Van Nes. Wit.: Gerrit Van Nes, Catarina Chroesbeek.

Geertruy, of John Dunnevan and Hope Hunt. Wit.: Geurt and Anna Schoonhoven.

Apr. 18. Eytje, of Antony D. Bratt and Christina Lagranzie. Wit.: Hendrik Halenbeek, Elizabeth Hellen.

June 7. Catarina, of Johannes Kidnie and Geertruy Van der Werken. Wit.: Roelof and Catrina Van der Werken.

Martha, of Richard and Martha Oliver. Wit.: Robbert and Maregrieta Grannel.

David, of Philip, Jr., and Maria Freest. Wit.: David and Abigal Freest.

Christopher, of Abram Jeets and Antje Ridder. Wit.: Christophel and Catalina Jeets.

Philip, of Ciljan Renselaar and Ariaantje Schuyler. Wit.: Nicholaas and Maria Schuyler.

June 8. Henderick, of John Raily and Lena Barber. Wit.: John Barber, Rachel Levisse.

June 14. Hue, of Cornelius Mecmannus and Rebecca Northun. Wit.: John and Nel. Darby.

Wouter, of Johannis Mob and Rebecca Borhead. Wit.: Abram and Mareytje Funda.

1747

Elsje, of Thomas Smith and Maria Berret. Wit.: Robbert Berret, Barentje Tebbits.

June 21. Antony, of Zeybrand Van Schaick, Jr., and Anatje Roseboom Wit.: Joh. and Elsje Roseboom.

Jacob, of Timothy Towhay and Elizabeth Jones. Wit.: Antony Bratt, Willemtje Brat.

Joseph, of Gerrit Van Zanten and Antje Van den Berg. Wit.: Joseph and Anna Van Zanten.

Cornelius, of Andries Huyck and Gerritje Valkenburg. Wit.: Reyer and Mareytje Schermerhoorn.

June 28. Sara, of Jacobus Hilton and Judie Marten. Wit.: Joseph and Anna V. Santen.

July 12. Andries, of Hue Wilson and Anna Townsley. Wit.: Folkerd and Catrina Van den Berg.

Wyntje, of Johannes Ludloff, Jr., and Geertruy Bratt. Wit.: Jan and Hilletje Bratt.

Johannes, of Lucas Hoogkerk and Rebecca Funda. Wit.: Hendrick and Maria Funda.

John, of Richard Cartwright and Anna Beesley. Wit.: John and Liddy Beesly.

July 19. Elizabeth, of Willem V. Buren and Teuntje V. den Bergh. Wit.: Petrus and Marritje V. den Bergh.

Rachel, Anna, of Franciscus and Maritje Lansing. Wit.: Cornelis and Rachel Lewisson, Jan and Lysbeth Van Arnhem.

July 26. Jacob, of Jacob Blyker and Margrieta Ten Eyck. Wit.: Hendrick Ten Eyk, Antje Blyker.

Aug. 2. Jannitje, of Albert Van der Zee and Antje Van Wie. Wit.: Harmen and Elsje Hun.

Levinus, of Abram J. Lansing and Catarina Livenson. Wit.: Willem and Mareytje Livenson.

Aug. 9. Anna, Mary, of John and Catharina Bryand. Wit.: Howel Wiljams, Nelly Ferrel, Thomas Powl.

John, of John Hinde and Annatje Thomas. Wit.: Daniel Obreyn, Mary Doole.

Mary, Jane, of Hue Dillon and Judith Dunagoe. Wit.: Thomas Fall, David Harp, Jane Fitsmorris.

Jacob, of Johannes Schefer and Elisabet Danels. Wit.: Jacob and Doritie Sheefer.

John, of William Rodgers and Mary Wite. Wit.: Dirick Brat Van Schoonover, Rachel Liverson.

Aug. 16. Elizabeth, of Jacobus Radloff and Catharina Bovie. Wit.: Joseph and Margarietha Radloff.

Anna, of Thomas Wiljams and Maria Van Hoezen. Wit.: Hendrick Wiljams, Jennickje Van Hoezen.

Aug. 23. Catarina, of Roeloff Du Voe and Elizabeth Golden. Wit.: Pieter Hogg, Catharina Du Voe.

Maria, of Abram Van Vrancken and Dirkje Criegier. Wit.: Samuel and Anatje Criegier.

Catharina, of Zacharias Haas and Geesje Witbeek.
Wit.: Danel and Alida Marrh.

Pieter Waldron, of Johannes Jeets and Rebecca Waldron.
Wit.: Willem and Elizabeth Waldron.

Maria, of Robbert Sanders and Elizabeth Schuyler.
Wit.: Barent Sanders, Catharina Schuyler.

Aug. 30. Geertruy, of Harmanus Wendel and Catarina
V. Vegten. Wit.: Evert Wendel, Engeltje V. Vegten.

Oct. 25. Catalina, of Abram Witbeek and Anna Van
Deuzen. Wit.: Jacob and Maritje Witbeek.

Marthen, of Adam Winne Gardenier and Jannitje
Gardenier. Wit.: Gerardus and Mareytje Chroesbeek.

Rebecca, of Pieter and Sarah D. Germo. Wit.: Matheus
and Rebecca D. Germo.

Lena, of Benjamin Winne and Rachel Van Arnhem.
Wit.: Johannes Becker, Jr., Cornelia Van Hoezen.

Mareytje, of Gysbert Van Zanten and Margarieta Carn.
Wit.: David Van Zanten, Mareytje Fleysburg.

Hester of Nicholaas Fisscher and Annatje Tymissen.
Wit.: Cornelis and Mareytje Tymissen.

Elizabeth, of Hendrick Funda and Catrina Chroesbeek.
Wit.: Wouter Chroesbeek, Neeltje Brat.

Benjamin, of Isaac Hansen and Mareytje Brat. Wit.:
Benjamin and Magdalena Brat.

Elsje, of Joachim Staats and Elizabeth Schuyler. Wit.:
Ciljan and Ariaantje Renselaar.

Frederick, of Johannes Meynerson and Maria Oostrander.
Wit.: Abram Meynertsen, Maria D. Wandelaar.

Gerrit, of Abram J. Lansing and Elizabeth Coeper.
Wit.: Gerrit J. Lansing, Jannitje Waters.

Catarina, of Harmen Gansevoort and Magdalena Douw.
Wit.: Johanes Gansevoort, Catrina Douw.

Johannes, of Andries Van Wie and Lena Arnhem.
Wit.: Johannes and Netje[?] Van Arnhem.

Jacob, of Edward Hogil and Mareytje Egmond. Wit.:
Jacob Egmond, Maria Lewis.

Fransis, of Pieter Hogil and Catrina Vosburgh. Wit.:
Pieter and Geertruy Schuyler.

Nov. 1. Margarieta, of Barent Van Buuren and Cataleyntje Schermerhoorn. Wit.: Abram and Jannitje
Vinnagel.

Bernardus, of Johannes Evertsen and Susannah Lagransie. Wit.: Corn. Van den Bergh, Ariaantje Bratt.

Johannes, of Frans Winne and Angenietje Van Wie.
Wit.: Jan and Catalyntje Winne.

Tanneke, of Hendrick Van Buuren and Annatje Salberge.
Wit.: Gerrit Isaac and Arriaantje Lansing.

Antony, of Hendrick Ten Broeck and Annatje Van
Schaick. Wit.: Antony and Mareytje Van Schaick.

1747

Nov. 8. Mary, of Robert and Margret Miller. Wit.: George and Ann Brown.

Mareytje, of Antonie Bovie and Catarina Van der Werken. Wit.: Jacob Barway, Catrina Bovie.

Hendrick, of Barent Hendrickze Ten Eyk and Lena Rykman. Wit.: Henderick and Margrietje Ten Eyk.

Nov. 22. Susanna, of Tobias and Maria Noordman. Wit.: Jacobus Van Colesh [?], Catrina V. B. Zanders.

Neeltje, of Jacobus Schuyler and Geertruy Staats. Wit.: Gerrit Staats, Annatje Fisscher.

Pieter, of Johannes V. Deuzen and Mareytje Winne. Wit.: Pieter Winne, Rachel Van Alen.

Brechje, of Evert Zeger and Sarah Orchard. Wit.: Hendrick Zeger, Zeyntje Orchard.

Treyntje, of Cornelius Waldron and Jannitje Van Nes. Wit.: Johannes and Rebecca Jeets.

Dec. 6. Jannicke, of Abram H. and Elizabeth Wendel. Wit.: Evert J. and Geesje Wendel.

Sarah, of John Fryer and Annatie Van Zanten. Wit.: Johannes and Sarah V. Santen.

Dec. 13. Margret, of Henry and Margret Cunningham. Wit.: William and Catarina Van den Berg.

Abram, of Johannis T. Witbeek and Eva Waldron. Wit.: Hendrick and Geertruy Van Buren.

Jannitje, of Willem Hogen, Jr., and Susannah Lansing. Wit.: Gerrit I. and Ariaante Lansing.

Dec. 20. Richard, of Willem Hilton and Margarieta Jones. Wit.: Joh. V. Zanten, Mary Hilton.

Abram, of Abram Valkenburg and Neeltje Gardenier. Wit.: Joh. M. and Femmitje Beekman.

Nicholaas, of Isaac Halenbeek and Gerritje Van Woerd. Wit.: Nicholaas and Dirkje Van Woerd.

Samuel, of Edward Cetin [?] and Isabel Marchal.

Dec. 25. Maria, of Teunis Slingerland and Angenietje Witbeek. Wit.: Hendrick Wiljams, Rachel Slingerland.

Isaac, of Johannes Van der Poel and Annatje Staats. Wit.: Phillip Schuyler, Geertruy Lansingh.

Pieter, of Jacob Bogaart, Jr., and Mareytje Jeets. Wit.: Pieter P. and Rebecca Bogaart.

Dec. 26. Folkerdt, of Jonas Oothoud and Elizabeth Lansing. Wit.: Folkerd Oothoud, Catarina Lansing.

Catalina, of Hendrick Van Ness and Margrieta Winne. Wit.: Gerrit and Catarina Van Ness.

Dec. 27. Teunis, of Willem Van Slyk and Catarina Van Schaick. Wit.: Zeybrand V. Schack, Jr., Annatje V. Schaick.

Elbertje, of Abram Fonda and Elbertje Van Alen. Wit.: Corn. Van Alen, Catarina Bratt.

1748
1748, Jan. 3. Angnietje, of Hendrick Van Slyk and Elizabeth V. Bethuizen. Wit.: Hend. V. Wie, Hillitje Van Wie.

Abraham, of Roelief Van der Werken and Hannaje Vosburg. Wit.: Abraham Lansing, Catrin Lanseseuw.

Peter, of Peter Docks and Geertruw De Voew. Wit.: Jacob Docks, Angenitje De Voew.

Cornelius, of Wilhelmus, Jr., an Angenitie Van de Bergh. Wit.: Wilhelmus and Geesje Van de Bergh.

Johannes, of Johannes Van Wie and Gerritie Wendel. Wit.: Johannes Hannesse Wendel, Aryaenje Van Veghten.

Jan. 10. Nathaniel, of William and Mary Wildin. Wit.: Nathaniel Plot, Marg. Moor.

Margarieta, of Jacob Hartzing and Maria Pruym. Wit.: Hendrick and Dirkje Gerzen.

Catarin, of Evert Siksberry and Elsje Egmond. Wit.: Nicholaas and Catarina Egmond.

Jan. 14. Anna, of Hendrick Burgert, Jr., and Catarina Huyck. Wit.: Lambert and Anna Radloff.

Jan. 24. Anna, of Jacob Ouderkerk and Neeltje Knoet. Wit.: Joh. and Lena Ouderkerk.

Anthony, of Benjamin Van Vegten and Annatje Bogardus. Wit.: Wouter Chroesbeek, Jannitje Bogardus.

Elizabeth, of Lucas Witbeek and Geertruy Lansing. Wit.: Gerrit and Neeltje Lansing.

Johannes, of Staats Zeger and Susanna Brat. Wit.: Johannes Zeger, Mareytje Brat.

Cornelius, of Michal Besset and Elizabeth Schermerhoorn. Wit.: Hend. M. and Marrytje Roseboom.

Maria, of Johannes J. Lansing and Mareytje Huyk. Wit.: Cornelius and Catarina Ouderkerk.

Jan. 31. Geertje, of Rykhard Bovie and Mareytje Huyk. Wit.: Abram Bovie, Alida V. Woert.

Margrieta, of Willem Hogen and Pietertje Douw. Wit.: Hitchius and Margarieta Holland.

Feb. 14. Elizabeth, of John McCarty and Anna Dorson. Wit.: John Tool, Neeltje Fissher.

Feb. 21. Gerritje, of Nicolaas Bleecker, Jr., and Margarieta Roseboom. Wit.: Hendrick Blycker, Elsje Roseboom

Gerrit Teunisse, of Bernardus Brat, Jr., and Catarina Van Vegten. Wit.: Daniel Brat, Jr., Feytje Esselstyn.

Feb. 24. Elnor, of Patrick and Margaret Fallon. Wit.: Math. Morrus, Elizabeth Morris, John Philip Ann.

Feb. 28. Magdalena, of Douwe Bogert and Willemtje Brat. Wit.: Abram, Jr., and Magdalena Bogert.

March 6. Abram, of Isaac Vosburg and Catarina Van Woert. Wit.: Willem Vosburg, Engeltje V. Vegten.

Catalyntje, of John McCag and Alida Barhead. Wit.: John Barhead, Mareytje Chroesbeek.

1748

Samuel, of Samuel Burn and Helena Pruym. Wit.: Jacob Hanse, Elisabeth Burn.

March 13. Anna, of Cornelius Ouderkerk and Catarina Huyk. Wit.: Johannes I. and Mareytje Lansing.

Johannes, of Gerrit Van Alen and Catarina Van Wie. Wit.: Frans and Angenietje Winne.

John, of Adriaen Bratt and Selia Van Zanten. Wit.: Johannes Douw, Gilgond Lewis.

March 20. Anna, of Christiaan La Gransie and Mareytje Evertsen. Wit.: Corn. and Ariaantje V. Sandvoord.

Hendrick, of Jacob J. Lansing and Huybertje Jeets. Wit.: Hendrick and Annatje Lansing.

March 27. Seth, of James Stanhouse and Anna Margarieta Vedder. Wit.: Reyer Schermerhoorn, Hillegonda Vedder.

John, of Gey and Elizabeth Young. Wit.: Jan and Elizabeth Van Arnhem.

Maria, of Johannes Zeger and Mareytje Brat. Wit.: Jacob Van Woerdt, Maritje V. Woerdt.

Jacob, of Gerrit Muzzelis and Margarieta Blycker. Wit.: Antony Blyker, Catrina Muzzlis.

Jacobus, of Dirk Brat Van Schoonhoven and Folkje Van den Berg. Wit.: Geurt and Anna V. Schoonhoven.

Apr. 3. Elizabeth, of Roelof Kidney and Engeltje Burger. Wit.: Isaac Fryer, Maretje Winne.

Cornelia, of Jacobus Peiter [or Perker] V. Benthuyzen and Sarah Cooper. Wit.: Obediah Cooper, Annatje Lansing.

Apr. 8. Maria, of Abram Vinnagel and Jannitje Van Buuren. Wit.: Johs. and Elizabeth Vinnagel.

Apr. 17. Johannes, of Roelof Van der Werken and Geertruy Funda. Wit.: Teunis and Maria Fielde.

Heyltje, of Coenraat and Elizabeth Regtmeyr. Wit.: Joh. Regtmeyer, Heyltje Streedels.

Hendrik, of Johannes H. Ten Eyck and Sarah Ten Broeck. Wit.: Hend. and Marg. Ten Eyk.

Apr. 24. Catharina, of Fedie Meginnie and Sara Haas. Wit.: Richd. and Sarah Cartwright.

Catharina, of Albert Brat and Anna Karel. Wit.: Geurt and Elizabeth Brat.

May 1. Dirkje, of Willem Winne and Maria De Wandelaar. Wit.: Adam and Gerritje Winne.

Elizabeth, of Hendrik Gardenier and Eva Van Valkenburg. Wit.: Marten Beekman, Elizabeth Johnson.

May 8. Zusannah, of Adam Bratt and Lydia Zeger. Wit.: Staats and Zusannah Zeger.

Jennicke, of Johannes and Rachel Van der Heyden. Wit.: Joh. V. Renselaar, Annatje Douw.

Evert, of Johannes Lansing and Ariaantje Wendel. Wit.: Evert and Engeltje Wendel.

1748

Daniel, of John Reyley and Lenah Barber. Wit: Isaac Fox and wife.

May 15. Maria, of Samuel Wood and Mareytje Schans. Wit.: Hendrick Schans and the mother.

William, of Josuah Brouks and Geesje Bont. Wit.: Thomas and Annatje Flight.

Rachel, of Folkert Van den Berg and Catarina Huyck. Wit.: Wilhelmus and Angenietje V. d. Berg.

May 29. Geysbert, of Geysbert Klaauw and Neeltje Sckerm. Wit.: Hendrick Bulsing, Alida Goewey.

Dirk, of Gerardus Groesbeek and Maria Ten Broek. Wit.: John Groesbeek, Elizabeth Renselaar.

June 5. Garrit, of Simon Springsteen and Maria Zeeger. Wit.: Isaac Lansing, Maria Roseboom.

Barent, of Joh. Ruth Bleecker, and Elizabeth Staats. Wit.: Barent Staats, Margarieta Collins.

Anthony, of Wouter Chroesbeek and Maria Bogardus. Wit.: Benj. V. Vegten, Jannitje Bogardus.

June 12. Alida, of Beniamin Goewey and Catrina Van den Berg. Wit.: Johannes Goewey, Angenieta Van den Berg.

Rachel, of Daniel P. Winne and Jannitje D. Foreest. Wit.: Pieter D. and Rachel Winne.

Pieter, of Jeromus Van Valkenburg and Maria Van Buuren. Wit.: Pieter and Ariaantje D. Wandelaar.

Charles, of Lambartus V. Valkenburg and Jacameyntje Burns. Wit.: Gerrit and Deborah Staats.

June 19. Johannes, of Thomas Morral and Hester De Mos. Wit.: Bernardus and Catarina Brat.

Johannes, of Evert Van Alen and Margrieta Vergerls. Wit.: Jacobus V. Alen, Jr., Sarah Maarsen.

June 26. Petrus, of Cornelius Teymissen and Maria Livertse. Wit.: Bastiaen Tymensen, Anna Fisher.

Johannis, of Tomas Seger and Josina Wieler. Wit.: Johannis and Brechtie Seger.

July 3. Jacob, of Gerrit Staats and Deborah Beekman. Wit.: Barent Staats, Magdalena Lansing.

Gerrit Reyersen, of Hendrick Gerritsen and Dirkje Thymesen. Wit.: Elbert and Anna Gerritsen.

July 10. Christoffel, of Abraham Jets and Antie De Ridder. Wit.: Christoffel Jets, Huybertje Lancen.

Johannes, of Henderik Bulsing and Catlyna Goewey. Wit.: Johannes and Alida Goewey.

Abraham, of Eldert Van der Poel and Maragrieta Vinhagen. Wit.: Abraham and Anna Van der Poel.

Jannetie, Maragrieta, of Reikert Van Vranken and Anna Truex. Wit.: Cornelus Van Sleyk, Sara Truex, Maas and Derkie Van Vranken.

July 17. Sara, of Reynier Van Hoesen and Cornelia Bekker. Wit.: Johannis Bekker, Sara Van Aarlen.

1748

Deborah, of Reykaard Hansen and Catarina Ten Broek.
Wit.: Gerrit and Magtel Lansing.
July 24. Marte, of Johannis Gog [?] and Geertruy Van
Beuren. Wit.: Pieter and Maria Van Beuren.
Engeltje, of Lambert Cool and Maria Kidney. Wit.:
William and Pietertje Hogen.
July 31. Elsje, of Jacob I. Lansing and Marritje Ebberts.
Wit.: Gerrit I. Lansing, Jannitje Waters.
Johannis, of Pieter De Wandelaar and Ariaantje Van
Buuren. Wit.: Joh. and Elizath. D'Wandelaar.
Maria, of Zebrant G. Van Schaick and Alida Roseboom.
Wit.: Robt. Lansing, Eva Roseboom.
Aug. 7. Susanna, of Richard Cartwright and Anna
Beesli. Wit.: John and Lidia Beesli.
Geysbert, of Willem Van den Berg and Susanna Van
Iveren. Wit.: Cornelius and Mareytje V. den Berg.
John, of John and Joanna Purnel.
Aug. 14. Simon, of Jurrie Coen and Anna Erhart.
Wit.: Johannes and Barber Coen.
Jacob, of Adriaan Quackenbosch and Elizabeth Knoet.
Wit.: Joh. and Maretje Knoet.
Mary, of Jacob Egmond and Mary Lewis. Wit.: William
and Ellenor Taylor.
Maria, of Bastiaan Teymensen and Maieke Ouderkerk.
Wit.: Jacameyntie Ouderkerk, Johannes Knickerbak-
ker.
Petrus, of Petrus and Mareitie Van den Berg. Wit.:
Gerrit and Angenietie Van den Berg.
Aug. 28. Daniel, of John Davie and Elizabeth Wyn-
gaard. Wit.: Benj. Moor, Anna Du Puy.
Thomas, of Thomas Beecraft and Mary Bun. Wit.:
Thomas and Anna Flyt.
Sep. 4. Anna, of William Burch and Mary Christiaan-
sen. Wit.: John Tool, Neeltje Fisscher.
David, of David Van Planck and Catarina Boom. Wit.:
Johannes and Anna Boom.
Sep. 11. Nicolaas, of Johannis Jac. Lansingh and
Catharina Schuyler. Wit.: Harmanus Schuyler, Elisabet
Haas.
Rachel, of Jan Derent [?] and Anna Devoe. Wit.: Jan
and Catrina Devoe.
Oct. 23. Catarina, of Abraham Dewever and Anna
Kerni. Wit.: Cornelius and Catarina Ouderkerk.
Philip, of Cornelius Muller and Maria Van Hoezen. Wit.:
Philip Muller, Geertruy Goewey.
Pieter, of Wouter Chroesbeek and Jannetje Bogaart.
Wit.: Pieter and Rebecca Bogaart.
Jan Gerritsen, of Wessel Van Schaick and Maria Gerritsen.
Wit.: Jacob V. Schaick, Jr., Rachel Van den Berg.

1748

Henderickje, of Isaac Lansing and Annatje Van Woerd. Wit.: Jacob and Alida V. Woerd.

Antje, of Jan Sperry and Francyntje Knoet. Wit.: Walran and Annatje Knoet.

Alida, of Willem Liversen and Mareytje Funda. Wit.: Isaac Funda, Leybetje Knickebacker.

Elizabeth, of Thomas Coeper and Elizabeth V. Buuren. Wit.: Corn. and Magdalena V. Buuren.

Magdalena, of Folkert Douw and Anna De Peyster. Wit.: Harmen and Magdalena Gansevoort.

Margrieta, of Johannes Douw and Jannitje Bogaart. Wit.: Hend. Bogaart, Doortje Witbeek.

Teunis, of Gerrit G. Van den Berg and Angnietjen Lievessen. Wit.: Corn. Teymensen, Mareytje Lieverse.

Eva, of Jacobus V. Valkenburg and Margrieta Redloff. Wit.: Joh. and Mareytje Redloff.

Elizabeth, of Isaac Muller and Elizabeth Kittle. Wit.: Barent Vrooman, Elizab. V. Valkenburg.

Nicholaas, of Jacobus Clement and Jannitje V. Woerd. Wit.: Nich. and Dirkje V. Woerd.

Margrieta, of Robert Wendel and Catarina Winne. Wit.: Philip Freest, Marg. V. Ness.

Jonathan, of William and Sara Bickroft. Wit.: Thomas and Mareytje Bickroft.

Susanna, of Cornelis Van den Berg and Anneke V. Vrancken. Wit.: Corn. V. den Berg, Antje V. Aalsteyn.

Oct. 30. Engeltje, of Frans Clauw and Catalyntje Bording. Wit.: Salomon Goedewey, Catalyntje Hansen.

Hillitje, of Hendrick H. Van Wie and Johanna Gardenier. Wit.: Hendrick and Hilletje V. Wie.

Antje, of Adam Winne and Gerritje Schermerhoorn. Wit.: Hend. and Mareytje Schermerhoorn.

Nov. 6. Hendrick, of Hendrick Van Hoezen and Catalyntje Van den Berg. Wit.: Reynier V. Hoezen, Folkje V. den Berg.

Gerritje, of Gerritje I. Lansing and Ariaantje Beekman. Wit.: Joh. Beekman, Jr., Rachel Slingerland.

Cornelia, of Samuel Gardenier and Barentje Barhead. Wit.: Joh. and Jacomyntje Bloemendal.

Nov. 20. Abraham, of Nicholaas Cuyler and Maria Schuyler. Wit.: Jeremia Schuyler, Margarita Cuyler.

Dec. 4. Margarieta, of Jacob Van Woerd and Hendrikje Oothout. Wit.: Corn. Ouderkerk, Maritje Oothoud.

Cornelia, of Jacob Cooper and Josina Orhard. Wit.: Thomas and Cornelia Cooper.

Anna, of Teunis Van Vegten and Cornelia Knickerbacker. Wit.: Joh. and Neeltje Knickerbacker.

Pieter, of Hendrick Jong and Catharina Landman. Wit.: Pieter Schuyler, Elizabeth Renselaar.

Dec. 11. Thomas, of Evert Zeger and Sara Orchard. Wit.: Roelof and Hillitje Zeger.

Dec. 18. Ann, of John and Catharine Bryan. Wit.: William Gordon, Catharine Dugon, Margret Porsess.

Jan, of Roelof Du Vou and Elizabeth Golden. Wit.: Andries and Elizabeth V. Woert.

Dec. 23. Samuel, of Daniel Morril and Alida Doxie. Wit.: Joh. and Rebecca Muzelius.

Dec. 25. Adam, of Roelof Fur and Barber Koen. Wit.: Adam Koen, Frena Meyer.

Catarina, of Jacob Sogwinjewane and Maria Magdalena. Wit.: Nich. I. and Margarieta Is. Lydius.

1748/9, Jan. 1. Lena, of Pieter Hoogteling and Anna Beckers. Wit.: Willem and Lena Hoogteling.

Jan. 8. Abraham, of Joh. Van den Berg and Maria Van Ness. Wit.: Dirk and Cornelia Brat.

Jilles, of Jilles De Garmo and Rachel Evertsen. Wit.: Joh., Jr., and Catarina De Garmo.

Maria, of Pieter Van Buuren and Maria Van der Poel. Wit.: Joh. and Maria V. Buuren.

Jan. 15. Willem, of Karel Marinus and Margarieta V. Boute. Wit.: Tieleman and Hester V. Schelluyne.

Catarina, of Thomas Willis and Rachel Radloff. Wit.: Jacobus and Catarina Radloff.

Elizabeth, of John and Mary Scot. Wit.: Joh. and Ariaantje Lansing.

Franciscus, of Pieter Marschal and Annatje Flensburg. Wit.: Willem and Emmitje Gaal.

Catarina, of Marten Bucley and Isabel Wilsen. Wit.: James and Catarina Wilsen.

Jan. 22. Mary, of William and Rebecca Gorden. Wit.: Jon Jonson, Persile Dyon.

Elizabeth, of Arent V. Deuzen and Treyntje Waldron. Wit.: Willem and Elizabeth Waldron.

Evert, of Johannes Evertsen and Susanna Lagransie. Wit.: Evert Evertsen, Maria Berret.

Lea, of Daniel Kittel and Catar. Valkenburg. Wit.: Lambert and Maria Valkenburg.

Jacob, of Johannes Pruyn and Jannitje V. Aalstyn. Wit.: Reynier and Pietertje V. Aalsteyn.

Feb. 5. Gerrit, of Dirk Van Aarsdalen and Geysbertje De Grauw.

Johannis, of Roel. Van de Werken and Annaje Vosburg. Wit.: Johannis V. d. Werken, Geertruy Vosburg.

Maria, of Pieter Martin and Elizabeth Burns. Wit.: Jacobus and Judith Hilton.

Feb. 19. Simon, of William Brombley and Lena Boom. Wit.: Jurrian and Anna Koen.

Ephraim, of Antony An. Brat and Wyntje Bogardus. Wit.: Ephraim and Angenietje Bogardus.

1749

Elizabeth, of Dirk Van der Heyden and Elizabeth Wendel. Wit.: Jacob and Alida Van der Heyden.

Anneke, of Adam Jeets and Annatje Gerritsen. Wit.: Gerrit and Huybertje Lansing.

Feb. 26. Baltus, of Andries Van Slyk and Maria Benthuysen. Wit.: Hendrick Van Slyk, Lydia Beesley.

March 5. Nelli, of Patrick Clark and Cornelia Walderon. Wit.: William and Nelli Waldron.

Joseph, of David Van Santen and Ariaantie Fort. Wit.: Johannis Van Santen, Anna Redlie.

John, of Gerrit Jac. Lansingh and Jannetie Waters. Wit.: John and Sara Waters.

William, of Cornelius Walderon and Jannitie Vanes. Wit.: Johannis To. Witbeek, Catarina Brat.

March 12. Mareytje, of Omi Lagransie and Mareytje Van Brakelen. Wit.: G. and Mareytje V. Brakelen.

Margret, of Patrick and Margret Fallon. Wit.: Patrick Fagen, Rojoice Crafford.

1749, Apr. 3. Barent Staats, of William Salsbury and Teuntje Staats. Wit.: Jochim Staats, Annaatje Fisher.

Apr. 9. Elizabeth, of Cornelius Macmannus and Rebecca Norton. Wit.: Lochlan Oyl, Elizabeth Norton.

Cornelius, of Hendrick Van Wie and Catarina Waldron. Wit.: Gerrit and Mareytje Waldron.

Johannis, of Jacobus V. Valkenburg and Catarina Turk. Wit.: Andries and Gerritje Huyck.

Apr. 16. Sarah, Margareta, of Robert Lansing and Zarah Van Schaick. Wit.: Zebrand and Alida V. Schaick, Joh. G. and Reykje Roseboom.

Alida, of Isaac Funda, Jr., and Cornelia De Foreest. Wit.: Isaac and Alida Funda.

Apr. 23. Guy, of William Young and Catarina Funda. Wit.: William and Margaret Crannel.

Catalyntje, of Dirk Brat V. Schoonhoven and Folkje Van den Berg. Wit.: Gysbert and Catalyntje V. d. Berg.

May 28. Catarina, of Christoffel Quin and Elizabeth Carlin. Wit.: John Lewis, Mary Carlin.

Antie, of Staats V. Sandvoort and Wilmptie Brat. Wit.: Cornelius V. Sandvoort, Cornelia Brat.

Frederik, of Johannes Menerse and Maria Oostrander. Wit.: Abraham Meinerse, Maria Winnen.

Elisabet, of Gerrit Cor. Van der Berg and Maragrieta Van Vegten. Wit.: David A. Schuyler, Maria Ten Broek.

Henderik, of Johannes Ten eick and Sara Ten broek. Wit.: Henderik and Maragrieta Teneik.

Maragrieta, of Hitchen and Maragrieta Holland. Wit.: Edward Colns, Maragrieta Collens.

Lachel, of Cornelius M. and Cornelia Van der berg. Wit.: Rutcher V. der berg, Weintie Van ieveren.

1749

Jacob, of Reynier Van Aalsteyn and Cornelia Vanderberg. Wit.: Hans and Jannittie Pruym.

Lena, of John Reyley and Lena Barber. Wit.: Lucas and Engeltie Van Vegten.

Catarina, of Phillip de Foreest and Rachel Vannes. Wit.: Jesse and Neeltie de Foreest.

June 4. Elsie, of Samuel and Neeltie Staats. Wit.: Jochum Staats, Elisabet Bleyker.

June 11. Johannis, of Henderick and Susanna Meyer. Wit.: Hend. and Frena Springer.

Celiaan, of Cornelius V. Berg and Rachel Ridder. Wit.: Adam and Anna Jets.

Angenietie, of Jacob Beurum and Sara Bronk. Wit.: Johan Gansevoort, Commertie Bronk.

Abraham, of Hendrik Spoor and Rebecka Valkenburg. Wit.: Jacob and Catarina Chroesbeek.

June 18. Rebecca, of Wouter Knickerbacker and Elizabeth Funda. Wit.: Harmen Knickerbacker, Rebecca Hoogkerk.

July 2. Nicolaas, of Pieter Degarmoo and Sara Gardenier. Wit.: Nicolaas and Rachel Gardenier.

Maragrieta, of Tomas Smit and Maria Bergen. Wit.: William Freyer, Malli Berret.

July 9. Willem, of Willem Hellen and Elizabeth Halenbeek. Wit.: Daniel and Dorothea Halenbeek.

Abraham, of Isak A. Vosburg and Catarina Van Woert. Wit.: William Vosburg, Engeltie Van Vegten.

Catarina, of Jan Devoe and Feythie Van der Kar. Wit.: Isaak and Catrina Devoe.

July 16. Neeltje, of Geysbert Van Brakelen and Maria Van Antwerpen. Wit.: Symon Veder, Maria Van Aalsteyn.

Petrus, of Harmen Gansevoort and Magdalena Douw. Wit.: Folkert P. Douw, Elje Gansevoort.

July 23. Anna, of Seth and Christina, pros. Wit.: Seth and Anna, pros.

Samuel, of Abram V. Vrancken and Dirkje Cregier. Wit.: Bastiaan and Jannitje Cregier.

Sara, of Gerrit Ther. Van Slyk and Annatie Turk. Wit.: Herry Beser, Maria Rykse.

Archabls, of Robbert Lathrigd and Elisabeth Hopsens. Wit.: William Henke [?], Jannitie Schot.

Cathrina, of Kelean Van renselaar and Areaantie Schuyler. Wit.: Hendrik Renselaar, Helena——.

Cathrina, of Andries Van Wie and Lena Van Arene. Wit.: Hendrik and Mareytie Van Wie.

July 30. Maria, of Pieter Lansing and Elizabeth Wendel. Wit.: Joh. Lansing, Marg. Schuyler.

Alida, of Abram I. Funda and Maria V. Schoonhoven. Wit.: Isaac Funda, Leybetje Knickerbacker.

1749

Catalyntje, of Henderick G. Van Nes and Margarita Winne. Wit.: Gerrit Van Nes, Catarina Chroesbeek.

Aug. 6. Levinus, of Abram I. Lansing and Catarina Liversen. Wit.: Willem Liversen, Maria Funda.

Catarina, of Jonathan Broeks and Rebecca Fotton. Wit.: John and Femmitje Kidney.

Tomas, of Johannes Mol and Rebecca Barheid. Wit.: Thomas Barhead, Alida Funda.

Johannes, of Henderick Albrecht and Elizabeth Folent. Wit.: Jacob Maasen, Engeltje Schermerhoorn.

Aug. 20. Sara, of Isak Hanson and Maria Bratt. Wit.: Hans Hanson, Jr., Nellitie Bratt.

Andries, of Johannes Redley and Geertruy Brat. Wit.: Andries and Mareytje Bratt.

Abraham, of Pieter Hogen and Catarina Bosburg. Wit.: Abram and Geertje Bosburg.

Aug. 27. Barnabas, of Hugh Cordegon and Catharine Miller. Wit.: Laughland Dogal, Josie Crafford.

Susanna, of William Merriday and Hilletie Brat. Wit.: William Hogen, Maragrieta Holland.

Annatje, of Gozen Van Schaick and Majeke Van den Berg. Wit.: Wynant and Annatje Vn. den Berg.

Richard, of Richard Jencens and Margrat Norten. Wit.: William Norten, Mary Lamb.

Sep. 3. Isaac, of Henderick Beekman and Annatje Swits. Wit.: Joh. M. Beekman, Maria Swits.

Benjamin, of Benjamin Hilton and Mary Prys. Wit.: Staats Santvoord, Jannitje V. Vranken.

Sep. 10. Elisabet, of Gerret Van Vranken and Susanna Ebbertse. Wit.: Johannes and Sara Van Vranken.

Tam, of Albaan, of H. B., and Bet, of M. V. I. Wit.: Franck, of Groesbeeck, and Diaan, of Reynier.

Sep. 24. Maria, of Michael Philips and Margarita Wyngaart. Wit.: James Philips, Mareytje Wyngaart.

Sep. 26. William Winselow, of Robbert Crannell and Aryaantje Bovie. Wit.: William and Maragrita Crannell. :

Mary, of Jacob Eckbers and Mary Ruis. Wit.: William and Annener Tarrer.

Annatie, of Abram Mol and Titie Barhead. Wit.: Jacobus and Lidia Mol.

Thomas, of Thomas Williams and Maria Van hoesen. Wit.: Edward and Elisebeth Williams.

Jacob, of Johannes Beekman and Debora Van Schaayk. Wit.: Marte and Catharina Beekman.

Antonie, of Jacob Tenyk and Cathrina Cuyler. Wit.: Barent C. and Gerritje Tenyk.

Oct. 1. Elsje, of Gerrit I. and Elsje Lansing. Wit.: Johannes Roseboom, Elizabeth Oothout.

1749
Oct. 8. Isack, of Jacob Ouderkerk and Neeltje Clup.
Wit.: Cornelius and Cathrina Ouderkerk.
Maria, of Gerrit Van Alen and Cathrina Van Wie.
Wit.: Jan Van Deusen, Maria Winne.
Oct. 15. Wyntje, of Jan Brat and Catarina Funda.
Wit.: Andries and Maria Brat.
Henderickje, of Barent and Catalyntje Van Buuren.
Wit.: Will. and Teuntje V. Buren.
Elizabeth, of Tam, of Joh. Beekman, and Tzerth, of A.
V Alen. Wit.: Jefta, of H., Wendel and Diana, of
Stevenson.
Oct. 22. Johannes, of Andries Huyck and Maria V.
Deuzen. Wit.: Teunis and Elizabeth V. Woerdt.
Margarita, of Johannes Douw and Jennitje Bogaart.
Wit.: Abram and Leentje Douw.
Maria, of Robert Zanders and Elizabeth Schuyler.
Wit.: Pieter Schuyler, Elizabeth Groesbeek.
Anneke, of Jacob Bogaart, Jr., and Maria Jeets. Wit.:
Adam and Annetje Jeets.
Nicholaas, of Abram Valkenburg and Neeltje Gardenier.
Wit.: Hend. Gardenier, Heyltje Cradel.
Maria, of Marten Hogen and Rachel Slingerland. Wit.:
Teunis Slingerland, Maria Hogen.
Robert, of Jacobus Hilton and Jude Marten. Wit.:
John V. Renselaar, Margarita Livingston.
Nov. 5. Pieter, of Pieter Van Alen and Annatje V.
Benthuysen. Wit.: Abram V. Benthuysen, Sarah Han-
sen.
Elizabeth, of Jack, serv. of Isaack Lagrange and Anna
V. Loon. Wit.: Isack, of Roseboom, and Cate, of B.
Zanders.
Nov. 12. John, of Abram I. Lansing and Elizabeth
Cooper. Wit.: Thomas Coper, Sarah Cooper.
Ariaantje, of Harmanus Wendel and Catarina V.
Vegten. Wit.: Lucas V. Vegten, Lena Wendel.
Nov. 19. John, of Henry Baschasche and Sofia Mag-
dalena. Wit.: William Gordon, Mary Miles.
Daniel, of Isaac Halenbeek and Gerritje Van Woerd.
Wit.: Daniel and Dorothea Halenbeek.
Johannes, of Abram H. and Elizabeth Wendel. Wit.:
Hermanus and Helena Wendel.
Abram, of Jan Van Arnhem and Elizabeth Lansing.
Wit.: Abram and Alida Van Arnhem.
Geertruy, of Gerardus Lansing and Maria Wendel.
Wit.: Johannis, Jr., and Geertruy Lansing.
Nov. 26. Patrick, of Patrick Flat and Elenor Viele.
Wit.: Joh. and Rachel De Peyster.
Sara, of John Fryer and Annatje Van Zanten. Wit.:
Joh. and Sara Van Zanten.

1749
Dec. 3. Pieter, of Andries Ten Eyck and Anna Ema. Coeyeman. Wit: Jacob C. Ten Eyck, Schalotta E. Coeyeman.

Johannes, of Henderick Van Buuren and Annatje V. Salisbury. Wit.: Folkert and Annatje Douw.

Jacob, of Jacob Van der Heyden and Maria Halenbeek. Wit.: Dirk and Alida Van der Heyden.

Dec. 10. Johannes, of Pieter, Jr., and Geertruy Schuyler. Wit.: Philip Schuyler, Elisabeth Zanders.

Catarina, of Jacobus Van der Poel and Neeltje Huyck. Wit.: Willem Groesbeek and Catarina Van der Poel.

Dec. 17. Geesje, of Johannes Dingmanse and Mareytje Muller. Wit.: Jacob and Seyntje Coeper.

Cathalyna, of Harmen Hun and Elssie Lansing. Wit.: Thomas La——, Elsjie Hun.

Dec. 25. Annatje, of Johannes Jeets and Rebecca Waldron. Wit.: Jacob and Huybertje Lansing.

Dec. 31. Neeltje, of Petrus and Maria, pros. Wit.: Henderick and Leah, pros.

Marritje, of Willem Vosburgh and Christina Van Woerd. Wit.: Isaac and Catarina Vosburg.

Cornelius, of Cornelius Sandvoord and Ariaantje Brat. Wit.: Cornelius Sandvoord, Cornelia Brat.

Baltus, of Henderick Van Slyk and Elizabeth Benthuyzen. Wit.: Richard and Johanna Cartwright.

LIST OF ABBREVIATIONS.

A., Albany.
A. City, Albany City.
A. Co., Albany County.
b., B., born or banns.
bapt., baptized.
C., Claverack.
Can., Canistagioene.
cert., certificate.
ch., chn., child, children.
Col. R., Colony Rensselaerswyck.
dau., daughter.
decd., deceased.
Do., Dominie (Reverend).
H. M., Half Moon.
h., house.
Ire., Ireland.
K., Kinderhook.
King., Kingston.
L., License.
l., living.
Ma., ma., Married.
N. Y., New York.
Pros., proselyte, proselytes.
R., Rensselaerswyck.
R. D., Reformed Dutch.
Reg., Registered.
Sch., Schenectady.
Scha., Schag., Schaghticoke.
Wid., widr., widow, widower.
Wit., Witness, witnesses.
y. d., unmarried woman.
y. m., unmarried man.

Johannes, of Sam. and Anna Rettelief, means Johannes *child* of Sam. and Anna Rettelief, etc., etc.

INDEX.

There was some question as to the best mode of preparing this index, inasmuch as there are so many varieties in spelling surnames as well as baptismal names. Those entering the names appear to have exercised their own judgment as to orthography, and frequently varied it, without apparent reason, though referring to the same person. If all the names were indexed separately, just as they appear in the records, with the original spelling, the work of tracing family lineages would be greatly increased. It was determined, therefore, to embrace under one heading all names probably belonging to the same family, indexing them, as far as practicable, under the form now in commonest use. Sometimes, where two distinct family names were much confused, like Barheit and Barrett, Van Eps and Van Ness, etc., they have been indexed under one heading. It is also to be observed that most of the early Dutch families were not regularly entered under their family name until many years had passed. They were mostly known by their patronymics; for instance, the Heemstraats will have to be looked for, sometimes, under Dirks or Takels, the Groesbeeks under Claasze, the Vander Poels under Wynandsz, the Van Deusens under Teuisz or Harpers, the Bloomingdales, Van Burens and Vroomans under Meesz or Maas, the Van Bergens under Gerrits, etc., etc. During this period, persons would sometimes be entered in the record under their patronymic and family name; at other times, under their family name only. For instance, Cornelis Maasze Bloemendaal would at times be entered as Cornelis Bloemendaal. In indexing, he was indexed throughout as Cornelis, without considering the Maasze, because the name was really Cornelis Bloemendaal, son of Maas. Gerrit Theunisse Van Slyk was indexed nnder Gerrit Van Slyk, etc., etc. Where a person had a double name, like Dirk Brat Van Schoonhoven, he was usually indexed as Dirk Van Schoonhoven, because the second name was not likely to be continually entered in the record. Appended is a list of the most numerous variations:

Aarnold, Aarnhoud, Ernhoud, Aarnoud, Aarhnout.

Armstrong, Harenstrong, Armstrongh, Aremstran.

Barheyt, Barhead, Barreith, Barith, Berryt, Barrith, Barrit Berret, Barheit, Borhead, Barheid, Berrith, Berheit, Barhayt.

Barroway, Barrewey, Barreway, Barway, Barrewe.

Basset, Basteth, Bestid, Bestidt, Bessed, Bessid, Basset, Basseth, Bessett.

Bath, Badt, Bedt, Baart, Bart, Beth, Bidt.

Beasely, Beesley, Beesli, Bezely, Beesly.

Becker, Bekker, Beckers, Bekkers.

Bleecker, Bleeker, Blyker, Bleekers, Bleyker, Blycker, Bleker, Bleiker.

Bloemendaal, V. Bloemendaal, Bloemendal, Blommendaal.

Bogert, Bogaert, Bogaart, Bogaard, Bogaardt, Van den Bogaart, Boogert, Bogardt.

Bovie, Bovy, Boy, Bovi.

Bratt, Brat, Brad, Bradt, Brats.

Brooks, Broeks, Broek, Brouks.

Brownley, Brommely, Bromly, Brombly.

Bunsing, Buntingh, Bulsen, Bulsem, Bulsin, Bulsing, Buusen, Bonting.

Coeyeman, Koeymans, Cojeman, Kojeman, Coeymans.

Collins, Collings, Colns, Collens.

Cooper, Couper, Koeper, Coeper, Coper.

Courtnie, Kerni, Cornier, Courtir.

Creddok, Credit, Creddisch, Cradik.

Crannell, Crellen, Crannill, Crannel, Crennen.

Cregier, Criegier, Crigier, Criger, Crieger.

Cuyler, Cuylder, Cuylers, Cuiler.

Danielson, Dennel, Donnels, Danniels, Danielse, Dennielse, Daniels, Danels.

De Foreest, Foreest, D. Foreest, Freest, Vreest, D. Vreest.

De Garmo, Gardemo, Garmoy, D. Garmoy, De Garamo, Garnoy, D. Germo, Degarmoo.

De Peyster, D. Peyster, Peyster, De Peister.

Dereth, Dret, Duret, Derent.

De Ridder, Ridder, Ridders, D. Ridder.

De Voew, De Vous, Devoe, Du Fou, Du Voe, D. Fou, d. Fou, D. Vou, De Voe, Devou, De Vous, Vous, Du Vou.

De Wandelaar, d. Wandelaar, De Wandelaars, Wandelaar, D. Wandelaar.

Doxsie, Doxs, Dogs, Dockzie, Doxat, Doxe, Doxie, Doxy, Dockzy, Dokse, Doksie, Docks, Dox.

Dunbar, Tumbarr, Tam Baarn, Tum Bar, Tombaar, Turnbarn, Dumbar, Dumbarr, Dumbaer.

Ecberts, Eckbertsen, Ebberts, Eckberssten, Eckberts, Egbertse, Ebbertse, Egberson, Ebberse, Eckbers.

Flensburg, Glensburgh, Flensburgh, Vlensburgh, Fleysburg.

Gerritsen, Gerritse, Gerritzen, Gerzen, Gerritz, Gerritze.

Goewey, Goewyk, Goewyck, Goedewey.

Grannel, Grannie, Grennel, Grennie.

Greveraat, Greveraad, Grevenraad, Grevenraadt, Greverard, Greveraart, Grevaad.

Groesbeck, Groesbeek, Chroesbeek, Kroesbeek.

Hansen, Hanzen, Hanszen, Hanse, Hanze, Hansse, Hanson.

Hilton, Hilten, Hillen, Hilden, Hildon.

Hogan, Hogin, Hogen, Hoogen.

Hoog, Hogh, Hoogh, Hog, Hogg.

Holland, Hollandt, Hollant, Holl.

Hoogkerk, V. Hooghkerke, V. Hooghkerk, Van Hoogkerk, Hooghkerk, Hoogkerke, V. Hoogkerk, Houwkerk.

Hoogtelink, Hooghtelink, Hooghteelingh, Hoogteelink, Hooghtelingh, Hooghteling, Hooghteeling, Hoogteeling, Hoogtelinck, Hoogtelink, Hoogtieling, Hoogteling, Hoogetelink, Hooghtelinck.

Huyck, Huyk, Heuck, Huick, Huygh.

Jansen, Janse, Johnson, Jansze, Jonson.

Kidney, Kithnie, Kitnie, Kidny, Kitney, Kidnie.

Kittelheyn, Ketelhuyn, Ketelluyn, Ketelheyn, Kittelheym.

Knickerbacker, Knikkerbacker, Knickerbakker, Knickerbackker Knickkerbackker, Knikkerbakker, Knickebakker, Knikkaback, Knikkebakker, Knikkabakker.

La Grange, La Gransie, Lagranzie, Lagransie, Le Gransie.

Lansing, Lansingh, Lansen, Lanseseuw, Landzing, Landsing, Lancen.

Lievense, Lievessen, Lievens, Liverson, Livenson, Liversen, Lieves, Livertse, Liverse, Levisse.

Lents, Lins, Linds, Lindts.

Loux, Loek, Louk, Louck.

Maarten, Maerten, Marten, Martyn, Martin.

Maassen, Maarze, Maarsen, Maessen, Maarse, Maason, Maarzen, Maartzen.

Mackans, Makansch, Makans, Maknans.

Macluur, Makluur, Makluys, Maklier, Makler, Maklur.

Mahanney, Mohennie, Mahanni.

Marselis, Marcelis, Marsselis, Marcelius.

Marshal, Marchal, Marschal, Merschel.

Meynertsen, Meinerse, Meyndertsen, Meinderts, Meynerson, Menerse.

Miln, Milt, Mil, Millin, Miles.

Morrel, Marl, Morall, Morril, Morral.

Muzelius, Muzzlis, Muzzelis, Muzzelius, Muselis.

Nichols, Nikkels, Nickels, Nicolls, Nicles.

Norton, Norten, Northen, Narden, Nordin, Northun.

Olvert, Olphert, Olivert, Oliver, Olivier, Olfert, Olfer.

Oostrander, V. Oostrander, Oostrand, Van Oostrander, Oostrande, Oostrandt.

Pemberton, Pemperton, Pemlethon, Pammerton, Pamerton, Pemmetshon.

Quackenbos, Quackenbosch, Quakkenbos, Quackinbos, Quakkenbosch, Quakkbos, Quack.

Rattelief, Ratdelief, Rettelief, Radelif, Radelief, Redlie, Radloff, Redley, Redlef, Rittelief, Radelif, Redloff, Ratlif, Raadly, Ratliff, Raedtly.

Reyley, Raily, Rylief, Rely.

Rightmeyer, Regtmeyer, Rigtmeyer, Richtmeyer, Rigtmyer, Rechsmider, Rechtmayer, Regtmeyr.

Rodgers, Rodgiers, Radtgert, Roetsels.

Roseboom, Rozeboom, Rooseboom, Rozenboom, Rooseb.

Rommelie, Rumbly, Ramsly, Romblic.

Rycksen, Ryksen, Rykse, Ryder.

Salisbury, Salsberry, Van Saltzberg, Salberge, V. Salisbury Van Salsbergen, Saltzberg, Saltzbergh, Salsbury.

Sanders, Zandertse, Sandertz, Zanders, Zandertsen, Sandertse.

Scherp, Sÿerp, Schjerp, Sharp, Sjerp, Scharp.

Schreydel, Scheyldel, Schrodel, Schriddel, Schredel, Schrattel, Schreyder, Schreyddel, Scherrette.

Schuyler, Schuylder, Schuyldert, Schuiler.

Schyans, Schians, Schjans, Schyaensch, Schiaens, Schants, Schiaensch, Schans, Schiaey, Schia, Schyarch, Schyarh.

Seskby, Siskby, Siksberry, Seksby.

Sheefer, Scheber, Schieber, Schever, Schefer.

Slingerland, Slingerlant, Slingerlandt, Slingerl.

Springsteen, Sprinksteen, Sprinckstien, Sprincksteen.

Stenhouse, Steenhuysen, Stenhuys, Stanhouse.

Teller, Teiller, Teyllier, Tellar.

Ten Broeck, Ten Broek, T. Broek, Ten Brooks, Tenbroek.

Ten Eyck, T. Eyck, Ten Eyk, T. Eyk, Ten Eik, Tenyk, Teneik, Teneick.

Tymensen, Tymissen, Tymense, Thymonson, Teymensen, Tymonsen, Teymissen, Tymes, Thymesen.

Van Aalsteyn, V. Aalsteyn, V. Alstein, Van Aalstyn, Van Aalstein, Van Alsteyn, V. Aalstyn, Van Alstein.

Van Antwerpen, V. Antwerpen, V. Antwerp, Van Antwerpe.

Van Arnhem, V. Arnhem, V. Aarnheim, Van Aarnem, Van Aernem, Van Arnem, Van Arnham, Van Aarnoms, Van Aarnheim, Arnhem, Van Arene.[1]

Van Benthuysen, V. Benthuysen, Van Benthuizen, Van Benthuyse, Benthuyzen, V. Bethuizen, V. Benthuyzen, Benthuysen.

Van Brakel, V. Brakelen, Van Brakele, Van Brakelen.

Van Brug, Van Brugh, V. Brugh, Verbrugh.

Van Buren, Van Buuren, V. Buuren, Van Bueren, V. Buren, Van Beuren, Van Buire, V. Buire.

Van Corlaar, Corlaar, Van Coddelaar, V. Corlaar.

Van den Berg, V. D. Berg, V. D. Bergh, V. d. Berg, V. d. Berk,

[1]The further corruption of this name in one family is interesting. Beginning as *Van Aarnhem* in the Albany records, we find in our MS records of Walpeck, New Jersey, on p. 111, the baptism of Elizabeth, child of John *Van Arnum* and Sarah Dupuy, born January 22, 1791; on p. 117, on December 26, 1792, the baptism of Susannah, child of John *Van Arnum*, and Sarah Depuy, born August 17, 1792; and in our records of Deer Park, (formerly Minisink,) Vol. II, p. 321, we find the baptism of Osee, child of John *Van Orman* and Sarah Depuy, in June, 1794, born May 12, 1794; on p. 328, Benjamin, child of John *Van Arnom* and Sarah Depuy, baptised 1800, born June 1, 1800; and on p. 339, Abraham, child of John *Van Norman* and Sarah Depuy, baptised probably 1807, born June 8, 1802. The name being further changed by dropping the Van, it is difficult to trace the *Norman* family back to *Aarnhem*, and the origin of the name may seem to be *Normandy*.

V. Bergen, Van den Bergh, Van d. Berg, Van Bergen, V. d. Berck, V. Den Bergh, V. D. Berch, Van de Bergh, Van den Berk, Van der Berk, Vanderberg, V. Berg, V. den Berg, Van der Bergh, Van der Berg, Van den Berck.

Van der Heyden, V. D. Heyde, V. d. Heyde, Vander Heiden, Van der Heyde, V. d. Heide, Van dr Heiden.

Van der Kar, V. d. Kar, V. d. Karre, V. D. Karre, V. Der Karre, Van D. Karre.

Van Der Poel, V. D. Poel, Van der Poel, V. d. Poel.

Van der Werken, V. D. Werke, Van der Werriken, V. d. Werken, V. D. Werk, Van dr Werriken, Van de Werke, Van der Werpe, V. dr Werken, Van der Werke, Van de Werken.

Van der Zee, V. d. Zee, V. D. Zee, Van d. Zee.

Van Deusen, V. Deusen, Van Deuzen, V. Deuze, V. Deuzen, Van Deuse.

Van Driessen, Van Driesen, V. Driesen, Van Driess.

Van Hoesen, Van Hoezen, V. Hoesen, Van Noezen, Van hoesen, V. Hoezen.

Van Ness, Van Eps, V. Nes, Van Es, V. Ess, Vanes, V. Ness, Van Nes, Vannes.

Van Olinda, V. Olinde, V. Olinda, V. d. Linde, Van Olinde, Van der Linde, Van O'Linde.

Van Rensselaer, Van Renzelaar, Renselaar, V. Rensselaar, Van Rensselaar, Rensselaar, Renzelaar, Van Renselaar, Van Rentzlaar, V. Rensselaer, V. Renselaar, Van renselaar.

Van Santvoord, V. Santvoord, V. Sandvoord, V. Sandvoort, Sandvoord, Van Sandvoort, Santvoord.

Van Schaick, V. Schaick, Van Schaik, V. Schayk, Schaik, V. Schaik, Van Schayk, Van Schayck, V. Schayck, Van Scaick, Van Schaick, Van Schaayk, Van Schack.

Van Schelluyn, Van Schelluyne, V. Schelluyn, V. Schelluyne, Van Schelluynen.

Van Schoonhoven, V. Schoonhoven, Schoonhoven, Van Schoonoven, Van Schoonover, Van Schoonhooven.

Van Slyck, Van Slyk, Van der Slyk, Van Sleyk, V. Slyk, V. Slyck.

Van Valkenburg, Van Valkenburgh, V. Valckenburg, Valkenburg, Valkenburgh, Van Valckenburgh, V. Valkenburgh, Valckenburg, V. Valkenburg.

Van Vegten, V. Vegten, Van Veghten, Van Vegte, V. Vechten, V. Veghten, Van Vechten, Van Veghte.

Van Vranken, V. Franken, Van Francken, Van Vrancken, V. Vrancken, Van Franken, Van Vranke, Van Franke.

Van Wie, V. Wie, V. Wyen, Verwie, Van Weed.

Van Woerdt, V. Woerdt, V. Woert, Van Woerd, Van Woert, V. Woerd, Van Wourdt, Van Woerden.

Van Yveren, V. Yveren, Van Ieveren, Van Iveren, V. Jeveren, V. Iveren, V. Yvere, Van Yvere, Van Yeveren, Van ieveren.

Van Zanten, V. Santen, V. Zanten, Van Santen.

Vedder, Veeder, Veder, Veders, Feder.
Verplanck, V. Plank, Verplank, Van Planck.
Viele, Vile, Vielde, Fiele.
Vinhagen, Vinhagel, Vinagel, Vinnagel, Finnagel.
Visser, Fisher, Visscher, Vischjer, Fisscher, Visjer, Fischer, Visschjer, Visher, Fissher.
Waldron, Walderom, Waldrom, Walran, Waldren, Walderon, Walrom, Walron.
Wells, Waals, Wels, Wales, Welsch.
Wieler, Wielaar, Wielaer, Wieler, Wielar, Wiele.
Williams, Wiljams, Williaems, Willems.
Wilkenson, Willekens, Welkens, Willis.
Wyngaart, Wyngaard, Wyngaards, Wyngaert, Wyngaardt, Wyngaerd.
Yates, Jeets, Jets, Jates, Yets, Jetz, Jaits, Yeets, Yeats, Yaets, Jaets, Joets, Jaats, Jetz, Iets, Yets, Yoets, Yerkes.
Young, Jongh, Jong, Joungh.
Zeeger, Seeger, Zeger, Seger, Zegers, Zeegers.
Zichelson, Sikkels, Zikkels, Zilchelson, Sikkel, Sikkelson.

Aarnold, Aarhnout, Jacob, Jacobus, 80, 82, 83, 84, 95.
   Margrieta, 80, 82, 83, 84, 95.
Aarscherd, Aalschirt, Zara, 14, 99.
Aartsier, Josyna, 87.
Abeel, Christoffel, Christ., Chr., 16, 22, 27, 36, 44, 54, 66, 82.
   M., 44.
   Margrieta, Margrietje, Marg., 16, 27, 36, 54, 66, 82, 113.
   Maria, 22.
Abramse, Anthony, 79, 81, 82.
   Catharyna, 79, 81, 82, 91.
   Japik, 71.
   Johannes, 9, 82, 91.
   Neeltje, 8.
   Rachel, 7.
Ackerson, John, 30.
   Maria, 30.
Albertsen, Roelef, 24.
Albrecht, Henderick, 127.
Anderson, Margrieta, 7.
Ann, John Philip, 119.
Appel, Anna, 25.
   Joh., 25.
Archel, Mary, 20.
   Tho., 20.
Armstrong, Harenstrong, Catharyn, Catr., 40, 61.
   John, Jan, 33, 40, 52, 61.
Bacblado, Sjeems, 87.
   Zara, 87.
Banker, Chr., 55.

E., 47.
Elyz., 16, 36, 55.
Evert, 16, 30.
G., 47.
Gerardus, 71.
Gerr., Ger., 55, 62.
M., 47.
Maria, Mar., 53, 55, 62, 71.
Willem, Will., 18, 71.
Banks, James, Jeems, Jems, 17, 22, 28, 41.
Bantly, Bankly, Jonathan, 6, 61.
   Orsel, 61.
Barber, John, 115.
   Lena, 115, 121, 126.
Barckley, Anna, 17.
Barheyt, Barhead, etc., Alida, 119.
   Anna Maria, 65.
   B. 47.
   Barentje, 6, 123.
   Catalyna, Cat., 18, 27.
   Christina, 89.
   Hieronymus, 98.
   John, 119.
   Maddel, 22.
   Maria, Malli, 74, 84, 95, 116, 124, 126.
   R., 67.
   Rachel, 17, 80.
   Rebecca, 97, 109, 115, 127.
   Robbert, 7, 65, 74, 84, 95, 114, 116.
   Teuntje, 107.
   Thomas, 127.

Crannell,—*Continued.*
　Robert, Rob., 15, 22, 127.
　William, Will., 2, 22, 76, 125,
　　127.
Creddok, Credit, Isaac, 79, 95,
　　98.
　J., 54.
　Maria, Marytje, 79, 95, 98.
Cregier, Criegier, Anatje, 116.
　Bastiaan, 126.
　Dirkje, 12, 116, 126.
　G., 51.
　Geertr., 21, 25, 30, 37, 41.
　Jannitje, 126.
　Johan Jurry, 11.
　S., 51.
　Samuel, Sam., 21, 25, 30, 37,
　　41, 114, 116.
Crispel, Anthony, 4.
Crooks, William, 7.
Cunningham, Henry, 118.
　Margret, 118.
Cuyler, Cuylder, A., 62.
　Abraham, Abr., 14, 17, 19,
　　31, 53, 63, 108.
　C., 59.
　Cathalyna, Catharina, Cath.,
　　etc., 6, 31, 33, 34, 38, 42,
　　43, 47, 53, 55, 58, 59, 63,
　　64, 67, 68, 69, 75, 77, 82,
　　86, 90, 91, 92, 100, 102,
　　111, 127.
　Christ., Chr., 44, 47.
　Cornelis, Corns, Corn., 2, 20,
　　32, 33, 42, 44, 50, 53,
　　57, 58, 59, 63, 67, 75, 77,
　　78, 84, 86, 87, 91, 92, 107.
　Elyz., Elsie, 4, 16, 29, 31, 33,
　　58.
　Eva, 50.
　H., 34, 47.
　Hendrick, Henrik, Hendr.,
　　16, 17, 23, 38, 50, 52, 62,
　　78, 100, 108.
　J. A., 64.
　John, Johannes, Johs., Joh.,
　　Jo., 2, 16, 17, 25, 29, 31, 33,
　　38, 40, 43, 47, 50, 53, 58, 59,
　　67, 82, 90, 100, 101, 108.
　M., 34, 64.
　Margarita, Margrieta, Marg.,
　　17, 23, 38, 53, 89, 114, 123.
　Maria, 4, 17, 20, 41, 43, 47, 53.
　Nicholaas, Nikolaas, Nic.,
　　15, 62, 108, 123.
　Sara, 3, 25, 30, 33.
Danielson, Donnels, Charles,
　　Cherl, 20, 65, 66, 75, 86.
　Elizabeth, 66, 86, 110, 114,
　　116.

Matje, 74.
Symen, 74.
Darby, John, 115.
　Nel., 115.
Davis, Davie, James. Jam., 3.
　John, 15, 122.
Decker, C., 6.
De Foreest, Foreest, A., 43, 67.
　Abigail, Abig., Ab., 28, 31,
　　53, 61, 64, 87, 115.
　Abraham, Abr., 3, 28, 31, 49,
　　51, 62, 77, 91, 100, 108.
　Catharina, 11.
　Cornelia, 92, 111, 125.
　D., 43, 67.
　David, Da., 31, 53, 61, 87,
　　115.
　Gerrit, 80.
　J., 39, 42, 51, 60, 64, 67.
　Jannetje, Jantje, 14, 80, 110,
　　121.
　Jesse, Jisse, 16, 19, 31, 34, 37,
　　51, 55, 64, 82, 112, 126.
　Johannes, Johs., Joh., 1, 26,
　　32, 35, 43, 48, 65, 66, 73,
　　80, 87.
　M., 39, 59, 60.
　Maria, Mary, Marytje, Mar.,
　　26, 32, 35, 43, 48, 51, 65,
　　66, 73, 80, 87, 115.
　N., 42, 64.
　Neeltie, Neelt., 16, 19, 31, 34,
　　37, 51, 82, 83, 112, 126.
　Philip, 14, 92, 115, 123, 126.
　Rebecka, Rebecca, Reb., 49,
　　51, 62, 77, 91, 100, 108.
　Sara, 31.
De Garmo, Gardemo, Catharina,
　　52, 124.
　D., 45.
　Dirk, 53.
　Eckbertie, Ebbertje, Eckb.,
　　Eck., 16, 21, 37, 41, 45, 53,
　　57, 66, 67.
　G., 5.
　Grietie, 40.
　J., 41.
　Jillis, Jill., 24, 31, 56, 73, 124.
　Johannes, Hannes, Johs.,
　　Joh., 16, 21, 22, 37, 41, 42,
　　49, 56, 66, 67, 101, 124.
　M., 37, 44, 53.
　Matthys, Matheus, Math., 24,
　　35, 76, 88, 100, 117.
　P., 40.
　Pieter, 117, 126.
　R., 42, 44, 48.
　Rachel, 56, 73.
　Rebecka, Reb., 24, 35, 45,
　　53, 76, 88, 100, 117.

De Garmo,—*Continued.*
Richd., 3.
Sarah, 117.
Z., 48.
Zyte, 42.
De Grauw Geysbertje, 124.
De Groot, Rebecca, 7.
D. Lamether, Christ., 25.
Claude, 25.
Delmont, Delmond, Abraham,
12, 62.
Elizabeth, Elyz., 46, 62, 83.
Mart., 17, 46.
De Levil, Hopie, 99.
John, 99.
De Long, Margriet, 61.
Sjems, 61.
De Mes, De Mos, Hester, 12, 121.
Denninson, Elyz., El., 36, 39.
J., 36.
De Peyster, A., 47.
Anna, Annatie, Annaatje,
12, 26, 30, 34, 53, 56, 62,
79, 106, 114, 123.
Johannes, John, Johs., Joh.,
18, 30, 53, 62, 79, 87, 97,
108, 128.
Rachel, 128.
Dereth, Derent, Anna, Annaatje,
61, 67, 78, 87, 95.
John, Johan, Jan, 5, 61, 67,
78, 87, 95, 110, 122.
De Ridder, Ridder, A., 43.
Anna, Annaatje, Antje, 14,
23, 25, 34, 37, 43, 44, 57,
61, 70, 81, 87, 94, 101, 102,
112, 115, 121.
C., 5.
Cath., 37, 55.
Cornelis, Corn., 1, 4, 23, 27,
52, 86, 92.
G., 44.
Gerrit, Gerr., 16, 25, 34, 37,
70, 101, 112.
Gerrittie, Gerritje, 54, 86.
H, 37, 43, 57.
Hendrik, Hendr., 23, 55, 61,
63, 81, 87, 94, 102.
Hilletie, Hilletje, Hill., 55,
63, 67, 69, 78, 81, 86,
101.
Killiaan, Kil., 67, 93.
Maria, 6, 43.
R., 4.
Rachel, 113, 126.
S., 57.
Simon, Symen, Symeon, 5,
55, 69, 86, 101.
Susanna, Sus., Zantje, 16,
23, 27, 103.

De Voew, Angenitje, 119.
Anna, Annatje, 110, 122.
Bechje, 94.
Catharina, Catrina, Chath.,
18, 116, 122, 126.
Fytje, Fydtje, 68, 78, 94.
G., 61.
Geertruid, Geertruw, Geertr.,
6, 57, 110, 119.
Isaac, 87, 126.
Jan, 5, 18, 34, 38, 68, 78, 94,
104, 122, 126.
Jannetje, Jantie, 87, 99, 106.
M., 5.
Marretje, 11.
R., 61.
Roelof, 11, 68, 94, 106, 116,
124.
Willem, 106.
De Wandelaar, d. Wandelaar, 4.
Agnietje, Angenitje, 50, 110.
Ariaantje, 121.
Elizath., 122.
Hannes, Joh., 66, 122.
Maria, 65, 117, 120.
Pieter, 65, 121, 122.
Rebecca, 66, 112.
Sara, Zara, 2, 53.
Dewever, Abraham, 122.
Dilling, John, 12.
Dillon, Hue, 116.
Dingmanse, Johannes, 129.
Dogal, Laughland, 127.
Doin, Sjeems, 83.
Dolvin, Hoop, 74.
Donnowa, Dunnevan, Donno-
wac, Jan, John, 71, 115.
Hopie, Hoop, 71, 76.
Doole, Mary, 116.
Dorson, Anna, 119.
Doty, Jabes, 12.
Douw, Douwe, Abraham,
Abram, Abr., Abm., 3.
42, 51, 59, 66, 70, 86, 90,
107, 128.
Andries, 19.
Anna, Annaatje, 19, 35, 44,
46, 51, 58, 59, 61, 70, 73
76 77, 85, 90, 94, 96, 97
104, 108, 114, 120, 129.
Catrina, 117.
Dorothee, 3, 30.
Elizabeth, Elyz., 4, 114.
F., 59.
H., 46.
Henricus, Hendr., 19, 30, 32,
50, 54, 64.
Jannetje, Jan., 79, 95, 102,
114.
Johannes, Joh., 69, 79, 86,

Hogil,—*Continued.*
Edward, 12, 97, 117.
Francis, 95.
Johannis, 95.
Maria, 97, 103.
Pieter, 97, 113, 117.
Holland, Alida, 59, 62, 81, 113.
Edward, Edoald, Edw., 24,
27, 47, 56, 62, 64, 95.
Francis, 95.
Henry, 3, 27, 28, 39, 50, 62,
115.
Hitchius, Hitchen, Hitsen,64,
119, 125.
Jenny, Jeen, 17, 39.
Magdal., Magd., 27, 47.
Maragrieta, Margarieta, 119,
125, 127.
Mary, 64.
Rits., 47.
Sealy,Zelia,2,18, 22,35,50,58.
Tho., 22.
Hondt, Geertruy, 60.
Hooftmensch, Catharina, 2.
Hoog, Hogh, Catharyna, 72.
Johannes, John, 7, 72, 108.
Pieter, 116.
Will., 25.
Hoogkerk, Houwkerk, 3.
J., 25.
L., 25, 35.
Lucas, 5, 56, 66, 75, 76, 77,
87, 92, 104, 116.
M., 3.
Mar., Maria, 35, 52.
Rebecca, 76, 77, 87, 92, 126.
Sara, Zara, 62, 75.
Hoogtelink, 3.
B., 3.
Beertie, 33.
C., 44.
Catharina, Tryntje, 13, 102,
105, 114.
Coenraad, 102, 115.
Cornelia, 11, 108.
Dorothea, 101.
H., 33, 44.
Henderik, Hendr, 3, 115.
Hest., 44.
Jonathan, 63.
Lena, 26, 33, 61, 63, 84, 101,
108, 114, 115, 124.
Maria, Marytje, 102, 115.
Pieter, 124.
Rachel, 14, 109.
Theunis, 101.
W., 33, 114.
Willem, William, Will., 26,
61, 63, 84, 101, 108, 115,
124.

Hopsens, Elisabeth, 126.
Hortje, Daniel, 61.
Horttie, Marie, 61.
Housie, D., 49.
Maria, 49.
Houst, Elisabet, 109.
Hue, Mary, 112.
Hun, Hunn, Adriaan, 62.
Anna, Johanna, Annaatje,
22, 30, 49, 51, 59, 60, 61,
68, 76, 78, 80, 96, 102, 105.
Catalyna, 2.
D., 55, 64.
Dirk, Dirck, 22, 46, 61, 62,
76, 85, 90, 97, 109.
Elyz., Elsje, Elsjie, 64, 73,
78, 97, 114, 116, 129.
Harmen, 5, 73, 78, 90, 97,
116, 129.
Hendrikje, 62, 97.
Johannes, Hannes, Johs.,
Joh., 1, 22, 27, 30, 46, 49,
59, 60, 61, 64, 68, 76, 78,
83, 93, 105.
M., 55.
Margreta, Margrietje, Marg.,
46, 52, 62, 76, 77, 85, 90,
109.
Mayke, Mayeke, Maike, 22,
23, 28, 46, 61, 64, 110.
Hunt, Hoop, Hope, 54, 115.
Hus, Lena, 111.
Hutje, Mally, 71.
Huyck, Andries, Andr., 20, 65,
86, 88, 90, 98, 114, 116,
125, 128.
Anna, 19.
Burger, 84, 114.
Catharyna, Catarina, 8, 83,
91, 98, 100, 102, 106, 110,
111, 119, 120, 121.
Christina, Chr., 8, 45.
Corns., 9.
Gerritje, 125.
Isaak, Isaac, 9, 89.
Johannes, Hannes, Joh.,
9, 26, 83, 91, 102, 110,
114.
Magdalena, Lena, Mad., 26,
62, 63, 90.
Maria, Marytje, 13, 20, 119.
Neeltje, Nelletje, 10, 86, 89,
98, 129.
Rachel, 114.
Willem, 1, 19.
Huyser, Maria, 1.
Huzzon, Huzon, Daniel, 69.
Mary, 69.
Immerik, Maria, 14.
Isaacs, Neeltje, 63.

Oothout,—*Continued*
Hendr., 23, 48.
Hendrickie, Hendrickje, 1,
111, 123.
Jan, 3, 19, 24, 26, 29, 34, 35,
37, 40, 47, 51, 53, 60, 72,
82, 93, 104.
Johs., 40.
Jonas, 11, 93, 102, 118.
Lammetje, 81.
M., 47, 60.
Maria, Maritje, Marretje,
Marr., 35, 40, 51, 72, 82,
93, 123.
Volkert, Folkerd, 92, 118.
Orchard, Orhard, Ochert, Josina,
Zeyntje, 118, 123.
Sara, 106, 118, 124.
Ouderkerk, A., 5.
Aaltie, 2.
Abr., 31.
Anna, Annaatje, 1, 7, 49, 53,
74, 105, 111.
Ariaentie, 20.
Bata, 9.
Cathrina, Catarina, Catharina, Catharyna, 77, 83,
87, 88, 93, 95, 102, 110,
119, 122, 128.
Cornelis, Cornelius, Corns.,
Corn., 8, 69, 77, 83, 87,
88, 93, 95, 102, 105, 106,
110, 119, 120, 122, 123, 128.
Eldert, 21.
Fydtje, 100.
Helena, Lena, Hel., 21, 61,
70, 71, 80, 87, 119.
Isaac, Isak, 12, 105, 106.
Jacameyntie, 122.
Jacob, 119, 128.
Jannetje, Jann., 23, 37, 38,
77.
Johannes, Hannes, Joh.,
Johs., 5, 23, 29, 37, 49,
50, 61, 70, 77, 80, 87, 104,
111, 119.
Marie, Marytje, Mayken,
Maieke, 13, 77, 89, 122.
Mettie, 31.
Willem, 77, 89.
Oyl, Lochlan, 125.
Paal, William, 71.
Pamberton, Pemperton, J., 59.
Jeremiah, Jeremy, Jer., 19,
37, 46, 49, 54.
M., 49, 59.
Marr., 19, 20, 37, 46.
Pareois, John, 22.
Mary, 22.
Pat Blado, James, 8.

Pearson, Paarsen, Jannetie,
Jann., 30, 69.
Japik, Jac., 30, 69.
Peers, Anna, 34.
Pels, Abr., 32.
Evert, 22, 62.
Judikje, 64.
Rachel, Rach., 32, 53.
Perre, Jasowe, 1.
Perry, Johannes, 15.
Philips, James, 127.
Michael, 15, 127.
Pieterson, William, 108.
Pinhaarn, Marytie, 106.
Plot, Nathaniel, 119.
Poin, Johannes, 76.
Maria Geertruy, 76.
Porsess, Margret, 124.
Potman, Elizabeth, 9.
Potton, J., 51.
R., 51.
Powl, Thomas, 116.
Provoost, Johannes, 6.
Pruyn, Pruym, A., 41.
Alida, 4, 24, 28, 31, 45, 54,
75, 80, 81, 87, 103.
Arent, 28, 29, 47, 49.
Catharina, Cathar., Cat., 6,
23, 28, 36, 41, 42, 45, 47,
54.
Christyna, 6.
Elsje, 14, 81, 94, 101.
Emilie, 28.
Franciscus, Frank, Frans,
Fr., 2, 17, 24, 28, 31, 42,
45, 52, 53, 54, 64, 65, 75,
76, 81, 86, 87, 103.
Helena, 120.
Jacob, 53.
Jannittie, 126.
Johannes, Hans, Joh., 28,
81, 92, 124, 126.
M., 42, 46.
Magdalena, 9.
Margarita, M a r g r i e t j e,
Marg., 17, 24, 28, 52, 65,
76, 86.
Maria, Marytje, Mar., 10,
23, 28, 31, 48, 53, 72, 82,
88, 95, 119.
Samuel, Sam., 28, 31, 46.
Prys, Elizabeth, 12.
Josyna, 50, 56, 63, 69, 76,
104.
Maria, Mary, 12, 127.
Maria Anne, 12.
Purnel, Joanna, 122.
John, 122.
Pycket, Hagar, 1.
Quackenbos, A., 59.

Schuyler,—Continued.
  36, 38, 45, 59, 61, 75, 88,
  95, 99, 106, 112, 117, 123,
  128, 129.
  Rachel, 114.
  Susanna, Sus., 21, 31, 42,
    50, 56, 73, 74, 108, 113.
Schyans, etc., C., 55.
  Catharyna, Catr., Cath., 9,
    18, 24, 34, 45, 64, 107.
  Christiaan, Christ., Chr., 18,
    24, 28, 34, 45, 55, 64, 91,
    107.
  David, 14, 107.
  Hendrick, 121.
  Mary, Maritje, Mareytje,
    5, 17, 107, 121.
  Will., 17.
Sckerm, Neeltje, 121.
Seskby, Siksberry, Anna, 79.
  Elsje, 75, 86, 97, 103.
  Evert, 75, 86, 97, 103, 119.
  Marrytje, 75.
  Nicolaas, 103.
  William, Willem, 8, 75, 79.
Sheefer, Schieber, Doritie, 116.
  Hendrik, 75, 96.
  Jacob, 116.
  Johannes, 114, 116.
  Maria, Marytje, 75, 96.
Shuckburgh, Mary, 115.
  Richard, 115.
Siabbets, Bar., 59.
Skinner, Elizabet, 87.
Slingerland, Slingerl., A., 49, 59.
  Aegje, 75.
  Anna, Annaatje, 25, 34, 42,
    46, 72, 81, 94, 108.
  Arent, 113.
  C., 48.
  Cornelia, Corn., 29, 33, 40,
    63, 72, 76, 87, 99.
  Elizabeth, Elyz., 5, 64, 113.
  Engeltie, 34.
  Eva, 7, 49, 66.
  Hester, Hest., 33, 42, 44,
    93, 99.
  J., 49, 59.
  Johannis, Hannes, Johs.,
    Joh., 25, 34, 42, 46, 48,
    72, 75, 81, 93, 94, 108.
  Lena, 5.
  Rachel, 84, 85, 118, 123,
    128.
  Sara, 4.
  Theunis, Th., 16, 29, 33, 34,
    40, 42, 48, 54, 63, 66, 76,
    84, 87, 93, 99, 113, 118,
    128.
Sluyter, Cornelia, 5.

Smit, Smith, Smidt, Barber,
    106.
  Ephraim, 9.
  J., 5.
  Margrietje, 61.
  Sjeems, 61.
  Thomas, Tomas, 116, 126.
Sparten, Rachel, 63.
Sperry, Jan, 123.
Speysser, John, 5.
Spoor, Bar., 24.
  Cor., 4.
  Hendrik, Hendricus, 79,
    104, 126.
  Johannes, Johs., 53, 79.
  Maria, Maretie, 18, 53.
  Rebecca, 79, 104.
Springer, A., 67.
  Daniel, Danis, Dennis, 65,
    74, 83.
  Frena, Fryna, 97, 100, 114,
    126.
  Hendrik, Henderick, Hend.,
    97, 100, 112, 114, 126.
  J., 67.
  Mary, Maria, 65, 74, 83.
Springsteen, Abr., 62.
  Antje, 62.
  Macht., 62.
  Marytje, 63, 77, 85, 100.
  R., 5.
  Reyer, 63, 77, 85, 100, 111.
  Symeon, Simon, 14, 110,
    121.
Staats, Staets, Abram, 113.
  Anna, Annaatje, 2, 13, 61,
    75, 89, 106, 118.
  Ariaantje, 53.
  B., 44.
  Barent, Bar., 13, 18, 34, 37,
    61, 79, 89, 90, 94, 104,
    110, 113, 121.
  Catharyna, Cath., 4, 6.
  Deborah, 121.
  Elizabeth, 13, 79, 86, 90, 95,
    99, 110, 121.
  Geertruyd, Geertruy, 107,
    118.
  Gerrit, 86, 118, 121.
  Isaac, 2, 34, 52, 61, 78, 89.
  Isabella, Isabelle, 18, 47.
  Jacob, 18, 36, 47.
  's Jeertje, 6.
  Joachim, Jochem, 8, 66, 75,
    78, 79, 90, 99, 107, 117,
    125, 126.
  Js. [probably Is. for Isaac],
    41.
  Maria, Marytje, 34, 37, 41
    50, 61, 78, 89.

168

Waldron,—*Continued.*
Cornelia, Corn., 4, 105, 125.
Cornelis, Corns., Corn., 22,
26, 29, 32, 46, 62, 73, 87,
94, 98, 107, 109, 114, 118,
125.
Elizabeth, Elyz., El., 15, 23,
29, 38, 48, 58, 63, 66, 71,
89, 94, 106, 117, 124.
Engeltie, Engelt., 22, 29, 32,
38, 56, 73, 86, 109.
Eva, 10, 62, 109, 118.
Gerrit, 86, 125.
Jannetie, Jannitje, 54, 62,
73, 87, 94, 98.
Mareytje, 125.
Neeltje, Nelli, 114, 125.
Pieter, Peter, Piter, 13, 89,
94, 106.
Rebecka, 7, 73, 109, 117, 129.
W., 38, 48, 58.
Willem, William, Will., 15,
23, 29, 54, 66, 71, 89, 97,
106, 117, 124, 125.
Walte, Jane, 105.
Walters, Jacoba, 32.
Waters, Waaters, J., 51.
Jannetje, 8, 117, 122, 125.
John, Jan, 16, 27, 47, 52, 78,
125.
Sara, 16, 22, 27, 35, 47, 59,
65, 125.
Weiss, G., M., 4.
Wells, etc., Annaatje, 100.
Elyz., El., 22, 25.
James, Sjeems, Jems, 25,
100, 109.
Welsch, John, 13.
Wendell, Wendel, Wendels,—, 4.
Abraham, Abram, Abr., 6,
10, 44, 47, 51, 74, 77, 87,
88, 91, 94, 98, 100, 101,
102, 108, 118, 128.
Anna, Annaatje, 7, 16, 22,
26,28,33,37,38,42,43,44,
52, 53, 58, 66, 71, 81, 84,
88, 93, 94, 102, 104, 115.
Ariaantje, 120.
Assuerus, 35.
Catharyna, Cathalina, Catal.,
Chath., Cath., 2, 11, 15, 17,
23, 24, 33, 53, 55, 61, 64,
65, 73, 75, 77, 93, 98, 99,
100, 101, 104, 106, 108,
109, 113.
E., 42.
Elizabeth, Elyz., 10, 17, 32,
53, 71, 72, 73, 76, 77, 82,
88, 102, 108, 113, 115, 118,
125, 126, 128.

Engeltie, Engelt., Eng., 23,
33, 42, 54, 120.
Ephraim, Epram, Ephr., 17,
26, 38, 42, 65, 66, 70, 74,
81, 94, 102, 107.
Evert, 6, 23, 47, 52, 54, 69,
72, 80, 82, 87, 102, 108,
115, 117, 118, 120.
Geertruy, 74, 83, 91.
Geesje, 108, 118.
Gerritje, Gerretje, 12, 108,
119.
H., 128.
Helena, Lena, Hel., 37, 45,
68, 77, 82, 94, 97, 103,
115, 128.
Hermanus, Harm., 11, 37,
38, 87, 93, 100, 107, 117,
128.
Isack, Isaac, 15, 17, 24, 33,
55, 64, 74, 77, 86.
J. E., 61.
Jacob, Japik, Jac., 3, 28, 35,
37, 42, 45, 52, 58, 64, 68,
77, 84, 88, 93, 94, 97, 103,
106, 113.
Johannes, Hannes, Jan, Joh.,
Johs., 16, 17, 26, 28, 32,
40, 44, 52, 53, 54, 68, 71,
72, 103, 119.
M., 3, 47.
Maria, Marritje, Maicke,
Marr., 35, 51, 87, 104, 107,
128.
Philip, Ph., 42, 69.
Robbert, Rob., Ro., 4, 53,
61, 71, 73, 101, 115, 123.
Susanna, Zuzanna, Zantje,
Sus., 5, 47, 63, 69, 80, 87,
93, 96, 103, 111.
Westerlo, Eiland, 1.
White, Weith, Wite, Dirk, 98.
Grees, Greesje, 77, 98.
Mary, 7, 105, 116.
Richard, 77, 83.
Wieler, Wielaar, Cath, 20, 24.
Elizabeth, 73, 99.
Evert, 16, 20, 21, 87.
Helena, 16.
John, 99.
Josyna, Josina, 73, 121.
Margrieta, 73, 84.
Maria, Marytje, 16, 21, 87.
Samuel, 73, 84.
Wildin, Mary, 119.
William, 119.
Wilkenson, Willis, Elizabeth,
61, 70, 83, 99.
Thomas, 61, 70, 83, 90, 115,
124.

Witbeek,—*Continued.*
J., 67.
Jacob, Japik, 12, 56, 103, 117.
Jan, Johannes, Hannes, Joh., Johs., 1, 10, 20, 26, 28, 36, 37, 42, 53, 55, 64, 70, 85, 88, 89, 91, 95, 97, 109, 118, 125.
Jannetje, 88, 95.
Jonas, 3, 70.
Jonathan, 7, 64, 80, 89, 103, 111.
L., 5, 38.
Lena, 9, 79, 108.
Leendert, Leend., 55, 68, 78.
Lucas, 113, 119.
Magtel, 80, 89, 103.
Maria, Maritje, Mayke, 28, 79, 89, 94, 95, 103, 117.
Mart., 26.
Melchert, 88, 95, 99, 103, 104.
Rachel, Racheltje, 26, 64, 89, 91.
Thomas, 94.
Tobias, 53, 103.
Woedkok, Woutkok, Dirk, 96.
Jan., 21.
Rachel, 21.
Zara, 96.
Wood, Samuel, 121.
Worgsmans, Wurgsmans, Anna, 83, 96.
Hannes, 83, 96.
Wyngaart, Abraham, Abram, Abr., 3, 7, 23, 34, 43, 71, 72, 84, 89.
Anna, Annaatje, 23, 43, 50, 58, 107.
Christyna, Christyntje, 68, 73, 80, 89, 108.
Elizabeth, Ely., 15, 43, 71, 72, 84, 89, 122.
Gerrit, 50, 73, 81, 107, 108, 111.
Johannes, Hannes, Johs., Joh., 1, 23, 32, 38, 41, 43, 46, 53, 63, 73, 80.
Lucas, Luykas, Luc., 25, 102, 106, 107, 108.
M., 41, 44, 46, 67.
Magtel, Magdel, Macht., Mach., 7, 32, 34, 111.
Mar., 23, 38.
Margarita, Margrietje, Margriet, 15, 50, 81, 97, 99, 103, 107, 127.
Maria, Mareytje, 32, 63, 73, 127.
Sara, 3, 25, 28, 105.

Yates, Jeets, Abraham, Abram, 115, 121.
Adam, 4, 45, 49, 57, 59, 77, 91, 96, 104, 113, 114, 125, 126, 128.
Anna, Annaatje, Annatie, 57, 77, 91, 106, 109, 113, 126, 128.
Cathalina, Cathalyntje, Catharyna, Catlena, Catal, Cat., 10, 24, 39, 40, 73, 77, 96, 103, 105, 109, 110, 115.
Christoffel, Christ., Chr., 24, 39, 40, 57, 73, 77, 96, 103, 109, 115, 121.
E., 45.
Elizabeth, y.
Eva, 40.
H., 62.
Hendrika, Hendr., Hend., 16, 25, 35, 40, 44, 48, 56.
Huybertje, 7, 120.
J., 45.
Ji., 62.
Johannes, John, Johs., 7, 73, 85, 86, 101, 109, 117, 118, 129.
Joseph, Jos., 7, 16, 25, 35, 40, 44, 48, 62, 91.
Maria, 11, 31, 109, 118, 128.
Rebekka, Rebecca, 86, 101, 118.
Robert, 24.
Ylingh, Evert, 1.
Yorck, Dan., 69.
Mary, 69.
Young, Elizabeth, 120.
Gey, 120.
Hendrik, 14, 113, 123.
W., 59.
William, 125.
Zeeger, Anatje, 112.
B., 45, 64.
Breggie, Bregje, Brefje, Brechtie, Brechie, 20, 27, 35, 49, 51, 56, 73, 75, 76, 106, 121.
Elizabeth, 11, 112.
Evert, 14, 87, 99, 106, 118, 124.
Gerrit, 88, 96.
Hendrick, 118.
Hillitje, 124.
J., 64.
Johannes, Joh., Johs., 20, 27, 35, 45, 49, 51, 56, 73, 76, 101, 106, 119, 120, 121.
Lydia, 10, 104, 112, 120.
Maria, 14, 88, 96, 101, 110, 111, 121.

Records of the Reformed Dutch Church of Albany, New York

Part 4
1750-1764

Excerpted from
Year Book of The Holland Society
of New York (1907)

RECORDS OF THE REFORMED DUTCH CHURCH OF ALBANY, N. Y.

MARRIAGES, 1750 TO 1762.

[For abbreviations see page fronting Index.]

1749/50, Feb. 3. With License. Harmen Fisher, y. m., of Sch., and Hester Van Iveren, y. d., of A.

Feb. 6. Married after three proclamations by Rev. Berkenmeyer, Gerrit Borgard, y. m., of Kinderhook, and Antje I. Lagrangie, y. d.

Feb. 6. **B.** Gerrit Quackenbosch, y. m., b. at Nist., l. at Saratoga, and Catarina De Voe, y. d., b. at Half Moon, l. in Col. R.

1750, March 30. **B.** John Wilson, y. m., and Barber Tievetorp, y. d., both of A.

May 7. **B.** Joseph Baley, y. m., and Debora Springer, y. d., both l. at A.

June 12. **L.** Philip Coneyn, y. m., and Commertje Bronck, y. d., both of Kogsackie.

June 15. **Ma.** after 3 pr. Barent Hogen, y. m., and Geertje Huyck, y. d., both from Hosanck.

June 16. **L.** Isaac I. Truax, y. m., and Maria Wyngaard, y. d., both from A. Co.

June 17. **Ma.** after 3 pr. Henderick Wendel, y. m., and Catalina Van Schaick, y. d., both from Col. R.

June 22. **Ma.** Johannes Gardenier, y. m., and Maria Woodkock, y. d., both from K.

June 28. **L.** Johannes Jansen, y. m., and Jannitje Schermerhoorn, y. d., both of Schot. in A. Co.

Aug. 19. **Pr.** Isaac De Voe, b. and l. at the H. M., and Mareytje Van Olinden, y. d., b. at Nist., l. near Schag.

Aug. 25. **L.** Wynant Vanden Berg, widr., and Catrina Groesbeek, wid., both of A.

Sep. 7. **L.** Tobias Ten Eyck, y. m., of Sch., and Rachel De Peyster, y. d., of A.

Nov. 10. **L.** Schiboleth Bogardus, y. m., and Elizabeth Van de Werken, y. d., both of A., in presence of Elder Jacob H. Ten Eyck.

1

Dec. 2. **L.** Johannes Gansevoort, y. m., of A., and Maria Douw, y. d., of Col. R.

Dec. 10. **Ma.** Johannes Fonda, y. m., of Col. R., and Elizabeth Ouderkerk, y. d., of the H. M.

1751, June 15. **Ma.** Johannes Backer, y. m., and Rebecca Bogaart, y. d., both of A.

June 22. **L.** Lucas Yeets, y. m., and Sarah Van Zanten, y. d., both of A.

June 29. **L.** Hendrick Bogaart, y. m., and Engeltje Van Schaak, y. d., both of A.

July 7. **Ma.** after 3 **B.** Johannes Post, y. m., and Frena Meyer, y. d., both of A.

July 7. **Ma.** after 3 **B.** Isaac Fort, y. m., of Schag., and Sara Viele, y. d., of Stillewater.

July 18. **Ma.** after 3 **B.** Casparus Lodewyck, y. m., and Maria Spoor, y. d., both of Schot.

July 24. **L.** Bastyaen Bisscher and Engeltje Van den Berg, both of A.

July 24. **L.** Jacob Van Wagenen, of N. Y., and Neeltje Visscher, of A.

Aug. 17. After 3 pr. by Do. I. Oglevie Eng. preacher in this City: Thomas Arche, y. m., of Normans Kill, and Mary Lewis, y. d., of the Verreberg.

Aug. 18. After 3 pr. by Do. Oglevie Eng. preacher in this City: William Carson of the garrison in this City, and Lydia Coda of this City.

Sep. 14. **L.** Jacob Van Schaick, y. m., and Catarina Cuyler, y. d., both of A.

Sep. 21. **L.** Anthony Van Schaick, y. m., and Christina Van Schaick, y. d., both of A.

Sep. 21. After 3 pr. Anthony Slingerlandt, y. m., of Col. R., and Claertje Cloet, y. d., of Nist.

Sep. 28. After 3 pr. Johanes Koen, y. m., of the Col. and Hillitje Zeger, y. d., of A.

Sep. 29. After 3 pr. John Hoar, of Schot., and Maria Bourch, of A.

Oct. 3. After 3 pr. Albert Van der Werken, y. m., of the H. M., and Maria Quackenbosch of the Draagplaets.

Oct. 6. After 3 pr. Michael Landtman, y. m., and Maria Brouwer, y. d., both of Hosack.

Oct. 6. **L.** Coenraedt Loeck, y. m., of A. Co., and Geertruy Van Deuzen, y. d., of A.

Oct. 27. **L.** Johannes D. Garmo, y. m., and Annatje Kettel, y. d., both of A. Co.

Nov. 8. After 3 pr. Cornelis DuBois, y. m., of Katskill, and Catarina Van der Poel, y. d., of K.

Nov. 10. After 3 **B.** Jacob Arnel [?], y. m., of Norman's Kill, and Anna Mug, y. d., of A.

Nov. 16. **L.** Matthew Mynderson, y. m., and Sarah Rykman, y. d., both of A.

Nov. 22. **L.** Abraham Van den Bergh, y. m., and Rachel Liverse, y. d., both of A. Co.

Nov. 29. **L.** Geysbert Marselis, y. m., and Catalina Wendel, y. d., both of A.

Dec. 6. **L.** Pieter Bloemendal, y. m., of A., and Christina Legrange, y. d., of the N. K., A. Co.

Dec. 30. After 3 **B.** Abner Roberts, y. m., of N. E., and Geertje Vosburgh, y. d., of Hosunck.

1751/2, Jan. 7. **L.** Pieter Gansevoort, y. m., and Gerritje Ten Eyck, y. d., both of A.

Jan. 14. **L.** Lambert Van Aalsteyn, y. m., of K., and Alida Coneyn, y. d., of C.

Jan. 18. After 3. **B.** Johannes Claesse Van Vrancken, y. m., of Nist., and Maria Potman, y. d., of Sch.

Jan. 30. **L.** Harmen Livessen, y. m., and Annatje Van Schoonhoven, y. d., both of H. M., A. Co.

Feb. 7. After 3 **B.** Luycas Wesselse, y. m., of K., and Annatje Van der Poel, wid., of the Col.

Feb. 9. After 3 **B.** John Phillips, y. m., and Maria Middleton, y. d., both of Sch.

Mar. 22. After 3 **B.** Abram Coeper, y. m., of A., and Catarina Oostrander, y. d., of Col. R.

Mar. 23. After 3 **B.** Thomas Wood, y. m., of New Ark, and Catarina Gardenier, y. d., of K.

1752, Mar 30. **L.** Abraham Mebie, widr., of Sch., and Catalina Roseboom, wid.

Apr. 9. **L.** Simon Johannissen Veder and Catalina Veder, both of N. K.

Apr. 19. **L.** Volkert Douw and Rachel Bogaert, both of A.

Apr. 25. **L.** Jesse Winne, y. m., and Anatje Van den Bergh, y. d., both of A. Co.

Apr. 25. After 3 **B.** Mattheus Boom, y. m., and Maria Hilton, y. d., both of this City.

May 10. **L.** Anthony Van der Zee, widr., of A., and Anatje Van Ness, y. d., of Col. R.

May 16. After 3 **B.** Johannes Redlof, Jr., y. m., and Anna Meccans, y. d., both of Col. R.

May 18. **L.** Antony Flensburg, y. m., and Annatje Redley, y. d., both of this place.

May 28. Jacob Roelefse, y. m., and Maria Ouderkerk, wid., both of A. Co.

June 6. **L.** John Danielson, y. m., and Geertruy Hilton, y. d., both of A.

June 9. After 3 **B.** Petrus Vosburg, y. m., and Anna Brouwer, y. d., both of Hosunk.

June 20. **L.** Adam Van Alen, widr., of K., and Maria Rooseboom, y. d., of A.

June 27. **L.** Robert Lansing, widr., of A., and Catarina Ten Broeck, wid. of Ephraim Van Vegten, of C.

July 2. **L.** David Abeel Jr., y. m., of A., and Neeltje Van Bergen, y. d., of Katskil.

Aug. 6. **L.** Arie Oothout, y. m., and Treyntje Van Aalsteyn, wid., both of Col. R.

Aug. 18. **L.** William Pemberton, y. m., and Sarah Drowley, y. d., both of A.

Aug. 22. **L.** Abraham Peek, y. m., and Catarina Van Sante, y. d., both of A.

Aug. 25. **L.** Petrus Hoffman, y. m., of Dutches Co., and Catarina Van Aalsteyn, y. d., of K.

Aug. 26. **Ma.** Cornelius Muller, y. m., and Cornelia Esselsteyn, y. d., both of C.

Sep. 17. **L.** Hugo Viele, widr., and Elizabeth Van Veghte, wid., both of Schag.

Sep. 27. **L.** Johannes Cloet, y. m., of A., and Sarah Van Arnhem, y. d., of Col. R.

Sep. 27. **L.** Peter De Garmo, y. m., of A., and Geertruy Cregier, y. d., of Nist.

Nov. 9. **B.** Pieter Redlof, y. m., of A., and Catalina Redlof, y. d., of Na.

Nov. 10. **L.** David Verplanck, widr., and Catarina Boom, both of A. Co.

Nov. 11. **L.** James Adams, y. m., and Margarita Hegeman, y. d., both of Na.

Nov. 12. **L.** Isaac A. Kip, y. m., and Neeltje Brat, y. d., both of A.

Nov. 18. **L.** Abraham Fort, y. m., and Sarah Van Woert, y. d., both of A. Co.

Nov. 22. **L.** Johannes Groesbeek, y. m., and Elisabeth Van Brakelen, y. d., both of Schag.

Nov. 24. **L.** Cornelius Groot, y. m., and Mareytje Van Vranken, y. d., both of A. Co.

Nov. 24. **L.** Arent Van Antwerpen, y. m., of Sch., and Elisabeth Groot, y. d., of Nist.

Dec. 21. **L.** Dr. Henricus Van Dyck, y. m., of A., and Margarita Douw, y. d., of R.

Dec. 23. **L.** David Groesbeek, y. m., and Catarina Veder, y. d., both of A.

1753, Jan. 4. **L.** Johannis Vosburgh, y. m., and Annatje Van Alen, y. d., both of K.

Jan. 5. **L.** Lucas Wyngaart, y. m., and Catarina Van Aalsteyn, wid. of Adam Van Alen, both of K.

Jan. 23. **L.** Abraham Oostrander, y. m., of Es., and Elisabeth Oostrander, y. d., of Col. R.

Feb. 20. After 3 **B.** Jan Decker, y. m., and Annatje Schils, y. d., both b. and l. at M. L.

Mar. 4. After 3 **B.** Gerrit Rosa, y. m., of Es. and Annatje Becker, y. d., of K.

Mar. 5. After 3 **B.** John Williams, y. m., of Scho., and Maria Leisch, y. d., of Col. R.

Mar. 5. **L.** Stephanus Van Schaick, y. m., and Janintje Brat, y. d., both of A.

Mar. 10. **L.** Pieter De Wandelaar, widr., and Annatje Van Veghten, wid., both of A.

Mar. 23. After 3 **B.** Adriaan Brat, widr., and Maria Meckans, y. d., both of Col. R.

Apr. 2. After 3 **B.** John Bel, widr., of C., and Mary Burnham, wid. of A.

Apr. 14. **L.** Isaac Deforeest, y. m., of A., and Alida Fonda, y. d., of Col. R.

Apr. 27. **L.** Johannes Loeck, y. m., of Na., and Geesje Legrange, y. d., of N. K.

May 5. **L.** Pieter Goewey, y. m., and Maria Young, y. d., both of Col. R.

May 8. **L.** Harmanus I. Wendel, y. m., and Barber Brat, y. d., both of A.

May 13. After 3 **B.** Alexander Martin, y. m., and Anna Philipse, y. d., both of A.

June 2. **L.** Jacob Vollenwyder, y. m., and Maria Brat, y. d., both of Nist.

June 7. **L.** Henderick Williams, y. m., and Franseyna Cloet, y. d., both of A. Co.

June 8. **L.** Hendrick Van Dyck, y. m., and Engeltje Mebie, y. d., both of Sch.

June 30. After 3 **B.** Johannes Muller, y. m., b. at A., l. in Col. R., and Sarah Van Ieveren, y. d., b. and l. in Col. R.

Sep. 5. **L.** Gerrit Roerbach, y. m., of N. Y., and Alida Visscher, y. d., of A.

Sep. 7. **L.** Daniel M'Kenny, y. m., of A. Co., and Margarita Stenhouse, y. d., of A.

Sep. 22. **L.** Johannes Huyck, y. m., and Gerritje Jansen, y. d., both of Schot.

Oct. 6. **L.** Johannes Knoet, y. m., and Jannitje Ouderkerk, y. d., both of A. Co.

Oct. 6. **L.** Geysbert Fonda, y. m., and Elsje Douw, y. d., both of A.

Oct. 14. **B.** Jacob Smit, y. m., of Saratoga, and Mareytje Smit, y. d., of the H. M.

Oct. 19. **L.** Joachim Van Slyck, y. m., of K., and Cornelia Van Valkenburgh, y. d., of Schot.

Oct. 20. **L.** Alexander Lansing, y. m., and Abigail Verplank, y. d., both of A.

Nov. 20. **L.** Reyer Schermerhoorn, y. m., of Schot., and Dirkje Van Buren, y. d.

Dec. 9. After 3 **B.** Dirk Brat, widr., of Nist., and Catarina Heypelaar, b. in Sweden, l. in Col R.

Dec. 30. **L.** Johannes Clement, y. m., and Rachel Redlof, y. d., both of A. (see Jan. 5, 1754).

1754, Jan. 1. After 3 **B.** Jacob Goewey and Eva Brat, wid. of John Morris, both of Col. R.

Jan. 5. **L.** Johannes Clement, y. m., and Rachel Redley, y. d., both of A. (see Dec. 30, 1753).

Jan. 12. After 3 **B.** Andries Gardenier, y. m., and Margarita Goewey, y. d., both of A.

Jan. 12. **L.** Pieter Brat, y. m., and Jacomeyntje Bloemendal, y. d., both of A.

Jan. 24. After 3 **B.** Hendrick Rou, y. m., of C., and Hilletje Clerk, y. d., of K.

Jan. 29. After 3 **B.** Elias Truex, y. m., and Ariaantje Jansen, y. d., both of the N. K.

Jan. 31. **L.** Jacobus Van Cortlandt, y. m., of N. Y., and Elisabeth Cuyler, y. d., of A.

Feb. 1. After 3 **B.** Isaac Van Vranken, y. m., of Nist., and Claartje Brat, y. d., of Col. R.

Feb. 1. After 3 **B.** Isaac Van Aalsteyn, y. m., and Anna Maria Seyvert, y. d., both of Saratoga.

Feb. 1. **L.** Claas DeGraef, y. m., and Catalina Truex, y. d., both of Sch.

Feb. 13. **L.** Johannes Beekman, y. m., of A., and Maria Nichols, y. d., of Col. R.

Feb. 18. After 3 **B.** Ephraim Moor, y. m., of C., and Christina Salsbergen, y. d., of Col. R.

Feb. 25. After 3 **B.** Roelof Seger, widr., and Lydia Harty, y. d., both of A.

Feb. 28. **L.** Dirk Van der Heyden, y. m., of the Draagplaets, and Margarita Kettel, y. d., of Schag.

Mar. 15. After 3 **B.** Henderick Poster, y. m., and Rachel Fitsgereld, both of Schot.

May 5. After 3 **B.** Jillis Winne, y. m., of this City, and Tietje Van Woert, of Col. R.

May 12. After 3 **B.** Johannes Barnhead, y. m., and Christina Huyck, y. d., both of Hosunck.

July 6. **L.** Rutger Van den Bergh, y. m., of A. Co., and Maria Van den Bergh, y. d., of A.

Aug. 5. After 3 **B.** David Augsburger, y. m., and Anna Elisabeth Scheldin, y. d., both b. in Ger., l. at A.

Aug. 23. **L.** Johannes Van Sandten, Jr., y. m., and Margarita Wilkenson, y. d., both of A.

Sep. 7. After 3 **B.** Gerrit Bovie, y. m., b. at the H. M., l. at Hosunck and Ariaantje Brouwer, y. d., b. at A., l. at Hosunck.

Sep. 4. **L.** Harmanus Schuyler, y. m., of A., and Christina Tenbroeck, y. d., of C.

Sep. 14. **L.** Wouter De Foreest, y. m., and Engeltje Brat, y. d., both of A.

Sep. 20. After 3 **B.** Dirk Van der Willigen, y. m., and Sara Laura, y. d., both of Na.

Oct. 26. After 3 **B.** David Springer, y. m., and Margarita Oliver, y. d., both of A.

Nov. 2. **L.** Jonathan Hoogteling, y. m., and Jannitje Slingerlandt, y. d., both of Na.

Nov. 2. **L.** Jacob Loeck, y. m., and Alida Goewey, y. d., both of A. Co.

Nov. 2. After 3 **B.** John Car, y. m., of Sco., and Margarita Bovie, y. d., of Nist.

Nov. 2. **L.** Frederick Cloet, y. m., and Maritje Ridder, y. d., both of Saratoga.

Nov. 2. **L.** Nicholaes Cloet, y. m., and Ariaantje Ridder, y. d., both of Saratoga.

Nov. 10. After 3 **B.** John Bourn, y. m., and Rachel Chidester, y. d., both of Ft. Masachuset at Hosac.

Nov. 27. **L.** Louis Van Antwerpen, y. m., and Henderica Funda, y. d., both of Schag.

Dec. 6. After 3 **B.** David Brat, y. m., and Treyntje Lang, y. d., both of Na.

Dec 18. **L.** Johannes Schuneman, preacher, and Anna Maria Van Bergen, y. d., both of Katskil.

Dec. 26. After 3 **B.** Johannes Van der Werken, y. m., and Mareytje Tefoe, y. d., both of H. M.

1755. Jan. 5. After 3 **B.** Reykert Redlof, y. m., and Maria Oliver, y. d., both of Na.

Mar. 7. After 3 **B.** Tobias Lent, y. m., and Anatje Van Tessele, y. d., both of the Manor of Cortland.

Mar. 29. After 3 **B.** Roelof Mackerie, y. m., and Catarina Bovie, y. d., both of A.

Mar. 30. After 3 **B.** Johan Henrich Winckler, widr., and Anna Catarina Hiserin, y. d., both of Ger.

Apr. 5. **L.** William Nichols, y. m., of Col. R., and Femmetje Beekman, y. d., of A.

Apr. 19. **L.** John Dunbar, y. m., and Helena Gerritse Lansing, y. d., both of A.

May 10. **L.** Folkert Van den Bergh, Jr., y. m., and Neeltje Waldron, y. d., both of A.

May 11. **L.** Gerrit Dirkse Becker, y. m., and Eva Hogen, y. d., both of A.

May 20. After 3 **B.** Henderick H. Gardenier, y. m., of K., and Maria Goewey, y. d., of A.

July 28. **L.** Johannis Groesbeek, y. m., and Mareytje Viele, y. d., both of Schag.

Sep. 7. **L.** Philip I. Schuyler, y. m., and Catarina Van Renslaer, y. d., both of A.

Sep. 20. **L.** Peter Williams and Elisabeth Funda, both of A.

Oct. 23. **L.** Abraham Meyndertse, y. m., and Cathrina Oostrander, y. d.

Nov. 2. After 3 **B.** George Clachry and Obedience Carpenter.

1756. Jan. 5. After 3 **B.** Matthys Hooghteeling, y. m., and Ariaantje Van der See, y. d., both of Na.

Jan. 15. After 3 **B.** Adriaan Brat, widr., and Lydia Van Aalsteyn, y. d., both of Na.

Jan. 29. **L.** Barent Ten Eyck, y. m., and Elsje Cuyler, y. d., both of A.

Feb. 6. **L.** Tobias Ten Eyck, y. m., of A., and Judithje Van Buren, y. d., of Schot.

Feb. 7. **L.** Samuel Pruyn, y. m., and Neeltje Ten Eyck, y. d., both of A.

Feb. 9. After 3 **B.** Christiaan Gerhart, y. m., and Anna Barbara Leererin, y. d., both of Ger.

Feb. 15. After 3 **B.** Philip Trender, widr., soldier of Col. Dunbar's Regt., and Elisabeth Martin, widow of A.

Feb. 17. After 3 **B.** Tam Hecket and Elisabeth Christiaanse.

Mar. 4. **L.** Johannes Van Arnhem, y. m., and Alida Van der Heyden, y. d., both of A. Co.

Mar. 13. **L.** Henderick Van der Werken, y. m., and Maria Viele, y. d., both of A. Co.

Apr. 2. After 3 **B.** Timmothy Connor, a soldier, and Mary Day.

Apr. 8. After 3 **B.** A soldier and a female called Nancy.

Apr. 13. **L.** Jonas Oothout, widr., and Elisabeth Vinnagel, y. d., both of A. Co.

May 1. After 3 **B.** Albartus Digmanse, y. m., of K., and Geertruy Ham, y. d., of A.

May 7. After 3 **B.** Daniel Bernardusse Brat, y. m., and Willempje Brat, y. d., both of A.

May 25. After 3 **B.** Albartus Bloemendal, y. m., and Maria Oostrander, y. d., both of A.

May 28. After 3 **B.** John Baker, a soldier, and Catharina Davis.

June 2. After 3 **B.** James Maccray, widr., a soldier in the govt's service, and Honer Dalley, wid., both b. in Ire., l. here.

July 15. **L.** Rev. Thomas Romein, y. m., Min. of the Gospel at Jamaica, L. I., N. Y., and Margarita Frielinghuysen, y. d. of A.

July 24. **L.** Teunis Brat, y. m., and Catalina Van Ness, y. d., both of A.

July 24. **L.** Jacob Deforeest, y. m., and Tryntje Brat, y. d., both of A. Co.

Aug. 28. After 3 **B.** Tam and Bet, servants of Jacob Loeck.

Sep. 17. **L.** Jacob Jacobse, y. m., and Maria Evertse, y. d., both of A.

Sep. 18. After 3 **B.** Evert Van den Bergh, y. m., and Anatje Lansing, y. d., both of A. Co.

Oct. 9. **L.** Lewis Hugose Viele, y. m., and Maria Viele, y. d., both of Schag.

Oct. 25. **B.** John Ferrel, y. m., b. in Ire., and Rachel Loyd, wid., b. at Charlestown, S. C., both l. near this place.

Oct. 25. After 3 **B.** Jacobus Fisher, y. m., of the Raritans, and Rachel Jochumse Van der Heyden, y. d., of A.

Nov. 23. After 3 **B.** Henderick Stronck, y. m., and Elisabeth Hermich, y. d., both b. in Germ., l. here.

Dec. 4. **L.** Abraham Slingerlandt, y. m., and Rebecca Viele, y. d., both of A. Co.

Dec. 20. After 3 **B.** Alexander Brown, y. m., and Christina Bowman, wid., both of Sco.

1757. Jan. 13. After 3 **B.** Adam Koen, y. m., b. at Schie. and Maria Vander Hoef, y. d., b. at N. Y., both l. in Col. R.

Jan. 13. After 3 **B.** Baltus Bacchus, y. m., b. at Rynbeek, and Barber Koen, y. d., b. at Schie.

Jan. 29. After 3 **B.** George Young, y. m., and Catarina Litcher, y. d., both of the Plain.

Jan. 29. After 3 **B.** John Crannel, y. m., and Volkje Van Aalsteyn, y. d., both of A. Co.

Jan. 30. After 3 **B.** George Mulligan, soldier of Gen. Otway's Regt., and Ellenor Wright.

Feb. 1. After 3 **B.** John Weaver, y. m., of Ger., and Catarina Crovin, wid., of Philadelphia.

Feb. 14. **L.** James Philip Crowa, y. m., musician of Daniel Webb's Regt., and Maria Kidney, y. d., of A.

Feb. 20. After 3 **B.** James Crow, soldier of Gen. Otway's Regt., and Ellenor Darby, wid.

Mar. 3. **L.** Johannis Egberson, y. m., and Catarina Van Wie, y. d., both of A. Co.

Mar. 5. **L.** Cornelius Livesse, y. m., and Cornelia Brat, y. d., both of A.

Mar. 18. After 3 **B.** Johannis P. Funda, y. m., and Dirkje Winne, y. d., both of A. Co.

Mar. 27. After 3 **B.** Alexander McOwen, of the 42d Regt., and Anna Slatery.

May 28. **L.** Jacob Loeck, y. m., and Rachel Hogen, wid., both of A. Co.

June 5. After 3 **B.** Jacob Cloet, y. m., of Nist., and Sara Goewey, y. d., of A. Co.

June 9. **L.** Henderick Wendel, y. m., and Maria Lansing, y. d., both of A.

June 18. **L.** Johannis Spoor, y. m., and Magdalena Bogaart, y. d., both of A.

July 7. **L.** Gosen Van Schaick, y. m., and Elisabeth Wendel, y. d., both of A.

July 9. **L.** Adriaan Quackenbos, y. m., and Volkje Van den Bergh, y. d., both of A. Co.

July 15. After 3 **B.** Gerrit Seger, Jr., y. m., and Wyntje Oliver, y. d., both of A. Co.

July 31. After 3 **B.** Nicolaes Brouwer and Maria Boom, both of A. Co.

Aug. 27. **L.** Andries Van Schaak, y. m., and Alida Hogen, y. d., both of A.

Sep. 15. **L.** Frans Wine, widr., and Maritje Lorway, wid., both of A. Co.

Sep. 30. After 3 **B.** Isaac Oostrander, y. m., and Elisabeth Meekans, y. d., both of A. Co.

Oct. 8. **L.** Hugh Denison, y. m., of N. Y., and Rachel Van Valkenburgh, y. d., of A.

Nov. 6. After 3 **B.** George Rushton and Margaret Adams, both b. in Eng., l. here.

Nov. 10. **L.** Jacob Viele, y. m., and Catarina Coddington, y. d., both of A. Co.

Nov. 11. **L.** Pieter Liverse, y. m., and Maria Funda, y. d., both of the Oak Groves of Mamre in A. Co.

Nov. 13. After 3 **B.** Francis Nicholson of Hamburg, sergt. in the Royal American Regt., and Catarina, wid. of Johannis Abramson, of A.

Nov. 16. **L.** Gerrit T. Slingerlant, y. m., and Eghje Van der See, y. d., both of Na.

Nov. 18. **L.** Jacobus Abeel, y. m., of A., and Abigael Van Buren, y. d., of Papsknee.

Nov. 18. **L.** Jacob Van Arnhem, y. m., and Anatje Van Vranken, y. d., both of A. Co.

Nov. 19. **L.** Folkert Douw, y. m., and Anatje Wendel, y. d., both of A.

Nov. 26. After 3 **B.** Johannes Goewey, y. m., and Maria Van Ieveren, y. d., both l. here.

Dec. 10. **L.** Cornelis Van Veghten, y. m., of Schag., and Anatje Knickerbacker, y. d., of A.

Dec. 15. John Frasier of the 42d Regt. and Isabella Polsum, dau. of David of the same Regt., by order of Lieut. Col. Grant.

Dec. 30. After 3 **B.** Johannis Heemstraet, y. m., and Elisabeth Bovie, y. d., both of Nist.

Dec. 31. After 3 **B.** Henderick Milton, widr., and Rachel Norton, y. d., both of A. Co.

1758. Jan. 13. After 3 **B.** Johannis Oliver, y. m., and Maritje Siksby, y. d., both of A. Co.

Mar. 4. After 3 **B.** Johannis Winne, y. m., and Saintje Ridder, y. d., both of A. Co.

Apr. 11. **B.** Frans Ruso, y. m., b. in Flanders, and Maria Palsin, y. d., b. in the Paltz, both l. in A. Co.

Apr. 22. After 3 **B.** Johan Pieter Claes, y. m., and Clara Margarita Curtin, y. d., both of A. Co.

May 1. After 3 **B.** Marmaduke Eakin, soldier of the 44th Regt., and Elizabeth Extraim.

May 13. **L.** Albert Van der Werken, Jr., y. m., and Anna Winne, y. d., both of A. Co.

May 19. **L.** Jacob Degarmo, y. m., of A., and Fytje Becker, y. d., of Na.

June 2. **L.** William Sole and Margarita Philips, wid., both of this city.

July 1. **L.** Abraham Fort, y. m., and Eva Benneway, y. d., both of A. Co.

July 15. **L.** Dirk Van der Heyden, y. m., and Sara Wendel, y. d., both of A. Co.

July 22. **L.** Dirk Swart, y. m., and Jannetje Van der See, y. d., both l. here.

Aug. 19. **L.** Abraham Wemp, y. m., of Sch., and Antje Van den Bergh, y. d., of A.

Sep. 3. After 3 **B.** William Maccue and Mary Burk, both of A.

Sep. 17. After 3 **B.** Hieram Weston and Maria Brown, both of A.

Sep. 28. **L.** Wynant Volkertse Van den Bergh, y. m., and Mareytje Van den Bergh, y. d., both of A. Co.

Sep. 28. After 3 **B.** Gerrit Johannisse Vandenbergh, y. m., and Alida Gerritse Vandenbergh, y. d., both of H. M.

Oct. 1. After 3 **B.** James Milton and Elisabeth Marchal, both l. here.

Oct. 1. After 3 **B.** John Van Tile and Charity Cartwright, both l. here.

Oct. 15. After 3 **B.** John Walley, y. m., and Charlotte Smith, y. d., both l. here.

Oct. 15. After 3 **B.** Emanuel Strobel, y. m., and Helena Burn, wid., both l. here.

Oct. 21. **L.** Dirk Van Veghten, y. m., and Alida Knickerbacker, y. d., both of A.

Oct. 22. After 3 **B.** Thomas Scot and Mary Reed, both l. here.

Oct. 29. **Ma.** at Schie. **L.** Do. Johan Maurits Goetschius and Catarina Heger, y. d., of Schie.

1759, March 2. **Ma.** by order, William Jackson, soldier of the 55th Regt., and Barbara Miller.

Mar. 4. **L.** John Fryer, y. m., and Elisabeth Van Woert, y. d., both of A.

Mar. 12. **L.** Barent Van Benthuysen, y. m., of Rynbeck, and Geertruy Halenbeck, y. d., of Klinkenbergh.

Mar. 21. **B.** Andrew Wright, soldier of the 55th Regt., and Margaret Cahoun.

May 6. **B.** Henry Edwards, of the 46th Regt., and Rachel White, wid., both at present l. here.

—— **Ma.** by order of the Officer: John Hilton of the Inniskilling Regt., and Margaret Barret, both at present at A.

May 24. **L.** John Glen, Jr., y. m., and Catarina Veder, y. d., both of A.

June 30. **B.** Johannes Oothout, y. m., and Elisabeth Van Woert, y. d., both of A. Co.

July 7. **L.** William Verplanck, y. m., and Lydia Liversen, y. d., both of A.

July 20. **L.** Jacob Moore, y. m., of C., and Maria Witbeek, y. d., of A. Co.

July 24. After 3 **B.** William Spuyver, y. m., and Elisabeth Heynsin, y. d., both b. in Ger., l. here.

1758 [*sic*], Nov. 26. **B.** William Pheland, y. m., and Maria Welsh, wid., both b. in Ire., l. here.

Nov. 28. **L.** Pieter Rykman, y. m., of A., and Lidia Van den Bergh, y. d., of A. Co.

Dec. 2. **L.** Francis Winne, y. m., and Anneke Viele, y. d., both of A.

Dec. 9. **L.** Johannis S. Quackenbosch, y. m., and Jannitje Viele, y. d., both of A. Co.

Dec. 17. **B.** James Mac Mullen and Margaret Mannen, both b. in Ire., now l. here.

Dec. 23. **L.** Cornelius Van Buren, y. m., of A. Co., and Majeke Hun, y. d., of A.

Dec. 24. **L.** Jacobus Van Sant, y. m., and Maria Broecks, y. d., both of A.

1759, Jan. 5. **L.** Johannis Fonda, y. m., and Eeghje Van der See, y. d., both of A. Co.

Jan. 13. **L.** Bastiaan Cregier, y. m., and Maria Fonda, y. d., both of A. Co.

Jan. 27. After 3 **B.** Isaac Vosburg, widr., of A., and Catarina Taat, y. d., of East Camp.

Feb. 4. **B.** Richard Kiskhop, of the Royal Artillery, and Mary Cambel, both at present l. here.

Aug. 4. **L.** David Scot, y. m., and Maria Wendel, y. d., both of A.

Aug. 8. **L.** Timothy O'Conner and Elisabeth Loteridge, wid., both of A.

Aug. 12. After 3 **B.** Johannis Kerner, y. m., and Susanna Hogin, y. d., both of A.

Aug. 16. **L.** Reynier Van Ieveren, y. m., and Debora Fielding, y. d., both of A.

Aug. 18. **L.** William Hun, y. m., and Sara Deforest, y. d., both of A.

Aug. 27. **B.** Arthur Colliger, soldier of the 11th Regt., and Maria Wilkenson, both l. at A.

Aug. 6 [*sic*], After 3 **B.** Abraham Vanderkar, y. m., and Margarita Tevoe, y. d., both of the H. M.

Aug. 8. **L.** Johannis Van Wie and Magdalena Loeck, y. d., both of A. Co.

Aug. 9. After 3 **B.** Lodewick Ensel, y. m., and Elisabeth Moor, y. d., both l. here.

Aug. 10. **L.** William Tayler and Maria Hopkins, both l. here.

Aug. 15. **L.** John Vielen, y. m., and Geesje Slingerlant, y. d., both of A.

Aug. 15. **L.** Henderick Vanness and Magdalena Vrooman, y. d., both of A.

Oct. 24. **L.** James Bloodgood and Lidea Van Valkenburgh, both of A.

Oct. 25. **L.** Geysbert Van San. . . . , and Rebecca Winne, both of A.

Nov. 1. **L.** Petrus Binnewie and Maria Fort, both of A.

1760, Oct. 18. **L.** Abraham Myndersse and Catharina Lansingh, both of A.

Oct. 19. Upon cert. of **B.** at Sch. by Do. B. Vrooman: Johannes Beetdely [or Beddely] and Margarita Passaste.

Oct. 21. **L.** Dinnes Ackerson and Lenea Slingerland, both under A.

Oct. 25. **L.** Petrus Jacob Van Woort and Rachel Redder, both of A.

Nov. 7. After 3 **B.** John Walker, y. m., b. in Dutchess Co., and Jannetje Burns, b. at Hosack, both l. on R. Manor.

Nov. 18. After 3 **B.** Willem Deinhart and Anna Althuize, l. at H. M.

Dec. 3. **L.** St. [?] Benneway and Gertruy Bovire, both of A. Co.

Dec. 4. **L.** John Cockran and Gertruide Schuyler, wid., both of A.

Dec. 6. **L.** Philip Young and Hanna Seckels, both of A.

Dec. 6. **L.** Courset Vedder and Neeltje Bourch, both of A.

Dec. 8. **L.** Harman Levison and Catharina Winne, both at A.

Dec. 26. **L.** Barent Vosbergh and Annatje Gerritse, both of A.

Dec. 26. **L.** Albert Slingerland and Elisabeth Moke, both of A.

Dec. 27. **L.** Isaac Slingerland and Eva Van Woert, both of A.

Dec. 31. **L.** David Hoogthaling and Hillegond Van der Zee, both of A.

1761, Jan. 8. **L.** Hermannus Ruiter and Mary Marselees, both of A.

Jan. 29. **L.** John J. Bleecker and Gerretje Van Schaik, both of A.

Feb. 1. **L.** Volckert Dawson and Gertruy Denison, wid., both of A.

Feb. 5. **L.** Geysbert Marselees and Anna Staats, both of A.

Feb. 20. **L.** Charles McKay and Moycke Ouderkerk, both near A.

Feb. 21. **B.** Jacob Moor and Cath. Claassen, both near A.

Mar. 3. **L.** Barent Romans and Mary Wendel, both near A.

Mar. 3. **B.** Hannesch Wiesch [?] and Elisabeth Hoghe.

Mar. 3. **L.** Abraham Lyle and Jane Van Alen, both of A.

Mar. 5. **L.** Jochem Isaac Staats and Geesje Veder, both of A.

Apr. 13. **B.** Hendrik Dennys and Mary Machauds [?]

Apr. 16. **B.** Hendrick Zeger and Margarita Koen, both of A.

Apr. 16. **L.** Martin Randall and Catharina Van de Bogart, wid., of A.

May 11. **B.** Antony Bartse and Elisabeth Fischer, of N. J.

May 11. **B.** Johannes Van Wielen of K., and Josina Van d. Hoef, of N. Y.

May 12. **B.** William McColloch and Margaretha McDaniels, both of Ire.

May 13. **B.** Jacobus Olfert and Annatje Sichsby, of Na.

May 13. **L.** Hendrick Van Aarnhem and Susanna Winne, both of A. Co.

June 1. **B.** Henry Mayer and Mary [?] Monre, of A. Co.

June 3. **L.** Gerardus Beekman of N. Y., and Anna Douw, of A. Co.

June 5. **L.** Simon De Foreest and Nancy McGinnis.

June 5. **L.** Walter Groesbeek and Alida Qwakkenbusch.

June 12. **L.** Jacob Kloet and Maria Lansing, of A. Co.

June 19. **L.** Isak Lansing and Anna Van Arnhem, at the h. of Abraham Van Arnhem.

July 17. **L.** Christoph Jets and Catharina Lansing.

July 28. **B.** Jonas Macnel [?], of Sco., and Marytje Kemmel, of O. E.

Aug. 2. After 3 **B.** Samuel Fouler, of O. E., and Marytje V. der Hoef, of A.

Aug. 8. **L.** Abraham Verplank and Mary Bogaart, of A.

Aug. 15. **L.** Daniel Winne and Catharina Hooghteling, of R.

Aug. 16. **L.** Archelaus Lynd and Mary Dovebach, of A.

Aug. 22. **L.** Abraham Yetz and Jannetje Brat, of A.

Aug. 27. **L.** Thomas Hun and Elizabeth Wendel, both of A.

Sep. 10. **L.** Martin Van Buren, y. m., and Hendrickje Van Buren, y. d., both of this Co.

Sep. 25. **L.** Gerrit V. Oostrander and Christina Van d. Berg, both of this Co.

Oct. 25 **L.** Johannes Lansing and Catharina Burhans, both of A.

Nov. 4. **B.** Arent Bekker, y. m., of Schie. and Margaretha, Balsing, y. d., of Na.

Nov. 14. **L.** George Dickson, y. m., of A., and Lena Kidney, y. d.

Nov. 20. **L.** Thomas Hun and Bata Van Deusen, both of A.

Nov. 20. **L.** Simon Van Antwerpen and Maria Denbach, both of this Co.

Nov. 21. **L.** Wilhelm V. den Berg and Annatje Van der Werken, wid., both of A.

Nov. 23. **L.** Abraham Douw and Catharina Lansing, both of A.

Nov. 25. **L.** Dirk Ten Broek, y. m., and Annatje Douw, both of A.

Nov. 26. **L.** Garret Waldrom, y. m., of the H. M., and Catharina Van den Berg, y. d., of the Bight, both of this Co.

Dec. 6. **L.** Wilhelmus Smit and Hanna Brat, both of A.

Dec. 12. **L.** John Ouderkerk and Annatje Van Ness, both of A.

Dec. 30. **L.** Nicolaas V. den Berg and Maria Van den Berg, of A. Co.

Dec. 27. After 3 **B.** David York and Susanna Grennel.

1762, Jan. 7. **L.** John Van Vegten and Anna Williams, both of A.

Jan 22. After 3 **B.** William Gaaf and Murry Hees, of Ire.

Jan 22. **L.** Goschen Van Schaik and Margareta Schuyler, both of A.

Jan 27. After 3 **B.** Abraham Van Esch and Antje De Ridder, both of H. M.

Jan. 30. **L.** Jacob H. Lansing and Maria Ouderkerk, both of this Co.

Feb. 2. After 3 **B.** Michael Fruy and Engeltje Van de Kar, of the H. M.

Feb. 18. After 3 **B.** Henry Northen and Margrita Van de Werken, of the H. M.

Feb. 27. After 3 **B.** Nicolaus Rechter and Maria Hindermond, of Na.

Feb. 27. After 3 **B.** Izak Vedder and Sara Bonds, of Nisthisom [?]

Mar. 13. **L.** Pieter Simons Veder and Maria Van den Bergh, both of A.

Mar. 18. After 3 **B.** Yzak Fryhout and Elisabeth Ruiter, of the H. M.

Mar. 31. After 3 **B.** William Venton and Anna Egmond, both of Col. R.

Apr. 1. **L.** Abraham Kuiler, y. m., and Catharina Wendel, y. d., both of A.

Apr. 4. **L.** Jacobus Hilten and Sara Barnton, both of A.

Apr. 26. After 3 **B.** John Rap and Mally Wilzon.

May 28. **L.** John I. Fort and Elyzabeth Qwakkenbusch, both of Schag.

June 1. After 3 **B.** Cornelis——, y. m., of Neapatmos, and Maria Sidley, of Germ., l. at A.

June 3. **L.** of C. Colden. Pieter Roozeveld, of N. Y., and Eliz. Frielinghuizen, wid., of A.

June 12. **L.** John Ten Broeck, y. m., and Sara Ganzevoort, y. d., both of A.

June 27. **L.** Jacob Fransen Z——, y. m., of the Colony, and Jannetje Visscher, y. d., of A.

July 21. **L.** Pieter W. Douw, y. m., and Rykje Van Schaick, y. d., both of A.

Sep. 10. **L.** Gerrit Van Wie and Catharina Lansing, of A. Co.

Sep. 11. **L.** William Winne, Jr., and Huibertje Yets, y. d., both of A.

Sep. 11. **B.** Frans Van der Werken and Geertruid Van Olinda.

——— **L.** Hendrik R. Lansing and Maria Marselies, both of A.

Oct. 13. **L.** Johannes V. d. Kar and Hilletje Van der Zee, both of A. Co.

Oct. 16. **L.** Gerrit V. d. Berg, y. m., and Alida Van den Berg, y. d., both of A.

Oct. 22. **L.** Jacob Kool, y. m., of Ulster Co., and Jannetje Witbeek, y. d., of A. Co.

Oct. 22. **L.** Gerrit Visscher, y. m., of A., and Alida Fonda, y. d., of the Bight.

Oct. ——. **L.** Pieter Scharp, Jr., y. m., and Catharine Berreger, y. d., of Col. R.

* **L.** Johannes Folkens, y. m., and Marry Smit, wid., of A. Co.

* **B.** Andries Wederwaks, y. m., and Catharina Reisdorp, y. d., of A. Co.

* **L.** Robert Winne, y. m., and Hillegonda Van Franken, y. d., both of this Co.

* **L.** Hendrik Brat, y. m., of A., and Agnieta Van Wie, y. d., of the Co.

* Date torn in the original.

17

* After 3. **B.** Andries Beessing and Jannetje Brat, of Na.
* **L.** Casparus Pruin, y. m., and Catharina Groesbeek, both of A.
* **L.** Volkert Van Vechten, y. m., and Jannetje Hun, y. d., both of A.
Dec. 17. **L.** Henry Schermerhoorn, y. m., and Cornelia Lansing, y. d., both of A. Co.
Dec. 17. **B.** Mattheus Flensburg and Christina Schneider, both of Col. R.

BAPTISMAL RECORD, 1750 TO 1762.

1749/50, Jan. 7. Helena, ch. of Henderick Gardenier and Maria Digmanse. Witnesses: Jacob and Sara V. Bloemendaal.
Jacob, of Lucas Hoogkerk and Rebecca Funda. Wit.: Wouter Knickerbacker, Maria Schoonhoven.
Jan. 14. Geertruy, of Symon Veder and Annatje V. Antwerpen. Wit.: Evert I. and Geesje Wendel.
Johannes, of Johannes Van der Heyden, Jr., and Catarina Van Brakelen. Wit.: Joh. and Rachel V. der Heyden.
Harmanus, of Jacob H. Ten Eyck and Anaatje Wendel. Wit.: Evert Wendel, Jr., Catarina Cuyler.
Jan. 21. Nicolaes, of Johanis Quackenbos and Rachel Gardenier. Wit.: Andries and Sara Gardenier.
Cornelius, of Antony Van Yveren and Maria Van den Bergh. Wit.: Cornelius and Catharina Van den Bergh.
Luycas, of Harme Bursscher and Sara Wyngaert. Wit.: Luycas Wyngaert, Sara Rykman.
Jacb[?], of Johannes Jac. Lansingh and Maria Huyk. Wit.: Abraham and Alida Van Armen.
Jan. 28. Philip, of Cornelius Schermerhoorn and Marytje Winne. Wit.: Adam Winne, Gerritje Schermerhoorn.
Abram, of Abram Witbeek and Anna Van Deuzen. Wit.: Joh. Witbeek, Annatje Jeets.
Feb. 4. Henderick, of Willem Van Buuren and Teuntje Van den Berg. Wit.: Harm. [?] Van Buuren, Geertruy V. Buuren.
Lena, of Melchert V. Deuzen and Neeltje Quackkenbosch. Wit.: Jacob and Catalyntje Witbeek.
Feb. 18. Annatje, of Philip Hansen and Geertruy Van Ness. Wit.: Hend. Van Ness, Rachel De Foreest.
Daniel, of Cornelius Winne and Catarina Van den Berg. Wit.: Pieter and Rachel Winne.
Johannes, of Gerardus Groesbeek and Maria Ten Broek. Wit.: Pieter Schuyler, Margarita Ten Broek.

* Date torn in the original.

1750

Barent Staats, of Jacobus Schuyler and Geertruy Staats. Wit.: Barent and Deborah Staats.

Neeltje, of Jochim Staats and Elizabeth Schuyler. Wit.: Gerrit Staats, Annatje Fisscher.

Feb. 25. Adam, of Staats Zeger and Susannah Brat. Wit.: Jan and Mareytje Brat.

March 4. Thomas, of Pieter Jones and Abigail Winne. Wit.: Isaac Verplanck, Margarita Hilton.

Hendrick Van Wie, of Albert Van der Zee and Antje Van Wie. Wit.: Hend. and Hillitje Van Wie.

Mar. 11. Maria, of John David and Elisabeth Wyngaert. Wit.: Johannes and Maria Wyngaert.

Rachel, Annatie, of Frederik Gerritsen and Maria Tok. Wit.: Johannes Peyster, Rachel De Pyster, Volkert and Annatie Douw.

Staats, of Adam Brat and Lydia Seger. Wit.: Johannes Seger, Ariaentie Lansing.

Barent, of Pieter d'Wandelaar and Arriaantje Van Buuren. Wit.: Pieter Winne, Elsje Douw.

Teunis, of Cornelius Tymissen and Mareytje Livissen. Wit.: Gerrit V. d. Berg, Angenitje Lievissen.

Mar. 18. Daniel, of Benoni Smith and Mary Springer. Wit.: Joh. Zeger, Deborah Springer.

Mar. 18. Thomas, Gerrit, of Lucas Witbeek and Geertruy Lansing. Wit.: Abram and Jannitje Witbeek, Johannis and Engeltje Lansing.

Christophel, of Pieter Jeets and Sarah Van Aalsteyn. Wit.: Chris. and Catal. Jeets.

Mar. 25. Annatje, of Abram de Weever and Annatje Carnin. Wit.: Isaac and Annatje Lansing.

Jacobus, of Henderick N. Gardenier and Eva V. Valkenburg. Wit.: Jacobus and Elizabeth V. Renslaar.

Annatje, of Antony Brat and Christina Lagrangie. Wit.: Mathys and Annatje Van Loon.

Samuel, of Thomas Dox and Elizabeth Van Woerd. Wit.: Gerardus Groesbeek, Heyltje Schuttel.

1750, Barent, of Benjamin Van den Berg and Annatje Vinnagel. Wit.: Joh. Vinnagel, Mar. V. d. Berg.

Apr. 1. Maria, of Andries Huych and Gerritje Valkenburg. Wit.: Joh. and Anna Huyk.

Apr. 8. Frances, of Renselaar Nichols and Elizabeth Salisbury. Wit.: Joh. V. Renselaar, Anna Douw.

Apr. 15. Cornelius, of Cornelius Van Ness and Susanna Swits. Wit.: Hend. and Annatje Beekman.

Apr. 22. Margarita, of Johannes Van der Poel and Annatje Staats. Wit.: Isaac and Maria Staats.

Apr. 29. Anna, of Gerrit Muzzelius and Margarita Blyker. Wit.: Antony, Jr., and Anna Blyker.

1750

May 6. Nicholaas, of Wouter Groesbeek and Maria Bogardus. Wit.: Jacob and Neeltje Groesbeek.

May 13. Neeltje, of Gerrit Staats and Debora Beekman. Wit.: Barent Staats, Annaatje Fischer.

Thomas of Jacob Witbeek and Catalyna Van Deusen. Wit.: Abram Witbeek, Geertruy Van Buuren.

Eechje, of Teunis Slingerland and Angenitje Witbeek. Wit.: Harmen Van der Zee, Angenitje Schot.

May 20. Alida, of Wilhelmus and Angnitje V. d. Berg. Wit.: Gerrit W. V. d. Berg, Alida Van den Berg.

Henderick, of Rykard Hansen and Catarina Ten Broeck. Wit.: Petrus and Annatje Douw.

May 24. Rachel, of Douwe Bogaart and Willemptje Brat. Wit.: Cornelius Van den Berg, Barber Brat.

Roelof, of Lambert Cool and Mareytje Kidney. Wit.: James and Rebecca Allin.

May 27. Willem, of Jan and Lena Burn. Wit.: Jan and Maria Burn.

Magdalena, of Folkert Douw and Anna De Peyster. Wit.: Harmen and Magdalena Gansevoort.

June 2. Magdalena, of Abram and Catarina Lansing. Wit.: Jacob Lansing, Elizabeth Oothout.

Abram, of Henderick Lansing and Anna Ouderkerk. Wit.: Jacob I. and Huybertje Lansing.

June 3. Antje, of Isaac Ouderkerk and Hesje Van Arnhem. Wit.: Walran and Annatje Knoet.

June 17. Gerardus, of Gerrit Knoet and Marritie Heemstraat. Wit.: Johannes and Lena Ouderkerk.

Isaac, of Abraham Vrooman and Mareytje Verplank. Wit.: Isaac Verplank, Marrietie Winne.

Johannes, of Jacob Van Woert and Elisabeth Post. Wit.: Jacob Van Woert, Annatie Lansing.

Pieter, of Frans Winne and Angnietie Van Wie. Wit.: Daniel and Jannitje Winne.

John, of Benjamin and Mary Williams. Wit.: John and Anna Fryer.

June 31 [sic]. Benjamin, of Jacob I. Lansing and Maria Egberts. Wit.: Egbert and Maria Egberts.

Sara, of Reykert Bovie and Maria Huyck. Wit.: Frederick Cas, Sara Van Woerd.

July 7. Rachel, of Franciscus Lansing and Maria Liversen. Wit.: Harmen and Rachel Liversen.

July 12. Maria, of Jacob Viele and Eva Fort. Wit.: Lodovicus Viele, Jacomeyntje Ouderkerk.

July 22. Geertruy, of Johannes Lansing and Ariaentie Wendel. Wit.: Johannes, Jr., and Geertruy Lansing.

July 29. Feytie, of Nicolaes Liversen [?] and Elisabeth Van der Kar. Wit.: Edward and Maria Williaems.

1750

Elisabeth, of Thomas Morral and Esther Demas. Wit.: Antonus A. and Wyntie Brat.

Wilhelmus, of Robert Van den Berg and Catarina Brando. Wit.: Caspar and Rachel Collier.

Aug. 5. Sara, of Abram De Foreest and Rebecca Van Antwerpen. Wit.: Thomas and Margarita Coeper.

Aug. 12. Geertruy, of Nicholaas Fisscher and Anna Teymissen. Wit.: David Van der Heyden, Neeltje Ten Eyck.

Heyltje, of Philip Muller and Geertruy Goewey. Wit.: Jacob Muller and Angenietje.

Hester, of Dirk Van der Heyden and Elizabeth Wendel. Wit.: Robert Wendel, Hester Van der Heyden.

Aaltje, of Jacob Harse and Mareytje Pruym. Wit.: Frans Pruym, Jr., Aaltje Binmaar.

Aug. 19. Wyntie, of Dyrick and Mareytie Brat. Wit.: Jan and Hilligonte Brat.

Aug. 26. Maria, of Jacob Coeper and Josina Oarchard. Wit.: John and Rachel De Peyster.

Sep. 2. Folkert, of Jonas Oothout and Elizabeth Lansing. Wit.: Folkert and Catarina Oothout.

Eldert, of Bastiaan Tymissen and Majeke Ouderkerk. Wit.: Eldert and Hester Tymissen.

Reinier, of Folkert Van Hoesen and Alida Muzzelius. Wit.: Ebbert and Cornelia Van Hoesen.

Sep. 16. Hilletje, of Henderick H. Van Wie and Johanna Gardenier. Wit.: Dirk and Margarita Hun.

Marten, of John Trotter and Annatje Hogen. Wit.: Jurrian and Maria Hogen.

Nov. 4. Annatje, of Martin Bucley and Catarina Oothout. Wit.: Harmen and Elsje Hun.

Teunis, of Wouter and Hester Slingerland. Wit.: Abram Slingerland, Engeltje Witbeek.

Lena, of Johannes I. Lansing and Catarina Schuyler. Wit.: Jacob and Lena Lansing.

Maritje, of Johannes S. Bruyn and Jannitje Van Aalsteyn. Wit.: Frans and Alida Pruym.

Pieter, of Pieter Knoet and Ariaantje Van Vranken. Wit.: Pieter and Catarina Schuyler.

Martina, of William Hogen, Jr., and Susanna Lansing. Wit.: Teunis Fisscher, Annatje Hogen.

Jannitje, of John Williams and Cornelia Bogardus. Wit.: Wouter Groesbeek, Annatje Van Vegten.

Janneke or Sanneke, of Abram Jeets and Antje Ridder. Wit.: Claas Van den Berg, Gerritje Ridder.

Ebbitje, Rachel, twins of Gerrit G. Van den Berg and Angenitje Liversen. Wit.: Willem and Teuntje Van Buren, Leendert Gansevoort, Lidia Liversen.

Marten, of Patrick Clark and Cornelia Walderon. Wit.: Pieter and Nellie Waldron.

1750-1751

Annatje, of Michael Besset and Lybetje Schermerhoorn. Wit.: Johannes and Annatje Besset.

Margritje, of Rykert Van Vrancken and Annatje Truex. Wit.: Maas and Dirkje V. Vranken.

Hendericus, of Bernardus Brat, Jr., and Catarina Van Vegten. Wit.: Johannes V. V. Schoonmaker, Rebecca Brat.

Anna, of Gerrit Lansing, Jr., and Wyntje Van den Berg. Wit.: Gerrit and Engeltje Lansing.

John, of Jacobus Van Benthuyzen and Sara Coeper. Wit.: Richard and Annatje Cartwright.

Nov. 18. Barent, of Johannes R. Bleeker and Elizabeth Staats. Wit.: Barent Staats, Margarita Collins.

Andries, of Cornelis Ouderkerk and Cataria Huyck. Wit.: Johannes and Sara V. Arnhem.

Nov. 25. Neeltje, of Isaac Funda, Jr., and Cornelia De Foreest. Wit.: Philip and Rachel De Foreest.

Folkert, of Johannes Douw and Jannitje Bogaart. Wit.: Jonas Witbeek, Catarina Bogaart.

Dec. 2. Nicholaes, of Jacobus Clement and Jannitje Van Woerd. Wit.: Andries and Elizabeth V. Woerd.

Angnitje, of Daniel S. and Rebecca V. Antwerpen. Wit.: Simon and Annatje Veder.

Albert, of Adriaan Brat and Celia Van Zanten. Wit.: Albert Brat, Catarina Viele.

Dec. 25. Sara, of Willem Van Zanten and Alida Smith. Wit.: Joh. and Sara Van Zanten.

Alida, of Hendrik Gerritsen and Dintie Tymese. Wit.: Jacob and Maria Hans.

1750/1, Jan. 6. Annatje, of Benjamin Goewey and Catarina Van den Berg. Wit.: Jacobus and Elizabeth V. Renselaar.

Ephraim, of Antony A. Brat and Wyntje Bogardus. Wit.: Cornelius and Ariaantje Sandvoort.

Rebecca, of Staats Van Sandvoort and Willimpje Brat. Wit.: Antony and Rebecca Brat.

Reynier, of Willem Van den Berg and Susanna Van Ieveren. Wit.: Antony and Pietertje Van Iveren.

Jan. 13. Catalyntje, of Seybrant Van Schayck and Jannitje Bogaart. Wit.: Jacob Bogaart, Alida Van Schaick.

Elizabeth, of Douwe I. Funda and Aaltje Van Buuren. Wit.: Abram and Maria Funda.

Abram, of Evert Wendel and Elizabeth Van Schaik. Wit.: Henderick and Catelyntje Wendel.

Gerrit, of Cornelis Van Ness and Aliada Van Woert. Wit.: Jan and Marytje Van Ness.

Isaac, of Henderick Funda and Catarina Groesbeek. Wit.: Wouter and Elizabeth Knickerbacker.

1751
Feb. 17. Eve, of Christopher Quint and Elizabeth Corlen. Wit.: William and Seyntje Hogen.

Sara, of Arent Slingerland and Jacomeyntje Van der Volgen. Wit.: Antony Slingerland, Elizabeth Van der Volgen.

Abram, of Isaac Ouderkerk and Mary Foster. Wit.: Jacobus V. Renslaer, Elizabeth Van Renslaer.

Teunis, of Pieter T. Van Slyck and Anna Rykse. Wit.: Willem Van Slyck, Eytje Siksberry.

Celia, of Johannes Redlof, Jr., and Geertruy Brat. Wit.: Rykard and Catarina Redlof.

Elizabeth, of Johannes Evertsen and Susanna Lagrange. Wit.: Gerrit I. and Jannitje Lansing.

Feb. 20. Gideon, of Nicas and Neeltje, pros. Wit.: Nicas and Christina, pros.

Pieter, of Johannes Seger and Maria Pros [?]. Wit.: Johannes De Peyster, Anna Douwe.

Mar. 3. Rachel, of Pieter D.' Garmo and Sara Gardenier. Wit.: Adam and Anna Jeets.

Thomas, of John Reyley and Helena Barber. Wit.: Gerrit Van Vranken, Elizabeth V. Renslaer.

Mar. 10. Anna, of Edward Hogen and Maria Egmond. Wit.: Thomas Lansing, Catarina Egmond.

Mar. 17. Annatje, of Cornelis M. V. Denberg and Cornelia Van Denberg. Wit.: Wynant C. and Annatje V. denberg.

Catalyntje, of Reynier Van Aalsteyn and Cornelia Van den berg. Wit.: Cornelis M. and Catalyntje Van den berg.

Wyntje, of Evert Zeger and Sara Oachard. Wit.: Henderck Zeger, Catarina Pietersen.

Catarina, of Henderick I. Van Wie and Mareytje Loeck. Wit.: Frans and Angenitje Winne.

1751, Mar. 24. Rykard, of Johannes Peersen and Alida Van Vranken. Wit.: Gerrit and Maria Van Vranken.

Simon, of Johannes Van Antwerpen and Catarina Veder. Wit.: Daniel and Rebecca Van Antwerpen.

Sara, of Johannes Meynertse and Maria Oostrande. Wit.: Marten Meynertsen, Sara Vroman.

Johannes, of Johannes Knickerbacker and Rebecca Funda. Wit.: Harmen and Rebecca Knickerbacker.

Mar. 31. Wyntje, of Albert Brat and Anna Corn. Wit.: Adriaan Brat, Celia Van Zanten.

Sara, of Gozen Van Schaick and Majeke Van den Berg. Wit.: Gerrit Van Schaick, Gerritje Ridder.

Apr. 5. Geertje, of Johannes Huyck and Catarina Bevier. Wit.: Jacob Ten Eyck, Marritje Van Woerd.

Hendrick, of Andries Huyck and Nelletje Bovie. Wit.: Johannes and Catarina Redlof.

1751

Apr. 7. Jannitje, of Pieter Waldron and Neeltje Lansing. Wit.: Isaac and Jannitje Lansing.

Apr. 21. Jacob, of Isaac I. Truex and Maria Wyngaart. Wit.: Jacob Truex, Elizabeth Lagrange.

Susanna, of Henderick Wendel and Catalyntje Van Schaick. Wit.: Gosen and Majeke Van Schaick.

Apr. 28. Margarita, of Roelof Turx [?] and Barbara Koen. Wit.: Johannes Koen, Hilletje Zeger.

Eldert, of Johannes Funda and Elizabeth Ouderkerk. Wit.: Johannes and Sophia Ouderkerk.

Elizabeth, of Henderick Jong and Catarina Lantman. Wit.: Lucas Van Vegten, Maria Lantman.

May 5. Samuel, of Roelof De Voe and Elisabeth Golden. Wit.: Isaac and Cornelia Funda.

Catalina, of Weynant Van den Berg and Catarina Van Ness. Wit.: Henderick V. G. Van Ness, Catarina Lansing.

May 12. Meyndert, of Seybrant G. Van Schaick and Alida Roseboom. Wit.: Joh. Beekman, Maria Roseboom.

Catarina, of Robert Wendel and Catarina Winne. Wit.: Jesse De Foreest, Sara Wendel.

May 19. Catarina, of Teunis Hoogteeling and Dorothee Vanden Berk. Wit.: Jacob C. Ten Eyck, Catarina Van Zanten.

Abram, of Jacobus Fort and Marritje Oosterhout. Wit.: Jacob and Eva Viele.

Gerrit, of Evert Siksberry and Elsje Egmond. Wit.: Gerrit and Ariaantje Lansing.

Elizabeth, of William Salisbury and Teuntje Staats. Wit.: Renselaer and Elizabeth Nichols.

May 26. Johannes, of Jurryen Koen and Andrasina Erhart. Wit.: Adam Koen, Adriana Jansen.

David, of Samuel Burn and Magdalena Pruyn. Wit.: Samuel Pruyn, Jr., Geertje Vosburg, Jr.

Angenitje, of Cornelis Muller and Maria Van Hoesen. Wit.: Leendert Muller, Alida Van Hoesen.

Johannes, of Harmen I. Fischer and Hester Van Iveren. Wit.: Johannes Fischer, Elizabeth Fisher.

Gerrit, of Pieter Hoogteeling and Anna Becker. Wit.: Gerrit and Ariaantje Becker.

May 27. Magtel, of Symon Springsteen and Maria Seeger. Wit.: Teunis and Magtel Fischer.

June 2. Geertruy, of Christiaan Haver and Engeltje Van de Werken. Wit.: Jacob Van de Werken, Maria Ouderkerk.

Alida, of Johannes Vanden Berg and Maria Van Ness. Wit.: Henderick and Geertruy Van Buren.

Daniel, of David Van Zanten and Ariaantje Fort. Wit.: Jacob and Catarina Beljew.

1 51

June 9. Lidia, of Andries Van Slyk and Maria Van Benthuysen. Wit.: Henry Beesly, Cornelia Rykman.

Catarina, of Johannes Gansevoort and Maria Douw. Wit.: Pieter and Catarina Gansevoort.

June 30. Nicholaes, of Kiljan Van Renslaer and Ariaantje Schuyler. Wit.: Harmanus Schuyler, Elizabeth Staats.

Johannes, of Johannes I. Wendel and Sara Bergen. Wit.: Isaac and Maria Swits.

July 7. Femmitje, of Jacob I. Lansing and Maria Egberts. Wit.: Egbert and Maria Egberts.

Machtel, of Adriaan Quackenbosch and Elizabeth Knoet. Wit.: Joh. and Magtel Quackenbosch.

Leendert, of Jan Van Buuren and Sara Bronck. Wit.: Leendert and Anna Bronck.

July 14. Johannes, of Gysbert Clauw and Neeltje Scherp. Wit.: Philip and Geertruy Muller.

Albert, of Isaac Hansen and Maria Brat. Wit.: Isaac De Foreest, Geertruy Van Ness.

Leendert, of Harmen Gansevoort and Magdalena Douw. Wit.: Joh. and Maria Gansevoort.

Aug. 4. Samuel, of William Bromley and Lena Boom. Wit.: Samuel Boom, Anna Arnhout.

Matheus, of Robert Cranel and Ariaantje Bovie. Wit.: Matheus and Nellitje Bovie.

Aug. 14. Gerrit, of Jacob Van Schaick and Geertje De Ridder. Wit.: Gerrit and Sara Van Schaick.

Aug. 18. Johannis, of Philip Foreest and Maria Bloemendal. Wit.: Joh. and Jacomyntje Bloemendal.

Aug. 25. Thomas, of John Lady and Catrina Oliford. Wit.: Richard and Martin Oliford.

Elizabeth, of Petrus and Catrina Hogil. Wit.: Harmen and Rachel Liverse.

Rachel, of Johannes and Rebecca Mor. Wit.: Petrus and Elizabeth Schuiler.

David, of Daniel Winne and Janntje Defreest. Wit.: David and Abigal De Freest.

Sep. 1. Barbara, of John Wilson and Barbara Dieppendorp. Wit.: Jacob and Annatje Deippendorp.

Sep. 7. Helena, of Isaac Lancen and Annaatje Van Worten. Wit.: Johannes and Sara Van Aarnam.

Sep. 15. Catrina, of Marta [sic] Defreest and Tanneca Winna. Wit.: Daniel and Jannetje Winna.

Sep. 22. Geertruy, of John E. Wendell and Maria Catarina Van Sandvoort. Wit.: Abram and Elizabeth Wendel.

Cornelis, of Henderick Van Buuren and Anatje Van Salsbergen. Wit.: Cornelis and Magdalena Van Buuren.

Elsje, of Abraham Jacobse Lancen and Elizebeth Kopper. Wit.: Jacob, Jr., and Marritje Lancen.

Sep. 29. Eva, of Hendrick Albrecht and Elisabeth Foland. Wit.: Coenraat and Cornelia Hoogteeling.

Naning, of Jacob Van der Heyden and Maria Halenbeek. Wit.: Naning and Maria Halenbeek.

Catarina, of Rykart Hansen and Catarina Ten Broeck. Wit.: Cornelis and Christyntje Ten Broek.

Oct. 7. Margarita, of Roelof and Anna Van der Werken. Wit.: Albert and Maria Van der Werken.

Abraham, of Frederick and Debrah Voert. Wit.: Jacob and Ephra Feeling.

Nancy, of Johannes David and Elizabeth Wyngaert. Wit.: Jacob Sickelson, Machtal Wyngaart.

Oct. 27. Christiaen, of Pieter Kasselman and Elisabeth Weasen. Wit.: Henderick and Sophia Magdalena Paschase.

Engeltje, of Arent Van Deusen and Treyntje Waldron. Wit.: Coenraed and Geertruy Loeck.

Susanna, of Willem Hellen and Elisabeth Halenbeek. Wit.: Hend. and Dorothea Halenbeek.

Pieter, of Henderick G. Van Ness and Margarita Winne. Wit.: Marten and Sara Winne.

William, of Benjamin Hilton and Maria Prys. Wit.: Wil. and Hilletje Van Antwerpen.

Nov. 10. Elisabeth, of Patrick Clark and Cornelia Waldron. Wit.: Arent Van Deusen, Elisabeth Waldron.

Catarina, of Folkert P. Douw and Anna De Peyster. Wit.: Petrus and Catarina Douw.

Annatje, of Barent Lewis and Catarina Van Slyck. Wit.: Barent Van der Poel, Antje Beckers.

Elizabeth, of Willem Van Slyck and Catarina Van Schaick. Wit.: Antony and Elizabeth Van Schaick.

Catalyntje, of Henderick Van Slyck and Elizabeth Van Benthuysen. Wit.: Andries and Anatje Van Slyck.

Nov. 17. Alida, of Henderick Van Wie and Catarina Waldron. Wit.: Willem G. and Maria Van den Berg.

Catalyntje, of Pieter Lansing and Elizabeth Wendel. Wit.: Joh. I. Lansing, Sarah Glen.

Abraham, of Isaac Ouderkerk and Hesje Van Arnhem. Wit.: Abraham and Alida Van Arnhem.

Nov. 24. Adriaan, of Marten Buckly and Catrina Oothout. Wit.: Johannes and Annaatje Hun.

Elizabeth, of Tuinnis Van Woort and Elizebeth Van Duisen. Wit.: Jacob Van Woort, Annatje Van Duisen.

Isaac, of John Makkleen and Catrina Van Duisen. Wit.: John and Catrina Renselaar.

Catrina, of Adam De Manse and Jannetje De Voy. Wit.: Peter and Englje Brat.

Henderick, of Philip Hanse and Geertery Van Ess. Wit.: Wiliam Gruisbeek, Catalina Van Ess.

Jacobus, of Dirk Brat Van Schoonhoven and Volkje Van den Berg. Wit.: Guirt and Annatje Van Sch'hoven.

Dec. 1. Anna, of Gerardus Groesbeek and Maria Ten Broeck. Wit.: Pieter Schuyler, Elizabeth Van Renslaer.

Dec. 8. Catalina, of Philip De Foreest and Rachel Van Ness. Wit.: Cornelis and Catalina Van Ness.

Dec. 15. Matheus, of Bastiaen Fisscher and Engeltje Van den berg. Wit.: Cornelis M. and Catalina Van den berg.

Dec. 22. Rebecca, of Andries Gardenier and Catarina De Garmo. Wit.: Matheus and Rebecca De Garmo.

Dec. 26. Teunis, of Gerrit T. Van Slyck and Anna Turk. Wit.: Richard and Anna Cartwright.

Dec. 29. Lambert, of Petrus Burgert and Eva Huyck. Wit.: Lambert Redloff, Rachel Van Deusen.

Johannes, of Jacob Rosevelt and Regina Frisera. Wit.: Ernst and Catarina Bacchus.

Johannes, of Jonathan Witbeek and Gerritje Oostrande. Wit.: Johannes and Elisabeth Oostrande.

1751 2, Jan. 5. Marten, of Pieter Van Buuren and Maria Van der poel. Wit.: Johs. and Eytje Van Buuren.

Catarina, of Dirk Van der Heyden and Elisabeth Wendel. Wit.: Abraham and Sara Wendel.

Rebecca, of Cornelius Van Sandvoort and Ariaantje Brat. Wit.: Antony and Rebecca Brat.

Jan. 19. Elisabeth, of Johannes Jansen and Jannitje Schermerhoorn. Wit.: Roelof and Elisabeth Jansen.

Dirck, of Pieter Van Vrancken and Neeltje Groot. Wit.: Andries and Maria Van Vrancken.

Frans, of Bernardus Harse and Catarina Pruyn. Wit.: Jacob and Maria Harse.

Jan. 30. Maria, Scharlotta, twins of Andries Ten Eyck and Anna Margarita Coëjeman. Wit.: Samuel and Catarina Coejeman, John and Gerritje Barclay.

Feb. 2. Henderick, of Willem Van Buren and Teuntje Van den Berg. Wit.: Barent and Catalyntje Van Buren.

Pieter, of Henderick Van Renslaer and Elisabeth Van Brugge. Wit.: Folkert P. Douw, Helena Wendel.

Cornelis, of Teunis Slingerlant and Angenietje Witbeek. Wit.: Joh. and Annatje Slingerland.

Susanna, of Henderick and Susanna Meyer. Wit.: Johannes and Frena Post.

Anthony, of Staats Van Sandvoort and Willempje Brat. Wit.: Antony A. and Ariaantje Brat.

Christopher, of Jacob Bogart, Jr., and Maria Jeets. Wit.: Jacob and Catalina Groesbeek.

Feb. 9. Jannitje, of Gerrit Van der Poel and Catarina Hoes. Wit.: Melchior Van der Poel, Maria Van Buren.

1752

Marten Cornelissen, of Barent Van Buren and Ariaantje Van der Poel. Wit.: Johs. and Eytje Van Buren.

Feb. 23. Elisabeth, of Isaac Vosburg and Catarina Van Woert. Wit.: Teunis and Elisabeth Van Woert.

Cornelis, of Abram De Wever and Anna Carnen. Wit.: Jan and Catalyntje Winne.

Catarina, of Robert Sanders and Elisabeth Schuyler. Wit.: John Sanders, Catarina Schuyler.

Rachel, of Pieter De Garmo and Sara Gardenier. Wit.: Adam Jeets, Heyltje Schriedel.

Margarita, of Roelof Zeger and Margarita Arnoldt. Wit.: Jacobus and Anna Arnoldt.

Alida, of Andries Van Wie and Helena Van Arnhem. Wit.: Frans and Alida Pruyn.

Johanna, of Pieter Marschal and Anna Flensburg. Wit.: Johs. Flensburg, Jr., Margarita Hun.

Andries, of Henderick H. Van Wie and Johanna Gardenier. Wit.: Arie and Eyta Gardenier.

Sara, of John Fryar and Anna Van Santen. Wit.: Johs. and Sara Van Santen.

Schibboleth, of Schibboleth Bogardus and Catarina Van der Werken. Wit.: Pieter and Weyntje Bogardus.

Mar. 8. Joseyna, of Evert Segher and Sara Aertshert. Wit.: Johannes Segher, Catrina Pieterse.

Mar. 15. Cornelis, of Henderick N. Gardenier and Eva Volkenburgh. Wit.: Andries A. and Gerritje Huyck.

Mar. 22. Arent, of Wouter and Hester Slingerlant. Wit.: Arent and Jannitje Slingerlant.

Magdalena, of John Reyley and Magdalena Barbar. Wit.: Gerardus and Maria Groesbeek.

1752, Mar. 29. Johannes, of Philip Muller and Geertruy Goedewey. Wit.: Johs. and Jannitje Goedewey.

Sarah, of Marten Meynersen and Sara Ryckman. Wit.: Abram Meynersen, Elsje Gansevoort.

Gerrit, of Jochim Staats and Elisabeth Schuyler. Wit.: John R. and Elisabeth Bleecker.

Apr. 9. Christina, of Jan Brat and Susanna Zeger. Wit.: Meyndert and Elisabeth Frederick.

Apr. 12. Elisabeth, of Willem Winne and Maria De Wandelaar. Wit.: Pieter DeWandelaar, Elisabeth Van Woert.

Rachel, of Pieter Knoet and Ariaantje Van Vrancken. Wit.: Isaac and Rachel Van Vrancken.

Apr. 19. Jacob, of Johannes Post and Frena Meyer. Wit.: Henderik Post, Catarina Beekman.

Apr. 26. Jacob, of Jacobus Arnold and Anna Mook. Wit.: Jacob and Frena Mook.

Johannes, of Daniel Morril and Alida Dox. Wit.: Folkert and Anna Douw.

1752

Elisabeth, of Geysbert Van Zanten and Margarita Carel.
Wit.: Geurt and Elisabeth Brat.

Dirkje, of Adam Winne and Gerritje Schermerhoorn.
Wit.: Henderick and Dirkje Van Buren.

Gerrit, of Johannis I. Lansing and Maria Huyck. Wit.:
Henderik Lansingh, Anna Lansing.

Hester, of Bastiaen Tymissen and Majeke Ouderkerk.
Wit.: Henderik and Dirkje Gerritse.

May 3. Dorothea, of Henderick Bogaart and Engeltje
Van Schaak. Wit.: Stephanus Van Schaak, Jannitje
Douw.

May 10. James, of Thomas Holland and Christina
Barhead. Wit.: Robert and Ariaantje Lansing.

Catarina, of Johannes Neiber and Anna Maria Folin.
Wit.: Alida Van der Heyden.

Rachel, of Cornelis Tymissen and Maria Liversen. Wit.:
Leendert and Maria Gansevoort.

Johannes, Catarina, of George Folemsbey and Jannitje
Valkenburg. Wit.: Joh. Valkenburg, Margarita Spoor,
Pieter and Bregje Schuyler.

Deborah, of Gerrit Staats and Deborah Beekman. Wit.:
Gerrit A. and Magtel Lansing.

Catarina, of Jacobus Van der Poel and Neeltje Huyck.
Wit.: Lucas and Anna Wesselsen.

May 17. Anna, of Samuel and Neeltje Staats. Wit.:
Joachim Staats, Anna Fischer.

Johannis, of Henderick Van Buren and Aaltje Winne.
Wit.: Joh. and Eytje Van Buren.

May 22. Jennicke, of Jacob Ouderkerk and Neeltje
Kloet. Wit.: Johannes and Alida Kloet.

Isaac, of Abram I. Funda and Maria Van Schoonhoven.
Wit.: Isac I. and Alida Funda.

Sara, of Abram Becker and Elisabeth Van Olinden.
Wit.: Johannes Becker, Jr., Sara Van Arnhem.

May. 29. Christina, of Henderick Litzert and Anna
Huyck. Wit.: Gerrit Bovie, Christina Huyck.

Engeltje, of Thomas Van Valkenburg and Rachel
Van den Berg. Wit.: Gerrit and Geertruy Van den
Berg.

Maria, of Andries Huyck and Cornelia Van Deusen.
Wit.: Teunis Van Woert, Elisabeth Van Deusen.

Rachel, of Willem Claeuw and Christina Huyck. Wit.:
Burger, Jr., and Jannitje Huyck.

Maria, of Staats Zeger and Susanna Brat. Wit.:
Johannes De Peyster, Anna Douw.

Anna, of Pieter Backis and Eva Maria Miller. Wit.:
Johan Jurrie and Anna Pruimer.

Daniel, of Johannes Flensburg and Cornelia Hoogteeling.
Wit.: Johannes, Jr., and Anna Flensburg.

1752

Pietertje, of Pieter Jeets and Sara Van Aalsteyn. Wit.: Reynier and Pietertje Van Aalsteyn.

Elisabeth, of Abram Coeper and Catarina Oostrande. Wit.: Johs. and Elisabeth Oostrande.

June 7. David, of Joost Bernard and Christina Hemmer. Wit.: David Pots, Catrina Daats.

Rachel, of Jacob Egmond and Maria Luwis. Wit.: Annaetje and Folkert Douw.

June 14. Patrick, of Pieter Martin and Elisabeth Burns. Wit.: John and Geertruy Danels.

Dirkje, of Cornelius Schermerhorn and Maria Winne. Wit.: Peter, Jr., and Rachel Winne.

Aaltje, of Johannes Fonda and Elizabeth Ouderkerk. Wit.: Isaac Dowe Fonda, Jackameyntje Bloemendaal.

June 21. James, of Daniel Macmichael and Sara Maselius. Wit.: Staats Van Santfort, Willempje Brat.

Rebecca, of Mattys Van den Berck and Rebecca Hendrikse. Wit.: Rikkart and Catarina Van Santen.

Petrus, of Johannis and Eva Van Valkenburg. Wit.: Lambert Van Valkenburg, Jannetje.

Maria, of Melchart Van der Poel and Margarita Vinhaagen. Wit.: Johannis Vinhaagen, Maria Van den Berg.

Goosen, of Antony Go. and Cristina Van Schaick. Wit.: Antony Van Schaick, Debora Beekman.

Gerrit, of Dirk Van Aarsdalen and Geysbertje De Grauw. Wit.: Isaac and Maria Ouderkerk.

July 6. Gerrit, of William Vosburg and Cristina Van Woert. Wit.: Tuinis and Elizabeth Van Woert.

Engeltje, of Johannis Jatch and Rebecca Waldron. Wit.: Johannis Tho. Witbeek, Catarina Van Renselaar.

Johannis, of Harmanus Wendel and Catarina Van Vegten. Wit.: Philip and Maria Van Vechten.

Cornelius, of Abraham Jac. Lansen and Catarina Lievense. Wit.: Cornelius Lievense, Marritje Lansen.

July 10. Antony, of Egbert B. Egberts and Maria Linch. Wit.: Jacob and Helena Fischer.

July 12. Rachel, of Lambert Kool and Maria Kidney. Wit.: Johannes and Femmitje Kidney.

Pieter, of Thomas Dox and Elizabeth Bekker. Wit.: Pieter Schuylder, Geertruy De Voe.

Catarina, of Harmen Lieverse and Anna Van Schoonhoven. Wit.: Willem and Maria Lieverse.

Anna, of Abram Van den Berg and Rachel Lieverse. Wit.: Weynant and Catarina Van den Berg.

July 19. Cornelia, of Andries Huyck and Nellitje Bovie. Wit.: Johannes Glen, Susanna Litscher.

Cornelius, of Antony Van Jeveren and Maria Van den Berg. Wit.: Volkert and Catarina Van den Berg.

1752

July 26. Elisabeth, of Antony Slingerlant and Claertje Cloet. Wit.: Gerrit Slingerlant, Jannitje Van der Zee.

Susanna, of Simon I. and Catalyntje Veder. Wit.: Meyndert and Elisabeth Veder.

Ábram, of Abram and Catarina Lansing. Wit.: Gerrit A. and Jannitje Lansing.

Aug. 2. Geertruy, of Martinus Cregier and Sara Van Vranken. Wit.: Bastiaen and Jannitje Cregier.

Johannis, of Mattheus Boom and Maria Hilton. Wit.: Johannes and Cornelia Preys.

Johannis, of Hendrik Milton and Jannetje Ejvens. Wit.: Dirk and Jannetje Van der Kar.

Catarina, of Gerrit Van Aalen and Catarina Van Wie. Wit.: Johannis and Gerritje Van Wie.

Aug. 16. Michel, of Michel Philips and Maragrita Wyngaart. Wit.: Jacobus Sickels, Jetra Kidny.

Jannetje, of Johannis Ph. Witbeek and Eva Waldron. Wit.: Jacob and Catalyntje Witbeek.

Mechtel, of Gerrit Quakkenbos and Catarina De Voy. Wit.: Albert and Maritje Van der Werken.

Catarina, of Wessel Van Schaick and Maria Gerritson. Wit.: Sybrant V. Schaick, Jr., Maria Ten Broek.

Aug. 23. Salomon, of Benjamin Goewey and Catarina Van den Bergh. Wit.: Salomon and Margarita Goewey.

Aug. 26. Jurrie, of Willem Phillip and Eva Church. Wit.: Jurrie Church, Catarina Weest.

Benjamin, of Michel Herder and Maria Rees. Wit.: Benjamin Rees, Geertruy Witbeek.

Thomas, of Lucas Witbeek and Catarina Carter. Wit.: Teunis Oosterhout, Eva Conyn.

Michel, of Johannes Lant and Sara Winne. Wit.: Michel Herder, Maria Rees.

Henderickje, of Pieter Kool and Alida Digmanse. Wit.: Leendert and Henderickje Conyn.

George, of Kneel Macdonald and Anna Dovie. Wit.: Michel and Mareytje Smit.

Rachel, of Willem Muller and Rachel Halenbeek. Wit.: Johannes Muller, Feytje Halenbeek.

Aug. 30. Engeltje, of Abram Mol and Tietje Barhead. Wit.: Jacob and Pallie Van Woert.

Isaac, of Reyer Springsteyn and Helena. Wit.: Johannes and Debora Beekman.

Cornelia, of Wilhelmus and Angenietje Van den Berg. Wit.: Gerrit and Maria Van den Berg.

Gerraddus, of Henderik Bulsen and Catelyna Goewey. Wit.: Gerraddus Groesbeek, Elizabeth Renselaar.

Nov. 7. Elisabeth, of Gerrit Van Vrancken and Susanna Egberts. Wit.: Isaac and Jennike Van Vranken.

1752

Emmitje, of Johannis Perry and Francyntje Knoet.
Wit.: Wouter and Neeltje De Foreest.

Nov. 12. Anna, of Harmen Fischer and Sara Wyngaert.
Wit.: Harmen Fisscher, Jr., Hester Fischer.

Johannes, of David Verplanck and Catarina Boom.
Wit.: Isaac Verplank, Catarina Brat.

Margarita, of Johannes Koen and Hillitje Zeger. Wit.:
Roelof Zeger, Barber Koen.

Francyntje, of Johannes I. Wendel and Sara Bergen.
Wit.: Abram and Francyntje Bergen.

Barent, of Johannes R. Bleecker and Elisabeth Staats.
Wit.: Edward and Margarita Collins.

Marritje, of Pieter Van Slyk and Anna Van Vranken.
Wit.: Nicholaes and Dirkje Van Vranken.

Eva, of Hendericus Beekman and Anna Swits. Wit.:
Geysbert and Anna Muzzelius.

Dirk, of Jan De Voe and Feytje Van der Kar. Wit.:
Dirk and Magdalena Van der Kar.

Obediah, of Jacob Coeper and Joseyna Orchard. Wit.:
Evert and Anna Lansing.

Maas, of Reykert Van Vranken and Anna Truex. Wit.:
Johannes and Anna Knoet.

Johannes, of Pieter Bloemendal and Christina Lagrange.
Wit.: Johannes Bloemendal, Maria Deforeest.

Nov. 19. Elisabeth, of Michael Lantman and Maria
Brouwer. Wit.: Johannes and Elisabeth Lantman.

Samuel, of Johannes S. Pruyn and Jannitje Van Aalsteyn. Wit.: Jacob and Maria Pruyn.

Nov. 26. Margarita, of Albert Van der Werken and
Maria Quackenbosch. Wit.: Andries and Elisabeth Van
Woert.

Dec. 3. Maria, of Pieter Gansevoort and Gerritje Ten
Eyck. Wit.: Harmen and Magdalena Gansevoort.

Thomas, of Thomas Wood and Catarientje Gardenier.
Wit.: Jacob and Seina Cooper.

Dec. 24. Catârina, of Isaac De Voy and Maritje V.
drlinden. Wit.: Isaac Vosburg, Geerteruy Van de Linden.

Cristina, of ,Jacobus Schuiler and Geerteruy Staats.
Wit.: Isaac and Maria Staats.

Jacob, of Antony Eb. Brat and Maria Van Aalstyn.
Wit.: Renier V. Aalstien, Sara Jetch.

Dec. 31. William, of Thomas Willis and Rachel Redlof.
Wit.: Johannes and Catarina Redlof.

Gerrit, of Cornelis I. Van den Bergh and Catarina Ridder.
Wit.: Cornelis C. Van den Berg, Maria Ridder.

Johannes, of Barnet Hug and Geertje Huyck. Wit.:
Johannes Burnhout, Maria Van der Heyden.

Catarina, of Johannes Huyck and Catarina Bovie.
Wit.: Jacob and Catalyntje Groesbeek.

1753

1753, Jan. 7. Maria, of Abraham Vroman and Maria Verplanck. Wit.: Cornelis Vroman, Engeltje Sield.

Henderick, of Cornelis Muller and Maria Van Hoesen. Wit.: Folkert Van Hoesen, Folkje Van den Berg.

Jan. 14. Abraham, of Johannes Perse and Alida Van Vranken. Wit.: Abram and Catarina Lansing.

Nicholaes, of Johannes Fort and Maria Van Vranken. Wit.: Gerrit Van Vranken, Saintje Egbertse.

Bata, of Teunis Van Woert and Elisabeth Van Doesen. Wit.: Jacob Van Woert, Neeltje Gardenier.

Leendert, of Johannes Gansevoort and Maria Douw. Wit.: Leendert and Catarina Gansevoort.

Margrita, of Meyndert Veder and Elisabeth Douw. Wit.: Pieter Winne, Elsje Douw.

Jan. 17. Phillip, of Phillip Conyn and Commertje Bronk. Wit.: Petrus and Catarina Conyn.

Feb. 4. Geertruy, of Cornelis Van Deusen and Leah Oostrander. Wit.: Cornelis Maarsen, Catarina Oostrander.

Wouter, of Antony Van der See and Anna Van Ness. Wit.: Albertus Becker, Sanneke Van Ness.

Harmen, of Thomas Williams and Maria Van Hoesen. Wit.: Edward and Maria Williams.

Feb. 11. Eldert, of Nicholaes Fisscher and Anna Tymessen. Wit.: Wilhelmus Van Antwerpen, Alida Van der Heyden.

Abraham, of Luycas Witbeek and Geertruy Lansing. Wit.: Johannes and Maria Witbeek.

Leendert, of Dirk Wesselse Ten Broek and Catarina Conyn. Wit.: Leendert and Emmitje Conyn.

Feb. 16. Catarina, of Killiaan Van Renslaer and Ariaantje Schuyler. Wit.: Henderick Van Renslaer, Helena Wendel.

Mar. 1. Annatje, of David Abeel, Jr., and Neeltje Van Bergen. Wit.: Gerrit Van Bergen, Catalyntje Abeel.

Jacobus, of Lambert Valkenburg and Catarina Van Vechten. Wit.: Teunis and Maria Van Vegten.

Mar. 8. Celia, of Johannes Redlof, Jr., and Anna Meccans. Wit.: Johannes Redlof, Judickje Jeets.

Mar. 11. Margarita, of Anthony Flensburg and Anna Redlof. Wit.: Johannes Flensburg, Cornelia Hoogteeling.

Catarina, of Frans Winne and Angenietje Van Wie. Wit.: Henderik I. Van Wie, Helena Lansing.

Cornelis, of Abram Jeets and Anna De Ridder. Wit.: Kiljaan and Gerritje De Ridder.

Maria, of Patrick Clark and Cornelia Waldron. Wit.: Pieter and Treyntje Brat.

Anna, of Johannes Knickerbacker and Rebecca Funda. Wit.: Geysbert and Elisabeth Funda.

1753

Mar. 14. Coenraat, of Johannes De Voe and Maria Keller. Wit.: Andries and Nellitje Huyck.

Mar. 18. Jacobus, of Jacobus Hilton and Judith Martin. Wit.: Willem and Alida Van Sante.

Susanna, of Daniel Halenbeek and Henderikje Hilton. Wit.: Gerrit Halenbeek, Elisabeth Hellen.

Johannes, of Abram Peek and Catarina Van Santen. Wit.: Gerrit and Antje Van Santen.

Apr. 1. Elsje, of Willem Hogen, Jr., and Susanna Lansing. Wit.: Harmen Hun, Rachel Hogen.

Apr. 8. Marten Cornelisse, of Barent Van Buren and Ariaantje Van der Poel. Wit.: Pieter and Mareyt Van Buren.

Frederick, of Johannes Meynerse and Maria Oostrande. Wit.: Abram Meynerse, Maria Winne.

Apr. 15. Jannitje, of Simon Springstien and Maria Seeger. Wit.: Johannes and Deborah Beekman.

Elizabeth, Engelje, of Johannes Van Antwerp and Cathrina Vedder. Wit.: Joh. Groesbeek, Eliz. Van Brakel.

Elizab., of Frederick Fort and Deborah Van Stande. Wit.: Maria and Petrus Belleway.

Maria, of Jacob Hasse and Maria Prume. Wit.: Hend. and Cath. Prume.

Peter, of Marthe De Forest and Jennetje Winne. Wit.: Pet. Winne, Maria Van Deussen.

Henderick, of Bastiaan Thiel and Catarina Ruyter. Wit.: Gerrit Van den Bergh, Catarina Daat.

Apr. 22. Anna, of John Danels and Geertruy Hilton. Wit.: Reykert and Maria Hilton.

Apr. 23. Magdalena, of Henderick I. Van Wie and Maria Loeck. Wit.: Jacob and Helena Loeck.

May 6. Sara, of Willem Van Santen and Alida Smit Wit.: Johannes Van Santen, Anna Freyer.

Jacob, of Abram H. and Elisabeth Wendel. Wit.: Jacob H. and Anna Ten Eyck.

Isaac, of Isaac Funda and Cordelia De Foreest. Wit.: Wouter and Elisabeth Knickerbacker.

Catalyntje, of Jacob I. Lansingh and Huybertje Jeets. Wit.: Jacob and Catalyntje Groesbeek.

May 13. Gerrit, of Henderick Wendel and Catalyntje Van Schaick. Wit.: Jacob Van Schaick, Elisabeth Van Renslaar.

Dorothea, of Jacobus Van Benthuysen and Sarah Coeper. Wit.: Henry Beesley, Lydia Crispel.

Arent, of Johannes Van Deusen and Maria Winne. Wit.: Arent Van Deusen, Treyntje Waldron.

May 20. Catalina, of Johannes Van Schaick and Alida Bogaart. Wit.: Pieter and Alida Schuyler.

1753

Pieter, of Robert Van Deusen and Catarina Van Alen.
Wit.: Henderick Bogaart, Jannitje Douw.

Burger, of Burger Huyck and Jannitje Hogeboom.
Wit.: Wynant and Volkje Van den Berg.

Johannes, of Henderick Jong and Catarina Lantman.
Wit.: Johannes Lantman, Susanna Litcher.

Engeltje, of Johannes Mol and Rebecca Barhead. Wit.:
Jacob and Catalyntje Groesbeck.

May 27. Abram, of Gerrit Van der Poel and Catarina
Hoes. Wit.: Barent, Jr., and Ariaantje Van Buren.

Pieter, of Johannes Hoes and Geertruy Van Buren.
Wit.: Pieter and Maria Van Buren.

Cornelia, of Abram I. Lansing and Elisabeth Coeper.
Wit.: Evert and Anna Lansing.

Machtel, of Harmen Hun and Elsje Lansing. Wit.:
Teunis and Machtel Fisscher.

June 3. Anna Margarita, of Coenraet Nellinger and
Anna Tiel. Wit.: Jurry and Anna Snyder.

Christiaen, of Christiaen Haver and Engeltje Van de
Werken. Wit.: Joh. Jurry and Anna Primer.

Jacob, of Cornelis Van Ness and Alida Van Woert.
Wit.: Jacob and Tietje Van Woert.

Mattheus, of Reynier Van Aalsteyn and Cornelia Van
den berg. Wit.: Rutger and Engeltje Van den Berg.

June 10. Johanna, of Gysbert Merselis and Catalina
Wendel. Wit.: Gerrit and Johanna Merselis.

Edward, of James Wells and Anna Groem. Wit :
Joseph Wells, Maria Danielson.

Jacobus, of James Taylor and Rachel Hoogkerk. Wit.:
Daniel Halenbeek, Henderikje Hilton.

June 17. Johannes, of Harmanus Van Salsberg and
Tannike Carick. Wit.: Johs. and Jobje Van Salsberg.

Anthony, of David Van Santen and Ariaantje Fort.
Wit.: Anthony Flensburg, Annatje Redlof.

Elisabeth, of Cornelis I. Muller and Teuntje Van Valkenburg. Wit.: Joh. I. Valkenburg, Dorothe Halenbeek.

Philip, of Coenraedt Loeck and Geertruy Van Deusen.
Wit.: Henderick Van Wie, Maria Loeck.

Willem, of David Groesbeek and Catarina Veder. Wit.:
David and Maria Groesbeek.

Willem, of Pieter Waldron and Neeltje Lansing. Wit.:
Willem and Elisabeth Waldron.

Catalina, of Willem Van den Berg and Susanna Van
Ieveren. Wit.: Brat Van Schoonhoven, Volkje Van
den Berg.

June 24. Johannes, of Pieter Jones and Abigal Winne.
Wit.: Kiljaan and Rachel Winne.

Gerrit, of Johannis Zeger and Maria Brat. Wit.: Gerrit
and Anna Zeger.

1753

Cornelia, of Gozen Van Schaick and Majeke Van den Berg. Wit.: Cornelis M. and Cornelia Van den Berg.
Rykert, of Henderick Van den Bergh and Treyntje Hoogteeling. Wit.: Robert and Catarina Van den Berch.
Marten, of Marten Buckley and Catarina Oothout. Wit.: Dirk Hun, Margarita Hogen.
Johannes, of John Jacob Harty and Margarita Pieterse. Wit.: Johannes Koen, Hilletje Zeger.
July 1. bo. May 10. Johanna, of Samuel Gardenier and Barentje Barhead. Wit.: Robert and Reykje Roseboom.
Ryckert, of Petrus Hilton and Machtel Wyngaart. Wit.: Reykert and Maria Hilton.
Anna, of Isaac Ouderkerk and Maria Foster. Wit.: Jacob Van Woert, Elisabeth Foster.
Ariaantje, of David Verplank and Catarina Boom. Wit.: Jacob and Alida Ten Eyck.
July 8. Magdalena, of Isaac Hansen and Maria Brat. Wit.: Isaac Kip, Nellitje Brat.
Magdalena, of Jonas Oothout and Elisabeth Lansing. Wit.: Gerrit A. and Elsje Lansing.
July 14. Alida, of Samuel Burn and Helena Pruyn. Wit.: Johannes and Christina Vande Werken.
Abraham, of Petrus Vosburg and Anna Brouwer. Wit.: Abraham and Geertje Vosburg.
July 22. Rebecca, of Philip Deforeest and Maria Bloemendal. Wit.: Jan and Catarina Brat.
July 29. Geertruy, of Wouter Groesbeek and Jannitje Bogaart. Wit.: David Groesbeek, Rachel Van Ness.
Willem, of James Adams and Margarita Hegeman. Wit.: Johannes Becker, Margarita Wilkeson.
Aug. 3. Stephanus, of Jacob Viele and Eva Fort. Wit.: Pieter Viele, Catarina Van Schaick.
Aug. 5. Joachim, of Hieronimus Van Valkenburg and Maria Van Buuren. Wit.: Joachim Van ——, Corn. V. Valkenburg.
Sara, of Geysbert Van Brakelen and Maria Van Antwerpen. Wit.: Wouter and Catarina De Freest.
Aug. 12. Elizabeth, of Johannes Wilms and Cornelia Bogardus. Wit.: Pieter Wilms, Elisabeth.
Geertje, of Pieter Hog and Catarina Vosburgh. Wit.: Nicolaes Cuyler, Catarina Winne.
Aug. 19. Jacob, of Jacob I. Lansing and Marritje Egbertse. Wit.: Abram and Catarina Lansing.
Jacob, of Johannes I. Lansing and Catarina Schuyler. Wit.: Gerrit I. Lansing, Jannitje Waters.
Johannes, of Marten Evert and Catarina Steur. Wit.: Johannes Wie, Maria Duyvebach.
Aug. 26. Maria, of Schibboleth Bogardus and Catarina Van der Werken. Wit.: Johannes and Geertruy Kidney.

1753

Johanna, of Henderick Beesley and Maria Noble. Wit.: Richard and Johanna Cartwright.

Sep. 2. Salomon, of Johannes Goewey and Elisabeth Jong. Wit.: Salomon and Margarita Goewey.

Sep. 9. Abigail, of Isaac Funda and Saintje De Foreest. Wit.: Daniel and Jannitje Winne.

Pieter, of Daniel P. Winne and Jannitje DeForeest. Wit.: Joh. and Maria Van Deusen.

Johannes, of Johannes Cloet, Jr., and Sarah Van Arnhem. Wit.: Johan and Anna Cloet.

Gerrit, of Gerrit Lansing, Jr., and Wyntje Van den Berg. Wit.: Cornelis M. Van den Berg, Cornelia Van Aalsteyn.

Sep. 22. Dorothea, of Stephanus Van Schaak and Jannitje Brat. Wit.: Andries and Engeltje Van Schaak.

Obediah, of Abram Coeper and Catarina Oostrander. Wit.: Thomas and Margarita Coeper.

Henderick, of Harmen Gansevoort and Magdalena Douw. Wit.: Pieter Gansevoort, Catarina Douw.

Geertruy, of Henderick Gerritse and Dirkje Tymissen. Wit.: Bastiaan and Hester Tymissen.

Sep. 29. Abraham, of Ebbener Robbese and Geertie Vosburg. Wit.: Isack Vosburg, Cataleyna Van Berg.

Dirk, of Cornelus Groot and Maria Van Vranken. Wit.: Abraham Groot, Rachel De Graaf.

Cornelus, of Jan Van Buren and Sara Bronk. Wit.: Hendrik and Geertruy Van Buren.

Oct. 7. Meyndert, of Harmen I. Visscher and Hester Van Ieveren. Wit.: Meyndert and Ariaantje Van Ieveren.

Oct. 14. Eldert, of Cornelis Tymissen and Maria Lieversen. Wit.: Nicholaes and Maritje Groot.

Samuel, of Willem Bromley and Lena Boom. Wit.: Samuel Boom, Annatje Aarnout.

Oct. 21. Hans Jirg, of Jacob and Regina Rosenberg. Wit.: Hans Jirg and Anna Bremer.

Bartholomeus, of Thomas Van Valkenburg and Rachel Van den Berg. Wit.: Willem and Maria Nikkels.

Hans Pieter, of Hans Nicolaas Eygelsheymel and Marregreta Mildring. Wit.: Jan Water, Ester Winne.

Oct. 28. Catarina, of Philip Hansen and Geertruy Van Ness. Wit.: Isaac Hansen, Catarina DeForeest.

Nov. 3. Elisabeth, of Jacob Fort and Marritje Oosterhout. Wit.: Corn. and Elis. Oosterhout.

Nov. 11. Johannes, of Gerardus Groesbeek and Maria Ten Broek. Wit.: Abram and Margarita Ten Broek.

Alida, of Gerrit Van Vranken and Maria Fort. Wit.: Johannes and Alida Cloet.

Catarina, of Albert Brat and Anna Carn. Wit.: Geurt Brat, Jannitje Hoogteeling.

1753

Jacobus, of John Davis and Elisabeth Wyngaert. Wit.: Johannes and Magtel Wyngaert.

Geesje, of Reykert Huyck and Jacomeyntje Van Deuse. Wit.: Jacobus and Lydia Valkenburg.

Johan Frederick, of Christophel Hugter and Catarina. Wit.: Johannes Post, Alida Van der Heyden.

Anna, of Henderic Alberecht and Elisabeth Foland. Wit.: Johannes Post, Frena Meyer.

Nov. 18. Jacob, of Johannes Janse and Janitje Schermerhoorn. Wit.: Corn. Schermerhoorn, Maria Winne.

Abraham, of Abram Valkenburg and Neeltje Gardenier. Wit.: Wessel Van Schaick, Neeltje Beekman.

Cornelis, of Jacob Quackenbosch and Catarina Huyck. Wit.: Johannes and Debora Beekman.

Abraham, of Andries Van Wie and Lena Van Arnhem. Wit.: Jacob and Alida Van Arnhem.

Dec. 9. Nicholaes, of Cornelis Van den Berg and Anneke Van Vranken. Wit.: Pieter and Ariaantje Van Woert.

Cornelius, of Henricus Van Dyk and Margarita Douw. Wit.: Petrus Douw, Maria Van Dyk.

Elisabeth, of Anthony E. Brat and Maria Van Aalsteyn. Wit.: Egbert and Elisabeth Brat.

Judithje, of Barent and Catalina Van Buuren. Wit.: Maas and Judikje Van Buren.

Marten, of Robert and Catarina Wendel. Wit.: Benjamin and Rachel Winne.

Annatje, of Jacob Cooper and Josina Oarchard. Wit.: Evert and Annatje Lansing.

Elisabeth, of Harmanus Wendel and Barbara Brat. Wit.: Barent and Elisabeth Brat.

Gerrit, of Wilhelmus and Angenietje Van den Berg. Wit.: Willem and Maria Van den Berg.

Philip, of Johannes Loeck and Geesje Legarange. Wit.: Jacob and Magdalena Loeck.

Dec. 16. Elisabeth, of Andries Van Vrancken and Maria Groot. Wit.: Johannes and Anne Cloet.

Barent, of Robert Sanders and Elisabeth Schuyler. Wit.: Barent Sanders, Geertruy Schuyler.

Elisabeth, of Pieter De Wandelaer and Anna Bogardus. Wit.: Willem and Maria Winne.

Majeke, of Isaac Ouderkerk and Hester Van Arnhem. Wit.: Cornelis Ouderkerk, Catarina Huyck.

Ariaantje, of J. and Frena Moock. Wit.: Jacob Arnel, Ariaantje Lansing.

Margarita, of Jacob Arnold and Anna Mook. Wit.: Jacob and Annatje Arnold.

Dec. 23. Maria, of Abram and Elisabeth Oostrande. Wit.: Johannes Oostrande, Maria Seylant.

1753-1754
Willem, of Pieter Hoogteeling and Anna Becker. Wit.: Coenraet and Cornelia Hoogteeling.
Dec. 30. Willem, of Jacob and Maria Van de Werken. Wit.: Douwe and Aaltje Funda.
Maria, of William Burch and Maria Christiaanse. Wit.: Bastiaan and Dirkje Fisscher.
Margarita, of Abraham Fort and Sara Van Woert. Wit.: Jacob I. and Elisabeth Van Woert.
1754, Jan. 1. Jurrie Jacob, of David Sornberger and Christina Louwer. Wit.: Pieter Lodewyk, Christina Rous.
Rachel, of Renselaer Nichols and Elisabeth Salisbury. Wit.: Harmen and Magdalena Gansevoort.
Jan. 6. Henderick, of Frederick Gerritse and Maria Tock. Wit.: James Tock, Anna Reyn.
Jan. 13. Johan Henderick, of Jacob ——bel and Elisabeth Humbert. Wit.: F. H. Winkel, Elisabet.
Jan. 22. Margrita, of Willem Snyder and Barber Klapper. Wit.: Henderick and Margarita Kels.
Heyltje, of Jacob and Heyltje Muller. Wit.: Stephanus and Geertruy Muller.
Maria, of Henderick Stoppelbeen and Elsje Smit. Wit.: Willem and Eva Phillip.
Cornelis, of Pieter Hogeboom and Heyltje Van Deusen. Wit.: Jeremias and Jannitje Hogeboom.
Jeremias, of Coenraet Smit and Jannitje Hogeboom. Wit.: Jacob and Heyltje Muller.
Jan. 24. Margarita, of Michael Rine and Joseyna Clerk. Wit.: Laurens Decker, Christina Vosburgh.
Jan. 27. Alexander, of Alexander Martin and Annatje Phlipse. Wit.: Johannes and Eefje Beekman.
Anthony, of Isaac A. Kip and Nelletje Brat. Wit.: Isaac Kip, Annatje Wendel.
Feb. 3. Catarina, of Pieter De Garmo and Sara Gardenier. Wit.: Andries Gardenier, Catarina De Garmo.
John, of Gerrit I. Lansing and Jannitje Waters. Wit.: John and Sara Waters.
Feb. 10. Johannes, of Jacob and Maria Smit. Wit.: Gerrit I. Lansing, Catarina Waters.
Feb. 18. John, of William Perry and Elisabeth Gardenier. Wit.: Mattheys and Margarita Lauer.
William, of Robert Turner and Rebecca Gardenier. Wit.: William and Elisabet Perry.
Annatje, of Henderick Jans and Catarina Ham. Wit.: Casper and Annatje Ham.
Feb. 24. Wouter, of Arent Slingerlant and Jacomeyntje Van der Volgen. Wit.: Jonathan Hoogteling, Jannitje Van der See.
Frans, of Bernardus Harse and Catarina Pruyn. Wit.: Samuel Pruyn, Alida Van Arnhem.

1754

Nanning, of Jacob Van der Heyden and Maria Halenbeek. Wit.: David and Geertruy Van der Heyden.

Maria, of Lewis Viele and Anatje Quackenbosch. Wit.: Teunis and Maria Viele.

Mar. 3. Catarina, of John Wilson and Barber Diependal. Wit.: Johannes and Sara Ten Eyck.

Christopher, of Jacob Bogaert, Jr., and Maria Jaets. Wit.: Abram and Antje Jaets.

Maria, of Ryckert Hansen and Catarina Ten Broeck. Wit.: David A. and Maria Schuyler.

Mar. 10. John, of Teunis Slingerlant and Angenietje Witbeek. Wit.: John and Elisabeth Williams.

Geertruy, of Henderick Van Buren and Anatje Salsbergen. Wit.: Wessel Van Schaick, Anna Quackenbosch.

Johannes, of Joseph Flensburgh and Elisabeth Veeling. Wit.: Joh. and Cornelia Flensburgh.

Mar. 11. Anna, of Michael Schoemaker and Catarina Oatner.

Mar. 17. Sara, of Jan Van Ness and Majeke Van den Bergh. Wit.: Abram and Antje Jeats.

Machtel, of Jonathan Witbeek and Gerritje Oostrander. Wit.: Tobias and Lea Witbeek.

Mar. 24. Magrita, of Pieter Goewey and Maria Jong. Wit.: Salomon and Alida Goewey.

Johannes, of Cornelis Sprong and Margarita Schans. Wit.: Johannes Renslaer, Catarina V. Renslaer.

Maria, of Willem Jong and Catalyntje Fonda. Wit.: Johannes Fonda, Cornelia Brat.

Franseyna, of Jacob Ouderkerk and Neeltje Knoet. Wit.: Wouter and Neeltje De Foreest.

Rebecca, of Staats Van Sandvoort and Willemtje Brat. Wit.: Anthony and Rebecca Brat.

Mar. 27. Johannes, of Johannes Van der Werken and Christina Pruyn. Wit.: Harm. and Catarina Wendel.

Mar. 31. Margarita, of Pieter Martin and Elisabeth Burns. Wit.: Robert and Maria Berrit.

Apr. 7. Gerrit, of Anthony and Claartje Slingerlant. Wit.: Gerrit and Marritje Knoet.

Cornelia, of Reykert Bovie and Maria Huyck. Wit.: Jacob and Catalyntje Groesbeek.

Jacob, of Johannes Knoet and Jannitje Ouderkerk. Wit.: Adriaan and Elisabeth Quackenbosch.

Henderick, of Henderick Gardenier and Eva Valkenburgh. Wit.: Wessel and Maria Van Schaick.

Apr. 14. Cornelia, of Henderick G. Van Wie and Catarina Waldron. Wit.: Pieter Brat, Engeltje Waldron.

Anna, of Jacobus G. Van Schaick and Geertje Ridder. Wit.: Henderick De Ridder, Annatje Ridder.

Anna, of Johannes Post and Frena Meyer. Wit.: Cornelis and Catalina Cuyler.

Apr. 22. Jeremias, of Pieter Lansing and Elisabeth Wendel. Wit.: Gerardus Lansing, Margarita Livingston.

Antje, of Cornelius Van Santvoort and Ariaantje Brat. Wit.: Staats and Willemje V. Santvoort.

Maria, of Jesse Winne and Anatje Van den Berg. Wit.: Wouter and Neeltje De Foreest.

Pieter, of Adriaan Brat and Mareytje Meckans. Wit.: Staats and Saintje Seger.

May 5. Cornelis, of Henderick Willemse and Francyntje Knoet. Wit.: Jacob Knoet, Anna Goewey.

May 12. Bata, of Dirk Heemstraat and Maria Barreway. Wit.: Johannes Heemstraat, Anna Quackenbosch.

Helena, of Johannes Funda and Elisabeth Ouderkerk. Wit.: Abram and Susanna Ouderkerk.

John De Peyster, of Folkert P. Douw and Anna De Peyster. Wit.: Tobias and Rachel Ten Eyck.

May 16. Anna, of Gerardus Lansing and Maria Wendel. Wit.: Henderick F. Oothout, Elsje Hun.

June 23. Elisabeth, of Martinus Cregier and Sara Van Vranken. Wit.: Jacob Van Vranken, Maria Wyngaert.

Johannes, of Johannes I. and Ariaantje Lansing. Wit.: Johannes Lansing, Engeltje Wendel.

Engeltje, of the same. Wit.: Abram E. and Elisabeth Wendel.

Henderick, of Johannes H. Ten Eyck and Sarah Ten Broeck. Wit.: Henderick and Margarita Ten Eyck.

Catalina, of Willem Winne and Maria De Wandelaer. Wit.: Jan and Catalina Winne.

Leendert, of Johannes Gansevoort and Maria Douw. Wit.: Leendert and Catarina Gansevoort.

Lavinus, of Franciscus and Martge Lansing. Wit.: Abraham and Catharina Lansing.

June 30. Jesse, of Philip De Vares and Rachel De Fares. Wit.: Jesse and Neltie Defares.

Gerrit, of Gerret Gerretsen Van der Bergh and Anganietie Van der Bergh. Wit.: Gerret V. der Bergh, Annatie De Wandelaar.

July 4. Eva, of Harmanus Van Aalsteyn and Anna Cat. Pesinger. Wit.: Philip and Geertruy Schuyler.

July 7. Lena, of Abram Quackenbosch and Bata Ouderkerk. Wit.: Johannes and Debora Beekman.

Anna, of Henderick Ten Broeck and Anna Van Schaick. Wit.: Antony G. and Christina Van Schaick.

Jacobus, of Jacob I. Van Woert and Elisabeth Fort. Wit.: Gillis Winne, Tietje Van Woert.

Johannes, of Jan Brat and Saintje Seger. Wit.: Pieter and Catalyntje Redlof.

Pieter, of Abram Bogaart and Maritje Besset. Wit.: Pieter Bogaart, Jannitje Groesbeek.

July 14. Jacob, of Isaac Lansing and Anna Van Woert. Wit.: Henderik and Anna Lansing.

Anna, of Antony G. and Christina Van Schaick. Wit.: Antony and Maria Van Schaick.

Jacob, Alida, of Dirk Van der Heyden and Elisabeth Wendel. Wit.: David and Geertruy Van der Heyden, Jacob and Alida Ten Eyck.

Coenraedt, of Pieter Gansevoort and Gerritje Ten Eyck. Wit.: Jacob C. and Gerritje Ten Eyck.

July 22. Elisabeth, of Albert Van der See and Antje Van Wie. Wit.: Gerrit Slingerlant, Anatje Ridder.

Catarina, of Abram Van den Berg and Rachel Liverse. Wit.: Willem Liverse, Maritje Lansing.

Maria, of Benjamin Goewey and Catarina Van den Berg. Wit.: Rutger and Maria Van den Berg.

Willem, of Evert Siksberry and Elsje Egmond. Wit.: John and Anna Fryer.

July 29. Hendericus, of Willem Hellen and Elisabeth Halenbeek. Wit.: Gerrit and Henderikje Halenbeek.

Aug. 5. Geertie, of Isack A. Vosburg and Catrina Van Woert. Wit.: Philip and Mareytie Van Vegten.

Maaja [?], of Jan F. Canker and Johanna Wyser. Wit.: Teunis and Mareytie Viele.

Johannis, of Johannis Perse and Alida V. Franken. Wit.: Johannis and Marragrieta Brat.

Aug. 12. Rachel, of James Wilson and Maria Van der Heyden. Wit.: Broeks and Rachel Farmer.

Philip, of Joachim Staats and Elisabeth Schuyler. Wit.: Harmanus Schuyler, Catarina Lansing.

Margrieta, of Johannes Redlof, Jr., and Anna Meccans. Wit.: Abram Ten Broeck, Elisabeth.

Aug. 20. Hannes, of Gerret Quakenbos and Catrina Devou. Wit.: Derk Van der Hyden, Margritie Kittel.

Coenrad, of Andres Denyk and Anatie Melia. Wit.: Barent and Gerretie Denyk.

Neeltie, of Hannes Groesbeek and Elisabeth Van Brakel. Wit.: Hannes Groesbeek, Jr., Neeltie Brat.

Susanna, of Harmen Liversen and Anatie Schoonhoven. Wit.: Philip V. Schoonhoven, Rachel Fischer.

Aug. 25. Catarina, of Pieter Bacchus, Jr., and Anna Vegen. Wit.: Johan Ernst Bacchus, Catharina Schever.

Johannes, of Pieter Bacchus and Eva M. Mullering. Wit. Jacob Rosenberg, Regina Fritzer.

Jacob, of Hermanus Wendell and Catarina V. Vegten. Wit.: Jacob Hendric Deneyk, Anna Dennyk.

Aug. 29. Hester, of Andries Gardenier and Catarina De Garmo. Wit.: Jillis and Jannitje Funda.

1754

Elisabeth, of Lodewyk Potman and Elisabeth Soets. Wit.: Hannes and Barbara Kits.

Aug. 30. Geertruy, of Harmen F. Fisscher and Catarina Brouwer. Wit.: Cornelis and Sara Smith.

Sep. 8. Geertruy, of Nicholaes and Jannitje Van Vranken. Wit.: Olderick and Ariaantje V. Vranken.

Johannes, of Johannes Koen and Hillitje Seger. Wit.: Johannes and Brechje Seger.

Johannes, of Jacob Frey and Alida Barhead. Wit.: Johannes and Frena Post.

Rachel, of Albert Van der Werken and Maria Quackenbosch. Wit.: Jacob and Geertje Van Schaick.

Willempje, of Isaac Hansen and Maria Brat. Wit.: Philip Hansen, Neeltje De Foreest.

Annatje, of Dirk Van der Heyden and Margarita Kittel. Wit.: David and Geertruy Van der Heyden.

Cornelia, of Abram Cooper and Catarina Oostrander. Wit.: Evert and Annatje Lansing.

Sep. 15. Geertruy, of Adam Van Vranken and Ariaantje Knoet. Wit.: Adriaan Quackenbosch, Elisabeth Knoet.

Henderick, Anna Margarita, of Willem Hen Urhib and Maria Hartman. Wit.: Pieter and Maria Binnewe, John Devenpoort, Eva Binnewe.

Geertruy, of Roelof Van der Werken and Anna Vosburg. Wit.: Harmen and Annatje Londersey.

Geertje, of Willem Vosburg and Christina Van Woert. Wit.: Jacob and Marritje Van Woert.

Treyntje, of Patrick Clark and Cornelia Waldron. Wit.: Pieter Funda, Treyntje Van Deusen.

Henderick, of Evert Seger and Sara Orchard. Wit.: Henderick and Joseyna Seger.

Sep. 22. Abram, of Frederick Cloet and Machtel Quakenbosch. Wit.: Abram Van Vranken, Dirkje Cregier.

Johannes, of Samuel Agesen Brad and Annatie Manzen. Wit.: Johannes and Annatie Mantz.

Matheus, of Gerret V. Ter Poel and Catarina Hus. Wit.: Jacob V. Schayk, Geertie Ridder.

Marritie, of Abraham Weever and Annatie Kernin. Wit.: Hannes and Marritie V. Ter Berg.

Sep. 29. Anna, of Gerrit Staats and Devorah Beekman. Wit.: Joachim and Elisabeth Staats.

Johannis, of Petrus Hilton and Machteld Wyngaard. Wit.: Johannis and Maria Wyngaart.

Engeltje, of Pieter Bloemendal and Christina Lagransie. Wit.: Jacobus and Engeltje Lagransie.

Oct. 6. Maria, of Johannis and Maria. Wit.: Hendrick and Maria.

Levinus, of Willem Liverse and Maria Funda. Wit.: Pieter and Catarina Liverse.

1754
Oct. 13. Samuel, of Abram Van Vranken and Dirkje Cregier. Wit.: Bastiaen and Jannitje Cregier.

Douwe, of Isaac D. Funda and Saintje Deforeest. Wit.: Douwe and Aaltje Funda.

Jan, of Adriaan Brat and Celia Van Sante. Wit.: Jan and Catarina Brat.

Annitje, of Cornelis Van den Berg and Elisabeth Pieterse. Wit.: Jan and Margarita Olvert.

Gerrit, of Folkert Van Hoesen and Alida Masselis. Wit.: Johannes and Catarina Van Renslaer.

Oct. 20. Geertruy, of Gerrit Van Vranken and Susanna Egbertse. Wit.: Johannis Van Vraken [sic], Maria Van Vranken.

Rachel, of Valentyn Reffenaar [?] and Catrina. Wit.: Johannis Fonda, Rachelje Beekman.

Jacobus, of Roelef Zeger and Lydia Hertie. Wit.: Johannis Zeger, Margarita Hartje.

Hendrikus, of Andrias H. Gardenier and Maragrieta Houwy. Wit.: Hendrik H. Gardinier, Maritje Houwy.

Oct. 27. Teunis, of Bastiaan Fischer and Engeltje Van den Bergh. Wit.: Teunis and Machteld Fischer.

Maria, of Johannes Huyck and Catarina Bovie. Wit.: Johannes I. and Maria Lansing.

Nov. 3. Annatje, of Cornelis W. Van den Berg and Maria Vielen. Wit.: Wynant C. Vanden Berg, Catarina Van Ness.

Daniel, of Johannes Flensburg and Cornelia Hoogteling. Wit.: Johannes Van Santen, Sara Jeets.

Nov. 10. Johannes, of Willem Kerchener and Christina Harmsin. Wit.: Jacob and Frena Mook.

Johannes, of Henderick Freydach and Christina Deppen. Wit.: Henderik and Frena Springer.

Rebecca, of Johannes Degarmo and Anna Kittel. Wit.: Mattheus Degarmo, Rebecca Van Arnhem.

Nov. 24. John Collins, of Hitchin Hollant and Margaret Collins. Wit.: Philip Lansing, Neeltje Douw.

Mattheus, of Corn. M. and Cornelia Van den Berg. Wit.: Gerrit G. Lansing, Catalina Van den Berg.

Catarina, of Jacob Van Schaick, Jr., and Catarina Cuyler. Wit.: Sybrant Van Schaik, Jr., Annatje Roseboom.

Neeltje, Elisabeth, twins of Johannes Knickerbacker and Rebecca Funda. Wit.: Wouter and Neeltje Knickerbacker, Gerrit Marselis, Pollie Funda.

Machteld, of Michael Philips and Margarita Wyngaert. Wit.: Petrus Hilton, Elisabeth Davis.

Jesse, of Wouter De Foreest and Engeltje Brat. Wit.: Jesse and Neeltje Deforeest.

Dec. 1. Cornelis, of David Groesbeek, Jr., and Catarina Veder. Wit.: Harmen I. Fisscher, Hester Van Ieveren.

1754-1755
Dec. 8. Franciscus, of Barent Hogen and Geertje Huyck. Wit.: Edward Hogin, Maria Egmont.

Dec. 15. Geysbert, of Dirk Brat Van Schoonhoven and Folkje Van den Bergh. Wit.: Willem and Susanna Van den bergh.

Sara, of Evert Wendel and Elisabeth Van Schaick. Wit.: Abram Ten broeck, Elisabeth Renslaar.

Geysbert, of Weynant Van den Bergh and Catarina Van Ness. Wit.: Wilhelmus and Geertje Van den berg.

Dec. 22. Martinus, of Isak Du Foe and Mareytje Van der Linde. Wit.: Martinus V. d. Linden, Elisabeth Doxs.

Johannes, of Pieter Garmoe and Gertruy Kregier. Wit.: Johannes and Ebertie Garmoe.

Jannitje, of John Reyley and Helena Barber. Wit.: Pieter and Antje Jeets.

Dec. 26. Nicholaes, of Kiljaan Van Renslaer and Ariaantje Schuyler. Wit.: Johannes and Catarina Lansing.

Elisabeth, of Reykart Van Vranken and Anna Truex. Wit.: Isaac and Elisabeth Van Arnhem.

1755, Jan. 1. Johannis, of Simon Veder and Anna Van Antwerpen. Wit.: Gerrit I. and Jannitje Lansing.

Annatje, of Johannis Clement and Rachel Redlof. Wit.: Joseph and Antje Clement.

Willem, of Johannes F. Witbeek and Eva Waldron. Wit.: Willem and Elisabeth Waldron.

Jan. 5. Johannis, of Henderick H. Van Wie and Johanna Gardenier. Wit.: Gerrit Slingerlant, Catarina Van Wie.

Adriaan, of Staats Seger and Susanna Brat. Wit.: Adriaan and Maria Brat.

Staats, of Simon Springsteen and Maria Seger. Wit.: Johannes and Maria Seger.

Jan. 26. Pieter, of Antony and Weyburgh Eyter. Wit.: Pieter and Eva Maria Backis.

March 12. Sara, of Cornelus S. Van Nes and Alida V. Woert. Wit.: Gerrit K. and Maieke V. Nes.

Johannes, of Jacob Van der Heyden and Lea Brouwer. Wit.: Johannes V. d. Heyden, Maria Van der Heyden.

Johannes Simonsche, of Simon and Cathalyntje Veder. Wit.: Isaac and Maria Switts.

Daniel, of Adam Winne and Gerritje Schermerhoorn. Wit.: Willem and Maria Winne.

Cathalyntje, of Rutger and Maria Van den Berg. Wit.: Gerrit G. and Weyntje Lansing.

Wilhelmus, of Marten Meyndertse and Sarah Reykman. Wit.: Albert and Annaatje Reykman.

Lena, of Johannes Lansing and Maria Huyk. Wit.: Abraham and Lena Lansing.

March 28. Johannis, of Johannis Bernhart and Christina Huyck. Wit.: Henderick Bernhart, Ariaantje Brouwer.

1755

Jacob, of Pieter Jeets and Sara Van Aalsteyn. Wit.: Adam Jeets, Cornelia Van den Bergh.

March 30. Margarita, of Dirk Brat and Catarina Hybelaar. Wit.: Cornelis Van den Berg, Anneke Van Vranken.

Johannis, of Johannes Seger and Catarina Pieterse. Wit.: Johannis, and Brechje Seger.

Alida, of Cornelis Ouderkerk and Catarina Huyck. Wit.: Isaac D. and Saintje Funda.

Simon, of Lewis Van Antwerpen and Henderickje Funda. Wit.: Abram De Foreest, Rebecca Van Antwerpen.

Apr. 6. Catarina, of Henderick Jong and Catarina Lantman. Wit.: Benjamin Goewey, Engeltje Van Veghten.

Apr. 13. Joseph, of Abram Peek and Catarina Van Santen. Wit.: Jacobus Clement, Jannike Van Woert.

Apr. 20. Willem, of Roelof Devoe and Elisabeth Golden. Wit.: Jacob Van Woert, Geertruy Dox.

Willem, of Pieter Waldron and Neeltje Lansing. Wit.: Willem and Elisabeth Waldron.

Catarina, of Bastiaan Tiel and Catarina Ruyter. Wit.: Pieter and Geertruy Schuyler.

Apr. 27. Leendert, of Cornelis Muller and Maria Van Hoesen. Wit.: Johannis and Sara Muller.

Johannis, of Johannis S. Pruyn and Jannitje Van Aalsteyn. Wit.: Antony E. Brat, Catalyntje Winne.

May 4. Nicholaes, of Matheus Boom and Josseyna Seger. Wit.: Nicholaes Boom, Hillitje Koen.

May 11. Abraham, of Johan Ernst Tevoe and Maria Keller. Wit.: Joh. Van de Werken, Maria Tevoe.

May 18. Barentje, of Thomas Smit and Maria Barret. Wit.: John and Anna Husan.

Catalyntje, of Samuel Burn and Helena Pruyn. Wit.: Joh. Depeyster, Anna Brat.

Rebecca, of Abram Bogaart and Maritje Besset. Wit.: Pieter and Magdalena Bogaart.

Geertje, of Henderick Funda and Catarina Groesbeek. Wit.: Jacob and Catalyntje Groesbeek.

June 22. Maria, of Daniel Halenbeek and Henderickje Hilton. Wit.: Reykert and Maria Hilton.

Nicholaes, of Harmanus Schuyler and Christina Ten broeck. Wit.: Johannes Schuyler, Elisabeth Staats.

Eva, of Gerrit Van Alen and Catarina Van Wie. Wit: Daniel P. Winne, Jannitje Deforeest.

June 26. Jacob, of Jillis Truex and Ariaantje Jansen. Wit.: Jacob Truex, Elisabeth Lagrange.

July 4. Jannitje, of Henderick Bogaart and Engeltje Van Schaak. Wit.: Johannis Douw, Jannitje Brat.

July 6. Douwe, of Johannes Funda and Elisabeth Ouderkerk. Wit.: Abram Funda, Susanna Deforeest.

1755

July 13. Sara, of Johannis Van Santen and Margarita Wilkensen. Wit.: Johs. Van Santen, Sara Jeets.

July 27. Barent, of Johannis Muller and Sara Van Ieveren. Wit.: Cornelis and Cornelia Van Ieveren.

Willem, of Cornelis Van Ness and Susanna Swits. Wit.: Philip and Rachel Deforeest.

Cornelia, of Henderick I. Van Wie and Maria Loeck. Wit.: Gerrit W. Van den Berg, Catarina Winne.

Lena, of Abram I. Lansingh and Elisabeth Coeper. Wit.: Abram and Catarina Lansingh.

July 30. Isaac, of Andries Van Wie and Helena Van Arnhem. Wit.: Isaac Ouderkerk, Anna Van Arnhem.

Aug. 3. Esther, of Thomas Wilson and Rachel Redlof. Wit.: Philip Redlof, ——— Valkenburg.

Jesse, of Isaac Funda, Jr., and Cornelia Deforeest. Wit.: Jesse and Neeltje Deforeest.

Aug. 10. Elisabeth, of Harmen I. Fisher and Hester Van Ieveren. Wit.: Reynier Van Ieveren, Annatje Nieukerk.

Aug. 17. Willem, of Jan and Feytje Devoe. Wit.: Johannis Van Santen, Jannitje Van der Kar.

Joris, of Johannis I. Wendel and Sarah Bergen. Wit.: Evert Wendel, Jacomeyntje Betom.

Aug. 24. Neeltje, of Isaac Deforeest and Alida Funda. Wit.: Jesse and Neeltje Deforeest.

Aug. 27. Jacobus, of John Davids and Elisabeth Wyngaert. Wit.: Johannis and Margarita Wyngaert.

Aug. 31. Machtel, of Adriaan Quackenbos and Elisabeth Cloet. Wit.: Sybrant and Machtel Quackenbos.

Wyntje, of Johannis Cloet and Jannitje Ouderkerk. Wit.: Johannis Muller, Sarah Van Ieveren.

Barent, of Johannis Van der Werken and Christina Pruyn. Wit.: Isaac and Anatje Lansing.

Evert, of Nicholaes Cloet and Ariaantje Ridder. Wit.: Johannis and Fryncyntje Perry.

Nicholaes, of Pieter Degarmo and Sara Gardenier. Wit.: Andries and Sara Gardenier.

Sep. 3. Angenitje, of Leendert Muller and Marritje Van Ness. Wit.: Jacob and Angenitje Muller.

Sep. 7. Dorothe, of Johs. Henrick Hendermont and Anna Catarina. Wit.: Joh. Jurrie Claver, Sus. [?] Cat. Sweertveger.

Killiaan, of Jillis Winne and Tietje Van Woert. Wit.: Killiaan and Dirkje Winne.

Sep. 21. Margarita, of Henderick Richard and Annatje Huyck. Wit.: Philip and Susanna Schuyler.

Marten, of Willem Hogen, Jr., and Susanna Lansing. Wit.: John Trotter, Maria Hogen.

1755

David, of Marten Deforeest and Tanneke Winne. Wit.: Philip and Maria Deforeest.

Gerardus, of Johannis Cloet and Catarina Lansing. Wit.: Jacob and Machtel Cloet.

Sep. 28. Rutger, of Teunis Van Woert and Elisabeth Van Deusen. Wit.: Isaac Vosburgh, Christina Van Woert.

Neeltje, of Jonathan Hoogteeling and Jannitje Slingerlant. Wit.: Storm Van der Zee, Lybetje Slingerlant.

Philip, of Henderick Alberecht and Elisabeth Folant. Wit.: Henderick Post, Rachel Fitsgeerels.

Oct. 23. Jacobus, of Johannes R. [?] Bleyker and Elizabeth Staats. Wit.: Jacobus Bleyker, Anna Roorbach.

Lambert, of Anthony Flensburgh and Anna Reddley. Wit.: Lambert and Anna Riddley.

Johannes, of Teunis Van Vegten and Cornelia Cnikkerbacker. Wit.: Harmen and Rebecca Cnikker Backer.

Albartus, of James and Margriet Adams. Wit.: Albartus Becker, Catharina Backer.

Philip, Salomon, of Jacob Lock and Alida Hocci (dec'd). Wit.: Johannes and Jeesje Lock, Salomon and Sara Hoccy.

Tjerk Harmse, of Johannes Beekman and Maria Nicoll. Wit.: Marten Beekman, Lena Visscher.

Isaac, of Isaac Ouderkerk and Hester Van Aarnhem. Wit.: Douwe and Alida Fonda.

Folkert, of Willem Van den Berg and Susanna Van Ieveren. Wit.: Folkert and Neeltje Van den Berg.

Nov. 9. Adam, of John Van der Heyden and Catarina Brown. Wit.: Dirk and Margarita Van der Heyden.

Gerrit, of Gosen Van Schaick and Majeke Van den Berg. Wit.: Pieter and Catarina Viele.

Nov. 22. Sara, of Abner Roberts and Caatje Vosburgh. Wit.: Pieter Vosburg, Annatje Brouwer.

Nov. 23. Catalyntje, of Henderick I. Wendel and Anna Magenis. Wit.: Pieter and Elisabet Lansing.

Margarita, of Henderick Blycker and Catalyntje Cuyler. Wit.: Henderic Cuyler, Margarita Blycker.

Nov. 30. Engeltje, of Johannis Van de Werken and Mareytje Devoe. Wit.: Martinus and Margarita Lydius.

Anatje, of Barant C. Van Buren and Ariaantje Van der Poel. Wit.: Melchert and Margarita Van der Poel.

Marten, of Benjamin Van Buren and Cornelia Salsbury. Wit.: Johannis and Maria Gansevoort.

Dirk, of Jacobus Hilton and Judith Martin. Wit.: William and Anna Fryar.

Melchert, of Gerrit Van der Poel and Catarina Hoes. Wit.: Melchert Van der Poel, Catarina Coeper.

Dec. 7. Johannis, of Pieter Marschal and Annatje Flensburg. Wit.: Joseph and Annatje Flensburg.

1755-1756
Mareytje, of Anthony Van der See and Anatje Van Ness.
Wit.: Wouter and Anatje Ridder.
Maria, of Jacob I. Lansingh and Marritje Egberts. Wit.:
Johannis I. and Catarina Lansing.
Pieter, of Robert Sanders and Elisabeth Schuyler. Wit.:
Johannis Lansing, Maria Sanders.
Johannis, of Johannis Seger and Maria Brat. Wit.:
Staats Seger, Susanna Brat.
Dec. 14. Cornelia, of Jacob Quackenbos and Catarina
Huyck. Wit.: Jacob Van Arnhem, Anatje Brat.
Rebecca, of Douwe I. Funda and Aaltje Van Buren.
Wit.: Lucas Hoogkerk, Annatje Knickerbacker.
Dec. 21. Nicholaes, of Geysbert Funda and Elsje Douw.
Wit.: Nicholaes Funda, Rebecca Knickerbacker.
Anthony, of Gerrit Bovie and Ariaantje Brouwer. Wit.:
Anthony and Catarina Bovie.
Catarina, of Johannes N. Groesbeek and Maria Viele.
Wit.: Hugo and Anneke Viele.
Dec. 28. Daniel, of Pieter Goewey and Maria Jong. Wit.:
Johannis and Elisabeth Goewey.
Maria, of Frederick Cloet and Maria Ridder. Wit.:
Walraven and Anatje Cloet.
Arent, of Cornelis Van Deusen and Leah Oostrander.
Wit.: Johs. Meynerse, Maria Oostrander.
1756, Jan. 1. Sara, of Henderick Wendel and Cata-
lyntje Van Schaick. Wit.: Evert and Elisabeth
Wendel.
Jan. 4. James, of Joseph Flensburgh and Elisabeth
Veder. Wit.: Abram and Catarina Peek.
Jan. 18. Jacob, of Gerrit Quackenbos and Catarina
Devoe. Wit.: Abram I. Lansing, Geertruy Van Olinden.
Storm, of David Brat and Treyntje Langh: Wit.:
Storm Brat, Sophia Ziele.
Jan. 25. Cathrina, of Johannis V. Schaik and Alida
Bogart. Wit.: Pieter and Sara Viele.
Geurt, of Finschen Bennewe and Annatie Bovie. Wit.:
Phlip and Nelletie Bovie.
Johannis Depeyster, of Folkert P. Douw and Anna
Depeyster. Wit.: John Barclay, Maria Gansevoort.
Feb. 1. Johannis, of Geysbert Marselis and Catalyntje
Wendel. Wit.: Evert I. and Annatje Wendel.
Feb. 8. Harmanus, of Henderick Van Buren and
Annatje Van Salsbergen. Wit.: Casparus and Marritje
Witbeek.
Feb. 15. Dorothea, of Stephanus Van Schaak and
Jannitje Brat. Wit.: Hendrick Bogert, Engeltje Van
Schaak.
Geertruy, of Johannis Redlof and Annatje Meccans.
Wit.: Geurt and Elisabeth Brat.

1756
Feb. 22. Sophia Christina, of Nicholaes Pitman and Anna Margarita Pit. Wit.: Jurrie Hen Staten, Sophia Christina.

Engeltje, of Philip I. Schuyler and Catarina Van Renslaar. Wit.: Joh. Van Renslaer, Margarita Livingston, Annatje, of Evert Lansing and Annatje Coeper. Wit.: Gerrit E. and Cornelia Lansing.

Mar. 1. Elisabeth, of Barent Van Buren and Catalyntje Schermerhorn. Wit.: Hugo and Elisabeth Viele.

Mar. 3. Engeltje, of Johannis Everse and Susanna Lagrange. Wit.: Simon and Catalyntje Veder.

Mar. 7. Nicholaes, of Arent Slingerlant and Jacomeyntje Van der Volgen. Wit.: Jacob and Eva Viele.

Jacob, of Jacob Bogaert, Jr., and Mareytje Jeets. Wit.: Wouter and Jannitje Groesbeek.

Mar. 21. Rachel, of Johannes Meynerse and Maria Oostrander. Wit.: Tobias and Lea Witbeek.

Karel, of Dirk Heemstraat and Maria Barreway. Wit.: Matthys and Elisabeth Bovie.

Maria, of Henricus Van Dyck and Margarita Douw. Wit.: Petrus Douw, Maria Van Dyck.

Rachel, of David Van Santen and Ariaantje Fort. Wit.: Gerrit Van Santen, Jannitje Hoogteeling.

Mar. 28. Margarita, of Johan Henrick and Elisabeth Leycher. Wit.: Philip Schuyler, Antje Van den Bergh.

Rachel, of Cornelis Tymissen and Maria Liversen. Wit.: Leendert Gansevoort, Lydia Liversen.

Anna, of Schiboleth Bogardus and Catarina Van de Werken. Wit.: Jacob and Cornelia Bogardus.

Apr. 4. Pieter, of Jesse Winne and Anatje Van den Bergh. Wit.: Gosen Van Schaick, Majeke Van den Bergh.

Abraham, of Jacob Ouderkerk and Neeltje Cloet. Wit.: Cornelis Van Ness, Alida Van Woert.

Alida, of Andries H. Gardenier and Margarita Goewey. Wit.: Jacob Loeck, Sarah Goewey.

Henderick, of Henderick H. Gardenier and Maria Goewey. Wit.: Anderies Gardenier, Elisabeth Van Renslaer.

Apr. 5. Maria, of Michael Herder and Maria Rees. Wit.: Benjamin B. Rees, Maria Herder.

Sarah, of Johannis I. Van Hoesen and Sarah Rees. Wit.: Arent and Charlotte Van der Kar.

Apr. 7. James, of John Wilson and Barber Diependorf. Wit.: Pieter, Jr., and Helena Bogaart.

Apr. 18. Catarina, of Petrus Vosburgh and Annatje Brouwer. Wit.: Roelof Merkel, Ariaantje Brouwer.

Apr. 25. Jochim, of Dirk V. D. Heyden and Margrieta Kittel. Wit.: Hans and Annatie D. Garmo.

Johannes, of Pieter De Wandelaar and Annatie Bogardus. Wit.: Johannis D. Wandelaar, Rebecka Knikkebakker.

1756

May 2. Evert, of Evert Siksbey and Elsje Egmont.
Wit.: Edward Hogg, Maritje Siksbey.
May 9. Sara, of Joseph Van Santen and Maria Brouwer.
Wit.: Johannis Van Santen, Annatje Fryer.
Isaac, of Pieter Lansingh and Elisabeth Wendel. Wit.:
Henricus and Margarita Van Dyck.
Andries, of Johannis Marselis and Neeltje Gardenier.
Wit.: Meyndert Marselis, Sara Gardenier.
Willem, of Johannis Erhart and Christina Wies. Wit.:
John Perry, Francyntje Cloet.
May 16. Johannis, of Reykert Redlof and Maria Oliver.
Wit.: Johannis and Catalyntje Redlof.
May 21. Isaac, of Wouter and Hester Slingerlant. Wit.:
Isaac Kip, Geesje Slingerlant.
May 27. Annatje, of Jacob Viele and Eva Fort. Wit.:
Petrus and Maria Binneway.
May 30. Staats, of Staats Seeger and Susanna Brat.
Wit.: Gerrit and Engeltje Seeger.
Engeltje, of Coenraet Loeck and Geertruy Van Deusen.
Wit.: Jan Van Deusen, Maria Winne.
June 20. Thomas, of Pieter Williams and Elisabeth
Funda. Wit.: John and Angenietje Williams.
June 27. Robert, of John Dunbar and Helena Lansing.
Wit.: Gerrit and Maria Dunbar.
June 28. Jean, of John Riddle and Mary Creaton. Wit.:
Gilbert Croesbey, Ellenor McComes.
July 4. Farquard, of Alexander McPharson and Anna
Maccantash. Wit.: James Farcharson, Elisabeth Anderson.
Read, of Anguis McDearwith and Margaret Cambell.
Wit.: Peter Stewart, Elisabeth Grant.
Catarina, of Daniel B. and Willempje Brat. Wit.: Barnardus, Jr., and Catarina Brat.
Storm, of Albert Brat and Magdalena Lang. Wit.:
Peter and Cornelia Brat.
July 9. Johannis, of Gerrit Van Sante and Hester
Winne. Wit.: Johannis and Elisabeth Van Santen.
July 11. Catarina, of Henderick Sans and Catarina
Ham. Wit.: Petrus Ham, Maria Sans.
July 18. Elisabeth, of Jacobus Arnold and Anna Moock.
Wit.: Jacob Moock, Anna Cock.
July 25. Catarina, of Cornelis Sprong and Margarita
Schans. Wit.: Henderick and Catarina Schans.
Elisabeth, of Abram and Elisabeth Oostrander. Wit.:
Petrus and Elisabeth Oostrander.
Sarah, of Anthony Van Ieveren and Maria Van den Bergh.
Wit.: Willem and Susanna Van den Bergh.
Aug. 1. Alida, of Henderic Bulsing and Catalina Goewey.
Wit.: Johannis and Elisabeth Goewey.

1756

Geertruy, of Johannis I. Lansing and Ariaantje Wendel. Wit.: Pieter Lansingh, Elisabeth Wendel.

Aug. 6. Duncan, of John Mackentise and Elenor Mac-Neel. Wit.: John Maccalm, Laughlin Mackentash.

Aug. 8. Evert, of Nicholaes and Jannitje Van Vrancken. Wit.: Harmen and Dirkje Van Vrancken.

Willem, of Daniel Winne, Jr., and Jannitje Deforeest. Wit.: Willem, Jr., and Dirkje Winne.

Aug. 15. Catalyntje, of Gerrit Lansing, Jr., and Wyntje Van den Bergh. Wit.: Rutger Lansing, Catalyntje Van den Bergh.

Aug. 22. Annelse, of Diderich Schever and Maria Marg. Hennerich. Wit.: Henrick Strouck.

Lydia, of Jan Brat and Susannah Seger. Wit.: Adam and Christina Brat.

Jesse, of Philip Deforeest and Rachel Van Ness. Wit.: Wouter and Cornelia Deforeest.

Aug. 29. Sara, of Jacob Coeper and Josyna Orchard. Wit.: Obediah and Hester Coeper.

Sep. 5. Anatje, of Jacobus Van Benthuysen and Sara Coeper. Wit.: Obediah and Cornelia Lansing.

Sept. 12. Maria, of Abram Coeper and Catarina Oostrande. Wit.: Johannis and Maria Meynerse.

Alida, of Adriaan Brat and Maria Meccans. Wit.: Johannis and Anatje Redlof.

Pietertje, of Anthony E. Brat and Maria Van Aalsteyn. Wit.: Reynier and Cornelia Van Aalsteyn.

Catarina, of Harmanus Wendel and Catarina Van Veghten. Wit.: Harmanus Cuyler, Elisabeth Wendel.

Sep. 14. John, of James McDonald and Margaret Nevels. Wit.: John Grant, Alexander Brown, Elisabeth Steward.

Sep. 19. Petrus, of Teunis C. Slingerlant and Angenietje Witbeek. Wit.: Thomas and Maria Williams.

Machtel, of Petrus Hilton and Anna Broecks. Wit.: William and Maria Hilton.

Geertruy, of Albert Van de Werken and Maria Quackenbosch. Wit.: Roelof and Anna Van de Werken, Maria [?] Viele.

Sep. 26. Catarina, of Gerardus Groesbeek and Maria Ten Broek. Wit.: Johannis H. Ten Eyck, Catarina Schuyler.

Oct. 3. Sara, of Albartus Bloemendal and Maria Oostrander. Wit.: Maas Bloemendal, Huybertje Jeets.

Johannis, of Bastiaen Teymissen and Majeke Ouderkerk. Wit.: Pieter Viele, Jannitje Ouderkerk.

Susanna, of Patrick Clerk and Cornelia Waldron. Wit.: Folkert and Neeltje Van den Bergh.

Oct. 4. John, of Donald and Catarina Mc Donald.

Oct. 10. Saar, of Sem Thomas and Brit, serv. Wit.: Jephta and Bet, serv.

Oct. 17. Gerrit, of Dirk Becker and Eva Hoogen. Wit.: Arent and Feytje Becker.

Oct. 24. James, of William and Elisabeth Harris. Wit.: Marten Meynertse, Sanneke Ryckman.

Maria, of Martinus Cregier and Sara Van Vranken. Wit.: Abram Van Vranken, Dirkje Cregier.

Jean, of James and Mary Frasier. Wit.: John McCay.

Oct. 24. Thomas, of Thomas Owen and Elisabeth Norman. Wit.: Thomas Owen, Francis Richardson.

Oct. 31. Nicolaes, of Andrew Montour and Sara. Wit.: Martinus and Sara Maria Lydius.

Nov. 2. Elisabeth, of Thomas Macfarland and Catarina Kincheler. Wit.: Jean Kennedy, Elisabeth Webster.

Daniel, of Hugh McNaughten and Judith McDonalds. Wit.: Daniel and Hannah McDonalds, John Woodhouse.

Nov. 5. John, of William Monro and Hester Blackfield. Wit.: Edward Wilkenson, Anna Van Ieveren.

Nov. 6. James, of George Sattin and Ginnit Steward. Wit.: James and Susanna Chandler.

William, of John Tailor and Susanna Baxter. Wit.: John Recubite, Daniel McFarland, Susanna Lovely.

Nov. 7. Genny, of John Matthison and Margaret Sudderland. Wit.: Matthew Matthison, Isabella Maccloud.

Nov. 14. Petrus, of Robert Crannel and Ariaantje Bovie. Wit.: Petrus Crannel, Maria Hilton.

Angenietje, of Daniel Winne and Elisabeth Dox. Wit.: Roelof Merckel, Geertruy Van Olinden.

Rebecca, of Johannis Yates and Rebecca Waldron. Wit.: Abram and Antje Yates.

Franciscus, of Edward Hogen and Maria Egmont. Wit.: John Crannel, Folkje Van Aalsteyn.

Joachim, of Johannis Degarmo and Anna Kittil. Wit.: Dirk I. Vanderheyden, Margarita Kittel.

Nov. 15. John Edward, of John Burton and Elisabeth Yoll. Wit.: William Bidlow, William Car, Sara Emerson.

Nov. 20. Johannis, of Joachim Staats and Elisabeth Schuyler. Wit.: Johannis Lansing, Geertruy Van Renslaer.

Jacob, of Gerrit Staats and Deborah Beeckman. Wit.: John and Aefje Beeckman.

Nov. 21. Margarita, of Jacob Van Schaick, Jr., and Catarina Cuyler. Wit.: Henderick and Margarita Cuyler.

Cornelia, of Wilhelmus, Jr., and Angenietje Van den Bergh. Wit.: Gerrit Van den Bergh, Catarina Winne.

Nov. 28. Philip, of Johannes I. Lansing and Catarina Schuyler. Wit.: Kiljaen Van Renslaer, Catarina Lansing.

1756-1757

Elbert, of Henderick Gerritse and Dirkje Tymissen. Wit.: Abram Van Deusen, Maria Van Schaick.

Dec. 5. Eva, of Theodorus Frielinghuysen and Elisabeth Sims. Wit.: Jacob and Geertruy Isabella Roseboom.

Dec. 12. Clemens, of John Manypenny and Darky Kendy. Wit.: John Manypenny, Mary Knowlan.

Maria, of Abram Peeck and Catarina Van Santen. Wit.: Jacobus Clement, Jennike Van Woert.

Abraham, of Gerrit I. Lansing and Jannitje Waters. Wit.: Abraham I. and Elisabeth Lansing.

Dec. 25. Elisabeth, of Barent Hogen and Geertje Huyck. Wit.: Cornelis Van Veghten, Geertje Litcher.

Elisabeth, of Jonathan Witbeek and Gerritje Oostrande. Wit.: Petrus Oostrande, Maria Meynerse.

1757, Jan. 9. Elisabeth, of Cornelis Groot and Maria Van Vrancken. Wit.: Robert and Elisabeth Sanders.

Jan. 16. Benjamin, of Isaac Kip and Nellitje Brat. Wit.: Benjamin and Magdalena Brat.

David, of Isaac D. Funda and Susanna Deforeest. Wit.: David and Abigael Deforeest.

Isaac, of Johannis Funda and Elisabeth Ouderkerk. Wit.: Jan and Catarina Brat.

Jan. 18. Abner, of Abner Roberts and Catarina Vosburg. Wit.: Petrus Vosburg, Anatje Brouwer.

Jan. 23. Margarita, of Abram and Anna Dewever. Wit.: Nicholaes and Ariaantje Cloet.

Annatje, of Daniel and Rebecca Van Antwerpen. Wit.: Cornelis and Catarina Ten Broeck.

Jan. 30. Johannis, of Johannis Mook and Barbar Beekman. Wit.: Christopher Hegeman, Joseph and Justina Pinter.

Jean, of Patrick Caseway and Mary Craig. Wit.: John Graham, William Hanna, Mary Chase, Matty Grain.

Elisabeth, of Lewis Viele and Anatje Quackenbos. Wit.: Seybrant and Elisabeth Quackenbos.

Feb. 6. Johannis, of Jonas Oothout and Elisabeth Vinnagel. Wit.: Johannis Vinnagel, Mareytje Van den Berg.

Alida, of Johannis Cloet, Jr., and Sara Van Arnhem. Wit.: Johannis Van Arnhem, Alida Van der Heyden.

Dirk, of Wouter Deforeest and Engeltje Brat. Wit.: Dirk and Cornelia Brat.

Feb. 13. Coenraadt, of Johannis Koen and Hillitje Seger. Wit.: Jacob Ten Eyck, Jannitje Lansing.

Maria, of John Williams and Cornelia Bogardus. Wit.: Edward and Maria Williams.

Abram, of Abram I. Lansing and Elisabeth Coeper. Wit.: Abram ar.d Catarina Coeper.

1757

Feb. 14. Marten, Jacob, of Philip Hofman and Elisabeth Clerck. Wit.: William Martin, Jacob, Cumbringer, Catarina Midcaf, Margaret McCloud.

Feb. 20. Thomas, of William and Francis Hartley. Wit.: Thomas Tatton, Daniel Maccan, Jane Gardener.

Johannis, of Jacob Frets and Margarita Ernstfrets. Wit.: Nicholaes and Maria Margarita Eygelseymer.

Feb. 27. Willem, of Willem Bromley and Helena Boom. Wit.: Willem and Sara Pemperton.

Mar. 6. Jacob, Helena, of Harmanus Wendel and Barbara Brat. Wit.: Henderick, Helena, Evert and Catarina Wendel.

Mar. 18. Elisabeth, of Pieter Bacchus and Eva Maria Miller. Wit.: Storm and Elisabeth Van der See.

Mar. 27. Catarina, of Abram Van den bergh and Rachel Liverse. Wit.: Cornelis Liverse, Helena Lansing.

Apr. 3. Susanna, of Abram I. Funda and Maria Van Schoonhoven. Wit.: Dirk Brat Van Schoonhoven, Susanna Van Schoonhoven.

April 8. Gerritje, of Pieter Gansevoort and Gerritje Teneyck. Wit.: Barent Teneyck, Elisabeth Brat.

Petrus, of Bastiaan Diel and Catarina Ruyter. Wit.: Pieter Hogen, Catarina Vosburgh.

Apr. 10. Geertruy, of Johannis T. Witbeek and Eva Waldron. Wit.: Johannis Jeets, Rebecca Waldron.

Margarita, of Isaac Hansen and Maria Brat. Wit.: Isaac Kip, Jannitje Brat.

Apr. 17. Abraham, of Willem Vosburgh and Christina Van Woert. Wit.: Abraham and Geertje Vosburgh.

Mattheys, of Rutger and Maria Van den Bergh. Wit.: Cornelis M. and Catalyntje Van den Bergh.

May 22. Cornelis, of Staats Van Santvoort and Willempje Brat. Wit.: Cornelis Van Santvoort, Jacoba Truex.

Jacob, of Philip Muller and Geertruy Goewey. Wit.: Leendert and Marritje Muller.

Renier, of Johannis Pruyn and Jannitje Van Aalsteyn. Wit.: Renier Van Alsteyn, Cornelia Van den bergh.

May 29. Johannis, of Pieter Hoogteeling and Annatje Beckers. Wit.: Johannis G. and Elisabeth Roseboom.

Gerritje, of Isaac Fort and Sara Viele. Wit.: Louis and Maria Viele.

May 31. Coenraadt, of Tobias C. Ten Eyck and Judithje Van Buren. Wit.: Jacob and Gerritje Ten Eyck.

June 5. Catarina, of Roelof Devoe and Elisabeth Golden. Wit.: Cornelis Van den berg, Catarina Ridder.

Henderick, of Harmen Gansevoort and Magdalena Douw. Wit.: Pieter Gansevoort, Catarina Douw.

1757

Thomas, of Johannis Seger and Catarina Pieterson
Wit.: Thomas Seger, Catarina Pieterson.

June 12. Jan, Henderick, of Albert Brat and Anatje
Carn. Wit.: Jan Brat, Catarina Funda, Henderick and
Margarieta Carn.

Elisabeth, of Harmen I. Fisher and Hester Van Ieveren
Wit.: Renier and Anatje Van Ieveren.

June 19. Maria, of Johannis Flensburgh and Cornelia
Hoogteling. Wit.: Gerrit Van Santen, Antje Van den
Bergh.

Rebecca, of Teunis Brat and Catalyntje Van Ness. Wit.:
Staats Van Santvoord, Willempje Santvoord.

June 26. Christina, of Johannis Speulman and Christina Huyck. Wit.: Nicholaes and Marritje Van Woert.

Willempje, of Douwe Bogaart and Willempje Brat.
Wit.: Johannis Becker, Jr., Maria Bogaart.

July 10. Franciscus, of Samuel Pruyn and Neeltje
Teneyck. Wit.: Franciscus and Alida Pruyn.

July 13. Jacobus, of Dirk Brat Van Schoonhoven and
Folkje Van den Bergh. Wit.: Geurt and Maria Van
Schoonhoven.

July 15. Levinus, of Cornelis Liverse and Cornelia Brat.
Wit.: Abram and Catarina Lansing.

July 17. Margarita, of Henderick Van der Werken and
Maria Viele. Wit.: Albert Vander Werken, Jannitje Viele.

July 24. Lucas Wyngaart, of Simon I. and Catalina
Veder. Wit.: Johs. Wendel, Sara Van Bergen.

Douwe, of Lewis Van Antwerpen and Henderickje Funda.
Wit.: Douwe and Maria Funda.

Anna, of Johannis I. Lansing and Maria Huyck. Wit.:
Jacob I. and Huybertje Lansing.

Rebecca, of Abraham Deforeest and Rebecca Van
Antwerpen. Wit.: Philip and Rachel Deforeest.

July 31. Johan Henrick, of Isaac Miller and Geertruy
Driessin. Wit.: Johan Henric Broun, Ester Brounin.

Benjamin, of Jacob I. Lansing and Marritje Egbertse.
Wit.: Marten and Geertruy Beekman.

Annatje, of Johannis Gansevoort and Maria Douw.
Wit.: Petrus and Annatje Douw.

Jacob, of Jillis Winne and Tietje Van Woert. Wit.:
Jacob and Elisabeth Van Woert.

Aug. 7. Johannis, of Willem Van Santen and Alida.
Wit.: Johannis Van Santen, Sara Yeats.

Wynant, of Evert Van den Bergh and Annatje Lansing.
Wit.: Wynant and Cornelia Van den Berg.

Elisabeth, of Cornelis W. Van den Berg and Maria Viele.
Wit.: Gerrit and Catarina Viele.

Aug. 11. Elisabeth, of Philip I. Schuyler and Catarina
Renslaer. Wit.: Cortlant and Cornelia Schuyler.

Aug. 14. Pieternelle, of Vincent Benneway and Antje Bovie. Wit.: Matthys and Pieternella Bovie.

Abraham, of Johannis Van Arnhem and Alida Van der Heyden. Wit.: Abraham Van Arnhem, Sarah Cloet.

Aug. 17. Ann, of William Gillilon and Anna Doff. Wit.: John Corner, Ann Ray.

Aug. 21. Barbara, of George Hoffman and Maria Carnin. Wit.: Abraham Vosburgh, Johanna Wolfgang.

Geertje, of Johannis Groesbeek and Elisabeth Van Brakelen. Wit.: Wouter Groesbeek, Alida Knickerbacker.

Maria, of Jacobus Fisher and Rachel Van der Heyden. Wit.: Dirk and Bata Van der Heyden.

Aug. 28. Sara, of Isaac Lansing and Annatje Van Woert Wit.: Jacob and Lybethje Van Woert.

Johannis, of Henderick Seger and Elisabeth Haver. Wit.: Johannis and Gerrebrech Seger.

Angenietje, of Johannis Muller and Sara Van Ieveren. Wit.: Leendert and Marritje Muller.

Sep. 4. Barber, of Andries Van Vranken and Maria Groot. Wit.: Johannis and Margrieta Brat.

Sep. 11. Teunis, of Bastiaan T. Fisher and Engeltje Vandenbergh. Wit.: Teunis and Machtel Fisher.

Albartus, of James Adams and Margaret Hegeman. Wit.: Albartus and Catarina Becker.

Maria, of Thomas Dox and Elisabeth Becker. Wit.: Jonathan and Jude Marrel.

Sep. 13. Mary, of John Grenal and Johanna Macmana. Wit.: William Horcoat, Johanna Macmana.

Sep. 18. Nicolaes, of Pieter Degarmo and Sara Gardenier. Wit.: Wessel and Mareytje Van Schaick.

Gerardus, Catarina, of Abram Becker and Elisabeth Van Olinde. Wit.: Gerardus and Geertruy Van Olinda, Abram I. and Catarina Lansing.

Maria, of Abram and Catarina Vinnagel. Wit.: Johannis Vinnagel, Elisabeth Oothout.

Sep. 25. Jochum, of Bernardus Brat and Eva Van Petten. Wit.: Bernardus, Jr., and Catarina Brat.

Oct. 2. Maria, of Henderick Strouk and Elsje Herwich. Wit.: Jacob Herwich, Maria Strouk.

Teunis, of Abram Slingerlant and Rebecca Viele. Wit.: Albert and Geesje Slingerlant.

Oct. 4. Morris, of Morris and Margaret Humphreys. Wit.: John Hops, Isaac Coops, Barbara Michal.

Henry, of Walter Riddle and Margaret Brown. Wit.: James King, Elisabeth Smith.

Oct. 9. Cornelis, of Nicholaes Brouwer and Mareytje Boom. Wit.: John and Anatje Fryer.

1757

Oct. 16. Maria, Teunis, of Gerrit Gerritse Vandenberg and Angenietje Liverse. Wit.: Petrus and Ebbetje Vandenbergh, Cornelis and Maria Tymissen.

Anthony, of Cornelis Sandvoort and Ariaentje Brat. Wit.: Teunis Brat, Catalina Van Ness.

Celia, of Adriaan Brat and Lydia Van Aalsteyn. Wit.: Johannis and Annitje Van Santen.

Abraham, of Gerrit Quackenbos and Catarina Devoe. Wit.: Jacob Van Woert, Geertruy Dox.

Nov. 4. Andries, of Johannis Redlof and Annatje Meccans. Wit.: Isaac Van Oostrande, Elisabeth Meccans.

Nov. 6. Elisabeth, of Frederick Gerritse and Maria Dock. Wit.: Pieter and Elisabeth Lansing.

Gerrit, of Nicholaes Cloet and Ariaantje Ridder. Wit.: Gerrit and Anna Ridder.

Jannitje, of Willem Hellen and Elisabeth Halenbeek. Wit.: Gerrit and Dorothea Halenbeek.

Philip, of Henderick I. Van Wie and Mareytje Loeck. Wit.: Johannis Loeck, Geesje Lagrange.

Sara, of Cornelis G. Van Ness and Alida Van Woert. Wit.: Abram and Alida Van Ness.

Catarina, of Petrus Vosburgh and Annatje Brouwer. Wit.: Pieter Hul, Catarina Redlof.

Nov. 13. Maria, of Johannis Funda and Dirkje Winne. Wit.: Pieter Funda, Catalina Young.

Gerrit, of Gosen Van Schaick and Majeke Vandenberg. Wit.: Evert and Elisabeth Wendel.

Nov. 20. Jan, of Isaac Devoe and Maria Van Olinde. Wit.: Jan Dox, Maria Coerteny.

Abraham, of Roelof Van der Werken and Anatje Vosburgh. Wit.: Abraham and Geertje Vosburgh.

Johannis, of Dirk Heemstraet and Mareytje Barroway. Wit.: Johannis Heemstraat, Elisabeth Van der Volgen.

Samuel, of Harmanus Schuyler and Christina Tenbroeck. Wit.: Dirk and Maria Tenbroeck.

Nov. 27. Machtel, of Pieter Waldron and Neeltje Lansing. Wit.: Teunis and Machtel Fisher.

Sara, of Johannis Van Santen and Margarieta Wilkenson. Wit.: Johannis and Sara Van Santen.

Dec. 11. Jellis, of Francis Cribel and Anna Palsin. Wit.: Jellis Winne, Maria Dauvenbach.

Johannis, of Pieter Hogen and Catarina Vosburg. Wit.: Johannis Hogen, Anneke Vandenbergh.

* Dec. 18. Geertruy, of Christiaan Jacobi and Margarita Hogen. Wit.: Johannis and Catarina Cuyler.

James, of Thomas Willis and Rachel Redlof. Wit.: William and Rebecca Sutherland.

* Dec. 18. 1757, to Feb. 26, 1758, appear after Aug. 1, 1763, in the record.

1757-1758

William, of !John Crannel and Folkje Van Aalsteyn. Wit.: Robert and Ariaantje Crannel.

Dec. 25. Abraham, of Pieter Jeets and Sara Van Aalsteyn. Wit.: Abraham and Antje Jeets.

Daniel, of Pieter Goewey and Maria Joung. Wit.: Johannis and Elisabeth Goewey.

Dec. 26. Angenita, of Charles Sulliman and Dorathea Luther. Wit.: Patrick Clark, Geesje Slingerlant.

1758, Jan. 1. Helena, of Jacob Lansing and Huybertje Jeets. Wit.: Isaac and Anatje Lansing.

Jan. 15. Helena, of Henderick Alderecht and Elisabeth Folent. Wit.: Maas and Helena Bloemendal.

Antje, of Gerrit Seger and Wyntje Olvert. Wit.: Reyckert and 'Mareytje Redlof.

Philippus, of Marten Deforeest and Tannike Winne. Wit.: Isaac and Sanitje Funda.

Rachel, of Jacob and Mareytje Smit. Wit.: Wilhelmus and Anatje Smit.

Jan. 22. Nicholaes, of Henderick Blycker, Jr., and Catalina Cuyler. Wit.: Johannis N. Bleycker, Margarita Cuyler.

Abraham, of Johannis Cloet and Catarina Lansing. Wit.: Abraham and Annatje Lansing.

John, of John Allen and Ellenor Sullivan. Wit.: William Ga . . . . , Elisabeth Ber . . .

Jan. 29. Joris, of Johannis Wendel and Sarah Bergen. Wit.: Simon I. and Catalyntje Veeder.

Jacob Visscher, of Egbert B. Egberts and Maria Lynch. Wit.: Isaac Swits, Geertruy Beekman.

Feb. 20. Catarina, of William Jong and Helena Funda. Wit.: Pieter Funda, Catarina Brat.

Pieter, of Frederick Conckkel. Wit.: Pieter and Jacomina Brat.

Feb. 19. Debora, of Robert Sanders and Elisabeth Schuyler. Wit.: Steven and Engeltje Schuyler.

Feb. 26. Catalina, of John David and Elisabeth Wyngaert. Wit.: Petrus Hilton, Catalina Wyngaart.

Alida, of Johannis Van der Werken and Christina Pruyn. Wit.: Jacob and Anneke Van Arnhem.

Rutger, of Teunis Van Woert and Elisabeth Van Deusen. Wit.: Johannis and Helena Van Deusen.

David, of Dirk Van der Heyden and Margarita Kittel. Wit.: James and Rachel Fisher.

Gerrit Vandenberg, of Benjamin Goedewey and Catarina Vandenberg. Wit.: Gerrit and Alida Vandenberg.

Anthony, of Arent Slingerlant and Jacomeyntje Van de Volgen. Wit.: Albert Van der See, Claertje Cloet.

Johannis, of Baltus Bacchus and Barber Koen. Wit.: Johannis and Catarina Bacchus.

1758

Elsje, of Kiljaan Van Renslaer and Ariaantje Schuyler. Wit.: Hermanus and Christina Schuyler.

Mar. 5. Timothy, of Henderick I. Wendel and Anna Maginnes. Wit.: Henderick and Margarita Van Dyck.

Elisabeth, of George Young and Catarina Litcher. Wit.: Pieter and Catarina Hog.

Jacob, of Adam Koen and Maria Vanderhoef. Wit.: Jacob and Francyntje Coeper.

Maria, of Johannes Loeck and Geesje Lagrange. Wit.: Henderick and Maria Van Wie.

Dorothee, of Andries Van Schaak and Alida Hogen. Wit.: Steven and Engeltje Van Schaak.

Mar. 12. Jenney, of Henrich Hoenderman and Catarina Margarita. Wit.: Isaac Slingerlant, Jenne Hollant.

Geesje, of Cornelis Muller and Maria Vanhoesen. Wit.: Egbert and Elsje Vanhoesen.

Mar. 19. Johannis, of Henderick Litser and Annatje Huyck. Wit.: Johannis Hogen, Catharina Lansing.

Maria, of Abraham Sixby and Eva Bacces. Wit.: Teunis Accessen, Catarina Waters.

Mar. 26. Johannis, of Henderick Keyser and Catarina Izellerin. Wit.: Johannis Van Orden, Elisabeth Smithin.

Jonathan, of Petrus Hilton and Annatje Broecks. Wit.: Philip Redlof, Femmetje Kidney.

Apr. 2. Maria, of Johannis Seger and Maria Brat. Wit.: Adam Brat, Engeltje Seger.

John, of Philip Lansing and Elsje Hun. Wit.: Johannis, Jr., and Geertruy Lansing.

Apr. 9. Mareytje, of Henderick and Elisabeth Leycher. Wit.: Dirk Schelpher, Marytje Duyvebach.

Catalyntje, of Anthony Van der See, and Annatje Van Ess. Wit.: Philip and Rachel Deforeest.

Geertruy, of Pieter Degarmo and Geertruy Cregier. Wit.: Bastiaan and Jannitje Cregier.

Apr. 16. Geysbert, of Adam Van Alen and Maria Roseboom. Wit.: Ahasuerus and Catarina Roseboom.

Margarita, of Johannis H. Teneyck and Sara Tenbroeck. Wit.: Abram and Margarita Tenbroeck.

Apr. 23. Arent, of Reykert Redlof and Mareytje Oliver. Wit.: Arent Devoe, Anatje Fryer.

Baertje, of David Brat and Treyntje Lang. Wit.: Christiaan Lang, Baertje Hoogteeling.

Leyntje, of Geysbert Funda and Elsje Douw. Wit.: Pieter Winne, Margarita Douw.

Apr. 30. Margarita, of Johannis Van de Werken and Maria Defoe. Wit.: Johannis Devoe, Maria Keller.

Johannis, of Johannis Devoe and Maria Keller. Wit.: Roelof and Annatje Van der Werken.

1758

May 7. Catarina, of Jacob Egmont and Maria Lewis. Wit.: Pieter and Catarina Crannel.

Storm, of Matthys Hoogteeling and Ariaantje Van der See. Wit.: Harmen Vander See, Helena Vrooman.

Catarina, of Jonas Oothout and Elisabeth Vinnagel. Wit.: Henderick and Henderickje Bogaart. (See below after Oct. 14, 1759.)

*May 14. Willem, of Frederick Cloet and Machtel Quackenbos. Wit.: Nicholaes Cloet, Ariaantje Ridder.

Pieter, of Stephanus Schuyler and Engeltje Van Venchten. Wit.: Pieter and Catarina Schuyler.

May 28. Elisabeth, of Gerrit and Eegje Slingerlant. Wit.: Wouter and Hester Slingerlant.

Mareytje, of Isaac Valk and Mareytje Warner. Wit.: Pieter and Catarientje Brat.

Gerrit, of Wessel Van Schaick and Maria Gerritse. Wit.: Adam Jeets, Catalina Witbeek.

Jurrie, of Jurie Scharp, Jr. Wit.: Coenraat and Magdalena Scharp.

June 11. Johannis, of Johannis Funda and Elisabeth Ouderkerk. Wit.: Johannis and Sophia Ouderkerk.

Alida, of Jacob Van Arnhem and Anneke Van Vranken. Wit.: Johannis and Alida Van Arnhem.

June 19. John, of Chrismas Howel and Margaret. Wit.: Archibald Mattelvray, Patarick Macnel, Catharina Kowley, Ellenor Bown.

June 24. Christian, of Walter and Ann Anderson. Wit.: —— Ferguson, Mary Ferguson.

June 25. Jesse, of Isaac Deforeest and Alida Funda. Wit.: Philip and Cornelia Deforeest.

Mary, of Isaac Copes and Mary Maccloud.

July 16. Henderick, of Philip Hansen and Geertruy Van Ness. Wit.: Cornelis and Antje Vandenbergh.

Casparus, of John Huson and Anna Cock. Wit.: Casparus and Frena Cock.

Jacob, of Jillis Winne and Fieytje Van Woert. Wit.: Jacob and Elisabeth Van Woert.

July 21. Catalina, of Willem Winne and Mareytje Dewandelaar. Wit.: Jan and Catalina Winne.

July 30. Cornelia, of Jacob Quackenbos and Catarina Huyck. Wit.: John and Sara Cloet.

Johannis, of Johannis Oliver and Maritje Siksbie. Wit.: Jacobus Oliver, Wyntje Seger.

Aug. 6. Johannis, of Johannis Lansing and Ariaantje Wendel. Wit.: Gerardus and Maria Lansing.

John, of Benjamin Hopkins and Mary Rickeby. Wit.: Anthony Halenbeek, Elisabeth Brat.

* May 14 to Aug. 20 appears after Oct. 14, 1759, in the records.

1758
Aug. 10. Margaret, of James Wilson and Martha Welsh.
Wit.: Archibald ——, Jennet Miller.
Aug. 13. David, of Jacob Deforeest and Treyntje Brat.
Wit.: Philip Deforeest, Maria Bloemendal.
Matthys, of Cornelis Mat. and Cornelia Vandenberg.
Wit.: Reinier and Cornelia Van Aalsteyn.
Aug. 20. Andries, of Isaac Oostrande and Elisabeth
Meccans. Wit.: Johannis and Celia Redlof.
Jacob, of Henderick Wendel, Jr., and Maria Lansingh.
Wit.: Harmanus I. and Helena Wendel.
Geysbert, of Folkert Vandenbergh and Neeltje Waldron.
Wit.: Cornelis and Catalyntje Vandenberg.
*Aug. 27. Frederick, of Jacob Ouderkerk and Neeltje
Cloet. Wit.: John Parie, Francyntje Cloet.
Angnietje, of Frans Winne and Marritje Hoogteeling.
Wit.: Johannis and Lena Van Wie.
John, of Patrick Clark and Cornelia Waldron. Wit.:
William and Maria Hogen.
Johannis, of Henderick Funda and Catarina Groesbeek.
Wit.: Johannis and Elisabeth Groesbeek.
Margarita, of Jacobus Abeel and Ebbitje Van Buren.
Wit.: David and Catalina Abeel.
Aug. 29. Lewis, of Lewis and Ann Macferson. Wit.:
Collom and Ann Macferson.
Sep. 3. Geertruy, of Pieter Lansing and Elisabeth
Wendel. Wit.: Pieter Schuyler, Maria Lansing.
Sep. 10. Eva, of Theodorus Frielinghuysen and Elisa-
beth Sims. Wit.: Jacob Roseboom, Susanna Catarina
Oglevie.
Geertruy, of Simon and Anatje Veeder. Wit.: Daniel
and Rebecca Van Antwerpen.
Sep. 12. Johannis Casparus, of Johannes and Elisabeth
Walter. Wit.: Henrick and Sophia Reriker, Casparus
Hart.
Sep. 16. Napier, of Gabriel Christie and Sarah Steven-
son.
Sep. 17. Johannis, of Folkert A. Douw and Annatje
Wendel. Wit.: Evert I. and Annatje Wendel.
Anna, of Geysbert Marselis and Catalina Wendel. Wit.:
Johannis M. and Eva Roseboom.
Sep. 21. Joshua, of Joshua and Nathie North. Wit.:
Patrick McNab, Duglas Fergwesson, Margaret Suther-
land, Mary Anderson.
Sep. 24. Sophia, of Albert Brat and Magdalena Lang.
Wit.: Jan Brat, Mareytje Vander Wilgen.
Margarita, of Philip I. Schuyler and Catarina Van Ren-
slaar. Wit.: Jeremiah Van Renslaer, Geertruy Renslaer.

* Aug. 27 to and including five entries of Oct. 15 appears after
Aug. 1, 1763, in the records.

1758

Geertruy, of Wouter Groesbeek and Jannitje Bogaart.
Wit.: Jacob Bogaert, Mareytje Groesbeek.
Andries, of Henderick Schans and Catarina Ham. Wit.:
Jeremias Schans, Marietje Ham.
Mareytje, of Cornelis I. Van den Berg and Catarina
Ridder. Wit.: Johannis and Susanna Winne.
Daniel, of Daniel B. and Willipe Bratt. Wit.: Daniel
and Jannetie Bratt.
Oct. 1. Abraham, of Henderick Wendel and Catalyntje
Van Schaick. Wit.: Henderick Van Ness, Jannetje
Waldron.
Neeltje, of Philip Deforeest and Rachel Van Ness. Wit.:
Isaac and Neeltje Deforeest.
Oct. 15. Catalina, of Johannis R. Bleeker and Elisabeth
Staats. Wit.: Gerrit Staats, Margarita Collins.
Machteld, of Johannis Heemstraat, Jr., and Elisabeth
Bovie. Wit.: Matthys and Geertruy Bovie.
Jannitje, of Johannis I. Goewey and Maria Van Ieveren.
Wit.: Johannis and Geertruy Goewey.
Bregje, of Thomas Zeger and Judith Hooglang. Wit.:
Johannes and Brejge Zeger.
Thomas, of Pieter Jones and Abigail Winne. Wit.:
Willem and Margarita Hilton.
Margarita, of Pieter Crannel and Catarina Egmont. Wit.:
Robert and Margarita Crannel. (See note after Oct. 14,
1759, below.)
Oct. 22. Willem, of Henderick Miller and Rachel
Norton. Wit.: Willem Norton, Annatje Teller.
Nov. 4. Sarah, of Johannis Van Santen, Jr., and Mar-
garita Wilkinson. Wit.: Johannis Van Santen, Sarah
Jates.
Nov. 5. Anna, of Henderick Van Dyck and Margarita
Douw. Wit.: Folkert P. and Anna Douw.
Susanna, Jacob, of Dirk Vanderheyden and Elisabeth
Wendel. Wit.: Levinus and Susanna Winne, Johannis
Van Arnhem, Rachel Fisher.
Nov. 12. Elisabeth, of Barent Hog and Geertje Huyck.
Wit.: Jacob Groesbeek, Annatje Van Vechten.
Machteld, of Albert Van der Werken and Mareytje
Quackenbosch. Wit.: Joh. I. and Maria Lansing.
Nov. 19. Willempje, of Cornelis Van Santvoort and
Ariaantje Brat. Wit.: Teunis Brat, Catarina Van
Ness.
Maria, of Frans Roeso and Maria Palsin. Wit.: Johan-
nis Van Wie, Margarita Pelsin.
Dec. 3. Salomon, of Pieter Goewey and Mareytje Jong.
Wit.: Benjamin and Catarina Goewey.
Wilhelmus, of Cornelis Vandeusen and Lea Oostrande.
Wit.: Pieter Brat, Jacomina Bloemendal.

1758-1759

Dec. 10. Mary, of Daniel Bruce and Jean Wilson. Wit.: William Bruce, Geertruyd Vosburgh.

Angenietje, of Leendert Muller and Marritje Vanness. Wit.: Philip and Geertruy Muller.

Dec. 17. Samuel, of Samuel Couenoven and Catalyntje Wyngaart. Wit.: Sacharias and Annatje Sickels.

Dec. 24. Maria, of Adriaan Brat and Maria Meccans. Wit.: Pieter and Catalyntje Redlof.

Dec. 31. Elisabeth, of Gerrit Van Vranken and Susannah Egbertse. Wit.: Albert Slingerlant, Maria Wyngaart.

Dirk, of Cornelis Groot and Maria Van Vranken. Wit.: Harman Van Vranken, Alida Cloet.

Eytje, of Tobias C. Teneyck and Judith Van Buren. Wit.: Johannis and Eytje Vanburen.

1759, Jan. 7. Dirk, of Anthony Slingerlant and Claertje Cloet. Wit.: Dirk and Geertruy Cloet.

Dirk, of Jacob Vanderheyden and Maria Halenbeek. Wit.: Naning and Rachel Fisher.

Alida, of Johannis Van Arnhem and Alida Vanderheyden. Wit.: Abraham and Anatje Van Arnhem.

Jan. 14. Maria, of Gerrit Vandenbergh and Alida Van Ness. Wit.: Wynant and Maritje Vandenberg.

Jacob, of Meyndert Veder and Elisabeth Douw. Wit.: Geysbert Fonda, Catalyntje Veder.

James, of John Griffith and Jennet. Wit.: John Sullivan, Samuel and Mary Stit.

Jan. 21. Robert, of William Soul and Margaret Wyngaart. Wit.: John and Elisabeth Davis.

Teunis, of Abraham and Elisabeth Oostrander. Wit.: Johannis and Mareytje Meynerse.

Jacob, of Maas Bloemendal and Helena Schermerhoorn. Wit.: Albertus Bloemendal, Hillitje Scot.

Elisabeth, of Dirk Van Veghten and Alida Knickerbacker. Wit.: Wouter and Elisabeth Knickerbacker.

Jan. 28. Ariaantje, of Nicholaes and Jannitje Van Vranken. Wit.: Gerrit Van Vranken, Annatje Scherp.

Petrus, of Johannis Flensburgh and Cornelia Hoogteeling. Wit.: Frans Winne, Mareytje Hoogteeling.

Maria, of Frederick Knoet and Mareytje Ridder. Wit.: Martinus and Sarah Lydius.

Feb. 11. Eytje, of John Donbar and Helena Lansing. Wit.: Johannis I. and Catarina Lansingh.

Christopher, of William Norton and Mary Baylie. Wit.: John Norton, Rachel Milton.

Rebecca, of Johannis Spoor and Magdalena Bogaart. Wit.: Pieter and Willimpje Bogaart.

Annatje, of Albert Van de Werken and Annatje Vandenbergh. Wit.: Wynant and Catarientje Vandenbergh.

1759

Annitje, of Anthony Flensburgh and Annatje Redlof.
Wit.: Lambert and Annitje Redlof.

Feb. 25. Martin, of Martin Buckley and Rachel Redlof.
Wit.: Roger Buckley, Henderickje Oliver.

Petrus, of Teunis Slingerlant and Angenietje Witbeek.
Wit.: Thomas and Cornelia Williams.

Pieter, of Pieter Bogaart and Barber Van Vranken.
Wit.: Jacob Bogaart, Jannitje Groesbeek.

Mar. 4. Elisabeth, of Jacobus Fisher and Rachel
Vanderheyden. Wit.: Johans and Maria Vanderheyden.

Mar. 11. Petrus, of Robert Crannel and Ariaantje
Bovie. Wit.: Pieter and Catarina Crannel.

Mar. 18. Isaac, of Abram I. Lansingh and Elisabeth
Coeper. Wit.: Isaac and Catarina Lansing.

Obediah, of Jacob Coeper and Josyna Orchard. Wit.:
Jacobus Parker Benthuysen, Sara Van Benthuysen.

Catarina, of Pieter Gansevoort and Gerritje Ten Eyck.
Wit.: Leendert and Catarina Gansevoort.

Elisabeth, of Frederick Gerritse and Maria Tuck. Wit.:
Pieter and Elisabeth Lansing.

Mar. 25. Nicholaes, of Pieter Williams and Elisabeth
Fonda. Wit.: Gisbert Fonda, Rebecca Knickerbacker.

Neeltje, of Gerrit Staats and Debora Beekman. Wit.:
Johannis and Annatje Roerback.

Mar. 31. Maria, of Dirck Wemp and Rebecca Van
Arnhem. Wit.: Nicholaes Becker, Cornelia Van Arnhem.

Apr. 1. Mareytje, of Abraham Vandenbergh and Rachel
Liverse. Wit.: Wynant W. Vandenberg, Mareytje Vandenbergh.

Anna, of Johannis Cloet and Sara Van Arnhem. Wit.:
Jan Ouderkerk, Bata Cloet.

Apr. 5. Gerrit, of Abram Peek and Catarina Van Santen.
Wit.: Reyker and Rachel Van Santen.

Apr. 8. Catarina, of Gerardus Groesbeek and Maria
Tenbroeck. Wit.: Robert and Elisabeth Sanders.

Wilhelmus, of Pieter Rykman and Lydia Vandenbergh.
Wit.: Albert and Annatje Rykman.

Apr. 22. Catarina, of Pieter Backes and Eva Maria
Muller. Wit.: Johannis and Catarina Hen Winkel.

May 6. Louis, of Isaac Fort and Sara Viele. Wit.:
Louis and Maria Viele.

Anna, of Johan Pieter Claas and Clara Margarita Curtin.
Wit.: Willem Heyns, Anna Catarina Clasin.

Jacob, of Willem Vandenbergh and Saintje Van Ieveren.
Wit.: Meyndert and Saintje Van Ieveren.

Johannis, of Johannis Cloet and Jannitje Ouderkerk.
Wit.: Meyndert Ouderkerk, Geertruy Quackenbos.

May 20. Coenraat, of David Sarnberger and Christina
Lauwer. Wit.: Tobias and Leah Witbeek.

1759
May 24. Rachel, of Gerrit Van Santen, Jr., and Hester Winne. Wit.: Benjamin and Rachel Winne.

May 27. Willem, of Barent and Catalyntje Van Buren. Wit.: Cornelis and Majeke Vanburen.

Jacobus, of Melchert Vanderpoel and Margarita Vinnagel. Wit.: Jacobus and Catarientje Vinnagel.

June 3. Catarina, of Matthias Boom and Joseyntje Seger. Wit.: Willem and Helena Bromley.

Rebecca, of Teunis Brat and Catalyntje Van Ness. Wit.: Staats and Willimpje Van Santfoort.

June 17. Neeltje, of Benjamin and Annatje Vandenbergh. Wit.: Barent and Geertruy Vandenbergh.

Joachim, of Johannis Degarmo and Annatje Kittel. Wit.: Dirk Vanderheyden, Margarita Kittel.

Margarita, of Dirk M. Vanderheyden and Sarah Wendel. Wit.: Mathys and Margarita Vanderheyden.

Matthys, of Rutgert and Maria Vandenbergh. Wit.: Gerrit W. and Alida Vandenbergh.

June 19. Elisabeth, of Mark and Francis Freeman. Wit.: William Baxter, Elenor Cornwal, Jane Drennen.

June 24. Folkert, of Weynant F. and Marritje Vandenberg. Wit.: Adriaan and Folkje Quackenbos.

Jacobus, of Johannis Vanderwerken and Dirkje Van Aalsteyn. Wit.: Johannis and Maria Brat.

Johannis, of Jacob Viele and Eva Fort. Wit.: Johannis and Francyntje Fort.

Johannis, of Emanuel Strobel and Helena Burn. Wit.: Pieter and Geertruy Degarmo.

Ryckert, of Willem Hilton and Elisabeth Broecks. Wit.: Petrus and Anne Hilton.

Johan Philip, of Jurrian Henrik Stater and Maria Rosina Renitsen. Wit.: Philip Kerner, Johan P. Kefer, Maria Catarina Kemerin.

Catarina, of Abraham and Catarina Freehold. Wit.: Jacob and Margarita Anold, John and Catarina Stricker.

July 1. Elisabeth, of Johannis S. Quackenbos and Jannitje Viele. Wit.: Seybrant Quackenbos, Neeltje Deforeest.

Alida, of Jacob Loeck and Rachel Slingerlant. Wit.: Pieter and Maria Goewey.

July 1. Sarah, of Gerrit I. Lansing and Jannitje Waters. Wit.: Jacob I. Lansing, Catarina Waters.

Susanna Catarina of Christian Kerhart and Anna Barbara Walfin. Wit.: Carel Moesel, Susanna Catarina.

Johanna Chalotta of Johan Philip Oost and Maria Elisabeta. Wit.: Charles Connor, Michael Meyer, Johanna Conner, Chalotta Bockin.

July 8. Elisabeth, of William Sutherland and Elisabeth. Wit.: Peter Mongomery, Martha Morrison, Ellenor Bovie.

1759

July 15. Anna Rosina, of Harmanus Van Aalsteyn and Catarina Pesinger. Wit.: Sophereyn Pesinger, Jannitje Brat.

Pieter Coejeman, of Andries Ten Eyck and Anna Marg. Coejeman. Wit.: Andries and Majeke Witbeek.

Elsje, of Johannis I. Lansingh and Catarina Schuyler. Wit.: Kiljaan and Aariaantje Renselaer.

Pieter of Johannis P. Funda and Dirkje Winne. Wit.: Daniel Winne, Mareytje Vandeusen.

Isabella, of Jephta and Isabella. Wit.: Jephta and Sara.

July 22. Margaret, of James Burnside and Debora Janse. Wit.: Gloud and Margaret Burnside.

Eytje, of Maas Van Buren and Catalyntje Van Valkenburgh. Wit.: Johannis and Eytje Vanburen.

July 29. Catarina, of Gerrit Quackenbos and Catarina Devoe. Wit.: Isaac Devoe, Rachel Ridder.

Maria, of William Berry and Elisabeth Roseboom. Wit.: John G. and Elsje Roseboom.

Gerrit, of William Hogen, Jr., and Susanna Lansingh. Wit.: Dirk Becker, Neeltje Waldron.

Aug. 5. Teunis, of Lewis Viele and Anatje Quackenbos. Wit.: John and Catarina Viele.

Maria, of Gerrit Seger and Wyntje Oliver. Wit.: Adam and Christina Brat.

Aug. 12. Abraham, of Barent C. Vanburen and Ariaantje Vanderpoel. Wit.: Tobias and Leah Witbeek.

Aug. 19. Neeltje, of Pieter Degarmo and Sara Gardenier. Wit.: Johannis Marselis, Neeltje Gardenier.

Aug. 22. Mary Anne, of William Chace and Mary Stone. Wit.: William Pemberton, William Maccue, Anne Gillilon, Elisabeth Stedman.

Aug. 26. John, of John Walley and Anne Smith. Wit.: William Hellen, Christina Erhart.

Douwe, of Isaac Funda and Susanna Deforeest. Wit.: Abraham and Majeke Funda.

Sep. 4. Catarina, of Willem Urlob and Maria Aug. Hartmanin. Wit.: Willem Heyns, Catarina Scheverin.

Sep. 9. Margaret, of Moses Cambel and Elisabeth Comes. Wit.: George and Anne Brown, Catarina Macuan.

Oct. 7. Johannes, of Samuel and Catryn Ryckensonn. Wit.: John Smit, Sarah Donnels.

Abraham, of Abraham Fonda and Maria Schoonhoven. Wit.: Wouter Knikkerbacker, Anna Van Victen.

Thomas, of Pieter Jones and Abigael Winne. Wit.: Willem and Margarit Hilton.

Oct. 14. (See above Oct. 7) Johannes, of Samuel and Catryn Ryckenson. Wit.: John Smit, Sarah Donnel.

1758–1759–1760

Abraham, of Abraham Fonda and Maria Schoonhoven. Wit.: Wouter Knikkerbacker, Anna Van Victen. (The following entries, including the first six entries in 1760, appear after Aug. 1, 1763, in the records.)

1758 or 1759, Oct. 21. Jonathan, of Jonathan and Margarita Witbeek. Wit.: Casparus and Maria Witbeek.

Catarina, of Frans and Anna Crevel. Wit.: Rachel Douw.

Oct. 15. Catarina, of Harme Gansevoort and Magdalena Douw. Wit.: Henderik and Margarita Van Dyck.

John, of John Freyer and Elizabeth Van Woert. Wit.: Jacobus and Jenneke Clement.

Abraham, of Johannes Fonda and Elizabeth Ouderkerk. Wit.: Jacob and Maajeke Fonda.

Kilyaan, of Frans Winne and Anneke Viele. Wit.: Kilyaan and Dirkje Winne.

Oct. Catarina, of Abraham Becker and Elizabeth Van Olinda. Wit.: Abraham and Catarina Lansing.

Nov. Johannes, of Daniel Winne and Jannetje De Foreest. Wit.: David and Maria Deforeest.

Jacomyna, of Bastiaan Teymisse and Maayeke Ouderkerk. Wit.: Lowis and Maria Viele.

Nov. 25. Dirk, of Pieter Hoogteling and Anna Becker. Wit.: Dirk Becker, Eva Hogen.

Sarah, of Jacob G. Van Schaik and Geertje Ridder. Wit.: Pieter and Catharina Viele.

Henderik, of George Yong and Catharina Litcher. Wit.: Pieter and Mary Hoewey.

Johannes, of Henderik Van Wie, Jr., and Maria Loek. Wit.: Daniel Winne, Jr., Lena Van Wie.

1759. Nov. 25. Johannes, of Cornelius G. Van Nes and Alida Van Woert. Wit.: Lowis and Rebecca Van Woert.

Gysbert, of Volkert Vandenberg and Neeltje Waldron. Wit.: Cornelius V. d. Berg, Maria Van Yveren.

Elsje, of Cornelius Van Buren and Maayeke Hun. Wit.: Harme and Elsje Hun.

Jacobus, of Evert Zeger and Sarah Orged. Wit.: Jacob and Josina Coeper.

1760. Jan. Johannes, of Ph. Lansing and Elsje Hun. Wit.: Johs. Hun, Ariaantje Lansing.

Annatje, of Jochim Staats and Elisabeth Schuyler. Wit.: John Roorebag, Cristina Schuyler.

Douwe, of Pieter and Maarya Liverse. Wit.: Isack D. and Susanna Fonda.

Elisabet, of Benjamin Goewy and Catrina Van D. berg. Wit.: Johs. and Elisabet Goewy.

Geertruy, of Stephanus Schuyler and Engeltje V. Vegte. Wit.: Luycas and Marya V. Vegte.

1760

Rutger, of Willem Vosburg and Cristina Van Wart. Wit.: Cathrina Vosburg, Piter Williams.

Jan. 4. Sara, of Rynier Van Ivere and Debora Filden. Wit.: Piter Willins, Hariaantje Van Ivere.

Teunus, of Derk Swart and Janetje Van der See. Wit.: Teunus and Rachel Swart.

Isack, of Jolus Crannell and Folkje Van Aalstyn. Wit.: Wynant V. Aelstyn, Folkje Vandenberg.

Jan. 6. Johannes, of Nicolaas Brouwer and Marya Boom. Wit.: Abraham Boom, Magdalena Bromly.

William, of Roelof De Voe and Elisabeth Golden. Wit.: Willem Smit, Janetje Bratt.

Sara, of Abraham Fort and Eva Bennewe. Wit.: Petrus Van Woert, Rabekka Fort.

bo. Nov. 1758. Myndert, of Jan P. Bratt and Susanna Seger. Wit.: Symon Jo. Veder, Annaje Staats.

1760, Jan. 13. bo. Jan. 12. Johannes, of Lawis V: A: werp and Hendrikje Vanbeure. Wit.: Symon and Marya Defreest.

bo. and ba. Jan. 13. Myndert, of Johannis Marcelus and Neeltje Gardinier. Wit.: Gerret and Alida Marcelus.

Jan. 29. Annaatje, of Jan Gerse Yates and Cataleyntje Hoewey. Wit.: Adam Yates, Maria Van Scaik.

Feb. 3, bo. Feb. 1. Derk, of Abra. Van der Kar and Margrita De Voet. Wit.: Derk and Magdalena V. Der Kar.

bo. Jan. 22. Marya, of Samuel Pruyn and Neeltje Ten Eyk. Wit.: Jacob Ten Eyk, Alida Fischer.

Mar. 9, bo. Feb. 28. Margrita, of Willm. Van Sante and Alida Smith. Wit.: Willm. Hilton, Margrita Jones.

bo. Feb. 22. Daniel, of Derk Joc. Van D. hyde and Margrita Kittle. Wit.: Jan. and Catrina Dret.

bo. Feb. 8. Catrina, Margarita, twins of Johanes Post and Frena Myer. Wit.: Johs. Glen, Anna Harsen, Gerardus Lansing, Elisabet Groesbeek.

bo. Feb. 18. Geertruy, of Petrus Vosburg and Anaatje Brouwer. Wit.: Isack Vosburg, Catrina Daart.

bo. Feb. 23. Cornelia, of Johanes Muller and Sara Van Ivere. Wit.: Cornelus and Cornelia Van Jevere.

bo. Feb. 12. Andris, of Johanes Ja. Lansing and Marya Huyk. Wit.: Andris and Gerritje Huyk.

bo. Feb. 29. Jacob of Jelles Winne and Fitje Van Woert. Wit.: Isack Ja. Lansing, Anna Van Woert.

bo. Feb. 8. Marya, of Derk Bekker and Eva Hogen. Wit.: Johs. and Marya Hogen.

bo. Feb. 29. Hendrikie, of Hendr. Is. Bogert and Barber Marcelus. Wit.: Isack Bogert, Hendrikje Oothout.

bo. Feb. 14. Jesse, of Isack Is. Fonda, and Cornelia Freest. Wit.: Ph. and Neeltje Deforeest.

1760
bo. Mar. 4. Petrus, of Abra. Slingerlant and Rabecka Viele. Wit.: Teunes and Catrina Viele.

Elsje, of Harmanus Schuyler and Cristina Tenbroeck. Wit.: Johs. Ja. Lansing, Catrina Schuyler.

bo. Feb. 5. Johs., of Luykas Witbeek and Geertruy Lansing. Wit.: Johs. Lansing, Ariaantje Wendel.

bo. Feb. 5. Folkert, of Cornelus Muller and Marya Vanhoese. Wit.: Harmen and Bregje Van Hoese.

Susanna, of Jan Fonda and Egje Van der Se. Wit.: Cornelus and Cornelia Vandeberg.

bo. and ba. Mar. 10. Teunes, of Staats V. Santfort and Willimpje Brat. Wit.: Teunes Brat, Catlyna Van Es.

Apr. 11, bo. Mar. 19. Magdalena, of Cristiaan Jacobi and Margrita Hogen. Wit.: Will. Soul, Margrita Wyngaart.

bo. Mar. 25. Isaac, of Piter Hog and Catrina Vosburg. Wit.: Isack Vosburg, Catrina Daart.

bo. Mar. 21. Elisabeth, of Teunes Van Woert and Elisabeth Vandeusen. Wit.: Jacob Ja. Van Woert, Elisabeth Fort.

bo. Apr. 4. Fredrik, of Jacob Ouderkerk and Neeltje Cloet. Wit.: Piter Cloet, Areaantje Van Vranken.

Apr. 13, bo. Feb. 29. Willem, of Marte Freest and Tanneke Winne. Wit.: Willem P. and Rachel Winne.

bo. Feb. 19. Johannes, of Hendrik Fonda and Catrina Groesbeek. Wit.: Johanes Groesbeek, Anna Van Vegte.

Apr. 15. Wilhelmus, of Jacob and Marya Smith. Wit.: Johannes and Elisabeth Smith.

Apr. 29. Antony, of Cornelis Liverse and Cornelia Bratt. Wit.: Antony and Rabecka Bratt.

May 5, bo. June 3 [sic]. Gysbert, of Derk Brat V. Schohove and Folkie Vandeberg. Wit.: Folkert G. Van Denberg, Neeltje Waldrom.

bo. June 3[sic]. Rynier, of Harman J. Fischer and Hester Van Jevere. Wit.: Rynier Van Jevere, Dabora Fielden.

bo. May 4. Ariaantje, of Willm. Verplank and Liedia Liverse. Wit.: Isack and Ariaantje Verplank.

May 5, bo. May 29 [sic]. Petrus Dow of Hendr. Van Dyk and Margrita Dow. Wit.: Folkert P. Dow, Anna De Peyster.

May 18, bo. May 15. Catrian, of Hendrik Bleeker, Jr., and Catlyna Cuyler. Wit.: Jacob Van Schajek, Jr., Catrina Cuyler.

bo. May 8. Janetje, of Johs. J. Goewey, Jr., and Marya Van Yvere. Wit.: Johannes and Geertruy Goewy.

bo. Apr. 15. Samuel, of Pieter Garmo and Geertruy Bragier. Wit.: Martynus and Janetje Bragier.

bo. May 16. Hendrik, of Andris Gardinier and Sara Hanse. Wit.: Hendrik Gardinier, Marya Goewy.

70

bo. May 9. Gysbert of Johanes Groesbeek and Elizabeth Van Brakele. Wit.: Abra. Defreest, Rabecka Van Antwerp.

May 24, bo. Apr. 25. Marya of Johs. Jo. Van D. Werke and Marya De Voe. Wit.: Piter Hoog, Catrina Vosburg.

June 19, bo. June 9. Barent of John R. Bleeker and Elisabeth Staats. Wit.: Jochom Staats, Elisabet Schuyler.

Willim of Jacobus P. Van Benthuyse and Sara Coeper. Wit.: Jacob and Josina Coeper.

bo. June 14. Folkert of Symon J. and Catlyna Veder. Wit.: John Glen, Jr., Catrina Veder.

bo. May 19. Catrina of Jacob D. Garmo and Fytje Bekker. Wit.: Jelles De Garmo and Rachel Evertsen.

bo. May 19. Isack of David Quakenbos and Catrina Huyk. Wit.: Isack Quackenbos, Rabecka Groot.

Anaatje of Nicolas Cloet and Ariaantje Ridder. Wit.: Walran and Anna Cloet.

bo. Apr. 19. Derk of Johs. G. Cloet and Catrina Lansing. Wit.: Gerardus and Elisabet Cloet.

June 25, bo. June 14. Wynant of Cornelus W. Van D. berg and Marya Viele. Wit.: Abra. Van Denberg, Rachel Liverse.

Marya of Gerrit Van Deberg and Angenietje Liverse. Wit.: Jacobus Abeel, Ebbetje Van Beure.

bo. May 28. Rykert of Jacob Van Aarnem and Annaatje Van Vranke. Wit.: Rykert and Christina Van Vranke.

Johannes of Cornelus Sprong and Margrita Shawns. Wit.: Jeremia Shawns, Elisabeth Bratt.

July 17, bo. July 9. Elizabeth of Robert Sanders and Elizabeth Schuyler. Wit.: Abraham Ten Broeck, Elizabeth Van Renslaar.

bo. July 16. Gerret of Gerrit G. Lansing and Wyntje Van D. berg. Wit.: John G. Lansing, Sara Burger.

bo. July 7. Jacob of Antony E. Bratt and Marya Van Aalstyn. Wit.: Stephanes Van Schajik, Jannetje Bratt.

Aug. 3. Margrita of Adam Roek and Marya Van der Hoef. Wit.: Johannes Roek, Hillitje Seger.

Sep. 9. bo. Sep. 4. Leena or Helena of Abraham Ja. Lansing and Elisabeth Coeper. Wit.: Johannes J. Lansing, Catrina Schuyler.

bo. Aug. 18. Rachel of Johannes P. Fonda and Derkje Winne. Wit.: Daniel Winne, Marya Van Deuse.

bo. Aug. 31. Pitertje of Rynier Van Aelstyn and Cornelia Van Denberg. Wit.: Piter Yates, Saara Van Aalstyn.

Magtel of Bastiaen Teus. Fischer and Engeltje Vandenberg. Wit.: Gerrit T. and Derkje Fisher.

Matys of Derk M. Van Derhyde and Sara Wendel.
Wit.: Matys Van Derhyde, Margrita Bratt.

bo. Sep. 2. Sara Hendrika of Hendrik Is. Wendel and
Anaatie Makgin. Wit.: Capt. Henry Shombr—, Elisabeth Macgin.

*Oct. 19. Maria of Quiliaan (Kiliaan) Van Renzelaar
(Rensselaar) and Arriaantje Schuyler (Schuiler). Wit.:
Catharina Tenbroek (Ten Broek), Petrus Douwe (Douw).

Johannatje (Jannetje) of Johannes and Christina Van
der Werke. Wit.: Gerardus Van der Linde (Gerard V.
Olinde), Elisabeth Bekker.

Maria of Folckert (Folkert) P. Douwe (Douw) and Anna
De Peister. Wit.: Elisabeth Douwe (Douw), Johannes
(Johannis) Gansevoort (Ganzevoord).

Maria of Hendrik Van Nes and Magdalena Vroman.
Wit.: Gysbert and Elsje Fonda.

Oct. 26. Helena of Hermannus (Hermanus I.) Jacob
Wendel and Barbara Brat. Wit.: Hendrik and Helena
Wendel.

Nov. 2. Rachel of Izak Van Oostrander and Elisabeth
Makans (Mahans). Wit.: William Venten (Venton),
Annatje Egmond.

Rebecca of Abraham Couper (Koeper) and Catharina
(V.) Oostrander. Wit.: Tobias and Lea Witbeek.

Gerrit of Gozen Van Schaik and Maieken Van den Berg
(Maaike V. d. Berg). Wit.: Gerrit and Marytje Van
Schaik.

Nov. 9. Simon of Pieter Jordens and Elisabeth Diersaat
(Dierhart). Wit.: Simon and Margarita Charles.

Jannetje of Izak De Voe and Marytje V. der Linde (Van
Olinde). Wit.: Daniel V. der Linde (Van Olinde),
Elisabeth Bekker.

Nov. 11. Evert of Jan Olver and Marytje Siksby.
Wit.: Evert and Ernstje Siksby.

Christopher (Christoffer) of Hendrick Kaatsbah (Kaatsbach) and Eva De Voe. Wit.: Hans De Voe, Marytje
Koller (Keller).

Nov. 15. Frederik of Christiaan Keller and Elisabeth
Baches (Christiaan and Elisabeth Keller). Wit.: Frederick (Frederik) Baches, Grietje Koen.

Maria of Daniel Halenbeek and Catharina Kwakenbosch (Kwakkenbusch). Wit.: Jacob Gosen Van Schaik,
Debora Van Schaik.

Cathalyntje of Corn. Mathys Van d. Berg (Cornelis M.

* Vol. III. of the original records appears to have a duplicate set of
entries from this date to and including Aug. 1, 1763. Where these
entries differ from the first the difference is shown in parentheses. For
title page see end of records, page 104.

1760

Van den Bergh) and Cornelia Van d. Berg (Van den Bergh). Wit.: Rutgert and Marytje V. d. Berg (Maria Van den Berg).

Johannes of Nanning Vischer (Visscher) and Catharyntje (Catharina) Wendel. Wit.: Johannes and Annatie (Annatje) Roerbach.

Nov. 23. Catharina of Wynand and Marytje V. d. Berg (Van den Berg). Wit.: Adriaan Kwackkenbosch (Kwakkenbusch), Folkje Van den Berg.

Thomas of Thomas and Elisabeth Eivry. Wit.: Samuel Sembly, Judith Nauts (Naues).

Nicolaus (Nicolaas) of Stephanus (Stefanus) Van Schaak and Jannetje Brat. Wit.: Hendrik Bogaart (Bogert), Engeltie (Engeltje) Van Schaak.

Nicolaus (Nicolaas) of Eduard Hogil (Hoghil) and Maria Egmond. Wit.: Pieter Grennel, Hester Lansing.

Nov. 30. Hendrik of Antony Briesch and Catharyntje Jetz (Yetz). Wit.: Johannes Jetz (Yetz), Wyntje Briesch.

Hendrik of Hendrick Milten (Hendrik Milton) and Rachel Naarten (Northen). Wit.: Hendrik Naarten (Northen), Marry Seau.

Eduard of Eduard and Nanny (Marry) Beins (Beirt). Wit.: Henry Robinson, Meebel (Mabel) Forbiesch.

Jacob of Jacob Bogaart and Marytje Jetz (Yetz). Wit.: Wouter and Jannetje Groesbeek.

Catharina Barbara of Adam and Magdalena Ramter (Ramzer). Wit.: Christiaan Gerard, Anna Barbara Carmontel (Carmousel).

Johan Christopher (Christoffer) of Conrad (Coenraad) and Christina Vrydag. Wit.: Johan Richter, Christopher Doppe (Christoffer Depper).

Dec. 7. Gertruid (Geertruid) of Petrus Pietersen (Pieterssen) and Rebecca Montagne. Wit.: St. Bennewe (Pieter Benneway), Gertrui (Geertruid) Bovie.

Maria of Johannes Spoor and Magdalena Bagaart (Bogart). Wit.: Gerrit De Buur (Ten Baar), Maria Spoor.

Dirk of Willem Hunze (Hanssen) and Sara De Freest (De Foreest). Wit.: Dirk Hun, Margarietje Hogen (Margarita Hoghing).

Dec. 11 (14). Patrik of Patrik and Mally Weit (Wheit). Wit.: Jek Ros (Jacob Ross), Caty (Catharina) McKinsy.

Arriantje (Arriaantje) of Pieter Hoogteling (Hoogtheling) and Annatje Bekkens (Annaatje Bekkers). Wit.: Jacob Degarmo (de Garmo), Fytje Bekkers.

Johnatan (Jonathan) of Jan (John) and Phebe (Phoebe) Kidny. Wit.: Willem and Annatje Hilten (Hilton).

1760–1761

Aris (Ary) of Hendrik Van Wie and Johanna Gardenier. Wit.: Jacob and Catharyntje (Catharina) Fily (Fiely).

Gerrit of Gerrit I. Lansing (Gerrit Langsingh) and Jannetje (Annatje) Waters. Wit.: Jacob Lansing (Lansingh), Marrytje Ebbertze (Marytje Egbertz).

Pieter of Pieter Bryaart (Bogart, Jr.,) and Barber (Barbara) Franke. Wit.: Jacob Bogaart (Bogart, Jr.,) Jannetje Groesbeek.

Anna of William and Elisabeth Green. Wit.: Thomas Devenpoort, Elisabeth V. d. Werken.

Dec. 21. Margarita of Albert V. d. Werken (Van der Werken) and Annatje V. d. Berg (Vanden Berg). Wit.: Abraham V. d. Berg (Bergh), Elisabeth V. d. Werken.

Marytje of Johannes Pery and Francyntje Kloet (Knoet). Wit.: Wynand V. d. Berg, Maria Ridder.

Maria of Andries Van Schaik and Alida Hogen (Hoghing). Wit.: Willem and Susanna Hogen (Hoghing).

Martha of Willem Sohl (William Solch) and Margarita Wyngaard (Wyngaerd). Wit.: Jelles Garman, Rachel Degarmau (Jelles and Rachel De Garmo).

1761, Jan. 4. Derk (Dirk) of Wouter De Vreest (Wouther De Foreest) and Engeltje Brat. Wit.: Derk (Dirk) and Cornelia Brat.

Jan. 18. Marytje of Johannis (Johannes) Oothout and Elisabeth V. (Van) Woert. Wit.: Jan Oothout, Marytje Wendel.

Eva of Gysbert Marselius (Marselees) and Cathalina Wendel. Wit.: Gerrit Marselius (Marselies), Geesje Wendel.

Hannes (Hannis) of Dirk Heemstraat and Marytje Barrewe (Baruere). Wit.: Philip and Margarietje (Margarita) Barrewe (Barruer).

Jan. 25 at Sch. Jacob of Johannes Gelen and Catharina Veder. Wit.: Hendrik and Elisabeth (Elisabet) Gelen.

Feb. 1. Christina of Johannes and Dorothea Stroop. Wit.: Filip and Catharina Kerner.

Annatje of Hadriaan Brat and Marytje Macans (Maerus). Wit.: Hannes and Catharyntje Redly.

Simon of Wouter De Ridder and Anneke V. d. Berg. Wit.: Simon De Ridder, Annatje (De) Ridder.

Feb. 15. Lavinus of Abraham V. d. Bergh (V. d. Berg) and Rachel Liverson (Levison). Wit.: Franciscus and Marrytje (Marytje) Lansing.

Jan of Philip (Filip) and Elsje Lansing. Wit.: Jan and Arriaantje Lansing.

Robert of Hendrik I. Wendel and Maria Lansing. Wit.: Robert Lansing, Marytje Roseboom (Rooseboom).

1761

bo. Jan. 8. Jacob of Maas Van Buren and Cathalyntje V. Valkenburg. Wit.: Jan Wenne (Winne), Cathalyntje Van Buren.

Feb. 22. Annatje of Philip De Verreest (Filip de Foreest) and Rachel Van Esch. Wit.: Anthony and Annatje Van der Zee.

Mar. 1. Susanna of Johan Pieter (P.) Claassen and Clara Margaretha (Marg.) Kortsen (Contjer). Wit.: Johannes Horn (Honn), Marytje Triesepach (Duivebach).

Mar. 4. Bate (Batha) of Nicolaus (Nicolaas) and Claartje Knoet. Wit.: Johannes and Elisabeth Heemstraat.

Annatje of Benjamin Onixeid(?) (Onreid?) and Cornelia V. (Van) Arnhem. Wit.: Abraham and Elisabeth (Elisabet) Bekker.

Mar. 8. Maria of David and Margarita Springer. Wit.: Pieter and Cathalyntje Redly (Redley).

Gerrit of Frerik (Freerik) Knoet and Marytje Ridder (Ridders). Wit.: Hansje Vroman, Antje Ridders.

Hendrik of Johannnes Eversen and Susanna Lagransy (Le Gransy). Wit.: Jilles (Jelles Charmo) and Rachel Charmau (Garmo).

Mar. 15. Elisabeth of Hannes Goewey and Elisabeth (Maria) Young. Wit.: Hendrik Gardenier, Marytje Goey (Goewey).

Elisabeth of Pieter Goewy (Goewey) and Maria (Elisabeth) Young. Wit.: Hendrik Young, Marytje Lidde(?) (Lidye).

Joseph of Mattys (Matthias) and Catharina Horn. Wit.: Joseph PrnAar(?) (Pindar), Catharina Salbergerin (Salsbarry).

Pietertje of Johannis (Johannes) Pruin and Jannetje V. Aalstein (Aalstein). Wit.: Pieter Yetz, Sara Van Aalstein.

Cornelia of John Vile and Geesje Slingerland. Wit.: Wouter and Hesje Slingerland.

Yzak (Izaac) of Gerrit Kwackenbusch (Kwakkenbusch) and Catharina du (De) Voe. Wit.: Izak Lansing (Izaac Lanzing), Anna Van Woerd (Woert).

(Mar. 16) Coenraad of Pieter Ganzevoort and Gerritje Ten Eyke (Eick). Wit.: Jacob Ten Eyk (Eik), Elsje Ten Eick née Kuilers (Elsje Kuiler).

(Mar. 23) Jacob of Izak Vosburg and Catharina Staats. Wit.: Jacob R. V. Woerd (Van Woert), Annatje Vosburg.

Annatje of Wynand V. d. Berg and Maria Ridder. Wit.: Gozen Van Schaik, Mayke V. d. Berg (Maayke Van d. Berg).

1761

Apr. 6. Johannes of Izak (Izaac) Fonda and Susanna Verreest (Foreest). Wit.: Johannes Fonda, Engeltje Visscher.

Matheus (Mattheus) of Johannes d'Charmau (John De Garmo) and Annatje Kittel. Wit.: Pieter and Hester De Charmau (de Charmo).

Apr. 12 (14). Cornelia of Jan Ten Baar and Lena Lansing. Wit.: Johannes Spoor, Cornelia Ten Baar.

Bata of Hannes and Elisabeth Heemstraat. Wit.: Nicolaus (Nicolaas) and Claartje Kloet.

May 3. Margarita of Pieter Rykman and Lydia V. d. Berg. Wit.: Gerrit C. and Margarita Van d. Berg (V. d. Berg).

Jacob of Johannes V. Aarnhem (Arnhem) and Alida V. d. Heide. Wit.: Dirk V. der (Van d.) Heide, Elisabeth Wendel.

Jacob Hendrik of Jacob Corsel (Jacob and Eva Korzel). Wit.: Hendrik and Dorothea Snyder (Schnyder).

Jacob of Johannes Fonda and Elisabeth Ouderkerk. Wit.: Pieter Levison, Maria Fonda.

Filip of Michael and Elisabeth Wageman (Wagenaar). Wit.: Filip Kenner (Kerner), Sara Hughen.

David of Johannes Flensburg and Cornelia Hoogteling. Wit.: Rykert and Rachel V. (Van) Santen.

Eduard of Johannes and Jannetje Waker. Wit.: Abraham Waker, Elisabeth V. d. Werken.

May 10. Petrus of Johannes and Catharina Huik. Wit.: Gerrit V. d. (Van den) Berg, Annatje V. d. (Van der) Werken.

May 27. Anna Margarita of Jurjen and Anna (Annatje) De Fou (Voe). Wit.: Abraham and Margarita V. d. (Van der) Kar.

May 31. Batje (Baatje) of Matthias and Batje (Bata) Bouvie (Bovie). Wit.: Dirk and Margarita V. d. (Van der) Heide.

Elisabeth of Melchior and Elisabeth Feil. Wit.: Izak (Izaac) and Elisabeth V. (Van) Arnhem.

Lena of Matthias and Arriaantje Hoogteling. Wit.: Coenraad Hoogteling, Saartje Gansevoort (Ganzevoord).

June 4. Johannetje (Jannetje) of Dirk and Rebecca Webb (Whebb). Wit.: Jelles and Titje (Fytje) Wenne (Winne).

June 7. Egje of Teunis and Agneta Slingerlant (Theunis and Agnietje Slingerland). Wit.: Gerrit Slingerlant (Slingerland), Agnitje (Agnietje) Brat.

Hendrikje of Harmen and Rebecca Fort. Wit.: Jelles and Titje (Fytje) Wenne (Winne).

Cathalina of Pieter and Sara Jetz (Yetz). Wit.: Jacob and Cathalyntje Groesbeek.

1761

June 13. Catharina of Jurjen and Catharina Scherp. Wit.: Philip (Filip) and Catharina Kenner (Kerner).

Harman (Harmen) of Cornelis V. (Van) Vechten and Annatje (Van Vechten). Wit.: Barent (Van Buren) and Cathalyntje V. Buren.

June 21. Maria Barbara of Hendrik and Sophia Berker (Berger). Wit.: Hendrik Berriger, Maria B. (Barbara) Kenniger (Berriger).

Machtel of Albert V. d. Werken and Marytje (Maria V. d. Werken). Wit.: Hannes Lansing (and wife Maria), Marytje V. Huiser.

June 22. Martha of Pieter and Cathalyntje (Catharina) Redley (Redlif). Wit.: Jan (John) Olfer, Rachel Redley (Redlif).

Annatje of Johannes Redley (Redlif) and Catharina (Redlif) V. Huiser. Wit.: Adriaan and Marytje Brat.

July 5. Elisabeth, of Caspar and Margareta (Margarita) Jang (Sarry). Wit.: Carel Morssel, Catharina Morslyn (Morsslyn).

Tryntje of Abraham Piek (Peek) and Catharina (Peek). Wit.: Thomas Kouper (Coeper), Margaritje (Margareta) V. Antwerpen.

Gerrit of Gerrit Jo. (J.) and Alida V. d. Berg. Wit.: Abraham Van Esch, Christyntje V. d. Berg.

July 12. Gerrit of Leonard (Leendert) and Marrytje (Marytje) Muller. Wit.: Corn. (Cornelis) and Alida V. (Van) Esch.

Frederik of Frans (Fredrik) Roos and Marytje Borrs (Borns). Wit.: Balth. and Jannetje Brat.

Johannes of Mathias and Josyntje Boom. Wit.: Hannes and Hilletje Koe (Koen).

July 19. Jacob of Hannes and Marytje Defou (de Voe). Wit.: Hendrik Kaatsbaan, Eva defou (de Voe).

July 26. Pieter of Barent Hoghil and Geertje (Hoghil). Wit.: Pieter and Sara De Charmau (De Garmo).

Aug. 1. Cornelia of Philip (Filip I.) Schuiler and Christina Renselaar. Wit.: John Braatstrit (Braatstreet), El. (Judith) Bayert, wife of Jerem. Renselaar.

Aug. 2. Jacobus of Johan Redly (John Redlif) and Margarita (Redlif). Wit.: Jacobus and Catharina Redly (Redlif).

Aug. 9. Abraham of Abraham V. d. Kar and Margarita (V. d. Kar). Wit.: Hans and Marytje V. d. Werken.

Egje of Jacob and Rachel Kloet (Kloek). Wit.: Hendrik and Marytje Van Wie.

Aug. 16. Abraham of Barent Vosburg and Annatje Gerritsen (Gerritzen). Wit.: Pieter and Elisabeth (Elisabet) Vosburg.

1761

Cornelia of Izak (Izaac) and Marytje Valk. Wit.: Coenraad and Cornelia Hoogteling.

Annatje of Filip Jong (Young) and Annatje Siphes (Sipkes). Wit.: Sacharias Siphes (Zacharias Sipkes), Elisabeth Davits (Davis).

Aug. 30. Johannes (Joannes) of Abraham and Elisabeth Oostrander (V. Oostrander). Wit.: Tobias and Maria Witbeek.

Hendrikje of Petrus and Rachel Van Woert. Wit.: Jelles and Titje (Fytje) Wenne (Winne).

Sep. 6. Johannes of Izak Fort and Saartje (Sara) Vile. Wit.: Johannes and Margarita Fort.

bo. Sep. 5. Johannes of Hendrik Bogaart and Barbara Marselis (Marselees). Wit.: Gysbert and Johanna Marsselees (Gysbert Marselies, Johanna Marselees).

Sep. 13. Cornelia of Michael V. d. Koek and Cornelia V. (Van) Esch. Wit.: Jonas and Elisabet Oothout (Jonas Oothout and wife Elisabet).

Sep. 20. Sara of Izak and Annatje Lansing. Wit.: Jacob Van Woert, and wife Elisabeth.

Elisabeth of Harmen and Judith Qwakkenbusch (Kwakkenbusch). Wit.: Adriaan and Elisabeth Kwakkenbusch.

Antony of Cornelis (V.) Sandvoort and Adriana Brat. Wit.: Staats (Van) Sandvoort, Willemje (Willemtje) Brat.

Antje of Jacob Olfer and Annake (Annatje) Siksby. Wit.: Rykert and Marytje Redly (Redlif).

Sep. 25. Marytje of Dirk and Jannetje Swartte (Swart). Wit.: Antony Van der Zee, Antje Yetz.

Sep. 27. Cornelis of Hendrik Meyer and Maria Morry. Wit.: Hendrik and Dorothea Snyer.

Jacob of Jacob Mook and Cathar. (Catharina) Claassen. Wit.: Jacobus and Annatje Arnhout (Aarnhout).

Lyntje of Gysbert Fonda and Elsje Douwe (Douw). Wit.: Pieter W. and Margarieta (Margarita) Douwe (Douw).

Oct. 4. Rebecca of Bernardus Brat and Eva V. (Van) Petten. Wit.: Daniel and (wife) Rebecca V. Antwerpen.

Oct. 11. Annatje (Annetje) of Albert and Elisabeth Slingerland. Wit.: Abraham and Geesje Slingerland.

Sara of Marten and Sara Meinersen (Meinerssen). Wit.: Abraham (Abrah.) and Maria Meinerse (Meinersse).

Gerrit of Benjamin and Catharina Goe (Goey). Wit.: Gerrit and Alida V. d. Berg.

Alida of Rutger and Maria V. d. Berg. Wit.: Wilhelmus and Agnita V. d. Berg.

Gysbert of Corn. (Cornelis) G. and Elisabeth V. d. Berg. Wit.: Gerrit and Tryntje V. d. Berg.

1761

Jan of Gerrit, Jr., (Gerrit) and Wyntje Zeeger. Wit.: Jan and Annaatje (Annatje) Hoessen.

Oct. 18. Margarietje (Margarita) of Bastiaan and Catharina Dile. Wit.: David York, Sara Winne.

Sara of Hannes and Margarietje V. Santen (Margarita Van Santen). Wit.: Willem and Alida V. Santen (Van Santen).

Johannes of Dirk Matthysse (Math.) V. d. Hoeve (Heide) and Sara Wendel. Wit.: Robert Wendel, Wid. Jannetje (Jannitje) Kuiler, née Beekman.

Oct. 15 (sic). Margarita of Hendrik V. Schaak and Jannetje Holland. Wit.: Ritcher (Hutschen) Holland, Jannetje V. Schaaik (Van Schaak).

Oct. 25. Jacobus Van Slyk of Filip Reyley and Jannetje V. (Van) Slyk. Wit.: Jacobus Van Slyk, Cathalyna Brat (Bratt).

Teunis (Theunis) of Johannes Quackenbusch (Kwakkenbusch) and Jannatje Vile. Wit.: Teunis (Theunes) and Catharina Vile.

Oct. 29 (27). William of William and Ann (Anna) Erl. Wit.: Elisabeth Kimmons (Cimmons).

Nov. 1. Coenraad of Jonathan Hoogtheling (Hoogteling) and Jannetje Slingerland. Wit.: Dirk and Fytje V. d. Kar.

Lena of David Hoogteling and Hilletje V. d. See (Van der Zee). Wit.: Daniel Winne, Catharina Hoogtheling (Hoogteling).

Maria of Jacob V. d. Heide and Maria Halenbeek. Wit.: Johannes V. Arnhem (Aarnem), Mary (Maria) Halenbeek.

Johannes (Joannes) of Tobias Ten Eick (Eik) and Judith V. Buren. Wit.: Barent Ten Eick (Eik), Gerritje Ten Eick, wife of P. Gansevoord (Gerritje Ganzevoord née Ten Eick).

Nov. 7 (8). Jonathan of Petrus Hilten and Annatje Broek (Broeks). Wit.: Jonathan and Rebecca Broeks.

Jacomyntje of Petrus Bennewe and Maria Fort. Wit.: Jan Fort, Sara Vile.

Nov. 14. Lavinus of Pieter Lievjson (Levison) and Maria Fonda. Wit.: Franciscus and Maria Lansing.

Elisabeth of Dirk and Alida Van Vechten (Alida of Dirk Van Vechten and Annatje Knikkerbakker). Wit.: Wouter and Annetje (Annatje) Knickerbacker (Knikkerbakker).

Cornelia of Isak (Yzak) Slingerland and Eva Van Woerd. Wit.: Abraham Slingerland, Rebecca Vile.

Nov. 21. Willem of Jacobus Abeel and Egbertje V. (Van) Buren. Wit.: Cornelis and Teuntje (Theuntje) Van Buren (V. Buren).

Barent of Folkert Dorschen and Geertruit (Geertruid) Hilten. Wit.: Isak and Marytje Swits (Yzak and Maria Zwitz).

Georgius Mathias (Mattias) of Jacob Kinmer (?) and Maria Barbara (Maria B.). Wit.: David Enosch (E.) Couper, Maria Enish (Enoch).

Susanna of Hendrik V. Arnhem (Aarnem) and Susanna Wenne (Winne). Wit.: Lavinus and Susanna Wenne (Winne).

Nov. 26 (28). Geertje of Wilh. and Agnita V. d. Berg. Wit.: Gerrit V. d. Berg, Engeltje Waldrom.

Dec. 6. Johannes of Johannes and Catharina Fester (Jester). Wit.: Carel and Catharina Morssel.

Dirk of Hermanus Schuyler (Schuiler) and Christyntje Ten (T.) Broek. Wit.: Quiliaan Van Rensselaar (Kiliaan V. Renzelaar), Arriaantje Schuiler.

Rebecca of Jelles Wenne (Winne) and Titje Van Woerd (Titie Van Woert). Wit.: Frans Wenne (Winne), Anneke (Annatje) Viele.

John of Franciscus and Sara Hoghil. Wit.: Hans (Goeey) and Elisabeth Goue (Goey).

Dec. 13. Daniel of Hendrick (Hendrik) and Maria Young. Wit.: Hannes and Maria Goee (Goeey).

(Maria of John and Sara Spek. Wit.: Thoon and Maria Spek).

Dec. 20. Elisabeth of Robert Sanders and Elisabeth Schuiler. Wit.: Philip P. Schuiler, Elisabeth Rensselaar, wife of A. Ten Broek (Elisabeth Ten Broek).

Neeltje of Hannes Coon (Koen) and Hilletje Zeger. Wit.: Johannes and Neeltje Douw.

Dec. 25. Jan of Willem Hilten and Elisabeth Broek (Broeks). Wit.: Jan Fadden (Tadden), Wina Church.

Dec. 26. Cornelius (Cornelis) of Frans and Marytje Winne. Wit.: Adam and Gerritje Winne.

Dec. 27. Cornelia of Gerrit Ten Rau (?) (Baar) and Cathalyntje But (Cathalina Brat). Wit.: Lavinus and Cornelia Ten Baar.

Dec. 30. Maria of Gerrit Bouvie (Bovie) and Arriaantje Bovie. Wit.: Vincent Binnewe (Bennewee), Geertruid Bouvie.

Sara Rachel Regina, of Mr. and N. Canner (Kanner). Wit.: John and Rachel Regina Farrel.

1762, Jan. 10. Ruben of Steven Schuyler (Stefen Schuiler) and Engeltje Van (V). Vechten. Wit.: Filip Van (V.) Vechtten, Elisabeth Sanders.

Daniel of Daniel Tevston (Irvsson), Jr., and Marytje Barret (Barrel). Wit.: Daniel and Maria Tevsten (Irvsson).

1762

Jan. 13. Jannetje of Hermanus Van (V.) Aalstein and Catharina Peesing (Peessing). Wit.: Andries Pesing (Peessink), Betje Valk.

Jan. 17. Annatje of Johannes and Elisabeth Fryer. Wit.: Jacob R. Van Woerd (Woert), Marytje Gardenier.

Isak (Izaac) of Willem Vosburg and Christina Van Woerd (Woert). Wit.: Willem V. d. Berg, Annatje Vosburg.

Jan. 24. Hendrik of Teunis (Theunis) Brat and Cathalyntje (Catharina) Van Esch. Wit.: John and Anna Van Esch.

Elisabeth of John (Jan) Knoet and Sara V. Arnhem (Aarnem). Wit.: Isak (Izak) H. Lansing, Anna V. Arnhem.

Jan. 31. Lena of Tobias Van (V.) Salsbergen and Margarita V. Salsbergen. Wit. John Rooseboom (Roozeboom), Elisabeth V. Schelluine.

Nicholaas (Nicolaas) of Wouter N. and Alida Groesbeek. Wit. Johannis and Marytje (Johans and Maria) Groesbeek.

Wyntje of Daniel and Willemtje Brat. Wit. Antony and Marytje Brat.

Willem of Folkert V. d. Berg and Neeltje V. Berg (V. d. Berg). Wit. Willem and Elisabeth Waldrom.

Feb. 7. Frerik of Hendrik and Vincentje Williams. Wit. Frerik and Marytje (Maria) Knoet.

Chatarina (Catharina) of Hannes Treal (?) (Freal) and Elze Mueret (Elsje Mucret). Wit. Jacob and Catharina Fryhout.

Hendrik (Willem Hendrik) of Willem and Maria Arlok ('Arlok). Wit. Hendrik Kadser (Rodger), Barbara Hermanns.

Anna of Harmanus (Hermanus) Kuiler and Barbara Marselees. Wit. Gerrit and Margarietje (Margaret) Marselees.

Feb. 11. bo. Jan. 7. Nicolaas of Joost and Margarita Acker. Wit. Nicholaas, Jr., and Geertruid Acker.

Feb. 14. bo. Jan. 31. Jacob of Hannes Bernard and Christina Huber. Wit. Jacob Van Woert, Lena Boom.

bo. Jan. 26. Teunis (Theunis) Vile of Louis Vile and Annatje Kwackenbosch (Anna Kwakkenbusch). Wit. Teunis (Theunis) and Catharina Vile.

bo. Jan. 17. Johannes of Jurjen Steen and Lea V. d Hoef. Wit. Adam Coon (Koen), Marytje (Maria) V. d. Hoef.

bo. Jan. 16. Pieter of Barent Romans and Maria Wendel. Wit. Robert and Elisabeth Wendel (Wendell).

Feb. 17. bo. Jan. 29. Theuntje of Barent C. Van

1762

Buren (Barent V. Buren) and Arriaantje Vander Poel
(V. d. Poel). Wit. Gerrit Vanden Berg, Marytje Van
Buren (Gerrit V. d. Berg, Maria Van Buren).

Feb. 28. bo. Same Date. Catharina of Frans Winne
and Anneke Vile. Wit. Hugo and Saartje (Sara)
Vile.

Mar. 14. bo. Mar. 1. Willem of Timotheus Van (V.)
Dyk Rendel and Catharina V. Antwerpen. Wit. Helmus
Van (V.) Antwerpen, Geertruid V. d. Linde.

3 Weeks old. Christofel (Christoffer) of Willem and
Mary (Maria) Northen. Wit. Hendrik and Mally
Denison (Denyson).

bo. Mar. 3. Eva of Dirk and Margarita V. d. Heide.
Wit. Daniel and Saara (Sara) Kittel.

4 Weeks and 1 day old. Catharyntje (Catharina) of
Michal (Michael) and Marytje Landman. Wit. Ebner
(Abner) and Geertje Robertson.

bo. Feb. 27. Geurt of Arriaan (Adriaan) and Lydia
Brat. Wit. Geurt Brat, Elisabeth Raren (Elisabet
Karen).

bo. Mar. 6. Isak (Izaac) of Willem Fryer and Hanna
Fennel. Wit. Isak (Izaac) and Catharina Fryer.

bo. Feb. 12. Mattheus of Hannes and Margarita
Wideman. Wit. Mattheus Kohler (Kokler), Anna
Kokler.

Mar. 18. bo. Feb. 16. Annatje of Daniel and Catharina
De Voe. Wit. Jurjen and Annatje De Voe.

Mar. 21. bo. Mar. 1. Hermanus of Curzet and Neeltje
Vedder. Wit. Hermanus and Catharyntje (Catharina)
Vedder.

bo. Feb. 24. Metje of Johannes La Grance (Legrancy)
and Elisabeth Merois (Meroy). Wit. Cornelis (Van)
Sandvoort and wife (and wife N. Brat).

bo. Mar. 14. Philip (?) or Fitye (?) (Filip) of Andries
H. and Saartje (Sara) Gardenier. Wit. John and
Cathalyntje Hansen (Hanssen).

Mar. 24. bo. Mar. 10. Maria of Pieter and Susanna
Winne. Wit.: Wynand and Marytje V. d. Berg.

Mar. 27. bo. Mar. 21. Catharina of Hendrik and Elsje
Stronk. Wit. Frederik (Frerik) Neidhart, Catharina
Herwick (Harwich).

Apr. 4. bo. Apr. 1. Johannes of Cornelis and Marytje
Muller. Wit. John Goue (Goeey), Marytje Goeue
(Goey).

Apr. 18. bo. Mar. 19. Petrus of Izak S. (Izaac J.)
Trouex and Marytje Wyngaard. Wit. Petrus Hilten
(Hilton), Margarita Wyngaard.

bo. Mar. 14. Arriaantje of Pieter Hoogteling and.

1762

Annatje Bekker. Wit. Jacob De Garmau (De Garmo), Gesje Bakkers (Getje Bekkers).

Apr. 25. bo. Mar. 16. Alida of Louis and Hendrikje V. (Van) Antwerpen. Wit. Isak (Izaac) and Alida De Foreest.

bo. Apr. (March) 4. Abigail of Jacob Foreest and Catharyntje (Catharina). Wit. Marten and Tanneke Foreest.

May 2. Jacob of Nicolaas Hunger and Anna Catharina (Anna C.). Wit. Jacob Michels (Micheels), Anna Elisabet (El.) Barbara.

bo. Mar. 26. Gerrit of Melchert and Margarytje (Margarita) V. d. Poel. Wit. Gerrit V. d. Poel, Marytje V. Buren.

bo. Apr. 10. Lea of Jonathan and Gerritje Witbeek. Wit. Tobias and Lea Witbeek.

bo. Apr. 30. Johannis of Gysbert and Rebecca V. Santen. Wit. Hannes and Elisabeth V. Santen.

May 7. bo. Apr. 29. (27) Cornelia of Patrik Klark (Patric Clark) and Cornelia Waldrom. Wit. Jacob C. Ten Eik (Ten Eick), Anna Waldrom.

May 9. bo. Apr. 4. Lavinus of Jan and Susanna Wenne (Winne). Wit. Robert and Susanna Winne.

bo. Apr. 1. Jacob of Evert and Elsje Siksby. Wit. Johannis (Johannes), Jr., and Hesse (Hester) Lansing.

May 16. bo. May 14. Jacob of Jacob Bogaart and Maria Yetz. Wit. Douwe and Willempje (Willemje) Bogaart.

bo. May 10. Johannetje (Jannetje) of Jan G. Yetz and Cathalyntje Goue. (Cathalina Goeey) Wit. Filip and Geertruid Muller.

bo. May 16. Annatje of Abraham Lansing and Elisabet Kouper (Couper). Wit. Christoffer Joh. (J.) Yetz (Yaetz), Catharina Lansing.

bo. May 9. Jochum of Patrik and Jannetje MakKenti (Patrik Mc Kinsy and Jannetje Makkinsy). Wit. Hermanus V. Aalstein, Lydia Brat.

May 20. bo. May 16. Barent of Gerrit and Debora Staats (Debora Beekman). Wit. Jochim (Jochum) Staats, Elisabeth Schuiler.

May 23. bo. Mar. 12. Rachel of Gysbert and Hester Bosch. Wit. Abraham and Mayke (Maaike) Oothout.

bo. May 14. Jacobus of Hugo Denyson and Rachel V. Valkenburg (Valkenburg). Wit. Jacobus and Margarita V. Valkenburg (Valkenburg).

bo. May 14. Bregje of Evert and Sara Zeger. Wit. Johannes and Bregje Zeger.

bo. May 1. Rachel of Franciscus Kenel (Cruel) and

1762

Annatje Bulsing. Wit. Folkert Douw, Rachel Bogaart (Bogart).

May 25. bo. May 18. Robert of William and Margarita Hesty. Wit. William Kerby, Hanna Millet.

May 30. bo. May 2. Johannes (Johan) Christoffer of Wilhelm and Justina Kirchner. Wit. Christoffer Dipper, Johanna (Johan) Richter.

bo. May 16. Barbara of Hendrik and Rachel Milton. Wit. John Milton, Mally Mekyoun (Mc Goun).

bo. May 6. Catharina of Martin De Foreest and Tanneke Winne. Wit. Daniel and Jannetje Winne.

bo. May 27. Annatje of Pieter and Catharina Hoghil. Wit. Ebner (Abner) Roberts, Annatje V. d. Berg.

bo. May 25. Jesse of Izak (Izaac) De Foreest and Alida Fonda. Wit. Philip and Neeltje De Foreest.

June 6. bo. June 4. Abraham of Evert and Annatje Vanden Berg (V. d. Berg). Wit. Abraham and Rachel V. d. Berg.

bo. Apr. 7. Engeltje of Jan and Susanna Brat. Wit. Hannes Lang, Engeltje Zeger.

June 13. bo. June 10. Maria of Cornelis Van (V.) Deusen and Lea V. Oostrander. Wit. Albertus Bloemendal, Lena Lansing.

June 27. bo. May 30. Margarita of Nicolaas and Marya Rechter (Nicolaas Richter and Maria Hindermond). Wit. Johannes and Margarita Rechter (Richter).

bo. May (June) 25. Gerrit of Gysbert Marselis (Merselis) and Annatje Staats. Wit. Gerrit and Margarita Marselis (Merselis).

bo. May (June) 25. Annatje of Filip and Elsje Lansing (Elsje Hun). Wit. Thomas and Elisabet (Elisabeth) Hun.

bo. May (June) 5. Johannes of Jacobus Arnold and Anna Mook. Wit. Hendrik Mook, Catharina Claassen.

June 28. Gerardus of Gerrit Kwakenbusch (Kwakkenbus) and Catharina De Voe. Wit. Wouter Ridder, Anneke V. d. Berg.

July 4. bo. June 13. Geertruid of Jacob Kwakkenbusch and Catharina Huik. Wit. Rykert and Christina V. Franken.

bo. June 18. Willem of Charl Makay and Mayke Ouderkerk (Charles Mc Kay and Maayke Ouderkerk). Wit. Jacob and Marytje (Maria) V. d. Werken.

bo. May 15. Maria of Rykert and Marytje Bovie. Wit. Cornelis and Alida Van Esch.

bo. June 30. Sara of Pieter Williams and Elisabeth Fonda. Wit. Reynier and Arriaantje Van Yveren (V. Yveren).

1762

July 11. bo. July 6. Sara of Abraham (Abrahm) and Catharina Meinersse. Wit. Marten and Maria Meinersse.

July 18. bo. June 28. Lena of Laurens and Margarita Reisdorp (Reisdorf). Wit. Pieter and Lena Scherp.

bo. June (July) 17. Machteld (Machtel) of Bastiaan T. and Engeltje Visscher. Wit. Gerrit T. and Dirkje Visscher.

bo. July 18. Hendrik of Daniel and Catharina Halenbeek. Wit. Jacob and Dorothee (Dorothea) Halenbeek.

July 29. bo. July 3. Rebecca of Simon De Foreest and Mary Megginnis (Maria McGinnis). Wit. Abraham (Abrm) and Maria De Foreest.

Aug. 1. bo. July 26. Catharina of Reignier and Debora Van Yveren. Wit. Georg and Catharina Filding (Fylden).

bo. July 31. Gerrit of Pieter Rykman and Lydia V. d. Berg. Wit. Gerrit and Margarita V. d. Berg.

bo. July 31. Johannis of John and Elisabeth Davis. Wit. Filip and Annatje Young.

(Aug. 21. Santje of Abraham, Jr., and Antje Yates. Wit. I. V. d. Berg, R. Bogert.)

bo. July 11. Jacob of Dirk and Marytje Heemstraat. Wit. Jan and Jannetje Droit (Duret).

bo. July 27. Adrianus Hogeland (Adriaan) of Thomas Zeger and Judith Hogeland. Wit. Roelof Zeger, Lydia Hartje.

bo. July 27. Catharina of Frederik and Muely (Mally) Gerritsen (Gerritze), Wit. Balthus Van (Baltes V.) Benthuizen, Catharina Meclerny (Mc Lerny).

Aug. 7. (Sep. 8) bo. July 31. Frans of Christiaan Jacobi (Jacobz) and Margarita Hoging (Hoghing). Wit. Jacob and Syntje Couper.

Jacob of Jacob and Maria Barbara (Maria B.) Smit. Wit. Filip and Maria Catharina (Maria C.) Kerner.

bo. Aug. (Sep.) 2. Anna of Samuel Pruin and Neeltje Ten Eick (Ten Eik). Wit. Casparus and Alida Pruin.

Sep. 5. bo. Aug. 31. Daniel of David York and Susanna Grell. Wit. Wilhelmus and Agnietje (Agnita) V. d. Berg.

bo. Aug. 31. Johannes of Hendrik and Maria V. d. Werken. Wit. Roelef and Geertruid V. d. Werken.

bo. Sep. 4. Fytje (Titie) of Hannes Marselis (Mercelis) and Neeltje Gardenier. Wit. Gerrit and Alida Marselis (Merselis).

bo. Aug. 16. Sofia of Jacob and Anna Bernhard. Wit. Hannis Rikkard, Sofia Bertel (Hannes Rikkart, Sofia Bartel).

bo. Aug. 1. Johannes of ——— (Hannes) Lynd and

1762

Marytje (Maria) Duivebach. Wit. Christiaan and Widow Duivebach.

bo. Aug. 26. Barent of Filip and Geertruid Muller. Wit. Barent Gove (Gouey), Marytje (Maria) Gardenier.

bo. Aug. 26. Cathalyntje of Thomas Hun and Barentje V. Deusen. Wit. Dirk and Margarita Hun.

bo. Aug. 29. Barent of Marten and Hendrikje V. Buren. Wit. Barent and Cathalyntje V. Buren (V. Burent).

Sep. 12. bo. Aug. 22. Marten of Jan and Folkje Grennel. Wit. Jan and Marytje (Maria) Van Aalstein (V. Aalstein).

bo. Sep. 8. Gerritje of Wynand V. d. Berg and Maria De Ridder. Wit. Evert and Gerritje De Ridder.

bo. Aug. 21. Barent of Johannes and Sara Muller. Wit. Martinus V. Yvern (—— Van Yveren) Maria Govey (Gouey).

bo. and ba. Sep. 18. Margarita of Hendrik R. Lansing and Mary Marselees (Merselis). Wit. Robert and Marytje (Maria) Lansing.

Sep. 19. bo. Sep. 13. Thomas of Johannes L. and Elisabet (Elisabeth) Redly. Wit. Thomas and Elisabeth Wilkeson.

bo. Sep. 14. Sara of Gerrit V. Santen and Hester Winne. Wit. Johannes and Elisabeth (Elisab.) V. Santen.

bo. Sep. 5. Martinus of Hannes I. (Hannes) and Engeltje Witbeek. Wit. Harmen V. d. See, Lena Vroman.

Magdalena of Abraham and Annatje Wever. Wit. Jan and Cathalyntje Wenne (Winne).

Oct. (3) bo. Sep. 19. Rebecca of Simon V. Antwerpen and Maria Ten Baar. Wit. Daniel and Rebecca V. Antwerpen.

bo. Sep. 4. Johannes of Hannes V. d. Werken and Marytje De Voe. Wit. Albart (Albert) and Marytje V. d. Werken.

bo. Sep. 15. Johannes of Hannes and Elisabeth Groesbeek. Wit. Jacob and Cathalyntje Groesbeek.

bo. Sep. 20. Petrus Douw of Gerardus Beekman and Anna Douw. Wit. Petrus Douw, Magdalena Gensevoo (Gansevoort).

bo. Sep. 18. Hendrik of Salomo and Geertruy (Geertruid) Bulsing. Wit. Hendrik and Cathalyntje Bulsing.

Oct. (Sep.) 16. bo. Oct. (Sep.) 12. Elsje of Pieter Ganzevoort and Gerritje Ten Eyk (Eick). Wit. Johannes and Annatje Ganzevoort.

bo. Oct. (Sep.) 12. Hendrik of Jacobus Burker V.

Benthuizen and Sara V. Benthuizen (Jacobus P. and Sara V. Benthuisen). Wit. John and Rebecca Trotter.

bo. Oct. (Sep.) 11. Rachel of Willem and Lydia Verplank. Wit. Cornelis and Marytje (Maria) Timesen (Tymessen).

Oct. 24. bo. Sep. 5. Samuel of John Walker and Jannetje Waker. Wit. Jacob Knoet, Margarita Boom (Borns).

Susanna of Dirk V. d. Heide and Elisabeth Wendel. Wit. Nanning Visscher (Visser), Alida Ten Eik (Eick).

bo. Sep. 30. Obadiah (Obadia) of Abraham Couper and Catharina Oostrander. Wit. Thomas and Margarita Couper.

Oct. 31. bo. Oct. (Sep.) 30. Lydia of John (Joan) Van Vechten and Annatje Williams. Wit. Folkert and Neeltje V. Vechten.

Oct. 31. bo. Oct. 30. Rebecca of Jacobus and Mally Van Santen (V. Santen). Wit. Jonathan and Nansy (Nensy) Broeks.

bo. Oct. 29. Hendrik, (and) Cornelis, of Dirk Brat V. Schoonhoven (Dirk B. Van Schoonhoven) and Folkje V. Schoonhoven. Wit. Hendrik and Susanna V. Schoonhoven, Cornelis and Sanne (Sanna) V. d. Berg.

bo. Oct. 5. Rachel of Johannes S. (Johannes J.) and Maria Lansing. Wit. Franciscus and Marytje (Franc and Maria) Lansing.

bo. Oct. 30. Abraham of Jacob and Annatje V. Arnhem. Wit. John (Joan) and Sara Knoet.

bo. Oct. 29. Elisabeth of Gerrit and Christina Oostrander (V. Oostrander). Wit. Hannes (Hans) and Elisabeth Oostrander (V. Oostrander).

Seven Weeks old. Abraham of Hendrik and Catharina Young. Wit. Waldraat and Marytje (Walraad and Maria) Kryger.

Nov. 7. bo. Oct. 12. Annatje of Abraham (Abrm) Van Esch and Antje Ridder. Wit. Evert and Anneke Ridder.

bo. Nov. 3. Willem of Henry Northen and Margarita (Margar.) V. d. Werken. Wit. Gozen V. Schaik, Jannetje Brat.

Nov. 15. bo. Oct. 15. Elisabeth of Hendrik and Margarita Zeger. Wit. Thomas and Turkje (Jurkje) Zeger.

Nov. 22. bo. Nov. 16. Cornelia of Theunis and Elisabeth (Elisabet) V. Woert. Wit. Thomas and Bata Hun.

Dec. 6. bo. Dec. 4. Barent of Hannes Goey (Goeey) and Maria Van Yveren (V. Yveren). Wit. Cornelis and Cornelia Van Yveren (V. Yveren).

Dec. 12. Four Weeks old. Annatje of Johannes

1762

Fonda and Elisabeth Ouderkerk. Wit. Eldert Van Woert (V. Woerd), Rebecca Fonda.

bo. Dec. 5. Annatje of Pieter and Cath. (Catharina) Crennel. Wit. Rutger and Wyntje Lansing.

bo. Dec. 10. Johannes of Jeremias Van Renzelaar (Jeremia V. Renzelaar) and Judith Bajert. Wit. Johannes and Geertruid Van (V.) Renzelaar.

Dec. 17. bo. Dec. 8. Marten of Hannes Van (V.) Buren and Marytje Briesch. Wit. Thomas and Marytje (Maria) Williams.

Dec. 19. bo. Dec. 15. Theunis of John Vilen (Joan Vile) and Geesje Slingerland. Wit. Theunis and Catharina Vile.

Five Weeks old. Eva of Matthias (Mathias) and Arriaantje Hoogteling (Hoogteeling). Wit. Albert V. d. See (Vander Zee), Leentje Ganzevoord (Ganzevoort).

Six Weeks old. Coenraad of Coenraad and Christina Frydag. Wit. Coenraad and Maria Schraay.

Dec. 20. bo. Nov. 6. Elisabeth of Wilhelmus and Annatje Smit. Wit. Johannis and Elisabeth Smith (Joannes and Elisabet Smit).

Dec. 25. bo. Dec. 18. Petrus of Petrus Pieterssen (Pietersen) and Rebecca Montagne. Wit. Matthias Bovie, Nelly Montagne.

bo. Dec. 13. Abraham of Abraham and Rebecca Slingerland. Wit. Wouter and Hester Slingerland.

Dec. 31. bo. Nov. 13. Hugo of Johannis and Marytje (Joannes and Maria) Groesbeek. Wit. Louis and Maria Vile.

MARRIAGE RECORD—1763 AND 1764.

1763, Jan. 8. L. Edward Davis and Jannetje Duret, both of A.

Jan. 20. L. Jacob Rozeboom, y. m., and Hester Lansing, y. d., both of this city.

Feb. 5. B. Frederick Olver and Tryntje V. d. Berg, y. p., of Niskatha.

Mar. 12. L. James Scharpe, y. m., and Hanna Wendel, wid. of A.

Mar. 15. L. Adam Fonda and ——— Briesch, y. d., of this Co.

Mar. 16. B. Efraim Vroman, y. m., and Christina Zwartte, y. d., both b. and l. at Schie.

Mar. 17. B. Adam Vroman, y. m., and Jannetje Fiele, y. d., both b. and l. at Schie.

Mar. 26. L. Cornelis J. Kuiler, y. m., and Anna Wendel, y. d., both of this City.

1763

Mar. 26. **L.** Abraham Fonda, y. m., and Maria Ouderkerk, y. d., both of A. Co.

Apr. 12. **L.** Richard Ellen, y. m., and Marry Regan, y. d., of A.

Apr. 16. **B.** Jurjen Christoffer Bregt, y. m., and Maayke Oothout, y. d., both l. in Col. R.

Apr. 29. **L.** Stephen Schuyler, y. m., and Helena Ten Eyck, y. d., both of this City.

May 7. **L.** John Vischer, y. m., and Elisabeth Brat, y. d., of A.

May 19. **L.** John Roozeboom, y. m., and Susanna Veder, y. d., of A. Co.

May 22. **B.** John Duret and Sara Rivvison of the Col.

June 4. **L.** John Van Esch and Rebecca Bogaart, y. p., of the Col.

June 11. **B.** Johannes V. Oostrander and Marritje Van Aalstein, y. p., of the Col.

June 11. **L.** Arent Bekker and Annatje V. Woert, y. p., of A. Co.

July 12. **L.** William Kittle and Ann Tol, of A. Co.

Aug. 13. **L.** Albertus Bloemendal and Annetje Harsens, both of A.

Aug. 16. **B.** Hendrik Ruiter and Rebecca Staats, both of Hosak.

Aug. 20. **L.** Wouter De Foreest and Alida Kloet, both of the Col.

Sep. 10. **L.** Harmen Van Hoesen, Jr., and Tryntje Witbeek, y. d., both of A. Co.

Sep. 29. **L.** Harmen Groesbeek, y. m., and Marytje Bennewie, y. d., both l. at Schag.

Sep. 31 (sic). **L.** John Van Aalstein, y. m., and Lena Scherpe, y. d., both of the Col.

Same Date. **L.** Albert Slingerland and Christina Van Vranken, y. d., l. in the Col.

Oct. 28. **L.** Izaac Hoogkerk, y. m., and Rachel Van Santen, y. d., both of A.

Oct. 29. **L.** Wouter Kwakkenbusch, y. m., and Bata Knoet, y. d., of the Col.

Nov. 5. **B.** Jacob Heemstraat and Cathar. Duret, of the Col.

Nov. 22. **L.** Isaac Roos, y.m., and Maria Van Franken, of this Co.

Dec. 2. **L.** Abrabam Schuyler, y. m., and Eva Beekman, y. d., of this City.

Dec. 28. **L.** John Fiele and Elisabeth Ackerson, y. p., of Schie.

Dec. 30. **B.** Matheus Brouwer and Annatje Ouderkerk, y. p., of Hosak.

1764
1764, Jan. 21. **L.** Johannes M. Beekman, widr., and Elisabeth Douw, y. d., of this place.

Feb. 4. **L.** Anthony Brat, widr., and Mally V. Deuzen, y. d., of this City.

Feb. 12. **B.** Frederik Bekker and M. Coen, l. at N. K.

Feb. 23. **L.** Jeremias V. Renzelaar, y. m., of N. Y. and Lena Lansing, y. d., of this City.

Feb. 23. **L.** Johannes Groesbeek and Maria Groesbeek, of Schag.

Feb. 25. **L.** Wouter Bekker, y. m., and Annatje De Ridder, both of A.

Feb. 28. **B.** George Mindel (?), y. m., and Margarita Spikens (?), wid., both of the Col.

Mar. 3. **L.** Matheus De Garmo, y. m., and Marytje Groesbeek, both of the Col.

Mar. 5. **L.** Jacob Cuiler, y. m., and Lydia V. Vechten, y. d., of A.

Mar. 7. **L.** William Monbrut, y. m., and Marytje De Forest, y. d., both of A. Co.

Mar. 11. **L.** Thomas Lansing, y. m., and Neeltje De Foreest, y. d., both of this City.

Mar. 25. **L.** Matheus Aarsen, y. m., and Bregje Van Hoesen, y. d., both of this City.

Mar. 25. **L.** John Van Valkenburg, y. m., and Elisabeth Meindertsen, y. d., of this City.

Mar. 28. **L.** John Taylor, y. m., and Margarita Valkenburg, y. d., of this City.

Apr. 10. **L.** Abraham Cuyler, y. m., and Jannetje Glen, y. d., both of this City.

June 3. **L.** William Rogers and Geertruy Reily, y. p., of A.

June 4. **L.** Jacob Harssens and Alida Groesbeek, y. p., of this City.

June 5. **B.** Duncan McGrigar and Rose Dlaan (or Dean), y. p., of this City.

June 9. **B.** Wendel Hillebrants and Geertruid Visbach, y. p., of this City.

June 10. Cert. by **B.** Crannel: Marten Everts and Cathar. Chester, both of this City.

June 11. **B.** William Wright and Sara Pladdo.

June 15. **B.** by D. V. Antwerpen "voorlezer" at Schaktkoo, Jonathan Marl, y. m., and Debora Van Deuzen, y. d., l. at Qenkhack.

June 15. **B.** Ma. by the same "voorlezer", Abraham Sherp, y. m., and Jacomyntje Van Deuzen, l. at Qenkhack.

June 20. **B.** Pieter Michelt and Marytje Bosch, y. p., of the Col.

1764

June 25. **L.** Christiaan Dovebach, y. m., and Cathalyna Deforeest, y. d., of this place.

June 26. **L.** Ryckert Van Vranken, widr., and Catharina Dunbar, y. d., l. in the Col.

July 8. **B.** Ma. at Schie. Jacob Heger and Cornelia Vroman, of Schie.

July 17. **L.** Gerrit Van Yveren and Catharina Bogart, y. p., of this City.

Aug. 5. **L.** Dirk Van Vechten and Cathalyna Van Esch, y. p., at Schag.

Aug. 21. **B.** Evert V. d. Bergh and Marytje Ouderkerk, y. p., at Saratoga.

Sep. 2. **B.** Zacharias Hendrik Haan and Annatje Hezy, at Niskatha.

Sep. 9. **L.** Johannes Ganzevoort and Evje Beekman, both of this City.

Oct. 7. **L.** of Sep. 19, Hendrik V. Renzelaar, and Alida Bratt, y. p., of the Colony.

Oct. 14. **L.** of Aug. 22. John J. Hanzen and Geertruid Slingerland, y. p., both of this City.

Oct. 24. **L.** Cornelis Glen, y. m., of the City and Elisabeth Nichols, y. d., of the Col.

Oct. 27. **L.** Rutgert Lansing, y. m., and Susanna V. Schoonhoven, y. d., of A. Co.

Nov. 2. **B.** Gerrit Brat and Lena Hoogteling, of Niskatha.

Nov. 2. **L.** Jacob Lansing and Willimpje Winne, y. p., of the Col.

Nov. 2. **L.** Nanning Vischer and Lena Lansing, both of A. Co.

Nov. 14. **B.** Hannes Ruiter and Elisabeth Pestr, both of Hosac.

Nov. 14. **B.** Hannes Hoghil and Elisabeth Leek, both of Hosac.

Nov. 16. **L.** Casparis Conyn, y. m., of C. and Tryntje Van Wie, y. d., of the Col.

Nov. 20. **B.** Barent Zepperlein and Margarita Wheger, y. p., of Hos.

Nov. 29. **L.** Arent Van Antwerp and Hester Krugier, y. p., of Nist.

Dec. 10. **B.** Daniel Van Olinda and Marytje Van der Werken, y. p., of H. M.

Dec. 17. **B.** Joan Georg Witrel and Maria Barbara Nicolaassen, y. p., of the Boght.

Dec. 24. **L.** Gozen Van Schaik and Catharina Bleecker, y. p., of this City.

Baptismal Record, 1763 and 1764.

1763. Jan. 2. Catharina Margarita of Jacob and Cathar. Cortel. Wit. Andries and Catharina Fyt.

Jan. 9. bo. Jan. 2. Cornelia of Albert V. d. Werken and Annatje V. d. Berg. Wit. Cornelis M. and Cornelia V. d. Berg.

bo. Dec. 19, 1762. Cathalyntje of Cornelis and Annatje Bulsing. Wit. Hendrik and Cathalyntje Bulsing.

(Jan. 16), bo. Nov. 14. Annatje of Abrahm Fryer and Jannatje Hetzil (Hetsel). Wit. Cornelis and Mally V. Aalstein.

bo. Dec. 8. Susanna of Jan and Evje (Eevje) Fonda. Wit. Cornelis M. and Cornelia V. d. Berg.

Jan. 25 (23), bo. Jan. 22. 1763. Maria of Willem and Marytje V. d. Berg. Wit. Gerrit and Aaltje V. d. Berg.

bo. Dec. 21, 1762. Sara of Philip and Lena Van Esch. Wit. Marten (Martin) and Sara Winne.

bo. Jan. 19, 1763. Gerlyn of Abraham Verplank and Marytje Bogaart (Bogert). Wit. Izak G. (Izak) and Arriaantje Verplank.

Jan. 30. bo. Dec. 30, 1762. Hendrik of Izak and Annatje Lansing. Wit. Hendrik Lansing, Catharina Ouderkerk.

Feb. 1 (2), bo. Dec. 30, 1762. Hendrik of Abraham and Catharina Kuiler (Abraham Kuiler and Catharina Wendel). Wit. Hendrik and Margarita Kuiler.

Feb. 6, 1763. bo. Dec. 30, 1762. Wynand of Willem and Annatje V. d. Bergh (Willem V. d. Berg and Annatje Vosburg). Wit. Wynand and Cathalyntje V. d. Berg.

Feb. 27. bo. Jan. 23, 1763. Christiaan of Albert and Magdalena Brat. Wit. David Brat, Tryntje Lang.

bo. Jan. 28. Cornelis of Gerrit Waldrom and Catharina V. d. Berg. Wit. Pieter and Geertje Waldrom.

bo. Feb. 18. Jacob of Izak Slingerland and Eva Van Woerd (Woert). Wit. Izak and Annatje Lansing.

bo. Jan. 23. Gerardus of Jacob Knoet and Maayke Lansing. Wit. Hannes and Elisabet Knoet.

bo. Feb. 22. Hester of Pieter De Garmoo and Sara Gardenier. Wit. Mattheus and Hester De Garmoo.

bo. Feb. 23. George Mathias (Mathys) of Matthyas (Mathias) and Anna Koeler. Wit. Jerk (Izak) and Elisabeth (Elisabet) Hildebrand.

bo. Jan. 11. Sara of Harmen and Rebecca Fort. Wit. Jacob J. (Jacob I. Van Woert) and Elisabeth V. Woert.

bo. Jan. 15. Arent of Johannes (Johannis) Olfer and Marytje Siksby. Wit. Izak (Hogingh) and Jannetje Hoging (Hoghing).

1763

bo. Feb. (Jan.) 23. Cornelis of John and Sara Ten Broek (John Ten Broek and Sara Ganzevoort). Wit. Cornelis (T. Broek) and Maria Ten Broek.

Mar. 6. bo. Jan. 30, 1763. Catharina of Nicolaas and Claartje Knoet. Wit. Jacob and Catharina Van (V.) Schaik.

bo. Feb. 14. David of Cornelius (Cornelis) Sprong and Margarita Haans (Margaret 'Jaans). Wit. Andries Witbeek, Alida Brat.

Mar. 13. bo. Mar. 10. Gerrit (and) Ytje of Gerrit Van Wie and Catharina Lansing. Wit. Isac (Izak) Lansing, Annatje Van (V.) Woerd, Jacob Lansing, Lena Van (V.) Arnhem.

Mar. 20. Christina of Johannes Everson and Susanna Lagranse (Le Gransy). Wit. Simon J. and Cathalyntje Veder.

bo. Mar. 14 (19). Hannes Wyngaart (Wyngaard) of William Fool (Tool) and Margarita Wyngaert (Wyngaard). Wit. Hannes and Margarita Wyngaert.

bo. Mar. 19. Hendrik of Jacob G. V. Schaik and Geertje Ridder. Wit. Evert De Ridder, Geertje Waldrom.

Mar. 30. bo. Mar. 1. Christiaan of Hannes and Christina Lang. Wit. Pieter and Engeltje Zeger.

Apr. 3. Agnita of Daniel Winne and Catharina Hoogteeling (Hoogteling). Wit. Gerrit Winne, Lena V. Arnhem.

bo. Mar. 29. Willem of Nicolaas and Marytje Brouwer. Wit. Hannes V. Santen, Antje Hilton (Hilten).

Apr. 17. bo. Apr. 16. Harmanus, of Hendrik Wendel and Maria Lansing. Wit. Abraam (Abhm.) Kuiler, Jr., Barbara Wendel.

Apr. 24. bo. Apr. 21. Maria of Gozen V. (Van) Schaik and Maayke V. d. Berg. Wit. Nicolaas V. d. Berg, Sara V. Schaik.

bo. Apr. 17. Maria of Casparus Pruin and Catharina Groesbeek. Wit. David and Cathalyntje Groesbeek.

May 2 (1). bo. Apr. 30. Philippus (Filippus) of Cornelis W. (Cornelis) V. d. Berg and Maria Vile. Wit. Gerrit (Viele) and Catharina Vile.

bo. Apr. 29. Arriaantje of Jacob De Garmo and Fytje Bekker. Wit. Dirk Bekker, Eva Hoghink (Hoghing).

bo. Apr. 10. Hester, of Hans V. Aarnhem (Arnhem) and Alida V. d. Heide. Wit. Jacob and Maria V. d. Heide.

May 8. Two Months old. Pieter of Izak V. Oostrander and Elisabeth McKans. Wit. Cobus Van Etten, Hanna Gengbort (Pengbort).

bo. Apr. 10. Andries of Adriaan Brat and Marytje

1763

McKans. Wit. Abraham (Abrhm.) and Antje Yets (Yaets).

bo. Apr. 7. Philip of Hendrik V. (Van) Wie and Marytje Louk (Maria Loek). Wit. Coenraat (Coenraad) Loek, Geertruid V. Deusen.

Five Weeks old. Abraham of Hendrik and Eva Katsenbach (Katzenbach). Wit. Hanes (Hannes) and Elisabeth Oothout.

May 15. Six Weeks old. Zacharias of Johannes H. Smit (Smith) and Margarita Weitman. Wit. Zacharias Smit (Smith), Anna Maria (Anna M.) Pender.

bo. Mar. 18. Maria of Melchert and Elisabeth Veil. Wit. Lodewyk and Maria B. Snyer.

Seven Weeks old. Nicolaas of Cobus Olfer and Annatje Siksby. Wit. Nicolaas and Marytje Siksby.

May 22. Four weeks old. Jonathan of Frans and Marytje Winne. Wit. Coenraad and Cornelia Hoogteling.

bo. May 14. Hannes of Yzak (Izak) and Cath. Vosburg. Wit. Hannes and Arriaantje Staats.

bo. May 17. Geertruid of Pieter and Geertruid de Garmo (Pieter De Garmo and Geertruid Garmo). Wit. Bastiaan Cruger, Anna Crugier (Bastiaan and Anna Crugier).

Six Weeks old. Johannes of Pieter Claas and Clara Marg. Clasen (Pieter and Clara M. Claassen). Wit. Jacob Mook, Cathar. Morney (Horney).

June 4. Martinus of Hendrik Loek and Neeltje Scherp (Sjerp). Wit. Jelles and Tytje Winne.

June 5. Four weeks old. Yzaac (Izaac) of Yzac (Izak) de Foe (de Voe) and Maria V. d. Linde. Wit. Cornelis V. d. Berg, Claartje Knoet.

bo. May 26. Geertruit (Geertruid) of Peter (Pieter) Veder and Marytje V. d. Berg. Wit. Simon and Annatje Veder.

Five weeks old. Willem of Rykert Redly (Redlif) and Marytje Olfert. Wit. Pieter and Cathalyntje Redly (Redlif).

bo. May 18 (28). Cornelia of Willem Hun and Sara de Foreest. Wit. Yzak (Izaac) Fonda, Neeltje de Foreest.

June 12. bo. May 13. Neeltje of Adam Been and Catharina Freer. Wit. Adam Zouthart (?) (Zoufhart), Neeltje Freer.

bo. May 7. Johannetje of Pieter de (De) Wandelaar and Annatje Bogardus. Wit. Harmen Knikkerbacker, Femmetje Switz (Zwitz).

June 14. bo. Mar. 22. Johan Nicolaas of Johannes Eger and Catharina Young. Wit. Abm. Schuiler, Evje Beekman.

1763

June 19. bo. May 22. Jacob of Abraham Fort and Eva Bennewee (Bennewe). Wit. Jacob J. (I.) and Elisabeth Van Woert (V. Woert).

bo. May 27. Pieter of Wouter Groesbeek and Alida Kwakkenbusch. Wit. Pieter and Sara Kwakkenbusch (Kwakkenbus).

bo. the Monday after Pentecost. Jacob of Jurjen (S.) Scherp ('Serp), Jr., and Catharina Fleegring (Fleegering). Wit. Jurjen and Barbara Scherp ('Sjerp).

bo. June 9. Quiliaan of Quiliaan V. Renselaar (Renzelaar) and Arriaantje Schuiler. Wit. Folkert P. Douw, Geertuid V. Renselaar (Renzelaar).

Nine Weeks old. Maria of Joseph and Susanna Robbinson. Wit. Matthias (Mathys) and Anna Koehler (Koeler).

bo. June 13. Lyndje of Folkert Douw and Marytje Kadwees (Katwas). Wit. Abraham and Margarita Douw.

June 26. Four weeks old. Johannes of Matheus Flensburg and Christina Schever (Schneider). Wit. Johs Flensburg, Rachel V. Santen.

bo. June 23. Sara of Gerrit Lansing and Jannetje Waters. Wit. Robert S. (I) Yetz (Yats), Tryntje Waters.

bo. June 3. Dirk of Dirk V. d. Heide and Sara Wendel. Wit. John and Rachel V. d. Heide.

Four weeks old. Jacobus of Hans and Cathar. Redif. Wit. Jacobus and Catharina Redlif.

July 3. Four Weeks old. Cornelis (Cornelius) of Barent Hogh and Geertje Huik. Wit. Hannes and Elisabeth Groesbeek.

bo. June 13. Pieter of Johs Fonda and Dirkje Winne. Wit. John and Egje Fonda.

Four Weeks old. Catharina of Samuel Hehner and Rebecca Feller. Wit. Freder. and Elisabet Schefer.

William of Thomas and Christ Edwrson (Edwison). Wit. Berning Winterseer (Wintersen), Jenny (Jennit) Lottersing.

July 11. bo. July 5. Anna Dorothea of Johs. Jurjen Kenner and Susanna Mc Kenny (Mc.Kenry). Wit. Coenraad Rouby (Roby), Sara Roby (Robby).

Aug. 1. bo. July 30. Geertruid of Jacob Roseboom and Hester Lansing. Wit. Jacob and Machtelt Roseboom.

bo. July 2. Jacob of Johan Thyes Pork and Catharina (Cathar.) Keveling. Wit. Jacob V. d. Heide, Elisabeth Winne.

bo. Yesterday (July 31). Johannes of Hermanus. Schuiler (Schuler) and Christina Ten (T.) Broek. Wit. Jochum Staats, Elisab Bogart (Ridgart).

1763

Aug. 11, bo. Aug. 7. Maria, of Cornelis Zwitz and Catharina Schuiler. Wit.: Izaac and Maria Zwitz.

bo. Aug. 9. Thomas, of Willem V. Santen and Alida Smit. Wit.: Gerrit Jr. and Hester V. Santen.

Aug. 14, bo. July 10. Frina, of Jacob Mook and Cathar. Claassen. Wit.: Pieter and Annatje Hoogteling.

bo. July 30. Balthasar, of Jacob Heller and Elisabeth Hellering. Wit.: Balthas Brat, Maria Hoghing.

Aug. 21, bo. Aug. 19. Elisabeth, of Cornelis V. Vechten and Annatje Knikkerbakker. Wit.: Wouter and Elisabeth Knikkerbakker.

Aug. 28, bo. Aug. 21. Filip, of Steven Schuyler and Engletje V. Vechten. Wit.: Filip and Margarita Schuiler.

bo. July 31. Abraham, of Michael Landman and Marytje Brouwer. Wit.: Gerrit Lansing, Jannetje Waters.

Sep. 4, bo. Aug. 3. Joannes, of Jonathan Hoogteling and Jannetje Slingerland. Wit.: Jan Brat, Maria Ter Willigen.

bo. June 10. Arriaantje, of Gerrit Kwakkenbusch and Cathar. de Voe. Wit.: Leendert Muller, Gerritje Ridder.

Sep. 11, bo. Aug. 15. Cornelia, of Gerrit Fort and Catharina V. Aalstein. Wit.: Cornelis and Cornelia V. Yveren.

Sep. 18, bo. Sep. 15. Annatje, of Thomas Hun and Elisabeth Wendel. Wit.: Johannes Hun, Elsje Lansing.

bo. Aug. 16. Pieter, of Pieter, Goey and Maria Young. Wit.: Theunis and Elisabeth V. Woert.

bo. Sep. 13. Elisabeth, of Folkert V. d. Berg and Neeltje Waldrom. Wit.: Will. Patr. Clerq, Cornelia Clerq.

Sep. 25, bo. Sep. 22. Catharina, of Hermanus Wendel and Barbara Brat. Wit.: Abraham Kuiler, Catharina Wendel.

bo. Sep. 23. Thomas, of Johs. Van Santen, Jr., and Margarita Wilkeson. Wit.: Thomas and Elisabeth Wilkeson.

bo. Sep. 6. Aaltje, of Pieter Levison and Maria Fonda. Wit.: Abraham Fonda, Marytje Ouderkerk.

bo. Sep. 21. Neeltje, of John Visscher and Elisabeth Brat. Wit.: Nanning Visscher, Alida Roerbach.

Sep. 29, ba. at Schahtko, bo. July 27. Jacob of John Davenpoot and Hendrikje Bennewie. Wit.: Petrus and Marytje Bennewie.

Sep. 29, at Schahtko. Sybrand, of Harmen and Judith Kwakkenbusch. Wit.: Sybrand Kwakkenbusch, Annatje Vile.

Oct. 2. Three weeks old. Margarita, of Johs. and Margr. Steel. Wit.: Hannes and Mary Bekker.

1763

Six weeks old. Hendrik, of Hannes and Santje Landman.
Wit.: Hansje and Elisabeth Brat.

bo. Sep. 28. William, of Frans Hoghil and Sara Young.
Wit.: Jacob V. Woert, Elisabet Fort.

bo. Sep. 26. Hendrik, of Hendrik Bleeker, Jr., and
Cathalina Kuiler. Wit.: Abraham and Catharina Kuiler.

bo. Sep. 28. Hendrik, of Abraham J. (or S.) Yaets and
Jannetje Brat. Wit.: Josef and Jurkje Yaets.

Oct. 6, bo. July 1. Elisabeth, of Nicolaas Eger, Jr., and
Geertruid Young. Wit.: Hendrik and Elisabeth Tyts.

Oct. 7, bo. Oct. 6. Lena, of Johannes S. Lansing and
Catharyntje Burhans. Wit.: Robert Lansing, Marytje
Wendel.

bo. Oct. 4. Joannes, of John R. Bleeker and Elisabeth
Staats. Wit.: Gerrit and Debora Staats.

bo. Oct. 7. Joannes, of Hendrik V. Arnhem and Susanna
Winne. Wit.: Yzak V. Arnem, Willemtje Winne.

bo. Sep. 28. Maria, of Jacobus Scherp and Annatje
V. Ginnis. Wit.: Thomas and Arriaantje Scherp.

bo. Oct. 4. Symon, of Wouter De Ridder and Anneke
V. de Berg. Wit.: Symon and Hilletje De Ridder.

Oct. 8. John Braadstreet, of Philip Schuyler and
Cathar. B. Renzelaar. Wit.: John Braadstreet, Judith
V. Renzelaar.

Oct. 9, bo. Sep. 27. Willem, of John Northen and
Elisabet de Voe. Wit.: Willem Northen, Mally
Beel.

bo. Oct. 7. Susanna, of Pieter Waldrom and Neeltje
Lansing. Wit.: William Hoghing, Susanna Lansing.

Three Weeks old. Alexander, of Hannes Oothout and
Elisabeth V. Woert. Wit.: Arent and Antje Bekker.

Oct. 16, bo. Oct. 15. Jenneke, of John Bleeker and
Antje V. Schaik. Wit.: Jacob and Geertje Bleeker.

bo. Oct. 12. Dirkje, of Barent Vosburg and Annatje
Gerritsen. Wit.: Hendrik and Dirkje Gerritse.

Thomas, of Thalm and Rachel Willes. Wit.: Thomas
and Rachel Willes.

Oct. 23, bo. Oct. 17. Johannes, of Folkert V. Vegten
Jannetje Hun. Wit.: Efraim and Neeltje V. Vechten.

Oct. , bo. Oct. . Johannes, of Jan Duret and Sara
Rivison. Wit.: Joannes Marselis, Christina Slingerland.

bo. Oct. 19. Abraham, of Jacobus Kool and Jannetje
Witbeek. Wit.: Abraham Witbeek, Geertruy Van
Buren.

bo. Oct. 2. Maria, of Albert Slingerland and Elisabeth
Mook. Wit.: Cobus Arnold, Annatje Slingerland.

bo. Oct. 27. Cornelia, of Eduard Davis and Jannetje
Duret. Wit.: John and Lena Davids.

bo. Oct. 7. Joannes of Frederik Olfer and Cathar. V. d. Berg. Wit. John and Marytje Olfer.

Nov. 13. bo. Nov. (sic.) 13. Hendrik of Johs. Redlif and Margarita Passage. Wit. Hendrik Passage, Elisabeth Redlif.

bo. Oct. 14. Abraham of Harpert Lansing and Marytje Visscher. Wit. Evert V. d. Berg, Annatje Lansing.

bo. Nov. 6. Cathalina of Christoffer Yaetz and Catharina Lansing. Wit. Johs. and Rebecca Yeatz.

bo. Nov. 8. Filip of Philip Young and Annatje Sickens. Wit. Lambert Sikkens, Eva Young.

bo. Oct. 4. Jacob of Hendrik Alberagt and Elisabeth Folland. Wit. Maas and Lena Bloemendal.

bo. Nov. 12. Hendrikje of Jelles Winne and Titje Van Woert. Wit. Jacob and Lybetje V. Woert.

Nov. 20. bo. Nov. 18. Johanna of Hendrik J. Bogaart and Barbara Merselis. Wit. Johannes M. and Eva Rozeboom.

bo. Nov. 18. Johannes of Coenraad and Sara Roube. Wit. Johs. and Christina Rof.

Nov. 27. bo. Oct. 4. Frany of Philip Coenraads and Frany Clomb. Wit. Joost Hervy, Elisabeth Clomb.

bo. Oct. 22. Anthony of Jacob Van Schaik and Catharina Kuiler. Wit. Wessel and Maria V. Schaik.

bo. Oct. 26. Debora of Johannes J. Beekman and Maria Sanders. Wit. John and Debora Sanders.

Dec. 11. bo. Dec. 8. Gerrit of Gysbert Merselis and Annatje Staats. Wit. Gerrit and Margarita Merselis.

bo. Dec. 1. Maria of John V. Aalstein and Lena Scherp. Wit. Wynand and Marytje V. Aalstein.

bo. Dec. 17. (sic.) Maria of Jacob Bogaart and Marytje Yets. Wit. Jacob and Hubertje Lansing.

bo. Dec. 25. Annatje of Gerrit Visscher and Alida Fonda. Wit. Hendrik Fonda, Cathar. Groesbeck.

bo. Dec. 5. Annatje of Andries Peessing and Jannetje Brat. Wit. Sefring Peessing, Lena Hoogteling.

bo. Dec. 29. (sic.) Elisabeth of Johannes Redlif and Elisabeth Wilkeson. Wit. Thomas and Elisabeth Wilkeson.

Dec. 10. bo. Nov. 23. Nicolaas of Thyas Boom and Josyntje Zeger. Wit. Johs. and Sara Zeger.

1764. Jan. 2. bo. Oct. 22, 1763. Annatje of Henry Young and Maria Ledger. Wit. Abraham Fonda, Marytje Ouderkerk.

Jan. 8. bo. Dec. 6, 1763. Annatje of Abraham Boom and Dorothea Cunnigans. Wit. Mathys and Lena Boom.

bo. Jan. 4. Catharina of Cornelis Cuiler, Jr., and Annatje Wendel. Wit. Johannes Cuiler, Elsje Ten Eik.

1764

bo. Jan. 1. Jacobus of Balthes V. Benthuisen and Sara Vile. Wit. Jacobus Perker V. Benthuisen, Sara Couper.

bo. Jan. 4. Johannes of Steven Schuiler and Lena Ten Eik. Wit. Filip Schuiler, Geertruid Cachron.

Jan. 15. bo. Jan. 11. Abraham of Johannes Knoet, Jr., and Sara V. Aarnhem. Wit. Abraham and Helena V. Aarnhem.

Jan. 22. bo. Dec. 19, 1763. Elisabeth of Hendrik H. Van Wie and Johanna Gardenier. Wit. Jacob C. Ten Eik, Jenneke Clement.

bo. Jan. 21, 1764. Maria of Johs. Vile and Geesje Slingerland. Wit. Theunis and Catharina Vile.

Feb. 4. bo. Oct. 31, 1763. Catharina of Matthias Bovie and Maria Wendel. Wit. John Mc Linnen, Marytje Janssen.

bo. Jan. 8, 1764. Annatje of Adam Zonfeld and Neeltje Freer. Wit. David and Annatje Ben.

bo. Jan... Geertuid of Andries H. Gardenier and Sara Hanssen. Wit. Johs. Ph. and Cathar. Hanssen.

bo. Jan. 9. Lydia of Gerrit Zeger and Wyntje Olfer. Wit. Hannes and Christina Lang.

bo. Feb. 1. Maria of Hannes Spoor and Lena Bogaart. Wit. Gerrit Ten Baar, Maria Spoor.

Feb. 4. bo. Jan. 12. Lavinus of Pieter Winne and Susanna V. d. Berg. Wit. Robert Winne, Hillegonda V. Franken.

bo. Jan. 3. Margarita of Gerrit Ten Baar and Cathalyntje Brat. Wit. Johs. and Margarita Brat.

bo. Dec. 23. (1763) Elisabeth of Hendrik Meyer and Maria Morris. Wit. Adam and Magdalena Remsy.

bo. Jan. 18, 1764. Cathalina of Rutgert and Maria V. d. Berg. Wit. Gerrit, Jr., and Wyntje Lansing.

Feb. 11. bo. Jan. 20. Folkje of Hannes Ostrander and Marytje V. Aalstein. Wit. Corn. and Cathal. V. Aalstein.

bo. Feb. 6. Johannes of Abrm. Meinerssen and Cath. Lansing. Wit. Thomas and Maria Lansing.

Four Months old. Sara of William Connely and Elisabeth Kelly. Wit. Gerrit and Abra. V. d. Berg.

Feb. 20. bo. Feb. 13. Johannes of Benjamin Goey and Catharina V. d. Berg. Wit. Hendrik and Marytje Gardenier.

Feb. 26. bo. Feb. 22. Jacob of Albert Bloemendal and Anna Harssens. Wit. Maas and Helena Bloemendal.

Four Weeks old. Geertje of Harmen Levison and Catharina V. d. Berg. Wit. Wilhelm and Agnietje V. d. Berg.

1764

bo. Feb. 20. Evert of Gysbert Merselis and Cathalyntje Wendel. Wit. Abraham N. and Annatje Wendel.

bo. Jan. 14. Gerrit of Arent Bekker and Antje V. Woert. Wit. Dirk Bekker, Eva Hoghink.

Feb. 29. bo. this day. Hadriaan Hoogeland of Thomas Zeger and Judith Hogeland. Wit. Roelef Zeger and wife Lydia Hartje.

Mar. 4. Elsje of Nicolaas Rechter and Maria Hoenemond. Wit. Hans Hillebrand, Elsje Rechter.

Mar. 11. bo. Feb. 12. Sara of Arent Bekker and Margar. Balsing. Wit. Wouter Bekker, Annatje Ridder.

bo. Mar. 4. Wynant of Wynant W. V. d. Berg and Maria De Ridder. Wit. Cornelis W. V. d. Berg, Maria Vile.

Mar. 18. bo. Mar. 3. Coenraad of Jacob Herman and Barbara Vos. Wit. Coenraad Herman, Elisabeth Zegert.

bo. Mar. 13. Josef of Abram Peek and Catharina V. Santen. Wit. Yzak Hoogkerk, Rachel V. Santen.

Mar. 25. bo. Feb. 18. Maria of Willem Northen and Mally Belly. Wit. Pieter Brat, Engeltje Waldrom.

bo. Mar. 10. Pieter of John David and Elisabeth Wyngaard. Wit. Petrus Hilton, Nensy Broeks.

Apr. 8. bo. Apr. 3. Hendrik of Frans Cruel and Annatje Baltz. Wit. Hendrik V. Dyk, Margarita Douw.

bo. Apr. 4. Egbert of Stefanus V. Schaak and Jannetje Brat. Wit. Egbert Brat, Elisabeth Lansing.

bo. Mar. 17. Wynand of Cornelis M. and Cornelia V. d. Berg. Wit. Wynand W. and Marytje V. d. Berg.

Apr. 11. bo. Mar. 14. Cornelis of Wilhelmus V. Deuzen and Christina Kittel. Wit. Cornelis V. Deuzen, Lea Van Deuzen.

bo. Apr. 7. Pieter of Maas Bloemendal and Catharina Steenberg. Wit. Pieter Brat, Catharina Viele.

Apr. 15. Almost three months old. Petrus of Gerrit Boevie and Arriaantje Brouwer. Wit. Petrus Marten, Neeltje Foreest.

bo. Mar. 12. Daniel of Daniel and Willempje Brat. Wit. Hannes and Elisabeth Brat.

Apr. 20. bo. Apr. 18. Maria of Pieter Yatz and Sara V. Aalstein. Wit. Hannes S. and Jannetje Pruin.

Apr. 22. bo. Mar. 25. Abraham of Pieter Van Buren and Maria V. d. Poel. Wit. Benjamin and Annatje V. d. Berg.

bo. Mar. 23. Rachel of Marten Foreest and Tanneke Winne. Wit. John and Marytje V. Deuzen.

Apr. 29. bo. Mar. 15. Sara of Simon de Foreest and Mally Mc Ginnis. Wit. William and Sara Mc Ginnis.

May 6. bo. Apr. 12. Geertruid of Hendrik Ruiter and Rebecca Dorth. Wit. Hannes Ruiter, Arriaantje Dorth.

1764

bo. Apr. 10. Annatje of Jacob Lansing and Marytje Ouderkerk. Wit. Jacob Knoet, Maayke Lansing.

bo. Mar. 28. Pieter of Johannes Fonda and Elisabeth Ouderkerk. Wit. Johs. P. Fonda, Dirkje Winne.

Elisabeth of Johannes Coen and Hilletje Zeger. Wit. Andries Fright, Elisabeth Dithmaal.

bo. Six Weeks ago. Lydia of Hannes Zeger and Marytje Brat. Wit. Gerrit and Marytje Brat.

bo. Mar. 3. Anthony of Jurjen de Voe and Anna Kelder. Wit. Anthony and Christina V. Schaik.

May 13. bo. Apr. 18. Laurens of Andries Wederwaks and Catharina Reisdorf. Wit. Laurens and Margarita Reisdorf.

bo. Apr. 21. Johannes of Albert V. d. Werken and Marytje Kwakkenbusch. Wit. Izak and Annatje Lansing.

bo. May 13. Adam of Jan G. Yats and Cathalyntje Goey. Wit. Christoffer Yaetz, Hubertje Lansing.

Anna Maria of Stefanis Koolhamer and Anna B. Freelich. Wit. Marten Freelich, Anna Maria.

bo. Apr. 22. Christoffer of Martin Freelich and Anna Maria Hagedoorn. Wit. Christofer and Anna Barbara Cremer.

Jacob of David and Anna Mary Any. Wit. Jacob and Maria Vretz, David Rouetz, Maria Roetze.

bo. Apr. 15. Huibertje of Willem Winne, Jr., and Hubertje Yaetz. Wit. Lucas and Judike Yaetz.

bo. Mar. 9. Annatje of Petrus V. Woert and Rachel Ridder. Wit. John and Antje Vroman.

bo. Mar. 24. Gerrit of Johannes Winne and Santje Ridder. Wit. Cornelis and Catharina V. d. Berg.

June 3. bo. May 7. Catharina of Melchert Fyl and Elisabeth Rickart. Wit. Johs. V. Arnhem, Alida V. d. Heide.

bo. May 1. Sara of David Ben and Annatje Garner. Wit. Staats and Willempje Santvoort.

bo. May 3. Bata of Jacob Kwakkenbusch and Catharina Huik. Wit. Frerik Knoet, Machtel Kwakkenbusch.

July 1. bo. the 27th. (sic.) Johan Pieter of Hannes Harh and Catharina Poossing. Wit. John and Christina Raf.

bo. Apr. 20. Benjamin of John Walker and Jannetje Born. Wit. Daniel and Elisabeth Van Olinda.

bo. May 29. Arriaantje of Pieter Hoogteling and Annatje Bekker. Wit. Arent and Antje Bekker.

bo. June 10. Dirk of Jacob Foreest and Catharyntje Brat. Wit. Pieter Brat, Engeltje Waldrom.

July 15. bo. June 12. Hubert of Abraham and Elisabeth Ostrander. Wit. Hubert and Sara Ostrander.

bo. July 4. Rachel of Thomas Hun and Baatje V. Deuzen. Wit. Willem Hun, Saratje de Foreest.

1764

July 29 bo. July 24. Maria of Petrus Hilton and Annatje Broeks. Wit. Willem and Elisabeth Hilton.

July 31. bo. July 27. Hendrik of Gerrit Staats and Debora Beekman. Wit. John R. Bleecker, Maria Beekman.

Aug. 5. bo. Three Weeks ago. Dirk of Michael Fry and Engeltje V. d. Kar. Wit. Dirk and Magdalena V. d. Kar.

bo. July 21. Elisabeth of Francis Nichols and Margarita V. Renzelaar. Wit. Renzelaar and Elisabeth Nichols.

bo. June 23. Willem of Johannes and Marytje Groesbeek. Wit. Gerrit and Marytje Groesbeek.

bo. July 15. Margarita of Jurgen Steen and Lena V. Troef. Wit. Hendr. and Margarita Zeger.

bo. July 28. Annatje of Evert and Annatje V. d. Berg. Wit. Cornelis and Marytje V. d. Berg.

bo. June 21. or 4. Wouter of Johan Fonda and Egje V. d. Zee. Wit. Cornelis V. d. Zee, Catharina Waters.

Aug. 12 bo. Aug. 8. Rachel of Gysbert V. Santen and Rebecca Winne. Wit. Benjamin and Rachel Winne.

bo. July 20. Bata of Hannes Heemstraat, Jr., and Elisabeth Bovie. Wit. Jacob Heemstraat, Jr., Catharina Duret.

Aug. 19. bo. July 22. Annatje of Jacob Pest and Annatje Jaart. Wit. Izaac and Catharina Vosburg.

bo. Aug. 13. Johannes of Isaac Roza and Marytje V. Franken. Wit. Geurt Roza, Catharina V. Franken.

bo. June 26. Annatje of Robert Winne and Hillegonda V. Franken. Wit. Rykert V. Franken, Annatje V. Arnhem.

bo. Aug. 19. Abraham of Pieter Winne Douw and Rykje Van Schaik. Wit. Abraham and Catharina Douw.

bo. Aug. 5. Joannes of Anthony Briesch and Catharyntje Yaets. Wit. Christoffer Yaets, Catharina Lansing.

Aug. 26 bo. Aug. 22. Folkert of Harmen V. Houzen and Catharyntje Witbeek. Wit. Meinard and Alida V. Houzen.

bo. Aug. 22. Christoffer of Jacobus Abeel and Egbertje V. Buuren. Wit. Egbert Willet, Catharyntje Abeel.

bo. Aug. 25. Yzaac of Jacob Lansing and Jannetje Fisscher. Wit. Theunis and Machtelt Visscher.

Aug. 29 bo. Aug. 28. Elsje of Pieter Ganzevoord and Gerritje Ten Eick. Wit. John and Sara Ten Broek.

Sep. 5. bo. Sept. 1. Meinart of Gerrit V. Yveren and Catharyntje Bogert. Wit. Reinier and Arriaantje Van Yveren.

bo. Sep. 3. Fieter of Wouter Kwakkenbusch and Bata Knoet. Wit. Pieter and Margarita Kwakkenbusch.

1764

Sep. 9. bo. Aug. 22. Adam of Hannes and Christina Lang. Wit. Adam and Marytje Brat.

bo. Aug. 12. Johannes of William Pengburn and Elisabeth Bogert. Wit. John and Marytje Brat.

bo. July 22. Jacob of Harmen Fort and Rebecca V. Woert. Wit. Yzaac and Annatje Lansing.

bo. July 24. Jacob of Wouter N. Groesbeek and Alida Kwakkenbusch. Wit. Pieter Groesbeek, Cathalyntje Yaetz.

Sep. 15. by Do. Vroman. Margarita, of Roelef M. V. d. Werken and Cornelia V. Aalstein. Wit. Evert and Maria V. d. Berg.

Sep. 16. Johannes of Christiaan Duivebach and Cathalyna De Foreest. Wit. Archelaus Lynd, Catharina Duivebach.

Sep. 23. bo. Sep. 1. Elisabeth of John V. d. Werken and Dirkje V. Aalstein. Wit. Yzaac Fryhout, Elisabeth Ruyter.

bo. Aug. 6. Casparus of Hannes I. Witbeek and Engeltje Vroman. Wit. Theunis and Agnietje Slingerland.

Sep. 29. bo. Sep. 4. Elisabeth of Charles McKay and Maayke Ouderkerk. Wit. Hendrik V. d. Kar, Elisabeth V. Woert.

bo. Sep. 13. Frederik of Abraham Freest and Jannetje Hetcher. Wit. Frederik Berringer, Margarita Zufeld.

bo. Sep. 15. Arriaantje of Salomon Bulsing and Geertruid Knoet. Wit. Pieter and Arriaantje Knoet.

bo. Aug. 22. Johannes of John and Margar. Bell. Wit. Johannes and Klaartje Kloet.

bo. Aug. 26. Hugo of Frans Winne and Anneke Viele. Wit. Louis and Maria Vile.

Oct. 7. bo. Sep. 6. Johannes of Hendrik V. d. Werken and Maria Vile. Wit. Roelef V. d. Werken, Geertruid Fonda.

bo. Sep. 15. Lea of Abraham Couper and Catharina V. Oostrander. Wit. Jonathan and Gerritje Witbeek.

bo. Oct. 1. Franciscus of Johannes S. Pruin and Jannetje V. Aalstein. Wit. Samuel and Neeltje Pruin.

bo. Oct. 5. Willem of Folkert V. d. Berg and Neeltje Waldrom. Wit. Willem and Elisabeth Waldrom.

Oct. 14. bo. Sep. 28. Storm of Gerrit Slingerland and Egje V. d. Zee. Wit. Jacob Loek, Rachel Slingerland.

bo. Sep. 6. Elisabeth of Arent Slingerland and Jacomyntje V. d. Volgen. Wit. Dirk and Sara V. d. Wilgen.

bo. Oct. 9. Jacob of Johs. Fryer and Elisabeth V. Woert. Wit. Jacob V. Woert, Susanna Ouderkerk.

bo. Oct. 6. Sara of Cornelis Bulzing and Annatje Konzaal. Wit. Hans and Sara Konzales.

1764

bo. Oct. 10. Agnietje of Philip Muller and Geertruy Goey. Wit. Jan. G. and Cathalyntje Yaets.

bo. Oct. 9. Nicolaas of Gysbert Fonda and Elsje Douw. Wit. Pieter Williams, Elisabeth Fonda.

Oct. 21. bo. Oct. 19. Johan, Wendel, twins of Mathys and Anna Koegler. Wit. Johs., Elisab., Wendel and Geertruid Hillebrand.

bo. Sep. 25. Margarita of Frederik and Maria Zoup. Wit. Nicolaas and Margarita Folder.

Oct. 28. bo. Oct. 22. Margarita of Johs. V. Valkenburg and Elisabet Meinerssen. Wit. Jacobus and Margarita V. Valkenburg.

Nov. bo. Oct. 16. Christina of Christiaan and Elisabeth Bender. Wit. Willem and Christina Zobel.

bo. Oct. 12. Annatje of Gerrit Waldrom and Catharina V. d. Berg. Wit. Corn. V. d. Berg, Marytje Viele.

bo. this day. Johannes of Hendrik Lansing and Maria Marselis. Wit. Gysbert and Cathal. Merselis.

bo. Oct. 24. Evert of Christoffer Yaets and Catharina Lansing. Wit. Evert and Annatje Lansing.

Nov. 11. bo. Nov. 3. Maria of Michael and Margarita Warner. Wit. Coenraad and Maria Seraay.

bo. Nov. 10. Theunis of Yzaac Slingerland and Eva V. Woert. Wit. Albert and Christina Slingerland.

bo. Oct. 19. Joan of Tobias V. Salsbergen and Margarita Bont. Wit. Wilhelmus and Agnietje V. d. Berg.

Nov. 18. bo. Nov. 14. Antje of Herculeus Lynd and Marytje Duivebach. Wit. Jan Ouderkerk, Cathal. Foreest.

bo. Nov. 14. Rebecca of Pieter Bogert, Jr., and Barbara V. Franken. Wit. Wouter Groesbeek, Jannetje Bogert.

Nov. 25. bo. Nov. 3. Johannes of Abraham V. d. Kar and Marg. Devoe. Wit. Hendrik and Jannetje V. d. Kar.

Dec. 2. bo. Oct. 16. Nicolaas of Jacob Smith and Barbara Craften. Wit. Nicolaas and Anna M. Veller.

bo. the 28th (sic) Hendrikus of John Visscher and Elisabeth Brat. Wit. Hendrik V. Renzelaar, Rebecca Bratt.

Dec. 9. bo. Nov. 17. Robert of John Crennel and Folkje V. Aalstein. Wit. Pieter and Catharina Crennel.

Dec. 16. bo. Oct. 1. Abraham of Coenraad Frydag and Christina Debt. Wit. Abraham and Engeltje Wendel.

bo. Dec. 11. Willem of Yzaac Fryer and Elisabeth Hilton. Wit. Willem and Margar. Hilton.

Dec. 23. bo. Nov. 15. Elisabeth of Hermanus V. Aalstein and Catharina Petinger. Wit. Storm Bratt, Margar. Pettinger.

Dec. 23. bo. Dec. 18. Maria of Abraham Schuyler and Eva Beekman. Wit. David and Maria Schuyler.

1764

bo. Nov. 28. Maria of Frederik Raaf and Elisabeth Daalhamer. Wit. Johs. and Maria Raaf.

bo. Nov. 13. Coenraad of Daniel Winne and Catharina Hoogteling. Wit. Coenraad Hoogteling, Cornelia Bratt.

bo. Nov. 25. Charlotte of Dirk and Fytje V. d. Kar. Wit. Dirk and Geertruid V. d. Kar.

Geertruid of Hannes V. d. Werken and Marytje de Voe. Wit. Roelef and Geertruid V. d. Werken.

bo. Dec. 26. (sic) Elisabeth of Frans Hoghil and Sara Young. Wit. Theunis and Elisabeth V. Woert.

bo. Dec. 8. Annatje of Jacob V. Arnem and Annatje V. Franken. Wit. Maas and Catharyntje V. Franken.

bo. Dec. 29. (sic) Annatje of Wendel and Geertruid Hillebrands. Wit. Mathys Koegher, Anna Koegler.

❦ ❦ ❦

The title-page of old Volume III. of the Albany Church Records is as follows (translated):

Baptismal, Marriage, Membership and Consistory Book

of the

Reformed Nether-Dutch Congregation

at

New-Albany

Commencing from October XIX of this year MDCCLX or 1760 with the first ministration of

D⁰· EILARDUS WESTERLO. (*See ante, p. 71*)

LIST OF ABBREVIATIONS.

A. Albany.
A. City Albany City.
A. Co. Albany County.
b. B. born or banns.
bapt. baptized.
C. Claverack.
Can. Canistagioene.
cert. certificate.
ch. chn. child children.
Col. R. Colony Rensselaerswyck.
dau. daughter.
decd. deceased.
Do. Domine (Reverend).
H. M. Half Moon.
h. house.
Ire. Ireland.
K. Kinderhook.
King., Kingston.
L. License.
l. living.
Ma. m. Married.
N. Y. New York.
Pros. proselyte proselytes.
R. Rensselaerswyck.
R. D. Reformed Dutch.
Reg. Registered.
Sch. Schenectady.
Scha. Schag. Schaghticoke.
Wid. widr. widow widower.
Wit. Witness witnesses.
y. d. unmarried woman.
y. m. unmarried man.
"Jacob, of Lucas Hoogkerk " means Jacob, *child* of Lucas Hoogkerk.

INDEX

In these records will be found many ways of spelling surnames as well as baptismal names, those entering the names having exercised their own judgment as to orthography, and frequently varied it, though referring to the same person. If all the names were indexed separately, in accord with the original spelling, the work would be greatly increased. It was determined, therefore, to embrace under one heading all names probably belonging to the same family, indexing them, as far as practicable, under the form now in commonest use. Sometimes, where two distinct family names are much confused, like Barheit and Barrett, Van Eps and Van Ness, etc., they have been indexed under one heading. Most of the early Dutch families were not regularly entered under their family names, but mostly under their patronymics. For instance, the Heemstraats will be found sometimes under Dirks or Takels, the Groesbeeks under Claasze, the Vander Poels under Wynandsz, the Van Deusens under Teuisz or Harpers, the Bloomingdales, Van Burens and Vroomans under Meesz or Maas, the Van Bergens under Gerrits, etc., etc. During this period, persons would sometimes be entered under both patronymic and family names, and at other times under family names only. For instance, Cornelis Maasze Bloemendaal would at times be entered as Cornelis Bloemendaal. In indexing, he is indexed throughout as Cornelis, without considering the Maasze; Gerrit Theunisse Van Slyk is indexed under Gerrit Van Slyk, etc., etc. Appended is a list of the most numerous variations:

Arnold, Aarnout, Anold, Arnoldt, Arnel, Aarnhout, Arnhout.
Backes, Bacchus, Bacces, Baches, Backis.
Barhead, Barnhead, Berrit, Barret.
Barreway, Barroway, Barrewe, Baruere, Barruer.
Beckers, Bekker, Bekkens, Bekkers.
Bennewee, Bennewie, Binnewe, Belleway, Benneway, Bennewe, Binnewie, Binnewey.
Berger, Berriger, Berker, Berreger.
Bleecker, Bleeker, Bleycker, Bleyker, Blycker, Blyker.
Bogert, Bogart, Bogaart, Bogaert, Bagaart, Van de Bogart.
Bovie, Boevie, Bouvie, Bovire.
Bulsing, Balsing, Bulzing, Bulsen.
Burn, Burns, Bourn, Born, Borrs, Borns.
Carn, Carnen, Carnin, Kernin.
Clasen, Clasin, Claas, Claes, Claassen.
Clark, Clerq, Clerck, Clerk, Klark.
Coon, Coen, Koe, Koen.
Cooper, Couper, Coeper, Koeper, Kouper, Kopper.
Crannel, Crennel, Cranel, Crellen.
Cregier, Kregier, Krugier, Cruger, Crugier, Kryger.
Danielson, Donnel, Donnels, Danels.

De Forest, Deforest, De Foreest, Deforeest, Foreest, DeFreest, Defreest, De Fares, Defares, DeVares, Verreest, de Foreest, De Verreest, De Vreest, Freest.

De Garmo, Degarmo, D. Garmo, Garmo, Garmoe, De Garmoo, de Charmo, Garmau, de Garmo, Charmo, Degarmau, Charmau, d'Charmau, De Charmau.

De Peyster, Depeyster, De Pyster, Peyster.

De Ridder, Ridders, Ridder, Redder.

De Voe, Devoe, Defoe, De Vou, Du Foe, De Voy, De Fou, Defou, du Voe, de Foe, de Voe.

De Wandelaar, D. Wandelaar, De Wandelaer, d.Wandelaar, Dewandelaar, Wandelaar.

Diependorf, Dieppendorp, Deippendorp, Diependal.

Dovebach, Dauvenbach, Duivebach, Duyvebach.

Egberts, Egbertse, Egberson, Ebbertze, Egbertz.

Everson, Evertse, Evertsen, Evert, Everse, Everts, Eversen.

Filding, Fylden, Filden, Fielden.

Foland, Folland, Folant, Folent, Folin.

Fryer, Freyar, Freer, Fryar, Frey, Fry, Freyer.

Gansevoort, Ganzevoort, Ganzevoord, Gensevoo.

Gerritson, Gerritse, Gerritsen, Gerritze, Gerritzen.

Goewey, Goewy, Goedewey, Houwy, Hoewey, Gove, Govey.

Goe, Goeey, Goue, Goee, Goeue, Goey, Gouey.

Hanssen, Hanse, Hans, Hansen, Hanzen, Hunze.

Harsen, Harse, Harsens, Harssens, Hasse.

Hillebrant, Hillebrands, Hillebrants, Hildebrand.

Hoghing, Hogingh, Hoghink, Hoogen, Hogen, Hogin.

Hogg, Hogh, Hog, Hug, Hoghe.

Hoogteling, Hoogthaling, Hooghteeling, Hooghteling, Hoogtheling, Hoogteeling.

Huyck, Huych, Huyk, Huik.

Katsenbach, Katzenbach, Kaatsbach, Kaatsbah, Kaatsbaan.

Kittle, Kittil, Kittel, Kettel.

Knickerbacker, Knikkebakker, Cnickerbacker, Cnicker Backer.

Kohler, Kokler, Koeler, Koehler, Koegler, Koegher.

Le Grange, Legrange, La Gransie, Lagrangie, Legarange, Lagrange, Lagrancy, Le Grancy, La Grance, Legrancy, Lagrance, LeGransy.

Lansing, Langsingh, Lansingh, Lancen, Lansen, Lanzing.

Lieversen, Liverse, Liverson, Levison, Liversen, Livessen, Livesse, Lieverse, Lievissen, Livissen, Lievjson.

Litser, Litscher, Litzert, Litcher, Leycher.

Louk, Loek, Lock, Loeck.

Maccan, Meckans, Meekans, Meccans, Makans, Mahans, Macans, McKans.

Macuan, Maccue, Mekyoun, McGoun.

McGinnis, Megginnis, Maginnes, Magenis.

Marcelus, Maselius, Merselis, Masselis, Marselis, Marselies, Marselees, Marselius, Mercelis.

Meynertsen, Meynersen, Meynerse, Meyndertse, Meinersen, Meinerssen, Meinersse, Meynertse, Myndersse, Mynderson.

Michelt, Michels, Micheels, Michal.

Nichols, Nicholson, Nikkels, Nicoll.

Oliver, Olfer, Olver, Olfert, Olvert, Oliford.

Oostrander, Oostrande, Ostrander, V.Oostrander, Van Oostrander, Van Oostrande.

Pesinger, Peessing, Peesing, Pesing, Peessink, Poossing.

Philips, Philipse, Phillip, Phlipse.

Pieterson, Pietersen, Pieterse, Pieterssen.

Quackenbos, Quackenbosch, Quackkenbosch, Quakenbosch, Quakkenbos, Quakenbos, Qwakkenbusch, Quackenbusch, Kwackenbosch, Kwakenbosch, Kwackkenbosch, Kwakkenbus, Kwakkenbusch, Kwackenbusch.

Redlof, Redloff, Redley, Redly, Reddley, Riddley, Redif, Redlif.

Richard, Richardson, Rickart, Rikkard, Rikkart.

Roerbach, Roorbach, Roerback, Roorebag.

Roseboom, Rooseboom, Roozeboom, Rozeboom.

Rouby, Roby, Robby, Roube.

Salsbury, Van Salsberg, Van Salsbergen, Salisbury, Salsbergen, V. Salsbergen, Salsbergerin, Salsbarry.

Scherp, Scharp, Scharpe, Scherpe, Sjerp, Serp, Sherp.

Schuyler, Schuylder, Schuler, Schuiler.

Siksby, Siksbey, Sixby, Siksberry, Sichsby.

Snyder, Snyer, Schnyder, Schneider.

Soul, Sohl, Solch, Sole.

Ten Broeck, Tenbroeck, Tenbroek, T. Broek.

Ten Eyck, Teneyck, Ten Eik, Ten Eyk, Ten Eyke, Ten Eick, Deneyk, Dennyk, Denyk.

Tymessen, Timesen, Tymese, Tymissen, Teymisse, Teymissen.

Van Aalstyn, Van Alsteyn, Van Aelstyn, V. Aelstyn, V. Aalstien, V. Aalstein, Van Aalstein, Aalstein.

Van Arnhem, Van Aarnhem, V. Arnhem, Van Armen, Van Aarnam, V. Aarnem, V. Aarnhem, Van Aarnem.

Van Benthuyse, Van Benthuizen, Van Benthuyzen, Benthuysen, V. Benthuisen, V. Benthuizen.

Van Buren, Vanburen, Van Buuren, Vanbeure, V. Buren, V. Burent, V. Buuren.

Van Den Bergh, Van den Bergh, Van den Berg, Van d. Berg, V. d. Berg, V. den Berg, V. d. Bergh, Van Denberg, V. Denberg, Vandenberg, Vandeberg, Vandenbergh, V.denberg, Van denBerch, Van den Berck, Van den Berk, Van der Bergh, V. der Bergh, V. Ter Berg, Van Bergen, Van Berg.

Van der Heyden, Vanderheyden, Van der Hyden, V.d. Heyden, V.der Heyden, V. d. Heyden, Van D. hyde, V. d. Heide, V. der Heide, Van Derhyde.

Van der Hoef, Vanderhoef, Van d. Hoef, V. d. Hoef, V. d. Hoeve.

Van der Kar, Vanderkar, Van de Kar, V. d. Kar.

Van der Linde, V. d. Linde, V. d. Linden, V. der Linde, V. drlinden, Van de Linden.

Van der Poel, Van der poel, V. d. Poel, V. Ter Poel.

Van der Werken, Van de Werken, Van D. Werke, Van der Werke, V. d. Werken.

Van der Zee, Van der See, Van der Se, V. d. See.

Van Deusen, Van Deuzen, Van Deuse, Van Deussen, V. Deuzen, Vandeusen, V. Deusen, Van Doesen, Van Duisen.

Van Hoesen, Van Hoese, Vanhoosen, Vanhoese, V. Houzen, V. Huiser, Hoesen.

Van Ness, Vanness, Van Nes, V. Nes, Van Es, Van Ess, Van Esch, V. Esch.

Van Olinda, Van Olinde, Van Olinden, V. Olinde.

Van Renselaar, Van Renslaar, Van Renslaer, V. Renselaar, V. Renslaar, V. Renslaer, Renslaar, Renselaar, Renselaer, Renslaer, V. Renzelaar, Van Renzelaar, Rensselaer, V. Renzelaar, Van Renzelaar.

Van Sandvoort, Van Santfoort, Van Santvoort, Van Santvoord, Van Santfort, V. Santvoort, V. Santfort, Santvoord, Sandvoord, Sandvoort, Santvoort.

Van Schaick, Van Schaik, Van Scaik, Van Schaak, Van Schayck, Van Schajek, Van Schajik, V. Schaick, V. Schayk, V. Schaik, V. Schaaik, V. Schaak.

Van Schoonhoven, Van Sch'hoven, V. Schoonhoven, V. Schohove, Schoonhoven.

Van Valkenburgh, Van Valkenburg, V. Valkenburg, Valkenburg, Valkburgh.

Van Vechten, Van Veghten, Van Vegten, Van Veghte, Van Vegte, Van Venchten, Van Victen, V. Vegten, V. Vegte.

Van Vranken, Van Vrancken, Van Vraken, V. Vranken, Van Franken, V. Franken.

Van Woert, Van Woerd, Van Wart, Van Worten, Van Woort, V. Woert, V. Woerd.

Van Yveren, Van Yvere, Van Ivere, Van Iveren, Van Ieveren, Van Jevere, Van Jeveren, V. Yveren, V. Yvern.

Van Zanten, Van Santen, Van Sandten, Van Sant, Van Sante, V. Santen.

Viele, Vielen, Vilen, Vile, Veil, Fiele, Fiely, Fily, Fyl, Feil.

Visscher, Visser, Visher, Fisscher, Fischer, Fisher.

Wilkenson, Wilkensen, Wilkinson, Wilkesen.

Williams, Willemse, Wilms, Williaems.

Winne, Wenne, Wine, Winna.

Wyngaard, Wyngaart, Wyngaerd, Wyngaert.

Yates, Yeats, Yets, Yeets, Yetz, Jaets, Jatch, Jates, Jetch, Jeats, Jets, Jeets, Jetz, Yaetz, Yats, Yaets, Yatz.

Zeger, Seger, Seeger, Segher, Zegert.

Zichelson, Sickelson, Sickels, Seckels, Sikkens, Sickens.

Bruce, 63.
Bruin, Bruyn (see Pruyn), 20.
Bryart, 73.
Buckley, 20, 25, 35, 64.
Bulsing, Balsing, 15, 30, 50, 83, 91, 99, 102.
Burch, Bourch, 2, 13, 38.
Burger, Burgert, Borgart, 1, 26, 70.
Burhans, 15, 96.
Burk, 11.
Burnhout, Burnham, 5, 31.
Burns, Borrs, 7, 11, 13, 19, 23, 29, 35, 39, 45, 65, 76, 86, 100.
Burnside, 66.
Burscher, 17.
Burton, 52.
But, 79.
Cachron, 98.
Cahoun, 12.
Cailjer, Cailyer, Collier, 20.
Cambell, Cambel, Kemmel, 12, 14, 50, 66.
Canker, 41.
Canner, Kanner, 79.
Car, 7, 52.
Carel, 28.
Carick, 34.
Carlin, Corlen, 22.
Carmontel, Carmousel, 72.
Carn, Carnin, 18, 27, 36, 42, 55, 56.
Carpenter, 8.
Carson, 2.
Cartwright, 11, 21, 26, 36.
Carter, 30.
Cas, 19.
Caseway, 53.
Chandler, 52.
Charles, 71.
Chase, Chace, 53, 66.
Chester, 89.
Chidester, 7.
Christiaanse, 8, 38.
Christie, 61.
Church, 30, 79.
Claasen, Clasin, 11, 14, 64, 77, 83, 93, 95.
Clachry, 8.
Clark, Clerk, Klark, 6, 20, 25, 32, 38, 42, 51, 54, 58, 61, 74, 82, 95.
Clauw, Claeuw, 24, 28.
Claver, 46.
Clement, 6, 21, 44, 45, 53, 67, 98.
Cloet, Kloet, 2, 4, 5, 7, 9, 14, 28, 30, 36, 37, 42, 46, 47, 48, 49, 50, 53, 56, 57, 58, 60, 61, 63, 64, 69, 70, 73, 75, 76, 88, 102.
Clomb, 97.
Cock, 50, 60.
Cockran, 13.

Coda, 2.
Coddington, 10.
Coejeman, 26, 66.
Coenraads, 97.
Colliger, 13.
Collins, 21, 31, 43, 62.
Comes, 66.
Conckel, 58.
Coneyn, Conyn, 1, 3, 30, 32, 90.
Connely, 98.
Conner, Connor, 8, 65.
Contjer, 74.
Cool, Kool, 16, 19, 29, 30, 96.
Coon, Koe, 2, 9, 14, 23, 31, 35, 42, 45, 53, 58, 59, 71, 76, 79, 80, 89, 100.
Cooper, Kopper, 3, 20, 21, 24, 29, 31, 33, 34, 36, 37, 42, 46, 47, 49, 51, 53, 59, 64, 67, 70, 71, 78, 82, 84, 86, 98, 102.
Coops, Copes, 56, 60.
Corner, Corn, 22, 56.
Cornwal, 65.
Corsel, Korzel, Cortel, 75, 91.
Couenoven, 63.
(Courtnie), Coerteny, 57.
Craften, 103.
Craig, 53.
Crannel, Crellen (see Grannel), 9, 24, 52, 58, 60, 62, 64, 68, 87, 89, 103.
Creaton, 50.
Cregier, Kryger, 4, 12, 30, 40, 42, 43, 44, 52, 59, 86, 90, 93.
Cremer, 100.
Crevel, 67.
Cribel, 57.
Crispel, 33.
Croesby, 50.
Crovin, 9.
Crow, 9.
Crowa, 9.
Cruel, 82, 99.
Cumbringer, 54.
Cunnigans, 97.
Curtin, 11, 64.
Cuyler, Kuiler, 2, 6, 8, 16, 17, 35, 40, 43, 47, 51, 52, 57, 58, 69, 74, 78, 80, 87, 89, 91, 92, 95, 96, 97.
Daalhamer, 104.
Daats, Daat, Daart, 29, 33, 68, 69.
Dalley, 8.
Danielson, Donnel, Donnels, Daniels, 3, 29, 33, 34, 66.
Darby, 9.
Davenpoot, Devenpoort, 42, 73, 95.
Davis, Davids, David, 8, 18, 37, 43, 46, 58, 63, 77, 84, 87, 96, 99.

Records of the Reformed Dutch Church of Albany, New York

Part 5
1765-1771

Excerpted from
Year Book of The Holland Society
of New York (1908)

RECORDS OF THE REFORMED DUTCH CHURCH OF ALBANY, N. Y.

MARRIAGES, 1765 TO 1771.

[For abbreviations see page fronting Index.]

1765, Jan. 3. **L.** Jacobus V. Schoonhoven, y. m., of H. M., and Elisabeth Cloet, y. d., of the Boght.

Jan. 12. **L.** Bastiaan Crugier, widr. of Nis., and Dirkje Fisscher, y. d., of A.

Jan. 20. **B.** Rykert Van Santen and Sara Hilton, y. p. of this city.

Feb. 22. **L.** Gerrit V. Buren and Marritje Witbeek, y. p. of A. Co.

Feb. 24. **L.** Jacob Van Schaik and Maria Van Buuren, y. p. of A. Co.

Mch. 6. **B.** Johan Otto Rham and Cath. Barbara Hoogstratterin, of this City.

Mch. 12. **L.** Isaak Bekker and Elisabeth Wendel, y. p. of A. Co.

Mch. 24. **B.** Barent Goey and Rachel Oostrander.

Mch. 24. **B.** Dirck Benson and Marytje Wyngaard.

Apr. 8. **B.** Hendrik Crennel and Jacomyntje Bloemendal, of the Col.

Apr. 20. **B.** Johannes Gonzalus and Machtelt Van Heemstraat, of Nist. in Col. R.

Apr. 21. **L.** Philip P. Schuiler, y. m., of the Col., and Annatje Wendell, y. d., of the City.

Apr. 22. **L.** Barent Vischer, y. m., and Sara Vischer, y. d., both of this City.

Apr. 23. **L.** Frederick Meinertse and Elisabeth Waldrom, y. p. of this City.

May 5. **B.** Alexander Bulzing and Alida Oothout, y. p. of the Col.

May 11. **B.** Baltes Bratt and Elisabeth Foller, y. p. of the Col.

May 11. **L.** George Lanck and Mary Shaw, y. p. of this City.

I

May 30. **B.** Meinard V. Hoesen and Geertruy Vinhagel, y. p. of the Col.

June 17. **B.** Petrus Maerthen and Elisabeth Creller, at Hos.

June 21. **L.** George Wray and Catharina Ten Broek, y. p. of this City.

June 29. **L.** of June 5. Cornelis Van den Bergh and Maayke Ouderkerk, y. p. of A. Co.

July 13. **L.** of June 20. John Groesbeek and Aaltje Van Aarschem, y. p. of this City.

July 24. **L.** of Apr. 29. Meinard Rozeboom and Geertruid Zwits, y. p. of this City.

July 28. **L.** Philip Wendel and Cathalina Groesbeek, y. p. of this City.

Aug. 9. **L.** of July 8. Johannes Brat and Sarah Van Antwerpen, both of Schach.

Sep. 9. **L.** of July 12. Hendrik Oothout and Lydia Douw, y. p. of A. Co.

Sep. 12. **L.** of Aug. 14. Johannes Brat, y. m., of the City, and Maayke Fonda, y. d., of the Col.

Sep. 21. **L.** of Aug. 27. Gerrit Van Nes and Sara du Garmo, y. p. of Schach.

Sep. 28. **L.** of Sep. 9. David Groesbeek and Sara Winne, y. p. of this City.

Oct. 5. **L.** of Sep. 10. Aaron Bratt and Geertruy Taaltzame, y. p. of A. Co.

Oct. 8. **B.** Johannes Smitt and Margarita Peesseling, y. p. of Niskatha.

Oct. 9. **B.** Frerik Fox and Lydia Van Aalstein, l. at Schoh.

Oct. 10. **L.** of Sep. 24. Lowis Van Woert and Catharina Van den Bergh, y. p. of A. Co.

Oct. 16. **B.** at Schach. Marthen Boschkerk and Maria Cantelin, y. p. of Qenkehack.

Nov. 3. **L.** Gerrit Groesbeek and Jannetje Van Slyk.

Nov. 10. **L.** Thomas Barret and Elisabeth V. Santen, y. p. of this City.

Nov. 17. **L.** Henry Van Renselaar and Rachel Douw, y. p. of A. Co.

Nov. 17. **B.** Hendrik Riddeke and Elisabeth Wells, both of A. Co.

Nov. 23. **B.** Lodewyk Sikker and Christina Fratsen, y. p. of Col. R.

Dec. 3. **B.** Johan Louis Foetje and Trina McGie, of this City.

Dec. 26. **B.** William Rhigel and Charlotta Phaff.

Dec. 31. **B.** Theunis Krankheit and Margarita Husen, of Niskatha.

1766, Jan. 1. **L.** of Oct. 31, '65. Yzaac Fonda and Rebecca Groesbeek, y. p. of A. Co.

1766

Jan. 20. **B.** Christoffel Lansing, y. m., and Sara Van Schaik, y. d., both b. and l. in Col. R.

Feb. 15. **B.** Storm Bratt and Dorothea Van Aalstein, y. p., b. at Schie., l. at Nitkatha.

Mar. 22. **B.** Bernardus Halenbeek and Neeltje Clerk, y. p. of this City.

Mar. 30. **B.** Arent Bratt and Jannetje Hoghingh, y. p. of this City.

Apr. 20. **B.** Casparus Van Wie and Jannetje Winne, both of the Col.

May 11. **B.** Hendrik Briesch and Arriaantje Vinhagel, y. p. of the Col.

May 22. **B.** Andries Goey and Gloriana Gyouwy, y. p. of the Col.

July 3. **L.** of Sir Henry Moor. Nicolaas Michael and Barbara Hoofaul, both of A. Co.

July 13. **L.** of June 17. Thomas Lotteridge and Maria Bratt, y. p. of this City.

July 19. **L.** Christofel Yeates and Catharina Waters, y. p. of this place.

Aug. 9. **L.** Nicolaas Merselis and Margarita Groesbeek, y. p. of this City.

Aug. 24. **B.** Joost Harwich and Christina Filips.

Aug. 31. **L.** Yzaac Fonda and Francyntje Perry, both of Col. R.

Oct. 12. **B.** Philip Harwich and Elizabeth M. Rhyff, both of the Col.

Oct. 16. **L.** Pieter Witbeek and Maria V. Alen, at Niskatha.

Oct. 17. **L.** Nicolaas Groesbeek and Geertruy Waldrom, of A. Co.

Oct. 21. **B.** Petrus V. Ostrander and Sara Bovie, of Hosak.

Nov. 7. **L.** Hendrik Mersselis and Marytje de Foreest, y. p. of this City.

Nov. 13. **B.** Joseph V. Santen and Rebecca De Garmo, y. p. of the Col.

Nov. 15. **B.** Yzaac Dox and Lena de Voe, y. p. of H. M.

Nov. 20. **B.** Cornelis V. d. Zee and Annatje Veder, y. p. of Niskatha.

Nov. 27. **B.** Thomas Wheger and Elisabeth Harwich, y. p. of the Col.

Dec. 5. **L.** Daniel V. Antwerpen and Dirkje Winne, y. p. of this City.

Dec. 10. **L.** of Nov. 24. James Williams and Mary O'Conner, y. p. of this City.

Dec. 11. **B.** Gerrit Zeger and Maria Pangborn, y. p. of Niskatha.

Dec. 12. **L.** of Dec. 1. Anthony Halenbeek and Cornelia Cooper, y. p. of this City.

Dec. 17. **L.** Wilhelmus Mancius and Annatje Ten Eick, y. p. of this City.

Dec. 19. **B.** Cornelis Vroman and Elisabeth Huigh, y. p. of this place.

Dec. 23. **L.** Wouter Qwackenbusch, widr. of the Col., and Catharina Roseboom, y. d., of the City.

1767, Jan. 8. **L.** Cornelis V. d. Berg, y. m., and Catharina Lansing, y. d., of Col. R.

Jan. 17. **B.** Carel Dirksen and Margarita Borns.

Jan. 17. **B.** Willem Dirksen and Margarita V. d. Werken.

Jan. 17. **L.** Pieter Schuyler, Jr., and Geertruy Lansing, y. p., of this City.

Jan. 23. **L.** Andries Douw, y. m., and Catharina de Foreest, y. d., of this City.

Jan. 26. **B.** Jacob Pest and Margarita Mellery, y. p. at Hosac.

Jan. 29. **L.** Ignas Kip and Annatje V. Vechten, y. p. at Schach.

Jan. 31. **L.** Nicolaas Sharp and Lena Hogeboom, y. p. of A. Co.

Feb. 1. **B.** Nicolaas Klein and Elisabeth Coughlen, y. p. of this City.

Feb. 6. **L.** Efraim Van Vechten and Annetje Wendel, y. p. in this City.

Feb. 14. **L.** Maas V. Buren and Rebecca Bogert, y. p. of A. Co.

Feb. 22. **L.** Gozen Van Schaick and Maria Bumney, y. p. of this City.

Mar. 4. **L.** Jacob G. Lansing and Neeltje Rozeboom, y. p. of this City.

Apr. 14. **L.** John Tingue and Maria Johanna Lieter, y. p. of this City.

Apr. 16. **B.** Abraham Sickels and Maria Rannel.

May 5. **B.** Coenraad Cremer and Margarita Prispen, y. p. of Saratoga.

May 20. **L.** William Van Wie and Jannetje Lansing, y. p. of this City.

May 22. **L.** Hendrik Ten Eick and Margarita Douw, y. p. of this City.

May 30. **B.** Lowis Brine and Catharina Bendell.

June 27. **L.** Andrew Sharp and Hanna Sedam, both of A. Co.

July 22. **L.** James Dole and Anna Van Santvoort, y. p. of this City.

July 31. **L.** John Bratt and Gerritje Lansing, y. p. of this City.

Aug. 1. **L.** John Nicolaas Claver and Susanna Merriday, y. p. of A. Co.

1767 – 1768

Aug. 3. **B.** Jacob Boomhouwer and Sara Kimmel, of the Col.

Aug. 20. **B.** Jesse Tolb and Maria Viele, y. p. of A. Co.

Aug. 24. **L.** Barent Staats and Antje Winne, y. p. of the Col.

Aug. 29. **B.** John Singers and Cornelia Richter, both of this place.

Oct. 8. **L.** Gosen Van Schaik and Elsje Roseboom, y. p. of A. Co.

Oct. 10. **L.** Wynand Van Aalstein and Margarita Reisdorp, y. p. of A. Co.

Oct. 11. **B.** Thomas Clump and Margarita Davis.

Oct. 13. **B.** John Olfer and Clara Syffers, y. p. of A. Co.

Oct. 15. **L.** Lavinus Dunbar and Margarita Harssen, y. p. of this place.

Oct. 17. **B.** Eduard Connel and Saartje Poolter.

Oct. 18. **L.** Abraham Hoogkerk, y. m., and Anna Hilton, y. d., both of this City.

Nov. 3. **B.** Adam Wiegant and Elisabeth Wageman, y. p. of this City.

Nov. 5. **L.** Gerrit A. Roseboom and Elsje Roseboom, y. p. of this City.

Nov. 6. **L.** Nicolaas Drury and Catharina Smith, y. p. of A. Co.

Nov. 7. **L.** Yzaac Hogen and Maria Gerritsen, y. p. of this City.

Dec. 10. **L.** Augustinus Sharp and Maria V. Aalstein, y. p. of A. Co.

Dec. 11. **L.** Cornelius Van Scherluyne and Elisabeth Roseboom, y. p. of this City.

Dec. 12. **L.** Michael Basset and Marytje Van Franken, y. p. in this City.

Dec. 13. **B.** John Pieter Rieseker and Mary Chapman.

Dec. 19. **B.** Yzac Legransy and Jacomyntje Knolb, y. p. of A. Co.

Dec. 25. **L.** Nanning Halenbeek and Alida Ten Eyck, y. p. of A. Co.

Dec. 27. **B.** by R. Crenny. John Knoet and Mary Wills.
J^b Stalker, Clerk in the Meeting:

Dec. 29. **B.** Thom^s Kannon and Mary Gilmore.

1768, Jan. 5. **B.** Christoffer Visscher and Johanna S. Canker, both of the Colony.

Jan. 9. **L.** Pieter Waldron Witbeek and Rachel Van den Bergh, y. p. of the Co.

Feb. 24. **L.** Philip Van Renzelaar and Maria Sanders, y. p. of this place.

Feb. 27. **L.** Gerrit A. Lansing and Cathalina Van Aalstein, y. p. of this City.

1768–1769
Feb. 30. **B.** John Jansen and E. Pengborn, y. p. of Nitkatha.

Mar. 10. **B.** Gerrit Lansing and H. Scherp, y. p. of Qenkhack.

May 27. **L.** Petrus Ham and Maria Mitchel, both of the Col.

June 15. **B.** Jacob Wormer and Maria Alles, both l. at Schach.

June 26. **L.** Jacob Lansing and Dorothea Levison, y. p. of this Co.

June 26. **B.** Robert Lithgou and Dorothea Thomson, both of this City.

July 12. **L.** Lucas Salsbury and Maria Van Buuren, y. p. l. in this Co.

Aug. 24. **L.** Isaac J. V. Aarnem and Catharina Van Wie, y. p. of the Col.

Oct. 7. **L.** John Visscher and Jannatje Pearce, y. p. of A. Co.

Oct. 8. **L.** Coenraad Le Grange and Annatje Le Grange, y. p. of A. Co.

Nov. 16. **B.** John McLong and Anna Scharp, of Cambridge.

Nov. 20. **B.** James Donneway and Elsje Smith, both of this City.

Nov. 23. **L.** John Wilver and Maria Cooper, y. p. of A. Co.

Dec. 10. **L.** Jacob Fonda and Dirkje Visscher, y. p. of A. Co.

Dec. 11. **B.** Hendrik Bulsing and Cornelia Marus.

Dec. 22. **B.** Theunis Coover and Susanna Cristen, of the Col.

Dec. 31. **L.** Balthes Benthuizen and Elisabeth Rumney, both of this City.

1769, Jan. 7. **L.** John Ryley and Cathalina V. d. Bergh, y. p. l. in the Col.

Jan. 12. **L.** Cornelis Wendel and Annatje Lansing, y. p. of this City.

Jan. 20. **L.** Philip Deforeest and Maayke Van Nest, of this City.

Jan. 21. **B.** Yzaac Trouex and Christina Pelleger, of Norman's kill.

Feb. 4. **B.** Andries Bratt and Annatje V. d. Kar, of Niskatha.

Feb. 6. **B.** Frans Van der Werken, y. m., of H. M., and Christina Barmhert, of Hos.

Feb. 26. **L.** Anthony Groesbeek and Cathalyna De foreest, y. p. of this City.

Mar. 1. **L.** Johannes Knickerbakker and Elisabeth Winne, y. p. of the City.

1769 – 1770

Apr. 4. **B.** John Wilkinson and Ann Mashel, y. p. of this City.

Apr. 14. **L.** Abraham Ten Eick and Annatje Lansing, y. p. of this City.

May. 6. **L.** Hendrik Jo. Lansing and Helena Winne, y. p. of the Col.

May. 6. Eldert Ouderkerk and Elisabeth Fonda, both of the Col.

May 7. **B.** Abraham Oothout and Martha Benneway, y. p. of the Col.

May 27. **L.** Samuel Gardenier and Hilletje Van Wie, y. p. of this Co.

May 27. **L.** Obadia Cooper and Anna V. d. Berg, y. p. of this City.

July 2. **L.** Cornelis Waldrom and Alida Groen.

July 11. **L.** Johs Wies (?) and Mary Peet.

July 15. **L.** Johs Pruin and Geertje Ten Eick, y. p. of this City.

Sep. 27. **L.** John Ten Broek and Gerritje Roseboom, y. p. of this Co.

Sep. 28. **B.** Richard Pangborn and Cathalyna V. Etten, y. p. at Nitkatha.

Nov. 9. **L.** John Amory and Neeltje Staats, y. p. of A. Co.

Nov. 14. **B.** Johannes Heiner and Catharina Theter.

Nov. 14. **B.** Johannes Teter and Elisabeth Heyner, y. p. of the Col.

Nov. 19. **B.** Guy Young and Dirkje Winne, y. p. of this City.

Nov. 30. **L.** Gerrit V. d. Berg and Rebecca Fonda, y. p. of A. Co.

Dec. 5. **L.** Gerrit Rykman, y. m., of this City, and Elisabeth Van Buuren, y. d., of A. Co.

Dec. 10. **L.** Pieter Van Deusen and Catharina Van Wie, y. p. of A. Co.

Dec. 16. **B.** Pieter Bratt and Margarita Fry, y. p. at Nitkatha.

Dec. 23. **L.** Cristoffel Miller and Jannatje Crugier, y. p. of Nist.

1770, Feb. **B.** John Van Wurmer and Francyna Ouderkerk, y. p., both of Hosak.

Feb. 13. **B.** Andries Trouex and Cathalyntje Maris, y. p., both of the Colony.

March 2. **L.** Cornelis Eckerson and Rebecca Van Santvoort, y. p., both of this County.

March 5. **B.** Barent Van Yveren and Rebecca Bratt, y. p., both of this County.

March 11. **L.** Lavinus Lansing and Catharina Van der Heide, y. p., both of the Colony.

1770

March 14. **B.** Gerardus V. Olinde and Catharina V. Oostrander, y. p., at Hosak.

March 18. **B.** Hannes Hevelis and Annatje Adams, y. p., both of the Colony.

April 9. **L.** Hermanus A. Wendel and Christina Van den Bergh, y. p., both of this place.

May 14. **L.** Leendert Ganzevoort and Hester Cuyler, y. p., both of this City.

May 14. **B.** Nicholaas Yeraleman and Jannetje Waldron, y. p., both of this City.

May 20. **B.** Daniel Winne and Alida V. d. Bergh.

May 20. **L.** Johannes F. V. d. Bergh and Maayke Ouderkerk, y. p., both of Half Moon.

May 26. **L.** David De Foreest and Elisabeth Witbeek, y. p., both of the Colony.

June 8. **L.** Johannes Merselis and Margarita V. d. Bergh, y. p., both of this County.

June 9. **L.** William Dunbar and Elisabeth Van Deusen, y. p., both of this City.

June 10. **B.** Joh⁵ Benson and Cathalyna V. Aalstein, y. p., both of the Colony.

June 10. **B.** Pieter Bratt and Jannetje Springsteen, y. p., both of the Colony.

June 20. **L.** John V. Woert, Jr., and Cathalyntje Lansing, y. p., both of the Colony.

June 20. **L.** Hendrik B. Ten Eick and Catharina Sanders, y. p., both of this City.

June 27. **L.** Dirk Van Vegten and Petertje Yates, both of Albany Co.

June 27, **B.** Hannes Connel, y. m., and Maria Magown, y. d., both liv. at Half moon.

June 31. **B.** Willem Bratt and Arriaantje Mook, y. p., both of Niskatha.

July 7. **B.** Theunis Hoogteling and Lena Hoogteling, at Niskatha.

July 13. **B.** Evert Janssen and Antje Le granssie, both of the Norman's-kill.

Oct. 8. On certif. by Rev. Clark. Robert Joed and Margarita Allen, y. p., both of this County.

Oct. 8. On certif. by Joh⁵ Groesbeek. Robert Williams and Jennit Conclin, y. p., both of this County.

Oct. 22. **B.** Frans Miller and Elisabeth Channel, y. p., both of the Colony.

Oct. 27. **B.** Joseph Bratt and Wyntje Bratt, y. p., both at Niskatha.

Nov. 8. James Miller and Alida Hay.

Nov. 8. Daniel Whildy and Annetje Simon.

Nov. 23. Franciscus Mershall and Geertruy Van Deuzen.

Dec. 9. Koenrad Harwich and Magdalena Meyers.

1770–1771

Dec. 23. John V. Benthuisen and Geesje Van Hoesen, y. p., both of this place.

Dec. 29. L. Yzaac Fonda and Jenneke Claassen, y. p., both of this County.

1771, Jan. 11. L. Herman Hofman, y. m., of Dutchess Co., and Catharina Douw, y. d., of this Place.

Jan. 11. L. Nicolaas Hofman, y. m., of Dutchess Co., and Ede Sylvester, y. d., of this City.

Jan. 19. L. Andries Roui and Rebecca Lodowick, y. p., both of this County.

Jan. 22. B. Andries Meyer and Catharina Ronkel, y. p., both of the Colony.

Jan. 27. B. by D? Vroman. Johannes Van Wie and Alida Van Wie, y. p., both of this County.

Feb. 3. B. Hendrik Louis and Marytje Davis, y. p., both of this City.

Feb. 10. L. Gerrit Visscher and Rachel V. d. Berg, y. p., both of this Place.

Feb. 10. B. Jacob Springer and Maria Snyder, y. p., both of the Colony.

May 1. L. William Staats and Anna Yates, y. p., both of this Place.

May 19. L. Jacob V. Deuzen and Elsje Lansing, y. p., both of this place.

July 1. (?) B. Martinus V. d. Werken and Marytje Winner, y. p., both at Saratoga.

July 1. L. William Ludlow and Catharina V. Renzelaar, y. p., of this County.

July 8. L. Bernardus Everzen and Martina Hoghing, y. p., both of this City.

July 20. B. Evert Oothout and —— Davenpoort, y. p., both of the Colony.

Aug. 20. L. Abraham D. Fonda and Hendrikje Lansing, y. p., both of the Colony.

Aug. 24. L. Andrew Abel and Johanna Marshal, y. p., both of this County.

Sept. 20. L. Hendrik V. Schoonhoven and Aaltje V. d. Berg, y. p., both of the Half moon.

Sept. 22. B. Thomas J. Witbeek and Elisabeth Reisdorp, y. p., both of the Colony.

Oct. 1. L. Gerrit A. Lansing and Agnietje Bratt, y. p., both of this City.

Oct. 8. B. Nathanael Semborn and Elisabeth De Foe, y. p., both of Schaaktko.

Oct. 28. B. Anthony Dirk and Anna Barbara Brustin, of this County.

Nov. 7. L. Pieter Brook and Santje Wendels, y. p., both of this City.

1771m. 1765b.

Nov. 11. **B.** Paulus Jeems and Annatje Krankheid, of the Colony.

Nov. 24. **L.** Gysbert V. d. Berg and Jannetje Witbeek, y. p., both of the Colony.

Nov. 24. **B.** Abraham Witbeek and Annatje V. Schaik, both of the Colony.

Nov. 26. Jan. Dox and Maria De Voe, y. p., both of the Half Moon.

Nov. 26. **L.** Hendrik Waldron and Margareta V. Franken, both of the Colony.

Dec. 13. **L.** Joh⁵ Hanssen and Elisabeth V. d. Heide, y. p., both of this place.

Dec. 26. **L.** Joh⁵ V. Hoesen and Anna V. Deusen, y. p., both of this City.

BAPTISMAL RECORD, 1765 TO 1771.

1765, Jan. 6, bo. Jan. 3. Albert, of Pieter Rykman and Lydia V. d. Berg. Wit.: Gerrit and Hester Rykman.

bo. Nov. 30. (1764) Theunis, of Dirk I. (or T.) Van Vechten and Cathalyntje Van Esch. Wit.: Cornelis and Annatje V. Vechten.

Jan. 13, bo. Jan. 12. (1765) Alida, of Casparus Pruin and Catharina Groesbeek. Wit.: Samuel and Neeltje Pruin.

bo. Nov. 18. (1764) Anna, of Philip Heiner and Eva Trever. Wit.: Frerik Concher, Anna Cancher.

bo. Jan. 6. (1765) Joannes, of Pieter and Anna Merschel. Wit.: Joannes Flensburg, Francyntje Perry.

bo. Jan. 8. Annatje, of Abraham Bogart and Marrytje Besset. Wit.: Michelt and Lybetje Besselt.

bo. Jan. 9. Annatje, of Johannes V. Santen and Margarytje Wilkenson. Wit.: John Fryer, Annatje V. Santen.

Jan. 27, bo. Jan. 22. Meinard, of Reinier Van Yveren and Debora Fildon. Wit.: Gerrit V. Yveren, Hester Fisscher.

Feb. 3, bo. Jan. 30. Cornelia, of Simon V. Antwerpen and Maria Dunbar. Wit.: Gerrit and Cornelia Dunbar.

bo. Jan. 30. Annatje, of Hendrik Kwakkenbusch and Margarita Oothout. Wit.: Pieter and Bata Kwakkenbusch.

Feb. 10, bo. Dec. 31. (1764) Margarita, of Joost Acker and Margarita Wever. Wit.: Hannes Acker, Catharina Youngen.

Feb. 17, bo. Jan. 24. Heiltje, of Johannes Muller and Sara Van Yveren. Wit.: Philip Muller, Geertruid Goey.

bo. Jan. 12. Anna Maria, of Barent and Marg. Neer. Wit.: Nichel. and Anna Maria Veller.

1765

bo. Feb. 11. Egbert, of Antony Brat and Mallytje V. Deuzen. Wit.: Egbert and Elisabeth Brat.

Feb. 17, bo. Feb. 15. Cornelia, of Johannes Goey and Maria Van Yveren. Wit.: Martinus V. Yveren, Sara Muller.

Feb. 24, bo. Jan. 24. Jannetje, of Jan Brat and Sanne Zegers. Wit.: John and Elsje Rozeboom.

bo. Feb. 17. Gerrit, of Hannes Groesbeek and Elisabeth V. Brakelen. Wit.: Gerrit and Catharina V. Brakelen.

bo. Feb. 20. Gerrit, of Johannes Knoet and Sara V. Aarnhem. Wit.: Johs. and Barbara Knoet.

Mar. 3, bo. Mar. 1. Jacob, of Abraham Kuiler and Catharina Wendel. Wit.: Hermanus and Lena Wendel.

Folkje, of Jek, Serv. of Johs. Roozeboom and Sara Spek. Wit.: Will, serv. of Claas V. d. Bergh, and Marra, serv. of Hannes Lansing.

Mar. 17, bo. Feb. 22. Catharina, of Gerrit Oostrander and Christina V. d. Bergh. Wit.: Burger and Catharina V. d. Berg.

Mar. 24, bo. Mar. 17. Christoffel, of Daniel Ertzenberger and Regina Cath. Leonard. Wit.: Johs. and Ester Maria Mendlein.

Mar. 24, ba. at home on account of sickness. bo. Mar. 23. David, of Samuel Strenger and Rachel V. d. Heide. Wit.: David and Geertruy V. d. Heiden.

Mar. 31, bo. Mar. 29. Albertus, of Wouter Bekker and Annatje Ridder. Wit.: Wouter Ridder, Jannetje Swart.

bo. Mar. 23. Dirk Brat, of Dirk Brat V. Schoonhoven and Folkje V. d. Berg. Wit.: Abraham Fonda, Rachel Fisscher.

Apr. 5, bo. Apr. 1. Johannes, of Wouter De Foreest and Alida Kloet. Wit.: John and Sara Cloet.

Seven Weeks old. Jannatje, of Hendrik Daniels and Maria Northen. Wit.: Philip and Jannetje Reyly.

Apr. 7. Four weeks old. Barent, of Wilhelmus Smith and Annatje Brat. Wit.: Barent A. and Annatje Bratt.

bo. Mar. 4. Gerrit, of Herbert Lansing and Marytje Visscher. Wit.: Gerrit and Wyntje Lansing.

Apr. 14, bo. Mar. 2. Storm, of David Hoogteling and Hilletje Van der Zee. Wit.: Matthys Hoogteling, Arriaantje V. d. Zee.

bo. Apr. 11. Catharina, of Cornelis V. Deuzen and Lea Oostrander. Wit.: Gerardus Lansing, Maria Wendel.

Apr. 21, bo. Mar. 31. Johannes, of Jacob Heemstraat and Cath. Duret. Wit.: Hannes and Elisabeth Heemstraat.

Apr. 28, bo. Mar. 15. Gerritje, of Tobias Ten Eick and Juditje V. Buren. Wit.: Maas and Cathalyntje V. Buuren.

1765

bo. Mar. 25. Annatje, of Albert V. d. Zee and Marytje V. d. Kar. Wit.: Hannes and Annatje Bekker.

May 5, bo. Apr. 16. Johannes, of Johs Jacobs Lansing and Maria Huik. Wit.: Yzak J. and Anna Lansing.

bo. May 1. Jacobus, of Rykert V. Santen and Sara Hilton. Wit.: Petrus and Judikje Hilton.

bo. May 2. Rachel, of Anthony Flensburg and Annatje Radly. Wit.: Hannes Clement, Rachel Redly.

May 12, bo. Apr. 21. Margarita, of Abraham Boom and Dorothea Cunningam. Wit.: Barent Goey, Rachel V. Oostrander.

bo. May 8. Magdalena, of Johs Ten Broek and Sara Ganzevoort. Wit.: Harmen and Magdalena Ganzevoort.

May 14, bo. Apr. 2. Rachel, of Evert V. d. Berg and Marytje V. d. Werken. Wit.: Abraham and Antje Wimp.

May 16, bo. May 13. Sara, of Jacob Harssen and Alida Groesbeek. Wit.: Jacobus and Geertruid Groesbeek.

May 19, bo. May 2. Jochum, of Adriaan Brat and Lydia V. Aalstein. Wit.: Hermanus V. Aalstein. Catharina Beelzinger.

bo. May 18. Hendrik, of Gerrit Van Wie and Catharina Lansing. Wit.: Hendrik Brat, Agnietje Van Wie.

bo. Apr. 29. Barbara, of John V. Aalstein and Lena Scherp. Wit.: Jurjen and Barbara Sherp.

bo. May 17. Jacob, of Dirk and Margarita V. d. Heide. Wit.: Mathys Bovie, Baatje V. d. Heiden.

May 26, bo. May 21. Lucas, of Cornelis Muller and Marytje V. Hoezen. Wit.: Hannes and Jannetje Pruin.

bo. May 1. Tobias, of Jonathan Witbeek and Gerritje Oostrander. Wit.: Tobias and Lea Witbeek.

bo. May 10. Catharina, of Abraham Slingerland and Rebecca File. Wit.: Johs. Quakkenbusch, Jannetje Vile.

June 2, bo. May 5. Alida, of Andries V. Slyk and Marytje V. Benthuizen. Wit.: Folkert P. and Annatje Douw.

bo. May 28. Theunis, of Gerrit Visscher and Alida Fonda. Wit.: Bastiaan Crugier, Neeltje Fischer.

June 9, bo. May 30. George, of Evert Zeger and Sara Orchard. Wit.: Thomas Zeger, Judike Hoogland.

June 23, bo. May 26. Andries, of Mathys Flensburg and Christina Snyder. Wit.: Frans and Marytje Winne.

bo. June 17. Cathalina, of Abraham C. Cuiler and Jannetje Glen. Wit.: Filip Schuyler, Elisabeth V. Cortland.

bo. June 20. Hendrikus, of Hendrik Renselaar and Alida Brat. Wit.: Quiliaan V. Renzelaar, Elisabeth Visscher.

bo. June 10. Catharina, of Yzaac Vosburg and Catharina Staats. Wit.: Theunis and Elisabeth V. Woert.

1765

June 23. Elisabeth, of John and Mary Adams. Wit.: Philip and Alida Reyly.

bo. June 22. Petrus, of Hannes Zoufeld and Sara Freer. Wit.: Petrus Freer, Cath. Scherzver.

June 30, bo. June 3. Margarita, of Marten and Hendrikje V. Buuren. Wit.: Bernardus Brat, Catharina Bratt.

bo. June 11. Pieter, of Andries Peessing and Jannetje Brat. Wit.: Pieter Bratt, Catharina V. Aalstein.

bo. June 28. Jacob, of Samuel Pruin and Neeltje Ten Eik. Wit.: Barent and Alida Ten Eick.

bo. June 4. Abraham, of Abraham de Wever and Annatje Kerner. Wit.: Leendert and Marritje Muller.

July 7, bo. July 6. Anthony, of Theunis Brat and Cathalyntje Van Esch. Wit.: Cornelis and Hadriana Van Santvoort.

July 14, bo. June 20. Maria, of Tobias V. Buuren and Cathalyntje Witbeek. Wit.: Pieter M. and Maria Van Buuren.

July 21, bo. July 16. Gerlyn, of Willem Verplank and Lydia Levison. Wit.: Abraham Verplank, Abigail Lansing.

July 23, at home. John Braadstreet, of Philip J. Schuyler and Catharina V. Renzelaar. Wit.: John Braadstreet, Judith V. Renzelaar.

Aug. 4, bo. July 16. Jacobus, of Jacobus V. Etten and Annatje Pengbang. Wit.: Hannes and Wyntje Redlif.

bo. July 6. Geurt, of Jacobus V. Schoonhoven and Elisabeth Knoet. Wit.: Geurt V. Schoonhoven, Maria Fonda.

Aug. 4, bo. July 12. Agnietje, of Hendrik Van Wie and Marytje Lock. Wit.: Gerrit Winne, Racheltje Slingerland.

Aug. 11, bo. July 3. Wouter, of Jonathan Hoogteling and Jannetje Slingerland. Wit.: Wouter and Hester Slingerland.

bo. July 20. Jochum, of Daniel Kittel and Sara V. Schaik. Wit.: Dirk and Margarita V. d. Heide.

bo. July 24. Abraham, of Yzaac H. Lansing and Annatje V. Aarnem. Wit.: Johannes and Alida V. Aarnem.

Aug. 18, bo. Seven weeks ago. Anna, of Hannes Eiby and Margarita Heene. Wit.: Philip and Anna Feller.

bo. July 19. Jonathan, of Pieter Hoogteling and Annatje Bekker. Wit.: David Hoogteling, Marytje Winne.

bo. June 26. Catharina, of Adam Beem and Catharina Freer. Wit.: Johs Freer, Catharina Dop.

Aug. 25, bo. Aug. 12. Elisabeth, of Daniel Halenbeek and Catharina Quakkenbusch. Wit.: Johs. and Elisabeth Quakkenbusch.

Five weeks old. Eva, of John Streler and Marytje Elva. Wit.: Yzac and Antje Hoghing.

1765

bo. Aug. 21. Alida, of Yzaac De Foreest and Alida Fonda. Wit.: Douw Fonda, Annatje Knikkerbakker.

Sep. 1, bo. Aug. 30. Elisabeth, of Abraham Peek and Cath. V. Santen. Wit.: Yzaac Hoogkerk, Rachel V. Santen.

bo. Aug. 8. Hendrik, of Theunis Slingerland and Agnietje Witbeek. Wit.: John and Agnietje Scott.

bo. Aug. 7. Harmen, of Dirk and Alida V. Vechten. Wit.: Cornelis V. Vechten, Elisabeth Vile.

Sep. 8, bo. Aug. 9. Antje, of Roelef Merky and Catharina Bovie. Wit.: Sam. and Geertruy Bennewie.

bo. Aug. 12. Abraham, of Hannes Landman and Santje Litger. Wit.: Jan and Saartje Van Buuren.

Neeltje, of Michel Landman and Marytje Brouwer. Wit.: Yzaac and Catharina Vosburg.

bo. Aug. 5. Annatje, Maria, twins of Nicolaas Brouif (?) and Marytje Pook. Wit.: Petrus and Nency Hilton, Mathys Boom, Jannetje Lansing.

bo. Sep. 6. Sara, of Johs Lansing V. and Catharina Burhans. Wit.: Hendrik and Maria Lansing.

bo. Aug. 14. Hadriaan, of Albert Brat and Magdalena Lang. Wit.: Mathys Hoogteling, Arriaantje V. d. Zee.

bo. Sep. 7. Yzaac, of Hendrik Y. (?) Bogaart and Barbara Marselis. Wit.: Yzaac and Catharina Bogart.

bo. Sep. 5. Gerrit, of Hendrik Van Esch and Lena Vroman. Wit.: Gerrit Van Esch, Maria Lansing.

Sep. 15. Matheus, of Philip Bovie and Geertruy V. d. Berg. Wit.: Mathys and Nelletje Bovie.

bo. Sep. 8. Johannes, of Eduard Davis and Jannetje Duret. Wit.: Yzaac Roza, Margarita V. d. Werken.

bo. Sep. 1. Annetje, of Evert V. d. Berg and Annatje Lansing. Wit.: Gozen V. Schaik, Maayke V. d. Berg.

Sep. 22, bo. Aug. 27. Daniel, of Harmen Kwakkenbusch and Judith Marl. Wit.: Pieter and Elisabeth Dox.

bo. Aug. 20. Margarita, of Cornelis Zwitz and Catharina Schuyler. Wit.: Anthony and Margarita Ten Eick.

Sep. 29, bo. Sep. 3. Lydia, of Gerrit Brat and Lena Hoogteling. Wit.: Adam Brat, Marytje Bratt.

bo. Sep. 19. Cornelia, of Johannes Hanssen and Geertruy Slingerland. Wit.: Wouter and Hester Slingerland.

bo. Sep. 3. Antje, of Ryckert Redly and Marytje Olver. Wit. Gerrit Zeger, Wyntje Olver.

Oct. 6, bo. Sep. 5. Johannes, of Yzaac Oostrander and Elisabeth McKans. Wit.: Johs. and Wyntje Redly.

bo. Sep. 17. Yzaac, of Jan Duret and Sara Revison. Wit.: Yzaac Dox, Annatje Smitt.

bo. Sep. 1. Judike, of Barent C. and Arriaantje V. Buuren. Wit.: Casparus and Geertruy Witbeek.

1765

bo. Sep. 29. Willem, of Folkert G. V. d. Berg and Neeltje Waldrom. Wit.: Patrik and Cornelia Clerk.

Oct. 11, bo. Oct. 9. Catharina, of Stephanus Schuyler and Engeltje V. Vechten. Wit.: Hermanus and Annatje Wendel.

Oct. 20, bo. Oct. 23. Elisabeth, of Johs Knoet and Jannetje Ouderkerk. Wit.: Johs. and Lena Ouderkerk.

bo. Oct. 11. Maria, of Cornelis W. V. d. Bergh and Maria Viele. Wit.: Gozen V. Schaik, Maayke V. d. Bergh.

Oct. 20, bo. Sep. 25. Philip, of Hannes Ruiter and Elisabeth Perst. Wit.: Coenraad Perst, Margarita Dauw.

Oct. 27, bo. Oct. 7. Christiaan, of Cornelis Strong and Margarita 'sJans. Wit.: John McLannon, Marytje 'sJaans.

bo. Oct. 18. Paulus, of Paulus and Elisabeth Hoogstrasser. Wit.: Jeems and Anna Maria Abbet.

bo. Oct. 24. Catharina, of Johannes Ganzevoort and Evje Beekman. Wit.: Pieter and Gerritje Ganzevoort.

Nov. 3, bo. Oct. 25. Nicolaas, of Johs. J. Redlif and Margarita Passage. Wit.: David and Maria Gyssen (or Gipsen).

bo. Oct. 6. Geertruid, of Arent V. Antwerpen and Hester Crugier. Wit.: Martinus and Sara Crugier.

bo. Oct. 9. Philip, of Hannes and Cath. Redlif. Wit.: Philip Redlif, Elisabeth Cankelin.

bo. Oct. 26. Barent, of Folkert Daassen and Geertruy Hilton. Wit.: Yzaac and Geertruy Zwits.

bo. Oct. 6. Barbara, of Pieter Sjerp and Catharina Berringer. Wit.: Jurjen and Barbara Sherp.

Nov. 3. Sara, of Johannes Conzalus and Machtel Heemstraat. Wit.: Yzaac and Francyntje Mills.

Nov. 10, bo. Nov. 3. Dirck, Elisabeth, twins of Abraham Ten Broek and Elisabeth Renzelaar. Wit.: Dirk and Margarita Ten Broek, Stephen Van Renselaar, *Patroon*, Catharina Livingston.

bo. Nov. 10. Andries, of Frerik Meinerssen and Elisabeth Waldrom. Wit.: Abraham Meinersse, Sara Vroman.

bo. Oct. 7. Elisabeth, of Frerik Olver and Tryntje V. d. Berg. Wit.: Cornelis and Elisabeth V. d. Bergh.

Nov. 17, bo. Oct. 26. Hendrik, of Jacobus Aurnel, Jr., and Annatje Mook. Wit.: Pieter Daniels, Anna Aurnel.

bo. Nov. 10. Annatje, of Frerik Knoet and Marytje Ridder. Wit.: Lavinus Winne, Antje Berry.

bo. Sep. (?) 26. Lena, of Johs Flensburg and Cornelia Hoogteling. Wit.: David Hoogteling, Hester V. Santen.

bo. Nov. 11. Cornelis, of Wynand V. d. Berg and Maria De Ridder. Wit.: Abrm. and Antje Yates.

bo. Oct. 25. Catharina, of Arent Bekker and Antje V. Woert. Wit.: Hans and Annatje Bekker.

Nov. 24. Daniel, of Pieter Goey and Maria Young. Wit.: Hannes and Elisabeth Goey.

bo. Oct. 31. Willem, of Johs. Strook and Dorothea Canner. Wit.: Sent V. and Geertruy Bennewie.

Dec. 1, bo. Nov. 19. Theunis, of John Vile and Geesje Slingerland. Wit.: Theunis Vile, Wyntje Bratt.

bo. Nov. 26 or 27. Margarita, of Andries H. Gardenier and Sara Hansen. Wit.: Willem Hun, Sara de Foreest.

bo. Nov. 26. Quiliaan, of Jellis Winne and Titje V. Woert. Wit.: Quiliaan and Dirkje Winne.

bo. Nov. 27. Catharina, of Hermanus J. Wendel and Barbara Brat. Wit.: Abraham and Catharina Kuyler.

bo. Nov. 7. Jacob, of Leenert Muller and Marritje V. Esch. Wit.: Johs. and Maria Goey.

bo. Nov. 27. Tobias, of Steven J. Schuyler and Leentje Ten Eick. Wit.: Tobias Rykman, Leena Ten Eick.

Dec. 8, bo. Oct. 27. Hendrik, of Jacob Knoet and Maayke Lansing. Wit.: Yzaac Lansing, Annatje V. Arnhem.

bo. Nov. 25. Annatje, of Nanning Vischer and Lena Lansing. Wit.: Gerardus Knoet, Alida Visscher.

Catharina, of Nicholaas Rechter and Maria Hendermond. Wit.: Hendrik and Catharina Hendermond.

Dec. 15, bo. Nov. 18. Gerrit, of Rutger Lansing and Susanna V. Schoonhoven. Wit.: Gerrit and Wyntje Lansing.

bo. Dec. 9. Marytje, of Cornelis V. Vechten and Annatje Knickerbaker. Wit.: Gerrit and Alida Visscher.

Dec. 22, bo. Dec. 18. Simon, of Wouter De Ridder and Anneke V. d. Berg. Wit.: Wouter Bekker, Annatje Ridder.

Dec. 25, bo. Nov. 16. Alexander, of David Scott and Marytje Wendel. Wit.: John Groesbeek, Aaltje V. Aarnhem.

bo. Nov. 4. Catharina, of Maas Van Buuren and Cathalyntje Valkenburg. Wit.: Barent and Elsje Ten Eick.

Dec. 29, bo. Oct. 10. Hendrik, of Hendrik Albrecht and Elisabeth Voland. Wit.: Samuel Tayler, Jennith Bertly.

1766, Jan. 2, bo. Dec. 29, (1765). Jacobus, of Gerardus Beekman and Anna Douw. Wit.: Folkert P. and Catharina Douw.

bo. Dec. 30, (1765). Sara Winne, of Pieter Crennel and Catharina Egmond. Wit.: Cornelis and Maria Cadmus.

Jan. 5, bo. Dec. 20, (1765). Adam, of Philip Coenraad and Frony Clumm. Wit.: Adam Coenraad, Elisabeth Clumm.

bo. Dec. 5. Cornelis, of Hannes Oothout and Elisabeth V. Woert. Wit.: Jurjen Breght, Maayke Oothout.

Jan. 12, bo. Jan. 5, (1766). Hendrikje, of Gerrit van

1766

Yveren and Catharina Bogert. Wit.: Yzaac Bogart, Maria Bogert.

bo. Dec. 6, (1765). Petrus, of David York and Susanna Creller. Wit.: Andries Goey, Annatje Creller.

Jan. 18, bo. Oct. 29, (1765). Annatje, of Mathys and Marytje Bovie. Wit.: Abraham V. d. Heide, Hendrikje Rykman.

bo. Dec. 5, (1765). Catharina, of Balthes Bratt and Ronne Foller. Wit.: Arent and Marg. Bekker.

bo. Jan. 10, (1766). Elisabeth, of Johs. Fryer and Elisabeth V. Woert. Wit.: Theunis and Elisabeth V. Woert.

bo. Dec. 22, (1765). Hugo, of David Ben and Annatje Gerner. Wit.: Cornelis and Willempje Santvoort.

Jan. 26, bo. Dec. 26, (1765). Willem, of Gerrit V. Buuren and Marritje Witbeek. Wit.: Cornelis and Maayke V. Buuren.

bo. Jan. 19, (1766). Cathalyna Sophia, of Philip Cuiler and Sara Cuyler. Wit.: Hendrik Kuyler, Elisabeth V. Cortland.

bo. Nov. 20, (1765). Theunis, of Adam and Neeltje Zonfeld. Wit.: Abraham Kerner, Antje Santvoort.

Samuel, of Dirk Benson and Marytje Wyngaart. Wit.: Willem Vosburg, Neeltje Merselis.

bo. Jan. 20. Gysbert, of Pieter Williams and Elisabeth Fonda. Wit.: Johs. Knickerbacker, Elsje Fonda.

Feb. 2, bo. Jan. 28. Magdalena, of Christiaan Jacobi and Margarita Hoghing. Wit.: William and Lena Brommely.

Feb. 2, bo. Jan. 10. Theunis, of Jacob F. Lansing and Jannetje Vischer. Wit.: Bastiaan I. and Engeltje Vischer.

bo. Jan. 26. Johannes, of Barent Goey and Rachel V. Oostrander. Wit.: Johs and Geertruy Goey.

bo. Jan. 24. Hendrik, of Alexander Bulsing and Aaltje Oothout. Wit.: Hendrik and Cathalyntje Bulsing.

bo. Jan. 31. Maria, of Gysbert G. Merselis and Annatje Staats. Wit.: Yzaac and Maria Staats.

bo. Feb. 1. Maria, of Hermanus Schuyler and Christina Ten Broek. Wit.: Hendrik and Margarita V. Dyk.

Feb. 9, bo. Jan. 27. Roelef, of John and Phebe Kidny. Wit.: Jacob Kidny, Catharina Broeks.

bo. Feb. 1. Johannes, of Jacob V. Schaik and Marytje V. Buuren. Wit.: Christoffel Lansing, Sara V. Schaik.

bo. Jan. 28. Marytje, of Gysbert and Hester Bosch. Wit.: Pieter Michelt, Marytje Bosch.

bo. Jan. 14. Susanna, of Jacob Mook and Catharina Claassen. Wit.: Pieter and Claartje Claassen.

Feb. 16, bo. Feb. 11. Sara, of Albertus Bloemendal and Anna Harssen. Wit.: Maas and Lena Bloemendal.

bo. Jan. 29. Elsje, of Hendrik Stroink and Elsje Harwich. Wit.: Philip and Anna Harwich.

1766
Feb. 23, bo. Jan 21. Petrus, of Cornelis G. V. Esch and
Alida Van Woert. Wit.: Ysaac and Annatje Lansing.
bo. Feb. 21. Dirkje, of John Van Esch and Hester
Gerritzen. Wit.: Hendrik and Dirkje Gerritsen.
bo. Jan. 22. Bastiaan, of Pieter Garmo and Geertruy
Crugier. Wit.: Bastiaan Garmo, Sara Fisscher.
bo. Feb. 2. Geertruid, of Mathys Bovie, Jr., and Bata
V. d. Heide. Wit.: Sim and Geertruy Bennewee.
Mar. 10, bo. Feb. 23. Annatje, of Johs. Arnold and
Annatje Hillebrand. Wit.: Wendel and Geertruy Hille-
brand.
bo. Feb. 13. Johannes, of Jacob Olfer and Annatje
Siksby. Wit.: Jurjen Hoghing, Cathalyntje Hun.
Mar. 16, bo. Dec. 25. (1765). Hester, of Albert Slinger-
land and Elisabeth Mook. Wit.: Albert V. d. Zee, Annatje
Veder.
bo. Mar. 13. Cornelis, of Pieter Veder and Marytje
V. d. Berg. Wit.: Cornelis and Cornelia V. d. Berg.
bo. Mar. 12. Margarita, of Johs. V. Valkenburg and
Elisabeth Meinerssen. Wit.: Jacob and Margar. V. Val-
kenburg.
bo. Mar. 13. Geertruid, of Philip Lansing and Elsje
Hun. Wit.: Gerardus and Maria Lansing.
bo. Mar. 13. Anna, of Pieter Ganzevoort and Gerritje
Ten Eik. Wit.: Johs. and Evje Ganzevoort.
Mar. 27, bo. Mar. 23. Hendrik, of Barent Vosburg and
Annatje Gerritsen. Wit.: Gerrit Greveraad, Marytje Ger-
ritsen.
Mar. 29, bo. Feb. 28. Maria, of Jacob Lansing and
Maria Ouderkerk. Wit.: Baas and Elisab. V. Woert.
Mar. 30, bo. Mar. 1. Jenneke, of Jacobus Kool
and Jannetje Witbeek. Wit.: Cornelis and Cathalyntje
Cool.
Apr. 6, bo. Mar. 3. Johannes, of Johannes Fryer and
Catharina Kernryk. Wit.: Hendrik V. Aarnhem, Santje
Winne.
bo. Mar. 23. Catharina, of Philip P. Schuyler and
Annatje Wendel. Wit.: Pieter and Engeltje Schuyler.
bo. Mar. 7. Gerrit, of Abraham V. Esch and Antje
Ridder. Wit.: Leendert Muller, Marritje V. Esch.
Apr. 13, bo. Mar. 16. Folkert, of Meinert V. Hoezen
and Geertruy Vinhagel. Wit.: Herman and Tryntje V.
Hoezen.
Elisabeth, of Frans Grewel and Annatje Balsing. Wit.:
Johs. M. and Elisabeth Beekman.
bo. Mar. 8. Johannes, of Jacob Roozeboom, Jr., and
Hester Lansing. Wit.: Jacob and Rykje Roseboom.
bo. Apr. 13. Abraham, of George Dean and Annetje
V. Deuzen. Wit.: Cornelis Cadmus, Annatje Lansing.

1766

Apr. 20, bo. Apr. 13. Dirk, of Johs. Hun and Catharina Viele. Wit.: Dirk and Margarita Hun.

bo. Mar. 28. Elisabeth, of Hannes Oostrander and Marrytje V. Aalstein. Wit.: Petrus and Elisabet Oostrander.

bo. Apr. 18. Lambert, of Johs. Redly and Elisabeth Wilkeson. Wit.: Lambert Redlif, Annatje Flensburg.

bo. Apr. 15. Philip, of Stephanus V. Renselaar and Catharina Levingston. Wit.: Abraham Ten Broek, Elizabeth Van Renzelaar.

Apr. 27, bo. Apr. 13. William, of Francis Nichols and Margarita V. Renzelaar. Wit.: Hendrik and Alida V. Renzelaar.

bo. Apr. 19. Gerardus, of Yzaac du Voe and Marytje V. Olinde. Wit.: Gerardus V. Olinde, Lena du Voe.

bo. Mar. 20. Evert, of Philip Wendel and Cathal. Groesbeek. Wit.: David Scott, Susanna Lansing.

May 4, bo. Apr. 11. Marritje, of Pieter Levison and Maria Fonda. Wit.: Abraham V. d. Berg, Rachel Levison.

May 11, bo. May 4. (?) Johannes, of Hendrik Bleecker, Jr., and Cathalina Cuyler. Wit.: Gerrit and Geertruy Rozeboom.

May 18, bo. Apr. 8. Annatje, of Albert V. d. Zee and Marytje V. d. Kar. Wit.: Dirk and Fytje V. d. Kar.

May 18, bo. Apr. 25. Johan Pieter, of Johan P. and Clara M. Claassen. Wit.: Jurg. Mich. Read, Anna Redin.

May 25, bo. May 1. Maria, of Melchert V. d. Berg and Margarita Vinhagel. Wit.: Johs. Vinhagel, Marytje V. d. Berg.

bo. May 3. Maria, of Thomas Willis and Rachel Redlif. Wit.: John Redlif, Nency Willis.

bo. May 20. Maria, of Albert Slingerland and Christina V. Franken. Wit.: Gerrit and Marytje V. Franken.

bo. May 19. Gysbert, of Cornelis M. and Cornelia V. d. Berg. Wit.: Bastiaan I. and Engeltje Visscher.

June 1, bo. Apr. 27. Cornelis, of Johs Fonda and Elisabeth Ouderkerk. Wit.: Johs and Marytje Bratt.

bo. May 28. Abigail, of Yzaac D. Fonda and Susanna Foreest. Wit.: Philip Foreest, Maria Bloemendal.

bo. May 13. Johannes, of Christoffer Yaets and Catharina Lansing. Wit.: Pieter and Catharyntje Yaets.

June 9, in the house. Margarita, of Harmen (?) Fort and Rebecca V. Woert. Wit.: John and Margar. V. Seissen.

June 15, bo. June 1. Abraham, of John Northen and Elisabeth de Voe. Wit.: Cornelis W. V. d. Bergh, Marytje Viele.

bo. May 26. Johannes, of Hendrik Meyer and Maria Snyer. Wit.: Balthes Geroni, Maria Snyder.

1766

bo. June 15. Jacobus, of Christoffer Lansing and Sara
V. Schaik. Wit.: Jacob and Hubertje Lansing.

bo. June 15. Jacobus, of Christoffer Lansing and Sara
V. Schaik. Wit.: Jacob and Hubertje Lansing.

bo. May 3. Marytje, of Jurjen Scherp and Catharina
Fliegery. Wit.: Pieter and Catharina Sherp.

bo. June 1. Maria, of Meinard Rozeboom and Geertruy
Switz. Wit.: Hendrik M. and Maria Roozeboom.

June 15, bo. May 14. Ryckert, of Gerrit V. Franken and
Alida Reyly. Wit.: Pieter and Barbara Bogaart.

June 22, bo. June 16. Rhebecca, of Yzaac Hoogkerk
and Rachel V. Santen. Wit.: Lucas and Alida Hoogkerk.

July 6, bo. July 5. Maria, of John D. Groesbeek and
Aaltje V. Aarnhem. Wit.: David and Catharina Groesbeek.

bo. June 11. Franciscus, of Daniel Winne and Catharina
Hoogteling. Wit.: Frans Winne, Marytje Hoogteling.

bo. June 22. Andries, of Filip Muller and Geertruy
Goey. Wit.: Andries Goey, Jeny Young.

bo. June 29. Gerrit, of Rutger and Maria V. d. Berg.
Wit.: Benjamin and Catharina Goey.

bo. July 4. Johannes, of Yzaac Slingerland and Eva V.
Woert. Wit.: Jacob and Marg. V. Woert.

bo. June 29. Jacobus, of Philip Young and Annatje
Sickels. Wit.: Gerrit and Catharina Viele.

bo. July 1. Hugo, of Balthes V. Benthuisen and Sara
Viele. Wit.: Hugo and Elisabeth Viele.

July 6, bo. June 3. Abraham, of Johs V. Aarnhem and
Alida V. d. Heiden. Wit.: John Knoet, Sara V. Aarnem.

bo. May 16. Elisabeth, of John Fonda and Egje V. d.
Zee. Wit.: Olfert V. d. Zee, Jr., Annatje Veder.

July 13, bo. May 10. Yzaac, of Johan Melchert Fyle
and Elisabeth Hansinger. Wit.: Barent and Anna M.
Zippersleyn.

bo. June 4. Jacob, of Willem Orloop (?) and Maria Hartman. Wit.: Willem and Christina Zabel.

July 18, bo. Apr. 6. Geertruy, of Jurjen Bickers and
Eva Rickert (or Staring). Wit.: Jacob and Margarita
Bleecker.

July 20, bo. July 15. Annatje, of Arent Bratt and
Jannetje Hoghing. Wit.: Simon and Annatje Veder.

bo. July 13. Sara, of Maas Bloemendal, Jr., and Helena
Schermerhoorn. Wit.: John Scott, Elisabeth Williams.

bo. June 30. Johannes, of Casparus Witbeek and Geertruy V. d. Berg. Wit.: Johs. and Rachel Witbeek.

bo. July 17. Jannetje, of Abraham J. Yaets and Jannetje
Brat. Wit.: John Williams, Elisabeth Bratt.

bo. July 12. Elisabeth, of Gozen V. Schaik and Maayke
V. d. Berg. Wit.: Evert Wendel, Elisabeth V. Schaik.

1766

July 25, bo. July 21. Abraham, of Abraham Wever and Annatje Kernel. Wit.: Hercules Lendt, Marytje Duivebach.

July 27, bo. July 22. Ryckert, of Pieter Bogart and Barbara V. Franken. Wit.: Dirk and Alida V. Franken.

bo. the 13th. Marytje, of Gerzer (?) Vedder and Neeltje Bords. Wit.: James Canon, Annatje Bords.

bo. the 22. Anthony, of Johs A. Bratt and Maayke Fonda. Wit.: Staats Santvoort, Willempje Bratt.

Aug. 3, bo. July 28. Catharina, of Andries Wederwaker and Catharina Reisdorf. Wit.: Hannes Snyder, Catharina Wederwax.

bo. July 27. Annatje, of Jacob Heemstraat and Catharina (?) Duret. Wit.: Ned. and Jannetje Davids.

bo. Aug. 2. Hendrikje, of Louis V. Woert and Catharyntje V. d. Berg. Wit.: Yzac J. and Annatje Lansing.

Aug. 10, bo. Aug. 3. Pieter, of Pieter Jones and Abigail Winne. Wit.: Bernardus and Cathar. Bratt.

bo. Aug. 9. Jacobus, of Yzaac V. Valkenburg and Annatje V. d. Berg. Wit.: Jacobus and Margarita V. Valkenburg.

bo. June 6. Abraham, of Jacob V. Olinde and Elisabeth Schermerhoorn. Wit.: Jurjen and Maria Wessel.

bo. Aug. 3. Johannes, of Johs. V. Santen and Margarita Wilkeson. Wit.: Thomas Barreth, Elisabeth V. Santen.

Aug. 10, bo. July 1. Andries, of Johs. Smit and Margar. Peettinger. Wit.: Jurjen and Lena Steers.

Aug. 17, bo. Aug. 15. Jacob, of Abraham C. Cuyler and Jannetje Glen. Wit.: John, Jr., and Elisabeth Glen.

bo. Aug. 14, Johannes, of Jacob Cuyler and Lydia V. Vechten. Wit.: Johannes and Elsje Cuyler.

bo. July 11. Johannes, of Hendrik Briesch and Arriaantje Vinhagel. Wit.: Johs. Vinhagel, Wyntje Briesch.

Aug. 24, bo. Aug. 18. Annatje, of Yzaac Roza and Marytje V. Franken. Wit.: Ryckert and Marg. V. Franken.

bo. Aug. 22. Hermanus, of Philip Reyly and Jannetje V. Slyk. Wit.: Hermanus and Geertruy V. Slyk.

Aug. 31, bo. Aug. 25. Annatje, of Barent and Sara Vischer. Wit.: Johs. and Annatje Boerbach.

Sep. 7, bo. Aug. 2. Catharina, of Annias McKentasch and Ebbetje V. d. Berg. Wit.: Abrm Yaets and Wife.

bo. Aug. 12. Ryckert, of Simon Fort and Annatje V. Franken. Wit.: Dirk and Alida V. Franken.

Sep. 14, bo. Aug. 23. Willem, of Jacob Herman and Barbara Vos. Wit.: Coenraad Herman, Elisabeth Vos.

bo. Sep. 13. Pieter, of Petrus Hilton and Annatje Broeks. Wit.: Pieter and Annatje Broeks.

Sep. 18, bo. Sep. 12. Cathalyntje, of John David and

1766

Elisabeth Wyngaard. Wit.: Yzaac Trouex, Cathalyna Maas.

Sep. 21, bo. Aug. 19. Ebbetje, of John Bell and Margarita Souper. (Touper?) Wit.: Christiaan and Rosina Souper. (Touper?).

bo. Sep. 17. Pieter, of Frans Winne and Anneke Viele. Wit.: Jelles and Fytje Winne.

bo. Aug. 24. Lena, of Wilhelmus V. Deuzen and Christina Kittel. Wit.: John J. and Maria Beekman.

bo. Sep. 3. Pieter Brat, of Jacob Foreest and Catharina Bratt. Wit.: Pieter and Vrouwtje Bratt.

bo. Sep. 16. Cathalyna, of Hendrik Qwakkenbusch and Margarita Oothout. Wit.: Hannes Oothout, Elisabeth Staats.

bo. Sep. 13. Jonas, of Hendrik Oothout, Jr., and Lydia Douw. Wit.: Jonas Oothout, Rachel Douw.

Sep. 23, bo. Sep. 21. Catharina, of Abraham Coeper and Cathar. V. Oostrander, dec'd. Wit.: Johannes(?) Witbeek, Lea V. Ostrander.

Sep. 28, bo. Sep. 6. Hendrik, of Hendrik Lygher and Anna Elisabeth Lycher. Wit.: Willem H. Oorlop, Barbara Herman.

bo. Sep. 3. Cornelis, of Cornelis V. d. Berg and Maayke Ouderkerk. Wit.: Wouter and Anneke Ridder.

Oct. 5. Jacob, of Samuel and Rebecca Hegher. Wit.: Nicol. and Anna Maria Failler.

Oct. 5, bo. Oct. 2. Catharina, of Theunis V. Woert and Elisabeth V. Deuzen. Wit.: Stephanus Schuyler, Engeltje V. Vechten.

Johannes, of Michael and Maria Ryckert. Wit.: Nicolaas and Anna M. Faillor.

bo. July 13. Elisabeth, of Jurj. H. and Maria R. Stater. Wit.: Paul and Elisabeth Hoogstrasser.

bo. Sep. 3. Maria Catharina, of Jacob and Elisabeth Heller. Wit.: Pieter and Maria Bratt.

Oct. 12. Maria, of William Denton and Annatje Egmond. Wit.: John Bornside, Mary Egmond.

bo. Oct. 11. Hendrik, of Bernardus Halenbeek and Neeltje Clark. Wit.: Gerrit and Susanna Halenbeek.

bo. Sep. 14. Jannetje, of Marten Foreest and Janneke Winne. Wit.: Daniel and Jannetje Winne.

bo. Sep. 20. Hendrik, of Cornelis Bulsing and Annatje Gonzales. Wit.: Hendrik and Cathal. Bulsing.

Oct. 19, bo. Sep. 28. Maria, of Gerrit Ten Baar and Cathalyntje Brat. Wit.: Simon V. Antwerpen, Maria Ten Baar.

bo. Sep. 18. Arriaantje, of Pieter Hoogteling and Annatje Bekkers. Wit.: Arent and Antje Bekker.

1766

bo. Sep. 13. Lydia, of Gerrit Zeger and Wyntje Olfer.
Wit.: Johs. and Annatje Fryer.

Nov. 2. Maria, of Yzaac Trouex and Maria Wyngaert.
Wit.: Johs. and Maria Wyngaert.

Nicolaas, of Hans Wederman and Margarita Follerin.
Wit.: Mathys and Anna Coegler.

bo. Oct. 31. Eva, of Harmen V. Hoezen and Catharina
Witbeek. Wit.: Johs. and Eva Witbeek.

bo. Oct. 10. Maria, of William Pengborn and Elisabeth
V. d. Bogert. Wit.: Gerrit Zeger, Mary Pengborn.

bo. Oct. 4. Jurjen, of Hannes Eiby and Margar. Heener.
Wit.: Jurjen and Cath. Scherp.

bo. Oct. 16. Johannes, of Willem Northen and Mally
Beely. Wit.: John and Elisab. Northen.

bo. Nov. 1. Lena, of Jacob Lansing and Willempje
Winne. Wit.: Jacob and Hubertje Lansing.

Nov. 9, bo. Sep. 17. Jacob, of Albert V. d. Werken and
Marytje Kwakkenbusch. Wit.: Martinus Lydius, Claartje
Knoet.

bo. Oct. 16. Coenraad, of Hannes Lang and Christina
Bratt. Wit.: Coenraad and Cornelia Hoogteling.

Nov. 16, bo. Nov. 9. Annatje, of Theunis Vischer and
Barbara Fonda. Wit.: Gysbert Fonda, Rebecca Knickerbacker.

bo. Oct. 23. Lydia, of Hermanus V. Aalstein and Cathar.
Peeshinger. Wit.: Adriaan Bratt, Lydia V. Aalstein.

bo. Nov. 14. Robert, of Hendrik Lansing and Maria
Mersselis. Wit.: Hendrik Wendel, Rykje Rozeboom.

Nov. 23, bo. Nov. 7. George, of Hannes Hoghil and
Sara Young. Wit.: George Young, Catharina Litzer.

Nov. 30, bo. Oct. 15. Abraham, of Abrm. Siksby
and Egje Ackers. Wit.: Theunis V. d. Zee, Christina
Bacchus.

bo. Nov. 29. Anna, of Johs. Johs. Bleecker and Gerritje
V. Schaik. Wit.: Sybrand and Anna V. Schaik.

Dec. 6, bo. Dec. 4. Catharina, of Benjamin Goey and
Catharina V. d. Berg. Wit.: Gerrit W. V. d. Berg, Alida
Goey.

bo. Dec. 3. George, of Michael Warner and Margarita
Schrey. Wit.: Coenraad and Maria Schrey.

Dec. 14, bo. Nov. 16. Wyntje, of Mathys Boom, Jr., and
Josyntje Zeger. Wit.: Thomas and Judike Zeger.

Dec. 21, bo. Nov. 13. Dirk, of Frederik and Maria
Zoup. Wit.: Dirk and Eva Bekker.

bo. Dec. 18. Quiliaan, of Daniel Winne and Jannetje
Banker. Wit.: Quiliaan and Dirkje Winne.

Dec. 25, bo. Dec. 22. Annatje, of Frerik Meinerssen
and Elisabeth Waldron. Wit. Abram and Sara Meinerssen.

1767, Jan. 5, bo. Nov. 9. (1766). Elisabeth, of Jacob V. Arnhem and Annatje V. Franken. Wit.: Yzaac and Annatje Lansing.

Jan. 11, bo. Oct. 11. (1766). Kiliaan, of Evert V. d. Berg and Marytje V. der Werken. Wit.: Kiliaan Ridder, Antje Yates.

Jan. 18, bo. Jan. 14. Rachel, of John Louis Voetje and Trina Voetje. Wit.: Theunis and Machtel Visscher.

bo. Oct. 19. (1766). Maria, of Abraham Fryer and Jannetje Hetsel. Wit.: John J. and Maria Beekman.

bo. Jan. 1. Johannes, of Abraham Boom and Dorothea Cunningham. Wit.: Nicolaas Brouny, Marytje Boom.

bo. Dec. 18. (1766). Elisabeth, of Abraham and Elisabeth Oostrander. Wit.: Petrus Oostrander, Gerritje Witbeek.

bo. Jan. 17. Sander, of Gerrit J. Lansing and Jannetje Waters. Wit.: Sander and Abigail Lansing.

bo. Dec. 7. Douwe, of Yzaac Fonda and Rebecca Groesbeek. Wit.: Yzaac and Alida Foreest.

Jan. 25, bo. Jan. 18. (1767). Johannes, of Johs Visscher and Elisabeth Bratt. Wit.: Johs. and Annatje Roerbach.

bo. Jan. 21. Catharina, of Casparus V. Wie and Jannetje Winne. Wit.: Pieter and Alida Van Wie.

bo. Nov. 19. (1766). Lavinus, of John Winne and Susanna Ridder. Wit.: Lavinus and Susanna Winne.

bo. Dec. 18. Wynand, of Gerrit Waldrom and Catharina V. d. Berg. Wit.: Wynand and Cathal. V. d. Berg.

Rebecca, of Christiaan and Ann Duivebach. Wit.: Thomas and R. Couper.

Jan. 26. Willempje, of Jacob and Cath. Quackenbusch. Wit.: Staats and Willemptje Santvoort.

Jan. 29, bo. Jan. 8. Margarita, of Dirk I. (or T.) V. Veghten and Cathalyntje V. Esch. Wit.: Philip and Lena V. Esch.

Feb. 1, bo. Dec. 31. (1766). Sara, Matheus, twins of Pieter DeGarmo and Lena Bomp. Wit.: Joseph V. Santen, Rebecca and Matheus Garmo, Marytje Groesbeek.

bo. Dec. 30. Annatje, of John Huson and Annatje Koch. Wit.: Folckert P. and Annatje Douw.

Feb. 8, bo. Feb. 4. (1767). Johannes, of Roelef Zeger and Lydia Hartje. Wit.: Thomas and Judike Zeger.

bo. Jan. 29. Catharina, of William and Christina Dobel. Wit.: Jurmet (?) and Barbara Cremer.

bo. Feb. 4. Johannes, of James and Mary Abbet. Wit.: John and Christina Bhaff.

bo. Jan. 29. Michael, of Jurjen and Lena Sting. Wit.: Anthony and Cornelia Halenbeek.

Feb. 15, bo. Jan. 27. Maria, of Pieter and Maria Michel. Wit.: Gysbert and Hester Bosch.

1767

bo. Feb. 13. Cornelis, of Jacob Abeel and Eybetje V. Buuren. Wit.: Cornelis and Maayke V. Buuren.

bo. Jan. 21. Whillem, of Matheus and Christina Flensburg. Wit.: Whillem Flensburg, Christina Boucher (?).

Feb. 15, bo. Jan. 3. Elisabeth, of Hannes and Barbara Mook. Wit.: Andries and Elisab. Fyt.

bo. Feb. 12. Maria, of Robert Yates and Jannetje V. Esch. Wit.: Joseph R. and Maria Yates.

bo. Sep. 15. Johanna, of Willem Sharp and Neeltje Zerdam. Wit.: Loys Van Woert, Neeltje Rozeboom.

Feb. 11, during evening Service, bo. Feb. 10. Annatje, of Christoffer Yates and Catharina Waters. Wit.: Adam and C. Yates.

Feb. 15, bo. Jan. 19. Geertruy, of Yzaac Dox and Lena de Voe. Wit.: Jan and Geertruy Dox.

Feb. 23, bo. Feb. 6. Marytje, of John Crennel and Folkje V. Aalstein. Wit.: Willem V. Aalstein, Sara Downal.

Feb. 25, bo. Feb. 9. Margarita, of Jacob Pess and Annatje Shaat. Wit.: Abm. Vosburg, Margarita Shaat.

bo. Jan. 30. Annatje, of Abraham Fort and Eva Benneway. Wit.: Harmen Groesbeek, Marytje Benneway.

bo. Feb. 3. Stephanus, of Loys Viele and Annatje Qwackenbusch. Wit.: John Viele, Geesje Slingerland.

Mar. 1, bo. Feb. 4. Catharina, of Storm Bratt and Dorothea V. Aalstein. Wit.: Pieter and Catharina Bratt.

Mar. 4, bo. Mar. 2. Marten Beekman, of Abraham Schuyler and Eva Beekman. Wit.: Marten and Geertruy Beekman.

Mar. 4, bo. Mar. 2. Annatje, of Pieter Yates and Sara Aalstein. Wit.: Hannes and Rebecca Yates.

Mar. 22, bo. Mar. 19. Hendrik, of Jacob V. Schaik and Catharina Cuyler. Wit.: Abraham and Elisabeth Cuyler.

bo. Mar. 21. Johannes, of Jacobus V. Santen and Maria Brooks. Wit.: John and Annatje Fryer.

bo. Mar. 17. Catharina, of Herculeus Lynd and Marytje Duivenbach. Wit.: Christiaan and Catharina Duivebach.

Mar. 25, bo. Feb. 26. Neeltje, of Arent V. Antwerpen and Hester Crugier. Wit.: Harmen and Neeltje V. Antwerpen.

Mar. 29, bo. Feb. 15. Cathalyntje, of Salomo Bulsing and Geertruy Knoet. Wit.: Hendrik Bulsing, Annatje Smith.

Elisabeth, of Whilliam Soul and Margarita Wyngaard. Wit.: Andries J. Trouex, Cathal. Wyngaert.

bo. Mar. 25. Sybrand, of Pieter W. Douw and Rykje V. Schaik. Wit.: Sybrand and Alida V. Schaik.

bo. Mar. 26. Harmen, of Joannes Ten Broek and Sara Ganzevoort. Wit.: Harmen and Magdalena Ganzevoort.

Apr. 5, bo. Mar. 13. Elisabeth, of Hannes V. der Werken

1767
and Maaytje de Voe. Wit.: John Northen, Elisabeth de Voe.

bo. Feb. 27. Hendrik, of Abraham V. d. Kar and Margarita de Voe. Wit.: Gozen V. Schaik, Catharina de Voe.

Apr. 12, bo. Apr. 4. Cornelia, of Abraham V. d. Berg and Rachel Levison. Wit.: Cornelis and Cornelia V. d. Bergh.

bo. Feb. 21. Petrus, of Jurjen and Margarita Cremer. Wit.: Petrus and Catharina Sharp.

Apr. 17, bo. Jan. 30. Anna, of Everhard and Magdalena Wheger. Wit.: Jacob and Anna C. Proest. (?).

bo. Feb. 11. Anna, of Jacob and Rezina B. Wheger. Wit.: Johs. Parent, Anna Baart.

bo. Mar. 6. Lodewyk, of Hannes and Anna Baart. Wit.: Lodewyk and Maria B. Snyer.

Apr. 19, bo. Mar. 13. Marytje, of John V. Aalstein and Lena Sharp. Wit.: Wynand and Marytje V. Aastein.

bo. Mar. 30. Rachel, of Gerrit Oostrander and Christina V. d. Berg. Wit.: Hendrik Oostrander, Elisabeth Knickerbacker.

bo. Mar. 22. Pieter, of Gerrit V. d. Poel and Cathar. Hoes. Wit.: Pieter N. V. Buuren, Marytje V. d. Poel.

bo. Mar. 30. Jacob, of Nicolaas Sharp and Lena Hogeboom. Wit.: Jurjen and Barbara Sharp.

bo. Mar. 17. Lambert, of Johs. Redly and Elisabeth Wilkeson. Wit.: Lambert Redly, Annatje Flensburg.

Whilliam and Susanna, twins of Evan and Cathar. Thomas.

Apr. 26, bo. Apr. 12. Whouter, of Anthony V. Slingerland and Saartje Knoet. Wit.: Whouter and Hesje Slingerland.

May 3, bo. Feb. 5. Philip, of Philip and Eva Heiner. Wit.: Johs Eedel, Grietje Heiner.

bo. Apr. 2. Adam, of Frans Winne and Marytje Hoogteling. Wit.: Willem and Antje Winne.

bo. Apr. 29. Confort, of John Ostrander and Anna Wolssen.

Catharina, of Baltes and Barbara Bakker. Wit.: Michel and Annatje Reek.

bo. Feb. 26. Marytje, of Daniel and Willempje Bratt. Wit.: Wouter and Marytje Groesbeek.

bo. May 2. Barent Sanders, of Johs. J. Beekman and Maria Sanders. Wit.: John Sanders, Sara Glen.

bo. Apr. 1. Elisabeth, of Hendrik and Grietje Zeger. Wit.: Roelef and Lydia Zeger.

May 10, bo. May 7. Maria, of Jochum Staats and Geesje Veder. Wit.: Yzaac and Maria Staats.

bo. Apr. 28. Lena, of Gerrit Slingerland and Egje V. d. Zee. Wit.: John and Geertruy Hanssen.

1767
bo. Mar. 3. Catharina, of Hannes Heemstraat and Elisabeth Bovie. Wit.: Frans Bovie, Machteld V. Franken.
bo. May 8. Benjamin, of Gysbert V. Santen and Rebecca Winne. Wit.: Benjamin and Hester Winne.
May 17, bo. Mar. 14. Yzaac, of Hendrik Young and Catharina Landman. Wit.: Yzaac Vosburg, Catharina Staats.
bo. Apr. 25. Jacob, of Hannes Muller and Sara V. Yveren. Wit.: Gerrit and Alida V. d. Berg.
May 17, bo. Apr. 26. Marytje, of Zacharias Berringer and Anna Fallor. Wit.: Nicholaas and Marytje Fallor.
bo. Apr. 16. Abraham, of Johannes Knoet, Jr., and Sara V. Aarnhem. Wit.: Yzaac and Elisabeth V. Aarnhem.
May 24, bo. Apr. 22 Hermanus, of Hendrik and Anna Haan. Wit.: Michel and Barbara Nicolas, Jacob Wagenaar.
bo. May 20. Margarita, of Hannes Haan and Catharina Boosten. Wit.: John and Marg. Tileman.
bo. May 20. Margarita, of Andrew and Elisabeth Wreight.
bo. May 8. Elsje, of Joh. Olfer and Marritje Siksby. Wit.: Evert and Elsje Siksby.
June 7, bo. Apr. 30. Sara, of Jacob G. V. Schaik and Geertje Ridder. Wit.: Hannes and Alida V. Schaik.
bo. Apr. 25. Abraham, of Dirk M. V. d. Heiden and Sara Wendel. Wit.: Dirk and Elisabeth V. d. Heiden.
bo. May 16. Marritje, of Nanning Visscher and Lena Lansing. Wit.: Frans and Marritje Lansing.
June 28, bo. June 1. Cornelia, of Nicolaas Rechter and Maria Hoenermond. Wit.: Christoffel Reine, Cornelia Regter.
bo. June 26. Jannetje, of Andries Goe and Florena Jung. Wit.: Jan Gerrisse Fels, Catalyntje Van Schaik.
bo. May 23. Nicolaas, of Baltus Brat and Rosina Follert. Wit.: Nicolaas and Margrietje Follert.
July 5, bo. Apr. 18. Johan Andreas, of Alexander and Margarita Kwee. Wit.: Andreas and Elisab. Fyt.
Johanna, of Jacobus Hoogteling and Gerritje Penboring. Wit.: Jan Bratt, Johanna Penborn.
July 8, bo. July 7. Margarita, of Pieter Rykman and Lydia V. d. Bergh. Wit.: Cornelis and Margarita V. d. Bergh.
July 12, bo. July 11. Wilhelmus, of Marten Meinerssen and Sara Rykman. Wit.: Pieter Rykman, Cornelia Prys.
bo. July 9. Philip, of Wouter De Foreest and Alida Knoet. Wit.: Philip and Cathar. de Foreest.
July 19, bo. June 6. Johannes, of Barent and Maria B. Neer. Wit.: Hannes and Barbara Ronkel.
bo. July 22. Marritje, of Pieter and Catharina Hogh. Wit.: Hendrik and Marytje Groveraad.

1767
bo. July 7. Elisabeth, of Thomas and Elisabeth Borrus. Wit.: Elisabeth Brous.

July 26, bo. Jan. 2. Maria, of Hannes Zoufeld and Elisab. Freer. Wit.: Adam Been, Cathar. Freer.

July 29, bo. July 26. Cornelis, of Dirk B. V. Schoonhoven and Folkje V. d. Berg. Wit.: Cornelis and Susanna V. d. Bergh.

bo. July 28. Elisabeth, of Folkert G. V. d. Berg and Neeltje Waldrom. Wit.: Whillem Waldrom, Elisabeth Meinerssen.

bo. July 22. Francis, of Pieter Silvester and Jannetje V. Schaak. Wit.: Elias and Anna Brevoort.

Aug. 2, bo. June 28. Meinard, of Wouter N. Groesbeek and Alida Qwakkenbusch. Wit.: Meinard Qwakkenbusch, Elisabeth Winne.

Aug. 5, bo. Aug. 1. Meinard, of Johannes 5 (V.?) Lansing and Catharina Burhans. Wit.: Pieter and Elisabeth Lansing.

Aug. 9, bo. Aug. 5. Gerardus, of Gerardus Beekman and Anna Douw. Wit.: Johs. and Annatje De Peyster.

Aug. 16, bo. July 22. Jochum, of John Hunter and Eva V. Aalstein. Wit.: Joseph Bratt, Marg. Brianside.

bo. July 13. Aaltje, of Johannes A. Brat and Maayke Douwe. Wit.: Yzaac and Santje Fonda.

bo. July 17. Margarita, of Johannes Coen (?) and Hilletje Zeger. Wit.: John and Susanna Merriday.

Aug. 22, bo. Aug. 15. Catharina, of John and Sara Spek. Wit.: Jo, *Negro of Johs. Hansse*, Sara Spek.

bo. July 23. Annatje, of Simon de Foreest and Maria McGennis. Wit.: Jacobus and Annatje Schaap.

bo. July 15. Catharina, of Gerrit Van Buuren and Marritje Witbeek. Wit.: Lucas and Geertruy Witbeek.

bo. Aug. 1. Maria, of Jonathan Witbeek and Gerritje Oostrander. Wit.: Adam and Gerritje Winne.

Aug. 29, bo. Aug. 20. Frerik, of Hannes Zeger and Marytje Bratt. Wit.: Thomas Zeger and wife.

Aug. 29, bo. Aug. 28. Gerrit, of Dirk Benson and Maria Wyngaart. Wit.: Albert Slingerland, Marritje Vcsburgh.

bo. Aug. 24. Abraham, of Hendrik Daniels and Mally McGuyen. Wit.: Abraham and Elisabeth Ten Broek.

bo. Aug. 27. Catharina, of Gerrit V. Wie and Catharina Lansing. Wit.: Casparus Conyn, Tryntje Van Wie.

Sep. 6, bo. Aug. 16. Annatje, of Abraham Sickels and Maria Cannel. Wit.: Zacharias Sickels, Annatje Young.

bo. Aug. 5. Thomas, of Jacobus P. V. Benthuisen and Sara Cooper. Wit.: Thomas and Margarita Cooper.

bo. Aug. 28. Cornelia, of Abraham Slingerland and Rebecca Viele. Wit.: Yzaac and Eva Slingerland.

1767

Sep. 13, bo. Aug. 29. Andries, of Adriaan Bratt and Lydia V. Aalstein. Wit.: Anthony Bratt, Soekje Merriday.

bo. Sep. 12. Pieter, of Johannes Goey, Jr., and Maria Van Yveren. Wit.: Hendrik and Marytje Gardenier.

bo. the 13th. Arriaantje, of Gerrit Van Yveren and Catharina Bogert. Wit.: Pieter and Hilletje Williams.

Sep. 16, bo. Sep. 14. Hendrik, of Anthony Halenbeek and Cornelia Cooper. Wit.: Gerrit and Susanna Halenbeek.

bo. Sep. 27. Franciscus, of Casparus Pruin and Catharina Groesbeek. Wit.: Samuel and Alida Pruin.

Sept. 16. Cornelius, of Eduard Davis and Jannetje Duret. Wit.: Staats and Willempje V. Santvoort.

Harmanus, of Hendrik Wendel and Maria Lansing. Wit.: Hendrik and Barbara Lansing.

Annatje, of Wendel Hillebrand and Geertruy Visbach. Wit.: Jacob Hildebrand, Elisabeth Visbach.

Eva, of Gysbert Mersselis and Cathalyntje Wendell. Wit.: Hendrik and Johanna Merselis.

Sep. 30, bo. Sep. 3. Gerrit Theunissen, of Anthony Briesch and Catharyntje Yats. Wit.: Gerrit I. Briesch, Engeltje Yates.

Oct. 2, bo. Sep. 8. Coenraad, of Arent Coen and Marytje V. d. Hoeven. Wit.: Roelef and Lydia Zeger.

bo. Sep. 1. Tobias, of Jan Droit and Sara Levingston. Wit.: Jacob V. Woert, Neeltje Mersselis.

bo. Sep. 8. Annatje, of Wilhelmus Smith and Annatje Bratt. Wit.: Pieter and Geertruy De Garmo.

Oct. 11, bo. Aug. 23. Jacobus, of James Bamnitz and Franceyntje Cahoen. *These are Presbyterians and therefore without witnesses.*

bo. Oct. 9. Dirck, of Jacob Cuyler and Lydia V. Vechten. Wit.: Gerrit and Margarita V. d. Bergh.

bo. Oct. 8. Helena, of Hendrik V. Aarnhem and Susanna Winne. Wit.: Abraham V. Aarnhem, Helena Lansing.

Oct. 16, bo. Oct. 13. Whillem, of Willem V. Santen and Alida Smith. Wit.: Thomas Bareuth, Elisab. V. Santen.

Oct. 18, bo. Oct. 15. Hendrik, of Willem Van Wie and Jannetje Lansing. Wit.: Hendrik Wm. and Cathar. V. Wie.

Oct. 18, bo. Oct. 10. Maayke, of Alexander Bulsing and Alida Oothout. Wit.: Jurjen C. Breght, Maayke Breght.

bo. Oct. 14. Dirk, of Pieter and Vrouwtje Bratt. Wit.: Jacob De Foreest, Catharyntje Bratt.

bo. Aug. 27. Whilliam, of Whilliam and Elisabeth Wens. Wit.: Jacob Mook, Elisab. Winne.

Oct. 20, bo. Sep. 2. Theunis, of Hendrik V. d. Werken and Maria Viele. Wit.: Louys and Annatje Viele.

1767

Oct. 25, bo. Oct. 19. Yzaac, of Cornelis Zwits and Catharina Schuyler. Wit.: Meinert Rozeboom, Geertruy Zwitz.

bo. Sep. 27. Cornelia, of Gerrit Bratt and Lena Hoogteling. Wit.: Coenraad and Cornelia Hoogteling.

bo. Sep. 29. Hendrik, of Johannes J. Lansing and Maria Huik. Wit.: Jacob J. and Jannetje Lansing.

bo. Oct. 22. Marritje, of Jacob F. Lansing and Jannetje Fischer. Wit.: Nanning and Lena Visscher.

Nov. 1, bo. Oct. 25. Rykert, of Folkert Daassen and Geertruy Hilten. Wit.: Petrus Hilton, Annatje Hilten.

Nov. 4, bo. Nov. 2. Gerrit, of Nicolaas Mersselis and Margarita Groesbeek. Wit.: Gerrit and Margarita Mersselis.

Nov. 8, bo. Nov. 1. Sara, of John M'Carree and Eva Beekman. Wit.: Nicolaas Cuyler, Catharina Ten Eick.

bo. Nov. 6. Maria, of Hannes V. Santen and Margarita Wilkeson. Wit.: John Wilkeson, Saartje Fryer.

Nov. 11, bo. Nov. 10. Paulus, of Patrik Clark and Cornelia Waldron. Wit.: Gerrit Halenbeek, Elisab. V. Deuzen.

Nov. 15, bo. Nov. 1. Coenraad, of Carel Durk and Margarita Borns. Wit.: Anthony Durk, Elisabeth Clump.

bo. Nov. 11. Neeltje, of Jacob J. Schermerhoorn and Elisabeth Whitaker. Wit.: Michel and Lybetje Besset.

Nov. 18, bo. Nov. 15. Marthen, of Johannes M. Beekman and Elisabeth Douw. Wit.: Marten and Geertruy Beekman.

Nov. 24, bo. Nov. 13. Alexander, of Joseph Stalker and Elisabeth Bails, decd. *Presbyterians.*

Nov. 25, bo. Nov. 24. Sara, of Barent Vischer and Sara Visscher. Wit.: Bastiaan H. and Sara Visscher.

bo. Nov. 18. Abraham, of Willem V. d. Berg and Annatje Vosburg. Wit.: Adriaan Qwakkenbusch, Margarita Dirkssen.

Nov. 29, bo. Nov. 28. Robert, of Hendrik R. Lansing and Maria Mersselis. Wit.: Hendrik and Maria Wendell.

bo. Nov. 25. Anna, of Johs. and Anna Judita Mack. Wit.: Mathys and Anna Coughler.

Dec. 6, bo. Nov. 28. Anna Dorothea, of Johs. Kerner and Susanna Haak. Wit.: John and Christina Bhaff.

bo. Nov. 29. Elisabeth, of Nicolaas and Elisabeth Clein. Wit.: Mathys Kughler, Anna Coughler.

Dec. 6, bo. Nov. 1. Sara, of Abraham V. Esch and Antje Ridder. Wit.: Nicolaas V. d. Berg, Aaltje V. Esch.

Dec. 9, bo. Nov. 23. Abraham, of Christoffer Hegerman and Elisabeth Copper. Wit.: Abraham and Catharina Douw.

bo. Dec. 8. Gerrit, of Johannes Spoor and Magdalena Bogert. Wit.: Jan Winne, Marritje Bogert.

bo. Dec. 5. Elisabeth, of Abraham C. Cuyler and Jannetje Glen. Wit.: Hendrik Kuyler, Margarita Low.

Dec. 13, bo. Dec. 10. Magdalena, of Johannes Hanssen and Geertruy Slingerland. Wit.: Benjamin and Marytje Hanssen.

bo. Dec. 11. Gerrit, of Daniel V. Antwerpen and Dirkje Winne. Wit.: Wilhelmus and Hilletje V. Antwerpen.

bo. Dec. 10. Robert, of Lavinus Ten Baar and Margarita Hanssen. Wit.: Willem Ten Baar, Cathar. V. Franken.

bo. Dec. 12. Philip, of Hermanus Schuyler and Christina Ten Broek. Wit.: Folkert P. and Annetje Douw.

Dec. 16, bo. Dec. 13. Georgius Wilhelmus, of Wilhelmus Mancius and Annatje Ten Eick. Wit.: Casparus and Cornelia Mancius.

Dec. 25, bo. Dec. 20. Yzaac, of Edward Willet and Maria Gail. Wit.: Elbert and Cathalyna Willet.

bo. Dec. 23. Elisabeth, of Cornelis V. Vechten and Annatje Knikkerbakker. Wit.: Wouter and Elisabeth Knickerbakker.

bo. Dec. 24. Cathalyntje, of Hendrik V. Esch and Magdalena Vroman. Wit.: Gerrit Groesbeek, Jannetje V. Slyk.

Dec. 27, bo. Dec. 25. Bernardus, of Albertus Bloemdal and Anna Hanssen. Wit.: Jacob and Catharina Hanssen.

1768, Jan. 1, bo. Nov. 20. (1767). Rebecca, of Jans S. Qwakkenbusch and Jannetje Viele. Wit.: Abraham and Rebecca Slingerland.

Jan. 3. (1768). Anneke, of Wouter Ridder and Anneke V. d. Berg. Wit.: Maas and Santje V. d. Berg.

Maria, of George Lain and Mary Shaw. Wit.: Lucas and Marytje V. Vechten.

Jan. 6, bo. Jan. 4. Eldert, of Johs. Fryer and Elisabeth V. Woerd. Wit.: Eldert V. Woert, Sofia Ouderkerk.

Jan. 10. Christina, of Hendrik and Elsje Strong. Wit.: Coenraad and Christina Harwich.

bo. Jan. 2. Catharina, of Abraham Fonda and Maria Ouderkerk. Wit.: Cornelis V. d. Berg, Maayke Ouderkerk.

Jan. 12, bo. Jan. 11. Annatje, of Yzaac Vosburg and Catharina Staats. Wit.: Jacob Pest, Annatje Staats.

Jan. 16, bo. Dec. 14. (1767). Vincent, of Benjamin Springer and Hendrikje Olfer. Wit.: Vincent and Geertruy Benneway.

bo. Oct. 2. James, of David Ben and Annatje Ganner. Wit.: James Dole, Antje V. Santvoort.

Johannes, of Jurjen and Mary Witsel. Wit.: John and Barbara Clint.

Jan. 16, bo. Dec. 5. Catharina, of Barent and Margarita Zipperlein. Wit.: Johs. and Catharina Snyder.

bo. Sep. 9. (1767). Willem, of Adam Sjoufeld and Neeltje Joufeld. Wit.: Ebner and Geertje Robberson.

Jan. 24, bo. Jan. 10. (1768). Maria Elisabeth, of Jacob and Mareillys Hoogstrasser. Wit.: Paulus and Elisabeth Hoogstrasser.

bo. Dec. 24 (1767). Elisabeth, of Johs. and Margarita Strell. Wit.: Jurjen Hoghen, Elisab. Wageman.

Jan. 27, bo. Nov. 9. (1767). Jacob, of Jacob Pest and Catharina Mellingtown. Wit.: Jacob and Anna Pest.

Jan. 31, bo. Jan. 20. (1768). Philip Jeremias, of Philip Schuyler and Catharina Renzelaar. Wit.: Robert V. Renzelaar, Barbara Schuyler.

Feb. 3, bo. Jan. 28. Antje, of Ryckert V. Santen and Sara Hilton. Wit.: Gerrit and Antje V. Santen.

bo. the 2d. Margarita, of Abraham Kuyler and Catharina Wendell. Wit.: Jacob and Catharina V. Schaik.

bo. Feb. 2. Catharina, of Alexander and Rachel Smith. Wit.: Stephen and Catharina V. Renzelaar.

Feb. 9. at the Half Moon, bo. Nov. 23. (1767). Martha, of Willem and Martha Baxter. Wit.: Nicolaas V. d. Bergh, Catharina Levison.

bo. Sep. 19. (1767). Willem, of Robert and Immetje Taylor. Wit.: Schibboleth and Catharina Bogardus.

Feb. 9, bo. Nov. 19. Joannes, of Joseph Cancklin and Rebecca Robinson. Wit.: Johannis and Mary Cancklin.

bo. Sep. 12. Phebe, of Johannes Taylor and Sara Wibry. Wit.: Josua and Margarita Taylor.

Abraham, of John Walker and Jannetje Burn. Wit.: Willem and Alida Levison.

Feb. 10, bo. Jan. 18. (1768). Christiaan, of Cornelis Sprong and Margarita S'Jans. Wit.: John McLannon, Marytje S'Jans.

bo. Feb. 7. Abraham, of Thomas Hun and Elisabeth Wendel. Wit.: Efraim and Geertruy Wendell.

bo. Feb. 5. Meinard, of Jellis Winne and Titje V. Woert. Wit.: Yzac and Eva Slingerland.

bo. the 24th. Philip, of Stephen J. [?] Schuyler and Helena Ten Eick. Wit.: Philip and Catharina Schuyler.

Feb. 14, bo. Jan. 13. Frerik, of Johs Stroop and Dorothea Cannon. Wit.: Philip Kerner, Marg. Dauber.

Feb. 21, bo. Jan. 25. Johannes, of Albert Bratt and Magdalena Lang. Wit.: Johs Lang, Christina Bratt.

Feb. 28, bo. Feb. 23. Maas, of Henrik Crennel and Jacomyntje Bloemendal. Wit.: Maas and Catharina Bloemdal.

bo. Feb. 23. Jacob, of Michael Nicolas and Maria B. Wagenaar. Wit.: Jacob Hildebrand, Maria Wagenaar.

bo. Feb. 12. Jacob, of Johan Otto Rham and Catharina Hoogstrasser. Wit.: Jacob and Elisab. Hoogstrasser.

1768

Mar. 2.   Johannes, of John Redlif and Margar. Passagie. Wit.: Philip Redly, Engeltie Kool.

bo. Feb. 28.   Neeltie, of Johannes Groesbeek and Elisabet V. Brakelen.   Wit.: Hendrik Fonda, Catharina Groesbeek.

Mar. 6, bo. Mar. 3.   Thomas, of Jacob Coeper and Sinah Orchart.   Wit.: Abraham Koeper and Elisabeth Lansing.

Mar. 9, bo. the 5th.   Francis, of Charles and Mary Follet. Wit.: James and Lydia Bloodgood.

bo. the 8th.   Gerrit, of Johannes E. Bratt and Gerritje Lansing.   Wit.: Isaac G. and Arriaantje Lansing.

bo. the 9th.   Sara, of Johs. V. Valkenburg and Elisab. Meinerssen.   Wit.: Abraham and Marytje Meinerssen.

Mar. 13, bo. the 11th.   Willem, of Isaac Hoghing and Marrytje Gerritsen.   Wit.: Willem, Jr., and Susanna Hoghing.

Mar. 13, bo. the 12th.   Leenert, of Pieter Gansevoort and Gerritje Ten Eick.   Wit.: Harmen and Magdalena Gansevoort.

bo. Mar. 8.   Johannes, of Hendrik J. V. Renselaar and Rachel Douw.   Wit.: Johannes and Geertruy V. Renselaar.

Mar. 13, bo. Jan. 23.   Marrytje, of Jacob Knoet and Jenneke Steenbergen.   Wit.: Salomon and Geertruy Bulsing.

Mar. 20, bo. Feb. 20.   Jacob, of Lodowyk Sickker and Christina Vretje.   Wit.: Jacob and Margarita Vretje.

bo. Feb. 23.   Phebe, of Willem R. Hilton and Elisabeth Brooks.   Wit.: Pieter and Phebe Broeks.

bo. Feb. 18.   Elisabeth, of Pieter Hoogteling and Annatie Bekkers.   Wit.: Harmen and Santie (or Leentie) Gansevoort.

Mar. 23, bo. Mar. 4.   Elisabeth, of Jacob V. Schaik and Marytje V. Buren.   Wit.: Marten and Elisabeth V. Buuren.

bo. Feb. 6.   Willem, of David Hoogteling and Hilletje V. d. Zee.   Wit.: Pieter and Lena Hoogteling.

bo. Feb. 14.   Catharina, of Hannes and Annatie Bekker. Wit.: Anthony and Annatie V. D. Zee.

Mar. 23, bo.   , 26.   Folkert, of Andries Douw and Catharina Foreest.   Wit.: Folkert and Rachel Douw.

bo. the 20th.   Elisabeth, of Michel Basset and Marytje V. Franken.   Wit.: Michel and Elisabeth Besset.

Mar. 27, bo. the 26th.   Ryckert, of Albert Slingerland and Christina V. Franken.   Wit.: Ryckert and Catharina V. Franken.

bo. . . . . 27.   Annatje, of Christoffer Yates and Catharyntje Waters.   Wit.: Adam and Catharyntje Yates.

Apr. 10, bo. . . ., 10.   Ryckert, of Johs. and Catharina Redlif.   Wit.: Rykert and Marytie Redlif.

34

Frerik, of Hendrik Albraght and Elisabeth Folland. Wit.: Joh and Anna Huson.

bo. . . . 13. Jacobus, of Hendrik Briesch and Arriaantje Vinnagel. Wit.: Jacobus and Elisabeth Vinhagel.

May .1, bo. . . . 17. Hendrik, of Andries H. Gardenier and Saartje Hanssen. Wit.: Philip Foreest, Marg. Hanssen.

bo. . . . 23. Cornelis, of Cornelis Muller and Marytje V. Hoesen. Wit.: Folkert V. d. Berg, Geesje V. Hoesen.

bo. . . . 28. Geertruy, of Jacob Roseboom and Hester Lansing. Wit.: Jacob and Machtel Rooseboom.

bo. . . . 25. Cornelis, of Frerik Olfer and Tryntje V. D. Berg. Wit.: Cornelis and Elisabeth V. D. Berg.

May 15, bo. Apr. 11. Jacob, of Joost Harwich and Christina Filips. Wit.: Hendrik and Elsje Strong.

bo. Apr. 13. Catharina, of Jacob Foreest and Tryntje Bratt. Wit.: Wynand and Grietje V. Aalstein.

bo. May 3. Anna, of Harmanus J. Wendel and Barbara Bratt. Wit.: Cornelis and Annatje Cuyler.

bo. Apr. 23. Jacob, of William Venton and Annatje Egmond. Wit.: Jacob Hogh, Mary Egmond.

Petrus, of Cornelis V. Esch and Alida V. Woert. Wit.: Izac and Annatje Lansing.

bo. Apr. 13. Gerrit, of Christoffer Yates and Catharina Lansing. Wit.: Obedia and Annatje Lansing.

bo. May 1. Archelaus, of Archelas Lynd and Marytje Duivebach. Wit.: Cornelis Douw, Marytje V. Driessen.

May 22, bo. Mar. 14. Annatje, of Pieter Goey and Maria Yong. Wit.: Andries and Florene Goey.

May 22, bo. Apr. 7. Saartje, of Hannes Smith and Neeltje Larreway. Wit.: Dirk and Saartje V. d. Wilgen.

bo. May 13. Marytje, of Christiaan Jacobi and Margarieta Hoghing. Wit.: Jacob and Annatje Hoghing.

May 23, bo. May 15. Engeltje, of Maas Bloemendal and Helena Schermerhoorn. Wit.: Samuel and Helena Schermerhoorn.

May 29, bo. Jan. 29. Annatje, of Rykert Bovie and Marytje Huik. Wit.: James and Antje Dole.

bo. May 26. Arriaantje, of Abraham Verplank and Marytje Bogert. Wit.: Sanders J. and Abigail Lansing.

bo. Apr. 18. Hesther, of Johs. H. Beekman and Hendrikje V. Buuren. Wit.: Marthen, Jr., and Annatje Beekman.

Annatje, of Frans Gruwel and Annatje Balsing. Wit.: Johs Douw, Marg. Viele. (?).

June 5, bo. May 5. Elisabeth, of George and Catharina Young. Wit.: Johs. and Elisab. Goey.

bo. May 23. Johannes, of Stephen Schuyler and Engeltje V. Vechten. Wit.: Hermanus and Catharina Wendel.

bo. . . . 5. George, of Reignier V. Yveren and Debora Fielden. Wit.: George Fildon, Santje V. Yveren.

June 5, bo. Apr. 20. Barbara, of Jurjen Scharp and Catharina Fleegting. Wit.: Nicolaas Scharp, Lena Scherp.

bo. May 30. Philippus, of Yzac Fonda and Santje Foreest. Wit.: Philip and Maria Foreest.

June 19, bo. May 26. Gerrit, of Casparus Witbeek and Geertruy V. d. Berg. Wit.: Benjamin and Annatje V. d. Bergh.

bo. . . . 19. Dirk, of Thomas Hun and Baatje V. Deuzen. Wit.: Dirk and Margarita Hun.

bo. Apr. 16. Jacobus, of Benjamin V. Etten and Heyltje Vredenburg. Wit.: Jacobus V. Etten, Annatje Pengborn.

June 26, bo. June 5. Jacob, of Melchior File and Elisabeth Hunsinger. Wit.: Jacob and Rosina R. Wheger.

July 3, bo. June 29. Yzaac, of Bastiaan I. Visscher and Engeltje V. d. Berg. Wit.: Gerrit, Jr., and Wyntje Lansing.

bo. June 9. Maria, of Barent Goey and Rachel V. Ostrander. Wit.: Abraham Schuyler, Eva Beekman.

July 10, bo. June 2. Maria, of Jan Fonda and Egje V. d. Zee. Wit.: Philip and Maria Foreest.

July 12, bo. Jan. 12. Cornelis, of Nicolaas Leek and Marritje Snyder. Wit.: Cornelis and Alida V. Esch.

July 14, bo. Mar. 30. Dorothe, of Daniel Halenbeek and Catharina Quakkenbosch. Wit.: Gerrit Halebeek, Elisabeth Hellen.

July 17, bo. June 16. Sara, of Leendert Muller and Marritje V. Esch. Wit.: Abraham V. Esch, Antje De Ridder.

bo. June 26. Theunis, of Theunis I. Visscher and Marytje Timessen. Wit.: Bastiaan and Dirkje Crugier.

Wynand, of Albert V. d. Werken and Annatje V. d. Berg. Wit.: Cornelis V. d. Berg, Marytje Viele.

bo. June 18. Claasje, of David Schot and Marytje Wendel. Wit.: Yzac and Elisabet V. Arnem.

July 19, bo. July 10. Maria, of Jacobus Cool and Jannetje Witbeek. Wit.: Theus and Annatje Nieuwkerk, Margarita V. d. Berg.

July 24, bo. July 6. Bata, of Jacob Heemstraat and Catharina Duret. Wit.: Dirk and Annatje Knoet.

bo. June 16. Johannes, of Hendrik Ruiter and Rebecca Dath. Wit.: Johs. and Elisab. Bratt.

bo. Apr. 22. Hendrik, of Hendrik Young and Marytje Lidzer. (?) Wit.: Gerrit and Jannetje Lansing.

bo. the 29th. Aaltje, of Hendrik Oothout and Lydia Douw. Wit.: Folkert Douw, Elisabeth Oothout.

bo. July 23. Claasje, of John D. Groesbeek and Aaltje V. Aarnem. Wit.: David and Marytje Schott.

1768

bo. July 21. Cornelis Erasmus, of Pieter W. Yates and Ann Mary Hellem. Wit.: Johs. and Rebecca Yates.

bo. June 24. Cornelis, of Jacob Van Olinde and Elisabeth Schermerhoorn. Wit.: Jurjen and Grietje Gremer.

July 24, bo. July 2. Wouter, of Dirk V. Vechten and Alida Knickerbacker. Wit.: Johs and Elisa Cath. Knickerbacker.

bo. June 25. Yzaac, of Johs. Fort and Elisabeth Kwakkenbusch. Wit.: Harmen and Lena Ganzevoort.

July 27, bo. July 3. Catharina, of Daniel Winne and Catharina Hoogteling. Wit.: Johannes and Catharina Winne.

bo. July 23. Susanna, of Frerik Meinerssen and Elisabeth Waldrom. Wit.: Pieter and Neeltje Waldrom.

bo. July 26. Rebecca, of Abraham Hoogkerk and Antje Hilton. Wit.: Lucas and Alida Hoogkerk.

Aug. 1, bo. July 17. George, of Hendrik Milton and Rachel Northen. Wit.: George and Margarita Mendel.

bo. July 29. Jacobus, of Dirk Schuyler and Maria V. Deusen. Wit.: David Schuyler, Catharina V. Deuzen.

Aug. 4. Aletteke, of Hendrik Katzebach and Eva De Voe. Wit.: John and Elisab. Northen.

Aug. 8, bo. . . . 24. Annatje, of Hannes V. d. Werken and Marytje De Voe. Wit.: Abraham Vosburg, Annatje V. Schaik.

bo. July 21. Helena, of Jacob H. Lansing and Marytje Ouderkerk. Wit.: Yzaac and Annatje Lansing.

bo. Aug. 4. William, of Nicolaas Claver and Susanna Merriday. Wit.: Johs. and Hilletje Merriday.

bo. Aug. 6. Staats Van Santvoort, of James Dole and Antje V. Santvoort. Wit.: Staats and Willempje V. Santvoort.

Aug. 14, bo. July 23. Willem, of Johannes Fonda and Elisabeth Ouderkerk. Wit.: Bastiaan Timessen, Maayke Ouderkerk.

bo. Aug. 13. Matheus, of Anthony Flensburg and Annatje Redley. Wit.: Johs. and Annatje Flensburg.

bo. Aug. 4. Eva, of Jacob de Garmo and Fytje Bekker. Wit.: Dirk Bekker, Eva Hoghing.

bo. . . . 14. Johannes, of Efraim V. Vechten and Annatje Wendel. Wit.: Folkert and Jannetje V. Vechten.

Aug. 17, bo. Aug. 15. Elisabeth, of Stephen Van Renzelaar and Catharina Livingston. Wit.: Abraham and Elisabeth Ten Broek.

bo. Aug. 14. Alida, of Christoffer Lansing and Sara V. Schaik. Wit.: Johs. and Alida V. Schaik.

Aug. 21, bo. Aug. 13. Hendrik, of Francis Nichols and Margarita Renzelaar. Wit.: Jeremias V. Renzelaar, Catharina Wendell.

1768

bo. July 15. Dirk, of Jacob Knoet and Maayke Lansing. Wit.: Willem and Sara Hun.

bo. July 17. Abraham, of Abraham Peek and Catharina V. Santen. Wit.: Staats V. Santvoort, Willempje Bratt.

Aug. 29, bo. July 23. Agnietje, of Harmen Groesbeek and Marytje Benneway. Wit.: Pieter and Annatje de Wandelaar.

bo. June 9. Wouter, of Albert V. d. Zee and Marytje V. d. Kar. Wit.: Wouter and Anneke Ridder.

Sep. 11. Catharina, of Mathias Bovie and Bata V. d. Heide. Wit.: Frans Bovie, Elisabeth Heemstraat.

Sept. 11. Mathias, of Philip Bovie and Geertruy V. d. Berg. Wit.: Matthias and Petronella Bovie.

Margarita, of Gysbert Mersselis, Jr., and Anna Staats. Wit.: Johannes and Margarita Merselis.

Gerrit, of Jacob G. and Neeltje Roseboom. Wit.: Gerrit and Jannetje Lansing.

Oct. 7, bo. Sep. 17. Anna, of Hendrik Ten Eick, Jr., and Margarita Douw. Wit.: Jacob H. Ten Eick, Anna Wendel.

bo. Sep. 8. Gerrit, of Rutger and Maria V. d. Berg. Wit.: Gerrit W. and Alida V. d. Berg.

bo. Sep. 18. Zeferinus, of Harmanus V. Aalstein and Catharina Peessinger. Wit.: Anthony Bratt, Geertje (or Grietje) Batterstein.

bo. Sep. 15. Hendrik, of Gerrit Visscher and Alida Fonda. Wit.: Yzaac and Annatje Fonda.

bo. Sep. 29. Nicolaas, of Gysbert Fonda and Elsje Douw. Wit.: Pieter and Elisabeth Williams.

bo. . . . 16. Benjamin, of Lavinus Winne and Marytje Lansing. Wit.: Benjamin and Lena Winne.

bo. . . . 17. Pieter, of Pieter Jones and Abigail Winne. Wit.: Mathys Boom, Marritje Winne.

Gysbert, of Hendrik Klaauw and Elisabeth Halenbeek. Wit.: Cornelis and Maria Groot.

bo. . . . 11. Catharina, of Hendrik and Margarita Qwakkenbusch. Wit.: Wouter Qwakkenbusch, Catharina Du Mont.

Oct. 9, bo. Aug. 22. Rykert, of Rykert Redley and Marytje Olfert. Wit.: Hannes and Cathar. Redley.

bo. Aug. 27. Arriaantje, of Maas V. Buren and Cathalyntje Valkenburg. Wit.: Tobias Ten Eick, Judike V. Buuren.

bo. Sep. 3. Neeltje, of Folkert V. Vechten and Jannetje Hun. Wit.: Efraim V. Vechten, Annatje Wendel.

bo. Sep. 24. Cornelis, of Pieter Levison and Maria Fonda. Wit.: Harmen Levison, Cathar. V. d. Berg.

Oct. 16, bo. Sep. 23. Annatje, of Johannes Ruyter and Elisab. Pest. Wit.: Jacob and Annatje Pest.

1768

bo. July 20. Hendrik, of Johs. Scholtz and Elisab. Dath. Wit.: Willem Waldrom, Elisab. Vos.

bo. Aug. 29. Cornelia, of Pieter Waldrom and Rachel V. d. Berg. Wit.: Cornelis M. and Cornelia V. d. Berg.

bo. Sep. 5. Coenraad, of Christiaan Couper and Anna Marg. Strong. Wit.: Frederik C. and Maria Neidhart.

bo. Sep. 14. Cornelia, of Willem Flensburg and Christina Backer. Wit.: Hansje and Cornelia Flensburg.

bo. . . . 16. Rebecca, of Frans Winne and Anneke Viele. Wit.: Douwe and Dirkje Winne.

Oct. 19, bo. Sep. 10. Lydia, of William Pangborn and Elisabeth V. d. Bogert. Wit.: Richard and Lydia Pengborn.

Oct. 19. Elisabeth, of Hannes Smith and Margarita Peessinger. Wit.: Balthes and Elisabeth Halkes.

Oct. 23, bo. Sep. 13. Rebecca, of Gysbert Bosch and Hester Ryck. Wit.: Johs. V. Esch, Rebecca Bogert.

bo. Sep. 22. Lydia, of Hannes Lang and Christina Bratt. Wit.: Pieter and Susanna Bratt.

bo. Oct. 19. Maria, of Robert Yates and Jannetje V. Esch. Wit.: Joseph and Maria Yates.

bo. Oct. 3. Maria, of Wynant V. d. Berg and Francyntje Kloet. Wit.: Frerik Kloet, Maria De Ridder.

bo. this day. Catharina, of Lowys Van Woert and Catharina V. d. Berg. Wit.: Adriaan and Folkje Qwakkenbusch.

Oct. 26, bo. Oct. 23. Cornelia, of Bernadus Halenbeek, and Neeltje Clark. Wit.: Patrick Clark, Neeltje Waldrom.

Oct. 30, bo. Sep. 17. Maria, of Jacob Lansing and Alida Levison. Wit.: Willem Levison, Alida Fonda.

bo. July 31. Maria, of Hannes Burn and Geertje Smitt. Wit.: Jurjen Breght, Maayke Oothout.

Nov. 2, bo. Nov. 1. Johannes, of Samuel Pruin and Neeltje Ten Eick. Wit.: Johannes Pruin, Geertje Ten Eick.

Nov. 3, bo. Sep. 30. Wyntje, of John Bell and Margar. Touper. Wit.: Gerrit G. and Wyntje Lansing.

Nov. 6, bo. Oct. 6. Johannes, of Johannes Ostrander and Marritje V. Aalstein. Wit.: Jonathan and Gerritje Witbeek.

Nov. 6, bo. Oct. 18. Elisabeth, of Jeremias 'S Jans and Lou Adams. Wit.: Christiaan Abrahamse, Margarita Strong.

Nov. 9, bo. Nov. 8. Johannis, of John J. Bleeker and Gerritje V. Schaik. Wit.: Sybrand V. Schaik, Geertruy Wendell.

Nov. 13, bo. Nov. 11. Whilliam, of John Thing and Maria Lucy. Wit.: Johs. and Eva Roseboom.

bo. Nov. 11. Maria, of Johannes Ten Broek and Sara Gansevoort. Wit.: Cornelis and Maria Ten Broek.

39

Nov. 27, bo. Nov. 21. Machtel, of John J. Beekman and Maria Sanders. Wit.: Gerrit A. and Ruth Lansing.

Dec. 4, bo. Oct. 29. Andries, of Johan P. Claas and Clara M. Cortin. Wit.: Douwe Bogert, Wyntje Bratt.

Dec. 7, bo. Dec. 5. Arriaantje, of Philip V. Renzelaar and Maria Sanders. Wit.: Quiliaan and Catharina V. Renselaar.

Martinus, of Hannes Witbeek and Engeltje Vroman. Wit.: David Hoogteling, Leentje Ganzevoort.

Dec. 11, bo. Nov. 11. Pieter, of Gerrit Waldrom and Cath. V. d. Berg. Wit.: Cornelis Waldrom, Alida Goey.

Dec. 21, bo. Nov. 10. Elisabeth, of Johs. V. Aarnem and Alida V. d. Heide. Wit.: John and Lena V. Wie.

bo. Dec. 13. Jannetje, of Cornelis V. Deuzen and Lea Oostrander. Wit.: Abraham Kuyler and Jannetje Glen.

Dec. 23, bo. Dec. 22. Pieter, of Barent Vosburg and Annatje Gerritsen. Wit.: Philip Lansing, Elsje Hun.

Dec. 25, bo. Dec. 4. Cornelis, of Alexander Bulsing and Alida Oothout. Wit.: Jan Oothout, Marritje Wendel.

bo. Nov. 24. Johannes, of Meinard V. Hoesen and Geertruy Vinhagel. Wit.: Johs. and Elisab. Vinhagel.

Dec. 26. Annatje, of Cornelis J. V. d. Bergh and Catharina Ridder. Wit.: Wynand and Maritje V. d. Bergh.

Phebe, of Nicolaas and Margarita Hart. Wit.: Wilhelmus and Hillegonda V. Antwerpen.

1769, Jan. 4, bo. . . . 29. Jacobus, of Pieter Hilton and Judith Bareuth. Wit.: Abraham Hoogkerk, Judith Hilton.

Joachim, of Gerrit Staats and Catharina Cunningam. Wit.: Barent Visscher, Annatje Schuyler.

Jan. 8, bo. Dec. 31. (1768). Regina, of Daniel Ersberger and Regina Loetling. Wit.: John Leener, Cornelia Rigter.

Jacob, of Jacob and Annetje Wagenaar. Wit.: Michel and Barbara Nicholas.

Jan. 11, bo. Jan. 11. (1769). Margarita, of John Northen and Elisab. De Voe. Wit.: Henry Northen, Margar. V. d. Werken.

bo. Jan. 10. Susanna, of John Visscher and Elisabeth Bratt. Wit.: Bernardus Bratt, Alida V. Renzelaar.

Jan. 15, bo. . . . Nov. 18, (1768). Machtel, of Tobias V. Buren and Catharina Witbeek. Wit.: Jonathan Witbeek and wife.

Jan. 18, bo. Jan. 6. (1769). Debora, of Daniel and Martha Nengel.

Jan. 22, bo. Jan. 20. Dirk, of Cornelis Van Schelhune and Elisabeth Roseboom. Wit.: Hendrik H. Rozeboom, Elisabeth V. Schelluine.

bo...26. Jacob, of Yzaac Lensing and Annaatje V. Aarnem. Wit.: Jacob and Marytje Lansing.

1769

Jan. 28, bo. Dec. 31. (1768). Annatje, of Adam Vroman and Jannetje Viele. Wit.: Johs. and Baatje Hun.

bo. Jan. 24 (1769). Yzaac, of Jan V. Aalstein and Lena Scharp. Wit.: Johs. and Folkje Grenny.

Feb. 1, bo. Jan. 18. Daniel, of Johs. Fonda and Dirkje Winne. Wit.: Daniel Winne, Jannetje Foreest.

Balthes, of Joris and Christina Bussing. Wit.: Balthes Kern and wife.

bo. May 27. (1768). Elisabeth, of Jurjen De Voe and Cathar. Keller. Wit.: John Northen, Elisab. De Voe.

Feb. 5, bo. Feb. 3 (1769). Catharina, of Hendrik Bleecker and Catharina Kuyler. Wit.: Jacob V. Schaik, Elisab. Kuyler.

bo. Dec. 11. (1768). Willem, of Mathys Hoogteling and Arriaantje V. d. Zee. Wit.: David and Catharyntje Bratt.

bo. Nov. 16. Jannetje, of Yzaac Fonda and Rebecca Groesbeek. Wit.: Wouter Knickerbacker, Jannetje Groesbeek.

Feb. 25. (1769). Quiliaan, of Hendrik Renselaar and Alida Bratt. Wit.: Philip Renzelaar, Maria Sanders.

Feb. 26, bo. Feb. 6. Anna, of Pieter Schuyler and Geertruy Lansing. Wit.: Gerardus and Maria Lansing.

bo. Feb. 1. Johannes, of Cornelis Bulsing and Annatje Conzalus. Wit.: Johs Conzalus, Machtel Heemstraat.

bo. Feb. 6. Annatje, of Obadia V. Benthuisen and Annatje Bumney. Wit.: Jacobus V. Benthuisen, Sara Cooper.

Mar. 1, bo. Jan. 29. Marytje, of Marten De Foreest and Janneke Winne. Wit.: Willem and Marytje Winne.

bo. Jan. 29. Annetje, of Cornelis V. d. Berg and Maayke Ouderkerk. Wit.: Yzaac Ouderkerk, Marytje Winne.

Mar. 3, bo. Feb. 13. Helena, of Cornelis W. V. d. Berg and Maria Viele. Wit.: Mathew V. Keuren, Helena Viele.

Mar. 7, bo. Mar. 3. Johannes, of Dirk Benson and Marytje Wyngaart. Wit.: Johs. Mersselis, Christina V. Franken.

bo. Mar. 6. Elisabeth, of Hannes and Cathar. Hall. Wit.: Nicolaas and Elisab. Klein.

Catharina, of Caspar Houshek and Elisab. Shousek. Wit.: Andries and Cath. Whyght.

Mar. 14, bo. Mar. 10. Jannetje, of Arent Bratt and Jannetje Hoghing. Wit.: Yzaac and Martina Hoghing.

Hendrik, Gerritje, twins of Laurens Scharp and Geesje Schermerhoorn. Wit.: Hendrik M. and Marytje Rozeboom, Johs. and Annatje Davis.

Mar. 18, bo. Jan. 23. Hendrik, of Hendrik Meyer and Maria Murry. Wit.: Hannes and Susanna Meyer.

1769
bo. Jan. 25. Johannes, of Dirk V. d. Wilgen and Saartje Larreway. Wit.: Jan and Marytje Bratt.

bo. Feb. 6. Cornelis, of Pieter Waldrom and Antje Ouderkerk. Wit.: Evert Waldrom, Jannetje V. Esch.

bo. Feb. 24. Abraham, of Christiaan Duivebach and Cathalyntje De Foreest. Wit.: Willem Monbrugh, Marytje De Foreest.

Mar. 22, bo. Mar. 18. Annatje, of Nicolaas Brouwer and Marytje Boom. Wit.: Pieter Hilton, Sara Fryer.

Mar. 25, bo. Mar. 19. Eva, of Philip and Annatje Young. Wit.: Philip Viele, Marytje Davis.

bo. Feb. 10. Cornelia, of Yzaac V. Valkenburg and Engeltje V. d. Berg. Wit.: Hannes Vinhagel, Baatje Valkenburg.

Mar. 30, bo. Mar. 21. Willem, of Daniel Winne and Jannetje Banker. Wit.: Willem and Annatje Banker.

Apr. 2, bo. Apr. 1. Folkert, of Harmen V. Hoesen and Tryntje Witbeek. Wit.: Matheus Aalstein, Bregje V. Hoesen.

bo. Feb. 20. Cornelis, of Johs. Oothout and Elisabeth S. V. Woert. Wit.: Willem and Christina Vosburg.

bo. . . . 30. Rachel, of Maas Bloemendal and Catharina Steenberg. Wit.: David Foreest, Jr., Wyntje Bratt.

Apr. 2, bo. . . . 31. David, of Abraham Schuyler and Eva Beekman. Wit.: David and Maria Schuyler.

Apr. 5, bo. Apr. 3. Johannes, of Johs. V. Santen and Margar. Wilkeson. Wit.: Thomas Barret, Elisab. V. Santen.

bo. the 30th. Laurens, of Jurjen and Mary Cremer. Wit.: William and Charlotte Bhyly.

the 4th. Yzaac, of Eduard and Maria Willet. Wit.: Elbert and Cathalina Willet.

Susanna, Rachel, twins of John Ostrander and Anna Wolfen.

Apr. 8, bo. Mar. 1. Thomas, of Joseph and Sara Shaw. Wit.: Thomas and Cath. Kerl.

bo. Mar. 11. Sara, of Gerrit and Wyntje Zeger. Wit.: Frerik and Tryntje Olfer.

bo. Mar. 6. Magdalena, of Mathys and Josyntje Boom. Wit.: Roelef and Lydia Zeger.

Apr. 15, bo. . . . 27. Yzaac, of Wynand V. Aalstein and Margarita Reisdorf. Wit.: Johs. and Lena V. Aalstein.

bo. Apr. 13. Nicolaas, of Abraham Kuyler and Margarita Wendel. Wit.: Nicolaas and Jannetje Cuyler.

bo. Sep. 10. (1768). Benjamin, of Benjamin and Ame (?) Shaw. Wit.: Christoffer and Catharina Yates.

Apr. 23, bo. Apr. 19. (1769). Maria, of Yzaac De Foreest and Alida Fonda. Wit.: Bastiaan Crugier, Alida Fonda.

Apr. 23, bo. Mar. 20. Jurjaan, of Hendrik and Margarita Zeger. Wit.: Jurjen and Annatje Koen.

Apr. 26, bo. Apr. 1. Bartholomeus, of Nicolaas Scherp and Lena Hogeboom. Wit.: Pieter and Catharina Scherp.

bo. Apr. 23. Maria, of Hermanus Schuyler and Christina Ten Broek. Wit.: Hendrik and Margarita V. Dyck.

Apr. 30. Johannes, of Pieter Winne and Susanna V. d. Berg. Wit.: Nicolaas and Aaltje V. d. Berg.

bo. Mar. 15. Maria, of Johs Flensburg and Cornelia Hoogteling. Wit.: Gysbert V. Santen, Rebecca Winne.

bo. Apr. 26. Annetje, of Wouter de Foreest and Alida Knoet. Wit.: Wilhelmus V. Antwerpen, Barbara Knoet.

May 4, bo. . . . 27. Joachim, of Barent Staats and Antje Winne. Wit.: Joachim and Elisabeth Staats.

May 7, bo. Apr. 11. Maria, of Nicolaas Richter and Maria Hoendermond. Wit.: Baltes Kern, Maria Snyder.

bo. Apr. 8. Catharina, of Cornelis and Fytje V. Salsburry. Wit.: Johs. and Jannitje V. Salsburry.

bo. Apr. 11. Rykert, of Robert Winne and Hillegondje V. Franken. Wit.: Rykert V. Franken, Catharina Ten Baar.

May 15. Willem, of Abraham and Annetje Wever. Wit.: Yzaac and Eva Slingerland.

May 16, bo. May 3. Theuntje, of Marten and Hendrikje V. Buuren. Wit.: Cornelis and Maayke V. Buren.

May 28, bo. Apr. 19. Lydia, of Adam Bratt and Maria McCans. Wit.: Gerrit and Mary Zeger.

May 28, bo. Apr. 24. Pieter, of Lucas Salsburry and Marytje V. Buren. Wit.: Pieter M. and Marytje V. Buuren.

bo. May 25. Sara, of Johs Kloet, Jr., and Sara V. Aarnem. Wit.: Johs Kloet, Helena Lansing.

May 31, bo. May 3. Johannes, of Gerrit Ten Baar and Cathalyntje Bratt. Wit.: Johs. and Margarita Bratt.

June 4, bo. May 1. Coenraad, of Matheus and Christina Flensburg. Wit.: Arent and Antje Bekker.

bo. Apr. 22. Frerik, of Arent and Marg. Bekker. Wit.: Matheus V. Deuzen, Marytje Hoghing.

bo. Apr. 14. Jacob, of Balthes Bratt and Rosina Foller. Wit.: Jacob and Cath. Bratt.

Femmetje, of Jacobus Hoogteling and Charity Peng Barn. Wit.: Hannes and Marytje Zeger.

June 18, bo. May 20. Elisabeth, of Pieter Hoogteling and Annatje Bekker. Wit.: Hannes and Leentje Gansevoort.

bo. June 12. Hubertje, of Abraham Y. Yaets and Jannetje Bratt. Wit.: Willem Winne, Jr., Judike Yates.

bo. June 13. Jan V. Aarnem, of Jacob Lansing and Willempje Winne. Wit.: Lavinus and Maria Winne.

1769

June 25, bo. June 22. Samuel, of Bastiaan Crugier and Dirkje Fischer. Wit.: Martinus and Sara Crugier.

bo. June 5. Andries, of Andries Peessinger and Jannetje Bratt. Wit.: Jelles and Fytje Winne.

June 21, [sic], bo. Mar. 28. Gerrit, of Thoms Peebles and Elisabeth Bratt. Wit.: Anthony and Annatje V. Schaik.

bo. June 15. Hendrik, of Albert V. d. Werken and Marytje Kwakkenbusch. Wit.: Hendr. V. der Werken, Maria Viele.

July 21, bo. May 19. Adam, of Johs. Ackerson and Engeltje Vroman. Wit.: Daniel and Jannetje Winne.

July 2, bo. June 26. Johannes, of Thoms. Witbeek and Janneke Rees. Wit.: Pieter W. and Rachel Witbeek.

bo. the 2d. Helena, of Johs. 5 (V.?) Lansing and Catharina Burhans. Wit.: Robert Lansing, Marytje Wendel.

bo. the 3d. Johannes, of Barent and Arriaantje V. Buren. Wit.: Marten and Annatje V. Buren.

bo. the 31st. Johanna, of Theunis Bratt and Cathal V. Esch. Wit.: Johs Bratt, Maayke Fonda.

July 5, bo. the 3d. Margarita, of Jacobus Abeel and Ebbetje V. Buren. Wit.: Hendrik V. Dyck, Cathalyntje Willet.

July 9, bo. the 7th. Cornelis, of Abraham C. Cuyler and Jannetje Glen. Wit.: Hendrik and Elisab. Glen.

July 15, bo. June 26. Andries, of Andries Wederwax and Catharina Reisdorp. Wit.: Andries and Susanna Michel.

bo. the 11th. Hendrik, of Casparus V. Wie and Jannetje Winne. Wit.: Hendrik and Catharina V. Wie.

bo. the 8th. Thomas, of Johs. Reyly and Cathalyntje V. d. Berg. Wit.: Folkert and Neeltje V. d. Berg.

bo. June 3. Annatje, of John and Susanna Winne. Wit.: Hendrik and Susanna V. Aarnem.

July 15, bo. June 21. Daniel, of Abraham and Marg. V. d. Kar. Wit.: Gozen and Marytje V. Schaik.

July 23, bo. the 19th. Franciscus, of Casparus Pruin and Catharina Groesbeek. Wit.: Samuel and Alida Pruin.

Aug. 6, bo. July 10. Margarita, of Jacob Smith and Barbara Smit. Wit.: Johs. and Catharina Heildrig.

bo. the 31st. [sic]. Sara, of Balthus V. Benthuysen and Elisabeth Bumney. Wit.: Frans Winne, Anneke Viele.

Aug. 12, baptized at the Spring and on the way. (bij de Fontein en op weg gedoopt.) bo. June 23. Annatje, of Andries Snyder and Annetje Hannes. Wit.: Mathias and Catharina Clockenaar.

Aug. 12, at the Spring and on the way. David and Petrus, of Jacob and N. Cool.

bo. July 9. Annatje, of Petrus Ham and Marytje Michel. Wit.: Caspar and Marytje Ham.

44

1769

Aug. 15, bo. July 19. Benjamin, of Pieter M. and Maria
V. Buuren. Wit.: Maas and Cathar. V. Buren.

Maria, of Adam Coen and Marytie V. d. Hoef. Wit.:
Jacob Kimmich, Maria Doozer. (?)

Maria, of Jurjen Steen and Lena V. d. Hoef. Wit.:
Hendrik Wheeler, Syntje V. d. Hoef.

Machtel, of Johs I. Fisscher (?) and Annatje Pearsse. (?)
Wit.: Bastiaan and Engeltje Visscher.

bo. the 23d. Frans, of Johs. and Elisab. Heemstraat.
Wit.: Frans and Machtel Bovie.

bo. the 9th. Marytje, of James Donneway and Elsje
Smitt. Wit.: James and Mag. Green.

Aug. 20, bo. the 18th. Catharina, of Gerrit V. Yveren
and Catharina Bogert. Wit.: Hendrik Y. Bogert, Hester
Visscher.

bo. the 5th. Margarita, of Hannes and Barbara Backes.
Wit.: Hendrik and Margar. Zeger.

bo. the 19th. Josina, of Anthony Halenbeek and Cornelia Cooper. Wit.: Jacob and Josina Cooper.

bo. the 22d. Frerik, of Pieter Scharp and Catharina
Berringer. Wit.: Jurjen Berringer, Rachel Gardenier.

bo. the 19th. Petrus, of Johannes M. Beekman and
Elisabeth Douw. Wit.: Petrus and Magdalena Douw.

Aug. 28, bo. the 21st. Cathalyntje, of John David and
Elisabeth Wyngaart. Wit.: Izaac J. Trouex, Cathal.
Wyngaart.

bo. the 24th. Johannes, of Yzaac Slingerland and Eva
V. Woert. Wit.: Jacob and Margareta V. Woert.

bo. July 10. Harmen, of Wouter N. Groesbeek and
Alida Qwakkenbusch. Wit.: Willem and Marytje Winne.

bo. the 28th. Douwe, of Jacob Fonda and Dirkje
Visscher. Wit.: Isaac and Susanna Fonda.

Sep. 3, bo. the 31st. [sic]. Gerrit, of Gysbert V. Santen
and Sara Hilton. Wit.: Yzaac Hoogkerk, Rachel V.
Santen.

Sep. 4, bo. Aug. 20. Johannes, of Pieter and Lena De
Garmo. Wit.: Abraham and Annatje De Garmo.

Sep. 6, bo. the 6th. Maria, of Barent J. Ten Eick and
Sara Cadmus. Wit.: Jacob and Alida Ten Eick.

Sep. 6, bo. the 6th. Johannes, of Barent and Sara
Visscher. Wit.: Johs. and Elisabeth Visscher.

Sep. 10. Johannes, of Joseph and Geertruy Redly.
Wit.: Abraham and Marytje Vroman.

bo. the 3rd. Gerrit, of Gysbert V. Santen and Rebecca
Winne. Wit.: Gerrit and Hester V. Santen.

Sep. 17, bo. the 16th. Anna, of Gerardus Beekman and
Annatje Douw. Wit.: Folkert and Racheltje Douw.

bo. Aug. 17. Maria, of Augustinus Scherp and Maria
V. Aalstein. Wit.: Willem V. Aalstein, Geesje V. Hoesen.

1769

Sep. 23, bo. the 20th. Rykert, of Pieter V. Bogert and Barbara V. Franken. Wit.: Rykert V. Franken, Barbara Knoet.

bo. Aug. 25. Harmen, of Theunis Visscher and Barbara Fonda. Wit.: Harmen and Saartje Visscher.

Oct. 1, bo. the 19th. [sic]. Daniel, of Abraham Sickels and Maria Kanner. Wit.: Philip Young, Christina Kanner.

bo. the 27th. Martinus, of Pieter De Garmo and Geertruy Crugier. Wit.: Martinus and Geertruy Crugier.

bo. the 30th. Dirkje, of Yzaac Hoghing and Marytje Gerritzen. Wit.: Barent and Annatje Vosburg.

bo. the 10th. Jacob, of Pieter and Catharina Crennel. Wit.: Jacob Hoghing, Annatje Hoghil.

Oct. 8. Cathalyntje, of Hendrik Bulsing and Cornelia Marus. Wit.: Alex. Bulsing, Alida Oothout.

bo. Sep. 3. Hester, of Cornelis V. d. Zee and Annatje Veder. Wit.: Dirk Bekker, Eva Slingerlands.

Oct. 8, bo. Sep. 8. Elisabeth, of Abraham Boom and Dorothee Cunningham. Wit.: Samuel Boom, Catharina Veltman.

Albert, of Theunis Slingerland and Agnietje Witbeek. Wit.: Jacob Look, Matie Hoghin.

Oct. 13, bo. Sep. 20. Willem, of Daniel Winne and Catharina Hoogteling. Wit.: Pieter Hoogteling, Annatje Bekker.

Oct. 15, bo. Aug. 5. Lena, of Gerrit Slingerland and Egje Vander Zee. Wit.: Albert V. d. Zee, Cornelia Prys.

bo. Sep. 17. Alida, of Johs. E. Lansing and Maria Staats. Wit.: Johannes Staats, Elsje Lansing.

Oct. 29, bo. the 23d. Pieter, of Pieter Rykman and Lydia V. d. Berg. Wit.: Marten Meinerssen, Sara Rykman.

bo. Sep. 27. Machtel, of Jacob F. (?) Lansing and Jannetje Visscher. Wit.: Bastiaan Crugier, Dirkje Visscher.

bo. the 8th. Wyntje, of Adriaan Bratt and Lydia V. Aalstein. Wit.: Johs. and Hillegonda Bratt.

bo. the 23d. Maria, of Nicolaas Marsselis and Margarita Groesbeek. Wit.: Gerardus Groesbeek, Maria Ten Broek.

bo. the 19th. Gerrit, of Cornelis Wendell and Annatje Lansing. Wit.: Gerrit and Wyntje Lansing.

bo. the 7th. Neeltje, of Johannes J. Lansing and Maria Huyk. Wit.: Samuel and Neeltje Pruin. [*Sometimes it is impossible to decide whether it is Pruin or Bruin. The writing is rather poor throughout.*]

bo. the 25th. John Waters, of Christoffer A. (?) Yates and Catharina Waters. Wit.: John Waters, Jannetje Lansing.

Nov. 5, bo. Oct. 25. Gysbert, of Joseph V. Santen and Rebecca De Garmo. Wit.: Hendrik and Marytje V. Santen.

Nov. 12. Matheus, of Johs. and Marg. Streel. Wit.: Willem and Elisab. Hilton.

Nov. 22, bo. Oct. 12. Hanna, of John Maby and Christina Tremper.

Nov. 19, bo. Oct. 17. Reynier, of Johs. Muller and Sara V. Yveren. Wit.: Barent V. Yveren, Marritje (Bruin or) Pruin.

bo. the 17th. Catharina, of Abraham Ten Eick and Annatje Lansing. Wit.: Jacob and Catharina Ten Eyck.

Nov. 26, bo. the 17th. George, of Nicolaas and Elisab. Clein. Wit.: Johs. Holt, Catharina Bower.

Nov. 26, bo. the 19th. Sara, of Johs, Jr., and Maria Goey. Wit.: Jan. G. and Cathalyntje Yates.

bo. the 24th. Margarita, of Hendrik Crennel and Jacomyntje Bloemendal. Wit.: William W. Crennel, Geertruy Bloemendal.

Dec. 10, bo. Nov. 19. Catharina, of John and Immetje V. Salsbergen. Wit.: Jacob and Elisabeth V. Salsbergen.

Dec. 13, bo. the 12th. Anna, of Wilhelmus Mancius and Annatje Ten Eyck. Wit.: Jacob H. and Anna Ten Eyck.

bo. Oct. 9. Alida, of Yzac J. Van Aarnem and Catharina Van Wie. Wit.: John A. and Lena Van Wie.

Dec. 13, bo. the 11th. Rykert, of Yzaac Rosa and Marytje Van Franken. Wit.: Johs Van Woert, Jannetje Van Franken.

bo. the 12th. Daniel, of Jelles Winne and Fytje Van Woert. Wit.: Daniel and Jannetje Winne.

Dec. 17, Marytje, of Jacob C. and Gerritje Schermerhoorn. Wit.: Philip and Marytje Schermerhoorn.

bo. Nov. 26. Christina, of Gerrit Bratt and Lena Hoogteling. Wit.: Johannes Lange, Christina Bratt.

Dec. 24. Jacob, of Hendrik and Elsje Strong. Wit.: Coenraad and Anna Harwich.

Dec. 23 [sic], bo. the 25th. Maria, of Folkert Daassen (Dawson) and Geertruy Hilton. Wit.: Cornelis and Catharina Switz.

bo. Nov. 16. Bastiaan, of Johannes Conzalus and Machtel Heemstraat. Wit.: Bastiaan and Engeltje Fisscher.

bo. the 18th. Engeltje, of Patrik Clark and Cornelia Waldrom. Wit.: William Waldrom, Engeltje V. Deuzen.

bo. the 23d. Rachel, of Philip Foreest and Maayke V. d. Berg. Wit.: Andries and Catharina Douw.

1770, Jan. 3, bo. the 30th. Pieter, of Gerrit Van Wie and Catharina Lansing. Wit.: Pieter and Alida Van Wie.

bo. the 17th. Maria, of Cornelis Vroman and Lena Huyk. Wit.: Abraham and Marytje Vroman.

Jan. 7, bo. Nov. 1 (1769). Annatje, of Johs J. Qwakken-

1770

busch and Jannetje Viele. Wit.: Adriaan and Folkje Qwakkenbusch.

Jan. 7, bo. the 5th. Elisabeth, of Cornelis Basset and Engeltje Cool. Wit.: Michel Besset, Marritje Bogert.

bo. Dec. 21. Margarita, of John Crennel and Folkje V. Aalstein. Wit.: Hendrik and Jacomyntje Crennel.

Jan. 10, bo. the 5th. Susanna, of Hannes Wiesch and Maria Biesch. Wit.: Jacob Van Woert, Elisabeth V. Woert.

bo. Dec. 15 (1769). Maria, of Abraham Slingerland and Rebecca Viele. Wit.: Johs. and Nenny Ouderkerk.

Jan. 14, bo. the 11th. Cornelia, of Lavinus Ten Baar and Margarita Hanssen. Wit.: Willem and Cornelia Ten Baar.

Jan. 21, bo. Dec. 30. (1769). Pieter, of Pieter and Maria S. Kimmel. Wit.: Philip and Anna M. Dark.

bo. Oct. 19. Catharina, of Benjamin Burt and Elizab. Hoghils. Wit.: Abraham and Geesje Hoghil.

bo. Sep. 29. Christina, of Jurjen Scharp and Catharina Slegers (?) Wit.: Johs. and Cathar. Heidely.

bo. the 1st. Jurjen, of Johs. and Catharina Heidely. Wit.: Cornelis and Maria Sluyter.

bo. Dec. 1. Maria, of John Viele and Geesje Slingerland. Wit.: Pieter and Vrouwtje Bratt.

bo. the 19th. Margarita, of Hendrik Wendell and Maria Lansing. Wit.: Cornelis Cuyler, Marytje Lansing.

Jan. 30 (1770), bo. Dec. 14. (1769). Gerardus, of Jacobus V. Schoonhoven and Elisab. Knoet. Wit.: Gerardus and Alida Knoet.

Jan. 29, bo. the 2d. Johannes, of Robert Tayler and Immetje Hendrikse. Wit.: Abraham and Margarita V. d. Kar.

bo. July 9. (1769). Sara, of Michiel V. d. Koek and Maria Alles. Wit. Gysbert and Hester Bosch.

Jan. 30. (1770). Philip Frederik, of Laurens and Anna Maria Cry. Wit.: Philip J. and Marg. Kerner.

bo. Nov. 10. Elisabeth, of Adam Soufeld and Neeltje Freer. Wit.: Jurjen Berringer, Elisabeth Beem.

Jan. 31, bo. Oct. 12. Thomas, of Jacob Pejo and Catharina Mellendong. Wit.: Hendrik Ruyter, Christina Dath.

bo. Dec. 8. Elisabeth, of Frederik Bernard and Sophia Zeel. Wit.: David Bernard, Catharina Zeel.

bo. Dec. 13. Anny, of Abraham V. d. Heide and Annatje Borrhais. Wit.: Vincent Benneway, Geertruy Bovie.

bo. the 23d. Willem, of Daniel G. V. Antwerpen and Dirkje Winne. Wit.: Willem and Marytje Winne.

Feb. 4, bo. Sep. 13. Daniel, of Hannes Devoe and Marrytje Keller. Wit.: Hendrik and Marg. Northen.

1770

bo. the 28th. Margarita, of Pieter W. Yates and Ann Marg. Hellens. Wit.: John Hellens, Annatje Yaits.

bo. the 25th. Jacob, of Wendel Hillebrand and Geertruy. Wit.: Jurjen and Elsje Hildenbrand.

Feb. 7. Johannes, of Johs. and Jannetje Danielson. Wit.: Nicolaas V. d. Bergh, Catharina Levison.

Feb. 8, bo. Nov. 12, (1769). Jenneke, of Pieter and Catharina Hoghil. Wit. Francis Hoghil, Jannetje Ouderkerk.

Feb. 8, bo. the 7th. Lavinus, of Hendrik V. Aarnem and Susanna Winne. Wit.: Johs. and Elisabeth Winne.

Feb. 11, bo. Jan. 7. Pieter, of Salomo Bulsing and Geertruy Knoet. Wit.: Nicolaas and Elisab. Knoet.

Feb. 14, bo. Jan. 28. Pieter, of Christoffer J. Yates and Cathar. Lansing. Wit.: Abraham and Engeltje Yates.

Feb. 18, bo. Dec. 24, (1769). Hendrik, of Joseph Boskerk and Santje Wendell. Wit.: Hendrik and Cathalyntje Wendel.

bo. the 14th. Thomas, of Thomas Watson and Catharina Veltman. Wit.: Cornelis and Rebecca V. Santvoort.

Feb. 21, bo. Jan. 22. Maayke, of Gerrit Oostrander and Christina V. d. Berg. Wit.: Philip De Foreest, Maayke V. d. Berg.

bo. the 9th. Wouter, of Wouter and Hester Slingerland. Wit.: Theunis Slingerland, Rebecca Viele.

Mar. 4, bo. Feb. 5. Jacobus, of Abraham Oothout and Martha Benneway. Wit.: Abraham and Maria Fonda.

bo. the 10th. William, of Gerrit Zeger and Mary Bengwood. Wit.: Philip Look, Sara Pengborn.

Mar. 7, bo. the 4th. Jorena, of John Fryer and Elisabeth Van Woert. Wit.: Hannes and Maria Wiesch.

bo. the 1st. Abraham, of John (*Negro of Joh. Rozeboom*) and Sara Spek. Wit.: Abraham, (*serv. of S. Kip*,) Mary Spek.

Mar. 11, bo. the 4th. Cornelis, of Cornelis Waldrom and Alida Goey. Wit.: Willem and Jannetje Waldrom.

Mar. 14, bo. the 9th. Gerrit, of Hendrik Y. Bogert and Barbara Mersselis. Wit.: Hendrik Mersselis, Marytje Lansing.

bo. the 12th. Claasje, of John D. Groesbeek and Aaltje V. Aarnem. Wit.: David and Marytje Scott.

Mar. 21, bo. the 6th. Rebecca, of Jacob Schermerhoorn and Elisab. Whitaker. Wit.: Willem Schermerhoorn, Engeltje Besset.

bo. the 21st. Jannetje, of Theunis Visscher and Marytje Simessen. Wit.: Bastiaan and Maayke Simessen.

Mar. 23, bo. the 17th. Margarita, of Hendrik Qwakkenbusch and Margarita Oothout. Wit.: Johs. and Cornelia Qwackenbusch.

1770

Mar. 28, bo. the 23d. Margarita, of Hannes V. Santen and Margarita Wilkeson. Wit.: Johs. L. Redly, Sara V. Santen.

bo. the 26th. Willem, of Johs. J. Redly and Margarita Passagie. Wit.: Johs. Passagie, Nency Willis.

bo. the 27th. Theunis, of Albert Slingerland and Christina V. Franken. Wit.: Yzaac and Eva Slingerland.

Apr. 1, bo. the 28th. Lyntje, of Hendrik Ten Eick, Jr., and Margarita Douw. Wit.: Abraham Douw, Elsje Fonda.

Apr. 8, bo. the 1st. Philip, of Andries H. Gardenier and Saartje Hanssen. Wit.: Anthony Groesbeek, Cathalyntje Foreest.

bo. Mar. 14. Hendrik, of Jeremias 'sJans and Loys Adams. Wit.: Johs Witbeek, Annatje Sjans.

Apr. 15, bo. M...18. Jacobus, of Jonathan Witbeek and Gerritje V. Oostrander. Wit.: Johs. and Cathalyntje Winne.

bo. Mar. 13. Jurjen, of Jacob Smith and Elisabeth Vinkel. Wit.: Jan and Magdalena V. Aalstein.

Apr. 18. Hermanus, of Arent V. Antwerpen and Hester Criegier. Wit.: Daniel and Rebecca V. Antwerpen.

Apr. 22, bo. Mar. 25. Petrus, of Philip Heiner and Eva Dryver. Wit.: Frerik and Johanna Canker.

Apr. 28, bo. the 8th. Gysbert, of Wynand W. V. d. Berg and Francyntje Knoet. Wit.: Abraham and Rachel V. d. Berg.

May 2, bo. the 28th. Susanna, of Michel Besset and Marytje V. Franken. Wit.: Gerrit and Susanna V. Franken.

May 6, bo. the 3d. Maria, of Lavinus Winne and Maria Lansing. Wit.: Johs. and Maria Lansing.

Johannes, of Piete and Maria Goey. Wit.: Johannes and Maria Goey.

bo. Apr. 29. Wilhelmus, of Gerrit Rykman and Elisab. V. Buuren. Wit.: Johs. and Cornelia Prys.

May 9, bo. the 5th. Margarita, of John L. and Frina Voetje. Wit.: Johs. M. and Eva Roseboom.

May 13, bo. Mar. 19. Aletteka, of Hermanus V. Salsbergen and Janneke Canck. Wit.: William Borrowee, Elisabeth V. Salsbergen.

May 16, bo. the 12th. Johannes, of Johs. Valkenburg and Elisabeth Meinerssen. Wit.: Maria and Sara Meinerssen.

May 27, bo. the 10th. Catharina, of Wouter Bekker and Annatje Ridder. Wit.: Wouter and Anneke Ridder.

June 2, bo. Apr. 20. Annatje, of Andries Bratt and Annatje V. d. Kar. Wit.: Albert and Annatje Bratt.

June 9, bo. May 10. Annatje, of Yzaac Oostrander and

Elisabeth McCans. Wit.: Gerrit V. d. Berg, Margarita Redly.

June 17. Annatje, of Harmen Fort and Rebecca V. Woert. Wit.: Yzac and Hendrikje Lansing.

Arriaantje, of Hendrik Biddeke and Elisab. Knoet. Wit.: Hendrik Jackson, Saartje Knoet.

bo. May 17. Bregje, of Johs Coen and Hilletje Zeger. Wit.: Thomas and Catharina Zeger.

June 27, bo. the 22d. Catharina, of Jacob Cuyler and Lydia v. Vechten. Wit.: John and Susanna Cuyler.

June 27, bo. the 25th. (or 23d.) Johs, of John W. Claver and Susanna Merriday. Wit.: Elbert and Cathal. Willet.

Hendrik and Margarita, of Pieter Ganzevoort and Gerritje Ten Eick. Wit.: Anthony Ten Eyck, Johs., Evje and Marytje Gansevoort.

June 31 [sic], bo. the 2d. Annatje, of Eldert V. Woert and Elisabeth Fonda. Wit.: Jacob V. Woert, Susanna Ouderkerk.

June 31, [sic]. Rachel, of Andries Douw and Catharina Foreest. Wit.: Anthony and Cathalyntje Groesbeek.

bo. the 15th. Marrinus, of Fransje Gruwel and Annatje Bulsing. Wit.: Martin Bratt, Lena (?) Beekman.

July 8, bo. June 21. Barent, of Barent V. Yveren and Rebecca Bratt. Wit.: Cornelis and Cornelia V. Yveren.

bo. June 12. Lena, of Hannes and Barbara Mook. Wit.: Nicholaas Rechter, Lena Bitman.

July 11, bo. the 13th. Jobje, of Benjamin V. Buuren and Cornelia Salsburry. Wit.: Nicolaas and Elsje Staats.

bo. the 8th. Aaltje, of Yzaac D. Fonda and Susanna Foreest. Wit.: Hannes and Maayke Bratt.

July 17. Maria, of Obadia V. Benthuisen and Annatje Rumney. Wit.: Jonathan Rumney, Maria V. Schaik.

July 19, bo. the 15th. Rachel, of Ned. Davis and Jannetje Duret. Wit.: Rykert and Margarita V. Franken.

July 22, bo. the 21st. Engeltje, of Hendrik J. Renselaar and Rachel Douw. Wit.: Philip and Catharina Schuyler.

Johannes, of Johs. and Annatje Bekker. Wit.: Wouter Ridder, Cathalyntje Hanssen.

bo. June 19. Phebe, of Josua Taylor and Claartje Knoet. Wit.: Johs. and Nenny Ouderkerk.

July 25, bo. June 10. Cornelis, of Evert V. D. Berg and Marytje V. D. Werken. Wit.: Cornelis V. D. Berg, Neeltje Pruin.

July 29, bo. the 23d. Gerrit, of Willem V. Wie and Jannetje Lansing. Wit.: Yzaac and Arriaantje Lansing.

bo. the 26th. Maria, of John Emry and Neeltje Staats. Wit.: Stephen and Hester de Lancee.

bo. the 1st. Elisabeth, of Obadia Cooper and Annatje V. d. Berg. Wit.: Thomas and Margarita Cooper.

1770

Aug. 3, bo. July 3. Marytje, of Willem Flensburg and Christina Bakker. Wit.: Jacobus and Maria V. Santen.

bo. the 2d. Jacob, of Hendrik J. and Lena Lansing. Wit.: Jacob and Hubertje Lansing.

bo. the 2d. Catharina, of Albert Bloemendal and Annatje Hanssen. Wit.: Samuel and Neeltje Pruin.

Aug. 19, bo. the 13th. Frans, of Christiaan Jacobi and Margarita Hoghing. Wit.: Abraham and Marg. Cuyler.

bo. July 20. Johannes, of Jan Fonda and Egje V. d. Zee. Wit.: Johs. Fonda, Dirkje Winne.

Aug. 26, bo. July 28. Wilhelmus, of Johs and Catharina Heener. Wit.: Hans and Elisabeth Dater.

bo. the 3d. Neeltje, of Meinert and Geertruy V. Hoesen. Wit.: Hendrik and Arriaantje Briesch.

bo. the 25th. Antje, of Yzaac Hoogkerk and Rachel V. Santen. Wit.: Rykert V. Santen, Saartje Hilton.

Aug. 29, bo. the 28th. Elisabeth, of Philip V. Renselaar and Maria Sanders. Wit.: Hendrik B. and Catharina Ten Eick.

Aug. 29, bo. the 27th. Jannetje, of Wouter Ridder and Anneke V. d. Berg. Wit.: Abraham and Antje Yates.

Sep. 10, bo. the 30th. Andries, of Stephanus V. Schaik and Jannetje Bratt. Wit.: Cornelia and Alida V. Schaik.

Sep. 16, bo. Aug. 16. Sara, of Johs. E. Zeger and Sara Brooks. Wit.: Evert and Sara Zeger.

bo. the 14th. Annatje, of Wouter De Foreest and Alida Knoet. Wit.: Wilh. V. Antwerpen, Barbara Knoet.

bo. the 14th. Catharina, of John and Marie Tingly. Wit.: William Hoghing, Annatje Shipboy.

Sep. 19, bo. the 7th. Hester, of Johs. V. d. Berg and Maayke Ouderkerk. Wit.: Yzaac and Hester Ouderkerk.

Sep. 30, bo. the 11th. Margarita, of Zacharias Berringer and Anna Feller. Wit.: Jurjen and Elisabeth Berringer.

Oct. 4, bo. the 2d. Arriaantje, of Jacob Roseboom and Hester Lansing. Wit.: Yzaac and Arriaantje Lansing.

Oct. 7. Catharina, of Lavinus Lansing and Catharina V. d. Heide. Wit.: Abraham and Catharina Lansing.

bo. Sep. 10. Jacobus, of Jacob V. Olinda and Elisabeth Schermerhoorn. Wit.: Cornelis and Elisabeth V. Schelluyne.

Oct. 19, bo. Sep. 8. Elisabeth, of Hendrik Ruyter and Rebecca Dath. Wit.: Johs Daath, Elisabeth Ruyter.

Oct. 10, bo. the 8th. Abraham, of George Dean and Anneke V. Deuzen. Wit.: Jacob and Engeltje V. Deuzen.

bo. the 8th. Willem Waldrom, of Folkert G. V. d. Berg and Neeltje Waldrom. Wit.: Willem Waldrom, Elisabeth Dunbar.

Oct. 10, bo. the 8th. Pietertje, of Nicolaas Jeronymun and Jannetje Waldrom. Wit.: Hendrik Hieronymun, Elisabeth Meinersse.

Oct. 14, bo. Oct. 12. Jonas, of Hendrik Oothout and Lydia Douw. Wit.: Jonas and Elisabeth Oothout.

bo. Aug. 24. Catharina, of Hannes Stroop and Dorothea Cannes. Wit.: Hannes Canne, Susanna Haak.

Oct. 17, bo. July 18. Marytje, of Barent Hoghen and Geertje Huik. Wit.: Abraham N. and Margarita Cuyler.

Oct. 18. Henry, of Hendrik Young and Catharina Keller. Wit.: Pieter and Mary Young.

bo. Oct. 21. Annatje, of Frerik Knoet and Marytje Ridder. Wit.: Abraham and Antje Yates.

Oct. 22, bo. Apr. 14. Neeltje, of Hannes Zoufel and Sara Freer. Wit.: Arent Zoufel, Neeltje Freer.

Oct. 24, bo. the 21st. Jacobus, of Abraham Hoogkerk and Antje Hilton. Wit.: Pieter and Judith Hilton.

Engeltje, of Coenraad Vrydag and Christina Deppe. Wit.: Philip and Engeltje Wendel.

Oct. 28, bo. the 23d. Willem, of Dirk Benson and Maritje Wyngaart. Wit.: Willem and Christina Vosburg.

bo. the 25th. Antje, of Archelaus Lynd and Marytje Duivenbach. Wit.: Christoffer Yaets, Catharyntje Waters.

Oct. 31, bo. the 30th. Margarita, of Hendrik R. Lansing and Maria Mersselis. Wit.: Robert and Maria Lansing.

bo. Mar. 15. Cornelis, of Jacob Heener and Magdalena Creller. Wit.: Cornelis V. Esch, Alida V. Woert.

Nov. 4, bo. Oct. 8. Jonathan, of Samuel Hagedoorn and Sofia Rees. Wit.: George Mendel, Lea Knoet.

bo. Oct. 1. Johannes, of John Leenert and Cornelia Richter. Wit.: Johs. and Marg. Rechter.

bo. Oct. 12. Adam, of Pieter Bratt and Margarita Fry. Wit.: Gerrit and Lena Bratt.

Nov. 7, bo. Oct. 30. Albert, of Wilhelmus Smith and Annatje Bratt. Wit.: Jacob V. Woert, Saartje Bogardus.

bo. Oct. 18. Elisabeth, of Cornelis Sprong and Margareta Sjans. Wit.: Hendrik V. Dyck, Margarita Douw.

Nov. 14, bo. the 9th. Cathalyna, of Ysaac Y. Trouex and Susanna Roseboom. Wit.: Cornelis V. Schelluyne, Elisabeth Roseboom.

bo. the 9th. Maria, of Pieter Hilton and Judith Berrit. Wit.: Thomas and Maria Berrit.

Nov. 22, bo. the 20th. Catharina, of Dirk Schuyler and Maria V. Deuzen. Wit.: Johs. Roerbach, Geertruy Schuyler.

Nov. 26, bo. Oct. 25. Marytje, of Gerrit V. d. Berg and Rebecca Fonda. Wit.: Petrus and Marytje V. d. Bergh.

Dec. 2, bo. the 26th. Tryntje, of Willem Ten Baar and Elisabeth V. Deuzen. Wit.: Arent and Engeltje V. Deuzen.

bo. the 5th. Whillem, of Hendrik Milton and Rachel Northen. Wit.: John Northen, Elisab. Devoet.

1770—1771

bo. Oct. 13. Neeltje, of Willem Pangborn and Elisabeth V. d. Bogert. Wit.: Gerrit and Mary Zeger.

Dec. 5, bo. the 3d. Helena, of Abraham Cuyler and Catharina Wendel. Wit.: Hendrik Wendel, Anna Cuyler.

Dec. 12, bo. Nov. 21. Margarita, of Adam Bratt and Maria McCans. Wit.: Marten Meinerssen, Lydia Rykman.

Dec. 20. Yzaac, of Bernardus Halenbeek and Neeltje Clark. Wit.: Nicolaas Halenbeek, Maria Clerk.

Dec. 26, bo. the 24th. Susanna, of Frerik Meinerssen and Elisab. Waldrom. Wit.: Pieter Waldrom, Neeltje Lansing.

Dec. 30, bo. the 25th. Elisabeth, of Eduard and Mary Willet. Wit.: Harmen and Elsje Hun.

bo. Nov. 6. Christoffel, of Anthony Briesch and Tryntje Yaets. Wit.: Pieter Yates, Annatje Yaets.

1771, Jan. 7, bo. the 2d. Johanna, of Cornelis Zwits and Catharina Schuyler. Wit.: Samuel and Elisabeth Schuyler.

Jan. 10, bo. Nov. 20th. Dirck, of Joh[s]. V. Aarnem and Alida V. d. Heide. Wit.: Jacob and Elisabeth V. d. Heide.

bo. the 2d. William, of Barent Goey and Rachel V. Oostrande. Wit.: Jonathan and Catharyntje V. Oostrander.

Jan. 14, bo. Dec. 5 Marytje, of Leendert Muller and Marytje V. Esch. Wit.: Nicolaas V. d. Berg, Aaltje V. Esch.

Jan. 17, bo. the 13th. Aaltje, of Joh[s]. Bratt and Maayke Fonda. Wit.: Staats and Willempje Santvoort.

bo. Dec. 10. Catharina, of Joh[s]. Oostrander and Marritje V. Aalstein. Wit.: Harmen and Cathar. V. Hoesen.

bo. the 12th. Jacob, of Wilhelmus Mancius and Annatje Ten Eick. Wit.: Jacob and Anna Ten Eick, Hendrik and Margarita Ten Eick.

Jan. 21, bo. Nov. 20. Hendrik, of Jacob Mook and Cathar. Claassen. Wit.: Hendrik Mook, Wyntje Redly.

Jan. 24, bo. Dec. 27. Eva, of Pieter W. Witbeek and Rachel V. d. Berg. Wit.: Thomas and Jannetje Witbeek.

bo. the 20th. Yzaac, of Joh[s]. Hanssen and Geertruy Slingerland. Wit.: Albert and Saartje Hanssen.

Jan. 27, bo. Dec. 27. Casparus, of Petrus Ham and Marytje Michel. Wit.: Folkert V. Vegten, Annatje 'sJans.

bo. Dec. 31. Elisabeth, of Jacob and Marytje Lansing. Wit.: Charles and Maayke McCay.

Jan. 30, bo. the 27th. Cathalyntje, of Bastiaan I. Visscher and Engeltje V. d. Berg. Wit.: Gerrit G. and Wyntje Lansing.

Jan. 30, bo. the 5th. Jannetje, of Gerardus V. Olinde and Catharina V. Oostrander. Wit.: Martinus and Sara Bekker.

1771

bo. the 30th. Willem, of Gerrit Groesbeek and Jannetje V. Slyck. Wit.: Nicolaas and Geertje Groesbeek.

bo. the 4th. Saartje, of Symon D. V. Antwerpen and Maria Ten Baar. Wit.: Joh^s. and Saartje Bratt.

Feb. 3, bo. Dec. 23. Lena, of Cornelis Vroman and Lena Huyk. Wit.: Lodewyk and Lena Huyk.

bo. Jan. 5. Maayke, of Alexander Bulsing and Aaltje Oothout. Wit.: Meinert Oothout, Annatje V. Schaik.

bo. Oct. 6. Willem, of Richard Pengborn and Cathalyntje V. Etten. Wit.: Joh^s. Zeger, Sara Pangborn.

bo. Jan. 10. Theuntje, of Hannes Springer and Jannetje Bont. Wit.: Casparus and Geertruy Witbeek.

Feb. 7, bo. the 10th. Edward, of Jacobus Zwart and Nelly Whitaker. Wit.: James Whitaker, Elisabeth V. Steenbergen.

Feb. 7, bo. the 6th. Maria, of Frans Winne, Jr., and Anneke Viele. Wit.: Jacob P. and Maria Bogert.

Feb. 11, bo. Nov. 11. Jan, of Yzaac Dox and Lena De Voe. Wit.: Jan and Catharina De Voe.

bo. Dec. 26. Catharina, of Hermanus V. Aalstein and Cathar. Peessinger. Wit.: Pieter Brat, Cathar. Bratt.

bo. Jan. 16. James, of George Leen and Mary Shaw. Wit.: Anthony and Cathalyntje Groesbeek.

Feb. 14, bo. . . . . 2. Maria, of James McCarray and Maria Hoghing. Wit.: Joh^s. McCarree, Alida V. Schaak.

bo. Nov. 31. David, of Pieter Hoogteling and Annatje Bekker. Wit.: Harmen and Lena Ganzevoort.

Feb. 14, bo. Nov. 22. Cathalyntje, of Philip V. Esch and Lena Ten Broek.

Feb. 16, bo. Aug. 1. Jacobus, of Johannes Hoghil and Elisabeth Leek. Wit.: James and Marrytje Perrot.

Feb. 17, bo. Jan. 16. Beertje, of Johannes Lange and Stine Bradt. Wit.: Albert Bradt and wife. Lena Lange.

bo. Dec. 10. Seintje, of Hendrik Wieler and Seintje Vander Roef. Wit.: Jurgen Steen, Lea Vander Roef.

Sabina, of Hannes Smidt and Margriet Beessinger. Wit.: Cristiaan Hellegaas, Maria Beessinger.

bo. the 14th. Maria, of Abraham Schuyler and Eva Beekman. Wit.: Joh^s. M. Beekman, Elisabeth Douwe.

Feb. 24, bo. the 22. Jacob, of Anthony Halenbeek and Cornelia Cooper. Wit.: Jacob and Janna Cooper.

bo. the 14th. Joseph, of Abraham Peek and Catharina V. Santen. Wit.: Joh^s. Redlif, Hester Winne.

bo. the 11th. Rebecca, of Cornelis Groot and Marritje Rykse. Wit.: Philip and Maria V. Rensselaar.

Gerrit, of John Bell and Margarita Duper. Wit.: Gerrit and Elsje Lansing.

Feb. 27, bo. Oct. 6. Marytje, of Henry Young and Marytje Fletcher. Wit.: Andries and Glorena Goey.

1771

bo. this day. Catharina, of Abraham N. (?) Cuyler and Margarita Wendel. Wit.: Robert Wendel, Marytje Romans.

March 3, bo. the 1st. Nanning, of Johannes Visscher and Elisabeth Bratt. Wit.: Barent and Saartje Visscher.

bo. the 27th. Catharina, of Joh⁵. Horn and Catharina Poossen. Wit.: Wilhelmus and Agnietje V. d. Berg.

bo. Jan. 31. Alida, of Gerrit V. Esch and Evje Scherp. Wit.: Jacob and Sara V. Esch.

Susanna, of Pieter Zeger and Annatje Howk. Wit.: Gerrit Zeger, Mary Pangborn.

bo. . . . 26. Magdalena, of Leendert Gansevoort and Hester Kuyler. Wit.: Harmen and Magdalena Ganzevoort.

March 6, bo. the 2d. Johannes, of Johannes Visser and Annatje Pearsse. Wit.: Jacobus and Alida Pearsse.

bo. Feb. 20. Jacob, of Hannes Primmer and Mary Pauwel. Wit.: Jacob Simmon, Catharina Roozenberger.

bo. Dec. 13. Wouter, of Yzaac Fonda and Rebecca Groesbeek. Wit.: Pieter Groesbeek and Elisab. Knickerbacker.

bo. the 1st. Roelef, of William McCanterisch and Geertruy Kidney. Wit.: Roelef Cool, Elisabeth Kidney.

bo. Jan. 10. Neeltje, of Theunis and Lena Hoogteling. Wit.: Jonathan Hoogteling, Jannetje Slingerland.

bo. Feb. 6. Joachim, of Gerrit Staats and Cathalina Cunningham. Wit.: Nicolaas Staats, Maria Salsburry.

bo. the 5th. Jacob, of Louys Van Woert and Catharina V. d. Berg. Wit.: Jacob and Elisabeth V. Woert.

bo. Nov. 22. Johannes, of Daniel and Catharina Halenbeek. Wit.: Joh⁵ and Elisabeth Qwakkenbusch.

March 10. Martyje, of Johan P. Claas and Clara M. Curteen. Wit.: Nicholaas and Marytje Richter.

March 27, bo. the 26th. Johannes, of Johannes Ten Broek and Sara Ganzevoort. Wit.: Pieter, Jr., and Anna Ganzevoort.

bo. the 1st. Johannes, of Jacob Foreest and Catharyntje Bratt. Wit.: Harmen V. Hoezen, Catharyna Witbeek.

April 6, bo. March 7. Philippus, of David Foreest and Elisabeth Witbeek. Wit.: Philip and Maria Foreest.

April 14, bo. March 7. Hannes, of Hannes Michel and Sara Church. Wit.: Andries and Catharina Wederwax.

Gysbert, of Laurens Claauw and Annatje Bord. Wit.: Daniel and Annatje Mershal.

bo. the 8th. Alida, of Rutger and Maria V. d. Berg. Wit.: Gerrit and Alida V. d. Berg.

April 20, bo. March 5. Cathalyna, of Johannes Fonda and Dirkje Winne. Joh⁵. Ouderkerk, Nenny V. Esch.

April 24, bo. March 9. Helena, of Jacob V. Aarnhem and Annatje V. Franken. Wit.: Abraham J. V. Aarnhem, Maria Winne.

56

April 28, bo. the 1st.   Arent, of Frerik Olfer and Catharyntje V. d. Berg.   Wit.: Rykert and Martyje Redly.

bo. March 12.   Johannes, of Robert Winne and Hillegonda V. Franken.   Wit.: Hendrik V. Aarnem, Susanna Winne.

bo. March 14.   Zacharias, of Jurgen Kernryk and Marga. Rockenfeller.   Wit.: Zacharias Berringee, Anne Felle.

April 28, bo. March 31.   Sara, of Abraham and Elisabeth Oostrander.   Wit.: Maas and Cathar. Bloemendal.

May 8, bo. March 30.   Johannes, of Arent Bratt and Jannetje Hoghing.   Wit.: John. V. Antwerpen, Catharina Wheight.

May 9, bo. Apr. 14.   Abraham, of Gerrit Waldron and Catharina V. d. Berg.   Wit.: Abraham V. d. Berg, Rachel Levison.

bo. Apr. 7.   Sarrtje, of Pieter Bratt and Jannetje Springsteen.   Wit.: Gerrit and Christina Bratt.

May 12.   Pieter, of Willem Oorlof and Maria Hartman. Wit.: Pieter and Christina Bouman.

May 12, bo. Apr. 14.   Yzaac, of Pieter Levison and Maria Fonda.   Wit.: Gerrit V. d. Berg.   Wit.: Rebecca Fonda.

May 15, bo. the 4th.   Elisabeth, of Philip P. Schuyler and Annatje Wendel.   Wit.: Steven Schuyler, Maria V. Renzelaar.

bo. the 11th.   Wouter, of Anthony Groesbeek and Cathalyntje Foreest.   Wit.: Wouter Groesbeek, Catharina Fonda.

May 19.   Maria, of Jacob and Maria E. Hoogstrasser. Wit.: Johan. O. Bam, Maria E. Bauman.

bo. Apr. 26.   Jannetje, of Arent Becker and Antje V. Woert.   Wit.: Dirk Bekker, Annatje Hoghing.

bo. Apr. 18.   Alida, of Yzac V. Arnem and Catharina V. Wie.   Wit.: Johs. and Lena V. Wie.

May 20, bo. the 19th.   Theodorus, of Cornelis V. Schelluyne and Elisabeth Roseboom.   Wit.: Abrm. Roseboom, Elisabeth V. Schelluyne.

May 22, bo. Apr. 7.   Elisabeth, of Pieter Bekker and Anna Acker.   Wit.: Johannes and Annatje Bekker.

May 26, bo. Feb. 25.   Catharina, of Joseph Shaw and Sara Duitscher.   Wit.: Quiliaan and Catharyntje V. Renzelaar.

bo. Apr. 15.   Abraham, of Hannes V. d. Werken and Marytje de Voe.   Wit.: Abraham and Margarita V. d. Kar.

bo. the 20th.   Johannes V. Schaik, of Christoffel Lansing and Sara V. Schaik.   Wit.: Johs. and Cathalyntje V. Schaik.

bo. March 17.   Pieter, of John Daniels and Jannetje Leevi.   Wit.: Hendrik and Marytje Greveraad.

May 29, bo. the 27th.   John, of James Donneway and Elsje Smith.   Wit.: Johs. and Susanna Donneway.

1771

bo...25. Anna, of John Bleiker and Gerritje V. Schaik. Wit.: Gerrit Roozeboom, Anna C. V. Schaik.

June 3, bo. the 29th. Douwe, of Maas V. Buuren and Rebecca Bogert. Wit.: Douwe and Willempje Bogert.

bo. the 23d. Elisabeth, of Joh^s. O. Rham and Catharina Hoogstrasser. Wit.: Paul and Elisabeth Hoogstrasser.

bo. Apr. 30. Johannes, of Hendrik Katsbach and Eva De Voe. Wit.: Joh^s. and Anna Barent.

The following six children were baptised on June 7 at Steen Babier. (Stone Arabia?)

June 7, bo. Oct. 12. Marytje, of John Wendell and Elisab. Young. Wit.: Robert Wendell and Marytje Romans.

bo. Feb. 8. Catharina, of Frans Hoghil and Sara Young. Wit.: Adam Beem, Cath. Free.

bo. Apr. 4. Elisabeth, of Carel Dark and Margar. Barent. Wit.: Coenraad and Elisab. Dark.

bo. March 3. Jochum, of Abraham V. d. Heide and Annatje Borrhee. Wit.: Joseph and Selly Norris.

bo. Oct. 8. Jacob, of Jacob Kitsholt and Femmetje V. Yveren. Wit.: Joh^s. and Marytje V. d. Werken.

bo. May 7. Sara, of Ebenezer Roberts and Catharina Vosburg. Wit.: Abraham Hoghil, Margar. V. d. Werken.

June 8, bo. Feb. 20. Maria, of Jurjen De Voe and Elisabeth Dunnig. Wit.: Johan Ernst and Marytje De Voe.

June 12, bo. May 17. Nicolas, of Nanning Visscher and Sara Lansing. Wit.: Gerrit G. V. Franken, Geertruy Visschers.

June 13, bo. May 28. Hendrik, of Johannes Zebo and Anna M. Rokkefeller. Wit.: Emrik Plas, Geertruy Rokkefeller.

June 16, bo. the 11th. Margarita, of Cornelis Ackerson and Rebecca V. Santvoort. Wit.: Thomas and Mary Ackerson.

bo. May 28. Jacob, of Marten Foreest and Thanneke Winne. Wit.: Reignier and Cornelia V. Aalstein.

June 16, bo. May 29. Johannes, of Maas and Cathalyntje V. Buuren. Wit.: Hendrik and Aaltje V. Buuren.

July 7, bo. Jan. 23. Rebecca, of Petrus Hilton and Annatje Broek. Wit.: Abraham Aets and Elisabeth Broeks.

bo. Apr. 4. Magdalena, of Melchert File and Elisab. Hunpriger. (or Hunsinger.) Wit.: Maas and Cath. Bloemendal.

bo. June 28. Jacobus, of Johannes V. Benthuisen and Geesje V. Hoesen. Wit. Abrah. Cooper, Sarah V. Benthuisen.

July 10, bo. June 10. Jacob, of Joh^s. H. Groesbeek and Marytje Vielen. Wit.: Pieter and Annatje De Wandelaar.

July 12, bo. the 10th. Meinard, of Barent Vosburg and Annatje Gersen. Wit.: Gysbert and Elsje Fonda.

bo. the 5th. Elisabeth, of Cornelis V. Deusen and Lea V. Oostrander. Wit.: Joh[s]. and Elisabeth Roseboom.

July 14, bo. the 26th. Johannes, of Nicolaas Richte and Maria Hoendemond. Wit.: Joh[s]. and Marya Richte.

bo. the 23. Margarita, of Baltes Bratt and Rosina Follert. Wit.: Nicolaas and Marg. Follert.

bo. June 8. Eva, of Casper and Elisab. Dauzer. Wit.: Adam Heins and Eva Buik.

July 21, bo. the 20th. Johannes, of Pieter Bratt and Vronntje Brat. Wit.: Hendrik and Tryntje Waldrom.

July 24, bo. the 15th. Arriaantje, of Reynier V. Yveren and Debora Fielden. Wit.: Gerrit Roseboom, Catharina V. Yveren.

bo. the 23d. Maria, of Philip Lansing and Elsje Hun. Wit.: Pieter and Elisabeth Lansing.

July 28, bo. June 30. Alida, of Cornelis Bulsing and Annatje Conzal. Wit.: Joh[s]. and Alida Bulsing.

July 28, bo. the 25th. (died.) Robert Sanders, of Hendrik B. T. Eick and Catharina Sanders, (decd.) Wit.: Philip V. Renzelaar, Maria Sanders.

Aug. 1, abt. 6 yrs. old. Susanna, of H. Kerrel and Judikje Hun. Wit.: Harmen and Elsje Hun.

Aug. 4, bo. July 2. Barent, of Adam Vroman and Jannetje Viele. Wit.: Hendrik and Cathalyntje Bleeker.

bo. the 27th. Gerrit, of Gerrit Visscher and Rachel V. d. Berg. Wit.: Gerrit and Agnietje V. d. Berg.

bo. the 28th. Margarita, of James Greers and Margarita Smith. Wit.: Jeremy V. Renselaar, Lena Lansing.

Aug. 11, bo. July 7. Susanna, of David Scott and Marytje Wendel. Wit.: Philip and Santje Wendell.

Pieter, of John Spak and Sara Spek. (colored.) Wit.: John Son, Nency.

Aug. 14, bo. the 13th. Alida, of Harmen V. Hoesen and Tryntje Witbeek. Wit.: John V. Benthuisen, Geesje V. Hoesen.

Aug. 18, bo. July 7. Elisabeth, of Willem Northen and Mary Malburg. Wit.: Willem Ten Baar, Elisab. V. Deusen.

bo. the 26th. Hendrik, of Jacob Springer and Margr. Snyder. Wit.: Hans and Catharina Hoorn.

bo. the 15th. Barbara, of Johannes Mersselis and Margarita V. d. Berg. Wit.: Hermanus Kuyler, Marg. (?) Mersselis.

bo. the 25th. Bregte, of Hendrik Zeger and Grietje Coen. Wit.: Roelef and Lydia Zeger.

bo. the 30th. Margarita, of Mathys Boom and Josyntje Zeger. Wit.: Hendrik and Margar. Zeger.

Jacobus, of Rykert Redly and Marytje Olfer. Wit.: Johannes and Wyntje Redly.

Aug. 21, bo. this day.   Johannes, of Hendrikus Mersselis and Maria Foreest.   Wit.: Gysbert Merselis, Eva Rooseboom.

bo. this day.   Harmen, of Jacob Fonda and Dirkje Visscher.   Wit.: Harmen and Maria Visscher.

Aug. 25, bo. the 24th.   David, of Casparus Pruin and Catharina Groesbeek.   Wit.: David and Sara Groesbeek.

bo. the 18th.   Helena, of John and Alida Van Wie. Wit.: Yzaac V. Aarnem, Catharina V. Wie.

bo. the 23d.   David, of Hannes Wiesch and Maryntje Riesch.   Wit.: Joh⁵. and Elisab. Fryer.

bo. the 22d.   Philip, of Hermanus Schuyler and Christina Ten Broek.   Wit.: Philip and Catharina Schuyler.

The following five children were baptized at the Half Moon, on Aug. 28.

Aug. 28, bo. the 17th.   Lowys, of Louys V. Antwerpen and Hendrikje Fonda.   Wit.: Pieter Viele, Elisabeth Fonda.

bo. the 8th.   Wouter, of Wouter N. Groesbeek and Alida Qwakkenbusch.   Wit. Wouter and Catharina Groesbeek.

bo. July 29.   Dorothe, of Simon Foreest and Maria McGinnis.   Wit.: Abraham and Sara Foreest.

bo. July 19.   Magdalena, of John Walker and Jannetje Burns.   Wit.: Harmen and Catharina Levison.

bo. July 16.   Hester, of Gysbert Bos and Hester Rycke. Wit.: Dirck Citko, Hester Coek.

Sept. 1.   Ysaac, of Willem V. Aalstein and Cathar. Hogeboom.   Wit.: Joh⁵. Crennel and Volkje V. Aalstein.

Catharina, of Jurjen Berringer and Elisab. Beem.   Wit.: Adam and Catharina Beem.

Sept. 4, bo. July 31.   Abraham, of Hermanus A. Wendel and Christina V. d. Berg.   Wit.: Abraham and Susanna Wendell.

Sept. 8, bo. Aug. 16.   Margarita, of Michel Lauer and Janneke V. Buuren.   Wit.: Jurjen J. and Margarita Lauenberger.

bo. Sept. 2.   Willem, of Robert and Jannetje Yates. Wit.: Willem V. Esch, Geertruy Schuyler.

bo. the 23d.   Marytje, of Abraham Sickels and Marytje Cannel.   Wit.: Joh⁵. G. Lansing and wife.

Sept. 14, bo. the 15th.   Annatje, of Franciscus Mershal and Geertruy V. Deuzen.   Wit.: Pieter and Annatje Mershal.

bo. Aug. 10.   Jacob, of Willem Bratt and Arriaantje Mack.   Wit.: Balthus Bratt, Annatje Palsing.

Sept. 21, bo. the 13th.   Willem, of Jacob V. Schaik and Marytje V. Buuren.   Wit.: Cornelis and Maayke V. Buuren.

bo. Aug. 27. Johannes, of Lucas V. Salsburry and Marytje V. Buuren. Wit.: Benjamin and Cornelia V. Buuren.

bo. the 19th. Daniel, of Barent Staats and Antje Winne. Wit.: Adam and Catherina Winne.

bo. the 18th. Willem, of Pieter Crennel and Catharina Egmond. Wit.: Robert and Arriaantje Crennel.

bo. Aug. 29. Margarita, of Wynand V. Aalstein and Margar. Reisdorp. Wit.: Laurens and Margarita Reisdorp.

bo. the 11th. Cathalyna, of Guy Young and Dirkje Winne. Wit.: Joh⁸. Fonda, Margarita V. Woert.

bo. Aug. 17. Douwe, of Joh⁸. Fonda and Elisabeth Ouderkerk. Wit.: Abraham Fonda and Hendrikje Lansing.

Sept. 29, bo. the 14th. Hadriaan, of Joseph and Wyntje Bratt. Wit.: Hadriaan and Lydia Bratt.

bo. the 22d. Hendrikje, of Yzaac Slingerland and Eva V. Woert. Wit.: Jelles and Fytje Winne.

Sept. 26, bo. the 12th. Gerritje, of Thomas Peobles and Elis. Bratt. Wit.: John Barclay, Marg. Ten Eick. *Baptized at Half Moon.*

bo. the 13th. Abraham, of Piete Waldrom and Antje Ouderkerk. Wit.: Joh⁸. V. d. Berg, Marytje Ouderkerk. *Baptized at Half Moon.*

Oct. 3, bo. Sept. 15. Johan Frederik, of Christoffer Visscher and Anna Canke. Wit.: Johan. Fred. and Johanna Louysa Canker.

bo. the 14th. Cousina, of Petrus Coen and Marytje Welch. Wit.: Carel and Grietje Dirk.

Oct. 4, bo. the 21st. Maria Magdalena, of Jacob Frederik and Christina Metske. Wit.: Jacob and Lena Metske.

Oct. 5, bo. the 27th. Cornelia, of Pieter W. Yates and Anna Mary Helms. Wit.: Benjamin and Rebecca Hilton.

bo. the 14th. Johannes, of Daniel Winne and Cathar. Hoogteling. Wit.: Joh⁸. and Catharina Winne.

bo. the 2d. Maria, of Johannes Cool and Annatje Daniel. Wit.: Lambert and Marritje Cool.

bo. the 27th. Jeremie, of Stephen Schuyler and Engeltje V. Vechten. Wit.: Pieter and Annatje Schuyler.

Oct. 25, bo. the 4th. Geertruy, of Joh⁸. Goey, Jr., and Maria V. Yveren. Wit.: Joh⁸. and Heiltje Muller.

bo. Nov. 17. Sybrand, of Joh⁸. J. Qwakkenbusch and Jannetje Viele. Wit.: Wouter Knickerbakker, Elisab. Knikkerbakker.

Oct. 27, bo. the 21st. Abraham, of Abraham Eights and Catharina Brooks. Wit.: Pieter Broeks, and Mary Eights.

Oct. 30, bo. Sept. 19. Arriaantje, of David Hoogteling and Hilletje V. d. Zee. Wit.: Harmen and M. Lena Gansevoort.

Nov. 3, bo. Oct. 6. Maria, of Carel Toll and Marytje Kittel. Wit.: Cornelis and Marytje V. d. Berg.

1771

Nov. 3, bo. Sept. 22. Benjamin, of Anthony V. Veghten and Marytje Fonda. Wit.: Pieter and Annatje De Wandelaar.

Nov. 6, bo. the 3d. Hendrik, of Yzaac Hoghing and Marytje Gerritse. Wit.: Hendrik and Marytje Greveraad.

Nov. 9, bo. Oct. 5. Yzaac, of John V. Aalstein and Lena Scherp. Wit.: Pieter and Cathar. Scherp.

bo. Oct. 9. David, of Joh[s]. Crever and Marytje Nelmer. Wit.: Andries and Margar. Miller.

bo. the 8th. Johannes, of Joh[s]. V. Santen and Marg. Wilkeson. Wit.: Thomas Barrheut, Elisab. V. Santen.

bo. Oct. 12. Marytje, of Gerrit Zeger and Marytje Pengborn. Wit.: John Jansen, Johanna Pangborn.

bo. the 7th. Pieter, of Johs. P. and Cornelia Qwakkenbusch. Wit.: Pieter and Catharina Qwakkenbusch.

Nov. 12. Abraham, of Johannes Knoet and Jannetje Ouderkerk. Wit.: John and Sara Knoet.

Jacobus, of Jacobus Forster and Jennith Jenkins. Wit.: Jacobus and Catharina Forster.

bo. the 9th. Arriaantje, of Hendrik Jackson and Sara Knoet. Wit.: Gerrit and Cath. Viele.

Nov. 16, bo. Oct. 28. Cathalyntje, of Christoffer J. Yates and Catharina Lansing. Wit.: Willem and Annatje Staats.

bo. Oct. 27. Lea, of Joseph Boskerk and Santje Wendel. Wit.: Gerrit and Saartje Wendel.

Dec. 1, bo. Nov. 8. Gerrit, of Gysbert V. Santen, Jr., and Rebecca Winne. Wit.: Gerrit and Hester V. Santen.

Dec. 4, bo. the 2d. Philip, of Philip Young and Annatje Sickels. Wit.: Philip Redly, Lucy Bedcok.

Dec. 4, bo. the 1st. Hendrik Demont, of Hendrik Staats and Maria Dumont. Wit.: John and Catharina Dumont.

bo. Oct. 30. Maria, of Abraham Boom and Dorothea Cunningham. Wit.: John and Sara Trotter.

Dec. 8, bo. the 5th. Johannes, of Theunis (?) Visscher and Marytje Simessen. Wit.: Eldert and Hester Simessen.

bo. the 6th. Johannes, of Hendrik Louis and Marytje Davids. Wit.: Daniel and Annatje Davids.

bo. the 3d. Anna, of Nicolaas Mersselis and Margar. Groesbeek. Wit.: Gysbert and Annatje Mersselis.

Dec. 11, bo. the 10th. Ysaac, of Nicolaas Halenbeek and Jannetje Willes. Wit.: Hendrik Halenbeek, Santje Hellen.

bo. the 9th. Sara, of John J. Beekman and Maria Sanders. Wit.: John S. and Sara Glen.

bo. Nov. 8. Maas, of Cornelis V. d. Berg and Maayke Ouderkerk. Wit.: Maas V. d. Berg, Margaritha Waldrom.

Dec. 18, bo. Nov. 1. Leendert, of Hendrik Meyer and Maria Snyder. Wit.: Leendert and Agnietje V. Buuren.

1771

bo. the 11th.   Arriaantje, of Folkert Dawson and Geertruy Hilton.   Wit.: Pieter Hilton and Sara Fryer.

Margarita, of Jelles Winne and Tietje V. Woert.   Wit.: Rachel Louis and Marg. V. Woert: Douwe and Cath. Winne.

bo. the 15th.   Sara, of Christoffer A. Yates and Catharina Water.   Wit.: Gerrit and Jannetje Lansing.

bo. Nov. 28.   Cornelis, of Nicolaas Groesbeek and Geertje Waldrom.   Wit.: Evert and Jannetje Waldrom.

Dec. 22, bo. Nov. 29.   Johannes, of Daniel V. Olinde and Marytje V. d. Werken.   Wit.: Johannes V. d. Werken, Christina Pruin.

Dec. 22, bo. the 20th.   John, of Rutger Bleeker and Catharina Elmendorp.   Wit.: John R. and Elisabeth Bleeker.

Dec. 29, bo. the 28th.   Thomas, of Daniel Yousen and Mary Barreth.   Wit.: Thomas and Elisabeth Barrith.

bo. the 18th.   Daniel, of Daniel Ertsberger and Fegine Leenerien.   Wit.: Joh^s. Richter, Anna M. Leenerien.

bo. the 11th.   Willem, of John Knickerbakker and Elisabeth Winne.   Wit.: Willem and Marytje Winne.

INDEX

Heemstraat, 11, 15, 21, 27, 35, 37, 40, 44, 46.
Heene, Heener, 13, 23, 51, 52.
Hegerman, 30.
Hegher, 22.
Heidely, Heildrig, 43, 47.
Heiner, Heyner, Heins, 7, 10, 26, 49, 58.
Hellegaas, 54.
Hellem, Hellen, Hellens, Heller, Helms, 22, 35, 36, 48, 60, 61.
Hendermond (see Hoendemond).
Hendrickse, 47.
Herman (see Hartman).
Hetsel, 24.
Hevelis, 8.
Heyner (see Heiner).
Hieronymun, Jeronymun, 51.
Hildebrand, Hildenbrand, Hillebrand, 18, 29, 32, 48.
Hilten, Hilton, 1, 5, 12, 14, 15, 21, 30, 32, 33, 36, 39, 41, 44, 46, 51, 52, 57, 60, 62.
Hoendemond, Hoendermond, Hoenermond, Hendermond, 16, 27, 42, 58.
Hoes, 26.
Hofman, 9.
Hogeboom, 4, 26, 42, 59.
Hogen, Hogh, Hoghen, Hoghin, Hoghing, Hoghingh, 3, 5, 9, 13, 17, 18, 20, 27, 32, 33, 34, 36, 40, 42, 45, 51, 52, 53, 54, 56, 61.
Hoghil, Hoghils, 23, 45, 47, 48, 54, 57.
Holt, 46.
Hoofaul, 3.
Hoogkerk, 5, 14, 20, 36, 39, 44, 51, 52.
Hoogland, 12.
Hoogstrasser, Hoogstratterin, 1, 15, 22, 32, 56, 57.
Hoogteling, 8, 11, 13, 14, 15, 20, 22, 23, 26, 27, 30, 33, 36, 39, 40, 42, 45, 46, 54, 55, 60.
Hoorn, Horn, 55, 58.
Houshek (see Shousek).
Howk, Huigh, Huik, Huyk, 4, 12, 30, 34, 45, 46, 52, 54, 55.
Hun, 16, 18, 19, 32, 35, 37, 39, 40, 53, 58.
Hunpriger, Hunsinger, Hansinger, 20, 35, 57.
Hunter, 28.
Husen, Huson, Yousen, 2, 24, 34, 62.
Huyk (see Howk).
Jackson, 50, 61.
Jacobi, 17, 34, 51.
Jansen, Janssen, 'sJans, S'Jans, Sjans, 6, 8, 15, 32, 38, 49, 52, 53, 61.

Jeems, 10.
Jek, 11.
Jenkins, 61.
Jeronymun (see Hieronymun)
Joed, 8.
John, Son Nency (?), 58.
Jones, 'sJaans, 15, 21, 37.
Joufeld (see Zoufel).
Jung (see Young).
Kanner, Kannon (see Canne).
Katsbach, Katzebach, 36, 57.
Keller, 40, 47, 52.
Kerl, Kern, Kernel, Kerner, Kernryk, Kerrel, 13, 17, 18, 21, 30, 32, 40, 41, 42, 47, 56, 58.
Kidney, Kidny, 17, 55.
Kimmel, Kimmich, 5, 44, 47.
Kip, 4, 48.
Kitsholt, 57.
Kittel, 13, 22, 60.
Klaauw (see Claas).
Klein (see Clein).
Kloet (see Cloet).
Knickerbacker, Knickerbaker, Knickerbakker, Knikkerbakker, 6, 14, 16, 17, 23, 26, 31, 36, 40, 55, 60, 62.
Knoet, 5, 11, 13, 15, 16, 20, 23, 25, 26, 27, 33, 35, 37, 42, 45, 47, 48, 49, 50, 51, 52, 61.
Knolb, 5.
Koch, Coek, 24, 59.
Koen (see Coen).
Koeper (see Cooper).
Kool (see Cool).
Krankheid, Krankheit, 2, 10.
Kughler (see Coegler).
Kuiler, Kuyler (see Cuyler).
Kwakkenbusch (see Quackenbusch).
Kwee, 27 (Goe?).
Lain (see Leen).
Lanck, Lang, Lange, 1, 14, 23, 32, 38, 46, 54.
Landman, 14, 27.
Lansing, Lensing, 3, 4, 5, 6, 7, 8, 9, 11, 12, 13, 14, 16, 17, 18, 19, 20, 21, 23, 24, 27, 28, 29, 30, 33, 34, 35, 36, 37, 38, 39, 40, 42, 43, 45, 46, 47, 48, 49, 50, 51, 52, 53, 54, 56, 57, 58, 59, 60, 61, 62.
Larreway, 34, 41.
Lauenberger, 59.
Lauer, 59.
Leek, 35, 54.
Leen, Leener, Leenerien, Leenert, Lain, 31, 39, 52, 54, 62.
Leevi, 56.
Le Grange, Legranssie, Legransy, 5, 6, 8.
Lendt (see Lynd).

Records of the Reformed Dutch Church of Albany, New York

Part 6
1772-1779

Excerpted from
Year Book of The Holland Society
of New York (1922/23)

RECORDS OF THE REFORMED DUTCH CHURCH OF ALBANY, N. Y.

MARRIAGES—1772 TO 1779.

1772, Jan. 18. **L.** Johannes Groesbeek and Anna Davenport, y. p., at Schaktko.

Jan. 21. **B.** Hendrik Clumb and Elisabeth Thoudel, (?) y. p., both of the Colony.

Jan. 27. **L.** Francis Salisbury and Elsje Staats, y. p., both of this County.

Jan. 28. **L.** Martin Egberson and Sinea Schermerhoorn, y. p., both of this County.

Feb. 13. **B.** Ysaac Hoogteling and Rachel Ploeg, y. p., at New Foundland.

March 14. **L.** Samuel Marll and Rachel Gardenier, y. p., both of this County.

March 24, with certif. of Rev. W. Andrew, Richard Tilleman and Sarah Morrel, y. p., both of this County.

June 8. **B.** Ephraim Bennet and Geertruy Bloemendal, in the Colony.

July 8. **L.** Martin C. Witbeek and Mirita V. d. Bergh, of this County.

July 9. **L.** Philip Loek and Magdalena Van Wie, y. p., at Niskatha.

I

July 18. **L.** Abraham Verplank and Hendrikje Lansing, y. p., of this place.

Aug. 30. **L.** John Bratt and Elisabeth Bratt, y. p., both of this place.

Sept. 6. **L.** Barent V. d. Berg and Marytje Blam (?), y. p., both of this place.

Sept. 27. **B.** Jacob Van Loon and Christina Schuyler, y. p., both of this place.

Sept. 28.. **L.** James Halenbeek and Ytje Bratt, both of this County.

Oct. 27. **L.** Daniel V. Antwerp and Gerritje Witbeek, y. p., both of this County.

1773, Jan. 2. **L.** Pieter J. Bogert and Saartje Van Schaak, y. p., both of this place.

Feb. 8. **B.** by Thomas Knowlton at N. Bethlehem. James Harring and Christina Koen, Rensselaer Manor.

Feb. 14. **B.** Abrhm Wendel and Alida Fonda, at Senehaitk (?).

Feb. 23. **B.** Petrus Sheer and Maria De Voe, at Half Moon.

March 2. **L.** Hendrik Greveraad and Marytje Van Driessen, y. p., both of this City.

March 2. **B.** Willem Hoogteling and Maria Bloemendaal, living in the Colony.

March 7. **B.** Nicolaas Siksby and Cornelia Cooper, of the Colony.

April 8. **L.** Anthony E. Bratt and Alida Van Schaak, of this City.

May 15. **B.** Cornelis Brouwer and Elisabeth Visbach, y. p., both in this City.

June 1. **B.** Simon V. d. Koek and Lavyntje V. d. Hoef, Half Moon.

June 5. **L.** Gerrit J. Lansing and Alida Fonda, of this County.

June 6. **L.** Cornelis Douw and Catharina V. Schaik, of this place.

June 7. **B.** Hendrik Wieler and Bregje Boom, of Niskatha.

Aug. 7. **B.** Theunis Van Slyk and Annaatje Cooper, of this County.

Aug. 21. **L.** Isaac Johnson and Anna Romney, y. p., both of this County.

Aug. 25. **B.** Abraham Fransisco and Hester Van der Coek, at the Half Moon.

Sept. 19. **B.** Uldrick Brouwer and Cornelia Beever, both in this County.

Sept. 22. **L.** Henry Van Buuren and Anna Van Schaik, of Saratoga.

Oct. 18. **L.** Zefrinus Peetinger and Maria Young, y. p., both of this City.

Oct. 22. **L.** Gerrit Winne and Anna Viele, y. p., both of the County.

Oct. 27. **B.** Zebuloss Cabols and Catharina Schouerman, y. p., both of this County.

Oct. 30. **L.** Henry Van Hoesen and Elisabeth Evertsen, y. p., both of Albany.

Nov. 7. **L.** John V. Esch and Margarita Van Woert, y. p., of Albany.

Nov. 16. **L.** Albert Meeby and Maria Hoghen, y. p., of this County.

Dec. 1. **L.** Yzaac Bogert and Cathalina Hun, y. p., of this city.

Found upon a piece of paper pasted in the original: (On one side:) Sir. Marriage is intended between James Harrington of New Bethlehan, Manor Reynslor, Albany County, of the one part and Christeen Koones of the other part, Manor Rynslor and County aforesaid. And you are hereby desired to publish the Bands, January 17th, 1773. (On the other side:) (Addressed) To Mr. Knowlton.

These two young people is lawfully by me Thomas Knowlton publickly in meaten U r 11 Sabaths runing.

JACOB HARRINTON,
WILLLOM BARMONE.

1774, Jan. 2. **B.** Matheus Clerk and Immetje Page, liv. in this County.

Jan. 4. **B.** Johs. Vander Werken and Sarah Van Dessel, y. p., of the Colony.

Jan. 28. **B.** Wilhelmus Freelig and Elisabeth Van der Zee, y. p., of the Colony.

Feb. 6. **L.** Abraham Staats and Cornelia Lansing, y. p., of this County.

Feb. 20. **B.** Andries Wilzon and Geertruy Van Ostrander, y. p., of the Colony.

Feb. 22. **B.** Abraham Poels and Dorothea Shutter, y. p., of the Colony.

Mar. 30. **L.** Folkert Oothout and Jannetje Bogert, y. p., of this County.

Apr. 22. **B.** Johs. Meerthen and Maria Freelich, y. p., of this County.

May 21. **B.** Hermanus Van Salsburry and Alida Scherp, y. p., of the Colony.

May 29. **L.** Gerrit Witbeek and Immetje Perry, y. p., of this County.

June. **B.** Johs. Salmsby and Eva Spoor, y. p., liv. at Schotak.

July 16. **B.** John Kames and Mary Dorruck, of the Colony.

Aug. 8. **B.** Martin Van Buren and Jannetje Holliday, of the Colony.

Aug. 28. **L.** Jacob G. Lansing and Femmetje Lansing, y. p., of this City.

Sept. 11. **B.** Abraham Ouderkerk and Aaltje Ouderkerk, y. p., of the Colony.

Oct. 29. **B.** Jacob Bovie and Rebecca Cronke, y. p., of this County.

Nov. 3. **B.** Albert Halenbeek and Sara Slingerland, y. p., of the Colony.

Nov. 20. **L.** Ephraim Van Vechten and Susanna Hoghing, of this City.

Dec. 11. **B.** Daniel McCloud and Margery McQueen.

Dec. 11. **B.** John McDonnall and Margery McDonnal, all of the Wittekill.

Dec. 26. **B.** Johs. Bulsing and Mally Wilzon, in the Colony.

Dec. 31. **L.** Pieter Van Wie and Abigail V. d. Berg, y. p., of the Colony.

1775, Jan. 12. **L.** John M. V. Aalstein and Dirkje Winne, y. p., of this County.

Feb. 2. **B.** Reyer Schermerhoorn and Marytje Bever, in this County.

May 13. **L.** Pieter Winne and Maria Oosterhout, y. p., of the Colony.

May 12. **B.** Samuel Canover and Nency Petton, in the Colony.

June 1. **B.** Pieter Zeger and Marytje Hoogteling, y. p., at Niskatha.

June 4. **L.** Pieter De Foreest and Pietertje Van Aalstein, y. p., of the Colony.

June 15. **B.** Michael Cooms and Elisabeth Jong, y. p., of the County.

June 22. **L.** Gerrit A. V. d. Berg and Anna 's Jans, y. p., of the Colony.

June 25. **L.** Folkert V. Vechten and Elisabeth V. d. Berg, y. p., of the Colony.

July 16. **B.** Alexander Mills, of Tryon County, and Jannet Grant, of this City.

July 19. **L.** Eilardus Westerlo and Catharina V. Rensselaer, née Livingston.

Aug. 2. **L.** John G. Van Schaik and Anna Van Schaik, y. p., of this County.

Aug. 17. **B.** Pieter Coens and Catharine Still, y. p., of the Colony.

Aug. 17. **B.** Court H. Ludolph and Jenneke Jakson, y. p., of this City.

Sept. 23. **B.** Jacobus Van Valkenburg and Catharina Siksby, of this County.

Sept. 24. **L.** Pieter Winne and Helena Bogert, of this County.

Oct. 1. **L.** John Oosterhout and Agnieta Winne, y. p., of the Colony.

Oct. 1. **L.** Martin Vinhagel and Judith Carrol, y. p., of the Colony.

Nov. 5. **L.** Jacobus Van Franken and Geertruy Fonda, y. p., of this County.

Dec. 15. **L.** Philip Bovie and Eva Sharp, y. p., of this County.

1776, Jan. 11. **L.** John J. Sabriskie, of Hakkensak, and Leentje Lansing, of Albany, y. p.

Jan. 21. **B.** Hendrik Kerker and Charlotte Craff, y. p., at Niskgioenen.

Jan. 25. **B.** Barent Meinzert and Polly Lister, y. p., of the Colony.

Feb. 1. **L.** Donald Fisher, of N. Y., and Elizabeth Munroe, y. d., of the Wittekill.

Feb. 10. **L.** John A. Lansing and Elisabeth Fryer, y. p., of this City.

Feb. 3. George Brown and Mally Hilton.

Feb. 3. Jacob Quackenbusch and Catharina de Voe.

Feb. 18. **L.** Anthony Ten Eyck and Maria Egbert, y. p., of this City.

Feb. 18. **L.** Jacob Jac. Bleecker and Elisabeth Wendell, y. p., of this City.

Feb. 19. **B.** John Obryan and Cath. Boom; Thoms Brown and Jannetje Le Granzy; John V. Tuylen and Marie Dauber, of the Colony.

Feb. 19. **B.** Samuel Bromely and Maria Spoor, of the City.

Feb. 21. **B.** Efraim Nolton and Elisabeth Baker, of the Colony.

Feb. 26. **B.** Martinus Van Yveren and Cornelia V. Schaik, y. p., of the Colony.

Feb. 28. **B.** John Siksby and Alida Bont, y. p., of the Colony.

Mar. 7. **B.** John Lawrence and Mindret Williamson, y. p., of New Bethlehem.

Mar. 30. **L.** Hermanus Ten Eyck and Margarita Bleecker, y. p., of this City.

Apr. 12. **B.** Johs. Rendell and Catharina Broekshaven.

Apr. 18. **B.** Johns. Shipley and Helena Gardinier.

Apr. 19. **B.** Johs. Witbeek and Catharina 's Jans.

Apr. 21. **B.** Pieter Grant and Catharina Commings.

May 9. **L.** Hendrik Bratt and Mary Eight.

May 18. **B.** David White and Margaret Reynard, of the army.

May 18. **B.** Wouter V. d. Zee and Mary Beck, of the Colony.

May 19. **B.** Antony Poel and Elisabeth Janssen, of Schotak.

May 25. **B.** Carel Shaver and Celia Redly, of the Colony.

May 26. **B.** William Lappius and Elly Van Deuzen.

June 14. **B.** William Gilberts and Esther Nilson, of this city, both.

July 6. **B.** Jacobus Van Valkenburg and Jannetje Jumens, of Schotak.

July 17. **B.** Thomas Pendell and Immetje V. Salsburry, of the Colony.

Aug. 4. **B.** Johs. Hoogherk and Elisabeth Martin, y. p., of this City.

Aug. 24. **L.** Abraham Halenbeek and Maria Pruin, of this County.

Aug. 25. **B.** William Brown and Polly Cadogan, y. p., of this County.

Oct. 6. **B.** Hendrik Muller and Catharina Ostrander, both of this County.

Oct. 8. James McCally and Wid. Edgelton, of Schenectady.

Oct. 20. **B.** Abraham Poel and Catharina Breesie, y. p., in R'wyck.

Oct. 20. **B.** Andries Ostrander and Catharina Valkenburg, of Kinderhook.

Nov. 28. Upon certif. of his Col. J. Visscher, John Mehony and Elisabeth Green.

Nov. 24. **B.** Willem Brezie and Catharina V. Deusen.

Dec. 10. **B.** Alexander Forsight and Mally Frasier, y. p., living here.

Dec. 21. **L.** Nanning Visscher and Agnietje Van Buuren, y. p., of this County.

Dec. 26. **B.** Gerrit A. Lansing and Elisabeth Wynkoop.

1777, Jan. 1. Certif. of Col. P. Ganzevoort, John Brown and Margaret Scott, of the Army.

Jan. 1. **B.** Elias Conkling and Hannah Lang, y. p., of Nistigioenen.

Jan. 12. **B.** Frederick Meinerszen and Machtelt Witbeek, y. p., of this County.

Jan. 16. **B.** John Evert and Nency Howard, y. p., of this City.

Jan. 19. **L.** Reynier Van Yveren and Rebecca De Foreest, y. p., of this County.

Jan. 21. **B.** Wouter Slingerland and Maria Prys, y. p., of the Colony.

Jan. 26. **B.** Abraham Witbeek and Elisabeth Lansing, y. p., of the Colony.

Feb. 10. **B.** Willem V. d. Werken and Maria Bogardus, y. p., of the Half Moon.

Feb. 10. **B.** Willem Waldron and Margaret V. d. Werken, y. p., of the Half Moon.

Feb. 12. **B.** Jochem V. Hoevenberg and Susanna Clerk, y. p., of this City.

Feb. 22. **B.** Abraham Van Wie and Jacomyntje Borhans, y. p., of the Colony.

Feb. 23. **B.** Arent V. Deuzen and Margaret McCloud, y. p., of this City.

Feb. 24. **B.** Johs. Sanders, Jr., of Schenectady and Debora Sanders, y. d., of this City.

Feb. 24. **B.** Henry Cortreght and Jinny Steel, of Schenectady.

Mar. 2. **B.** Abraham Gardenier and Eva Lewis, liv. in Tryon Co.

Mar. 9. **B.** Pieter Yates and Mary Petten, y. p., of the Colony.

Mar. 9. **B.** Izac Seaman and Margriet Tilman, y. p., of this City.

Mar. 16. **B.** William Tarberd and Anna Young, y. p., of this City.

Mar. 30. **B.** Jacob Van Woert and Sara Van Ness, y. p., of the Colony.

May 2. **B.** Johs. V. d. Berg and Marytje Hoes, y. p., of this County.

May 7. **B.** Robert Gray and Susanna La Grange, y. p., of this County.

May 14. **L.** of Gov. Livingston, Johs. De Wandelaar and Gerritje Ganzevoort, y. p., of this City.

May 28. **B.** John Betty and Elisabeth Daniels, y. p., of the Colony.

May 31. **B.** Theunis W. Slingerland and Rachel Bogert, y. p., of this County.

June 7. **B.** Nicolaas Siksby and Engeltje Vroman, y. p., of Pightawee (?).

June 9. **B.** Cornelis Janssen and Lydia Car, y. p., of Kinderhook.

June 10. **B.** Bernard Neeker and Catharina Heyde, y. p., of the Colony.

June 15. **B.** Thomas Low and Geertje Vosburg, y. p., of the Colony.

June 19. **B.** Zacharias Sickels and Catharina Cheirs, y. p., of this City.

June 29. **B.** Cornelis Gardenier and Antje V. Slyck, y. p., of Schotak.

June 29. **B.** Daniel Bratt and Christina Bakeman, y. p., of the Colony.

June 29. **B.** Johs. V. Esch and Neeltje de Foreest, y. p., at Claverak.

July 13. **B.** Frans Pruin and Maria V. Esch, y. p., of this City.

Aug. 17. **B.** Isaac Oostrander and Sara Herrington.

Sept. 15. **B.** William Coeny and Elisabeth King.

Sept. 27. **B.** Jurjen Honsiker and Anna Smith.

Nov. 6. **B.** Yzac Sturges and Sally Smith.

Nov. 9. **B.** John Graham and Maria Fryer.

Nov. 15. **B.** William Colebride and Hester Van Deusen.

Nov. 18. **B.** Matheus Poel and Elisabeth Shutter.

Nov. 23. **B.** Oliver Stitson and Jany Anderson.

Nov. 30. **B.** Alexander Cameron and Margaret Murray.

Nov. 30. **B.** Samuel Warren and Sally Ames.

Nov. 30. **B.** William Abbot and Margaret Jackson.

Dec. 10. **B.** Daniel Morrison and Eleonor Fraser.

Dec. 25. **B.** Jurjen Lerk and Jannetje V. Buren.

Dec. 25. **B.** Jerson Valenbee and Elisabeth Witbeek.

Dec. 25. **B.** Coenraad Coens and Christina Omfrie.

1778, Jan. 9. **B.** Johs. Ryan and Mary Robinson.

Jan. 7. **B.** William Lacy and Janneke Salsbury.

Jan. 7. **B.** Cornelis Wynkoop and Anna Ganzevoort.

Jan. 10. **B.** Jacob Lansing and Susanna Fonda.

Jan. 11. **B.** Reinier Vanden Bergh and Elisabeth Vinhagen.

Jan. 12. **B.** Pieter Ganzevoort and Catharina V. Schaik.

Jan. 18. **B.** Patrick Philips and Sarah Culberton.

Jan. 19. **B.** Mathys Klegner and Susannah Wilsy.

Jan. 20. **B.** Johs. Vosmer and Polly McCegg.

Jan. 20. **B.** Stephen Owen and Tytje Mersselis.

Jan. 24. **B.** Joseph Welch and Margarita Gurschey.

Feb. 10. **B.** John Williamson and Maria Love.

MARR. UPON BANNS:

Feb. 10. John Cosdan and Alida Nisbert.

Feb. 15. Hiskias Van Norden and Engeltje Loek.

Mar. 2. Pieter V. Buuren and Dorothea Poel.

Mar. 3. Jabis Landers and Hanna Herrington.

Mar. 8. Jacobus Velentbee and Rachel Barheidt.

Mar. 8. Hendrik Gardenier and Elisabeth Huyck.

Mar. 8. John Van Alen and Maria Look.

Mar. 15. Luther Throwbridge and Elisabeth Tillman.
Mar. 21. Anthony Drissee and Eleanor Alder.
Mar. 29. John Lewis Welch and Eunice Murray.
Apr. 5. Elisa Smith and Alida Bulsing.
Apr. 8. Roelef Huyck and Rachel Dickson.
      James Melonay and Abby Brouwer.
      Charles D. Whitley and Elisabeth Willis.
Apr. 19. John Banker and Geertruy Jacobi.
Apr. 20. Roelef Janssen and Maria Wats.
Apr. 21. Abraham Shutter and Catharine Salsbury.
Apr. 26. Samuel Cuddy and Lydia Bratt.
      Samuel Verbank and Mary Rodgers.
      James Ray and Sara Mumpford.
      William Brown and Jane Read.
May 3. John Johnson and Nancy Davenport.
May 8. John Bounds and Mary Fisher.
May 9. Johs. V. Rensselaer and Frences Nichols.
May 24. Edward Comptton and Maria V. Schaik.
May 28. John Sabrisky and Dorothea Bogert.
June 4. Charles McCarty and Dorcas Ward.
June 7. Philip de Foreest and Annatje V. Deuzen.
June 14. Leonard Weyland and Agnieta Miller.
July 6. Alexander Campbell and Mary McMullen.
July 7. Valentyn Denick and Barbara Moor.
July 20. Lewis Grant and Majorey Fayer.
Aug. 12. John V. Antwerp and Cathalina Yates.
Aug. 14. Gerardus Lansing and Margarita Richards.
Aug. 16. Hendrik Lewis and Jannetje Helling.
Aug. 20. Thomas Knowlton Adams and Mary Barnum.
Sept. 5. Thomas Haddock and Catharine Connerly.
Sept. 8. Johannes Muller and Maria Fonda.
Sept. 10. Jan De Voe and Annatje Conner.
Sept. 22. Kiliaan Bont and Maria Beevins.
Sept. 25. —— Roun and Geertruy Shup.
Oct. 4. Isaac V. Aalstein and Margarita V. Aalstein.
Oct. 28. Jurjen Claann and Christina Springsteen.
Nov. 8. John Graham and Debora Staats.
Nov. 29. John Hoogan and Annatje White.
Dec. 4. John Fatten and Catharine V.d. Werken.
      Abiah Chagweek and Peggy Wilson.
Dec. 7. Albert Hansen and Engeltje Hansen.
Dec. 26. Humphrey Hardgrave and Jane Wats.

1779, Jan. 6. Nicholaas Slingerland and Mary Halen-
beek.
Jan. 16. Mathew Daly and Mary Brown.
James King and Martha Raly.
Jan. 18. Yzac Foreest and Marytje Greveraad.
Jan. 28. Isaac Larreway and Sara Heemstraat.
Jan. 31. John Albrech and Resina Briesch.
Feb. 6. Frederik Brown and Polly Ramsey.
Feb. 7. Samuel Gart and Ann Carney.
Feb. 7. Jochum V.d. Heiden and Elisabeth Smith.
Feb. 14. Thoms. Foster and Nelly Bourrighs.
Joseph Prindell and Anna Springsteen.
Alexander McGriger and Betsy McVie.
Feb. 16. Josua English and Elisabeth Brogden.
Feb. 20. Marten Wendel and Maria Winne.
Feb. 21. David Getens and Catharine Hewes.
John McKay and Margaret Thomson.
Feb. 28. Joseph Gardener and Oner Thomsen.
Mar. 8. Gerrit P. Van Vrancken and Maria Burch.
Mar. 7. John McClean and Catharina Sarter.
Gerrit Hoogteeling and Annatje Oosterhout.
Mar. 21. John Gates and Geertruy V. Vrancken.
Bethuel Washburn and Gerritje Bratt.
Mar. 19. Henry Herritz and Barber Tholl.
Mar. 28. Christiaan Fero and Catharina Levison.
Mar. 29. Henry Shutter and Jannetje Hindermond.
Apr. 4. Henry Chambers and Rachel V. Santen.
Apr. 11. Isaac Yz. Fonda and Antje V. Santvoord.
Apr. 18. Theunis Abr. Slingerland and Margarita
Hanssen.
May 2. Wouter Moll and Catharina Peek.
Daniel Owens and Elisabeth Springsteen.
George Robertson and Susy Hofman.
MARR. WITH BANNS:
May 16. Himloke Woodruff and Maria Lansing.
Samuel Veeder and Neeltje Koert (or Koen)
May 30. Willem Sibree and Rebecca Yates.
Othonia Preston and Rachel Archerd.
June 2. Richard Robeson and Hanna Stuard.
June 12. Willem Larraway and Sara Wynkoop.
July 4. Pieter W. Groesbeek and Alida V. Aarnem.
July 10. Evert Evertsen and Elisabeth Goey.

July 10. Francis Harssen and Rebecca Spoor.
July 12. Daniel Flensburg and Catharine Hoogteling.
Jacob Shutter and Margarita Howard.
July 13. Cornelis V. Ostrander and Margarita Muller.
July 19. Eduard Chinn and Margarita J. Livingston.
July 25. Nathaniel Henry and Mary Williams.
Harpert V. Deuzen and Geertruy Witbeek.
Aug. 1. James Halstede and Susanna Miller.
Jesse De Foreest and Rebecca Van Santen.
Aug. 8. John M. Kinsy and Hanna Burnett.
Aug. 15. Carel Heemstraat and Geertruy V.d. Werken.
Jacob Springsteen and Rachel Cool.
Sept. 2. John Miller and Hannah Bratt.
Oct. 14. Joseph Haswell and Mary Mark.
Oct. 15. Thomas Brower and Sara Fairfield.
Oct. 22. Dirk Flensburg and Alida V.d. Werken.
Oct. 17. Willem Witbeek and Catharina De Foreest.
Nov. 7. Henry Cool and Jannetje Springsteen.
Wilhelmus Mook and Hester Frederik.
Nov. 21. Volkert V.d. Berg and Maria Vinhagen.
Nov. 22. Gerrit Staats and Elisabeth Low.
Yzac Fonda and Sara Wynkoop.
Dec. 8. Thomas Eesterly and Bata Van Woert.
Dec. 25. David Foreest and Susanna Fonda.
Dec. 27. James Penkerton and Mary Marshall.

BAPTISMAL RECORD—1772 TO 1779.

1772, Jan. 5. bo. Dec. 7. Jurjen of Nicolaas Scherp and Lena Hogeboom. Wit. Jurjen and Catharina Scherp.

Jan. 8. bo. Oct. 27. Margarita of Ignas Kip and Annatje V. Vegten. Wit. Dirk V. Vegten, Pietertje Yates.

bo. Dec. 9. Cathalyntje of Dirk V. Vegten and Pietertje Yates. Wit. Ignas Kip, Annatje V. Vegten.

bo. Nov. 15. Jacob of Harmen Qwakkenbusch and Judike Marl. Wit. Samuel Marl, Elisab. Knikkerbacker.

Jan. 10. bo. Dec. 2. Willem of Everhard Weger and Magdalena Neufll. Wit. Gothfreed Enaks, Margaretha Enan.

Jan. 13. bo. Nov. 22. Maria of Nanning Halenbeek and Alida Ten Eick. Wit. Samuel and Neeltje Pruin.

1772

Jan. 16. bo. the 4th. Hendrik of Jacobus Abeel and Egbertje V. Buuren. Wit. Gerrit and Elisabeth Rykman.

bo. the 12th. Annatje of Willem V. Santen and Alida Smith. Wit. John and Annatje Fryer.

Jan. 20. bo. Dec. 14. Elisabeth of Johannes Oothout and Elisabeth V. Woert. Wit. Pieter and Elisabeth Williams.

Jan. 23. Dirk of Lavinus Lansing and Catharina V. d. Heide. Wit. Dirk and Elisab. V. d. Heide.

Jan. 26. bo. Dec. 18. Marytje of Harman Fort and Rebecca V. Woert. Wit. Jacob and Elisabeth V. Woert.

bo. Dec. 30. Cornelis Cadmus of Hendrik Crennel and Jacomina Bloemendal. Wit. Cornelis and Maria Cadmus.

Feb. 2. bo. the 1st. Jacobus of John Davis and Elisabeth Wyngaard. Wit. Philip and Annatje Young.

Feb. 2. bo. the 8th. Hilletje of Richard Pengburn and Cathalyntje V. Etten. Wit. Benjamin and Heyltje V. Etten.

Feb. 12. bo. the 1st. Benjamin of Cornelis Waldrom and Alida Goey. Wit. Benjamin Goey, Catharina V. d. Berg.

bo. Jan. 1. Catharina of Eldert V. Woert and Elisabeth Fonda. Wit. Hendrik and Catharina Fonda.

Feb. 19.. bo. the 17th. Jacob of Abraham Ten Eick and Annatje Lansing. Wit. Jacob Lansing, Lena V. Renzelaar.

Feb. 23. bo. the 17th. Elisabeth of Johs. V. Woert, Jr., and Cathalyna Lansing. Wit. Jacob and Elisabeth V. Woert.

March 1. bo. Feb. 2. Francyntje of Johs. Conzalus and Machtel Heemstraat. Wit. John Visscher, Annatje Persse.

March 4. bo. the 3d. Maria of Bathus V. Benthuisen and Elisabeth Romney. Wit. Benjamin and Maria Rumney.

Susanna of Will. Serv. of P. Schuyler and Brit. Serv. of Abm. Ten Broek. Wit. Susan serv. of Madame V. Renselaar.

March 8. bo. Feb. 13. Catharina of Hannes and Catharina Redlif. Wit. Willem Willis, Rachel Redlif.

March 11. bo. Feb. 19. Lydia of Jurjen Steen and Lea V. der Hoef. Wit. Roelef and Lydia Zeger.

March 15. bo. the 13th. Neeltje of Nicolaas Hieralymon and Jannetje Waldrom. Wit. Willem and Neeltje Waldrom.

March 15. bo. the 1st. Andries of Hendrik V. Ostran-

1772

der and Maria V. d. Bergh. Wit. Benjamin and Maria V. d. Berg.

bo. Feb. 20. Maria of Wynand W. V. d. Berg and Francyntje Knoet. Wit. Gerrit and Jannetje Lansing.

March 17. Johannes of Daniel and Willempje Bratt. Wit. Johs. Ja. and Catharina Lansing.

March 18. bo. Feb. 23. Zacharias of Adam Schonfeld and Neeltje Freer. Wit. Zachary and Annatje Neet.

March 22. bo. the 21st. Yzaac of Gysbert G. Mersselis and Anna Staats. Wit. Jocham and Elisab. Staats.

bo. Jan. 31. Cornelis of Salomo Bulsing and Geertruy Knoet. Wit. Cornelis and Annatje Bulsing.

April 1. bo. the 29th. David of Willem Groesbeek and Catharina V. Deuzen. Wit. David and Sara Groesbeek.

April 4. bo. March 31. Annatje of Albert Slingerland and Christina V. Franken. Wit. Hendrik and Margarita Waldrom.

April 7. bo. March 29. Maria of Philip Muller and Geesje V. Hoesen. Wit. Harmen Muller, Elsje V. Hoesen.

April 11. bo. March 12. Cornelis of Pieter Simessen and Geertruy Crugier. Wit. Cornelis and Marytje Simessen.

bo. Feb. 26. Pieter of Jan Don and Marytje de Voe. Wit. Samuel Don, Jannetje V. d. Kar.

bo. Feb. 20. Catharina of Abraham K. V. Vlek and Gerritje Contyn. Wit. Matheus and Catharina Contyn.

bo. the 8th. Martinus of Hermanus Hofman and Catharina Douw. Wit. Martinus and Alida Hofman.

April 19. bo. March 30. Alida of Johs. J. Lansing and Maria Huik. Wit. Johs. and Sara Knoet.

April 26. bo. the 20th. Machtel of Yzaac Roza and Marytje V. Franken. Wit. Gerrit and Catharina Viele.

bo. the 20th. Annatje of Abraham Yaetes and Jannetje Bratt. Wit. Pieter and Annatje de Wandelaar.

bo. the 20th. Margarita of Gerrit A. Lansing and Agnietje Bratt. Wit. Bernardus Bratt, Marytje Williams.

May 3. bo. March 23. Cornelis of Hannes Muller and Sara V. Yveren. Wit. Cornelis Muller, Rebecca V. Yveren.

bo. the 29th. Jan of John D. Groesbeek and Aaltje V. Aarnem. Wit. Yzac and Elisabeth V. Aarnem.

May 7. bo. the 5th. Marten of Johannes M. Beekman

1772
and Elisabeth Douwe. Wit. Marten and Geertruy Beekman.

May 12. bo. Apr. 4. Wynand of Albert V. d. Werken and Annatje V. d. Berg. Wit. Abraham and Rachel V. d. Berg.

May 14. bo. the 7th. Andries of Andries H. Gardenier and Saartje Hanssen. Wit. Hannes Mersselis, Neeltje Gardenier.

May 7. bo. the 16th. Anna of Gerrit Rykman and Elisabeth V. Buuren. Wit. Pieter Rykman, Lydia V. d. Berg.

May 17. bo. Mch. 1. Harmen of Cornelis V. Vegten and Annatje Knickerbacker. Wit. Dirk and Alida V. Vegten.

Robert of Johs. Crennel and Folkje V. Aalstein. Wit. Cornelis and Alida V. d. Berg.

May 24. bo. Apr. 27. Johannes of Andries Goey and Glorena Young. Wit. Hans Goey, Elisab. Young.

May 27. bo. the 18th. Johannes of Hendrik and Cathalyna Bleeker. Wit. Johannes Beekman, Elisabeth Cuyler.

bo. the 25th. Hendrik of Andries Abel and Annatje Marshal. Wit. Hendrik Abel. Cathalyna Groesbeek.

May 31. bo. the 5th. Jan of Evert Oothout and Margarita Davenpoort. Wit. Sander and Alida Bulsing.

bo. Mch. 30. Alida of Pieter Goey and Maria Young. Wit. Cornelis Waldrom, Alida Goey.

bo. May 1. Susanna of Hannes Zeger and Sara Pangburn. Wit. Adam and Marytje Zeger.

June 7. bo. Feb. 25. Gerrit of Jacob G. V. Schaik and Geertje Ridder. Wit. Gozen and Maayke V. Schaik.

Whillem of John Rheyly and Cathal. V. d. Berg. Wit. Willem and Santje V. d. Berg.

bo. the 5th. Maria of John McCanne and Eva Beekman. Wit. Robert Yates, Catharina Been.

June 8. bo. the 6th. Maria of Hermanus Wendel and Barbara Bratt. Wit. Hendrik and Marytje Wendell.

bo. the 2d. Catharina of Hendrik Q. V. Renselaar and Alida Bratt. Wit. William St. Lodlo, Elsje Rensselaar.

June 10. bo. the 9th. Robert of Lavinus Dunbaar and Margarita Hanssen. Wit. Simon and Marytje V. Antwerpen.

June 29. bo. Apr. 1. Catharina of Matheus Brouwer and Annatje Ouderkerk. Wit. Yzaac and Catharina Huyk.

1772

June 28. Catharina of Cornelis Wendel and Annatje Lansing. Wit. Hermanus H. Wendel, Annatje Schuyler.

Elisabeth of John Amory and Neeltje Staats. Wit. Joachim and Elisabeth Staats.

July 8. bo. the 8th. Jellis of Daniel Winne and Jannetje Banker. Wit. Jellis and Fytje Winne.

July 12. bo. June 17. William of Francis Salisbury and Elsje Staats. Wit. William Salisbury, Theuntje Staats.

July 18. bo. the 18th. Maria of Nicolaas Claver and Susanna Merridey. Wit. Gerrit and Catharina Viele.

July 20. bo. June 26. Margarita of Joseph V. Santen and Rebecca DeGarmo. Wit. Yzaac Hoogkerk and Rachel V. Santen.

bo. June 27. Johannes of Gerrit V. Oostrander and Christina V. d. Berg. Wit. Abraham and Elisab. V. Oostrander.

bo. the 19th. Sara of Gerrit V. Yveren and Catharina Bogert. Wit. Martin Meinerssen, Debora V. Yveren.

July 23. bo. June 9. Susanna of Hendrik V. Schoonhoven and Aaltje V. Esch. Wit. Gerrit Van Schoonhoven, Maria Fonda.

July 27. Helena of Gerrit Van Wie and Catharina Lansing. Wit. John Ten Baar, Helena Lansing.

Lena of John and Lena Ofens. Wit. Barent and Hendrikje V. Buuren.

bo. Mch. 2. Johannes of Petrus Benneway and Marytje Fort. Wit. Frans Winne, Anneke Viele.

July 31. bo. Mch. 1. Jacob of Yzaac Ouderkerk and Annatje Rodgers. Wit. Abraham Hoghil, Eliabeth Baarh.

Aug. 2. bo. July 30. Johannes of Lavinus Winne and Maria Lansing. Wit. Jacob and Lena Lansing.

Wyntje of John J. Fonda and Evje V. d. Zee. Wit. Theunis V. d. Zee, Wyntje Lansing.

Aug. 5. bo. June 27. Maria of Jacob A. Lansing and Alida Levison. Wit. Willem and Catharina Levison.

Aug. 9. bo. the 5th. Margarita of Nicolaas Klein and Elisabeth Couglen. Wit. Pieter and Lydia Rykman.

Aug. 16. bo. the 13th. Jonathan of Pieter Broeks and Francyntje Wendel. Wit. Jonathan Broeks, Maria V. Santen.

Aug. 16. bo. Aug. 10. Wyntje of Barent V. Yveren and Rebecca Brat. Wit. Johs. and Maayke Bratt.

1772

Aug. 19. bo. Aug. 17. Yzaac of Wouter De Foreest and Alida Knoet. Wit. Yzaac and Neeltje Foreest.

Aug. 22. bo. May 16. Johannes of Willem Groen and Cathalyntje Borns. Wit. John Berry, Marritje de Wever.

Aug. 30. bo. the 26th. Rachel of Jacob de Garmo and Fytje Bekker. Wit. Jellis and Rachel De Garmo.

bo. the 22d. Elisabeth of Abraham Ten Broek and Elisabeth V. Renselaar. Wit. Gerardus Groesbeek Catharina V. Renselaar.

bo. the 10th. Rachel of Jan and Selly Duret. Wit. Johs. and Cath. V. Woert.

Sept. 13. bo. the 11th. Brand Schuyler of Cornelis Zwits and Catharina Schuyler. Wit. Johs. and Elisabeth Bleeker.

bo. the 7th. Catharina of Hendrik Ten Eyck, Jr., and Margarita. Wit. Abraham and Catharina Douw.

Sara of Dick and Maria (slaves) Tham and Susanna.

Sept. 14. Catharina of Leendert Gansevoort and Hester Cuyler. Wit. Johs. Beekman, Jannetje Cuyler.

Sept. 16. bo. the 1st. Margarita of Hendrik Daniels and Mally McCyoung. Wit. George Mendel, Margar. Northern.

Sept. 23. bo. the 22d. Margarita of John Mersselis, Jr., and Margarita V. d. Berg. Wit. Gerrit C. and Margarita V. d. Berg.

Sept. 30. James of James Goarley and Annatje Schuyler. Wit. Dirk and Maria Schuyler.

Oct. 2. bo. Sept. 2. Douwe of Abraham D. Fonda and Hendrikje Lansing. Wit. Yzaac Fonda, Santje Foreest.

Oct. 6. bo. Sept. 27. Lena of Johs. and Elisabeth Fryer. Wit. Edward and Jannetje Davids.

Nov. 1. bo. Oct. 1. Jacobus Barker of Obadia Van Benthuysen and Annatje Rumney. Wit. Baltes and Sara V. Benthuisen.

bo. Oct. 18. Jacob of Albertus Bloemendal and Anna Harssen. Wit. Casparus and Catharina Pruin.

bo. Oct. 11. Hendrik of Hendrik V. d. Werken and Maria Viele. Wit. Cornelis Waldrom, Alida Goey.

bo. Oct. 22. Johannes of Theunis Bratt and Cathalyntje V. Esch. Wit. Johs. Bratt, Anna V. Santvoort.

bo. Oct. 30. Samuel of Edward and Mary Willet. Wit. Theunis and Mechtelt Visscher.

1772-1773

Nov. 8. bo. the 1st. Yzaac of Willem Staats and Annatje Yates. Wit. Yzaac and Maria Staats.

bo. the 1st. Jacobus of Johs. V. Valkenburg and Elisab. Meinersse. Wit. James and Lydia Bloodgood.

Nov. 18. bo. Nov. 7. Alida of Barent and Sara Visscher. Wit. Jacob and Dirkje Fonda.

Nov. 11. bo. Oct. 20. Christiaan of Jacermo 'S. Jans and Lois Adams. Wit. Samuel and Neeltje Pruin.

Nov. 25. bo. the 1st. Margarita of Gerrit Ten Baar and Cathalyntje Bratt. Wit. Johs. V. Franken, Alida Bratt.

bo. the 21st. Jacob of Jacob Cuyler and Lydia V. Vechten. Wit. Dirk and Elisabeth V. Vechten.

Dec. 6. bo. Dec. 2. Aaltje of Andriew Douw and Catharina Foreest. Wit. Hendrik and Lydia Oothout.

Dec. 20. bo. the 18th. Cornelis of Hendrik Waldrom and Margar. V. Franken. Wit. Cornelis Waldrom, Alida Goey.

Dec. 20. bo. Oct. 27. Elisabeth of Mathys Boom and Rosyntje Zeger. Wit. Jacob Kidny, Elisab. Fort.

Dec. 25. bo. the 4th. Folkert Douw of Hendrik Oothout and Lydia Douw. Wit. Andries and Rachel Douw.

bo. the 24th. Willem of Yzaac Vosburg and Catharina Staats. Wit. Philip and Geertruy Wendel.

1773, Jan. 6. bo. the 3d. Thomas of George McDole and Catharina Zeger. Wit. Thomas and Judike Zeger.

Jan. 10. bo. Oct. 9. Willem of Johs. Fonda and Dirkje Winne. Wit. Willem P. Winne, Jannetje V. Aalstein.

Jan. 17. bo. Nov. 19. Laurens of Joseph Boskerk and Santje Wendel. Wit. Gerrit and Saartje Wendel.

bo. the 17th. Petrus of Daniel Mershal and Elisabeth Conchron. Wit. Pieter and Annatje Mershal.

Jan. 20. bo. Aug. 18. Wynand of Pieter Th. Winne and Cathalyntje V. d. Berg. Wit. Abrah. and Rachel V. d. Berg.

bo. Nov. 20. Willem of Nicholaas Groesbeek and Geertje Waldrom. Wit. Gerrit and Jannetje Groesbeek.

Marytje of Jacob Man and Cathar. Smith. Wit. James and Elsje Donneway.

bo. the 19th. Marritje of Jacob V. Deuzen and Elsje Lansing. Wit. Anthony Bratt, Rachel V. Deuzen.

Jan. 24. bo. the 2d. Michael of Johannes Heidly and Catharina Zegerin. Wit. Cornelis Sluiter, Maria Zigerin.

1773

bo. Dec. 31. Hendrik Ten Eyck of Stephen J. Schuyler and Lena Ten Eick. Wit. Barent H. and Lena Ten Eick.

bo. the 7th. Machtel of Marten C. Witbeek and Maria V. d. Berg. Wit. Jonathan Witbeek, Cathal. V. Buuren.

Jan. 24. bo. the 20th. Robert Sanders of Philip Renselaar and Maria Sanders. Wit. Pieter and Debora Sanders.

Jan. 27. bo. the 24th. Alida of Johs. V. Santen and Margar. Wilkeson. Wit. Willem and Alida V. Santen.

Jan. 31. bo. Dec. 5. Whillem of Paulus James and Annetje Crankheid. Wit. Willem and Elisab. Crankheid.

bo. Dec. 4. Gerrit of Johs. Land and Christina Bratt. Wit. Garret and Lena Bratt.

Feb. 3. bo. Nov. 22. Maria of Gerrit V. Esch and Egje Scherp. Wit. Abraham and Neeltje V. Esch.

bo. Oct. 20. Dirk of Jacobus Zwart and Neeltje Whitaker. Wit. Dirk Zwart and wife.

Feb. 7. bo. Jan. 6. Cornelis of George Leen and Mary Shaw. Wit. Hugo and Elisab. McManus.

bo. Jan. 31. Anna of Hendrik J. V. Renselaar and Rachel Douw. Wit. Folkert and Anna Douw.

bo. the 31st. Abraham of George Dean and Annetje V. Deuzen. Wit. Rachel, Jacob and Engeltje V. Deuzen, Anthony and Pietertje Bratt.

Feb. 17. bo. the 13th. Franciscus of Pieter and Vrouwtje Brat. Wit. Johs. and Wyntje Bratt.

bo. the 9th. Cathalyntje of Reynier V. Yveren and Annatje Hoghil. Wit. Anthony and Marytje V. Yveren.

Feb. 28. bo. the 6th. Salomo of Alexander Bulsing and Aaltje Oothout. Wit. Salomo Bulsing, Geertruy Knoet.

bo. the 24th. Sofia of John Redley and Margarita Passagie. Wit. Robert and Arriaantje Crennel.

bo. Jan. 8. Dirk of Jacob V. Olinde and Elisabeth Schermerhoorn. Wit. Rykert and Cathar. V. Franken.

March 2. David and Helena of John Lansing and Catharyntje Burhans. Wit. Jacob and Lena Lansing, Robt. Lansing, Marytje Wendels.

Mch. 7. bo. Feb. 9. Theunis of Abraham and Elisabeth Oostrander. Wit. Johs. and Maria Ostrander.

bo. Feb. 4. Catharina of Johs. Bratt and Margarita Daath. Wit. Bernardus and Catharina Bratt.

Mch. 14. bo. Feb. 15. Maria of Abraham N. Cuyler

1773

and Margarita Wendel. Wit. Nicolaas Cuyler, Elisabeth Staats.

Mch. 17. bo. Jan. 29. Renselaar of Philip Schuyler and Catharina V. Renzelaar. Wit. Stephen and Engeltje Schuyler.

bo. the 15th. Bastiaan of Matheus Visscher and Lydia Fryer. Wit. Bastiaan and Engeltje Visscher.

Mch. 20. bo. Feb. 21. Alida of Yzaac Fonda and Rebecca Groesbeek. Wit. Louys and Hendrikje V. Antwerpen.

Mch. 20. bo. the 26. Susanna of Anthony Halenbeek and Cornelia Cooper. Wit. Daniel and Susanna Halenbeek.

bo. the 24th. Petrus of Jacob V. Loon and Cathalyntje Schuyler. Wit. Petrus and Dirkje V. Loonen.

Mch. 31. bo. the 25th. Johannes of Jacob Roozeboom and Hester Lansing. Wit. Jacob and Machtel Rozeboom.

Apr. 9. bo. the 5th. Abraham of Gysbert Fonda and Elsje Douw. Wit. Abraham and Catharina Douw.

bo. the 9th. Cornelis of Yzaac J. Trouex and Susanna Roseboom. Wit. Cornelis and Elisabeth V. Schelluyne.

Apr. 11. bo. Mch. 5. Adam of Gerrit Zeger and Marytje Pengborn. Wit. Adam and Marytje Zeger.

bo. Feb. 25. Yzaac of John DeVoe and Magdalena File. Wit. Yzaac V. Aarnem, Elisabeth File Aarnem.

Apr. 12. bo. Mch. 25. Lucas of David Foreest and Elisabeth Witbeek. Wit. Lucas and Geertruy Witbeek.

bo. the 10th. Anna of Wilhelmus Mancius and Annatje Ten Eick. Wit. Jacob H. and Anna Ten Eick.

Apr. 21. bo. the 1st. Jacob of Jacob Foreest and Frenkje Bratt. Wit. Yzaac Fonda, Santje Foreest.

bo. the 16th. Abraham of Johs. Knoet, Jr., and Sara V. Aarnem. Wit. Abraham V. Aarnem, Alida Knoet.

Apr. 23. bo. the 1st. Catharina of Michel Lauer and Janneke Van Buuren. Wit. Caspar and Catharina Lauer.

May 2. bo. Apr. 30. Abraham of Dirk Benson and Marytje Wyngaart. Wit. Hendrik Waldrom, Geertje Vosburg.

bo. the 26th. Debora of Cornelis Schelluyne and Elisabeth Roseboom. Wit. Yzaac J. Trouex, Cathal. Schuyler.

bo. Mch. 23. Jacob and Elisabeth of Hendrik V. Aarnem and Susanne Winne. Wit. Jacob V. Aarnem, Cathar. Veder, Robert and Elisab. Winne.

1773
May 8. Dorothea of John Sullivan and Elisab. Cooper.
Wit. Charles and Agnes Sullevan.

May 9. Annaatje of Johannes Coen and Christina Bratt.
Wit. Gerardus and Annatje Beekman.

Annatje of Obadia Lansing and Cornelia V. Benthuisen.
Wit. Johs. and Annatje Lansing.

Abraham of Cornelius Vroman and Lena Huyk. Wit.
Arent Bekker, Geertruy Vroman.

Petrus of Johannes Ten Broek and Sara Gansevoort.
Wit. Leendert Gansevoort, Rachel Douw.

May 12. bo. the 11th. Andries of Samuel Marll and
Rachel Gardenier. Wit. Johs. V. Esch, Rebecca Gardenier.

May 12. bo. the 10th. Maria of Hendrik Staats and
Maria Dumont. Wit. Yzaac and Maria Staats.

bo. the 9th. Willem Van Deuzen of Dirk Schuyler and
Maria V. Deuzen. Wit. Willem and Catharina Van
Deuzen.

May 16. Folkert of Cornelis Sprong and Marg. 'S Jans.
Wit. Folkert and Annatje Douw.

bo. the 14th. Cornelia of Pieter W. Yates and Any Mary
Helmer. Wit. Cornelis V. Schaak Jr., Engeltje Van
Schaak.

May 19. bo. May 3. Melchert of Melchert Fyle and
Elisab. Harssinger. Wit. Yzaac and Elisabeth V. Aarnem.

bo. the 17th. Hendrik of Hendrik Wendel and Maria
Lansing. Wit. Abraham and Catharina Cuyler.

bo. April 11. Catharina of Philip G. Viele and Maria
Bratt. Wit. Gerrit and Catharina Viele.

May 22. bo. Apr. 13. Jacobus of Pieter Vroman and
Wyntje Redly. Wit. Pieter and Geertruy De Garmo.

May 26. bo. the 24. Alida of Hendrik Greveradt and
Marytje V. Driessen. Wit. Elbert and Marytje Greveradt.

May 30. bo. the 30th. Pieter of Willem (or Pieter) V.
Wie and Jannetje Lansing. Wit. Pieter and Cornelia V.
Wie.

Willem of John Wendel and Elisabeth Young. Wit. Guy
and Marytje Young.

Cornelis of Michael Besset, Jr., and Marytje V. Franken.
Wit. Michel Besset, Engeltje V. Hoesen.

June 6. bo. the 2d. Willempje of Cornelis Ackerson and
Rebecca Sandvoort. Wit. Staats and Willempje V. Sandvoort.

1773

June 10. bo. Apr. 18. Jacob of Jacob Van Aarnem and Annatje V. Franken. Wit. Hendrik and Margarita Waldrom.

June 12. bo. May 14. Jacob of Adam Vroman and Jannetje Sille. Wit. Pieter and Engeltje Zwart.

June 22. bo. May 28. Maria of Abraham Van Esch and Antje Ridder. Wit. Jacob V. Schaik, Geertje Ridder.

June 23. bo. the 19th. Folkert of Matheus Aarsen and Breggie Van Hoesen. Wit. Gerrit and Alida Van Hoesen.

bo. the 19th. Robert of Willem Dunbaar and Elisabeth Van Deusen. Wit. John Dunbaar, Lena Lansing.

bo. May 5. Hendrik of Francis Hoghil and Sara Young. Wit. Yzaac and Catharina Van Aarnem.

June 27. bo. May 6. Cathalyntje of Michiel Landman and Marytje Brouwer. Wit. Robert and Arriaantje Crennel.

bo. the 22d. Annatje of Edward Davis and Jannetje Duret. Wit. Johs. and Elisab. Fryer.

July 4. bo. June 7. Catharina of Daniel Winne and Catharina Hoogteling. Wit. Johs. Van Wie, Magdal. Loek.

bo. June 6. Johannes of Johs. V. d. Berg and Maayke Ouderkerk. Wit. Wynand and Maritje V. d. Berg.

Lydie of Johs. Snyder and Maria Cool.

July 7. bo. the 3d. Abraham of Hermanus A. Wendel and Christina V. d. Berg. Wit. Abraham and Tanneke Wendel.

Loth of Loth and Sara (slaves). Wit. Abraham and Pye.

Yzaac of Arent I. (?) Bratt and Jannetje Hoghing. Wit. Willem and Susanna Hoghing.

July 11. bo. June 5. Folkje of Louys Van Woert and Catharyntje V. d. Berg. Wit. Adriaan and Folkje Qwakkenbusch.

July 16. bo. the 15th. Hendrik of Abraham Cuyler and Catharina Wendel. Wit. Johs. Beekman and Elisabeth Cuyler.

bo. the 10th. Geertruy of Abraham Schuyler and Eva Beekman. Wit. Eilardus Westerlo, Annatje Beekman.

bo. the 17th. Johannes of John Tingy and Maria Lutz. Wit. Philip and Geetruy Muller.

1773

bo. June 11. Magdalena of Jonas Kinter and Maria Ering. Wit. Michel, Elisabeth and Sara Ering.

bo. June 19. Jacob of Petrus V. Ostrander and Catharina Erig. Wit. Jacob and Jacomyntje Ostrander.

bo. June 11. Catharina of Harmen Ering and Elisabeth Wolff. Wit. Mathys and Magdalena Keeler.

bo. July 8. Catharina of Samuel Ering and Saartje Oostrander. Wit. Jonas Kniter, Marytje Ering.

bo. the 12th. David of David and Any Smith. Wit. Johs. and Annatje Husen.

bo. June 5. Cornelis of Franciscus Marshal and Geertruy V. Deuzen. Wit. Cornelis and Lea V. Deuzen.

July 25. bo. the 20th. Sara of Hendrik I. Lansing and Helena Winne. Wit. Gerrit and Hester V. Santen.

bo. June 26. Geertruy of Philip P. Schuyler and Annatje Wendel. Wit. Harmanus and Geertruy Wendel.

July 28. bo. the 27th. Rachel of Frans Winne and Anneke Viele. Wit. Daniel and Jannetje Winne.

bo. June 16. William of Nicholaas Staats and Maria Salisbury. Wit. William and Teuntje Salsbury.

bo. the 26th. Hibertje of Christoffer Lansing and Sara Van Schaik. Wit. Jacob I. Lansing, Willempje Winne.

Aug. 1. bo. July 31. Joseph of Rykert V. Santen and Sara Hilton. Wit. Hannes Redly and Annetje Flensburg.

bo. July 4. Geertruy of Abraham Boom and Dorothee Cunningam. Wit. Barent Staats, Elisab. Wendell.

Aug. 8. bo. the 7th. Lucas of Abraham Hoogkerk and Antje Hilton. Wit. Yzaac and Rachel Hoogkerk.

Aug. 18. bo. the 13th. Jacob of Pieter J. Bogert and Saartje Schaik. Wit. Jacob and Marytje Bogert.

Aug. 22. bo. July 25. Claasje of David Scott and Marytje Wendel. Wit. Yzaac and Elisabeth V. Aarnem.

bo. the 10th. Maria of Gerardus Beekman and Annatje Douwe. Wit. Hendrik and Margarita Van Dyk.

bo. the 20th. Jacob Glen of Abraham C. Cuyler and Jannatje Glen. Wit. John and Catharina Glen.

Aug. 25. bo. June 23. Johannes of Leendert Muller and Marytje V. Esch. Wit. Johs. and Sara Muller (at the Half Moon).

bo. July 11. Margarita of John Daniels and Jannetje Dennison. Wit. Harman and Catharina Levison.

1773

bo. July 3d. Sara of Thomas Andrew and Rachel Ostrander. Wit. Johs. Ostrander and Sara Concklin.

Sept. 1. bo. the 20th. Johannes Beekman of John McCrea and Eva Beekman. Wit. John I. and Debora Beekman.

Sept. 5. bo. the 1st. Cathalyntje of Philip Wendel and Geertruy Vosburg. Wit. John Groesbeek, Marytje Scott.

bo. the 2d. Rebecca of John Visscher and Elisabeth Bratt. Wit. William and Geertruy Groesbeek.

Sept. 12. bo. June 16. David of Pieter Bekker and Annatje Akkerson. Wit. David and Maria Bekker. (Baptized at Saratoga.)

Sept. 12. bo. Aug. 30. Annatje of Martinus V. d. Werken and Marytje Winne. Wit. Albert and Annatje V. d. Werken. (Baptized at Saratoga.)

bo. the 9th. Rebecca of Cornelis V. Vegten and Annatje Knickerbakker. Wit. Dirk and Alida Van Vegten. (Bp. at Saratoga.)

Sept. 15. Johannes of Hannes Wiesch and Maria Riesch. Wit. Guy Young, Dirkje Winne.

bo. the 9th. Sara of Frerik Meinarssen and Elisabeth Waldrom. Wit. Nicolaas Hieronymal, Jannetje Waldrom.

Sept. 19. bo. Aug 31. Jacob of Johs. Olfer and Marritje Siksby. Wit. Gerrit and Elsje Siksby.

Oct. 3. bo. the 28th. Aaltje of Albertus Bloemendal and Anna Harssen. Wit. Johs. and Geertje Pruin.

Oct. 15. bo. the 29th. James of Hendrik Jakson and Sara Knoet. Wit. Johs. and Jannetje Jakson.

Oct. 17. Evert of Gerrit Waldrom and Cath. V. d. Berg. Wit. Gerardus and Marytje Lansing.

bo. Sept. 7th. Helena of Eldert V. Woert and Elisab. Fonda. Wit. Johs. and Elisab. Fryer.

bo. the 14th. Johannes of John P. and Cornelia Qwakkenbusch. Wit. Johs. and Marg. Qwakkenbusch.

Oct. 24. bo. the 19th. Rachel of Thomas Hun and Baatje V. Deuzen. Wit. Willem and Saratje Hun.

Oct. 27. bo. the 23d. Quiliaan of Guy Young and Dirkje Winne. Wit. Frans and Anneke Winne.

bo. the 19th. Catharina of Folkert V. d. Berg and Neeltje Waldrom. Wit. Jacob and Baatje V. Yveren.

Oct. 31. bo. the 19th. John Daniels of John Cool and Annatje Daniels. Wit. John Daniels, Geertruy Daaschen.

1773-1774
Nov. 3. bo. Oct. 11. Harmen of Jacob D. Fonda and Dirkje Visscher. Wit. Bastiaan and Saartje Visscher.

Nov. 7. bo. the 5th. Sybrand of John J. Bleeker and Gerritje V. Schaik. Wit. Wessel and Marytje V. Schaik.

bo. the 4th. Aaltje of Johs. A. Bratt and Maayke Fonda. Wit. Staats and Willempje Santvoort.

bo. Oct. 17. Annatje of Pieter W. Witbeek and Rachel V. d. Berg. Wit. Obadia and Annatje Cooper.

bo. Oct. 16. Alida of Rutger and Maria V. d. Berg. Wit. Gerrit W. and Alida V. d. Berg.

Nov. 10. bo. Nov. 3. Joseph of Robert Yates and Jannetje V. Nes. Wit. Gerrit J. and Jannetje Lansing.

bo. the 8th. Alida of John V. Benthuisen and Geesje V. Hoesen. Wit. Johs. V. Hoezen, Engeltje V. Deusen.

bo. the 6th. Folkert of Reynier V. Hoezen and Engeltje Cool. Wit. Gerrit and Alida Van Hoesen.

bo. Oct. 31. Magdalena of James Green and Margarita Smith. Wit. Dirk Ten Broek, Magdalena Stevenson.

Nov. 21. bo. Oct. 8. Evert of Pieter Waldrom and Antje Ouderkerk. Wit. Gerrit Waldrom, Cath. V. d. Berg.

Dec. 1. bo. the 27th. Hendrik of Hendrik V. Wie and Marytje Merthen. Wit. Pieter and Catharina Van Wie.

Dec. 5. bo. Oct. 27. Evert of Johs. E. Lansing and Maria Staats. Wit. Obadia Lansing, Cornelia V. Benthuisen.

Dec. 12. bo. the 3d. Maria of Jacob Schermerhoorn and Annatje Stroop. Wit. Storm and Racheltje Bratt.

bo. the 11th. Alida of Casparus Pruin and Catharina Groesbeek. Wit. Johs. and Geertje Pruin.

Dec. 12. bo. Nov. 29. Johannes of Ephraim Bennet and Geertruy Bloemendal. Wit. John and Rebecca Foreest.

bo. Nov. 7. Sara of Abraham D. Fonda and Hendrikje Lansing. Wit. Abraham Verplank, Lena Lansing.

bo. Nov. 22. Alexander of Christoffer J. Yates and Catharina Lansing. Wit. Hendrik and Cornelia Schermerhorn.

Dec. 22. bo. the 14th. Elisabeth of Wilhelmus Smith and Annatje Bratt. Wit. Jacob Bogardus, Cornelia Bratt.

1774, Jan. 9. bo. the 1st. Johannes of Gozen Van Schaick and Maria Ten Broek. Wit. Johs. and Elisabeth Ten Broek.

1774

bo. Dec. 31. Jacobus of Abraham Sikkels and Marytje Connel. Wit. Andries and Marytje Viele.

bo. the 6th. Theunis of Johs. I. Visscher and Annatje Peirce. Wit. Bastiaan and Dirkje Crugier.

Jan. 12. bo. the 7th. Abraham of Johs. Schram and Eva Valkenburg. Wit. Yzac D. Fonda, Susanna Foreest.

bo. Dec. 3. Maria of Johs. Goey and Maria V. Yveren. Wit. Andries Goey and Marytje Gardenier.

bo. the 9th. Jacob Lansing of Johs. Van Woert and Cathalyntje Lansing. Wit. Jacob and Willempje Lansing.

Jan. 16. bo. the 15th. Neeltje of Wouter De Foreest and Alida Cloet. Wit. Thomas Lansing, Neeltje Foreest.

bo. Dec. 17. Cornelia of Gerrit Lansing and Alida Fonda. Wit. Yzaac Fonda, Francyntje Cloet.

bo. Nov. 10. Matheus of Abraham K. Van Vlek and Margarita Conteyn. Wit. Peter and Elisabeth Conteyn.

Jan. 21. bo. Nov. 22. Margarita of Anthony Dark and Barbara Brues. Wit. Coenraad and Elisabeth Dark.

Jan. 21. bo. Dec. 19. Elisabeth of Coenraad Ham and Anne Morris. Wit. Carel Dark, Margarita Baals.

Jan. 26. bo. Nov. 19. Margarita of Gerrit Staats and Catharyntje Cunningham. Wit. Johs. and Eva Ganzevoort.

bo. the 23d. Gerrit of Yzaac Jansen and Annetje Rumny. Wit. Gerrit Jansen, Alida Van Schaik.

bo. the 18th. Maria of James Dunnewy and Elsje Smith. Wit. James and Margarita Green.

bo. Dec. 24. Albert of Abraham Slingerland and Rebecca Viele. Wit. Theunis and Christina Slingerland.

bo. the 11th. Cathalyna of Barent Staats and Antje Winne. Wit. Gerrit Staats, Dirkje Winne.

Feb. 3. bo. the 30th. Andries Witbeek of Daniel G. V. Antwerpen and Gerritje Witbeek. Wit. Pieter and Maayke Witbeek.

bo. the 29th. Marytje of John Berry and Catharina Pikket. Wit. Abraham and Antje Yates.

bo. Jan. 29. Jannetje of Philip Muller and Geertruy Goey. Wit. Andries and Glorena Goey.

bo. Jan. 27. Sara of Simon D. V. Antwerpen and Maria Dunbar. Wit. Johs. and Sara Bratt.

bo. the 1st. Jannetje of Barent Goey and Rachel Ostrander. Wit. Salomo Goey and Elisabeth Santvoort.

1774
Feb. 7. bo. Dec. 27. Christoffer of Abraham Coens and Annatje Hegeman. Wit. Christoffer Koens, Maria Coens.

Roelef of Johs. V. d. Werken, Jr., and Marytje DeVoe. Wit. Jurjen and Margarete Cremer.

bo. Jan. 29. Johannes of Hendrik Oostrander and Maria V. d. Berg. Wit. Petrus Ostrander, Lea Witbeek.

Feb. 7. bo. Jan. 16. Engeltje of Hans Conzalus and Machtel Heemstraat. Wit. Pieter Veder, Marytje V. d. Berg.

Feb. 16. bo. Aug. 4. William of John Downal and Lydia Donnam. Wit. Pieter and Annatje Mershal.

bo. the 2d. Barent of Casparus Witbeek and Geertruy V. d. Berg. Wit. Barent and Engeltje V. Valkenburg.

Feb. 20. bo. Jan. 21. Pieter of William Hoogteling and Marytje Bloemendal. Wit. Theunis and Lena Hoogteling.

bo. the 10th. Elisabeth of Nicolaas Hieralymon and Jannetje Waldrom. Wit. Harmen and Elsje Hun.

Feb. 23. Alida of Jacob V. Schaik and Marytje V. Buuren. Wit. John and Cathalyntje Groesbeek.

Feb. 27. Antje of Frederik Olfer and Catharina V. d. Berg. Wit. Gerrit and Wyntje Zeger.

Mar. 2. bo. Feb. 23. Gerardus of Nicolaas Mersselis and Margarita Groesbeek. Wit. Abrm. Ten Broek, Elisabeth Groesbeek.

Mar. 20. bo. Feb. 7. Elsje of Nicolaas Siksby and Cornelia Cooper. Wit. Evert and Elsje Siksby.

bo. the 17th. Hendrik of Cornelis Waldrom and Alida Goey. Wit. Hendrik Waldrom, Margarita V. Franken.

Mar. 23. bo. the 20th. Maria of Frans Strup and Catharina de Wever. Wit. Bastiaan and Engeltje Visscher.

bo. Feb. 20. Theuntje of Gerrit Rykman and Elisabeth V. Buuren. Wit. Gerrit G. V. d. Berg, Theuntje V. Buren.

Mar. 27. bo. Feb. 28. Roelef of Johs. V. d. Werken and Annatje Bogardus. Wit. Roelef V. d. Werken, Wyntje Bogardus.

Apr. 13. bo. the 12th. Johannes Hun of Philip Lansing and Elsje Hun. Wit. Thomas and Elisabeth Hun.

Apr. 13. bo. the 16th. Hendrikje of Yzac Slingerland and Eva V. Woert. Wit. Jelles and Tysje Winne.

bo. the 12th. Annatje of John Mersselis, Jr., and Margareta V. d. Berg. Wit. Gysbert and Annatje Marsselis.

Apr. 17. bo. Mar. 12. Margarita of Jeremias S. Jans

1774

and Loys Adams. Wit. Folkert V. Vegten and Geertruy Groesbeek.

bo. the 16th. Catharina of Johs. V. Hoezen and Engeltje V. Deuzen. Wit. Arent V. Deuzen, Elisabeth Dunbaar.

Apr. 24. bo. the 3d. Coenraad of Gerrit Brat and Lena Hoogteling. Wit. Daniel Winne, Cathar. Hoogteling.

bo. the 20th. Petrus of Daniel Marshal and Elisabeth Cachron. Wit. Pieter and Annatje Mershal.

Apr. 27. bo. the 27th. Meinert of Barent Vosburg and Annatje Gerritsen. Wit. Gysbert and Elsje Fonda.

May 8. bo. Apr. 4. Tobias of Jacobus and Jannetje V. Salsbergen. Wit. Hermanus and Tanneke V. Salsbergen.

bo. the 3d. Dirk of Cornelis and Elisabet V. Schelluine. Wit. Abraham Roseboom, Susanna Truex.

bo. Apr. 11. Lea of Samuel Hagedoorn and Sophia Rees. Wit. Johs. and Maria Knoet.

May 15. bo. Apr. 5. Rebecca of Hendrik Crennel and Jacomyna Bloemendal. Wit. Cornelis and Lea V. Deusen.

bo. the 17th. Rachel of Jurjen Steen and Lea V. Froef. Wit. Jacob and Rachel Loek.

May 29. bo. Feb. 11. Geertje of Hendrik V. Buuren and Annatje V. Schaik. Wit. Jacob and Geertje V. Schaik.

June 1. bo. May 29. Johannes of Hermanus Cuyler and Elisabeth V. Bergen. Wit. Jacob and Catharina Cuyler.

June 5. bo. May 11. Willem of Jacob H. Lansing and Marytje Ouderkerk. Wit. Yzaac Ouderkerk, Elisabeth Bratt.

June 10. bo. Apr. 30. Elisabeth of Jan Hansen and Elisabeth V. d. Heide. Wit. Dirk and Elisabeth V. d. Heide.

June 15. bo. the 13th. Geertruy of Hendrik Ten Eyck and Margarita Douw. Wit. Wilhelmus and Annatje Mancius.

June 19. bo. May 13. Andries of Petrus Ham and Marytje Michell. Wit. David and Sara Groesbeek.

June 22. bo. May 31. Dirkje of Herms. V. Aalstein and Cathar. Beessinger. Wit. Adriaan and Celia Bratt.

bo. May 19. Hesther of Joseph V. Santen and Rebecca De Garmo. Wit. Albert Bratt, Elisab. V. Santen.

June 26. bo. the 19th. Annatje of Andries Abel and Annatje Mershal. Wit. Pieter and Annatje Mershal.

1774
Herry of Bill and Brit (slaves). Wit. Mink and Sanne Spek.

July 3. bo. June 28. Maria of Abraham T. Eik and Annatje Lansing. Wit. Jacob J. and Femmetje Lansing.

bo. the 1st. Cornelia of Baltes V. Benthuisen and Elisab. Rumney. Wit. Obadia and Cornelia Lansing.

July 17. Cathalyna of Jacobus Abeel and Ebbetje V. Buuren. Wit. Elbert and Cathalyna Willet.

bo. the 11th. Jannetje of Cornelis Douw and Catharina V. Schaik. Wit. Johs. and Jannetje Douw.

July 22. bo. the 17th. Johannes of Jacob Roseboom, Jr., and Hester Lansing. Wit. Jacob Roseboom, Machteld Rykman.

July 31. bo. the 13th. Maria of Evert Oothout and Marg. Davenpoort. Wit. Onfry and Maria Davenpoort.

July 31. bo. the 24th. Evje of John J. Beekman and Maria Sanders. Wit. Johs. and Evje Gansevoort.

bo. the 27th. Andries of Hendrik V. Woert and Catharina Eats. Wit. Jacob V. Woert, Jente Clement.

Aug. 6. bo. the 1st. Elisabeth of Nicolaas Claver and Susanna Merriday. Wit. Johs. Merselis, Neeltje Gardenier.

Aug. 9. bo. July 17. Jacobus of Hendrik V. Schoonhoven and Aaltje V. Esch. Wit. Dirk B. V. Schoonhoven Folkje V. d. Berg.

Aug. 13. Hermanus of Johs. V. d. Berg and Eva V. Aalstein. Wit. Hermanus and Cath. V. Aalstein.

Aug. 17. bo. July 22. Johannes of Anthony Briesch and Cath. Yates. Wit. Willem Staats and Elisab. Yates.

Aug. 21. bo. the 17th. Femmetje of Cornelis Zwits and Catharina Schuyler. Wit. Marten H. Beekman, Geertruy Roseboom.

Aug. 28. bo. July 21. Maria of Marten and Annatje V. Buuren. Wit. Pieter M. and Maria V. Buuren.

bo. the 16th. Yzaac of Andries Peesinger and Jannetje Bratt. Wit. Johs. and Catharina Lansing.

bo. the 9th. Salomo Van Vechten of Hendrik V. Renselaar and Alida Bratt. Wit. Johs. and Elisabeth Vischer.

bo. the 23d. David of Lavinus Winne and Maria Lansing. Wit. David Groesbeek, Sara Winne.

Aug. 31. bo. the 4th. Daniel of Marten Foreest and Tanneke Winne. Wit. Jan and Marytje Winne.

1774

Sept. 4. bo. Aug. 17. Elisabeth of Jan Dox and Marytje De Voe. Wit. Christoffer Remsier, Catharina De Voe.

Sept. 11. bo. Aug. 2. Catharina of Daniel C. Winne and Alida V. d. Berg. Wit. Harmen and Cathar. Levison.

Sept. 11. bo. the 9th. Rebecca of Johs. J. Wendel and Alida Hoogkerk. Wit. Lucas and Rachel Hoogkerk.

bo. Aug. 12. Christiaan of Laurens Snyder and Elisab. Heggerty. Wit. Yzaac and Francyntje Fonda.

bo. the 9th. Daniel of Abrah. I. Yates and Jannetje Bratt. Wit. Anthony E. and Alida Bratt.

bo. the 9th. Pieter Edmund of Rutgert Bleeker and Catharina Elmendorp. Wit. John and Margarita Elmendorp.

Sept. 14. bo. Aug. 13. Neeltje of Cornelis and Fytje V. Salsbergen. Wit. Jonathan Cannik, Catharina V. Salsbergen.

Sept. 18. bo. Aug. 6. Rachel of Yzaac Valkenburg and Engeltje V. d. Berg. Wit. Casparus Witbeek, Geertruy V. d. Berg.

bo. Aug. 18. Abraham of James Flin and Jannetje Vroman. Wit. Jacobus and Geertruy Vroman.

Sept. 26. bo. the 22d. Elisabeth of Henry Louys and Mary Davids. Wit. John and Elisabeth Davies.

bo. the 19th. Sara of Gysbert V. Santen and Rebecca Winne. Wit. Willem and Alida V. Santen.

bo. the 18th. Jonas of Folkert Oothout and Jannetje Bogert. Wit. Hendrik and Elisab. Oothout.

Sept. 31. bo. Sept. 9. Petrus of Gerrit V. d. Berg and Rebecca Fonda. Wit. Gerrit Visser, Rachel V. d. Berg.

bo. Aug. 10. Evert of Johs. Zeger and Sara V. d. Hoef. Wit. Evert and Sara Zeger.

Oct. 7. bo. Sept. 13. Johannes of Wynand and Marritje V. d. Berg. Wit. Johs. and Maayke V. d. Berg.

Oct 14. bo. the 13th. Harmen of Yzaac Bogart and Cathalyntje Hun. Wit. Harmen and Elsje Hun.

Oct. 16. bo. Sept. 23. Rykert of Hendrik Waldrom and Margarita V. Franken. Wit. Rykert and Catharyntje V. Franken.

Oct. 19. bo. the 3d. David of John Danielson and Jenith Leen. Wit. John and Anna V. d. Werken.

bo. Sept. 17. Yzaac of Jelles V. d. Berg and Maayke Ouderkerk. Wit. Yzaac and Elisabeth Ouderkerk.

1774-1775
Oct. 23. bo. Sept. 12. Annatje of Obadia V. Benthuisen and Annatje Rumney. Wit. Abrah. Cooper, Sara Benthuisen.

bo. the 16th. Rebecca of Jonathan Brooks and Elisabeth Bratt. Wit. Abrah. and Catharina Aets.

Oct. 30. bo. the 23d. Christina of Nicolaas Klein and Elisab. Coochler. Wit. David and Nancy Smith.

bo. the 6th. Annatje of Cornelis Vroman and Lena Huyk. Wit. Pieter Staats Zeger, Annatje Huyk.

Nov. 20. bo. Oct. 5. Marytje of Benjamin Overbach and Jenneke Oosterhout. Wit. Wilhelmus Oosterhout, Marytje Dekker.

bo. Oct. 20. Maayke of Pieter Levison and Marytje Fonda. Wit. Johs. Bratt, Maayke Fonda.

bo. the 9th. Rebecca of Willem Staats and Annatje Yates. Wit. Anthony and Tryntje Briesch.

Nov. 22. bo. the 18th. Meinard of Jelles Winne and Tietje Van Woert. Wit. Yzaac and Eva Slingerland.

Nov. 26. bo. the 24th. David of John Groesbeek and Cathalyna V. Schaik. Wit. David and Sara Groesbeek.

Nov. 30. bo. the 26th. Harmen of Barent and Sara Visscher. Wit. Theunis and Barbara Visser.

Dec. 4. bo. Nov. 6. Maria of James Harrington and Christina Coens.

Dec. 19. bo. Nov. 2. Pieter of Johs. Lang and Christina Bratt. Wit. Piete and Margarita Bratt.

bo. the 13th. Bernardus of Hendrik Brat and Annatje Davids. Wit. Bernardus and Catharina Bratt.

bo. the 8th. Josyna of Anthony Halenbeek and Cornelia Cooper. Wit. Thomas and Margar. Cooper.

bo. Nov. 5. John of John Redly and Marytje Egmond. Wit. Hans and Catharyntje Redly.

1775, Jan. 1. bo. Dec. 29. Maria of Pieter Van Deuzen and Lena Van Wie. Wit. Hendrik and Maria Van Wie.

Jan. 4. bo. Dec. 12. Elisabeth of Abrahm. Cuyler and Margarita Wendel. Wit. Yzaac and Elisabeth Bekker.

bo. Dec. 28. Andries of John and Alida Van Wie. Wit. Abraham and Lena Van Wie.

Jan. 8. bo. Nov. 5. Catharina of Micheel Laner and Tanneke V. Buuren. Wit. Casper Laner, Catharina Snyder.

1775

bo. Nov. 15. Heiltje of Jeremias Muller and Catharina Moor. Wit. Folkert and Jannetje V. Vegten.

bo. the 5th. Rachel of Anthony Groesbeek and Cathal. De Foreest. Wit. Andries and Cathar. Douw.

Jan. 10. bo. Nov. 26. Elisabeth of Jacobus Zwart and Neely Whitaker. Wit. Eduard and Elisabeth Whitaker.

bo. the 10th. Petrus of Jacob Van Loon and Christina Schuyler. Wit. Dirk and Geertruy Schuyler.

Jan. 15. bo. the 7th. Yzaac of Abraham Staats and Cornelia Lansing. Wit. Yzaac and Eva Staats.

bo. Dec. 13. Susanna of Jacobus V. Schoonhoven and Elisabeth Knoet. Wit. Rutger Lansing and Susanna Fonda.

Jan. 18. bo. the 13th. Christina of Johs. Fryer and Elisabeth V. Woert. Wit. Willem and Christina Vosburg.

Jan. 22. bo. the 20th. Alida of Jacob Pruin, Jr., and Hendrikje V. Buuren. Wit. Samuel and Neeltje Pruin.

bo. the 20th. Hendrik of John V. Esch and Margarita V. Woert. Wit. Theunis and Cathalyntje Bratt.

Jan. 25. bo. June 5. Theunis of Gerrit and Egje Slingerland. Wit. Adriaan and Lydia Bratt.

bo. the 21st. Garritje of Maas Bloemendal and Lena Schermerhoorn. Wit. Cornelis and Lea V. Deuzen.

bo. the 20th. Cornelis of Gerrit Van Wie and Cathar. Lansing. Wit. Cornelis and Cornelia Van Wie.

bo. the 24th. Leendert of Johannes and Sara Ten Broek. Wit. Leendert and Hester Ganzevoort.

Feb. 8. bo. the 1st. Daniel of Samuel Marll and Rachel Gardenier. Wit. Daniel Marll, Judik Qwakkenbusch.

Feb. 12. bo. Jan. 21. Jacob of Mathys Boom and Josyntje Zeger. Wit. Jacob Shutter, Elisab. Fight.

bo. Dec. 7. Johannes of John Voorhees and Jannetje V. Ist. Wit. Thomas and Arriaantje Burnside.

Feb. 15. bo. the 2d. Maria of Matheus V. Deuzen and Cornelia V. Wie. Wit. John and Marytje V. Deuzen.

Feb. 19. bo. the 12th. Marytje of Christoffer Yates and Cathar. Waters. Wit. John G. and Annatje Yates.

Mar. 5. bo. Feb. 18. Glen of Jacob Cuyler and Lydia V. Vechten. Wit. Abraham C. Cuyler, Jannetje Glen.

bo. Feb. 7. Abraham of Hendrik Oothout and Lydie Douw. Wit. Abrah. and Margarita Oothout.

Mar. 15. bo. the 10th. John Perry of Gerrit Witbeek and Immetje Perry. Wit. Yzac and Francyntje Fonda.

1775

Mar. 19. bo. the 15th. Marinus of Eduard Willet and Mary Galen. Wit. Elbert and Sara Willet.

bo. the 18th. Abraham of Abrah. Lansing and Elsje Rensselaar. Wit. Abrah. and Catharina Douw.

bo. the 15th. Petrus of Johs. M. Beekman and Elisabeth Douw. Wit. Petrus and Catharina Douw.

Mar. 26. bo. Feb. 23. Martinus of Bastiaan Crugier and Dirkje Fisscher. Wit. Pieter and Geertruy De Garmo.

bo. Feb. 6. Evert of Obadia Lansing and Cornelia V. Benthuisen. Wit. Christoffer Yaets, Catharina Lansing.

bo. the 22d. Lucas of Yzaac Hoogkerk and Rachel V. Santen. Wit. Abrm. Hoogkerk, Antje Hilton.

Mar. 29. bo. the 25th. Marytje of Nicolaas Halenbeek and Jannetje Willis. Wit. Willem and Marytje Willes.

Apr. 2. bo. Feb. 21. Annatje of Hendrik Bulsing and Neeltje Maas. Wit. Pieter and Geertruy Schuyler.

bo. Mar. 4. Geertruy of Cornelis V. Buuren and Mally Ofens. Wit. Hendrik and Magdal. V. Buuren.

Apr. 9. Johannes of Dirk V. d. Willegen and Saartje Larraway. Wit. John and Maaytje Bratt.

Apr. 14. bo. the 11th. Wouter of John Knoet and Sara V. Aarnem. Wit. Wouter De Foreest, Alida Knoet.

Apr. 16. bo. Mar. 19. Folkje of Gerrit V. Oostrander and Christina V. d. Berg. Wit. Adriaan Qwakkenbusch, Folkje V. Hoesen.

bo. the 11th. Catharina of Dirk Benson and Marytje Wyngaart. Wit. Gerrit and Geertje Vosburg.

Apr. 16. bo. Mar. 20. Maria of David Foreest and Elisabeth Witbeek. Wit. Johs. and Rebecca De Foreest.

Apr. 31. bo. Mar. 26. Gerrit of Joseph Boskerk and Santje Wendel. Wit. Cornelis and Cathar. Douw.

May 7. bo. Mar. 20. Aaltje of Abraham D. Fonda and Hendrikje Lansing. Wit. Pieter Levison, Maria Fonda.

May 10. bo. the 9th. Catharina of Gerrit Groesbeek and Jannetje V. Slyk. Wit. Jacob and Catharina V. Schaak.

May 14. Pieter of Hendrik Riddeker and Elisab. Knoet. Wit. Salomon Bulsing, Geertruy Knoet.

bo. Apr. 11. Maria of John Sullivan and Elisabeth Cooper. Wit. Jacob Scotter, Annatje Cooper.

May 17. Pieter of Robert Winne and Hillegonda V. Franken. Wit. Pieter and Susanna Winne.

1775

May 21. bo. Apr. 2. Johannes of Johs. Fonda and Dirkje Winne. Wit. John and Saartje V. Buuren.

bo. the 19th. Robert of Johs. Lansing (5) and Catharyntje Burhans. Wit. Johs. J. and Cath. Lansing.

Hendrikus of John Schoonmaker and Aaltje Burhans. Wit. Hendrik Burhans, Tempe Demant.

May 28. bo. the 25th. Rachel of Andries Douw and Catharina De Foreest. Wit. Philip and Maayke De Foreest.

June 4. bo. Apr. 19. Dirkje of Jacob Fr. Lansing and Jannetje Visscher. Wit. Gerrit and Rachel Visscher.

June 11. Bregje of Hendrik Weeler and Bregje Boom. Wit. John O'Brian, Cathar. Boom.

bo. Apr. 24. Cornelia of Mathew Flensburg and Christina Snyder. Wit. Johs. and Cornelia Flensburg.

June 11. bo. May 23. Anthony of James Young and Anna Snyder. Wit. Adrian (?) Bratt, Elis Fight.

June 14. bo. May 7. Abraham of Hendrik Feero and Maria Vredenburg. Wit. Abrah. Vredenburg, Cathar. Buys (?)

bo. June 10. Gerrit of Jacob De Garmo and Fytje Bekker. Wit. Gerrit Bekker, Geertruy Soup.

June 18. bo. the 16th. Celia of Johs. V. Santen and Maria Wilkeson. Wit. Thoms. Barreuth, Elis. V. Santen.

bo. May 7. Elisabeth of William Pengburn and Elis. V. d. Bogert. Wit. Johs. and Elis. Davies.

bo. Mar. 23. Hendrikus of Salomo and Arriaantje Du Boy. Wit. Hendrikus Du Boy, Jannetje Hoogteling.

Mar. 27. John of Alexander Bulsing and Alida Oothoud. Wit. Evert Oothout, Margar. Davenpoort.

June 21. bo. Feb. 12. Francis of Abrah. Bloodgood and Elisab. V. Valkenburg. Wit. James and Lydia Bloodgood.

June 25. bo. the 7th. Barent Bratt of Philip G. Viele and Marytje Bratt. Wit. Nicolaas and Barbara Bratt.

bo. the 17th. Hester of Cornelis Brouwer and Elisabeth Visbach. Wit. Wendel Hildebrand, Geertruy Visbach.

July 9. bo May 24. Petrus of Thomas Ismy and Elis. Palmatier. Wit. Pieter Palmatier, Sara Swartwoud.

bo. Apr. 5. Elisabeth of John Hunter and Eva V. Aalstein. Wit. Hendrik and Marg. Zeger.

July 14. bo. the 11th. Elisabeth of Obadia Cooper and Annatje V. d. Berg. Wit. Thomas and Margar. Cooper.

1775

July 16. bo. the 15th. Annatje of Gerrit A. Lansing and Catharina Zwart. Wit. Evert W. and Maria Zwart.

July 20. bo. the 18th. Marritje of Jacob V. Deuzen and Elsje Lansing. Wit. Anthony Bratt, Rachel V. Deuzen.

July 30. bo. the 23d. Abraham Cuyler of Leendert Gansevoort and Hester Cuyler. Wit. Nicolaas and Jannetje Cuyler.

bo. the 27th. Jacob of Pieter and Sara Bogert. Wit. Jacob and Marytje Bogert.

bo. the 5th. Magdalena of Albert Bratt and Elisab. Chambers. Wit. Gerrit and Sophia Bratt.

bo. the 25th. Petrus of Franciscus Mershall and Geertruy V. Deuzen. Wit. Petrus and Annatje Mershall.

bo. the 25th. Geertruy of Dirk Schuyler and Mary V. Deuzen. Wit. Abrm. V. Deuzen. Neeltje Schuyler.

Aug. 6. Hilletje of Dirk A. V. d. Kar and Hilletje Muller. Wit. Yzac and Lena Dox.

bo. July 8. Maria of Jermy 'S Jans and Lena Adams. Wit. Johs. and Cathal. Groesbeek.

Yzac of Jesse Feerguil and Mary Gerritsen. Wit. William and Susanna Hoghing.

Aug. 13. bo. the 7th. Benjamin of Casparus Van Wie and Jannetje Winne. Wit. Lavinus and Hester Winne.

Aug. 20. bo. July 20. Lodewyk of Hannes Huyk and Lena Beekman. Wit. Lodewyk and Lena Huyk.

Aug. 27. bo. July 30. Philip Cortland of Stephen Schuyler and Lena Ten Eyk. Wit. Philip and Catharina Schuyler.

bo. the 13th. Hendrik of Gerrit Reyer and Jannetje V. Slyk. Wit. Balthus and Elisab. V. Benthuysen.

Sept. 16. bo. July 31. Jacobus of Jacobus Cool and Jannetje Witbeek. Wit. Eilardus and Catharina Westerlo.

Sept. 6. bo. the 3d. Hendrik of Yzac Vosburg and Cathar. Staat. Wit. Hendrik Staats, Geertje Vosburg.

Sept. 10. bo. the 8th. Hendrik of Abraham Schuyler and Eva Beekman. Wit. Dirk and Maria Schuyler.

Sept. 11. Bo. Apr. 21. Alida of Willem Seathon and Cathy Connik.

Sept. 17. bo. the 12th. Yzaac of Abraham Veder and Sara Hanssen. Wit. Johs. and Marytje Hanssen.

Sept. 20. bo. the 15th. Annatje of Reinier V. Yveren and Debora Viele. Wit. Hendrik Lansing, Anna V. Yveren.

1775

bo. the 17th. Arriaantje of Philip V. Rensselaar and Maria Sanders. Wit. Guiliaan and Maria V. Rensselaar.

bo. the 7th. Maria of Robert Hilton and Elisabeth Bontjes. Wit. Abrahm. and Antje Hoogkerk.

Sept. 24. bo. the 20th. Wouter of Johs. and Cornelia Qwakkenbusch. Wit. Wouter and Sophia Qwakkenbusch.

Sept. 27. bo. the 26. Abraham of Pieter W. Winne and Rykje V. Schaik. Wit. Abrah. and Catharina Douw.

bo. Aug. 24. Wyntje of Gerrit T. Briesch and Geertruy Groesbeek. Wit. Anthony and Tryntje Briesch.

Oct. 1. bo. the 23d. Adriaantje of Theunis Bratt and Cathalyntje V. Esch. Wit. Cornelis and Antje V. Santvoort.

Oct. 8. bo. Sept. 12. Pieter of Hendrik V. Santen and Catharina De Garmo. Wit. Rykert and Sara V. Santen.

bo. the 6th. Yzac of Philip Wendell and Geertruy Vosburg. Wit. Yzac and Cath. Vosburg.

bo. the 4th. Hendrik of Hendrik V. Hoesen and Elisabeth Evertsen. Wit. Philip Muller, Geesje V. Hoesen.

Oct. 8. bo. the 6th. Agnietje of Barent Bogart and Alida V. d. Berg. Wit. Wilhelmus and Agnietje V. d. Bergh.

Oct. 4 at home. bo. Sept. 2. Marytje of Cornelis Sprong and Mary 'S Jans. Wit. Christ. Abrahams, Cath. 'S Jans.

Oct. 5. bo. July 12. Barent of Abrah. V. d. Heide and Annatje Boorhas. Wit. Eilsa and Elisabeth Adams.

Oct. 13. bo. Aug. 30. Helena of Daniel Fr. Winne and Catharina Hoogteling. Wit. Gerrit and Lena Bratt.

bo. the 10th. Jacob Viele of Frans Winne and Annatje Viele. Wit. Jacob and Catharina Viele.

Oct. 15. Rebecca of Pieter Brooks and Francyntje Winne. Wit. Jacobus V. Santen, Phebe Wyngaart.

bo. the 13th. Lydia of Johs. Mersselis, Jr., and Margarita V. d. Berg. Wit. Cornelis V. d. Berg, Lydia Rykman.

Oct. 22. bo. the 16th. Thomas of Johs. Wilkes and Annatje Mershal. Wit. Thomas Wilks, Maria Wilkes.

Johanna of Theunis Bratt and Cathalina V. Esch. Wit. Johs. Ouderkerk, Anna V. Esch.

Oct. 25. Catharina of Johs. Redly and Maria Passagee. Wit. Willem Pemberton, Hester Willes.

Nov. 4. bo. Oct. 27. Gerardus of Gerardus Beekman and Annetje Douw. Wit. Harmen Gansevoort, Elisabeth Douw.

1775

bo. Oct. 6. Petrus of Abrm. and Elisabeth V. Oostrander. Wit. Hendrik Ostrander, Maria V. d. Berg.

bo. Oct. 21. Jannetje of Arent Aarsen and Aaltje Qwakkenbusch. Wit. Stephen and Jannetje V. Schaak.

Nov. 8. bo. the 7th. Willem of Guy Young and Dirkje Winne. Wit. Zepherinus Peesinger, Marytje Young.

Nov. 12. bo. the 4th. Samuel of Eduard S. Willet and Sara Fryer. Wit. Elbert and Cathalina Willet.

bo. the 2d. Andries of Jelles Trouex and Nency McKinsy. Wit. Andries Trouex, Catharina Wyngaert.

Nov. 19. Nency of Daniel Cumming and Elisab. Grant.

Nov. 26. bo. Sept. 25. Johannes of Pieter W. Witbeek and Rachel V. d. Berg. Wit. Abm. and Annatje Witbeek.

George of James Warren and Mary Crosby. Wit. George McDonald, Mary Cumming.

Nov. 29. bo. Oct. 23. Stephanus of Abrm. Slingerland and Rebbeca Viele. Wit. Stephen and Jannetje V. Schaak.

bo. the 29th. Jannetje of Nicolaas Hieralymon and Jannetje Waldrom. Wit. Folkert and Jannetje V. Vegten.

Dec. 3. bo. Oct. 8. Andries of Pieter Vroman and Wyntje Redly. Wit. Gerrit and Cath. Viele.

bo. Oct. 21. Jonathan of Theunis and Lena Hoogteling. Wit. Willem and Marytje Winne.

Dec. 10. bo. the 7th. Cornelia of Albert Slingerland and Christina V. Franken. Wit. Yzac and Eva Slingerland.

bo. Oct. 31. Margarita of Abrahm. V. d. Poel and Dorothea Shutter. Wit. Melchert and Margar. V. d. Poel.

bo. Oct. 16. Nicolaas of Johs. P. Claas and Clara M. Cortin. Wit. Johs. Leonards, Cornelia Richters.

bo. Nov. 7. Daniel of Pieter Winne, Jr., and Maria Oosterhout. Wit. Daniel Winne, Jannetje De Foreest.

bo. the 8th. Wyntje of Cornelis Wendell and Annatje Lansing. Wit. Reynier V. Yveren, Cathalyna Lansing.

Dec. 13. bo. the 8th. Louys of Louys Obryen and Catharina Rendell. Wit. Martinus Rendell, Anna Young.

bo. the 11th. Geertruy of James Dunway and Elsje Smith. Wit. Pieter and Marytje Scherp.

bo. Oct. 29. Barbara of Augustinus Scherp and Maria V. Aalstein. Wit. Jurjen and Barbara Sherp.

Dec. 17. bo. the 7th. Abraham of Hendrik Wendel and Maria Lansing. Wit. Abraham Roseboom, Catharina Jieldon.

1775-1776

Dec. 20. bo. the 13th. Elisabeth of Johs. I. Visscher and Annatje Persse. Wit. Andries and Elisabeth Trouex.

Dec. 31. bo. the 24th. Gerrit of Jacob G. and Femmetje Lansing. Wit. Gerrit and Jannetje Lansing.

bo. the 26th. Susanna of John Ostrander and Anna Wolssen. Wit. Abrahm. and Jannetje C. Cuyler.

bo. the 29th. Elias of Eduard Davids and Jannetje Droit. Wit. Johs. and Elisab. Fryer.

bo. the 23d. Maria of Pieter W. Yates and Ann Mary Helms. Wit. Benjamin Hilton, N. Hoaksly.

1776, Jan. 1. bo. Dec. 6. Adam of Jeremias Pemberton and Susanna Bratt. Wit. Samuel Lodeman, Elisab. Pemberton.

Jan. 7. bo. Dec. 22. Cornelia Lynch of Philip Schuyler and Catharina V. Rensselaar. Wit. Stephen J. Schuyler, Cornelia Livingston.

Jan. 14. bo. May 26. Ann of Willem Bell and Ann Wallis.

bo. Dec. 15. Martinus of Gerardus V. Olinde and Cath. Ostrander. Wit. Martinus V. Olinde, Sara V. Oost (or Voast).

Jan. 21. bo. Dec. 7. Cathalyna of Hannes Bulsing and Mally Wilson. Wit. Hendrik and Cathalyntje Bulsing.

Jan. 21. bo. Dec. 24. Jacobus of Hendrik V. Schoonhoven and Aaltje V. Esch. Wit. Dirk B. V. Schoonhoven, Folkje V. d. Berg.

Jan. 23. bo. Dec. 15. Susanna of Piete Landman and Sara V. Santen. Wit. Harmen and Susanna Landman.

Jan. 28. bo. Dec. 8. Hendrik of Gerrit Staats and Catharina Cunningam. Wit. Johs. and Maria Beekman.

bo. the 20th. Yzac of Willem V. Wie and Jannetje Lansing. Wit. Yzac Lansing, Hester Roseboom.

bo. the 15th. Annatje of John V. Alen and Maria Lansing. Wit. Barent and Annatje V. Alen.

Helena of Hannes Wiesch and Marytje Riesch. Wit. Eduard Davis, Lally Bell.

Feb. 4. bo. the 1st. Catharina of Hendrik Staats and Maria Dumont. Wit. Johs. duMont, Catharina V. Deuzen.

Feb. 7. bo. the 2d. Anthony of James Halenbeek and Ytje Bratt. Wit. Anthony and Elisabeth Bratt.

Feb. 11. bo. Dec. 24. Alida of Eldert V. Woert and Elisab. Fonda. Wit. Gerrit and Rachel Visscher.

1776
Feb. 13. Christoffel and Adam of Christoffel Yates and Catharina Waters. bo. the 9th. Wit. Josef, Jannetje, Jan G. and Cathal Yates.

Feb. 13. bo. Jan. 5. Yzac of Abrah. and Alida Ouderkerk.

Elisabeth of Pieter Burnside and Maria de Lange.

Feb. 18. Petrus of Hans Meisserger and Antje V. d. Berg. Wit. Cornelis G. (?) and Elisab. V. d. Berg.

Feb. 21. bo. the 14th. Annatje of Edmund Butler and Nency Tilson. Wit. Fredrik Meinerssen, Anna Flensburg.

Feb. 25. bo. Jan. 29. Adam of George Berringer and Elisabeth Been. Wit. Adam and Cathar. Been.

bo. Feb. 5. Evert of Nicolaas Siksby and Cornelia Cooper. Wit. Jacobus Valkenburg, Cathar. Siksby.

Feb. 28. bo. the 5th. Jacob of John Redlif and Marytje Egmond. Wit. David Gibson, Mary Egmond.

Mar. 3. bo. Feb. 6. Margarita of Thoms. Burnside and Arriaantje T. Eyk. Wit. Andries and Elis. Stoll.

bo. Feb. 10. Frina of Jacob Springer and Marytje Snyder. Wit. Hans and Cathar. Hoom.

Mar. 10. bo. Feb. 6. Anny of Yzac Fryer and Elisabeth Hilton. Wit. Mathys and Lydia Visscher.

Mar. 17. bo. the 11th. Willem of Casparus Pruin Catharina Groesbeek. Wit. Johs. and Cathalyntje Groesbeek.

Mar. 20. bo. the 19th. Pieter of Gerrit Rykman and Elisabeth V. Buuren. Wit. Marten and Sara Meinerssen.

bo. Feb. 29. Johannes of Gerrit Lansing and Alida Fonda. Wit. Lavinus Winne, Maryn Lansing.

Mar. 24. bo. Jan. 31. Bata of Johs. Conzalus and Machtel Heemstraat. Wit. Dirk and Annatje Knoet.

Mar. 31. bo. the 23d. Maria of Albertus Bloemendal and Anna Harssen. Wit. Philip V. Rensselaar, Maria Sanders.

(A leaf in the original had been bound wrong).

Apr. 7. bo. the 3d. Johannes of Wouter de Foreest and Alida Kloet. Wit. Johs., Jr., and Alida Kloet.

Apr. 7. bo. the 4th. Cornelis of Cornelis V. Zandvoort, Jr., and Cornelia V. Wie. Wit. Cornelis and Annatje V. Sandvoort.

bo. the 5th. Jacob of John V. Esch and Margarita V. Woert. Wit. Yzac and Annatje Lansing.

1776

Apr. 18. bo. Jan. 20. Mary of Alexander Chesny and Jane McMolly.

Apr. 17. bo. the 9th. Jurjen of Coenraad Sharp and Elisabeth Staats. Wit. Jurjen and Barbara Sharp.

Apr. 21. bo. the 12th. Susanna of Johs. Coen and Christina Brat. Wit. Jeren. Pemberton, Sus. Bratt.

Apr. 28. bo. the 19th. Robert of Matheus Aarsen (or Harsen) and Bregje V. Hoesen. Wit. Philip V. Rensselaer. Maria Sanders.

bo. the 27th. Arent of Willem Ten Baar and Elisabeth V. Deuzen. Wit. Arent and Engeltje V. Deuzen.

bo. the 24th. Johannes of Pieter Qwakkenbusch and Maria Shifley. Wit. Wouter, Margarita and Catharina Qwakkenbusch.

May 5. Yzaac of Yzac Slingerland and Eva V. Woert. Wit. Theunis Slingerland, Geertruy Hanssen.

bo. Apr. 30. Margarita of Johs. N. Bleecker and Margarita V. Deuzen. Wit. Hendrik and Margarita Bleecker.

May 11. Jane of George Rodgers and Eleonore Morry.

May 12. bo. the 9th. Elisabeth of Henry Lewis and Marytje David. Wit. Johs. and Elisab. David.

bo. Mar. 22. Engeltje of Folkert Oothout and Jannetje Bogert. Wit. Hendrik and Dorothe Bogert.

bo. the 6th. Rensselaer of Eilardus Westerlo and Catharina Livingston. Wit. Stephen and Elisabeth Van Rensselaer.

May 19. bo. the 3d. Elisabeth of Hendrik Daniels and Maria McCowl. Wit. Willem Northen, Elisabeth McManus.

bo. the 6th. James of James Tounsel and Rachel Gardenier. Wit. Hans E. and Sara Zeger.

May 26. bo. the 19th. Sybrand of Gozen V. Schaik and Maria Ten Broek. Wit. Meinard and Maria V. Schaik.

bo. May 5. Geertruy of Michel Bessett and Marytje V. Franken. Wit. Gerrit and Geertruy V. Franken.

bo. May 1. Barent of Hendrik Oostrander and Maria V. d. Berg. Wit. Barent V. d. Berg, Marytje Ham.

June 5. bo. Dec. 3. Johannes of Hendrik Finke and Annatje Cocks.

bo. May 10. Jacobus of Jacobus Proper and Eva Althouser. Wit. Willem Bartel, Geertruy Rees.

1776
June 9. bo. May 12. Annatje of Petrus Ham and Marytje Michel. Wit. Barent V. d. Bergh, Marytje Ham.

bo. the 5th. Abeltje of John J. Bleicker and Ann Elisabeth Schuyler. Wit. Jacobus Bleecker, Abeltje Bleeker.

bo. the 5th. Maria of Nicolaas Mersselis and Margarita Groesbeek. Wit. Gerardus and Elisabeth Groesbeek.

June 19. bo. May 26. Elisabeth of Abraham Sickels and Maria Conner. Wit. John and Maria Beekman.

June 23. bo. May 14. Andries of Gerrit A. V. d. Bergh and Annatje 'S Jans. Wit. Barent V. d. Bergh, Maryke Ham.

bo. May 3. Theuntje of Hendrik V. Buuren and Annatje V. Schaik. Wit. Gerrit Rykman, Elisab. V. Deuzen.

June 24. bo. May 25. Willem of Willem Brazee and Elisab. Salsbury. Wit. Jacobus and Jannetje Salsbury.

June 26. bo. the 5th. Engeltje of Jacob Foreest and Tryntje Bratt. Wit. Jesse and Saratje Foreest.

July 7. bo. June 17. George of Hendrick Milton and Rachel Northen. Wit. Johs. and Margarita Jankins.

July 14. bo. June 17. Robert of Hendrik Crennel and Jacomyntje Bloemendal. Wit. Philip and Maayke de foreest.

bo. the 10th. Benjamin of Hendrik J. Lansing and Helena Winne. Wit. David Groesbeek, Sara Winne.

bo. the 7th. Elisabeth of Hendrik V. Wie and Maria Merthen. Wit. Eduard Willet, Elisabeth Merthen.

bo. the 8th. Margarita of Willem Adams and Hester Willis. Wit. Nicolaas Halenbeek, Margar. Pruin.

bo. the 10th. Pieter of Hendrick Jackson and Sara Knoet Wit. Pieter Knoet, Margar. Jakson.

July 17. Jannetje of Thomas Pendell and Immetje Salsbury. Wit. Cornelis V. Salsburry, Fytje Salsburry.

July 21. bo. June 26. Antje of Reyer Schermerhoorn and Dirkje V. Buuren. Wit. Barent and Antje Staats.

bo. June 25. Barbara of Nicolaas Sherp and Lena Hogeboom. Wit. John and Magdalena V. Aalstein.

bo. the 15th. Pieter of Philip P. Schuyler and Annatje Wendell. Wit. Pieter Schuyler, Cornelia Livingston.

bo. the 18th. Margarita of Abraham Ten Broek and Elisabeth V. Rensselaer. Wit. John and Catharina Livingston.

July 28. bo. June 23. Wilhelmus of Johs. Oosterhout

1776

and Agnietje Winne. Wit. Wilhelmus Oosterhout, Marytje Decker.

bo. July 6. Annatje of Christoffer I. Yates and Catharina Lansing. Wit. Jacob V. Aalstein, Annatje Lansing.

July 28. bo. July 5. Alida of Yzac J. V. Aarnem and Catharina V. Wie. Wit. Johs. and Alida Van Wie.

July 31. bo. the 27. Johannes of John D. Groesbeek and Cathalyntje V. Schaik. Wit. Johs. and Alida V. Schaik.

bo. the 4th. Cathalina of Pieter de Foreest and Pieterje V. Aalstein. Wit. Reignier and Cornelia V. Aalstein.

Aug. 4. bo. Aug. 1. Anna of Balthes V. Benthuisen and Elisabeth Rumny. Wit. Obadia V. Benthuisen, Anna Rumney.

bo. July 10. Elisabeth of Jan Dox and Marytje de Voe. Wit. Jan and Catharina devoe.

bo. June 29. Wessel of John Gerritse and Anna V. Schaik. Wit. Wessel and Maria V. Schaik.

Aug. 11. bo. the 6th. Abraham of Johs. Lansing and Elisabeth Fryer. Wit. Gerrit and Elisabeth Lansing.

Aug. 14. bo. the 12th. Barent of Hermanus Wendell and Barbara Bratt. Wit. Elisabeth Bleecker.

Aug. 18. bo. the 16th. Abraham of Frans Stuip and Catharine de Wever. Wit. Abraham and Annatje de Wever.

Aug. 21. bo. July 31. Susanna of Arent J. Vedder and Jannetje Hoghing. Wit. Marthen Hoghing, Jannetje V. Vechten.

bo. the 18th. Johannes of Cornelis Douw and Catharina V. Schaik. Wit. Johs. and Alida V. Schaik.

Johannes of John Wendell and Elisabeth Young. Wit. Guy Young.

Aug. 27. bo. the 25th. Annatje of Frerik Meinerssen and Elisabeth Waldrom. Wit. Frerik Meinerssen, Elisabeth V. Valkenburg.

Sept. 2. bo. Aug. 27. Sara of Johs. J. Wendell and Alida Hoogkerk. Wit. Johs. Wendell, Francyntje Broeks.

Sept. 2. bo. Aug. 21. Catharina of Cornelis Zwits and Catharina Schuyler. Wit. Abrahm. Schuyler, Eva Beekman.

Sept. 4. bo. Aug. 30. Salomon of Cornelis Waldrom and Alida Goey. Wit. Salomon and Marytje Goey.

bo. Aug. 11. Johannes of Alexander Green and Catharyntje Waldrom. Wit. Johs. Waldrom, Annatje Eneen.

1776

Sept. 8. bo. the 6th. Johannes Yates of Willem Staats and Annatje Yates. Wit. Cornelis V. Schaik, Rebecca Yates.

bo. Sept. 2. John of Connel Farguson and Mary McCarn.

Sept. 10. bo. Aug. 22. William of Stephen Bell and Elisabeth Kidny.

Sept. 22. bo. the 15th. Johannes of Jacob Roseboom and Hester Lansing. Wit. Barent H. Ten Eyk, Machtel Roseboom.

bo. the 18th. Yzac of Yzac Bogert and Cathalina Hun. Wit. Hendrik and Barbara Bogert.

bo. Aug. 5. Johannes of John J. Fonda and Fitje V. d. Zee. Wit. Johs. P. and Dirkje Fonda.

bo. Aug. 6. Catharina of Johs. V. Buuren and Annatje V. d. Poel. Wit. Matheus and Catharina V. d. Poel.

bo. the 20th. Jannetje of Hendrik Waldrom and Margarita V. Franken. Wit. Casparus and Jannetje V. Wie.

bo. Aug. 9. Jacobus of Gerrit Knoet and Sara Abel. Wit. Jurjen and Alida Abel.

Sept. 25. bo. the 21st. Engeltje of Harmen V. Hoezen and Catharina Witbeek. Wit. Cornelis V. Schaak, Elisabeth Yates.

Oct. 6. bo. Sept. 31. Elisabeth of Cornelis Brouwer and Elisab. Visbach. Wit. Wendel Hillebrand, Geertruy Visbach.

Oct. 6. bo. Sept. 6. Rebecca of Ephraim Bennet and Geertruy Bloemendal. Wit. Henry and Jacomyntje Crennel.

bo. Aug. 31. Yzac of Benjamin V. Etten and Catharina Ell. Wit. Maas and Catharina Bloemendal.

bo. Sept. 6. Jonathan of Hermanus V. Salsbergen and Janneke Canik. Wit. Jonathan Canik, Jannatje V. Buuren.

bo. Sept. 14. Sara of Johs. V. Benthuisen and Geesje (?) V. Hoesen. Wit. Harmen and Catharina V. Hoezen.

Oct. 9. bo. Aug. 31. Joseph of Hugh McChesny and Janna Plum.

bo. the 7th. Catharina of Eduard Connel and Sara Polten. Wit. Hans and Catharina Hoorn.

Oct. 13. bo. Sept. 18. Cornelia of Barent V. Yveren and Rebecca Bratt. Wit. Hannes and Sara Muller.

1776

Willem of Rykert V. Santen and Sara Hilton. Wit. Robert and Elisab. Hilton.

Oct. 21. bo. the 15th. Hubertje of Johs. V. Woert and Cathalyntje Lansing. Wit. Christoffer and Saartje Lansing.

bo. the 20th. Elisabeth of John. Tinky and Maria Luyts. Wit. Meinard and Maria Roseboom.

bo. the 15th. Petrus of Jacob Hilton and Sara Barrington. Wit. Pieter V. Deuzen, Catharina V. Wie.

Margarita of Nicolas and Elisab. Ligthhall. Wit. Nicolas and Marg. Klein.

Nov. 3. bo. Oct. 6. Johannes of Salomo Goey and Elisabeth Santvoord. Wit. Johs. and Elisabeth Goey.

Johannes Bratt of Willem Hoogteling and Maria Bloemendal. Wit. Pieter and Vrouwtje Bratt.

Nov. 3. bo. Sept. 17. Johannes of Jacob Forster and Jennith Jinkins. Wit. Johs. and Elisab. Jinkins.

Nov. 6. bo. the 23d. Abraham of Abraham Ten Eyck and Annatje Lansing. Wit. Coenraad and Charlotte Ten Eyck.

Nov. 10. Rebecca of Johs. Hoogkerk and Margarita Meerthen. Wit. Abrah. and Antje Hoogkerk.

Susanna of John Wilson and Marytje Bratt. Wit. Gerrit and Sofia Bratt.

bo. Oct. 5. Catharina of Johs. Witbeek and Catharina S'Jans. Wit. Hendrik and Claartje S'Jans.

Nov. 17. bo. Oct. 13. Douwe of Abrah. D. Fonda and Hendrikje Lansing. Wit. Yzac and Santje Fonda.

bo. Oct. 14. Margarita of Benjamin Post and Catharina V. Norden. Wit. Benjamin and Sara V. Norden.

bo. the 8th. Hendrik of Pieter V. Wie and Ebbetje V. d. Berg. Wit. Gerrit and Catharina V. Wie.

Lena of — Zwaartveger and — Hener. Wit. Jacob Hener, Mary Creller.

Nov. 24. bo. the 17th. Johannes of Samuel Pruin and Neeltje Hadfield. Wit. Jacob and Marytje Pruin.

bo. Oct. 26. Barent of Martinus V. Yveren and Cornelia V. Schaik. Wit. Cornelis and Cornelia V. Yveren.

Hester of Hendrik V. Aernem and Susanna Winne. Wit. Yzac V. Aarnheim, Catharina V. Wie.

bo. the 17th. Rachel of Lavinus Winne and Maria Lansing. Wit. Jacob and Willempje Lansing.

1776
bo. the 27th. Jacobus of Obadia Lansing and Cornelia
V. Benthuisen. Wit. Abm. Cooper, Sara V. Benthuisen.

Nov. 24. bo. Oct. 19. Cornelia of Johs. Oostrander and
Marytje V. Aalstein. Wit. Cornelis and Cornelia V.
Yveren.

Nov. 27. bo. Oct. 30. Willem of Zephrinus Peessinger
and Marytje Young. Wit. Guy Young, Dirkje Winne.

Dec. 1. bo. Nov. 24. Gerrit of Anthony Halenbeek and
Cornelia Cooper. Wit. Gerrit Halenbeek, Jennit Hellen.

bo. Nov. 12. Hendrik of Philip Look and Magdalena V.
Wie. Wit. Hendrik and Marytje V. Wie.

bo. Nov. 27. Maria of Abraham Hoogkerk and Antje
Hilton. Wit. Robert Hilton, Elisabeth Burgess.

Dec. 4. bo. Nov. 1. Jacobus of Gerrit Theunissen and
Geertruy Groesbeek. Wit. Johs. and Elisabeth Visscher.

bo. Nov. 30. Sara of John Sabrisky and Leentje Lansing.
Wit. John and Catharina Lansing.

Dec. 8. bo. the 5th. Nicolaas of Nicolaas Klein and
Elisabeth Kohler. Wit. Hannes and Hilletje Miller

Catharina of Abrah. Wendell and Elisabeth Winne. Wit.
Abrm. N. and Margarita Cuyler.

bo. Nov. 15. Rachel of Mathias Bovie and Baatje V. d.
Heiden. Wit. Gerrit and Geertruy V. Franken.

bo. Nov. 11. Yzac of Gerrit V. d. Berg. and Rebecca
Fonda. Wit. Abrm. D. Fonda, Hendrikje Lansing.

bo. the 7th. Yzac of Johs. Hanssen and Geertruy Slingerland. Wit. Albert and Sara Hanssen.

Dec. 11. John Witbeek of Folkert V. Vegten and Elisab.
V. d. Berg. Wit. John Witbeek, Lena V. Vechten.

Dec. 15. bo. Nov. 17. Rebecca of Henry Will and Magdalena Han. Wit. Paul and Elisab. Hoogstrasser.

Dec. 18. bo. the 14th. Catharina of Anthony Ten Eyck
and Maria Egberts. Wit. Jacob C. and Catharina Ten
Eyck.

bo. the 13th. Jacob of John Bleecker and Gerritje V.
Schaik. Wit. Jacob and Margarita Bleecker.

bo. the 7th. Cornelia of Wilhelmus Smith and Annatje
Bratt. Wit. Pieter and Geertruy Groesbeek.

bo. the 3d. Hilletje of Nicolaas Claver and Susanna
Merriday. Wit. Hadriaan Bratt, Hilletje Merriday.

Dec. 22. bo. the 14th. Rebecca of Johannes Bratt and
Maayke Fonda. Wit. Gerrit and Rebecca V. d. Berg.

1776-1777

Dec. 22. bo. the 19th. Maria of Henry Height and Margarita Smith. Wit. Philip G. and Maria Viele.

Dec. 25. bo. the 1st. Robert of Gerrit Ten Baar and Cathalyntje Bratt. Wit. Jelles and Tietje Winne.

bo. Oct. 18. Alida of Meinard V. Hoezen and Geertruy Vinhagel. Wit. Johs. and Engeltje V. Hoezen.

Dec. 29. bo. the 6th. Margarita of Pieter Sharp and Catharina Berringer. Wit. Jacob and Marytje Berringer.

1777, Jan. 5. bo. the 1st. Johannes of Andries Abel and Annatje Marshal. Wit. Johs. Flensburgh, Annatje Marshal.

bo. the 1st. Dirk of Johannes Hoes and Maria Qwakkenbusch. Wit. Thoms. and Josina Witbeek.

bo. Dec. 31. Dirk of Dirk and Marytje Benson. Wit. John and Elisab. Fryer.

Jan. 8. John of Pieter McCluren and Margaret Thomson.

Jan. 10. bo. Sept. 11. Annatje of Arent Heens and Elisabeth Freelig. Wit. Jacob and Annatje Heens.

Jan. 12. bo. Dec. 2. Geesje of Jeremus Muller and Catharina Moor. Wit. John Prys and wife Cornelia.

bo. Oct. 4. Jobje of Johs. and Immetje Salsbury. Wit. Benj. and Cornelia V. Buren.

bo. Oct. 21. Evert of Abraham Oothout and Maria Dox. Wit. Evert and Margarita Oothout.

Jan. 15. bo. the 12th. Johannes of Samuel Marll and Rachel Gardenier. Wit. Johs. Marll, Rebecca Dox.

bo. the 8th. Rachel of Lucas Taylor and Celia Bratt. Wit. Hadriaan and Lydia Bratt.

bo. Nov. 21. Johannes of Hendrik Stronk and Elsje Harbich. Wit. Hendrik and Eva Plass.

Jan. 17. bo. the 7th. Catharina of John Bates and Mary Butler. Wit. Daniel Martin, Cath. Sullivan.

Jan. 19. bo. Sept. 22. Jacobus of Jeremias 'S Jans and Loys Adams. Wit. Jacobus and Elis. Vinhagel.

bo. Dec. 10. Gerrit of Cornelis V. Buren and Jannetje V. d. Poel. Wit. Gerrit V. d. Poel, Catharina Brodie.

bo. Dec. 17. Annatje of Martinus V. d. Werken and Geertje V. d. Berg. Wit. Gerrit Vosburg, Marg. V. d. Werken.

bo. Dec. 23. Pieter Nicolaas of Nicolaas Louw and Sarah Low. Wit. Quiliaan V. Renselaar, Mary Low.

1777
Jan. 26. Marten of Daniel Roos and Baatje Ponk. Wit.
Marten C. and Marytje Witbeek.

Jan. 29. bo. June 11. Cathalyntje of Gysbert V. Yveren
and Mary Canke. Wit. Frederik and Johanna Canke.

Feb. 5. Margaret of John and Sara Jackson.

Feb. 9. bo. the 1st. Engeltje of Pieter and Vrouwtje
Bratt. Wit. Bastiaan Visscher, Engeltje V. d. Berg.

Feb. 12. bo. Dec. 29. John of David Jamus and Mary
V. d. Werken. Wit. Albert and Marytje V. d. Werken.

bo. the 8th. Alida of Barent and Sara Visscher. Wit.
Jacob D. and Dirkje Fonda.

Feb. 16. bo. the 13th. Abraham of Hendrik V. Woert
and Catharina Eyghts. Wit. Abraham Eights, Elisab.
Hilton.

bo. Jan. 13. Alida of Salomo Bulsing and Geertruy
Knoet. Wit. Gerardus and Alida Bulsing.

bo. Jan. 24. Benjamin of Richard Pengborn and Cathal.
V. Etten. Wit. Hans and Rebecca V. Etten.

bo. Dec. 30. Fytje of Yzac Dox and Lena Devoe. Wit.
Michel Fry, Fytje Devoe.

bo. the 8th. Hendrik of John Otts and Catharina de
Ram. Wit. Hendrik and Elisab. Lychert.

Feb. 19. Maria of Frerick C. Neidhart, and Maria
Stronk. Wit. Hendrik and Maria Stronk.

bo. Jan. 25. Jochum of Nicolaas Staats and Maria Salsbury. Wit. Barent and Antje Staats.

Maria of Joseph Teabear and Debora Smith.

Feb. 22. bo. Dec. 14. Elisabeth and Margaret of James
McKee and Mary Logan.

Feb. 23. bo. Dec. 22. Neeltje of Yzac Ouderkerk and
Annatje Rodgers. Wit. Jacob and Neeltje Ouderkerk.

bo. Jan. 30. Andries of Hendrik Oothout and Lydie
Douwe. Wit. Andries and Cathar. Douw.

Feb. 23. bo. Dec. 27. John of John Hannway and
Hester Hampton (?). Wit. Johs. Mahon (?), Elis.
Greene.

Feb. 24. bo. Apr. 8. Hester of Yzac V. Aarnem and
Freela (?) Runnels. Wit. Benj. and Rachel Winne.

Feb. 27. bo. Jan. 31. Marya of Jacob V. Schaik and
Marytje V. Buuren.

Cornelis and Catharina Douw.

1777

bo. the 22. Pieter of Gerrit Rykman and Elisabeth V. Buren. Wit. Marten Meinerssen, Sara Rykman.

bo. the 23d. Anthony of Wouter V. d. Zee and Marytje Peek. Wit. Anthony V. d. Zee, Annatje V. Esch.

Mar. 2. bo. Feb. 5. Anneke (or Tanneke) of Tobias and Jannetje V. Buren. Wit. Harms and Tanneke V. Buren.

Mar. 5. bo. Dec. 29. Maria of Hendrik Staaf and Maria Jones.

Mar. 9. bo. Dec. 28. John of Timothy Hutton and Jane McCherny. Wit. George and Mary Hutton.

bo. Jan. 9. Josia of Hosea Lincoln and Else Corral. Wit. Neal Shaw and Mary de Klein.

Mar. 12. bo. the 10th. Elisabeth of Obadia V. Benthuisen and Annatje Rumny. Wit. Baltes and Elisabeth V. Benthuisen.

bo. the 2d. Jacob of Jacobus Bleecker, Jr., and Elisabeth Wendel. Wit. Johs. H. Ten Eyck and Geertruy Wendell.

Mar. 16. bo. the 8th. Egbert of Anthony E. Bratt, Alida Hoghing. Wit. Egbert and Elisab. Bratt.

Mar. 17. bo. Nov. 20. Elisabeth of Patrik Farguson and Anna Forbes.

Mar. 23. bo. the 18th. Jenny of Mathias de Camp and Mary Mollens. Wit. Elisabeth Smith.

Mar. 23. bo. Dec. 4. Jane of William Dale and Catharina M. Gurrah.

Mar. 26. bo. Jan. 26. Martha of Robert Henry and Elisabeth Vernor.

Mar. 31. bo. the 27th. William of William and Mary Thomson.

Apr. 2. bo. Feb. 25. William of William Burnside and Mary Hudson.

Robert of James Boyd and Jane McMaster.

Apr. 5. bo. the 4th. John of William Luteridge and Anna de Wever. Wit. Jurrie (?) or Janus and Catharina Struys.

Apr. 13. bo. Mar. 1. Sara of Benjamin Overbach and Jenneke Oosterhout. Wit. Hendrik and Annatje Oosterhout.

bo. Dec. 31. Caspar of Jacobus and Jannetje Salisbury. Wit. Richard Cook, Geertruy Salsbury.

Apr. 16. bo. the 12th. Maria of Hendrik Muller and

1777

Catharina V. Ostrander. Wit. Philip Muller, Geesje V. Hoesen.

Apr. 20. bo. Mar. 10. Johannes of Philip Luke and Aitje Vander Spaan. Wit. Johannes Luke, Geesje La Grange.

Apr. 23. bo. the 17th. Sara of Jellis Winne and Fytje V. Woert. Wit. David and Sara Groesbeek.

bo. the 21st. Elisabeth of Barent Vosburg and Annatje Gerritse. Wit. Thomas T. (?) and Elisabeth Hun.

bo. Mar. 13. Abraham of John E. Lansing and Maria Staats. Wit. Abrahm and Elisab. Staats.

May 4. bo. Apr. 18. Gerritje of Barent Staats and Antje Winne. Wit. Nicolaas and Maria Staats.

May 4. bo. the 1st. Tanneke of Cornelis and Fytje V. Salsbergen. Wit. Tobias and Jannetje V. Buuren.

bo. the 14th. Cathalyntje of Alexander Bulsing and Aaltje Oothout. Wit. Hendrik Bulsing, Cathalyntje Green.

bo. the 2d. Johan Georg of John and Susanna Kernel. Wit. Coenraad and Sara Rubse.

May 8. bo. Mar. 14. David of William Pangburn and Elis. Bogert.

bo. Apr. 28. John of William Geberis and Hester Nelson.

bo. the 3d. Elsje of Pieter de Reemer and Elsje Barrington. Wit. Henry and Mary Greveraad.

May 11. bo. Apr. 17. Anna of Johs. Bulsing and Mally Wilson. Wit. Gerard and Marytje Lansing.

bo. Apr. 18. Marytje of Maas V. Buuren and Rebecca Bogart. Wit. Abrm. and Magdal. Verplank.

May 14. bo. May 13. Anna of Wilhelmus Mancius and Anna Ten Eyck. Wit. Henry and Anna Ten Eyck.

bo. Apr. 18. Catharina of Nanning Fisher and Agnietje Van Beuren. Wit. John Nanning Fisher, Geesje Wendell.

bo. Apr. 13. James of Jonathan Petit and Agnes Riddle.

May 18. bo. Apr. 26. Margariet of John Leenders and Cornelia Rechteren. Wit. Charles and Christina Newman.

bo. Apr. 14. Andries of Andries Meyer and Cath. Ronkel. Wit. Andries and Maria Meyer.

bo. Apr. 31. Nicolaas of Hendrik Riddekel and Elisab. Knoet. Wit. Nicolaas Knoet, Rose Hervey.

May 19. bo. Apr. 14. Petrus of Petrus Ostrander and Catharina Ering. Wit. Johs. V. Oostrander, Marytje V. Deuzen.

1777

bo. Apr. 19. Neeltje of Jacob V. Olinde and Elisab. Schermerhoorn. Wit. Cornelis Schelluine, Tanneke Truex.

May 26. bo. Apr. 20. Johannes of Herbert Lansing and Maria Fisher. Wit. Johans. Fisher, Eva Snyder.

bo. Apr. 30. Cornelius of Simeon Veele and Neeltje Palmatier. Wit. Cornelius Veele, Arriaantje Hageman.

May 21. bo. the 19. John of James and Elisabeth Livingston. Wit. John Ten Eyck, Catharina Livingston.

May 22. bo. Apr. 25. Elisabeth of Daniel V. Olinde and Marytje V. d. Werken. Wit. Martinus de Voe, Marytje V. Olinde.

bo. Apr. 27. Elisabeth of Petrus Scheer and Catharina De Voe. Wit. Matheus and Christina Scheer.

May 29. bo. the 24th. Cathalyna of Hermanus Ten Eyck and Margarita Bleecker. Wit. Hendrik and Cathalyna Bleecker.

bo. Apr. 27. Susanna of Cornelis V. d. Berg and Maayke Ouderkerk. Wit. Yzac and Susanna Fonda.

June 5. bo. May 31. Geertruy of Barent Goey and Rachel Ostrander. Wit. Philip and Heiltje Muller.

bo. May 27. Philip of Hendrik Q. V. Rensselaer and Alida Bratt. Wit. Leendert Gansevoort, Maria V. Rensselaer.

bo. the 4th. Elsje of Hendrik T. Eyck and Margarita Douw. Wit. Gysbert and Lyntje Fonda.

bo. May 31. Rebecca of Joseph Fairchild and Marytje Gerritsen. Wit. Nicolaas and Jannetje Hieralymon.

June 8. bo. May 31. Hendrik of Johs. and Alida Van Wie. Wit. Gerrit and Catharina V. Wie.

June 9. Abraham of Pieter Janssen and Elisabeth Huik. Wit. Cornelis Janssen, Lydia Car.

bo. May 18. Rebecca of Salomo and Arriaantje du Bois. Wit. Johs. de Boy, Rebecca Tapper.

June 19. bo. May 25. Heiltje of John De Voe and Margarita Redly. Wit. Johs. de Voe, Magdalena Fyle.

bo. the 16th. Pieter Sanders of Philip V. Rensselaer and Maria Sanders. Wit. John and Elisabeth Sanders.

bo. the 14th. Cornelis of Pieter Rykman and Lydia V. d. Berg. Wit. Folkert and Maria V. d. Berg.

bo. May 12 . Geertruy of Midbury V. Hoezen and Antje Bevings. Wit. Jacobus and Geertruy Vroman.

1777

June 23. Jannetje of Johs. Schermerhoorn and Margarita Folksby. Wit. Jacobus and Catharina Folksby.

June 25. bo. Jan. 26. Gerrit of John Winne and Susanna Ridder. Wit. Petrus and Rachel V. Woert.

June 26. bo. May 16. Neely of Jacob Pest and Jannetje Vredenburg. Wit. Pieter Bartel, Nelly Vredenburg.

June 28. bo. the 16th. John of Joseph Hall and Johanna Patterson.

Aug. 17. bo. the 2d. James of David and Maria Gibson. Wit. William and Hester Adams.

bo. July 8. Christina of Joost Herwich and Christina Philip. Wit. Hendrik and Marytje Strong.

bo. July 18. Elisabeth of Philip Harwich and Susanna Walton. Wit. Hendrik and Elisabeth Strong.

Aug. 20. bo. July 9. Lena of Williams Flensburg and Christina Bakker. Wit. Pieter Flensburg, Saartje V. Santen.

Aug. 20. bo. June 20. Marten of Lucas Salsbury and Marytje V. Buren. Wit. Marten and Theuntje V. Buren.

Aug. 24. bo. the 13. Pieter of Gysbert Bosse and Hester Ryke. Wit. Jacob and Maria Cool.

bo. June 24. Leendert of Johs. H. Beekman and Hendrik V. Buren. Wit. Leendert and Sara Van Buuren.

Aug. 31. bo. the 4th. Franciscus of Jacob Fr. Lansing and Jannetje Visscher. Wit. Franciscus and Marritje Lansing.

bo. the 29th. Johannes of Wendel Hillebrand and Geertruy Visbach. Wit. Jurgen and Elsje Hildebrands.

Sept. 28. bo. the 18th. Johannes of Hendrik Bratt and Annatje Davids. Wit. Johs. and Elisabeth Davids.

Jacobus of Johs. Vinhagen and Baatje Valk. Wit. Jacobus and Marytje Vinhagen.

Maayke of Pieter Bogert and Saartje V. Schaik. Wit. Gosen and Maayke Van Schaik.

bo. the 8th. Johannes of Johs. V. Esch and Margar. V. Woert. Wit. John and Annatje Ouderkerk.

bo. the 9th. Robert of Abraham Cuyler and Margareta Wendel. Wit. Robert and Catharina Wendel.

bo. the 4th. Petrus of John Fort and Elisab. Kwakkenbusch. Wit. Petrus and Marytje Benneway.

Oct. 1. bo. Apr. 8, 1775. Cornelia of Nicolaas Brouwer and Sara Drake. Wit. William Conklin, Jane Brouwer.

1777
bo. May 10. Nicolaas of William Concklin and Jane Brouwer. Wit. Thomas and Ann Hilton.

bo. the 28th. Annatje of Andries Gardenier and Sara Hansen. Wit. Theunis and Cathalyntje Bratt.

Oct. 1. bo. the 27th. Petrus of Leendert Muller and Annatje V. Esch. Wit. Gerrit and Elisabeth Rykman.

bo. the 28th. Geertruy of John Cool and Annatje Daniel. Wit. Folkert Daarsen, Nency Hilton.

Oct. 5. bo. Sept. 12. Hendrik of Anthony Vroman and Margarita Arnel. Wit. Jacob and Anna Arnel.

bo. Sept. 14. Hester of Gysbert V. Santen and Rebecca Winne. Wit. Gerrit and Hester Van Santen.

bo. Sept. 12. Petrus of Petrus Ostrander and Antje Denmarken. Wit. Johs. and Catharina Van Oostrander.

bo. Aug. 28. Wilhelmus of Pieter Winne and Maria Osterhout. Wit. Wilhelmus Osterhout, Marytje Dekker.

bo. Sept. 10. Cornelis of Meinert Oothout and Maria Siksby. Wit. Yzac and Eva Slingerland.

bo. the 3d. Ludovicus of Stephanus Viele and Sara Toll. Wit. Ludovicus Viele, Eva Toll.

Oct. 8. bo. Sept. 29. Maria of Frerik Meinerssen and Machtel Witbeek. Wit. Hendrik Ostrander, Marytje V. d. Berg.

bo. Sept. 14. Zacharias of Zacharias Fuller and Femmy de Foy. Wit. Michel Diderick, Cath. Fallor.

Nov. 2. bo. Oct. 30. Judike of Theunis V. Vechten and Elisab. de Wandelaar. Wit. Theunis V. Vechten, Judike Ten Broeck.

Nov. 6. bo. Oct. 10. Cornelia of Obadia Cooper and Annatje V. d. Berg. Wit. Cornelis and Cornelia V. d. Berg.

Nov. 9. bo. Oct. 27. Willem of Johs. Fryer and Elisab. V. Woert. Wit. Dirk and Marytje Benson.

bo. Oct. 27. Franciscus of Nanning Visher and Lena Lansing. Wit. Lavinus Lansing, Catharina V. d. Berg.

Nov. 9. bo. Oct. 2. Geertruy of Lavinus Dunbar and Margarita Hanssen. Wit. Andries and Sara Gardenier.

bo. Aug. 23. Hendrik of Andries Bratt and Annatje V. d. Kar. Wit. Hendrik and Tempe Burhans.

bo. the 2d. Rachel of Casparus Van Wie and Jannetje Winne. Wit. Gysbert and Rebecca Van Santen.

1777
Marytje of Hendrik Hendermond and Baatje Smith. Wit. Pieter Sharp.

Cornelis of Willem Groesbeek and Catharina V. Deuzen. Wit. Cornelis Groesbeek, Marytje Schuyler.

bo. Sept. 2. Lena of Johs. Burhans and Tempe V. Northen. Wit. Philip and Lena Look.

bo. the 4th. Tobias V. Vechten of Jacob Cuyler and Lydia V. Vechten. Wit. Gosen and Maria Van Schaik.

Nov. 14. bo. July 13. Benjamin of William Carr and Sara Wilson. Wit. Joseph Taylor, Mary Sloan.

bo. the 9th. Daniel of Cornelis V. Aalstein and Maria Goey. Wit. Daniel and Annatje V. Aalstein.

Nov. 17. bo. Sept. 1. Johannes of Johs. W. Wendel and Maria Tratter. Wit. Anthony Bratt, Annatje Tratter.

bo. Nov. 11. Johannes of Pieter Broeks and Francyntje Wendel. Wit. John I. and Alida Wendell.

bo. Oct. 15. Anna of Hendrik Koch and Maria Young. Wit. Johs. and Anna Huson.

Tobias of Dick and Maria (Slaves) Tobias and Beth.

Nov. 26. bo. Oct. 17. Geertruy of James Donway and Elsje Smith. Wit. Abrahm and Alida Fonda.

Nov. 23. bo. the 21st. Gerrit of Ary Le Gransy and Maria V. Antwerpen. Wit. Abrahm and Jannetje Yates.

bo. Apr. 29. Willem of Timotheus Bushing and Jannetje Crosby.

Nov. 26. bo. the 23d. Sara of Robert Hilton and Elisabeth Burges. Wit. John and Maria Burges.

Nov. 29. bo. Aug. 9. John of Hugh and Rosanna Mc-Muller. Wit. Johs. McMuller, Nancy McGregor.

Nov. 30. bo. the 1st. Cornelia of Stephen J. Schuyler and Lena Ten Eyck. Wit. Pieter Schuyler, Geertruy Lansing.

Dec. 3. bo. Nov. 14. Isabella of Pieter Atkison and Ann Griffin. Wit. John Watson, Isabella White.

Dec. 12. Elisabeth of Arent V. Deuzen and Mary Mc-Cloud. Wit. Frans Marshal, Geertruy V. Deuzen.

Dec. 14. bo. the 13th. Hendrik Du Mont of Hendrik Staats and Maria Du Mont. Wit. Jochum Yz. and Elisabeth Staats.

Mathias of Mathys Boom and Syntje Zeger. Wit. Conraad Coen, Elly Watson.

bo. the 6th. Abraham of Gerrit A. Lansing and Elisabeth Wynkoop. Wit. Abraham and Elisabeth Lansing.

Dec. 25. bo. the 21st. Cathalina of Philip Wendel and Geertruy Vosburg. Wit. John and Cathalina Groesbeek.

bo. the 23d. Jacobus of Jacob V. Loonen and Cathalyntje Schuiler. Wit. Abrm. and Eva Schuyler.

Dec. 26. bo. Oct. 24. Jane of Alexander Forfeight and Mary Fraser.

Dec. 28. bo. the 5th. Andries of Abrah. V. Wie and Jacomyntje Burhans. Wit. Johs. and Alida V. Wie.

Dec. 28. bo. the 23d. Rebecca of Abrahm. Eights and Catharyntje Brooks. Wit. Jacobus V. Santen, Phebe Brooks.

1778, Jan. 2. Jelles of Evert Janssen and Antje Le Gransy. Wit. Jelles and Annatje Legransy.

bo. Dec. 17. Christiaan of Andrew Downall and Cath. Thompson.

bo. Nov. 5. William Abraham of William Cane and Elisabeth Dox.

Jan. 4. bo. Oct. 20. Abraham of John Schoonmaker and Aaltje Burhans. Wit. Abrahm. V. Wie, Jacomyntje Burhans.

bo. Dec. 29. George of David Patterson and Phebe Cox.

bo. Dec. 17. Margaret of John Brown and Marg. Wilson.

bo. the 1st. Folkert of Andries Douw and Catharina Foreest. Wit. Hendrik Oothout, Rachel Douw.

bo. the 2d. Jane Ann of Udny (?) Hay and Margriet Smith.

Catharina of Nicholas Sigsby and Cornelia Cooper.

Jan. 11. bo. Dec. 12. Anthony of Daniel Brad and Christina Beekman. Wit. Jonathan and Elizabeth Brooks.

Willempje of Barent Bogert and Alida Van de Bergh. Wit. Amos Van Beuren, Willempje Bogert.

Jan. 12. bo. Jan. 7. Matheus of Collin Gibson and Ellin Story.

bo. Sept. 7. Lydia of Jacob Zeger and Maria Crosby. Wit. Roelef and Lydia Zeger.

Jan. 14. bo. Dec. 13. Geertruy of David Foreest and Elisabeth Witbeek. Wit. Gerrit and Immetje Witbeek.

1777-1778
bo. Nov. 19. Rachel of Jacob Qwakkenbusch and Catharina De Voe. Wit. Jan De Voe, Catharina Qwakkenbusch.

bo. Nov. 8. Catharina of Gerardus Knoet and Sara Abel. Wit. Johs. Knoet, Lena Lyn.

bo. Dec. 18. Jacob of Willem V. d. Werken and Marytje Bogardus. Wit. Jacob and Marytje Lansing.

bo. Sept. 6. Alexander of George Dool and Catherina Zeger. Wit. Adriaan and Lydia Bratt.

Jan. 15. bo. Nov. 28. Elisabeth of Marten Auringer and Christine Sheer. Wit. Maas V. d. Berg, Cath. Sheer.

bo. Aug. 28. Maria of Samuel Bell and Jane McChesnee. Wit. Maas V. d. Berg, Cath. Sheer.

Jan. 18. bo. Dec. 14. Elisabeth of Theunis and Lena Hoogteling. Wit. Willem Hoogteling, Maria Bloemendal.

Jan. 19. bo. the 16th. Lucretia of John Bartel and Elisab. Trouex. Wit. Pieter and Mally Bartel.

Jan. 21. Allen of Ezechiel Ensign and Abigail Gibbs. Wit. John Graham, Mary Loodman.

bo. the 2d. Ralf of Lucas Cassiday and Rachel Cool. Wit. John and Engeltje Cool.

bo. July 23, 1776. Hannah of Ralph Watson and Hannah Hart. Wit. Thomas Smith Diamont.

Jan. 24. bo. Jan. 8. Nancy of Thomas Patridge and Mary McGuire. Wit. Mary Davis.

Jan. 31. bo. Oct. 21. Hannah of John Hartwell and Mary Holiday.

Feb. 1. bo. the 31st. Harmen of Philip Muller and Geesje V. Hoesen. Wit. Harmen Muller, Sara Downer.

Catharina of Lodewyk Obrian and Catharina Rendel. Wit. Coenraad and Sara Rubie.

bo. Dec. 28. Gerrit of Philip G. Viele and Maaytje Bratt. Wit. Catharina Viele.

bo. the 30th. James of James Smith and Elisabeth Allen.

Feb. 4. bo. the 1st. Johannes of Johs. Van Santen and Margarita Wilkeson. Wit. Thomas Bareith, Elisabeth V. Santen.

Annatje of Johs. Ostrander and Marritje V. Deuzen. Wit. Hendrik and Annatje Van Deuzen.

Sara of Johs. Ten Broek and Sara Ganzevoort. Wit. Cornelis D. Wynkoop, Catharina Gansevoort.

Feb. 8. Maria of Franciscus Marshal and Geertruy V. Deuzen. Wit. Wilhelmus and Maria V. Deuzen.

1778

Feb. 11. bo. Jan. 13. Cathalyntje of Daniel Winne and Catharina Hoogteling. Wit. Johs. and Cathalyntje Winne.

Feb. 15. bo. the 10th. Hendrik of Johannes Bleecker and Margarita V. Deuzen. Wit. Willem and Catharina V. Deuzen.

bo. the 9th. Annatje of Eduard S. Willet and Sara Fryer. Wit. John Fryer, Lydia Fisscher.

bo. the 12th. William of Bernardus Everssen and Martina Hoghen. Wit. William and Susanna Hoghen.

Feb. 22. bo. Jan. 10. Jacob of Coenraad and Charlotte Ten Eyck. Wit. Abraham and Annatje Ten Eyck.

bo. the 13th. Maria of William B. Hilton and Margarita Gladdon. Wit. Dirk and Maria Schuyler.

Feb. 22. bo. Jan. 3. Petrus of Johs. Wiesch and Maria Rees. Wit. John and Maria Think.

Feb. 25. bo. Jan. 22. Adam of Jurjen Hansikker and Anna Smith. Wit. Samuel and Rebecca Hainer.

bo. the 24th. Johannes of Hendrik V. Hoesen and Elisabeth Evertsen. Wit. Bernardus and Susanna Eversen.

bo. Jan. 26. Johannes of Marten Egbertson and Josina Schermerhoorn. Wit. Jacob Schermerhoorn and Lena Bloemendal.

bo. Jan. 10. James of Abraham Bloodgood and Elisabeth V. Valkenburg. Wit. John and Margarita Taylor.

Mar. 1. Cornelis of John W. Schermerhoorn and Cathalyntje Valkenburg. Wit. Jacob and Gerritje Schermerhoorn.

bo. Feb. 17. Maria of Leendert Ganzevoort and Maria V. Rensselaer. Wit. Johannes Ganzevoort, Maria Van Rensselaer.

Mar. 11. bo. Feb. 28. Maria of Reignier Ja V. Yveren and Rebecca De Foreest. Wit. Philip and Maria de Foreest.

Ann of Jacob and Anna Wennel. Thomas Hume, Mary Whitvoot, Marg. Davids.

Mar. 15. bo. Jan. 22. James of James Bell and Mary McCarly.

Mar. 20. bo. the 19th. John of John Squince and Jane Nixon. Wit. Davis Whitley, Johs. Rob, Elisabeth Willis.

Mar. 25. bo. the 17th. Catharina of Jacob and Elisabeth V. Schaik. Wit. Willem and Elisabeth Elzevoort.

1778

Mar. 29. bo. the 3d. Samuel of Mathew Hall and Jane Young.

bo. the 18th. Jany of Gregory Grant and Margareth Echad.

Apr. 1. bo. Mar. 19. Tabitha of Gerrit Heyer and Jannetje V. Slyk. Wit. John V. Benthuisen, Cathalyna V. Slyk.

bo. Mar. 24. Catharina of Pieter Webber and Catharina Warn. Wit. John and Cornelia Prys.

bo. the 27th. Eva of James Bloodgood and Lydia Valkenburg. Wit. John Verner, Margarita Taylor.

Apr. 12. bo. Mar. 11. Jacob of Andries Miller and Margarita Kets. Wit. Jacob and Catharina Foreest.

bo. Mar. 19. Lea of Joseph Boskerk and Susanna Wendel. Wit. Cornelis and Catharina Douw.

Mar. 1. George of Jeroom Vallensby and Elis. Witbeek. Wit. George Valensby, Jannetje V. Valkenburg.

bo. Mar. 10. Johannes of Wouter Mol and Cornelia Cool. Wit. Jacobus and Hendrikje Mol.

Sara of Timotheus Bushing and Jannetje Crosby. Wit. Edmund Kingsland, Marten Norwich.

bo. Sept. 12. James of John Graham Obryan and Nancy Davenpoort. Wit. Elisabeth Thompson.

Apr. 19. Arriaantje of Johs. Arnoud and Elisab. Buis. Wit. Cornelis and Antje V. Santvoort.

Apr. 25. bo. Mar. 25. Abraham of Abraham V. d. Poel and Marytje Bekker. Wit. Philip Shever, Rachel Valkenburg.

Apr. 26. bo. the 22. Nicolaas of Nicolaas Hieralomon and Jannetje Waldrom. Wit. Hendrik and Maria Van Wie.

bo. the 24th. Cathalina of Jacob Pruin and Hendrikje V. Buuren. Wit. Barent and Cathalyntje Van Buuren.

May 3. bo. Mar. 23. Catharina of Coenraad Harwig and Magdalena Meyer. Wit. Philip and Susanna Herwig.

May 6. bo. Apr. 19. Willem of Gerrit Staats and Catharina Cunningham. Wit. Jochum and Geesje Staats.

bo. the 4th. Pieter of Johs. De Wandelaar and Gerritje Gansevoort. Wit. Pieter and Annatje De Wandelaar.

May 2. bo. Apr. 1. Alida of Johs. Springer and Jannetje Bont. Wit. John Siksby, Geesje Bont.

1778

William of Willem Smith and Mary Corker. Wit. William Morris, Susanna Noble.

May 13. bo. Apr. 22. Geertruy of Samuel Witbeek and Rebecca Buys. Wit. Gerrit R. and Geertruy Gerritsen.

May 15. bo. Dec. 12. Sara of Nicolaas Clement and Rachel Garmo. Wit. Johs. and Neeltje Mersselis.

May 16. bo. Apr. 23. Alexander of Alexander Zegers and Mary Potter.

May 12. bo. 11th. Jenet and Isabel of William Faulkner and Margarita Anderson.

May 20. bo. May 13. Annatje of John A. Lansing and Elisabeth Fryer. Wit. Isaac and Annatje Fryer.

bo. May 17. Lyntje of Peter W. Douw and Ryckie Van Schaik. Wit. Abraham Douw, Elsje Fonda.

bo. the 15th. Cortland of Philip Schuyler and Catharina V. Rensselaer. Wit. Robert V. Rensselaer, Geertruy Cochron.

bo. Jan. 23. Guy of Stephen Tuttle and Mary Graham. Wit. Marten Gerritse, V. Bergen, Sara Trotter.

May 24. bo. the 1st. Margarita of Abrahm. V. d. Poel and Dorothea Shutter. Wit. Melchert and Margarita V. d. Poel.

bo. the 10th. Helena of Elisa Smith and Alida Bulsing. Wit. Hendrik and Cathalina Bulsing.

bo. Apr. 12. Maria of John Wally and Sibylla Appelis. Wit. Jacob and Margarita Henry.

May 31. bo. the 16th. John of Zachariah Sickels and Catharina Sheers. Wit. David Scot, Mary Wendal.

June 12. bo. May 22. Margaret of Cornelius Cummings and Hanna Swels. Wit. John Duncan, Nelly Bros.

June 15. Thomas of James and Jenny Stuart.

bo. the 15th. Folkert of Johs. Van Hoesen and Engeltje V. Deusen. Wit. Harmen and Tryntje V. Hoesen.

June 24. bo. Feb. 24. Maria of Jan de Voe and Lena Fyle. Wit. George and Maria Hutton.

bo. the 5th. Johannes of Willem Lappius and Alida V. Deusen. Wit. Johs. V. Ostrander, Marritje V. Deusen.

bo. the 23d. Lucas of Gerrit Witbeek and Immetje Perry. Wit. Lucas and Geertruy Witbeek.

June 28. bo. May 8. Jacob of Eldert V. Woert and Elisabeth Fonda. Wit. Jacob V. Woert, Elisabeth Fryer.

1778

July 1. bo. the 27th. Jelles of Jacob Winne and Susanna Evertse. Wit. Jelles and Fietje Winne.

July 5. bo. June 14. Jan of Jan Voorhees and Jannetje V. Ist. Wit. Jan and Saartje Van Ist.

July 6. John of William Brown and Jane Ridder.

July 8. Isabell of Duncan Farguson and Isabella Erneston.

July 12. bo. the 8th. Sara of Johs. V. Woert and Cathalyntje Lansing. Wit. Jacob and Sara V. Woert.

July 17. bo. June 24. Willem of Abrm. Sickels and Maria Connal. Wit. Nicolaas Ietzal, Maria Casey.

July 15. bo. the 11th. Yzac of Willem V. Wie and Jannetje Lansing. Wit. Yzac and Arriaantje Lansing.

July 22. bo. the 18th. Rachel and Elisabeth of Jacob V. Deuzen and Elsje Lansing. Wit. Stuart Deane, Rachel V. Deuzen, Gerrit and Elisabeth Lansing.

Catharina of William Coeny and Elisabeth King. Wit. Wouter V. d. Zee, Margarita Coony.

Pieter Sanders of Philip V. Rensselaer and Maria Sanders. Wit. Hendrik Q. and Alida V. Rensselaer.

July 28. bo. the 9th. Laurens of Laurens Chambers and Fenny Thoff.

July 29. bo. the 28th. Johannes of John D. Groesbeek and Cathalyntje V. Schaik. Wit. Johs. and Alida V. Schaik.

bo. the 23d. Hans Burhans of Johs. V. Lansing and Catharina Burhans. Wit. Robt. Lansing, Marytje Wendell.

bo. the 27th. John of John Berry and Elisabeth Meinerssen. Wit. John and Marytje Berry.

July 30. bo. May 30. Margarita of John Wards and Margarita Burnsides.

Aug. 5. Thomas of John Corrny and Brejge Zeger. Wit. Thomas and Judike Zeger.

Aug. 6. bo. July 11. Jane of William Deal and Caty McGaharry.

Aug. 8. bo. Mar. 13. Guy of Abraham Mills and Margt. Briston.

Aug. 9. bo. the 4th. Christina of John Thompson and Jennet Wilson.

bo. the 2d. Willem of Volkert Dawson and Geertruy Hilton. Wit. Jacob and Sara Hilton.

1778

bo. July 1. Cornelis of Hendrik Schermerhoorn and Cornelia Lansing. Wit. Joh. and Marytje Lansing.

Aug. 12. bo. July 9. Andries of Thoms. Burnside and Arriaantje Ten Eyck.

Aug. 14. bo. July 22. John of Samuel Beety and Catharina Clensy.

Aug. 16. bo. the 7th. Gerrit of Jacob Roseboom and Hester Lansing. Wit. Leendert Ganzevoort, Gerritje Bratt.

bo. the 8th. Gerrit of Yzac Hoogkerk and Rachel V. Santen. Wit. Ryckert V. Santen, Saartje Hilton.

Marytje of Jacob C. and Gerritje Schermerhoorn. Wit. Philip Schermerhoorn, Dorothea Muller.

bo. the 14th. Cornelis of Eduard Davis and Jannetje Dreit (?). Wit. Staats and Willempje Santvoord.

bo. the 14th. Nicolass of Nicolass Clein and Elisabeth Cogby. Wit. David and Nanny Smith.

Aug. 19. bo. the 16th. Elisabeth of John Finky and Maria Luits. Wit. Lavinus and Maria Winne.

bo. July 22. John of Hugh Deniston and Rachel V. Valkenburg. Wit. John and Margret. Taylor.

bo. the 21st. Maayke of Martinus V. Yveren and Cornelia V. Schaik. Wit. Gosen and Maayke V. Schaik.

bo. the 18th. Elisabeth of Johs. Hoogkerk and Margarita Marten. Wit. Hendrik V. Wie, Marytje Marten.

Aug. 26. bo. Aug. 23. Catharina of Eilardus Westerlo and Catharina Livingston. Wit. Johannes Ten Eyck, Sara Ten Broek.

Sept. 2. bo. Aug. 8. Rachel of Christoffer Oly and Eleonoor Kern. Wit. Thomas and Rachel Christiana Whitbeek.

bo. Aug. 25. Jurjen of Coenraad Sherp and Elisabeth Staats. Wit. Augustinus and Marytje Scherp.

Sept. 5. bo. Aug. 6. George of James Colwell and Elisabeth Barents.

Sept. 6. bo. Aug. 10. Jannetje of Hannes V. Buuren and Annate V. d. Poel. Wit. Cornelis and Jannetje Van Buuren.

bo. Aug. 12. Daniel of Jurjen Stark and Jannetje V. Buuren. Wit. Matheus and Elisabeth Poel.

bo. Aug. 2. Daniel of Mathys Flensburg and Christina Snyder. Wit. Daniel Flensburgh, Sara V. Santen.

1778

bo. Aug. 31. Willem of Pieter Hilton and Elisabeth Eights. Wit. Willem and Margarita Hilton.

Sept. 9. bo. July 13. Hendrik of Christiaan Cooper and Anna Marg. Strong. Wit. Hendrik and Elsje Strong.

Sept. 13. bo. Aug. 24. Catharina of Jacobus V. Franken and Geertje Fonda. Wit. Hendrik Fonda, Annatje Visscher.

bo. Aug. 18. Annatje of Jeremie S'Jans and Loys Adams. Wit. Gerrit and Annatje V. d. Berg.

bo. Aug. 21. Catharina of Petrus Ham and Marytje Michel. Wit. Johs. and Catharina Witbeek.

Sept. 16. bo. Aug. 23. Joachim of Nicolaas Staats and Maria Salsbury. Wit. Barent and Antje Staats.

bo. Aug. 26. Catharina of Benjamin V. Etten and Catharina Erl. Wit. Jurjen and Annatje Housekker.

Sept. 19. bo. the 10th. John of Thomas Brown and Jane Mordan. Wit. John and Any Allen.

Sept. 20. bo. the 9th. Elisabeth of Hendrik V. Ostrander and Maria V. d. Berg. Wit. Abraham and Elisabeth V. Ostrander.

bo. Aug. 27. Annatje of Daniel Young and Elisabeth V. d. Kar. Wit. Andries Bratt, Annatje V. d. Kar.

bo. the 8th. Sara of Johannes Muller and Sara V. Yveren. Wit. Martinus and Cornelia V. Yveren.

bo. Apr. 8. Archibald of Archibald Kemmel and Christina Starrenberg.

Sept. 27. bo. the 4th. Gerrit of Obadia Lansing and Cornelia Benthuisen. Wit. Jacob and Annatje Van Aalstein.

bo. the 2d. Coenraad of Jurjen Berringer and Elisabeth Beem. Wit. Philip and Christina Berringer.

Oct. 6. bo. Sept. 12. Sara of Hendrik V. Schoonhoven and Aaltje V. Esch. Wit. Jacob V. Woert, Sara V. Esch.

Oct. 14. bo. Sept. 27. George of George Rodgers and Eleonore Murray.

bo. Sept. 19. Yzac of Gerrit Lansing and Alida Fonda. Wit. Yzac Fonda and Cornelia Hun.

Oct. 18. bo. the 7th. Cathalyntje of Christoffer Lansing and Sara V. Schaik. Wit. John Groesbeek, Cathalyntje V. Schaik.

Rebecca of John Northen and Elisabeth De Voe. Wit. Hugo and Rebecca McManus.

1778

bo. Sept. 11. Maria of Philip P. Schuyler and Annatje Wendel.

bo. Sept. 29. Maria of Stuart Deane and Pieterje Bratt. Wit. Anthony Bratt, Marytje Conynton (or Compton).

bo. Sept. 26. Andries of Hendrik Oothout and Lydia Douw. Wit. Andries and Catharina Douw.

Oct. 18. bo. the 12th. Cathalyna of Hermanus Ten Eyck and Margarita Bleecker. Wit. Hendrik and Cathalyna Bleecker.

bo. the 9th. Hermanus of Jacob Bleecker and Elisabeth Wendel. Wit. Hermanus and Barbara Windel.

Oct. 25. bo. the 21st. Hendrik of Willem Staats and Annatje Yaets. Wit. Hendrik and Elisabeth Staats.

bo. the 22d. Hester of Theunis Slingerland and Rachel Bogert. Wit. Wouter and Hester Slingerland.

bo. the 1st. Helena of Johs. Oosterhout and Agnietje Winne. Wit. Daniel Winne, Catharina Hoogteling.

Oct. 26. bo. the 20th. William of Pieter Sharp and Marg. Donneway.

bo. Sept. 2. Marytje of Johs. Bulsing and Mally Wilson. Wit. Pieter Schuyler, Geertruy Lansing.

Oct. 28. bo. Sept. 22. Cornelis of Willem Waldrom and Margarita V. d. Werken. Wit. Pieter Waldrom, Vroutje Bratt.

bo. the 26th. Alida of Reynier V. Hoesen and Engeltje Cool. Wit. Matheus and Bregje Aarssen.

Rachel of Louys V. Woert and Catharina V. d. Berg. Wit. Adriaan and Folkje Quakkenbusch.

bo. the 26th. Joseph of John Brogden and Margaret Kelly. Wit. William Colbeth, John Rendell, Catharina Fairchild, Isabella Watson.

Oct. 30. bo. Sept. 31. Maria of Johs. Weeler and Marytje Cooper. Wit. Thomas Orchard, Bregje Zeger.

Nov. 1. bo. Oct. 22. William of James Green and Margarita Smith. Wit. Pieter W. Yates, Maria Holiday.

bo. Sept. 28. Pieter of Jan Dox and Marytje Devoe. Wit. Samuel Dox, Jannetje V. d. Kar.

Nov. 1. bo. Oct. 11. Lydia of John Denny and Penella Lydie. Wit. Abm. and Anna Ten Eyck.

bo. Oct. 25. Annatje of Mathew Visscher and Lydia Fryer. Wit. John Fryer, Sara Wyllet.

1778
Nov. 2. bo. Oct. 25. William of Jack (?) Donaldson and Margret Richey.

Nov. 8. bo. the 6th. Cornelis of Cornelis Brower and Elisabeth Visbach. Wit. Gysbert and Lyntje Fonda.

bo. the 6th. Arent of Willem Ten Baar and Elisabeth V. Deusen. Wit. Arent and Engeltje V. Deusen.

Nov. 22. bo. Nov. 11. Arriaantje of Abraham A. Lansing and Elsje V. Rensselaer. Wit. Guiliaan and Maria V. Rensselaer.

bo. Oct. 20. Salomo of Adam Potman and Catharina Meyers.

Nov. 28. bo. the 10th. James of John Crosier and Agnes Darrich.

Nov. 29. Arent Leendert of Arent Aarssen and Aaltje Qwakkenbusch. Wit. Leendert Bleeker, Gerritje Lansing.

bo. the 27th. Willem of Petrus Qwakkenbusch and Maria Shipfield. Wit. Wouter and Cornelia Qwakkenbusch.

bo. the 20th. Benjamin of Baltes V. Benthuisen and Elisabeth Rumney. Wit. Hendrik and Maria Fonda.

bo. the 18th. Dirk of Johs. V. Petten and Wyntje Knoet. Wit. Arent and Fytje Vedder.

Dec. 2. bo. Oct. 13. Catharina of Pieter Claas and Clara Marg. Courdin. Wit. Jacob, Jr., and Anna Mook.

Dec. 4. bo. Oct. 8. Annatje of Coenraad Coert and Anna Stafford.

Dec. 6. Richard of Richard Tilman and Sara Marel. Wit. Hendrik and Annatje Bratt.

Dec. 16. bo. the 7th. Gerrit of Pieter Van Wie and Egbertje V. d. Berg. Wit. Theunis and Marytje V. d. Bergh.

Geertruy of Abrahm. Kip and Saartje Hanssen. Wit. Pieter and Marytje Veder.

bo. Nov. 29. Margarita of Albert and Engeltje Hanssen. Wit. John Hanssen, Geertruy Slingerland.

Dec. 20. bo. Oct. 23. Elsje of Jacobus Valkenburgh and Catharina Sixby. Wit. Nicholas and Cornelia Sixby.

bo. Dec. 15. Pieter of Philip Lansing and Elsje Hun. Wit. Gerardus and Margaret Lansing.

bo. Nov. 18. Andries of Johannes Radley and Maritje Egmont. Wit. John Ward, Wyntje Radley.

Dec. 27. bo. Nov. 8. Sarah of Gerrit Theunis Breese

1778-1779
and Geertruid Groesbeek. Wit. David and Sarah Groesbeek.

Dec. 30. bo. Oct. 11. James White of Lewis Barrington and Jane White. Wit. Volkert and Geertruy Dawson.

bo. Dec. 27. Annatje of Jacob Lansing and Susanna Fonda. Wit. Isaac and Annatje Lansing.

bo. Dec. 21. Petrus of Isaac Slingerland and Eva Van Woert. Wit. Jacob Winne, Sussanna Evertse.

Dec. 16. bo. Aug. 7. Maria of Coenraad Legrange and Ann Legrange. Wit. Cornelis V. Santvoort, Arriaantje Gready.

Dec. 26. bo. the 3d. Jacomyntje of Jonathan Oostrander and Lea Ostrander. Wit. Jacob and Jacomyntje V. Ostrander.

Dec. 29. bo. Nov. 29. Marten of Pieter Foreest and Pietertje V. Aalstein. Wit. Martin and Janneke Foreest.

Dec. 30. Jacob Hendrik of Hendrik Kescher and Maria B. Schaltren. Wit. Jacob Foett, Margar. Hoop.

1779, Jan. 3. bo. Dec. 30. Johs. V. Wie of Philip Loek and Magdalena V. Wie. Wit. Hiskia V. Norden, Engeltje Look.

bo. Nov. 16. Cornelis of Johs. V. d. Berg and Eva V. Aalstein. Wit. Andries and Jannetje V. Aalstein.

Jan. 6. bo. the 3d. Rebecca of John V. Esch and Margarita V. Woert. Wit. Jacob and Marytje Bogert.

Jan. 9. bo. Oct. 29. Gerrit of Robert Gray and Susanna Legrange.

Jan. 10. bo. the 4th. Pieter of Willem Low and Elisabeth Daniels. Wit. Pieter and Annatje Daniels.

Jan. 13. bo. Dec. 3. Cornelis of Cornelis V. d. Berg and Rebecca Fonda. Wit. Petrus V. d. Berg, Marytje Fort.

bo. Dec. 6. Cornelis of Andries Ouderkerk and Annatje Fero. Wit. Yzac Ouderkerk, Elisabeth Bratt.

bo. the 8th. Obadia of Anthony Halenbeek and Cornelia Cooper. Wit. Obadia and Saartje Cooper.

Jan. 16. bo. the 11th. William of Robert McChesnut and Mary Cannum.

bo. Nov. 15. Yzac of Hugh McChesnut and Johanna Plumb.

Jan. 17. bo. the 11th. Hendrik of Lavinus Winne and Maria Lansing. Wit. Jacob and Lena Lansing.

1779

bo. the 9th. Geertruy of Wendell Hillebrand and Geertruy Visbach. Wit. Cornelis and Elisabeth Brower.

Caty of Alexander Clark and Nency Clark. Wit. Duncan McMullan, Nency Stuart, Jennie Grant.

Jan. 20. bo. the 10th. Joseph of Charles Follet and Mary Bloodgood. Wit. Thoms and Mary Diamond.

bo. Dec. 29. Cornelia of Evert V. d. Berg and Jannetje V. Schaik. Wit. Cornelis and Cornelia V. d. Berg.

bo. the 6th. Catharina of Johs. Stevenson and Magdalena Douw. Wit. John and Mary Douw.

Jan. 21. Christina of James Mitchel and Mary Cameron. Wit. Hugh and Mary Frazier.

Jan. 22. bo. the 16th. James of John Easton and Janet Rutherford.

Jan. 24. bo. the 19th. Stephanus of Frans Winne, Jr., and Annake Viele. Wit. Willem and Saraatje Hun.

bo. Dec. 28. Cornelia of John and Jannetje Salsbury. Wit. Cornelis and Jobje Salsbury.

Jan. 27. bo. the 26th. John of Johannes J. Wendell and Alida Hoogkerk. Wit. Abraham and Anatje Hoogkerk.

bo. the 23d. Pieter Martin of Hendrick Van Wey and Maria Martin. Wit. Johs. Hoogkerk, Janet Martin.

bo. the 24th. Ann of John Williamson and Mary Love. Wit. David and Ann Smith.

Jan. 29. Robert of Collin and Mary Farguson.

Jan. 30. bo. Oct. 8. Jane of William Ebbet and Mary Jackson.

Feb. 7. bo. the 2d. Theunis of Albert Slingerland and Christina V. Franken. Wit. John Hanssen, Geertruy Slingerland.

bo. June 15. Meinard of Barent V. Yveren and Rebecca Bratt. Wit. Meinard V. Yveren, Sara Muller.

Feb. 10. bo. Aug. 29. Thomas of Pieter and Susanna Johnson.

Feb. 14. bo. Jan. 1. Anneke of Abraham D. Fonda and Hendrikje Lansing. Wit. Yzac and Annatje Lansing.

Feb. 17. bo. the 13th. Theunis of Johannes T. Visscher and Annatje Pierce. Wit. Gerrit and Rachel Visscher.

bo. Jan. 31. Sara of Johs. Grahams and Maria Fryer. Wit. William de Wit, Sara Graham.

Feb. 21. bo. the 19th. Elsje of Hendrik Ten Eik and Margarita Douwe. Wit. Gysbert and Elsje Fonda.

1779
Feb. 23. bo. Jan. 14. John Frerik of Frerik Santhagen and Charlotte Ross. Wit. Francis McKinzy, Ally Watson.

Feb. 24. bo. Feb. 9. Henry of John Bancker and Geertruy Jacobi. Wit. Jacob Kidney, Elisabeth Jacobi.

bo. Jan. 14. John Frerik of Frerik Santhagen and Charlotte Ross. Wit. Francis McKinsy, Ally Watson.
(Repetition in the record.)

Feb. 28. bo. Jan. 30. Jan Dirkson of Yzac V. Aarnem and Catharina V. Wie. Wit. Abrahm. V. Aarnem, Anneke Rogers.

bo. the 23d. Niccolaas of Samuel Marll and Rachel Gardenier. Wit. Nicolaas Gardenier, Cathalyntje Bogert.

bo. Feb. 5. Hendrik of Laurens V. Cleef and Cathalyntje Jackson. Wit. Hendrick and Sara Jackson.

bo. Jan. 5. Agnes of James Boyd and Jane McMaster.

Mar. 3. bo. Jan. 4. Willem of Pieter Levison and Maria Fonda. Wit. Wilhelmus and Agnietje V. d. Berg.

bo. Feb. 23. Maria Van Rensselaer of Abraham Ten Broek and Elisabeth Van Rensselaer. Wit. Stephen Van Rensselaer, Maria Groesbeek.

Mar. 7. bo. Jan. 19. Bernardus Brat of Thomas Lottridge and Mary Brat. Wit. John B. and Margaret Brat.

bo. Mar. 6. Maus of Hendrik Waldron and Margareta Van Vrancken. Wit. Maus R. and Christina Van Vrancken.

Mar. 7. bo. Feb. 23. George of Richard Welch and Eva Great. Wit. George and Hannah Rider.

Mar. 10. bo. Mar. 4. Johannes Lansing of John Jacob Zabriskie and Lena Lansing. Wit. Nicolas J. and Elsje Lansing.

bo. the 5th. Catharina of William Brown and Mary Cadogan. Wit. Bernard Cadogan, Catharina McFarling.

bo. Feb. 18. Anatje of John Vischer and Elisabeth Brat. Wit. John R. and Elisabeth Bleeker.

Mar. 17. bo. the 12th. Andries of Andries Abel and Annatje Marshal. Wit. Daniel and Elisabeth Marshell.

bo. the 11th. Susanna of Pieter Broeks and Francyntje Wendel. Wit. Johs. and Elsje Wendel.

Mar. 21. bo. the 9th. Abraham of William Lothridge and Anna de Wever. Wit. William Crennel, Martitje de Wever.

Mar. 24. bo. the 15th. Willem of Frederick Myndertse

1779

and Elisabeth Waldron. Wit. Willem Van Wie, Jannetje Lansing.

bo. Feb. 12. David of Peter Winne and Maria Oosterhout. Wit. David Winne, Neeltje Deforeest.

bo. Feb. 7. Sussanah of Staats Brat and Maria Zeeger. Wit. Gerrit Zeger, Mary Pangburn.

Mar. 26. bo. Feb. 27. Hannah of Robert McCallan and Jane Williams.

Alexander of David Allan and Jennet Steward.

Mar. 28. Robert of Robert Wildring and Nency Herrington. Wit. John Cary, John Skeffington, Mally Miller.

Mar. 30. bo. Feb. 15. Albert of David Chambers and Margarita V. d. Werken. Wit. Albert and Maarytje Van Der Werken.

Apr. 1. Margaret of Robert Campbell, Sara McDavid.

Apr. 2. bo. the 22d. Neeltje of Andries H. Gardenier and Sara Hanssen. Wit. Andries and Catharina Douw.

bo. the 26th. Maria of Albertus Bloemendal and Anna Hanssen. Wit. Philip and Maria V. Rensselaer.

Apr. 4. bo. Jan. 9. Samuel of Timothy Hutton and Jane May Chestny. Wit. Joseph Maychestney, Elisabeth Phile.

Apr. 7. bo. Mar. 27. Johannes of John Redlif and Margarita Passagie. Wit. Joseph Passagie, Elisabeth Jacobi.

bo. Feb. 27. Thomas of William de Wit and Hester Dykman. Wit. John Graham, Mary Fryer.

bo. the 6th. William of Daniel McBead and Rachel McCantisch.

Apr. 9. bo. Apr. 1. Margareth of Robert Campbell and Sara M. David.

Apr. 10. bo. Mar. 6. Susanna of Thomas Roes and Catharina Saranto. Wit. Robert Davis, Mary Zeger.

Apr. 11. bo. Mar. 15. Catharina of Gerrit V. d. Berg and Annatje s'Jans. Wit. Hendrik 'Jans, Catharina J'ans.

bo. Mar. 23. Jonathan of Johs. Witbeek and Catharina J'ans. Wit. Jonathan and Gerritje Witbeek.

Apr. 14. bo. Mar. 22. Johannes of Hendrik Crennel and Jacomyna Bloemendal. Wit. Johs. Crennel, Fytje Marsselis.

Apr. 14. bo. Feb. 17. Catharina of Cornelis V. Buuren and Jannetje V. d. Poel. Wit. Gerrit and Catharina Poel.

1779

Apr. 17. bo. Sept. 19, 1778. Jane of Philip Gregory and Margaret Herring.

Apr. 18. bo. Mar. 19. Nicolas of John Leonart and Cornelia Rechter. Wit. Johs. and Else Hillingbrand.

Margaret of Daniel Cummings and Abigail Grant.

Apr. 22. bo. Mar. 1. Johannes of Carel Shever and Sara Redly. Wit. John de Voe, Magdalena File.

Apr. 24. Martha of John McClesky and Mary Nengels.

Apr. 26. bo. the 21st. Anthony of John G. and Annatje V. Schaik. Wit. Anthony and Christina V. Schaik.

bo. the 1st. Johannes of Sobrinus Peesinger and Marytje Young. Wit. Johs. Miller, Marytje Fonda.

Robert and Duncan of James Paal and Anna McEwen.

Apr. 29. bo. Mar. 16. John of Robert Gray and Elisabeth Drummer.

Apr. 28. bo. the 20th. Elisabeth of Gerrit Rykman and Elisabeth V. Buren. Wit. Yzac and Cathalyntje Bogert.

May 2. bo. Apr. 3. Rebecca of Willem Hoogteling and Maria Blooomendal. Wit. Gerrit Hoogteling, Annatje Oosterhout.

May 3. Francis of William David and Ruth North. Wit. Francis Dougten.

bo. Apr. 9. Margarita of Nicolaas Sherp and Lena Hogeboom. Wit. Johs. and Maria Lewis.

May 5. bo. Mar. 16. Maria of Johs. V. d. Heiden and Annatje Price. Wit. Isaac Price, Maria V. Schaak.

bo. Apr. 7. Hermanus of Hermanus V. Aalstein and Catharina Peessing. Wit. Gerrit Bratt, Lena Hoogteling.

bo. Jan. 3. Magdalena of Johs. Rosenberg and Annatje Crespsel. Wit. Johs. and Christina Lang.

May 7. bo. Feb. 6. Elisabeth of Johs. Sherp and Jerissa (?) North. Wit. Herms. Salsbery, Alida Sherp.

May 9. Gerrit of Michel Besset and Marytje V. Franken. Wit. Gerrit and Susanna V. Franken.

bo. the 2d. Catharina of Johan Otto Ram and Catharina Hoogstrasser. Wit. Johs. and Sara Knoet.

May 12. bo. the 2d. Simon of Louis Grant and Margaret Frasier.

May 15. bo. the 2d. Christina of Dirk Benson and Marytje Wyngaart. Wit. Willem and Christina Vosburg.

May 16. Christina of Nen (Slaves) Jack and Jenne.

1779

bo. the 19th. Barent of Jacob Y. and Geertruy Schermerhoorn. Wit. Meinard and Marytje Roseboom.

bo. Apr. 3. Hendrik of Hendrik Bulsing and Neeltje Marus. Wit. Cornelis V. Aalstein, Maria Goey.

bo. the 12th. John of John Jackson and Sara Lundy.

May 19. bo. the 14th. Johannes of Jonathan Brooks and Elisabeth Bratt. Wit. Johs. Bratt, Saartje V. Santen.

bo. Apr. 6. Johannes of Leendert Weyland and Agnietje Muller. Wit. Johs. and Sara Muller.

May 23. Cornelia of Johs. Olfer and Catharina V. d. Berg. Wit. Johs. Olfer, Antje Zeger.

May 30. bo. the 3d. Elisabeth of Barent J. Staats and Antje Winne. Wit. Philip and Annatje Staats.

May 30. bo. the 26th. Willem Barrinton of Jacob Hilton and Sara Barrinton. Wit. Thoms. Hilton, Catharina Druly.

bo. the 29th. Judike of Abrah. Hoogteling and Antje Hilton. Wit. Johs. Hoogkerk, Margarita Meerthen.

bo. Apr. 18. Egbert of Anthony Ten Eyck and Maria Egbertson. Wit. Benjamin and Maria Egberts.

bo. Apr. 11. Willem of Reyer B. Schermerhoorn and Marytje Beevers. Wit. Leendert and Neelte Schermerhoorn.

bo. the 21st. Catharina V. Deuzen of Willem Groesbeek and Catharina V. Deusen. Wit. Willem and Cornelia V. Deuzen.

bo. the 27th. Nency of Johs. Stuart and Jane Kemmel.

bo. the 24th. John Kemmel of Alexander Kemmel and Mary McMullen.

June 2. bo. Mar. 23. Susanna of Dirk and Cathalyntje Schermerhoorn. Wit. Marten and Cathalyntje Egbertson.

bo. May 14. Catharina of Hendrik Feero and Maria V. Vredenburg. Wit. Christiaan Feero, Catharina Levison.

bo. May 10. Christoffer of Christoffer J. Yates and Catharina Lansing. Wit. Willem Seebry, Rebecca Yates.

bo. May 9. Cathalyntje of Jacob V. Aalstein and Annatje Lansing. Wit. Reignier and Cornelia V. Aalstein.

June 6. bo. Apr. 10. Johannes of Cornelis and Fytje V. Salsbury. Wit. Hermanus V. Salsbury, Hannah Kannel.

June 6. bo. May 17. Catharina of Matheus Poel and Elisabeth Shutter. Wit. Gerrit and Annatje Poel.

Margaret of Johs. Erwin and Mary Thomson.

1779

June 9. bo. May 6. Willem of Jurjaan Hoghing and Annatje White. Wit. Willem Hoghing, Annatje Everssen.

bo. May 20. Maria of Meinard V. Hoesen and Geertruy Vinhagen. Wit. Johannes and Baatje Vinhagen.

bo. Feb. 13. Dirk of John McMichell and Engeltje Kidney. Wit. Felix Meyer, Phebe Wyngaert.

June 10. bo. Apr. 25. Sara of Stephen Turtle and Maria Grahams. Wit. Leendert Ganzevoort, Jr., Debora Grahams.

June 13. bo. the 7th. Pieter of Cornelis Waldron and Alida Goey. Wit. Pieter and Vrouwtje Bratt.

bo. May 22. Alida of Jonathan Kannik and Margarita Perry. Wit. Willem Burwell, Annatje Perry.

bo. the 7th. Marytje of Anthony Groesbeek and Cathalyntje Foreest. Wit. Pieter and Annatje de Wandelaar.

June 20. bo. May 24. Johannes of Johs. Heemstraat and Elis. Bovie. Wit. Michel and Marytje Besset.

bo. the 16th. Karel of Frans Snip and Cath. de Wever. Wit. William and Annetje Lotteridge.

bo. the 11th. Sofia of Johs. Bras and Lena Shafner. Wit. Hendrik and Maria Koek (?)

June 23. bo. the 19th. Engeltje of Pieter and Vrouwtje Bratt. Wit. Bastiaan and Machtelt Visscher.

June 31. bo. the 4th. Neeltje of Reignier V. d. Berg and Elisabeth Vinhagen. Wit. Johs. Vinhagen, Baatje Valkenburgh.

July 8. Elisabeth of Yzac Sturges and Sally Hardy.

July 10. bo. June 25. Abraham of John Sullivan and Elisabeth Cooper. Wit. Abraham Cooper, Lena V. Buuren.

June 13. Yzac of Johs. W. Trouex and Magdalena Huiser. Wit. Yzac and Marytje Trouex.

bo. the 8th. Catharina V. Deuzen of William Koolbrat and Hester V. Deusen. Wit. Willem and Maria V. Deusen.

July 14. bo. the 7th. Marytje of Wouter V. d. Zee and Marytje Peet. Wit. Dirk and Jannetje Zwart.

July 15. bo. June 28. Robert of John Willis and Jane Brett.

Aug. 11. bo. July 4. Yzac Hegeman of Thoms. Esmy and Elisabet. Palmetier. Wit. Yzac Hegeman, Neeltje DeGraaf.

1779
bo. June 12. Arriaantje of Simon Viele and Neeltje Palmetier. Wit. Reinert (?) Viele, Annatje Palmetier.

Aug. 14. bo. Sept. 7. Debora of Christoffer Sickel and Neeltje Fynhout. Wit. Hannes and Hester Sikkels.

bo. June 9. Elisabeth of William Collen and Elisabeth Brett.

Aug. 16. bo. July 5. John of Samuel Bell and Jane McChesnut.

Aug. 17. bo. Apr. 18. Jan of Jacob Buis and Gouda Annis. Wit. Jan and Catharina Bratt.

Aug. 18. bo. June 18. Meinert of William Pengburn and Elisabeth V. d. Bogert. Wit. Meinert and Rachel Swarthout.

bo. Nov. 27. Lydia of John Gavin and Mary Pengburn. Wit. Hans. Nostrand, Lydia Pengburn.

Aug. 18. bo. the 17th. Hester of Barent Vosburg and Annatje Gerritse. Wit. Yzac Foreest, Marytje Greveraad.

bo. July 23. Marthen of Philip Foreest and Annatje V. Deusen. Wit. Marthen and Janneke Foreest.

bo. the 19th. Rebecca of Josua Colwell and Annatje Broadin. Wit. Dirk and Marytje Schuyler.

Aug. 22. bo. July 3. Anna Catharina of Hendrik Perkley and Anna Cooglar. Wit. Jacob Perkley, Catharina Hendriks.

Cathalyne of Nicolaas Richter and Maria Hindermond. Wit. Casparus and Catharina Pruin.

bo. the 14th. Anna of Thomas Hilton and Nency Cadoghan. Wit. Pieter and Elisabeth Hilton.

Aug. 25. bo. July 21. John of Philip Rees and Eleonora Calligon. Wit. John Collinger, Elisabeth Colwell.

July 16. bo. June 11. Gerrit of John V. Alen and Maria Look. Wit. Willem and Catharina V. Alen.

bo. the 2d. Debora of Joseph Hall and Johanna Patterson. Wit. Daniel and Maria V. Antwerpen.

July 18. bo. June 24. Elisabeth of George McDool and Catharina Zeger. Wit. Johs. and Cornelia Leonard.

bo. June 6. Christina of Zacharias Berringer and Anna Faller. Wit. Philip and Christina Berringer.

bo. June 21. Elisabeth of Salomo Bulsing and Geertruy Cnoet. Wit. Hendrik and Elisabeth Riddeker.

July 21. bo. the 19th. Maria of Jacob G. and Femmetje Lansing. Wit. Jacob Lansing, Lena Rensselaer.

1779

Daniel of Eduard Conner and Sara Proeltenry. Wit. Daniel and Jannetje Winne.

July 25. bo. the 22d. Annatje of Elia Arnold and Geertruy Groesbeek. Wit. Gysbert Groesbeek, Annatje V. Antwerpen.

bo. June 18. Elisabeth of Jan de Voe and Annatje Conner. Wit. Hendrik and Geertruy V. d. Kar.

bo. the 19th. Susanna of Jesse Fairchild and Marytje Gerritsen. Wit. Jurjen and Elsje Hoghen.

bo. June 25. Catharina of Benjamin Sevenbach and Jenneke Oosterhout. Wit. Christiaan Service, Catharyntje Hoevenbael.

bo. June 15. Albert of Hendrik Bratt and Marytje Arnold. Wit. Albert Bratt, Annetje Arnold.

July 28. bo. the 20th. Gerrit of Jacob Halenbeek and Ytje Bratt. Wit. Gerrit and Cornelia Halenbeek.

Aug. 1. bo. July 29. Hendrik of Cornelis V. Santvoort, Jr., and Cornelia V. Wie. Wit. Pieter V. Wie, Ebbetje V. d. Bergh.

Aug. 8. bo. June 22. Alexander of Alexander Bulsing and Alida Oothout. Wit. Evert and Jannetje V. d. Bergh.

bo. July 16. Catharina of Benjamin Post and Catharina V. Northen. Wit. Andries and Elisabeth V. Wie.

Aug. 25. bo. the 20th. Joseph of Cornelis Cuyler and Jannetje Yates. Wit. Jacobus and Maria Taylor.

bo. the 16th. Thomas of James Donneway and Elsje Smith. Wit. Eduard Wallet, Saartje Willer.

Aug. 29. bo. the 21st. Elisabeth of Hendrik V. Woert and Catharina Agths. Wit. Gozen V. Schaick, Catharina Ten Broeck.

bo. the 26th. Anthony of Johs. Brat and Sara Wendel. Wit. Theunis and Cathalyntje Bratt.

bo. July 25. Johan Joost of Hendrik Strunck and Elsje Harwich. Wit. Joost and Christina Harwich.

Aug. 29. bo. July 22. Margarita of Jacobus Abeel and Egbetje V. Buuren. Wit. David and Catharina Abeel.

Sept. 4. bo. July 16. Susanna Hains of James Aherrin and Mary Hains.

bo. Aug. 29. Catharine of Hugh McKinsey and Maron McCloud.

bo. Aug. 15. Magdalena of Cornelis V. Buuren and Maria Owen. Wit. Pieter and Dorothea V. Buuren.

1779

bo. Aug. 26. Lena of Abraham Ten Eyck and Annatje Lansing. Wit. Jeremie and Lena V. Rensselaer.

bo. Aug. 28. Neeltje of Efraim V. Vechten and Susanna Hoghen. Wit. Hendrikus and Lydia V. Vechten.

bo. July 28. Elisabeth of Jacobus V. Schoonhoven and Elisabeth Knoet. Wit. Garardus and Annatje Knoet.

Sept. 29. bo. Aug. 28. Johannes of Hendrik V. Rensselaer and Alida Bratt. Wit. Johs. and Elisabeth Visscher.

Sept. 30. bo. July 17. Johs. of Salomo and Arriaantje du-Boy. Wit. Johs. duBoy, Rebecca Tapper.

bo. the 28th. William of James Fuller and Jane Keitl.

Oct. 3. Johannes of Arent Bratt and Jannetje Hoghen. Wit. John and Geertruy Veder.

bo. Sept. 1. Jelles of Evert Janssen and Antje Le Gransy. Wit. Jelles and Annatje Legransy.

bo. Sept. 12. Harmen of Pieter Ganzevoort and Catharina V. Schaik. Wit. Harmen and Santje Ganzevoort.

bo. Sept. 15. Antje of Rykert V. Santen and Sara Hilton. Wit. Johs. and Cornelia Flensburg.

Oct. 3. bo. Aug. 24. Sara of Manning Visscher and Agnietje V. Buuren. Wit. Johs. and Sara V. Buuren.

bo. Sept. 3. Catharina of Matheus V. Deusen and Cornelia V. Wie. Wit. Pieter and Catharina V. Buuren.

bo. Sept. 24. Daniel of Hendrik Bratt and Annatje Davids. Wit. Daniel and Willempje Bratt.

bo. Sept. 28. Gosen of Pieter Bogert and Sara V. Schaik. Wit. Gosen and Maayke V. Schaik.

bo. Sept. 28. Robert of William Talbot and Annatje Young. Wit. Philip Young, Sosky Merriday.

Christiaan of Johs. Legrange and Maria Knoll. Wit. Ary and Jacomyntje Legrange.

Oct. 4. Martha of Elisa Hungerfor and Cosia (or Sofia) Conger.

Oct. 6. bo. Aug. 23. Martinus of Hannes V. Ostrander and Marritje V. Aalstein. Wit. Martinus and Cornelia V. Yveren.

bo. Sept. 21. Christina of Willem Breezy (?) and Catharina V. Deuzen. Wit. Wilh. and Christiana V. Deuzen.

Oct. 17. bo. Sept. 23. Abraham of Abrahm. Lansing and Annatje V. d. Berg. Wit. Abraham and Rachel V. d. Berg.

1779

bo. the 9th. John of Bethuel Wasburn and Gerritje Lansing. Wit. Anthony and Alida Bratt.

bo. Sept. 2. Jacob of John Wolly and Sibilla Apley. Wit. Mathys Coegler, Catharina Henry.

bo. Sept. 20. Lydia of Lucas Taylor and Celia Bratt. Wit. Adriaan and Eva Bratt.

bo. Sept. 14. Annatje of Nicolaas Siksby and Cornelia Cooper. Wit. Jacobus Olfer, Annatje Cooper.

Oct. 17. bo. the 3d. Jannetje of Abrahm. V. Wie and Jacomyntje Burhans. Wit. Hendrikus Burhans, Tempe De Mont.

bo. Sept. 15. John of Benjamin Bulsing and Elisab. Moor. Wit. Hendrik and Neeltje Bulsing.

Oct. 22. bo. the 20th. Jacob of Christoffer Bogert and Rebecca Winne. Wit. Jacob and Marytje Bogert.

Oct. 12. bo. Aug. 14. James of George Bradshaw and Elisab. M. Killips., at Stillwater.

Oct. 24. bo. the 22d. Christoffer of Hendrik J. Lansing and Helena Winne. Wit. Christoffer and Sara Lansing.

bo. Sept. 10. Ann of Efraim Hudson and Hanna Claus. Wit. Moses Hudson, Susan Claus.

Oct. 31. bo. the 26th. Lyntje of Pieter W. Douw and Rykje V. Schaik. Wit. Folkert and Maria Douw.

bo. the 24th. Hermanus of Jacob Bleecker, Jr., and Elisabeth Wendel. Wit. Hermanus and Barbara Wendell.

bo. Sept. 9. Mary of Patrick Kellinic and Susanna Raw. Wit. Helmus and Charity Raw.

bo. the 15th. Frederik of George Visscher and Maria Ruthen. Wit. Hendrik and Maria V. Wie.

Nov. 3. bo. the 22d. Elisabeth of John Malony and Elisabeth Erskine. Wit. Anthony Custika, Polly Holliday.

Thomas of Thomas Clum and Margarita Davies. Wit. Bernard and Elis. Winterskeer.

Margaret of James Foot and Elisabeth Williams. Wit. Thomas and Margaret Clumm.

Nov. 14. bo. Oct. 26. Cattrina of Abraham Sikels and Maria Connor. Wit. Peter Gansevoort, Cattrina V. Schoiick.

Nov. 14. bo. the 12th. John of John Wilkkinson and Hanna Marshal. Wit. Johannis Radly, Elizabeth V. Zante.

bo. Oct. 25. Helena of Johannis Oosterhoud and Angenitie Winne. Wit. Daniel Winne, Cattrina Hoogteling.

1779
bo. Oct. 19. Harman of Timothy Bussing and Jane Crossby.

Nov. 21. Margarita of John Everts and Nency Howard. Wit. Jacob S. Hutter, Margarita Howard.

bo. the 20th. Catharina of John Ten Broeck and Sara Ganzevoort. Wit. Cornelis and Magdalena Ten Broeck.

bo. Oct. 21. Elisabeth of Folkert Oothout and Jannetje Bogert. Wit. Abrahm. and Margarita Oothout.

Dec. 5. bo. Oct. 25. James of William Karr and Sara Wilson.

bo. Nov. 23. Annatje of Johs. Lansing and Elisabeth Fryer. Wit. Ysac and Annatje Fryer.

bo. the 1st. Maria of Johs. de Wandelaar and Gerritje Ganzevoort. Wit. Pieter and Gerritje Ganzevoort.

bo. Nov. 22. Jennet of Jacob V. d. Heiden and Jennet Livingston. Wit. Samuel and Rachel Stringer.

Dec. 12. bo. the 7th. Henry of John and Thelia Young. Wit. Henry and Maria Coch.

Dec. 23. Maria of Bartholomeus Sleighter and Catharina Boyl. Wit. John Ruthel, Johs. Former, Mally Brown.

Dec. 25. bo. the 8th. Benjamin of Cornelis V. Aalstein and Marytje Goey. Wit. Cornelis and Alida Waldrom.

bo. the 9th. Tobias of Gosen V. Schaik and Maria Ten Broek. Wit. Jacob and Lydia Cuyler.

Dec. 25. bo. the 11th. Samuel of Abrah. Halenbeek and Maria Pruin. Wit. Samuel and Neeltje Pruin.

bo. the 10th. Jacob Ten Eyck of Wilhemus Mancius and Annatje Ten Eyck. Wit. Hermanus and Margarita Ten Eyck.

bo. Oct. 31. David of Gerrit Hoogteling and Annatje Oosterhout. Wit. Theunis and Lena Hoogteling.

bo. No. 14. John of John Flynn and Catharina Keerselbers. Wit. Christoffer and Annatje Miller.

bo. Sept. 25. Catharina of Maria Wendell and Marytje Winne. Wit. Robert and Catharina Wendell.

Dec. 26. bo. the 18th. Anna of John and Cornelia Qwakkenbusch. Wit. Hendrik and Elisabeth Qwakkenbusch.

Dec. 31. bo. Nov. 15. Nency of Robt. Thomson and Agnes Webner.

bo. Oct. 10. Mary of Alexander Breace and Elisabeth Cavel.

INDEX

of the

MARRIAGE AND BAPTISMAL REGISTER

of the

REFORMED PROTESTANT DUTCH CHURCH OF ALBANY
1772-1779

INDEX

*Indicates that name appears more than once on page.

Brogden, Elisabeth 11; John 62; Joseph 62.
Bromley, Samuel 6.
Brooks, Broeks, Catharyntje 54; Elizabeth 54; Francyntje 42; Johannes 53, 69; Jonathan 16*, 31, 54, 69; Phebe 54; Pieter 16, 36, 53, 66; Rebecca 31, 36; Susanna 66.
Bros, see Bras.
Brouwer, Brower, Abby 10; Catharina 15; Cornelia 51; Cornelis 2, 34, 43, 63*, 65; Elisabeth 43, 65; Hester 34; Jane 51, 52; Marytje 22; Matheus 15; Nicolaas 51; Thomas 12; Uldrick 3.
Brown, Catharina 66; Frederik 11; George 6; John 7, 54, 59, 61; Mally 75; Margaret 54; Mary 11; Thomas, Thoms 6, 61; William 7, 10, 59, 66.
Brues, Barbara 26.
Buis, Elisab. 57; Jacob 71; Jan 71.
Bulsing. Alexander 19, 34, 49, 72*; Alida 10, 15, 47*, 58; Annatje 14, 33; Anna 49; Benjamin 74; Cathalyna 38, 58; Cathalyntje 38, 49; Cornelis 14*; Elisabeth 71; Gerardus 47; Hannes 38; Hendrik 33, 38, 49, 58, 69*, 74; John 34, 74; Johs 4, 49, 62; Marytje 62; Neeltje 74; Salomo 14, 19*, 47, 71; Salomon 33; Sander 15.
Burch, Maria 11.
Burgess, Burges, Elisabeth 45, 53; John 53; Maria 53.
Burhans, Borhans, Aaltje 34, 54; Catharina 59; Catharyntje 19, 34; Hendrik 34, 52; Hendrikus 74; Jacomyntje 8, 54*, 74; Johs 53; Lena 53; Tempe 52.
Burnett, Hanna 12.
Burnside, Andries 60; Arriantje 32; Elisabeth 39; Margarita 39, 59; Pieter 39; Thoms, Thomas 32, 39, 60; William 48*.
Burwell, Willem 70.
Bushing, see Bussing.
Bussing, Harman 75; Sara 57; Timotheus, Timothy 53, 57, 75; Willem 53.
Butler, Annatje 39; Edmund 39; Mary 46.
Buys, (?) Cathar. 34; Rebecca 58.
Cabols, Zebuloss 3.
Cachron, see Cochron.
Cadmus, Cornelis 13; Maria 13.
Cadogan, Cadoghan, Bernard 66; Mary 66; Nency 71; Polly 7.

Calligon, Eleanora 71.
Cameron, Alexander 9; Mary 65.
Campbell, Kemmel, Alexander 10, 69; Archibald 61*; Jane 69; John 69; Margaret 67*; Robert 67*.
Cane, William 54; William Abraham 54.
Canke, Frederick 47; Johanna 47; Mary 47.
Cannik, Canik, Connik, Kannik, Alida 70; Cathy 35; Janneke 43; Jonathan 30, 43, 70.
Cannum, Mary 64.
Carney, Ann 11.
Carr, Car, Karr, Benjamin 53; Lydia 8, 50; James 75; William 53, 75.
Carrol, Judith 5.
Cary, John 67.
Casey, Maria 59.
Cassiday, Lucas 55; Ralf 55.
Cavel, Elisabeth 75.
Chagweek, Abiah 10.
Chambers, Albert 67; Elisab. 35; David 67; Henry 11; Laurens 59*.
Cheirs, Catharina 8.
Chesny, see McChesney.
Chinn, Eduard 12.
Claann, Jurjen 10.
Claas, Claus, Clauz, Catharina 63; Hanna 74; Johs. P. 37; Nicolaas 37; Pieter 63; Susan 74.
Clark, Clerk, Alexander 65; Caty 65; Matheus 3; Nency 65; Susanna 7.
Claver, Elisabeth 29; Hilletje 45; Maria 16; Nicolaas 16, 29, 45.
Clein, see Klein.
Clement, Jentje 29; Nicolaas 58; Sara 58.
Clensy, Catharina 60.
Cloet, Kloet, Alida 26, 39*; Francyntje 26; Johs. Jr. 39.
Clumm, Clumb, Clum, Hendrik 1; Margaret 74; Thomas 74*.
Cnoet, see Knoet.
Coch, see Koch.
Cochron, Cachron, Conchron, Elisabeth 18, 28; Geertruy 58.
Cocks, see Cox.
Coegler, see Kohler.
Coen, Coens, Koen, Koens, Koones, Koert, Coert, Abraham 27; Annaatje 21, 63; Christeen 3; Christina 2, 31; Christoffer 27*; Conraad, Coenraad 9, 53, 63; Johannes 21; Johs. 40; Maria 27; Neeltje 11; Pieter 5; Susanna 40.
Coeny, see Coony.

Cogby, Elizabeth 60.
Colbeth, *see* also Colebride, and Koolbrat, William 62.
Colebride, *see* also Colbeth and Koolbrat, William 9.
Collen, Elisabeth 71; William 71.
Collinger, John 71.
Colwell, Elisabeth 71; George 60; James 60; Josua 71; Rebecca 71.
Compton, Comptton, *see* also Conynton, Edward 10; Marytje 62.
Commings, *see* Cummings.
Conchron, *see* Cochron.
Conkling, Concklin, Conklin, Elias 7; Nicolaas 52; Sara 24; William 51, 52.
Conger, Cosia (or Sofia) 73.
Connel, Connal, Kannel, Catharina 43; Eduard 43; Hannah 69; Maria 59; Marytje 26.
Conner, Connor, Annatje 10, 72; Daniel 72; Eduard 72; Maria 41, 74.
Connerly, Catharine 10.
Connik, *see* Cannik.
Conover, Samuel 4.
Conteyn, Contyn, Catharina 14; Elisabeth 26; Gerritje 14; Margarita 26; Matheus 14; Peter 26.
Conynton, *see* also Compton, Marytje 62.
Conzalus, Bata 39; Engeltje 27; Francyntje 13; Hans 27; Johs. 13, 39.
Coochler, *see* Kohler.
Cooglar, *see* Kohler.
Cook, Richard 48.
Cool, Cornelia 57; Engeltje 25, 55, 62; Geertruy 52; Jacob, Jacobus 35*, 51; Henry 12; John 24, 52, 55; John Daniels 24; Maria 22, 51; Rachel 12, 55.
Cooms, Michael 5.
Coony, Coeny, Catharina 59; William 9, 59; Margarita 59.
Cooper, Abm. Abrah., Abraham 31, 45; 70; Annatje 2, 25, 33, 74; Christiaan 61; Cornelia 2, 20, 27, 31, 39, 45, 52, 54, 64, 74; Elisabeth, Elisab. 21, 33, 34, 70; Hendrik 61; Margar. 31, 34; Marytje 62; Obadia 25, 34, 52, 64; Saartje 64; Thomas 31, 34.
Corker, Mary 58.
Corral, Else 48.
Corrny, John 59; Thomas 59.
Cortin, Courdin, Clara M. 37; Clara Marg. 63.
Cortreght, Henry 8.

Cosdan, John 9.
Couglen, Elisabeth 16.
Courdin, *see* Cortin.
Cox, Cocks, Annatje 40; Phebe 54.
Craff, Charlotte 5.
Crankheid, Annatje 19; Elisab. 19; Willem 19.
Creller, Mary 44.
Cremer, Jurjen 27; Margarete 27.
Crennel, Arriaantje 19, 22; Cornelis, Cadmus 13; Hendrik 13, 28, 41, 67; Henry 43; Jacomyntje 43; Johannes 67; Johs. 15, 67; Rebecca 28; Robert 15, 19, 22, 41; William 66.
Crepsel, Annatje 68.
Cronke, Rebecca 4.
Crosby, Crossby, Jane 75; Jannetje 53, 57; Maria 54; Mary 37.
Crosier, James 63; John 63.
Crugier, Bastiaan 26, 33; Dirkje 26; Geertruy 14; Martinus 33.
Cuddy, Samuel 10.
Culberton, Sarah 9.
Cummings, Cumming, Commings, Catharina 6; Cornelius 58; Daniel 37, 68; Margaret 58, 68; Mary 37; Nency 37.
Cunningham, Cunningam, Catharina 38, 57; Catharyntje 26; Dorothee 23.
Custika, Anthony 74.
Cuyler, Abrahm., Abraham 21, 22, 31, 38, 51; Abraham C. 23, 32; Abrm., Abraham N. 19, 45; Catharina 21, 28; Cornelis 72; Elisabeth 15, 22, 31; Glen 32; Hendrik 22; Hermanus 28; Hester 17, 35; Jacob 18*, 28, 32, 53, 75; Jacob Glen 23; Jannetje 17, 35; Jannetje C. 38; Johannes 28; Joseph 72; Lydia 75; Maria 19; Margarita 45; Nicolaas 20, 35; Robert 51; Tobias V. Vechten 53.

Daarsen, *see* Dawson.
Daaschen, *see* Dawson.
Daath,*see* Dark.
Dale, Deal, Jane 48, 59; William 48, 59.
Daly, Mathew 11.
Daniels, Daniel, Danielson, Downall, Andrew 54; Annatje 24, 52, 64; Christiaan 54; David 30; Elisabeth 8, 40, 64; Hendrik 17, 40; John 23, 24, 27, 30; Margarita 17, 23; Pieter 64; William 27.
Danielson, *see* Daniels.
Dark, Daath, Anthony 26; Carel 26;

Druly, Catharina 69.
Drummer, Elisabeth 68.
Droit, Dreit, *see* Duret.
du Bois, Du Boy, de Boy, Arriaantje 34, 50, 73; Hendrikus 34*; Johs. 50, 73; Rebecca 50; Salomo 34, 50, 73.
Dumont, du Mont, Du Mont, De Mont, Demant, Johs. 38; Maria 21, 38, 53; Tempe 34, 74.
Dunbar, Dunbaar, Elisabeth 28; John 22; Geertruy 52; Lavinus 15, 52; Maria 26; Robert 15, 22; Willem 22.
Duncan, John 58.
Dunway, Dunnewy, *see* Donneway.
Duret, Droit, Dreit, Jan 17; Jannetje 22, 38, 60; Rachel 17; Selly 17.
Dykman, Hester 67.

Easton, James 65; John 65.
Eats, *see* Yates.
Ebbet, Jane 65; William 65.
Echad, Margareth 57.
Edgelton, (Wid:) 7.
Eesterly, Thomas 12.
Egberts, Egbert, *see* Egbertson.
Egbertson, Egberson, Egberts, Egbert, Benjamin 69; Cathalyntje 69; Johannes 56; Maria 6, 45, 69*; Marten, Martin 1, 56, 69.
Egmond, Egmont, Mary 39; Marytje, Maritje 31, 39, 63.
Eights, Eight, *see* Yates.
Ell, Catharina 43.
Elmendorp, Catharina 30; John 30; Margarita 30.
Elzevoort, Elisabeth 56; Willem 56.
Enaks, Gothfreed 12.
Enan, Margaretha 12.
Eneen, Annatje 42.
English, Josua 11.
Ensign, Allen 55; Ezechiel 55.
Ering, Erig, Catharina 23*, 49; Elisabeth 23; Harmen 23; Maria 23; Marytje 23; Michel 23; Samuel 23; Sara 23.
Erl, Catharina 61.
Erneston, Isabella 59.
Erskine, Elisabeth 74.
Erwin, Johs 69; Margaret 69.
Esmy, Ismy, Petrus 34; Thomas 34, 70; Yzac 70; Yzac Hegeman 70.
Evertse, Evertsen, Everssen, Eversen, Evert, Everts, Annatje 70; Bernardus 56; Elisabeth 3, 36, 56; Evert 11; John 7, 75; Margarita 75; Susanna 56, 59, 64; William 56.
Eyghts, *see* Yates.

Fairchild, Catharina 62; Jesse 72; Joseph 50; Rebecca 50; Susanna 72.
Fairfield, Sara 12.
Fallor, Faller, Anna 71; Cath. 52.
Farguson, Collin 65; Connel 43; Duncan 59; Elisabeth 48; Isabell 59; John 43; Mary 65; Patrik 48; Robert 65.
Fatten, John 10.
Faulkner, Isabel 58; Jenet 58; William 58.
Fayer, Majorey 10.
Feerguil, Jesse 35; Yzac 35.
Feero, Fero, Abraham 34; Annatje 64; Catharina 69; Christiaan 11, 69; Hendrik 34, 69.
Fight, Elis. 34; Elisab. 32.
File, Fyle, *see* Viele.
Finke, Finky, Elisabeth 60; Hendrik 40; Johannes 40; John 60.
Finky, *see* Finke.
Fisscher, Fisher, *see* Vischer.
Flensburg, Anna 39; Annetje 23; Cornelia 34*, 73; Daniel 12, 60*; Dirk 12; Johs. 34, 46, 73; Lena 51; Mathys, Mathew 34, 60; Pieter 51; William 51.
Flynn, Flin, Abraham 30; James 30; John 75*.
Foett, Jacob 64.
Folksby, Catharina 51; Jacobus 51; Margarita 51.
Follet, Charles 65; Joseph 65.
Fonda, Aaltje 33; Abraham 20, 53; Abrah. D., Abraham D. 17, 25, 33, 44, 45, 65; Alida 2*, 20, 26, 39, 53, 61; Anneke 65; Catharina 13; Dirkje 18, 43, 47; Douwe 17, 44; Elisab., Elisabeth 13, 24, 38, 58; Elsje 28, 58, 65; Francyntje 30, 32; Geertje 61; Geertruy 5; Gysbert 20, 28, 50, 63, 65; Harmen 25; Hendrik 13, 61, 63; Isaac Yz. 11; Jacob 18; Jacob D. 25, 47; Johannes 34, 43; John J. 16, 43; Johs. 18, 34; Johs. P. 43; Lyntje 50, 63; Maayke 25, 31, 45; Maria 10, 16, 33, 63, 66; Marytje 31, 68; Rebecca 30, 45, 64; Sara 25; Santje 44; Susanna 9, 12, 32, 50, 64; Willem 18; Wyntje 16; Yzac, Yzaac 12, 17, 20*, 26, 30, 32, 44, 50, 61; Yzaac D. 26.
Foot, James 74; Margaret 74.
Forbes, Anna 48.
Foreest, *see* De Foreest.
Forfeight, Alexander 54; Jane 54.
Former, Johs. 75.

Hoghil, Abraham 16; Annatje 19; Francis 22; Hendrik 22.

Hoghing, *see* Hoghen.

Holliday, Holiday, Jannetje 4; Maria 62; Mary 55; Polly 74.

Honsiker, Hansikker, Housekker, Adam 56; Annatje 61; Jurjen 9, 56, 61.

Hoogan, *see* Hoghen.

Hoogkerk, Abrahm., Abrm., Abraham 23, 33, 36, 44, 45, 65; Alida 30, 42, 65; Anatje, Antje 36, 44, 65; Elisabeth 60; Gerrit 60; Johs. 7, 44, 60, 65, 69; Lucas 23, 30, 33; Maria 45; Rachel 23, 30; Rebecca 44; Yzac, Yzaac 16, 23, 33, 60.

Hoogstrasser, Catharina 68; Elisab. 45; Paul 45.

Hoogteling, Abrah. 69; Cathar., Catharina 22, 28, 36, 56, 62; Catharine 12; Cattrina 74; David 75; Elisabeth 55; Gerrit 11, 68, 75; Jannetje 34; Johannes Bratt 44; Jonathan 37; Judike 69; Lena 27, 28, 37, 55, 68, 75; Marytje 5; Pieter 27; Rebecca 68; Theunis 27, 37, 55, 75; William, Willem 2, 27, 44, 55, 68; Yzaac 1.

Hoom, Cathar. 39; Hans 39.

Hoop, Margar. 64.

Hoorn, Catharina 43; Hans 43.

Housekker, *see* Honsiker.

Howard, Margarita 12, 75; Nency 7, 75.

Hudson, Ann 74; Efraim 74; Mary 48; Moses 74.

Huik, *see* Huyck.

Hume, Thomas 56.

Hun, Cathalina 3, 43; Cathalyntje 30; Cornelia 61; Elisabeth 27, 49; Elsje 27*, 30, 63; Harmen 27, 30; Rachel 24; Saraatje, Saratje 24, 65; Thomas 24, 27; Thomas T. (?) 49; Willem 24, 65.

Hungerfor, Elisa 73; Martha 73.

Hunter, Elisabeth 34; John 34.

Husen, Huson, Anna, Annatje 23, 53; Johs. 23, 53.

Husier, Magdalena 70.

Hutter, Jacob S. 75.

Hutton, George 48, 58; John 48; Maria 58; Mary 48; Samuel 67; Timothy 48, 67.

Huyck, Huyk, Huik, Annatje 31; Catharina 15; Elisabeth 9, 50; Hannes 35; Lena 21, 31, 35; Lodewyk 35*; Maria 14; Roelef 10; Yzac 15.

Ietzal, Nicolaas 59.

Ismy, *see* Esmy.

Jackson, Jakson, Cathalyntje 66; Hendrik 24, 41, 66; James 24; Jannetje 24; Jenneke 5; John 47, 69*; Johs. 24; Margar., Margaret 9, 41, 47; Mary 65; Pieter 41; Sara 47, 66.

Jacobi, Elisabeth 66, 67; Geertruy 10, 66.

James, Jamus, David 47; John 47; Paulus 19; Whillem 19.

Jamus, *see* James.

Jankins, *see* Jinkins.

Jans, Jansen, Janssen, 'S Jans, s'Jans, 'Jans, J'ans, Abraham 50; Anna 5; Annatje 41, 61, 67; Cath. 36; Catharina 6, 44, 67*; Christiaan 18; Claartje 44; Cornelis 8, 50; Elisabeth 6; Evert 54, 73; Gerrit 26*; Hendrik 44, 67; Jacermo 18; Jacobus 46; Jelles 54, 73; Jeremias 27, 46; Jeremias S. 27; Jeremie 61; Jermy 35; Marg. 21; Margarita 27; Maria 35; Mary 36; Pieter 50; Roelef 10; Yzaac 26.

Jieldon, Catharina 37.

Jinkins, Jankins, Elisab. 44; Jennith 44; Johs. 41, 44; Margarita 41.

Johnson, Isaac 2; John 10; Pieter 65; Susanna 65; Thomas 65.

Jones, Maria 48.

Jong, Elisabeth 5.

Jumens, Jannetje 6.

Kames, John 4.

Kannel, *see* Connel.

Kannik, *see* Cannik.

Karr, *see* Carr.

Keeler, *see* Kohler.

Keerselbers, Catharina 75.

Keitl, Jane 73.

Kellinic, Mary 74; Patrick 74.

Kelly, Margaret 62.

Kemmel, *see* Campbell.

Kerker, Hendrik 5.

Kern, *see* Kernel.

Kernel, Kern, Eleanoor 60; Johan Georg 49; John 49; Susanna 49.

Kescher, Hendrik 64; Jacob Hendrik 64.

Kets, Margarita 57.

Kidney, Kidny, Elisabeth 43; Engeltje 70; Jacob 18, 66.

Killips, Elisab. M. 74.

King, Elisabeth 9, 59; James 11.

Kingsland, Edmund 57.

Legrange, *see* La Grange.
Le Gransy, Legransy, *see* La Grange.
Leonards, Leonard, Leonart, Cornelia 71; John 68; Johs. 37, 71; Nicolas 68.
Lerk, Jurjen 9.
Levison, Alida 16; Cathar. 30; Catharina 11, 16, 23, 69; Harman 23, 30; Maayke 31; Pieter 31, 33, 66; Willem 16, 66.
Lewis, Louys, Elisabeth 30, 40; Eva 8; Hendrik 10; Henry 30, 40; Johs. 68; Maria 68.
Ligthhall, Elisab. 44; Margarita 44; Nicolas 44.
Lincoln, Hosea 48; Josia 48.
Lister, Polly 5.
Livingston, Catharina 5, 40, 41, 50, 60; Cornelia 38, 41; Elisabeth 50; Gov. 8; James 50; Jennet 75; John 41, 50; Margarita J. 12.
Lodeman, Loodman, Mary 55; Samuel 38.
Lodlo, William St. 15.
Loek, Look, Luke, Engeltje 9, 64; Hendrik 45; Jacob 28; Johannes 49*; Johs. V. Wie 64; Lena 53; Magdal. 22; Maria 9, 71; Philip 1, 45, 49, 53, 64; Rachel 28.
Logan, Mary 47.
Look, *see* Loek.
Lottridge, Lothridge, Lotteridge, Lutheridge, Abraham 66; Annetje 70; Bernardus Brat 66; John 48; Thomas 66; William 48, 66, 70.
Louys, *see* Lewis.
Love, Maria 9; Mary 65.
Low, Louw, Elisabeth 12; Mary 46; Nicolass 46; Pieter 64; Pieter Nicolass 46; Sara 46; Thomas 8; Willem 64.
Ludolph, Court. H. 5.
Luke, *see* Loek.
Lundy, Sara 69.
Luteridge, *see* Lottridge.
Lutz, Luits, Luyts, Maria 22, 44, 60.
Lychert, Elisabeth 47; Hendrik 47.
Lydie, Penella 62.
Lyn, Lena 55.

McBead, Daniel 67; William 67.
McCallan, Hannah 67; Robert 67.
McCally, James 7.
McCanne, John 15; Maria 15.
McCantisch, Rachel 67.
McCarly, Mary 56.
McCarn, Mary 43.
McCarty, Charles 10.
McCegg, Polly 9.

McCherny, Jane 48.
McChesny, McChesnee, McChesnut, Chesny, Maychestney, May Chesny, Alexander 40; Hugh 43, 64; Jane 55, 71; Jane May 67; Joseph 43, 67; Mary 40; Robert 64; William 64; Yzac 64.
McClesky, John 68; Martha 68.
McClean, John 11.
McCloud, Daniel 4; Margaret 8; Maron 72; Mary 53.
McCluren, John 46; Pieter 46.
McCowl, Maria 40.
McCrea, John 24; Johannes Beekman 24.
McCyoung, Mally 17.
McDavid, Sara 67*.
McDole, George 18; Thomas 18.
McDonald, McDonnal, McDonnall, George 37; John 4; Margery 4.
McDool, Elisabeth 71; George 71.
McEwen, Anna 68.
McGaharry, Caty 59.
McGregor, McGriger, Alexander 11; Nancy 53.
McFarling, Catharina 66.
McGuire, Mary 55.
McKay, John 11.
McKee, Elisabeth 47; James 47; Margaret 47.
McKinsy, McKinsey, McKinzy, Catharine 72; Francis 66; Hugh 72; Nency 37.
McManus, Elisab., Elisabeth 19, 40; Hugo 19, 61; Rebecca 61.
McMaster, Jane 48, 66.
McMichell, Dirk 70; John 70.
McMolly, Jane 40.
McMullen, McMullan, Duncan 65; Mary 10, 69.
McMuller, Hugh 53; John 53; Johs. 53; Rosanna 53.
McQueen, Margery 4.
McVie, Betsy 11.
Maas, Neeltje 33.
Mahon, (?) Johs. 47.
Malony, *see* Melonay.
Man, Jacob 18; Marytje 18.
Mancius, Anna 20, 49; Annatje 28; Jacob Ten Eyck 75; Wilhelmus 20, 28, 49, 75.
Mark, Mary 12.
Marll, Marl, Marel, Morrel, Andries 21; Daniel 32*; Johannes 46; Johs. 46; Judike 12; Niccolaas 66; Samuel 1, 12, 21, 32, 46, 66; Sara 1, 63.
Marshal, Mershal, Mershall, Annatje 15, 18, 27, 28*, 35, 36, 46*, 66; Cornelis 23; Daniel 18, 28, 66;

Elisabeth 66; Franciscus 23, 35, 55; Frans 53; Hanna 74; Maria 55; Mary 12; Pieter 18, 27, 28*; Petrus 18, 28, 35*.

Marsselis, see Mersselis.

Martin, Marten, Daniel 46; Elisabeth 7; Janet 65; Margarita 60; Maria 65; Marytje 60.

Marus, Neeltje 69.

Maychestney, see McChesny.

Meeby, Albert 3.

Meerthen, Johs. 4; Margarita 44, 69.

Mehony, John 7.

Meinerssen, Meinersse Meinerszen, Meinarssen, Meinzert, Myndertse, Annatje 42; Barent 5; Elisabeth, Elisab. 18, 59; Frederick 7, 66; Fredrik 39; Frerik 24, 42*, 52; Maria 52; Marten 16, 39, 48; Sara 24, 39; Willem 66.

Meinzert, see Meinerssen.

Meisserger, Hans 39; Petrus 39.

Melonay, Malony, Elisabeth 74; James 10; John 74.

Mendel, George 17.

Merriday, Hilletje 45; Sosky 73; Susanna 16, 29, 45.

Mershal, or Mershall, see Marshall.

Mersselis, Marsselis, Annatje 27*; Fytje 67; Gerardus 27; Gysbert 27; Gysbert G. 14; Hannes 15; John Jr. 17, 27; Johs. 29, 58; Johs. Jr. 36; Lydia 36; Maria 41; Margarita 17; Neeltje 58; Nicolaas 27, 41; Tytje 9; Yzaac 14.

Merthen, Elisabeth 41; Maria 41; Marytje 25.

Meyer, Meyers, Andries 49*; Catharina 63; Felix 70; Magdalena 57; Maria 49.

Michell, Michel, see Mitchel.

Miller, see also Muller, Agnieta 10; Andries 57; Annatje 75; Christoffer 75; Hannes 45; Hilletje 45; Jacob 57; John 12; Johs. 68; Mally 67; Susanna 12.

Mills, Abraham 59; Alexander 5; Guy 59.

Milton, George 41; Hendrick 41.

Mitchel, Michel, Michell, Christina 65; James 65; Marytje 28, 41, 61.

Moll, Mol, Hendrikje 57; Jacobus 57; Johannes 57; Wouter 11, 57.

Mollens, Mary 48.

Mook, Anna 63; Jacob Jr. 63; Wilhelmus 12.

Moor, Barbara 10; Catharina 32, 46; Elisab. 74.

Mordan, Jane 61.

Morrel, see Marll.

Morris, Anne 26; William 58.

Morry, Eleanore 40.

Morrison, Daniel 9.

Muller, see also Miller, Agnietje 69; Cornelis 14*; Dorothea 60; Geertruy 22; Geesje 46; Hannes 14, 43; Harmen 14, 55*; Heiltje 32, 50; Hendrik 7, 48; Hilletje 35; Jannetje 26; Jeremias 32; Jeremus 46; Johannes 10, 23, 61; Johs. 23, 69; Leendert 23, 52; Margarita 12; Maria 14, 48; Petrus 52; Philip 14, 22, 26, 36, 49, 50, 55; Sara 23, 43, 61, 65, 69.

Mumpford, Sara 10.

Munroe, Elizabeth 5.

Murray, Eleonore 61; Eunice 10; Margaret 9.

Myndertse, see Meinerssen.

Neeker, Bernard 8.

Neet, Annatje 14; Zachary 14.

Neidhart, Frerick C. 47; Maria 47.

Nelson, Nilson, Esther 6; Hester 49.

Nengels, Mary 68.

Neufll, Magdalena 12.

Newman, Charles 49; Christina 49.

Nichols, Frences 10.

Nilson, see Nelson.

Nisbert, Alida 9.

Nixon, Jane 56.

Noble, Susanna 58.

Nolton, Efraim 6.

North, Ruth 68; Jerissa 68.

Northern, see Van Norden.

Norwich, Marten 57.

Nostrand, see Van Nostrand.

O'Brian, Obryan, Obrian, Obryen, Catharina 55; James 57; John 6, 34; John Graham 57; Lodewyk 55; Louys 37*.

Ofens, John 16; Lena 16*; Mally 33.

Olfer, Antje 27; Cornelia 69; Frederik 27; Jacob 24; Jacobus 74; Johs. 24, 69*.

Oly, Christoffer 60; Rachel 60.

Omfrie, Christina 9.

Oosterhout, Osterhout, Oosterhoud, Annatje 11, 48, 68, 75; Helena 62, 74; Hendrik 48; Jenneke 31, 48, 72; Johannis 74; John 5; Johs. 41, 62; Maria 4, 37, 52, 67; Welhelmus 31, 41, 42, 52.

Oothout, Oothoud, Aaltje 19, 49; Abrah., Abraham 32*, 46, 75; Alida 34, 72; Andries 47, 62; Cornelis 52; Elisab., Elisabeth

Catharina 40, 55; Cornelia 24, 36, 63, 75; Elisab., Elisabeth 51, 75; Folkje 22, 62; Harmen 12; Hendrik 75; Jacob 6, 12, 55; Johannes 24, 40; John 75; John P. 24; Johs. 24, 36; Judik 32; Marg. 24; Margarita 40; Maria 46; Petrus 63; Pieter 40; Rachel 55; Sophia 36; Willem 63; Wouter 36*, 40, 63.

Radley, Radly, Redley, Redly, Redlif, Andries 63; Catherina 13, 36; Catharyntje 31; Celia 6; Hannes 13, 23; Hans 31; Jacob 39; Johannes 63, 67, 74; John 19, 31*, 39, 67; Johs. 36; Margarita 50; Rachel 13; Sara 68; Sofia 19; Wyntje 21, 37, 63.

Raly, *see* Rheyly.

Ram, *see* de Ram.

Ramsey, Polly 11.

Raw, Charity 74; Helmus 74; Susanna 74.

Ray, James 10.

Read, Jane 10.

Rechter, *see* Richters.

Rechteren, *see* Richters.

Redlif, *see* Radley.

Redly, Redley, *see* Radley.

Rees, Geertruy 40; John 71; Maria 56; Philip 71; Sophia 28.

Remsier, Christoffer 30.

Rendell, Rendel, Catharina 37, 55; John 62; Johs. 6; Martinus 37.

Rensselaar, *see* Van Rensselaer.

Reyer, Gerrit 35; Hendrik 35.

Reynard, Margaret 6.

Rheyly, Raly, John 15; Martha 11; Whillem 15.

Richards, Margarita 10.

Richey, Margret 63.

Richters, Richter, Rechter, Rechteren, Cathalyne 71; Cornelia 37, 49, 68; Nicolaas 71.

Riddeker, Riddekel, Elisabeth 71; Hendrik 33, 49, 71; Nicolaas 49; Pieter 33.

Ridder, Rider, Antje 22; Geertje 15, 22; George 66; Hannah 66; Jane 59; Susanna 51.

Riddle, Agnes 49.

Riesch, Maria 24; Marytje 38.

Rob, Johs. 56.

Robertson, George 11.

Robeson, *see* Robinson.

Robinson, Robeson, Mary 9; Richard 11.

Rodgers, Rogers, Annatje 16, 47; Anneke 66; George 40, 61*; Jane 40; Mary 10.

Roes, *see* Roos.

Romney, *see* Rumney.

Ronkel, Cath. 49.

Roos, Roes, Roza, Daniel 47; Machtel 14; Marten 47; Susanna 67; Thomas 67; Yzac 14.

Roseboom, Rozeboom, Roozeboom, Abraham 28, 37; Elisabeth 20; Geertruy 29; Gerrit 60; Hester 38; Jacob 20*, 29, 43, 60; Jacob, Jr. 29; Johannes 20, 29, 43; Machtel 20, 43; Maria 44; Marytje 69; Meinard 44, 69; Susanna 20.

Rosenberg, Johs. 68; Magdalena 68.

Ross, Charlotte 66.

Roun, —— 10.

Roza, *see* Roos.

Rubse, Rubie, Coenraad 49, 55; Sara 49, 55.

Rumney, Rumny, Romney, Anna 2, 42; Annatje 17, 26, 31, 48; Benjamin 13; Elisab. 29; Elisabeth 13, 42, 63; Maria 13.

Runnels, Freela (?) 47.

Ruthel, John 75.

Ruthen, Maria 74.

Rutherford, Janet 65.

Ryan, Johs. 9.

Ryke, Hester 51.

Rykman, Anna 15; Cornelis 50; Elisabeth 13, 52, 68; Gerrit 13, 15, 27, 39, 41, 48, 52, 68; Lydia 16, 36; Machteld 29; Pieter 15, 16, 39, 48, 50; Sara 48; Theuntje 27.

Sabrisky, Sabriskie, see Zabriskie.

Salisbury, Salsberry, Salsbury, Salsbury, V. Salsbergen, V. Salsbury, V. Salsburry, Caspar 48; Catharine 10; Catharina 30; Cornelia 65; Cornelis 30, 41, 49, 65, 69; Elisab. 41; Francis 1, 16; Fytje 30, 41, 49, 69; Geertruy 48; Hermanus 4, 28, 43, 69; Herms 68; Immetje 6, 41, 46; Jacobus 28, 41, 48; Janneke 9; Jannetje 28, 41, 48, 65; Jobje 46, 65; Johannes 69; John 65; Johs. 46; Jonathan 43; Lucas 51; Maria 23, 47, 61; Marten 51; Neeltje 30; Tanneke 28, 49; Teuntje 23; Tobias 28; William 16*, 23.

Salmsby, Johs. 4.

Sanders, Debora 8, 19; Elisabeth 50; John 50; Johs., Jr. 8; Maria 19, 29, 36, 39, 40, 50, 59; Pieter 19.

Santhagen, Frerik 66; John Frerik 66.

Terwilliger, V. d. Willigen, Dirk
33; Johannes 33.
Theunissen, Gerrit 45; Jacobus 45.
Think, John 56; Maria 56.
Thoff, Fenny 59.
Tholl, see Toll.
Thomson, Thomsen, Thompson,
Cath. 54; Christina 59; Elisa-
beth 57; John 59; Margaret 11,
46; Mary 48, 69; Nency 75;
Oner 11; Robt. 75; William 48*.
Thoudel (?), Elisabeth 1.
Throwbrige, Luther 10.
Tilleman, Tillman, Tilman, Elisa-
beth 10; Margriet 8; Richard 1,
63*.
Tilson, Nency 39.
Tingy, see Tinky.
Tinky, Tingy, Elisabeth 44; Johan-
nes 22; John 22, 44.
Toll, Tholl, Barber 11; Eva 52;
Sara 52.
Tounsel, James 40*.
Tratter, Trotter, Annatje 53; Maria
53; Sara 58.
Trotter, see Tratter.
Truex, Trouex, Andries 37*,38; Cor-
nelis 20; Elisab., Elisabeth 38,
55; Jelles 37; Johs. W. 70;
Marytje 70; Susanna 28; Tan-
neke 50; Yzac 70*; Yzaac J. 20*.
Tuttle, Turtle, Guy 58; Sara 70;
Stephen 58, 70.

Valenbee, see Vallensby.
Valk, Baatje 51.
Valkenburg, see Van Valkenburg.
Vallensby, Valenbee, Velentbee,
George 57*; Jacobus 9; Jeroom
57; Jerson 9.
Veeder, Veder, Vedder, Abraham
35; Arent 63; Arent J. 42;
Cathar. 20; Fytje 63; Geertruy
73; John 73; Marytje 63; Pieter
27, 63; Samuel 11; Susanna 42;
Yzaac 35.
Velentbee, see Vallensby.
Verbank, Samuel 10.
Vernor, Verner, Elizabeth 48; John
57.
Verplank, Abrm., Abraham 2, 25,
49; Magdal. 49.
Viele, Veele, File, Fyle, Phile,
Andries 26; Anna 3; Annake
65; Annatje 36; Anneke 16, 23;
Arriaantje 71; Barent Bratt 34;
Cath., Catharina 14, 16, 21*, 36,
37, 55; Cornelius 50*; Debora
35; Elisabeth 67; Gerrit 14, 16,
21, 37, 55; Jacob 36*; Lena 58;
Ludovicus 52*; Magdelena 20,

50, 68; Maria 17, 46; Marytje
26; Melchert 21*; Philip G. 21,
34, 46, 55; Rebecca 26, 37;
Reinert 71; Simeon 50; Simon
71; Stephanus 52.
Vinhagel, see Vinhagen.
Vinhagen, Vinhagel, Baatje 70;
Elis. 46; Elisabeth 9, 70; Geer-
truy 46, 70; Jacobus 46, 51*;
Johannes 70; Johs. 51, 70; Maria
12; Martin 5; Marytje 51.
Visbach, Elisabeth 2, 34, 43, 63;
Geertruy 34, 43, 51, 65.
Vischer, Visscher, Visher, Visser,
Fisscher, Fisher, Alida 18, 47;
Anatje 66; Annatje 61, 62;
Barbara 31; Barent 18, 31, 47;
Bastiaan 20*, 25, 27, 47, 70;
Catharina 49; Col. J. 7; Dirkje
25, 33; Donald 5; Elisabeth 29,
38, 45, 73; Engeltje 20, 27;
Franciscus 52; Frederik 74;
George 74; Gerrit 30, 34, 38, 65;
Harmen 31; Jannetje 34, 51;
Johans 50; Johannes T. 65;
John 13, 24, 66; John Nanning
49; Johs. 29, 45, 73; Johs. I.
26, 38; Lydia 39, 56; Machtelt
70; Manning 73; Maria 50;
Mary 10; Matheus 20; Mathew
62; Mathys 39; Mechtelt 17;
Nanning 7, 49, 52; Rachel 34,
38, 65; Rebecca 24; Saartje 25;
Sara 18, 31, 47, 73; Theunis 17,
26, 31, 65.
Voorhees, Jan 59*; Johannes 32;
John 32.
Vosburg, Barent 28, 49, 71; Cath.
36; Christina 32, 68; Elisabeth
49; Geertje 8, 20, 33, 35; Geer-
truy 24, 36, 54; Gerrit 33, 46;
Hendrik 35; Hester 71; Mein-
ert 28; Willem 18, 32, 68; Yzaac
18, 35, 36.
Vosmer, Johs. 9.
Vredenburg, Van Vredenburg,
Abrah. 34; Jannetje 51; Maria
34, 69; Nelly 51.
Vroman, Abraham 21; Adam 22;
Andries 37; Annatje 31;
Anthony 52; Cornelis 31; Cor-
nelius 21; Engeltje 8; Geertruy
21, 30, 50; Hendrik 52; Jacob
22; Jacobus 21, 30, 50; Jannetje
30; Pieter 21, 37.
V. Aalstein, Andries 64; Annatje 53,
61; Benjamin 75; Cath. 29;
Cathalyntje 69; Cornelia 42, 69;
Cornelis 53, 69, 75; Daniel 53*;
Dirkje 28; Eva 29, 34, 64;
Folkje 15; Hermanus 29, 68*;

tina 68; Cornelia 6, 44, 60; Cornelis 43*; Cornelis, Jr. 21; Elisabeth 56; Engeltje 21; Geertje 28; Gerrit 15; Gerritje 25, 45; Gozen, Gosen 15, 25, 40, 51, 53, 60, 72, 73, 75; Jacob 22, 27, 28, 33, 47, 56; Jacob G. 15; Jannetje 37*, 65; Johannes 25; John G. 5, 68; Johs. 42*, 59; Maayke 15, 51, 60, 73; Maria, Marya 10, 40, 42, 47, 53, 68; Marytje 25; Meinard 40; Ryckie, Rykje 36, 58, 74; Saartje 2, 23, 51; Sara 23, 61, 73; Stephen 37*; Sybrand 40; Tobias 75; Wessel 25, 42.

Van Schelluyne, V. Schelluyne, V. Schelluine, Schelluyne, Schelluine, Cornelis 20*, 28, 50; Debora 20; Dirk 28; Elisabeth 20, 28.

Van Schoonhoven, V. Schoonhoven, Dirk B. 29, 38; Elisabeth 73; Gerrit 16; Hendrik 16, 29, 38, 61; Jacobus 29, 32, 38, 73; Sara 61; Susanna 16, 32.

V. Slyck, Van Slyk, V. Slyk, Antje 8; Cathalyna 57; Jannetje 33, 35, 57; Theunis 2.

V. Tuylen, John 6.

Van Valkenburg, V. Valkenburg, Valkenburg, Baatje 70; Barent 27; Cathalyntje 56; Catharina 7; Elisabeth 34, 42, 56; Elsje 63; Engeltje 27; Eva 26; Jacobus 5, 6, 18, 39, 63; Jannetje 57; Johs. 18; Lydia 57; Rachel 30, 57, 60; Yzaac 30.

Van Vegten, V. Vegten, V. Vechten, Alida 15, 24; Annatje 12*; Cathalyntje 12; Cornelis 15, 24; Dirk 12*, 15, 18, 24; Elisabeth 18; Ephraim, Efraim 4, 73; Folkert 5, 28, 32, 37, 45; Harmen 15; Hendrikus 73; Jannetje 32, 37, 42; John Witbeek 45; Judike 52; Lena 45; Lydia 18, 32, 53, 73; Neeltje 73; Rebecca 24; Theunis 52*.

Van Vlek, Abraham K. 14, 26; Catharina 14; Matheus 26.

V. Oost (or Voast), Sara 38.

Van Vrancken, V. Franken, V. Francken, Annatje 22; Cathar., Catharina 19, 61; Catharyntje 30; Christina 14, 37, 65, 66; Geertruy 11, 40, 45; Gerrit 40, 45, 68; Gerrit P. 11; Hillegonda 33; Jacobus 5, 61; Johs. 18; Margarita, Margareta, Margar. 18, 27, 30, 43, 66; Marytje 14,

21, 40, 68; Maus R. 66; Rykert 19, 30; Susanna 68.

V. Vredenburg, see Vredenburg.

Van Wie, V. Wie, Van Wey, Abraham, Abrahm., Abrah., 8, 31, 54, 74; Alida 31, 42, 50, 54; Andries 31, 54, 72; Benjamin 35; Casparus 35, 43, 52; Catharina 25, 42, 44*, 50, 66; Cornelia 21, 32*, 39, 72, 73; Cornelis 32*; Elisabeth 41, 72; Gerrit 16, 32, 44, 50, 63; Helena 16; Hendrick, Hendrik 25*, 31, 41, 44, 45, 50, 57, 60, 65, 74; Jannetje 43, 74; John 31; Johs. 22, 42, 50, 54; Lena 31*; Magdalena 1, 45, 64; Maria 31, 57, 74; Marytje 45; Pieter 4, 21*, 25, 44, 63, 72; Pieter Martin 65; Rachel 52; Willem 21, 38, 59, 67; Yzac 38, 59.

Van Woert, V. Woert, Abraham 47; Alida 38; Andries 29; Bata 12; Cath., Catharina 13, 17; Eldert 13, 24, 38, 58; Elisab., Elisabeth 13*, 32, 52, 72; Eva 27, 40, 64; Folkje 22; Fytje 49; Helena 24; Hendrik 29, 47, 72; Hubertje 44; Jacob 8, 13*, 29, 58*, 59, 61; Jacob Lansing 26; Johs. 17, 26, 44, 59; Johs., Jr. 13; Louys 22, 62; Margar., Margarita 3, 32, 39, 51, 64; Petrus 51; Rachel 51, 62; Rebecca 13; Sara 59*; Tietje 31.

Van Yveren, V. Yveren, Anna 35; Annatje 35; Anthony 19; Baatje 24; Barent 16, 43, 44, 65; Cathalyntje 19, 47; Cornelia 43, 44, 45, 61, 73; Cornelis 44, 45; Debora 16; Gerrit 16; Gysbert 47; Jacob 24; Maayke 60; Maria 26, 56; Martinus 6, 44, 60, 61, 73; Marytje 19; Meinard 65*; Rebecca 14; Reynier 7, 19, 35, 37; Reynier, Jr. 56; Sara 14, 16, 61; Wyntje 16.

V. Zandvoort, see Van Santvoort.

Van Zante, V. Zante, V. Santen, Alida 19*, 30; Annatje 13; Antje 73; Celia 34; Elis., Elisab., Elisabeth 28, 34, 55, 74; Gerrit 23, 52; Gysbert 30, 52*; Hendrik 36; Hester, Hesther 23, 28, 52*; Jacobus 36, 54; Johannes 55; Johs. 19, 34, 55; Joseph 16, 23, 28; Margarita 16; Maria 16; Pieter 36; Rachel 11, 16, 33, 60; Rebecca 12, 52; Ryckert, Rykert 23, 36, 44, 60, 73; Saartje 51, 69; Sara 30, 36, 38, 60; Willem 13, 19, 30, 44.

Waldron, Waldrom, Alida 75; Benjamin 13; Catharyntje 42; Cornelis 13, 15, 17, 18*, 27, 42, 62, 70, 75; Elisabeth 24, 42, 67; Evert 24, 25; Geertje 18; Gerrit 24, 25; Hendrik 14, 18, 20, 22, 27*, 30, 43, 66; Jannetje 13, 24, 27, 37, 43, 57; Johs. 42; Margarita 14, 22; Maus 66; Neeltje 13, 24; Pieter 25, 62, 70; Rykert 30; Salomon 42; Willem 7, 13, 62.
Wallet, Eduard 72.
Wallis, Ann 38.
Wally, John 58; Maria 58.
Walton, Susanna 51.
Ward, Wards, Dorcas 10; John 59, 63; Margarita 59.
Warn, *see* Warren.
Warren, Warn, Catharina 57; George 37; James 37; Samuel 9.
Washburn, Wasburn, Bethuel 11, 74; John 74.
Waters, Cathar., Catharina 32, 39.
Wats, Jane 10; Maria 10.
Watson, Ally 66; Elly 53; Hannah 55; John 53; Isabella 62; Ralph 55.
Webber, Catharina 57; Pieter 57.
Webner, Agnes 75.
Weeler, Wieler, Willer, Bregje 34; Hendrik 2, 34; Johs. 62; Maria 62; Saartje 72.
Weger, Everhard 12; Willem 12.
Welch, George 66; John Lewis 10; Joseph 9; Richard 66.
Wendel, Wendell, Wendels, Wendal, Windel, Wennel, Abrah., Abraham 2, 22*, 37, 45; Alida 53; Ann 56*; Annatje 23, 41, 62; Barbara 62, 74; Barent 42; Cathalina 54; Cathalyntje 24; Catharina 16, 22, 45, 51, 75*; Cornelis 16, 37; Elisab., Elisabeth 6, 23, 48, 62, 74; Elsje 66; Francyntje 16, 53, 66; Geertruy 18, 23, 48; Geesje 49; Gerrit 18; Harmanus 15, 23; Hermanus 42, 62, 74; Hermanus A. 22; Hermanus H. 16; Hendrik 15, 21*, 37; Jacob 56; Johannes 42, 53; Johannes J. 65; John 21, 42, 65; John I. 53; Johs. 42, 66; Johs. J. 30, 42; Johs. W. 53; Margareta 51; Margarita 20, 31; Maria 15, 75; Marten 11; Mary 58; Marytje 15, 19, 23, 59; Philip 18, 24, 36, 54; Rebecca 30; Robert 51, 75; Saartje 18; Santje 18, 33; Sara 42, 72;

Susanna 57; Tanneke 22; Willem 21; Wyntje 37; Yzac 36.
Wennel, *see* Wendel.
Westerlo, Catharina 35, 60; Eilardus 5, 22, 35, 40, 60; Rensselaer 40.
Weyland, Johannes 69; Leendert 69; Leonard 10.
Whitaker, Eduard 32; Elisabeth 32; Neeltje 19; Neely 32.
White, Annatje 10, 70; David 6; Isabella 53; Jane 64.
Whitley, Charles D. 10; Davis 56.
Whitvoot, Mary 56.
Wieler, *see* Weeler.
Wiesch, Hannes 24, 38; Helena 38; Johannes 24; Johs. 56; Petrus 56.
Wildring, Robert 67*.
Wilkes, Johs. 36; Maria 36; Thomas 36*.
Wilkeson, Wilkkinson, John 74*; Margar., Margarita 19, 55; Maria 34.
Wilkkinson, *see* Wilkeson.
Will, Henry 45; Rebecca 45.
Willer, *see* Weeler.
Willes, *see* Willis.
Willet, Wylett, Wyllet, Annatje 56; Cathalina 37; Cathalyna 29; Eduard 33, 41; Eduard S. 37, 56; Edward 17; Elbert 29, 33, 37; Marinus 33; Mary 17; Samuel 17, 37; Sara 33, 62.
Williams, Elisabeth 13, 74; Jane 67; Mary 12; Marytje 14; Pieter 13.
Williamson, Ann 65; John 9, 65; Mindret 6.
Willis, Willes, Elisabeth 10, 56; Hester 36, 41; Jannetje 33; John 70; Marytje 33; Robert 70; Willem 13, 33.
Wilson, Wilzon, Andries 3; Jennet 59; John 44; Mally 4, 38, 49, 62; Marg. 50; Peggy 10; Sara 53, 75; Susanna 44.
Wilsy, Susannah 9.
Winne, Abraham 36; Agnietje 5, 42, 62; Angenitie 74; Anneke 24; Antje 26, 49, 69; Benj. 47; Cathalyntje 56*; Catharina 22, 30; Daniel 16, 22, 23, 28, 37*, 56, 62, 72, 74; Daniel C. 30; Daniel Fr. 36; David 29, 67*; Dirkje 4, 18, 24*, 26, 34, 37, 45; Elisab., Elisabeth 20, 45; Fietje 59; Francyntje 36; Frans 16, 23, 24, 36; Frans, Jr. 65; Fytje 16; Gerrit 3, 51; Helena 23, 36, 41, 74; Hendrik 64; Hester 35; Jacob 59, 64; Jacob Viele 36;

Records of the Reformed Dutch Church of Albany, New York

Part 7
1780-1789

Excerpted from
Year Book of The Holland Society
of New York (1924/25)

RECORDS OF THE REFORMED DUTCH CHURCH OF ALBANY, N. Y.

MARRIAGES—1780 TO 1789

1780, Jan. 9. William W. Crennell and Mary Eman.
Jan. 9. Daniel McMollen and Sara Words.
Feb. 6. Francis Hoghil and Cornelia De Foreest.
    John V. Salsbergen and Margarita V. Salsbergen.
Feb. 14. Johs. Brower and Marytje De Wever.
Feb. 20. Hendrick Huick and Rachel Barheat.
Feb. 27. David Foreest and Rachel V.d.Heide.
Feb. 28. David Winne and Maria Spaan.
Mar. 5. Dirck V. Vechten and Catharina Spoor.
Mar. 11. Bastiaan Visscher and Anna Grahams.
Mar. 12. George Hodson and Elisabeth McBenton.
Apr. 8. Gerrit Poel and Margarita Wilson.
Apr. 10. Joseph Dennison and Maria Schoonmaker.
    Nicolas Christman and Maria Christman.
    Johs. V. d. Poel and Geertruy V. Buuren.
Apr. 16. Gerrit Becker and Maria Wynkoop.
Apr. 27. Thoms. Ashley and Margareth Gibson.
May 9. Ebenezer Wands and Mary Hunter.
May 10. Ruben Conger and Lena de Voe.
May 12. Gerrit Brower and Antje Zeger.

I

May 14. John V. Emburgh and Annatje Flensburg.
May 21. Alexander Kirkland and Catharina Steel.
May 28. Wynand V. d. Berg and Annatje Cooper.
June 4. Cornelis Brower and Jacomyntje Meck.
Willm. McCloghlin and Rachel Cole.
July 25. David Winne and Geertruy Groesbeck.
Aug. 4. Yzac V. Wie and Neeltje Ooosterhout.
Aug. 7. Jannes Philips and Margarita Passagie.
Aug. 12. Hendrik V. Deusen and Neeltje Brummetje.
Sept. 24. John Staats and Jane McClannen.
Sept. 25. Pieter Adir, of Schenectady, and Alida Van Slyck, of Cocksackie.
Oct. 1. Jeremia Lansing and Helena Wendel.
Oct. 1. John Sheer and Catharina Qwakkenbush.
Oct. 8. Stephen Durham and Susanna Cool.
Oct. 14. Thomas Reed and Hanna Edgar.
Oct. 15. Lavinus Lansing and Maria Parssen.
Oct. 22. Hendrik Huyk and Mary Bell.
Oct. 29. Jacobus Peek and Catharina Meeby.
Nov. 12. John Norris and Mary Herod.
Nov. 15. Charles Bodeman and Nency Holles.
Nov. 19. John V. Sant and Elisabeth V. Sant.

MARR. WITH BANNS:

Nov. 20. Nicholaas V. Rensselaer and Elsje V. Buuren.
Nov. 24. Robert Haswell and Sara Mark.
Yzac Mark and Mary Haswell.
Nov. 27. Robert Dunbar and Annatje Slingeland.
Dec. 14. Richard Lush and Lyntje Fonda.
Colonel Alex. Hamilton and Elisabeth Schuyler.
Dec. 17. John Schulter and Margarita Jacobi.
Marthin Kuyler and Margarita Hargans.
Yzaac D. Verplank and Helena Hoogteling.
1781, Jan. 1. Thomas McMoris and Chrysill Schott.
Jan. 7. Elisa Crane and Ruth Philips.
Jan. 14. Henry New Meyer and Mary Forlow.
Jan. 14. Dirk Foreest and Rebecca Bratt.
Jan. 21. John Thompson and Janny McFarson.
Feb. 11. Hendrik Loodwyk and Leena Huyck.
Feb. 18. John V. d. Poel and Isabell Daggelis.
Coenraad F. Ten Eyck and Geertje Ten Eyck.
Feb. 21. John Berhart and Mary Wheeler.

Mar. 12. James McCogtreen and Dolly Ramsey.
Apr. 8. John Andrie and Jenny McClarming.
Pieter Dox and Nency Rendell.
John Lansing and Cornelia Ray.
Apr. 16. Arthur Banks and Sara Lommis.
Apr. 29. John Waters and Dorothea V. Benthuisen.
May 20. Pieter Chadden and Sara Hoogteling.
June 8. Obadia Cooper and Lena Albrecht.
June 10. Willem Touper and Maria Hilton.
Jurjen Poel and Jannetje Brezie.
June 22. Andries Wessels and Geertruy Cloet.
June 24. Evert Olfert and Rebecca Cooper.
June 28. Obadia Cooper and Lena Helbrig.
July 4. Dirk Hanssen and Lysie Low.
Karel Racosham and Sara Becker.
July 8. Jacobus McChesny and Cornelia Ten Baar.
John Boom and Sibyll Johnston.
July 18. John Folsom and Elisabeth File.
July 29. Thomas V. Aalstein and Arriaantje V. Deusen.
Aug. 19. Arthur Hasswell and Mary Coghtree.
Sept. 6. Jonathan Butler and Martha Williams.
Nov. 11. John Johnson and Abigail Collins.
Nov. 22 (?). Thomas Watt and Christina Webster.
Nov. 12. Andrew Conyn and Charlotta McHay.
Nov. 18. Jacobus Pearse and Maria V. d. Berg.
Dec. 2. John Stuard and Henry (sic) Stuard.
Dec. 16. George Grant and Margareth Killy.
Dec. 25. Pieter V. Antwerp and Susanna Band.
1782, Jan. 20. John Ten Eyck and Maria Douw.
Jan. 30. Adam Rosman and Annatje Decker.*
John Hay and Margarita Hutton.*
Feb. 12. Silvester Ryly and Thige(?) Schermerhoorn.
Feb. 17. Benjamin Fox and Martha Andries, widow.
Mar. 4. Abrm. V. d. Kar and Margarita V. d. Kar.
Mar. 31. Matheus V. Aalstein and Rachel De Foreest.
Apr. 21. Hendrick V. d. Poel and Tanneke Mulder.
May 13. Carl Fred. Salomo Frederic, V. D. M., and
Sara Zieglern.
June 24. Moses Dearling and Jenny (or Fenny) Fletter.
June 29. Johs. Rose and Margaret Mill.

---

* In the Manor of Livingston.

4

Aug. 17. David Flensburg and Maria Smitt.
Oct. 6. John V. Sante and Mary Burgess.
          John Segers and Rebecca Witbeek.
Oct. 25. James Wilks and Catharina Schoonmaker.
          Henry Hart and Elisabeth Visscher.
Nov. 3. Robert Clerk and Agness Cogtrie.
Nov. 18. Jacobus Bleecker and Rachel V. Sant.
Nov. 28. Storm Hoogteeling and Jannetje V. d. Willigen.
Dec. 8. Dirk Hunn and Annatje Lansing.
Dec. 29. Nicolaas V. d. Bogert and Margarita Flens-
          burg.
1783, Jan. 26. William Winne and Maria Bekker.
Jan. 27. Jacobus V. d. Poel and Maria Mulder.
          Simon Belsah and Debora Davis.
Feb. 9. Joseph Juwell and Nency Dennels.
          John Godfreed and Bridged Boom.
Feb. 10. Adam V. Ostrander and Catharina Proper.
          Pieter Proper and Maria Hays.
Feb. 23. Maas V. Franken and Geertruy Veder.
Feb. 24. James Hunter and Catharina Cassen.
Mar. 16. William Foreest and Abigail Foreest.
Apr. 27. Jonathan Hilton and Cornelia V. Antwerpen.
May 4. Jacobus Lagrance and Arriaantje Truex.
May 26. Hendrik Brezier and Cornelia V. Buren.
June 5. Casparus Witbeek and Cornelia Dunbar.
June 11. James Wand and Margaret Burnside.
June 16. Andrew Hannah and Elisabeth Rickert.
July 13. William Loudon and Mary Dickins.
July 20. Henry Wheeler and Margarita Blancker.
Aug. 18. Pieter Cooper and Anna Strong.
Aug. 30. Jacobus Fonda and Willempje Bogert.
Sept. 2. Hendrik Eversson and Hendrikje Winne.
Sept. 10. Martinus Reess and Lena Jacobi.
Sept. 13. John Boom and Annatje Brower.
Oct. 13. Harpert Witbeek and Geertruy Wendell.
Oct. 19. John Fonda and Cornelia Hunn.
          William Papham (Popham?) and Mary
          Morris.
Oct. 26. Jacob Miller and Geertruy Veeder.
Nov. 5. Johs. Freer and Annatje Eyly.
Nov. 9. Jacobus Redliff and Maria Otman.

Nov. 24. Jurjen Springsteen and Sara Springsteen.
Nov. 30. David Wever and Elisabeth Collington.
Dec. 4. Cornelis Groesbeek and Annatje V. Antwerp.
Dec. 20. William Camble and Rhode Philips.
Dec. 22. Pieter Ginter and Elisabeth Frisby.
Dec. 24. Pieter Flensburg and Maria Becker.
Wlm. McIntosh and Heron.
1784, Jan. 1. Gysbert Groesbeek and Cornelia Valkenburgh.
Jan. 11. Jeremia Pennel and Annatje Hilton.
Cornelis V. Schaak and Willempje Hanssen.
Jan. 18. Johs. Vollumsbury and Catharina V. Schaik.
William McMaris and Mary Fare.
Jan. 22. Coenraad Noorman and Catharina Tayler.
Jan. 23. Andries Beveridge and Isabella Cumming.
Feb. 1. Yzac Moll and Jannetje Schermerhoorn.
Reinier Van Yveren and Elisabeth Ostrander.
Feb. 4. Jacob A. Lappius and Maria De Foreest.
Feb. 8. Abraham Lansing and Maria Bloodgood.
William Davie and Jannetje Relyea.
Feb. 19. Ysaac Bell and Maria V. Buren.
Feb. 20. Geertruy Miller(?) and Geertruy Warner.
Jacob Arnhout and Maria Slingerland.
Mar. 22. Wouter Hoogteling and Jannetje Adering.
Mar. 24. Johs. Bloemendal and Catharina Sharp.
Abraham V. Buuren and Neeltje V. d. Bergh.
Apr. 4. Jacob Fonda and Aletta Willet.
Apr. 9. Leendert Muller and Maria Strong.
Apr. 22. Nicholas Lansing, preacher in the Manor of Livingston, and Dorcas Sara Dickinson.
May 4. Henry Ridliff and Elisabeth Jacobs.
Joseph Hagemans and Rebecca Coenes.
May 16. Frans Winne and Leena Flensburg.
May 18. Cornelis Bloemendal and Lena Reisdorp.
May 20. Abraham V. Vechten and Catharina Schuyler.
May 30. Daniel Clement and Rachel Milton.
June 9. Jonathan Freeman and Mary Haines, widow Haren.
July 18. Barent Ridder and Nency Ryn.
July 22. Pieter Davies and Elisabeth Calwell.
July 25. Cornelius Ray and Elisabeth Elmendorp.

Aug. 15. John Hilton and Elisabeth Bleek.
Aug. 22. Nicholaas Hoghil and Catharina Valkenburgh.
Aug. 28. John Rumney and Rachel Meinerssen.
Oct. 4. William Robeson and Dirkje V. Hoesen.
Oct. 8. Yzaac I. Fryer and Catharina V. Wie.
Oct. 14. Thomas Farmer and Catharine Manson.
Oct. 24. Dirk J. De Foreest and Maria Fonda.
Nov. 4. Richard Fin and Margaret Black.
Nov. 10. Jacobus Redlif and Susanna Claas.
          George Remsay and Grisswell Coultrek.
Nov. 11. Jacob Albrecht and Anna Arnhout.
Nov. 12. Samuel McGiffy and Susanna Robison.
Dec. 14. John Gillifs and Jane Cannell.
Dec. 18. Sybrand Quackenbusch and Elisabeth V. Schaak.
Dec. 26. Alexander M. Donaldson and Jane Mitchell.
Dec. 27. Alexander Lavety and Elisabeth Riddel.
1785, Jan. 2. Pieter Slingeland and Maria V. d. Werken.
Jan. 11. Storm Hoogteeling and Martha Watson.
Feb. 8. John McPherson and Jane Mill, wid. Henry.
Feb. 12. Cornelis V. Wie and Nancy Schenklin.
Feb. 16. Johs. Hoogteling and Catharina Van Alen.
Feb. 17. James Hall and Mary Malword.
Feb. 27. Henrikus Oosterhout and Catharina Warrant,
          wid. of James Burnside.
Mar. 10. John Brat and Wyntje Bratt.
Mar. 26. Hermanus A. Wendell and Catharine H.
          Wendell.
Apr. 21. Nanning Visscher and Alida Fonda.
Apr. 26. William Reside and Janny McDaniel.
May 2. Richard Sill and Elisabeth Nicols.
May 4. Hendr. V. Ist and Maria Ten Eyck.
May 9. John V. Aernem and Hester V. Aarnem.
May 16. Moses Woodworth and Maria Northen.
May 17. Philip Berringer and Catharine Meyers.
May 21. Michael Levy and Bata Heemstraat.
June 21. Abraham V. Fyn and Hester Carpenter.
July 7. Gerrit Poel and Cornelia Muller.
July 11. Johs. M. Flensburg and Catharina Becker.
July 16. Thomas MeLoy and Wyntje Snyder.
Aug. 14. Samuel Hannan and Agness Malhilh.
Oct. 15. John Foet and Loys Cummins.

Nov. 14. Hendrik V. Aalstein and Rebecca Van Aalstein.
Nov. 29. Hendrik Bratt and Elisabeth V. d. Berg.
Dec. 8. John Henry and Christy Henrys.
Dec. 11. William Henry and Anna Alexander.
Dec. 14. Hendrik Benthuisen and Cathalina Hunn.
Dec. 18. Pieter Fero and Jane Van Deusen.
1786, Jan. 3. Arent Slingerland and Annatje Aarnout.
Jan. 4. Mathias Falkenburg and Bertha Bratt.
Jan. 19. John Price and Annatje Peesinger.
    Henry Yates and Rachel V. Zanten.
    John Wards and Mary Warren.
Feb. 12. Johannes V. d. Werken and Catharina Slingerland.
Feb. 23. Philip Redlif and Newman Hall.
Mar. 4. Nicolaas H. Groesbeek and Jacomyntje Fort.
Mar. 6. Jacob I. Schermerhoorn and Rachel Gardenier.
Mar. 14. Hendrik Slingerland and Eva Van der Zee.
Mar. 17. Jacob I. Pruin and Neeltje Foreest.
Apr. 29. Nicolas Tiets and Elisabeth Johnson.
May 28. Hendrik H. V. Rensselaer and Cornelia V. Aalstein.
June 5. Abraham Vrydag and Hannah Beeby.
June 26. Gillis Bett and Sara V. Yveren.
June 22. John Daniel Winne and Agness V. Wie.
Aug. 7. Evert Mersselis and Sara V. Benthuisen.
Sept. 6. Thomas Coeper and Lea Cooper.
Sept. 13. William Thomson and Isabell Frasier.
Sept.15. Anthony V. Santvoort and Maria Roff.
Sept. 17. Yzaac Huyk and Hanna Platt.
Oct. 3. Theodorus V. Wyk Graham and Magdalena Ten Broeck.
    Reinier Pruin and Jannetje Goey.
Nov. 20. Matthew Halliday and Catharina Cooper.
1787, Jan. 23. Hendrik Visscher and Alida Lansing.
Jan. 31. Gerrit Marsselis and Machteld Visscher.
Feb. 11. Pieter Bloemendal and Barber Sherp.
Feb. 13. Michael Parkley and Anna Warner.
Feb. 27. Dirk Hogeboom and Jemima Keane.
Mar. 4. Jacob Veeder and Catharine Spaan.
Mar. 14. John Roberts and Catharine Smith.

Apr. 8. Anthony Bradt and Geertruy V. d. Bergh.
Apr. 16. Benjamin Winne and Elisabeth Basset.
Apr. 21. Gerrit J. Lansing and Maria V. Aernem.
Apr. 24. Jurjen Pickert and Maria Freeligh.
May 28. Gerrit Goey and Egje Look.
June 5. Nicolaas Halenbeek and Maria Shutt.
Aug. 5. Benjamin V. Santen and Sarah Visscher.
Aug. 9. Jacob Chr. Lansing and Rachel Verplank.
Aug. 30. John G. V. Santen and Leentje Lansing.
Sept. 2. Gerrit R. Lansing and Alida Foreest.
Sept. 18. John B. Schuyler and Elisabeth V. Rensselaer.
Nov. 7. Abraham Vosburgh and Sara Bulsingh.
Nov. 11. William Capron and Mary Northen.
Dec. 2. Martin C. V. Buuren and Theuntje V. Buuren.
Barent Bleecker and Sara Lansingh.
Dec. 9. Pieter W. Witbeek and Marritje Pruyn.
Dec. 23. John De P. Douwe and Deborah Beekman.
Dec. 25. Jacob Fryer and Agnietje Muller.
1788, Jan. 1. Christiaan Arnhout and Phebe Wary.
Mar. 3. James Waldrom and Ytje Ten Eyck.
Mar. 14. Andries Bartell and Sophia Bartell.
Mar.16. Yzac Trouex and Tanneke Bleecker.
Mar. 18. Abraham Groot and Margarita Zeeker.
May 19. Hermanus Vedder and Elisabeth Bassett, by
Certif. from Rev. Mr. Romaine, of Schenec-
tady.
May 21. Adam Long and Eleanor Groesbeek, by Certif.
from their parents.
May 25. William Vrendenburgh and Dorothea Turell,
by certif. of publication in Albany.
May 25. John Gui and Petritie Jerolomon, by certif. of
their respective parents.
June 2. Guliam D. Winne and Sarah Connolly, by con-
sent of Guardians.
July 7. George Ramsay and Christian Smith, Certif.
July 9. John Jac. Lansingh and Arriaantje Verplank.
Aug. 18. Garret Groosbek and Widow Abraham Ver-
plank.
Aug. 12. Micheel Halenbeek and Neeltje Hoogteeling.
Aug. 16. Arent Tinhout and Catharina Tonser.
Sept. 29. Abraham Quakkenbush and Elisabeth Le-
grange.

Oct. 18. Cornelis V. d. Bergh and Anna V. Woert.
Nov. 2. Abraham Wieler and Maria Bernhard.
Nov. 4. Johannis Proper and Charity Lint (?).
Nov. 13. Nathan Wood and Neby Hynds.
Nov. 17. Charles Morgan and Sarah Heyer.
Dec. 3. Theunis Visscher, Widr., and Elsje Roseboom, wid.
1789, Jan. 31. Isaac Bogart and Tina Vischer, by cons. of Pars.
Feb. 6. John T. Cuyler and Jenny Ray.
Mar. 25. Barent Staats and Catharina Cuyler.
Mar. 26. Aaron Asburn and Mary Wels.
Apr. 2. James V. Schoonhooven and Mary Spoor.
Apr. 9. Jacob Sharp and Arriaantje V. Yveren.
Apr. 27. Archelaus Lint and Elisabeth Proper.
July 1. John Jauncey and Elsey (?) Cuyler.
    Philip Schuyler and Miss Van den Bergh.
July 13. John V. Deursen and Antje Witbeek.
Aug. 14. John Johnson and Helena Lottrige.
Sept. 1. Christoffer Lang and Maria Raff.
Sept. 6. Jacobus Hilton and Catharina Friar.
Sept. 26. Gerrit V. Alen and Magdalena Van Wie, wid. of Philip Look.
Oct. 1. Willem Stover and Elisabeth Halenbeek.
Oct. 14. John McMullan and Jennet Wands.
Oct. 15. Peter De Foreest and Barbara V. Aalstein.
Nov. 9. Henry Truax and Miss Yeates.
Nov. 12. William Crennel and Catharina Valentyn.
Nov. 13. John Slingerland and Hester Slingerland.
Nov. 17. Johannes Klabert and Christina Strunk.
Nov. 24. Isaac Crennel and Maria Morris.
Dec. 2. Peter Schuyler and Caty Cuyler.
Dec. 6. Charles Winne and Hannah Switz.
Dec. 9. William Robertson and Elhanah Freyeer.
    Saunders Lansing and Caty Ten Eyck.
Dec. 12. Cornelius Winkoop and Miss Forcey.
Dec. 14. James Seger and Maria Trooper.

BAPTISMAL RECORD—1780 TO 1789

1780, Jan. 2. bo. Nov. 29. Annatje of John Beekman and Hendrikje V. Buuren. Wit. Johs. M. Beekman, Elisabeth Douw.

Jan. 16. bo. Dec. 6. Yzac of Yzac Fonda Yz. and Antje V. Santvoort. Wit. Yzac and Francyntje Fonda.

Jan. 17. bo. Dec. 13. David of James Mc Alpin and Margarita Bratt.

bo. the 1st. Jacomyntje of Johs. V. Ostrander and Marritje V. Deuzen. Wit. Jacob and Jacomyntje V. Ostrander.

Jan. 23. bo. Dec. 11. Lydia of Christiaan Boonards and Annatje Freelich. Wit. Dirk and Sara V. d. Willigen.

bo. Dec. 23. Mary of Robert Venton and Margaret Adams. Wit. Thomas and Mary Venton.

bo. the 20th. Ann of Hunlock Woodruff and Maria Lansing. Wit. Abraham and Annatje Ten Eyck.

Jan. 24. Mary of Alexander Young and Elisabeth Sneed.

Jan. 29. Ann of James Milligan and Isabella Kemmel.

Jan. 30. bo. Dec. 23. Sofia of Rykert Kerkenaer and Annatje V. Aalstein. Wit. Eduard Brant, Margarita Kerkenaar.

Feb. 3. bo. Jan. 13. George of Jonathan Pettit and Agness Riddle. Wit. Henry Finn.

Feb. 6. bo. Jan. 18. Maria of Abrahm. Eight, and Catharina Brooks. Wit. Hendrik and Catharina V. Woert.

bo. Jan. 7. Jacob of Daniel Schermerhoorn and Maria V. d. Poel. Wit. Jacob and Gerritje Schermerhoorn.

bo. Jan. 24. Cornelia of Obadia V. Benthuisen and Hanna Rumney. Wit. Obadia and Cornelia Lansing.

bo. Jan. 8. Hendrik of Johannes Aarnout and Elisabeth Buys. Wit. Pieter and Geertruy de Garmo.

bo. Jan. 4. Annatje of Wilhelmus Rouw and Geertruy Schuuk. Wit. Pieter Raauw, Marytje Schuuk.

Feb. 18. bo. Jan. 1. John of John Haswell and Mary Holliday.

Feb. 20. bo. Jan. 30. Stephanus of Jeremie Muller and Catharina Moor. Wit. Stephanus and Catharina Muller.

bo. Jan. 12. Gerrit Theunissen of Folkert V. Vechten and Elisabeth V. d. Berg. Wit. Gerrit and Margarita V. d. Berg.

1780

bo. Feb. 4. John Henry of Eduard Compstead and Mary V. Schaik. Wit. Anthony and Alida Bratt.

Feb. 20. bo. the 8th. Rebecca of John V. Esch and Margarita V. Woert. Wit. Cornelis and Cathalyntje V. d. Berg.

bo. Jan. 16. Eva of Gysbert V. d. Berg and Jannetje Witbeek. Wit. Hannes and Eva Witbeek.

bo. the 18th. Jannetje of Abraham G. Lansing and Tanneke Yates. Wit. Jacob G. and Femmetje Lansing.

Coenraad of Coenraad Burger and Catharina Mook. Wit. Hendrik and Elisabeth Mook.

bo. Dec. 17. Margarita of Cornelis V. d. Zee and Annatje Veder. Wit. Jacob and Alida Look.

bo. Dec. 23. Nicolaas of Daniel Bratt and Christina Beekman. Wit. Christoffer and Maria Beekman.

Pemberton of John Cool and Annatje Daniels. Wit. William Pemberton, Geertruy Dawson.

Feb. 21. Sara of John Ross and Mary Russel. Wit. Abrm. Sunts, Rachel Clement.

bo. Jan. 16. Abraham of Hendrik Muller and Cath. V. Ostrander. Wit. Abraham and Elisabeth Ten Broeck.

Rachel of Denys McCarty and Nency Homes. Wit. Abraham and Elisabeth V. Deuzen.

bo. July 15. Elisabeth of Samuel Lancaster and Sara Warren.

Feb. 27. bo. Dec. 15. Sara of Judlow Cranker and Neeltje De Garmo. Wit. Johs. E. and Maria Lansing.

bo. Jan. 5. Geertje of Eldert V. Woert and Elisabeth Fonda. Wit. Jacob and Geertje V. Franken.

bo. Feb. 21. Philip of John Foreest and Elbertje V. Aalstein. Wit. Philip Foreest, Maria Bloemendal.

Feb. 27. bo. Feb. 2. Gerritje of Frerik Meinerssen and Machteld Witbeek. Wit. Jonathan and Gerritje Witbeek.

bo. Dec. 27. Nicolaas of George Rees and Anna Bulloks. Wit. Philip Rees, Nelly Calligan.

bo. Jan. 31. Immetje of Franciscus Marshal and Geertruy V. Deuzen. Wit. Daniel and Elisabeth Marshall.

Mar. 5. Hendrik of Johs. Albrecht and Rosina Buis. Wit. Johs. and Rebecca V. Etten.

Mar. 19. bo. the 5th. Jan Dirkse of Abrahm. Y. V. Aarnem and Anneke Bogert. Wit. Jacob Lansing, Willempje Winne.

1780
bo. the 13th. Mary and Jennet (twins) of Alexander McGriger and Ebbie McVie.

Mar. 26. bo. the 22d. Helena of Johs. V. Woert and Cathalyntje Lansing. Wit. Hendrik and Helena Lansing.

bo. the 1st. Samuel of Joseph McChesney and Mary Monnex.

Mar. 27. bo. Feb. 11. Johan Pieter of Samuel Roos and Elisabeth Rees. Wit. Johs. and Elisabeth Kemp.

Apr. 2. bo. Feb. 28. Annatje, of Gysbert V. Santen and Rebecca Winne. Wit. John and Lydia Fryer.

bo. Mar. 3. Rachel of Christoffer Oly and Cornelia Kerl. Wit. Johs. and Rachel Witbeek.

bo. Feb. 25. Christina of Gerrit Ostrander and Christina V. d. Berg. Wit. Hendrik V. Hoesen, Elisabeth Eversen.

Apr. 9. bo. the 1st. Arriaantje of John N. Bleecker and Margarita V. Deuzen. Wit. Johs. M. V. Harlingen, Elisabeth V. Deuzen.

bo. Mar. 10. Catharina of Andries Beessinger and Jannetje Bratt. Wit. Hermanus and Catharina V. Aalstein.

Apr. 9. bo. Mar. 22. Christina of Saml. Witbeek and Rebecca Buis. Wit. Zacharias and Christina Shoek.

bo. the 4th. Jacobus of Jacob V. Loon and Christina Schuyler. Wit. Johs. V. Loon, Maria Schuyler.

Apr. 16. bo. Mar. 15. Jacobus of Obadia Lansing and Cornelia V. Benthuisen. Wit. Baltes and Elisabeth V. Benthuisen.

bo. Mar. 4. Elisabeth of Andries Trouex and Cathal. Wyngaerd. Wit. John and Elisabeth Davis.

bo. the 6th. Pieter of Gerrit V. Wie and Cath. Lansing. Wit. Pieter V. Wie, Egbertje V. d. Berg.

Apr. 16. bo. Jan. 17. Catharina of Evert Oothout and Margarita Davenpoort. Wit. Gerrit and Immetje Witbeek.

Margarita of Andries Ouderkerk and Annatje Fero. Wit. David Fero, Margarita Freelig.

Hendrik of Hendrik Hindermond and Baatje Smith. Wit. Hendrik and Tempe Burhans.

bo. Mar. 14. Jacob of Benjamin Van Etten and Catharina Earl. Wit. Jacob and Lea Elmendorp.

Apr. 23. bo. Mar. 12. Antony of Anthony Briesch and Cathalina Yates. Wit. Adam and Neeltje Fonda.

1780

bo. Mar. 9. Gerrit of Jacobus V. Valkenburg and Catharina Siksby. Wit. Gerrit Siksby, Marritje Olfer.

bo. Feb. 15. Reinier of John Reyley and Cathalina V. d. Berg. Wit. Reinier V. d. Berg, Elisabeth Vinhagen.

Apr. 26. Hendrik of Eldert Groot and Alida Gerritsen. Wit. Barent and Annatje Vosburg.

Apr. 30. bo. Mar. 9. Marytje of Johs. Bulsing and Mally Wilson. Wit. Archibld and Grace Rutherford.

Apr. 30. bo. the 23d. Cornelis of Arent V. Deuzen and Margarita McCloud. Wit. Cornelis and Lea V. Deuzen.

bo. Mar. 30. Jurjen of Augustinus Sharp and Marytje V. Aalstein. Wit. Coenraad and Elisabeth Sharp.

May 7. bo. Apr. 10. Catharina of Nicolaas Claver and Susanna Merridith. Wit. Andries Viele, Cathalyntje Hanssen.

May 14. bo. the 3d. Pieter of Pieter Broeks and Francyntje Wendel. Wit. Mathew and Lydia Visscher.

bo. the 12th. Sara of John Grahams and Debora Staats. Wit. Gerrit and Catharina Staats.

bo. Apr. 12. Barent of Stephen J. Schuyler and Lena Ten Eyck. Wit. Johs. Ten Eyck, Sara Ten Broeck.

May 21. Antje of Gerrit V. d. Poel and Margarita Wilson. Wit. Matheus and Elisabeth V. d. Poel.

bo. the 15th. Annatje of Pieter Groesbeek and Alida V. Aarnem. Wit. Albert and Marytje Slingerland.

bo. the 6th. Tryntje of John and Alida V. Wie. Wit. Casparus and Tryntje Conyn.

bo. the 15th. Lena of John Passagie and Margarita Crumm. Wit. Johs. and Margarita Redly.

bo. the 1st. Tanneke of Jurjen Herrick and Jannetje V. Buuren. Wit. Pieter and Dorothea V. Buuren.

bo. the 7th. Cornelis of Jacob Cuyler and Lydia V. Vechten. Wit. Cornelis and Jannatje Cuyler.

May 28. bo. the 21st. Christina of Dirck Benson and Marytje Wyngaard. Wit. Eduard and Jannetje Davies.

June 4. bo. May 27. Catharina of Hendrik Will and Margarita Haan. Wit. John and Catharina Maley.

June 11. bo. May 14. Philip of Hans Berringer and Annatje Valentyn. Wit. Philip and Christina Berringer.

June 18. bo. the 14th. Catharine of Eduard S. Willet and Sara Fryer. Wit. Marinus and Maria Willet.

1780

bo. the 13th. Susanna of Ary Evert Everssen and Elisabeth Goey. Wit. Ary and Maria Le Grange.

bo. Jan. 5. Andries of Casp. Halenbeek and Hilletje Sharp. Wit. Andries and Elisabeth Sharp.

bo. May 14. Thomas of Efraim Bennet and Geertruy Bloemendal. Wit. David and Elisabeth Foreest.

June 25. bo. May 27. Margarita of Johs. Schoonmaker and Aaltje Burhans. Wit. Hendrikus and Tempe Burhans.

bo. May 24. Susanna of Johs. Lang and Christina Bratt. Wit. Staats and Marytje Bratt.

bo. the 19th. Margarita of Nicolaas Mersselis and Margarita Groesbeek. Wit. Johs. and Annatje Mersselis.

June 27. bo. May 24. Johannes of Jurjen Steen and Lea Van Roef. Wit. Joh. and Annatje Zeger.

June 28. bo. Apr. 27. Catharina of Edmund Pengburn and Maria V. Ostrander.

July 2. bo. June 23. Sara of Hendrik Koek and Maria Young. Wit. Marten and Sara Meinersse:1.

bo. May 6. Catharina of Jacob Johs. V. Schaik and Marytje V. Buuren. Wit. Cornelis Douw, Catharina V. Schaik.

July 7. bo. June 7. Abraham of Pieter Dox and Cathalyntje Lansing. Wit. Garrit Mersselis, Rebecca Dox.

July 8. bo. Feb. 9. Elisabeth of Daniel Owens and Elisabeth Springsteen. Wit. Johs. Orwort, Ebigl. Clenzy.

July 9. bo. June 16. Matheus of Hannes Conzalus and Machtel Heemstraat. Wit. Matheus and Lydia Visscher.

July 10. bo. June 15. John of James Boyd and Jane McMaster.

July 16. bo. the 6th. Abraham of John Siksby and Lea Davenpoort. Wit. Yzac and Catharina V. Aarnem.

bo. the 10th. Pieter of Theunis Th. V. Vechten and Elisabeth de Wandelaar. Wit. Pieter and Annatje de Wandelaar.

bo. the 6th. Nicolaas of Christoffer Beekman and Maria Thowman. Wit. Daniel and Christina Bratt.

bo. the 10th. Lucas of Johs. Hoogkerk and Margaritha Marthen. Wit. Yzac and Rachel Hoogkerk.

bo. the 8th. Johannes of Bernardus Everssen and Martina Hoghing. Wit. Evert and Elisabeth Evertsen.

July 23. bo. June 28. Hendrik of Johs. Milton and Rosina Shoekat. Wit. Hendrik Milton, Rachel Northen.

1780
bo. June 20. Eduard of Hendrik Chambers and Rachel V. Santen. Wit. Eduard Bratt, Margar. Kerkenaer.

July 26. bo. May 30. Sara of Willm. Johnson and Margarita Knets(?). Wit. Christoffer and Catharina Rof.

July 30. Maria of Jacob Kim and Elisabeth Fort. Wit. Wendell Hildebrand, Marytje Kim.

bo. the 22d. Johannes Evertsen of Jacob Winne and Susanna Everssen. Wit. Johs. Evertsen, Hendrikje Winne.

bo. the 29th. Cornelia of Barent Bogert and Alida V. d. Berg. Wit. Cornelis and Geertje V. d. Berg.

Aug. 1. bo. July 9. Richard of Thomas Sickels and Mary Norwood.

bo. July 15. Mary of Francis Rawert and Carolina Beever.

Aug. 13. bo. July 20. Sara of Thomas Hook and Catharina Crane. Wit. Thomas and Elisab. Cunningham.

bo. the 1st. Cornelis of Gerrit Staats, Jr., and Elisabeth Low. Wit. Barent and Antje Staats.

bo. the 6th. Geertruy of Harmen V. Hoesen and Catharina Witbeek. Wit. Gysbert and Jannetje V. d. Berg.

bo. July 17. Nicolaas of Andries Bratt and Annatje V. d. Kar. Wit. Albert and Marytje V. d. Zee.

Aug. 20. bo. July 25. Jacob of Joh. Voorhees and Jannetje V. Ist.

bo. the 11th. Johs. of John Coldin and Alida V. Wurmer. Wit. Cornelis V. Wurmer, Alida Nesbith.

bo. the 13th. Catharina of Barent Goey and Rachel V. Ostrander. Wit. Johs. and Marytje Muller.

bo. July 22. Arriaantje of Hendrik Mook and Elisabeth Heller. Wit. Jacobus and Annatje Arnhout.

bo. the 12th. Judike of John Cormey and Bregje Zeger. Wit. Samuel Veeder, Neeltje Coen.

bo. June 21. Tanneke of Johs. Fonda and Dirkje Winne. Wit. Marten and Tanneke Foreest.

Aug. 24. bo. the 3d. Yzac of Petrus Sheer and Cath de Voe. Wit. Jan and Jannetje De Voe.

bo. the 12th. Daniel of Cornelis Caghill and Hanna Russell. Wit. Rachel Clement.

Aug. 27. bo. the 21st. Wynand of Hendrik V. Hoesen and Elisabeth Evertsen. Wit. Martinus Sharp and Sara Downing.

1780

Aug. 27. bo. the 22d. Margarita of Jan Miller and Annatje Bratt. Wit. Johs. and Sara Knoet.

bo. the 20th. Rebecca of Pieter W. Yates and Anna M. Helmes. Wit. Pieter Fiers, Mary Mag. Tibout.

bo. the 20th. Gosen of Jacob and Elisabeth V. Schaik. Wit. Gosen and Elsje V. Schaik.

bo. the 6th. Magdalena of Coenraad Harwich and Magdalena Meyer. Wit. Philip Meyer, Vrome Walter.

bo. Aug. 26. Arriaantje of Leonard Gansevoord, Jr., and Maria V. Rensselaer. Wit. Abrahm. A. and Elsje Lansing.

Aug. 31. bo. the 19th. Mary of Hugh McAdams and Catharina Gerritson.

Sept. 3. bo. the 27th. Elisabeth of Thomas Easterly and Bata V. Woert. Wit. Theunis and Elisabeth V. Woert.

Sept. 17. bo. Aug. 13. Rebecca of Philip Viele and Marytje Bratt. Wit. Cornelis and Eva V. d. Berg.

bo. Aug. 29. Maria of John Fingy and Maria Finky. Wit. Hannes and Marytje Muller.

bo. Aug. 24. Cornelia of Barent V. Yveren and Rebecca Bratt. Wit. Cornelis and Cornelia Van Yveren.

bo. the 8th. Maria of Jacob Yz. Lansing and Susanna Fonda. Wit. Abraham and Maria Fonda.

Sept. 21. bo. Apr. 18. Nicolaus of Theodorus Smith and Caty Simson. Wit. George Starr, Lena Samson.

Sept. 22. bo. July 5. Catharina of Willem Tiets and Maria M. Cregeler. Wit. Jacobus Tiets, Maria Cregeler.

Sept. 23. bo. the 19th. Christina of John McVie and Mary M. Donald.

Sept. 24. bo. Aug. 14. Andries of Hermans V. Salsbergen and Alida Scherp. Wit. Andries and Elisabeth Scherp.

bo. the 4th. Maria of Pieter Webber and Catharina Ward. Wit. Johs. and Catharina Qwakkenbusch.

bo. Aug. 27. Gerrit of Lucas Salsbergen and Marytje V. Buuren. Wit. Cornelis and Fytje V. Salsbergen.

bo. Aug. 27. Pieter of Johs. Poel and Geertruy V. Buuren. Wit. Pieter and Maria V. Buuren.

Jennet of Willem Love and Elisabeth Danielson. Wit. Andries Viele, Susanna Claver.

Oct. 1. bo. Sept. 18. Maria of Rutger Bleecker and Catharina Elmendorp. Wit. Petrus and Maria Elmendorp.

bo. Sept. 19. Bernardus of Frans Harssen and Rebecca Spoor. Wit. Albertus and Anna Bloemendal.

1780

bo. Sept. 24. Susanna of Nicolaas Hieralymon and Jannetje Waldrom. Wit. Johs. and Engeltje V. Hoesen.

bo. Aug. 24. Marytje of Pieter Zeeger and Annatje Huik. Wit. Staats and Marytje Bratt.

Oct. 5. bo. Aug. 11. John of William Loth and Nency Jackson.

Oct. 8. bo. Sept. 14. Sara of Hendrik and Annatje Zeger. Wit. Evert Zeger, Bregje Zeeger.

Oct. 15. bo. Sept. 26. Annatje of John Grahams and Mary Fryer. Wit. Eduard and Sara Willet.

bo. June 30. Pieter of James Flyn and Jannetje Vroman(?). Wit. Pieter and Lena Winne.

bo. Sept. 8. Anthony of Johannes Bratt and Saartje Wendel. Wit. Theunis and Cathalyntje Bratt.

Oct. 17. bo. July 4. Jacob of Jacobus Springsteen and Rachel Cole.

Oct. 22. bo. Sept. 25. Johannes of Gerrit Staats and Catharina Cunningham. Wit. Johs. Grahams and Debora Staats.

Oct. 25. Rebecca of Andries Bouman and Lea Oosterhout. Wit. Gerrit and Annatje Visscher.

Oct. 29. bo. Sept. 20. Willem of Pieter V. Wie and Ebbetje V. d. Berg. Wit. Willem and Jannetje V. Wie.

bo. the 27th. Margarita of John Banker and Geertruy Jacobs. Wit. Lavinus and Catharina Winne.

bo. the 26th. David of Nicolaas Cleyn and Elisabeth Cougler. Wit. David and Nenny Smith.

Oct. 31. bo. Sept. 2. Jacob Truex of Johs. Evertsen and Jennet White. Wit. Nency Burhans.

Nov. 5. Annatje of Johs. Fletcher and Syntje Zeeger. Wit. Hendrik and Annatje Zeger.

Nov. 12. bo. the 6th. Maria of Johs. Brouwer and Marytje de Wever. Wit. Saml. and Lydia Stringer.

bo. Sept. 10. Jacobus of Cornelis Vroman and Lena Hogh. Wit. Jacobus and Geertruy Vroman.

bo. the 11th. Mary of Joh. Blackny and Marg. McCay.

bo. July 22. Alida of Pieter Bratt and Margarita Fery. Wit. Andries and Aaltje Bratt.

Nov. 19. bo. the 9th. Rachel of Zacharias Sickles and Catharina Sheerum. Wit. Nanning and Rachel Visscher.

1780
Nov. 24. bo. Apr. 27. Pieter of Benjamin Bruster and
Margarita Goey. Wit. Pieter Goey, Mary Young.

Nov. 26. bo. Oct. 21. Bastiaan of Willem Goodbrood
and Barbara Coen. Wit. Martin and Elisabeth Heeugier.

bo. the 21st. Wouter of Jesse De Foreest and Rebecca
V. Santen. Wit. Wouter and Neeltje de Foreest.

bo. Oct. 7. Nicolaas of Cornelis Brouwer and Cathalyntje
McManus. Wit. Johs. and Marritje Brouwer.

bo. Oct. 24. Quiliaan of Philip V. Rensselaer and Maria
Sanders. Wit. Abraham and Elsje Lansing.

Dec. 3. bo. No. 2. Timotheus of Timothy Huston and
Jane McChesny. Wit. Yzac and Antje Fonda.

bo. Nov. 21. Anthony of Anthony Halenbeek and Cornelia Cooper. Wit. Eduard Willet and Ytje Brett.

Dec. 6. bo. Oct. 10. Sara of Christiaan Pender and
Elisabeth Cramer. Wit. Henry Newman, Sara Zyler.

Dec. 7. bo. Nov. 2. Cathalyntje of Gerrit Wendel and
Machtel Heemstraat. Wit. Gerrit and Aaltje Lansing.

bo. Nov. 15. Sara of Martinus Cruger and Cathalyntje
Foreest. Wit. Bastiaan and Dirkje Crugier.

Dec. 9. bo. Nov. 21. Willem of Petrus Qwakkenbusch
and Mary Sheffield. Wit. Wouter and Cornelia Qwakkenbusch.

bo. Nov. 30. Joseph of Lodewyk Obryan and Catharina
Rendell. Wit. Joseph and Elisabeth Clyn.

bo. Nov. 17. Stephen of Philip P. Schuyler and Annatje
Wendell.

Dec. 13. bo. Nov. 10. Eduard of Frans Hoghil and Cornelia Foreest. Wit. Reynier and Annatje V. Yveren.

Dec. 17. bo. the 10th. Arriaantje of William Winzelo
Crannel and Marytje Emans. Wit. Robert and Arriaantje
Crennel.

bo. Nov. 16. Maria of Evert V. d. Berg and Janetje V.
Schaik. Wit. Gerrit Witbeek, Maria V. Schaik.

bo. Nov. 14. Helena of Jacob I. Lansing and Jannetje
Visscher. Wit. Lavinus and Maria Lansing.

Dec. 22. bo. Nov. 16. Anna Margarita of Abrahm.
Hoogteling and Annatje Buys. Wit. Hannes and Anna M.
Muller.

Dec. 24. bo. the 16th. Agnietje of Casparus V. Wie and
Jannetje Winne. Wit. Hendrikus and Maria Bratt.

1780-1781

bo. the 22d. Abraham of Jacob V. Deuzen and Elsje Lansing. Wit. Abraham Lansing, Engeltje V. Deusen.

bo. Nov. 28. Abraham of Theunis E. Slingerland and Margarita Hanssen. Wit. Abraham and Rebecca Slingerland.

bo. Nov. 7. Catharina of Jacob V. Olinda and Elisabeth Schermerhoorn. Wit. George Ray, Catharina T. Broek.

bo. the 20th. Anthony of Stuart Dean and Pietertje Bratt. Wit. Anthony and Alida Bratt.

Dec. 26. bo. Oct. 27. Frederik of Nicolaas and Maria Christman. Wit. Frederik Raff (?), Elisabeth Pillington.

bo. Nov. 28. Pieter of Hans Christman and Cath. Docksteder. Wit. Pieter and Geertruy Schuyler, Hendrik and Elisabeth Lycher.

bo. Nov. 4. Margarita of Johs. Burk(?) and Elisabeth Riemsnyder. Wit. Fred Wals, Marg. Kerker(?).

Dec. 29. bo. Oct. 30. Isabella of Hugh McChesny and Johanna Plumb(?).

bo the 5th. Samuel of John McChesny and Cat. Heens.

bo. the 6th. Adam Winne of Hans Van Aalstein and Dirkje Winne. Wit. Adam and Catharina Winne.

Dec. 29. bo. Oct. 22. Catharina of Stephen Derham and Susanna Cool. Wit. David Chatfield, Nency Cunningham.

bo. Nov. 19. Job of Uzia Congel and Mary Hungerford.

Dec. 30. bo. Nov. 8. Hugh of Mordac McCloud and Christina Rose. Wit. Hugh and Marg. Frasier.

Dec. 31. bo. Nov. 25. Elisabeth of Zepherinus Koch and Elisabeth Hall. Wit. Hendrik and Maria Koch.

bo. Oct. 14. Andries of Wilhelmus Heermans and Antje Snissen. (?). Wit. Wynand and Annatje V. d. Berg.

1781, Jan. 7. bo. Nov. 30. Maria of Johs. Oosterhout and Agnetje Winne. Wit. Pieter Winne, Marytje Oosterhout.

bo. Nov. 13. Jannetje of Thoms. Brown and Sara Fairchild. Wit. Christiaan and Elizabeth La Grange.

bo. Dec. 24. Annatje of Andries Douw and Catharina Foreest. Wit. Anthony and Cathalyntje Groesbeek.

Jan. 10. bo. Dec. 14. John of Thoms. Burghes and Mary Geyer. Wit. John and Mary Burghes.

Jan. 11. bo. Nov. 31. James of John McClosky and Mary Nengels.

1781

Jan. 14. bo. Dec. 27. Elisabeth of Gerrit Heyer and Jannetje V. Slyk. Wit. Theunis and Sofia V. Slyk.

bo. the 7th. Annatje of Cornelis Brouwer and Elisabeth Visbach. Wit. Gerardus and Annatje Beekman.

bo. Jan. 5. Judike of John J. Wendell and Alida Hoogkerk. Wit. Matheus and Lydia Visscher.

bo. Nov. 25. Jannetje of David Winne and Marytje Spaan. Wit. Daniel and Jannetje Winne.

Jan. 15. bo. Dec. 15. Mary of John Cummings and Isabella McCay.

bo. May 9, 1779. William of Normand and Elenor McDonald.

Jan. 19. bo. Jan. 1. Elisabeth of Wilm. Hardin and Any Dodg. Wit. Johs. and Elisabeth Hood.

Feb. 18. bo. the 11th. Anthony of Pieter and Vrouwtje Bratt. Wit. Johs. and Sara Bratt.

bo. July 30. Yzac of Milbury V. Hoezen and Antje Beeving. Wit. Adam and Santje Vroman.

Feb. 19. bo. Nov. 6. Margaret of Willem Ebbet and Mary Jackson.

bo. Jan. 17. James of James Pawl and Ann McEwan.

Feb. 22. bo. Apr. 27, 1780. Johs., of David Allen and Janet Stuart.

Feb. 25. bo. Jan. 26. Pieter of Judlof Krankert and Neeltje Gardenier. Wit. Hendrik Schermerhoorn, Cornelia Lansing.

bo. Jan. 27. Wilhelmus of Gerrit Hoogteling and Annatje Oosterhout. Wit. Wilhelmus and Marytje Oosterhout.

bo. the 22d. Maria of Willem Staats and Annatje Yates. Wit. Jochum Staats, Annatje Mersselis.

bo. the 11th. Daniel Flensburg of Daniel Marshall and Elisabeth Cochran. Wit. Franciscus and Geertruy Marshall.

bo. Oct. 18. Mary of Leonard Chambers and Fenny Kief. Wit. Arthur Kief, Caty Obryan.

Feb. 26. bo. Dec. 23. Jeremia of Joseph Springsteden and Elisabeth Matthews. Wit. Jeremia and Christina Springstede.

Feb. 26. bo. Jan. 22. Elisabeth of George Rodgers and Eleonor Murray.

bo. the 16th. Lavaruke of John Way and Hilletje Muller. Wit. Hendrik and Marytje Gardenier.

1781

Mar. 3. bo. Dec. 20. Alexander of John McMullen and Agness Gordon.

Mar. 4. Catharina Rensselaer of Philip Schuyler and Catharina Rensselaer. Wit. Genl. Washington, James Rensselaer, Mrs. Washington, Margarita Schuyler.

bo. Jan. 24. Rebecca of Hendrik V. d. Kar and Antje Williams. Wit. Dirck V. d. Kar, Catharina de Voe.

Mar. 5. bo. Feb. 16. Roelef of Stephen Bell and Elisabeth Kidney.

Jan. 21. Gerrit of Abraham Staats and Cornelia Lansing. Wit. Garrit and Annatje Lansing.

bo. the 11th. Susanna of David Fonda and Catharina Ten Broek. Wit. Yzac and Susanna Fonda.

bo. Dec. 22. Margarita of George Berringer and Elisabeth Been. Wit. Pieter and Catharina Shirp.

bo. Dec. 8. Rosina of Balthes Bratt and Rosina Fullering. Wit. Hendrik and Elisabeth V. Hoesen.

bo. Oct. 17. Johannes of Joseph V. Santen and Rebecca Garmo. Wit. Hendrik and Tempe Burhans.

Feb. 1. bo. Jan. 8. Yzac of Nicolaas Muller and Cathal. Gardenier. Wit. Johs. and Elis. Muller.

Feb. 2. Sofia Regina of Hendrik Riddeker and Elis. Kloet. Wit. Pieter and Sofia Riddeker.

Feb. 4. bo. Jan. 20. Abraham of Johs. Visscher and Annatje Pearce. Wit. Lavinus and Marytje Lansing.

Feb. 4. bo. Jan. 28. Antje of Gerrit Witbeek and Immetje Perry. Wit. John L. Witbeek, Maria Perry.

bo. Jan. 31. Franciscus of Jacob Pruin and Hendrikje V. Buren. Wit. Casparus and Catharina Pruin.

bo. Dec. 28. Gosen of Martinus V. Yveren and Cornelia V. Schaik. Wit. Gosen and Marytie V. Schaik.

Feb. 5. bo. Oct. 5. Robert of Johs. Warns and Marg. Burnside. Wit. Daniel and Lena Hoogteling.

bo. Jan. 5. David of Daniel Winne and Cath. Hoogteling.

Feb. 11. bo. Jan. 6. Eva of Gerrit Becker and Marytje Wynkoop. Wit. Jacob and Fytje Garmo.

bo. the 9th. Jacob of Hermanus T. Eick and Margarita Bleecker. Wit. Hendrik T. Eyck, Annatje Mancius.

bo. Dec. 25. Lyne of Abraham Bloodgood and Elisab. V. Valkenburg. Wit. Hugh and Rachel Denison.

bo. Dec. 25. Neeltje of Johs. Schermerhoorn and Bata

1781

V. Valkenburg. Wit. Meinard and Geertruy V. Hoesen.

bo. Jan. 16. Catharina of Folkert V. d. Berg and Marytje Vinhagen. Wit. Abraham and Catharina Vinhagen.

Feb. 12. bo. Oct. 2. Caty of Efraim Holbrook and Esther Johnson. Wit. Jeremia and Christoffer Springsteede.

Feb. 16. bo. Oct. 2. Daniel of Neal Gillazny and Mary Jackson.

Mar. 11. bo. Feb. 27. Maria of Willem Groesbeek and Catharina V. Deuzen. Wit. Dirk and Maria Schuyler.

bo. Feb. 12. Marytje of Gerrit Lansing and Alida Fonda. Wit. Noah Jellet, Lena Lansing.

Mar. 14. Margarita of James Flored and Margarita Steen. Wit. Hendrik and Annatje Zeeger.

Mar. 17. bo. the 1st. Mary of Robt. Haswell and Sarah Mark.

Mar. 18. bo. the 10th. John of John Daniels and Sofia Hilton. Wit. Folkert and Geertruy Dashon.

bo. the 11th. Jannetje of Cornelis Douw and Catharina V. Schaik. Wit. Folkert Oothout, Dorothea Zabrisky.

Mar. 25. bo. the 9th. John of Thoms. Lotteridge and Maria Bratt. Wit. William and Mary Philips.

Apr. 1. bo. Mar. 18. Maria of John Berry and Elisabeth Meinerssen. Wit. Frerik and Machteld Meinerssen.

bo. Mar. 29. Hermanus of Cornelis Wendel and Annatje Lansing. Wit. Johs. H. and Geertruy Wendell.

Apr. 7. bo. Mar. 26. Thomas of James Green and Margarita Smith. Wit. Thomas Bareuth, Elisab. Hilton.

bo. Feb. 25. Maria of Johs. E. Lansing and Maria Staats. Wit. Christoffer and Catharina Yates.

bo. Feb. 11. Hendrik of Hendrik Oothout and Lydia Douw. Wit. Folkert and Jannetje Oothout.

bo. the 5th. Johannes of Wendel Hildebrand and Geertruy Visbach. Wit. Cornelis and Elisabeth Brouwer.

bo. Mar. 23. Geertruy of John Martins and Cath. Beemus. Wit. Philip Meyer, Geertruy Bovie.

Apr. 4. bo. Mar. 2. Dirk of Carel Heemstraat and Geertruy V. d. Werken. Wit. Johs. and Rachel V. d. Werken.

Apr. 15. bo. the 14th. Sara of Lavinus Winne and Maria Lansing. Wit. David and Sara Groesbeek.

Apr. 15. bo. Mar. 8. Lena of Willem Hoogteling and Maria Bloemendal. Wit. Johs. and Arriaantje Hoogteling.

1781

bo. the 13th. Angus of Alexander Kemmel and Mary McMuller.

Apr. 16. bo. the 13th. Pieter of Jeremie Lansing and Lena Wendell. Wit. Pieter and Elisabeth Lansing.

Apr. 21. bo. Nov. 3. Elisabeth of John Nightingale and Elisabeth Neithhall.

Apr. 22. bo. Jan. 10. Evert Swart of Willem V. Benthuisen and Margarita Conklin. Wit. Baltes V. Benthuisen, Elisabeth Rumney.

bo. Mar. 20. Alida of Gerrit V. d. Berg and Rebecca Fonda. Wit. Jacob and Dirkje Fonda.

bo. the 18th. Lena of Jacob Roseboom and Hester Lansing. Wit. Barent H. and Lena Ten Eyck.

bo. Mar. 7. John of Jurjaan Hoghing and Annatje Wite. Wit. Jacob Look and Violet White.

bo. the 18th. Margaret of Francis McKinsy and Ellison Watson.

Apr. 26. bo. Mar. 19. Andries of Maas V. d. Berg and Catharina Sheer. Wit. Andries and Elisabeth Sheer.

Apr. 28. bo. Feb. 9. William of Henry Millar and Mary McCarty. Wit. Abigail Clench.

April 29. bo. Mar. 26. Yzac of Abraham Lansing and Annatje V. d. Berg. Wit. Jacob and Susanna Lansing.

bo. the 4th. Douwe of Theunis W. Slingerland and Rachel Bogert. Wit. Barent and Willempje Bogert.

bo. the 21st. Aaltje of John D. Groesbeek and Cathalyntje V. Schaik. Wit. Yzac and Elisabeth V. Aarnem.

Apr. 29. bo. the 24th. Arriaantje of Abrahm. A. Lansing and Elsje V. Rensselaer. Wit. Quiliaan and Maria V. Rensselaer.

May 6. bo. Mar. 13. Abraham of Pieter V. Buuren and Dorothea Shutter. Wit. Matheus and Elisabeth Poel.

bo. the 1st. Harmen of Samuel Marl and Rachel Gardenier. Wit. Harmen Qwakkenbusch, Elisabeth Fyle.

bo. Mar. 27. Robert of Robt. Kemmel and Sara McDavid.

May 12. bo. the 9th. Alida of Johs. V. Hoesen and Engeltje V. Deusen. Wit. Matheus and Bregje Aerssen.

bo. Apr. 11. Eva of Willem Witbeek and Catherina Foreest. Wit. Pieter and Rachel Witbeek.

May 25. bo. Mar. 20. Jacob of Jacob McDonald and Lydia Pengburn.

1781

May 27. bo. Mar. 26. Simon of Hendrik Zeger and Marg. Coen. Wit. John Cortney (?), Annatje Zeger.

bo. Apr. 15. Maria of John de Voe and Annatje Conner. Wit. Ned Davies and Marytje Conner.

bo. Mar. 20. Jacob of Jacob McDonald and Lydia Pengburn. (Repetition.)

bo. Apr. 21. Thomas of Thoms. Haslet and Margt. Gibson.

bo. Apr. 15, 1776, Alexander; bo. Feb. 1, 1778, Margaret; bo. Dec. 4, 1780, William, of Price Kemmel and Margaret Clark.

June 2. bo. Apr. 31. Helena of Yzac V. Wie and Neeltje Oosterhout. Wit. Yzac and Catharina V. Aernem.

bo. Mar. 20. John of Elias Willard and Catharina Livingston. Wit. Johannes and Sara Ten Eyck.

June 2. bo. May 7. Catharina of Matheus Poel and Elisabeth Shutter. Wit. Gerrit and Margarita Poel.

bo. May 10. Petrus of Hendrik Crennel and Jacomina Bloemendal. Wit. Nicolaas Hoghen, Annatje Crennel.

June 8. bo. Apr. 13. William of Alexander Kemmel and Catharina Steel.

June 10. bo. May 31. Agnietje of Cornelis and Cathalyntje V. d. Berg. Wit. Wilhelmus and Agnietje V. d. Berg.

June 15. bo. Jan. 21. Elisabeth of Thoms. Mackelwayn and Jenny Mackelwayn.

June 19. bo. the 14th. Jenny of John Stuart and Jane Kemmel.

June 20 or 23. bo. Apr. 16. William of Joseph Stalker and Anna Albrecht.

bo. May 9. Hilletje of Ruben Conger and Lena de Voe.

bo. Jan. 30. Lydia of Job Shawman and Any Conger.

June 24. bo. the 22d. Catharina of Hendrik V. Wie and Maria Merthen. Wit. Cornelis J. and Ytje V. Wie.

Maria of Willem de Wit and Hester Rykman. Wit. Pieter and Mary Qwakkenbusch.

June 28. bo. Aug. 20. John of Neal McCay and Catharine McKinzy. Wit. John Grant and Nency McDonald.

July 1. bo. June 1. Hendrik of Cornelis Huyk and Hester Gardenier. Wit. Hendrik and Maria Huyk.

July 3. bo. June 12. Mary of Pieter Sharp and Mary Donneway.

1781

July 4. Annatje of Thoms. King and Jannetje Krankheit. Wit. Stephen and Elisab. Bell.

July 8. bo. June 12. David of Christiaan Fero and Catharina Levison. Wit. Hendrik and Maria Fero.

bo. the 1st. Abraham Trouex of Albert Slingerland and Christina V. Franken. Wit. Maas V. Franken, Marytje Slingerland.

July 15. bo. the 5th. Joachim of John Staats and Jenny McClallen. Wit. Philip and Annatje Staats.

July 22. bo. June 31 (?). Ann of Alexander Thomson and Nelly Grant. Wit. John Thomson, Barbara Grant.

bo. the 15th. John of Joseph Hall and Johanna Pettison.

bo. June 22. Jacob of George McDoles and Catharine Zeger. Wit. Jacob and Rachel Look.

Alexander of Daniel McClance(?) and Rachel McKentisch. Wit. Gregor Grant.

bo. the 20th. Malcom of Pieter McDougal and Catharina Thomson.

Catharina of John and Sara Cregg. Wit. Jacob Bauh, Hanna Bacchus.

July 29. bo. the 25th. Elisabeth of John Gates and Geertruy V. Franken. Wit. Michel and Marytje Besset.

bo. the 20th. Hendrik of Balthes V. Benthuisen and Elisabeth Rumney. Wit. Hendrik V. Benthuisen, Catharyntje Winne.

bo. the 4th. Evert of Wynand V. d. Berg and Annatje Cooper. Wit. Evert and Jannetje V. d. Bergh.

bo. the 8th. Reinier of Pieter Foreest and Pietertje V. Aalstein. Wit. Reinier and Cornelia V. Aalstein.

July 29. bo. the 24th. Theunis of Dirk de Foreest and Rebecca Bratt. Wit. Theunis and Cathalyntje Bratt.

bo. the 26th. Gysbert of Elia Arnold and Geertje Groesbeek. Wit. Gysbert and Sara V. Brakelin.

Aug. 12. bo. July 6. Elisabeth of Abrah. Veder and Neeltje Schuyler. Wit. Simon Veder, Susanna Roseboom.

bo. July 19. Elisabeth of Meinard V. Hoesen and Geertruy Vinhagen. Wit. Gerrit Marsselis, Rebecca Dox.

bo. June 25. John of Salomo Sharp and Rachel Halenbeek. Wit. Andries Sharp, Elisabeth Goey.

Aug. 19th. bo. the 15th. Cornelis of Cornelis Cuyler and Jannetje Yates. Wit. Jacob and Lydia Cuyler.

1781

bo. the 16th. Sara of Pieter de Riemer and Elsje Barbington. Wit. Pieter Wabber, Sara Barbington.

bo. the 5th. Marytje of Nicolaas V. d. Berg and Catharina Waldron. Wit. Gerrit and Marytje Waldrom.

bo. the 17th. Theunis of Johs. Hanssen and Geertruy Slingerland. Wit: Abraham and Rebecca Slingerland.

bo. July 28. Maria of Reynier V. Hoesen and Engeltje Cool. Wit. William and Rachel McGlochum.

Sept. 2. bo. Aug. 24. Andrew Van Schaak of Eduard Compstone and Mary V. Schaak. Wit. Anthony Bratt (or V. Schaak), Alida Bratt.

bo. Aug. 2. Willem of Hendrikus Burhans and Tempe Du Mont. Wit. John B. and Neeltje Du Mont.

bo. Aug. 23. John Sanders of John Jac. Beekman and Maria Sanders. Wit. John, Jr., and Debora Sanders.

bo. Aug. 19. Andries of Yzaac J. V. Aarnem and Catharina V. Wie. Wit. Abraham and Jacomyntje Van Wie.

Sept. 4. bo. Aug. 29. Elisabeth of Alexander Clark and Nency Grant. Wit. John Grant, McCovie, Caty McMuller.

Sept. 9. bo. the 1st. Jannetje of Obadia Cooper and Annatje V. d. Berg. Wit. Abrah. Cooper, Marytje Veder.

bo. Aug. 9. Johannes of Jacob J. Lansing and Maria Knipp. Wit. Lavinus and Maria Winne.

bo. Aug. 3. Maria of Charles McCoy and Maayke Ouderkerk.

bo. July 18. Nency of William McCullogh and Elisabeth Bride.

Sept. 16. bo. Aug. 24. Christina of Philip de Foreest and Annatje V. Deusen. Wit. Wilhelmus and Christina V. Deuzen.

bo. the 9th. Maria of William Talbert and Annatje Young. Wit. Frans and Rebecca Harssen.

bo. the 10th. Harmen of Johs. de Wandelaar, Jr., and Gerritje Gansevoort. Wit. Theunis and Elisabeth V. Vechten.

Sept. 20. bo. the 16th. Christina of Daniel McDonal and Nency McGrieger. Wit. Gregory Grant, Margaret Orchard.

Oct. 6. bo. Sept. 29. James of James Mitcher and Mary McGrieger.

1781

bo. Sept. 25. Neeltje of Frerik Meinerssen and Elisabt. Waldrom. Wit. Folkert and Jannetje V. Vechten.

bo. Sept. 23. Elisabeth of Johs. V. Imburg and Annatje Flensburg. Wit. Nicolaas and Jannetje Jeralemons.

bo. Aug. 27. Abraham of Alexander Bulsing and Alida Oothout. Wit. Jellis and Tietje Winne.

Oct. 14. bo. the 12th. John of Richard Leish and Syntje Fonda. Wit. Stephen Lush, Elsje Fonda.

Oct. 16. bo. Sept. 8. Elisabeth of Ebenezer Ward and Marytje Hunter.

Oct. 21. bo. Sept. 8. Catharina of Robert Winne and Hillegond V. Franken. Wit. Albert and Christina Slingerland.

bo. the 14th. Wouter of Pieter Groesbeek and Alida V. Aarnem. Wit. David and Geertruy Winne.

bo. the 18th. Abraham of Abrahm. Hoogkerk and Antje. Hilton. Wit. Abraham and Jannetje Yates.

bo. Sept. 12. Cornelis of Yzac Fonda and Antje V. Santvoort. Wit. Cornelis and Willempje V. Santvoort.

Oct. 23. bo. Sept. 15. William of Joseph McChesny and Margarita Mullenhicks.

Oct. 28. bo. Sept. 25. Coenraad of Jacob Elmendorp, Jr., and Lea Bloemendal. Wit. Coenraad and Sara Elmendorp.

Oct. 31. bo. Sept. 27. John of Joseph Haswell and Mary Mark.

Nov. 11. bo. Oct. 13. Anna of Abraham Fonda and Hendrikje Lansing. Wit. Yzac Lansing, Annatje V. Woert.

Lucas of Andries Wesselsen and Geertruy Knoet. Wit. Lucas and Annatje Wesselsen.

bo. the 10th. Cornelia of Gerrit Rykman and Elisabeth V. Buren. Wit. John and Cornelia Price.

bo. Oct. 6. Annatje of John Droit and Sara Revison. Wit. Jacob V. Woert, Cornelia V. Antwerpen.

bo. Oct. 1. Hendrik of Folkert Oothout and Jannetje Bogart. Wit. Cornelis V. Schaak, Marytje Comstone.

bo. Oct. 27. Charlotte of Daniel Young and Elisabeth V. d. Kar. Wit. Hans Muller, Marytje Fonda.

Nov. 12. July 24. John of James McCastry and Dolly Ramser.

1781-1782

Dec. 3. Hendrikje of Johs. V. Woert and Cathalyntje Lansing. Wit. Jelles and Fytje Winne.

bo. the 26th. Gerrit of Cornelis Waldrom and Alida Goey. Wit. Gerrit Goey, Gerritje V. d. Berg.

Dec. 13. bo. Nov. 26. Gerritje of John N. Bleecker and Margarita V. Deuzen. Wit. Nicolaas and Cathalyntje Bleecker.

bo. Nov. 23. Wessel of Pieter Gansevoort and Catharina V. Schaik. Wit. Wessel and Marytje V. Schaik.

bo. Nov. 20. Anna of Albertus Bloemendal and Anna Harssen. Wit. .Frans and Rebecca Harssen.

Dec. 16. bo. Nov. 10. David of Andries Ouderkerk and Annatje Fero. Wit. Christiaan Fero, Catharina Levison.

bo. Nov. 4. Jacobus of Jacobus V. Schoonhoven and Elisabeth Kloet. Wit. Jacobus and Alida Fonda.

Dec. 18. Catharina of Price Kemmel and Margarita Clark.

bo. Nov. 22. Maria Lansing of Hunlok(?) Woodruff and Maria Lansing. Wit. Jacob Lansing, Lena V. Rensselaer.

Dec. 18. bo. Nov. 26. Elisabeth of James Burnside and Catharina Warren.

bo. Nov. 9. Jane of Thoms. Burnside and Arriaantje T. Eyck.

Dec. 23. bo. the 21st. Johannes of Jacob V. Woert, Jr., and Sara V. Esch. Wit. Philip and Maayke Foreest.

Dec. 27. bo. Nov. 10. Lena of John Benson and Cathal. V. Aalstein. Wit. Gerrit Peek, Marytje V. Aalstein.

Dec. 30. bo. Oct. 19. Stephen of William Colbrecht and Esther V. Deuzen. Wit. Aaron Aarsen, Cornelia V. Deuzen.

bo. the 21st. Jacob Sanders of Jacob G. and Femmetje Lansing. Wit. Jacob and Elsje Lansing.

Dec. 25. bo. the 23d. George Ray of John Ten Broek and Sara Ganzevoort. Wit. George and Catharina Ray.

1782, Jan. 6. bo. Oct. 14. Pieter of Andries Sitzer(?) and Sara Allen. Wit. Wilhelmus Row, Geertruy Soop.

Joseph of David See and Leentje Snyder. Wit. James Young and Annatje Snyder.

Jan. 13. bo. Dec. 10. Cornelia of Mathys Flensburg and Christina Snyder. Wit. Johs. and Cornelis Flensburgh.

bo. the 3d. Abraham of Gerrit A. Lansing and Elisabeth Wynkoop. Wit. Johs. Lansing and Sara Fonda.

1782

Jan. 9. bo. Dec. 25. Johs. of Jacob Buis and Cath. Oothout. Wit. Hannes Albrecht, Resina Buis.

Jan. 11. Joseph and Jane and Elisabeth, triplets, of Andrew Schenklin.

Jan. 20. Cathalyna of Jacob and Geertje Schermerhoorn. Wit. Jacob and Hendrikje Pruin.

bo. the 4th. Catharina of William V. Wie and Jannetje Lansing. Wit. John and Alida Van Wie.

bo. Oct. 12. Catharina of Willem Larraway and Sara Wynkoop. Wit. Johs. and Catharina Wynkoop.

bo. the 12th. Cathalyna of Anthony Groesbeek and Cathalyna Foreest. Wit. John V. Esch, Marytje Pruin.

bo. the 6th. Maria of John G. and Annatje V. Schaick. Wit. Anthony and Annatje Ten Broeck.

Jan. 20. bo. the 1st. Laurens of Frederick Haak and Margarita Scheffer. Wit. Laurens and Maria Frank.

Jan. 27. bo. the 12th. Abraham Yates of Abraham G. Lansing and Susanna Yates. Wit. Abraham, Jr., and Antje Yates.

bo. Dec. 23. Dirk of Jacob Dirk Vander Heydn and Jannetje Yates. Wit. Johannes Van Aernem, Elisabeth Van der Heyden.

bo. Jan. 19. Elisabeth of Jacob Hilton and Sara Barrington. Wit. Barent Dassen and Elisabeth Baily.

Jan. 27. bo. Dec. 11. James of Coenraad Coen and Ann Stafford.

bo. June 10. John of John Watkins and Judith Livingston. Wit. Eduard Livingston, Elisabeth Watkins.

Jan. 21. bo. at Livingston Manor, William of John J. Burrick and Margarita Bratt(?).

Jan. 21. bo. at Livingston Manor. Margaret of John Moor and Christina McKinly.

Feb. 5. bo. Mar. 19. Susanna of Stephen Meyer and Catharina Bernard.

Feb. 7. bo. Oct. 1. Margarita of Pieter Hilton and Judith Bareuth. Wit. Daniel and Margarita Husher.

Feb. 10. bo. Nov. 23. Casparus of William Borrowel and Elisabeth Salsbury. Wit. Jonathan Cannik, Margarita Perry.

bo. the 2d. William of Arent Bratt and Jannetje Hoghing. Wit. Jurjen and Elsje Hoghing.

1782

Feb. 3. bo. Sept. 17. Francis of Francis Jackson and Charlotte Glove. Wit. Henry Molling, Mary Holliday.

Feb. 11. bo. Dec. 22. Philip of Alexander Hamilton and Elisabeth Schuyler. Wit. Philip and Catharina Schuyler.

Feb. 13. bo. Oct. 25. Maria of Eduard Connel and Sara Powlton.

bo. Jan. 22. Annatje of Nanning V. d. Heiden and Catharina Levison. Wit. Harmen and Catharina Levison.

Feb. 22. bo. Dec. 20. Petrus of Pieter Tilton and Margarita Yhl. Wit. Abraham and Margarita V. d. Kar.

Feb. 25. bo. Dec. 7. Jan of Meinard Oothout and Maria Siksby. Wit. Wynand and Annatje V. d. Berg.

bo. the 19th. Elisabeth of Abraham Eight and Catharina Broocks.

bo. the 14th. Elisabeth of Hendrik V. Woert and Cath. Eight.

Mar. 9. bo. Feb. 28. Catharina of Evert Evertsen and Elisabeth Goey. Wit. Benjamin and Catharina Goey.

bo. Feb. 23. Willem of Johs. Lansing and Elisabeth Fryer. Wit. John and Catharina Fryer.

bo. Nov. 22. Pieter of Damas Palmentier and Elisab. Bertley. Wit. Cornelis Bareit, Maria Owen.

Mar. 8. bo. Feb. 3. Catharina of Evert Olver and Rebecca Cooper. Wit. Nicolaas and Cornelia Siksby.

Jeromie of Abrahm. Cuyler and Margarita Wendel. Wit. Pieter and Geertruy Schuyler.

Joh. T. Broeck of David Fonda and Catharina T. Broek. Wit. Gosen and Maria V. Schaick.

Mar. 12. bo. Sept. 7. Sarah of Thoms. Beely and Olive Hall.

Mar. 13. bo. Nov. 22. Thomas of Benjamin Russel and Rachel Bank. Wit. Hudson.

Mar. 24. bo. the 2d. Maria of Theunis E. Slingerland and Margaret Hanssen. Wit. Johs. and Maria Hansse.

Mar. 31. bo. the 23d. Willem of James Donway and Elsje Smith. Wit. Pieter and Marytje Sharp.

bo. the 22d. Petrus of John V. Esch and Margarita V. Woert. Wit. Fytje Winne.

bo. the 13th. Benjamin of Obadia V. Benthuisen and Annatje Rumney. Wit. Gosen and Maria V. Schaik.

Apr. 7. bo. the 3d. Annatje of Frans Struys (or Stuip) and Catharina Wever. Wit. Hannes and Marritje Brower.

1782

Apr. 14. bo. Mar. 6. Sara of Obadia Lansing and Cornelia Benthuisen. Wit. Hendrik and Sara V. Benthuisen.

bo. the 17th. Lea of Franciscus Marshall and Geertruy V. Deuzen. Wit. Wilhelmus and Christina V. Deuzen.

bo. the 20th. Catharina of Johs. Witbeek and Catharina s'Jans. Wit. Petrus and Marytje Ham.

bo. the 10th. Lea of Arent V. Deuzen and Marg. McCloudy. Wit. Gerard Lansing, Lea Ostrander.

Margarita of Charles Smith and Mary Asurne(?). Wit. Johs. and Isabell V. d. Poel.

bo. Feb. 3. Jannetje of Hendrik Bulsing and Neeltje Marus(?). Wit. Evert and Jannetje V. d. R——.

Apr. 21. bo. the 16th. Abraham of Marten V. Buuren and Jannetje Holiday. Wit. Abraham and Jennetje (or Teuntje?) V. Buuren.

Apr. 28. bo. the 13th. Annatje of Lewis Barrington and Margarita Adams. Wit. Marg. Adams.

bo. the 4th. Douwe of Theunis W. Slingerland and Rachel Bogert. Wit. Barent and Willempje Bogert.

May 5. bo. Apr. 16. Elisabeth of Gerrit Staats, Jr., and Elisabeth Low. Wit. Philip and Annatje Staats.

bo. Apr. 4. Hendrik of Gerrit V. d. Berg and Annatje s'Jans. Wit. Joh. and Jane Staats.

May 11. Catharina Douw of Leendert Gansevoort, Jr., and Maria V. Renselaer. Wit. Folkert P. and Catharina Douw.

May 12. bo. Apr. 4. Joseph of John M. Donald and Lydia Pengburn.

May 19. bo. the 8th. Quiliaan of Nicolaas V. Rensselaar and Elsje V. Buuren. Wit. Hendrik and Alida V. Rensselaar.

bo. Apr. 17. Susanna of Reignier V. d. Berg and Elisabeth Vinhagen. Wit. Gysbert and Susanna V. d. Berg.

bo. the 14th. Jelles of Christoffer Bogert and Rebecca Winne. Wit. Jelles and Fytje Winne.

May 26. bo. Apr. 30. Alida of Johs. Visscher and Elisabeth Bratt. Wit. Hendrik and Alida V. Rensselaar.

bo. Apr. 13. Marytje of Nicolaas Siksby and Cornelia Cooper.

bo. Apr. 26. Gerrit of Joseph Boskerk and Susanna Wendel. Wit. John and Cathalyntje Groesbeek.

bo. Mar. 17. Eva of Willem Flensburg and Christina

1782

Boeches. Wit. Jesse and Rebecca Foreest.

June 2. bo. May 26. Catharina of Dirk Hanssen and Lena Low. Wit. Johs. J. and Catharina Beekman.

bo. Aug. 3, 1777, Lachelin; bo. Aug. 5, 1781, Daniel, of Daniel Watson and Isabella Bosse.

June 8. bo. May 12. Elisabeth of Arthur Haswell and Mary Coughtry.

June 9. bo. Mar. 26. James of David Allen and Jennet Stuard.

bo. Apr. 13. Peter of William Patterson and Mary McEntee.

bo. Mar. 8. Cornelia of Mulbury Van Hoesen and Antje Bevens. Wit. Frans Van Hoesen and Gertruy Schermerhorn.

June 11. bo. May 19. Elisabeth of John McKenny and Elisabeth McCarty. Wit. John Ja. Beekman, Mary Saunders.

July 28. Joachim of Barent Staats and Antje Winne. Wit. Joachim and Elisabeth Staats.

Aug. 3. bo. July 6. Hendrik of Pieter Hanssen and Rachel Fonda. Wit. John and Engeltje Fonda.

Aug. 18. bo. the 2d. Albert of Carel Heemstraat and Geertruy V. d. Werken. Wit. Yzak and Elisabeth Ouderkerk.

Aug. 24. bo. July 29. Jannetje of Benjamin Hoevenbach and Jenneke Osterhout. Wit. Piete Winne, Mary Oosterhout.

Jaapik of Jacob and Saar (serv.). Wit. Dick and the mother.

Aug. 30. bo. the 28th. Rachel of Hendrik I. Lansing and Helena Winne. Wit. Jacob and Willempje Lansing.

bo. the 23d. Simon of Wilhelmus V. Deuzen and Rachel Pietersen. Wit. Arent and Catharina V. Deusen.

Sept. 5. bo. July 31. Margaret of James Pawl and Ann McCewen.

bo. Aug. 10. John of Jacob Mook and Mary McGee.

bo. the 4th. Reynold and Alexander, of Mordach McCloud and Christian Rose.

Sept. 5. bo. Aug. 8. Rebecca of David Foreest and Elisabeth Witbeek. Wit. Reinier and Rebecca V. Yveren.

1782

John of Alexander McGreeger and Appy M. Veen.

Sept. 12. bo. Aug. 26. Anna of John Fulson and Elisabeth File.

bo. the 7th. Samuel Stringer of Stephen Lush and Lydia Stringer. Wit. Samuel and Rachel Stringer.

bo. the 6th. Maria of Bernardus Evertsen and Martina Hoghen. Wit. Jurjaan Hoghen, Maria Charless.

Sept. 20. bo. Aug. 31. Cornelis of Cornelis V. Aalstein and Marytje Goey. Wit. Pieter and Gerritje V. Aalstein.

bo. the 3d. Alida of Jacobus V. Franken and Geertje Fonda. Wit. Gerrit I. and Rachel Visscher.

bo. Aug. 16. Evert of Philip Wendell and Geertruy Vosburg. Wit. David and Marytje Scott.

Sept. 28. bo. Aug. 9. Rachel of Cornelis V. d. Zee and Annatje Veder. Wit. Andries and Elisabeth Van Wie.

Oct. 6. bo. the 30th. Elisabeth of John Williams and Mary Love. Wit. Christiaan and Margarita Erin.

June 16. bo. May 29. Johannes of Johs. V. Benthuysen and Geesje V. Hoesen. Wit. Obadia and Cornelia Lansing.

June 16. bo. the 12th. Frans of Quiliaan Winne and Maria Perry. Wit. Frans and Anneke Winne.

June 23. bo. May 30. William of Andrew Collins and Charlotte M. Hart.

June 23. bo. the 18th. Pieter of Joh. De Garmo and Margarita Wendell. Wit. Pieter and Geertruy De Garmo.

bo. the 8th. Rachel of Pieter V. Deuzen and Catharina V. Wie. Wit. Willem and Jannetje Winne.

bo. May 12. Janneke of David Foreest and Rachel V. d. Heide. Wit. Marten and Tanneke Foreest.

bo. May 24. John of Robt. Ten Baer and Annatje Slingerland. Wit. John and Lena Ten Baer.

bo. May 20. Elisabeth of Hendrik Oothout and Lydia Douw. Wit. Gerrit and Ruth Lansing.

June 29. bo. the 24th. Dirkje of Jacob V. Loonen and Christina Schuyler. Wit. Abraham and Neeltje Veder.

July 3. bo. Apr. 5. Ann of Timothy Bussing and Jane Crosby.

July 8. bo. the 3d. Abraham of Johs. Brower and Marritje de Wever. Wit. Frans and Catharina Stoop.

July 14. bo. June 12. Jesse of Joh. V. Esch and Neeltje de Foreest. Wit. Philip and Maayke Foreest.

1782

bo. June 5. Wyntje of Gerrit Brower and Antje Zeger. Wit. Jan and Marytje Zeger.

bo. the 2d. Gysbert of Dirk Benson and Marytje Wyngaerd. Wit. Johs. and Marytje Finky.

July 20. bo. the 18th. Jacob of Jacob V. Schaik and Elisabeth Berry. Wit. Gerrit and Jannetje Groesbeek.

July 20. bo. the 17th. Coenraad of Abraham Ten Eyck and Annatje Lansing. Wit. Coenraad and Charlotte Ten Eyck.

bo. the 16th. Maria of Thomas Easterly and Bata V. Woert. Wit. Philip and Maria V. Renselaer.

July 28. bo. the 26th. Wyntje of Pieter Dox and Cathalyntje Lansing. Wit. Gerrit and Wyntje Lansing.

bo. the 20th. Hendrik of John and Cornelia Qwakkenbush. Wit. Hendrik and Elisabeth Qwakkenbush.

Oct. 11. John Brasler of Thomas Sickles and Mary Norwood. Wit. John V. Ingen.

Oct. 13. bo. Sept. 12. Christina of Daniel Bratt and Christina Beekman. Wit. Joh. Bratt, Ytje Halenbeek.

bo. the 11th. Jannetje of Yzac Bogert and Cathalina Hunn. Wit. Folkert and Jannetje V. Vechten.

bo. the 12th. Joseph of John Gates and Geertruy V. Vranken. Wit. John and Annatje Visscher.

Oct. 20. bo. Sept. 22. Johannes of Johs. Sicksby and Lea Davenport. Wit. Meinard and Marytje Oothout.

bo. the 3d. Cornelis of Aaron and Elsje Austin. Wit. William and Hester Colberth.

Oct. 27. bo. Sept. 15. Arriaantje of Philip Schuyler and Anna Wendell. Wit. Johs. and Catharina Wendell.

Oct. 28. bo. the 22d. Jacob and Agnieta of Cornelis V. d. Berg and Cath. Bogert. Wit. Jacob and Marytje Bogert, Will. and Agnietje V. d. Berg.

Nov. 3. bo. Oct. 19. Stephanus of Nicolaas Mersselis and Margarita Groesbeek. Wit. Abraham and Elisabeth Ten Broeck.

bo. Oct. 7. John of William Duer and Catharina Alexander. Wit. George Rose, Catharina Lawrence.

Nov. 10. bo. Sept. 26. Meinard of Gozen V. Schaik and Maria T. Broeck. Wit. Hendrik and Maria Roseboom.

Nov. 17. bo. the 7th. Annatje of Theunis T. V. Vechten

1782-1783
and Elisabeth de Wandelaar. Wit. Pieter and Annatje De
Wandelaar.

Dec. 1. bo. Nov. 30. Sarah of Jacob Y. Lansing and
Susanna Fonda. Wit. Abraham and Hendrikje Fonda.

bo. Nov. 30. Elisabeth of Johs. Hoogkerk and Margarita
Marthen. Wit. Hendrik and Maria V. Wie.

Dec. 8. bo. Nov. 10. Evert of Gerrit Bekker and
Marytje Wynkoop. Wit. Evert and Saartje Wynkoop.

Dec. 15. bo. the 9th. Jacob of Cornelis Brouwer and
Elisabeth Visbach. Wit. Wendel and Geertruy Hildebrand.

bo. Nov. 12. Alida of Jacob V. Aarnem and Maria V.
Deuzen. Wit. Johannes and Elisabeth V. Aarnem.

Dec. 22. bo. the 9th. Lydia of Eduard S. Willet and Sara
Fryer. Wit. Martha and Lydia Visscher.

Dec. 29. bo. the 15th. Magdalena of Pieter W. Yates
and Ann Mary Helms. Wit. John Hawill, Mary Magd.
Tibout.

1783, Jan. 26. bo. the 14th. Catharina of Zelotes Watson and Catharina Wynkoop. Wit. James and Abigail
Watson.

Feb. 9. bo. Jan. 11. Eduard of George Vischer and
Maria Reddin. Wit. Theunis and Marytje V. d. Berg.

bo. the 8th. Bastiaan of Johannes I. Visscher and Annatje
Pearssen. Wit. Bastiaan and Machtel Visscher.

bo. Jan. 20. Philip of Philip V. Rensselaer and Maria
Sanders. Wit. Leendert and Maria Gansevoort.

bo. Jan. 14. Lucretia of Willem Groesbeek and Catharina
V. Deuzen. Wit. Abraham and Lucretia V. Deuzen.

Feb. 16. bo. Jan. 14. Cornelis of John Schoonmaker and
Alida Burhans. Wit. Johs. and Tempe Burhans.

bo. Jan. 17. Wilhelmus of Yzac Van Wie and Neeltje
Oosterhout. Wit. John Oosterhout, Elisabeth Cluet.

Feb. 23. bo. the 16th. Petrus of Pieter Qwakkenbusch
and Mary Sheffield. Wit. Philip de Foreest, Margarita
Qwakkenbush.

bo. the 2d. Margaret of Hendrikus Burhans and Temperance Dumont. Wit. Willem V. Norden DuMont, Jannetje Schoonmaker.

Mar. 2. bo. Feb. 16. Alida of Johs. J. Wendel and Alida
Hoogkerk. Wit. Jacobus and Alida Fonda.

1783
bo. Feb. 13. Cornelis of Cornelis Cuyler and Jannetje Yates. Wit. Jacob and Lydia Cuyler.

Mar. 9. bo. Jan. 29. Johannes of Frerik Meinerssen and Machtel Witbeek. Wit. Abraham and Rachel Meinerssen.

bo. the 3d. Elsje of Dirk Lush and Lyntje Fonda. Wit. Gysbert and Elsje Fonda.

Mar. 16. bo. the 6th. Jannetje of Gerrit Heyer and Jannetje V. Slyk. Wit. Hendrik and Marytje Lansing.

Mar. 23. bo. the 11th. Maria of Philip Muller and Geesje V. Hoesen. Wit. Martinus and Maria Sharp.

bo. the 19th. Cathalina of Dirk Hunn and Hanna Lansing. Wit. Thomas and Neeltje Lansing.

bo. the 13th. Johanna of Eilardus Westerlo and Catharina Livingston. Wit. I. H. Livingston, Margarita Jones.

Mar. 30. Mary of Thoms. Harsslet and Margaret Gibson. Wit. Samuel, Marg. and Antje Rock.

bo. the 16th. Anna of Hermanus T. Eyck and Margarita Bleeker. Wit. Wilhelmus V. Buuren, —— Mancius, Margarita T. Eyck.

Apr. 6. bo. the 22d. Ezechiel of Henry Hart and Elisabeth Visscher. Wit. Reynier and Hester Visscher.

bo. Feb. 21. Abraham of Johs. Poll and Isabella Douglas. Wit. Melchert and Margarita Poel.

Apr. 13. bo. Feb. 5. Hendrik of Johs. Fonda and Alida Levison. Wit. Hendrik and Maria Fonda.

bo. Mar. 11. Catharina of Benjamin Bulsing and Elisabeth Moor. Wit. Jacob Wendell, Catharina Schuyler.

Apr. 18. bo. the 13th. Johannes of Johs. Pruin and Arriaantje Verplank. Wit. Jacob and Marritje Pruin.

Apr. 20. bo. the 10th. James Wynkoop of Gerrit Lansing and Elisabeth Wynkoop. Wit. James and Alida Wynkoop.

Apr. 27. bo. the 20th. Maayke of Gerrit V. Schaik and Christina Berringer. Wit. Gosen and Elisabeth V. Schaik.

May 4. bo. Apr. 16. Albert and Michel, of Hendrik Acker and Margarita Land. Wit. Jerom. Valenbeek, Elisabeth and Jonathan Witbeek, Cath. Cooper.

bo. Mar. 17. Cornelia of David Flensburg and Maria Stratt(?). Wit. Mathys Flensburg, Saartje V. Santen.

May 11. bo. Apr. 18. Abraham of Nicolas Fort and Catharina V. d. Berg. Wit. Abraham and Annatje Lansing.

1783

May 18. bo. Apr. 15. Cornelia of Jacob and Aaltje Schermerhoorn. Wit. Andries and Cornelia Schermerhoorn.

bo. the 11th. Lavinus of Lavinus Winne and Maria Lansing. Wit. Cornelis Groesbeek, Catharina V. Wie.

May 25. bo. the 18th. Catharina of Willem Staats and Annatje Yates. Wit. Anthony and Catharina Briesch.

bo. the 9th. Thomas of Anthony Halenbeek and Cornelia Cooper. Wit. Jacob and Rosina Cooper.

May 25. bo. the 5th. Hendrik Wendel of Johs. Bratt and Sara Wendel. Wit. Hendrik and Cathalina Wendell.

May 25. bo. the 17th. Benjamin of James Williams and Maria O'Conner. Wit. Benjamin Williams, Sara O'Conner.

May 29. bo. the 25th. Willempje of Johs. V. Woert and Cathalyntje Lansing. Wit. Jacob and Willempje Lansing.

May 31. bo. Apr. 19. Ridgart of Jeremias Muller and Catharina Moor. Wit. Johs. and Catharina Muller.

bo. the 30th. Douwe of Barent Bogert and Alida V. d. Berg. Wit. Pieter Winne, Willempje Bogert.

June 8. bo. May 15. Catharina of Willem Hoogteling and Maria Bloemendal. Wit. Jesse and Rebecca Foreest.

June 15. bo. May 19. Maria of Christiaan Fero and Catharina Levison. Wit. Pieter and Maria Levison.

bo. May 16. Lucas of Lucas V. Salsberghen and Maria V. Buren. Wit. Abraham Poel and Judik V. Buren.

bo. May 12. Geesje of Joh. V. Alen and Maria Look. Wit. Hannes and Geesje Look.

June 22. bo. May 20. Margarita of Hendrik Shutter and Jannetje Hindermond.

June 30. bo. the 18th. Samuel of William Fuller and Rebecca Forgess. Wit. Samuel and Rachel Stringer.

bo. the 4th. Alida of Lavinus Lanssing and Marytje Perrser. Wit. Johs. and Annatje Visscher.

bo. the 10th. Jannetje of Cornelis V. Buren and Maria Owens. Wit. Melchert Poel, Cornelia Hoes.

July 6. bo. June 16. Heiltje of Hannes V. Etten and Geertruy Redlif. Wit. Benjamin and Heiltje V. Etten.

July 6. bo. the 30th. Harmen of Samuel Marll and Rachel Gardenier. Wit. Sybrand and Neeltje Qwakkenbusch.

bo. June 10. Rachel of James Denison and Lena Lansing. Wit. Hugh and Isabella Denison.

1783

July 15. bo. June 12. Barbara of Matheus Poel and Elisabeth Shutter. Wit. Abrah. Shutter, Geertruy Salsbury.

bo. June 19. Gerrit of Pieter Bratt and Margarita Fry. Wit. Arent V. Deusen, Lydia Bratt.

bo. the 13th. Robert of Johs. Lansing and Cornelia Ray. Wit. Robert Ray, Jannetje Lansing.

July 20. bo. May 31. Joseph de Peister of James Blanchet and Margaret de Peister.

July 28. bo. the 26th. Maas of Jacob Bloemendal and Margarita Roller. Wit. Maas and Lena Bloemendal.

bo. June 21. Theodosia Bartow of Aaron Burr (?) and Theodosia Bartow.

bo. the 23d. Caty of Jacob Trouex and Catharina Dacksteder. Wit. William Mover, Caty Trouex.

Aug. 3. bo. July 16. Margarita of Joseph V. Santen and Rebecca De Garmo. Wit. Rykert and Jannetje (or Saartje?) V. Santen.

bo. July 26. John of Benjamin Simmons and Annatje Mentley. Wit. John and Cathalyntje Groesbeek.

Aug. 10. bo. July 29. Peter of Joseph Clyne and Hannah Tolhammer. Wit. Peter and Polly Tolhammer.

bo. May 29. Johnson of Ephraim Holebrock and Esther Johnson.

bo. Aug. 4. Gerrit of Abraham G. Lansingh and Susanna Yates. Wit. Gerrit and Sara Lansingh.

Aug. 10. bo. July 27. Hunlocke of Hunlocke Woodruff and Maria Lansingh. Wit. Jacob and Phebe Lansingh.

bo. July 9. Anthony of Anthony Ten Eyck and Maria Egberts. Wit. Abraham and Anna Ten Eyck.

bo. July 6. David of John De Foreest and Elbertje Van Aalstyne. Wit. Elisabeth Witbeek. David D. Foreest.

Aug. 17. bo. the 7th. Annatje of Harpert V. Deusen and Geertje Witbeek. Wit. Harpert and Marritje Witbeek.

bo. July 4th. Hannah of Benjamin Goodhart and Jannetje Adley. Wit. John Ward, Bregje Zeger.

bo. the 8th. Marytje of Baltes Pratt and Resina Foller. Wit. Frans and Marytje Ruson.

bo. July 25. Adam of Johs. S. Zeger and Saartje Pengburn. Wit. Pieter and Annatje Zeger.

Aug. 24. bo. the 20th. Jeremia of John Luther and Elisabeth Roller. Wit. Jers. and Lena V. Rensselaer.

1783

bo. the 19th. Sara of Jacobus Bleecker and Rachel V. Santen. Wit. Gerrit and Hester V. Santen.

bo. the 17th. Joseph of Abraham Blodgood and Elisabeth V. Valkenburg.

Aug. 31. bo. the 27th. Catharina of Abraham Lansing and Elsje V. Rensselaar. Wit. Johs. J. and Catharina Lansing.

bo. the 24th. Gerrit Theunissen of Hendrikus Bratt and Annatje Davidson. Wit. Gerrit Bratt, Marytje Loveridge.

bo. July 24. Phebe of John M. Michell and Engeltje Kidney. Wit. Rykert Hilton, Christina Brook.

bo. the 14th. Maria of Albert and Engeltje Hanssen. Wit. Benjamin Hanssen, Marytje Bratt.

Aug. 31. bo. the 6th. David of Johs. Oosterhout and Agnietje Winne. Wit. David Winne, Geertruy Groesbeek.

bo. July 29. Gerrit of Jurjaan Hoghing and Annatje White. Wit. Marten and Elsje Hoghingh.

Sept. 17. bo. the 29th. Andrew V. Schaik of Eduard Comstone and Mary V. Schaak. Wit. Stephen V. Schaak and Wife.

bo. Aug. 4. Mathys of Abraham Hoogteling and Annatje Bruss. Wit. Theunis and Rachel Hoogteling.

bo. Aug. 30. Pieter of Robert Yates and Jannetje V. Nesh. Wit. Pieter and Geertruy Schuyler.

Sept. 21. bo. June 20. Nency of Willm. Ebbet and Mary Jackson. Wit. George Ramsey, Nency Stonert.

Sept. 28. bo. the 25th. Wessel of Johs. T. Broeck and Sara Gansevoort. Wit. Pieter, Jr., and Catharina Ganzevoort.

Oct. 5. bo. the 3d. Margarita of Johs. Helmer and Catharina Muller. Wit. Willem and Margarita Cunningham.

bo. June 11. Anna of Thoms Hadik and Catharina Conny.

Maria of John (or Isaac?) Obrian and Hanna. Wit. John and Catharina Obrian.

bo. Sept. 5. Franciscus of Cornelis Winne and Elis V. d. Bogert. Wit. Pieter and Magdalena Winne.

Oct. 10. bo. the 1st. Blandina of Rutger Bleecker and Catharina Elmendorp. Wit. Jacobus Brower, Blandina Elmendorp.

1783

Oct. 12. bo. the 10th. Willem of Johs. V. Santen and Margarita Burghess(?). Wit. Johs. and Alida V. Santen.

bo. the 7th. Thomas of Pieter Dox and Nency Rendell. Wit. Gerardus and Elisabeth Groesbeek.

Oct. 19. bo. the 3d. John of John Way and Hilletje Millar. Wit. Jacob Miller, Martha Way.

bo. the 5th. Johs. of Wilh. V. Deusen and Rachel Pietersse. Wit. Johs. and Abigail V. Deusen.

Oct. 26. bo. the 12th. Anthony of Hendrikus Bratt and Maria Eight. Wit. Stuart Dean, Alida Bratt.

bo. Sept. 28. Maria of William Sebring and Rebecca Yates.

bo. the 14th. Catharina of Frans Hanssen and Rebecca Spoor. Wit. Jacob Hanssen, Maria Spoor.

bo. the 8th. Dirckje of Jacob V. Loon and Christina Schuyler. Wit. Abraham and Eva Schuyler.

Nov. 2. bo. Oct. 27. Elsje of Wendell Hildebrand and Geertruy Visbach. Wit. Cornelis and Elisabeth Brower.

bo. the 4th. Johs. Jurjen of Andries Harick and Elisabeth Warner. Wit. Jurjen and Catharine Warner.

bo. Oct. 31. Gerrit of Johs. S. Lansing and Catharina Burhans. Wit. Hendrik and Marytje Lansing.

bo. Oct. 20. Samuel Stringer of Stephen Lush and Lydia Stringer. Wit. Samuel and Rachel Stringer.

bo. Oct. 15. Leendert of Pieter Ganzevoort and Catharina V. Schaik. Wit. Leendert and Hester Ganzevoort.

Nov. 9. bo. Oct. 14. Margarita of Valentine Casparus and Rebecca Snyder. Wit. John and Margarita Jenkins.

bo. Oct. 24. Rosina Catharina of Charles F. Brown and Maria C. Ramsey. Wit. Joh. H. Werffenbach, Catharina Ramsey.

bo. the 6th. Hermanus of Jeremias Lansing and Helena Wendell. Wit. Hermanus and Barbara Wendell.

Nov. 9. bo. the 7th. Elisabeth of Douwe Fonda and Catharina Ten Broek. Wit. Johs. Oothout, Margarita T. Broeck.

Nov. 23. bo. the 14th. John of Balthes V. Benthuisen and Elisabeth Rumney. Wit. John Rumney, Sara Valkenburg.

Nov. 30. bo. the 23d. Wouter of Dirck de Foreest and

1783

Rebecca Bratt. Wit. Jesse De Foreest, Rebecca V. Santen.

Oct. 13. Engeltje of John Everts and Nency Howards. Wit. Gerrit and Rachel Visscher.

Dec. 7. bo. Nov. 6. Hugh Bennys of Willm. Colebrecht and Hester V. Deusen. Wit. William and Ann V. Deusen.

bo. Oct. 3. Stephen Rensselaer of Stephen J. Schuyler and Helena T. Eyck. Wit. Stephen and Margarita V. Rensselaer.

bo. Sept. 30. Jannetje of Henry McKinsy and Elisabeth V. Aalstein. Wit. Pieter Pessinger, Jannetje V. Aalstein.

bo. Sept. 23. Maria Catharina of Josiah Crane, Jr., and Carolina Walters. Wit. Thoms. and Catharina Hook.

bo. Aug. 29. James of Thoms Burnside and Arriaantje T. Eyck.

Dec. 14. bo. the 6th. Lena and Johannes, twins, of Jacob Roseboom and Hester Lansing. Wit. Barent H. and Lena T. Eyck, Gerardus and Elisabeth Bancker.

bo. Oct. 23. Pieter of Stuart Deane and Pietertje Bratt (decd.). Wit. Alida Bratt.

bo. the 10th. Margarita of Jacob Pruin and Hendrikje V. Buren. Wit. Jacob Schermerhoorn, Alida Foreest.

bo. Nov. 25. Maria of Theunis A. Slingerland and Margarita Hanssen. Wit. Albert Hanssen, Maria Bratt.

Dec. 21. bo. Nov. 12. Gerrit of Harmen V. Hoesen and Catharina Witbeek. Wit. Reignier and Engeltje V. Hoesen.

Dec. 21. bo. Nov. 12. Elsje of John Wagenaar and Elisabeth Smith. Wit. Jacob and Elsje V. Deusen.

bo. the 16th. Annatje of Maas V. Franken and Geertruy Veeder. Wit. Ryckert V. Franken, Margarita Waldrom.

bo. Nov. 10. Johannes Burhans, of Abrm. V. Wie and Jacomyntje Burhans. Wit. Johs. and Tempe Burhans.

Dec. 23. bo. Nov. 21. Hendrik of John Voorhees and Jannetje V. Ist.

Dec. 28. bo. Nov. 2. Pieter of Johs. V. Valkenburg and Annatje Reisdorp. Wit. Wynand and Margarita V. Aalstein.

bo. Nov. 5. Johannes of Evert Olfer and Rebecca Cooper. Wit. Johs. and Marytje Oliver.

bo. Nov. 8. Johannes of Obadiah Lansing and Cornelia V. Benthuisen. Wit. John Lansing, Maria Staats.

1784

1784, Jan. 11. bo. Nov. 31. Cornelis of Pieter V. Buuren and Dorothea Shutter. Wit. Cornelis and Jannetje V. Buuren.

bo. Dec. 15. Sarah of Gerrit Rykman and Elisabeth V. Buren. Wit. Wilhelmus and Janneke Rykman.

Jan. 18. bo. July 6. Alida of Gerrit I. Briesch and Geertruy Groesbeek. Wit. Hendrik and Alida Rensselaer.

bo. the 8th. Hannah of William Salbert and Johanna Young. Wit. Saml. and Rachel Marl.

Jan. 25. bo. Dec. 23. Mary of John W. Wendell and Mary Frother. Wit. Sally Frother.

bo. Nov. 22. Robert of Absalom Woodworth and Catharina Sprong. Wit. Robert Woodworth.

bo. the 18th. Catharina of Evert Evertssen and Elisabeth Goey. Wit. Benjamin and Catharina Goey.

Feb. 22. bo. Jan. 27. Rachel of Pieter Winne and Maria Oosterhout. Wit. John Winne, Cathalyntje Hanssen.

bo. Jan. 25. Hester of William Borwell and Elisabeth Salsbury.

bo. the 7th. Maria of Jacobus Fonda and Willempje Bogert. Wit. Jacob Lansing, Maria Fonda.

bo. the 15th. Pieter of Jacob V. Woert and Sara V. Esch. Wit. Jacob and Elisabeth V. Woert.

bo. Jan. 22. Annatje of Jurjen Berringer and Elisabeth Beem. Wit. Johs. and Anna Berringer.

bo. the 2d. Arriaantje of Cornelis V. Santvoort and Cornelia V. Wie. Wit. Yzac and Antje Fonda.

Feb. 29. bo. Jan. 1. Willem of Daniel Young and Elisabeth V. d. Kar. Wit. Andries Bratt, Annatje V. d. Kar.

bo. Dec. 19. Lena of Yzac Owen and Arriaantje Hegeman. Wit. Cornelis and Maria V. Buren.

Mar. 7. bo. Feb. 19. Yzac of Theunis Slingerland and Rachel Bogert. Wit. Wouter W. and Geertruy Slingerland.

bo. the 25th. Margarita of Jacobus V. d. Poel and Marytje Muller. Wit. Melchert and Margarita V. d. Poel.

bo. Nov. 15. Hilletje of Salomo Sherp and Rachel Helenbeek. Wit. Caspar Halenbeek, Hilletje Scharp.

bo. Jan. 14. Hendrikje of Caspar Halenbeek and Hilletje Scharp. Wit. John and Margarita Halenbeek.

bo. Feb. 9. Hermanus of Joseph Salsbergen and Margarita Oetsenjans(?). Wit. Hermanus and Tanneke V. Salsbergen.

1784

bo. the 4th. Elisabeth of Eli Arnold and Geertruy Groesbeek. Wit. Johs. and Neeltje Groesbeek.

Mar. 14. bo. the 7th. Thomas of Thomas Easterly and Bata V. Woert. Wit. Cornelia V. Woert.

Mar. 21. bo. the 12th. Elisabeth of John N. Bleecker and Margarita V. Deuzen.

Mar. 28. bo. the 21st. Jacob of Johs. Lansing and Elisabeth Fryer. Wit. Jacob and Elsje V. Deusen.

bo. the 10th. Johannes of Johs. Brass and Lena Shaffner. Wit. Jonathan Kidny, Annatje Hilton.

bo. the 26th. Willem of Johs. Groesbeek and Cathalina V. Schaik. Wit. Casparus Pruin, Maria Groesbeek.

Apr. 4. bo. Mar. 27. Annatje of Nicolaas Hieralymon and Jannetje Waldrom. Wit. Pieter and Catharina V. Deusen.

bo. the 24th. Catharina of Frerik Meinerssen and Elisabeth Waldrom. Wit. Abram and Rachel Meinertsen.

bo. Mar. 7. Margarita of Hendrik V. Wie and Maria Marthen. Wit. Nicolaas Hieralymon, Lucretia Wright.

bo. the 2d. Elisabeth Richards of Leendert Gansevoort, Jr., and Maria V. Rensselaar. Wit. John M. and Elisabeth Beekman.

Apr. 11. bo. the 3d. Hendrik of Hendrik V. Woert and Catharina Eights. Wit. Mary Eights.

bo. the 5th. Nicolaas of Johs. Brower and Marytje de Wever. Wit. Willem and Marytje Brower.

bo. the 6th. Elisabeth of Andries Abel and Annatje Marshal. Wit. Samuel and Rachel Marl.

Apr. 12. bo. the 5th. Geertruy of Jacob J. Lansing and Jannetje Heyer. Wit. Johs. and Catharina Lansing.

Apr. 18. bo. the 13th. Jacob Pruin of Lewis Barrington and Margarita Adams. Wit. Margaret Pruin.

bo. the 6th. Letty of Zacharias Sickels and Catharina Sharer. Wit. John and Maria Groesbeek.

Apr. 25. bo. the 15th. John of John Staats and Jennet McClennen. Wit. Gerrit Rykman, Neeltje Visscher.

bo. Feb. 31st (sic). Jannetje of David Winne and Geertruy Groesbeek. Wit. Pieter Groesbeek and Leentje Bogert.

bo. the 10th. David of John Robinson and Geertje V. Petten.

May 2. bo. Apr. 23. Catharina of Dirk Benson and Marytje Wyngaart. Wit. Casparus and Jannetje V. Wie.

Barbara of Abrm. Shutter and Geertruy Vosburg. Wit. David Poel, Elisabeth Shutte.

1784

May 19. bo. the 5th. Annatje of Pieter J. Bogert and Saartje V. Schaik. Wit. Abraham and Annatje Witbeek.

bo. Mar. 13. Annatje of Johs. Milton and Resina Shoecat. Wit. Pieter and Rachel Witbeek.

May 16. bo. Apr. 3. Aaltje of Alexander Bulsing and Aaltje Oothout.

May 20. bo. Dec. 20. Richard of Daniel Hale and Catharina Dyckman.

bo. the 13th. Gerrit Lansing of Pieter Dox and Cathalyntje Lansing. Wit. Cornelis and Annatje Wendell.

bo. the 28th. Magdalena of Folkert Oothout and Jannetje Bogert. Wit. Hendrik and Lydia Oothout.

May 23. bo. Mar. 11. Wouter of Cornelis V. d. Zee and Annatje Veder. Wit. Theunis and Elisabeth Ackerson.

May 30. bo. the 23d. Catharina of Nicolaas V. d. Bogert and Margarita Flensburg. Wit. John and Annatje Flensburgh.

May 30. bo. the 7th. Rachel of Abraham Eights and Catharina Broecks.

bo. Mar. 31. Catharina of Cornelis V. Buren and Jannetje V. d. Poel. Wit. Jurjaan and Catharina Poel.

May 31. bo. the 7th. Tempe of Jeremiah Rendell and Geertruy Gardenier. Wit. Bastiaan and Engeltje Visscher.

bo. the 30th. Salomon of Cornelis V. Aalstein and Maria Goey. Wit. Gerrit Goey, Geertje V. d. Berg.

June 6. bo. Feb. 23. Pieter of Pieter Vroman and Wyntje Redlif. Wit. Archibald and Christina Camble.

bo. the 2d. Susanna of Hendrik Evertson and Hendrikje Winne. Wit. Jacob and Susanna Winne.

bo. May 31. Joseph of Daniel Marshall and Elisabeth Cochron. Wit. John and Maria Van Santen.

bo. Apr. 6. Harinah of Thoms. Hook and Catharina Crane.

July 15. bo. June 18. Sara of Christoffer Lansing and Sara V. Schaik. Wit. Jacobus Lansing.

bo. the 9th. Elisabeth of Jonathan Hilton and Cornelia V. Antwerp. Wit. Willem and Elisabeth Hilton.

bo. June 26. Benjamin of Johs. Hanssen and Geertruy Slingerland. Wit. Cornelis and Willempje V. Schaak.

bo. June 16. Alida of Cornelis Douw and Catharina V. Schaik. Wit. John and Alida V. Schaik.

1784
July 19. bo. May 29. Pieter of Hans Arnold and Elisabeth Brusch. Wit. Pieter and Annaatje Daniels.

bo. the 12th. Catharina of John Hartwich and Rachel Archer. Wit. Thomas and Margaret Archer.

July 19. bo. June 5. Sara of John Fonda and Cornelia Hun. Wit. William and Sara Hun.

bo. the 15th. Pieter of Christoffer Yates and Rebecca Winne. Wit. Pieter and Sara Bogert.

bo. the 16th. Catharina of Yzac Qwakkenbush. Wit. Catharina Gardinier, Samuel and Rachel Marl.

July 25. bo. June 27. Rachel of John Bloemendal and Catharina Sharp. Wit. Jurgen and Marytje Sharp.

bo. Mar. 20. Adam of Matheus Flensburgh and Christina Snyder. Wit. Jurjen and Annatje Hoghen.

bo. the 2d. Christiaan of Wilhelmus Cooper and Marytje Berringer. Wit. Pieter and Catharina Sharp.

Aug. 9. bo. May 24. Meinard of Barent V. Yveren and Rebecca Bratt. Wit. Pieter Bratt, Saartje V. Yveren.

Aug. 9. bo. July 21. Jacob of Bernardus Evertson and Martina Hogen. Wit. Hendrik and Elisabeth V. Hoesen.

Catharine Schuyler of Stephen V. Rensselaer and Margarita Schuyler. Wit. Philip and Catharina Schuyler.

bo. July 19. James Wynkoop of Gerrit A. Lansing and Elisabeth Wynkoop. Wit. Jacobus and Alida Wynkoop.

Aug. 15. bo. July 9. Jane of Johs. Bulsing and Marg. Wilson. Wit. James Bertly, Jane Thomsen.

Geertruy of Abrm. V. d. Poel and Catharina Brasie. Wit. Jurjen and Jannetje V. Poel.

bo. July 3. Wilhelmus of Reinier V. d. Bergh and Elisabeth V. Alen. Wit. Jacob V. d. Berg, Saartje V. Yveren.

bo. Apr. 16. Arriaantje of Gerrit Brouwer and Antje Zeger. Wit. Cornelis and Marytje Vroman.

Aug. 15. bo. July 19. Marten of Mathys V. Aalstein and Rachel De Foreest. Wit. Marten and Janneke Foreest.

July 17. Gerrit of Martinus V. Yveren and Cornelia V. Schaik. Wit. Gerrit and Christina V. Schaik.

bo. July 16. Johannes of David Berringer and Marg. P. Heiner. Wit. Johs. and Anna Berringer.

Aug. 15. bo. the 9th. Rachel of Hendrik Lansing and Helena Winne. Wit. Helena and Willemje Lansing.

bo. the 3d. Elisabeth of Lodewyk Obrien and Catharina

1784
Rendell. Wit. Jacob and Catharina Hermans.

bo. July 28. Wilhelmus of Cornelis V. d. Bergh and Catharina Bogert. Wit. Wilhelmus and Agnieta V. d. Berg.

bo. the 4th. Alida of Johs. V. Hoesen and Engeltje V. Deusen. Wit. John and Geesje V. Benthuise.

Aug. 22. bo. June 24. Margarita of Hendrik Rodey and Maria Smith. Wit. Pieter V. Buren, Hilletje V. d. Berg.

bo. July 8. Stephen of John Wally and Sibyl Appely. Wit. Stephen and Margarita V. Rensselaer.

bo. July 3. Matheus of Willem Flensburg and Christina Bauher. Wit. Matheus and Catharina Flensburg.

bo. the 15th. Geertruy of James Donneway and Elsje Smith. Wit. Hendrik and Barentje Hendemond.

bo. the 1st. Michael of Michael Besset and Maria V. Franken. Wit. John Gates, Elisabeth Besset.

Aug. 29. bo. July 30. Rachel of David Winne and Marytje Spaar(?). Wit. Pieter and Maria Winne.

bo. the 19th. David of Jacob V. d. Heiden and Jennet Livingston. Wit. David and Poyer V. d. Heiden.

Sept. 5. bo. Aug. 8. Elisabeth of Pieter Cooper and Anna Strong. Wit. Hendrik and Elsje Strong.

bo. Aug. 4. Hendrik of Joh and Immetje Salisbury. Wit. Hendrik and Hilletje V. Buren.

Sept. 12. John of Wilhelmus Mancius and Annatje T. Eyck. Wit. Cornelis E. Wynkoop, Cornelia Mancius.

bo. Aug. 18. Samuel of Edward Cumpston (?) and Mary V. Schaak.

Sept. 21. John of Pieter David and Elisabeth Colwell. Wit. John and Elisabeth David.

Harmen Visscher of Henry Hart and Elisabeth Visscher. Wit. John and Cornelia Price(?).

Sept. 27. bo. the 3d. Alida of Matheus Aarsen and Bregje V. Hoesen. Wit. Gerrit and Elsje Roseboom.

bo. Aug. 25. Cornelis of Pieter W. Witbeek and Rachel V. d. Berg. Wit. Pieter and Marytje Veder.

bo. Aug. 19. Hendrik of Nicholas Bleeker and Neeltje Staats. Wit. Hendrik and Cathalyntje Bleecker.

John of James Rood and Elisabeth Williams. Wit. Jacob De Garmo, Fytje Becker.

Oct. 3. bo. Sept. 7. Sara Hilton of Willem Cooper and

1784

Maria Hilton. Wit. Jacob and Sara Hilton.

bo. Sept. 12. Christina of Reynier V. Yveren and Elisabeth Oostrander. Wit. Gerrit and Christina Oostrander.

bo. Sept. 26. Benjamin of John Williamson and Mary Coop (?). Wit. Timothy and Maria Williamson.

bo. Sept. 22. Wilhelmus of Philip Foreest and Annatje V. Deusen. Wit. Cornelis and Lena V. Deusen.

Oct. 3. bo. Sept. 1. Marten of Willem and Abigail Foreest. Wit. Marten and Tanneke Foreest.

bo. Sept. 6. Samuel Provoost of Gerrit Staats, Jr., and Elisabeth Louw. Wit. Maria Low.

Oct. 7. bo. July 28. John of Alexander Boyd and Elisabeth Bocker.

Oct. 10. bo. Sept. 11. John of Johannes Poel and Elisabeth Douglas. Wit. John Douglass.

bo. Aug. 22. William of Moses Hudson and Amelia Upham. Wit. Ephraim and Elisabeth Hudson.

Oct. 17. bo. the 11th. John of Johs. Fryer and Maria Follewyser. Wit. John and Elisabeth Fryer.

bo. the 13th. Johannes T. Eyck of Philip Hilton and Sara Barmigton. Wit. John T. Eyck, Maria Douw.

bo. the 7th. Margarita of Jacobus Redly and Maria Otman. Wit. John and Margarita Redly.

bo. June 7. Yzak of Timotheus Bussing and Jannetje Crosby.

bo. the 19th. bapt. Oct. 21. Rebecca of William McManus and Mary Veher. Wit. Cornelis and Jemima Brower.

bo. Sept. 6. Hermanus of Johs. Wendel and Cathalina V. Benthuisen.

bo. Sept. 10. Abraham of Harpert Witbeek and Geertruy Wendell. Wit. Lucas V. Vechten, Engeltje Schuyler.

Louys of Thomas and Mercy. Serv. of I. V. Rensselaer.

Oct. 31. bo. Sept. 17. Willem of William Groesbeek and Catharina V. Deusen. Wit. Willem and Cornelia V. Deusen.

Oct. 31. bo. the 16th. Sara of Obadia V. Benthuisen and Annatje Rumney. Wit. Hendrik and Sara V. Benthuisen.

Nov. 12. bo. Oct. 30. Pieter of Jacob Daniels and Maria Riddel. Wit. Pieter and Annatje Daniels.

bo. Oct. 30. Annatje of Arent V. Deusen and Margarita McCloud. Wit. Jacob Cuyler, Jannetje V. Deuzen.

1784-1785

Nov. 27. bo. Sept. 10. Cornelia of Gysbert Groesbeek and Cornelia V. Valkenburg (decd.). Wit. Gerrit and Neeltje Groesbeek.

bo. Oct. 30. Johannes of John and Alida V. Wie. Wit. Yzac and Neeltje V. Wie.

bo. Oct. 31. Johannes of John P. and Cornelia Qwakkenbusch.

Dec. 5. bo. Nov. 9. Matheus of William W. Crennel and Marytje Eman. Wit. Nicolaas and Arriaantje Crennel.

bo. Nov. 9. Petrus of Pieter J. Qwakkenbusch and Mary Sheffield. Wit. Philip Foreest.

bo. Nov. 28. Maria of Cornelis Brouwer and Elisabeth Visbach. Wit. Pieter and Annatje Beekman.

Dec. 12. bo. Nov. 5. Engeltje of James V. Rensselaer and Cathalina Cortland. Wit. Philip and Catharina Schuyler.

Dec. 18. bo. the 4th. Ary of Jacobus Le Granzy and Annatje Visscher. Wit. Ary and Maria Le Granzy.

Dec. 25. bo. Nov. 22. Annatje of Gerrit Hoogteling and Annatje Oosterhout. Wit. Johs. and Arriaantje Hoogteling.

bo. Oct. 24. Mary of Arthur Hasswel and Mary Cofftree (?).

Dec. 26. bo. Nov. 19. Elisabeth of Willem Hoogteling and Maria Bloemendal. Wit. Gerrit Becker, Marytje Wynkoop.

1785, Jan. 2. bo. Nov. 31 (sic). John of Daniel Clemenger and Rachel Milton. Wit. John and Charlotte Milton.

bo. Dec. 28. Abraham Fonda of Jacob Y. Lansing and Susanna Fonda. Wit. Abraham and Penmet (?) Fonda.

Jan. 9. bo. Dec. 20. Annatje of Anthony Groesbeek and Catharina Foreest. Wit. Willem Hann and Catharina Douw.

bo. Sept. 15. Cornelis of Milburn V. Hoesen and Antje Beemus. Wit. Cornelis and Marytje Vroman.

bo. the 3d. Catharina of Cornelis Groesbeek and Annatje V. Antwerp. Wit. Willem and Catharina Groesbeek.

bo. Nov. 2. Annatje of Gerrit Staats and Catharina Cunningham.

Jan. 16. bo. the 8th. Anthony of John V. Imburgh and Annatje Flensburg. Wit. Christiaan and Annatje Pierce.

Jan. 23. bo. Dec. 20. Cornelia of Frans Winne and Lena

1785

Flensburg. Wit. David and Maria Flensburgh.

bo. Dec. 24. John of Yzac Moll and Jannetje Schermhoorn. Wit. John M. Kern(?), Gerritje Schermhoorn.

bo. the 2d. John Lansing of Cornelis Wendell and Annatje Lansing. Wit. Reinier and Rebecca V. Yveren.

Jan. 30. bo. Dec. 27. Jenny of Seth Miggs and Jemina Boskerk.

bo. Dec. 23. Anthony of Anthony T. Eyck and Maria Egberts. Wit. Anthony and Annatje Egberts.

Feb. 6. bo. Dec. 26. Maria of Yzac V. Wie and Neeltje Oosterhout. Wit. Hendrik Oosterhout, Cathy Warrens.

Feb. 13. bo. Jan. 8. Elisabeth of John Fulson and Elisabeth File.

Feb. 13. bo. Jan. 10. Jannetje of Johs. Hoogteling and Maria Mason. Wit. Coenraad and Neeltje Hoogteling.

bo. Jan. 26. Cathalyntje of Hendrik V. Hoesen and Elisab. Eversson. Wit. Evert and Elisabeth Evertson.

bo. Feb. 9. Willempje Bogert of Jacobus Fonda and Willempje Bogert. Wit. Barent and Willempje Bogert.

bo. the 10th. Maayke of Nicholas Rensselaer and Elsje V. Buuren. Wit. Cornelis and Maayke V. Buuren.

bo. Jan. 9. Cornelis of Leendert Muller and Maria Strong. Wit. Johs. and Catharina Muller.

bo. Jan. 10. Dirk of Jacob V. Schaayk and ------ Berry.

bo. Jan. 31. Geertruy of Jacobus V. d. Voort and Nency Krifer(?). Wit. Jacob and Cathalina V. Losner(?).

Feb. 20. bo. the 12th. Engeltje of Jesse De Foreest and Rebecca V. Santen. Wit. Pieter and Vrouwtje Bratt.

bo. Jan. 24. Johannes of Willem Witbeek and Catharina Foreest. Wit. Thomas and Elisabeth Witbeek.

Annatje of Evert Janssen and Antje Le Granzy. Wit. Jelles and Annatje Le Granzy.

Feb. 22. bo. Jan. 27. Jane of John Lansingh and Cornelia Ray. Wit. Jacob and Jannatje Lansingh.

Feb. 27. bo. the 4th. Jacob of Abraham Dingman and Lena Salsbury. Wit. Abraham Shutter, Geertruy Salsbury.

bo. the 22d. Maria of Cornelis Cuyler and Jannetje Yates. Wit. Joseph Yates, Catharina Meinerssen.

bo. the 19th. Mary of Dirck Lush and Lyntje Fonda. Wit. Stephen and Lydia Lush.

Mar. 3. bo. Feb. 24. Catharina of Frans Harssen and Rebecca Spoor. Wit. Jacob Harssen, Maria Spoor.

1785

bo. Feb. 4. Pieter of Hendrik V. Buuren and Hilletje Shutter. Wit. Pieter V. Buren, Dorothea Shutter.

Mar. 13. bo. the 3d. Margarita of Hendrik Redlif and Elisab. Jacobs. Wit. Johs. and Margarita Redlif.

bo. Feb. 17. Elias of Johs. Oosterhout and Agnietje Winne. Wit. Wilhelmus and Sarah Oosterhout.

Mar. 20. bo. the 5th. Johannes of Sylvester Cruiselaer and Maria Shram. Wit. Frederik Bratt, Helena Burhans.

bo. the 10th. William of William Fuller and Rebecca Forger. Wit. Jacob and Lydia Cuyler.

Mar. 31. Catharina Glen of John J. V. Rensselaer and Catharina Glen. Wit. John and Catharina Glen.

Apr. 3. bo. Mar. 19. Elisabeth of Albertus Bloemendal and Anna Harssen.

bo. Mar. 2. Magdalena of Frans Stoop and Catharina de Wever.

bo. Mar. 20. Cathalyna of Obadiah Cooper and Annatje V. d. Berg. Wit. Pieter Witbeek, Rachel Skidmore.

bo. Mar. 24. Sara of Jacobus Bleeker and Rachel V. Santen. Wit. Gerrit and Hester V. Santen.

Apr. 10. bo. Mar. 22. Alida of Johs. Hoogkerk (decd.) and Rachel(?) Masten. Wit. Yzac and Alida Hoogkerk.

bo. Mar. 27. Elsje of Dirk Hun and Annatje Lansing. Wit. Philip and Elsje Lansing.

bo. the 1st. Johannes of Johs. Pruin and Arriaantje Verplank. Wit. Jacob and Pietertje Pruin.

Apr. 11. bo. Apr. 4. Jacob Bogert of Abraham V. Aarnem and Anneke Bogert. Wit. Jacob and Maria Bogert.

Apr. 17. bo. the 7th. Arriaantje of Willem V. Wie and Jannetje Lansing. Wit. Jacob and Hester Roseboom.

bo. the 5th. Simon Veder of Arent Bratt and Jannetje Hoghing. Wit. Maas and Geertruy V. Franken.

Apr. 24. bo. the 19th. Evert of Cornelis Waldrom and Alida Goey. Wit. Gerardus and Margarita Lansing.

bo. Mar. 9. Lucas of Philip P. Schuyler and Annatje Wendel.

bo. the 22d. Engeltje of Dirk De Foreest and Rebecca Bratt. Wit. Jesse and Rebecca De Foreest.

May 1. bo. Apr. 2. Dirk of David Foreest and Santje Fonda. Wit. Dirk Foreest, Maria Fonda.

bo. Mar. 9. Judike of Abraham V. Vechten and Catharina Schuyler.

1785

bo. Mar. 21. Hendrik of Hendrik Oothout and Lydia Douw. Wit. Folkert and Jannetje Oothout.

May 8. bo. Mar. 18. Margarita of Hendrik Ronckel and Margarita Toeper. Wit. William and Maria Toeper.

May 31. bo. Mar. 8. Sara of Ruben Schuyler and Sara Fort. Wit. Stephanus and Engeltje Schuyler.

May 15. bo. the 13th. Jeremia V. Rensselaer of Abraham T. Eyck and Annatje Lansing. Wit. Jeremiah and Lena V. Rensselaer.

June 12. Pieter of Johs V. Woert and Cathal. Lansing. Wit. Jacob and Sara V. Woert.

Eduard of Nicholas Hoghil and Catharina Valkenburg. Wit. Jacob Hoghil, Annatje Barret(?).

June 12. Sara of Pieter M. Gibbet and Margarita Smitt. Wit. Sara Staats.

bo. May 28. Gerrit of John Gates and Geertruy V. Vranken. Wit. Sara Visscher.

bo. May 1. Willem of Philip and Margarita Kerner. Wit. Willem and Cath. Groesbeek.

June 26. bo. the 6th. Elisabeth of Eli Arnold and Geertruy Groesbeek. Wit. John and Neeltje Groesbeek.

bo. May 18. John of David Foreest and Rachel V. d. Heide. Wit. John V. d. Heide, Catharina V. Brakelen.

July 3. bo. June 4. Catharina of Yzac Poel and Maria V. Buuren. Wit. Jonathan Witbeek, Catharina Poel.

bo. the 22d. Sara of Lavinus Winne and Maria Lansing. Wit. David and Sara Groesbeek.

bo. June 13. Lydia of Gerrit Hyer and Jannetje V. Slyk.

bo. June 8. Abraham of Abr. Lansing, Jr., and Maria Bloodgood.

July 6. Geertruy of Nicolaas Mersselis and Margarita Groesbeek. Wit. Thomas and Elisabeth Hunn.

July 7. bo. May 1. Geertje of Petrus Ostrander and Antje Denemark. Wit. Jacob Wever, Geertje V. Vliet.

July 11. bo. June 3. Tryntje of Pieter Waldrom and Antje Ouderkerk. Wit. Nicolas Groesbeek, Geertje Waldrom.

bo. the 1st. Lea of Wilhelmus V. Deusen and Rachel Pieterson. Wit. Frans and Geertruy Marshall.

bo. June 7. Cornelis of Matheus V. d. Berg and Annatje Yates. Wit. Pieter W. and Rachel Witbeek.

1785

July 11. bo. June 8. Margarita of Daniel Bratt and Christina Beekman. Wit. Jurgen and Lena Huyk.

July 24. bo. the 23d. Arriaantje of Abraham A. Lansing and Elsje V. Rensselaer. Wit. Leendert, Jr., and Maria Ganzevoort.

bo. the 20th. Gerrit of Gerrit A. Lansing and Elisabeth Wynkoop. Wit. Cornelis Wynkoop, Sara Fonda.

bo. the 17th. Jacob Lansing of Jacob V. Deusen and Elsje Lansing. Wit. John Liswell, Annatje Lansing.

Aug. 18. bo. July 25. Maayke of Willem M'Coy and Geertje Levison. Wit. Charles and Maayke M'Coy.

Sept. 4. bo. Aug. 30. Yzac of David Fonda and Catharina T. Broeck. Wit. Yzac and Susanna Fonda.

Sept. 13. bo. July 13. Hunloke of Hunloke Woodruff and Maria Lansing.

Sept. 27. bo. Sept. 21. Cornelia of Willem Dunbar and Elisabeth V. Deusen. Wit. Levinus and Cornelia Dunbar.

Oct. 16. bo. the 13th. Cathalina of Philip Muller and Geesje V. Hoesen. Wit. Burger V. d. Bergh, Cathalina V. Hoezen.

bo. the 1st. Judike of Rykert V. Santen and Sara Hilton. Wit. Abraham and Antje Hoogkerk.

bo. the 2d. Benjamin of John Rumney and Rachel Meinersse. Wit. Gozen and Maria V. Schaik.

bo. Aug. 23. John of John Reyly and Cathalina V. d. Berg. Wit. John and Catharina V. Ostrander.

Oct. 21. bo. the 19th. Anna of Enoch Leonard and Maria V. Vechten.

Oct. 23. bo. Sept. 12. Abraham of Philip Wendell and Geertruy Vosburg. Wit. Abraham and Elisabeth Vosburgh.

Oct. 24. bo. the 23d. Obadia of Obadia Lansing and Cornelia Cooper. Wit. Christoffer and Catharina Yates.

Oct. 30. bo. Sept. 27. Pieter of Pieter Dox and Cathalina Lansing.

bo. Sept. 6. Johannes of Abraham Sickels and Marytje Connel. Wit. Nicholas and Susan Claver.

Nov. 1. bo. Oct. 8. Margarita of Jacobus Redlif and Susanna Claassen. Wit. Pieter and Maria Claassen.

Nov. 7. bo. Oct. 17. Sara of Hendrik and Annatje Zeger. Wit. George and Bregje Zeger.

bo. Sept. 10. Maria of Johs. Ouderkerk and Annatje Fero. Wit. Abraham and Alida Ouderkerk.

53

1785-1786
bo. Oct. 12. Elias of Hendrik Oosterhout and Caty Warren. Wit. Jurjen and Maria Oosterhout.

bo. Oct. 10. Maas of John(?) Bloemendal and Catharina Sharp. Wit. Pieter Bloemendal, Barbara Sharp.

Nov. 12. bo. Oct. 9. John of Andries Bratt and Annatje V. d. Kar. Wit. John Bratt, Susanna Merriday.

Nov. 20. bo. Oct. 23. Folkert of John H. Benthuisen and Geesje V. Hoesen. Wit. Matheus Aarssen, Bregje V. Hoesen.

bo. Oct. 17. Yzac of Abraham H. Fonda and Penina Petteson. Wit. Yzac and Maria Fonda.

bo. the 14th. Hendrik of Willem Gobbus and Maria Forry. Wit. Bastiaan and Engeltje Visscher.

Nov. 27. bo. Oct. 13. Jacob of Dirk Knoet and Rachel Lansing. Wit. Jacob and Maria Lansing.

bo. the 6th. William of Stephen Lush and Lydia Stringer. Wit. Richard and Lyntje Lush.

Nov. 27. bo. the 17th. Cornelis de Ridder of Abraham G. Lansing and Tanneke Yates. Wit. Abrm., Jr., and Antje Yates.

bo. the 24th. Willem of Pieter Dox and Nency Randell. Wit. William Childs, Annatje Ruby.

Dec. 11. bo. Nov. 4. Gerrit of Abraham V. Wie and Jacomyntje Burhans. Wit. John and Agnietje Van Wie.

bo. Nov. 4. Theunis of Theunis T. Vechten and Elisabeth de Wandelaar.

bo. the 8th. Jacob of Hendrik T. Eyck and Margarita Douw. Wit. Hermanus and Margarita T. Eyck.

bo. Sept. 21. Sara of Hendrik Van Ist and Maria T. Eyck.

Dec. 18. bo. Oct. 13. Johannes of Barent Muller and Cornelia Goey. Wit. Jacob and Sara Muller.

bo. Nov. 6. Catharina of Cornelis V. Wie and Anna Schenklin. Wit. Gerrit and Itha V. Wie.

Dec. 25. bo. the 4th. Hendrikus of Hendrikus Bratt and Annatje Davies. Wit. Johs. and Phebe Wyngaerd.

1786, Jan. 8. bo. Nov. 30. Maria of Philip Berringer and Catharina Meyer. Wit. Willem and Maria Cooper.

bo. Nov. 1. Jacobus of Hendrik Aernout and Jannetje V. Aalstein. Wit. Willem and Elisabeth Bradt.

bo. Nov. 23. Pieter and Margarita, twins, of Christiaan Fero and Catharina Levison. Wit. Levinus and Marritje Levison, David Fero, Margarita Freeleg(?).

1786

bo. Sept. 18. Maria of Gerrit Brouwer and Antje Zeger. Wit. Johs. and Celia Redlif.

bo. Dec. 23. Matheus of Samuel Marl and Rachel Gardenier. Wit. Sarah Cloet.

Jan. 8. bo. Dec. 16. Harmen Ganzevoort of Cornelis Wynkoop and Annatje Gansevoort. Wit. Harmen and Magdalena Ganzevoort.

Cornelis of Gerrit Rykman and Elisabeth V. Buren. Wit. Cornelis and Maayke V. Buuren.

bo. Dec. 16. John of William Benthuisen and Margarita Conklin. Wit. John and Geesje V. Benthuisen.

bo. Dec. 11. Engeltje of Christiaan LeGranzy and Elisabeth Freeman.

bo. Oct. 8. Engeltje of Cornelis V. d. Zee and Annatje Veder. Wit. Dirk Foreest, Maria Fonda.

Jan. 9. bo. Oct. 27. Lavinus of Marten Wendel and Maria Winne. Wit. Lavinus Winne, Catharina Wendell.

Jan. 15. bo. Dec. 15. Maria of Johs. Fonda and Alida Levison. Wit. Pieter and Maria Levison.

Jan. 29. bo. Dec. 26. Cathalina of Jurjan Hoes and Judike V. Buren. Wit. Jacob Pruin, Hendrikje V. Buren.

Jan. 29. bo. the 10th. Theunis of Johs. Bratt and Saartje Wendell. Wit. Theunis and Cathalina Bratt.

bo. Nov. 28. Dirkje of Barent Staats and Antje Winne. Wit. Gerrit V. Antwerp, Marytje Pruin.

Feb. 5. bo. Jan. 3. Rebecca of Theunis Slingerland and Margarita Hanssen. Wit. Pieter and Rebecca Slingerland.

bo. the 1st. Maria of Baltes V. Benthuisen and Elisabeth Rumney. Wit. John Rumney, Maria Gist.

Feb. 12. bo. Dec. 22. Elias of Hendrik Fero and Maria Vredenburg. Wit. Frans Still, Rosina Fero.

bo. Dec. 26. Pieter of Gerrit Poel and Caty Couwenhoven. Wit. Cornelis and Jannatje Poel.

Feb. 12. bo. the 7th. Rachel of Nanning H. Visscher and Alida Fonda. Wit. Maria Fonda.

Feb. 16. bo. Nov. 19. Piter of Jonathan Hilton and Maria Baldwin.

Feb. 26. bo. the 16th. Dorothea of Anthony Halenbeek and Cornelia Cooper. Wit. John and Dorothea Waters.

bo. Jan. 17. Maria of Alexander Bulsing and Aaltje

1786

Oothout. Wit. Cornelis and Maria Cadmus.

bo. Jan. 20. Daniel of Willem D. Winne and Marytje Beckers. Wit. Daniel and Jannetje Winne.

bo. Dec. 31. Rachel, of James Dennison and Hanna Lansing.

bo. the 21st. Hendrik of Hermanus T. Eyck and Margarita Bleecker. Wit. Nicolaas and Neeltje Bleecker.

bo. the 22d. Willem of Abraham Hoogkerk and Antje Hilton. Wit. Rykert and Sara V. Santen.

bo. Jan. 19. Johannes of Pieter Cooper and Anna Strunk. Wit. Willem and Marytje Cooper.

bo. Jan. 21. Rachel of Abraham Eight and Catharina Broecks.

Mar. 3. bo. May 1. Abraham and Jacob, twins, of Daniel Halenbeek, Jr., and Geertruy Snyder. Wit. Daniel and Catharina Halenbeek.

Mar. 5. bo. Feb. 1. Maria of Johs. Vinhagen and Bata Valkenburgh. Wit. Johs. and Cornelia Vinhagen.

Mar. 13. bo. Feb. 23. Willem of Johs. Brouwer and Marritje de Wever. Wit. Willem and Annatje Lotteridge.

bo. Dec. 28. Jacob of Johs. D. Groesbeek and Cathalina V. Schaik. Wit. Jacob V. Schaik, Claasje Groesbeek.

Mar. 19. bo. the 7th. Yzaac of John Y. Fonda and Cornelia Hun. Wit. Yzaac and Catharina Fonda.

Apr. 9. bo. the 2d. Sara of Johs. Brash and Lena Shaffners. Wit. Jacob and Baatje V. Yveren.

bo. Mar. 28. Elisabeth of John Hilton and Elisabeth Black. Wit. Rykert and Phebe Hilton.

bo. Feb. 25. Annatje of Abraham Lansing and Annatje V. d. Bergh. Wit. Jacob and Cornelia Slingerland.

bo. Mar. 28. Andries of Jacob Bloemendal and Margarita Roller. Wit. Andries and Alida Roller.

bo. the 2d. Annatje of John V. Bleecker and Margarita V. Deusen.

bo. Mar. 30. Johannes of Leendert Ganzevoort, Jr., and Maria Rensselaer. Wit. Leendert and Eva Ganzevoort.

Apr. 16. bo. Mar. 30. Catharina of Coenraad Sharp and Elisabeth Staats. Wit. Petrus and Catharina Staats.

bo. Mar. 3. Deborah of Jacob Kinny and Elisabeth Fort. Wit. Hendrik and Tempe Burhans.

bo. Apr. 14. Maria of John Fryer and Marytje Followyzer. Wit. Jacob and Maria Followyzer.

1786

bo. Mar. 25. William Nicolls of Richard Sill and Elisabeth Nicols. Wit. Francis and Margaret Nicoll.

Apr. 23. bo. Mar. 9. Catharina of David Berringer and Maria B. Heiner. Wit. Philip and Catharina Berringer.

bo. the 10th. Rachel of Johannes H. Wendell and Cathalyntje V. Benthiusen.

Apr. 31 (sic). bo. the 2d. Dirk of Samuel Pruin and Neeltje Hasevoet. Wit. Dirk and Marytje Groot.

Apr. 31 (sic). bo. Mar. 17. Johannes of Tjerk Schoonmaker and Cornelia Acker. Wit. Theunis and Engeltje Acker.

bo. Mar. 10. David of William Borreway and Elisabeth Salsbury. Wit. David Groesbeek.

bo. Mar. 19. Jacob of Valentyn Casparis and Rebecca Snyder. Wit. Jacob and Catharine Berringer.

May 7. bo. Mar. 30. Cornelia of Martinus V. Yveren and Cornelia V. Schaik. Wit. John and Maria Goey.

bo. Apr. 20. Maria Matilda of Philip V. Rensselaer and Maria Sanders. Wit. William and Maria Ludlow.

bo. Apr. 26. Theunis of Thomas Easterly and Bata V. Woert.

May 15. bo. the 3d. Elisabeth of John V. Santen and Margarita Burgess. Wit. Johs. and Annatje V. Santen.

bo. Apr. 9. Catharina of Jacobus V. d. Poel and Marytje Muller. Wit. Jeremie and Catharine Muller.

Johannes of Barent Young and Elis. Ryken. Wit. John and Delia Young.

bo. Apr. 30. Catharina of Jacob Johs. Lansing and Jannetje Heyer. Wit. Johs. I. and Catharina Lansing.

bo. the 7th. Rachel of Abraham Bloodgood and Elisabeth Valkenburg.

bo. Apr. 28. Johannes Yates of William Sibry and Rebecca Yates. Wit. Anthony and Marytje Briesch.

bo. May 5. Nicolaas of Cornelius V. Schaik and Willempje Hanssen. Wit. Stephen V. Schaak, Cornelia Hanssen.

May 21. bo. Apr. 20. Francis of Francis Still and Rosina Fero. Wit. Wilh. Fero, Maria Berrit.

May 21. bo. Apr. 27. Jesse of Yzac Fonda and Antje V. Santvoort. Wit. Yzac and Marytje Foreest.

bo. Apr. 23. Gerrit of Gerrit V. d. Bergh and Rebecca Fonda. Wit. Cornelis and Ebbetje V. d. Bergh.

57

1786
bo. Apr. 23. Pieter of Cornelis V. Buuren and Jannetje Poel. Wit. Pieter and Dorothe V. Buren.

bo. Apr. 16. Catharina of Cornelis V. Santvoort and Cornelia V. Wie.

bo. Mar. 12. Arriaantje of Thomas Burnside and Arriaantje T. Eyck.

bo. Apr. 16. Margarita of Gerrit V. Schaik and Christina Berringer. Wit. Willem Cooper, Marytje Berringer.

May 23. Cathalyntje of Pieter Foreest and Pietertje V. Aalstein. Wit. Jacob and Annatje V. Aalstein.

May 28. bo. the 14th. Jannetje of Jacob G. and Femmetje Lansing. Wit. John and Cornelia Lansingh.

June 2. bo. Mar. 24. Thomas of Thomas Hook and Catharina Crane.

June 5. bo. May 24. Yzac of Jacob Vosburgh and Hanna Robbison. Wit. Yzac and Catharina Vosburgh.

June 10. bo. Mar. 1. Debora of John Graham and Debora Staats. Wit. Barent Staats, Debora Beekman.

bo. May 3. Margarita of Gerrit V. d. Poel and Cornelia Muller. Wit. Melchert and Marytje V. d. Poel.

bo. June 3. Pieter of Jacob H. Wendell and Geertruy Lansing. Wit. Pieter and Elisabeth Lansing.

bo. the 1st. Annatje of Johs. A. Lansing and Elisabeth Fryer. Wit. John and Catharina Fryer.

June 18. bo. the 6th. Stephanus of Stephanus V. Rensselaer and Margarita Schuyler. Wit. Philip V. Rensselaer, Catharina Westerlo, née Livingston.

bo. May 22. Cornelia of Obadia Cooper and Lena Albrecht. Wit. Anthony and Cornelia Halenbeek.

bo. the 11th. Elisabeth of Gozen V. Schaik and Maria Ten Broeck. Wit. Hendrik and Elisabeth Qwakkenbusch.

June 25. bo. the 20th. Alida of Johannes V. Hoesen and Engeltje V. Deusen. Wit. Meinard and Geertruy V. Hoesen.

bo. May 30. Johannes of John F. and Wyntje Bratt. Wit. Reynier and Rebecca V. Yveren.

July 9. bo. June 16. Andries of Yzac Qwakkenbusch and Catharina Gardenier. Wit. Benjamin and Maria Winne.

July 23. bo. the 12th. Engeltje of Pieter Waldrom Yates and Anna M. Helmes. Wit. Corn. E. and Margarita Yates.

1786

July 30. John of John Liswell and Annatje Lansing.

Aug. 6. bo. Aug. 27, 1785, Jacobus V. d. Veer of Jaques Janssen and Catharina Beekman.

Aug. 16. bo. July 3. Yzac of Jacob Qwakkenbush and Catharina De Voe. Wit. Yzac and Lena Dox.

Aug. 20. bo. July 14. Margarita of Herms Salsbury and Alida Sharp. Wit. Arbahm. De Manssen, Lena Salsbury.

bo. the 14th. Elisabeth of Jeremias Lansing and Helena Wendell. Wit. Pieter and Elisabeth Lansing.

bo. the 1st. Catharina of Pieter Young and Eva Moor. Wit. Jesse and Rebecca de Foreest.

Aug. 22. bo. July 22. Gerrit of Storm Slingerland and Annatje Halenbeek. Wit. Arent Slingerland, Cornelia Viele.

Aug. 22. bo. Mar. 3. Abraham of Johs. Sharp and Jerisha North. Wit. Abrah. Shutter, Geertruy Salsbury.

Sept. 4. bo. Aug. 28. Abraham of Jacobus Fonda and Willempje Bogert. Wit. Nanning and Alida Visscher.

bo. Aug. 3. David of Petrus Fero and Jannetje V. Deusen. Wit. Hendrik and Maria Fero.

Sept. 17. Jacob of Carel Heemstraat and Geertruy V. d. Werken. Wit. Casparus V. Wie, Rebecca V. Santen.

bo. Aug. 23. John of Jurjaan Hoghing and Annatje White. Wit. Salomo Look, Alida King.

bo. Aug. 3. Maria of David Winne and Geertruy Groesbeek. Wit. Jonathan and Maria Winne.

bo. Aug. 8. Benjamin of Theunis Oostrander and Marritje V. Vliet. Wit. Benjamin V. Vliet, Lea Oostrander.

bo. July 13. Nicholas of John Boom and Annatje Brower. Wit. Johs. and Maria Brouwer.

bo. Aug. 15. Daniel of John Milton and Rosina Joucat Wit. Daniel Clemsy, Rachel Milton.

bo. the 7th. William of Hendrik V. Woert and Catharina Eights. Wit. Elisabeth Eights.

Sept. 24. bo. Aug. 14. Maria of Pieter Davids and Elisabeth Colvill. Wit. Cornelius and Elisabeth Glen.

bo. the 22d. Annatje of Jacob Pruin and Hendrikje V. Buren. Wit. Johs. and Geertruy Pruin.

bo. the 20th. Elisabeth of Willem Staats and Annatje Yates. Wit. Barent and Elisabeth Staats.

bo. Oct. 11. Corrtland of Stephen S. Schuyler and Lena Ten Eyck. Wit. Pieter Schuyler, Geertruy Lansing.

1786
Oct. 29. bo. the 3d. Maria of Thoms. Witbeek and Elisth. Rysdorp. Wit. Pieter W. and Geertruy Witbeek.

bo. Sept. 30. Abraham Witbeek of David Foreest and Elisth. Witbeek. Wit. Abraham and Elisabeth Witbeek.

bo. Sept. 10. Folkert of Folkert Oothout and Jannetje Bogert. Wit. Eduard Comstor, Aaltje Oothout.

Nov. 5. bo. Sept. 28. Maria of Gerrit Hoogteeling and Annatje Oosterhout. Wit. Pieter and Maria Winne.

bo. the 4th. Debora of Nicolaas Bleeker and Neeltje Staats. Wit. Gerrit and Catharina Staats.

bo. the 3d. Elisabeth of Hendrik V. Benthuysen and Cathalyntje Hunn. Wit. Thomas Hun, Baatje V. Deusen.

Nov. 12. Marten of Willem Witbeek and Catharina Foreest. Wit. Marten and Tanneke Foreest.

bo. the 4th. Maria of John Williams and Mary Coep. Wit. Benjamin Williams, Mary Huyg.

Nov. 19. bo. the 8th. Maria of Dirk Benson and Marytje Wyngaert. Wit. Abrhm. Vosburgh, Maria Slingerland.

bo. the 10th. Catharina of James Donneway and Elsje Smith. Wit. Jacob Man, Catharina Sharp.

Nov. 27. bo. the 1st. Maria of Jesse Foreest and Rebecca V. Santen.

Dec. 17. bo. the 2d. Abraham of Pieter W. Groesbeek and Alida Van Aarnem. Wit. Abraham V. Aarnem, Sara Knoet.

bo. the 2d. Barent of Douwe Levison and Annatje Visscher. Wit. John and Saartje Visscher.

bo. the 16th. Elisabeth of Jacob Y. Trouex and Catharina Dogsteder. Wit. John and Elis. Bartell.

Dec. 24. bo. Nov. 23. Hiskia of Jacobus Schoonmaker and Elisabeth Acker. Wit. Hiskia and Annatje Schoonmaker.

bo. Nov. 8. Jacob of Nicholas Siksby and Cornelia Cooper. Wit. Evert Olfer, Elsje Siksby.

Dec. 31. bo. the 2d. Philippus of Jacob Berringer and Catharina Heiner. Wit. Philip and Catharina Berringer.

bo. the 23d. Rachel of Jacob Muller and Geertruy Veeder. Wit. Peter and Cornelia Witbeek.

bo. the 25th. Hester of Arent W. Slingerland and Annatje Aarnoudt. Wit. Wouter Slingerland, Lena Hanssen.

1786-1787
bo. the 7th. Elisabeth of Hendrik Oothout and Lydia Douw. Wit. Gerrit Lansing, Judith Cadmus.

bo. the 18th. Petrus of Pieter Ganzevoort and Catharina V. Schaick. Wit. John Ten Broeck, Sara Ganzevoort.

bo. Nov. 5. Jan Gerritsen of Jacob D. V. d. Heiden and Jannetje Yates. Wit. John G. and Cathalina Yates.

1787, Jan. 7. bo. Dec. 22. Cathalina of Jacobus Bleecker and Rachel V. Santen. Wit. John R. Bleecker, Elisabeth Staats.

Jan. 14. bo. Dec. 12. Jannetje and Lena of Wouter Hoogteling and Jenny Addringtraen. Wit. Coenraad, Geertruy, Theunis and Lena Hoogteling.

bo. Dec. 1. Catharina of Harpert Witbeek and Geertruy Wendell. Wit. Cornelis and Annatje Wendel.

bo. Dec. 18. Maria of John Rumney and Rachel Meinerssen. Wit. Frerik Meinerssen, Machtel Witbeek.

bo. the 13th. Annatje of Abraham Lansing, Jr., and Maria Bloodgood.

bo. Nov. 19. Geertruy of John Witbeek and Lena V. d. Bergh. Wit. David and Elisabeth Foreest.

Jan. 19. bo. Jan. 29, 1786. Catharine of Pieter Firese and Mary Hunter.

Jan. 21. bo. the 15th. Yzac Lansingh of Nicholas Jeralymon and Jannetje Waldrom. Wit. Yzac and Cathalina Bogert.

bo. the 16th. Gerrit of Hendrik V. Wie and Maria Merthen. Wit. Gerrit and Catharina Van Wie.

bo. Dec. 16. Hendrik of Daniel Clemison and Rachel Milton. Wit. Hendrik and Rachel Milton.

bo. Dec. 17. Cornelia of Barent V. Yveren and Rebecca Bratt. Wit. Cornelis V. Yveren, Sara Muller.

Jan. 29. bo. Nov. 5. Jannetje of Frerik Meinerssen and Elisabeth Waldrom. Wit. Johs. Rumney.

bo. the 19th. Alida of Gerrit A. Lansingh and Elisabeth Wynkoop. Wit. Jacobus and Alida Wynkoop.

bo. the 20th. Simon of Maas V. Franken and Geertruy Veeder. Wit. Jochum and Geesje Staats.

Jan. 30. bo. the 10th. Mary of Stephen Lush and Lydia Stringer. Wit. Samuel and Rachel Stringer.

1787

Feb. 5. bo. Jan. 7. Tanneke of Philip Foreest and Annatje V. Deusen. Wit. Marten and Tanneke Foreest.

bo. Jan. 5. Geertruy of Yzaac Harsen and Maria Roller. Wit. John Luther, Elisab. Roller.

Feb. 11. bo. Jan. 27. Folkert Douw of Jacob Hilton and Sara Barrington. Wit. Folkert and Annatje Douw.

bo. Jan. 4. Alida of Yzaac V. Wie and Neeltje Oosterhout. Wit. Johs. and Agnieta Oosterhout.

bo. Jan. 12. Susan of Japik and Saar (salves).

Feb. 25. bo. Jan. 24. Lea of Pieter Roman and Catharine V. Deusen. Wit. Frans and Geertruy Marshall.

bo. the 2d. Elisabeth of John Bleecker and Jane Gilliland. Wit. John and Elisabeth Bleecker.

bo. the 17th. Johannes of Cornelis Groesbeek and Annatje V. Antwerpen. Wit. Daniel and Rebecca V. Antwerpen.

bo. the 14th. Abraham of Hendrik Yates and Rachel V. Santen. Wit. Abraham and Jannetje Yates.

bo. Jan. 28. Willem of George Berringer and Elisabeth Boehn. Wit. Willem and Marytje Cooper.

bo. the 9th. Sara of Yzac Yz. Fryer and Catharina V. Wie. Wit. David and Sara Groesbeek.

bo. the 5th. Gerritje of Jacob and Geertruy Schermerhoorn. Wit. Hendrik and Elisabeth Roseboom.

Feb. 19. bo. Jan. 26. Hannah of John Gates and Geertruy V. Franken.

Mar. 2. bo. Feb. 25. Annatje of Reynier V. Yveren and Elisabeth Ostrander. Wit. Jelles and Sara Bett.

bo. Feb. or Jan. 25. Tanneke of Abrhm. Lappieris and Maria Foreest. Wit. Marten and Tanneke Foreest.

Feb. 19. bo. Dec. 31. Anna of Jesse Toll and Maria Viele, at Saratoga.

bo. Jan. 14. Johannes of Hendrik V. d. Werken and Catharina Cremer (Half Moon). Wit. Jurjen and Rebecca Cremer.

Feb. 20. bo. Jan. 29. Lena of Johs. Rous and Alida V. Etten. Wit. Hendrik and Annatje V. d. Kar.

bo. Dec. 27. Elisabeth of Francis Latimore and Geertruy Esch.

Feb. 20. Elias of Jacob Schouten and Catharina Dox. Wit. Elias and Catharina Steenberger.

Mar. 4. Cornelia of John Ostrander, Jr., and Catharina Witzel. Wit. John and Cornelia Price.

1787

bo. Feb. 24. Sara and Geertruy (twins) of Dirk Hunn and Annatje Lansing. Wit. Willem and Sara Hunn, Abrm. and Geertruy Lansingh.

bo. Feb. 20. Tobias of David Fonda and Catharina T. Broeck. Wit. Alida V. Schaick.

Mar. 7. bo. Feb. 12. Sara of John Lansingh, Jr., and Catharine Ray. Wit. Robert Rays, the mother.

Mar. 18. bo. Feb. 25. Johannes of Jacob Van Loon and Christina Schuyler. Wit. Johannes V. Loon, Annatje Schuyler.

Mar. 25. bo. the 14th. Jacobus of Philip Redly and Nancy(?) Hall. Wit. Ary Van Vlieck and Mary V. Vlieck.

Mar. 28. bo. Feb. 21. Elisabeth of Jacob V. Schaick and Elizabeth Berry. Wit. The parents.

Apr. 1. bo. Mar. 4. Johannes of Andries (or Abraham?) Lansing and Annatje V. d. Berg. Wit. Johs. and Neeltje Lansing.

bo. Mar. 2. Margarita of Johs. Poel and Isabella Douglass.

Apr. 8. bo. Mar. 21. Susanna of John Thinky and Maria Louths. Wit. William Thinky, Cornelia Hanssen.

bo. Mar. 31. Willem of Johs. J. Pruin and Arriaantje Verplank. Wit. Willem and Lydia Verplank.

Apr. 15. bo. Mar. 15. Catharina of Thomas and Lea Cooper. Wit. Nicholas Siksby, Cornelia Cooper.

bo. the 8th. Yzaac of Jacob Yz. Lansing and Susanna Fonda. Wit. Yzaac and Annatje Lansingh.

Apr. 15. bo. Mar. 17. Pieter of John and Alida V. Wie. Wit. Pieter and Ebbetje V. Wie.

bo. the 7th. Robert of Arent V. Deusen and Margarita McCloud. Wit. Elisabeth V. Deusen.

The following three children were bapt. when the first sermon was preached in the Greinebusch.

Apr. 19. bo. Mar. 4. Catharina of Obadia Lansingh and Cornelia V. Benthuisen. Wit. Cathalina Yates.

bo. Mar. 23. Cornelia of Daniel Springsteen and Annatje Schermerhoorn. Wit. Hendrik and Cornelia Schermerhoorn.

bo. Feb. 15. Henry of Timothy McCarty and Rebecca Patin.

1787

Apr. 22. bo. the 19th. Hermanus of Hermanus A. and Catharina Wendell. Wit. Philip P. and Annatje Schuyler.

bo. the 16th. Cathalina of Evert Mersselis and Sara V. Benthuisen. Wit. John and Eva Mersselis.

bo. the 20th. Annatje of John Veder and Catharina Winne. Wit. Maas and Geertruy V. Vranken.

May 13. bo. Apr. 20. Elisabeth of John V. Emburgh and Annatje Flensburgh. Wit. Thomas V. Zandt, Pietertje Hieralemon.

bo. Mar. 24. Jannetje of John D. Winne and Agnietje V. Wie. Wit. Daniel Winne, Jannetje De Foreest.

bo. Apr. 7. Maas of William P. Hoogteling and Maria Bloemendal. Wit. Jurjaan Hoghen, Hannah White.

bo. May 8. Quiliaan V. Rensselaer of Abram A. Lansingh and Elsje V. Rensselaer. Wit. Quiliaan I. and Elisabeth V. Rensselaer.

bo. Mar. 31. Wouter of David De Foreest and Susanna Fonda. Wit. Wouter and Wyntje Fonda.

May 18. bo. Apr. 17. Maria of Pieter J. Qwakkenbush and Mary Sheffield.

May 27. bo. Apr. 17. Samuel of Jacob Schermerhoorn and Annatje Kennada. Wit. Samuel Schermerhoorn, Lena Bloemendal.

bo. Apr. 16. Gerrit of Willem Flensburgh and Christina Backer. Wit. Gerrit and Antje Brouwer.

bo. May 15. Adriaantje of Anthony V. Santvoort and Maria Ross (or Roff). Wit. Yzac and Antje Fonda.

bo. the 13th. Theunis of Hendrik Bratt and Elisabeth V. d. Berg. Wit. Theunis and Cathalina Bratt.

bo. May 10. Maria Matilda of Philip V. Rensselaer and Maria Sanders. Wit. William and Maria Ludlow.

June 10. bo. May 16. Gerrit of Frans Harssen and Rebecca Spoor. Wit. Hannes and Magdalena Spoor.

bo. the 1st. Alida of Theunis Visscher and Alida Lansing. Wit. Gerrit Visscher, Annatje Legrancy.

bo. May 19. Nicolaas of Michael Besset and Maria V. Franken. Wit. Lavinus Winne, Elisabeth Basset.

June 15. bo. May 10. Temperance of Hendrik Shutter and Jannetje Hindermond. Wit. Hendrik Burhans, Temperance Dumont.

June 18. bo. May 16. Maria of Cornelis Brouwer and Jemina McMannis. Wit. William and Maria Brouwer.

bo. May 22. Agnieta of Cornelis V. Wie and Annatje

1787

Shenklen. Wit. Carparus V. Wie, Jannetje Winne.

June 24. bo. May 20. Catharina of John E. Lansingh and Maria Staats. Wit. Jacob and Annatje V. Aalstein.

bo. the 13th. Lena of Abraham T. Eyck and Annatje Lansingh. Wit. Jeremiah and Lena V. Rensselaer.

July 1. bo. May 21. Maria Catharina of George Madole and Catharina Seeger. Wit. Johs. and Catharina Seaman.

July 1. bo. June 11. Stephen of Hendrik V. Rensselaar and Cornelia V. Aalstein. Wit. Stephen and Margarita V. Rensselaer.

July 5. bo. June 17. John of Nicolas Frank and Elisab. Fonda. Wit. Wouter and Wyntje Fonda.

bo. June 10. Margarita of Wilhs Hayner and Elis. Muller. Wit. Andries and Margarita Muller.

bo. the 21st. Jacob of Nicholas Hoghil and Catharina V. Valkenburgh. Wit. Jacob Sharp, Christina Valkenburgh.

bo. the 27th. Philip and Jacob of Frederick Hook and Margarita Schefer. Wit. Philip and Jacob Heiner, Cath. Struyk, Lea Countreman.

bo. May 21. Wilhelmus of Wendel Jager and Anna Maria Simmons. Wit. Salmo and Sarah Jager.

July 8. bo. June 16. Nicholas of Pieter Clapper and Margarita House. Wit. Nicholas and Marytje Wheeler.

July 15. bo. June 23. Johannes of Frans Hoghil and Cornelia de Foreest. Wit. Pieter and Catharina de Foreest.

bo. July 1. Pieter of Abraham Veeder and Saara Hanssen. Wit. Pieter and Maria Veeder.

July 22. bo. June 7. Debora of Dirk Hanssen and Helena Louw. Wit. Abrm. Schuyler, Maria V. Rensselaer.

Aug. 12. bo. July 23. Catharina of John H. Wendell and Cathalina V. Benthuizen.

Aug. 13. Johannes of John and Wyntje Bratt. In the house on account of sickness.

Aug. 19. bo. July 13. Obadia of Obadia Benthuisen and Hanna Crumney(?).

Aug. 26. bo. the 6th. Jannetje of Anthony Groesbeek and Cathalina Foreest. Wit. Stephen and Jannetje V. Schaik.

Aug. 26. bo. the 13th. John Lee of Richard Sill and Elisabeth Nicholas. Wit. Cornelis and Elisabeth Glen.

Aug. 30. bo. July 28. Abraham of Gosen V. Schaik and Maria T. Broeck.

1787

Aug 31. bo. the 26th. Cathalina of Johs. V. Woert and Cathalina Lansingh.

bo. the 27th. Jannetje of Reynier Pruin and Jannetje Goey. Wit. Marritje Pruin.

Sept. 9. bo. Aug. 29. Cathalina of Hendrik Staats and Antje Lot. Wit. Johs. I. Lott, Cathalina V. Sinderen.

Sept. 17. bo. the 11th. Hubertje of Hendrik I. Lansing and Helena Winne. Wit. Jacob and Hubertje Lansingh.

Sept. 25. bo. the 17th. Gerrit of Jacobus Legrange and Annatje Visscher. Wit. Gerrit Visscher, Rachel V. d. Bergh.

bo. Apr. 17. Johannes of Bethuel Washburn and Gerritje Lansingh. Wit. Ary Legrange, Maria V. Antwerpen.

Oct. 19. bo. Sept. 2. Philip of Nicolaas Bower and Annatje Bartel. Wit. Andries and Sophia Bartel.

bo. Sept. 16. Lydia of Gerrit Hyer and Jannetje V. Slyck.

Oct. 27. bo. the 5th. Jacob of Philip Berringer and Catharina Meyer. Wit. Jacob Berringer, Catharina Heener.

bo. Sept. 29. Maria of Hendrik Van Ist and Andries (sic) Ten Eyk.

bo. Sept. 30. David Scot of Philip Wendell and Geertruy Vosburg. Wit. David and Susanna Scot.

Nov. 4. bo. Oct. 8. Benjamin of Benjamin Post and Catharina V. Norden. Wit. Wilhelmus Post, Gerritje Mill.

Nov. 4. bo. Oct. 2. Geertruy of Cornelis and Lena Vroman. Wit. Jacobus and Geertruy Vroman.

bo. Sept. 16. Elisabeth of David Flensburg and Maria Smith. Wit. Daniel and Catharina Flensburgh.

bo. Sept. 3. Jacobus of Hendrikus Bratt and Annatje Davids. Wit. Jacobus and Cathalina Davids.

bo. Oct. 4. Barent of Barent Muller and Cornelia Goewy. Wit. John and Maria Goewy.

Nov. 11. bo. Sept. 16. Maria of Mulburry V. Hoesen and Antje Beevings. Wit. John Prys and Cornelia Rykmans.

bo. Oct. 3. Annatje of Quiliaan Winne and Maria Perny. Wit. Yzac and Francyntje Fonda.

Nov. 18. bo. Oct. 18. Catryn (?) of Gysbert V. d. Bergh and Jannetje Witbeek. Wit. Pieter W. and Eva Witbeek.

bo. Oct. 1. Johannes of Jacobus V. d. Voort and Annatje Schuyler. Wit. Johs. Johs. V. Schayk, Catharina Schuyler.

1787-1788

bo. Oct. 2. Cornelia of Gysbert Groesbeek and Elisabeth Groff. Wit. Gerrit and Neeltje Groesbeek.

Nov. 25. bo. the 3d. Maas of Cornelis Bloemendal and Lena Reisdorp. Wit. John and Catharina Bloemendal.

bo. Oct. 22. Maas of Pieter Bloemendal and Barbara Sharp. Wit. Jurjen and Christina Sharp.

bo. the 2d. Jonathan of Frederik Meinerssen and Machtel Witbeek. Wit. John and Catharina Witbeek.

bo. Nov. 20. Lavinus of Benjamin Winne and Elisabeth Basset. Wit. Lavinus and Maria Winne.

Dec. 9. bo. Nov. 17. John of Dirk Foreest and Maria Fonda. Wit. John and Egje Fonda.

Dec. 23. bo. Oct. 31. Abraham of Dirk Knoet and Rachel Lansingh. Wit. Noah Gillet, Leentje Lansingh.

bo. Nov. 24. Johannes of Johs. Brouwer and Marritje de Wever.

bo. Nov. 1. Elisabeth of Wilhelms Cooper and Anna M. Berringer. Wit. Jurgen Berringer, Elisabeth Beem.

bo. the 10th. Anna of Arent S. Veeder and Jannetje Hoghingh. Wit. John Veeder, Catharina Winne.

bo. Nov. 28. Margarita of Obadia Cooper and Annatje V. d. Bergh. Wit. Matheus and Annatje V. d. Bergh.

Dec. 25. bo. the 18th. Jacob of Pieter Dox and Cathalina Lansingh. Wit. Reignier and Rebecca V. Yveren.

Dec. 30. bo. Nov. 23. Dirk of Willem D. Winne and Maria Becker. Wit. Gerrit and Marytje Becker.

1788, Jan. 7. bo. Nov. 11. Margarita of Abraham Dingman and Lea Salsbury. Wit. Hendrik V. Buuren, Hilletje Shutter.

bo. Nov. 16. Cornelia of Obadia F. Cooper and Lena Albrecht. Wit. Anthony and Cornelia Halenbeek.

bo. Nov. 3. Annatje of Pieter C. Bronk and Elisabeth V. Wie. Wit. Andries V. Wie, Marytje V. d. Bergh.

bo. Dec. 5. Alida of Harmen V. Hoesen and Catharina Witbeek.

Jan. 13. bo. Nov. 24. Gerrit of Matheus Poel and Elisabeth Shutter. Wit. Gerrit and Catharina Poel.

bo. Dec. 3. Engeltje of Meinard Oothout and Maria Siksby. Wit. Nicholas and Engeltje Siksby.

bo. Dec. 15. Lea of Petrus Fero and Jannetje V. Deuzen. Wit. Cornelis V. Deuzen, Geertruy Marshall.

1788

Jan. 13. bo. Dec. 22. Catharina of Wynand E. V. d. Bergh and Annatje Cooper. Wit. Christoffel and Catharina Yates.

bo. Nov. 31. (sic). Anna of Loys Barrington and Margarita Adams. Wit. Margarita Pruin.

Abraham of John Lisswell and Annatje Lansingh. Wit. Gerrit Lansingh.

Jan. 15. bo. Jan. 4. Abraham of John Brass. Wit. Abraham E. Wendell, Margarita Rykman.

Jan. 20. bo. the 12th. Elisabeth of Jacob V. Woert and Sarah V. Esch. Wit. Jacob and Elisabeth V. Woert.

Hannah of Jack Jackson and Beth (slaves). Wit. Saar.

Jan. 25. bo. Dec. 9. Yzac of James Hoogteelink and Neeltje Palmentier.

Jan. 26. bo. Dec. 23. Pieter of Jan Voorhees and Susanna Dumont.

bo. Jan. 12. Jacob of Lavinus Winne and Maria Lansingh. Wit. Egbert V. Schaak, Marytje Winne.

bo. the 14th. Catharina of Thomas Easterly and Baatje V. Woert.

Feb. 3. bo. Dec. 21. Annatje of Ludowich Haines and Margarit Arnold.

bo. Nov. 29. Garrit of Malachi Vander Pool and Annatje Sager.

Rebecca of Peter Slingland and Mary Vander Veher(?).

bo. Jan. 16. Nicholas of John N. Bleecker and Margarit Van Deusen.

Feb. 10. bo. the 3d. Yzac of Jacob J. Pruin and Neeltje Foreest. Wit. Yzac and Maria Foreest.

bo. Dec. 29. Maria of Marten C. and Theuntje V. Buuren. Wit. Peter M. and Marytje V. Buuren.

bo. Jan. 22. Sibble of Abner Sharp and Cornelia Halenbeek. Wit. Henry and Annaatje Halenbeek.

Feb. 17. bo. Jan. 4. Maayke of Andries Ouderkerk and Annatje Fero. Wit. Cornelis and Maayke V. d. Berg.

Feb. 24. bo. Jan. 15. Theuntje of Abraham Meyer and Geesje Bont. Wit. Philip Springer, Jacomyntje Beeving.

bo. Jan. 30. Anna of Johan Mathys Snoek and Geertruy Rees. Wit. Martinus Levins, Christina Pulver.

bo. Jan. 16. Sara Rutger of Rutger Bleecker (decd.) and Catharina Elmendorp. Wit. Barent Bleecker, Sara Lansingh.

1788

Feb. 29. bo. the 4th. Cornelia of Mathias V. Aalstein and Rachel de Foreest. Wit. Jacob and Annatje V. Aalstein.

bo. the 21st. Bata of Johs. V. Valkenburgh and Annatje Reisdorp. Wit. Johs. Vinhagen, Bata V. Valkenburgh.

bo. Jan. 17. Annatje of Nicholas V. d. Berg and Hannah Clute. Wit. Walter de Ridder and wife.

Mar. 2. bo. Dec. 12. Ulpianus of Nicholas Snyder and Femmetje V. Sinderen. Wit. Ulpianus V. Sinderen.

Mar. 6. bo. Jan. 14. Abraham of Jacobus Parse and Maritie Vanden Bergh. Wit. Abraham Vanden Bergh and wife Annatie.

Mar. 9. bo. Jan. 17. Frerick of Abraham V. Wie and Jacomyntje Burhans. Wit. Frerik Bratt, Lena Burhans.

bo. Mar. 1. Lydia of James Lansingh and Rachel Verplank. Wit. Willem and Lydia Verplank.

Mar. 9. bo. Feb. 26. Jeremie of Jacobus V. d. Poel and Marytje Muller. Wit. Johannes and Lyntje Muller.

Mar. 16. bo. the 10th. John of Abraham G. Lansingh and Susanna Yates. Wit. John Lansingh, Sara Bleeker.

Mar. 24. bo. the 2d. Dirk of Jesse de Foreest and Rebecca V. Santen. Wit. Dirk and Rebecca Foreest.

Mar. 30. bo. the 23d. John of Theunis V. Vechten and Elisabeth de Wandelaar. Wit. John de Wandelaar, Gerritje Ganzevoort.

bo. the 18th. Abraham of Jacobus Fonda and Willempje Bogert. Wit. Nanningh Visscher, Alida Fonda.

bo. the 5th. Franciscus of Daniel Marshall and Elisabeth Cockeran. Wit. Franciscus and Geertruy Marshall.

Apr. 6. bo. Mar. 29. Rebecca of Benjamin V. Santen and Sara Visscher. Wit. Gysbert V. Santen, Rebecca Winne.

Apr. 13. bo. Mar. 5. Jacob of David Berringer and Maria Barbara Heiner. Wit. Jacob Heiner, Elisabeth Kanter.

bo. Mar. 18. Hendrik of Pieter Cooper and Annatje Strunck. Wit. Coenraad Cooper, Christina Strunk.

Apr. 27. bo. the 22d. Hendrik of John Bogert and Catharina T. Broeck. Wit. Yzac and Hendrikje Bogert.

May 4. bo. Mar. 22. Catalina of Matthias Van den Bergh and Annatje Yeetes. Wit. John and Catalina Yates.

bo. Apr. 1. Cornelia of Martinus Van Ever and Cornelia V. Schaick. Wit. John Gui, Mary Van Ever.

1788

May 11. bo. Mar. 28. Jonathan of Samuel Morrel and Rachel Gardenier.

bo. Apr. 30. Maragrite of Hermanus Ten Eyck and Maragrite Bleecker. Wit. Henry and Catarina Bleecker.

May 11. bo. Mar. 16. Alida of Israel Anthony and Elisabeth V. Arnum. Wit. Johannes V. Aarnem, Hester Ouderkerk.

bo. Apr. 28. Catrina of John Groesbeek and Catalina V. Schaick. Wit. Casparus and Maria Prime.

May 18. bo. Apr. 29. Catharine of Henry Van Voort and Catharina Eights. Wit. Maria Loriss(?).

bo. May 3. Christiana of Henry Waldron and Margaret Van Vranken. Wit. Albert and Annatie Slingerland.

bo. Apr. 30, 1785. Henry of Wilhelmus Osterhout and Jane Chrysler. Wit. Maarten and Henry Oosterhout.

May 25. bo. May 12. Caty of John C. Cuyler and Hannah Mayby. Wit. John Mayby, Caty Trimper.

bo. May 1. Benjamin of Benjamin V. Etten and Caty Earle. Wit. Cornelia Bloemendale, Helena Rysdorfe.

bo. May 3. John Depeyster of John Depeyster Ten Eyck and Maria Dowe.

bo. Apr. 22. Jannitie of Augustine Sharp and Mary Van Alstine. Wit. Knout Van Alstine, Margaret Rysdorf.

May 30. bo. the 19th. Engeltje of Gerrit Marsselis and Magdalena Visscher. Wit. Bastiaan and Engeltje Visscher.

June 1. bo. May 4. Jacob of John Flensburgh and Catharina Bekker. Wit. Pieter and Marytje Flensburgh.

bo. Apr. 23. Salomon of Salomo Goey and Elisabeth Sandvoort.

bo. the 25th. Martinus of John De Garmo and Margarita Wendell. Wit. Christoffer and Annatje Millar.

June 7. bo. May 7. Rebecca of Pieter Bogert and Sara V. Schaik. Wit. John V. Esch.

June 8. bo. Apr. 26. Elisabeth of Wendel and Annatje Hillebrands.

bo. May 10. Cathalyntje of Dirk De Foreest and Rebecca Bratt. Wit. Theunis and Cathalina Bratt.

bo. the 6th. Rachel of Jacob V. Deuzen and Elsje Lansingh. Wit. Catharina Wendell.

June 22. bo. May 29. Willem of Johs. V. Santen and Margarita Burgess.

1788

June 28. bo. Apr. 13. Eleonora of Arent Lynn and Phebe Woodruff. Wit. Francis and Eleonora Carbin.

June 30. bo. May 16. Christina of Pieter T. Bratt and Jannetje Springby. Wit. Jacob Kidny, Anna Kelly.

July 6. bo. June 24. Jacob of John G. V. Santen and Leentje Lansingh. Wit. Jacob Lansingh, Willempje Winne.

June 8. John of John J. Fryer and Maria Follewyzer. Wit. John Fryer, Elisabeth V. Woert.

bo. June 6. Margarita of John and Cornelia Qwakkenbush.

July 12. Ruben of John Leonard and Maria V. Vechten.

July 13. bo. the 3d. Theunis of Anthony Bratt and Geertje V. d. Bergh. Wit. Theunis and Cathalyntje Bratt.

Abraham of Thoby and Elisabeth (salves). Wit. Abraham and Sara.

July 20. bo. June 3. Jacob of John Reyly and Cathalyntje V. d. Bergh.

bo. the 3d. Maria of John Fonda and Cornelia Hunn. Wit. Hendrik and Maria Mersselis.

July 20. bo. June 26. Lea of Gerrit Lansing and Maria V. Deusen. Wit. Cornelis V. Deusen.

bo. the 13th. Abraham of Dirk Ten Broeck and Cornelia Stuivesand. Wit. Abraham Ten Broeck, Elisabet. V. Renselaer.

bo. the 14th. Philip of Jacob Fryer and Agnietje Muller. Wit. Jacob and Geertruy Muller.

bo. the 25th. Celia of John(?) Devoe and Marg. Redly. Wit. Charles Shaves(?), Celia Radly.

Aug. 16. Jelles of Peter Legrange and Judith Maas. Wit. Christiaan and Elisabeth Legrange.

Aug. 24. bo. the 20th. Barbara Cloet of Jacob Vosburgh and Annatje Robbertson. Wit. Barbara Cloet.

bo. the 9th. Jacobus of Willem V. Benthuisen and Margarita Conklin. Wit. Evert and Sara Mersselis.

bo. the 8th. Arriaantje of Evert Janssen and Antje Legrange. Wit. Jacobus and Arriaantje Legrange.

Aug. 31. bo. the 23d. Daniel of Anthony Halenbeek and Cornelia Cooper. Wit. Hendrik and Susanna Halenbeek.

Sept. 5. bo. Aug. 28. Gerrit of Nicolaas Bleecker and Neeltje Staats. Wit. Gerrit and Catharina Staats.

bo. Aug. 19. Alida of Barent Bogert and Alida V. d. Bergh.

1788

bo. July 12. Zacharias of Christiaan Burk and Tabitha Chissam. Wit. Zacharia and Hanna Berringer.

Sept. 7. bo. June 2. Elisabeth of Eldert V. Woert and Elisabeth Fonda. Wit. John and Elisabeth Fryer.

Sept. 13. bo. Aug. 5. Maria of Willem Northen and Cath. Livingston. Wit. Richard and Marytje Northen.

Sept. 13. bo. July 2. Catharina of Johs. H. Fonda and Aaltje Levison. Wit. Yzac and Santje Fonda.

bo. the 5th. Elisabeth and Maria of John A. Lansingh and Elisabeth Fryer. Wit. Leentje Lansingh, Polly (or Sally) Graham.

bo. Aug. 17. Willem of Abram. Vosburgh and Saartje Bulsingh. Wit. Willem and Christina Vosburgh.

Sept. 21. bo. Aug. 26. Susanna of Gerrit Lansingh and Alida Foreest (should be "Fonda"). Wit. Rutger Lansing, Maria Fonda.

Sept. 28. bo. the 19th. Rebecca of Hendrik Yates and Rachel V. Santen. Wit. Gysbert and Rebecca V. Santen.

Oct. 6. bo. Sept. 11. Marthen of Leendert Reisdorp and Jannetje Foreest. Wit. Marten and Tanneke Foreest.

bo. Sept. 27. Jacobus of Hendrik V. Benthuisen and Cathalina Hunn. Wit. Baltes and Sara V. Benthuisen.

bo. Sept. 2. Willem of Wynand V. d. Bergh and Maria Hickson. Wit. Willem and Annatje V. d. Bergh.

Oct. 12. bo. Oct. 7. Abraham of Pieter W. Groesbeek and Alida V. Aarnem. Wit. Gerrit and Sarah Cloet.

bo. Sept. 16. Magdalena of Abraham V. Thessel and Annatje Lansingh. Wit. Willem and Lena Lansingh.

bo. Sept. 26. Cornelia of Charles Dickenson and Elsje Lansingh. Wit. Hendrik and Cornelia Remsen.

Oct. 14. bo. the 12th. John of Anthony Santvoort and Maria Rhaff. Wit. John and Christina Rhaff.

Oct. 15. bo. Aug. 22. Rebecca of John McIntosh and Mary Smith. Wit. Dirk and Rebecca Hagedoorn.

Oct. 19. bo. Sept. 19. Charlotte of William Brouwer and Mary Marschalk.

Oct. 15. bo. Oct. 7. Geertruy of Andries Abeel(?) and Annatje Marshall. Wit. Frans and Geertruy Marshall.

bo. Oct. 14. Sara of Thomas V. Benthuysen and Nency Enax. Wit. Thomas and ——— Cooper.

bo. Sept. 29. Cathalina of John Milton and Recina

1788-1789
Chiceat. Wit. Cornelis W. and Cathalina V. d. Bergh.

Oct. 3. Peter of Douwe Levessen and Annatie Fisher. Wit. Peter and Maria Leversen.

bo. Sept. 26. Dorothea of Fulcher Oothout and Jannetie Bogart. Wit. Cornelius and Willempie V. Schaick.

Oct. 19. Egje of Walter Fonda and Catharina Fox. Wit. John Fonda.

Nov. 16. bo. Oct. 26. Philip of John B. Schuyler and Elisabeth V. Rensselaer. Wit. Philip and Catharine Schuyler.

Nov. 23. bo. Nov. 19. Johanna of David Fonda and Catharina T. Broeck. Wit. Jacob and Catharina Cuyler.

bo. Nov. 8. Robert Ray of John Lansingh, Jr., and Cornelia Ray. Wit. Cornelis Ray, Elisabeth and Catharine Elmendorp.

Nov. 31. bo. Oct. 31. John of John Gates and Geertruy V. Franken.

Dec. 5. bo. Nov. 30. Catharina of Johannes Goey and Pietertje Jeralymon. Wit. Cornelis Waldrom, Alida Goey.

Dec. 28. bo. Dec. 22. Pieter of Pieter Ganzevoort, Jr., and Catharina V. Schaick. Wit. John T. Broeck, Sara Ganzevoort.

bo. Dec. 15. Franciscus of John F. and Wyntje Bratt. Wit. Reignier and Rebecca V. Yveren.

1789. Jan. 4. bo. Oct. 30. Wilhelmus of Yzac V. Wie and Neeltje Oosterhout. Wit. Pieter Winne, Maria Oosterhout.

Jan. 11. bo. Dec. 29. Catharina of Pieter Koen and Lydia Duitscher. Wit. William and Catharina Northen.

bo. Dec. 13. Hester of Gerrit Rykman and Elisabeth V. Buren. Wit. Gerrit P. and Margarita Rykman.

bo. Jan. 2. Frans of John Veeder and Catharina Winne. Wit. Maria Winne.

bo. Dec. 30. Elisabeth of Gerrit A. Lansingh and Elisabeth Wynkoop. Wit. Jacob and Elsje Van Deusen.

Jan. 25. bo. Jan. 3. Elisabeth of Abraham Lappius and Maria de Foreest. Wit. Arent V. Antwerpen, Elisabeth V. Lappius.

bo. Nov. 12. Cathalina of Pieter and Elisabeth David. Wit. Asa Fort. Cathalyntje David.

1789
bo. Dec. 4. Maria of William W. Crennel and Maria
Eman. Wit. Andries and Maria Eman.

Feb. 9. bo. Dec. 6. Pieter of Jonas Simons and Elsje
Strunk. Wit. Pieter and Catharina Simons.

bo. Jan. 6. Elisabeth of Nicholas Sixby and Cornelia
Cooper. Wit. Salomo Wally, Elisabet. Sixby.

Feb. 5. Jane of Alexander Taylor and Jenny Brisby,
baptised at Saratoga.

Feb. 6. bo. Sept. 21. James of William Sprott and Margar. McCrieger, baptised at Saratoga.

bo. Sept. 22, 1786, John of John Lang and Elisab. Rob.

bo. June 19, 1788, Jane of John Lang and Elisab. Rob.

bo. May 8, 1787, Drew of William Lang and Betsy
Johnson.

Feb. 22. bo. Dec. 7. Gerrit of Cornelis V. Aalstein and
Marytje Goey. Wit. Gerrit Goey.

Feb. 22. bo. the 13th. Catharina of Jacob H. Wendell
and Geertruy Lansingh. Wit. Lucas and Maria V. Vechten.

bo. the 13th. Maria of John V. A. Lansingh and Arriaantje Verplank. Wit. Jacobus Fonda, Willempje Bogert.

bo. the 14th. ———— of James Elliot Thompson and
Gertrude Conner. Wit. Francis Conner and his wife Maria.

Mar. 1. bo. Feb. 19. Alida of Theunis G. Visscher and
Alida Lansingh. Wit. Gerrit Visscher and Annatje Le
Gransy.

Mar. 8. bo. Feb. 5. Gerritje of Barent Staats and Antje
Winne. Wit. Adam and Gerritje Winne.

Mar. 22. bo. Mar. 5. Margarita of James Dunneway
and Elsje Smith. Wit. John Christy and Marytje Smith.

bo. Mar. 12. Neeltje of Ely Arnold and Geertruy Groesbeek. Wit. Adam Long, Neely Groesbeek.

Mar. 29. bo. Mar. 20. John of Hendrik Evertsen and
Hendrikje Winne. Wit. Bernardus and Annatje Evertsen.

Apr. 12. bo. Mar. 30. Hendrik Roseboom of Yzaac
Trouex and Jenneke Bleecker. Wit. Hendrik Trouex, Deborah V. Schelluyne.

Apr. 26. bo. Feb. 2. Jurjen of John Bloemendal and
Catharina Sharp. Wit. Jurgen, Jr., and Christina Sharp.

bo. Mar. 11. Rachel of Hendrik Fero and Maria Vredenburgh. Wit. Rachel Vredenburgh.

bo. Mar. 21. Lansingh of Douwe Fonda and Machtel
Lansingh. Wit. Jacob Franse and Jannetje Lansingh.

1789

bo. Apr. 13. Neeltje of Dirk Hunn and Annatje Lansingh. Wit. Thomas Lansingh, Neeltje Pruin.

bo. Mar. 29. Stephen of Stephen Van Rensselaer and Margarita Schuyler. Wit. Philip S. V. Rensselaer, Catharina Livingston.

Apr. 26. bo. Feb. 15. Charlotte of John Bleecker and Jane Gilleland. Wit. James Bleecker, Charlotte Cuyler.

bo. Apr. 28. Hendrick of John D. Winne and Agnes V. Wie. Wit. Hendrick and Maria Van Wie.

bo. May 1. Daniel of Jafrinus(?) Passenger and Maria Young. Wit. Daniel and Elisabeth Young.

bo. Apr. ——. Elisabeth of Peter Van der Linden and Susannah Anthony. Wit. Cornelius Van der Linden, Catharina Fonda.

May 29. bo. May 10. Abraham of Paulus and Lea Cooper. Wit. Abraham Cooper, Lena V. Buuren.

bo. the 17th. Theunis of Hendrik Bratt and Elisabeth V. d. Bergh. Wit. Theunis Bratt, Cathalyntje V. Esch.

June 5. bo. May 31. Loreina of Reynier Pruin and Jannetje Goey. Wit. Loxeine Goey.

bo. May 28. Annatje of Richard Lush and Lyntje Fonda. Wit. Nicholas and Lyntje Fonda.

bo. June 1. Yzac of Willem Staats and Annatje Yates.

June 7. Alida of Carel Heemstraat and Geertruy V. d. Werken. Wit. Gerrit and Baatje Cloet.

June 14. bo. May 16. Gerrit of Theunis V. d. Bergh and Marytje Beeker. Wit. Gerrit and Marytje V. d. Bergh.

June 28. bo. the 21st. Elisabeth of Hermanus A. Wendel and Catharina Wendell. Wit. John and Susanna Wendell.

bo. the 24th. Engeltje of Gerrit G. Mersselis and Machtel Visscher. Wit. Bastiaan and Engeltje Visscher.

July 9. bo.June 23. Hester of Stephanus Viele and Zara Toll.

bo. Sept. 18, 1787, Elisabeth, bo. June 13, 1789, Johannes, of Frans Ruger and Janiette Jewel, baptized at Saratoga. Wit. John and Elisabeth Ruger, John and Theophila Jewel.

July 10. bo. May 8. Cornelius of Nicholas Van de Bergh and Janiette Waldrom. Wit. Johannes Waldrom and Alida V. d. Bergh.

bo. Apr. 28. Abyah of John Smith and Mary McDole.

July 9. bo. Feb. 28. Cornelius of Cornelius and Margaret

1789
McLean. Wit. John Winne, Caty Glasby.

July 12. bo. July 4. Pieter of Jacob Muller and Geertruy Veeder. Wit. Pieter and Marytje Veeder.

July 19. bo. June 4. Engeltje of Jacobus Schoonmaker and Elisabeth Ackerson. Wit. Adam and Engeltje Ackerson.

bo. June 2. Lena of Cornelis and Lena Vroman. Wit. Cornelis and Lena Vroman.

bo. June 28. Saartje of Simon Ter Willigen and Jannetje Coen. Wit. Dirk and Saartje Ter Willigen.

bo. June 22. David of Willem Hoogteeling and Maria Bloemendal. Wit. Pieter and Elisabeth Hilton.

July 27. bo. June 28. Elisabeth of Richard Canton and Catrina Boogena(?). Wit. Jacob and Elisabeth Nainar.

bo. July 24. Catharin Cuyler of Leonard Gansevorth and Hester Cuyler. Wit. Abraham Ten Broeck, Annatie Cuyler.

Aug. 9. bo. May 24. John of Gysbert Groesbeek and Elisabeth Graff. Wit. Johs. and Cornelia Groesbeek.

bo. June 26. John of Adam Long and Neeltje Groesbeek. Wit. Coenraad and Christina Long.

Aug. 16. bo. the 6th. Theunis of Johs. Pruin and Arriaantje Verplank. Wit. Gelyn Verplank, Rachel Lansingh.

Aug. 9. bo. July 12. Abraham of Johs. and Alida V. Wie. Wit. Abraham V. Wie, Jacomyntje Burhans.

Aug. 23. bo. July 27. Geertruy of Abraham Veeder and Neeltje Schuyler. Wit. Dirk and Annatje Schuyler.

bo. July 25. John of David Foreest and Elisab. Witbeek. Wit. John de Foreest, Elbertje V. Aalstein.

Aug. 30. bo. July 25. Pieter of David Foreest and Janneke Fonda. Wit. Pieter Foreest, Barbara V. Aalstein.

Aug. 30. bo. Aug. 26. Pieter of Nicolaas Hieralomon and Jenny Waldrom. Wit. Pieter Waldrom, Susan Meinersse.

Sept. 6. bo. June 13. Margarita of Martin Aurinjer and Maria Buis.

bo. Aug. 24. Garret of Charles Morgan and Sarah Neyer. Wit. Garret Neyer.

Oct. 18. bo. Sept. 26. Maria of John J. Lansingh and Annatje Marshall. Wit. Johs. and Maria Lansingh.

bo. Sept. 28. Abraham of Johs. H. V. d. Werken and Catharina Slingerland. Wit. Abrah. and Marytje Slingerland.

1789

bo. Sept. 19. Annatje of Johs. Brouwer and Marritje de Weever.

bo. Sept. 18. ———— of Isaac Deniston and Eleanor Visher.

bo. Sept. 30. ———— of John Van Inburgh and Hannah Flamsburgh. Wit. Hannah Van Imburgh.

Oct. 24. bo. Oct. 19. Garret of Nicholas Bleecker and Nellie Staats. Wit. Garret Staats, Catharina Cunninghs.

Oct. 25. bo. Sept. 16. Cornelis of Petrus Fero and Jannetje V. Deuzen. Wit. Cornelis and Elisabeth V. Deussen.

bo. Sept. 22. Catharina of Jacob Sharp and Arriaantje V. Yveren. Wit. Hendrik and Barbara Bogert.

Oct. 25. bo. Oct. 15. Barent of Jacob V. Loon and Christina Schuyler. Wit. Marten and Maria Schuyler.

Oct. 31. bo. Oct. 16. Mary of Thomas Van Benthuisen and Nancy Enochs.

bo. Sept. 30. Samuel of Edward Comptton and Mary Van Schaick.

bo. Sept. 10. Andreas of George Ten Eyck and Magdalena Upham.

Nov. 8. bo. the 6th. Magdalena of Abraham A. Lansingh and Elsje V. Rensselaar. Wit. Gerrit G. and Lena Lansingh.

bo. Oct. 25. Jacob and Alida (twins) of Jacob Y. Lansingh and Susanna Fonda. Wit. Nanningh and Alida Visscher.

Nov. 14. bo. Oct. 25. Philip(?) of Jonathan Hilton and Catharina Hansen. Wit. Levinus Timber, Catalina Hansen.

bo. Nov. 5. Johannes of Jacob Eversen and Hannah Slingerland. Wit. Jacob and Susannah Winne.

bo. Oct. 17. John of Matthew Trotter and Margaret Wendle.

bo. Sept. 30. Maria of Leonard Winnigh and Annatie Muller. Wit. Cornelius Vedder, Naltie Muller.

bo. Nov. 9. Dirck Brat of James Van Schoonhoven and Maria Spore. Wit. Cornelius and Volkia V. Schoonhoven.

bo. Oct. 21. James of James Legrange and Annatie Fisher. Wit. Arie Legrange.

bo. Oct. 18. Garret of Dirck Clute and Rachel Lansing.

bo. Sept. 2. Magdalena of Henry Lewis and Maria Davis.

1789

Nov. 15. bo. Oct. 12. Hetty of Jesse Foreest and Rebecca V. Santen. Wit. John V. Santen, Hetty Jones.

George W. Ray of John Cuyler and Jennet W. Ray. Wit. George W. Ray, Catharina T. Broeck.

Nov. 22. bo. Nov. 12. Nicolaas of John N. Bleecker and Margarita V. Deusen.

Nov. 22. bo. Nov. 13. Angeltie of Bernardus Everson and Martina Hogan. Wit. Arie Legrange, Maria V. Antwerp.

Nov. 29. bo. Oct. 26. Jannetje of Cornelis V. Wie and Annatje Shenklin. Wit. Gerrit V. Wie, Jannetje Lansingh.

Dec. 15. bo. Nov. 27. Engeltje of Isaac H. Bogert and Catalina Fisher. Wit. Bastian and Mackeltie Fisher.

INDEX

of the

MARRIAGE AND BAPTISMAL REGISTER

of the

REFORMED PROTESTANT DUTCH CHURCH OF ALBANY

1780-1789

* Indicates that name appears more than once on page.

William 5.
Cannell, Jane 6.
Cannik, Jonathan 29.
Canton, Elisabeth 75; Richard 75.
Capron, William 8.
Carbin, Eleanora 70; Francis 70.
Carpenter, Hester 6.
Casparus, Casparis, Jacob 56; Margarita 40; Valentine, Valentyn 40, 56.
Cassen, Catharina 4.
Chadden, Pieter 3.
Chambers, Eduard 15; Hendrik 15; Leonard 20; Mary 20.
Charless, Maria 33.
Chatfield, David 19.
Chiceat, Recina 72.
Childs, William 53.
Chissam, Tabitha 71.
Christman, Frederik 19; Hans 19; Maria 1, 19; Nicolas 1, 19; Pieter 19.
Christy, John 73.
Chrysler, Jane 69.
Claas, Susanna 6.
Claassen, Maria 52; Pieter 52; Susanna 52.
Clapper, Nicholas 64; Pieter 64.
Clark, Clerk, Alexander 26; Elisabeth 26; Margaret, Margarita 24, 28; Robert 4.
Claver, Catharina 13; Nicholaas 13, 52; Susan 52; Susanna 16.
Clemenger, Daniel 48; John 48.
Clement, Daniel 5; Rachel 11, 15.
Clemison, Daniel 60; Hendrik 60.
Clemsy, Daniel 58.
Clench, Abigail 23.
Clenzy, Ebigl 14.
Clerk, see Clark.
Cleyn, Clyn, Clyne, David 17; Elisabeth 18; Joseph 18, 38; Nicholaas 17; Peter 38.
Cloet, Cluet, Clute, Kloet, Baatje 74; Barbara 70; Elis., Elisabeth 21, 28, 35; Dirck 76; Garret 76; Geertruy 3; Gerrit 71, 74; Hannah 68; Sarah 54, 71.
Cluet, see Cloet.
Clute, see Cloet.
Clyn, see Cleyn.
Cochron, Cachron, Cockeran, Elisabeth 20, 44, 68.
Coen, Coenes, Koen, Barbara 18; Catharina 72; Coenraad 29; James 29; Jannetje 75; Marg. 24; Neeltje 15; Pieter 72; Rebecca 5.
Coep, Mary 59.
Coeper, see Cooper.

Cofftree, see Coghtree.
Coghtree, Cogtrie, Cofftree, Coughtry, Agness 4; Mary 3, 32, 48.
Colberth, Hester 34; William 34.
Colbrecht, Colebrecht, Hugh Bennys 41; Stephen 28; Willm, William 28, 41.
Coldin, John 15; Johs. 15.
Cole, Rachel 2, 17.
Collington, Elisabeth 5.
Collins, Abigail 3; Andrew 33; William 33.
Colwell, see Calwell.
Colvill, see Calwell.
Compstead, Eduard 11; John Henry 11.
Compstone, Comstone, Andrew Van Schaak 26, 39; Eduard 26, 39; Marytje 27.
Comstor, Eduard 59.
Compton, Edward 76; Samuel 76.
Congel, Job 19; Uzia 19.
Conger, Any 24; Hilletje 24; Ruben 1, 24.
Conklin, Margarita 23, 54, 70.
Connel, Eduard 30; Maria 30; Marytje 52.
Conner, Annatje 24; Francis 73; Gertrude 73; Maria 73; Marytje 24.
Connolly, Sarah 8.
Conny, Catharina 39.
Conyn, Andrew 3; Casparus 13; Tryntje 13.
Conzalus, Hannes 14; Matheus 14.
Cool, Engeltje 26; John 11; Pemberton 11; Susanna 2, 19.
Coop (?) Mary 47.
Cooper, Abrah. Abraham 26, 74*; Annatje 2, 25, 67; Cathalyna 50; Cath., Catharina 7, 36, 62; Christiaan 45; Cornelia 18, 31, 37, 54, 57, 59, 62, 66, 70, 73; Coenraad 68; Elisabeth 46, 66; Hendrik 68; Jacob 37; Jannetje 26; Johannes 55; Lea 7, 62, 74; Margarita 66; Maria 53; Marytje 55, 61; Obadia 3*, 26, 50, 57, 66; Obadia F. 66; Paulus 74; Pieter 4, 46, 55, 68; Rebecca 3, 30, 41; Rosina 37; Sara Hilton 46; Thomas 7, 62, 71; Wilhelmus 45, 66; Willem 46, 53, 55, 57, 61.
Cormey, John 15; Judike 15.
Cortland, Cathalina 48.
Cortney (?) John 24.
Coughtry, see Coghtree.
Cougler, Elisabeth 17.

Hart, Charlotte M. 33; Ezechiel 36; Harmen Visscher 46; Henry 4, 36, 46.
Hartwich, Catharina 45; John 45.
Harwich, Coenraad 16; Magdalena 16.
Hasevoet, Neeltje 56.
Haslet, Thomas 24*.
Haswell, Hasswell, Hasswel, Arthur 3, 32, 48; Elisabeth 32; John 10*, 27; Joseph 27; Mary 2, 22, 48; Robert 2, 22.
Hawill, John 35.
Hay, Hays, John 3; Maria 4.
Hayner, Margarita 64; Wilhs. 64.
Heemstraat, Albert 32; Alida 74; Bata 6; Carel 22, 32, 58, 74; Dirk 22; Jacob 58; Machtel 14, 18.
Heener, Catharina 65.
Heens, Cat. 19.
Heermans, Andries 19; Wilhelm 19.
Heeugier, Elisabeth 18; Martin 18.
Hegeman, Hagemans, Arriaantje 42; Joseph 5.
Heiner, Catharine 59; Jacob 64, 68; Maria B. 56; Maria Barbara 68; Marg P. 45; Philip 64.
Helbrig, Lena 3.
Heller, Elisabeth 15.
Helmer, Johs 39; Margarita 39.
Helmes, Helms, Anna M. 16, 57; Ann Mary 35.
Hendermond, see Hindermond.
Henry, Henrys, Christy 7; John 7; William 7.
Hermans, Catharina 46; Jacob 46.
Herod, Mary 2.
Herrick, Jurjen 13; Tanneke 13.
Heyer, see also Hyer, Elisabeth 20; Gerrit 20, 36; Jannetje 36, 43. 56; Sarah 9.
Hickson, Maria 71.
Hieralymon, Hieralomon, see Jerolomon.
Hildebrand, Hillebrands, Annatje 69; Elisabeth 69; Elsje 40; Geertruy 35; Johannes 22; Wendel, Wendell 15, 22, 35, 40. 69.
Hilton, Annatje 5, 43; Antje 27, 55; Elisab, Elisabeth 22, 29; 44*, 55, 75; Folkert Douw 61; Jacob 29, 47, 61; Jacobus 9; Johannes T. Eyck 47; John 6, 55; Jonathan 4, 44, 54, 76; Margarita 29; Maria 3, 47; Phebe 55; Philip 47, 76; Pieter 29, 54, 75; Rykert 39, 55; Sara 47, 52; Sofia 22; Willem 44.

Hindermond, Hendermond, Barentje 46; Hendrik 12*, 46; Jannetje 37, 63.
Hodson, George 1.
Hoes, Cathalina 54; Cornelia 37; Jurjen 54.
Hoevenbach, Benjamin 32; Jannetje 32.
Hogeboom, Dirk 7.
Hogen, see Hoghen.
Hogh, Lena 17.
Hoghen, Hogen, Hoghing, Hoginah, Annatje 45; Elsje 29, 39; Gerrit 39; Jannetje 29, 50, 66; John 23, 58; Jurjaan 33, 39; Jurjen 23, 29, 45, 58, 63; Martina 14, 33, 45, 77; Marten 39; Nicolaas 24.
Hoghil, Hoghel, Eduard 18, 51; Francis 1; Frans 18, 64; Jacob 51, 64; Johannes 64; Nicolas 6, 51, 64.
Hoghing, see Hoghen.
Holbrook, Holebrock, Caty 22; Efraim, Ephraim 22, 38; Johnson 38.
Holles, Nency 2.
Holliday, Holiday, Halliday, Jannetje 31; Mary 10 30; Matthew 7.
Homes, Nency 11.
Hood, Elisabeth 20; Johs 20.
Hoogkerk, Abrahm, Abraham 27*, 52, 55; Alida 20, 35, 50*; Antje 52; Elisabeth 35; Johs 14, 35, 50; Lucas 14; Rachel 14; Willem 55; Ysac 14, 50.
Hoogteling, Hoogteeling, Abrahm 18, 39; Anna Margarita 18; Annatje 48; Arriaantje 22, 48; Cath. Catharina 21, 37; Coenraad 49, 60; Daniel 21; David 75; Elisabeth 48; Geertruy 60; Gerrit 20, 48, 59; Helena 2; James 67; Jannetje 49, 60; Johs 6, 22, 48, 49; Lena 21, 22, 60*; Maas 63; Maria 59; Mathys 39; Neeltje 8, 49; Rachel 39; Sara 3; Storm 4, 6; Theunis 39, 60; Wilhelmus 20; Willem 22, 37, 48, 75; William P. 63; Wouter 5, 60; Yzac 67.
Hook, see also Huyck, Catharina 41; Frederick 64; Harinah 44; Jacob 64; Philip 64; Sara 15; Thoms, Thomas 15, 41, 44, 57*.
House, Margarita 64.
Howards, Nency 41.
Hudson, Elisabeth 47; Ephraim 47; Moses 47; William 47.

Huik, *see* Huyck.
Hungerford, Mary 19.
Hunn, Hun, Cathalina 7, 34, 36, 71; Cathalyntje 59; Cornelia 4, 45, 55, 70; Dirck, Dirk 4, 36, 50, 52, 62, 74; Elisabeth 51; Elsje 50; Geertruy 62; Neeltje 74; Sara 45, 62*; Thomas 51, 59; William, Willem 45, 62.
Hunter, James 4; Mary 1, 60; Marytje 27.
Husher, Daniel 29; Margarita 29.
Huston, Timotheus 18; Timothy 18.
Hutton, Margarita 3.
Huyck, Huyk, Huik, Haick, *see* also Hook, Annatje 17; Cornelis 24; Hendrik 1, 2, 24*; Jurjen 52; Leena, Lena 2, 52; Maria 24; Mary 59; Yzaac 7.
Hyer, Gerrit 51, 65; Lydia 51, 65.
Hynds, Neby 9.

Jackson, Francis 30*; Hannah 67; Jack 67; Mary 20, 22, 39; Nency 17.
Jacobi, Lena 4; Margarita 2.
Jacobs, Elisab., Elisabeth 5, 50; Geertruy 17.
Jager, Salmo 64; Sarah 64; Wendel 64; Wilhemus 64.
Janssen, Annatje 49; Arriaantje 70; Evert 49, 70; Jacobus v. d. Veer 58; Jaques 58..
Jauncey, John 9.
Jellet, *see* Gillet.
Jenkins, John 40; Margarita 40.
Jerolomon, Jeralemon, Jeralymon, Hieralymon, Hieralomon, Annatje 43; Jannetje 27; Nicholas 17, 27, 43*, 60, 75; Petritie 8; Pieter 75; Pieterje 63, 72; Susanna 17; Yzac Lansingh 60.
Jewel, Juwell, Janiette 74; John 74; Joseph 4; Theophila 74.
Johnson, Johnston, Betsy 73; Elisabeth 7; Esther 22, 38; John 3, 9; Sara 15; Sibyll 3; Willm 15.
Jones, Hetty 77; Margarita 36.
Joucat, Rosina 58.
Juwell, *see* Jewel.

Kanter, Elisabeth 68.
Keane, Jemima 7.
Kelly, Anna 70.
Kemmel, Alexander 23, 24*; Angus 23; Catharina 28; Isabella 10; Jane 24; Margaret 24; Price 24, 28; Robert 23*; William 24*.

Kemp, Elisabeth 12; Johs. 12.
Kennada, Annatje 63.
Kerkenaer, Margarita 10; Margar 15; Rykert 10; Sofia 10.
Kerker (?) Marg 19.
Kerl, Cornelia 12.
Kern (?), John M. 49.
Kerner, Margarita 51; Philip 51; Willem 51.
Kidney, Kidny, Elisabeth 21; Engeltje 39; Jacob 70; Jonathan 43.
Kief, Arthur 20; Fenny 20.
Killy, Margareth 3.
Kim, Jacob 15; Maria 15; Marytje 15.
King, Alida 58; Annatje 25; Thoms 25.
Kinny, Deborah 55; Jacob 55.
Kirkland, Alexander 2.
Klabert, Johannes 9.
Kloet, *see* Cloet.
Knets (?), Margarita 15.
Knipp, Maria 26.
Knoet, Abraham 66; Dirk 53, 66; Geertruy 27; Jacob 53; Johs 16; Sara 16, 59.
Koch, Elisabeth 19; Hendrick 19; Maria 19; Zepherinus 19.
Koek, Hendrik 14; Sara 14.
Koen, *see* Coen.
Krankert, Judlof 20; Pieter 20.
Krankheit; Jannetje 25.
Krifer (?) Nency 49.
Kuyler, *see* Cuyler.

La Grange, Lagrange, Le Grange, Le Granzy, Le Grancy, Annatje 49, 63, 73; Antje 49, 70; Arriaantje 70; Ary, Arie 14, 48*, 65, 76, 77; Christiaan 19, 54, 70; Elisabeth 8, 19, 70; Engeltje 54; Gerrit 65; Jacobus 4, 48, 65, 70; James 76*; Jelles 49, 70; Maria 14, 48; Peter 70.
Lancaster, Elisabeth 11; Samuel 11.
Land, Margarita 36.
Lang, Christoffer 9; Drew 73; Jane 73; John 73*, Johs 14; Susanna 14; William 73.
Lansing, Lansingh, Lanssing, Aaltje 18; Abr, Abraham 5, 18, 19, 23, 28, 36, 39, 51, 55, 62*; Abraham A. 16, 23, 52, 63, 76; Abraham Fonda 48; Abraham G. 11, 29, 38, 53, 68; Abraham, Jr. 51, 60; Abraham Yates 29; Alida 7, 37, 60, 63, 73, 76; Andries 62; Annatje 4, 21, 22, 34, 36, 49, 50, 51, 52, 55,

Lycher, Elisabeth 19; Hendrik 19.
Lynn, Arent 70; Eleonora 70.

McAdams, Hugh 16; Mary 16.
McAlpin, David 10; James 10.
McBenton, Elisabeth 1.
McCarty, Denys 11; Elisabeth 32;
    Henry 62; Mary 23; Rachel
    11; Timothy 62.
McCastry, James 27; John 27.
McCay, Isabella 20; John 24;
    Marg 17; Neal 24.
McCewen, Ann 32.
McChesney Hugh 19; Isabella 19;
    Jacobus 3; Jane 18; John 19;
    Joseph 12, 27; Samuel 12, 19;
    William 27.
McClallen, Jenny 25.
McClance (?), Alexander 25;
    Daniel 25.
McClannen, Jane 2.
McClarming, Jenny 3.
McClennen, Jennet 43.
McCloglin, William 2.
McClosky, James 19; John 19.
McCloud, McCloudy, Alexander
    32; Hugh 19; Marg, Margarita
    13, 31, 47, 62; Mordac, Mor-
    dach 19, 32; Reynold 32.
McCogtreen, James 3.
McCovie, —— 26.
McCoy, Charles 26, 52; Maayke
    52*; Maria 26; Willem 52.
McCrieger, Margar 73.
McCullogh, Nency 26; William 26.
McDaniel, Janny 6.
McDavid, Sara 23.
McDole, McDoles, George 25; Ja-
    cob 25; Mary 74.
McDonald, McDonal, Christina 26;
    Daniel 26; Elenor 20; Jacob
    23*, 24; Nency 24; Normand
    20 William 20.
McDougal, Malcom 25; Pieter 25.
McEntee, Mary 32.
McEwan, Ann 20.
McFarson, Janny 2.
McGee, Mary 32.
McGiffy, Samuel 6.
McGlochum, Rachel 26; William
    26.
McGriger, McGrieger, McGreeger,
    Alexander, 12 33; Jennet 12;
    John 33; Mary 12, 26; Nency
    26.
McHay, Charlotta 3.
McIntosh, John 71; Rebecca 71;
    Wlm 5.
McKenny, Elisabeth 32; John 32.
McKentisch, Rachel 25.
McKinly, Christina 29.

McKinsy, McKinzy, Catharina 24;
    Francis 23; Henry 41; Jan-
    netje 41; Margaret 23.
McLean, Cornelius 75*; Margaret
    75.
McManus, McMannis, Cathalyntje
    18; Jemima 63; Rebecca 47;
    William 47.
McMaris, William 5.
McMaster, Jane 14.
McMollen, McMullen, Alexander
    21; Daniel 1; John 9, 21.
McMoris, Thomas 2.
McMullen, see McMollen.
McMuller, Caty 26; Mary 23.
McPherson, John 6.
McVie, Christina 16; Ebbie 12;
    John 16.

Maas, Judith 70.
Mackelwayn, Elisabeth 24; Jenny
    24; Thoms 24.
Madole, George 64; Maria Catha-
    rina 64.
Maley, Catharina 13; John 13.
Malhilh, Agness 6.
Malword, Mary 6.
Man, Jacob 59.
Mancius, Annatje 21; Cornelia 46;
    John 46; Wilhelmus 46.
Manson, Catharine 6.
Mark, Mary 27; Sara, Sarah 2,
    22; Yzac 2.
Marl, Marll, Morrel, Harmen 23,
    37; Jonathan 69; Matheus 54;
    Rachel 42, 43, 45; Saml, Sam-
    uel 23, 37, 42, 43, 45, 54, 69.
Marschalk, Mary 71.
Marshal, Marshall, Annatje 43, 71,
    75; Daniel 11, 20, 44, 68;
    Daniel Flensburg 20; Elisa-
    beth 11; Franciscus 11, 20, 31,
    68*; Frans 51, 61, 71; Geer-
    truy 20, 51, 61, 66, 68, 71;
    Immetje 11; Joseph 44; Lea
    31.
Marsselis, see Mersellis.
Marthen, Merthen, Margarita 14,
    35; Maria 24, 43, 60.
Martins, Geertruy 22; John 22.
Marus (?) Neeltje 31.
Mason, Maria 49.
Masten, Rachel (?), 50.
Matthews, Elisabeth 20.
Mayby, Hannah 69; John 69.
Meck, Jacomyntje 2.
Meeby, Catharina 2.
Meinerssen, Meinersee, Meinertsen,
    Abram, Abraham 36, 43; Cath-
    arina 43, 49; Elisabeth 22;
    Frederik 66; Frerik 11, 22,

Johs. 34; Maria 30, 66; Marytje 31; Nicolaas 30, 31, 59, 62, 66, 73.

Sill, John Lee 64; Richard 6, 56, 64; William Nicolls 56.

Simmons, Simons, Anna Maria 64; Benjamin 38; Catharina 73; John 38; Jonas 73; Pieter 73*.

Simson, Caty 16.

Sitzer (?) Andries 28; Pieter 28.

Sixby, see Siksby.

's Jans, Annatje 31; Catharina 31.

Skidmore, Rachel 50.

Slingerland, Slingeland, Abrah., Abraham 19*, 26, 75; Abraham Trouex 25; Albert 13, 25, 27, 69; Annatje, Annatie 2, 33, 69; Arent 7, 58; Arent W. 59; Catharina 7, 75; Christina 27; Cornelia 55; Douwe 23, 31; Gerrit 58; Geertruy 26, 42, 44; Hannah 76; Hendrik 7; Hester 9, 59; Jacob 55; John 9; Maria 5, 30, 41, 59; Marytje 13, 25, 75; Rebecca 19, 26, 54*, 67; Pieter 6, 54, 67; Storm 58; Theunis 42, 54; Theunis A. 41; Theunis E. 19, 30; Theunis W. 23, 31; Wouter 59; Wouter W. 42,; Yzac 42.

Smith, Abyah 74; Baatje 12; Catharine 7; Charles 31; Christian 8; David 17; Elisabeth 41; Elsje 30, 46, 59, 73; John 74; Margarita 22, 31; Maria 46, 65; Mary 71; Marytje 73; Nenny 17; Nicolaus 16; Theodorus 16.

Smitt, Margarita 51; Maria 4.

Sneed, Elisabeth 10.

Snissen, (?) Antje 19.

Snoek, Anna 67; Johan Mathys 67.

Snyder, Annatje 28; Christina 28, 45; Geertruy 55; Leentje 28; Nicholas 68; Rebecca 40, 56; Ulpianus 68; Wyntje 6.

Soop, Geertruy 28.

Spaan, Catharine 7; Maria 1; Marytje 20.

Spaar, (?) Marytje 46.

Spoor, Spore, Catharina 1; Hannes 63; Magdalena 63; Maria 40, 49, 76; Mary 9; Rebecca 16, 40, 49, 63.

Springby, Jannetje 70.

Springer, Philip 67.

Springsteen, Cornelia 62; Daniel 62; Elisabeth 14; Jacob 17; Jacobus 17; Jurjen 5; Sara 5.

Springsteden, Springstede, Springsteede, Christina 20; Christoffer 22; Jeremia 20*, 22; Joseph 20.

Sprong, Catharina 42.

Sprott, James 73; William 73.

Staats, Abraham 21; Annatje 25, 31. 48; Antje 15; Barent 9, 15, 32, 54, 57, 58, 73; Cathalina 65; Catharina 13, 37, 55, 59, 70; Cornelis 15; Debora 13, 17, 57; Dirkje 54; Elisabeth 31, 32, 55, 58*, 60; Garret 76; Geesje 60; Gerrit 13, 17, 21, 48, 59, 70; Gerrit, Jr. 15, 31, 47; Gerritje 73; Hendrik 65; Jane 31; Joachim 25, 32*; Jochum 20, 60; Joh. 31; Johannes 17; John 2, 25, 43*; Maria 20, 22, 41, 64; Neeltje 46, 59, 70; Nellie 76; Petrus 55; Philip 25, 31; Samuel Provoost 47; Sara 51; Willem 20, 37, 58, 74; Yzac 74.

Schuuk, see v. Schaik.

Stafford, Ann 29.

Stalker, Joseph 24; William 24.

Starr, George 16.

Steel, Catharina 2, 24.

Steen, Johannes 14; Jurjen 14; Margarita 22.

Steenberger, Catharina 61; Elias 61.

Still, Francis 56*; Frans 54.

Stonert, Nency 39.

Stoop, Catharina 33; Frans 33, 50; Magdalena 50.

Stover, Willem 9.

Stratt, (?) Maria 36.

Stringer, Lydia 17, 33, 40, 53, 60; Rachel 33, 37, 40, 60; Saml, Samuel 17, 33, 37, 40, 60.

Strong, Anna 4, 46; Elsje 46; Hendrik 46; Maria 5, 49.

Strunk, Strunck, Anna 55; Annatje 68; Christina 9, 68; Elsje 73.

Struyk, Cath. 64.

Struys, Annatje 30; Frans 30.

Stuard, see Stuart.

Stuart, Henry 3; Janet Jennet 20, 32; Jenny 24; John 3, 24.

Stuivesand, Cornelia 70.

Sunts, Abrm. 11.

Switz, Hannah 9.

Talbert, Maria 26; William 26.

Taylor, Tayler, Alexander 73; Catharina 5; Jane 73.

Ten Baer, Cornelia 3; John 33*; Lena 33; Robt. 33.

Voorhees, Hendrik 41; Jacob 15; Jan 67; Joh. 15; John 41; Pieter 67.

Vosburg, Vosburgh, Abrhm, Abraham 8, 52, 59, 71; Annatje 13; Barbara Cloet 70; Barent 13; Catharina 57; Christina 71; Elisabeth 52; Geertruy 33, 43, 52, 65; Jacob 57, 70; Willem 71*; Yzac 57*.

Vredenburgh, Maria 54, 73; Rachel 73; William 8.

Vroman, Adam 20; Cornelis 17, 45, 48, 65, 75*; Geertruy 17, 65*; Jacobus 17*, 65; Jannetje 17; Lena 65, 75; Marytje 45, 48; Pieter 44*; Santje 20.

Vrydag, Abraham 7.

Van Aalstein, V. Aalstein, Van Alstine, Adam Winne 19; Annatje 10, 57, 64, 68; Barbara 9, 75; Cathal 28; Catharina 12; Cornelia 7, 25, 64, 68; Cornelis 33*, 44, 73; Elbertje 11, 38, 75; Elisabeth 41; Gerrit 73; Gerritje 33; Hans 19; Hendrik 7; Hermanus 12; Jacob 57, 64, 68; Jannetje 41, 53; Knout 69; Margarita 41; Marten 45; Matheus, Mathias, Mathys 3, 45, 68; Mary 69; Marytje 13, 28; Pieter 33; Pieterje 25, 57; Rebecca 7; Reinier 25; Solomon 44; Thomas 3; Wynand 41.

V. Aarnem, V. Aernem, V. Arnum, Abraham 11, 50, 59; Abraham Y. 11; Alida 13, 27, 35, 59, 71; Andries 26; Catharina 14, 24; Elisabeth 23, 35, 69; Hester 6; Jacob 35; Jacob Bogert 50; Jan Dirkse 11; Johannes 29, 35, 69; John 6; Maria 8; Yzac 14, 23, 24; Yzac J. 26.

Van Alen, Catharina 6; Elisabeth 45; Geesje 37; Gerrit 9; Joh. 37.

V. Antwerp, V. Antwerpen, Annatje 5, 48, 61; Arent 75; Cornelia 4, 27, 44; Daniel 61; Gerrit 54; Maria 65, 77; Pieter 3; Rebecca 61.

V. Benthuisen, V. Benthuysen, Benthuisen, Baltes, Balthes 12, 23, 25, 40, 54, 71; Benjamin 30; Cathalina 47, 64; Cathalyntje 56; Cornelia 10, 12, 31, 41, 62; Dorothea 3; Elisabeth 12, 59; Evert Swart 23; Folkert 53; Geesje 46, 54; Hen-

drik 7, 25*, 31, 47, 59, 71; Jacobus 70, 71; Johannes 33; John 40, 46, 54*; John H. 53; Johs. 33; Maria 54; Mary 76; Obadia 10, 30, 47, 64*; Sara 7, 31, 47*, 63, 71*; Thomas 71, 76; Willem, William 23, 54, 70.

V. Brakelin, Catharina 51; Gysbert 25; Sara 25.

V. Buskirk, see Buskerk.

V. Buuren, V. Buren, Abraham 5, 23, 31*; Catharina 44; Cornelia 4; Cornelis 37, 42*, 44, 49, 54, 57; Dorothe, Dorothea 13, 57; Elisabeth 27, 42, 54, 72; Elsje 2, 31, 49; Geertruy 1, 16; Hendrik 46, 50, 66; Hendrikje 10, 21, 41, 54, 58; Hilletje 46; Jannetje 13, 31, 37, 42; Judik, Judike 37, 54; Lena 74; Maayke 49, 54; Maria 16, 37, 42, 51, 67; Marten 31; Martin C. 8, 67; Marytje 14, 16, 67; Pieter 13, 16, 23, 42, 46, 50*, 57*; Peter M. 67; Theuntje 8, 67; Wilhelmus 36.

V. d. Berg, V. d. Bergh, Van den Bergh, Abraham 68; Agnieta 34, 46; Agnietje 24*, 34; Alida 15, 23, 37, 70, 74; Andries 23; Annatje 19, 23, 26, 30, 50, 55, 62, 66*, 68, 71; Annatie 68; Burger 52; Catalina 68; Cathalina 13, 52, 72; Cathalyntje 11, 24, 70; Catharina 22, 36, 67; Catryn (?) 65; Christina 12; Cornelis 9, 11, 15, 16, 24, 34, 46, 51, 56, 67; Cornelis W. 72; Cornelius 74; Ebbetje 17, 56; Egbertje 12; Elisabeth 7, 10, 63, 74; Eva 11, 16; Evert 18, 25*; Folkert 22; Geertje 15, 44, 70; Geertruy 8; Gerrit 10, 23, 31, 56*, 74*; Gerritje 28; Gysbert 11, 15, 31, 65; Hendrik 31*; Hilletje 46; Jacob 34, 45; Jannetje 15, 25; Lena 60; Maas 23; Maayke 67; Margarita 10; Maria 3, 5, 18; Maritie 68; Marytje 26, 35, 66, 74; Matheus 51, 66; Matthias 68; Neeltje 5; Nicholaas, Nicholas 26, 68, 74; Rachel 46, 65; Reinier, Regnier 13, 31, 45; Susanna 31*; Theunis 35, 74; Will 34; Willem 71*; Wilhelmus 24, 45, 46*; Wynand 2, 19, 25, 30, 71; Wynand E. 67.

V. d Bogert, Catharina 44; Elis 39; Nicolaas 4, 44.

natje 27; Baatje 67; Bata 16, 34, 43, 56; Cathalina 65; Catharina 10; Cornelia 43; Eldert 11, 71; Elisabeth 16, 30, 42, 67*, 70, 71; Geertje 11; Helena 12; Hendrik 10, 30, 43* 58; Hendrikje 28; Jacob 27, 42*, 51, 67*; Jacob, Jr. 28; Johannes 28; Johs. 12, 28, 37, 51, 65; Margarita 11, 30; Pieter 42, 51; Sara 51; Theunis 16; William 58; Willempje 37.

V. Wurmer, Alida 15; Cornelis 15.

Van Yveren, V. Yveren, Van Ever Annatje 18, 61; Arriaantje 9, 76; Baatje 55; Barent 16, 45, 60; Christina 47; Cornelia 16*, 56, 60, 68; Cornelis 16, 60; Gerrit 45; Gosen 21; Jacob 55; Martinus 21, 45, 56, 68; Mary 68; Meinard 45; Rebecca 32, 49, 57, 66, 72; Reinier, Reynier, Reignier 5, 18, 32, 47, 49, 57, 61, 66, 72; Saartje 45*; Sara 7.

V. Zanten, V. Zandt, Rachel 7; Thomas 63.

Wabber, *see* Webber.

Wagenaar, Elsje 41; John 41.

Waldrom, Waldron, Catharina 26; Christiana 69; Cornelis 28, 50, 72; Elisabeth 27, 43, 60; Evert 50; Geertje 51; Gerrit 26, 28; Henry 69; James 8; Jannetje, Janniette 17, 43, 60, 74; Jenny 75; Johannes 74; Margarita 41; Marytje 26; Pieter 51, 75; Tryntje 51.

Wally, John 46; Salomo 73; Stephen 46.

Wals, Fred 19.

Walter, Walters, Carolina 41; Vrome 16.

Wand, Wands, Ebenezer 1; James 4; Jennet 9.

Ward, Wards, Catharina 16; Ebenezer 27; Elisabeth 27; John 7, 38.

Warner, Anna 7; Catharine 40; Elisabeth 40; Geertruy 5; Jurjen 40.

Warns, Johs. 21; Robert 21.

Warrant, Catharina 6.

Warren, Warrens, Catharina 28; Cathy, Caty 49, 53; Mary 7; Sara 11.

Wary, Phebe 8.

Washburn, Bethuel 65; Johannes 65.

Washington, Genl. 21; Mrs. 21.

Waters, Dorothea 54; John 3, 54.

Watkins, Elisabeth 29; John 29*.

Watson, Abigail 35; Catharina 35; Daniel 32*; Ellison 23; James 35; Lachelin 32; Martha 6; Zelotes 35.

Watt, Thomas 3.

Way, John 20, 40*; Lavaruke 20; Martha 40.

Webber, Wabber, Maria 16; Pieter 16, 26.

Webster, Christina 3.

Wels, Mary 9.

Wendel, Wendell, Wendle, Abraham 52; Abraham E. 67; Alida 35; Anna 34; Annatje 18, 44, 50, 60; Barbara 40; Cathalina 37; Cathalyntje 18; Catharina 34, 54, 63, 64, 69, 73, 74; Catharine H. 6; Cornelis 22, 44, 49, 60; David Scot 65; Elisabeth 74; Evert 33; Francyntje 13; Geertruy 4, 22, 47, 60; Gerrit 18; Helena 2, 40, 58; Hendrik 37; Hermanus 22, 40, 47, 63; Hermanus A. 6, 63, 74; Jacob 36; Jacob H. 57, 73; Johannes H. 56; John 74; John H. 64; John J. 20; John Lansing 49; John W. 42; Johs. 34, 47; Johs. H. 22; Johs. J. 35; Judike 20; Lavinus 54; Lena 23; Margaret 76; Margarita 30, 33, 69; Marten 54; Mary 42; Philip 33, 52, 65; Pieter 57; Rachel 56; Saartje 17, 54; Sara 37; Susanna 31, 74.

Werffenbach, Joh. H. 40.

Wessels, Andries 3.

Wesselsen, Andries 27; Annatje 27; Lucas 27*.

Westerlo, Catharina 57; Eilardus 36; Johanna 36.

Wever, De Wever, Catharina 30, 50; David 5; Jacob 51; Marritje, Marytje 1, 17, 33, 43, 55, 66, 76.

Wheeler, Henry 4; Mary 2; Marytje 64; Nicholas 64.

White, Wite, Annetje, Annatje 23, 39, 58; Hannah 63; Jennet 17; Violet 23.

Wieler, Abraham 9.

Wilks, James 4.

Will, Catharina 13; Hendrik 13.

Willard, Elias 24; John 24.

Willet, Aletta 5; Catharine 13; Eduard 17, 18; Eduard S. 13, 35; Lydia 35; Maria 13; Marinus 13; Sara 17.

Williams, Antje 21; Benjamin 37*, 59; Elisabeth 33, 46; James 37; John 33, 59; Maria 59; Martha 3.

Records of the Reformed Dutch Church of Albany, New York

Part 8
1789-1809

Excerpted from
Year Book of The Holland Society
of New York (1926/27)

RECORDS OF THE REFORMED DUTCH CHURCH OF ALBANY, N. Y.

Marriages—1789 to 1804

MARR. WITH BANNS:

1790, Jan. 10.   Garret Van Wie and Maritie Slingerland.
Jan. 19.   Asa Foot and Catalyntie David.
Jan. 21.   Jacob Jacb. Lansingh and Annatje Qwackenbush.
Feb. 15.   Stephen Mosher and Phebe Joseline.
Feb. 15.   Elisha Wells and Elizabeth Joceline.
Mar. 6.   Matthew Bevie and Elizabeth Lansing.
Mar. 7.   Johannes Ja. Heemstraat and Catharina Weever.
Mar. 18.   Abraham Slingerland and Sarah Schoonmaker.
George Ganse and Jane Neal.
Mar. 21.   Barent Smith and Hannah Bell.
Apr. 18.   James Milwater and Abigail Gascon.
May 18.   Jacob Goes and Elisabeth Hoogteeling.
May 23.   Jacob Slingerland and Catharina V. Eevere.
May 24.   Coenraad Luke and Elisabeth Hillebrand.
May 31.   William Fosburgh and Jacob V. Schaick.
June 2.   Caleb Nex and Margaret Jolse.
Peter Morhouse and Sarah Sallard.
Garret Yeates and Cornelia Lansing.
July 18.   Barent TenEyck and Nancy Hofman, from this City.

July 24. Pieter Flensburgh and Frankje V. d. Bogert, from
Niskatha.
July 24. Baltis Heller and Ariantie Bratt.
July 29. Henry B. Hallenbake and Rachel Winne.
Aug. 13. Gerrit Becker and Arriaantje Hoogteeling.
Sept. 6. John Cely and Rewby Morehouse.
Sept. 8. Johannes Hydly and Anna Schermerhorn.
Jacob Smith and Anna Hydly.
Sept. 21. Pieter Frank and Elisabeth Shutter.
Sept. 24. David Ver Planck and Rachel Worden.
Oct. 2. Hermanus P. Schuyler and Mary Staats.
Oct. 5. John Schoonmaker and Magdalene Hansen.
Oct. 14. Revd. Samuel Smith and Elizabeth Van Vechten.
Oct. 21. John Pengburn and Catharina Mason.
Nov. 2. Joseph V. d. Bogert and Saartje V. Santen.
1800, Apr. 13. Gerrit Groesbeek and Jannetje Pruyn, widow
of Rynier Pruyn.
1796, Dec. 24. Daniel Morrell and Clashe Groesbeck.
1797, Jan. 9. Clark Jennings and Margaret Campbell.
Jan. 29. William Clark and Lovice Dunham.
Feb. 16. Harmanus P. Schuyler and Hester Beeckman.
Feb. 21. Ambrose Dorman and Catrine Woodbeck.
Solomon Hale and Rebecca Martin.
Mar. 8. Peter Van Bergen and Elizabeth Fryer.
Mar. 10. Andrew Ten Eick and Lucy Legrange.
Apr. 15. Daniel Steel and Elisabeth Van Benthuysen.
June 3. John Veeder and Catharina Delang.
June 22. Peter Long and Hannah Arnold.
June 24. John Bloore and Susan Van Schoonhoven.
July 2. Angus McDonald and Elen Monteith.
July 15. John Dunn and Francis Godsby.
July 16. John Kimmey and Jane Le Roy.
Aug. 22. John R. Todd and Clarissa Chesebrough.
Sept. 9. Wilhelmus Winney and Aefje Van der Zee.
Oct. 13. Brandt Schuyler Swits and Alida Van Schaick.
Nov. 8. James Chisholm and Eve McCloud.
Nov. 21. James McNish and Hannah Cowan.
Gardiner Avery and Huldah Russell.
Dec. 16. Amos Hitchcock and Margaret Charles.
Dec. 18. William McDermit and Nelly Consalb.
1798, Jan. 28. Garrit Rooseboom and Josina Hornbeck.

Feb. 20.   Charles Rosseter and Doratha Hart.
         Thomas Smith and Jane McElroy.
Feb. 24.   William Springstead and Catharine Vn. Deusen.
Mar. 1.   Conrodt Bunts and Elizabeth Williams.
June 9.   Cornelius Vn. Wie and Lydia Tayler.
June 17.   Jesse Mott and Sarah Forman.
June 28.   John Goodrich and Sarah Houghton.
July 3.   Isaac Hansen and Jane Cooper.
July 10.   Robert Austin and Mary Park.
Aug. 19.   Peter Slingerland and Garritie Bloomingdale.
Aug. 23.   Andrew Vroeman and Hannah Vroeman.
Sept. 6.   Edward Brown and Tabitha Hyer.
Sept. 23.   Nanning Marsaelis and Deborah De Graef.
Nov. 26.   Thomas C. Gardner and Willempe Bogart.
Dec. 1.   John Lotridge and Mary Read.
Dec. 19.   Peter W. Yates and Mary Terboss.
1799, Jan. 10.   Garrit De Garmo and Catharina Cooper.
Jan. 27.   Frances Marks Faten and Catharina Van Deusen
         Groesbeeck.
Feb. 14.   Gilbert Ackerman and Rachel De Garmo.
Feb. 26.   John McDermott and Margaret Barrington.
Apr. 21.   Joseph Beebe and Lydia Larroway.
May 28.   Peter Van Loon and Catharina Lusher.
May 30.   David Putnam and Jennet Angus.
July 13.   Charles Storer and Catharina Johnson.
Aug. 11.   Robert W. Dunbar and Eliza Muir.
Aug. 14.   James Carhartt and Susan Jerolumen.
Aug. 18.   Isaac Slingerlandt and Elisabeth Hines.
Aug. 31.   Hassel Brower and Maria Bloomingdale.
Sept. 10.   James Gourley and Lana Bromley.
Oct. 8.   Gideon Ackerman and Elizabeth Drurie.
Oct. 13.   Benjamin Holmsted and Catharine Van Schaick.
Oct. 15.   Cornelius Woodworth and Catalina Veeder.
Oct. 27.   Henry Hyer and Mary Fenton.
Nov. 9.   Samuel F. Brott and Nancy Cassada.
Nov. 17.   John Bleecker and Elizabeth Schuyler.
Nov. 23.   Philip Hoofman and Martha Graham.
Nov. 25.   Isaac D. Fonda and Martha Cooper.
Nov. 28.   John Cooper and Phoebe Vunck.
1800, Jan. 4.   Barent Goes and Batie Vin Hagen.
Jan. 11.   John Coe Carpenter and Sally Mead.

Jan. 12. Joseph Buckby and Susannah Betts.
Feb. 9. Jacob Burdoine and Hilletie Claver.
Mar. 9. Matthias Hauzs and Rachel Sickels.
July 11. William Driscol and Elizabeth Lansing.
July 20. Caleb Wright and Tirza Chapin.
Sept. 27. Benjamin De Witt and Eve Bloodgood.
Oct. 9. Robert S. Van Renssellaer and Catharine N. Bogart.
Oct. 18. David Rockett and Rose, serv. wom. of St. Renssellaer.
Oct. 30. James McCrackin and Elizabeth Larroway.
Nov. 11. John Smith and Nancy Davis.
Nov. 19. John W. Yates and Ann Metcalfe.
1801, Feb. 1. Salem Dutcher and Lydia Denney.
Feb. 2. Joseph Alston and Theodocia Burr.
Mar. 8. Benjamin Wheat and Lydia Goodrich.
Apr. 23. John I. Groesbeck and Maria Lansing.
Sept. 13. Anthony Brees and Rebecca Brown.
Sept. 26. Michael Rhyne and Catharina Pool.
Sept. 29. William Lloyd and Jane McCarmick.
John Bleecker, Jr., and Annatie Van Alen.
Oct. 24. Peter Pool and Elizabeth Le Roy.
Nov. 9. William Van Zandt and Eleanor Mynderson.
Dec. 1. Peter A. Hilton and Ester Groat.
Dec. 22. Henry Guest, Jr., and Elizabeth De Witt.
1802, Jan. 5. Michael Kilmartin and Harriet Arnthoudt.
Henry Arnthoudt and Catharina O'Brien.
John Evertson and Sarah Lansing.
Feb. 2. Cornelius Van Husen and Hannah Graham.
Feb. 3. Peter Brinckerhoff and Elizabeth Bleecker.
Feb. 7. Peter Mermie and Jane Battrin.
Feb. 11. Dirck A. Bratt and Agnes Humphrey.
Feb. 13. John Cutler and Mary Shears.
Mar. 1. Arthur Hotchkiss and Judith Hoofkirk.
Mar. 2. Jacob Rightenberg and Anna Wayman.
Mar. 9. George Davis Ovrin and Catharine Courtney.
Mar. 21. Thomas Omen and Rachel Denniston.
Aug. 3. Jacob S. Pruyn and Harriet Rooseboom.
Aug. 8. Thomas Hocknell and Catharine Van Wie.

REGISTER OF MARRIAGES BY JOHN M. BRADFORD.

1805, Dec. 30. Robert Adams and Mary Le Grange.

Dec. 31.   Asa Gardener and Helen A. Townsend.
1806, Mar. 18.   Rev. John H. Muer and Mary Lansing.
Mar. 27.   Cornelius W. Groesbeck and Jane Pruyn.
Apr. 1.   (Col'd.) Richard Thomson and Jane Johnson.
Apr. 10.   Jonathan Warner and Alida Pruyn.
June 10.   James Kane (Schoharie) and Jane Dounel.
July 11.   (Col'd.) Samuel Gassa and Dinah Yocksen.
Sept. 6.   Moses Kenyon and Elizabeth Staats.
Oct. 13.   John Q. Wilson and Maria Lush.
Oct. 25.   Benjamin Hansen, Jr. and Mary Slingerland.
Dec. 6.   William Moore and Anna Westervelt.
1807, Jan. 8.   Nanning I. or T. Visscher and Catherine G.
　　　　　　Van Rensselaer.
Jan. 10.   Henry W. Staats and Catharine Van Santvoord.
Jan. 14.   Henry Cedam and Lucy Goodwin.
Apr. 18.   Jeremiah Whalen and Elisabeth Bloomingdale.
Oct. 3.   Anthony Van Santvoord and Catherine Groesbeeck.
Oct. 31.   Henry Mac and Maria McDurmot.
Nov. 18.   William Roades and Maria Luther.
Dec. 26.   John B. Washburn and Cornelia Van Kleeck.
1808.   Jan. 2.   Ryer Schermerhorn and Gertrude Abel.
Jan. 25.   John Hare and Catharine Freeman.
Feb. 23.   Ralph Pratt and Eliza Witham.
Feb. 27.   Elisha Jones and Nancy Young.
Mar. 21.   John Eppes and Sally Field.
Mar. 31.   Gerrit Y. Lansing and Helena Ten Eycke.
Apr. 16.   Martin Van Alstein and Jane Lansing.
May 7.   Coenradt Baumes and Catherine Baugert.
May 18.   John R. Bleecker and Mrs. Hester Linn.
May 19.   Martte Evertsen and Eliza Tillghman.
May 30.   Wilm W. Frazer and Susannah Brannent.
May 31.   Samuel T. Burrows and Eliza Lansing.
June 12.   John Paddock and Mrs. Christiana Oliver.
June 21.   Christian Schrafford and Nancy Snyder.
June 23.   Cornelius Van Hoesen and Esther Ryan.
Sept. 18.   Asahel Felt and Fanny Ostrander.
Oct. 16.   John Whitney and Rachel Bounds.
Oct. 29.   John Humphreys and Mary H. Wallan.
Oct. 30.   Peter Willett and Helen Van Tassel.
Nov. 6.   James Robertson and Lilis Wilson.
Nov. 26.   Obadiah R. Van Benthuysen and Sarah Wood.

Dec. 1. Anthony Braadt and Sally Groesbeeck.
Dec. 10. John Evertsen and Alida Visher.
Dec. 10. Lee (?) Avery and Eliza Hooker.
Dec. 12. George Pearson and Judith Van Vechten.
COPIED FROM A DIFFERENT RECORD.
1791, Jan. 4. Nicholas Olford and Eltie Salsbury.
Jan. 5. Robert Martin and Elisabeth Utter.
Jan. 8. Abraham Bronck and Caty Radley.
Jan. 9. Mary Younglove and Rev. Jacob Harrington.
Jan. 10. Mott. Sallero and Margaret Monteath.
Jan. 12. Frederick V. Patten and Elisabeth Say.
Feb. 7. Garret Ryckman and Gertruy Lansing.
Feb. 11. James Winkoop and Catalina Dunbar.
Mar. 3. William Conger and Margaret McNab.
Mar. 12. Jacob V. Elten and Helena Shute.
1790, Nov. 25. Gulian V. Planck and Hannah De Forest.
Francis and Dina, serv. of John Fonda.
1791, Apr. 8. William Seger and Hannah Prenk.
Garrit Quakenbush and Elizabeth Banker.
May 8. Henderik Van Der Werken and Elisabeth Sturbergh.
June 3. Meindert Lansing and Mary Usher.
June 4. Peter Spawer and Maria Springsty.
June 25. Christiaan Miller and Maritie V. Schaic.
June 29. Daniel Sherred and Rachel Huick.
Aug. 28. Samuel Berter and Mary Nicholson.
Aug. 30. Francis Pruer (Pruyn?) and Cornelia Dunbar.
Sept. 6. Andreas Blass and Catharine V. Eller.
Sept. 6. Frederick Edigh and Caty Smith.
Sept. 7. John Burton and Eleanor Pangburn.
Nov. 5. John de Camp and Eva Widder.
Nov. 15. John Arnold and Cornelia Wilsie.
Nov. 17. Coenraad Wedeman and Anna Oliver.
Nov. 22. Jacob Strunk and Elisabeth Tater.
Nov. 20. Garret Clulo and Elisabeth Kane.
Nov. 30. Asa Hutchurson and Mary Turney.
Dec. 17. Egbert V. Schaer (Schaick?) and Maria Winnen.
Dec. 29. Daniel Firga and Mary Clarke.
1792, Jan. 6. Arnes Richard and Christina V. d. Berg (?).
Jan. 14. Mathias Younghans (?) and Margaret V. Litstine (?).

Jan. 30. Willm. Bower and Margaret V. Zandt.
Feb. 5. Willm. Evars and Elisabeth Calder.
Feb. 25. Thomas V. Zandt and Rebecca Hoghkerk.
Mar. 9. Abraham Hollenbeck and Sarah Schuler.
May 28. John Lyden and Anna Oliver.
May 28. Gilbert Sharp and Annatie Schoenmaker.
June 3. Henry Visher and Rebecca Bracoty.
June 9. Peter Burnier Vielee and Rachel Boesom.
June 16. Peter Lottridge and Sarah Bloomdal.
June 16. Willem Leach and Sarah Wales.
June 17. Joseph Solsbury and Geertruy Ornort.
July 3. James Hoghkirk and Alida V. Zandt.
Aug. 20. John Dale and Helena Boon.
Sept. 15. John Gross and Jane Rutherford.
Oct. 28. Thomas Lansing and Jannetie Hun.
Oct. 22. Willm. Pangbower and Ann Badgley.
Nov. 17. Jeremiah Springstee and Eleanor Burkley.
Nov. 17. Pieter Witbeek and Marritie V. Schaic.
Dec. 2. Garrit V. Zandt and Caty Hilton.
Dec. 7. John Connor and Helena Groots (?).
Dec. 7. Meindert V. de Bogert and Ann Smith.
Dec. 9. Anthony Brooks and Catalintie V. Huson.
Dec. 9. Richard Hilton and Elisabeth Norton.
Dec. 15. Thomas R. V. Zandt and Mary V. Zandt.
Dec. 25. Elisha Putman and Elsie Johnson.
1793, Jan. 6. Solomon Walley and Widow of Jacob Truax.
Jan. 6. Walter A. Groesbeek and Annatie Rykman.
Jan. 6. John Brats and Rebecca Binnet.
Apr. 22. Henry Mouny and Margaret Troisi.
Apr. 28. Philip Gardenier and Elisabeth V. Schaic.
Apr. 28. Samuel Nicol and Elisabeth Sile.
May 28. Christian Cooper and Catharine Deerstyne.
June 3. John V. D. Heyden and Mary Britt (?).
June 5. Garret Long and Chrystal Hoffman.
June 5. Peter Bulson and Rachel Smith.
June 20. Eduard Nelson and Christina Hoffman.
June 20. Abm. Slingerland and Henrietta Slingerland.
July 11. Philip Hoffman and Margaret Adams.
July 27. Edward Huister and Cateline Freyer.
July 27. Jacobus Kidney and Christina Casseman.
Aug. 5. Abm. Turk and Mary Truax.

Aug. 8.   John Kilmer and Sarah Raddock (?).
Aug. 8.   Willem Kilmer and Sarah Ostrander.
Aug. 10. Willem Hoghtiller and Hannah V. Waggoner.
Sept. 2. Hans Seger and Eleanor Esmy.
Sept. 2. Michael V. Hinter (or Huster) and Charity Bronk.
Sept. 7. George Coller and Catharine Obrien.
Nov. 3.   George Gerish and Eunice Packer.
Nov. 3.   Jacob and Gin, servants.
1794, Jan. 14.   Adam Countryman and Maria Hawk.
Jan. 14. John V. Alen and Margaret Bentie.
Jan. 21. John Arnhout and Mary Walley.
Jan. 21. Albert V. Etta and Anna Martins.
Jan. 28. William Roff and Christina Sicker.
Jan. 28. Obadiah Millar and Maria Millar.
Feb. 15. Andrew Ostrander and Catharina Van Wie.
Feb. 17. John V. Valkenburgh and Sarah V. der Bergh.
Feb. 17. David Thurstion and Margaret Philips.
Feb. 17. Philip Strunk and Elisabeth Coons.
Feb. 26. John Palmater and Jemima Hollenbeck.
Mar. 17. William Seaman and Mary Nicol.
Mar. 22. Adam Happal and Christina Thomson.
Mar. 31. Sybrant Dow and Lyntie Ten Eyk.
Apr. 1.   John Dykman and Maritie Palmatren.
Apr. 1.   John Rose and Martha Smith.
Feb. 23. Obadiah Miller and Maria Miller.
Feb. 26. Henry Slater and Lydia Hungerfordt.
1795, Jan. 8.   Garret Bogert and Margarit Pelse.
Apr. 3.   John Fort and Eva Marselis.
Apr. 4.   John S. Pruyn and Margaret Lansing.
Apr. 4.   Jacob Ten Eyck and Madgalene Gansevoort.
Apr. 24. Jonathan Brooks and Mary Hoghkirk.
May 19.   John Bassett and Anna Hun.
Sept. 15. Cornelis V. Denberg and Anna Ten Eyck.
Sept. 26. James Johnson and Mary Jackson.
Oct. 2.   Stephen Sweet and Elisabeth Mosier.
Oct. 7.   Samuel Mills (or Miller) and Phebe Stanton.
Oct. 10. Philip Devereax and Julia Conway.
Oct. 20. Evert Delamater and Mary Cole.
Nov. 11. David I. Verplank and Mary McClellyan.
Nov. 25. Samuel Price and Charlotte Jinnings.
Nov. 28. Amosa Ford and Gertrude Cole.

Nov. 30.   George Robb and Jennett McMillen.
Dec. 31.   Isaac Bratt and Elisabeth V. Deusen.
Aug. 9.   Henry Evertsen and Cornelia Slingerland.
1794, Nov. 23.   Douwe Fonda and Matilda Beekman.
　　　　　James Holmes and Ann Bulson.
1796, Jan. 9.   Gideon Hoppson and Margaret Fadden.
Jan. 14.   Hugh Boyd and Catalina Staats.
Jan. 19.   Adam Seger and Elisabeth Livingston.
Jan. 20.   Stephen Herreman and Sarah Paine.
Jan. 21.   Samuel Crane and Sarah Willis.
Jan. 25.   William White and Loisa Palmer.
Jan. 29.   Samuel Hopson and Hannah Van der Werken.
Feb. 13.   Cornelius Anthony and Mary Van der Werken.
Feb. 18.   Stephen McChestney and Christina Roff.
Feb. 24.   Mechal Ritter and Eunice Pettit.
Mar. 6.   William Lawrence and Mary Pruyn.
Mar. 24.   Robert Dunbar, Jr., and Alida Gravarit.
Apr. 2.   Christopher Passage and Elizabeth Moore.
June 6.   Charles Simons and Mary Osterhout.
June 30.   Joseph Lewis and Delia Wells.
　　　　　John Hallenbake and Antie Legrange.
July 10.   William Montgomery and Alida Hallenbake.
July 15.   Nicholas Rideker and Alida Bulsom.
July 16.   Henry Van Beuren and Magdelene Barhanse.
Aug. 25.   John McChestney and Rebecca Hoghkirk.
Sept. 5.   Francis Osterhout and Elizabeth Nodan.
Sept. 22.   Uriah Betts and Elizabeth Roceter.
Sept. 22.   Abraham Hun and Maria Gansevoort.
Sept. 25.   John Brinkerhoff and Gertrude Schuyler.
Oct. 2.   Francis Eagles and Mary Low.
Oct. 29.   John Schuyler, Jr., and Annatie Cuyler.
Nov. 10.   Isaac Passenger and Alida Bratt.
Nov. 20.   Dirck V. Den Bergh and Sophia Cromwell.
Dec. 5.   John Egan and Cornelia Quackenbuss.
Dec. 5.   Philip McIntire and Jane Clement.
Dec. 22.   Thomas Chadwick and Mary Outhout.
Dec. 26.   Daniel Bulson and Mary Armee.
Dec. 31.   Daniel Winne and Margaret Mool.
1797, Jan. 2.   Silas Palmer and Nancy Clarke.
Jan. 5.   James Vrooman and Johanna Watson.
Jan. 27.   Casper Ten Eyck and Levina Springstead.

1796, Dec. 24. Daniel Morrell and Clashe Groesbeek.
      Humphrey Platt and Maria Ertsberger.
1797, Jan. 9. Clark Jennings and Margaret Campbell.
Jan. 29. Willm. Clark and Lodice Dunham.
Mar. 9. Michal Shuter and Catharine Kirkner.
Mar. 10. John McMillen and Cornelia V. Wort.
Apr. 18. Thomas Willinger and Susan, servant of Abraham
    Ten Broeck.
Jan. 2. William Schooley and Anna Millar.
Apr. 22. Peter Schoonmaker and Eleanor Olinda.
.... 4. Nicholas Jerolome and Eva Becker.
May 25. John Smith and Cataline Witbeck.
July 1. John Tillman and Catharine Auley.
Aug. 11. John Jones and Rachel Oley.
      John A. Goey and Rachel De Forest.
Sept. 21. Aaron Oliver and Wealthy Bennet.
Sept. 28. Frederick Richmond and Margaret Brack.
      Richard Clery and Mary Robinson.
Oct. 9. Jonathan Tuttle and L. Zelpha Utter.
Oct. 29. Elias Kane and Deborah V. Schuyline.
Nov. 3. Thomas Millegan and Catharine Outhout.
Nov. 28. Roswell Nollen and Lydia Steen.
Dec. 29. John Earl and Hannah McCredy.
1798, Apr. 25. Lucas Hooghkerk and Mary Burton.
Apr. 27. James Neely and Hannah Vosburgh.
Sept. 25. Bernadus Bloomendale and Ann Shandland.
June 22. Richard Clute and Mary McMichal.
June 24. Peter Wuter (?) and Catharine Van Etta.
July 13. Edward Willet and Jane Orsen (?).
July 21. Andrew Passenger and Magdelene Seger.
Aug. 12. Bartholomew V. Alstine and Mary Snook.
Oct. 23. James Maky and Isabella Graham.
      James White and Rebecca Kinnear.
Dec. 22. Oliver Haight and Hannah Rowe.
1799, Feb. 5. Walter Clarke and Helena Van Wie.
Mar. 3. John Brown and Jane Brown.
Apr. 18. James Van Ingen and Elizabeth Schuyler.
Apr. 22. John B. Romeyn and Harriot Bleecker.
Apr. 12. Whiting Warner and Elizabeth Ostrander.
June 9. Henry Wheeler and Elizabeth Totham.
Oct. 2. Abraham Schoonmaker and Sarah Bender.

June 12. Hermanus Schuyler and Mary Deane.
June 22. Henry Bleecker and Elizabeth Metcalf.
Oct. 4. Samuel D. Taylor and Alley Yearsley.
Oct. 17. John Pangburne and Elizabeth Bronck.
Nov. 17. Benjamin Coe and Sarah Minderse.
Nov. 18. John Clark and Lucy Cleveland.
1800, Jan. 24. Hermanus V. Beuren and Sophia Miller.
　　　　Ruloph V. Der Werken and Margaret
　　　　Witbeck.
Jan. 31. Humphrey Outhout and Elisabeth Bulsom.
　　　　Philip Christ and Catharine Millar.
Feb. 17. James Van Hagen and Margaret Van Volkenburgh.
Apr. 10. William Van Alstyne and Margaret Sharpe.
May 1. Teunis Slingerland and Eleanor Van den Bergh.
May 11. Rosell Goodrich and Esther Hodge, of the Society
　　　　of Shakers.
July 1. Jonathan Vorst and Caty Shoft.
Aug. 14. Robert Waterson and Rebecca Abrahams.
Oct. 5. Abraham Shuter and Hannah Rechter.
Oct. 5. Abraham Sickels and Elisa Johnson.
Nov. 7. Philip Berringer and Volkie Ostrander.
Nov. 12. John Sicker and Latte Carker.
　　　　Elisha Kilburne and Eliza Raymond.
1801, Jan. 26. William Donnolly and Margaret Mills.
Feb. 22. Rossel Barber and Elisabeth Broom.
Apr. 25. Lambert V. Volkenburgh and Sarah Van den
　　　　Bergh.
Apr. 26. William C. Bussing and Catharine Oliver.
May 3. Martin Joy and Mary Cummings.
May 17. Jacob Ostrander and Nancy Haddock.
　　　　Abraham R. Ten Eyck and Annatie Visher.
July 25. John Broocks and Hannah Groesbeck.
July 30. Lawrence Hoghteling and Deborah Page.
July 31. John Lackey and Ann Cackle.
Aug. 8. Isaac Owens and Wintie Boom.
Aug. 9. Anthony Sanford and Rachel Groesbeck.
Aug. 25. Asa Douglass and Sarah Wyncoop.
Aug. 27. Abraham Arway and Sarah Kiff.
Oct. 18. Garret Hoogkirk and Sarah Ryckman.
　　　　Herman Knickerbaker and Harriot Lansing.
Nov. 2. Samuel Tucker and Elizabeth Johnson.

1802, Jan. 2.   Isaac Wells and Catharina Gravenbergh.
Jan. 25.   Ezra Thayer and Jane Douglass.
    William Donelly and Margaret Mills.
    John Hochnell and Clara Graham.
1802, Feb. 20.   George Dollar and Margaret Schoonmaker.
Feb. 28.   Samuel Leach and Phebe Lynn.
Apr. 17.   John D. Seger and Mary Fitch.
May 14.   Garret Nott and Jane Brown.
Jan. 25.   John Newson and Mary Washburn.
June 8.   Loring Simmons and Hannah Sturges.
June 10.   Thomas Gates and Esther Vincent.
June 29.   Isaac V. Den Bergh and Maria Fondey.
June 29.   John Clute and Alida V. Den Bergh.
Aug. 14.   Peter and Susan, servants.
Aug. 20.   Daniel Simmons and Emma, servants.
July 1.   Thomas Linacre and Margaret V. der Voort.
Sept. 9.   Peter Elmendorf and Elizabeth V. Renselaer.
    Joseph Bartoe and Maria Godfrey.
    Cornelius V. Schoonhoven and Rebecca V. Nest.
Oct. 15.   Henry Albert and Sarah Jones.
Oct. 23.   Thomas Wilkinson and Ann Hilton.
Nov. 20.   John Shaffer and Eva Eaker.
Sept. 26.   Henry Weaver and Margaret Rubey.
1803.   Jan. 3.   Epenitus White and Susan Fonday.
Jan. 7.   Christopher Dun and Hannah Allen.
Jan. 11.   Nathaniel Burdett and Elisabeth Reynolds.
Jan. 23.   John Mills and Elizabeth Horsefale.
Jan. 24.   Andrew Hollenbake and Angeltie Le Grange.
    James McCluskie and Jannitie Le Grange, 12
    years of age.
Feb. 20.   Jacob Van Loon and Maritie Van der Zee.
Feb. 20.   Asa H. Center and Elizabeth Heyer.
Mar. 6.   Jeremiah Luther and Maritie Shear.
1802, Sept. 11.   James Cameron and Mary Brower.
1803, Mar. 20.   Adam Blake and Sarah Richards.
Mar. 20.   Ephraim De Witt and Gertie V. Loon.
Apr. 9.   Isaac Van Wie and Christina Kittle.
Apr. 11.   James Richardson and Hannah Bartow.
June 1.   Abraham Weaver and Margaret Seacorne, alias
    Dunbar.
June 14.   Teunis Snook and Catharine Snyder.

June 12.   Stampshire Woods and Ann Douw.
June 19.   Valentine Austen and Abigail Catlin.
June 30.   John Pool and Christina Herrick.
July 5.   William Turner and Christina Van Deursen.
Aug. 23.   William Silvey and Mary Hawkins.
Sept. 21.   Sylvanus Palmer and Ann Gardinier.
Sept. 23.   Peter Redecker and Margaret Clute.
Sept. 25.   James Abbey and Phoebe Benson.
Oct. 4.   Charles Platt and Sarah Bleecker.
Oct. 22.   John Dox and Alida Van Woert.
Oct. 31.   Teunis Hemstreet and Catharina Chatterton.
Nov. 19.   John Meadon and Elisabeth Bell.
Nov. 26.   Henry Van Benthuysen and Elizabeth Van Woert.
Dec. 16.   John Bills and Margaret Hall.
Dec. 7.   Thomas G. Witbeck and Leah Marshal.
Dec. 24.   Yellis Bogert and Elizabeth Ryckman.
1804, Jan. 11.   Jacob Borttle and Elizabeth Post.
              Nathaniel Rogers and Elizabeth Hoekerman.
              Dirck Heemstraat and Maria Clute.
              John Angus and Gertrude Krank.
Feb. 17.   Peter Beekman and Majeke Van Renselaer.
Mar. 10.   Casparus Nehemiah and Margaret Dingman.
Apr. 8.   Lott Higgins and Margaret Harois.
Apr. 22.   Ezra Buckbee and Sophia Ochenpagh.
Apr. 30.   Philip W. Lake and Hannah Kilmore.
              Elijah Lion and Mary Dunleavy.
June 4.   Russel E. Post and Maria Esterly.
June 16.   Robert Gedney and Sarah Burris.
June 17.   Peter Milkins and Sarah Barhanse.
June 5.   James Sibley and Elizabeth Esterly.
June 20.   Jacob Hildenbrandt and Adriana Johanna Van
              Tiffelen.

1789, Dec. 15. bo. Oct. 26. Jane of Peter I. Bratt and Jane Springsly.

1790, Jan. 10. bo. Dec. 4. Evert of Andries Lansingh and Annatje V. d. Bergh. Wit: Wynand V. d. Bergh, Annatje Cooper.

bo. Oct. 18. Jane of George Thompson and Elizabeth Bratt. Wit: James Irwin, Eleanor Bratt.

bo. Dec. 13. Jonas of William Hainer and Elizabeth Muller. Wit: Jacob Hainer, Elizabeth Kenter (?).

Jan. 14. bo. Jan. 1. Levinus of Benjamin Winne and Elisabeth Bassett. Wit: Levinus Winne, Mary Lansing.

bo. Oct. 30. Jochum of Jacob Vedder and Catharina Spawn.

Jan. 17. bo. Jan. 11. Sarah of Benjamin V. Zandt and Sarah Visher. Wit: Sarah and Bastian Visher.

bo. Jan. 6. Mynert Marsilius of Peter Dox and Catalina Lansing. Wit: Rebecca Dox, Garret Marselius.

Jan. 24. bo. the 18th. Pieter of Jeremia Lansingh and Helena Wendell. Wit: John V. Alen, Maria Lansingh.

bo. Dec. 26. David of Dirk de Foreest and Maria Fonda. Wit: David and Susanna De Foreest.

Robin of Claas and Sarah (slaves). Wit: Orgen and Bett.

bo. Sept. 8. David of Minburry V. Hoesen and Antje Bevins. Wit: David Nyffer, Margarita V. Wagenen.

Jan. 31. bo. Jan. 9. Janitje of Francis Slingerland and Rachel Davis. Wit: Jannitje and Edward Davis.

bo. Jan. 3. Rebecca of Jacobus Fonda and Willempje Bogert. Wit: Maas and Rebecca V. Buuren.

Albertus of Hendrik V. Wageningen and Annatje Landman. Wit: Albertus Bekker, Hester V. d. Zee.

Feb. 7. bo. Jan. 7. James of James Hilton and Caty Freyer. Wit: William Hilton.

Feb. 10. bo. May 7. Cathrina of Philip Luke and Eistie Spawn. Wit: Jacob Vedder, Catharina Spawn.

Feb. 21. bo. Jan. 19. Jacob of Evert Everson and Elisabeth Goey.

bo. Jan. 19. Pieter of Gerrit Hoogteelingh and Annatje Oosterhout. Wit: John and Maria V. Alen.

1790
bo. Jan. 30. Hermanus of John H. Wendell and Catharina Benthuysen.

Feb. 28. bo. Jan. 2. Jellis of Robert Grey and Suzannah Legrange. Wit: Jacobus Legrange, Natie Fisher.

bo. Feb. 4. Martinus of Thomas Easterly and Bata V. Woert. Wit: the parents.

Feb. 28. bo. Feb. 10. Annatie of Jacob Freyer and Annatie Muller. Wit: John and Elisabeth Freyer.

bo. Feb. 22. Sarah of John Bogert and Cathrina Ten Broeck. Wit: John and Sarah Ten Broeck.

Mar. 7. bo. Feb. 1. Bernardus of Frans Harsingh and Rebecca Spoor. Wit: Bartje and Annatje Bloemendal.

bo. Jan. 21. Helena of Gerrit Lansingh and Helena V. Deusen. Wit: Noah and Helena Gillot.

bo. Jan. 19. Maria of William Adams and Hester Willison. Wit: Philip Willis, Peggy Adams.

Mar. 14. bo. Feb. 16. Laurens of Cornelis Bloemendal and Lena Reisdorp. Wit: Laurens and Margarita Reisdorp.

bo. Feb. 14. Catharina of Hendrikus Bratt and Annatje Davies. Wit: Daniel and Willempje Bratt.

bo. Feb. 1. Hendrik of Frederick Minerson and Elizabeth Waldron. Wit: Hendrick V. Wie and Mary Van Wie.

bo. Feb. 12. Maria of Abraham Bloodgood and Elizabeth V. Volkenburgh.

Mar. 16. bo. Feb. 8. Christina of John G. and Anna V. Schaick. Wit: Gerrit W. and Christina V. Schaick.

Mar. 21. bo. Feb. 21. Jannetje of Johs Goewey and Pietertje Hieralymon. Wit: Nicholas Hieralymon, Susanna Minerssen.

bo. Mar. 16. Hadrian of Jacob V. Woert and Sarah V. Esch. Wit: Hadriaan and Folkje Qwakkenbusch.

bo. Jan. 29. Rachel of Lavinus V. d. Bergh and Elisabeth Anthony.

bo. Feb. 5. Elizabeth of Aaron Slingerland and Hannah Arnold. Wit: John and Elizabeth Slingerland.

Apr. 3. bo. Mar. 4. Margrita of Jacobus V. d. Voort and Annatje Neghs. Wit: Hermanus Henry, Catharina Schuyler.

bo. Mar. 22. Willem of Barent G. Staats and Catharina Cuyler. Wit: Gerrit and Catharina Staats.

Apr. 11. bo. Apr. 3. Johannes of Jacob Bloemendal and Margarita Roller. Wit: Bernardus and Engeltje Bloemendal.

1790

bo. Apr. 10. Folkert Pieter of John De P. Douw and Debora Beekman. Wit: Folkert Douw, Annatje de Peister.

Apr. 18. bo. the 2d. Jelles of Daniel Winne and Hanna Zwits. Wit: Hendrik Everts, Hendrikje Winne.

bo. Feb. 28. Dirk of George Zeeger and Catharina V. d. Willigen. Wit: Dirk, Simon and Sara V. d. Willigen, Jennith Cook (?).

bo. the 3d. Jeremiah V. Rensselaer of Abraham Ten Eyck and Annatje Lansingh. Wit: Jermias V. Rensselaer, Lena Lansingh.

bo. Mar. 11. Jacob of Yzac Y. Fonda and Antje V. Santvoord. Wit: Yzaac Fonda, Cornelia Lansingh.

May 2. bo. Mar. 27. Freryk of Willem Cooper and Marytje Berringer. Wit: Gerrit V. Schaik, Christina Berringer.

bo. Mar. 9. Philip of Philip Wendell and Geertruy Vosburgh. Wit: John and Cathalina Groesbeek.

bo. Mar. 14. Annatje of Pieter Cooper and Annatje Stronk. Wit: Christiaan and Elisabeth Cooper.

bo. Apr. 14. William of Jacob A. Cuyler and Rebecca Cane. Wit: William and Elisabeth Cane.

bo. Apr. 13. Deborah of Jacob Pruin and Hendrikje V. Buuren.

May 9. bo. Mar. 16. Jeremias of Jacob Berringer and Catharina Heimer. Wit: Philip Heimer, Ann Maria Symon.

May 9. bo. Apr. 15. Franciscus of Lavinus I. Lansingh and Marytje Pearce. Wit: Jacob I. Lansingh, Jannetje Vischer.

May 16. bo. Apr. 14. Schuyler of Philip V. Rensselaer and Maria Sanders. Wit: Robert and Elisabeth V. Rensselaer.

bo. May 4. Died May 25. Stephen Van Renselaer of John B. Schuyler and Elisabeth V. Rensselaer. Wit: Stephen V. Rensselaer, Catharina Westerlo.

May 23. bo. March 26. Elisabeth of Nicolaas Siksby and Cornelia Cooper.

bo. Apr. 25. Tietje of Quiliaan Winne and Sara Kloet. Wit: Jelles and Tietje Winne.

bo. Apr. 1. Henry of Henry Barhanse and Temperance Dumond. Wit: Johannes Barhanse, Temperance V. Orden.

May 29. bo. Mar. 22. Catharina of Nicholas Frank and Elizabeth Fonda. Wit: Hannah and John Fonda.

1790
bo. Mar. 1. Isaac of Walter Van der Zee and Maria Peck. Wit: Isaac Hoogkirk, Rachel V. Zanten.

June 4. bo. May 12. Tanneke of Pieter Foreest and Pietertje V. Aalstein. Wit: Marten and Tanneke Foreest.

bo. Mar. 12. Jannitie of Garrit V. Wie and Mary Slinger-land. Wit: William V. Wie, Jannitie Lansing.

June 6. bo. May 3. Annatje of Martinus V. Yveren and Cornelia V. Schaick. Wit: Abrah. and Annatje Witbeek.

bo. May 2. Wouter of David Winne and Geertruy Groes-beek. Wit: Pieter Groesbeek, Alida V. Alen.

bo. May 28. Johannes of Jacob J. and Neeltje Pruyn. Wit: Johs. Pruyn, Marritje Witbeek.

bo. May 12. Catharina of Coenraad Sharp and Elisabeth Staats.

June 7. Jeremia and Geesje (Twins) of Richard Smith and Sophia Muller. In the house, owing to sickness.

bo. Mar. 25. Elizabeth Roe of Jacob Jeguor and Marigritta Dunbar. Wit: John Miller, Anna Berch.

bo. May 21. Catharine of James Radley and Mary Olmar. Wit: Catharina and Philip Waggenen.

bo. Mar. 28. Mary of Henry Bronk and Sarah Osterhout. Wit: Henry and Mary Osterhout.

bo. Apr. 11. Peter of William D. Winne and Mary Baker. Wit: Peter Winne, Mary Osterhout.

Mar. 31. Lewis of Lewis Barrington and Margaret Adams.

June 20. bo. May 22. Caty of Hendrick Arnold and Janneke V. Alstine. Wit: Andrew V. Alstyne, Mary Shutter.

bo. May 25. Jannitie of Christian Legrange and Elizabeth Freeman.

bo. June 6. John Jeremiah of John Jeremiah V. Rensselaer and Catharina Glen. Wit: John Glen, Judith Bruce.

bo. May 17. Abraham of Winens V. Den Bergh and Mary Nexson. Wit: William V. Den Bergh, Annatie Fosburgh.

bo. June 1. Eleanor of George Barringer and Elizabeth Pean. Wit: Jacob Barringer, Catharina Hainer.

bo. Apr. 19. Catharina of Jacob Hainer and Elizabeth Kenter. Wit: Philip Barringer, Catharine Meyers.

bo. June 2. Rachel of Dennis Clevison and Rachel Milton. Wit: Henry Milton, Rachel Norten.

June 29. bo. June 11. Mary of Philip Raidley and Susannah Seger. Wit: Garret Seger, Mary Pangburn.

1790

July 4. bo. May 31. Petrus of Isaac Van Alstyne and Barbara Sharpe. Wit: Peter Sharpe, Cathrina Barringer.

bo. June 11. Elizabeth of John Flamsborough and Catharina Baker.

July 11. bo. the 6th. Antje of Abraham G. Lansingh and Tanneke Yates. Wit: Cornelis C. V. d. Bergh, Antje Yates.

bo. July 2. Mary of David Fonda and Catharina Ten Broeck.

July 18. bo. June 28. Jannetje of Quiliaan D. Winne and Sara Connel. Wit: Willem and Fytje Winne.

bo. June 17. Yzac de Foreest of Gerrit R. (?) Lansingh and Alida Foreest. Wit: Yzac de Foreest, Marytje Greveraads.

bo. July 5. Sara of Jacobus Lansingh and Rachel Verplank. Wit: Christoffer and Hubertje Lansingh.

bo. June 19. Jacobus of John Arnot and Elisabeth Briese. Wit: Jacobus and Annatie Arnot.

bo. July 24. Margaret Stuyvesand of Dirck Ten Broeck and Cornelia Stuyvesand. Wit: Nicholas and Margaret Stuyvesand.

bo. July 7. James of John Boyd and Christina V. Deursen.

July 25. Rachel of Mathew Archards and Elisab. Murphy. Wit: John Artwich (?), Rachel Archard.

bo. July 19. John Ebenezer of William W. Waan and Edith Legrange.

bo. June 8, 1785, Maria of Jacob Wendel and Sarah Trotter. Wit: Henry Wendell, Maria Lansing.

Aug. 8. bo. Sept. 18, 1788. Ann of Jacob Wendel and Sarah Trotter. Wit: Hermanus Wendell.

Aug. 14. bo. July 21. Laurens of Leendert Reisdorp and Jannetje de Foreest. Wit: Laurens and Margarita Reisdorp.

bo. July 17. Margaret of Jacob Wendell and Sarah Trotter. Wit: Mathew Trotter, Margaret Wendell.

Aug. 22. bo. Aug. 17. Hannah of John Hilton and Elizabeth Black.

Aug. 29. bo. Aug. 12. Barbara of Johs Shewdy and Catharina Keizer. Wit: Philip Baker, Elisabeth Shewdy.

bo. July 29. Christopher William of Christophel Tilman and Lucy Tracy. Wit: John D. Dickenson.

bo. July 14. Sarah of Abraham Peck and Mary Hammond. Wit: William Peck, Barbara Snider.

1790

Sept. 3. bo. Aug. 4. Maria of Christoffel Bogert and Rebecca Winne.

bo. Aug. 19. Jane Ann of Sanders Lansing and Catharina Ten Eyck.

Sept. 5. bo. Aug. 23. Hadriaan of Anthony V. Santvoort and Maria Roff. Wit: Yzac Fonda, Antje V. Santvoort.

bo. Aug. 1. Gerrit of Willem V. Alen and Magdalena V. Wie. Wit: John V. Alen, Maria Look.

bo. Aug. 10. Jacob of Salomo Look and Lena Moock. Wit: Jacob and Alida Look.

bo. Aug. 8. Annatje of John V. Benthuysen and Geesje V. Hoessen. Wit: Willem and Sara V. Benthuysen.

bo. Aug. 14. Elisabeth of Hendrik Bulsingh and Maria Moor. Wit: Nicols Muller, Cathal. Bulsingh.

bo. Aug. 14. Hendrick of Peter Slingerland and Mary Waldron. Wit: Hendrick Van der Werken, Maragarita Waldron.

Sept. 5. bo. Sept. 2. Isaac of Jacob Slingerland and Caty V. Evere.

bo. Sept. 9. Helena of Garret Gui and Angie Look. Wit: Alida and Jacob Look

Sept. 13. bo. Aug. 2. Gerrit V. Santen of Jacobus Bleecker and Rachel V. Santen. Wit: Gerrit and Hester V. Santen.

John of George and Beth Orien. Wit: Jack and Diaan Jackson.

Sept. 19. bo. the 8th. Catharina of Johs Vosburgh and Elisab. Richmond. Wit: Pieter Muller, Cath. Richmond.

Sept. 14. bo. Aug. 18. David of Joseph Christon and Mary Brouwer. Wit: David and Catharina Hart.

bo. May 1. Elisabeth of Seth Price and Mary Gold.

Geertje of Pieter Stooner and Mary Freely.

bo. Aug. 16. Maria of Nichs Wurmer and Geertruy Vosburgh. Wit: Arent Wurmer, Maria V. Schaik.

bo. ult. June. John of Andries Huyk and Rachel Carr. Wit: Nichls and Betsy Huyk.

bo. Aug. 12. Margarita of Yzac Arnold and Gerritje Huyk. Wit: Andries and Rachel Huyk.

Sept. 23. bo. Aug. 4. Margaret of Abraham V. der Heyden and Maritie Sharp. Wit: Matthew V. Der Heyden, Mary Denken.

1790
Sept. 24. bo. Sept. 8. Engeltje of Peter S. Schuyler and Caty Cuyler. Wit: Stephen Schuyler, Angeltie V. Vechten.

Sept. 30. bo. Sept. 11. Jannitie of Samuel Pruyn and Eleanor Norsefield. Wit: John Pruyn, Engeltie Ver Plank.

Sept. 30. bo. Sept. 24. Annatie of John Guyer and Christina Roff (or Ross). Wit: Anthony Van Santvoort, Maria Roff.

bo. Aug. 31. Sarah of Hendrick Rumple and Margaret Hooper. Wit: John Bratt, Sarah Wendell.

bo. Sept. 16. Philip of Matthias Bevee and Elizabeth Lansing. Wit: Robert Crannel, Ariantie Bevie.

Oct. 8. bo. Sept. 3. Catharine of Teunis Visher and Elizabeth Groat. Wit: Abraham Groat, Elsie McKeney.

bo. Sept. 8. Cornelius Bassett of Hermanus Veder and Elizabeth Bassett.

Oct. 24. bo. Aug. 30. Abraham of Stuart Dean and Margaret Wheaten.

bo. Oct. 19. Catharina of Yzac V. Wie and Neeltje Oosterhout.

Oct. 31. bo. Oct. 4. Robert of Pieter Roman and Catharina V. Deusen.

bo. Sept. 26. Frederik of David Berringer and Maria B. Heyner. Wit: Pieter Heyner, Maria Canter.

bo. Oct. 4. Pieter of John V. Deusen and Antje Witbeek. Wit: Pieter and Catharina V. Deusen.

Nov. 21. bo. Nov. 5. Margarita of Jacob Jac. Lansingh and Annatje Qwakkenbush. Wit: Hendrik Qwakkenbush, Elisabeth Cuyler.

bo. Nov. 9. Rachel Douw of Leendert Ganzevoort and Maria V. Rensselaer. Wit: John de P. and Rachel Douw.

bo. Nov. 12. Abraham Verplank of John V. A. Lansingh and Arriaantje Verplank. Wit: Gerrit Groesbeek, Helena Lansingh.

Nov. 28. bo. the 17th. Maria of Hendrik V. Wie and Maria Mershen. Wit: Hendrik and Elisabeth V. Wie.

Apr. 17. bo. Apr. 2, 1791. James of Gerrit A. Lansing and Elizab. Wynkoop. Wit: Jacobus and Alida Wynkoop.

bo. Mar. 18. Catalyntie of Volkert S. Veeder and Ann Quakenb.

bo. Apr. 7. Ann Bleeker of Isaac Truax and Jane Bleeker. Wit: John Bleeker, Garritie V. Schaik.

bo. Apr. 7. Rosina of George Gantz and Jane Neal.

1791
bo. Apr. 6. Maria of Peter Gansevoort and Cath. V. Schaic. Wit: Goos and Maria V. Schaick.

Apr. 25. bo. Mar. 29. Susannah of Abrm. Lappary and Maritie de Foreest.

Apr. 30. bo. Mar. 25. Thomas Witbeck of Thomas Lowe and Gertrey Vosburg.

May 8. bo. May 5. Abraham of Jacob A. Wendel and Eve Swart. Wit: Hermanus A. and Catharine Wendel.

bo. Apr. 1. Joccim of Jacob Veeder, Cath. Spaan. Wit: Volkert Veeder, Annatie Quakenbusch.

bo. Apr. 11. Lyntie Dow of Richard Lush and Lyntie Fonda. Wit: Volkert Dow, Mary Codwine.

bo. Apr. 23. Mary of William Claver and Cath. Schuyler. Wit: Dirck Schuyler, Mary Claver.

May 1. bo. Apr. 7. Catharine of Baar Ten Eyck and An Hoffman. Wit: Volkert P. and Ann Dow.

May 11. bo. Apr. 7. Magdalene of Coonrath Luke and Eliz. Hellebrant. Wit: Wilm. and Magdalene V. Alen.

May 15. bo. Apr. 18. Rebecca of Abrm. Slingerland and Sarah Schoenmaker. Wit: Albert and Rebecca Slingerland.

May 17. bo. Apr. 9. Frederick of Peter Tetterly and Hannah Borsley. Wit: Frederick Borsley, Mary Torne.

May 22. bo. Apr. 27. Garrit Visher Dennison of Garrit Visher Dennison and Eleanir Visher.

May 31. bo. Feb. 1. Margarit of Mathias V. der Heyden and Mary Denker. Wit: Abrm. V. der Heyden, Maritie Sharp.

June 2. bo. May 29. Philip V. Vechten of Harmanus A. and Catharina Wendel. Wit: Lucas and Maritie V. Vechten.

June 3. bo. Mar. 30. Lydia of Solomon Yager and Sarah Price. Wit: John Price, Lydia Pools.

June 12. bo. May 24. John of Benjamin V. Ette and Catharine Erle. Wit: John and Sarah Sterbergh.

June 13. bo. May 2. Henry of Garrit Rykman and Elizabeth V. Beuren. Wit: Nicholas Ranselear, Eltie V. Beuren.

June 25. bo. June 18. Garrit of Eli Arnold and Gertroy Groesbeck. Wit: Lewis and Elizabeth Jermy.

June 26. bo. June —. Frances of John Lansing, Jr. and Cornelia Reay. Wit: Jacob G. and Faancer Lansing.

May 15. bo. Apr. 18. Jacob of Samuel Marcel and Rachal Gardenear.

1791
June 5. bo. May —. John of John V. Zand and Maria Burses.

bo. Apr. 7. Maritie of Jacob Livingston and Sarah House. Wit: Nicholas Wheeler, Maritie Decker.

bo. May 6. Maria of John Luther and Elizabeth Rowler. Wit: Nicholaas Rieben, Mary Hiendeman.

July 11. bo. May 28. Sarah of Andreas Ten Eyk and Ludie V. Esh.

bo. Jan. 11. William of Henry Mooth and Elizabeth Neller.

July 11. bo. May 7. Margarita of John Bleeker and Jane Gilleland. Wit: John R. and Elizabeth Bleeker.

bo. June 12. Maritie of Leonard Miller and Maritie Strunk. Wit: Jacob Strunk, Gatie Miller.

bo. June 17. Jacob of Jacob Lansing and Susannah Faida (Fonda).

July 25. bo. July 22. John of John Schoenmaker, Jr. and Magdalene Houser. Wit: John Schoenmaker, Alida Borhans.

July 11. bo. July 8. Mary of Hermanus Schuyler and Mary Staats. Wit: Henry Staats, Ann Lott.

July 25. bo. July 3. Anna Maria of John Tortler and Elizabeth Cribble.

July 31. bo. July 22. Margarit of Harmanus Ten Eyk and Margarit Bleeker.

Aug. 5. bo. June 26. Catharina Woters of Henry Truax and Ann Yeates. Wit: Christopher and Sarah Yeates.

Aug. 13. bo. July 12. Sophia of Peter Flamsborough and Maritie Becker.

bo. July 18. Cornelius of John Brower and Mary de Weaver.

Aug. 14. bo. July 29. Barent of Jacob V. Loon and Catharine Schuyler. Wit: Catharina Staats.

Elizabeth of Peter Koon and Lydia Dutcher. Wit: Mathew Harperns, Elizabeth Turry.

Aug. 21. bo. Aug. 13. Rachel of Obadiah Cooper and Annatie V. d. Bergh. Wit: Elizabeth Cooper.

bo. June 23. Anna of Garrit Merselis, and ———— Visher. Wit: Guisbert Merselis, Anna Staats.

Aug. 28. bo. Aug. 5. Garrit of John Groesbeek and Cornelia Batt. Wit: Gerrit Batt.

Sept. 2. bo. Sept. 1. Deborah of Nicholaas Bleeker and Eleana Staats.

1791

bo. Aug. 18. Maritie of Rynier Pruyn and Jannitie Goey. Wit: Peter and Cornelia Witbeck.

Sept. 3. bo. Aug. 2. Elizabeth of Jacob Sharp and Ariantie V. Everson. Wit: Nicholas and Helena Sharp.

bo. Aug. 22. Alida of James Funda and Willempie Bogert. Wit: Hennery Visher, Alida Funda.

Sept. 5. bo. July 28. Cornelius V. Vechten of Enoch Leman and Maritie V. Vechten.

Sept. 7. bo. Aug. 12. Isaac of Richard Pangburn and Catalina V. Etta. Wit: Isaac V. Etta, Lalia Radley.

Sept. 10. bo. May 8. Margarit of James E. Thomson and Gertroy Carmen. Wit: James Elliot, Margarit Whey (?).

bo. Aug. 27. William of John Fundey, Jr. and Cornelia Hun. Wit: William and Sarah Hun.

Oct. 20. bo. Sept. 19. John of Philip Boeringley and Catharina Meyer. Wit: William and Elizabeth Heiner.

bo. Aug. 27. John of John I. de Forest and Barbara V. Alstine. Wit: John and Helena V. Alstine.

bo. Sept. 28. Alida of James Legrange and Annatie Visher. Wit: Garrit I. and Rachel Visher.

bo. Oct. 16. Willim of William Staats and Hannah Yates.

bo. Oct. 1. William Belshaser of James V. Benthuyser and Elizabeth Herman.

Oct. 29. bo. Oct. 18. Mary of John Ostrander, Jr. and Catharine Wetsel. Wit: John G. Ostrander, Mary Hermann.

Oct. 30. bo. Aug. 25. Maria of Cornelius and Magdalena Vroman. Wit: Hendric and Mary Vroman.

bo. Sept. 1. Hendrick of John Muller and Catharina Strunk. Wit: Leonard and Maritie Miller.

bo. Sept. 29. Herry of Jacobus Schoenmaker and Elizabeth Atersen. Wit: Henry and Maria Schoenmaker.

Sept. 30. bo. June —. John of John Courtney and Mary Teeser. Wit: Harman Teeser, Mary Courtney.

Oct. 30. bo. Oct. 2. Mary Ann of Jurian Hogan and Hannah While.

Nov. 1. bo. Oct. 20. John of James Hallenbake and Eder Bratt. Wit: Anthony and Christina Broeks.

bo. Sept. 15. Magdalena of Obadiah V. Benthuysen and Johanna Rimley.

bo. Oct. 29. Margarit Pool of John Groesbeck and Cathalintie V. Schaik. Wit: David Groesbeck, Sarah Winne.

1791-1792

bo. Oct. 19. Catharina of Henderick V. Woert and Catharine Eights.

Nov. 20. bo. Nov. 6. Walter of John and Cornelia Quakenbuss. Wit: Walter and Catharina Quakenbuss.

Nov. 27. bo. Sept. 10. Mary of John Wheeler and Maria Hainer. Wit: Nicholas and Maria Wheeler.

bo. Oct. 27. Ann of Simon de Williga and Jane Coon. Wit: Coonrath and Ann Coon.

Nov. 30. bo. May 14, 1790. Sarah of John McMichael and Angeltie Kidney.

Dec. 12. bo. Oct. 20, 1791. James of Garrit Becker and Mary Wincoop.

bo. Nov. 1. James of James Wincoop and Cataline Dunbar. Wit: Jacob Wyncoop, Alida Wincoop.

Nov. 8. Mary of Dirk Soup and Mary Couverd.

Dec. 25. bo. Dec. 13. John of Dirk Hun and Ann Lansing. Wit: John E. and Mary Lansing.

Jan. 15, 1792. bo. Dec. 30, 1791. Henderick of Peter Riddeker and Elizabeth Snatt.

Jan. 14. bo. Dec. 12. Sarah of John Whoop and Haccost Barkley.

bo. Dec. 25. Magdelene of James V. Schoonhover and Maria Spoor.

Jan. 18. bo. Jan. 8, 1792. Alida of John Goey and Petertie Jerolomon. Wit: Cornelius and Alida Walden.

bo. Jan. 8. Richard of Samuel Benson and Mary Nicholson. Wit: Richard Benson, Mary Wingart.

bo. Dec. 27, 1791. David of Robert Wilson and Catharina Wilsie.

Feb. 5. bo. Oct. 28, '91. John of Nicholas Labagh and Eleaner Wilsie.

bo. Jan. 26, '92. Petrus Stuyvesant of Dirk Ten Broeck and Cornelia Stuyvesant. Wit: Petrus Stuyvesant, Margarit Livingston.

Catharine of Minardt Lansing and Mary Ustres.

bo. Jan. 21. William of Philip Radley and Herbe Hall. Wit: Nicholas Radley, Rachel Willis.

Feb. 5. bo. Jan. 16. Gertroy of Jacob Fryer and Hannatie Miller.

bo. Oct. 16. Peter of Cornelus Vedder and Caty V. Duicher. Wit: Peter and Mary Vedder.

1792
Feb. 12. bo. Feb. 1. Elizabeth of Jacob Cuyler and Rebacca Kane. Wit: William and Elizabeth Kane.

bo. Feb. 3. Jane of John H. Wendel and Catalina Benthuyser.

Feb. 21. bo. Feb. 6. Simon V. Antwerp of Jonathan Hilton and Catharina Hansen. Wit: Simon and Maria V. Antwerp.

Feb. 27. bo. Dec. 21. Eleana of Adam Yates and Margarit Cardenright.

Mar. 2. bo. Apr. 9, 1789. Dorothy of William Hilbing, Jr. and Susannah Hallenbake. Wit: Samuel and Catharina Hallenbake.

Mar. 3. bo. Feb. 2. Maritie of Teunis Slingerland and Maritie Malice.

bo. Feb. 14. Clartie of Walter Slingerland and Jocamintie Hallenbake.

bo. Feb. 22. Cornelius Switz of Daniel Winne and Johannah Switz. Wit: B. Schuyler Switz, Mary Switz.

Eleanor of Henry B. Hallenbake and Rachel Winne.

Mar. 7. bo. Feb. 3. Henry of Cornelius V. Wie and Anna Shantland. Wit: John and Alida V. Wie.

Mar. 12. bo. Mar. 4. Rebecca and Simon (Twins) of John Veeder and Catharina Winne. Wit: Rebecca and Hugh Winne, Joacins and Ghetie Staats.

bo. Dec. 11. Maritie of Adiean Brat and Maritie Arnhout.

Mar. 12. bo. Feb. 8. Levinus Winne of Henderick I. Lansing and Helena Winne. Wit: Levinus Winne, Maritie Lansing.

Mar. 15. bo. Mar. 4. William of John Giver and Magdalena Schermerhorn.

Mar. 18. bo. Feb. 12. John of Daniel Bratt and Christina Beekman.

bo. Mar. 5. Fikie of Henry Everson and Hendrica Winne. Wit: Yellis and Fikie Winne.

John of John Frank and Isabella Eesbester. Wit: James V. d. Woert, Susan Claver.

Apr. 22. bo. Mar. 16. Jane of George Seger and Catharine Terwilliger. Wit: Harm. and Jane Hoghteling.

bo. Apr. 15. Sanders of Abraham I. Lansing and Susannah Yates. Wit: Sanders Lansing, Jr., Catharina Ten Eyck.

1792

Apr. 8. bo. Mar. 4. Isaac Fonda of Peter Groesbeek and Alida V. Allen. Wit: Isaac and Rebecca Fonda.

Mar. 3. bo. Sept. 11, 1791. Richord of Claus and Sarah (slaves). Wit: John.

bo. Mar. 26. Elizabeth of Charles Morgan and Sarah Heyer.

Apr. 15. bo. Apr. 10. John Saunders of Kilian K. V. Ranselear and Margarit Saunders. Wit: John and Deborah Saunders.

Apr. 26. bo. June —. Jane of Barnhardus Evertson and Maritie Hogan. Wit: William and Johannah Evertson.

Apr. 13. bo. Apr. 14. John Earnest of John Earnest Coenrad Christian Miller and Maritie V. Schaick.

May 13. bo. Apr. 28. Charlotte of Thomas Easterly and Batta V. Voort.

May 20. bo. Apr. 28. Michal Bassett of Benjamin Winne and Elizabeth Bassett.

bo. Mar. 28. Hannah of Adam Finkelbach and Helena Finger.

bo. Feb. 6. Barent of Leonard Winning and Annanitie Miller. Wit: John and Annatie Berger.

June 4. bo. May 26. Casparus of Francis Prince and Cornelia Dunbar. Wit: Casparus and Mary Pruim.

bo. May 13. James Hindern of Jacob Hindern and Margarit Philips. Wit: Jacob and Margarit Hindern.

bo. Feb. 23. Mary of John Brice and Catie Lottridge. Wit: Thomas and Mary Lox.

bo. June 6. Garrit of Evert Evertson and Elizabeth Goe.

May 14. bo. Apr. 7. Elizabeth of Jacob Winne and Susanna Hoghtelon.

May 29. bo. Mar. 29. William Charley of John McDole and Eleanor Charley.

Apr. 4. bo. Mar. 9. John Fetter of Jonathan Elvendorff and Margarit Fetter.

June 16. bo. May 26. John of James Radley and Maria Otmann.

bo. May 1. Margarit of Lewis Barrington and Margarit Actan.

June 20. bo. May 29. John of Jonathan Radney and Hannah V. Zandt.

1792
bo. June 2. Daniel of James V. der Voort and Ann Schuyler. Wit: William Bordman, Gertroy Schuyler.

June 20, 1792. Lydia Booth, an adult.

bo. June 9. Guisbert of Evert Marselius and Sarah V. Benthuyser.

bo. May 3. Maria of Robert V. Duson and Gertruy Yager. Wit: Philip Heiner, Anna Maria Simon.

July 11. bo. June 11. Rebecca of Kilian de Winne and Sarah Connolly.

bo. July 13. Catharina Cuyler of Barnt G. Staats and Catharina Cuyler. Wit: Jacob Cuyler, Lydia V. Vechten.

Aug. 6. bo. July 25. Catharina Waters of Henry Truax and Anna Yates. Wit: James and Rebecca Hixer.

Sept. 2. bo. Aug. 1. Rebecca of John Hilton and Elizabeth Black.

bo. Aug. 13. Mary Schuyler of William Claver and Catharina Schuyler.

Aug. 6. bo. July 11. Elbert of Isaac Witbeck and Elizabeth V. Voert.

Aug. 15. bo. July 14. Mary of Peter Roman and Caty V. Deusen.

Sept. 14. bo. Aug. 12. Abraham Ten Eyk of Sanders Lansing and Catharina Ten Eyk.

Sept. 16. bo. Aug. 14. Rebecca of Jacob Berringer and Catharina Heiner. Wit: William Cooper, Ann Maria Berringer.

Sept. 16. bo. May 2. John Rudolff of John Crum and Catharina Rudolff.

bo. 'Sept. 2. William of Samuel Waters and Catharine Lent.

John of Samuel and Elizabeth Norton.

Oct. 19. bo. Sept. 21. Alida of Jacob Pruym and Eleanor De Forest.

Oct. 23. bo. Aug. 1. Catharina of Martin Hoffmann and Mary V. Benthuysen.

bo. Oct. 10. Garrit of John and Alida V. Wie.

Oct. 28. bo. Sept. 30. Margarit of Peter Young and Eva Mone.

bo. Aug. 28. John of Garrit Cluck and Elizabeth Kane.

Oct. 10. bo. Sept. 12. Catharine of Adam Couse and Margarit Snyder.

1792-1793
Nov. 12. bo. Oct. 13. Peter of Peter D. Winne and Mary Osterhout.

bo. Oct. 7. Sarah of Kilian I. Winne and Sarah Clute.

bo. Oct. 8. Henry of John Hock and Eltie Dunbar. Wit: Henry and Eltie V. Wie.

bo. Oct. 24. Walter of John V. Deurson and Antie Witbeck. Wit: Walter and Gertruy Witbeck.

bo. Oct. 18. Maria of Adam Winne and Christina Lagrange. Wit: Cornelious and Elizabeth Winne.

Dec. 1. bo. Nov. 16. Debora of Jacob Slingerland and Caty Everson.

David of Garrit V. Zandt and Caty Hilton.

Dec. 5. bo. Nov. 27. Jacob Jeremiah of Jeremiah Lansing and Helena Wendel.

Dec. 5. bo. Nov. 21. William of Robert Lottridge and Sarah Bloomendall. Wit: Bernhard Bloomendall, Hannah Lottridge.

Dec. 16. bo. Oct. 26. Mathew of John Flamsborough and Catharine Becker.

bo. Nov. 18. Stephen of Egbert V. Schaick and Maria Winne. Wit: Stephen V. Schaick, Jane Bratt.

bo. Nov. 18. Margarit of Christopher Eebigh and Sophia Radly. Wit: Christopher Passage, Catharine Radliff.

bo. Dec. 9. Hannah of James Hilton and Catharina Fryer. Wit: Abraham Lansing, Hannah Witbeck.

bo. Nov. 16. Wynand of Mathias V. Den Bergh and Annatie Yates. Wit: Obadiah and Cornelia Cooper.

bo. Sept. 26. Maria of Benjamin Winne and Annatie Bratt. Wit: Petrus and Maria Ecker.

bo. Oct. 18. William of John Leonard and Cornelia Rechter. Wit: Casparus and Marietie Prime.

bo. Nov. 24. Leonard of Mathias Huick and Rebecca Quackenbuss. Wit: Johannis and Cornelia Witbeek.

bo. Dec. 1. Johannis of Zacharias Harster and Rebecca Spore.

bo. Dec. 17. Jacob of Jacob J. Lansing and Annatie Quackenbuss. Wit: Jeremiah Ranselaer, Helena Lansing.

Jan. 4, 1793. bo. Oct. 25. Maritie of William Waldron and Catharina V. DerZee. Wit: Albert and Maritie V. Der Zea.

Jan. 6. bo. Oct. 19. Baltas of Nicholas Brett, and Lucy Britton.

1792-1793

bo. Dec. 16. Jacob of John Van Arnen Lansing, Ariantie V. Plank. Wit: Jacob Lansing, Willempie Winne.

Jan. 6. bo. Nov. 28. Rebecca of John V. Der Winter and Catharina Slingerland. Wit: Albert Slingerland, Rebecca Quackenbuss.

Dec. 1. Maria of John Bloomendall and Catharine Sharp. Wit: Abraham V. der Heyder, Maritie Sharp.

bo. Dec. 21. Maria of Willem Brawer and Margarit V. Zand.

bo. Dec. 16. Maria of Elias Mathias and Margarit Soop.

John of Barnard Varley and Rachel Bulson.

Maria of John V. Volkenburgh and Catharina Tingue.

Jan. 15. bo. Jan. 7. Hermanus of Nicholas Bleeker and Eleanor Staats.

bo. Nov. 23. Isaac Hogan of John Gorseley and Durckie Hogan. Wit: Jeremiah Hogan, Maritie Charles.

bo. Oct. 14. Bassett of John McMicheal and Angeltie Kidney.

bo. Dec. 29. Barent of Banjamine V. Zandt and Sarah Visher. Wit: John and Sarah Visher.

bo. Dec. 11. Henry of Mathew Troller and Margaret Wendell.

Jan. 14. bo. Dec. 1. Henry of Henry Yates and Rachal V. Zand.

Helena and Susannah of John Luther and Elizabeth Rowler. Wit: Jerem. V. Ranselear, Helena Lansing, Nicholas Clove, Susannah Marridick.

Jan. 30. bo. Dec. 18. Maria of John Schoonmaker and Magdeline Hansin. Wit: Isaac and Cornelis Hansin.

Jan. 30. bo. Oct. 24. Peter of Durck Hoghtiller and Antie V. Der Car.

Jan. 29. bo. Jan. 16. Hosiah of Anthony V. Santfort and Mary Roff.

Feb. 3. bo. Jan. 11. John of John W. V. Zand and Mary Burges.

bo. Jan. 3. Elizabeth of Thomas V. Zand and Rebeccah Hoghkirk. Wit: James and Mary V. Zand.

bo. Jan. 4. John of John Yates and Gertruy V. Vranken.

bo. Jan. 26. Philip of Hermanus P. Schuyler and Mary Staats.

1793

bo. Jan. 18. Jacob of Isaac Quakenbuss and Althumne Gardenier.

Feb. 13. John of John Shoudy and Catharina Keyser.

Feb. 17. bo. Feb. 1. Jacob of Jacob Bloomendall and Margarit Roller. Wit: Richard Vosburgh, Geritie Bloomendall.

bo. Feb. 4. Sedney Lewis of Peter V. Deuson and Lydia Brewslin. Wit: Philip and Catharine Waggens.

Feb. 20. bo. Jan. 31. Mathias of John V. Einburgh and Hannah Hamsburgh. Wit: Isaac and Rachel Hoghkirck.

Feb. 23. bo. Oct. 6, '92. David of Jonathan Winne and Annatie Becker.

bo. Feb. 18. Elizabeth of Jacob V. Woert and Sarah V. Nest. Wit: Jacob I. and Elizabeth V. Woert.

Feb. 26. bo. Jan. 5. Margarit of Peter Class and Annatie V. Esis.

Feb. 26. bo. Jan. 1. William of Isaac V. Etta and Celia Radly.

bo. Feb. 16. Garrit of Teunis G. Visher and Alida Lansing. Wit: Garrit and Rachel Visher.

bo. Jan. 18. Garrit of William Seger and Annatie Brant. Wit: Garrit and Mary Seger.

Mar. 3. bo. Feb. 10. Abraham of Garrit A. Lansing and Elizabeth Winkoop. Wit: Abraham A. Lansing, Helena Denisson.

Mar. 10. bo. Jan. 3. Hendrick of Laurence Winne and Annatie Chambers. Wit: Hendrick Chamber, Rachel V. Zand.

bo. Feb. 5. Edmund of John and Mary Victory.

bo. Mar. 3. Barbary of John Vosburgh and Elizabeth Richmund.

Mar. 31. bo. Mar. 7. Jeremiah of Barent Smith and Hannah Bel.

Mar. 31. bo. Feb. 20. John of John Osterhoudt and Mary Williamson. Wit: Isaac V. Wie, Eliann Osterhoudt.

Apr. 6. bo. Mar. 5. Barbara of Reuben Gaffers and Maria Furrie.

bo. Mar. 5. Harry of John and Elizabeth Jackson. Wit: George Onan, Elizabeth Jackson.

Magdalena of Abraham A. Lansing and Eltie V. Ranselear. Wit: Abraham D. Lansing and Christintie Voorheers.

1793

Apr. 14. bo. Mar. 8. Peter of Gilbert Sharp and Annatie Schoonmaker.

Gertruidie of Abraham V. Vechten and Catharina Schuyler.

Apr. 14. bo. Mar. 10. Abraham of James Fonda and Willempie Bogert. Wit: Nanning Visher, Alida Fonda.

bo. Feb. 9. Janitie of Abraham Slingerland and Sarah Schoonmaker. Wit: Henry Barhanse, Temperance Dumont.

bo. Mar. 23. Agnes of Wilhelmus Osterhout and Jane Schuyler. Wit: John Osterhout, Mary Williams.

Apr. 24. bo. Feb. 17. Henry of John Snyder and Mary Deerstine.

bo. Apr. 19. Gilbert Fonda of Richard Lush and Lyntie Fonda. Wit: Nicholas and Eltie Fonda.

May 5. bo. Apr. 26. Mary Lansing of Jacob Lansing and Alida Dawe.

bo. Apr. 25. Peter of Andreas Abel and Johannah Marshal. Wit: Mary and Annatie Abel.

May 14. Jane of John McCaughtry and Elizabeth Seabury.

May 21. bo. Mar. 12. Margarit of Joseph Salsbury and Margarit Oversandt.

bo. Apr. 19. Catharine of Frederick Ettich and Geertruy Smith. Wit: Robert and Catharine Smith.

bo. May 28. Peter of Jacob and Sarah (servants).

bo. May 12. Philip of Peter V. Durson and Catharine V. Wie. Wit: Abraham and Ann Hoghkirk.

bo. May 8. Ann of Jacobus Hoghkirk and Alida V. Zandt.

bo. Mar. 23. Hugh of John Taylor and Eleanor Naggy. Wit: John Camern, Mr. McDonald.

Apr. 21. bo. Apr. 25. Isaac of Teunis Slingerland and Rachel Davis.

June 2. bo. May 3. Magdelene of Isaac Quackenbuss and Catharine Banker.

May 15. Cornelius of Cornelius Bloomendall and Helena Rysdorp.

bo. Mar. 28. Elizabeth of Peter David and Elizabeth Caldwell.

June 14. bo. Mar. 20. Nancy of Garrit Staats and Anna Lowe.

June 16. bo. May 17. Martinus of Casparus Witbeck and Cornelia Dunbar.

1793
bo. May 21. Joseph of John V. Voorhees and Susannah Dumont.

bo. May 28. Elizabeth of Micheal Nin and Catharina Power. Wit: John and Catharina Ostrander.

bo. May 28. Mindert of Jacobus Legrange and Annatie Visher.

bo. June 3. Garrit of Henry Visher and Rebecca Brooks. Wit: Garrit Visher, Rachel V. De Bergh.

June 23. bo. May 20. Abraham of Peter Slingerland and Maritie V. D. Werken. Wit: Albert Slingerland, Maritie V. Wie.

July 7. bo. June 15. Maritie of Richard Vosburgh and Angeltie Bloomendall.

July 9. bo. June 17. Robert of Nicholas Crannel and Garritie V. D. Bergh. Wit: Robert Crannel, Harritie Bovie.

July 15. bo. Mar. 11. Sarah of Thomas Lawe and Charity Vosburgh. Wit: Abraham and Sara Vosburgh.

July 20. bo. July 10, 1793. Lambert and William of Samuel Norton and Elizabeth Radley.

bo. June 10. Catharine of Mark Lasher and Elizabeth Kilmer.

July 21. bo. July 5. Elizabeth of John Lansing, Jr. and Cornelia Ray. Wit: Cornelious Ray, Elizabeth Elmendorff.

bo. June 24. Robert Ray of John Brawer and Mary de Weax. Wit: John Lansing, Jr., Cornelia Ray.

July 27. bo. July 4. Sarah of Henry V. Benthuysen and Catalina Hun. Wit: Obadiah and Cornelia Lansing.

bo. July 8. Jacob of Aaron Slingerland and Hannah Arnhold. Wit: Isaac Slingerland, Eva V. Weah.

bo. Nov. 25, 1792. Rachel Maria of Isaac Brinkerhoff and Sophia Quackenboss.

Aug. 3. bo. July 27. Catharine of Peter Bloomendall and Barbara Sharp.

bo. July 18. Catharina of David Groesbeck and Elizabeth Burton. Wit: Wilm. Groesbeck, Cathar. Groesbeck.

bo. July —. Elisabeth of Jost Driesback and Caty Hoghstrosser.

Aug. 10. bo. July 5. Mindert of Abraham Veeder and Eleana Schuyler. Wit: Jacob Veeder, Catharina Shawn.

bo. July 21. Isaac of Isaac Truax and Jasie Bleaker. Wit: Henry Truax, Ann Yates.

1793
Aug. 21. Catharine of Garrit Gui and Achi Luke. Wit: Evert Evertson.

Aug. 24. bo. Aug. 4. Jeremiah of John I. V. Ranselaer and Catharina Sless. Wit: Robert V. Ranselear, Judith Bayard.

Aug. 25. bo. Aug. 7. Ryneer of John I. Pruyn and Ariantie V. Plank.

Aug. 24. bo. July 11. Catharine of Philip Wendel and Gertruy Vosburg.

Aug. 27. bo. Aug. 15. Hugh of Isaac Denison and Eleanor Visher. Wit: John Freyer, Ann Dennisson.

Sept. 4. bo. Aug. 4. Elizabeth of Baarent Bleaker and Sarah Lansing.

Sept. 9. bo. Aug. 22. Dorothy of Wilm. V. Benthuysen and Margarit Circuler.

bo. Aug. 30. Sarah of Garrit V. Zandt and Catharine Hilten.

bo. Sept. 1. Helena of Jacob and Janitie Lansing. Wit: Jeremiah V. Ranselear, Helena Lansing.

Oct. 27. bo. Oct. 13. Maria of Eli Arnold and Gertruy Groesbeck. Wit: Cornelious Groesbeck, Anatie V. Antwerp.

Nov. 3. bo. Oct. 16. Catalintie of Walter Groesbeck and Hannah Rykman. Wit: Anthony and Catalintie Groesbeck.

bo. Oct. 16. Elizabeth of William Norton and Catharina Livingston. Wit: Richard and Elizabeth Hilton.

Sept. 28. Maritie of Jacob P. Miller and Gertruy Veeder. Wit: Peter and Maritie Veeder.

bo. Oct. 18. Nicholas of John Gui and Petertie Gerolomer. Wit: Nicholas and Jane Gerolomer.

bo. Oct. 16. Simon of John Veeder and Catharina Winner.

Nov. 10. bo. Aug. 26. Eve of David Berringer and Mary Haner.

Nov. 10. bo. Oct. 22. Christiana of Jacob Everson and Hannah Slingerland. Wit: Albert and Cornelia Slingerland.

Nov. 16. bo. Oct. 26. Thomas of James V. Benthuysen and Elizabeth Hermann.

Dec. 8. bo. Nov. 22. Henry of John and Cornelia Quakenbush.

bo. Nov. 26. Stephen of John S. Schuyler and Catharina Cuyler. Wit: Stephen Schuyler, Helena Ten Eyk.

bo. June 3. Peter of Jacob Foster and Jane Iephers.

1793-1794

Nov. 23. bo. Oct. 27. John of James R. and Mary V. Zandt.

Dec. 1. bo. Nov. 25. Efice of Leonard Gansevoort, Jr., Mary V. Ranselaer. Wit: Peter and Magdalena Gansevoort.

bo. Nov. 9. Catrina of Hermanus A. and Catharine Wendel. Wit: Cornelious Wendel, Annatie Lansing.

bo. Nov. 12. Eleanor of Isaac V. Wie and Eleanor Osterhout.

Dec. 15. bo. Nov. 17. Margarit of Adam and Annatie Bratt.

Dec. 22. bo. July 22. John of John Buyse and Anne Rutherford.

bo. Oct. 19. Mary of Benjamin Winne and Elizabeth Bassett.

bo. Nov. 16. Catharine of Nicholas A. Quakenbush and Annatie Gansevoort. Wit: Nicholas Quakenbush.

bo. Oct. 28. Catharine of John Hoghtilling and Jane Barhanse. Wit: John and Maria V. Alen.

Dec. 22. bo. Nov. 29. William of George Carkner and Margarit Wediman.

bo. Sept. 5. Elizabeth of Henry Passage and Elizabeth Claus. Wit: Henry and Elizabeth Class.

bo. Oct. 13. Maritie of Teunes Slingerland and Maritie Neulie.

bo. Nov. 21. John of Jacob Frier and Annatie Miller.

bo. Dec. 10. Dirk of Dirk Hun and Anne Lansing.

1794, Jan. 3. bo. June 27. Hannah of Arent Bratt and Jane Hogar. Wit: Jurias Hogar, Mary Charles.

bo. Dec. 28. Elizabeth of Isaac Arnold and Sophia Philips. Wit: Isaac and Elizabeth Arnold.

bo. Dec. 13. William of Dennis Flamisham and Rachel Milton.

bo. Dec. 24. Wilhelmus of Edward Brunt and Margarit Kerkennonn.

bo. Dec. 8. Eltie of Jurian Hogan and Hannah White.

bo. Nov. 5. Mary of Garrit Lansing and Chrital Hoffman.

bo. Dec. 30. Alida of Jacob I. Lansing and Susanna Funda.

bo. Nov. 28. Jane of Peter Reddems and John (sic) Lodowic.

bo. Jan. 1, 1794. Elias of Lucas W. Veeder and Susannah W. Bratt.

1794

Jan. 3. bo. Jan. 4. (sic) Nicholas of William Radley and Margarit Cline. Wit: Nicholas and Elizabeth Cline.

Adam of John Beem and Sarah Tonkins.

bo. Jan. 30. Catharine of Francis Pruyne and Cornelia Dunbar. Wit: Casparus and Mary Pruyne.

bo. Jan. 9. Maria of Salomon Luhr and Helena Mohr. Wit: John and Maria Mohr.

bo. Sept. 2, '93. Elizabeth of John Freyer and Mary Johoier.

bo. Oct. 28. Jane of Zacharias Sickels and Catharina Shever.

bo. Dec. 11. Cornelious of Abraham Vosburgh and Sarah Bulson.

Feb. 12. bo. Dec. 31, '93. Sarah of Pet. Edmund Elmendorf and Eliza V. Renselear. Wit: Mary and Catharina Elmendorf, John R. Bleeker, Jr.

Dec. 18, '94 (sic). bo. Oct. 26, '92. Elizabeth and Abraham of Ozia Richards and Hannah Sickels. Wit: Abraham and Mary Sickels.

Feb. 15. bo. Jan. 13. Helena of John Winkoop and Harriet Bartay.

bo. Jan. 18. Tike of Henry Hollenbeck and Rachel Winne.

bo. Jan. 1. Johannah of Garrit Cluck and Elizabeth Kune.

bo. Sept. 11, '93. Margarit of Peter Koon and Ledia Dutcher. Wit: John Koon, Margarit Wise.

bo. Feb. 17, '94. John of James V. Schermerhorn* and Maria Spoor. Wit: Francis Hanser, Rebecca Spoor.

Feb. 15. bo. Feb. 13. Sarah of Richard I. Hilton and Elizabeth Norton.

bo. Feb. 9. Anne of Volkert Veeder and Anna Quackenbush.

bo. Feb. 24. Anne Usher of Mindert Lansing and Mary Usher.

bo. Feb. 18. Celia of Jonathan Kidney and Brunat V. Zandt.

Feb. 14. bo. Feb. 1. Levy of John Ostrander and Catharina Wetsel.

bo. Jan. 15. Miriam of Enoch Leonard and Maria V. Vechten.

---

*Somebody had written above this, in pencil, Schoonhoven.

1794
bo. Mar. 17. Godfrey Enoch of Thomas V. Benthuysen and Mary Enoch.

Apr. 14. bo. Apr. 4. Garret of John V. Zandt and Mary Barga.

Apr. 20. bo. Mar. 26. Margaret of Peter Roman and Caty V. Deuser.

bo. Apr. 25. John of Jacob Wendel and Eve Swart. Wit: John and Susannah Wendel.

July 24. bo. July 20. Charles of James V. Der Voort and Mary Schuyler.

May 11. bo. Apr. 13. Ghosen V. Schaick of John Ernest Conred Christian Miller and Maritie V. Schaick.

May 11. bo. Apr. 15. Thomas Diamond of John V. Allen and Mary Diamond.

Oct. 19. bo. Sept. 18. Caterlintie of Anthony T. Bratt and Gertruy V. den Bergh. Wit: Teuris and Caterlintie Bratt.

Oct. 19. bo. Sept. 27. Rachel of Garrat G. Visher and Rebecca Brooks.

bo. Oct. 10. Levinus of Egbert V. Schaick and Maria Winner. Wit: Levinus and Rachel Winner.

bo. Oct. 10. Abraham of Sybrant Dowe and Lyntie T. Eyck. Wit: Peter and Rykie Dowe.

Nov. 22. bo. Sept. 28. Catalina of Isaac Willet and Elizabeth V. Woert. Wit: John and Hyltie V. Woert.

Nov. 2. bo. Oct. 5. John of Jacobus Hoghkirk and Alida Van Zandt.

William of John Johnson and Helena Lottryde.

Nov. 12. bo. Oct. 24. Jacob of John H. Wendel and Càtalina V. Benthuisen.

Dec. 18. bo. Oct. 27. Stephen of Philip S. Schuyler and Rachel V. den Bergh.

Sept. 19. bo. Dec. 25 (sic). Cornelious Wynkoop of Garrita Lansing and Elizabeth Wynkoop.

bo. Dec. 12. Jacob of Jacob I. Prime and Eleanor De Forest.

Nov. 30. bo. Nov. 23. Kilian V. Renselear of Abraham Lansing and Eltie Van Renselear. Wit: Kilian and Ariantie V. Rensalear.

Dec. 14. bo. Nov. 23. Jannetie of Peter Groesbeck.

1794-1795
bo. Dec. 1. Elizabeth of Jacob I. Lansing and Annatie Quackenbuss. Wit: Jacob G. Lansing, Elizabeth Quackenbuss.

Feb. 14, 1795. bo. Jan. 17, 1795. Sarah and Cornelia of John Lansing, Jr. and Cornelia Ray. Wit: Sarah and Jane Lansing.

Feb. 18. bo. Jan. 25. Angelica of Peter S. Schuyler and Catharina Cuyler. Wit: Stephen Schuyler, Maria V. Vechten.

Feb. 14. bo. Jan. 30. Elizabeth of Richard S. Treat and Gertrude Stringer.

Mar. 14. bo. Feb. 13. Willempie of John V. A. Lansing and Harriot VerPlank. Wit: Jacob and Willempie Lansing.

Feb. 8. bo. Jan. 11. Mary of Isaac and Margaret Seaman.

Jan. 20. bo. Sept. 11. Philip of Harry Quilhot and Mary Lansing.

Jan. 1. bo. Nov. 28, 1794. Samuel A. of Abraham V. Vechten and Catharina Schuyler.

Mar. 22. Rachel of Benjamin Winne and Elizabeth Bussel Wit: John Cossley, Rachel Winne.

bo. Jan. 12. Richard of Andrew Marsel and Cornelia Slingerland.

Jan. 6. bo. Dec. 7, 1794. John of Daniel Marshal and Elizabeth Cochen.

Jan. 10. bo. Dec. 26. John of Eldert Fryer and Helena Melgen.

bo. Dec. 23. Mary of Garret Benser and Dolly Hoofman.

bo. Nov. 30. Thomas of Philip Radley and Naomi Hall.

bo. Nov. 13. Jane of John Skidmore and Ann Clarke.

bo. Mar. 29. Mary of John Ostrander and Mary Scott.

Jan. 10. bo. Apr. 9. Elizabeth of Jacob House and Catharine Snyder.

bo. May 5. Geesie of James V. Benthuysen and Mary Sima (?).

Mar. 14. bo. Mar. 4. Hannah of Gould Price and Hannah Walles.

Mar. 26. bo. Mar. 16. Sarah of Guy Canada and Margaret Paterson.

Apr. 9. bo. May 3. Christopher Lansing of Teunis G. Visher and Alida Lansing.

1795
May 14. bo. May 4. William of James Allen and Mary Hollenbake. Wit: William and Mary Claver.

May 31. bo. May 20. Elizabeth Maria of Dirck Ten Broeck and Cornelia Stuyvesant. Wit: Abraham Ten Broeck, Elizabeth V. Renselaer.

July 31. bo. June 15. Susannah of Isaac Denniston and Eleanor Visher.

Aug. 5. bo. Aug. 1. William of Philip Mowers and Hannah Coens.

Sept. 2. bo. Aug. 17. Peter Wicoff of John V. Voorhees and Elizabeth Wicoff.

Sept. 3. bo. May 3. Hendric of John H. V. Der Werken and Catharina Slingerland.

Sept. 5. bo. July 20. Henrietta of Jeremiah Randal and Gertray Gardinier.

Sept. 7. bo. Aug. 29. Gerritie of Isaac Truax and Janet (?) Bleecker. Wit: John J. Bleecker, Gerretie V. Schaick.

bo. June 16. Jane and James of William Robinson and Ierina Freyer.

Sept. 7. bo. Feb. 28. Catalina of John Bratt and Margaritta Winne. Wit: Teunis and Catalina Bratt.

bo. Feb. 23. Dowe Bogert of James Fonda and Willempie Bogert. Wit: Peter Winne, Magdalena Bogert.

June 28. bo. May 27. John of John V. der Pool and Gertruy V. Beuren.

July 10. bo. July 1. Cornelius of Jeremiah Schuyler and Jane Cuyler. Wit: John Cuyler, Catharina Glen.

July 11. bo. June 22. Glen of John I. V. Renselaer and Catharina Glen. Wit: John Glen, Catharina Veeder.

July 12. bo. June 14. Richard of James Hickson and Elizabeth V. Slyck.

July 21. bo. June 28. Garret of James R. and Mary V. Zandt.

bo. June 7. Ann of Peter David and Elizabeth Caldwel.

July 27. bo. July 3. Lawrence of Abraham Quackenbuss and Caty Radliff.

bo. July 8. Magdelene of Francis Harsin and Rebecca Spoor.

Aug. 3. bo. May 25. Abraham of George Bush and Mary Magee.

1795

Aug. 15. bo. July 22. Angus of Philip Dunbar and Susannah Angus.

bo. June 31. Hendric of George Ten Eyck and Magdalena Upham.

bo. May 22. James of James and Dinah (servs. of Stephen V. Renselaer).

Aug. 15. bo. June 5. Eltie of Teunis Vischer and Elizabeth Groot.

Aug. 22. bo. July 10. Philip of John Dingman and Catalina Springer. Wit: William McClenn (?), Christina Springer.

Aug. 29. bo. Aug. 7. Anthony of Isaac A. Quackenbuss and Catharina Baber.

bo. July 29. George of John Luker and Elizabeth Roller. Wit: George Benter, Barbara Roller.

bo. Aug. 19. Garret of Jacob Bloomendale and Margaret Roller (?).

Sept. 6. bo. Aug. 12. Anna of Volker A. Veeder and Annatie Quackenbuss.

bo. Aug. 22. William of William Pepper and Elizabeth Simpson.

bo. Aug. 15. Catharine of Jost Driesbach and Catharina Hoghstrasser.

Sept. 13. bo. Sept. 2. Elizabeth of John Vosburgh and Elizabeth Richmond.

bo. Aug. 20. ———— of William Fonda and Susannah Hollenbake.

Oct. 3. bo. Sept. 3. Elizabeth of Walter Groesbeck and Hannah Rykman. Wit: Eltie Van Renselaer.

bo. Sept. 27. Ann V. Renselaer of Leonard Gansevoort, Jr. and Mary V. Renselaer. Wit: Solomon V. Renselaer, Ann Stephenson.

bo. Oct. 1. George Clinton of Isaac Quackenbuss and Catharina Gardenier. Wit: Maus and Anne V. Vranken.

Sept. 21. bo. Oct. 1 (sic). Peter of Peter Marselis and Catharine Cennel. Wit:. Edward and Sarah Cennel.

Oct. 5. bo. Sept. 26. Sarah of John S. Pruyn and Margaret Lansing. Wit: John Bratt, Sarah V. Antwerp.

Oct. 14. bo. Sept. 27. Deborah Sanders of Kilian K. V. Renselaer and Margareth Sanders. Wit: Myndert S. Ten Eyck, Elsie Sanders.

1795
Oct. 16. Judith, bo. Mar. 17, 1794, Elizabeth, bo. Oct. 4, 1795 of Matthew Freyer and Susannah Carles.

Sept. 18. bo. the 15th. Susannah of Henry Truax and Anna Yeates.

Oct. 2. bo. the 17th. Maria of Philip Gardenier and Elizabeth V. Schaick.

Sept. 2. bo. Oct. 17th. Charles of Calvin Copley and Rachel Winne.

Nov. 1. bo. Oct. 14th. Catharine of Jacob Slingerland and Catharina V. Everen. Wit: Isaac Slingerland, Eva V. Woert.

Nov. 2. bo. Sept. 14. James of Walter P. Barheit and Catharina McGen.

Nov. 3. bo. Oct. 5. Sarah of John D. Groesbeck and Catalina V. Schaick. Wit: Christophel and Hybertie Lansing.

ba. July 6 by the Rev. Mr. De Ronde. bo. June 29. Henry of Cornelius V. D. Bergh and Annatie Ten Eyck. Wit: Henry and Lyntie Ten Eyck.

Nov. 14. bo. Oct. 22. John of Jacobus Hoghkerk and Alida V. Zandt.

Nov. 14. bo. Oct. 16. Abraham of Thomas V. Zandt and Rebecca Hoghkirk.

bo. Oct. 25. Charlotte of Charles Morgan and Sarah Heyer.

Nov. 14. bo. Oct. 10. Annatie of James V. Benthuysen and Elizabeth Hermans.

Nov. 12. bo. Aug. 12. Catalina of Jesse De Forest and Rebecca V. Zandt.

Nov. 27. bo. Oct. 23. Margaret of Garrit V. Allen and Ann Moody.

Nov. 29. bo. Nov. 12. Sarah Jordan of Thomas Guest and Gertrude Schuyler.

Dec. 20. bo. Nov. 21. Rebecca of Jonathan Ridney and Hannah V. Zandt.

Dec. 20. bo. Nov. 7. Gessie of David Winne and Alida V. Benthuysen.

Dec. 20. bo. Nov. 8. Gertrude of Peter Varley and Rachel Balsom. Wit: Solomon and Gertrude Balsom.

bo. Nov. 1. William of Garret Clute and Elizabeth Kane.

Dec. 21. bo. Nov. 17. James Parker of James and Hannah V. Benthuysen.

1795-1796

Dec. 10. bo. Nov. 15. John of Barnt G. Staats and Catharina Cuyler.

bo. and ba. Jan. 4, 1796. Hester Ganzevoort of Jacob Ten Eyck and Magdalena Gansevoort. Wit: Leonard Gansevoort, Hester Cuyler.

ba. Jan. 10. bo. Dec. 15, 1795. Benjamin of John Goewey and Petertie Jerolomon.

Jan. 19. bo. Dec. 6. William V. Bergen of Peter C. Adams and Catalina V. Bergen. Wit: Henry V. Bergen, Eleanor Salisbury.

Jan. 25. bo. Nov. 12. Rebecca of Albert Slingerlandand Susannah V. Nest.

Jan. 26. bo. Dec. 22. Nicholas of Henry Bulsom and Catharina Cater. Wit: Nicholas Ridcher, Alida Bulson.

Feb. 2. bo. Dec. 28. Abraham of Simeon and Cornelia Decker. Wit: John Fonda, Elties V. Deusen.

Feb. 9. bo. Aug. 24. Alexander of Philip G. Viele and Mary V. den Bergh. Wit: Nicholas V. d. Bergh, Catharina Waldrom.

Feb. 11. bo. Jan. 30. Magdalena Maria of Garret Bogert and Margaret Nexson.

Feb. 13. bo. Jan. 11. Garret of Casparus Witbeck and Cornelia Dunbar.

bo. Jan. 11. Catharine of Dirck Hilton and Mary V. Deuzen.

Feb. 15. bo. Nov. 12. Albertus of Storm Becker and Elizabeth Clute.

Feb. 17. bo. Dec. 27. Henry of John G. and Annatie V. Schaick.

Feb. 18. bo. Feb. 10. Catharina V. Ingen of Harmanus Ten Eyck and Margaret Bleecker. Wit: James V. Ingen, Catharina Bleecker.

Feb. 21. bo. Jan. 12. Gertrude of Peter Roman and Catharina V. Deusen.

Feb. 24. bo. Aug. 25, '95. Peter of Alexander Boyd and Elizabeth Becker.

Mar. 6. bo. Feb. 4. Ann Tilet of John V. Alen and Mary Diamond.

Mar. 26. bo. Mar. 5. Elizabeth of Jacob Fryer and Annanitie Muller.

1796
Mar. 26. bo. Feb. 13. Catalina of Garret Marselis and Machtel Visher. Wit: Isaac Bogert, Catalena Visher.

Mar. 31. bo. Feb. 29. Nicholas of Nicholas Quackenbush and Annatie Gansevoort.

Mar. 16. bo. Feb. 29. Andreas Dowe of Jacob Lansing, Jr. and Alida Dowe. Wit: Volkert and Catharina Dowe.

Apr. 3. bo. Mar. 2. Bernardus of Henry B. Hallenbake and Rachel Winne.

Apr. 10. Christina Louisa of Anthony V. Santford and Mary Roff. Wit: Christina Roff.

Apr. 24. bo. Mar. 31. Jacob of Jacob Evertson and Hannah Slingerland.

Apr. 30. bo. Apr. 4. Augustus V. Schaick of John Earnest Conrad Christian Miller and Maritie V. Schaick.

May 4. bo. Apr. 11. Elizabeth of Richard Smith and Sophia Millar.

May 8. bo. Feb. 29. William V. Bergen of Andrew N. Hermanse and Eleanor Van Bergen. Wit: Henry V. Bergen, Eleanor Salisbury.

May 15. bo. Apr. 30. Henrykie of Henry Evertson and Cornelia Slingerland.

Aug. 3. bo. May 21, John Cole of Evert (?) Delamater and Mary Cole.

bo. May 1. Reuben of Reuben Johnson and Ann Hartwich.

June 5. bo. Feb. 20. Robert of John Burns and Lydia Burch.

June 3. bo. Mar. 25. Abraham of Philip Wendel and Sarah Packart.

June 12. bo. May 17. Alida of Jacob I. Lansing and Susannah Fonda. Wit: Nanning Vischer, Alida Fonda.

June 12. bo. May 9. Mary of Abraham Bensen and Sarah Augerdon.

bo. Apr. 20. Teunis Van der Volgen of Isaac Lerway and Sarah Hemstraat.

June 20. bo. Apr. 7. Abraham of William Hermanse and Mary Scott.

bo. May 27. Christopher of Abraham G. Lansing and Susannah Yates. Wit: Abraham Yates, Jr., Jane Lansing.

July 10. bo. June 18. Elizabeth of Isaac Willett and Elizabeth Van Wort.

1796

July 17. bo. June 4. Eliza of William V. Benthuysen and Margaret Conklin.

July 19. bo. July 14. Catalina of Nicholas Bleecker and Eleanor Staats. Wit: Catalina Bleecker.

July 22. bo. July 14. Eleanor of Mindert Marsilius and Catharine Milderbergh. Wit: Andrew Marselis, Sarah Brower.

July 31. bo. July 29. Eleanor of John Bassett and Anna Hun. Wit: Francis and Eleanor Bassett.

Aug. 3. bo. June 18. Dirck V. Schuyline of John Brower and Mary de Weaver. Wit: Dirk and Deborah V. Schuyline.

Aug. 7. bo. Aug. 3. Janetie of Jacob I. Pruyne and Eleanor De Forest. Wit: Janitie Pruyne.

Aug. 8. bo. July 27. Barbara of John Eaton and Christian (sic) McArthur.

Aug. 21. bo. July 26. Winant of Winant V. Den Bergh and Mary Nexson.

bo. July 18. Johanna of Danill Winne and Alida Van Arnum. Wit: Fanny Switz.

Aug. 20. bo. July 1. Rebecca of John Guyer and Christina Roff. Wit: Anthony Sandford, Mary Roff.

Aug. 26. bo. June 5. Eleanor of Hermanus Vedder and Elizabeth Basset. Wit: Angeltie V. Husen.

Aug. 12. bo. Aug. 8. Abraham of Jacob A. Cuyler and Rebecca Kane.

Aug. 15. bo. July 20. Alida of Edward Cumsiston (?) and Mary Bratt.

Sept. 4. bo. July 15. Elizabeth of Peter Bulsom and Rachel Smith. Wit: Peter Walde, Elizabeth Smith.

Sept. 11. bo. July 21. Eleanor of John Johnson and Eleanor Lottridge.

Sept. 25. bo. Sept. 4. Sarah of James and Mary V. Zandt. Wit: Isaac and Rachel Hooghkirk.

Sept. 26. bo. Sept. 3. Margarit of Matthew Trotter and Margaret Wendel.

Oct. 2. bo. Sept. 1. William of Dennis Clamisher and Rachel Milton.

bo. Sept. 23. Catharine of Hermanus A. and Catarine Wendel.

bo. Sept. 10. John Henry Meyers of James Wincoop and Catalina Dunbar.

1796
bo. Aug. 27. John of John Hermanse and Elenor Sheffer.
Sept. 28. bo. Sept. 22, 1758. Caleb of James Studevant
and Mary Devenant.

Found on a loose piece of paper; an exact copy:
The son of Abram and Maria Brower Garrison named
Henry Garrison, born Nov. 9th, 1768.

Sept. 28, 1796. bo. Apr. 29, 1783. Susannah of Caleb
Studevant and Sarah Chandler.

bo. Feb. 29, 1788. Sarah. The same as above.

The following five children were baptised by Rev. Mr.
Johnson:

June 7. bo. Mar. 26. Maria of Peter E. Elmendorf and
Elizabeth V. Renselaer. Wit: Philip and Maria V. Renselaer.

Aug. 7. bo. July 8. Volkert of Luca W. Veeder and Susannah Pratt. Wit: Volkert Veeder.

Aug. 9. bo. July 29. Hermanus of Abraham V. Vechten
and Catharina Schuyler.

Aug. 9. bo. June 25. Robert of James Taulie and Maria
Yates. Wit: Robert Yates, Jannitie V. Ness.

Aug. 5. bo. Aug. 16. Sara of David Pruyn and Hebertie
Lansing. Wit: Christophel Lansing.

Oct. 8. bo. Sept. 17. Peter of Peter Dox and Nancy Randall. Wit: George Collier, Catharina O'Brian.

Oct. 8. bo. Oct. 4. Levinus of Francis Pruyne and Cornelia
Dunbar. Wit: Levinus and Margarit Dunbar.

Oct. 15. bo. Sept. 12. Edward of John Oatie (?) and Jane
Williams.

Oct. 15. bo. Sept. 23. Anna of Barnt Smith and Hannah
Bell.

bo. June 14. Margaret of Luther Troubridge and Elizabeth
Tillman.

Oct. 23. bo. Sept. 27. Rachel of Andrew Morill and Cornelia Slingerland.

Oct. 23. bo. Oct. 4. Peter of Jacob P. Bogart and Aulida
Bloomindale.

Nov. 5. bo. Oct. 5. Andrew of Christophel Nacoxs (?) or
Hawks (?) and Mary Passinger.

bo. Oct. 9. Winant of Nicholas Crannel and Garritie Van
den Bergh. Wit: Winant V. Den Bergh, Christintie Clute.

1796-1797
bo. Oct. 23. Benjamin and Jacob, twins, of Garret Goey and Akie Luke.

bo. Oct. 29. Jane Maria of John H. Wendell and Catalina Van Benthuysen.

Nov. 12. bo. Oct. 28. Isaac Van Arnum of John Franks and Elisabeth Eisbester. Wit: William Magarty, Classie Groesbeck.

bo. Oct. 28. Maria of Samuel Norton and Elizabeth Redley.

Nov. 20. bo. Nov. 15. Jacob of Jacob Van Woort and Sarah Van Nest. Wit: Jacob V. Woort, Rebecca Bogert.

bo. Oct. 27. Alexander of Daniel Sickels and Jennet Dunse. Wit: Samuel and Ann Hannah.

Nov. 27. Maria of Jack and Mary (slaves). Wit: Nicholas and Eltie Fonda.

Dec. 10. bo. Nov. 9. Gilbert of Garret Benson and Dorothy Hoffman.

Dec. 25. bo. Oct. 31. Maria of John Ostrander and Mary Scott.

bo. Sept. 24. Timothy of Jeronimus Turk and Elizabeth Bussing (?).

Dec. 5. bo. Nov. 18. Isaac Fonda of Peter Groesbeck and Alida V. Arnum.

1797, Jan. 3. bo. Dec. 25. Martina of John Slingerland and Susannah Evertson. Wit: Bernardus Evertson, Martina Hogan.

Jan. 22. bo. Dec. 29, 1796. Samuel Stringer of Richard S. Treat and Gertrude Stringer. Wit: Samuel Stringer, Rachel Van der Heyden.

Jan. 28. bo. Jan. 6. Jane of Isaac Bratt and Elizabeth V. Deursen.

Jan. 27. bo. Dec. 31. Elizabeth of Lewis Weaver and Elisabeth Derick. Wit: Charles and Margaret Derick.

bo. Sept. 11. Elizabeth of Baltus V. Sleyck and Anna Canine.

Feb. 5. bo. Jan. 15. Sarah of Peter Murphy and Caty Connel. Wit: Edward and Sarah Connel.

bo. Dec. 3, 1796. Catharine of Hendric T. Bratt and Elizabeth Van den Bergh.

Feb. 27. bo. Jan. 31. Ann De Peyster of John P. Dowe and Margaret Livingston. Wit: Henry Renselaer, Rachel Dowe.

1797
Feb. 6. bo. Sept. 12, 1795. Abraham Samuel Wh———— of Peter V. Deuser and Lydia Brewster. Wit: William and Catharina Groesbeck.

Mar. 12. bo. Feb. 17, 1797. Cornelia of William Fonda and Susannah Hollenbake.

Apr. 3. bo. Mar. 16. John Clute of Kilian I. Winne and Sarah Clute.

Jan. 24. bo. Dec. 12, 1796. ———————— of Philip S. Schuyler and Rachel V. Den Bergh. Wit: Stephen Schuyler, Maria V. Vechten.

Nov. 28, 1796. bo. Nov. 6. John Mayby of John C. Cuyler and Hannah Mayby. Wit: John and Catharina Mayby.

bo. Dec. 4, 1796. Isaac of James Fonda and Willempie Bogert. Wit: Jacob I. and Susannah Lansing.

Feb. 17. bo. Jan. 28, 1797. ———————— of William Talbert and Hannah Young.

Feb. 17. bo. Jan. 29. Charlotte of William Claver and Catharina Schuyler. Wit: John Clay, Elizabeth Claver.

Apr. 8. bo. Nov. 20. John of Edmond Hatfield and Jane Ranten.

Apr. 2. bo. Nov. 22. Henry of Dirck De Forest and Rebecca Bratt. Wit: Hendric Bratt and Elizabeth V. D. Bergh.

Apr. 7. bo. Mar. 25. Elizabeth of William Robinson and Javannah Freyer.

Apr. 9. bo. Mar. 24. Henry V. Renselaer of Cornelius Schermerhorn and Catharina V. Renselaer. Wit: Salomon and Hariot V. Renselaer.

Mar. 26. bo. Feb. 14. Philip of Jacob Millar and Gertrude Veeder. Wit: Philip and Nelletie (or Hilletie) Millar.

Apr. 10. bo. Mar. 17. Lansing of Teunis Visher and Alida Lansing. Wit: Christopher and Hubertie Lansing.

Apr. 17. bo. Mar. 25. Elizabeth of Garret Visher and Rebecca Brooks.

Apr. 23. bo. Mar. 22. Jane of Henry Yates and Rachel V. Zandt.

Apr. 15. bo. Mar. 25. Catalina of Eliaham L. Sandey and Rachel Hun.

bo. Apr. 6. Parker of James P. and Hannah V. Benthuysen.

bo. Jan. 6. Ann of Hugh Boyd and Catharina Staats.

bo. Mar. 6. James of John Grant and Mary Cumming.

1797
bo. Apr. 13. Catalina of George Collier and Catharina Obrien.

bo. Apr. 30. Richard of James Van der Woort and Ann Meggs.

bo. May 13. Walter (?) or Aaltie (?) of Lucas Hoogkirk and Eleanor De Forest.

bo. Mar. 13. Catharina of Thomas Watsen and Hannah Trever.

bo. Sept. 21, 1796. Jane Maria of John Keating and Jane Duryee (?).

bo. May 2, 1797. William of George Charles and Mary Price.

bo. Mar. 24. Anna of Jeremiah Rundle and Gertrude Gardenier. Wit: Andries and Annatie Gardenier.

bo. May 10. Garrit Teunis of Garret Teunis V. Vechten and Anna Merselis. Wit: John Merselis.

bo. July 6. Abraham Cuyler of Jacob Ten Eyck and Magdalene Gansevoort. Wit: Abraham Ten Eyck, Ann Lansing.

bo. June 29. Hubertus of Peter Roman and Catharine V. Deursen.

bo. June 22. ———— of Nicholas Riddeker and Hannah Balson.

bo. July 11. Dorothy of Egbert V. Schaick and Maria Winne. Wit: Stephen V. Schaick, Janitie Bratt.

bo. June 13. Willempie of John V. Zandt and Helena Lansing.

bo. Aug. 4. Cornelia of John Fondey, Jr. and Cornelia Hun.

bo. Oct. 20, 1788, Patty of William Carter and Ann Gasley.

bo. Oct. 5, 1790, Samuel of William Carter and Ann Gasley.

bo. May 18, 1797, Ward of William Carter and Ann Gasley.

bo. June 30, 1797. Stephen of John S. Schuyler and Caty Cuyler.

bo. July 20. Ann of Evert Evertson and Elizabeth Goey.

bo. Feb. 20, 1795, Margaret of William McBride and Elizabeth Chambers.

bo. June 17, 1797, George of William McBride and Elizabeth Chambers.

bo. Mar. 1. David of David Brownlow and Elspie Aikens.

bo. May 17. George of John Simpson and Catharina Douglass.

1797

bo. July 15. Garret of Stephen Pangburn and Sarah Iesle.

bo. Aug. 14. John of William Pipper and Elizabeth Simpson.

bo. Aug. 5. John of Abraham Quackenbuss and Catharina Redliff.

bo. Aug. 7. Elsie Lansing of Abraham Oake and Elizabeth De Assigne.

bo. Aug. 20. Robert Van Renselaer of Elisha Kane and Alida Van Renselaer.

bo. Sept. 15. Elizabeth Bayard of John I. V. Renselaer and Catharina Glen.

bo. Sept. 23. Cornelius of John Gates and Catharina V. Vranken.

bo. Oct. 11. Herman of Enoch Leonard and Maria V. Vechten.

bo. Sept. 28. Margaret of Abraham Benson and Sara Hogeboom.

bo. Oct. 10. William of Jonathan Kidney and Hannah V. Zandt.

bo. Sept. 25. Catalina of Nicholas Bleecker and Eleanor Staats.

bo. Sept. 23. Mary Ann of Jacob Legrange and Mary McCrea.

bo. Sept. 20. Maria of Walter Groesbeck and Ann Rykman.

bo. Feb. 17, 1795. Daniel of Peter Goey and Mary Milk (?).

bo. Sept. 3, 1790. Mary of Hendrik Robertson and Ann Weeger.

bo. Oct. 25, 1790. Maritie of Richard V. Zandt and Sarah Hilton. Wit: Isaac Hoogkirk, Rachel V. Zandt.

bo. Nov. 5, 1790. Elizabeth of Jacob Vosburgh and Hannah Robertson.

bo. Oct. 3, 1790. Annatie of John Freyer and Maritie Wolvisen.

bo. Nov. 20, 1790. Guisbert of Henry Yates and Rachel V. Zandt. Wit: Guisbert and Rebecca V. Zandt.

bo. Nov. 14, 1790. Andrew Truax of Jeremiah Raca and Ann McMillen.

bo. Dec. 1, 1790. Margaret of Barnt Smith and Hannah Bell. Wit: Wilhelmus Smith, Hannah Bratt.

1797

bo. Oct. 21, 1790. Eleanor of John Johnson and Helena Lottridge.

bo. Oct. 27, 1790. Baltus of Martin Crannel and Caty Brokus. Wit: Isaac Cranel, Mary Morris.

bo. Oct. 29, 1790. Folkie of Isaac Crannel and Mary Moris. Wit: Marten Crannel, Caty Brokus.

bo. Oct. 21, 1790. John of John Volkenburgh and Caty Tingue.

bo. Oct. 5, 1790. John of John Victory and Mary Pangburn. Wit: Benjamin Post, Caty Van Norden.

bo. Sept. 24, 1790. Abraham of Abraham Van Wie and Jacomintie Barhanse. Wit: Philip Crayselaer, Sarah Barhanse.

bo. Sept. 23, 1790. Susannah of Jacob Edigh and Margaret York. Wit: Frederik Edig, Caty Weaver.

bo. Dec. 25, 1790. Henry of Henry Waldron and Margaret V. Vranken.

bo. Oct. 6, 1790. Elizabeth Schuyler of Rev. Brand Schuyler Lupton and Ester Brown.

bo. Jan. 14, 1791. William Matthias of William Gaffers and Maria Fore (?). Wit: William Waggener, Caty Hendric.

bo. Jan. 20, 1791. William of William V. Benthuysen and Margaret Cochran.

bo. Sept. 24, 1790. Benjamin I. Stephenson of Isaac Warner and Elsie Van Loon. Wit: Benjamin Van Loon, Maikie Hook.

bo. Dec. 24. Mary of William Storn and Elizabeth Halenbake.

bo. Nov. 29. Peter of Peter Warner and Susannah Burger. Wit: Peter Livingston, Maritie Waldron.

bo. Feb. 18, 1791. Rebecca of Cornelius Groesbeck and Ann Van Antwerp. Wit: John B. Bratt, Sarah Van Antwerp.

bo. Sept. 1, 1790. Eleanor of John Bouvse and Ann Rutherford. Wit: William and Eleanor Rutherford.

bo. Nov. 13. Mary of William W. Crannel and Maria Emen. Wit: John and Temperance Barhanse.

bo. Oct. 20, 1790. Abraham of David De Forest and Susannah Fonda. Wit: John and Ann Fonda.

bo. Nov. 20. Eleanor of Anthony Groesbeck and Catalina de Forest. Wit: John V. Ness, Mary Devenhoff.

50

1797
bo. Nov. 6. Richard of Dirck Hanson and Helena Lowe.
bo. Dec. 12. John Banker of Isaac I. Quackenbuss and Caty Banker.
bo. Oct. 14. Aunah of James Buckhout and Margaret Britt. Wit: Baltes Britt, Aunah Tollot.
bo. Dec. 10. Peter of Peter Young and Eva Moore. Wit: Philip Coenrad, Hannah Colhammer.
bo. Dec. 12. Ann of David Neven and Margaret Waggener. Wit: John Wilclaar, Ann Waggener.
bo. Nov. 6. Ephraim of Asa Foot and Caty Davis.
bo. Jan. 1, 1791. Jacobus Stoutenburgh of Abraham Lansing and Margaret Bloodgood.
bo. Jan. 1. John of John V. Volkenburg and Hannah Rysdorf.
bo. Oct. 20, 1790. Rachel of Christian Bourke and Tabitha Chun. Wit: Archelaus Louw, Mary Dovenhoof.
bo. Dec. 14. John of Isaac Quackenbuss and Caty Gardenier. Wit: Philip Gardenier, Sartie V. Antwerp.
bo. Feb. 10, 1791. Hannah of Abraham Vosburgh and Sara Bulson. Wit: Cornelius and Ann Bulson.
bo. Jan. 9. Cornelia of Jacob Van Deurson and Eltie Lansing.
bo. Feb. 5, 1791. Angeltie of Evert Johnson and Ann Legrange.
bo. Feb. 15. Garret of John Lansing and Elizabeth Freyer. Wit: Garrit Lansing, Elizabeth Wincoop.
bo. Feb. 15. Mary, servant maid of Guisbert Fonda.
bo. Feb. 25. Cornelius of John Voorheis and Susannah Dumont.
bo. Feb. 15. Noble Caldwel David of Peter Nevin and Elizabeth Caldwell. Wit: Noble Caldwel, Elizabeth David.
bo. Jan. 2, 1790. Charles of May, servant maid of Guisbert Fonda. Wit: Nicholas Fonda.
bo. Dec. 28, 1790. John of Jacob Truax and Caty Doxtader. Wit: John and Cornelia Young.
bo. Oct. 23. Ann of Jacob Legrange and Ariantie Truax. Wit: Yellis Truax, Ann Cox.
Cornelius of John Bloomendal and Caty Sharpe. Wit: Cornelius Bloomendal, Helena Rys.
bo. Nov. 24. Peter of Simon Vander Look and Levintie Van der Hooker.

1797

bo. Aug. 26. Altie of Abraham Garresson and Jane Francisco.

bo. Oct. 20. Ann of Adam P. Winne and Christina Legrange. Wit: Coenraad and Eltie Legrange.

bo. Mar. 11, 1791. Garret of Dirck Rosaboom and Rhoda Dowey. Wit: Tuonis and Elsie Visher.

bo. Mar. 1. Sarah of Thomas V. Benthuysen and Ann Enochs.

bo. Feb. 17, 1791. William of Isaac Vosburgh and Elizabeth Barry.

bo. Mar. 9. Thomas of Henry V. Benthuysen and Catharina Hun. Wit: Dirck Hun, Hannah Lansing.

bo. Mar. 10. Sarah of Teunis Jafesh and Alida Lansing. Wit: Christopher and Elsie Lansing.

bo. Feb. 8. Sarah of William Norton and Catharina Livingston. Wit: Jacob and Sarah Livingston.

bo. Feb. 24. Jacob of Jacob Denbar and Margaret Crannel. Wit: Henry and Jamima Crannel.

bo. Mar. 18. Annanitie of Anthony Bratt and Geritie V. D. Bergh. Wit: Cornelius and Catalintie V. Den Bergh.

bo. Mar. 14. Garret of Abraham Lansing and Elsie V. Renselaer. Wit: Garrit A. Lansing, Anna Zabriske.

bo. Apr. 11, 1791. Mary of Memory Vieling and Sarah Steenbrander. Wit: Barnt Staats, Mary Winne.

bo. Oct. 22, 1797. Annatie Drett of Teunis Slingerland and Rachel Davis.

bo. Oct. 17. Elizabeth of Philip Wendel and Sarah Picker.

bo. Oct. 26. Sussanah of Robert Grey and Susannah Grant.

bo. Nov. 16. Grace of Francis Costigen and Jane Hageman.

bo. Nov. 2. Margaret of Thomas V. Zandt and Rebecca Hoghkirk.

bo. Aug. 11. Mary of Philip Liday and Hannah Bussing.

bo. Nov. 28. Henrietta of John Bogert and Christiana Vough.

bo. Oct. 15. Hendricke of Henry Evertson and Cornelia Slingerland.

bo. Nov. 12. Simon of Jost Driesbach and Catharina Hoogstrasser.

1797-1798

bo. Nov. 23. Alida Ten Eyck of John S. Pruyn and Margaret Lansing.

bo. Apr. 6, 1798. Elizabeth of John Bassett and Anna Hun. Wit: Thomas Hun, Elizabeth Wendel.

bo. Feb. 4. Stephen Williams of John Oahee (?) and Jane Williams.

bo. Mar. 15. Mary of Samuel Bensen and Mary Nicholson.

bo. Apr. 23. Cornelia of Dirk Ten Broeck and Cornelia Stuyvesant. Wit: Abraham and Margaret Ten Broeck.

bo. Mar. 3. Anne of Garret Clute and Elizabeth Kane.

bo. Mar. 15. Abraham of Jacob A. Cuyler and Rebecca Kane.

bo. Mar. 1. Gerrit of Barnt G. Staats and Catharina Cuyler.

bo. Apr. 27. Samuel Stringer of Richard S. Treat and Gertrude Stringer. Wit: Samuel Stringer and Alida Van der Heyden.

bo. May 4. Hendric Ten Eyck of Sybrant Dowe and Lyntie Ten Eyck.

bo. July 1. Gertrude of Abraham Van Vechten and Catharina Schuyler.

bo. July 5. Richard of Benjamin Middleton and Elizabeth Owens.

bo. July 7. John Van Woort of Isaac Willet and Elizabeth V. Woort.

bo. July 27. Rachel of Henry Hallenbake and Rachel Winne.

bo. Nov. 21. John Ouderkerk of Henry V. Ness and Christina Shelly.

bo. Nov. 12. Hendric of George Ten Eyck and Magdalena Uphan.

bo. May 3. Elizabeth of Henry Bulsom and Catharina Keeder (?).

bo. June 29. George of John I. V. Allen and Mary Diamond.

bo. Aug. 25, 1797. John of Henry A. Gardenier and Henriette V. Everson.

bo. Aug. 8, 1797. James of Peter David and Elizabeth Caldwell.

1798-1799

bo. Aug. 11, 1797. George Dunbar of Myndert Lansing and Mary Usher.

bo. June 15, 1796. Maria of Dirk Hansen and Helen Lowe.

bo. May 31, 1798. John Mildenburgh of Myndert Merselis and Catharina Mildenburgh.

bo. Aug. 12. Catharine of Daniel Winne and Alida V. Arnum.

bo. Oct. 17. Elizabeth of Elias Kane and Deborah V. Schuyline.

bo. Sept. 15, 1799. Abigail of Jeremiah Rendall and Gertrude Gardenier.

bo. Sept. 28, 1798. Elizabeth of Barnt Smith and Hannah Bell.

bo. Oct. 21. Hendric of Benjamin V. Wie and Majke Bogert.

bo. July 5. Jacob of William Powel and Charity Brower.

bo. Oct. 9. Lansing of Abraham V. Arnum and Maritie Lansing.

bo. Sept. 6. Elizabeth of Jacob Ertsberger and Lois Hungerford.

bo. Apr. 1. Rachel, of Andrias Morel and Cornelia Slingerland.

bo. Sept. 7. Ann Maria of Luther Trowbridge and Elizabeth Tilman.

bo. Oct. 31. Hannah of John Goey and Peter (sic) Jerolomon.

bo. July 10. John of John Goey and Pietertie De Forest.

bo. Jan. 26, 1799. Anntie of Abraham G. Lansing and Susannah Yates. Wit: Jane Lansing.

bo. Dec. 22, 1798. Samuel of Samuel Masel (?) and Clartie (?) Groesbeek.

bo. Jan. 29, 1799. Cataline of Isaac Quackenbuss and Catharine Gardenier.

bo. Feb. 9. Hannah of John Guest, Jr. and Sarah Williams.

bo. Feb. 29. James of Eldert Freyer and Helena McGee.

bo. Feb. 2. Susannah of William Talbert and Hannah Young.

bo. Feb. 7. Henry of Asa Foot and Catharina David.

bo. Mar. 25. Eleanor of Isaac Slover and Alida Whitlock.

bo. Mar. 9. William of William Colbreath and Hester Van Deursen. Wit: William Groesbeck, Catharina V. Deursen.

1798-1799

bo. May 21. Barbara of Gerrit Bogart and Margaret Nexsen.

bo. May 22. Madalena of James Van Schoonhoven and Mary Spoor.

bo. Apr. 25. Jacob of Jacob Ginning and Christiana Passagie. Wit: Matthias Casparus, Lydia Countryman.

bo. July 28. William of Samuel Norton and Elizabeth Radley.

bo. Aug. 24. Magdelene of William Pepper and Elizabeth Simpson.

bo. Dec. 1, 1798. Catharine Odell of Jacob Lent and Hannah Odell.

bo. Aug. 15, 1799. Gertruy of Nicholas Ridecker and Alida Bulsom.

bo. July 22, 1799. Alida of Jacobus and Alida V. Zandt.

bo. Aug. 16. Eleanor of Christopher Oley and Sarah V. Antwerp.

bo. Aug. 10. Mary of William Montgomery and Alida Hollenbake.

bo. Aug. 20. Christian Legrange of John Hallenbake and Ann Legrange.

bo. Aug. 18. John of John V. d. Lansing and Harriot Verplank.

bo. Sept. 7. John of Bernardus Bratt and Margaret Lyde.

bo. Sept. 7. Rebecca of Anthony Sanford and Mary Roff. Wit: Antie Sanford, Isaac I. Fonda.

bo. Aug. 27. Leah of Isaac Bratt and Elizabeth V. Deursen.

bo. Sept. 10. William of James Hilton and Catharine Freyer.

bo. Sept. 22. James of Jacob Lansing, Jr. and Alida Dowe.

bo. Oct. 23. Johannes of John I. Ouderkerke and Mary Sickle.

bo. Apr. 15. Andrew of Benjamin Bowman and Christina Dowland.

bo. May 22. Ephraim of James Reynolds and Margaret Jackson.

bo. Oct. 17. Mary of Elias Kane and Deborah Van Schuylyne.

bo. Nov. 10, 1799. Cornelius Veeder of Jacob P. Millar and Gertrude Veeder.

bo. Nov. 10. Jeremiah of Elizabeth and Ned (slaves). Wit: Rachel Oothout.

bo. Aug. 25. Christian of John Simpson and Catharine Douglass.

bo. Nov. 5. Henry of Philip Stunck and Elizabeth Cooper.

bo. Nov. 24. Abraham of Martinus Casparus and Catharine Countryman.

bo. Dec. 30. Margaret of Jacob Brown and Dinah V. Everen.

bo. Jan. 10, 1800. Catharine of Nicholas Bleeker and Eleanor Staats.

bo. Nov. 15, 1799. Henry Hollenbake of Abner Sharp and Cornelia Hollenbake.

bo. Oct. 12. Mahaley of Andreas Jones and Hannah Barnham.

bo. Dec. 17. Herman of Volkert V. Housen and Jane Young.

bo. Jan. 18, 1800. George of Denis Clemisham and Rachel Milton.

bo. Aug. 10, 1797. Catharine of John Grey and Catharine Osburn.

bo. Dec. 2, 1800. William of John Grey and Catharine Osburn.

bo. Feb. 24. Catharine of Jeremiah Sharp and Catharine Goey.

bo. Mar. 10. Richard of Enoch Leonard and Maria V. Vechten.

bo. Feb. 21. Rachel of Peter Owen (?) and Margaret Staats.

bo. Mar. 12, 1800. Joseph Caldwel of Peter David and Elizabeth Caldwel.

bo. Mar. 23. Maria and James of James Cornelinsse and Anna Vosburg.

bo. Mar. 4. George of Philip Carner and Hannah Crannel.

bo. Mar. 22. Samuel of Jacob Sharpe and Gertruy Aring.

bo. Feb. 22. Angeltie of Michal V. Schaick and Angeltie Truax.

bo. Feb. 25. Samuel of John I. Pruyne and Margaret Lansing. Wit: Neltie Pruyne.

bo. Mar. 6. Gertruy of Matthew Bevie and Elizabeth Lansing.

1800

bo. Mar. 7. Ambrose of Barnt G. Goey and Elizabeth Jones.

bo. Mar. 28. Hendrikie of William Lansing and Altie Fonda.

bo. Apr. 22. Gertrude of Peter Roman and Catharine V. Deursen.

bo. Mar. 17. Margaret of Thomas Milligan and Catharine Oothout.

bo. Apr. 27. Eva of Thomas Chadwick and Marietie Oothout.

bo. May 25. Judith of Abraham V. Vechten and Catharina Schuyler.

bo. May 20. John Henry of John Henry Denniston and Eleanor Fisher.

bo. May 28, 1800. Rachel of Jacobus Parse and Maria V. Den Berg.

bo. May 31. Sarah of John Karner and Jane Goey.

bo. Mar. 7. Maria of Henry Dierstyne and Caty Meor.

bo. May 7. Harriot Anne of William Williams and Maria Brown.

bo. June 9. Anne of John Ostrander and Fanny Consaul.

bo. June 4. Jacob of Isaac Willett and Elizabeth V. Woert.

bo. June 20. Cornelia of Thomas V. Benthuysen and Ann Enocks.

bo. June 2. Angelica of Jonathan Kidney and Hannah Van Zandt.

bo. July 2. Catharine of John I. Ostrander and Ann Muir.

bo. June 14. Stephen of Elisha Putnam and Esther Johnson.

bo. July 23. Gilbert of William Childs and Christina Horne.

July 27. bo. July 23. Maria of Abraham Hun and Maria Gansevoort. Wit: Leonard Gansevoort, Maria V. Renselaer.

bo. July 16. Helena of Joseph Wilson and Sarah Fonda.

June 19. Barbara of Jeremiah Lansing and Helena Wendel. Wit: Barbara Wendel.

bo. Apr. 1. Garret V. Everen of Peter A. (?) Bratt and Catharina V. Everen.

bo. Apr. 9. Matthew of Nicholas Crannel and Gerretie V. D. Berg.

bo. Apr. 7. John of Benjamin Wihne and Elizabeth Bassett.

1800

bo. Apr. 5. Rebecca of Gerret Clute and Elizabeth Kane.

bo. Aug. 17, 1794. Mary of Benjamin Middleton and Elizabeth Owens.

bo. Apr. 19, 1800. Stephen V. Renselaer of Jacob Slingerland and Cornelia V. Alstine.

bo. Jan. 28, 1799. Ann of John Veeder and Catharina Winne.

bo. Aug. 14, 1800. Eleanor of Christophel Oley and Sarah V. Antwerp.

bo. July 6, 1800. Catharine of John Brower and Maria Weaver.

bo. June 6. Isaac of Henry Evertson and Cornelia Slingerland.

bo. Aug. 25, 1799. Mary of Benjamin Maurice and Mary Justice.

bo. July 5, 1800. Nicholas of George Kline and Mary Claver.

bo. Nov. 24, 1799. Andrew of Obijah Hunt and Marian Dunn.

bo. July 12. Elizabeth of David Armer and Caty Bulsom.

bo. Aug. 16, 1799. Cornelia of Henry T. E. Schuyler and Sarah Visher. Wit: Stephen Schuyler, Helena Ten Eyck.

bo. Mar. 7, 1800. Peter of Abraham Quackenbush and Catharine Radliff. Wit: Peter Quackenbuss, Margarit Radliff.

bo. May 1. John of John Vosburg and Elizabeth Richmond. Wit: Elizabeth Claver.

bo. Jan. 26, 1799. Abraham of Thomas Dyer and Maria Cuyler.

David and Margaret of Francis C. Pruyn and Cornelia Dunbar. Wit: Levinus Winne, Margaret Hansen, David Pruyne, Hebertie Lansing.

bo. Feb. 28. Catharine Waters of Henry Truax and Anna Yates.

bo. July 28. Robert of David Bromlee and Elspy Aikens.

bo. Dec. 2. Alida of Jonathan Brooks and Mary Hoghkirk.

bo. Dec. 14, 1798. John Bleecker of Isaac Truax and Jannitie Bleecker. Wit: John Bleecker, Gerritie V. Schaick.

bo. Mar. 17, 1799. Rebecca of Lucas Hoghkirk and Mary Burton.

bo. Dec. 22. Philip of Philip Wendel and Sarah Packard.

1800

bo. Sept. 15. Stephen of George Charles and Mary Price.

bo. July 31, 1797. Jane of Isaac V. Arnum and Jane Jerolomon.

bo. Sept. 5, 1799. Abraham of Philip S. Schuyler and Rachel V. Den Bergh.

bo. Oct. 30, 1799. Benjamin of Egbert V. Schaick and Maria Winne

bo. Aug. 28, 1798. Margaret of James and Mary V. Zandt.

bo. Dec. 13, 1791. Pat of Baltus Hugnot and Phebe, serv. of Mary V. Alen.

bo. June 7, 1799. Jenny of Baltus Hugnot and Phebe, serv. of Mary V. Alen.

bo. June 7, 1799. Elizabeth of William Southarck and Nancy Grey. Wit: John and Rachel Taylor.

bo. Nov. 17. Philip Stephen V. Renselaer of Jacob A. Cuyler and Rebecca Kane.

bo. May 18. John Wendel of William M. Diamond and Rebecca Wendel.

bo. Mar. 13, 1797. Eliza of Reuben and Sarah Fuller.

bo. Apr. 28, 1800. Maria of Reuben and Sarah Fuller.

bo. July 30, 1800. Helena of Benjamin Lansing and Maria Timese.

bo. Aug. 8. Eliza Muir of Robert W. Dunbar and Eliza Muir.

bo. Jan. 4. Marian of Daniel Sickles and Jane Dox.

bo. Aug. 14. Mary Guest of John Musier and Sarah Guest.

bo. May 12. James of Henry Sickels and Effie Barré.

bo. Aug. 30. Margaret of Thomas Guest and Gertruy Schuyler.

bo. Aug. 15. Sarah of Andrew B. Bottle and Anna Catharina Kerle.

bo. Sept. 4, 1800. Dirckie of Martinus Krigier and Eva V. Den Berg.

bo. June 10. Walter of Dirck De Forest and Rebecca Bratt.

bo. Sept. 29. John of John V. Ness and Mary Sicker.

bo. Oct. 8. Mary of Jacob Hertsberger and Lois Hungerford.

bo. Sept. 15. Elizabeth of Sybrant Rittle (?) or Kettle (?) and Annatie Hinne. Wit: John Walsh, Elizabeth Winne.

1800-1801

bo. Oct. 25. Dirckie of Samuel Crigier and Mary Fairchild.

bo. Dec. 18. Maria of John Bassett and Annatie Hun. Wit: Abraham Hun, Maria Gansevoort.

bo. Dec. 6. Tichie of Daniel I. Winne and Alida V. Arnum.

bo. Dec. 3. Penelope of Robert Ausin and Mary Parks.

bo. Oct. 3. Philip of Leonard Reisdorp and Janitie De Forest.

bo. Dec. 24. Ann Maria of Christophel Hawk and Mary Passenger.

bo. Nov. 5. Myndert of Volkert Arson and Alida Van Huysen.

bo. Jan. 5, 1801. Stephen of David I. De Forest and Susannah Fonda.

bo. Dec. 3, 1800. Catharine of Jonathan and Leah Ostrander.

bo. Dec. 14, 1800. John of Daniel Morrel and Clausie Groesbeek.

bo. Dec. 9. Helena of Jacob House and Caty Snyder.

bo. Dec. 24. Catharine McKown of Silas Houghton and Hannah Boom.

bo. July 11. Benjamin of Benjamin Bowman and Christina Downey.

bo. Nov. 6. John Quackenbuss of Andreas Huyck and Rebecca Quackenbuss.

bo. Jan. 12, 1801. Barnt Sanders of Kilian K. V. Renselaer and Margaretta Sanders. Wit: Barnt and Sarah Sanders.

bo. Dec. 29, 1800. Charles Christopher of Luther Trowbridge and Elizabeth Tillman.

bo. Jan. 21, 1801. Yellis Winne of Henry B. Hollinbake and Rachel Winne.

bo. Feb. 3. Simon V. Antwerp of Christopher Olee and Sarah V. Antwerp.

bo. Feb. 17, 1801. George Washington of Simeon Dewit and Jane Varick.

bo. Jan. 2. Isaac Gilbert of Peter V. Deursen and Lydia Brewster.

bo. Oct. 19, 1798. Sarah of Winant V. Den Bergh and Mary Hixson.

bo. Feb. 7, 1801. James of Winant V. Den Bergh and Mary Hixson.

1800-1801

bo. Feb. 9. Myndert of Myndert Lansing and Mary Usher.

bo. Dec. 29, 1800. Gertrude of Dirck Volwider and Mary Van Vranken.

bo. Feb. 26, 1801. Catalina of John Witbeck and Sarah Crigier.

bo. Mar. 18. Isaac of Isaac Slover and Antie Whitlock.

bo. —————. Anna Davis of Daniel Bratt and Anna Bloomendale. Wit: Albertus Bloomendale, Margaret Bratt.

bo. Jan. 13, '01. Sarah of Jacob V. Benthuysen and Elizabeth Hermance.

bo. Feb. 13. William of Richard Hocknel and Jane McClarkland.

bo. Mar. 31. Eleanor of John R. Tillman and Gertrude Oley.

bo. Apr. 24. John of Peter V. Den Bergh and Elizabeth Freyer.

Apr. 13. Peter of William Tuper and Mary Hilton.

bo. Mar. 26. Elizabeth of William Montgomery and Alida Hillenbake.

bo. Dec. 23. Jacob of Richard Hilton and Elizabeth Norton.

bo. Apr. 3. Elizabeth of Barnt Smith and Hannah Bell.

bo. May 14. Jacob Ten Broeck of Abraham V. Vechten and Catharine Schuyler.

bo. Apr. 26. Adam of Henry Rose and Maritie Philips.

bo. Apr. 6. Sarah Margaret of Thomas Dyer and Maria Cuyler.

bo. June 6. Annatie of Teunis G. Visher and Alida Lansing.

bo. June 4. Guisbert of Garret G. Merselis and Machtel Visher.

bo. Oct. 1, 1800. Susannah of Lambert Cole and Ann Sawyer.

bo. June 17. Alexander of William Tillon and Margaret Hawk.

bo. July 4. William of Eldert Freyer and Helena McGee.

bo. July 18, 1801. Peter of Peter Murphy and Catharina Conner.

bo. Dec. 23, 1800 (?). Rachel of Randal McCollum and Elizabeth Matchel.

1801-1802

bo. July 27, 1801. Cornelis Glen of John I. Van Renselaer and Catharine Glen. Wit: Cornelius Glen, Elizabeth Nicoll.

bo. July 11. Louisa of John De Peyster Dowe and Margaret Livingston.

Susannah of George Ten Eyck and Magdalena Upham.

bo. Aug. 6. Cornelius V. Schullyne of Elias Kane and Deborah V. Schelluyne. Wit: Cornelius Van Schelluyne.

bo. Mar. 7. Sarah of Henry Yates and Rachel Van Zandt.

bo. Sept. 2. Isaac of Lucas I. Hoogkirk and Mary Burton.

bo. Aug. 31. Elizabeth of Asa Foot and Catharine Davis.

bo. Aug. 10. Rachel of Henry Milton and Elizabeth Smith. Wit: William and Mary Milton.

bo. Oct. 9. Abraham of Jacob Vosburgh and Hannah Robison.

bo. Oct. 27. Garret of Evert Evertson and Elizabeth Goey.

bo. Oct. 24. John of William Pepper and Elizabeth Simpson.

bo. Dec. 21. Isaac of William Vosburgh and Mary McDonald.

bo. Dec. 18. Daniel of Richard Fort and Maritie Levessee.

bo. Dec. 22. Isaac of John Brinkerhoff and Gertrude Schuyler.

bo. Dec. 17. John of John Goey and Pietertie Jerolomon.

bo. Nov. 11. Sarah of David Winne and Alida V. Benthuysen.

bo. Jan. 16, 1802. Maria of Abraham Hun and Maria Gansevoort. Wit: Leonard and Harriot Gansevoort.

bo. May 10, 1801. Jacob Ten Broeck of Abraham V. Vechten and Catharine Schuyler.

bo. Jan. 4, 1802. Herman of John B. Visher and Gertrude Dunbar.

bo. Sept. 18, 1801. John of John G. Van Zandt and Helena Lansing.

bo. Oct. 23, 1801. Helena of John and Ariantie Lansing.

bo. Jan. 25, 1795. Marian Charlotte of John Berry and Catharina Harbeck.

bo. Oct. 3, 1798. Helena Augusta of John Berry and Catharina Harbeck.

1801-1802

bo. Oct. 8, 1801. Joanne Catharine of John Berry and Catharina Harbeck.

bo. Oct. 18, 1801. Isaac Bogert of Matthew Freyer and Susannah Carles.

bo. Oct. 8, 1799. Cornelia of Walter Groesbeck and Hannah Ryckman.

bo. Dec. 29. Joseph Tunnicliff of Joseph Johnson and Batie Hemstraat.

bo. Jan. 3, 1802. Maria of Jacob Evertsen and Hannah Slingerland.

Jellis of Kilian I. Winne and Sarah Clute.

bo. Jan. 18. Samuel of Andrew Morrel and Cornelia Slingerland.

bo. Dec. 18, 1801. Peter of William Orlogh and Elizabeth Bowman.

bo. Jan. 9, 1802. Daniel of Bernardus Bratt and Margaret Night.

bo. Mar. 23. Eltie of Abraham D. Lansing and Christina Voorhees.

bo. Feb. 26. Abraham Hun of John Wands and Mary Warren.

bo. Aug. 28, 1796. Mary of Samuel Burrows and Esther Oaks.

bo. Jan. 10, 1799. John Wilcoxs of Samuel Burrows and Esther Oaks.

bo. Mar. 6, 1801. Ann Elize of Samuel Burrows and Esther Oaks.

bo. Dec. 1, 1801. John Cuyler of Peter S. Schuyler and Catharine Cuyler.

bo. Nov. 20, 1801. Lucas V. Vechten of Philip S. Schuyler and Rachel V. Den Bergh.

bo. Jan. 12, 1802. Johan of John Weide and Hannah Jansen.

bo. Oct. 4, 1801. Margaret of George Collier and Catharina Obrien.

bo. Jan. 29, '02. Helena of Richard Vosburgh and Angeltie Bloomendale.

bo. Nov. 6, 1801. Yellis of Kilian Winne and Angeltie Clute.

1802

bo. Nov. 20. John of Lambert V. Volkenburgh and Susannah V. Den Bergh.

bo. Nov. 20. David of Francis Pruyne and Cornelia Dunbar.

bo. Dec. 5. John of Reuben Fulten and Sarah Tuttle.

bo. Nov. 28. Margaret of William Talbet and Hannah Young.

bo. Oct. 2. John Carpenter of Philip S. Schuyler and Cynthia Carpenter.

bo. Jan. 8, 1802. Henry of James V. Der Woert and Nancy Neggs.

bo. Apr. 14. Solomon of John S. Goey and Mary Marshal.

bo. Apr. 22. Agnes of Henry T. Eyck Schuyler and Sarah Visher.

bo. Mar. 17. William of Abraham Lottridge and Elizabeth Shear.

bo. Apr. 15. Sarah of Jacob Kirker and Sarah Rubee.

bo. Apr. 19. George Henry of William Carnright and Catharina Kirker.

bo. Apr. 7. Mary of William Loyd and Jane McCarnock.

bo. May 5. Jacob of Paul Hoghstrasser and Catharina Snyder.

bo. Dec. 21, '01. William Tremper of John C. Cuyler and Hannah Mayby.

bo. May 3, '02. Eliza Margaret of Henry I. Bleecker and Mary Storm.

bo. Apr. 12. Jacob of John Arnhout and Mary Walley.

bo. Jan. 21, '01. Eva of Teunis Visher and Elizabeth Groat.

bo. June 1, '02. Abraham of Abraham Quackenbuss and Catharina Radliff.

bo. June 1. John of John Johnson and Elizabeth Marshal.

bo. May 23. Annatie of Isaac Bratt and Elizabeth V. Deursen.

bo. May 19. Nancy of William Burns and Bessy (serv. of Leonard Gansevoort.)

bo. June 20. Elizabeth of John Brooks and Hannah Groesbeck.

bo. May 30. Richard Joseph of Richard I. (?) Treat and Gertrude Shinger.

1802-1803

bo. July 28. Rebecca of Garrit Hoogkirk and Sarah Rykman.

bo. July 24. Sophia of Abraham Cark and Gloriana Merrit.

bo. June 16. Cornelius of Robert Dunbar and Hannah Slingerland.

bo. Aug. 24. William of William Radliff and Margaret Cline.

bo. Aug. 25. Abraham of Jacobus Hoghkirk and Alida V. Zandt.

bo. Sept. 9. Isaac of Philip Hoffman and Patty Graham.

bo. July 28. Abigail of Walter Clarke and Helena Van Wie.

bo. Aug. 21. John of William Montgomery and Alida Hallenbake.

bo. Oct. 18. Anna Helena Ouderkirk of John Van Ness and Maria Sicker.

bo. Oct. 11. Elizabeth Gertrude of Adam Russ and Elizabeth Lewis.

bo. Oct. 30. Bethuel Washburn of John Hughson and Maria Washburn.

Leah of Abraham and Nancy Profit.

bo. Nov. 12. Albertus of Hessel Brower and Mary Bloomendale.

bo. Nov. 8. John of John Bassett and Anna Hun. Wit: Eleanor Bassett, Peter Bonnett.

bo. Dec. 8. Sarah of Rutger V. Woert and Anna Lansing.

bo. Nov. 17. Sebastian of Martinus Crigier and Eva V. Den Berg.

bo. Jan. 5, 1803. Stephen Van Renselaer of John Bleecker and Elizabeth Van Renselaer. Wit: Stephen Van Renselaer, Catharina Livingston.

bo. Jan. 10. Gertrude of John Perry Witbeck and Sara Krigier.

bo. Oct. 7, 1802. Gertrude of Volkert Anson and Alida V. Heusen.

bo. Dec. 12. John Graham of Cornelius V. Husen and Hannah Graham.

bo. Dec. 31. Jane Ann of John H. Wendel and Cathalina Van Benthuysen.

bo. Jan. 16, 1803. Helena of John Schuyler and Catharina Cuyler.

1803

bo. Jan. 31. James of Wynant V. Den Bergh and Mary Hickson.

bo. Jan. 17. Jonathan of Nicholas Morrel and Elizabeth Brooks.

bo. Feb. 17. Elizabeth of William and Anne Collins.

bo. Feb. 6. Archibald of John I. V. Renselaer and Catharina Glen. Wit: Archibald and Judith Bruce.

bo. Feb. 4. Esther of Isaac A. Quackenbuss and Catharina Banker.

bo. Feb. 12. Isaac of Daniel I. Winne and Alida Van Arnum.

bo. Feb. 14. Catharine of David Pruyne and Hibertie Lansing. Wit: Casparus and Mary Pruyne.

bo. Feb. 17. Elizabeth of Arthur Hotchkiss and Judith Hoghkirk.

bo. Dec. 25, 1798. Adeline of Arthur Hotchkiss and Elizabeth Leavenworth.

bo. Oct. 27, 1782. Susannah of James and Mary LeGrange.

bo. Sept. 24, 1802 (?). Mary Ann of Thomas Guest and Gertrude Schuyler.

bo. Sept. 12. Maria of David I. Groesbeck and Harriot Crannel.

bo. Sept. 5. Sarah of Abraham G. Lansing and Susannah Yates. Wit: Barent Bleecker, Sarah Lansing.

bo. Nov. 15, 1802. Hester of Gerrit Roseboom and Josina Hallenbake.

bo. Apr. 5. Jane of Martin Joy (?) and Mary Cummings.

bo. Nov. 11. Andrew of Henry Abel and Elizabeth Patten.

bo. Sept. 28. Jane Ann of Henry Guest and Elizabeth De Wit.

bo. Oct. 20. Sarah of Peter Quackenbuss and Mary Radliff.

bo. Aug. 15. Mary of Evert Merselis and Sarah V. Benthuysen.

bo. Nov. 1. Sarah of John R. Bleecker and Eliza Ten Eyck Bridgen (?).

bo. July 24. Margaret of Isaac Dunneston and Eleanor Vischer.

bo. Feb. 15. Rachel of John A. (?) Freyer and Ann Deniston.

1803

bo. Jan. 31. Mary of Nicholas Crannel and Garretie V. Den Bergh.

bo. Mar. 8, 1803. William of Theunis Slingerland and Eleanor V. Den Bergh.

bo. Mar. 7. Maria Nottingham of Benjamin De Witt and Eve Bloodgood.

bo. Feb. 25. Ann Maria of Samuel Krigier and Maria Fairchild.

bo. Nov. 21, '02. Catharine Willard of Thomas W. Ford and Renette McWillard.

bo. Mar. 26, 1803. Henry of Henry Evertsen and Cornelia Slingerland.

bo. Apr. 3. Frances of Sanders Lansing and Catharine Ten Eyck.

bo. Feb. 11. Maria of Richard Hilton and Elizabeth Norton.

bo. May 22. Judik of Abraham V. Vechten and Catharina Schuyler.

bo. Mar. 22. James of Nicholas Frank and Elizabeth Fonda.

bo. July 22, 1802. Isaac Vosburgh of James Corneleysse and Hannah Vosburgh.

bo. June 14. Philip De Forest of John A. Goey and Rachel De Forest.

bo. Dec. 31, 1803. David of Francis Weighmeyer and Mary Quackenbuss.

bo. July 4. Margaret of Cornelius V. Schoonhoven and Rebecca V. Ness.

bo. July 21. Edmund Peter of Peter Edmund Elmendorf and Elizabeth Van Renselaer. Wit: Jeremiah Van Renselaer, Frances Nicoll.

bo. Mar. 29. Maria of George Charles and Mary Price.

bo. Aug. 4. Rynier of Lambert Van Volkenburgh and Susannah Van Den Bergh.

bo. July 10. Gilbert of Christopher Devoe and Maria Sharpe.

bo. July 18. Elizabeth of Joseph Johnson and Barbara Hemstraat.

bo. June 30. Jacob of Peter V. Loon and Sarah Wendel.

bo. June 26, 1791. Barnt of Jacob V. Loon and Catharina Schuyler.

1803

bo. Feb. 19, 1792. Cornelius of William Hoghteling and Maria Bloomendale.

bo. Mar. 27 (??). Catharine of Henry Bronk and Sarah Osterhout.

bo. Mar. 19 (??). Richard of Henry Scabugh (?) and Ann V. Alstine.

bo. 1803. Elbert Timesson of Benjamin Lansing and Maria Timesse.

bo. Mar. 10. Susannah of Jacob A. Wendel and Eva Swart.

bo. Aug. 2. Ann Maria of Matthew Trotter and Margarit Wendell.

bo. Aug. 17. Henry of George Milton and Mary Sturges.

bo. July 16. George of Henry V. Nest and Christina Shelley.

bo. Aug. 21. Elizabeth of Eldert Freyer and Eleanor Magee. Wit: Isaac Slingerland, Elizabeth Hinis (?).

bo. June 25. Henry of Abraham Bradt and Mary V. Husen.

bo. Aug. 26. Jacob of John Simons and Elizabeth Hertsbergher.

bo. Aug. 15. Jacob Lansing of John I. Groesbeck and Maria Lansing.

bo. Aug. 13. Gertrude of Lucas G. Witbeck and Emma Marshal.

bo. Aug. 27. Gertrude of John S. Goey and Mary Marshal.

bo. Aug. 30. Helena of Philip S. Schuyler and Cinthia Carpenter.

bo. Aug. 14. Judith of Henry Yates and Rachel V. Zandt.

bo. July 21. John of John W. Hilton and Elizabeth Black.

bo. May 31, 1803. Louysa of Elias Kane and Deborah V. Schiryline.

bo. Feb. 27. John of Jacob Miller and Gertrude Veeder.

bo. May 11, 1802. Jacob V. Voort of Jacob Freyer and Annenitie Miller.

bo. Sept. 18. William Groesbeck of Francis Mack Fallin and Catharine Groesbeck. Wit: David W. and Lucretia Groesbeck.

bo. Aug. 18. Ann and Catharine of Mathew Bevie and Elizabeth Lansing.

bo. Sept. 8. Sarah of Gerrit A. Lansing and Elizabeth Wynkoop.

1803-1804

bo. Oct. 19. Gertrude of Francis C. Pruyne and Cornliae Dunbar.

bo. Sept. 20, 1803. Catharine of Henry Harbeck and Deborah Cornice. Wit: John Harbeck, Hannah Lansing.

bo. Aug. 20. Harriot of Richard Waring and Eleanor V. Vechten.

bo. Nov. 9. John Bleecker of John V. Schaick and Margaret Bleecker. Wit: John Bleecker, Mary Ten Broeck.

bo. Sept. 31. John of Nicholas Tansel and Ann Dykman.

bo. Aug. 19. Ann Eliza of Isaac V. Arnum and Jane Jeroloman.

bo. May 2. Ann Maria of Isaac Hansen and Jane Cooper.

bo. Aug. 20. Elizabeth of Jeremiah Luther and Maria Shears.

bo. Oct. 17, 1803. Catharine of Stephen Van Renselaer and Cornelia Patterson. Wit: William Patterson, Euphemia White.

bo. July 16, 1800. Helena of Joseph Wilson and Sarah Fonda.

bo. Nov. 13, 1803. Henry of Henry Bleecker and Elizabeth Metcalf.

bo. June 26. Maria of Charles Malcom and Elizabeth Lewis. Wit: Maria Davis.

bo. Dec. 20. Peter of John Brooks and Hannah Groesbeck.

bo. Oct. 24. John of John Simpson and Catharine Douglass.

bo. Dec. 3. Maria of Ephraim De Witt and Diricke Van Loon.

bo. Dec. 9. James of Robert P. and Catharine Van Renselaer.

bo. Dec. 22. James of Teunis G. Visher and Alida Lansing.

bo. Jan. 2, 1804. Henry Fonda of Henry Visher and Rebecca Brooks.

bo. Nov. 27, 1803. Alida Wendel of William M. Diamond and Rebecca Wendel.

bo. Dec. 20. Jacob Lansing of Jacob Ten Eyck and Magdelena Gansevoort. Wit: Catharine Gansevoort.

bo. Aug. 20. Judith of Henry Yates and Rachel V. Zandt.

bo. Nov. 2. Jane of Isaac V. Wie and Christine Kettle. Wit: William V. Wie, Jane Lansing.

1803-1804

bo. Nov. 21, 1803. George Hinds of Isaac Slingerland and Elizabeth Hinds.

bo. Dec. 6. Gertrude of John B. Visher and Gertrude Dunbar.

bo. Oct. 6. Richard Henry of Barnt G. Staats and Catharine Cuyler.

bo. Dec. 26. Susannah of Lucas Hoghkirk and Mary Burton.

bo. May 3. Henry of Jacob A. Cuyler and Rebecca Kane.

bo. Mar. 16. Mary of Thomas C. Gardner and Willempie Bogert.

bo. Feb. 1. John of John V. Husen and Mary Freyer.

bo. Apr. 20. Elizabeth of David Armee and Catharine Bulsom.

bo. Apr. 15. Elizabeth of John Campbell and Cataline Bulsom.

bo. Dec. 23, 1801. Catharine of John Campbell and Cataline Bulsom.

bo. Oct. 3, 1802. Mary of John Holmes and Nancy Bulsom.

bo. Apr. 28, 1803. Cornelius V. Den Bergh of Garret De Garmo and Cornelia Cooper.

bo. June 24, 1796. Elizabeth of Charles Malcom and Elizabeth Lewis.

bo. Jan. 27, 1798. Renselaer of Charles Malcom and Elizabeth Lewis.

bo. Nov. 10, 1800. Charles of Charles Malcom and Elizabeth Lewis.

bo. Aug. 17, 1802. Elias of Charles Malcom and Elizabeth Lewis.

bo. Feb. 13, 1803. Guisbert of Hendric V. Schoonhoven and Cornelia Veder.

bo. Mar. 31. Henry of Peter Van Bergen and Elizabeth Freyer.

bo. Apr. 3. Francis of Sanders Lansing and Catharina Ten Eyck.

bo. Dec. 26. Alida of Jacob Bloemendale and Margaret Roller.

bo. Dec. 20. Helena Maria of Enoch Leonard and Maria V. Vechten.

bo. Oct. 21. Eunice of Philip Wendel and Sarah Packet.

1804

bo. Nov. 26. Harriot of Henry I. Bleecker and Mary Storm.

bo. Jan. , 1804. Maria of William Tooper and Mary Hilton.

bo. Dec. 18, 1803. James of Asa Foot and Catharine Davis.

bo. Mar. 10, 1804. Lewis of John Van Nest and Maria Sicker.

bo. Apr. 3. Volkert Dowe of Jacob Lansing, Jr. and Alida Dowe.

bo. Apr. 18. Walter of Abraham Van der Zee and Margaret V. Den Bergh.

bo. Sept. 8. Bridget of Joseph Barto and Mary Godfrey.

bo. May 5. Margaret of Henry B. Hallenbake and Rachel Winne.

bo. Mar. 29, 1804. Richard of William Bell and Elizabeth Van Vranken.

bo. May 22. Elizabeth of Peter Redecker and Mary Clute.

bo. Sept. 27. Julianna of Charles Magan and Sarah Heyer.

bo. Aug. 30. Cornelia of Jacob A. or N. Styles and Cornelia Ryckman.

bo. Aug. 23. Mary of David Melech and Maria Hughson.

bo. Sept. 2. Gerrit of Kilian I. Winne and Sarah Clute.

bo. Aug. 31. Anna of John Wendel and Catalina V. Benthuysen.

bo. Sept. 30, 1804. Goldsborough of Goldsborough Banyer and Maria Jay. Wit: Goldsborough Banyan, John Jay, Martha Banyer.

bo. Oct. 3. Hester of Henry Abel and Elizabeth Van Petten.

bo. July 27. Cornelius of Egbert Van Schaick and Maria Winne.

bo. Sept. 17. Bethuel Washburne of Jacob Lansing and Harriot Washburne.

bo. Oct. 11. Elizabeth of Henry Van Benthusen and Elizabeth V. Woert.

bo. Sept. 22. Philip of Lucas Hoghkirk and Eleanor De Forest.

bo. Oct. 16. John Rutse of John Bleecker and Elizabeth Van Rensselaer. Wit: James and Elizabeth Bleecker.

1804-1805

bo. Oct. 28. Emmitie of John Perry Witbeck and Sarah Cregier. Wit: Gerrit Witbeck.

bo. Nov. 11. Sarah of Myndert Lansing and Mary Usher. Wit: John Del Vecchio, Ann Usher.

bo. Sept.13. Hessel of Hessel Brower and Mary Bloomendale.

bo. Oct. 21. Charles of Gerrit Clute and Batie Bovie.

bo. Oct. 4. John of Thomas V. Zandt and Rebecca Hoghkirk. Wit: Jacobus and Mary V. Zandt.

bo. Aug. 15. Marian Stewart of William Crow and Margarit Dowe. Wit: Adam Rose, Elizabeth Lewis.

bo. Jan. 31. Sarah of John Grey and Catharine Osburne.

bo. Aug. 1. Dirk Groot of Garret V. Vranken and Mary Bell.

bo. Nov. 17, 1803. Margaret of Martin Joy and Mary Cumming.

bo. June 2, 1804. John of Robert Ashley and Dinah (serv. of Henry Outhout). Wit: Henry and Altie Outhout.

bo. Dec. 4. Dirk Bratt of Cornelius Van Schovenhoven and Rebecca V. Ness.

bo. Dec. 17. Alexander Hamilton of Gerrit Bogert and Margaret Nexson.

bo. Sept. 5. Angeltie of Aaron W. Slingerland and Hannah Arnaut.

bo. Nov. 7. —————— of Levinus L. Winne and Ann Visher.

bo. Feb. 15, 1804. Magdalene of Lewis Huick and Mary Luke.

bo. Feb. 16, 1805. Gerrit of Thomas G. Witbeck and Leah Marshal.

bo. Nov. 21, 1804. John of Isaac Bratt and Elizabeth Van Deursen.

bo. Oct. 10, 1804. Margaret V. D. Werken of Thomas Guest and Gertrude Schuyler.

bo. Mar. 26, 1805. Jane of Benjamin Van Wie and Magdelene Bogert. Wit: Casparus Van Wie, Jannitie Winne.

bo. Feb. 13. Nicholas of John N. Quackenbush and Nancy Smith.

bo. Feb. 3. Gerrit of Nicholas Jerolomon and Eva Becker.

bo. Mar. 6. William Patterson of Stephen Van Renselaer and Cornelia Patterson. Wit: Stephen V. Renselaer, Jr., Catharina Westerlo.

1796-1806

bo. July 5, 1803. Nancy of James Foster and Elizabeth Clinton.

bo. Nov. 25, 1804. Clinton of James Foster and Elizabeth Clinton.

bo. Mar. 4. Matthew of George Cline and Mary Claver.

bo. Apr. 16. Jacobus of Johannes Hildebrandt and Adriana Johanna Van Teffler.

bo. Jan. 26. Rebecca of Yellis Bogert and Elizabeth Rykman. Wit: Kilian and Rebecca Winne.

bo. Apr. 29. Myndert of Daniel I. Winne and Alida Van Arnum.

ba. Jan. 1, 1805 by Rev. Henry Ostrander. bo. Aug. 3, 1804. Elizabeth of John R. Bleecker and Eliza T. E. Bridgen. Wit: Barent and Elizabeth Bleecker.

ba. Apr. 8, 1805 by Rev. Christian Bork. bo. Mar. 23. Henry of Jacob A. Cuyler and Rebecca Kane.

ba. May 23 by Rev. Dr. Linn. bo. May 7. Abraham Lansing of Philip P. Van Rensselaer and Catharina Lansing. Wit: Abraham A. and Elsie Lansing.

ba. May 26 by Rev. Dr. Linn. bo. Apr. 7. Catalina of David I. Groesbeck and Harriet Crannell.

ba. Dec. 10, 1806. bo. June 1, 1801. William of Garret Groesbeek and Jannetje Goewey.

ba. Nov. 16, 1797. bo. Oct. 7, 1797. Richard of John Brinckerhoff and Gertrude Schuyler.

ba. Mar. 25, 1805. bo. Feb. 5, 1804. John of John Brinckerhoff and Gertrude Schuyler.

June 7, 1796. bo. Mar. 26, 1796. Maria of Peter Edmund Elmendorf and Elizabeth Vn. Rensselaer. Wit: Philip and Maria Vn. Rensselaer.

July 31. bo. July 29. Eleanor of Rev. John Bassett and Anna Hun. Wit: Francis and Eleanor Bassett.

Aug. 7. bo. July 8. Volkert of Lucas W. Veeder and Susannah Brat. Wit: Volkert Veder.

Aug. 9. bo. July 29. Hermanus of Abm. Vn. Vechten and Catharina Schuyler.

bo. June 25. Robert of James Fauly and Maria Yates.

Aug. 16. bo. Aug. 5. Sarah of David Pruyn and Hebertie Lansing. Wit: Christopher Lansing.

Oct. 23. bo. Oct. 4. Peter of Jacob P. Bogart and Aulida Bloomingdale.

1796-1797

Nov. 28. bo. Nov. 25. John Maley of John E. Cuyler and Hannah Maley. Wit: John and Catharine Maley.

Dec. 4. bo. Nov. 1, 1796. Isaac of James Funda and Willimpie Bogart. Wit: Jacob I. (or T.) and Susanna Lansing.

Jan. 22, '97. bo. Dec. 30, '96. Samuel Stringer of Richard S. Treat and Gertrude Stringer. Wit: Samuel Stringer, Lydia Lush.

Jan. 27, '97. bo. Dec. 31, '96. Elizabeth of Lewis Weaver and Elizabeth Derick. Wit: Charles and Margaret Derick.

Feb. 9. bo. Jan. 10, '97. Maria of Sanders Lansing and Catharina Ten Eyck.

Mar. 11. bo. Mar. 1. Ann of Garret Quackenboss and Elizabeth Banker.

Mar. 17. bo. Mar. 10. Rebecca of John Veeder and Catharine Winner.

Mar. 26. bo. Feb. 16. Rebecca of John Wilton and Elizabeth Black.

Apr. 1. bo. Jan. 31. Rynier of Myndert Veeder and Elizabeth Perry.

Apr. 2. bo. Mar. 10. John of Garrit A. Lansing and Elizabeth Wynkoop. Wit: John and Elizabeth Lansing.

June 4. bo. May 25. Margaret of Philip Dunbar and Susannah McIntosh. Wit: Lavinus and Margaret Dunbar.

bo. May 12. Sarah of Richard Fosbergh and Amilia Bloomendale. Wit: Garritie Bloomendale.

June 4. bo. May 10. Hannah of James Hilton and Catharine Fryer.

bo. Apr. 27. Gerlyn Verplanck of John Vn. Aernam Lansing and Harrietta Verplanck.

June 11. bo. May 11. Sarah of Jacob House and Catharine Snyder.

bo. Mar. 5. Nicholas of Isaac Quackenboss and Catharina Gardineer.

June 18. bo. June 9. Sarah of Benjn. V. Wie and Margaret Bogert. Wit: Abraham and Hannah Witbeek.

June 23. bo. May 28. Ann Jane of Jeremiah Schuyler and Jane Cuyler.

June 25. bo. June 3. Thomas of Willm. M. Diamond and Rebecca Wendell. Wit: Sarah Wendell.

bo. May 24. Elizabeth of Jonathan Cornick and Margaret Perry.

1797-1798
July 16. bo. June 29. Peter of Henry Fisher and Rebecca Brooks.
bo. June 23. John Hooghkerk of John McChesney and Rebecca Hooghkerk.
July 22. bo. July 1. Peter of Peter Vn. Bergen and Elizabeth Fryer.
July 23. bo. July 2. Margaret of Garrit R. Vn. Zandt and Catharine Hilton.
Aug. 6. bo. Dec. 10, 1796. Catlyna of George Pearson and Gitty Huyck.
Aug. 15. bo. Aug. 19, 1797. Sarah of John Lansing, Jr. and Cornelia Ray. Wit: Sarah Lansing.
Aug. 20. bo. July 28. Elizabeth of Jacobus Hooghkerk and Alyda Van Zandt.
Sept. 10. bo. May —. Susannah of James and Dinah (serv. of S. Vn. Ranselaer). Wit: Elizabeth, serv. of Mrs. Westerlo.
bo. Aug. 15. Mary of John Vn. Zandt and Mary Burges.
Sept. 10. bo. Aug. 20. John of Eldert Fryer and Helena McGee.
Sept. 17. bo. Aug. 23. Daniel of Peter Marshall and Hannah Bacon.
bo. Aug. 13. Evert of John Van der Mark and Cornelia Vn. Der Bargh.
Dec. 10. bo. Nov. 3. Alida of Solomon and Harriet Van Renssellaer.
ba. Feb. 4, 1798. bo. Jan. 4, 1798. Laura (or Laina) of Elisha Putnam and Ester Johnson.
Feb. 17. bo. Jan. 24. Daniel of Daniel Steele and Elizabeth Vn. Benthuysen.
Feb. 23. bo. Jan. 26. Garrit of Wilhelmus G. Rykman and Maria Funda.
bo. Jan. 15. Catlina of Peter A. Bratt and Catlina Vn. Everen.
Feb. 25. bo. Feb. 5. Sarah of Philip Gardinier and Elizabeth Vn. Schaick. Wit: Hannah Gardinier.
Mar. 4. bo. Jan. 13. John William of William Chapman and Elizabeth Lambert.
Mar. 25. bo. Feb. 16. Elizabeth of Volkert S. Veeder and Ann Quackenbush.
Apr. 8. bo. Mar. 10. Elizabeth of Jacob Bloomingdale and Margaret Ruller. Wit: Elizabeth and John Luther.

1798

May 19. bo. Mar. 30. Mary of Abrm. Herring and Elizabeth Ivers.

July 22. bo. June 22. John of John Van Emburgh and Hannah Flansburgh.

July 22. bo. June 20. Richard of Stephen Lush and Lydia Stringer.

July 25. bo. July 2. Mary Ann of Jared Skinner and Mary Drew.

July 29. bo. July 12. Robert of Thomas Milligan and Catharina Oathoudt. Wit: Robert Milligan, Mary McDonald.

bo. July 4. Ann of Lucas Hooghkerk and Eleanor Deforest.

Aug. 25. bo. Aug. 17. Ann Susan of Harmanus A. and Catharine Wendell.

Aug. 26. bo. Aug. 11. Margery of James Chisholm and Eve McCloud.

bo. Aug. 4. Elizabeth of William Brower and Margaret Van Zandt.

Aug. 29. bo. Aug. 22. Jacob of Garrit Roseboom and Josenah Hornbeck. Wit: Hester Roseboom.

Aug. 2. bo. Aug. 15. Schuyler of Schuler Swits and Alida Vn. Schaic.

Sept. 19. bo. Aug. 8. William of Christian Millar and Maria Vn. Schaick.

Sept. 17. bo. Aug. 31. Anna Matilda of Sebastian Visscher and Rosanna Shipboy.

Sept. 23. bo. June 30. Elizabeth of Jeremiah Voorhaas and Magdalena Terhune.

bo. May 11. Richd Bruster of John Manley and Richard (sic) Tuttle.

bo. Oct. 22, 1797. Samuel of Saml. B. Jones and Anna Bohannah.

bo. May 31, 1798. Mary of Garrit Van Voorst and Sarah Schermerhorn.

Sept. 30. bo. Aug. 20. Dirck of Thomas Guest and Gertrude Schuyler. Wit: Dirck and Margaret Schuyler.

Sept. 26. bo. Aug. 30. Maria Laidlie of John B. Johnson and Elizabeth Lupton.

Oct. 3. bo. Aug. 7, at N. York. Louisa of James Fairlie and Maria Yates.

Oct. 8. bo. Oct. 1. Angelica of Peter S. Schuyler and Catharine Cuyler.

1798-1799

Oct. 20. Sept. 25. Magdalen of James Fonda and Williampe Bogart. Wit: Peter and Magdalen Winner.

Oct. 27. bo. Oct. 24. Catalina of Jacob Van Loon and Catalina Schuyler. Wit: Abm. Veeder and wife, Neeltie Schuyler.

bo. June 18. Anna Gourlay of Jacobus Vn. De Voort and Nancy Schuyler. Wit: James Gourlay, Margaret Vn. De Werken, wife of Dirck Schuyler.

Nov. 4. bo. Oct. 1. David of James and Catharine Salsbury. Wit: Casparus and Catharina Salsbury.

bo. Sept. 10. Gertrude of John Salsbury and Alida Martin. Wit: Barent Witbeck, Mary Bell.

Nov. 11. bo. Oct. 7. Jacob of Isaac Wentworth and Elizabeth Hauver.

Dec. 1. bo. Nov. 11. Catalintie of Peter Van Loon and Sarah Wendell.

Dec. 31. bo. Nov. 26. Margaret Livingston of John D. P. Douw and Margaret Livingston. Wit: Mary Livingston.

Jan. 2, 1799. bo. Dec. 3, 1798. John of Mary and Thomas. Wit: Mary and John.

Jan. 20, 1799. bo. Oct. 10, 1798. Ann of John Franks and Isabella Isbister. Wit: Alletta Groesbeck.

Jan. 27. bo. Jan. 7. Augustus of John C. Cuyler and Hannah Maley.

Jan. 28. bo. Dec. 14, 1798. Benjamin of James and Hannah Vn. Benthuysen.

Mar. 1, 1799. bo. Feb. 2. Robert of Saunders Lansing and Catharina Ten Eyck. Wit: John Lansing, Jr. and wife, Cornelia.

Mar. 3. bo. Jan. 23. Catharina of Isaac Arnold and Sophia Phillips.

Mar. 10. bo. Feb. 21. Matthew of Robert Austin and Mary Parks.

Mar. 10. bo. May 15, 1797. Phillip Hooker of Thomas Hall and Mary Heledice. Wit: Philp. Hooker and wife.

Apr. 5. bo. Mar. 20. Susannah of James Le Grange and Maria McCray.

Apr. 24. bo. Mar. 27. Peter of John Bartholomew and Ann Frymire. Wit: Peter Beekman, Judith Van Vechten.

1799

May 5. bo. Apr. 10. Elizabeth of John Luther and Elizabeth Ruller. Wit: Elizabeth Claver, Nichs. Richter.

May 7. bo. Oct. 16, 1798. Mary Anna of Edmund Hatfield and Jennet Rankin.

May 20. bo. Apr. 17. Ann Mary of John and Rebecca King. Wit: P. W. Yates and wife.

May 26. bo. Apr. 25. Andrew McNeally of Wm. Laurence and Maria Perry.

May 29. bo. May 10. Bernardus of Evert Evertsen and Elizabeth Goewey. Wit: Bernardus and Hannah Evertsen.

May 30. bo. May 11. John Van Schaick of Teunis G. Visscher and Alida Lansing. Wit: Christn and Hybertie Lansing.

May 31. bo. May 9. Sarah of Henry Yates and Rachel Vn Zandt.

June 30. bo. June 12. Abraham of Abm Herring and Elizabeth Ivers.

July 16. bo. May 7. Samuel of Willm and Elizabeth (servs. of Mr. L. Gansevoort). Wit: Sarah, serv. of Mr. L. Gansevoort.

July 21. bo. June 29. John of John Hilton and Elizabeth Black.

Aug. 3. bo. June 19. Vernor of John T. Cuyler and Mary Vernor.

Aug. 4. bo. Aug. 2. John of Benjamin Hilton and Jemimah Van Volkenburg.

Aug. 11. bo. July 22. Teunis of Garrit G. Fisher and Rebecca Brooks. Wit: Garret T. and Rachel Fisher.

Aug. 30. bo. Aug. 1. Maria Van Vechten of John H. Wendell and Cathalina Van Benthuysen. Wit: Lucas and Maria Van Vechten.

Sept. 8. Baltus of Nicholas Wood and Sarah (former serv. of John Lansing). Wit: John, serv. of John Lansing.

bo. Aug. 18. John of David I. Groesbeek and Harriet Crannell. Wit: Letty Groesbeck.

bo. Aug. 18. Douwe of Thos. Champin Gardner and Willempe Bogart. Wit: Barent and Alida Bogart.

Sept. 9, 1799. bo. Oct. 9, 1798. Maria of Willm. Dana and Sarah Hall.

Sept. 23, 1799. bo. Feb. 1, 1798. David of David Hosford and Christiana Petree.

1799-1800

bo. Aug. 26, 1799. George Dunbar Usher of Myndert Lansing and Mary Usher. Wit: James Robeshon, and wife Hannah.

Sept. 30. bo. Sept. 12. Abm Schuyler of John Brinckerhoff and Gertrude Schuyler.

Oct. 6. bo. Sept. 13. Catharine of Jonathan Cowneck and Margaret Perry.

Oct. 27. bo. Oct. 11. Jacob of Garrit De Garmo and Cornelia Cooper. Wit: Isaac Hansen.

bo. Oct. 22. Jacob of Gilbert Ackerman and Rachel De Garmo.

Nov. 3. bo. Sept. 9. William of Garrit Kirk and Mary Prechard. Wit: Krinie Kirk.

bo. Oct. 4. Annatie of James Gourley and Lany Bromley.

bo. Sept. 20. Thomas of Joseph Beebe and Lydia Larroway.

Nov. 25. bo. Nov. 22. Catalina of Wilhelmus G. Ryckman and Maria Fonda. Wit: Albertie Phillips.

Dec. 6. bo. Nov. 2. Garrit of Henry Visscher and Rebecca Brooks. Wit: Garrit T. Visscher.

Dec. 15. bo. Dec. 13. John of Francis Mark Fatten and Catharina Groesbeck. Wit: Willm. and Catharine Groesbeck.

bo. Nov. 14. Sarah of John Graham and Gertrude Hilton.

bo. Nov. 5, 1798. George of John Johnson and Elizabeth Marshall.

Dec. 22. bo. Nov. 5, 1799. Sarah Eliza of William Johnson and Rebecca Hickson. Wit: Elizabeth Johnson.

Dec. 31. bo. Nov. 7. Isaac of Francis Costigan and Jane Hagaman.

Jan. 5, 1800. bo. Dec. 11, 1799. George of Henry A. Guardinier and Harrietta Van Yeveren.

Jan. 12. bo. Dec. 26. Elizabeth of Solomon and Harriet Van Renssellaer. Wit: Peter Edmund Elmendorp, Maria Van Renssellaer.

Jan. 12. bo. Sept. 8. Silas of David Lansing and Mercy Buckby.

Jan. 13. bo. Jan. 3. Anna of Jacob Ten Eyck and Magdalena Gansevoort. Wit: Abrahm. Ten Eyck, Jr., Judith Van Vechten.

1800

Jan. 15. bo. Dec. 28. Nicholas of Isaac Van Arnum and Jane Jeroluman.

bo. Dec. 22. Rachel of Garrit Goeway and Aighe Luke.

Feb. 2, 1800. bo. Feb. 12, 1799 (?). Angelica of Jeronimus Turk, Jr. and Elizabeth Bussing.

bo. Dec. 12, '99. Barbara of John Sylman and Doratha Roller. Wit: George Bender.

Feb. 9. bo. Dec. 30. Alida of Cornelius Schermerhorn and Catharina Van Renssellaer.

bo. Jan. 26, 1800. Catharine of James Van Ingen and Elizabeth Schuyler.

Feb. 11. bo. Jan. 18. Nicholas Cline of Willm Radliff and Margaret Cline.

Feb. 19. bo. Jan. 8. Isaac of John Slingerland and Susannah Evertson.

Feb. 23. bo. Jan. 15. Rachel Stringer of Richard S. Treat and Gertrude Stringer. Wit: Samuel Stringer.

bo. Feb. 13. Mary Ann of Jacob H. Wendell and Gertrude Lansing. Wit: Peter Lansing, Ann Van Allen.

Mar. 2. bo. Feb. 9. Sarah of David Winne and Alida Van Benthuysen.

Mar. 3. bo. Feb. 6. Christina of Andrew Morrell and Cornelia Slingerland.

Mar. 16. Richard Varick of Simeon DeWitt and Jane Varick.

bo. Feb. 13. Lydia of Richard Lush and Lyntia Fonda. Wit: Stephen and Lydia Lush.

Mar. 25, 1800. bo. Oct. 8, 1798. Catharine of Isaac Drurye and Elizabeth Van Wie.

Apr. 13. bo. Mar. 26. Agnes of Jacob Fryer and Agnes Miller.

June 3. bo. May 6. Wm. McGowen of Christian Ableman and Regina Kena.

June 4. bo. Aug. 2, '99. Archibald of James Thompson and Gertrude Conner. Wit: James and Rebecca Elliot.

June 8, 1800. bo. Apr. 25. Walter of Lucas Hoogkerk and Nelly (Eleanor) De Forest.

June 15. bo. May 5. Cornelia of Whiting Warner and Elizabeth Ostrander.

bo. Mar. 18. Maria of David Putnam and Jennet Angus.

1800

June 29. bo. June 9. Catharine of Abraham Benson and Sarah Hagadorn.

July 6. bo. Apr. 6. Elizabeth of Peter W. Yates and Mary Ter Bush. Wit: Catharine Hunt.

(It was intended to call this child, and she is called by her parents Catharine.)

July 8. bo. May 28. Catalina of Henry Bleecker and Elizabeth Metcalfe. Wit: Catalina Bleeker, Catalina Ten Eyck.

July 12. bo. May 6. Robert of Garret A. Lansing and Elizabeth Wyncoop.

July 20. bo. July 16. Richard Cuyler of Barent G. Staats and Catharina Cuyler. Wit: Jacob and Lydia Cuyler.

July 22, 1800. bo. Mar. 11, 1799. John Radley of Christopher Eadick and Sophia Radley.

July 27. bo. July 14. Mary Catharine of Paul Hoghstrasser and Catharina Snyder.

bo. July 7. Garrit of Hessel Brower and Maria Bloomingdale.

Aug. 17. bo. July 24. Rebecca of John Hilton and Elizabeth Black.

Sept. 1. bo. Mar. 9. Elizabeth of William Chapman and Elizabeth Lambert.

Sept. 7. bo. July 3. Maria of Abraham Cark and Glorianna Merritt.

Sept. 8. bo. Nov. 18, '99. William of William Brower and Margaret Van Zandt.

Sept. 14, 1800. bo. July 27. Mary Anna of Hermanus P. Schuyler and Maria Dean.

Sept. 17. bo. Sept. 5. Matthew of Sebastian Visscher and Rosannah Shipboy.

Sept. 28. bo. Sept. 19. Elizabeth of John Van Schaick and Margaret Bleecker. Wit: Mary Van Schaick.

Oct. 6. bo. Sept. 17. Henry of Henry Koon and Maria Kentee. Wit: Peter Kilman.

Oct. 9. bo. Sept. 24. Cornelia of Garrit Roseboom and Josena Hollenbeck. Wit: Cornelia Hollenbeck.

Oct. 13. bo. Aug. 19. Rutger of John R. Bleecker, Jr. and Eliza Atwood. Wit: John R. and Elizabeth Bleecker.

Oct. 18. bo. Sept. 10. Jacob of Francis Hamestraat and Helena Van Arnum.

1800-1801

Oct. 19. bo. Oct. 12. Margaret of Henry T. Bleecker and Mary Storm. Wit: John N. and Eliza Bleecker.

Oct. 28. bo. Sept. 16 or 14. Mary of John Lansing, Jr. and Cornelia Ray. Wit: Sanders and Catharina Lansing.

Oct. 12. bo. Sept. 15. William Lupton of John B. Johnson and Elizabeth Lupton.

Nov. 14. bo. Oct. 27. John of James LeGrange and Mary McCrea.

Nov. 14. bo. Sept. 4. Ephraim Gilbert of Isaac Hollenbeck and Catharine Rue.

Nov. 18. bo. Nov. 9. John of Nicholas Radliff and Catharine Gibsen. Wit: Mary Radliff.

Nov. 25. bo. Oct. 18. William of William Fonda and Susannah Hollenbeck.

Nov. 27. bo. Oct. 31. Alida of James Hoghkerk and Alida Van Zandt.

Dec. 8. bo. Dec. 2. Albert of Teunis Slingerland and Ellenor Van Den Bergh.

Dec. 14. bo. Dec. 8. Nancy of Robert Hubbard and Dinah. Wit: Rachel Oathoudt, Sr.

Dec. 24. bo. Nov. 23. Helena of Christopher Lansing and Abigail Hostrum. Wit: Helena Lansing.

Jan. 11, 1801. bo. Dec. 26. George of Matthias Hawes and Rachel Sickles.

Jan. 22. bo. Sept. 28. Margaret of John T. or I. Van Alen and Mary Diamond.

Feb. 1. bo. Nov. 25. Elizabeth of Stephen Miller and Christina Garner. Wit: Elizabeth and Godfrey Garner, Jr.

Feb. 5. bo. Jan. 26, 1800. Catharine of Hendrick Van Beuren and Toppie Salsburry. Wit: Harms Vn Beuren.

Feb. 22. bo. Feb. 1. Isaac Sturges of George Milton and Mary Sturges.

bo. Sept. 18, 1797. Benjamin Ledyard of Glen Cuyler and Mary Forman Ledyard.

bo. July 2, 1799. Richard Glen of Glen Cuyler and Mary Forman Ledyard.

Feb. 26. bo. Feb. 9, 1801. Philip Schuyler of James Van Ingen and Elizabeth Schuyler.

Mar. 6, '01. bo. Nov. 27, 1800. Peter Yates of David Harris and Mary Yates. Wit: Peter W. Yates.

1801

Mar. 8. bo. Jan. 22. Maria of Volkert S. Veeder and Ann Quackenboss.

Mar. 8. bo. Mar. 4. John of Isaac Hansen and Jane Cooper.

Apr. 3. bo. Mar. 12. Daniel of John Morrell and Rebecca Bratt.

Apr. 6. bo. Feb. 21. Maria of Sanders Lansing and Catharine Ten Eyck.

Apr. 12. bo. Jan. 26. Eleanor Van Cotts of Paul Clark and Rachel Vn Cotts. Wit: James Baker, Catalina Holenbeck.

July 5. bo. June 9. Helena of Jacob Bloomingdale and Margaretta Ruller.

July 10. bo. June 20. Gertrude of Jacob A. Wendell and Eva Swart.

Aug. 1. bo. May 4. John of Francis Costegan and Jane Hagaman.

Aug. 10. bo. Mar. 29. Jane Ann of Douw Winne and Anna Boice. Wit: Rebecca Winne.

Aug. 16. bo. June 27. Joseph of Benjamin Middleton and Elizabeth Owens.

bo. Aug. 6. Annatie of Garrit De Garmo and Cornelia Cooper. Wit: Obediah.

Aug. 21. bo. June 28. Catharina of Peter W. Yates and Mary Ter Bush.

Aug. 23. bo. Aug. 21. Peter and Sarah of Jacob Bogert and Alida Bloomingdale. Wit: Albertus Bloomingdale.

bo. July 28. Thomas of Thomas C. Gardner and Willimpie Bogert. Wit: Agnes Bogert.

Aug. 30. Peter Schuyler of John I. Cuyler and Mary Vernor.

Apr. 23, 1801. bo. Apr. 6, 1800. Richard of Gilbert Ackerman and Rachel De Garmo.

Sept. 20. bo. Aug. 22. Teunis of Rutger Van Woert and Annatie Lansing.

bo. Aug. 28. Peter of David Melich and Mary Hewson.

Oct. 17. bo. Oct. 12. Leonard Gansevoort of Jacob Ten Eyck and Magdalen Gansevoort. Wit: Leonard and Hester Gansevoort.

Oct. 25. bo. Oct. 23. Catharine Groesbeck of Francis M. Faten and Catharina V. D. Groesbeck. Wit: William and Catharina Groesbeck.

1801-1802

Nov. 7. bo. Sept. 24. Helletie of Joseph Kainer and Rachel Hallenbeck.

Nov. 15. bo. Aug. 9. Rebecca of Peter Marshall and Hannah Bacon.

Nov. 22. bo. Oct. 27. James Bloodgood of Benjamin DeWitt and Eve Bloodgood.

Nov. 29. bo. Oct. 22. Mary Ann of William M. Diamond and Rebecca Wendell.

bo. Oct. 25. Jonathan of Anthony Brooks and Catharine Van Huysen.

Jan. 2, 1802. bo. Nov. 3. Philip of Robert S. Van Rensselaer and Catharine N. Bogert. Wit: Maria Van Rensselaer.

bo. June 17, 1801. James of James Van Rensselaer and Elsie Schuyler.

Jan. 26, 1802. bo. Dec. 13, 1801. Hannah of Elias Johnson and Edith Le Grange. Wit: Anna Johnson.

Feb. 1. bo. Jan. 17. Henry of Barent G. Staats and Catharine Cuyler.

Feb. 2. bo. Dec. 22. Rachel of Nicholas Morrell and Elizabeth Brooks.

Feb. 7. bo. Dec. 27. Maria of James Gourdlay and Lany Bromley.

Feb. 8. bo. Nov. 10. Esther Rebecca of Walter and Henrietta Slingerland. Wit: Rebecca Slingerland.

Feb. 10. bo. Feb. 10. Jacob of Francis Waley and Elizabeth Arnthoudt.

Feb. 26. bo. Jan. 15. Helletie of John Hallenbeck and Anna LeGrange.

Mar. 14. bo. Feb. 19. Frances of Henry Fisher and Rebecca Brooks.

Mar. 18. bo. Mar. 1. Elizabeth of Nicholas Redecker and Alida Bulson. Wit: John Bulson. Eliza Halbert.

Mar. 27. bo. Mar. 11. Catharina of Whitehead Warner and Elizabeth Ostrander. Wit: John T. Ostrander.

Mar. 31. bo. Feb. 28. John of Benjamin Hilton and Jemima Van Volkenburgh.

Apr. 4. bo. Mar. 6. John of John Groesbeck and Maria Lansing.

bo. Jan. 29. Rachel of Frederick Brown and Elizabeth Hunter.

1802-1805

Apr. 12. bo. Mar. 23. Lawrence Fonda of Wilhelmus G. Ryckman and Maria Fonda. Wit: Cornelia Ryckman.

Apr. 25. bo. Mar. 29. Rensselaer of Solomon and Harriet Van Rensselaer. Wit: Maria and Robert S. Van Rensselaer.

May 9. bo. Apr. 18. Sarah Ann of William Van Zandt and Eleanor Mynderson.

bo. Apr. 4. Abraham of Lucas Hooghkerk and Eleanor De Forest.

bo. Mar. 10. Philip of Abrahm R. Ten Eyck and Ann Fisher.

May 10. bo. Apr. 14. Elizabeth of Gilbert Ackerman and Rachel De Garmo.

July 3. bo. Feb. 16. John of Amos Fuller and Catharine Smith.

July 6. bo. June 25. Catlina of John Merselis, Jr. and Alida Quackenboss.

July 16. bo. July 5. Anna of James and Mary Van Zandt.

July 21. bo. June 7. John of Philip Mower and Hannah Coons.

Sept. 4, 1802. bo. Jan 1, 1801. Rachel of Abm Profit and Nancy, free black woman, former serv. of Elias Kane.

Sept. 16. bo. June 6. Richard Goadsby of John Dunn and Frances Goadsby.

Sept. 26. bo. Aug. 3. Joab of Spencer Stafford and Dorotha Hallenbake.

bo. Aug. 2. Martha of James Baker and Catlina Hallenbake. Wit: John Van Hoevenbergh.

Aug. 14, 1805. bo. July 11. Ann of John T. and Maria Groesbeeck.

Aug. 18. bo. June 5. Lydia of Benjamin and Eve De Witt.

Sept. 15. bo. Sept. 5. Gertrude of Isaac and Jane Hanson.

Sept. 15. bo. Aug. 18. Cornelia of William and Dorothy Austin.

Oct. 26. bo. Aug. 28. Maria Harriet of Abraham and Catherine Van Vechten.

Oct. 28. bo. Sept. 8. Henry Young of John A. and Rachel Ghoewy.

Dec. 2. bo. Nov. 23. Samuel Stringer of Christopher C. and Ann Yates.

Dec. 4. bo. Nov. 8. Ann Elize of Garrit and Susannah Plumb.

1805-1806

Dec. 18, 1805. bo. Nov. 19, 1803. John of Abraham and Elizabeth Lottridge.

Dec. 18. bo. Nov. 17. Robert of Abraham and Elizabeth Lottridge.

Dec. 25, 1805. bo. Oct. 18, 1798. Anna of Daniel and Anna McKelvey.

Dec. 25. bo. Nov. 27. Peter Beeckman of Daniel and Phebe McKelvey.

Dec. 31. bo. May 28. Maria of Jeremiah and Maria Luther.

Dec. 31. bo. Aug. 25. Henry, no parents given.

Jan. 13, 1806. bo. Oct. 28. Samuel of Nicholas and Elizabeth Morrel.

Jan. 13, 1806. bo. Nov. 14, 1805. Samuel of Herman and Catherine Morrel.

Jan. 26. bo. Jan. 17. Harmen Gansevoort of Jacob and Magdalen Ten Eyck.

Jan. 30, 1806. bo. Dec. 15, 1797. David Eldridge of Jacob T. and Ann Cuyler.

Jan. 30, 1806. bo. Aug. 1, 1801. Lydia Ann of Jacob T. and Ann Cuyler.

Feb. 2, 1806. bo. Jan. 17, 1805. Richard March of Samuel and Mary Schuyler.

Feb. 6. bo. Nov. 14, 1805. Mary of Jacob and Fanny Van Ness.

Mar. 17. bo. Feb. 21. Anthony of Anthony and Catherine Brooks.

Apr. 6. bo. Jan. 30. Sarah of John R.' and Gertrude Tillman.

Apr. 6. bo. Feb. 28. Elisabeth of Lucas T. and Mary Hooghkerk.

Apr. 19. bo. Apr. 4. Nicholas Bogart of Catherine and Robert S. Rensselaer.

Apr. 20. bo. Mar. 22. Josiah of Matthew and Hester Burton.

Apr. 20. bo. Mar. 31. Benjamin of Garret and Cornelia De Garmo.

Apr. 23. bo. Nov. 2, 1806. (sic) Russell Edmund of Russell E. and Maria Post.

1806

May 7. bo. Apr. 14. William of John Y. and Maria Staats.

May 11. bo. Feb. 5. Sarah Ann of George and Mary Charles.

May 11. bo. Apr. 12. Alida of James and Alida Hooghkerk.

May 11. bo. Apr. 10. George Metcalf of Henry and Elizabeth Bleecker.

June 1. bo. Apr. 26. Van Vechten of Solomon V. and Harriet Van Renselaer.

June 28. bo. Apr. 17. Jacob Roseboom of Jacob S. and Henriette Pruyn.

June 29. bo. May 20. Mary Jane of Lawrence L. and Alida Van Kleeck.

July 6. bo. Nov. 6, 1805. Martin of Isaac and Mary Van Buskirk.

July 6. bo. May 16. James Franklin of Thomas and Margaret Linacre.

July 14. bo. June 19. Sally Ann of David W. and Ann Groesbeeck.

July 25. bo. May 30. Frederic of Sanders and Catherine Lansing.

Aug. 10. bo. July 15. Abraham of Henry and Rebecca Fisher.

Aug. 17. bo. June 29. Henry Van Putten of Henry and Elizabeth Able.

Aug. 17. bo. June 11. Martin Beeckman of John and Gertrude Brinkerhoff.

Sept. 7. bo. July 24. Sarah Ann of Killian and Sarah Winne.

Sept. 14. bo. Aug. 22. Catherine of Rensselaer and Jane Westerlo. Wit: Stephen Van Rensselaer, Catherine Westerlo.

Oct. 4. bo. June 3. Peter Kane of Gerrit and Elisabeth Clewett.

Oct. 5. bo. Sept. 2. Dorothy of Henry B. and Rachel Halenbake.

Oct. 19. bo. Aug. 5. Sarah of James and Catalina Wynkoop.

bo. Sept. 12. Henry Van Woert of Henry B. and Elisabeth Benthuysen.

Oct. 26. bo. Oct. 9. William Henry of James and Gertrude Van Ingen.

1806-1807

Nov. 18. bo. Oct. 6. Peter of Wilhelmus G. and Maria Ryckman.

Nov. 24. bo.·Nov. 8. James Bleecker of Charles and Sarah Platt.

Nov. 27. bo. Oct. 14. Philip of Stephen and Cornelia Van Rensselaer.

Nov. 30. bo. Nov. 3. Catharine of Cornelius and Rebecca Van Schoonhoven.

Dec. 22. bo. Nov. 20. Catherine of Adam and Elisabeth Russ.

Dec. 25. bo. Oct. 13. Anthony Groesbeeck of Anthony and Rachel Van Santvoort.

Jan. 4, 1807. bo. Dec. 12. William Groesbeeck of George and Mary Milton.

Jan. 16. bo. Oct. 1, 1806. Sarah of Francis and Jane Costigan.

Jan. 18. bo. Oct. 7, 1806. Elsie of Herman and Arrietta Knickerbacker.

Jan. 18. bo. Dec. 25, 1806. Cornelia of Thomas C. and Willelpie Gardner.

Jan. 25. bo. Dec. 21. Steven of James and Mary La Grange.

Jan. 25. bo. Dec. 25, 1806. Alida of Ch. C. and Ann Yates.

Feb. 24. bo. Jan. 17. Nanning Visscher of Levinus L. and Ann Winne.

Mar. 1. bo. Jan. 31. Ann Elizabeth of Benjamin and Eve De Witt.

Mar. 8. bo. Feb. 9. Gerrit Lansing of Cornelius and Anna Van Hussan.

Mar. 22. bo. Feb. 4. Mary of William and Mary Vusburgh.

Mar. 22. Peter of Thomas and Catalina Dox.

Apr. 2. bo. Feb. 4. Harriet of Jeremiah and Gertrude Smith.

Apr. 5. bo. Feb. 12. John Wendall of John and Alida Stillwell.

Apr. 5, 1807. bo. Nov. 22, 1806. Sarah of William M. and Rebecca Diamond.

Apr. 12. bo. Mar. 6. Maria of John and Maria Hewson.

Apr. 12. bo. Feb. 16. Alida of Lucas and Helen Hoghkerk.

1807

Apr. 14. bo. Feb. 10. Volkert Douw of Jacob and Alida Lansing.

Apr. 19. bo. Mar. 11. Catalina of David T. and Harriet Groesbeeck.

May 8. bo. Mar. 9. John of Andrew and Maria Van Antwerp.

May 28. bo. May 17. Alexander of Eldert and Lena Fryer.

May 21. bo. Mar. 24. Harriet Maria of Abm. and Catherine Van Vechten.

May 31. bo. Apr. 4. Eve of David and Margaret Schuyler.

May 25. bo. Apr. 23. Maria of B. and Magdalena Van Wie.

June 7. bo. Feb. 6. Catharina Maley of John C. and Hannah Cuyler.

June 24. bo. May 27. Margaret of Nicholas N. and Ann Quackenbush.

June 27. bo. Apr. 18. John Van Rensselaer of Peter E. and Elizabeth Elmendorf.

July 12. bo. June 11. Obadiah Cooper of Isaac and Jane Hansen.

July 19. bo. June 14. Elizabeth of Isaac and Elisabeth Bradt.

July 26. bo. June 14. Abraham Truax of Jacob and Hannah Evertsen.

bo. June 9. Margaret of Hugh and Maria Begley.

Aug. 9. bo. June 15. Agnes of John S. and Margaret Pruyn.

Aug. 23. bo. July 22. Magdalen of David and Mary Milich.

Sept. 20. bo. Aug. 22. Jacob of Henry and Gertrude Van Santvoort.

Oct. 4. bo. Sept. 15. Anna of Francis and Jane Costigan.

Oct. 2. bo. Sept. 14. Elizabeth of Jacob and Fanny Van Ness.

Oct. 7. bo. Sept. 17. Jacob Roseboom of Jacob and Henrietta Pruyn.

Oct. 19. bo. Sept. 25. Magdalen of James and Maria Van Schoonoven.

Oct. 19. bo. Sept. 25. Catherine of John N. and Nancy Quackenbush.

1807-1808

Oct. 25. bo. Oct. 11. Anna Maria of Abraham and Maria Hun.

Nov. 29. bo. Sept. 23. Amos Fuller of Isaac and Mary Van Buskirk.

Dec. 25. bo. Dec. 15. Gertrude of Benjamin and Maria Hansen.

Jan. 8, 1808. bo. Nov.·8. Thomas Loring of John and Mary Sharp.

Jan. 22. bo. Dec. 25. Maria of Teunis and Eleanor Slingerland.

Feb. 21. bo. Jan. 30, 1808. Charles Edwin of Paul and Catherine Hochstrasser.

Feb. 26. bo. Jan. 16. James of Peter and Catherine Murphy.

Mar. 13. bo. Jan. 15. Ann Eliza of John and Phebe Cooper.

Mar. 20. bo. Mar. 2. Elisabeth of David W. and Ann Groesbeck.

Apr. 17. bo. Mar. 31. Ann Eliza of Edward and Margaret Willett.

Apr. 21. bo. Mar. 22. Cornelia of Rensselaer and Jane Westerlo. Wit: John, Jr. and Cornelia Lansing.

May 1. bo. Mar. 21. William of James and Alida Hoghkirk.

June 19. Rachel of Lucas Hoghkirk.

June 20. bo. June 5. Maria of Francis C. and Cornelia Pruyn.

June 26. bo. May 31. Henry Van Wie of Matthew and Hester Burton.

June 30. bo. June 6. Jane Elizabeth of John A. and Rachel Goewhy.

July 2. bo. Mar. 27. Nicholas Bogart of Robert and Cathrine Van Rensselaer.

July 3. bo. June 10. Cornelius of John Brinkerhoff and Gertrude Schuyler.

July 3. bo. June 25. Cornelia of Thomas C. and Willempie Gardner.

July 3. bo. Apr. 15. Agnes of Wilhelmus and Sally Van der Bergh.

July 8. bo. June 13. Edward of Sanders and Catherine Lansingh.

1808

July 10. bo. June 5. Eliza of John T. and Ann Ostrander.
July 29. bo. June 7. Solomon of John and Petertie Goewhy.
July 29. bo. June 7. Nelly of John and Petertie Goewhy.
July 30. bo. July 17, Thomas of Samuel and Mary Schuyler.
bo. June 12. Anna Maria of Anthony and Cath. Van Santvoort.
Aug. 7. bo. June 12. Maria of Philip and Harriet Van Rensselaer.
Aug. 7. bo. July 13. Harriet of David T. and Harriet Groesbeeck.
Aug. 7. bo. June 27. David of John T. and Maria Groesbeeck.
Aug. 14. bo. May 10. Jane Ann Maria of Joseph and Triny Webber.
Aug. 14. bo. June 30. Sally Ann of Henry A. and Harriet Gardinier.
Aug. 28. bo. Aug. 2. Bernardus Evertsen of John Y. and Maria Staats.
Aug. 28. bo. June 24. Theodorus of Elias and Deborah Kane.
Sept. 11. bo. Aug. 13. Jellis of Daniel T. and Alida Winne.
Sept. 13. bo. Aug. 14. Henry B. of Isaac B. and Cornelia Halmbake.
Sept. 16. bo. Sept. 13. Jacob of Jellis, Jr. and Sally Winne.
Sept. 21. bo. Sept. 14. Thomas of Abraham and Maria Hun. Wit: John and Anna Bassitt.
Sept. 24. bo. Apr. 17. Isaac Van Santvoort of Isaac P. and Anna Truax.
Oct. 4. bo. Sept. 23. Mary of Gerrit and Susannah Plumb.
Oct. 9. bo. Aug. 28. Elisabeth of William and Maria Roades.
Oct. 10. bo. May 26. Cortland of Stephen and Cornelia Van Rensselaer.
Oct. 23. bo. Sept. 28. Peter of Henry and Rebecca Visher.
Oct. 26. bo. Oct. 20. Robert of Abm and Sarah Benson.
Nov. 6. bo. Oct. 10. William of Henry B. and Elisabeth Van Benthuysen.
Nov. 13. bo. Oct. 10. Rachel of Gerrit and Sally Hoghkirk.
Dec. 3. Angelica of Abm and Mary Bradt.

1808-1809

Dec. 5. bo. Oct. 19. Susannah of Abm and Jane Lansing.

Dec. 9. bo. Nov. 11. Mary of Philip and Harriet Miller.

Dec. 11. bo. Nov. 4. Louisa Ridgeley of John M. and Mary Bradford.

Dec. 11. bo. Oct. 27. Maria of David and Margaret Schuyler.

Dec. 18. bo. Sept. 20. Margaret Ann of Thomas and Margaret Linacre.

Dec. 25. bo. Oct. 14. Stephen of James and Mary Le-Grange.

Dec. 25. bo. Nov. 2. Cecilia of Jacob and Catharine Groesbeck.

Dec. 25. bo. June 22. Richard William of Nicholas and Phebe Brower.

Jan. 9, 1809. bo. Sept. 6. Mary Hugenin of Peter and Jane Gerbrantz.

Jan. 22, 1809. bo. Dec. 23, 1808. James of Adam and Elizabeth Russ.

Jan. 22. bo. Oct. 8. Elijah of John and Mary Van Ness.

Jan. 22. bo. Feb. 2, 1809. (sic) Jannett Eliza of John and Christiana Andrew.

Feb. 3. bo. Feb. 3. Rufus King of Solomon and Harriet Van Renselaer.

Feb. 6. bo. Dec. 19, 1808. Catherine Brinkerhoff of Gerrit and Margaret Benson.

Feb. 19. bo. Jan. 24. Rachel Norton of George and Mary Milton.

Feb. 26. bo. Jan. 6. Eleanor of George and Mary Charles.

Feb. 26. bo. Sept. 27, 1808. Sally of Sybrant and Nancy Kettle.

Feb. 26. bo. Jan. 22. Gertrude of James and Catharina Vosburgh.

Feb. 2. bo. Jan. 20. John of Corns. and Rebecca Van Schoonoven.

Mar. 12. bo. Jan. 19. Henry of John and Mary Sharp.

Mar. 12. bo. Jan. 14. Jeremiah of John and Jane Williams.

Mar. 13. bo. Feb. 1. William of James and Catalina Wynkoop.

INDEX

of the

MARRIAGE AND BAPTISMAL RECORD

of the

REFORMED PROTESTANT

DUTCH CHURCH OF ALBANY

1790-1809

* Indicates that name appears more than once on page.

Borsley, Frederick 21, Hannah 21.
Borttle, Jacob 13.
Bottle, Andrew B. 58; Sarah 58.
Bounds, Rachel 5.
Bourke, Christian 50; Rachel 50.
Bouvse, Eleanor 49; John 49.
Bovie, Batie 71; Harritie 32.
Bower, Willm 7.
Bowman, Andrew 54; Benjamin 54, 59;* Elizabeth 62.
Boyd, Alexander 41; Ann 46; Hugh 9, 46; James 18; John 18; Peter 41.
Brack Margaret 10.
Bracoty, Rebecca 7.
Bradford, John M. 91; Louisa Ridgeley 91; Mary 91.
Bradt, see Bratt.
Brannent, Susannah 5.
Brant, Annatie 30.
Bratt, Brats, Brett, Bradt, Braadt, Abraham, Abm. 67, 90; Adam 34; Alida 9; Adiean 25; Angelica 90; Ann Davis 60; Annanitie 51; Annatie 28, 34, 63; Anthony 6, 51; Anthony T. 36; Arent 34; Ariantie 2; Baltas 28; Bernardus 54, 62; Catalina, Catlina 38,* 74; Caterlintie 36;* Catharina, Catharine 15, 45; Daniel 15, 25, 60, 62; Dirck A. 4; Eder 23; Eleanor 14; Elizabeth 14, 88;* Garret V. Everen 56; Hannah 34, 48; Hendric 46; Hendric T. 45; Hendrikus 15; Henry 67; Isaac 9, 45, 54, 63, 71, 88; Jane 14, 28, 45; Janitie 47; John 7, 20, 25, 38, 39, 54, 71; John B. 49; Leah 54; Margarit, Margaret 34, 60; Maritie 25; Mary 7, 43, 90; Nicholas 28; Peter A. 56, 74; Peter I. 14; Rebecca 46, 58, 82; Susannah 72; Susannah W. 34; Teunis 38; Teuris 36; Willempje 15.
Brawer, John 32; Maria 29; Robert Ray 32; Willem 29.
Brees, Anthony 4.
Brett, see Bratt.
Brewslin, Lydia 30.
Brewster, Lydia 46, 59.
Brice, John 26; Mary 26.
Bridgen (?), Eliza Ten Eyck 65, 72.
Briese, Elizabeth 18.
Brinckerhoff, Brinkerhoff, Abm Schuyler 78; Gertrude 86; Isaac 32, 61; John 9, 61, 72,* 78, 86; Martin Beeckman 86; Peter 4; Rachel Maria 32; Richard 72.
Britt, Baltes 50; Margaret 50; Mary 7.
Britton, Lucy 28.
Broeks, see Brooks.
Brokus, Caty 49.*
Bromley, Bromlee, David 57; Lana 3; 78, 83; Robert 57.

Bronck, Bronk, Abraham 6; Catharine 67; Charity 8; Elizabeth 11; Henry 17, 67; Mary 17.
Brooks, Broocks, Broeks, Alida 57; Anthony 7, 23, 83, 85;* Catherine 85; Christina 23; Elizabeth 63, 65, 83; John 11, 63, 68; Jonathan 8, 57, 83; Peter 68; Rebecca 32, 36, 46, 68, 74, 77, 78, 83.
Broom, Elisabeth 11.
Brott, Samuel F. 3.
Brower, Brouwer, Albertus 64; Catharine 57; Charity 53; Cornelius 22; Dirck V. Schuyline 43; Elizabeth 75; Garrit 80; Hassel, Hessel 3, 64, 71,* 80; John 22, 43, 57; Mary 12, 19; Nicholas 91; Phebe 91; Richard William 91; Sarah 43; William 75, 80.*
Brown, Edward 3; Esther 49; Frederick 83; Jacob 55; Jane 10, 12; John 10; Margaret 55; Maria 56; Rachel 83; Rebecca 4.
Brownlow, David 47.*
Bruce, Archibald 65; Judith 17, 65.
Brunt, Edward 34; Wilhelmus 34.
Buckby, Buckbee, Ezra 13; Joseph 4; Mercy 78.
Buckhout, Aunah 50; James 50.
Bulsingh, Cathal 19; Elisabeth 19; Hendrik 19.
Bulsom, Bulson, Alida 9, 41, 54, 83; Ann 9, 50; Cataline 69;* Catharine 69; Caty 57; Cornelius 50; Elizabeth 11, 43, 52; Daniel 9; Henry 41, 52; John 83; Nancy 69; Nicholas 41; Peter 7, 43; Rachel 29; Sarah, Sara 35, 50.
Bunts, Conrodt 3.
Burch, Lydia 42.
Burdett, Nathaniel 12.
Burdoine, Jacob 4.
Burger, Susannah 49.
Burges, Mary 29, 74.
Burkley, Eleanor 7.
Burns, John 42; Nancy 63; Robert 42; William 63.
Burr, Theodocia 4.
Burris, Sarah 13.
Burrows, Ann Elize 62; John Wilcoxs 62; Mary 62; Samuel 62;* Samuel T. 5.
Burses, Maria 22.
Burton, Elizabeth 32; Henry Van Wie 89; Hester 85, 89; John 6; Josiah 85; Mary 10, 57, 61, 69; Matthew 85, 89.
Bussel, Elizabeth 37.
Bussing, Elizabeth 45, 79; Hannah 51; William C. 11.
Bush, Abraham 38; George 38.
Buyse, John 34.*

Cackle, Ann 11.
Calder, Elizabeth 7.
Caldwell, Elizabeth 31, 38, 50, 52, 55; Noble 50.
Cameron, Camern, James 12; John 31.
Campbell, Catharine 69; Elizabeth 69; John 69;* Margaret 2, 10.
Canada, Guy 37; Sarah 37.
Cane, Elizabeth 16; Rebecca 16; William 16.
Canine, Anna 45.
Canter, Maria 20.
Cardenright, Margarit 25.
Carhartt, James 3.
Cark, Abraham 64, 80; Maria 80; Sophia 64.
Carker, Latte 11.
Carkner, George 34; William 34.
Carles, Susannah 40, 62.
Carmen, Gertroy 23.
Carner, George 55; Philip 55.
Carnright, George Henry 63; William 63.
Carpenter, Cynthia, Cinthia 63, 67; John Coe 3.
Carr, Rachel 19.
Carter, Patty 47; Samuel 47; Ward 47; William 47.*
Casparus, Abraham 55; Martinus 55; Matthias 54.
Cassada, Nancy 3.
Casseman, Christina 7.
Cater, Catharina 41.
Catlin, Abigail 13.
Cedam, see Suydam.
Cely, John 2.
Cennel, Catharine 39; Edward 39; Sarah 39.
Center, Asa H. 12.
Chadwick, Eva 56; Thomas 9, 56.
Chambers, Chamber, Annatie 30; Elizabeth 47;* Hendrick 30.
Chandler, Sarah 44.
Chapin, Tirza 4.
Chapman, Elizabeth 80; John William 74; William 74, 80;
Charles, Eleanor 91; George 47, 58, 66, 86, 91; Margaret 2; Maria 66; Maritie 29; Mary 34, 86, 91; Sarah Ann 86; Stephen 58; William 47.
Charley, Eleanor 26.
Chatterton, Catharina 13.
Cheseborough, Clarissa 2.
Childs, Gilbert 56; William 56.
Chisholm, James 2, 75; Margery 75.
Christ, Philip 11.
Christon, David 19; Joseph 19.
Chun, Tabitha 50.
Circuler, Margarit 33.
Clamisher, Dennis 43; William 43.

Clark, Clarke, Abigail 64; Ann 37; Eleanor Van Cotts 82; John 11; Mary 6; Nancy 9; Paul 82; Walter 10, 64; Willm, William 2, 10.
Class, Claus, Elizabeth 34;* Henry 34; Margarit 30; Peter 30.
Claver, Charlotte 46; Elizabeth 46, 57, 77; Hilletie 4; Mary 21,* 38, 57, 72; Mary Schuyler 27; Susan 25; William 21, 27, 38, 46.
Clay, John 46.
Clement Jane 9.
Clemisham, Denis 55; George 55.
Clery, Richard 10.
Cleveland, Lucy 11.
Clevison, Dennis 17; Rachel 17.
Clewett, Elizabeth 86; Gerrit 86; Peter Kane 86;
Cline, Kline, Elizabeth 35; George 57, 72; Margarit, Margaret 35, 64, 79; Matthew 72; Nicholas 35, 57.
Clinton, Elizabeth 72.*
Clove, Nicholas 29.
Cluck, Garrit 27, 35; Johannah 35; John 27.
Clulo, Garret 6.
Clute, Angeltie 62; Anne 52; Charles 71; Christintie 44; Elizabeth 41; Garret, Gerret 40, 52, 57, 71; John 12; Margaret 13; Maria 13; Mary 70; Rebecca 57; Richard 10; Sarah 28, 46, 62, 70; William 40.
Cochen, Elizabeth 37.
Cochran, Margaret 49.
Codwine, Mary 21.
Coe, Benjamin 11.
Coenrad, Philip 50.
Coens, Hannah 38.
Colbreath, William 53.*
Cole, Gertrude 8; Lambert 60; Mary 8, 42; Susannah 60.
Colhammer, Hannah 50.
Coller, George 8.
Collier, Catalina 47; George 44, 47, 62; Margaret 62.
Collins, Anne 65; Elizabeth 65; William 65.
Conger, William 6.
Conklin, Margaret 43.
Connel, Caty 45; Edward 45; Sara 18, 45.
Conner, Connor, Catharina 60; Gertrude 79; John 7.
Connolly, Sarah 27.
Consalb, Nelly 2.
Consaul, Fanny 56.
Conway, Julia 8.
Cook (?), Jennith 16.
Coon, Ann, 24; Coonrath 24; Jane 24.
Coons, Elizabeth 5, 8; Hannah 84.

Cooper, Ann Eliza 89; Annatje 14, 16; Catharina 3; Christian 7, 16; Cornelia 16, 28, 69, 78, 82; Elizabeth 16, 22, 55; Freryk 16; Jane 3, 68, 82; John 3, 89; Martha 3; Obadiah 22, 28; Phebe 89; Pieter 16; Rachel 22; William 16, 27.

Copley, Calvin 40; Charles 40.

Corneleysse, Isaac Vosburgh 66; James 66.

Cornelinsse, James 55;* Maria 55.

Cornice, Deborah 68.

Cornick, Elizabeth 73; Jonathan 73.

Cossley, John 37.

Costigen, Costigan, Costegan, Anna 88; Francis 51, 78, 82, 87, 88; Grace 51; Isaac 78; Jane 87, 88; John 82; Sarah 87.

Countryman, Adam 8; Catharine 55; Lydia 54.

Courtney, Catharine 4; John 23;* Mary 23.

Couse, Adam 27; Catharine 27.

Couverd, Mary 24.

Cowan, Hannah 2.

Cowneck, Catharine 78; Jonathan 78.

Cox, Ann 50.

Crane, Samuel 9.

Crannel, Cranel, Baltus 49; Folkie 49; Hannah 55; Harriet, Harriot 65, 72, 77; Henry 51; Isaac 49;* Jamima 51; Margaret 51; Marten 49;* Mary 49, 66; Matthew 56; Nicholas 32, 44, 56, 66; Robert 20, 32;* William W. 49; Winant 44.

Crayselaer, Philip 49.

Cribble, Elizabeth 22.

Crigier, see also Krigier, Dirckie 58; Martinus 64; Samuel 58; Sarah 60, 71; Sebastian 64.

Cromwell, Sophia 9.

Crow, Marian Stewart 71; William 71.

Crum, John 27; John Rudolff 27.

Cumisiston (?), Alida 43; Edward 43.

Cummings, Mary 11, 46, 65, 71.

Cutler, John 4.

Cuyler, Abraham 43, 52; Ann 85;* Annatie 9; Augustus 76; Benjamin Ledyard 81; Catharina, Catharine 15, 27, 33, 37, 41, 52, 62, 64, 69, 75, 80, 83; Catharina Maley 88; Caty 20, 47; David Eldridge 85; Elisabeth, Elizabeth 20, 25; Glen 81;* Hannah 88; Henry 69, 72; Hester 41; Jacob 25, 27, 80; Jacob A. 16, 43, 52, 58, 69, 72; Jacob T. 85;* Jane 38, 73; John 38; John C. 46, 63, 76, 88; John E. 73; John I. 82; John Maley 73; John Mayby 46; John T. 77; Lydia 80; Lydia Ann 85; Maria 57, 60; Peter Schuyler 82; Philip Stephen V. Renselaer 58; Richard Glen 81; Vernor 77;

William 16; William Tremper 63.

Dale, John 7.

Dana, Maria 77; Willm. 77.

David, Ann 38; Catalyntie 1; Catharina 53; Elizabeth 31, 50; James 52; Joseph Caldwell 55; Peter 31, 38, 52, 55.

Davis, Davies, Annatje 15; Catharine 61, 70; Caty 50; Edward 14; Jannitje 14; Maria 68;* Nancy 4; Rachel 14, 31, 51.

Dawe, Alida 31.

Dean, Deane, Abraham 20; Maria 80; Mary 11; Stuart 20.

De Assigne, Elizabeth 48.

De Camp, John 6.

Decker, Abraham 41; Cornelia 41; Maritie 22; Simeon 41.

Deerstyne, Deerstine, Dierstyne, Catharine 7; Henry 56; Maria 56; Mary 31.

De Forest, Deforest, see also Foreest; Abraham 49; Catalina 40, 49; David 14,* 49; David I. 59; Dirk, Dirck 14, 46, 58; Eleanor 27, 36, 43, 47, 70, 75, 79, 84; Hannah 6; Henry 46; Jannetje 18; Janitie 59; Jesse 40; John 23; John I. 23; Maritie 21; Nelly 79; Pietertie 53; Rachel 10, 66; Stephen 59; Susanna 14; Walter 58; Yzac 18.

De Garmo, Annatie 82; Benjamin 85; Cornelia 85; Cornelious V. Den Bergh 69; Garrit, Gerrit 3, 69, 78, 82, 85; Jacob 78; Rachel 3, 78, 82, 84.

De Graef, Deborah 3.

Delamater, Evert 8, 42; John Cole 42.

Delang, Catharina 2.

Del Vecchio, John 71.

Denbar, Jacob 51.*

Denken, Mary 19.

Denker, Mary 21.

Denney, Lydia 4.

Dennison, Denisson, Denison, Deniston, Denniston, Ann 33, 65; Garrit Visher 21;* Helena 30; Hugh 33; Isaac 33, 38, 65; John Henry 56;* Margaret 65; Rachel 4; Susannah 38.

De Peyster, de Peister, Annatje 16.

Derick, Charles 45, 73; Elisabeth 45, 73; Margaret 45, 73.

De Ronde, Rev. Mr. 40.

Devenhoff, see also Dovenhoff, Mary 49.

Devenant, Mary 44.

Devereax, Philip 8.

Devoe, Christopher 66; Gilbert 66.

de Weaver, see Weaver.

De Weax, Mary 32.

de Williga, Ann 24; Simon 24.

De Witt, De Wit, Dewit, Ann Elizabeth 87; Benjamin 4, 66, 83, 84, 87; Elizabeth 4, 65; Ephraim 12, 68; Eve 84, 87; George Washington 59; James Bloodgood 83; Lydia 84; Maria 68; Maria Nottingham 66; Richard Varick 79; Simeon 59, 79.

Diamond, Alen 91; Alida Wendel 68; John Wendel 58; Mary 36, 41, 52, 81; Mary Ann 83; Rebecca 87; Sarah 87; Thomas 73; William M. 58, 68, 73, 83, 87.
Sarah 87; Thomas 73; William M. 58, 68, 73, 83, 87.

Dickenson, John D. 18.

Dierstyne, see Deerstyne.

Dingman, John 39; Margaret 13; Philip 39.

Dollar, George 12.

Donnolly, Donelly, William 11, 12.

Dorman, Ambrose 2.

Douglass, Douglas, Asa 11; Catharine, Catharina 47, 55, 68; Jane 12.

Douw, Dow, Dowe, Abraham 36; Alida 42, 54, 70; Ann 13, 21; Ann de Peyster 45; Catharina 42; Folkert 16; Folkert Peter 16; Hendric Ten Eyck 52; John D. P. 76; John De P. 16, 20; John De Peyster 61; John P. 45; Louisa 61; Margarit 71; Margaret Livingston 76; Peter 36; Rachel 20, 45; Rhoda 51; Rykie 36; Sybrant 8, 36, 52; Volkert 21, 42; Volkert P. 21.

Dounel, Jane 5.

Dovenhoof, see also Devenhoff, Mary 50.

Dow, see Douw.

Dowey, see Douw.

Dowland, Christina 54.

Downey, Christina 59.

Dox, Catalina 87; Jane 58; John 13; Mynert Marsilius 14; Peter 14, 44*, 87; Rebecca 14; Thomas 87.

Doxtader, Caty 50.

Drew, Mary 75.

Driesbach, Driesback, Catharine 39; Elisabeth 32; Jost 32, 39, 51; Simon 51.

Driscol, William 4.

Drurie, Drurye, Catharine 79; Elizabeth 3; Isaac 79.

Dumond, Dumont, Susannah 32, 50; Temperance 16, 31.

Dun, Dunn, Christopher 12; John 2, 84; Marian 57; Richard Goadsby 84.

Dunbar, Angus 39; Catalina, Cataline 6, 24, 43; Cornalie 68; Cornelia 6, 26, 31, 35, 41, 44, 57, 63; Cornelius 64; Eliza Muir 58; Eltie 28; Gertrude 61, 69; Lavinus, Levinus 44,

73; Margaret, Margarit 12, 44, 73;* Margarita 17; Philip 39, 73; Robert 64; Robert Jr. 9; Robert W. 3, 58.

Dunham, Lodice 10; Lovice 2.

Dunleavy, Mary 13.

Dunn, see Dun.

Dunneston, see Dennison.

Dunse, Jennet 45.

Duryee (?), Jane 47.

Dutcher, Lydia, Ledia 22, 35; Salem 4.

Dyer, Abraham 57; Sarah Margaret 60; Thomas 57, 60;

Dykman, Ann 68; John 8.

Eadick, Christopher 80; John Radley 80.

Eagles, Francis 9.

Eaker, Eva 12.

Earl, Erle, Catharine 21; John 10.

Easterly, Charlotte 26; Martinus 15; Thomas 15, 26.

Eaton, Barbara 43; John 43.

Ecker, Maria 28; Petrus 28.

Edig, Edigh, Frederick 6, 49; Jacob 49; Susannah 49.

Eesbester, Eisbester, Isbester, Elizabeth 45; Isabella 25, 76.

Eebigh, Christopher 28; Margaret 28.

Egan, John 9.

Eights, see Yates.

Eisbester, see Eesbester.

Elliot, James 23, 79; Rebecca 79.

Elmendorf, Catharina 35; Edmund 78; Edmund Peter 66; Elizabeth 32, 88; John Van Rensselaer 88; Maria 44, 72; Mary 35*; Peter 12; Peter E. 44, 72; Mary 35;* Peter 12; Peter E. mund 35, 66, 72, 78; Sarah 35.

Elvendorff, John Fetter 26; Jonathan 26.

Emen, Maria 49.

Enoch, Enochs, Enocks, Ann 51, 56; Mary 35.

Eppes, John 5.

Erle, see Earl.

Ertsberger, Elizabeth 53; Jacob 53; Maria 10.

Esmy, Eleanor 8.

Esterly, Elizabeth 13; Maria 13.

Ettich, Catharine 31; Frederick 31.

Evars, Willm. 7.

Evertson, Evertsen, Everson, Everts, Abraham Truax 88; Angeltine 14; Ann 47; Barnhardus, Bernardus 14, 26, 45, 77;* Caty 28; Christiana 33; Evert 14, 26, 33, 47, 61, 77; Fikie 25; Garret 26, 61; Hannah 77, 88; Hendrik 16; Hendricke 51; Henrietta 51; Henrietta V. 52; Henry 9, 25, 42, 51, 57, 66;* Henryke 42; Isaac 57; Jacob 14, 33, 42,* 62, 88;

Gassa, Samuel (Cold.) 5.
Gates, Cornelius 48; John 48; Thomas 12.
Gedney, Robert 13.
Gerbrantz, Jane 91; Mary Hugenin 91; Peter 91.
Gerish, George 8.
Gerolomer, Jane 33; Nicholas 33; Peertie 33.
Ghoewy, see Goey.
Gibsen, Catharine 81.
Gilleland, Jane 22.
Gillot, Helena 15; Noah 15.
Ginning, Jacob 54.*
Giver, John 25; William 25.
Glen, Catharine, Catharina 17, 38,* 48, 61, 65; Cornelius 61; John 17; 38.
Goadsby, Godsby, Frances 2; 84.
Godfrey, Maria 12; Mary 70.
Godsby, see Goadsby.
Goe, Elizabeth 26.
Goes, Barent 3; Jacob 1.
Goey, Goewey, Goeway, Ghoewy, Goewhy, Alida 24; Ambrose 56; Barnt G. 56; Benjamin 41, 45; Catharine 55; Daniel 48; Elisabeth, Elizabeth 14. 47, 61, 77; Garret, Garrit 45, 79; Gertrude 67; Hannah 53; Henry Young 84; Jacob 45; Jane 56; Jane Elizabeth 89; Jannetje, Jannitie 15, 23, 72; John 24, 41, 53,* 61,* 90;* John A. 10, 66, 84, 89; John S. 63, 67; Johs 15; Nelly 90; Peter 48; Petertie 90;* Philip DeForest 66; Rachel 79, 84, 89; Salomon, Solomon 63, 90; William 55.
Gold, Mary 19.
Goodrich, John 3; Lydia 4; Rosell 11.
Goodwin, Lucy 5.
Gorseley, Isaac Hogan 29; John 29.
Gourley, Gourlay, Gourdlay, Annatie 78; James 3, 76, 78, 83; Maria 83.
Graham, Clara 12; Hannah 4, 64; Isabella 10; John 78; Martha 3; Sarah 78; Patty 64.
Grant, James 46; John 46; Susannah 51.
Gravarit, Alida 9.
Gravenbergh, Catharina 12.
Greveraads, Marytje 18.
Grey, Gray, Catharine 55;* Jellis 15; John 55,* 71; Nancy 58; Robert 15, 51; Sarah 71; Susannah 51; William 55.
Groat, Abraham 20; Elizabeth 20, 63; Ester 4.
Groesbeek, Groesbeeck, Alletta 76; Ann 84, 86, 89; Anthony 33, 49; Catalina 72, 88; Catalintie 33;* Cathalina 16; Cathar 32; Catharina V. D. 82; Catharina Van Duersen 3; Catharine, Catharina 5, 32, 46,

67, 78,* 82, 91; Cecelia 91; Clartie (?), 53; Clashe, Classie 2, 10, 45; Clausie 59; Cornelia 62; Cornelious, Cornelius 33, 49; Cornelius W. 5; David 23, 32, 90; David I. 65, 72, 77; David T. 88, 90; David W. 67, 86, 89; Eleanor 49; Elizabeth 39, 89; Geertruy 17, 33; Gertroy 21; Gerrit, Garrit 2, 20, 22, 72; Hannah 11, 63, 68; Harriet 88, 90;* Isaac Fonda 45; Jacob 91; Jacob Lansing 67; Jannetie 36; John 16, 22, 23, 77, 83;* John D. 40; John I. 4, 67; John T. 90; Isaac Fonda 26; John T. 84; Letty 77; Lucretia 67; Margarit Pool 23; Maria 48, 65, 84, 90; Pieter, Peter 17, 26, 36, 45; Rachel 11; Rebecca 49; Sally 6; Sally Ann 86; Sarah 40; Walter 33, 39, 48, 62; Walter A. 7; William, Wilm 32, 46, 53, 72; 78, 82.
Groot, Elizabeth 39.
Groots (?), Helena 7.
Gross, John 7.
Guest, Dirck 75; Hannah 53; Henry 65; Henry Jr. 4; Jane Ann 65; John Jr. 53; Margaret 58; Margaret V. D. Werken 71; Mary Ann 65; Sarah 58; Sarah Jordan 40; Thomas 40, 58, 65, 71, 75.
Gui, Catharine 33; Garret, Garrit 19, 33; Helena 19; John 33; Nicholas 33.
Guyer, Annatie 20; John 20, 43; Rebecca 43.

Haddock, Nacy 11.
Hagadorn, Sarah 80.
Hageman, Hagaman, Jane 51, 78, 82.
Haight, Oliver 10.
Hainer, Haner, Catharina 17;* Jacob 14, 17; Jonas 14; Maria 24; Mary 33; William 14.
Halbert, Eliza 83.
Hale, Solomon 2.
Hall, Herbe 25; Margaret 13; Naomi 37; Philip Hooker 76; Philip 76; Sarah 77; Thomas 76.
Hallenbake, Halenbake, Halmbake, Hollenbeck, Hollenbake, Hollinbake, Holenbeck, Abraham 7; Alida 9, 54, 60, 64; Andrew 12; Bernardus 42; Catharina 25; Catlina 82, 84; Christian Legrange 54; Cornelia 55, 80, 90; Dorotha 84; Dorothy 86; Eleanor 25; Elizabeth 49; Ephraim Gilbert 81; Helletie 83; Henry 35; 52; Henry B. 2, 25,42, 59, 70, 86, 90; Isaac 81; Isaac B. 90; Jacamintie 25; James 23; Jemima 8; John 9, 23, 54, 83; Josina, Josena 65, 80; Margaret 70; Mary 38; Rachel 52, 83, 86; Samuel 25;

Neven, Nevin, Ann 50; David 50; Noble
 Caldwell David 50; Peter 50.
Newson, John 12.
Nex, Caleb 1.
Nexson, Nexsen, Margaret 41, 54, 71;
 Mary 17, 43.
Nicholson, Mary 6, 24, 52.
Nicol, Nicoll, Elizabeth 61; Frances 66;
 Mary 8; Samuel 7.
Night, Margaret 62.
Nin, Elizabeth 32; Michael 32.
Nodan, Elizabeth 9.
Nollen, Roswell 10.
Norsfield, Eleanor 20.
Norton, Norten, Elizabeth 7, 27, 33, 35,
 60, 66; John 27; Lambert 32; Maria
 45; Rachel 17; Samuel 27, 32, 45,
 54; Sarah 51; William 32, 33, 51,
 54.
Nott, Garret 12.
Nyffer, David 14.

Oahee (?), John 52; Stephen Williams
 52.
Oake, Abraham 48; Elsie Lansing 48.
Oaks, Esther 62.*
Oathout, Oathoudt, see Oothout.
Oatie, Edward 44; John 44.
O'Brien, Obrien, O'Brian, Catharine,
 Catharina 4, 8, 44, 47, 62.
Ochenpagh, Sophia 13.
Odell, Hannah 54.
Oley, Olee, Christophel 57; Christopher
 54, 59; Eleanor 54, 57; Gertrude
 60; Rachel 10; Simon V. Antwerp
 59.
Olford, Nicholas 6.
Olinda, Eleanor 10.
Oliver, Aaron 10; Anna 6, 7; Catharine
 11; Mrs. Christiana 5.
Olmar, Mary 17.
Omen, Thomas 4.
Onan, George 30.
Oosterhout, Osterhout, Osterhoudt, Ag-
 nes 31; Annatje 14; Eleanor 34;
 Eliann 30; Francis 9; Henry 17;
 John 30,* 31; Mary 9, 17,* 28;
 Neeltje 20; Sarah 17, 67; Wilhelmus
 31.
Oothout, Outhout, Oathout, Oathoudt,
 Altie 71; Catharine, Catharina 10,
 56, 75; Henry 71* Humphrey 11;
 Marietie 56; Mary 9; Rachel 55;
 Rachel Sr. 81.
Orien, Beth 19; George 19; John 19.
Orlogh, Peter 62; William 62.
Ornort, Geertruy 7.
Orsen (?), Jane 10.
Osburn, Osburne, Catharine 55,* 71.
Osterhout, see Oosterhout.
Ostrander, Andrew 8; Ann 56, 90;
 Catharine, Catharina 32, 56, 59;
 Eliza 90; Elizabeth 10, 79, 83;

Fanny 5; Henry, Rev. 72; Jacob 11;
 John 32, 35, 37, 45, 56; John G.
 23; John I. 56; John Jr. 23; John
 T. 83, 90; Jonathan 59; Leah 59;
 Levy 35; Maria 45; Mary 23, 37;
 Sarah 8; Volkie 11.
Otmann, Maria 26.
Ouderkerke, Johannes 54; John I. 54.
Outhout, see Oothout.
Oversandt, Margarit 31.
Ovrin, George Davis 4.
Owens, Owen (?), Elizabeth 52, 57,
 82; Isaac 11; Peter 55; Rachel 55.

Packart, Packard, Sarah 42, 57.
Packer, Eunice 8.
Packet, Sarah 69.
Paddock, John 5.
Page, Deborah 11.
Paine, Sarah 9.
Palmater, Palmatren, John 8; Maritie 8.
Palmer, Loisa 9; Silas 9; Sylvanus 13.
Pangbower, Willm 7.
Pangbour, Pangburne, Pengburn, El-
 eanor 6; Garret 48; Isaac 23; John
 2, 11; Mary 17, 49; Richard 23;
 Stephen 48.
Park, Parks, Mary 3, 59, 76.
Parse, Jacobus 56; Rachel 56.
Passage, Passagie, Christiana 54; Chris-
 topher 9, 28; Elizabeth 34; Henry
 34.
Passenger, Passinger, Andrew 10; Isaac
 9; Mary 44, 59.
Paterson, Patterson, Cornelia 68, 71;
 Margaret 37; William 68.
Patten, Elizabeth 65.
Pean, Elizabeth 17.
Pearce, Marytje 16.
Pearson, Catlyna 74; George 6, 74.
Peck, Abraham 18; Maria 17; Sarah 18;
 William 18.
Pelse, Margarit 8.
Pengburn, see Pangburn.
Pepper, John 61; Magdelene 54; Wil-
 liam 39,* 54, 61.
Perry, Elizabeth 73; Margaret 73, 78;
 Maria 77.
Pettit, Eunice 9.
Petree, Christiana 77.
Philips, Phillips, Albertie 78; Margaret,
 Margarit 8, 26; Maritie 60; Sophia
 34, 76.
Picker, Sarah 51.
Pipper, John 48; William 48.
Platt, Charles 13, 87; Humphrey 10;
 James Bleecker 87; Sarah 87.
Plumb, Ann Elize 84; Garrit, Gerrit
 84, 90; Mary 90; Susannah 84, 90.
Pool, Pools, Catharina 4; John 13;
 Lydia 21; Peter 4.
Post, Benjamin 49; Elizabeth 13; Maria

Strunk, Stronk, Annatje 16; Catharina 23; Jacob 6, 22; Maritie 22; Philip 8.
Studevant, Caleb 44;* James 44; Susannah 44.
Stunck, Henry 55; Philip 55.
Sturbergh, Elisabeth 6.
Sturges, Hannah 12; Mary 67, 81.
Stuyvesant, Stuyvesand, Cornelia 18, 24, 38, 52; Margaret 18; Nicholas 18; Petrus 24.
Styles, Cornelia 70; Jacob A. or N. 70.
Suydam, Cedam, Henry 5.
Sylman, Barbara 79; John 79.
Swart, Eve, Eva 21, 36, 67, 82.
Sweet, Stephen 8.
Swits, Switz, B. Schuyler 25; Brandt Schuyler 2; Fanny 43; Johannah 25; Mary 25; Schuler 75; Schuyler 75.
Symon, see Simons.

Talbert, Margaret 63; Susannah 53; William 46, 53, 63.
Tansel, John 68; Nicholias 68.
Tater, Elisabeth 6.
Taulie, James 44; Robert 44.
Taylor, Tayler, Hugh 31; John 31, 58; Lydia 3; Rachel 58; Samuel D. 11.
Ten Broeck, Abraham 10, 38, 52; Cathrina 15, 18; Cornelia 52; Dirck, Dirk 18, 24, 38, 52; Elizabeth Maria 38; John 15; Margaret Stuyvesand 18, 52; Mary 68; Petrus Stuyvesant 24; Sarah 15.
Ten Eyck, Ten Eick, Ten Eycke, Ten Eyk, Abraham 16, 47; Abraham Cuyler 47; Abrahm Jr. 78; Abraham R. 11, 84; Andreas 22; Andrew 2; Anna 8, 78; Annatie 40; Baar 21; Barent 1; Casper 9; Catalina 80; Catharine, Catharina 19, 21, 25, 27, 66, 69, 73, 76, 82; Catharina V. Ingen 41; George 39, 52, 61; Harmanus 22, 41; Harmen Gansevoort 85; Helena 5, 33, 57; Hendric 39, 52; Henry 40; Hester Ganzevoort 41; Jacob 8, 41, 47, 68, 78, 82, 85; Jacob Lansing 68; Jeremiah V. Rensselaer 16; Leonard Gansevoort 82; Lyntje, Lyntie 8, 36, 40, 52; Magdalen 85; Margarit 22; Myndert S. 39; Philip 84; Sarah 22; Susannah 61.
Terboss, Ter Bush, Mary 3, 79, 82.
Terhune, Magdalena 75.
Terwilliger, Catharine 25.
Tesser, Harman 23; Mary 23.
Tetterly, Frederick 21; Peter 21.
Thayer, Ezra 12.
Thomson, Thompson, Archibald 79; Christina 8; George 14; James 79; James E. 23; Jane 14; Margarit 23;

Richard (Cold.) 5.
Thurstion, David 8.
Tillgham, Eliza 5.
Tillman, Tilman, Christophel 18; Christopher William 18; Eleanor 60; Elizabeth 44, 53, 59; Gertrude 85; John 10; John R. 60, 85; Sarah 85.
Tillon, Alexander 60; William 60.
Timesse, Maria 58, 67.
Tingue, Catharina 29; Caty 49.
Todd, John R. 2.
Tollot, Aunah 50.
Tonkins, Sarah 35.
Tooper, Maria 70; William 70.
Torne, Mary 21.
Tortler, Anna Maria 22; John 22.
Totham, Elizabeth 10.
Townsend, Helen A. 5.
Tracy, Lucy 18.
Treat, Elizabeth 37; Rachel Stringer 79; Richard I. (?) 63; Richard Joseph 63; Richard S. 37, 45, 52, 73, 79; Samuel Stringer 45, 52, 73.
Trever, Hannah 47.
Troisi, Margaret 7.
Troller, Henry 29; Mathew 29.
Trotter, Ann Maria 67; Margarit 43; Matthew, Mathew 18, 43, 67; Sarah 18.*
Troubridge, Trowbridge, Ann Maria 53; Charles Christopher 59; Luther 44, 53, 59; Margaret 44.
Truax, Angeltie 55; Ann Bleeker 20; Anna 90; Ariantie 50; Catharina Woters, Catharine Waters 22, 27, 57; Gerritie 38; Henry 22, 27, 32, 40, 57; Isaac 20, 32,* 38, 57; Isaac P. 90; Isaac Van Santvoort 90; Jacob 7, 50; John 50; John Bleecker 57; Mary 7; Susannah 40; Yellis 50.
Tucker, Samuel 11.
Tuper, Peter 60; William 60.
Turk, Abm 7; Angelica 79; Jeronimus 45; Jeronimus Jr. 79; Timothy 45.
Turner, William 13.
Turney, Mary 6.
Turry, Elizabeth 22.
Tuttle, Jonathan 10; Richard 75; Sarah 63.

Upham, Uphan, Magdalena 39, 52, 61.
Usher, Ann 71; Mary 6, 35, 53, 60, 71, 78.
Ustres, Mary 24.
Utter, Elisabeth 6; L. Zelpha 10.

Varick, Jane 59, 79.
Varley, Barnard 29; Gertrude 40; John 29; Peter 40.
Veeder, Vedder, Veder, Abraham, Abm 32, 76; Anna 39; Anne, Ann 35, 57; Catalina 3; Cataलyntie 20; Catharina 38; Cornelia 69; Corne-